HOLT McDOUGAL

Algebra 1

Edward B. Burger

David J. Chard

Paul A. Kennedy

Steven J. Leinwand

Freddie L. Renfro

Tom W. Roby

Bert K. Waits

HOLT McDOUGAL

HOUGHTON MIFFLIN HARCOURT

Algebra 1 Contents in Brief

Printed in Canada

ISBN-13 978-0-030-99574-3

ISBN-10 0-030-99574-4

2 3 4 5 6 7 8 9 10 XXX 18 17 16 15 14 13 12 11 10

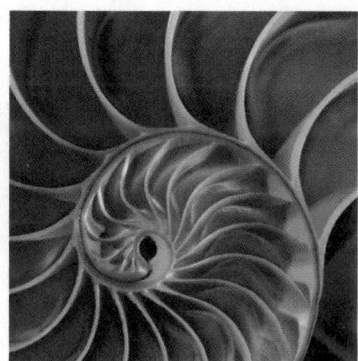

Cover photo: © James L. Amos/Corbis

AUTHORS

Edward B. Burger, Ph.D., is Professor of Mathematics at Williams College and is the author of numerous articles, books, and videos. He has won several of the most prestigious writing and teaching awards offered by the Mathematical Association of America. Dr. Burger has made numerous television and radio appearances and has given countless mathematical presentations around the world.

Freddie L. Renfro, MA, has 35 years of experience in Texas education as a classroom teacher and director/coordinator of Mathematics PreK-12 for school districts in the Houston area. She has served as a reviewer and TXTEAM trainer for Texas Math Institutes and has presented at numerous math workshops.

David J. Chard, Ph.D., is the Leon Simmons Dean of the School of Education and Human Development at Southern Methodist University. He is a past president of the Divison of Research at the Council for Exceptional Children, a member of the International Academy for Research on Learning Disabilities, and has been the Principal Investigator on numerous research projects for the U.S. Department of Education.

Tom W. Roby, Ph.D., is Associate Professor of Mathematics and Director of the Quantitative Learning Center at the University of Connecticut. He founded and directed the Bay Area-based ACCLAIM professional development program. He also chaired the advisory board of the California Mathematics Project and reviewed content for the California Standards Tests.

Paul A. Kennedy, Ph.D., is a professor and Distinguished University Teaching Scholar in the Department of Mathematics at Colorado State University. Dr. Kennedy is a leader in mathematics education. His research focuses on developing algebraic thinking by using multiple representations and technology. He is the author of numerous publications.

Bert K. Waits, Ph.D., is a Professor Emeritus of Mathematics at The Ohio State University and cofounder of T^3 (Teachers Teaching with Technology), a national professional development program. Dr. Waits is also a former board member of the NCTM and an author of the original NCTM Standards.

Steven J. Leinwand is a Principal Research Analyst at the American Institutes for Research in Washington, D.C. He was previously, for 22 years, the Mathematics Supervisor with the Connecticut Department of Education.

REVIEWERS

John Remensky
Mathematics Department Chair
South Park High School
South Park, PA

Raymond Seymour
Mathematics Department Head, retired
Kirby Middle School
San Antonio, TX

Jennifer J. Southers
Mathematics Teacher
Hillcrest High School
Simpsonville, SC

Jill Springer
Mathematics Teacher
Henderson County High School
Henderson, KY

Dr. Katherine Staltare
Mathematics Consultant & Graduate Level
    Course Developer
NYSUT, Effective Teaching Program
New York State

Pam Walker
Curriculum Teacher Specialist
Nacogdoches ISD
Nacogdoches, TX

Larry Ward
Mathematics Supervisor, retired
Carrollton-Farmers Branch ISD
Carrollton, TX

Carmen Whitman
Director, Mathematics for All Consulting
Pflugerville, TX

CONTRIBUTING AUTHORS

Carmen Whitman
Pflugerville, TX

Linda Antinone
Fort Worth, TX

FIELD TEST PARTICIPANTS

Len Zigment
Mesa Ridge High School
Colorado Springs, CO

Vicky Petty
Central Middle School
Murfreesboro, TN

John Bakelaar
Peebles Middle School
Jackson, MS

Carey Carter
Alvarado High School
Alvarado, TX

Preparing for Standardized Tests

Holt McDougal Algebra 1 provides many opportunities for you to prepare for standardized tests.

Test Prep Exercises

Use the Test Prep Exercises for daily practice of standardized test questions in various formats.

Multiple Choice—choose your answer.

Gridded Response—write your answer in a grid and fill in the corresponding bubbles.

Short Response—write open-ended responses that are scored with a 2-point rubric.

Extended Response—write open-ended responses that are scored with a 4-point rubric.

Test Tackler

Use the Test Tackler to become familiar with and practice test-taking strategies.

The first page of this feature explains and shows an example of a test-taking strategy.

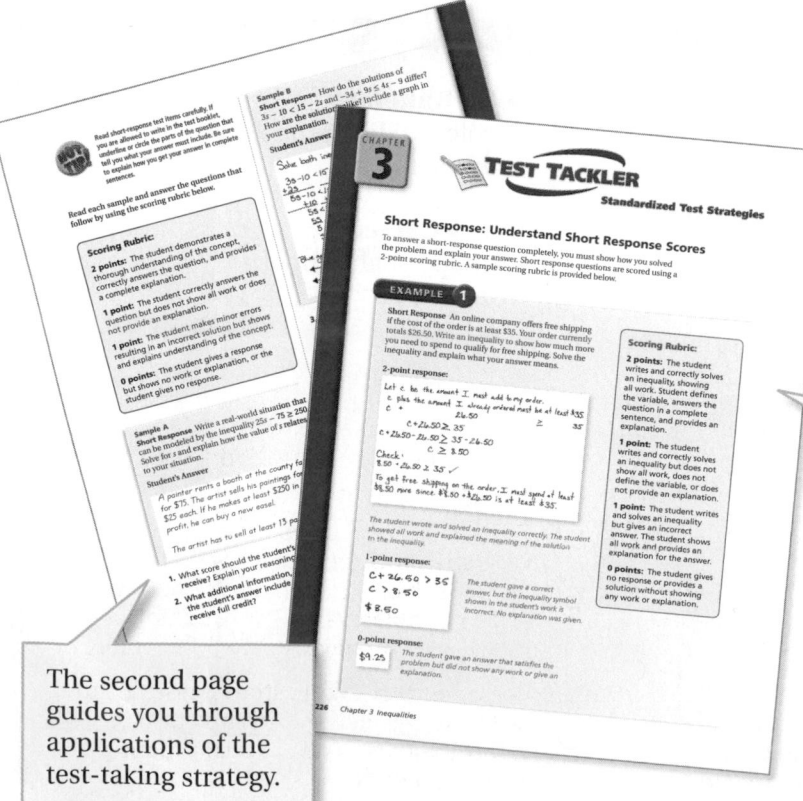

The second page guides you through applications of the test-taking strategy.

Standardized Test Prep

Use the Standardized Test Prep to apply test-taking strategies.

The Hot Tip provides test-taking tips to help you suceed on your tests.

These pages include practice with multiple choice, gridded response, short response, and extended response test items.

Countdown to Testing

Use the Countdown to Testing to practice for your state test every day.

There are 24 pages of practice for your state test. Each page is designed to be used in a week so that all practice will be completed before your state test is given.

Each week's page has five practice test items, one for each day of the week.

Test-Taking Tips

- ✔ Get plenty of sleep the night before the test. A rested mind thinks more clearly and you won't feel like falling asleep while taking the test.

- ✔ Draw a figure when one is not provided with the problem. If a figure is given, write any details from the problem on the figure.

- ✔ Read each problem carefully. As you finish each problem, read it again to make sure your answer is reasonable.

- ✔ Review the formula sheet that will be supplied with the test. Make sure you know when to use each formula.

- ✔ First answer problems that you know how to solve. If you do not know how to solve a problem, skip it and come back to it when you have finished the others.

- ✔ Use other test-taking strategies that can be found throughout this book, such as working backward and eliminating answer choices.

DAY 1

Which expression always represents an odd number when n is a natural number?

- (A) $n^2 + 1$
- (B) $2n + 1$
- (C) n^2
- (D) $n + 1$

DAY 2

Cell phone bills are based on a flat monthly fee and the number of minutes used. In the equation $c = 0.07m + 29.99$, what does the variable m represent?

- (F) The number of months billed
- (G) The total amount of the bill
- (H) The number of minutes used
- (J) The phone number

DAY 3

Which equation best describes the relationship between the number of astudents and the number of tables in the cafeteria?

Students (n)	Tables (t)
720	18
600	15
960	24

- (A) $n = 40t$
- (C) $t = 40n$
- (B) $n = 35t + 90$
- (D) $n = 45t - 90$

DAY 4

Which expression represents the verbal phrase "the sum of three times a number and five"?

- (F) $3(n + 5)$
- (G) $3 + n \cdot 5$
- (H) $3n + 5$
- (J) $3 + (n + 5)$

DAY 5

What is the next term in the pattern?

$$-3, 6, -12, 24, \_\_\_, \ldots$$

- (A) 30
- (B) 36
- (C) -32
- (D) -48

DAY 1

What is the next term in the pattern?

$$-1, \frac{1}{2}, -\frac{1}{4}, \frac{1}{8}, \underline{\quad\quad}, \ldots$$

Ⓐ $-\frac{1}{16}$

Ⓑ $-\frac{1}{10}$

Ⓒ $\frac{1}{10}$

Ⓓ $\frac{1}{16}$

DAY 2

Which expression is equivalent to $2(3x - 4) - 8x + 3$?

Ⓕ $2x + 11$

Ⓖ $-2x - 5$

Ⓗ $2x - 5$

Ⓙ $-2x - 11$

DAY 3

Based on the table, which inequality correctly shows the relationship between x and y?

x	2	3	5	6
y	−3	−8	−10	−9

Ⓐ $x > -y$

Ⓑ $2x < -y$

Ⓒ $x < -y$

Ⓓ $2x > -y$

DAY 4

The sum of three consecutive even numbers is 42. The sum can be represented by the equation $n + (n + 2) + (n + 4) = 42$. What does n represent?

Ⓕ The greatest number

Ⓖ The average of the numbers

Ⓗ The middle number

Ⓙ The least number

DAY 5

A job advertisement states that the position pays $12 an hour. Which equation represents the relationship between the salary s and the number of hours h worked?

Ⓐ $s = 12 + h$

Ⓑ $s = 12h$

Ⓒ $h = 12s$

Ⓓ $h = 12 + s$

DAY 1

Which expression is equivalent to 2^3?

(A) $2 \cdot 3$

(B) $3 + 3$

(C) $2 + 2 + 2$

(D) $2 \cdot 2 \cdot 2$

DAY 2

Which number is not a solution of $-7y + 19 < 75$?

(F) 13

(G) 0

(H) -2

(J) -8

DAY 3

Lydia received a gift card for $25.00 worth of smoothies from the Smoothie Spot. If the cost of each smoothie is $3.25, which table best describes b, the balance remaining on the gift card after she buys n smoothies?

(A)

n	b
1	$21.75
3	$15.25
4	$12.00
7	$2.25

(C)

n	b
1	$21.75
2	$18.50
5	$15.25
7	$12.00

(B)

n	b
2	$18.50
4	$12.00
6	$6.50
8	$0

(D)

n	b
2	$18.50
3	$15.25
5	$7.75
6	$4.50

DAY 4

The band is trying to raise money to take a field trip to the Rock and Roll Hall of Fame. They decide to sell sweatshirts. The equation for the amount of money a that they will make for selling t sweatshirts is $a = 22t - 350$. In order to make at least $2100, how many sweatshirts do the band members need to sell?

(F) 112

(G) 111

(H) 80

(J) 79

DAY 5

What is the solution to the equation $8x - 10 = 54$?

(A) 5.5

(B) 6.75

(C) 8

(D) 12

DAY 1

Which expression is equivalent to $2x(3x + 5) - x^2 + 8$?

(A) $-x^2 + 6x + 18$

(B) $5x^2 + 10x + 8$

(C) $10x + 14$

(D) $-x^2 + 16x + 8$

DAY 2

What is the value of $3x^2 - 5x + 2$ when $x = -4$?

(F) -66

(G) -26

(H) 30

(J) 70

DAY 3

Which graph matches the values from the table?

x	−3	−1	2	4
y	6	2	−4	−8

(A)

(C)

(B)

(D)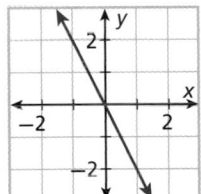

DAY 4

A rectangle has a length of 8 m and a width of 3 m. If a similar rectangle has a length of 22 m, what is its width?

(F) 58.67 m

(G) 17 m

(H) 8.25 m

(J) 9 m

DAY 5

Simplify the algebraic expression $4(x + 5) - 2(x + 5)$.

(A) $2x + 10$

(B) $2x + 30$

(C) $6x + 30$

(D) $-8x^2 - 200$

DAY 1

Which description of the relationship between x and y best represents the table below?

x	9	0	-6	1
y	3	0	-2	$\frac{1}{3}$

(A) The value of y is three times the value of x.

(B) The value of x is three more than the value of y.

(C) The value of x is three less than the value of y.

(D) The value of x is three times the value of y.

DAY 2

Claire's father is 6 years more than 3 times her age. If her dad is 39 years old, how old is Claire?

(F) 15 years old

(G) 11 years old

(H) 7 years old

(J) 6 years old

DAY 3

Which expression represents the phrase "four times the sum of a number and 2"?

(A) $4n + 2$

(B) $4(2n)$

(C) $4(n + 2)$

(D) $4 \cdot n + 2$

DAY 4

What is the solution to $-8x - 3 = -4x + 5$?

(F) -4

(G) -2

(H) 2

(J) 4

DAY 5

The cheerleaders are selling tickets to a pasta dinner to raise money for new competition outfits. They plan to charge $6 per person, and their total expenses for dinner are $135. Which value for the number of tickets sold would result in the cheerleaders not making a profit?

(A) 46

(B) 45

(C) 23

(D) 22

DAY 1

Which equation matches the data in the table?

x	3	1	−2	6
y	2	4	7	−1

Ⓐ $y = -x + 5$

Ⓑ $y = 2x - 1$

Ⓒ $y = x + 3$

Ⓓ $y = -3x + 11$

DAY 2

The drama club charges $3 admission to the one-act play festival. Their expenses are $115. In order for the club to make exactly $110 after expenses, how many people must attend the festival?

Ⓕ 39

Ⓖ 75

Ⓗ 114

Ⓙ 152

DAY 3

Melissa's brother is 6 years less than twice her age. The sum of her age and her brother's age is 27. Which equation best shows this information?

Ⓐ $x + (6 - 2x) = 27$

Ⓑ $x + (2x - 6) = 27$

Ⓒ $2x - 6 = 27$

Ⓓ $x = 2x - 6$

DAY 4

A rectangle has a length of 5 inches and a width of 3 inches. If a similar rectangle has a width of 15 inches, what is its length?

Ⓕ 5 inches

Ⓖ 9 inches

Ⓗ 15 inches

Ⓙ 25 inches

DAY 5

A bus company sells an annual bus pass for $8.50, and then charges a rider $0.25 per ride. Using the equation $c = 0.25b + 8.5$, how much will it cost for someone to ride the bus 38 times?

Ⓐ $118.00

Ⓑ $20.00

Ⓒ $18.00

Ⓓ $9.50

DAY 1

Daniel's recipe for 24 cookies calls for $2\frac{1}{2}$ cups of flour. How much flour will Daniel need to make 60 cookies?

- (A) 1 cup
- (B) $6\frac{1}{4}$ cups
- (C) $6\frac{1}{2}$ cups
- (D) $7\frac{1}{2}$ cups

DAY 2

What is the value of $2x^2 + 3x - 5$ when $x = -2$?

- (F) -7
- (G) -3
- (H) 5
- (J) 9

DAY 3

Which graph shows a line where each value of y is three more than half of x?

(A)

(C)

(B)

(D)

DAY 4

What is the solution to $2x + 8 < 3x - 4$?

- (F) $x < 12$
- (G) $x > \frac{12}{5}$
- (H) $x > 12$
- (J) $x < \frac{12}{5}$

DAY 5

Simplify the expression $3(5x - 8) + 2(4x - 1)$.

- (A) $23x + 26$
- (B) $23x + 22$
- (C) $23x - 22$
- (D) $23x - 26$

DAY 1

A swimming pool charges an annual $75 membership fee, and it costs $1.50 each time a member brings a guest. Which equation shows the yearly cost y in terms of the number of guests g?

- (A) $y = 75g + 1.5$
- (B) $y = -1.5g + 75$
- (C) $y = 1.5g + 75$
- (D) $y = 1.5g + 75g$

DAY 2

On a certain standardized test, the equation $s = 9q + 218$ is used to determine a student's score. In this equation, s is the score and q is the number of questions answered correctly. If the maximum score on the test is 650, how many questions are on the test?

- (F) 96 questions
- (G) 72 questions
- (H) 48 questions
- (J) 24 questions

DAY 3

If you belong to Lowell's Gym and plan to work out 82 times in a year, what is your total cost for the year?

Lowell's Gym	
Membership fee	$75
Workout fee (per visit)	$2

- (A) $89
- (B) $157
- (C) $164
- (D) $239

DAY 4

A publishing company must ship boxes of a particular book to bookstores around the country. The boxes used for shipping can hold a maximum of 35 pounds. If the company wants to ship at least 10 books per box, what is the maximum weight of a book that can be put in the box?

- (F) 3 pounds
- (G) $3\frac{1}{2}$ pounds
- (H) 4 pounds
- (J) 25 pounds

DAY 5

Which verbal description does not match the function $f(x) = -\frac{1}{3}x - 5$?

- (A) The function value is the difference between x times $-\frac{1}{3}$ and 5.
- (B) The function value is 5 less than the product of x and $-\frac{1}{3}$.
- (C) The function value is $-\frac{1}{3}$ of x subtracted from 5.
- (D) The function value is $-\frac{1}{3}$ of x decreased by 5.

DAY 1

Brian calculates the charge for each lawn he mows by using the function $f(t) = 10t + 5.5$, where t is the number of hours spent mowing the lawn. He always works for at least one full hour. Which statement cannot be inferred from this information?

Ⓐ Brian's hourly rate is $10.

Ⓑ Brian includes a charge of $5.50 for all lawns.

Ⓒ Brian uses $5.50 worth of gas for each job.

Ⓓ The minimum that Brian will make for each lawn is $15.50.

DAY 2

Which of the following relationships has a negative correlation?

Ⓕ A person's height and weight

Ⓖ The number of minutes spent studying and a test grade

Ⓗ The outside temperature and the number of layers of clothes a person wears

Ⓙ The number of years a person spent in school and the person's salary

DAY 3

The graph shows the value of a car over a period of years. Which of the following statements cannot be concluded from the graph?

Ⓐ The car started at a value of approximately $8400.

Ⓑ The car's value depreciates more quickly at the beginning, and then less quickly as time goes on.

Ⓒ The car is worth approximately $3000 when it is 5 years old.

Ⓓ The car should be sold before its worth drops below $2000.

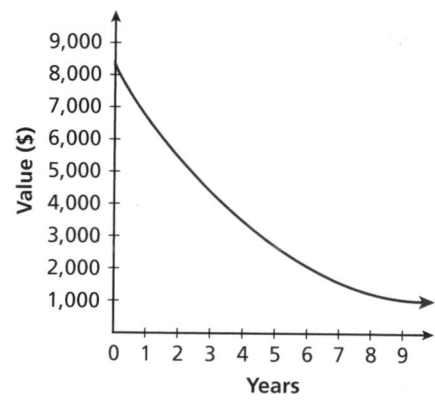

DAY 4

Which function best matches the table?

x	−3	0	3	6
y	2	4	6	8

Ⓕ $y = -\frac{2}{3}x$

Ⓖ $y = 2x + 4$

Ⓗ $y = \frac{2}{3}x + 4$

Ⓙ $y = \frac{1}{3}x + 3$

DAY 5

To change from degrees Celsius to degrees Fahrenheit, you can use the equation $f = \frac{9}{5}c + 32$. If the temperature is at least 55 degrees Fahrenheit, what inequality can you use to find the temperature in Celsius?

Ⓐ $55 \geq \frac{9}{5}c + 32$

Ⓑ $f \geq \frac{9}{5} \cdot 55 + 32$

Ⓒ $55 \leq \frac{9}{5}c + 32$

Ⓓ $f \leq \frac{9}{5} \cdot 55 + 32$

DAY 1

A function relating two quantities is $f(x) = \frac{1}{5}x + 6$. What will always be true based on this function?

A $f(x)$ will be less than x.

B If x is positive, then $f(x)$ will be positive.

C If x is negative, then $f(x)$ will be negative.

D $f(x)$ will be greater than x.

DAY 2

In the equation $p = -40q + 163$, which relationship between p and q is true?

F You cannot determine the relationship based on this information.

G q is dependent on p.

H p and q are independent of each other.

J p is dependent on q.

DAY 3

What is the equation of the line shown?

A $y = 2x$

B $y = -2x$

C $y = \frac{1}{2}x$

D $y = -\frac{1}{2}x$

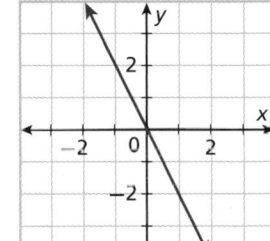

DAY 4

What is the solution to $-8x - 3 \geq -4x + 5$?

F $x \leq -2$

G $x \geq 2$

H $x \leq 2$

J $x \geq -2$

DAY 5

The sum of three consecutive integers is 54. What is the greatest of the three integers?

A 17

B 18

C 19

D 20

DAY 1

Darian has a picture that is 4 inches wide and 6 inches long. He wants to enlarge the picture so that it has a width of 18 inches. What is the length of the enlarged picture?

Ⓐ 27 inches

Ⓑ 24 inches

Ⓒ 20 inches

Ⓓ 12 inches

DAY 2

At a computer repair shop, the function $f(t) = 40t + 35$ is used to calculate fees, where t is the number of hours technicians spend working on the computer. If you pay $315 to get your computer repaired, how long did the technician work on repairing your computer?

Ⓕ 8.75 hours

Ⓖ 7.875 hours

Ⓗ 7.5 hours

Ⓙ 7 hours

DAY 3

The scatter plot shows the relationship between the size of a diamond in Carats and its retail price. What is the approximate retail price of a 0.30 Carat diamond?

Ⓐ $400

Ⓑ $600

Ⓒ $800

Ⓓ $1000

DAY 4

What is the next term in the pattern?

50, 10, 2, $\frac{2}{5}$, ___, ...

Ⓕ $\frac{1}{25}$

Ⓖ $\frac{2}{25}$

Ⓗ $\frac{2}{10}$

Ⓙ $\frac{1}{5}$

DAY 5

Which expression is equivalent to $5x - 35$?

Ⓐ $5(x - 35)$

Ⓑ $5(x - 7)$

Ⓒ $5(x + 35)$

Ⓓ $5(x + 7)$

DAY 1

Based on the information in the table, what is the relationship between the weight of the object and its volume?

Weight (lb)	2	5	8	12
Volume (in³)	0.5	1.25	2	3

A The weight is 1.5 more than the volume.

B The volume is 4 times the weight.

C The weight is 4 times the volume.

D The volume is 6 less than the weight.

DAY 2

What is the range of the function shown in the table?

x	1	3	5	8
$f(x)$	2	−2	0	2

F {1, 3, 5, 8}

G {4}

H {−2, 0, 2}

J {7}

DAY 3

Which graph shows a linear function?

A

C

B

D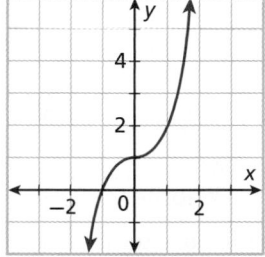

DAY 4

What is the solution to the equation $6(x − 9) = −12x + 36$?

F $x = 5$

G $x = 2.5$

H $x = −1$

J $x = −5$

DAY 5

Simplify the algebraic expression $5x − 2(4x − 3) + 7$.

A $−3x + 1$

B $13x + 13$

C $−3x + 13$

D $3x + 1$

DAY 1

The slope of a line is $-\frac{1}{4}$, and the y-intercept is –3. What is the equation of the line?

Ⓐ $x + y = -3$

Ⓑ $y = -\frac{1}{4}x + 1$

Ⓒ $y = -\frac{1}{4}x - 3$

Ⓓ $x - 4y = -3$

DAY 2

A taxi company charges a $2.50 fee per ride plus an additional $2.10 per mile traveled. If the taxi fee increases to $2.75, which characteristic of this function would change?

Ⓕ The slope

Ⓖ The x-intercept

Ⓗ The y-intercept

Ⓙ There would be no changes

DAY 3

Which description of the relationship between x and y best matches the graph below?

Ⓐ The value of y is 3 times the value of x.

Ⓑ The value of x is 2 more than the value of y.

Ⓒ The value of x is 2 less than the value of y.

Ⓓ The value of x is 3 times the value of y.

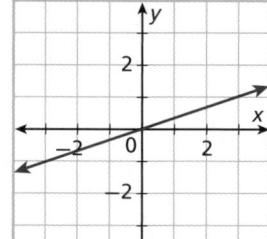

DAY 4

In which relationship are the two quantities independent of one another?

Ⓕ The amount of tax paid for an item and the price of the item

Ⓖ The number of snacks bought from a snack machine and the amount of money in the machine

Ⓗ The number of hours worked at $6.50 per hour and the amount of money earned

Ⓙ The age of a person and the number of televisions in his or her home

DAY 5

The linear function $f(x) = 3x + 15$ models the cost of renting x movies over the course of a year from a certain store. What range restrictions will there be if you graph this function?

Ⓐ $f(x) \geq 0$

Ⓑ $f(x) \geq 15$

Ⓒ $f(x) > 0$

Ⓓ $0 \leq f(x) \leq 15$

DAY 1

Which function matches the data in the table?

x	−3	2	5
$f(x)$	15	0	15

Ⓐ $f(x) = -3x + 6$

Ⓑ $f(x) = -5x$

Ⓒ $f(x) = x^2 - 2x$

Ⓓ $f(x) = 3x^2 - 12$

DAY 2

A consultant charges her clients for her services based on an equation relating the total bill $f(h)$ to the number of hours worked h. The best interpretation of this function $f(h) = 125h + 150$ is:

Ⓕ She charges $150 per hour plus a $125 flat fee.

Ⓖ She charges $125 per hour plus a $150 flat fee.

Ⓗ She charges $275 per hour.

Ⓙ Her hourly charges vary from $125 to $150 depending on the job.

DAY 3

Which situation best fits the graph below?

Ⓐ The height of a candle if it is lit, blown out, lit again, and blown out again

Ⓑ The distance a car drives if it is driven a while, stops at a light, driven again, then stopped

Ⓒ The amount of water in a tub if the faucet is turned on, turned off, turned on again, and then turned off again

Ⓓ The altitude of a person who hikes up a mountain, then stops for a snack, continues up the mountain, and then rests at the top.

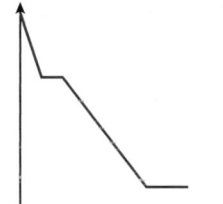

DAY 4

What is the range of the function $f(x) = 2x + 3$?

Ⓕ All real numbers

Ⓖ $f(x) \geq 3$

Ⓗ $f(x) \geq 0$

Ⓙ $f(x) \geq -3$

DAY 5

At Terry's TVs, profit is calculated using the equation $p = 0.4c - 125$, where p is the profit and c is the wholesale cost. If the company makes a profit of $375 on one TV, what is the wholesale cost of the TV?

Ⓐ $25

Ⓑ $937.50

Ⓒ $1250

Ⓓ $1062.50

DAY 1

Which graph shows a linear function?

(A)

(C)

(B)

(D)

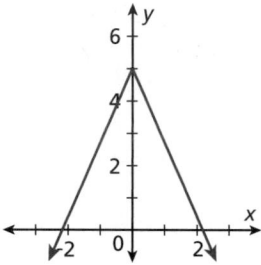

DAY 2

The relationship between which two quantities can be represented by a linear function?

(F) The volume of a cube and its side length

(G) The perimeter of a rectangle and its area

(H) The perimeter of an equilateral triangle and its side length

(J) The area of a square and its side length

DAY 3

Which equation represents a linear function with a slope of $\frac{2}{3}$?

(A) $y = \frac{3}{2}x$

(B) $y = \frac{2}{3}x + 4$

(C) $y = x + \frac{2}{3}$

(D) $y = \frac{2}{3}$

DAY 4

What are the x- and y-intercepts of $y = \frac{2}{5}x - 2$?

(F) x-intercept: –2; y-intercept: 5

(G) x-intercept: $\frac{2}{5}$; y-intercept: –2

(H) x-intercept: 0; y-intercept: –2

(J) x-intercept: 5; y-intercept: –2

DAY 5

A system of equations is set up to determine how many pounds of hazelnut coffee and how many pounds of Colombian coffee were mixed together to make a blend. The total mixture was 20 pounds of coffee. Which of the following is not a possible solution to the system?

(A) (7, 13)   (C) (11, 9)

(B) (32, –12)   (D) (1, 19)

DAY 1

If a graph shows the relationship between the amount of sand in the top of an hourglass y over time x, what quantity does the x-intercept represent?

(A) The amount of sand that is in the top of the hourglass originally

(B) The speed at which the sand passes to the bottom of the hourglass

(C) The height of the hourglass

(D) The amount of time it takes for all of the sand to pass to the bottom of the hourglass

DAY 2

Which equation represents a line parallel to the one shown?

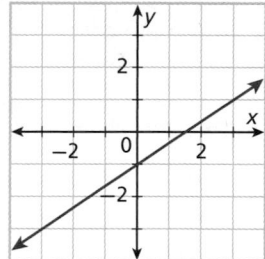

(F) $y = \frac{3}{2}x + 1$

(H) $y = \frac{2}{3}x + 1$

(G) $y = -\frac{3}{2}x - 1$

(J) $y = -\frac{2}{3}x$

DAY 3

Which situation best describes the graph shown if the x-axis represents time passed?

(A) The speed of a car as it accelerates

(B) The distance away from the finish as a person runs up a hill and then proceeds to run at a constant speed

(C) The amount of fuel remaining in a car's gas tank as the car travels at a constant speed

(D) The height of a baseball thrown upward and then rolled down a driveway

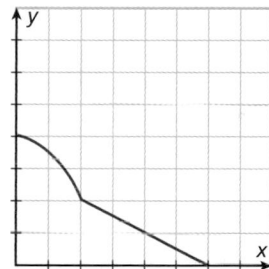

DAY 4

Your school is selling candles to raise money. If profit y is related to the number of items sold x, what are reasonable restrictions on the domain?

(F) $y \geq 0$

(G) No restrictions

(H) $x \geq 0$

(J) $0 \leq y \leq 2000$

DAY 5

What is the solution to the system of equations graphed below?

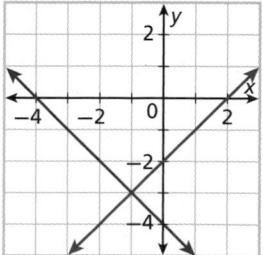

(A) $(-1, 3)$

(C) $(-3, -1)$

(B) $(-1, -3)$

(D) $(3, -1)$

DAY 1

A store manager increases the wholesale cost of an item by 35%. Which statement best represents the functional relationship between the wholesale cost of the item and the markup on the item?

(A) The markup is dependent on the wholesale cost.

(B) The wholesale cost is dependent on the markup.

(C) The markup and the wholesale cost are independent of each other.

(D) The relationship cannot be determined.

DAY 2

Which situation can best be represented by a linear function?

(F) The distance that an airplane is away from the airport as it comes in for a landing and time

(G) The distance traveled by a car moving at a constant speed and time

(H) The number of apples on a tree and the number of trees in the orchard

(J) The height from the ground of a person riding a roller coaster and time

DAY 3

The scatter plot shows the percent of households that own a car versus the household income. What is a reasonable estimate for the percent of households that own a car if the household income is $50,000?

(A) 50%

(B) 65%

(C) 77%

(D) 85%

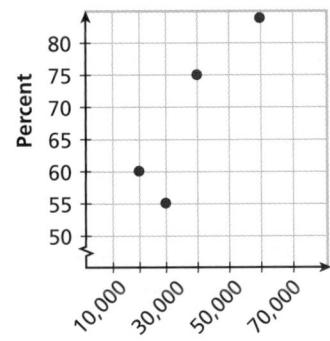

DAY 4

What is the slope of the line with equation $3x - 5y = 12$?

(F) -3

(G) $-\dfrac{3}{5}$

(H) $\dfrac{3}{5}$

(J) 3

DAY 5

Joy and a friend start a business. What linear function relates the total income and each partner's share of the profit based on the data in the table?

Total Income (t)	Profit Share (p)
$350.00	$50.00
$425.00	$87.50
$500.00	$125.00

(A) $p = \dfrac{1}{2}t - 125$

(C) $p = t - 300$

(B) $p = \dfrac{1}{4}t - 37.5$

(D) $p = \dfrac{1}{7}t$

DAY 1

What is the range of the function $f(x) = 2x^2 + 1$ if the domain is $\{-2, 0, 3\}$?

Ⓐ $\{1, 9, 19\}$ Ⓒ $\{-9, 1, 19\}$

Ⓑ $\{0, 8, 18\}$ Ⓓ $\{-2, 0, 3\}$

DAY 2

Which function has a y-intercept of -2 and a graph whose slope is $\frac{5}{4}$?

Ⓕ $5x + 4y = 2$ Ⓗ $y = -\frac{5}{4}x + 2$

Ⓖ $y = \frac{5}{4}x + 2$ Ⓙ $y = \frac{5}{4}x - 2$

DAY 3

The graph shows the relationship between a person's height and mass. Which of the following statements would be an invalid conclusion for this data?

Ⓐ The graph shows data for 20 people.

Ⓑ A person who is tall is likely to have a higher mass.

Ⓒ Two participants had a mass of 50 kg.

Ⓓ A person who has a low mass has a fast metabolism.

DAY 4

Which of the following cannot be represented by a linear function?

Ⓕ The amount of water w coming out of a dripping faucet over m minutes

Ⓖ The height h of a person over t years

Ⓗ The gross sales s made from the sale of c CDs priced at $14 each

Ⓙ The amount of sales tax on a purchase of d dollars if the rate is 6%

DAY 5

The graph shows the distance that a person is from home while driving at a constant speed. What quantity is represented by the y-intercept?

Ⓐ The speed at which the person is driving

Ⓑ The distance from home at the start

Ⓒ The amount of time it takes to get home

Ⓓ The distance from home at the end

DAY 1

Assuming that the graph below has the same *x*- and *y*-scale, which is the best estimate for the solution to the system?

- **A** $(-5, 10)$
- **B** $(-4, 2)$
- **C** $(3, -6)$
- **D** $(8, -4)$

DAY 2

What is the *y*-intercept of the function whose graph has a slope of $-\frac{1}{3}$ and passes through the point $(-6, 4)$?

- **F** 6
- **G** 2
- **H** -2
- **J** -6

DAY 3

Which graph shows a function from the family $f(x) = x^2$?

A

C

B

D

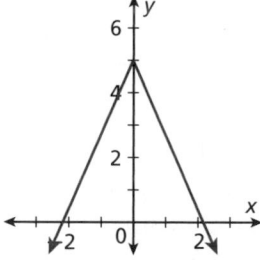

DAY 4

Miguel earns a 15% commission on his sales in addition to a salary of $500 a week. His earnings can be modeled by the equation $p = 0.15s + 500$. What restrictions on the values of *p* and *s* best fit this situation?

- **F** $p \geq 0$, *s* can be any value.
- **G** $s \geq 0$, *p* can be any value.
- **H** $s \geq 500$, $p \geq 0$
- **J** $s \geq 0$, $p \geq 500$

DAY 5

If $f(x) = \frac{1}{2}x$, what best describes the relationship between *x* and $f(x)$?

- **A** As the value of *x* increases by 1, the value of $f(x)$ will increase by 2.
- **B** As the value of *x* increases by 1, the value of $f(x)$ will remain the same.
- **C** As the value of *x* increases by 1, the value of $f(x)$ will increase by $\frac{1}{2}$.
- **D** The value of *x* will not affect the value of $f(x)$.

DAY 1

On Saturday, Suzie's Pretzel Stand sells a total of 12 items. Suzie charges $3 for a pretzel and $2 for a milkshake. If she took in $32 on Saturday, which system of equations can be used to determine how many pretzels and how many milkshakes were sold?

(A) $\begin{cases} 3x + 2y = 12 \\ x + y = 32 \end{cases}$ (C) $\begin{cases} 3x - 2y = 12 \\ x + y = 32 \end{cases}$

(B) $\begin{cases} 3x - 2y = 32 \\ x + y = 12 \end{cases}$ (D) $\begin{cases} x + y = 12 \\ 3x + 2y = 32 \end{cases}$

DAY 2

What is the slope of the line shown?

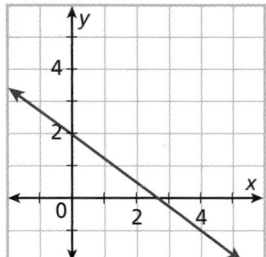

(F) $-\dfrac{4}{3}$ (H) $\dfrac{3}{4}$

(G) $-\dfrac{3}{4}$ (J) $\dfrac{4}{3}$

DAY 3

If the x-intercept of the function graphed below were to stay the same and the slope of the line decreased, what impact would that have on the y-intercept?

(A) The y-intercept will decrease.

(B) The y-intercept will remain the same.

(C) The y-intercept will increase.

(D) The y-intercept will double.

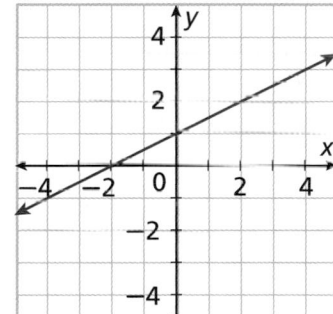

DAY 4

A system of equations is set up to determine the number of nickels and the number of quarters that Elissa has. Which ordered pair does not represent a valid solution to this system?

(F) (0, 15)

(G) (12, −5)

(H) (31, 4)

(J) (7, 0)

DAY 5

A gym membership costs $25 a month plus $3 per visit. This is modeled by the function $c = 3v + 25$, where c is the cost per month and v is the number of visits. If the slope of this function's graph were to increase, what would that mean about the prices that the gym charges?

(A) The gym raised its monthly fee.

(B) The gym lowered the cost per visit.

(C) The gym raised the cost per visit.

(D) The gym lowered its monthly fee.

DAY 1

Which of the functions, when graphed, will result in the most narrow parabola?

(A) $y = 5x^2$

(B) $y = \frac{1}{5}x^2$

(C) $y = x^2$

(D) $y = \frac{1}{2}x^2$

DAY 2

How do the graphs of the functions $f(x) = x^2 - 5$ and $g(x) = x^2 + 4$ relate to each other?

(F) The graph of $f(x)$ is 9 units to the left of the graph of $g(x)$.

(G) The graph of $f(x)$ is 1 unit below the graph of $g(x)$.

(H) The graph of $f(x)$ is 9 units below the graph of $g(x)$.

(J) The graph of $f(x)$ is 1 unit to the left of the graph of $g(x)$.

DAY 3

The graph shows the proposed balance in Jake's bank account if Jake saves an average of $15 a week. Which statement would not be true if the slope of the line were to increase?

(A) Jake is saving more money per week.

(B) Jake started with more money in his bank account.

(C) It will take less time for Jake's bank balance to reach $120.

(D) After 6 weeks Jake will have more than $90 in his bank account.

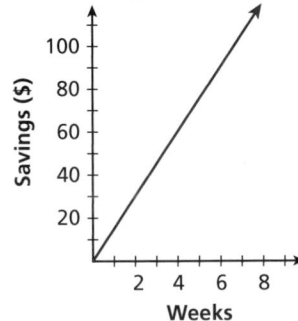

DAY 4

What are the roots of the function $f(x) = (2x - 1)(x + 5)$?

(F) $\frac{1}{2}$ and -5

(G) -1 and 5

(H) 1 and -5

(J) $-\frac{1}{2}$ and 5

DAY 5

For a typical shot in basketball, the ball's height in feet will be a function of time in seconds, modeled by an equation such as $h = -16t^2 + 25t + 6$. Which inequality shows the restrictions that should be put on the domain of this function?

(A) $t \leq 0$

(B) $h \leq 0$

(C) $h \geq 0$

(D) $t \geq 0$

DAY 1

What are the roots of the graphed function?

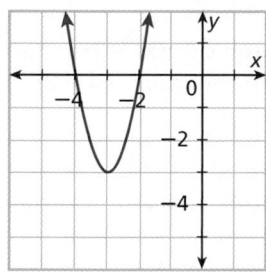

(A) 2 and 4

(C) −2 and 4

(B) −2 and −4

(D) 2 and −4

DAY 2

What is the range of the function shown?

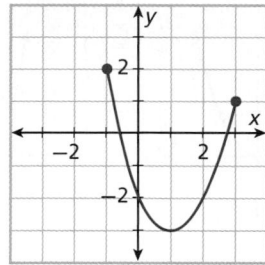

(F) $-2 < y < 3$

(H) $-3 \le y \le 2$

(G) $-3 < y \le 2$

(J) $-2 \le y \le 3$

DAY 3

The graph shows the height of a baseball from the time it is thrown until the time it hits the ground. What value is not shown on the graph?

(A) The amount of time that the ball was in the air

(B) The height at which the ball started

(C) The maximum height that the ball reached

(D) The speed at which the ball was thrown

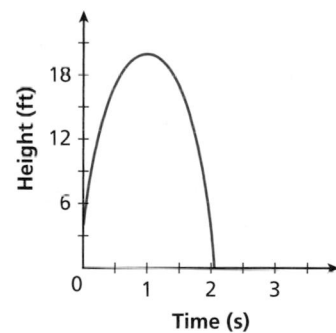

DAY 4

What are the solution(s) of the equation $x^2 - 10x - 24 = 0$?

(F) $x = -4, 6$

(G) $x = 2, -12$

(H) $x = -2, 12$

(J) $x = 4, -6$

DAY 5

What is the solution to the system of equations?

$$\begin{cases} 3x - 4y = 19 \\ y = 2x - 11 \end{cases}$$

(A) $(5, -1)$

(B) $(-5, -21)$

(C) $(5, 1)$

(D) $(-5, -8.5)$

DAY 1

Which graph shows a function $y = ax^2$ when $a > 1$?

(A)

(C)

(B)

(D)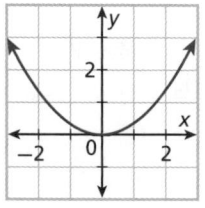

DAY 2

Which best describes the difference between the graphs of $f(x) = x^2$ and $g(x) = x^2 - 3$?

(F) The graph of $g(x)$ is translated 3 units up from the graph of $f(x)$.

(G) The graph of $g(x)$ is translated 3 units left from the graph of $f(x)$.

(H) The graph of $g(x)$ is translated 3 units right from the graph of $f(x)$.

(J) The graph of $g(x)$ is translated 3 units down from the graph of $f(x)$.

DAY 3

The graph shows the height of water coming out of a fountain over time. How many seconds pass before the water reaches the ground?

(A) 0

(B) 2

(C) 4

(D) 18

DAY 4

What is one solution to the equation $2x^2 + 7x + 3 = 0$?

(F) $x = 3$

(G) $x = \frac{1}{2}$

(H) $x = -\frac{1}{2}$

(J) $x = -1$

DAY 5

What is the solution to the system of equations $4x + 2y = -8$ and $x - 2y = 13$?

(A) $(25, 6)$

(B) $(1, 6)$

(C) $(-1, -6)$

(D) $(1, -6)$

DAY 1

Which is the parent function of the graph shown?

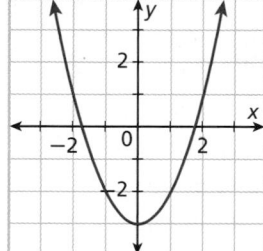

A $y = x$

B $y = |x|$

C $y = x^2$

D $y = x^3$

DAY 2

What is the *x*-intercept of the function shown?

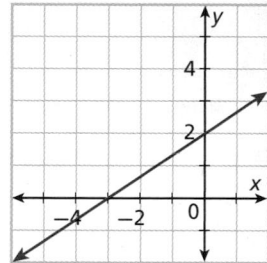

F $x = -3$

G $x = -2$

H $x = 2$

J $x = 3$

DAY 3

Which situation cannot be described by a linear function?

A The amount of commission earned on a sale if the commission rate is 12%

B The area of a square given its side length

C The cost of renting a car if the charge is $25 plus $0.15 per mile

D The amount paid for babysitting *h* hours if you charge $8.25 per hour

DAY 4

What is the equation of the line that passes through the points $(-4, 2)$ and $(-8, 8)$?

F $y = -\dfrac{3}{2}x - 4$

G $y = -\dfrac{3}{2}x - 20$

H $y = -\dfrac{3}{2}x - 8$

J $y = -\dfrac{3}{2}x + 4$

DAY 5

What is the slope of the line given the equation $3x - 4y = -8$?

A $m = 3$

B $m = 2$

C $m = \dfrac{3}{4}$

D $m = -3$

CHAPTER 1

Foundations for Algebra

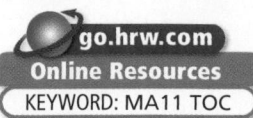

go.hrw.com
Online Resources
KEYWORD: MA11 TOC

Tools for Success

Reading and Writing Math

Reading Math 32, 34, 54

Writing Math 6, 33, 55

Vocabulary 3, 4, 9, 17, 23, 29, 35, 43, 49, 57, 62

Study Skills

Know-It Notes 15, 20, 21, 34, 40, 46, 47

Graphic Organizers 8, 17, 22, 28, 35, 42, 49, 56

Homework Help Online 9, 17, 23, 29, 35, 43, 49, 57

TEST PREP

Test Prep Exercises 11, 19, 25, 31, 37, 45, 51, 59

Multi-Step Test Prep 10, 18, 24, 30, 36, 38, 44, 50, 58, 60

College Entrance Exam Practice 67

Test Tackler 68

Standardized Test Prep 70

Equations

go.hrw.com
Online Resources
KEYWORD: MA11 TOC

Table of Contents

Tools for Success

CHAPTER
3

Inequalities

Tools for Success

Reading Math 172
Writing Math 170
Vocabulary 167, 168, 173, 208, 220

Study Strategy 169
Know-It Notes 171, 176, 182, 183, 204, 212, 213
Graphic Organizers 172, 179, 184, 192, 199
Homework Help Online 173, 179, 185, 193, 199, 208

Functions

CHAPTER

4

go.hrw.com
Online Resources
KEYWORD: MA11 TOC

Tools for Success

Reading and Writing Math

Reading Math 251, 276
Writing Math 241, 258
Vocabulary 231, 232, 237, 243, 253, 270, 279, 284

Study Skills

Know-It Notes 257, 267, 276, 277
Graphic Organizers 236, 242, 252, 260, 269, 278
Homework Help Online 237, 243, 253, 260, 270, 279

TEST PREP

Test Prep Exercises 239, 245, 255, 262, 273, 281
Multi-Step Test Prep 238, 245, 254, 261, 264, 272, 280, 282
College Entrance Exam Practice 289
Test Tackler 290
Standardized Test Prep 292

go.hrw.com
Online Resources
KEYWORD: MA11 TOC

Linear Functions

Tools for Success

Reading Math 324

Writing Math 344

Vocabulary 297, 298, 304, 310, 318, 333, 365, 373, 382

Study Strategy 299

Know-It Notes 302, 315, 316, 324, 330, 331, 345, 351, 361, 363, 369, 370, 371

Graphic Organizers 303, 309, 317, 327, 332, 339, 347, 355, 364, 372

Homework Help Online 304, 310, 318, 327, 333, 348, 355, 365, 373

Test Prep Exercises 306, 312, 321, 329, 335, 341, 350, 358, 367, 375

Multi-Step Test Prep 305, 312, 320, 329, 334, 340, 342, 349, 357, 366, 374, 376

College Entrance Exam Practice 387

Test Tackler 388

Standardized Test Prep 390

Systems of Equations and Inequalities

go.hrw.com
Online Resources
KEYWORD: MA11 TOC

Tools for Success

Reading and Writing Math

Writing Math 395
Vocabulary 393, 394, 400, 423, 432, 438, 444

Study Skills

Know-It Notes 404, 411, 414, 421, 429
Graphic Organizers 399, 407, 415, 423, 431, 437
Homework Help Online 400, 408, 415, 423, 432, 438

TEST PREP

Test Prep Exercises 401, 410, 417, 425, 434, 440
Multi-Step Test Prep 400, 409, 416, 424, 426, 433, 439, 442
College Entrance Exam Practice 449
Test Tackler 450
Standardized Test Prep 452

CHAPTER 7

Exponents and Polynomials

go.hrw.com
Online Resources
KEYWORD: MA11 TOC

Tools for Success

Factoring Polynomials

go.hrw.com
Online Resources
KEYWORD: MA11 TOC

Tools for Success

Reading Math 581
Writing Math 551
Vocabulary 541, 542, 544, 594

Know-It Notes 561, 578, 580, 588
Graphic Organizers 546, 554, 563, 571, 581, 588
Homework Help Online 547, 555, 564, 572, 582, 589

Test Prep Exercises 549, 557, 566, 574, 584, 590
Multi-Step Test Prep 549, 556, 565, 573, 576, 583, 590, 592
College Entrance Exam Practice 599
Test Tackler 600
Standardized Test Prep 602

CHAPTER 9

Quadratic Functions and Equations

Tools for Success

Reading Math 656

Writing Math 664

Vocabulary 607, 608, 614, 623, 645, 667, 675, 684

Study Strategy 609

Know-It Notes 612, 620, 621, 633, 635, 642, 650, 656, 663, 664, 670, 672, 674

Graphic Organizers 613, 623, 629, 636, 644, 653, 659, 666, 675

Homework Help Online 614, 623, 629, 637, 645, 653, 659, 667, 675

Test Prep Exercises 617, 625, 631, 639, 647, 655, 661, 669, 677

Multi-Step Test Prep 616, 625, 630, 638, 640, 646, 654, 660, 668, 677, 678

College Entrance Exam Practice 689

Test Tackler 690

Standardized Test Prep 692

Data Analysis and Probability

Tools for Success

Reading Math 702, 718, 745, 746

Writing Math 709

Vocabulary 695, 696, 705, 712, 720, 728, 740, 747, 754, 764, 774

Know-It Notes 738, 746, 751, 753, 760, 762, 763

Graphic Organizers 704, 711, 719, 727, 739, 747, 754, 763

Homework Help Online 705, 712, 720, 728, 740, 747, 754, 764

Test Prep Exercises 708, 714, 722, 730, 742, 749, 756, 766

Multi-Step Test Prep 707, 714, 722, 729, 734, 741, 748, 756, 766, 768

College Entrance Exam Practice 779

Test Tackler 780

Standardized Test Prep 782

CHAPTER
11

go.hrw.com
Online Resources
KEYWORD: MA11 TOC

Exponential and Radical Functions

Tools for Success

Reading and Writing Math

Reading Math 806
Writing Math 790
Vocabulary 787, 788, 793, 800, 809, 825, 832, 837, 850, 856

Study Skills

Study Strategy 789
Know-It Notes 799, 805, 806, 807, 815, 822, 823, 829, 830, 846, 850
Graphic Organizers 792, 799, 808, 816, 824, 832, 837, 842
Homework Help Online 793, 800, 809, 817, 825, 832, 837, 843, 850

TEST PREP

Test Prep Exercises 795, 802, 811, 819, 827, 834, 839, 845, 853
Multi-Step Test Prep 794, 801, 811, 818, 820, 826, 833, 838, 844, 852, 854
College Entrance Exam Practice 861
Test Tackler 862
Standardized Test Prep 864

Rational Functions and Equations

go.hrw.com
Online Resources
KEYWORD: MA11 TOC

Rational Functions and Expressions

Operations with Rational Expressions and Equations

Tools for Success

Reading Math 874
Writing Math 879
Vocabulary 867, 868, 875, 883, 890, 923, 930

Study Strategy 869
Know-It Notes 871, 873, 879, 882, 898, 900, 905, 913
Graphic Organizers 874, 882, 889, 901, 908, 917, 923
Homework Help Online 875, 883, 890, 902, 909, 917, 923

Test Prep Exercises 877, 885, 892, 904, 911, 919, 925
Multi-Step Test Prep 876, 884, 891, 896, 903, 910, 918, 924, 926
College Entrance Exam Practice 935
Test Tackler 936
Standardized Test Prep 938

WHO USES MATHEMATICS?

The Career Path features are a set of interviews with young adults who are either preparing for or just beginning in different career fields. These people share what math courses they studied in high school, how math is used in their field, and what options the future holds. Also, many exercises throughout the book highlight the different skills used in various career fields.

Career Path

go.hrw.com
Career Resources Online
KEYWORD: MA7 Career

Career Applications

Agriculture 677
Aquatics 644
Archaeology 124, 810
Architecture 622, 834
Aviation 86, 409, 928
Business 139, 433, 817
Careers 135, 303
City Planning 582
Communication 470, 877
Construction 109, 320, 890
Design 31
Economics 88
Education 24, 186, 200
Engineering 630, 875
Environmental Science 310
Farming 439
Finance 80, 409, 555
Landscaping 401
Law Enforcement 825
Manufacturing 124, 461
Marine Biology 616
Mechanics 875, 877
Medicine 463, 501
Meteorology 10, 209, 851
Military 439
Navigation 929
Nutrition 88, 148, 244
Photography 507, 517
Quality Control 739
Real Estate 131
Shipping 279
Technology 29, 766

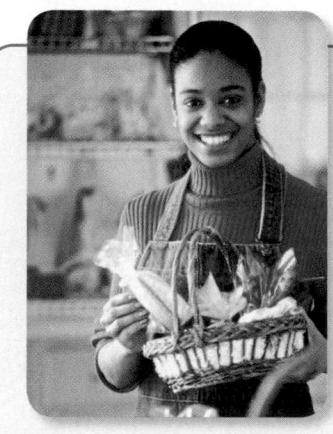

CULINARY ARTS *p. 202*
If you enjoy preparing food, you might be interested in a culinary arts program. Besides cooking, you can also learn business skills, like how to start and run your own catering business. See page 202 to find out what math courses will help prepare you for this career.

DATA MINING *p. 358*
Read the Career Path on page 358 to learn what courses a data mining major may take and what careers are available in this field. For example, do you like to keep track of sports statistics? If so, a background in data mining can help you find work with a professional sports team.

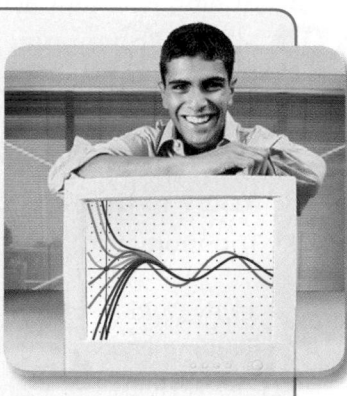

BIOSTATISTICS *p. 767*
The Career Path on page 767 describes the education and experience needed to be a successful biostatistician. One important job biostatisticians do is research and test medications to ensure that they are both effective and safe for human use.

WHY LEARN MATHEMATICS?

Links to interesting topics may accompany real-world applications in the examples or exercises. For a complete list of all applications in *Holt McDougal Algebra 1*, see page IN1 in the Index.

Find the given term of each arithmetic sequence.

Number Theory

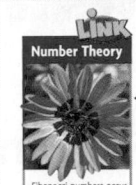

Fibonacci numbers occur frequently throughout nature. The number of petals on many flowers are numbers of the Fibonacci sequence. Two petals on a flower are rare but 3, 5, and even 34 petals are common.

34. 2.5, 8.5, 14.5, 20.5, …; 30th term

35. 189.6, 172.3, 155, 137.7, …; 18th term

36. $\frac{1}{4}, \frac{3}{4}, \frac{5}{4}, \frac{7}{4}$ …; 15th term

37. $\frac{2}{3}, \frac{11}{12}, \frac{7}{6}, \frac{17}{12}$ …; 25th term

38. Number Theory The sequence 1, 1, 2, 3, 5, 8, 13, … is a famous sequence called the Fibonacci sequence. After the first two terms, each term is the sum of the previous two terms.
  a. Write the first 10 terms of the Fibonacci sequence. Is the Fibonacci sequence arithmetic? Explain.
  b. Notice that the third term is divisible by 2. Are the 6th and 9th terms also divisible by 2? What conclusion can you draw about every third term? Why is this true?
  c. Can you find any other patterns? (*Hint:* Look at every 4th and 5th term.)

39. Entertainment Seats in a concert hall are arranged in the pattern shown.
  a. The numbers of seats in the rows form an arithmetic sequence. Write a rule for the arithmetic sequence.
  b. How many seats are in the 15th row?

Real-World LINKS

Animals 186

Art 565

Astronomy 10, 340

Automobiles 713

Biology 105, 311, **464**, 646, 891

Biology

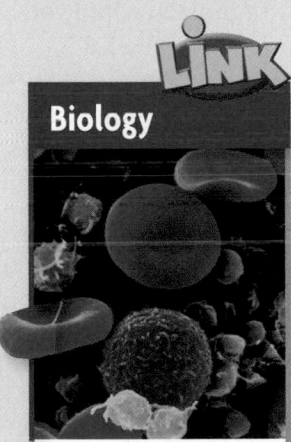

When bleeding occurs, platelets (which appear green in the image above) help to form a clot to reduce blood loss. Calcium and vitamin K are also necessary for clot formation.

Chemistry 209, 470

Diving 24

Ecology 271

Electricity 844

Engineering 624

Engineering

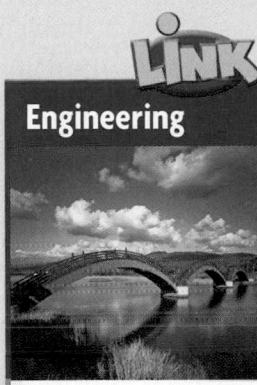

This arched bridge spans a river near the city of Yokote in northwestern Japan.

Geology 81, 424, 826

Health 180

History 97, 731, 765

Hobbies 374

Landscaping 401

Math History 58, 416, 526, 590, 834

Meteorology 851

Military 439

Music 548

Number Theory 280

Physics 660

Recreation 200

School 755

Science 356

Solar Energy 918

Sports 44, 125, 238, 518

Statistics 88

Technology 142, 773, 801

Transportation 254, 500

Travel 630, 910

Travel

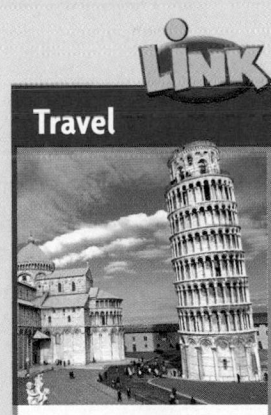

Building began on the Tower of Pisa, located in Pisa, Italy, in 1173. The tower started leaning after the third story was added. At the fifth story, attempts were made to correct the leaning. The tower was finally complete in 1350.

Focus on Problem Solving

The Problem-Solving Plan

To be a good problem solver you need a good problem-solving plan. Using a problem-solving plan along with a problem-solving strategy helps you organize your work and correctly solve the problem. The plan used in this book is outlined below.

UNDERSTAND the Problem

■ **What are you asked to find?**

Make sure you understand exactly what the problem is asking. Restate the problem in your own words.

■ **What information is given in the problem?**

List every piece of information the problem gives you.

■ **Is all the information relevant?**

Sometimes problems have extra information that is not needed to solve the problem. Try to determine what is and is not needed. This helps you stay organized when you are making a plan.

■ **Were you given enough information to solve the problem?**

Sometimes there simply is not enough information to solve the problem. List what else you need to know to solve the problem.

Make a PLAN

■ **What problem-solving strategy or strategies can you use to help you solve the problem?**

Think about strategies you have used in the past to solve problems. Would any of them be helpful in solving this problem?

■ **Create a step-by-step plan of how you will solve the problem.**

Write out your plan in words to help you get a clearer idea of how to solve the problem mathematically.

SOLVE

■ **Use your plan to solve the problem.**

Translate your plan from words to math. Show each step in your solution and write your answer in a complete sentence.

LOOK BACK

■ **Did you completely answer the question that was asked?**

Be sure you answered the question that was asked and that your answer is complete.

■ **Is your answer reasonable?**

Your answer should make sense.

■ **Could you have used a different strategy to solve the problem?**

Solving the problem again with a different strategy is a good way to check your answer.

■ **Did you learn anything that could help you solve similar problems in the future?**

You may want to take notes about this kind of problem and the strategy you used to solve it.

Using the Problem-Solving Plan

The feeder at an animal shelter needs 125 pounds of food to feed the rescued dogs for a month. A local grocery store is having a special—buy two 10-pound bags of dog food and get a 3.5-pound bag free. What is the fewest number of 10-pound bags the feeder can buy to have enough dog food for the month?

UNDERSTAND the Problem

List the important information in the problem.

At least 125 pounds of dog food are needed for one month.
If the feeder buys two 10-pound bags of dog food, she gets a 3.5-pound bag free.
What is the problem asking you to find?

The fewest number of 10-pound bags the feeder needs to buy to have 125 pounds of dog food.

Make a PLAN

Choose a strategy.

You can **make a table** to organize the number of bags purchased, the number of pounds in those bags, the number of free pounds, and the total number of pounds. Make a table and work out one column at a time until there are at least 125 pounds of food.

SOLVE

Use the strategy.

For every even number of bags, increase the number of free pounds by 3.5.

Number of Bags	1	2	3	4	5	6	7	8	9	10	11
Pounds	10	20	30	40	50	60	70	80	90	100	110
Free Pounds	0	3.5	3.5	7	7	10.5	10.5	14	14	17.5	17.5
Total Pounds	10	23.5	33.5	47	57	70.5	80.5	94	104	117.5	**127.5**

The fewest number of bags the feeder must buy is 11.

LOOK BACK

Check your answer.

Multiply the number of bags purchased by the weight of each bag. This is the number of pounds paid for: $11 \times 10 = 110$.

Then divide the number of bags purchased by 2, and multiply the whole number result by 3.5. This is the number of free pounds received because of the special: $11 \div 2 = 5.5$, $5 \times 3.5 = 17.5$.
Add the pounds: $110 + 17.5 = 127.5$.
The feeder only needs 125 pounds, so this is enough.

HOW TO STUDY ALGEBRA 1

This book has many features designed to help you learn and study effectively. Becoming familiar with these features will prepare you for greater success on your exams.

Learn

The **vocabulary** is listed at the beginning of every lesson.

Look for the **Know-It-Note** icons to identify important information.

Study the **examples** to apply new concepts and skills. Examples include stepped out solutions.

Test your understanding of examples by trying the **Check It Out** problems. Check your work in the Selected Answers.

Practice

Use a **graphic organizer** to summarize each lesson.

Refer to the examples from the lesson to solve the **Guided Practice** exercises.

If you get stuck, use the internet for **Homework Help Online**.

Review

Study and review **vocabulary** from the entire chapter.

Test yourself with **practice problems** from every lesson in the chapter.

Scavenger Hunt

Use this scavenger hunt to discover a few of the many tools in *Holt McDougal Algebra 1* that you can use to become an independent learner. On a separate sheet of paper, write the answers to each question below. Within each answer, one letter will be in a yellow box. After you have answered every question, identify the letters that would be in yellow boxes and rearrange them to reveal the answer to the question at the bottom of the page.

1. What is the first **Vocabulary** term in the Study Guide: Preview for Chapter 2?

□□□□□□□□

2. What keyword should you enter for **Homework Help** for Lesson 6-3?

□□□□□□

3. In Lesson 7-3, what is **Example 1** teaching you to find?

□□□□□□□□□ □□ □□□□□□

4. What are you asked to give an example of in the **Know-It Note** on page 563?

□□□□□□□□□

5. What college major is listed for the **Career Path** on page 567?

□□□□□□□□□□□□□□ □□□□□□□□

6. To what school subject is **Exercise 44** on page 470 linked?

□□□□□□□□□

7. In the **Study Guide: Review** for Chapter 10, what sport do Questions 4 and 5 refer to?

□□□□□□

8. In Chapter 5's **Test Tackler**, what multiple choice strategy is described?

□□□□□□□□□□ □□□□□□□□□□

FACT!

Algebra was used to build what ancient structures?

□□□□□□□□

Chapter

- Solve problems with real numbers.
- Make connections between verbal and algebraic representations.

Discovering the *"Magic"*

You can use the operations and properties in this chapter to complete a magic square.

go.hrw.com
Chapter Project Online
KEYWORD: MA7 ChProj

ARE YOU READY?

✓ Vocabulary

Match each term on the left with a definition on the right.

1. difference
2. factor
3. perimeter
4. area

A. the distance around a figure

B. a number that is multiplied by another number to form a product

C. a result of division

D. the number of square units a figure covers

E. a result of subtraction

✓ Whole Number Operations

Add, subtract, multiply, or divide.

5. $23 + 6$
6. $156 \div 12$
7. 18×96
8. $85 - 62$

✓ Add and Subtract Decimals

Add or subtract.

9. $2.18 + 6.9$
10. $0.32 - 0.18$
11. $29.34 + 0.27$
12. $4 - 1.82$

✓ Multiply Decimals

Multiply.

13. 0.7×0.6
14. 2.5×0.1
15. 1.5×1.5
16. 3.04×0.12

✓ Divide Decimals

Divide.

17. $6.15 \div 3$
18. $8.64 \div 2$
19. $7.2 \div 0.4$
20. $92.7 \div 0.3$

✓ Multiply and Divide Fractions

Multiply or divide. Give your answer in simplest form.

21. $\frac{3}{5} \times \frac{1}{2}$
22. $\frac{2}{3} \div \frac{1}{6}$
23. $\frac{7}{8} \times \frac{4}{7}$
24. $4 \div \frac{2}{3}$

✓ Add and Subtract Fractions

Add or subtract. Give your answer in simplest form.

25. $\frac{2}{5} + \frac{2}{5}$
26. $\frac{3}{8} - \frac{1}{8}$
27. $\frac{1}{2} + \frac{1}{4}$
28. $\frac{2}{3} - \frac{4}{9}$

Study Guide: Preview

Where You've Been

Previously, you

- learned words related to mathematical operations.
- identified numbers on a real number line.
- performed operations on whole numbers, decimals, and fractions.
- plotted points in the coordinate plane.

In This Chapter

You will study

- how to evaluate and simplify expressions.
- properties of the real number system.
- the order of operations.
- patterns formed by points plotted in the coordinate plane.

Where You're Going

You can use the skills in this chapter

- to form a solid foundation for the rest of this algebra course.
- in other classes, such as Biology, History, and Physics.
- to determine final costs, stock values, and profit.

Key Vocabulary/Vocabulario

additive inverse	inverso aditivo
coefficient	coeficiente
constant	constante
coordinate plane	plano cartesiano
irrational numbers	números irracionales
like terms	términos semejantes
origin	origen
rational numbers	números racionales
variable	variable

Vocabulary Connections

To become familiar with some of the vocabulary terms in the chapter, consider the following. You may refer to the chapter, the glossary, or a dictionary if you like.

1. The word **variable** comes from the word *vary*. What does *vary* mean? Which of the key vocabulary terms above has the opposite meaning?

2. Another word for *inverse* is *reverse*. The word *additive* relates to the operation of addition. What do you think an **additive inverse** is?

3. The prefix *ir-* means "not." What relationship do you think **rational numbers** and **irrational numbers** may have?

4. To *originate* means "to begin at." What do you think the **origin** of a coordinate plane is?

Reading and *Writing* **Math**

Reading Strategy: Use Your Book for Success

Understanding how your textbook is organized will help you locate and use helpful information.

Pay attention to the **margin notes.** Know-It Note icons point out key information. Writing Math notes, Helpful Hints, and Caution notes help you understand concepts and avoid common mistakes.

 **Know it!** *Note*

Writing Math
These expressions mean "2 times *y*":
$2y$ $2(y)$

Helpful Hint
A replacement set a set of numbers t can be substituted

Caution!
In the expression 5^2, 5 is the base because the nega

The **Glossary** is found in the back of your textbook. Use it as a resource when you need the definition of an unfamiliar word or property.

The **Index** is located at the end of your textbook. Use it to locate the page where a particular concept is taught.

The **Problem-Solving Handbook** is found in the back of your textbook. These pages review strategies that can help you solve real-world problems.

Glossary/Glos

 A ―――――――

ENGLISH
absolute value (p. 14) The absolute value of *x* is the distance from zero to *x* on a number line,

Index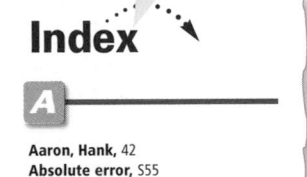

A ―――――――

Aaron, Hank, 42
Absolute error, 555
Absolute value, 14, 148
    equations, 148–149
    functions, 366–367

Problem Sol

Draw a Diagra
You can **draw a diagram**
the words of a problem are

 Try This

Use your textbook for the following problems.

1. Use the index to find the page where each term is defined: *algebraic expression, like terms, ordered pair, real numbers.*

2. What mnemonic device is taught in a Helpful Hint in Lesson 1-6, Order of Operations?

3. Use the glossary to find the definition of each term: *additive inverse, constant, perfect square, reciprocal.*

1-1 Variables and Expressions

Objectives
Translate between words and algebra.

Evaluate algebraic expressions.

Vocabulary
variable
constant
numerical expression
algebraic expression
evaluate

Why learn this?

Variables and expressions can be used to determine how many plastic drink bottles must be recycled to make enough carpet for a house.

Container City, in East London, UK, is a development of buildings made from recycled shipping containers.

A home that is "green built" uses many recycled products, including carpet made from recycled plastic drink bottles. You can determine how many square feet of carpet can be made from a certain number of plastic drink bottles by using *variables, constants,* and *expressions.*

A **variable** is a letter or symbol used to represent a value that can change.

A **constant** is a value that does not change.

A **numerical expression** may contain only constants and/or operations.

An **algebraic expression** may contain variables, constants, and/or operations.

You will need to translate between algebraic expressions and words to be successful in math. The diagram below shows some of the ways to write mathematical operations with words.

| Plus, sum, increased by | Minus, difference, less than | Times, product, equal groups of | Divided by, quotient |

EXAMPLE 1 Translating from Algebraic Symbols to Words

Give two ways to write each algebraic expression in words.

Writing Math

These expressions all mean "2 times *y*":
$2y$ $2(y)$
$2 \cdot y$ $(2)(y)$
$2 \times y$ $(2)y$

A $x + 3$
the sum of x and 3
x increased by 3

B $m - 7$
the difference of m and 7
7 less than m

C $2 \cdot y$
2 times y
the product of 2 and y

D $k \div 5$
k divided by 5
the quotient of k and 5

 Give two ways to write each algebraic expression in words.

1a. $4 - n$ **1b.** $\dfrac{t}{5}$ **1c.** $9 + q$ **1d.** $3(h)$

To translate words into algebraic expressions, look for words that indicate the action that is taking place.

Add	**Subtract**	**Multiply**	**Divide**
↑	↑	↑	↑
Put together, combine	Find how much more or less	Put together equal groups	Separate into equal groups

EXAMPLE 2 | **Translating from Words to Algebraic Symbols**

A Eve reads 25 pages per hour. Write an expression for the number of pages she reads in h hours.

h represents the number of hours that Eve reads.

$25 \cdot h$ or $25h$ *Think: h groups of 25 pages.*

B Sam is 2 years younger than Sue, who is y years old. Write an expression for Sam's age.

y represents Sue's age.

$y - 2$ *Think: "younger than" means "less than."*

C William runs a mile in 12 minutes. Write an expression for the number of miles that William runs in m minutes.

m represents the total time William runs.

$\dfrac{m}{12}$ *Think: How many groups of 12 are in m?*

 CHECK IT OUT!

2a. Lou drives at 65 mi/h. Write an expression for the number of miles that Lou drives in t hours.

2b. Miriam is 5 cm taller than her sister, who is m cm tall. Write an expression for Miriam's height in centimeters.

2c. Elaine earns $32 per day. Write an expression for the amount that she earns in d days.

To **evaluate** an expression is to find its value. To evaluate an algebraic expression, substitute numbers for the variables in the expression and then simplify the expression.

EXAMPLE 3 | **Evaluating Algebraic Expressions**

Evaluate each expression for $x = 8$, $y = 5$, and $z = 4$.

A $x + y$

$x + y = 8 + 5$ *Substitute 8 for x and 5 for y.*

$= 13$ *Simplify.*

B $\dfrac{x}{z}$

$\dfrac{x}{z} = \dfrac{8}{4}$ *Substitute 8 for x and 4 for z.*

$= 2$ *Simplify.*

 CHECK IT OUT!

Evaluate each expression for $m = 3$, $n = 2$, and $p = 9$.

3a. mn **3b.** $p - n$ **3c.** $p \div m$

EXAMPLE 4 *Recycling Application*

Approximately fourteen 20-ounce plastic drink bottles must be recycled to produce 1 square foot of carpet.

a. **Write an expression for the number of bottles needed to make *c* square feet of carpet.**

The expression $14c$ models the number of bottles needed to make c square feet of carpet.

Helpful Hint

A *replacement set* is a set of numbers that can be substituted for a variable. The replacement set in Example 4 is {40, 120, 224}.

b. **Find the number of bottles needed to make 40, 120, and 224 square feet of carpet.**

Evaluate $14c$ for $c = 40$, 120, and 224.

c	**14*c***
40	$14(40) = 560$
120	$14(120) = 1680$
224	$14(224) = 3136$

To make 40 ft² of carpet, 560 bottles are needed.
To make 120 ft² of carpet, 1680 bottles are needed.
To make 224 ft² of carpet, 3136 bottles are needed.

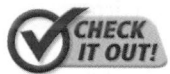

CHECK IT OUT!

4. To make one sweater, sixty-three 20-ounce plastic drink bottles must be recycled.

   a. Write an expression for the number of bottles needed to make *s* sweaters.

   b. Find the number of bottles needed to make 12, 25, and 50 sweaters.

THINK AND DISCUSS

1. Write two ways to suggest each of the following, using words or phrases: addition, subtraction, multiplication, division.

2. Explain the difference between a numerical expression and an algebraic expression.

3. **GET ORGANIZED** Copy and complete the graphic organizer. Next to each operation, write a word phrase in the left box and its corresponding algebraic expression in the right box.

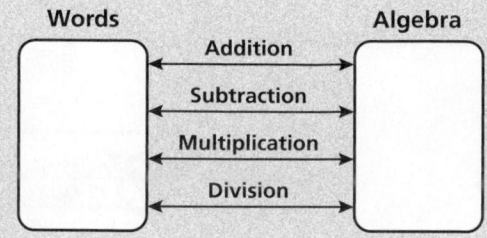

go.hrw.com
Homework Help Online
KEYWORD: MA7 1-1
Parent Resources Online
KEYWORD: MA7 Parent

GUIDED PRACTICE

1. **Vocabulary** A(n) ___?___ is a value that can change. (*algebraic expression*, *constant*, or *variable*)

SEE EXAMPLE 1
p. 6

Give two ways to write each algebraic expression in words.

2. $n - 5$ 3. $\dfrac{f}{3}$ 4. $c + 15$ 5. $9 - y$

6. $\dfrac{x}{12}$ 7. $t + 12$ 8. $8x$ 9. $x - 3$

SEE EXAMPLE 2
p. 7

10. George drives at 45 mi/h. Write an expression for the number of miles George travels in h hours.

11. The length of a rectangle is 4 units greater than its width w. Write an expression for the length of the rectangle.

SEE EXAMPLE 3
p. 7

Evaluate each expression for $a = 3$, $b = 4$, and $c = 2$.

12. $a - c$ 13. ab 14. $b \div c$ 15. ac

SEE EXAMPLE 4
p. 8

16. Brianna practices the piano 30 minutes each day.
    a. Write an expression for the number of hours she practices in d days.
    b. Find the number of hours Brianna practices in 2, 4, and 10 days.

PRACTICE AND PROBLEM SOLVING

Independent Practice

For Exercises	See Example
17–24	1
25–26	2
27–30	3
31	4

Extra Practice
Skills Practice p. S4
Application Practice p. S28

Give two ways to write each algebraic expression in words.

17. $5p$ 18. $4 - y$ 19. $3 + x$ 20. $3y$

21. $-3s$ 22. $r \div 5$ 23. $14 - t$ 24. $x + 0.5$

25. Friday's temperature was 20° warmer than Monday's temperature t. Write an expression for Friday's temperature.

26. Ann sleeps 8 hours per night. Write an expression for the number of hours Ann sleeps in n nights.

Evaluate each expression for $r = 6$, $s = 5$, and $t = 3$.

27. $r - s$ 28. $s + t$ 29. $r \div t$ 30. sr

31. Jim is paid for overtime when he works more than 40 hours per week.
    a. Write an expression for the number of hours he works overtime when he works h hours.
    b. Find the number of hours Jim works overtime when he works 40, 44, 48, and 52 hours.

32. **Write About It** Write a paragraph that explains to another student how to evaluate an expression.

Write an algebraic expression for each verbal expression. Then write a real-world situation that could be modeled by the expression.

33. the product of 2 and x 34. b less than 17   35. 10 more than y

36. This problem will prepare you for the Multi-Step Test Prep on page 38.

The air around you puts pressure on your body equal to 14.7 pounds per square inch (psi). When you are underwater, the water exerts additional pressure on your body. For each foot you are below the surface of the water, the pressure increases by 0.445 psi.

a. What does 14.7 represent in the expression $14.7 + 0.445d$?

b. What does d represent in the expression?

c. What is the total pressure exerted on a person's body when $d = 8$ ft?

37. Geometry The length of a rectangle is 9 inches. Write an expression for the area of the rectangle if the width is w inches. Find the area of the rectangle when the width is 1, 8, 9, and 11 inches.

38. Geometry The perimeter of any rectangle is the sum of its lengths and widths. The area of any rectangle is the length ℓ times the width w.

a. Write an expression for the perimeter of a rectangle.

b. Find the perimeter of the rectangle shown.

c. Write an expression for the area of a rectangle.

d. Find the area of the rectangle shown.

$\ell = 14$ cm

$w = 8$ cm

Complete each table. Evaluate the expression for each value of x.

39.

x	$x + 12$
1	
2	
3	
4	

40.

x	$10x$
1	
5	
10	
15	

41.

x	$x \div 2$
12	
20	
26	
30	

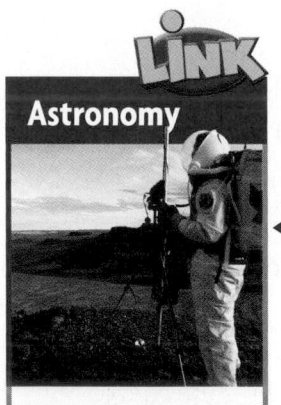

Astronomy

A crater on Canada's Devon Island is geologically similar to the surface of Mars. However, the temperature on Devon Island is about 37 °F in summer, and the average summer temperature on Mars is −85 °F.

42. Astronomy An object's weight on Mars can be found by multiplying 0.38 by the object's weight on Earth.

a. An object weighs p pounds on Earth. Write an expression for its weight on Mars.

b. Dana weighs 120 pounds, and her bicycle weighs 44 pounds. How much would Dana and her bicycle together weigh on Mars?

43. Meteorology Use the bar graph to write an expression for the average annual precipitation in New York, New York.

a. The average annual precipitation in New York is m inches more than the average annual precipitation in Houston, Texas.

b. The average annual precipitation in New York is s inches less than the average annual precipitation in Miami, Florida.

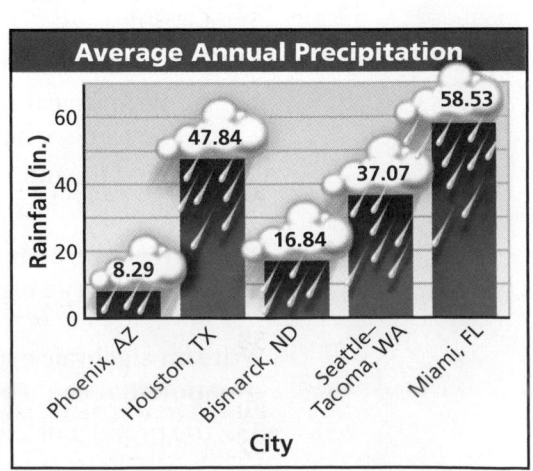

Average Annual Precipitation

Rainfall (in.)

Phoenix, AZ: 8.29
Houston, TX: 47.84
Bismarck, ND: 16.84
Seattle–Tacoma, WA: 37.07
Miami, FL: 58.53

City

44. Critical Thinking Compare algebraic expressions and numerical expressions. Give examples of each.

Write an algebraic expression for each verbal expression. Then evaluate the algebraic expression for the given values of *x*.

	Verbal	Algebraic	x = 12	x = 14
	x reduced by 5	x − 5	12 − 5 = 7	14 − 5 = 9
45.	7 more than x	■	■	■
46.	The quotient of x and 2	■	■	■
47.	The sum of x and 3	■	■	■

48. Claire has had her driver's license for 3 years. Bill has had his license for *b* fewer years than Claire. Which expression can be used to show the number of years Bill has had his driver's license?

Ⓐ 3 + b   Ⓑ b + 3   Ⓒ 3 − b   Ⓓ b − 3

49. Which expression represents *x*?

Ⓕ 12 − 5   Ⓗ 12(5)

Ⓖ 12 + 5   Ⓘ 12 ÷ 5

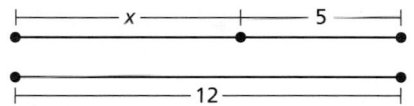

50. Which situation is best modeled by the expression 25 − *x*?

Ⓐ George places *x* more video games on a shelf with 25 games.

Ⓑ Sarah has driven *x* miles of a 25-mile trip.

Ⓒ Amelia paid 25 dollars of an *x* dollar lunch that she shared with Ariel.

Ⓓ Jorge has 25 boxes full of *x* baseball cards each.

CHALLENGE AND EXTEND

Evaluate each expression for the given values of the variables.

51. $2ab$; $a = 6$, $b = 3$ **52.** $2x + y$; $x = 4$, $y = 5$ **53.** $3x \div 6y$; $x = 6$, $y = 3$

54. Multi-Step An Internet service provider charges $9.95/month for the first 20 hours and $0.50 for each additional hour. Write an expression representing the charges for *h* hours of use in one month when *h* is more than 20 hours. What is the charge for 35 hours?

SPIRAL REVIEW

The sum of the angle measures in a triangle is 180°. Find the measure of the third angle given the other two angle measures. *(Previous course)*

55. 45° and 90°   **56.** 120° and 20°   **57.** 30° and 60°

Write an equivalent fraction for each percent. *(Previous course)*

58. 25%   **59.** 50%   **60.** 75%   **61.** 100%

Find a pattern and use it to give the next three numbers. *(Previous course)*

62. 4, 12, 20, 28, …   **63.** 3, 9, 27, 81, 243, …   **64.** 2, 3, 5, 8, 12, …

1-1 Technology LAB

Create a Table to Evaluate Expressions

You can use a graphing calculator to quickly evaluate expressions for many values of the variable.

Use with Lesson 1-1

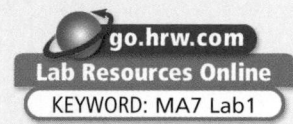

go.hrw.com
Lab Resources Online
KEYWORD: MA7 Lab1

Activity 1

Evaluate $2x + 7$ for $x = 25, 125, 225, 325,$ and 425.

1 Press **Y=** and enter **2X+7** for **Y1**.

2 Determine a pattern for the values of x.

The x-values start with 25 and increase by 100.

3 Press **2nd** **WINDOW** (TBLSET) to view the *Table Setup* window.

Enter **25** as the starting value in **TblStart=**.

Enter **100** as the amount by which x changes in **△Tbl=**.

4 Press **2nd** **GRAPH** (TABLE) to create a table of values.

The first column shows values of x starting with 25 and increasing by 100.

The second column shows values of the expression $2x + 7$ when x is equal to the value in the first column.

You can use the arrow keys to view the table when x is greater than 625.

Try This

1. Use the table feature of a graphing calculator to evaluate $5x - 7$ for $x = 4, 6, 8, 10,$ and 12.

   a. What value did you enter in **TblStart=**?

   b. What value did you enter in **△Tbl=**?

2. Use the table feature of a graphing calculator to evaluate $3x + 4$ for $x = -5, -1, 3, 7,$ and 11.

   a. What value did you enter in **TblStart=**?

   b. What value did you enter in **△Tbl=**?

You can also use a spreadsheet program to evaluate expressions.

Activity 2

Evaluate $2x + 7$ for $x = 3, 5, 7, 9,$ and 11.

1 In the first column, enter the values 3, 5, 7, 9, and 11.

	126	▼		f_x			
	A	B	C	D	E	F	G
1	3						
2	5						
3	7						
4	9						
5	11						
6							

2 Enter the expression in cell B1.

To do this, type the following:
= 2 * A1 + 7

	SUM	▼ X ✓	f_x =2*A1+7				
	A	B	C	D	E	F	G
1	3	=2*A1+7					
2	5						
3	7						
4	9						
5	11						
6							

3 Press Enter.

The value of $2x + 7$ when $x = 3$ appears in cell B1.

	B1	▼	f_x =2*A1+7				
	A	B	C	D	E	F	G
1	3	13					
2	5						
3	7						
4	9						
5	11						
6							

4 Copy the formula into cells B2, B3, B4, and B5.

Use the mouse to click on the lower right corner of cell B1. Hold down the mouse button and drag the cursor through cell B5.

	B1	▼	f_x =2*A1+7				
	A	B	C	D	E	F	G
1	3	13					
2	5	17					
3	7	21					
4	9	25					
5	11	29					
6							

For each row in column B, the number that is substituted for x is the value in the same row of column A.

	B2	▼	f_x =2*A2+7				
	A	B	C	D	E	F	G
1	3	13					
2	5	17					
3	7	21					
4	9	25					
5	11	29					
6							

You can continue the table by entering more values in column A and copying the formula from B1 into more cells in column B.

Try This

3. Use a spreadsheet program to evaluate $-2x + 9$ for $x = -5, -2, 1, 4,$ and 7.

   a. What values did you enter in column A?

   b. What did you type in cell B1?

4. Use a spreadsheet program to evaluate $7x - 10$ for $x = 2, 7, 12, 17,$ and 22.

   a. What values did you enter in column A?

   b. What did you type in cell B1?

Adding and Subtracting Real Numbers

Objectives
Add real numbers.

Subtract real numbers.

Vocabulary
real numbers
absolute value
opposites
additive inverse

Why learn this?
The total length of a penguin's dive can be determined by adding real numbers. (See Example 4.)

The set of all numbers that can be represented on a number line are called **real numbers**. You can use a number line to model addition and subtraction of real numbers.

Addition
To model addition of a positive number, move right. To model addition of a negative number, move left.

Subtraction
To model subtraction of a positive number, move left.
To model subtraction of a negative number, move right.

EXAMPLE 1 **Adding and Subtracting Numbers on a Number Line**

Add or subtract using a number line.

A $-3 + 6$

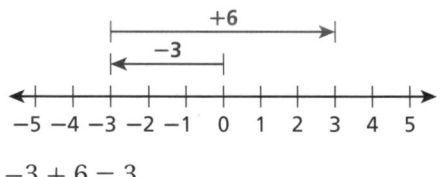

$-3 + 6 = 3$

Start at 0. Move left to −3.

To add 6, move right 6 units.

B $-2 - (-9)$

$-2 - (-9) = 7$

Start at 0. Move left to −2.

To subtract −9, move right 9 units.

 CHECK IT OUT! Add or subtract using a number line.

1a. $-3 + 7$ **1b.** $-3 - 7$ **1c.** $-5 - (-6.5)$

The **absolute value** of a number is its distance from zero on a number line. The absolute value of 5 is written as $|5|$.

5 units   5 units

$|5| = 5$

$|-5| = 5$

Know it!
Note

Adding Real Numbers

WORDS	NUMBERS	
Adding Numbers with the Same Sign Add the absolute values and use the sign of the numbers.	$3 + 6$ 9	$-2 + (-9)$ -11
Adding Numbers with Different Signs Subtract the absolute values and use the sign of the number with the greater absolute value.	$-8 + 12$ 4	$3 + (-15)$ -12

EXAMPLE 2 **Adding Real Numbers**

Add.

A $-3 + (-16)$
$(3 + 16 = 19)$
-19

Same signs: add the absolute values.
Both numbers are negative, so the sum is negative.

B $-13 + 7$
$(13 - 7 = 6)$
-6

Different signs: subtract the absolute values.
Use the sign of the number with the greater absolute value.

C $6.2 + (-4.9)$
$(6.2 - 4.9 = 1.3)$
1.3

Different signs: subtract the absolute values.
Use the sign of the number with the greater absolute value.

CHECK
IT OUT!
Add.
2a. $-5 + (-7)$ **2b.** $-13.5 + (-22.3)$ **2c.** $52 + (-68)$

Two numbers are **opposites** if their sum is 0. A number and its opposite are **additive inverses** and are the same distance from zero. They have the same absolute value.

Inverse Property of Addition

WORDS	NUMBERS	ALGEBRA
The sum of a real number and its opposite is 0.	$6 + (-6) = (-6) + 6 = 0$	For any real number a, $a + (-a) = (-a) + a = 0$

To subtract signed numbers, you can use additive inverses. Subtracting a number is the same as adding the opposite of the number.

Subtracting Real Numbers

WORDS	NUMBERS	ALGEBRA
To subtract a number, add its opposite. Then follow the rules for adding signed numbers.	$3 - 8 = 3 + (-8)$ $= -5$	$a - b = a + (-b)$

EXAMPLE 3 **Subtracting Real Numbers**

Subtract.

A $7 - 10$

$7 - 10 = 7 + (-10)$ *To subtract 10, add −10.*

$(10 - 7 = 3)$ *Different signs: subtract absolute values.*

-3 *Use the sign of the number with the greater absolute value.*

Helpful Hint

On many scientific and graphing calculators, there is one button to express the opposite of a number and a different button to express subtraction.

B $-3 - (-12)$

$-3 - (-12) = -3 + 12$ *To subtract −12, add 12.*

$(12 - 3 = 9)$ *Different signs: subtract absolute values.*

9 *Use the sign of the number with the greater absolute value.*

C $-\dfrac{1}{8} - \dfrac{3}{8}$

$-\dfrac{1}{8} - \dfrac{3}{8} = -\dfrac{1}{8} + \left(-\dfrac{3}{8}\right)$ *To subtract $\dfrac{3}{8}$, add $-\dfrac{3}{8}$.*

     Same signs: add absolute values.

$\left(\dfrac{1}{8} + \dfrac{3}{8} = \dfrac{4}{8} = \dfrac{1}{2}\right)$ *Both numbers are negative, so the sum is negative.*

$-\dfrac{1}{2}$

D $22.5 - (-4)$

$22.5 - (-4) = 22.5 + 4$ *To subtract −4, add 4.*

$(22.5 + 4 = 26.5)$ *Same signs: add absolute values.*

26.5 *Both numbers are positive, so the sum is positive.*

 Subtract.

3a. $13 - 21$ **3b.** $\dfrac{1}{2} - \left(-3\dfrac{1}{2}\right)$ **3c.** $-14 - (-12)$

EXAMPLE 4 *Biology Application*

An emperor penguin stands on an iceberg that extends 10 feet above the water. Then the penguin dives to an elevation of −67 feet to catch a fish. What is the total length of the penguin's dive?

elevation of iceberg	minus	elevation of fish
10	−	−67

$10 - (-67) = 10 + 67$ *To subtract −67, add 67.*

$ = 77$ *Same signs: add absolute values.*

The total length of the penguin's dive is 77 feet.

 4. What if...? The tallest known iceberg in the North Atlantic rose 550 feet above the ocean's surface. How many feet would it be from the top of the tallest iceberg to the wreckage of the *Titanic*, which is at an elevation of −12,468 feet?

1-2 Exercises

go.hrw.com
Homework Help Online
KEYWORD: MA11 1-2
Parent Resources Online
KEYWORD: MA7 Parent

GUIDED PRACTICE

1. Vocabulary The sum of a number and its ___?___ is always zero. (*opposite* or *absolute value*)

SEE EXAMPLE **1** p. 14

Add or subtract using a number line.

2. $-4 + 7$ **3.** $-3.5 - 5$ **4.** $5.6 - 9.2$ **5.** $3 - \left(-6\frac{1}{4}\right)$

SEE EXAMPLE **2** p. 15

Add.

6. $91 + (-11)$ **7.** $4\frac{3}{4} + \left(-3\frac{3}{4}\right)$ **8.** $15.6 + (-17.9)$ **9.** $-\frac{1}{16} + \frac{5}{8}$

SEE EXAMPLE **3** p. 16

Subtract.

10. $23 - 36$ **11.** $4.3 - 8.4$ **12.** $1\frac{1}{5} - 2\frac{4}{5}$ **13.** $\frac{7}{10} - \left(-\frac{2}{5}\right)$

SEE EXAMPLE **4** p. 16

14. Economics The Dow Jones Industrial Average (DJIA) reports the average prices of stocks for 30 companies. Use the table to determine the total decrease in the DJIA for the two days.

DJIA 1987	
Friday, Oct. 16	-108.35
Monday, Oct. 19	-507.99

PRACTICE AND PROBLEM SOLVING

Independent Practice

For Exercises	See Example
15–18	1
19–22	2
23–26	3
27	4

Extra Practice

Skills Practice p. S4
Application Practice p. S28

Add or subtract using a number line.

15. $-2 + 6$ **16.** $6 + (-2)$ **17.** $\frac{1}{4} - 12$ **18.** $-\frac{2}{5} + 6$

Add.

19. $-18 + (-12)$ **20.** $-2.3 + 3.5$ **21.** $-15 + 29$ **22.** $-4.8 + (-5.4)$

Subtract.

23. $12 - 22$ **24.** $-\frac{3}{4} - \left(-\frac{1}{4}\right)$ **25.** $38 - 24.6$ **26.** $\frac{2}{3} - \left(-\frac{1}{2}\right)$

27. Meteorology A meteorologist reported that the day's high temperature was 17 °F and the low temperature was -6 °F. What was the difference between the day's high and low temperatures?

Evaluate the expression $n + (-5)$ for each value of n.

28. $n = 312$ **29.** $n = 5.75$ **30.** $n = -\dfrac{7}{12}$ **31.** $n = -7\dfrac{2}{5}$

Add or subtract.

32. $-8 - 3$ **33.** $-9 + (-3)$ **34.** $16 - (-16)$ **35.** $100 - 63$

36. $5.2 - 2.5$ **37.** $-4.7 - (-4.7)$ **38.** $\dfrac{2}{5} - \dfrac{7}{8}$ **39.** $\dfrac{2}{5} - \dfrac{3}{10}$

40. Business A restaurant manager lost \$415 in business during the month of January. Business picked up in February, and he ended that month with a profit of \$1580.

     a. What was the manager's profit after January and February?

     b. What if...? The restaurant lost \$245 in business during the month of March. What was the manager's profit after January, February, and March?

Compare. Write $<$, $>$, or $=$.

41. $-4 - (-6)$ ▨ $-7 - 3$ **42.** $|-51|$ ▨ $|0|$ **43.** $3 - (-3)$ ▨ $0 - (-3)$

44. $-3 - 8$ ▨ $-22 + 11$ **45.** $|-10 + 5|$ ▨ $|-15|$ **46.** $9 + (-8)$ ▨ $-12 + 13$

47. Travel Death Valley National Park is located in California. Use the table to determine the difference in elevation between the highest and lowest locations.

Death Valley National Park	
Location	**Elevation (ft)**
Badwater	−282
Emigrant Pass	5,318
Furnace Creek Airport	−210
Telescope Peak	11,049

Critical Thinking Tell whether each statement is sometimes, always, or never true. Explain.

48. The value of the expression $-2 + n$ is less than the value of n.

49. When b is positive, the expression $-b + (-b)$ is equal to 0.

50. When x is negative, the value of the expression $x + 1$ is negative.

51. **///ERROR ANALYSIS///** Which is incorrect? Explain the error.

MULTI-STEP TEST PREP

52. This problem will prepare you for the Multi-Step Test Prep on page 38.

     a. A plane flies at a height of 1800 feet directly over a 150-foot-tall building. How far above the building is the plane? Draw a diagram to explain your answer.

     b. The same plane then flies directly over a diver who is 80 feet below the surface of the water. How far is the plane above the diver? Draw a diagram to explain your answer.

     c. Subtract the diver's altitude of −80 feet from the plane's altitude of 1800 feet. Explain why this distance is greater than 1800 feet.

53. Write About It Explain why addition and subtraction are called inverse operations. Use the following examples in your explanation:

$$8 + (-2) = 8 - 2 \qquad 8 - (-2) = 8 + 2$$

54. Which expression is equivalent to $|-3 + 5|$?

    Ⓐ $-3 - 5$ Ⓑ $-3 + 5$ Ⓒ $3 - 5$ Ⓓ $3 + 5$

55. At midnight, the temperature was -12 °F. By noon, the temperature had risen 25 °F. During the afternoon, it fell 10 °F and fell another 3 °F by midnight. What was the temperature at midnight?

    Ⓕ   0 °F   Ⓖ   3 °F   Ⓗ   12 °F   Ⓙ   24 °F

56. The table shows the amounts Mr. Espinosa spent on lunch each day one week. What is the total amount Mr. Espinosa spent for lunch this week?

Day	Monday	Tuesday	Wednesday	Thursday	Friday
Amount ($)	5.40	4.16	7.07	5.40	9.52

    Ⓐ $21.83   Ⓑ $22.03   Ⓒ $31.55   Ⓓ $36.95

CHALLENGE AND EXTEND

Simplify each expression.

57. $-1\frac{1}{5} + (-7.8)$ **58.** $-\frac{1}{5} + 2.1$ **59.** $9.75 + \left(-7\frac{3}{4}\right)$ **60.** $-2\frac{3}{10} + 8.5$

For each pattern shown below, describe a possible rule for finding the next term. Then use your rule to write the next 3 terms.

61. 14, 10, 6, 2, …   **62.** $-2, -\frac{8}{5}, -\frac{6}{5}, -\frac{4}{5}, …$

63. Geography Sam visited two volcanoes, Cotapaxi and Sangay, and two caves, Sistema Huautla and Sistema Cheve. Cotapaxi, in Ecuador, has an elevation of 19,347 ft. Sangay, also in Ecuador, has an elevation of 17,159 ft. The main entrance of Sistema Huautla, in Mexico, has an elevation of 5051 ft. The main entrance of Sistema Cheve, also in Mexico, has an elevation of 9085 ft. What is the average elevation of these places?

SPIRAL REVIEW

Write each number as a terminating or repeating decimal. *(Previous course)*

64. $\frac{3}{16}$ **65.** $\frac{2}{9}$ **66.** $\frac{15}{12}$ **67.** $\frac{4}{11}$

Divide each polygon into triangles to find the sum of its angle measures. (**Hint:** Remember that the sum of the angle measures in a triangle is 180°.) *(Previous course)*

68.   **69.**   **70.**

1-3 Multiplying and Dividing Real Numbers

Objectives
Multiply real numbers.

Divide real numbers.

Vocabulary
reciprocal
multiplicative inverse

Who uses this?
Hot-air balloon pilots can determine how far away from liftoff they will land by using multiplication. (See Example 4.)

When you multiply or divide two numbers, the signs of the numbers determine whether the result is positive or negative.

Numbers	Product/Quotient
Both positive	Positive
One negative	Negative
Both negative	Positive

Multiplying and Dividing Real Numbers

WORDS	NUMBERS	
Multiplying and Dividing Numbers with the Same Sign		
If two numbers have the same sign, their product or quotient is positive.	$4 \cdot 5 = 20$	$-15 \div (-3) = 5$
Multiplying and Dividing Numbers with Different Signs		
If two numbers have different signs, their product or quotient is negative.	$6(-3) = -18$ $(-7)2 = -14$	$-18 \div 2 = -9$ $10 \div (-5) = -2$

EXAMPLE **1** **Multiplying and Dividing Signed Numbers**

Find the value of each expression.

A $-12 \cdot 5$

-60 *The product of two numbers with different signs is negative.*

B $8\left(-\dfrac{5}{4}\right)$

$= \left(\dfrac{8}{1}\right)\left(-\dfrac{5}{4}\right) = -\dfrac{40}{4}$ *Multiply.*

$= -10$ *The quotient of two numbers with different signs is negative.*

 Find the value of each expression.

1a. $35 \div (-5)$ **1b.** $-11(-4)$ **1c.** $-6(7)$

Two numbers are **reciprocals** if their product is 1. A number and its reciprocal are called **multiplicative inverses** .

Inverse Property of Multiplication

WORDS	NUMBERS	ALGEBRA
The product of a nonzero real number and its reciprocal is 1.	$4 \cdot \dfrac{1}{4} = \dfrac{1}{4} \cdot 4 = 1$ $-3 \cdot \left(-\dfrac{1}{3}\right) = -\dfrac{1}{3} \cdot (-3) = 1$	For any real number a ($a \neq 0$), $a \cdot \dfrac{1}{a} = \dfrac{1}{a} \cdot a = 1$

To divide by a number, you can multiply by its multiplicative inverse.

EXAMPLE 2 **Dividing with Fractions**

Divide.

A $-\dfrac{4}{5} \div \left(-\dfrac{8}{15}\right)$

$$-\dfrac{4}{5} \div \left(-\dfrac{8}{15}\right) = -\dfrac{4}{5}\left(-\dfrac{15}{8}\right)$$ *To divide by $-\dfrac{8}{15}$, multiply by $-\dfrac{15}{8}$.*

$$= \dfrac{(-4)(-15)}{5(8)}$$ *Multiply the numerators and multiply the denominators.*

$$= \dfrac{60}{40} = \dfrac{3}{2}$$ *$-\dfrac{4}{5}$ and $-\dfrac{8}{15}$ have the same sign, so the quotient is positive.*

B $-4 \div 9\dfrac{1}{4}$

$$-4 : 9\dfrac{1}{4} = -\dfrac{4}{1} \div \dfrac{37}{4}$$ *Write 4 as a fraction with a denominator of 1. Write $9\dfrac{1}{4}$ as an improper fraction.*

$$= -\dfrac{4}{1} \cdot \dfrac{4}{37}$$ *To divide by $\dfrac{37}{4}$, multiply by $\dfrac{4}{37}$.*

$$= -\dfrac{4(4)}{1(37)} = -\dfrac{16}{37}$$ *-4 and $9\dfrac{1}{4}$ have different signs, so the quotient is negative.*

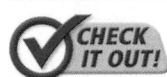 **Divide.**

2a. $-\dfrac{3}{4} \div (-9)$ **2b.** $\dfrac{3}{10} \div \left(-\dfrac{6}{5}\right)$ **2c.** $-\dfrac{5}{6} \div 1\dfrac{2}{3}$

The number 0 has special properties for multiplication and division.

Properties of Zero

WORDS	NUMBERS	ALGEBRA
Multiplication by Zero The product of any number and 0 is 0.	$\dfrac{1}{3} \cdot 0 = 0 \quad 0(-17) = 0$	$a \cdot 0 = 0 \quad 0 \cdot a = 0$
Zero Divided by a Number The quotient of 0 and any nonzero number is 0.	$\dfrac{0}{6} = 0 \quad 0 \div \dfrac{2}{3} = 0$	$\dfrac{0}{a} = 0 \quad (a \neq 0)$
Division by Zero Division by 0 is undefined.	$12 \div 0$ ✗ $\qquad \dfrac{-5}{0}$ ✗	$a \div 0$ ✗ $\qquad \dfrac{a}{0}$ ✗

E X A M P L E 3 Multiplying and Dividing with Zero

Multiply or divide if possible.

A $0 \div 16.568$ *Zero is divided by a nonzero number.*
   0 *The quotient of zero and any nonzero number is 0.*

B $63\dfrac{7}{8} \div 0$ *A number is divided by zero.*
                   Division by zero is undefined.
   undefined

C $1 \cdot 0$ *A number is multiplied by zero.*
   0 *The product of any number and 0 is 0.*

 Multiply or divide if possible.

3a. $0 \div \left(-8\dfrac{1}{6}\right)$ **3b.** $2.04 \div 0$ **3c.** $(-12{,}350)(0)$

E X A M P L E 4 *Recreation Application*

A hot-air balloon is taken for a 2.5-hour trip. The wind speed (and the speed of the balloon) is 4.75 mi/h. The balloon travels in a straight line parallel to the ground. How many miles away from the liftoff site will the balloon land?

Find the distance traveled at a rate of 4.75 mi/h for 2.5 hours. To find distance, multiply rate by time.

rate	times	time
4.75	•	2.5

$4.75 \cdot 2.5$
11.875

The hot-air balloon will land 11.875 miles from the liftoff site.

 4. What if...? On another hot-air balloon trip, the wind speed is 5.25 mi/h. The trip is planned for 1.5 hours. The balloon travels in a straight line parallel to the ground. How many miles away from the liftoff site will the balloon land?

THINK AND DISCUSS

1. Explain how to use mental math to find the missing value: $\frac{4}{5} \cdot ? = 1$.

2. GET ORGANIZED Copy and complete the graphic organizer. In each blank, write "pos" or "neg" to indicate positive or negative.

Multiplying and Dividing Numbers	
Multiplication	**Division**
pos × ☐ = pos	pos ÷ ☐ = pos
pos × ☐ = neg	pos ÷ ☐ = neg
neg × ☐ = neg	neg ÷ ☐ = neg
neg × ☐ = pos	neg ÷ ☐ = pos

1-3
Exercises

go.hrw.com
Homework Help Online
KEYWORD: MA11 1-3
Parent Resources Online
KEYWORD: MA7 Parent

GUIDED PRACTICE

1. **Vocabulary** How do you find the *reciprocal* of $\frac{1}{2}$?

SEE EXAMPLE 1
p. 20

Find the value of each expression.

2. $-72 \div (-9)$ 3. $11(-11)$ 4. $-7.2 \div 3.6$

SEE EXAMPLE 2
p. 21

Divide.

5. $5 \div \frac{5}{7}$ 6. $\frac{4}{5} \div \left(-\frac{7}{5}\right)$ 7. $-\frac{2}{3} \div \left(-\frac{1}{3}\right)$ 8. $-\frac{16}{25} \div \left(-\frac{4}{5}\right)$

SEE EXAMPLE 3
p. 22

Multiply or divide if possible.

9. $3.8 \div 0$ 10. $0(-27)$ 11. $0 \div \frac{2}{3}$ 12. $\frac{7}{8} \div 0$

SEE EXAMPLE 4
p. 22

13. **Entertainment** It is estimated that 7 million people saw off-Broadway shows in 2002. Assume that the average price of a ticket was $30. How much money was spent on tickets for off-Broadway shows in 2002?

PRACTICE AND PROBLEM SOLVING

Independent Practice

For Exercises	See Example
14–16	1
17–20	2
21–24	3
25	4

Extra Practice
Skills Practice p. S4
Application Practice p. S28

Find the value of each expression.

14. $-30 \div (-6)$ 15. $8(-4)$ 16. $-25(-12)$

Divide.

17. $-\frac{3}{20} \div \left(-\frac{1}{6}\right)$ 18. $\frac{3}{14} \div \frac{15}{28}$ 19. $-4\frac{1}{2} \div 1\frac{1}{2}$ 20. $2\frac{3}{4} \div \left(-1\frac{1}{2}\right)$

Multiply or divide if possible.

21. $0 \cdot 15$ 22. $-0.25 \div 0$ 23. $0 \div 1$ 24. $\frac{0}{1} \div 3$

25. **Weather** A cold front changes the temperature by -3 °F each day. If the temperature started at 0 °F, what will the temperature be after 5 days?

Multiply or divide.

26. $21 \div (-3)$ 27. $-100 \div 25$ 28. $-6 \div (-14)$ 29. $-6.2(10)$

30. $\frac{1}{2} \div \frac{1}{2}$ 31. $-3.75(-5)$ 32. $-12\frac{1}{2}(-3)$ 33. $17\left(\frac{1}{17}\right)$

34. **Critical Thinking** What positive number is the same as its reciprocal?

Evaluate each expression for $a = 4$, $b = -3$, and $c = -\frac{1}{2}$.

35. ab 36. $a \div c$ 37. bc 38. $c \div a$

Let p represent a positive number, n represent a negative number, and z represent zero. Tell whether each expression is positive, negative, zero, or undefined.

39. pn 40. pnz 41. $\frac{n}{p}$ 42. $-pz$

43. $-\frac{p}{n}$ 44. $-(pn)$ 45. $\frac{pn}{z}$ 46. $\frac{z}{n}$

Evaluate the expression $y \div \frac{3}{4}$ for each value of y.

47. $y = \frac{3}{4}$ **48.** $y = -\frac{9}{16}$ **49.** $y = \frac{3}{8}$ **50.** $y = -2\frac{1}{4}$

Evaluate the expression $\frac{1}{2} \div m$ for each value of m.

51. $m = -\frac{5}{2}$ **52.** $m = \frac{7}{8}$ **53.** $m = \frac{4}{9}$ **54.** $m = -5$

Diving

55. Education Benjamin must have 120 credit hours of instruction to receive his college degree. Benjamin wants to graduate in 8 semesters without attending summer sessions. How many credit hours must Benjamin take on average each semester to graduate in 8 semesters?

56. Diving An underwater exploration team is swimming at a depth of -20 feet. Then they dive to an underwater cave that is at 7 times this depth. What is the depth of the underwater cave?

Florida is home to more than 300 freshwater springs, some of which are explored by cave divers.

Multiply or divide. Then compare using $<$, $>$, or $=$.

57. $10\left(-\frac{1}{2}\right)$ ▥ $20 \div 4$ **58.** $16 \div (-2)$ ▥ $-2(-4)$ **59.** $-2\frac{2}{3} \div 3$ ▥ $5(-2.4)$

60. $20 \div 4$ ▥ $\frac{3}{4} \div \left(-\frac{1}{2}\right)$ **61.** $2.1(-3.4)$ ▥ $-3.4(2.1)$ **62.** $0\left(-\frac{3}{5}\right)$ ▥ $\frac{1}{2} \div \frac{1}{2}$

63. Critical Thinking There is a relationship between the number of negative factors and the sign of the product.

   a. What is the sign of the product of an even number of negative factors?

   b. What is the sign of the product of an odd number of negative factors?

   c. Explain why the number of negative factors affects the sign of the product.

   d. Does the number of positive factors affect the sign of the product? Explain.

Write each division expression as a multiplication expression.

64. $12 \div (-3)$ **65.** $75 \div 15$ **66.** $\frac{80}{-8}$ **67.** $\frac{-121}{11}$

Determine whether each statement is sometimes, always, or never true. Explain.

68. When t is negative, the expression $\frac{t}{10}$ is negative.

69. When n is positive, the expression $-6n$ is positive.

70. The value of the expression $4c$ is greater than the value of c.

71. Write About It The product of two factors is positive. One of the factors is negative. Explain how you can determine the sign of the second factor.

MULTI-STEP TEST PREP

72. This problem will prepare you for the Multi-Step Test Prep on page 38.

   a. You swam 20 feet in 5 seconds. Use the formula $r = \frac{d}{t}$ to determine how fast you were swimming.

   b. A diver descended at a rate of 15 feet per minute. Make a table to show the diver's depth after 1, 2, and 5 minutes.

   c. Show two ways to find how far the diver descended in 5 minutes. Remember that multiplication is repeated addition.

73. A recipe for lemonade calls for $1\frac{1}{2}$ cups of lemon juice per batch. Berto estimates that he can get about $\frac{1}{4}$ cup of lemon juice from each lemon that he squeezes. Lemons cost $0.45 each. What is the approximate amount Berto will need to spend on lemons to make a batch of lemonade?

    Ⓐ $0.70   Ⓑ $1.70   Ⓒ $2.70   Ⓓ $3.70

74. Robyn is buying carpet for her bedroom floor, which is a 15-foot-by-12-foot rectangle. If carpeting costs $1.25 per square foot, how much will it cost Robyn to carpet her bedroom?

    Ⓕ $68   Ⓖ $144   Ⓗ $180   Ⓙ $225

75. Short Response In music notation, a half note is played $\frac{1}{2}$ the length of a whole note. A quarter note is played $\frac{1}{4}$ the length of a whole note. In a piece of music, the clarinets play 8 half notes. In the same length of time, the flutes play x quarter notes. Determine how many quarter notes the flutes play. Explain your method.

CHALLENGE AND EXTEND

Find the value of each expression.

76. $(-2)(-2)(-2)$

77. $\frac{5}{7} \cdot \frac{5}{7}$

78. $5\left(-\frac{4}{5}\right)\left(-\frac{3}{4}\right)$

79. $\left|-\frac{1}{4}\right| \cdot |20|$

80. $5 \cdot 4 \cdot 3 \cdot 2 \cdot 1$

81. $\left|-\frac{2}{5}\right| \cdot \left|\frac{5}{2}\right|$

82. $\frac{1}{2} \cdot \frac{2}{3} \cdot \frac{3}{4} \cdot \frac{4}{5}$

83. $\left(-\frac{3}{4}\right)\left(-\frac{3}{4}\right)\left(-\frac{3}{4}\right)$

84. $|(-4)(-4)(-4)|$

For each pattern shown below, describe a possible rule for finding the next term. Then use your rule to write the next 3 terms.

85. $-1, 2, -4, 8, \ldots$

86. $\frac{1}{63}, -\frac{1}{21}, \frac{1}{7}, -\frac{3}{7}, \ldots$

87. $-5, 10, -15, 20, -25, \ldots$

88. $0.5, 0.25, 0.125, 0.0625, \ldots$

89. A cleaning service charges $49.00 to clean a one-bedroom apartment. If the work takes longer than 2 hours, the service charges $18.00 for each additional hour. What would be the total cost for a job that took 4 hours to complete?

SPIRAL REVIEW

Find the surface area of each rectangular prism. *(Previous course)*

90.

91.

92. A prepaid phone card has a credit of 200 minutes. Write an expression for the number of minutes left on the card after t minutes have been used. *(Lesson 1-1)*

Compare. Write $<$, $>$, or $=$. *(Lesson 1-2)*

93. $-12 + 7$ ▨ $10 + (-5)$

94. $|-14|$ ▨ -2

95. $|-7 + 11|$ ▨ $|-4|$

96. $-20 + (-35)$ ▨ $-35 - 20$

1-4 Powers and Exponents

Objective
Simplify expressions
containing exponents.

Vocabulary
power
base
exponent

Who uses this?
Biologists use exponents to model the growth patterns of living organisms.

When bacteria divide, their number increases exponentially. This means that the number of bacteria is multiplied by the same factor each time the bacteria divide. Instead of writing repeated multiplication to express a product, you can use a power.

A **power** is an expression written with an *exponent* and a *base* or the value of such an expression. 3^2 is an example of a power.

The base, 3, is the number that is used as a factor.

3^2

The exponent, 2, tells how many times the base, 3, is used as a factor.

When a number is raised to the second power, we usually say it is "squared." The area of a *square* is $s \cdot s = s^2$, where s is the side length.

When a number is raised to the third power, we usually say it is "cubed." The volume of a *cube* is $s \cdot s \cdot s = s^3$, where s is the side length.

EXAMPLE 1 Writing Powers for Geometric Models

Write the power represented by each geometric model.

A

There are 3 rows of 3 dots. 3×3
The factor 3 is used 2 times.

3^2

B

The figure is 4 cubes long, 4 cubes wide, and 4 cubes tall. $4 \times 4 \times 4$
The factor 4 is used 3 times.

4^3

✓ CHECK IT OUT! Write the power represented by each geometric model.

1a.

1b.

There are no easy geometric models for numbers raised to exponents greater than 3, but you can still write them using repeated multiplication or a base and exponent.

Reading Exponents			
Words	Multiplication	Power	Value
3 to the first power	3	3^1	3
3 to the second power, or 3 squared	$3 \cdot 3$	3^2	9
3 to the third power, or 3 cubed	$3 \cdot 3 \cdot 3$	3^3	27
3 to the fourth power	$3 \cdot 3 \cdot 3 \cdot 3$	3^4	81
3 to the fifth power	$3 \cdot 3 \cdot 3 \cdot 3 \cdot 3$	3^5	243

EXAMPLE 2 **Evaluating Powers**

Simplify each expression.

A $(-2)^3$

$(-2)(-2)(-2)$ *Use −2 as a factor 3 times.*

-8

Caution!

In the expression -5^2, 5 is the base because the negative sign is not in parentheses.
In the expression $(-2)^3$, −2 is the base because of the parentheses.

B -5^2

$-1 \cdot 5 \cdot 5$ *Think of a negative sign in front of a power as*

$-1 \cdot 25$ *multiplying by −1. Find the product of −1*

-25 *and two 5's.*

C $\left(\dfrac{2}{3}\right)^2$

$\dfrac{2}{3} \cdot \dfrac{2}{3}$ *Use $\dfrac{2}{3}$ as a factor 2 times.*

$\dfrac{2}{3} \cdot \dfrac{2}{3} = \dfrac{4}{9}$

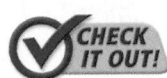 **CHECK IT OUT!** Simplify each expression.

2a. $(-5)^3$ **2b.** -6^2 **2c.** $\left(\dfrac{3}{4}\right)^3$

EXAMPLE 3 **Writing Powers**

Write each number as a power of the given base.

A 8; base 2

$2 \cdot 2 \cdot 2$ *The product of three 2's is 8.*

2^3

B −125; base −5

$(-5)(-5)(-5)$ *The product of three −5's is −125.*

$(-5)^3$

 CHECK IT OUT! Write each number as a power of the given base.

3a. 64; base 8   **3b.** −27; base −3

EXAMPLE **4** *Problem-Solving Application*

A certain bacterium splits into 2 bacteria every hour. There is 1 bacterium on a slide. If each bacterium on the slide splits once per hour, how many bacteria will be on the slide after 6 hours?

1 Understand the Problem

The **answer** will be the number of bacteria on the slide after 6 hours.
List the **important information:**
• There is 1 bacterium on a slide that divides into 2 bacteria.
• Each bacterium then divides into 2 more bacteria.

2 Make a Plan

Draw a diagram to show the number of bacteria after each hour.

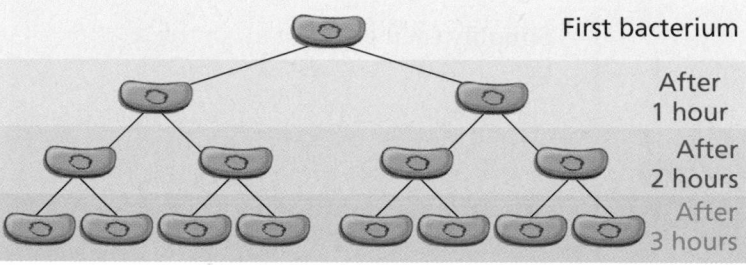

3 Solve

Notice that after each hour, the number of bacteria is a power of 2.

After 1 hour: $1 \cdot 2 = 2$ or 2^1 bacteria on the slide
After 2 hours: $2 \cdot 2 = 4$ or 2^2 bacteria on the slide
After 3 hours: $4 \cdot 2 = 8$ or 2^3 bacteria on the slide

So, after the 6th hour, there will be 2^6 bacteria.

$2^6 = 2 \cdot 2 \cdot 2 \cdot 2 \cdot 2 \cdot 2 = 64$ *Multiply six 2's.*

After 6 hours, there will be 64 bacteria on the slide.

4 Look Back

The numbers quickly become too large for a diagram, but a diagram helps you recognize a pattern. Then you can write the numbers as powers of 2.

 4. What if...? How many bacteria will be on the slide after 8 hours?

THINK AND DISCUSS

1. Express 8^3 in words two ways.

2. GET ORGANIZED Copy and complete the graphic organizer. In each box, give an example and tell whether the expression is positive or negative.

	Even Exponent	Odd Exponent
Positive Base		
Negative Base		

28   *Chapter 1 Foundations for Algebra*

go.hrw.com
Homework Help Online
KEYWORD: MA7 1-4
Parent Resources Online
KEYWORD: MA7 Parent

GUIDED PRACTICE

1. **Vocabulary** What does the *exponent* in the expression 5^6 tell you?

SEE EXAMPLE **1**
p. 26

Write the power represented by each geometric model.

2.

3.

4.
   9

   9

SEE EXAMPLE **2**
p. 27

Simplify each expression.

5. 7^2
6. $(-2)^4$
7. $(-2)^5$
8. $-\left(\dfrac{1}{2}\right)^4$

SEE EXAMPLE **3**
p. 27

Write each number as a power of the given base.

9. 81; base 9
10. 100,000; base 10
11. −64; base −4
12. 10; base 10
13. 81; base 3
14. 36; base −6

SEE EXAMPLE **4**
p. 28

15. **Technology** Jan wants to predict the number of hits she will get on her Web page. Her Web page received 3 hits during the first week it was posted. If the number of hits triples every week, how many hits will the Web page receive during the 5th week?

PRACTICE AND PROBLEM SOLVING

Independent Practice	
For Exercises	See Example
16–18	1
19–22	2
23–28	3
29	4

Extra Practice

Skills Practice p. S4

Application Practice p. S28

Write the power represented by each geometric model.

16.
   5

   5

17.
   3

   3   3

18.

Simplify each expression.

19. 3^3
20. $(-4)^2$
21. -4^2
22. $\left(-\dfrac{3}{5}\right)^2$

Write each number as a power of the given base.

23. 49; base 7
24. 1000; base 10
25. −8; base −2
26. 1,000,000; base 10
27. 64; base 4
28. 343; base 7

29. **Biology** Protozoa are single-celled organisms. *Paramecium aurelia* is one type of protozoan. The number of *Paramecium aurelia* protozoa doubles every 1.25 days. There was one protozoan on a slide 5 days ago. How many protozoa are on the slide now?

30. **Write About It** A classmate says that any number raised to an even power is positive. Give examples to explain whether your classmate is correct.

Compare. Write <, >, or =.

31. 3^2 ▢ 3^3
32. 5^2 ▢ 2^5
33. 4^2 ▢ 2^4
34. 1^9 ▢ 1^4
35. -2^3 ▢ $(-2)^3$
36. -3^2 ▢ $(-3)^2$
37. 10^2 ▢ 2^6
38. 2^2 ▢ 4^1

Write each expression as repeated multiplication. Then simplify the expression.

39. 2^3

40. 1^7

41. $(-4)^3$

42. -4^3

43. $(-1)^3$

44. $(-1)^4$

45. $\left(\dfrac{1}{3}\right)^3$

46. -2.2^2

 47. Geometry The diagram shows an ornamental tile design.

    a. What is the area of the whole tile?

    b. What is the area of the white square?

    c. What is the area of the two shaded regions?

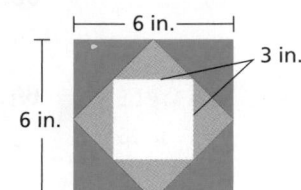

Write each expression using a base and an exponent.

48. $3 \cdot 3 \cdot 3 \cdot 3$

49. $6 \cdot 6$

50. $8 \cdot 8 \cdot 8 \cdot 8 \cdot 8$

51. $(-1)(-1)(-1)(-1)$

52. $(-7)(-7)(-7)$

53. $\left(\dfrac{1}{9}\right)\left(\dfrac{1}{9}\right)\left(\dfrac{1}{9}\right)$

54. Art A painting is made of 3 concentric squares. The side length of the largest square is 24 cm. What is the area of the painting?

55. Estimation A box is shaped like a cube with edges 22.7 centimeters long. What is the approximate volume of the box?

Write the exponent that makes each equation true.

56. $2^{\blacksquare} = 4$

57. $4^{\blacksquare} = 16$

58. $(-2)^{\blacksquare} = 16$

59. $5^{\blacksquare} = 625$

60. $-2^{\blacksquare} = -8$

61. $10^{\blacksquare} = 100$

62. $5^{\blacksquare} = 125$

63. $3^{\blacksquare} = 81$

64. Entertainment Mark and Becky play a coin toss game. Both start with one point. Every time the coin comes up heads, Mark doubles his score. Every time the coin comes up tails, Becky triples her score. The results of their game so far are shown in the table.

    a. What is Mark's score?

    b. What is Becky's score?

    c. What if...? If they toss the coin 50 more times, who do you think will win? Why?

Coin Toss Results	
Heads	**Tails**
✓	✓
✓	✓
✓	✓
✓	
✓	

65. Critical Thinking The number of zeros in powers of 10 follow a pattern.

    a. Simplify each of the following: 10^2, 10^3, 10^4.

    b. Explain what relationship you see between the exponent of a power of 10 and the number of zeros in the answer.

MULTI-STEP TEST PREP

66. This problem will prepare you for the Multi-Step Test Prep on page 38.

The formula $p = \dfrac{F}{A}$ shows that pressure p is the amount of force F exerted over an area A in square units.

    a. A 50-pound bag of flour sits on a block and exerts a force over an area of 100 in². What is the pressure exerted on the block by the bag of flour?

    b. A weight exerts 64 pounds on each square foot of a diver's body. What force is exerted on each square *inch* of the diver's body? (*Hint:* Determine how many square inches are in one square foot.)

67. Which of the following is equal to 9^2?

    (A) $9 \cdot 2$ (B) 27   (C) 3^4 (D) -9^2

68. Which expression represents the same value as the product $(-16)(-16)(-16)(-16)$?

    (F) $(-16)4$ (G) $(-16)^4$ (H) -16^4 (J) $-(16 \cdot 4)$

69. A number raised to the third power is negative. What is true about the number?

    (A) The number is positive.   (C) The number is even.

    (B) The number is negative.   (D) The number is odd.

70. A pattern exists as a result of raising -1 to consecutive whole numbers. Which is the best representation of the value of -1 raised to the 100th power?

$(-1)^n$	$(-1)^1$	$(-1)^2$	$(-1)^3$	$(-1)^4$	$(-1)^5$	$(-1)^6$
Value	-1	1	-1	1	-1	1

    (F) -1^{100} (G) -1 (H) 1   (J) 0

CHALLENGE AND EXTEND

Simplify each expression.

71. $\left(2^2\right)\left(2^2\right)\left(2^2\right)$ **72.** $\left(2^3\right)\left(2^3\right)\left(2^3\right)$ **73.** $\left(-4^2\right)\left(-4^2\right)\left(-4^2\right)\left(-4^2\right)$

74. Design The diagram shows the layout of a pool and the surrounding path. The path is 2.5 feet wide.

30 ft

30 ft

    a. What is the total area of the pool and path?

    b. What is the area of the pool?

    c. What is the area of the path?

    d. One bag of pebbles covers 10 square feet. How many bags of pebbles are needed to cover the path?

75. Exponents and powers have special properties.

    a. Write both 4^2 and 4^3 as a product of 4's.

    b. Write the product of the two expressions from part **a.** Write this product as a power of 4.

    c. Write About It Add the exponents in the expressions 4^2 and 4^3. Describe any relationship you see between your answer to part **b** and the sum of the exponents.

SPIRAL REVIEW

Find the mean of each data set by dividing the sum of the data by the number of items in the data set. *(Previous course)*

76. 7, 7, 8, 8   **77.** 1, 3, 5, 7, 9   **78.** 10, 9, 9, 12, 12

Give two ways to write each algebraic expression in words. *(Lesson 1-1)*

79. $5 - x$ **80.** $6n$ **81.** $c \div d$ **82.** $a + b$

Multiply or divide if possible. *(Lesson 1-3)*

83. $\dfrac{4}{5} \div \dfrac{8}{25}$ **84.** $0 \div \dfrac{6}{7}$ **85.** $-20(-14)$ **86.** $\dfrac{1}{2}\left(-\dfrac{4}{5}\right)$

Roots and Real Numbers

Objectives

Simplify expressions containing roots.

Classify numbers within the real number system.

Vocabulary

square root
principal square root
perfect square
cube root
natural numbers
whole numbers
integers
rational numbers
terminating decimal
repeating decimal
irrational numbers

Why learn this?

Square roots can be used to find the side length of a square garden when you know its area. (See Example 3.)

A number that is multiplied by itself to form a product is a **square root** of that product. The radical symbol $\sqrt{}$ is used to represent square roots. For nonnegative numbers, the operations of squaring and finding a square root are inverse operations. In other words, for $x \geq 0$, $\sqrt{x} \cdot \sqrt{x} = x$.

Positive real numbers have two square roots. The **principal square root** of a number is the positive square root and is represented by $\sqrt{}$. A negative square root is represented by $-\sqrt{}$. The symbol $\pm\sqrt{}$ is used to represent both square roots.

$$4 \cdot 4 = 4^2 = 16 \longrightarrow \sqrt{16} = 4 \longleftarrow \text{Positive square root of 16}$$

$$(-4)(-4) = (-4)^2 = 16 \longrightarrow -\sqrt{16} = -4 \longleftarrow \text{Negative square root of 16}$$

A **perfect square** is a number whose positive square root is a whole number. Some examples of perfect squares are shown in the table.

0	1	4	9	16	25	36	49	64	81	100
0^2	1^2	2^2	3^2	4^2	5^2	6^2	7^2	8^2	9^2	10^2

A number that is raised to the third power to form a product is a **cube root** of that product. The symbol $\sqrt[3]{}$ indicates a cube root. Since $2^3 = 8$, $\sqrt[3]{8} = 2$. Similarly, the symbol $\sqrt[4]{}$ indicates a fourth root: $2^4 = 16$, so $\sqrt[4]{16} = 2$.

EXAMPLE 1 **Finding Roots**

Find each root.

A $\sqrt{49}$

$\sqrt{49} = \sqrt{7^2}$ *Think: What number squared equals 49?*

$= 7$

B $-\sqrt{36}$

$-\sqrt{36} = -\sqrt{6^2}$ *Think: What number squared equals 36?*

$= -6$

C $\sqrt[3]{-125}$

$\sqrt[3]{-125} = \sqrt[3]{(-5^3)}$ *Think: What number cubed equals −125?*

$= -5$ $(-5)(-5)(-5) = 25(-5) = -125$

Find each root.

1a. $\sqrt{4}$ **1b.** $-\sqrt{25}$ **1c.** $\sqrt[4]{81}$

Writing Math

The small number to the left of the root is the *index*. In a square root, the index is understood to be 2. In other words, $\sqrt{}$ is the same as $\sqrt[2]{}$.

EXAMPLE **2** **Finding Roots of Fractions**

Find $\sqrt{\frac{1}{4}}$.

$$\sqrt{\frac{1}{4}} = \sqrt{\left(\frac{1}{2}\right)^2}$$ *Think: What number squared equals $\frac{1}{4}$?*

$$\sqrt{\frac{1}{4}} = \frac{1}{2}$$

CHECK IT OUT! Find each root.

2a. $\sqrt{\frac{4}{9}}$ 2b. $\sqrt[3]{\frac{1}{8}}$ 2c. $-\sqrt{\frac{4}{49}}$

Square roots of numbers that are not perfect squares, such as 15, are not whole numbers. A calculator can approximate the value of $\sqrt{15}$ as 3.872983346… Without a calculator, you can use the square roots of perfect squares to help estimate the square roots of other numbers.

EXAMPLE **3** *Gardening Application*

Nancy wants to plant a square garden of wildflowers. She has enough wildflower seeds to cover 19 ft². Estimate to the nearest tenth the side length of a square with an area of 19 ft².

Since the area of the square is 19 ft², then each side of the square is $\sqrt{19}$ ft. 19 is not a perfect square, so find the two consecutive perfect squares that 19 is between: 16 and 25. $\sqrt{19}$ is between $\sqrt{16}$ and $\sqrt{25}$, or 4 and 5. Refine the estimate.

4.3:	$4.3^2 = 18.49$	too low	$\sqrt{19}$ is greater than 4.3.
4.4:	$4.4^2 = 19.36$	too high	$\sqrt{19}$ is less than 4.4.
4.35:	$4.35^2 = 18.9225$	too low	$\sqrt{19}$ is greater than 4.35.

Since 4.35 is too low and 4.4 is too high, $\sqrt{19}$ is between 4.35 and 4.4. Rounded to the nearest tenth, $\sqrt{19} \approx 4.4$.

The side length of the plot is $\sqrt{19} \approx 4.4$ ft.

Writing Math

The symbol $\approx$ means "is approximately equal to."

CHECK IT OUT! **3.** Estimate to the nearest tenth the side length of a cube with a volume of 26 ft³.

Real numbers can be classified according to their characteristics.

Natural numbers are the counting numbers: 1, 2, 3, …

Whole numbers are the natural numbers and zero: 0, 1, 2, 3, …

Integers are the whole numbers and their opposites: …, −3, −2, −1, 0, 1, 2, 3, …

Writing Math

To show that one or more digits repeat continuously, write a bar over those digits.

1.333333333… = $1.\overline{3}$
2.14141414… = $2.\overline{14}$

Rational numbers are numbers that can be expressed in the form $\frac{a}{b}$, where a and b are both integers and $b \neq 0$. When expressed as a decimal, a rational number is either a *terminating decimal* or a *repeating decimal*.

- A **terminating decimal** has a finite number of digits after the decimal point (for example, 1.25, 2.75, and 4.0).

- A **repeating decimal** has a block of one or more digits after the decimal point that repeat continuously (where all digits are not zeros).

Irrational numbers are all real numbers that are not rational. They cannot be expressed in the form $\frac{a}{b}$ where a and b are both integers and $b \neq 0$. They are neither terminating decimals nor repeating decimals. For example:

0.10100100010000100000...   *After the decimal point, this number contains 1 followed by one 0, and then 1 followed by two 0's, and then 1 followed by three 0's, and so on.*

This decimal neither terminates nor repeats, so it is an irrational number.

If a whole number is not a perfect square, then its square root is irrational. For example, 2 is not a perfect square, and $\sqrt{2}$ is irrational.

The real numbers are made up of all rational and irrational numbers.

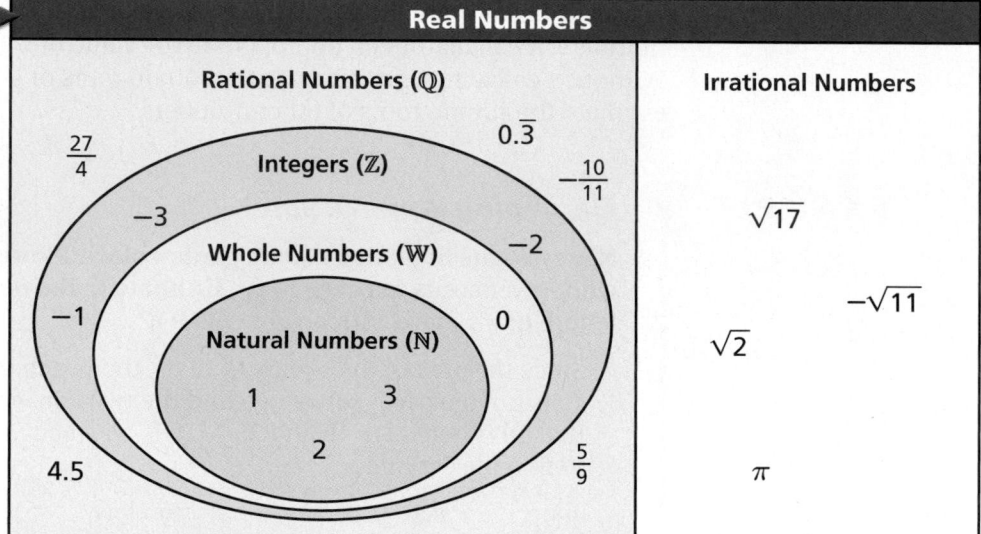

EXAMPLE 4   **Classifying Real Numbers**

Write all classifications that apply to each real number.

 A $\frac{8}{9}$

$\frac{8}{9}$ *is in the form* $\frac{a}{b}$*, where a and b are integers and b ≠ 0.*

$8 \div 9 = 0.8888...$
$\qquad = 0.\overline{8}$ $\frac{8}{9}$ *can be written as a repeating decimal.*

rational, repeating decimal

 B 18

$18 = \frac{18}{1}$ *18 can be written in the form* $\frac{a}{b}$*.*

$18 = 18.0$ *18 can be written as a terminating decimal.*

rational, terminating decimal, integer, whole, natural

 C $\sqrt{20}$

irrational   *20 is not a perfect square, so* $\sqrt{20}$ *is irrational.*

 Write all classifications that apply to each real number.

4a. $7\frac{4}{9}$ **4b.** -12

4c. $\sqrt{10}$ **4d.** $\sqrt{100}$

THINK AND DISCUSS

1. Write $\frac{2}{3}$ and $\frac{3}{5}$ as decimals. Identify what number classifications the two numbers share and how their classifications are different.

2. **GET ORGANIZED** Copy the graphic organizer and use the flowchart to classify each of the given numbers. Write each number in the box with the most specific classification that applies. $4, \sqrt{25}, 0, \frac{1}{3}, -15, -2.25, \frac{1}{4}, \sqrt{21}, 2^4, (-1)^2$

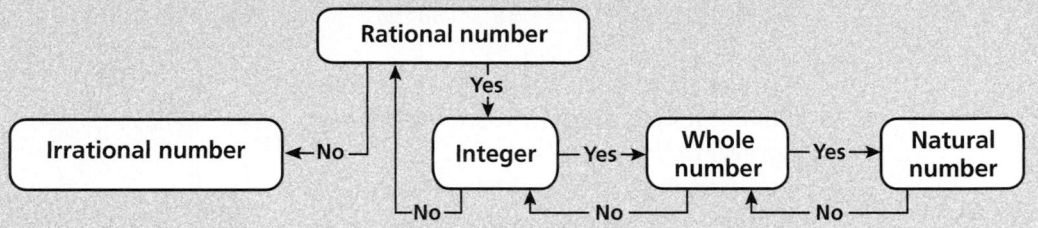

1-5 Exercises

go.hrw.com
Homework Help Online
KEYWORD: MA11 1-5
Parent Resources Online
KEYWORD: MA7 Parent

GUIDED PRACTICE

1. **Vocabulary** Give an example of a *square root* that is not a *rational number*.

Find each root.

SEE EXAMPLE **1**
p. 32

2. $\sqrt{64}$
3. $-\sqrt{225}$
4. $\sqrt[3]{-64}$
5. $\sqrt[4]{625}$
6. $\sqrt{81}$
7. $-\sqrt[3]{27}$
8. $-\sqrt[3]{-27}$
9. $-\sqrt{16}$

SEE EXAMPLE **2**
p. 33

10. $\sqrt{\frac{1}{16}}$
11. $\sqrt[3]{\frac{8}{27}}$
12. $-\sqrt{\frac{1}{9}}$
13. $\sqrt{\frac{9}{64}}$
14. $\sqrt{\frac{1}{36}}$
15. $\sqrt[3]{\frac{1}{64}}$
16. $-\sqrt{\frac{4}{81}}$
17. $\sqrt[3]{-\frac{1}{125}}$

SEE EXAMPLE **3**
p. 33

18. A contractor is told that a potential client's kitchen floor is in the shape of a square. The area of the floor is 45 ft². Estimate to the nearest tenth the side length of the floor.

SEE EXAMPLE **4**
p. 34

Write all classifications that apply to each real number.

19. -27
20. $\frac{1}{6}$
21. $\sqrt{33}$
22. -6.8

PRACTICE AND PROBLEM SOLVING

Find each root.

23. $\sqrt{121}$
24. $\sqrt[3]{-1000}$
25. $-\sqrt{100}$
26. $\sqrt[4]{256}$
27. $\sqrt{\frac{1}{25}}$
28. $\sqrt[4]{\frac{1}{16}}$
29. $\sqrt[3]{-\frac{1}{8}}$
30. $-\sqrt{\frac{25}{36}}$

31. An artist makes glass paperweights in the shape of a cube. He uses 68 cm³ of glass to make each paperweight. Estimate to the nearest tenth the side length of a paperweight.

Independent Practice

For Exercises	See Example
23–26	1
27–30	2
31	3
32–35	4

Extra Practice

Skills Practice p. S5

Application Practice p. S28

Write all classifications that apply to each real number.

32. $\dfrac{5}{12}$

33. $\sqrt{49}$

34. -3

35. $\sqrt{18}$

36. Geometry The cube root of the volume of a cube gives the length of one side of the cube.

a. Find the side length of the cube shown.

b. Find the area of each face of the cube.

Volume = 343 cm³

Compare. Write $<$, $>$, or $=$.

37. $8 \ \blacksquare \ \sqrt{63}$

38. $\sqrt{88} \ \blacksquare \ 9$

39. $6 \ \blacksquare \ \sqrt{40}$

40. $\sqrt{\dfrac{9}{25}} \ \blacksquare \ 0.61$

Travel During a cross-country road trip, Madeline recorded the distance between several major cities and the time it took her to travel between those cities. Find Madeline's average speed for each leg of the trip and classify that number.

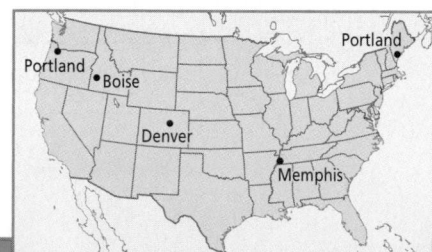

Madeline's Cross-Country Road Trip				
	Distance (mi)	Time (h)	Speed (mi/h)	Classification
41. Portland, ME, to Memphis, TN	1485	33	▨	▨
42. Memphis, TN, to Denver, CO	1046	27	▨	▨
43. Denver, CO, to Boise, ID	831	24	▨	▨
44. Boise, ID, to Portland, OR	424	9	▨	▨

Determine whether each statement is sometimes, always, or never true. If it is sometimes true, give one example that makes the statement true and one example that makes it false. If it is always true, explain. If it is never true, rewrite the statement so that it is always true.

45. Mixed numbers are rational numbers.

46. The decimal form of an irrational number is a repeating decimal.

47. A terminating decimal is a rational number.

48. A negative number is irrational.

49. Critical Thinking A positive number has two square roots, one that is positive and one that is negative. Is the same thing true for the cube root of a positive number? What about the fourth root of a positive number? Explain.

MULTI-STEP TEST PREP

50. This problem will prepare you for the Multi-Step Test Prep on page 38.

The equation $a^2 + b^2 = c^2$ relates the lengths of the sides of a right triangle. Sides a and b make the right angle of the triangle.

a. What is the value of c^2 when $a = 5$ and $b = 12$? Determine the square root of c^2 to find the value of c.

b. A diver is a horizontal distance of 50 feet from a boat and 120 feet beneath the surface of the water. What distance will the diver swim if he swims diagonally to the boat?

51. **Entertainment** In a board game, players place different-colored stones on a grid. Each player tries to make rows of 5 or more stones in their color while preventing their opponent(s) from doing the same. The square game board has 324 squares on it. How many squares are on each side of the board?

52. **Write About It** Explain why you cannot take the square root of a negative number but you can take the cube root of a negative number.

TEST PREP

53. Which point on the number line is closest to $-\sqrt[3]{36}$?

   Ⓐ A   Ⓑ B   Ⓒ C   Ⓓ D

54. What is the area of the figure at right?

   Ⓕ 24 cm^2 Ⓗ 104 cm^2

   Ⓖ 52 cm^2 Ⓙ 576 cm^2

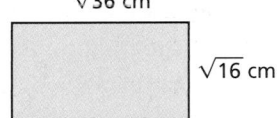

55. Which number is irrational?

   Ⓐ $-\sqrt{9}$ Ⓑ 4.0005

   Ⓒ $2.\overline{17}$ Ⓓ $\sqrt{40}$

56. The square root of 175 is between which two whole numbers?

   Ⓕ 11 and 12   Ⓖ 12 and 13   Ⓗ 13 and 14   Ⓙ 14 and 15

CHALLENGE AND EXTEND

Find each root.

57. $\sqrt{0.81}$ 58. $\sqrt{0.25}$ 59. $\sqrt[3]{-0.001}$ 60. $\sqrt{2.25}$

Evaluate each expression for $a = 9$ and $b = 7$.

61. $\sqrt{a+b}$ 62. $b\sqrt{a} - a$ 63. $\sqrt[4]{b+a} + ab$ 64. $\sqrt{ab+1}$

65. The *Density Property of Real Numbers* states that between any two real numbers, there is another real number.

   a. Does the set of integers have this property? Explain.

   b. Use the Density Property to write a convincing argument that there are infinitely many real numbers between 0 and 1.

SPIRAL REVIEW

Add or subtract. *(Lesson 1-2)*

66. $-14 + (-16)$ 67. $-\frac{1}{4} - \left(-\frac{3}{4}\right)$ 68. $25 - 17.6$

Multiply or divide. *(Lesson 1-3)*

69. $\frac{1}{8} \div \left(-\frac{2}{3}\right)$ 70. $(-2.5)(-8)$ 71. $-\frac{21}{6}$

Simplify each expression. *(Lesson 1-4)*

72. -3^4 73. $\left(-\frac{2}{5}\right)^3$ 74. 14^2 75. 4^3

MULTI-STEP TEST PREP

The Language of Algebra

Under Pressure Atmospheric pressure is 14.7 pounds per square inch (psi). Underwater, the water exerts additional pressure. The total pressure on a diver underwater is the atmospheric pressure plus the water pressure.

1. As a diver moves downward in the water, the water pressure increases by 14.7 psi for approximately every 33 ft of water. Make a table to show the total pressure on a diver at 0, 33, 66, and 99 ft below the surface of the water. At what depth would the total pressure equal 73.5 psi? Explain your method.

2. A diver is 40 ft below the surface of the water when a hot-air balloon flies over her. The hot-air balloon is 849 ft above the surface of the water. Draw a diagram and write an expression to find the distance between the diver and the balloon when the balloon is directly above her.

3. The diver swam 62.5 ft in 5 minutes. How fast was she swimming? What total distance will she have traveled after an additional 4 minutes if she maintains this same speed?

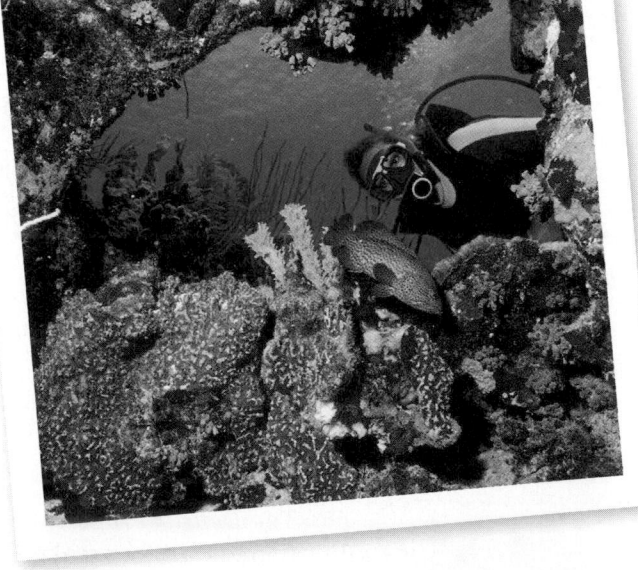

4. The total pressure on each square foot of the diver's body is given by the expression $2116.8 + 64.145d$, where d is the depth in feet. At a depth of 66 ft, what is the total pressure on each square foot of her body? What is the total pressure on each square *inch* of her body at this depth? How does your answer compare to your results for part **a?**

5. The diver realizes that she has drifted horizontally about 30 ft from the boat she left. She is at a depth of 40 ft from the surface. What is the diver's diagonal distance from the boat?

Quiz for Lessons 1-1 Through 1-5

1-1 Variables and Expressions

Give two ways to write each algebraic expression in words.

1. $4 + n$ **2.** $m - 9$ **3.** $\dfrac{g}{2}$ **4.** $4z$

5. Bob earns \$15 per hour. Write an expression for the amount of money he earns in h hours.

6. A soccer practice is 90 minutes long. Write an expression for the number of minutes left after m minutes have elapsed.

Evaluate each expression for $x = 3$, $y = 6$, and $z = 2$.

7. $y \div z$ **8.** xy **9.** $x + y$ **10.** $x - z$

1-2 Adding and Subtracting Real Numbers

Add or subtract.

11. $81 + (-15)$ **12.** $27 - 32$ **13.** $2 - \left(-1\dfrac{1}{4}\right)$ **14.** $-7 + (-14)$

15. Brandon's bank statement shows a balance of $-\$45.00$. What will the balance be after Brandon deposits \$70.00?

1-3 Multiplying and Dividing Real Numbers

Find the value of each expression if possible.

16. $9(-9)$ **17.** $6 \div \dfrac{3}{5}$ **18.** $9.6 \div 0$ **19.** $\left(-\dfrac{1}{2}\right)\left(-\dfrac{1}{2}\right)$

20. Simon drove for $2\dfrac{1}{2}$ hours to get from his house to the beach. Simon averaged 55 miles per hour on the trip. What is the distance from Simon's house to the beach?

1-4 Powers and Exponents

Simplify each expression.

21. $(-3)^2$ **22.** -3^2 **23.** $\left(-\dfrac{2}{3}\right)^3$ **24.** $\left(-\dfrac{1}{2}\right)^5$

25. The number of bytes in a kilobyte is 2 to the 10th power. Express this number in two ways.

1-5 Roots and Real Numbers

Find each root.

26. $\sqrt{225}$ **27.** $-\sqrt{49}$ **28.** $\sqrt[3]{8}$ **29.** $\sqrt{\dfrac{16}{25}}$

30. Mindy is building a patio that is in the shape of a square. The patio will cover 56 square yards. Find the length of a side of the patio to the nearest tenth of a yard.

Write all classifications that apply to each real number.

31. $\dfrac{1}{11}$ **32.** $\sqrt{12}$ **33.** $\sqrt{400}$ **34.** -6

1-6 Order of Operations

Objective
Use the order of operations to simplify expressions.

Vocabulary
order of operations

Who uses this?
Sports statisticians use the order of operations to calculate data. (See Example 5.)

A baseball player must run to first, second, and third bases before running back to home plate. In math, some tasks must be done in a certain order.

When a numerical or algebraic expression contains more than one operation symbol, the **order of operations** tells you which operation to perform first.

Know it! Note

Order of Operations	
First:	Perform operations inside grouping symbols.
Second:	Simplify powers and roots.
Third:	Perform multiplication and division from left to right.
Fourth:	Perform addition and subtraction from left to right.

Grouping symbols include parentheses ( ), brackets [ ], and braces { }. If an expression contains more than one set of grouping symbols, simplify the expression inside the innermost set first. Follow the order of operations within that set of grouping symbols and then work outward.

EXAMPLE 1 **Simplifying Numerical Expressions**

Simplify each expression.

A $-4^2 + 24 \div 3 \cdot 2$

$\begin{array}{ll} -4^2 + 24 \div 3 \cdot 2 & \textit{There are no grouping symbols.} \\ -16 + 24 \div 3 \cdot 2 & \textit{Simplify powers. The exponent applies only to the 4.} \\ -16 + 8 \cdot 2 & \textit{Divide.} \\ -16 + 16 & \textit{Multiply.} \\ 0 & \textit{Add.} \end{array}$

B $4\left[25 - (5-2)^2\right]$

$\begin{array}{ll} 4\left[25 - (5-2)^2\right] & \textit{There are two sets of grouping symbols.} \\ 4\left[25 - 3^2\right] & \textit{Perform the operation in the innermost set.} \\ 4\left[25 - 9\right] & \textit{Simplify powers within the brackets.} \\ 4 \cdot 16 & \textit{Subtract within the brackets.} \\ 64 & \textit{Multiply.} \end{array}$

Helpful Hint

The first letters of these words can help you remember the order of operations.

Please	Parentheses
Excuse	Exponents
My	Multiply/
Dear	Divide
Aunt	Add/
Sally	Subtract

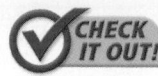 **CHECK IT OUT!** Simplify each expression.

1a. $8 \div \frac{1}{2} \cdot 3$ **1b.** $5.4 - 3^2 + 6.2$ **1c.** $-20 \div \left[-2(4+1)\right]$

EXAMPLE 2 **Evaluating Algebraic Expressions**

Evaluate each expression for the given value of x.

A $21 - x + 2 \cdot 5$ for $x = 7$

$21 - x + 2 \cdot 5$

$21 - 7 + 2 \cdot 5$ *First substitute 7 for x.*

$21 - 7 + 10$ *Multiply.*

$14 + 10$ *Subtract.*

24 *Add.*

B $5^2(30 - x)$ for $x = 24$

$5^2(30 - x)$

$5^2(30 - 24)$ *First substitute 24 for x.*

$5^2(6)$ *Perform the operation inside the parentheses.*

$25(6)$ *Simplify powers.*

150 *Multiply.*

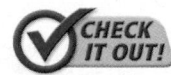 **CHECK IT OUT!** Evaluate each expression for the given value of x.

2a. $14 + x^2 \div 4$ for $x = 2$ **2b.** $(x \cdot 2^2) \div (2 + 6)$ for $x = 6$

Fraction bars, radical symbols, and absolute-value symbols can also be used as grouping symbols. Remember that a fraction bar indicates division.

EXAMPLE 3 **Simplifying Expressions with Other Grouping Symbols**

Simplify each expression.

A $\dfrac{-22 - 2^2}{5 - 3}$

$\dfrac{(-22 - 2^2)}{(5 - 3)}$ *The fraction bar acts as a grouping symbol. Simplify the numerator and the denominator before dividing.*

$\dfrac{-22 - 4}{5 - 3}$ *Simplify the power in the numerator.*

$\dfrac{-26}{5 - 3}$ *Subtract to simplify the numerator.*

$\dfrac{-26}{2}$ *Subtract to simplify the denominator.*

-13 *Divide.*

> **Helpful Hint**
>
> You may need to add grouping symbols to simplify expressions when using a scientific or graphing calculator.
> To simplify $\frac{2+3}{5-4}$ with a calculator, enter $(2 + 3) \div (5 - 4)$.

B $|10 - 5^2| \div 5$

$|10 - 5^2| \div 5$ *The absolute-value symbols act as grouping symbols.*

$|10 - 25| \div 5$ *Simplify the power.*

$|-15| \div 5$ *Subtract within the absolute-value symbols.*

$15 \div 5$ *Write the absolute value of -15.*

3 *Divide.*

 CHECK IT OUT! Simplify each expression.

3a. $\dfrac{5 + 2(-8)}{(-2)^3 - 3}$ **3b.** $|4 - 7|^2 \div (-3)$ **3c.** $3\sqrt{50 - 1}$

You may need to use grouping symbols when translating from words to numerical or algebraic expressions. Remember that operations inside grouping symbols are performed first.

EXAMPLE **4** **Translating from Words to Math**

Translate each word phrase into a numerical or algebraic expression.

Remember!

Look for words that imply mathematical operations.

difference →subtract
sum → add
product → multiply
quotient → divide

A one half times the difference of −5 and 3

$\frac{1}{2}(-5 - 3)$ *Use parentheses so that the difference is evaluated first.*

B the square root of the quotient of −12 and n

$\sqrt{\dfrac{-12}{n}}$ *Show the square root of a quotient.*

 4. Translate the word phrase into a numerical or algebraic expression: the product of 6.2 and the sum of 9.4 and 8.

EXAMPLE **5** *Sports Application*

Hank Aaron's last season in the Major Leagues was in 1976. A player's total number of bases can be found using the expression $S + 2D + 3T + 4H$. Use the table to find Hank Aaron's total bases for 1976.

HANK AARON 1976 Statistics	
Base Hits	**Number**
Single (S)	44
Double (D)	8
Triple (T)	0
Home run (H)	10

$S + 2D + 3T + 4H$

$44 + 2(8) + 3(0) + 4(10)$ *First substitute values for each variable.*

$44 + 16 + 0 + 40$ *Multiply.*

$60 + 0 + 40$ *Add from left to right.*

100 *Add.*

Hank Aaron's total number of bases for 1976 was 100.

 **5.** Another formula for a player's total number of bases is Hits + D + 2T + 3H. Use this expression to find Hank Aaron's total bases for 1959, when he had 223 hits, 46 doubles, 7 triples, and 39 home runs.

THINK AND DISCUSS

1. Explain whether you always perform addition before subtraction when simplifying a numerical or algebraic expression.

2. GET ORGANIZED Copy and complete the graphic organizer. In each box, show how grouping symbols can be placed so that the expression is equal to the number shown.

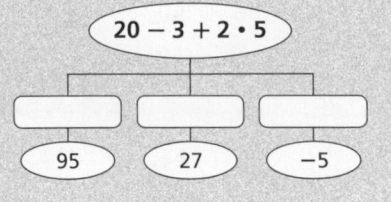

go.hrw.com

Homework Help Online
KEYWORD: MA7 1-6

Parent Resources Online
KEYWORD: MA7 Parent

GUIDED PRACTICE

1. **Vocabulary** Explain why the *order of operations* is necessary for simplifying numerical expressions.

SEE EXAMPLE 1
p. 40

Simplify each expression.

2. $5 - 12 \div (-2)$

3. $30 - 5 \cdot 3$

4. $50 - 6 + 8$

5. $12 \div (-4)(3)$

6. $(5 - 8)(3 - 9)$

7. $16 + \left[5 - \left(3 + 2^2\right)\right]$

SEE EXAMPLE 2
p. 41

Evaluate each expression for the given value of the variable.

8. $5 + 2x - 9$ for $x = 4$

9. $30 \div 2 - d$ for $d = 14$

10. $51 - 91 + g$ for $g = 20$

11. $2(3 + n)$ for $n = 4$

12. $4(b - 4)^2$ for $b = 5$

13. $12 + \left[20(5 - k)\right]$ for $k = 1$

SEE EXAMPLE 3
p. 41

Simplify each expression.

14. $24 \div |4 - 10|$

15. $4.5 - \sqrt{2(4.5)}$

16. $5(2) + 16 \div |-4|$

17. $\dfrac{0 - 24}{6 + 2}$

18. $\dfrac{2 + 3(6)}{2^2}$

19. $-44 \div \sqrt{12 \div 3}$

SEE EXAMPLE 4
p. 42

Translate each word phrase into a numerical or algebraic expression.

20. 5 times the absolute value of the sum of s and -2

21. the product of 12 and the sum of -2 and 6

22. 14 divided by the sum of 52 and -3

SEE EXAMPLE 5
p. 42

23. **Geometry** The surface area of a cylinder can be found using the expression $2\pi r(h + r)$. Find the surface area of the cylinder shown. (Use 3.14 for π and give your final answer rounded to the nearest tenth.)

$r = 3$ ft

$h = 7$ ft

PRACTICE AND PROBLEM SOLVING

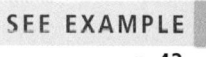

For Exercises	See Example
24–32	1
33–41	2
42–49	3
50–53	4
54	5

Extra Practice

Skills Practice p. S5

Application Practice p. S28

Simplify each expression.

24. $3 + 4(-5)$

25. $20 - 4 + 5 - 2$

26. $41 + 12 \div 2$

27. $3(-9) + (-2)(-6)$

28. $10^2 \div (10 - 20)$

29. $(6 + 2 \cdot 3) \div (9 - 7)^2$

30. $-9 - (-18) + 6$

31. $15 \div (2 - 5)$

32. $5(1 - 2) - (3 - 2)$

Evaluate each expression for the given value of the variable.

33. $-6(3 - p)$ for $p = 7$

34. $5 + (r + 2)^2$ for $r = 4$

35. $13 - \left[3 + (j - 12)\right]$ for $j = 5$

36. $(-4 - a)^2$ for $a = -3$

37. $7 - (21 - h)^2$ for $h = 25$

38. $10 + \left[8 \div (q - 3)\right]$ for $q = 2$

39. $(4r - 2) + 7$ for $r = 3$

40. $-2(11b - 3)$ for $b = 5$

41. $7x(3 + 2x)$ for $x = -1$

Simplify each expression.

42. $-4|2.5 - 6|$

43. $\dfrac{8 - 8}{2 - 1}$

44. $\dfrac{3 + |8 - 10|}{2}$

45. $\sqrt{3^2 - 5} \div 8$

46. $\dfrac{-18 - 36}{-9}$

47. $\dfrac{6|5 - 7|}{14 - 2}$

48. $\sqrt{5^2 - 4^2}$

49. $(-6 + 24) \div |-3|$

Translate each word phrase into a numerical or an algebraic expression.

50. the product of 7 and the sum of 2 and d

51. the difference of 3 and the quotient of 2 and 5

52. the square root of the sum of 5 and -4

53. the difference of 8 and the absolute value of the product of 3 and 5

54. Geometry The perimeter of a rectangle can be found using the expression $2(\ell + w)$. Find the perimeter of the rectangle shown.

$w = 4$ in.
$\ell = 8$ in.

55. Simplify each expression.

a. $50 + 10 \div 2$ **b.** $50 \cdot 10 - 2$ **c.** $50 \cdot 10 \div 2$

d. $50 \div 10 \cdot 2$ **e.** $50 - 10 \cdot 2$ **f.** $50 + 10 \cdot 2$

Translate each word phrase into a numerical or algebraic expression.

56. the difference of 8 and the product of 4 and n

57. 2 times the sum of 9 and the opposite of x

58. two-thirds of the difference of -2 and 8

59. the square root of 7 divided by the product of 3 and 10

Sports

60. Sports At the 2004 Summer Olympics, U.S. gymnast Paul Hamm received the scores shown in the table during the individual all-around competition.

2004 Summer Olympics Individual Scores for Paul Hamm						
Event	Floor	Pommel horse	Rings	Vault	Parallel bars	Horizontal bar
Score	9.725	9.700	9.587	9.137	9.837	9.837

a. Write a numerical expression to show the average of Hamm's scores. (*Hint:* The average of a set of values is the sum of the values divided by the number of values.)

b. Simplify the expression to find Hamm's average score to the nearest thousandth.

In 2004, Paul Hamm became the first American to win a gold medal in the men's all-around gymnastics competition at the Olympics. He won by a margin of 0.012 point.

61. Critical Thinking Are parentheses required when translating the word phrase "the sum of 8 and the product of 3 and 2" into a numerical phrase? Explain.

Translate each word phrase into a numerical expression. Then simplify.

62. the sum of 8 and the product of -3 and 5

63. the difference of the product of 3 and 5 and the product of 6 and 2

64. the product of $\frac{2}{3}$ and the absolute value of the difference of 3 and -12

MULTI-STEP TEST PREP

65. This problem will prepare you for the Multi-Step Test Prep on page 60.

a. Find the area of each face of the prism. Find the sum of these areas to find the total surface area of the prism.

3 in.
4 in.
5 in.

b. The total surface area of a prism is described by the expression $2(\ell w) + 2(\ell h) + 2(wh)$. Explain how this expression relates to the sum you found in part **a.**

c. Use the expression above to find the total surface area of the prism. Explain why your answers to parts **a** and **c** should be equal.

66. **Geometry** The area of a trapezoid is equal to the average of its bases times its height. Use the expression $\left(\frac{b_1 + b_2}{2}\right)h$ to determine the area of the trapezoid.

$b_1 = 4$ cm

$h = 6$ cm

$b_2 = 10$ cm

67. **Write About It** Many everyday processes must be done in a certain order to be completed successfully. Describe a process that requires several steps, and tell why the steps must be followed in a certain order.

68. Cara's family rented a car for their 3-day vacation to the Grand Canyon. They paid $29.00 per day and $0.12 for each mile driven. Which expression represents Cara's family's cost to rent the car for 3 days and drive 318 miles?

(A) $29 + 0.12(318)$

(B) $29 + 3 + 0.12 + 318$

(C) $29(3) + 0.12(318)$

(D) $3[9 + 0.12(318)]$

69. The perimeter of the Norman window shown is approximated by the expression $2(3 + 8) + 3.14(3)$. Which is the closest approximation of the perimeter of the window?

(F) 23.4 feet

(G) 28.4 feet

(H) 31.4 feet

(J) 51.4 feet

8 ft

6 ft

70. **Gridded Response** Simplify $\sqrt{\dfrac{54 - (-2)(5)}{20 - 4^2}}$.

CHALLENGE AND EXTEND

Simplify each expression.

71. $\dfrac{3 + 9 \cdot 2}{2 - 3^2}$

72. $\left[(-6 \cdot 4) \div (-6) \cdot 4\right]^2$

73. $\sqrt{\dfrac{8 + 10^2}{13 + (-10)}}$

74. Use the numbers 2, 4, 5, and 8 to write an expression that has a value of 5. You may use any operations, and you must use each of the numbers at least once.

75. Use the numbers 2, 5, 6, and 9 to write an expression that has a value of 1. You may use any operations, and you must use each of the numbers at least once.

76. If the value of $(\otimes + 5)^2$ is 81, what is the value of $(\otimes + 5)^2 + 1$?

77. If the value of $(\otimes + 1)^2 - 3$ is 22, what is the value of $(\otimes + 1)^2 - 5$?

SPIRAL REVIEW

Identify each angle as acute, right, obtuse, or straight. *(Previous course)*

78.

79.

80.

Add or subtract. *(Lesson 1-2)*

81. $51 - (-49)$

82. $-5 + \left(-1\frac{1}{3}\right)$

83. $-3 + (-8)$

84. $2.9 - 5.3$

Find each square root. *(Lesson 1-5)*

85. $\sqrt{64}$

86. $\sqrt{324}$

87. $\sqrt{\dfrac{36}{49}}$

88. $-\sqrt{121}$

Simplifying Expressions

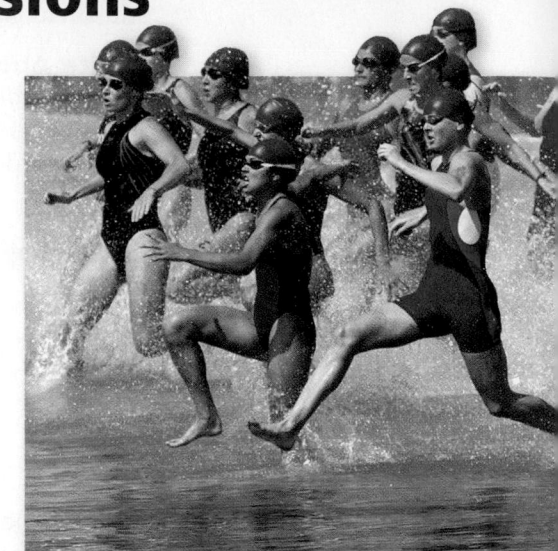

Objectives

Use the Commutative, Associative, and Distributive Properties to simplify expressions.

Combine like terms.

Vocabulary

term
like terms
coefficient

Who uses this?

Triathletes can use the Commutative, Associative, and Distributive Properties to calculate overall times mentally.

A triathlon is an endurance race that includes swimming, biking, and running. The winner is determined by adding the times for each of the three events.

The Commutative and Associative Properties of Addition and Multiplication allow you to rearrange an expression to simplify it.

Properties of Addition and Multiplication

WORDS	NUMBERS	ALGEBRA
Commutative Property You can add numbers in any order and multiply numbers in any order.	$2 + 7 = 7 + 2$ $3 \cdot 9 = 9 \cdot 3$	$a + b = b + a$ $ab = ba$
Associative Property When you are only adding or only multiplying, you can group any of the numbers together.	$(6 + 8) + 2 = 6 + (8 + 2)$ $(7 \cdot 4) \cdot 5 = 7 \cdot (4 \cdot 5)$	$(a + b) + c = a + (b + c)$ $(ab)c = a(bc)$

EXAMPLE **1** **Using the Commutative and Associative Properties**

Simplify each expression.

A $4 \cdot 9 \cdot 25$

$9 \cdot 4 \cdot 25$ *Use the Commutative Property of Multiplication.*

$9 \cdot (4 \cdot 25)$ *Use the Associative Property of Multiplication to make groups of compatible numbers.*

$9 \cdot 100$

900

B $25 + 48 + 75$

$25 + 75 + 48$ *Use the Commutative Property of Addition.*

$(25 + 75) + 48$ *Use the Associative Property of Addition to make groups of compatible numbers.*

$100 + 48$

148

Helpful Hint

Compatible numbers help you do math mentally. Try to make multiples of 5 or 10. They are simpler to use when multiplying.

Simplify each expression.

1a. $15\frac{1}{3} + 4 + 1\frac{2}{3}$ **1b.** $410 + 58 + 90 + 2$ **1c.** $\frac{1}{2} \cdot 7 \cdot 8$

Commutative and Associative Properties

I used to get the Commutative and Associative Properties mixed up.

To remember the Commutative Property, I think of people commuting back and forth from work. When people commute, they move. I can move the numbers around without changing the value of the expression.

For the Associative Property, I think of associating with my friends. They're the group I hang out with. In math, it's about how numbers are grouped.

The Distributive Property is used with addition to simplify expressions.

Distributive Property

WORDS	NUMBERS	ALGEBRA
You can multiply a number by a sum or multiply each addend by the number and then add. The result is the same.	$3(4+8) = 3(4) + 3(8)$	$a(b+c) = ab + ac$

The Distributive Property also works with subtraction because subtraction is the same as adding the opposite.

EXAMPLE 2   **Using the Distributive Property with Mental Math**

Write each product using the Distributive Property. Then simplify.

Helpful Hint

Break the greater factor into a sum that contains a multiple of 10.

A $15(103)$

$15(100 + 3)$ *Rewrite 103 as 100 + 3.*
$15(100) + 15(3)$ *Use the Distributive Property.*
$1500 + 45$ *Multiply.*
1545 *Add.*

B $6(19)$

$6(20 - 1)$ *Rewrite 19 as 20 − 1.*
$6(20) - 6(1)$ *Use the Distributive Property.*
$120 - 6$ *Multiply.*
114 *Subtract.*

CHECK IT OUT! Write each product using the Distributive Property. Then simplify.

2a. $9(52)$ **2b.** $12(98)$ **2c.** $7(34)$

The **terms** of an expression are the parts to be added or subtracted. **Like terms** are terms that contain the same variables raised to the same powers. Constants are also like terms.

Like terms   Constant

$$4x - 3x + 2$$

A **coefficient** is a number that is multiplied by a variable. Like terms can have different coefficients. A variable written without a coefficient has a coefficient of 1.

$1x^2 + 3x$

Coefficients

Using the Distributive Property can help you combine like terms. You can factor out the common factor to simplify the expression.

$$7x^2 - 4x^2 = (7 - 4)x^2 \qquad \textit{Factor out } x^2 \textit{ from both terms.}$$
$$= (3)x^2 \qquad\qquad \textit{Perform operations in parentheses.}$$
$$= 3x^2$$

Notice that you can combine like terms by adding or subtracting the coefficients and keeping the variables and exponents the same.

EXAMPLE 3 **Combining Like Terms**

Simplify each expression by combining like terms.

A $12x + 30x$

$12x + 30x$ *12x and 30x are like terms.*

    $42x$ *Add the coefficients.*

> **Caution!**
>
> Add or subtract only the coefficients.
> $6.8y^2 - y^2 \neq 6.8$

B $6.8y^2 - y^2$

$6.8y^2 - y^2$ *A variable without a coefficient has a coefficient of 1.*

$6.8y^2 - 1y^2$ *$6.8y^2$ and $1y^2$ are like terms.*

   $5.8y^2$ *Subtract the coefficients.*

C $4n + 11n^2$

$4n + 11n^2$ *4n and $11n^2$ are not like terms. Do not combine.*

 **CHECK IT OUT!** Simplify each expression by combining like terms.

3a. $16p + 84p$ **3b.** $-20t - 8.5t$ **3c.** $3m^2 + m^3$

EXAMPLE 4 **Simplifying Algebraic Expressions**

Simplify $2(x + 6) + 3x$. Justify each step with an operation or property.

	Procedure	Justification
1.	$2(x + 6) + 3x$	
2.	$2(x) + 2(6) + 3x$	Distributive Property
3.	$2x + 12 + 3x$	Multiply.
4.	$2x + 3x + 12$	Commutative Property of Addition
5.	$(2x + 3x) + 12$	Associative Property of Addition
6.	$5x + 12$	Combine like terms.

 CHECK IT OUT! Simplify each expression. Justify each step with an operation or property.

4a. $6(x - 4) + 9$ **4b.** $-12x - 5x + 3a + x$

1-7 Exercises

go.hrw.com
Homework Help Online
KEYWORD: MA7 1-7
Parent Resources Online
KEYWORD: MA7 Parent

GUIDED PRACTICE

1. Vocabulary The _____?_____ Property states the following: $(a + b) + c = a + (b + c)$. (*Associative*, *Commutative*, or *Distributive*)

SEE EXAMPLE **1**
p. 46

Simplify each expression.

2. $-12 + 67 + 12 + 23$ **3.** $16 + 2\frac{1}{2} + 4 + 1\frac{1}{2}$ **4.** $27 + 98 + 73$

5. $\frac{1}{3} \cdot 8 \cdot 21$ **6.** $2 \cdot 38 \cdot 50$ **7.** $50 \cdot 118 \cdot 20$

SEE EXAMPLE **2**
p. 47

Write each product using the Distributive Property. Then simplify.

8. $14(1002)$ **9.** $16(19)$ **10.** $9(38)$

11. $8(57)$ **12.** $12(112)$ **13.** $7(109)$

SEE EXAMPLE **3**
p. 48

Simplify each expression by combining like terms.

14. $6x + 10x$ **15.** $35x - 15x$ **16.** $-3a + 9a$

17. $-8r - r$ **18.** $17x^2 + x$ **19.** $3.2x + 4.7x$

SEE EXAMPLE **4**
p. 48

Simplify each expression. Justify each step with an operation or property.

20. $5(x + 3) - 7x$ **21.** $9(a - 3) - 4$ **22.** $5x^2 - 2(x - 3x^2)$

23. $6x - x - 3x^2 + 2x$ **24.** $12x + 8x + t - 7x$ **25.** $4a - 2(a - 1)$

PRACTICE AND PROBLEM SOLVING

Simplify each expression.

26. $53 + 28 + 17 + 12$ **27.** $5 \cdot 14 \cdot 20$ **28.** $6 \cdot 3 \cdot 5$ **29.** $4.5 + 7.1 + 8.5 + 3.9$

Write each product using the Distributive Property. Then simplify.

30. $9(62)$ **31.** $8(29)$ **32.** $11(25)$ **33.** $6(53)$

Simplify each expression by combining like terms.

34. $3x + 9x$ **35.** $14x^2 - 5x^2$ **36.** $-7x + 8x$ **37.** $3x^2 - 4$

Simplify each expression. Justify each step with an operation or property.

38. $4(y + 6) + 9$ **39.** $-7(x + 2) + 4x$ **40.** $3x + 2 - 2x - 1$

41. $5x - 3x + 3x^2 + 9x$ **42.** $8x + 2x - 3y - 9x$ **43.** $7y - 3 + 6y - 7$

44. Estimation Tavon bought a binder, 3 spiral notebooks, and a pen. The binder cost $4.89, the notebooks cost $1.99 each, and the pen cost $2.11. About how much did Tavon spend on school supplies?

45. Sports In a triathlon, athletes race in swimming, biking, and running events. The athlete with the shortest total time to complete the events is the winner.

Times from Triathlon			
Athlete	Swim (min:s)	Bike (min:s)	Run (min:s)
Amy	18:51	45:17	34:13
Julie	17:13	40:27	23:32
Mardi	19:09	38:58	25:32
Sabine	13:09	31:37	19:01

   a. Find the total time for each athlete. (*Hint:* 1 minute = 60 seconds)

   b. Use the total times for the athletes to determine the order in which they finished the triathlon.

Name the property that is illustrated in each equation.

46. $5 + x = x + 5$ **47.** $x - 2 = -2 + x$ **48.** $2 + (3 + y) = (2 + 3) + y$

49. $3(2r - 7) = 3(2r) - 3(7)$ **50.** $(2 + g) + 3 = 2 + (g + 3)$ **51.** $45x - 35 = 5(9x) - 5(7)$

 Geometry Give an expression in simplified form for the perimeter of each figure.

52.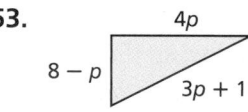
$2w$
w

53.
$4p$
$8 - p$
$3p + 1$

54.
$2s + 3$
$2s + 3$

55. Critical Thinking Evaluate $a - (b - c)$ and $(a - b) - c$ for $a = 10$, $b = 7$, and $c = 3$. Based on your answers, explain whether there is an Associative Property of Subtraction.

56. Write About It Describe a real-world situation that can be represented by the Distributive Property. Translate your situation into an algebraic expression. Define each variable you use.

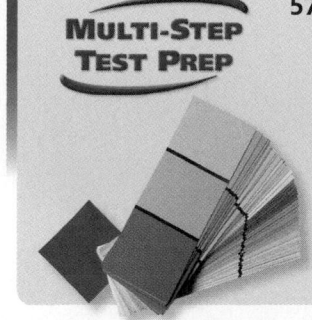

MULTI-STEP TEST PREP

57. This problem will prepare you for the Multi-Step Test Prep on page 60.

   a. The diagram shows a pattern of shapes that can be folded to make a cylinder. How is the length ℓ of the rectangle related to the circumference of (distance around) each circle?

   b. An expression for the circumference of each circle is $2\pi r$. Write an expression for the area of the rectangle.

   c. Write an expression for the total area of the figures. Leave the symbol π in your expression.

58. Ariel has 19 more CDs than her sister Tiffany has. Victor has 3 times as many CDs as Ariel has. Tiffany has x CDs. Which expression can be used to show how many CDs the three have in total?

   Ⓐ $19 + 3x$ Ⓑ $51 + 3x$ Ⓒ $76 + 3x$ Ⓓ $76 + 5x$

59. Which expression can be used to represent the perimeter of the rectangle?

   Ⓕ $16k$ Ⓗ $3k + 13$

   Ⓖ $32k$ Ⓙ $6k + 26$

$3 + k$

$2(k + 5)$

60. Which equation is an example of the Distributive Property?

   Ⓐ $(25 + 18) + 33 = 25 + (18 + 33)$ Ⓒ $33 \cdot 25 + 33 \cdot 18 = 33 \cdot (25 + 18)$

   Ⓑ $33 + (25 \cdot 18) = (25 \cdot 18) + 33$ Ⓓ $3 + 25 \cdot 33 + 18 = 18 + 33 \cdot 25 + 33$

CHALLENGE AND EXTEND

Simplify.

61. $4\big[3(x + 9) + 2\big]$

62. $-3\big[(x - 2) + 5(x - 2)\big]$

63. $(2b + 5) - (8b + 6) + 3(b - 2)$

64. $\frac{1}{2}\big[(10 - g) + (-6 + 3g)\big]$

65. Fill in the missing justifications.

Procedure	Justification
$11e - 7 - 3e = 11e + (-7) + (-3e)$	Definition of subtraction
$= 11e + (-3e) + (-7)$	**a.** _____?_____
$= \big[11e + (-3e)\big] + (-7)$	**b.** _____?_____
$= \big[11 + (-3)\big]e + (-7)$	**c.** _____?_____
$= 8e + (-7)$	**d.** _____?_____
$= 8e - 7$	Definition of subtraction

66. Fill in the missing justifications.

Procedure	Justification
$\dfrac{a + b}{c} = \dfrac{1}{c}(a + b)$	Definition of division
$= \dfrac{1}{c}(a) + \dfrac{1}{c}(b)$	**a.** _____?_____
$= \dfrac{a}{c} + \dfrac{b}{c}$	**b.** _____?_____

SPIRAL REVIEW

Give the area of the figure described. *(Previous course)*

67. square; $s = 6$ ft

68. parallelogram; $b = 7$ mm, $h = 13$ mm

Simplify each expression. *(Lesson 1-4)*

69. 2^6 **70.** 18^2 **71.** $-\left(\frac{1}{2}\right)^3$ **72.** $\left(-\frac{1}{2}\right)^2$

Simplify each expression. *(Lesson 1-6)*

73. $3 + 4 - 10 \div 2 + 1$ **74.** $\dfrac{8^2 - 6^2}{8^2 + 6^2}$ **75.** $2 - \big[6 - 8 \div (3 + 1)\big]$

Connecting Algebra to Geometry

Perimeter

The distance around a geometric figure is called the *perimeter*. You can use what you have learned about combining like terms to simplify expressions for perimeter.

A closed figure with straight sides is called a *polygon*. To find the perimeter of a polygon, add the lengths of the sides.

Example 1

A Write an expression for the perimeter of the quadrilateral.

Add the lengths of the four sides.

$$P = (a + 3) + (2a - 8) + (3a - 3) + (a - 1)$$

Combine like terms to simplify.

$$P = (a + 2a + 3a + a) + (3 - 8 - 3 - 1)$$

$$= 7a - 9 \qquad \text{\textit{This is a general expression for the perimeter.}}$$

B Find the perimeter of this quadrilateral for $a = 5$.

Substitute 5 for a.

$$P = 7(5) - 9 \qquad \text{\textit{Multiply; then subtract.}}$$

$$= 35 - 9$$

$$= 26 \qquad \text{\textit{This is the perimeter when } a = 5.}$$

Try This

Write and simplify an expression for the perimeter of each figure.

1.

$x + 2$
$3x$
$2x + 1$

2.
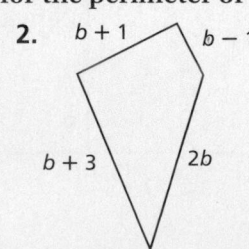
$b + 1$ $b - 1$
$b + 3$ $2b$

3.

$m + 1$
$2m - 1$

Find the perimeter of each figure for the given value of the variable.

4. $k = 3$

$k - 2$
$k - 1$
$k + 1$
$k - 1$
$k - 2$

5. $n = 10$

$3n - 1$
n
$3n - 1$

6. $y = 4$

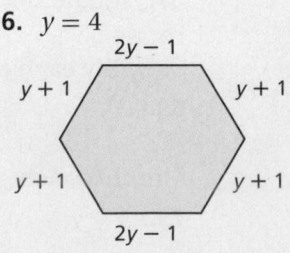
$2y - 1$
$y + 1$ $y + 1$
$y + 1$ $y + 1$
$2y - 1$

Combining like terms is one way to explore what happens to the perimeter
when you double the sides of a triangle or other polygon.

Example 2

**What happens to the perimeter of this triangle when you double the length of
each side?**

Write an expression for the perimeter of the smaller triangle.
Combine like terms to simplify the expression.

$(x - 1) + (2x - 1) + (x + 3)$

$(x + 2x + x) + (-1 - 1 + 3)$

$4x + 1$ *Perimeter of small triangle*

Double the length of each side of the triangle.

$2(x - 1) = 2x - 2$

$2(2x - 1) = 4x - 2$

$2(x + 3) = 2x + 6$

Find the perimeter of the larger triangle.
Combine like terms to simplify.

$(2x - 2) + (4x - 2) + (2x + 6)$ *Add the lengths of the sides.*

$(2x + 4x + 2x) + (-2 - 2 + 6)$ *Use the Associative and Commutative Properties of Addition and combine like terms.*

$8x + 2$ *Perimeter of large triangle*

Use the Distributive Property to show that the new perimeter is
twice the original perimeter.

$8x + 2 = 2(4x + 1)$

Try This

**Each set of expressions represents the side lengths of a triangle. Use the
Distributive Property to show that doubling the side lengths doubles the perimeter.**

7. $2p + 1$ **8.** $c - 1$ **9.** $w + 5$ **10.** $h - 2$

    $3p + 2$ $2c + 1$ $w + 5$ $3h$

    $5p$ $3c - 1$ $3w - 1$ $2h + 3$

Solve each problem.

11. Use the triangles in Example 2. Find the side lengths and perimeters for $x = 5$.

12. The sides of a quadrilateral are $2x - 1$, $x + 3$, $3x + 1$, and $x - 1$. Double the length
of each side. Then find an expression for the perimeter of the new figure.

13. What happens to the perimeter of this trapezoid when you triple the
length of each side? Use the variables a, b, b, and c for the lengths
of the sides. Explain your answer using the Distributive Property.

1-8 Introduction to Functions

Objectives
Graph ordered pairs in the coordinate plane.

Graph functions from ordered pairs.

Vocabulary
coordinate plane
axes
origin
x-axis
y-axis
ordered pair
x-coordinate
y-coordinate
quadrant
input
output

Why learn this?
You can use functions to determine how the cost of a caricature is affected by the number of people in the picture. (See Example 3.)

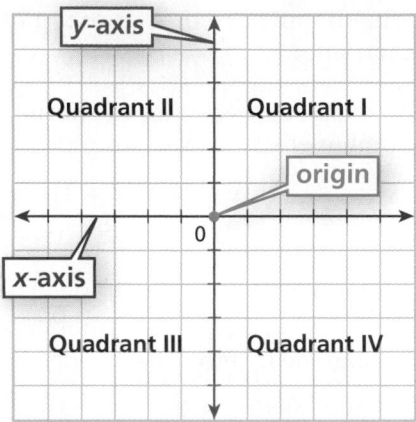

The **coordinate plane** is formed by the intersection of two perpendicular number lines called **axes**. The point of intersection, called the **origin**, is at 0 on each number line. The horizontal number line is called the **x-axis**, and the vertical number line is called the **y-axis**.

Points on the coordinate plane are described using ordered pairs. An **ordered pair** consists of an **x-coordinate** and a **y-coordinate** and is written (*x*, *y*). Points are often named by a capital letter.

EXAMPLE 1 **Graphing Points in the Coordinate Plane**

Graph each point.

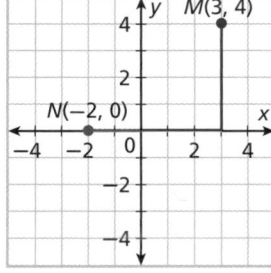

A *M*(3, 4)
Start at the origin.
Move 3 units right and 4 units up.

B *N*(−2, 0)
Start at the origin. Move 2 units left.

Reading Math

The *x*-coordinate tells how many units to move left or right from the origin. The *y*-coordinate tells how many units to move up or down.

CHECK IT OUT! Graph each point.
1a. *R*(2, −3)   **1b.** *S*(0, 2)   **1c.** *T*(−2, 6)

Look at the graph at the top of this lesson. The axes divide the coordinate plane into four **quadrants**. Points that lie on an axis are not in any quadrant.

EXAMPLE 2 **Locating Points in the Coordinate Plane**

Name the quadrant in which each point lies.

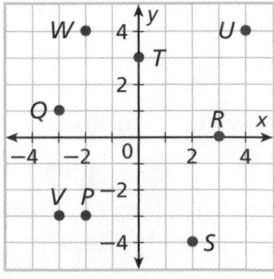

A *P*
Quadrant III

B *Q*
Quadrant II

C *R*
no quadrant (*x*-axis)

D *S*
Quadrant IV

CHECK IT OUT! Name the quadrant in which each point lies.
2a. *T*   **2b.** *U*   **2c.** *V*   **2d.** *W*

An equation that contains two variables can be used as a rule to generate ordered pairs. When you substitute a value for x, you generate a value for y. The value substituted for x is called the **input**, and the value generated for y is called the **output**.

Output   Input

$$y = 10x + 5$$

In a *function*, the value of y (the output) is determined by the value of x (the input). All of the equations in this lesson represent functions.

EXAMPLE 3   *Art Application*

A caricature artist charges his clients a $5 setup fee plus $10 for every person in a picture. Write a rule for the artist's fee. Write ordered pairs for the artist's fee when there are 1, 2, 3, and 4 people in the picture.

Let y represent the artist's fee and x represent the number of people in a picture.

Artist's fee	is	$5	plus	$10	for each	person.
y	$=$	5	$+$	10	$\cdot$	x

$y = 5 + 10x$

Number of People in Picture	Rule	Fee	Ordered Pair
x (input)	$y = 5 + 10x$	y (output)	(x, y)
1	$y = 5 + 10(1)$	15	$(1, 15)$
2	$y = 5 + 10(2)$	25	$(2, 25)$
3	$y = 5 + 10(3)$	35	$(3, 35)$
4	$y = 5 + 10(4)$	45	$(4, 45)$

Writing Math

The artist's fee is determined by the number of people in the picture, so the number of people is the input and the artist's fee is the output.

 CHECK IT OUT!

3. What if...? The artist increased his fees to a $10 setup fee plus $20 for every person. Write a rule for the new fee. Write ordered pairs for the fee when there are 1, 2, 3, and 4 people.

When you graph ordered pairs generated by a function, they may create a pattern.

EXAMPLE 4   Generating and Graphing Ordered Pairs

Generate ordered pairs for each function using the given values for x. Graph the ordered pairs and describe the pattern.

A $y = 4x - 3$; $x = -1, 0, 1, 2$

Input	Output	Ordered Pair
x	y	(x, y)
-1	$4(-1) - 3 = -7$	$(-1, -7)$
0	$4(0) - 3 = -3$	$(0, -3)$
1	$4(1) - 3 = 1$	$(1, 1)$
2	$4(2) - 3 = 5$	$(2, 5)$

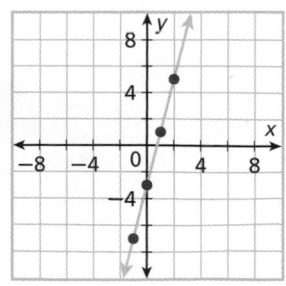

The points form a straight line.

Generate ordered pairs for each function using the given values for *x*. Graph the ordered pairs and describe the pattern.

B $y = 2x^2 + 1; x = -2, -1, 0, 1, 2$

Input	Output	Ordered Pair
x	*y*	(*x, y*)
−2	$2(-2)^2 + 1 = 9$	(−2, 9)
−1	$2(-1)^2 + 1 = 3$	(−1, 3)
0	$2(0)^2 + 1 = 1$	(0, 1)
1	$2(1)^2 + 1 = 3$	(1, 3)
2	$2(2)^2 + 1 = 9$	(2, 9)

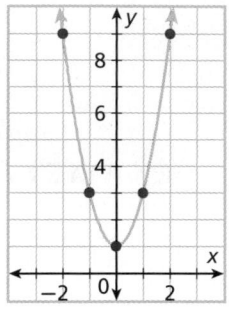

The points form a U shape.

C $y = |x + 3|; x = -5, -4, -3, -2, -1$

Input	Output	Ordered Pair
x	*y*	(*x, y*)
−5	$|-5 + 3| = |-2| = 2$	(−5, 2)
−4	$|-4 + 3| = |-1| = 1$	(−4, 1)
−3	$|-3 + 3| = |0| = 0$	(−3, 0)
−2	$|-2 + 3| = |1| = 1$	(−2, 1)
−1	$|-1 + 3| = |2| = 2$	(−1, 2)

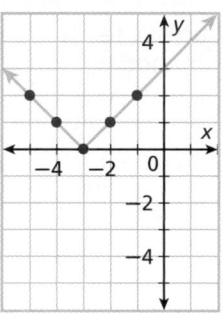

The points form a V shape.

 Generate ordered pairs for each function using the given values for *x*. Graph the ordered pairs and describe the pattern.

4a. $y = \frac{1}{2}x - 4; x = -4, -2, 0, 2, 4$

4b. $y = 3x^2 + 3; x = -3, -1, 0, 1, 3$

4c. $y = |x - 2|; x = 0, 1, 2, 3, 4$

In Chapter 4, you will learn more about functions. You will study the relationship between the shape of a graph and the rule that generates the ordered pairs.

THINK AND DISCUSS

1. Describe how to graph the ordered pair $(-3, 6)$.

2. Give an example of a point that lies on the *y*-axis.

3. GET ORGANIZED Copy and complete the graphic organizer. In each blank, write "positive" or "negative."

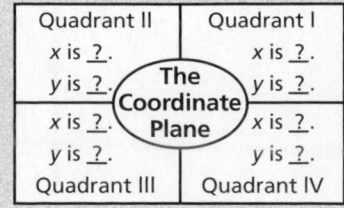

go.hrw.com
Homework Help Online
KEYWORD: MA7 1-8
Parent Resources Online
KEYWORD: MA7 Parent

GUIDED PRACTICE

1. **Vocabulary** Explain why the order in an *ordered pair* is important.

SEE EXAMPLE 1
p. 54

Graph each point.

2. $J(4, 5)$ **3.** $K(-3, 2)$ **4.** $L(6, 0)$ **5.** $M(1, -7)$

SEE EXAMPLE 2
p. 54

Name the quadrant in which each point lies.

6. A **7.** B **8.** C

9. D **10.** E **11.** F

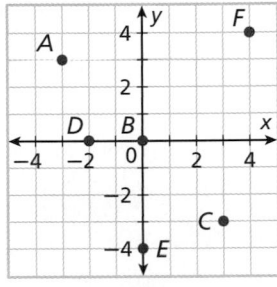

SEE EXAMPLE 3
p. 55

12. Multi-Step The number of counselors at a summer camp must be equal to $\frac{1}{4}$ the number of campers. Write a rule for the number of counselors that must be at the camp. Write ordered pairs for the number of counselors when there are 76, 100, 120, and 168 campers.

SEE EXAMPLE 4
p. 55

Generate ordered pairs for each function for $x = -2, -1, 0, 1$, and 2. Graph the ordered pairs and describe the pattern.

13. $y = x + 2$ **14.** $y = -x$ **15.** $y = -2|x|$ **16.** $y = \frac{1}{2}x^2$

PRACTICE AND PROBLEM SOLVING

Independent Practice

For Exercises	See Example
17–20	1
21–26	2
27	3
28–31	4

Extra Practice
Skills Practice p. S5
Application Practice p. S28

Graph each point.

17. $D(2, 8)$ **18.** $E(-2, -7)$ **19.** $F(0, -5)$ **20.** $G(4, -4)$

Name the quadrant in which each point lies.

21. X **22.** Y **23.** Z

24. R **25.** S **26.** T

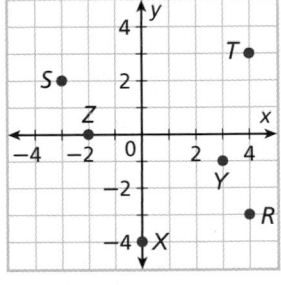

27. Multi-Step Jeremy's wages include a $500 base salary plus $\frac{1}{10}$ of his sales. Write a rule for the total amount of Jeremy's paycheck. Write ordered pairs for the amount of Jeremy's paycheck when his sales are $500, $3000, $5000, and $7500.

Generate ordered pairs for each function for $x = -2, -1, 0, 1$, and 2. Graph the ordered pairs and describe the pattern.

28. $y = 6 - 2x$ **29.** $y = -(x^2)$ **30.** $y = 3|x|$ **31.** $y = x^2 + 3$

Geometry Graph each point and connect them in the order they are listed. Connect the last point to the first. Describe the figure drawn.

32. $(-1, 1), (4, 1), (4, -4), (-1, -4)$ **33.** $(-6, 3), (2, -2), (-7, -3)$

34. $(4, 4), (6, 2), (5, -1), (3, -1), (2, 2)$ **35.** $(-6, 5), (4, 5), (4, 7), (-6, 7)$

36. Multi-Step The salary at Beth's company is $32,000 for someone with no experience and increases by $2700 per year of experience. Write a rule for the salary at Beth's company. Write ordered pairs for the salaries for employees with 0, 2, 5, and 7 years of experience.

37. This problem will prepare you for the Multi-Step Test Prep on page 60.

   a. A room decorator wants to purchase fabric. Each yard of fabric costs $2.90. Write a rule for the cost of the fabric. Let c equal the total cost and f equal the number of yards of fabric.

   b. Which variable is the input and which variable is the output?

   c. Make a table showing the cost of 1, 2, 3, 4, and 5 yards of fabric.

   d. How many whole yards can the decorator purchase if she has $21.00?

Write an equation for each rule. Use the given values for x to generate ordered pairs. Graph the ordered pairs and describe the pattern.

38. y is equal to 3 more than the absolute value of x; $x = -2, -1, 0, 1,$ and 2.

39. y is equal to the sum of one half of x and -3; $x = -4, -2, 0, 2,$ and 4.

40. y is equal to the sum of x squared and 1; $x = -5, -3, -1, 1, 3,$ and 5.

41. Business An events planner is preparing for a 5K race. She will buy enough water bottles for 50 volunteers, plus $1\frac{1}{2}$ times the number of runners who preregister for the race.

   a. Write an equation for the number of water bottles the planner should buy.

   b. Generate ordered pairs for the number of water bottles the event planner will buy for the following numbers of preregistered runners: 100, 150, 200, 250, and 300.

Give the coordinates of three points that fit the given description. Graph the points and describe the pattern.

42. The x-coordinate is 1 less than the y-coordinate.

43. The sum of the x-coordinate and y-coordinate is 5.

44. The x-coordinate is 2 times the y-coordinate.

45. The quotient of the x-coordinate and y-coordinate is 3.

46. Critical Thinking Lance wrote five ordered pairs for which the y-coordinate was the opposite of the x-coordinate. Then he graphed the ordered pairs. What pattern did the points make?

 47. Write About It Graph the point $(4, 2)$.

   a. How is graphing the point $(4, 2)$ different from graphing the point $(2, 4)$?

   b. How is graphing the point $(4, 2)$ different from graphing the point $(-4, -2)$?

48. ///**ERROR ANALYSIS**/// Two students graphed the point $(4, 6)$. Which is incorrect? Explain the error.

49. Generate ordered pairs for $y = x$, graph the points, and connect them to make a line. Do the same for $y = x + 2$ using the same values for x. How is the line for $y = x + 2$ different from the line for $y = x$?

50. Which equation could be used to generate the ordered pairs $(2, 7)$ and $(6, 9)$?

Ⓐ $y = 9 - x$ Ⓑ $y = \frac{3}{2}x^2 + 1$ Ⓒ $y = \frac{1}{2}x + 6$ Ⓓ $y = x + 5$

51. Which table of ordered pairs is generated when the values 1, 2, 3, and 4 are substituted for x in the equation $y = 2x - 4$?

Ⓕ
x	y
1	−3
2	−2
3	−1
4	0

Ⓖ
x	y
1	−2
2	0
3	2
4	4

Ⓗ
x	y
1	−2
2	0
3	1
4	2

Ⓙ
x	y
1	−3
2	−1
3	2
4	4

52. For which point on the graph is $x > \frac{7}{2}$ and $y < \frac{8}{3}$?

Ⓐ A Ⓒ C

Ⓑ B Ⓓ D

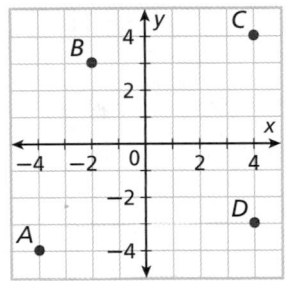

53. Which ordered pair describes the point $(2, 5)$ shifted 3 units right and 2 units down?

Ⓕ $(0, 8)$ Ⓗ $(5, 3)$

Ⓖ $(2, 3)$ Ⓙ $(5, 5)$

CHALLENGE AND EXTEND

Graph each point.

54. $W(x + 4, y - 8)$ for $x = 5$ and $y = 2$ **55.** $X(5 - x, y^2)$ for $x = -1$ and $y = 3$

56. $Y(x + y, y - x)$ for $x = 6$ and $y = 3$ **57.** $Z(xy, x^2y)$ for $x = -1$ and $y = 4$

58. Graph several ordered pairs that have an x-coordinate of 3. Describe the pattern.

59. Graph several ordered pairs that have a y-coordinate of 6. Describe the pattern.

60. Find the perimeter of a rectangle whose vertices have the coordinates $A(3, 6)$, $B(3, -2)$, $C(-1, -2)$, and $D(-1, 6)$.

61. **Multi-Step** The coordinates of three vertices of a rectangle are $J(-4, -2)$, $K(2, -2)$, and $L(2, 5)$. Find the coordinates of the fourth vertex. What is the area of the rectangle?

SPIRAL REVIEW

Give the name of each figure. *(Previous course)*

62.   **63.**   **64.**   **65.**

Write all classifications that apply to each real number. *(Lesson 1-5)*

66. $\sqrt{36}$ **67.** $\sqrt{6}$ **68.** $\frac{1}{9}$ **69.** -32

Simplify each expression. *(Lesson 1-7)*

70. $\frac{1}{5} \cdot 18 \cdot 25$ **71.** $x^2 + 3x$ **72.** $2a - b + a + 4b$

MULTI-STEP TEST PREP

The Tools of Algebra

Design Time Lori's family and Marie's family are redecorating a room in each other's home. They have three days for the decorating project, which will be filmed for a local TV show.

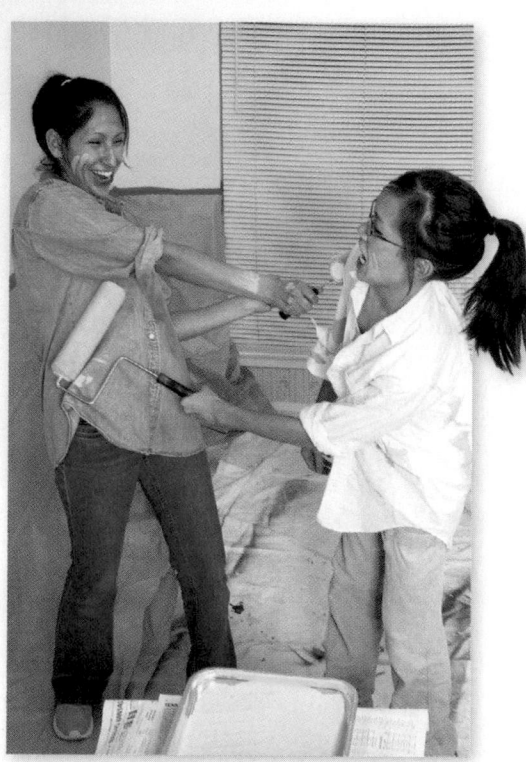

1. Lori decides to paint Marie's room a shade of blue. She measures the height and width of each wall in the rectangular room. She finds that two walls have a width of 12 feet and the other two have a width of 14 feet. The ceiling is 9 feet high. Find the area of each wall. Find the total area of all four walls plus the ceiling.

2. One gallon of paint covers 400 square feet. How many gallons are needed if Lori wants to apply 2 coats of paint to all the walls and the ceiling?

3. Lori decided to build a bedside table in the shape of a cylinder and cover all of its surfaces except the bottom with yellow fabric. The fabric costs $2.50 per square yard. The table has a radius of 1 foot and a height of 2 feet. What is the cost to cover the table? Use 3.14 for π.

1 ft

2 ft

4. Lori will fill a vase with multicolored beads and place it on the bedside table. The vase is in the approximate shape of a cone. The height of the vase is 10 inches, and the radius of the vase at the top is 3 inches. Find the volume of the vase. Use 3.14 for π. (*Hint:* The formula for the volume of a cone is $V = \frac{1}{3}\pi r^2 h$, where r is the radius of the cone and h is the height of the cone.)

3 in.

10 in.

5. Lori wants to create a border around the room using stickers. She can purchase a package of 5 stickers for $6.00. Make a table to show the cost of 1, 2, 3, 4, and 5 packages of stickers. Make another table to show the cost based on the number of stickers (not the number of packages). How many stickers can Lori purchase if she has $32 left in her budget?

READY TO GO ON?

Quiz for Lessons 1-6 Through 1-8

✓ 1-6 Order of Operations

Simplify each expression.

1. $-6 + 12 \div (-3)$

2. $30 - 9 + 4$

3. $(6 - 8) \cdot (7 - 5)$

4. $8 \cdot \left[8 - (4 - 2)\right]$

5. $\dfrac{23 - 3 \cdot 5}{4}$

6. $|3 - 9| \div 2 + 5$

Translate each word phrase into a numerical expression.

7. the quotient of 16 and the difference of 9 and -7

8. the product of 5 and the sum of 6 and 4

9. The area of a trapezoid can be found using the expression $\frac{1}{2}\left(b_1 + b_2\right)h$. Find the area of the trapezoid shown.

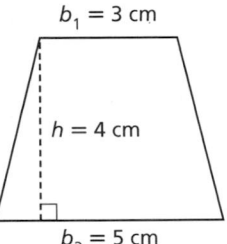

$b_1 = 3$ cm

$h = 4$ cm

$b_2 = 5$ cm

✓ 1-7 Simplifying Expressions

Simplify each expression.

10. $75 + 32 + 25$

11. $5 \cdot 18 \cdot 20$

12. $\dfrac{1}{4} \cdot 19 \cdot 8$

Write each product using the Distributive Property. Then simplify.

13. $7(67)$

14. $9(29)$

15. $17(18)$

16. $8(106)$

Simplify each expression by combining like terms.

17. $4k + 15k$

18. $x^2 + 22x^2$

19. $-2g + 5g$

Simplify each expression. Justify each step with an operation or property.

20. $3(x + 2) - 3x$

21. $x - 6x^2 + 3x + 4x^2$

22. $-2\left(3x + 2y + 4x - 5y\right)$

✓ 1-8 Introduction to Functions

Graph each point.

23. $A(0, -3)$

24. $B(-2, -3)$

25. $C(1, 4)$

Name the quadrant in which each point lies.

26. A

27. B

28. C

29. D

30. E

31. F

Generate ordered pairs for each function for $x = -2, -1, 0, 1,$ and 2. Graph the ordered pairs and describe the pattern.

32. $y = x^2 + 1$

33. $y = x - 1$

34. $y = -|x|$

35. $y = 3x + 3$

36. A swimming pool contains 30,000 gallons of water. The pool is drained at a rate of 100 gallons per minute. Write a rule for the amount of water in the pool when x minutes have gone by. Write ordered pairs for the amount of water in the pool when 30, 60, 90, and 120 minutes have gone by.

Vocabulary

Complete the sentences below with vocabulary words from the list above.

1. A(n) ___?___ is a value that does not change.

2. The ___?___ include the natural numbers and zero.

3. A(n) ___?___ is the numerical factor of a term that contains a variable.

4. The ___?___ is the point where the axes of a coordinate plane intersect.

1-1 Variables and Expressions (pp. 6–11)

EXAMPLES

■ Barbara has saved d dollars for a $65 sweater. Write an expression for the amount of money she still needs to buy the sweater.

$65 - d$ *Think: d dollars less than the price of the sweater.*

■ Evaluate $b - a$ for $a = 7$ and $b = 15$.

$b - a = 15 - 7$ *Substitute the values for*
     $= 8$ *the variables.*

EXERCISES

5. Grapes cost $1.99 per pound. Write an expression for the cost of g pounds of grapes.

6. Today's temperature is 3 degrees warmer than yesterday's temperature t. Write an expression for today's temperature.

Evaluate each expression for $p = 5$ and $q = 1$.

7. qp **8.** $p \div q$ **9.** $q + p$

10. Each member of the art club will make the same number of posters to advertise their club. They will make 150 posters total. Write an expression for how many posters each member will make if there are m members. Find how many posters each member will make if there are 5, 6, and 10 members.

1-2 Adding and Subtracting Real Numbers *(pp. 14–19)*

EXAMPLES

Add or subtract.

- $-4 + (-9)$

  $-4 + (-9)$ *The signs are the same.*

  $(4 + 9 = 13)$ *Add the absolute values and use*

  -13 *the sign of the numbers.*

- $-8 - (-3)$

  $-8 + 3$ *To subtract −3, add 3.*

  -5

EXERCISES

Add or subtract.

11. $-2 + (-12)$ **12.** $-6 + 1.4$ **13.** $9\frac{1}{4} + \left(-4\frac{3}{4}\right)$

14. $\frac{1}{2} - \frac{3}{2}$ **15.** $-8 - 16$ **16.** $6.7 - (-7.6)$

17. A trail starts at an elevation of 2278 feet. It descends 47 feet to a campsite. What is the elevation of the campsite?

1-3 Multiplying and Dividing Real Numbers *(pp. 20–25)*

EXAMPLES

Multiply or divide.

- $-12(9)$

  $-12(9) = -108$

- $-\frac{5}{6} \div \left(-\frac{3}{4}\right)$

  $-\frac{5}{6} \div \left(-\frac{3}{4}\right) = -\frac{5}{6}\left(-\frac{4}{3}\right)$

  $= \frac{(-5)(-4)}{6(3)}$

  $= \frac{20}{18} = \frac{10}{9}$

EXERCISES

Multiply or divide if possible.

18. $-5(-18)$ **19.** $0 \cdot 10$ **20.** $-4(3.8)$

21. $-56 \div 7$ **22.** $0 \div 0.75$ **23.** $9 \div 0$

Divide.

24. $4 \div \frac{4}{9}$ **25.** $-\frac{1}{2} \div \frac{3}{4}$ **26.** $\frac{6}{7} \div \frac{2}{5}$

27. An exercise program recommends that a person walk at least 10,000 steps every day. At this rate, how many steps would the person walk in 1 year?

1-4 Powers and Exponents *(pp. 26–31)*

EXAMPLES

- **Simplify** -3^4.

  $-3^4 = -1 \cdot 3 \cdot 3 \cdot 3 \cdot 3$ *Find the product of −1*

  $= -81$ *and four 3's.*

- **Write −216 as a power of −6.**

  $-216 = (-6)(-6)(-6)$ *The product of three*

  $= (-6)^3$ *−6's is −216.*

EXERCISES

Write each expression as repeated multiplication. Then simplify the expression.

28. 4^3 **29.** $(-3)^3$ **30.** $(-3)^4$

31. -5^2 **32.** $\left(\frac{2}{3}\right)^3$ **33.** $\left(-\frac{4}{5}\right)^2$

Write each number as a power of the given base.

34. 16; base 2   **35.** −1000; base −10

36. 64; base −8   **37.** 12; base 12

38. The interior of a safe is shaped like a cube with edges 9 inches long. What is the volume of the interior of the safe?

1-5 Roots and Real Numbers (pp. 32–37)

EXAMPLES

Find each root.

■ $-\sqrt{64}$

$8^2 = 64$

$-\sqrt{64} = -8$

■ $\sqrt{\dfrac{16}{81}}$

$\left(\dfrac{4}{9}\right)^2 = \dfrac{4}{9} \cdot \dfrac{4}{9} = \dfrac{16}{81}$

$\sqrt{\dfrac{16}{81}} = \dfrac{4}{9}$

■ Write all classifications that apply to -7.

$-7 = \dfrac{-7}{1} = -7.0$

rational number, terminating decimal, integer

EXERCISES

Find each root.

39. $\sqrt{36}$
40. $\sqrt[3]{64}$
41. $-\sqrt{49}$
42. $-\sqrt{144}$
43. $\sqrt{\dfrac{25}{36}}$
44. $\sqrt[3]{\dfrac{1}{27}}$

Write all the classifications that apply to each real number.

45. 21
46. 0
47. -13
48. 0.8
49. $\sqrt{3}$
50. $\dfrac{5}{6}$

51. A tabletop is shaped like a square with an area of 13 square feet. Find the length of one side of the table to the nearest tenth of a foot.

1-6 Order of Operations (pp. 40–45)

EXAMPLES

■ Simplify $18 - 3\left(\dfrac{15-7}{4}\right)^2$.

$18 - 3\left(\dfrac{15-7}{4}\right)^2$

$18 - 3\left(\dfrac{8}{4}\right)^2$ *Simplify the numerator.*

$18 - 3(2)^2$ *Simplify inside parentheses.*

$18 - 3 \cdot 4$ *Simplify powers.*

$18 - 12$ *Multiply.*

6 *Subtract.*

■ Evaluate $-5\sqrt{40 - x} + 12$ for $x = 4$.

$-5\sqrt{40 - 4} + 12$ *Substitute the value for x.*

$-5\sqrt{36} + 12$ *Simplify inside the square root symbol.*

$-5(6) + 12$ *Find the square root.*

$-30 + 12$ *Multiply.*

-18 *Add.*

EXERCISES

Simplify each expression.

52. $5 \cdot 4 + 3$
53. $17 + 3(-3)$
54. $[8 + (2 - 6)^2] \div 4$
55. $\dfrac{4^2 - 11}{10}$
56. $|12 - 3 \cdot 7| \cdot (-2)$
57. $\sqrt{4 \cdot 5 + 5} - 5$

Evaluate each expression for the given value of x.

58. $48 - x + 29$ for $x = 15$
59. $x + 4 \cdot 6 - 10$ for $x = -4$
60. $8(x - 8)^3$ for $x = 9$
61. $[(3 - x)^2 + 4] \div 2$ for $x = 7$

Translate each word phrase into a numerical or algebraic expression.

62. the sum of 8 and the product of 7 and -2
63. the quotient of 12 and the sum of 8 and 3
64. 4 times the square root of x less than 20
65. The expression $16t^2 + vt$ can be used to find the distance in feet traveled by a falling object. The initial speed is v (ft/s), and time is t (s). Find the distance traveled in 3 s by a falling object with an initial speed of 8 ft/s.

1-7 Simplifying Expressions (pp. 46–51)

EXAMPLES

Simplify each expression.

■ $-6f^2 - 8f + 3f^2$

$\qquad -6f^2 + 3f^2 - 8f$ *Commutative Property*

$\qquad -3f^2 - 8f$ *Combine like terms.*

■ $3x - 4y$

$\qquad 3x - 4y$ *There are no like terms.*

$\qquad$ *It cannot be simplified.*

■ $5x^2 - 3(x - 2) - x$

$\qquad 5x^2 - 3x - 3(-2) - x$ *Distributive Property*

$\qquad 5x^2 - 3x + 6 - x$ *Multiply.*

$\qquad 5x^2 - 3x - x + 6$ *Commutative Property*

$\qquad 5x^2 - 4x + 6$ *Combine like terms.*

EXERCISES

Simplify each expression.

66. $18 + 26 - 8 + 4$ **67.** $60 \cdot 27 \cdot \frac{1}{6}$

Write each product using the Distributive Property. Then simplify.

68. $13(103)$ **69.** $18(99)$

Simplify each expression.

70. $20x - 16x$ **71.** $2y^2 + 5y^2$

72. $6(x + 4) - 2x$ **73.** $-2(x^2 - 1) + 4x^2$

74. $-2y + 3y^2 - 3y + y$ **75.** $7y + 3y - a - 2y$

76. Rita bought a sandwich, 2 bottles of water, and an apple for lunch. The sandwich cost \$4.99, the bottles of water cost \$1.48 each, and the apple cost \$0.89. About how much did Rita spend on lunch?

1-8 Introduction to Functions (pp. 54–59)

EXAMPLES

■ Generate ordered pairs for the function using the given values for *x*. Graph the ordered pairs and describe the pattern.

$y = x + 2; x = -4, -3, -2, -1, 0$

Input	Output	Ordered Pair
x	*y*	(*x, y*)
−4	−4 + 2 = −2	(−4, −2)
−3	−3 + 2 = −1	(−3, −1)
−2	−2 + 2 = 0	(−2, 0)
−1	−1 + 2 = 1	(−1, 1)
0	0 + 2 = 2	(0, 2)

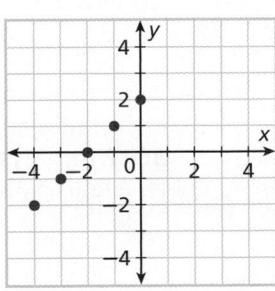

The points form a straight line.

EXERCISES

Graph each point.

77. $A(2, 3)$ **78.** $B(-1, 4)$

79. $C(0, 8)$ **80.** $D(5, -3)$

Name the quadrant in which each point lies.

81. R

82. S

83. T

84. U

85. V

86. W

87. The price of an item with tax is equal to the price of the item plus $\frac{1}{20}$ of the price. Write a rule for the price with tax. Write ordered pairs for the price with tax of items that cost \$2, \$15, \$30, and \$40.

88. Generate ordered pairs for the function $y = \frac{1}{4}x^2$ for $x = -4, -1, 0, 1,$ and 4. Graph the ordered pairs and describe the pattern.

CHAPTER TEST

Evaluate each expression for $a = 2$, $b = 3$, and $c = 6$.

1. $c - a$ **2.** ab **3.** $c \div a$ **4.** $\dfrac{c}{b}$ **5.** $b - a$

6. Give two ways to write $n - 5$ in words.

7. Nate runs 8 miles each week. Write an expression for the number of miles he runs in n weeks. Find the number of miles Nate runs in 5 weeks.

Add or subtract.

8. $-5 + 8$ **9.** $-3 - 4$ **10.** $4 + (-7)$ **11.** $7 - (-2)$

The table shows the lowest temperatures recorded in four states.

12. How much greater is the lowest temperature in Hawaii than the lowest temperature in Alaska?

13. How much greater is the lowest temperature in Texas than the lowest temperature in Nebraska?

Lowest Temperatures in Four States	
Location	Temperature (°F)
Prospect Creek, Alaska	−80
Camp Clarke, Nebraska	−47
Mauna Kea, Hawaii	12
Seminole, Texas	−23

Multiply or divide if possible.

14. $(-3)(-6)$ **15.** $-\dfrac{1}{2} \div \dfrac{1}{4}$ **16.** $12 \div (-3)$ **17.** $0 \div (-4)$

Simplify each expression.

18. 5^4 **19.** $\left(-\dfrac{4}{5}\right)^3$ **20.** 2^5 **21.** -6^2

Write all classifications that apply to each real number.

22. 30 **23.** $\sqrt{6}$ **24.** -12 **25.** $\dfrac{1}{2}$

Evaluate each expression for the given value of x.

26. $\dfrac{-2 - 6}{x^2}$ for $x = 2$ **27.** $8(x - 1)^2$ for $x = 11$ **28.** $22 + \left[-2(19 - x)\right]$ for $x = 7$

29. Does the phrase "2 times the sum of a number and 5" represent the same expression as the phrase "the sum of 2 times a number and 5"? Explain why or why not.

Simplify each expression.

30. $5\dfrac{1}{4} + 7 + 2\dfrac{3}{4}$ **31.** $-2(x + 5) + 4x$ **32.** $3x + 2x^2 - x$

Graph each point.

33. $W(1, -3)$ **34.** $X(-3, 0)$ **35.** $Y(5, 3)$ **36.** $Z(0, -2)$

37. Generate ordered pairs for $y = 2x - 1$ for $x = -2, -1, 0, 1, 2$. Graph the ordered pairs and describe the pattern.

COLLEGE ENTRANCE EXAM PRACTICE

FOCUS ON SAT*

The SAT is often used to predict academic success at the college level. SAT scores are used to compare the math and verbal reasoning skills of students from all over the world.

You may want to time yourself as you take this practice test. It should take you about 8 minutes to complete.

In each section of SAT questions, the easier questions are at the beginning of the section and harder questions come later. Answer as many of the easy questions as you can first, and then move on to the more challenging questions.

---

1. The number 0 is NOT an example of which of the following?

    (A) Real numbers

    (B) Rational numbers

    (C) Whole numbers

    (D) Integers

    (E) Natural numbers

---

2. A clothing store opens with 75 pairs of jeans on a sale table. By noon, 10 pairs have been sold. As of 2:00, another 8 pairs have been sold. A clerk then restocks with 12 pairs. Receipts show that 18 pairs of jeans were sold after 2:00. How many pairs of jeans are left at the end of the day?

    (A) 23

    (B) 27

    (C) 36

    (D) 51

    (E) 123

---

3. If Jack is three times as old as his sister Judy, which of the following expressions represents Jack's age if Judy is j years old?

    (A) $3 \div j$

    (B) $3j$

    (C) $j + 3$

    (D) $3 - j$

    (E) $\frac{1}{3}j$

---

4. Which of the following is equal to -3^4?

    (A) 81

    (B) 12

    (C) -12

    (D) -64

    (E) -81

---

5. What is the result after applying the following sequence of operations to a number n in the given order?

    1. Subtract 2.   3. Add 7.
    2. Divide by 3.   4. Multiply by -1.

    (A) $\frac{n-2}{3} + 7(-1)$

    (B) $\frac{(-n-2)+7}{3}$

    (C) $-\left(-\frac{2}{3} + 7\right)n$

    (D) $-\left(\frac{n-2}{3} + 7\right)$

    (E) $n - \frac{2}{3} + 7(-1)$

---

6. Which expression is equivalent to $8(6 + x)$?

    (A) $48x$

    (B) $8x + 14$

    (C) $8x + 48$

    (D) $x + 14$

    (E) $x + 48$

---

*SAT is a registered trademark of the College Board, which was not involved in the production of, and does not endorse, this product.

✎ TEST TACKLER

Standardized Test Strategies

Gridded Response: Fill in Answer Grids Correctly

When responding to a test item that requires you to place your answer in a grid, you must fill out the grid on your answer sheet correctly, or the item will be marked as incorrect.

EXAMPLE 1

Gridded Response: Simplify the expression $12^2 - 3(10 + 4)$.

$$12^2 - 3(10 + 4)$$
$$12^2 - 3(14)$$
$$144 - 3(14)$$
$$144 - 42$$
$$102$$

The expression simplifies to 102.

- Write your answer in the answer boxes at the top of the grid.
- Put only one digit in each box. Do not leave a blank box in the middle of an answer.
- Shade the bubble for each digit in the same column as the digit in the answer box.

EXAMPLE 2

Gridded Response: Evaluate the expression $ba \div c$ for $a = -7$, $b = 2$, and $c = -6$.

$$ba \div c$$
$$(2)(-7) \div (-6)$$
$$-14 \div (-6)$$
$$\frac{7}{3} = 2\frac{1}{3} = 2.\overline{3}$$

The expression simplifies to $\frac{7}{3}$, $2\frac{1}{3}$, or $2.\overline{3}$.

- Mixed numbers and repeating decimals cannot be gridded, so you must grid the answer as $\frac{7}{3}$.
- Write your answer in the answer boxes at the top of the grid.
- Put only one digit or symbol in each box. On some grids, the fraction bar and the decimal point have a designated box. Do not leave a blank box in the middle of an answer.
- Shade the bubble for each digit or symbol in the same column as the digit in the answer box.

On many grids you cannot grid a negative number because the grid does not include the negative sign. If you get a negative answer to a test item, you may need to recalculate the problem.

Read each sample and then answer the questions that follow.

Sample A
A student correctly evaluated an expression and got $\frac{8}{15}$ as a result. Then the student filled in the grid as shown.

1. What error did the student make when filling in the grid?

2. Explain how to fill in the answer correctly.

Sample B
The square root of 6.25 is 2.5. This answer is displayed in the grid.

3. What error did the student make when filling in the grid?

4. Explain how to fill in the answer correctly.

Sample C
A student correctly simplified the expression $2\frac{1}{8} + 3\frac{5}{8} + \frac{7}{8}$. Then the student filled in the grid as shown.

5. What answer does the grid show?

6. Explain why you cannot fill in a mixed number.

7. Write the answer $6\frac{5}{8}$ in two forms that could be entered in the grid correctly.

Sample D
A student added -10 and 25 and got an answer of 15. Then the student filled in the grid as shown.

8. What error does the grid show?

9. Another student got an answer of -15. Explain why the student knew this answer was wrong.

STANDARDIZED TEST PREP

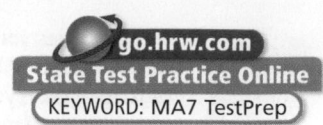

go.hrw.com
State Test Practice Online
KEYWORD: MA7 TestPrep

CUMULATIVE ASSESSMENT, CHAPTERS 1

Multiple Choice

1. Eric is collecting gifts for a charity event. He needs 150 gifts. So far he has collected x gifts. Which expression represents how many gifts Eric still needs to collect?

    (A) $150 + x$
    (C) $x - 150$
    (B) $150 - x$
    (D) $150 \div x$

2. An online store sells birdhouses for $34.95 each. For each order, there is a one-time shipping and handling fee of $7.50. Which expression can be used to represent the cost of ordering x birdhouses?

    (F) $x + 34.95 + 7.50$

    (G) $(34.95 + 7.50)x$

    (H) $7.50x + 34.95$

    (J) $34.95x + 7.50$

3. Which equation could have generated the table?

x	y
−2	5
−1	2
0	1
1	2
2	5

    (A) $y = -2x + 1$
    (B) $y = x + 1$
    (C) $y = |2x| + 1$
    (D) $y = x^2 + 1$

4. The equation $C = \frac{5}{9}(F - 32)$ relates the Celsius temperature C to the Fahrenheit temperature F. What is the Celsius temperature if the Fahrenheit temperature is −13 degrees?

    (F) $-45\,°C$
    (H) $-25\,°C$
    (G) $-39.2\,°C$
    (J) $-10.6\,°C$

5. Which equation is NOT true?

    (A) $55 + 27 + 45 = 100 + 27$

    (B) $5 \cdot 7 \cdot \frac{2}{5} = 2 \cdot 7$

    (C) $14(126) = 14(100) + 14(26)$

    (D) $31(152) = 30(150) + 1(2)$

6. The volume of a sphere with radius r is $\frac{4\pi r^3}{3}$. The radius of a ball is 4 inches. What is the volume of the ball in cubic inches?

    (F) 16π in³

    (G) $\frac{64\pi}{3}$ in³

    (H) $\frac{256\pi}{3}$ in³

    (J) $\frac{4096\pi}{3}$ in³

7. Which of the following real numbers is a terminating decimal?

    (A) π

    (B) $\frac{3}{2}$

    (C) $\frac{4}{9}$

    (D) $\frac{1}{3}$

8. At one time, a U.S. dollar had the same value as 11.32 Mexican pesos. To the nearest hundredth, how many Mexican pesos were equal to 16 U.S. dollars at that time?

    (F) 1.41 pesos

    (G) 4.68 pesos

    (H) 27.32 pesos

    (J) 181.12 pesos

9. Tickets to a festival cost $5.00 each, and lunch costs $8.50 per person. Renting a bus to and from the festival costs $47.00. Which expression gives the cost of *x* people going to the festival?

   (A) $5.00 + 8.50 + 47.00$

   (B) $5.00x + 8.50 + 47.00$

   (C) $5.00 + 8.50x + 47.00$

   (D) $5.00x + 8.50x + 47.00$

10. Tariq cut a rectangular piece of paper in half to make two triangles, as shown.

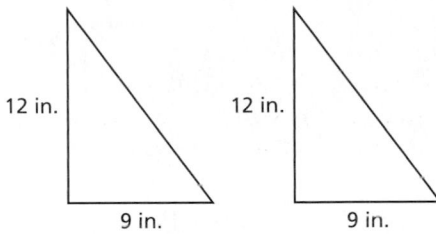

   What was the area of the rectangle?

   (F) 42 inches

   (G) 54 square inches

   (H) 72 inches

   (J) 108 square inches

Gridded Response

11. A scientist prepares 4 beakers of an acid solution. Each beaker contains 70.9 milliliters of the solution. How many milliliters of acid solution did the scientist prepare in all?

12. At an accident scene, an insurance inspector finds a skid mark 60 feet long. The inspector can determine how fast the car was going in miles per hour when the driver applied the breaks by using the expression $\sqrt{21d}$, where *d* is the length of the skid mark in feet. To the nearest tenth, what was the speed of the car that left the skid mark?

13. The area of a circle with radius *r* is πr^2. What is the area in square meters of the robot sumo-wrestling ring shown below? Use 3.14 for π. Round to the nearest tenth.

0.76 m

Short Response

14. Dee is using a coordinate plane to make a map of her town. Each square on the grid represents 1 square mile. She plots her house at the origin. Her school is 3 miles east and 2 miles north of her house.

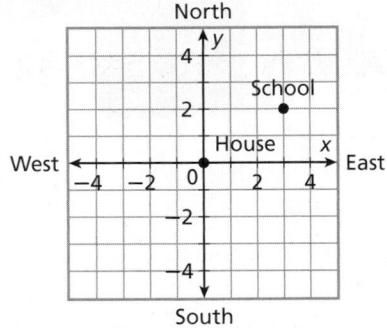

   a. Write an ordered pair to show where Dee plotted the point for her school.

   b. The post office is 4 miles east of Dee's house. Write an ordered pair to show where Dee should plot a point for the post office.

   c. The bank is 3 miles north and 3 miles west of the school. Which is closer to Dee's house, the post office or the bank? Explain your answer.

15. As part of a challenge problem, a math teacher writes the following expression on the board:

   $$-(-x).$$

   a. If *x* is 12, what is the value of the expression?

   b. If *x* is a negative number, is the value of the expression positive or negative? Explain how you found your answer.

   c. Simplify the expression.

Extended Response

16. Fatima enrolled in a traveler rewards program. She begins with 10,000 bonus points. For every trip she takes, she collects 3000 bonus points.

   a. Write a rule for the number of bonus points Fatima has after *x* trips.

   b. Make a table showing the number of bonus points Fatima has after 0, 1, 2, 3, 4, and 5 trips.

   c. Graph the ordered pairs from the table. Describe the pattern formed by the points.

   d. When Fatima has collected 20,000 bonus points, she gets a free vacation. How many trips does Fatima need to take to get a free vacation?

Equations

Chapter
FOCUS

- Use properties of equality.
- Choose procedures to solve equations efficiently.
- Write and solve equations to solve problems.

All in *Proportion*

A common use of equations and proportional relationships is the construction of scale models.

go.hrw.com
Chapter Project Online
KEYWORD: MA7 ChProj

ARE YOU READY?

✓ Vocabulary

Match each term on the left with a definition on the right.

1. constant
2. expression
3. order of operations
4. variable

    A. a mathematical phrase that contains operations, numbers, and/or variables

    B. a mathematical statement that two expressions are equivalent

    C. a process for evaluating expressions

    D. a symbol used to represent a quantity that can change

    E. a value that does not change

✓ Order of Operations

Simplify each expression.

5. $(7 - 3) \div 2$
6. $4 \cdot 6 \div 3$
7. $12 - 3 + 1$
8. $2 \cdot 10 \div 5$
9. $125 \div 5^2$
10. $7 \cdot 6 + 5 \cdot 4$

✓ Add and Subtract Integers

Add or subtract.

11. $-15 + 19$
12. $-6 - (-18)$
13. $6 + (-8)$
14. $-12 + (-3)$

✓ Add and Subtract Fractions

Perform each indicated operation. Give your answer in the simplest form.

15. $\frac{1}{4} + \frac{2}{3}$
16. $1\frac{1}{2} - \frac{3}{4}$
17. $\frac{3}{8} + \frac{2}{3}$
18. $\frac{3}{2} - \frac{2}{3}$

✓ Evaluate Expressions

Evaluate each expression for the given value of the variable.

19. $2x + 3$ for $x = 7$
20. $3n - 5$ for $n = 7$
21. $13 - 4a$ for $a = 2$
22. $3y + 5$ for $y = 5$

✓ Connect Words and Algebra

23. Janie bought 4 apples and 6 bananas. Each apple cost $0.75, and each banana cost $0.60. Write an expression representing the total cost.

24. A rectangle has a width of 13 inches and a length of ℓ inches. Write an expression representing the area of the rectangle.

25. Write a phrase that could be modeled by the expression $n + 2n$.

Study Guide: Preview

Where You've Been

Previously, you
- practiced using operations in algebra.
- used variables to represent quantities.
- wrote expressions to represent situations.
- simplified and evaluated expressions.

In This Chapter

You will study
- how to use inverse operations to solve equations containing variables.
- writing equations to represent situations.
- simplifying equations before solving.

Where You're Going

You can use the skills in this chapter
- to compare unit prices for consumer products.
- to calculate percentages in taxes, tips, interest, and commissions.
- to create or interpret scale models and drawings.
- to solve problems in science courses and all future math courses.

Key Vocabulary/Vocabulario

equation	ecuación
formula	fórmula
identity	identidad
indirect measurement	medición indirecta
literal equation	ecuación literal
percent	porcentaje
percent change	porcentaje de cambio
proportion	proporción
ratio	razón
unit rate	tasa unitaria

Vocabulary Connections

To become familiar with some of the vocabulary terms in the chapter, consider the following. You may refer to the chapter, the glossary, or a dictionary if you like.

1. The word **equation** begins with the root *equa-*. List some other words that begin with *equa-*. What do all these words have in common?

2. The word *literal* means "of letters." How might a **literal equation** be different from an equation like $3 + 5 = 8$?

3. One definition of **identity** is "exact sameness." An equation consists of two expressions. If an equation is an *identity*, what do you think is true about the expressions?

4. The word *per* means "for each," and the word *cent* means "hundred." How can you use these meanings to understand the term **percent**?

Reading and Writing Math

Study Strategy: Use Your Own Words

Explaining a concept using your own words will help you better understand it. For example, learning to solve equations might seem difficult if the textbook doesn't use the same words that you would use.

As you work through each lesson:

- Identify the important ideas from the explanation in the book.
- Use your own words to explain the important ideas you identified.

What Arturo Reads

To evaluate an expression is to find its value.

To evaluate an algebraic expression, substitute numbers for the variables in the expression and then simplify the expression.

A replacement set is a set of numbers that can be substituted for a variable.

What Arturo Writes

Evaluate an expression— find the value.

Substitute a number for each variable (letter), and find the answer.

Replacement set—numbers that can be substituted for a letter.

Try This

Rewrite each paragraph in your own words.

1. Two numbers are opposites if their sum is 0. A number and its opposite are on opposite sides of zero on a number line, but are the same distance from zero.

2. The Commutative and Associative Properties of Addition and Multiplication allow you to rearrange an expression to simplify it.

3. The terms of an expression are the parts to be added or subtracted. Like terms are terms that contain the same variables raised to the same powers. Constants are also like terms.

2-1 Algebra LAB

Model One-Step Equations

You can use algebra tiles and an equation mat to model and solve equations. To find the value of the variable, place or remove tiles to get the x-tile by itself on one side of the mat. You must place or remove the same number of yellow tiles or the same number of red tiles on both sides.

Use with Lesson 2-1

go.hrw.com
Lab Resources Online
KEYWORD: MA11 LAB2

KEY

 = 1

 = −1

 = x

REMEMBER

 = 0

Activity

Use algebra tiles to model and solve $x + 6 = 2$.

MODEL		ALGEBRA
	Model $x + 6$ on the left side of the mat and 2 on the right side of the mat.	$x + 6 = 2$
	Place 6 red tiles on both sides of the mat. This represents adding −6 to both sides of the equation.	$x + 6 + (-6) = 2 + (-6)$
	Remove zero pairs from both sides of the mat.	$x + 0 = 0 + (-4)$
	One x-tile is equivalent to 4 red tiles.	$x = -4$

Try This

Use algebra tiles to model and solve each equation.

1. $x + 2 = 5$ **2.** $x - 7 = 8$ **3.** $x - 5 = 9$ **4.** $x + 4 = 7$

Solving Equations by Adding or Subtracting

Objective
Solve one-step equations in one variable by using addition or subtraction.

Vocabulary
equation
solution of an equation

Who uses this?
Athletes can use an equation to estimate their maximum heart rates. (See Example 4.)

An **equation** is a mathematical statement that two expressions are equal. A **solution of an equation** is a value of the variable that makes the equation true.

To find solutions, *isolate the variable*. A variable is isolated when it appears by itself on one side of an equation, and not at all on the other side. Isolate a variable by using inverse operations, which "undo" operations on the variable.

An equation is like a balanced scale. To keep the balance, perform the same operation on both sides.

Inverse Operations

Add x. $\longleftrightarrow$ Subtract x.

EXAMPLE 1 Solving Equations by Using Addition

Solve each equation.

A $x - 10 = 4$

$$\begin{array}{rcl} x - 10 & = & 4 \\ +\,10 & & +\,10 \\ \hline x & = & 14 \end{array}$$

Since 10 is subtracted from x, add 10 to both sides to undo the subtraction.

Check $\quad\dfrac{x - 10 = 4}{\begin{array}{c|c} 14 - 10 & 4 \\ 4 & 4 \checkmark \end{array}}$

To check your solution, substitute 14 for x in the original equation.

B $\dfrac{2}{5} = m - \dfrac{1}{5}$

$$\begin{array}{rcl} \dfrac{2}{5} & = & m - \dfrac{1}{5} \\[2mm] +\dfrac{1}{5} & & +\dfrac{1}{5} \\[2mm] \hline \dfrac{3}{5} & = & m \end{array}$$

Since $\frac{1}{5}$ is subtracted from m, add $\frac{1}{5}$ to both sides to undo the subtraction.

Writing Math

Solutions are sometimes written in a *solution set*. For Example 1A, the solution set is {14}. For Example 1B, the solution set is $\left\{\dfrac{3}{5}\right\}$.

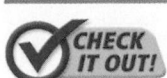 Solve each equation. Check your answer.

1a. $n - 3.2 = 5.6$ **1b.** $-6 = k - 6$ **1c.** $16 = m - 9$

EXAMPLE **2** **Solving Equations by Using Subtraction**

Solve each equation. Check your answer.

A $x + 7 = 9$

$$
\begin{array}{rr}
x + 7 = & 9 \\
-7 & -7 \\
\hline
x = & 2
\end{array}
$$

Since 7 is added to x, subtract 7 from both sides to undo the addition.

Check
$$
\begin{array}{c|c}
\multicolumn{2}{c}{x + 7 = 9} \\
\hline
2 + 7 & 9 \\
9 & 9 \checkmark
\end{array}
$$

To check your solution, substitute 2 for x in the original equation.

B $0.7 = r + 0.4$

$$
\begin{array}{rr}
0.7 = & r + 0.4 \\
-0.4 & -0.4 \\
\hline
0.3 = & r
\end{array}
$$

Since 0.4 is added to r, subtract 0.4 from both sides to undo the addition.

Check
$$
\begin{array}{c|c}
\multicolumn{2}{c}{0.7 = r + 0.4} \\
\hline
0.7 & 0.3 + 0.4 \\
0.7 & 0.7 \checkmark
\end{array}
$$

To check your solution, substitute 0.3 for r in the original equation.

 Solve each equation. Check your answer.

2a. $d + \dfrac{1}{2} = 1$ **2b.** $-5 = k + 5$ **2c.** $6 + t = 14$

Remember that subtracting is the same as adding the opposite. When solving equations, you will sometimes find it easier to add an opposite to both sides instead of subtracting. For example, this method may be useful when the equation contains negative numbers.

EXAMPLE **3** **Solving Equations by Adding the Opposite**

Solve $-8 + b = 2$.

$$
\begin{array}{rr}
-8 + b = & 2 \\
+8 & +8 \\
\hline
b = & 10
\end{array}
$$

Since −8 is added to b, add 8 to both sides.

 Solve each equation. Check your answer.

3a. $-2.3 + m = 7$ **3b.** $-\dfrac{3}{4} + z = \dfrac{5}{4}$ **3c.** $-11 + x = 33$

Student to Student **Zero As a Solution**

Ama Walker
Carson High School

I used to get confused when I got a solution of 0. But my teacher reminded me that 0 is a number just like any other number, so it can be a solution of an equation. Just check your answer and see if it works.

$$
\begin{array}{rr}
x + 6 = & 6 \\
-6 & -6 \\
\hline
x = & 0
\end{array}
$$

Check
$$
\begin{array}{c|c}
\multicolumn{2}{c}{x + 6 = 6} \\
\hline
0 + 6 & 6 \\
6 & 6 \checkmark
\end{array}
$$

EXAMPLE 4 *Fitness Application*

A person's maximum heart rate is the highest rate, in beats per minute, that the person's heart should reach. One method to estimate maximum heart rate states that your age added to your maximum heart rate is 220. Using this method, write and solve an equation to find the maximum heart rate of a 15-year-old.

Age	added to	maximum heart rate	is	220.
a	$+$	r	$=$	220

$$a + r = 220$$ Write an equation to represent the relationship.

$$15 + r = 220$$ Substitute 15 for a. Since 15 is added to r,
$$\underline{-15 \qquad -15}$$ subtract 15 from both sides to undo the
$$r = 205$$ addition.

The maximum heart rate for a 15-year-old is 205 beats per minute. Since age added to maximum heart rate is 220, the answer should be less than 220. So 205 is a reasonable answer.

 CHECK IT OUT!

4. What if...? Use the method above to find a person's age if the person's maximum heart rate is 185 beats per minute.

The properties of equality allow you to perform inverse operations, as in the previous examples. These properties say that you can perform the same operation on both sides of an equation.

Properties of Equality

WORDS	NUMBERS	ALGEBRA
Addition Property of Equality You can add the same number to both sides of an equation, and the statement will still be true.	$3 = 3$ $3 + 2 = 3 + 2$ $5 = 5$	$a = b$ $a + c = b + c$
Subtraction Property of Equality You can subtract the same number from both sides of an equation, and the statement will still be true.	$7 = 7$ $7 - 5 = 7 \quad 5$ $2 = 2$	$a = b$ $a - c = b - c$

THINK AND DISCUSS

1. Describe how the Addition and Subtraction Properties of Equality are like a balanced scale.

2. **GET ORGANIZED** Copy and complete the graphic organizer. In each box, write an example of an equation that can be solved by using the given property, and solve it.

GUIDED PRACTICE

1. **Vocabulary** Will the *solution of an equation* such as $x - 3 = 9$ be a variable or a number? Explain.

Solve each equation. Check your answer.

SEE EXAMPLE 1
p. 77

2. $s - 5 = 3$

3. $17 = w - 4$

4. $k - 8 = -7$

5. $x - 3.9 = 12.4$

6. $8.4 = y - 4.6$

7. $\frac{3}{8} = t - \frac{1}{8}$

SEE EXAMPLE 2
p. 78

8. $t + 5 = -25$

9. $9 = s + 9$

10. $42 = m + 36$

11. $2.8 = z + 0.5$

12. $b + \frac{2}{3} = 2$

13. $n + 1.8 = 3$

SEE EXAMPLE 3
p. 78

14. $-10 + d = 7$

15. $20 = -12 + v$

16. $-46 + q = 5$

17. $2.8 = -0.9 + y$

18. $-\frac{2}{3} + c = \frac{2}{3}$

19. $-\frac{5}{6} + p = 2$

SEE EXAMPLE 4
p. 79

20. **Geology** In 1673, the Hope diamond was reduced from its original weight by about 45 carats, resulting in a diamond weighing about 67 carats. Write and solve an equation to find how many carats the original diamond weighed. Show that your answer is reasonable.

PRACTICE AND PROBLEM SOLVING

Independent Practice

For Exercises	See Example
21–30	1
31–40	2
41–48	3
49	4

Extra Practice
Skills Practice p. S6
Application Practice p. S29

Solve each equation. Check your answer.

21. $1 = k - 8$

22. $u - 15 = -8$

23. $x - 7 = 10$

24. $-9 = p - 2$

25. $\frac{3}{7} = p - \frac{1}{7}$

26. $q - 0.5 = 1.5$

27. $6 = t - 4.5$

28. $4\frac{2}{3} = r - \frac{1}{3}$

29. $6 = x - 3$

30. $1.75 = k - 0.75$

31. $19 + a = 19$

32. $4 = 3.1 + y$

33. $m + 20 = 3$

34. $-12 = c + 3$

35. $v + 2300 = -800$

36. $b + 42 = 300$

37. $3.5 = n + 4$

38. $b + \frac{1}{2} = \frac{1}{2}$

39. $x + 5.34 = 5.39$

40. $2 = d + \frac{1}{4}$

41. $-12 + f = 3$

42. $-9 = -4 + g$

43. $-1200 + j = 345$

44. $90 = -22 + a$

45. $26 = -4 + y$

46. $1\frac{3}{4} = -\frac{1}{4} + w$

47. $-\frac{1}{6} + h = \frac{1}{6}$

48. $-5.2 + a = -8$

49. **Finance** Luis deposited $500 into his bank account. He now has $4732. Write and solve an equation to find how much was in his account before the deposit. Show that your answer is reasonable.

50. **///ERROR ANALYSIS///** Below are two possible solutions to $x + 12.5 = 21.6$. Which is incorrect? Explain the error.

A
$$x + 12.5 = 21.6$$
$$\underline{- 12.5 \quad - 12.5}$$
$$x = 9.1$$

B
$$x + 12.5 = 21.6$$
$$\underline{+ 12.5 \quad + 12.5}$$
$$x = 34.1$$

Write an equation to represent each relationship. Then solve the equation.

51. Ten less than a number is equal to 12.

52. A number decreased by 13 is equal to 7.

53. Eight more than a number is 16.

54. A number minus 3 is –8.

55. The sum of 5 and a number is 6.

56. Two less than a number is –5.

57. The difference of a number and 4 is 9.

58. Geology The sum of the Atlantic Ocean's average depth (in feet) and its greatest depth is 43,126. Use the information in the graph to write and solve an equation to find the average depth of the Atlantic Ocean. Show that your answer is reasonable.

Deepest Oceans and Seas

Greatest depth (ft) / Ocean or sea

Pacific Ocean 35,837
Atlantic Ocean 30,246
Indian Ocean 24,460
Caribbean Sea 22,788

59. School Helene's marching band needs money to travel to a competition. Band members have raised $560. They need to raise a total of $1680. Write and solve an equation to find how much more they need. Show that your answer is reasonable.

60. Economics When you receive a loan to make a purchase, you often must make a down payment in cash. The amount of the loan is the purchase cost minus the down payment. Riva made a down payment of $1500 on a used car. She received a loan of $2600. Write and solve an equation to find the cost of the car. Show that your answer is reasonable.

Geometry The angles in each pair are complementary. Write and solve an equation to find each value of x. (*Hint:* The measures of complementary angles add to 90°.)

61.

63°
$x°$

62.

$x°$
42°

63.

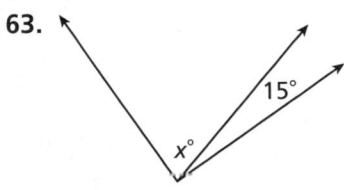

15°
$x°$

MULTI-STEP TEST PREP

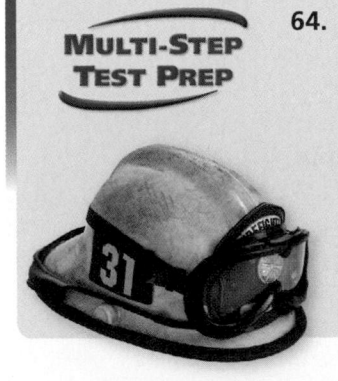

64. This problem will prepare you for the Multi-Step Test Prep on page 118.

Rates are often used to describe how quickly something is moving or changing.

a. A wildfire spreads at a rate of 1000 acres per day. How many acres will the fire cover in 2 days? Show that your answer is reasonable.

b. How many acres will the fire cover in 5 days? Explain how you found your answer.

c. Another wildfire spread for 7 days and covered a total of 780 square miles. How can you estimate the number of square miles the fire covered per day?

65. Statistics The range of a set of scores is 28, and the lowest score is 47. Write and solve an equation to find the highest score. (*Hint:* In a data set, the range is the difference between the highest and the lowest values.) Show that your answer is reasonable.

66. Write About It Describe a real-world situation that can be modeled by $x + 5 = 25$. Tell what the variable represents in your situation. Then solve the equation and tell what the solution means in the context of your problem.

67. Critical Thinking Without solving, tell whether the solution of $-3 + z = 10$ will be greater than 10 or less than 10. Explain.

68. Which situation is best represented by $x - 32 = 8$?

Ⓐ Logan withdrew $32 from her bank account. After her withdrawal, her balance was $8. How much was originally in her account?

Ⓑ Daniel has 32 baseball cards. Joseph has 8 fewer baseball cards than Daniel. How many baseball cards does Joseph have?

Ⓒ Room A contains 32 desks. Room B has 8 fewer desks. How many desks are in Room B?

Ⓓ Janelle bought a bag of 32 craft sticks for a project. She used 8 craft sticks. How many craft sticks does she have left?

69. For which equation is $a = 8$ a solution?

Ⓕ $15 - a = 10$ Ⓖ $10 + a = 23$ Ⓗ $a - 18 = 26$ Ⓙ $a + 8 = 16$

70. Short Response Julianna used a gift card to pay for an $18 haircut. The remaining balance on the card was $22.

a. Write an equation that can be used to determine the original value of the card.

b. Solve your equation to find the original value of the card.

CHALLENGE AND EXTEND

Solve each equation. Check your answer.

71. $3\frac{1}{5} + b = \frac{4}{5}$ **72.** $x - \frac{7}{4} = \frac{2}{3}$ **73.** $x + \frac{7}{4} = \frac{2}{3}$ **74.** $x - \frac{4}{9} = \frac{4}{9}$

75. If $p - 4 = 2$, find the value of $5p - 20$.   **76.** If $t + 6 = 21$, find the value of $-2t$.

77. If $x + 3 = 15$, find the value of $18 + 6x$.   **78.** If $2 + n = -11$, find the value of $6n$.

SPIRAL REVIEW

Multiply or divide. *(Lesson 1-3)*

79. $-63 \div (-7)$ **80.** $\frac{3}{7} \div \left(-\frac{4}{7}\right)$ **81.** $(-12)(-6)$

Give the side length of a square with the given area. *(Lesson 1-5)*

82. 225 m^2 **83.** 36 ft^2 **84.** 100 cm^2

Simplify each expression. *(Lesson 1-6)*

85. $8[-5 - (3 + 2)]$ **86.** $1 - [4^2 - (12 - 15)^2]$ **87.** $\frac{-12 + (-6)}{6}$

Area of Composite Figures

Connecting Algebra to

Geometry

Review the area formulas for squares, rectangles, and triangles in the table below.

Squares	Rectangles	Triangles
$A = s^2$	$A = \ell w$	$A = \frac{1}{2}bh$

A *composite figure* is a figure that is composed of basic shapes. You can divide composite figures into combinations of squares, rectangles, and triangles to find their areas.

Example

Find the area of the figure shown.

Divide the figure into a rectangle and a right triangle. Notice that you do not know the base or the height of the triangle. Use b and h to represent these lengths.

The bottom of the rectangle is 16 units long; the top of the rectangle is 8 units long plus the base of the triangle. Use this information to write and solve an equation.

$$\begin{aligned} b + 8 &= 16 \\ -8 \quad &\quad -8 \\ \hline b &= 8 \end{aligned}$$

The right side of the figure is 13 units long: 7 units from the rectangle plus the height of the triangle. Use this information to write and solve an equation.

$$\begin{aligned} h + 7 &= 13 \\ -7 \quad &\quad -7 \\ \hline h &= 6 \end{aligned}$$

The area of the figure is the sum of the areas of the rectangle and the triangle.

Area of rectangle
Area of triangle

$$A = \ell w + \frac{1}{2}bh$$
$$A = 16(7) + \frac{1}{2}(8)(6)$$
$$A = 112 + 24$$
$$A = 136 \text{ square units}$$

Try This

Find the area of each composite figure.

1.

2.

3.

Connecting Algebra to Geometry **83**

Solving Equations by Multiplying or Dividing

Objective
Solve one-step equations in one variable by using multiplication or division.

Who uses this?
Pilots can make quick calculations by solving one-step equations. (See Example 4.)

Solving an equation that contains multiplication or division is similar to solving an equation that contains addition or subtraction. Use inverse operations to undo the operations on the variable.

Remember that an equation is like a balanced scale. To keep the balance, whatever you do on one side of the equation, you must also do on the other side.

Inverse Operations
Multiply by x. ←→ Divide by x.

EXAMPLE **1** **Solving Equations by Using Multiplication**

Solve each equation. Check your answer.

A $-4 = \dfrac{k}{-5}$

$(-5)(-4) = (-5)\left(\dfrac{k}{-5}\right)$ *Since k is divided by −5, multiply both sides by −5 to undo the division.*

$20 = k$

Check $-4 = \dfrac{k}{-5}$ *To check your solution, substitute 20 for k in the original equation.*

-4	$\dfrac{20}{-5}$
-4	-4 ✓

B $\dfrac{m}{3} = 1.5$

$(3)\left(\dfrac{m}{3}\right) = (3)(1.5)$ *Since m is divided by 3, multiply both sides by 3 to undo the division.*

$m = 4.5$

Check $\dfrac{m}{3} = 1.5$ *To check your solution, substitute 1.5 for m in the original equation.*

$\dfrac{4.5}{3}$	1.5
1.5	1.5 ✓

 CHECK IT OUT! Solve each equation. Check your answer.

1a. $\dfrac{p}{5} = 10$ **1b.** $-13 = \dfrac{y}{3}$ **1c.** $\dfrac{c}{8} = 7$

EXAMPLE 2 **Solving Equations by Using Division**

Solve each equation. Check your answers.

A $7x = 56$

$$\frac{7x}{7} = \frac{56}{7}$$

$$x = 8$$

Since x is multiplied by 7, divide both sides by 7 to undo the multiplication.

Check $7x = 56$

$$\frac{7(8) \mid 56}{56 \mid 56 \checkmark}$$

To check your solution, substitute 8 for x in the original equation.

B $13 = -2w$

$$\frac{13}{-2} = \frac{-2w}{-2}$$

$$-6.5 = w$$

Since w is multiplied by −2, divide both sides by −2 to undo the multiplication.

Check $13 = -2w$

$$\frac{13 \mid -2(-6.5)}{13 \mid 13 \checkmark}$$

To check your solution, substitute −6.5 for w in the original equation.

 Solve each equation. Check your answer.

2a. $16 = 4c$ **2b.** $0.5y = -10$ **2c.** $15k = 75$

Remember that dividing is the same as multiplying by the reciprocal. When solving equations, you will sometimes find it easier to multiply by a reciprocal instead of dividing. This is often true when an equation contains fractions.

EXAMPLE 3 **Solving Equations That Contain Fractions**

Solve each equation.

A $\frac{5}{9}v = 35$

$$\left(\frac{9}{5}\right)\frac{5}{9}v = \left(\frac{9}{5}\right)35$$

$$v = 63$$

The reciprocal of $\frac{5}{9}$ is $\frac{9}{5}$. Since v is multiplied by $\frac{5}{9}$, multiply both sides by $\frac{9}{5}$.

B $\frac{5}{2} = \frac{4y}{3}$

$$\frac{5}{2} = \frac{4y}{3}$$

$$\frac{5}{2} = \frac{4}{3}y$$

$\frac{4y}{3}$ is the same as $\frac{4}{3}y$.

$$\left(\frac{3}{4}\right)\frac{5}{2} = \left(\frac{3}{4}\right)\frac{4}{3}y$$

$$\frac{15}{8} = y$$

The reciprocal of $\frac{4}{3}$ is $\frac{3}{4}$. Since y is multiplied by $\frac{4}{3}$, multiply both sides by $\frac{3}{4}$.

Solve each equation. Check your answer.

3a. $-\frac{1}{4} = \frac{1}{5}b$ **3b.** $\frac{4j}{6} = \frac{2}{3}$ **3c.** $\frac{1}{6}w = 102$

EXAMPLE 4 **Aviation Application**

The distance in miles from the airport that a plane should begin descending, divided by 3, equals the plane's height above the ground in thousands of feet. If a plane is 10,000 feet above the ground, write and solve an equation to find the distance at which the pilot should begin descending.

Caution!

The equation uses the plane's height above the ground in *thousands* of feet. So substitute 10 for *h*, not 10,000.

| Distance | divided by 3 | equals | height in thousands of feet. |

$$\frac{d}{3} = h$$ *Write an equation to represent the relationship.*

$$\frac{d}{3} = 10$$ *Substitute 10 for h. Since d is divided by 3, multiply both sides by 3 to undo the division.*

$$(3)\frac{d}{3} = (3)10$$

$$d = 30$$

The pilot should begin descending 30 miles from the airport.

CHECK IT OUT! **4. What if...?** A plane began descending 45 miles from the airport. Use the equation above to find how high the plane was flying when the descent began.

You have now used four properties of equality to solve equations. These properties are summarized in the box below.

Properties of Equality

WORDS	NUMBERS	ALGEBRA
Addition Property of Equality You can add the same number to both sides of an equation, and the statement will still be true.	$3 = 3$ $3 + 2 = 3 + 2$ $5 = 5$	$a = b$ $a + c = b + c$
Subtraction Property of Equality You can subtract the same number from both sides of an equation, and the statement will still be true.	$7 = 7$ $7 - 5 = 7 - 5$ $2 = 2$	$a = b$ $a - c = b - c$
Multiplication Property of Equality You can multiply both sides of an equation by the same number, and the statement will still be true.	$6 = 6$ $6(3) = 6(3)$ $18 = 18$	$a = b$ $ac = bc$
Division Property of Equality You can divide both sides of an equation by the same nonzero number, and the statement will still be true.	$8 = 8$ $\frac{8}{4} = \frac{8}{4}$ $2 = 2$	$a = b$ $(c \neq 0)$ $\frac{a}{c} = \frac{b}{c}$

2-2 Exercises

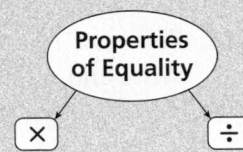
go.hrw.com
Homework Help Online
KEYWORD: MA7 2-2
Parent Resources Online
KEYWORD: MA7 Parent

GUIDED PRACTICE

Solve each equation. Check your answer.

SEE EXAMPLE **1**
p. 84

1. $\frac{k}{4} = 8$

2. $\frac{z}{3} = -9$

3. $-2 = \frac{w}{-7}$

4. $6 = \frac{t}{-5}$

5. $\frac{g}{1.9} = 10$

6. $2.4 = \frac{b}{5}$

SEE EXAMPLE **2**
p. 85

7. $4x = 28$

8. $-64 = 8c$

9. $-9j = -45$

10. $84 = -12a$

11. $4m = 10$

12. $2.8 = -2h$

SEE EXAMPLE **3**
p. 85

13. $\frac{1}{2}d = 7$

14. $15 = \frac{5}{6}f$

15. $\frac{2}{3}s = -6$

16. $9 = -\frac{3}{8}r$

17. $\frac{1}{10} = \frac{4}{5}y$

18. $\frac{1}{4}v = -\frac{3}{4}$

SEE EXAMPLE **4**
p. 86

19. **Recreation** The Baseball Birthday Batter Package at a minor league ballpark costs $192. The package includes tickets, drinks, and cake for a group of 16 children. Write and solve an equation to find the cost per child.

20. **Nutrition** An orange contains about 80 milligrams of vitamin C, which is 10 times as much as an apple contains. Write and solve an equation to find the amount of vitamin C in an apple.

PRACTICE AND PROBLEM SOLVING

Solve each equation. Check your answer.

21. $\frac{x}{2} = 12$

22. $-40 = \frac{b}{5}$

23. $-\frac{j}{6} = 6$

24. $-\frac{n}{3} = -4$

25. $-\frac{q}{5} = 30$

26. $1.6 = \frac{d}{3}$

27. $\frac{v}{10} = 5.5$

28. $\frac{h}{8.1} = -4$

29. $5t = -15$

30. $49 = 7c$

31. $-12 = -12u$

32. $-7m = 63$

33. $-52 = -4c$

34. $11 = -2z$

35. $5f = 1.5$

36. $-8.4 = -4n$

Independent Practice	
For Exercises	See Example
21–28	1
29–36	2
37–44	3
45	4

Extra Practice
Skills Practice p. S6
Application Practice p. S29

Solve each equation. Check your answer.

37. $\frac{5}{2}k = 5$

38. $-9 = \frac{3}{4}d$

39. $-\frac{5}{8}b = 10$

40. $-\frac{4}{5}g = -12$

41. $\frac{4}{7}t = -2$

42. $-\frac{4}{5}p = \frac{2}{3}$

43. $\frac{2}{3} = -\frac{1}{3}q$

44. $-\frac{5}{8} = -\frac{3}{4}a$

45. Finance After taxes, Alexandra's take-home pay is $\frac{7}{10}$ of her salary before taxes. Write and solve an equation to find Alexandra's salary before taxes for the pay period that resulted in $392 of take-home pay.

46. Earth Science Your weight on the Moon is about $\frac{1}{6}$ of your weight on Earth. Write and solve an equation to show how much a person weighs on Earth if he weighs 16 pounds on the Moon. How could you check that your answer is reasonable?

47. ///ERROR ANALYSIS/// For the equation $\frac{x}{3} = 15$, a student found the value of x to be 5. Explain the error. What is the correct answer?

 Geometry The perimeter of a square is given. Write and solve an equation to find the length of each side of the square.

48. $P = 36$ in.

49. $P = 84$ in.

50. $P = 100$ yd

51. $P = 16.4$ cm

Write an equation to represent each relationship. Then solve the equation.

52. Five times a number is 45.

53. A number multiplied by negative 3 is 12.

54. A number divided by 4 is equal to 10.

55. The quotient of a number and 3 is negative 8.

56. Statistics The mean height of the students in Marta's class is 60 in. There are 18 students in her class. Write and solve an equation to find the total measure of all students' heights. (*Hint:* The mean is found by dividing the sum of all data values by the number of data values.)

57. Finance Lisa earned $6.25 per hour at her after-school job. Each week she earned $50. Write and solve an equation to show how many hours she worked each week.

58. Critical Thinking Will the solution of $\frac{x}{2.1} = 4$ be greater than 4 or less than 4? Explain.

59. Consumer Economics Dion's long-distance phone bill was $13.80. His long-distance calls cost $0.05 per minute. Write and solve an equation to find the number of minutes he was charged for. Show that your answer is reasonable.

60. Nutrition An 8 oz cup of coffee has about 184 mg of caffeine. This is 5 times as much caffeine as in a 12 oz soft drink. Write and solve an equation to find about how much caffeine is in a 12 oz caffeinated soft drink. Round your answer to the nearest whole number. Show that your answer is reasonable.

Statistics

American Robert P. Wadlow (1918–1940) holds the record for world's tallest man— 8 ft 11.1 in. He also holds world records for the largest feet and hands.

Source: Guinness World Records 2005

Use the equation $8y = 4x$ to find y for each value of x.

	x	4x	8y = 4x	y
61.	−4	4(−4) = −16	8y = −16	
62.	−2			
63.	0			
64.	2			

65. This problem will prepare you for the Multi-Step Test Prep on page 118.

   a. The formula for the mean of a data set is mean $= \frac{\text{sum of data values}}{\text{number of data values}}$. One summer, there were 1926 wildfires in Arizona. Which value does this number represent in the formula?

   b. The mean number of acres burned by each wildfire was 96.21. Which value does this number represent in the formula?

   c. Use the formula and information given to find how many acres were burned by wildfires in Arizona that summer. Round your answer to the nearest acre. Show that your answer is reasonable.

Solve each equation. Check your answer.

66. $\frac{m}{6} = 1$ **67.** $4x = 28$ **68.** $1.2h = 14.4$ **69.** $\frac{1}{5}x = 121$

70. $2w = 26$ **71.** $4b = \frac{3}{4}$ **72.** $5y = 11$ **73.** $\frac{n}{1.9} = 3$

Biology Use the table for Exercises 74 and 75.

Average Weight			
Animal	At Birth (g)	Adult Female (g)	Adult Male (g)
Hamster	2	130	110
Guinea pig	85	800	1050
Rat	5	275	480

74. The mean weight of an adult male rat is 16 times the mean weight of an adult male mouse. Write and solve an equation to find the mean weight of an adult male mouse. Show that your answer is reasonable.

75. On average, a hamster at birth weighs $\frac{2}{3}$ the weight of a gerbil at birth. Write and solve an equation to find the average weight of a gerbil at birth. Show that your answer is reasonable.

 76. **Write About It** Describe a real-world situation that can be modeled by $3x = 42$. Solve the equation and tell what the solution means in the context of your problem.

77. Which situation does NOT represent the equation $\frac{d}{2} = 10$?

   Ⓐ Leo bought a box of pencils. He gave half of them to his brother. They each got 10 pencils. How many pencils were in the box Leo bought?

   Ⓑ Kasey evenly divided her money from baby-sitting into two bank accounts. She put $10 in each account. How much did Kasey earn?

   Ⓒ Gilbert cut a piece of ribbon into 2-inch strips. When he was done, he had ten 2-inch strips. How long was the ribbon to start?

   Ⓓ Mattie had 2 more CDs than her sister Leona. If Leona had 10 CDs, how many CDs did Mattie have?

78. Which equation below shows a correct first step for solving $3x = -12$?

   Ⓕ $3x + 3 = -12 + 3$ **Ⓗ** $3(3x) = 3(-12)$

   Ⓖ $3x - 3 = -12 - 3$ **Ⓙ** $\frac{3x}{3} = \frac{-12}{3}$

79. In a regular pentagon, all of the angles are equal in measure. The sum of the angle measures is 540°. Which of the following equations could be used to find the measure of each angle?

  Ⓐ $\dfrac{x}{540} = 5$ Ⓒ $540x = 5$

  Ⓑ $5x = 540$ Ⓓ $\dfrac{x}{5} = 540$

80. For which equation is $m = 10$ a solution?

  Ⓕ $5 = 2m$ Ⓖ $5m = 2$ Ⓗ $\dfrac{m}{2} = 5$ Ⓙ $\dfrac{m}{10} = 2$

81. Short Response Luisa bought 6 cans of cat food that each cost the same amount. She spent a total of $4.80.

  a. Write an equation to determine the cost of one can of cat food. Tell what each part of your equation represents.

  b. Solve your equation to find the cost of one can of cat food. Show each step.

CHALLENGE AND EXTEND

Solve each equation. Check your answer.

82. $\left(3\dfrac{1}{5}\right)b = \dfrac{4}{5}$ **83.** $\left(1\dfrac{1}{3}\right)x = 2\dfrac{2}{3}$ **84.** $\left(5\dfrac{4}{5}\right)x = -52\dfrac{1}{5}$

85. $\left(-2\dfrac{9}{10}\right)k = -26\dfrac{1}{10}$ **86.** $\left(1\dfrac{2}{3}\right)w = 15\dfrac{1}{3}$ **87.** $\left(2\dfrac{1}{4}\right)d = 4\dfrac{1}{2}$

Find each indicated value.

88. If $2p = 4$, find the value of $6p + 10$.   **89.** If $6t = 24$, find the value of $-5t$.

90. If $3x = 15$, find the value of $12 - 4x$.   **91.** If $\dfrac{n}{2} = -11$, find the value of $6n$.

92. To isolate x in $ax = b$, what should you divide both sides by?

93. To isolate x in $\dfrac{x}{a} = b$, what operation should you perform on both sides of the equation?

94. Travel The formula $d = rt$ gives the distance d that is traveled at a rate r in time t.

  a. If $d = 400$ and $r = 25$, what is the value of t?

  b. If $d = 400$ and $r = 50$, what is the value of t?

  c. What if...? How did t change when r increased from 25 to 50?

  d. What if...? If r is doubled while d remains the same, what is the effect on t?

SPIRAL REVIEW

Find each square root. *(Lesson 1-5)*

95. $\sqrt{144}$ **96.** $\sqrt{196}$ **97.** $\sqrt{625}$ **98.** $-\sqrt{9}$

Write and solve an equation that could be used to answer each question. *(Lesson 2-1)*

99. Lisa's age plus Sean's age is 17. Sean is 11 years old. How old is Lisa?

100. The length of a rectangle is 6 feet more than the width of the rectangle. The length is 32 feet. What is the width of the rectangle?

Solve each equation. Check your answer. *(Lesson 2-1)*

101. $2 = a - 4$ **102.** $x - 12 = -3$ **103.** $z - 5 = 11$ **104.** $-4 = x + 5$

2-3 Technology LAB

Solve Equations by Graphing

You can use graphs to solve equations. As you complete this activity, you will learn some of the connections between graphs and equations.

Use with Lesson 2-3

go.hrw.com
Lab Resources Online
KEYWORD: MA11 LAB2

Activity

Solve $3x - 4 = 5$.

1 Press **Y=** . In **Y₁**, enter the left side of the equation, $3x - 4$.

Y= 3 **X,T,θ,n** **−** 4 **ENTER**

In **Y₂**, enter the right side of the equation, 5.

Y= 5 **ENTER**

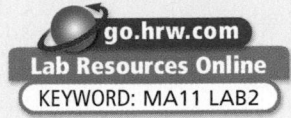

2 Press **GRAPH** . Press **TRACE** . The display will show the *x*- and *y*-values of a point on the first line. Press the right arrow key several times. Notice that the *x*- and *y*-values change.

3 Continue to trace as close as possible to the intersection of the two lines. The *x*-value of this point 2.9787…, is an approximation of the solution. The solution is about 3.

4 While still in trace mode, to check, press 3 **ENTER** . The display will show the *y*-value when $x = 3$. When $x = 3$, $y = 5$. So 3 is the solution. You can also check this solution by substituting 3 for *x* in the equation:

$$\begin{array}{r|l} \textbf{Check} \quad 3x - 4 &= 5 \\ \hline 3(3) - 4 & 5 \\ 9 - 4 & 5 \\ 5 & 5 \checkmark \end{array}$$

Try This

1. Solve $3x - 4 = 2$, $3x - 4 = 17$, and $3x - 4 = -7$ by graphing.

2. What does each line represent?

3. Describe a procedure for finding the solution of $3x - 4 = y$ for any value of *y*.

4. Solve $\frac{1}{2}x - 7 = -4$, $\frac{1}{2}x - 7 = 0$, and $\frac{1}{2}x - 7 = 2$ by graphing.

Solving Two-Step and Multi-Step Equations

Objective
Solve equations in one variable that contain more than one operation.

Why learn this?
Equations containing more than one operation can model real-world situations, such as the cost of a music club membership.

Alex belongs to a music club. In this club, students can buy a student discount card for $19.95. This card allows them to buy CDs for $3.95 each. After one year, Alex has spent $63.40.

To find the number of CDs *c* that Alex bought, you can solve an equation.

Cost of discount card
↓

Cost per CD → $3.95c + 19.95 = 63.40$ ← Total cost

Notice that this equation contains multiplication and addition. Equations that contain more than one operation require more than one step to solve. Identify the operations in the equation and the order in which they are applied to the variable. Then use inverse operations and work backward to undo them one at a time.

$$3.95c + 19.95 = 63.40$$

Operations in the Equation

❶ First *c* is **multiplied** by 3.95.

❷ Then 19.95 is **added**.

To Solve

❶ **Subtract** 19.95 from both sides of the equation.

❷ Then **divide** both sides by 3.95.

EXAMPLE **1** **Solving Two-Step Equations**

Solve $10 = 6 - 2x$. Check your answer.

$$10 = 6 - 2x$$
$$\underline{-6 \quad -6}$$
$$4 = \quad -2x$$
$$\frac{4}{-2} = \frac{-2x}{-2}$$
$$-2 = 1x$$
$$-2 = x$$

First x is multiplied by −2. Then 6 is added.

Work backward: Subtract 6 from both sides.

Since x is multiplied by −2, divide both sides by −2 to undo the multiplication.

Check

$10 = 6 - 2x$	
10	$6 - 2(-2)$
10	$6 - (-4)$
10	10 ✓

 Solve each equation. Check your answer.

1a. $-4 + 7x = 3$ **1b.** $1.5 = 1.2y - 5.7$ **1c.** $\frac{n}{7} + 2 = 2$

EXAMPLE 2 **Solving Two-Step Equations That Contain Fractions**

Solve $\dfrac{q}{15} - \dfrac{1}{5} = \dfrac{3}{5}$.

Method 1 Use fraction operations.

$$\dfrac{q}{15} - \dfrac{1}{5} = \dfrac{3}{5}$$

$$\underline{+\dfrac{1}{5} \quad +\dfrac{1}{5}}$$ *Since $\frac{1}{5}$ is subtracted from $\frac{q}{15}$, add $\frac{1}{5}$ to both sides to undo the subtraction.*

$$\dfrac{q}{15} = \dfrac{4}{5}$$ *Since q is divided by 15, multiply both sides by 15 to undo the division.*

$$15\left(\dfrac{q}{15}\right) = 15\left(\dfrac{4}{5}\right)$$

$$q = \dfrac{15 \cdot 4}{5}$$ *Simplify.*

$$q = \dfrac{60}{5}$$

$$q = 12$$

Method 2 Multiply by the least common denominator (LCD) to clear the fractions.

$$\dfrac{q}{15} - \dfrac{1}{5} = \dfrac{3}{5}$$

$$15\left(\dfrac{q}{15} - \dfrac{1}{5}\right) = 15\left(\dfrac{3}{5}\right)$$ *Multiply both sides by 15, the LCD of the fractions.*

$$15\left(\dfrac{q}{15}\right) - 15\left(\dfrac{1}{5}\right) = 15\left(\dfrac{3}{5}\right)$$ *Distribute 15 on the left side.*

$$q - 3 = 9$$ *Simplify.*

$$\underline{+3 \quad +3}$$ *Since 3 is subtracted from q, add 3 to both sides to undo the subtraction.*

$$q = 12$$

 CHECK IT OUT! **Solve each equation. Check your answer.**

2a. $\dfrac{2x}{5} - \dfrac{1}{2} = 5$ **2b.** $\dfrac{3}{4}u + \dfrac{1}{2} = \dfrac{7}{8}$ **2c.** $\dfrac{1}{5}n - \dfrac{1}{3} = \dfrac{8}{3}$

Equations that are more complicated may have to be simplified before they can be solved. You may have to use the Distributive Property or combine like terms before you begin using inverse operations.

EXAMPLE 3 **Simplifying Before Solving Equations**

Solve each equation.

A $6x + 3 - 8x = 13$

$$6x + 3 - 8x = 13$$

$$6x - 8x + 3 = 13$$ *Use the Commutative Property of Addition.*

$$-2x + 3 = 13$$ *Combine like terms.*

$$\underline{-3 \quad -3}$$ *Since 3 is added to $-2x$, subtract 3 from both sides to undo the addition.*

$$-2x = 10$$

$$\dfrac{-2x}{-2} = \dfrac{10}{-2}$$ *Since x is multiplied by -2, divide both sides by -2 to undo the multiplication.*

$$x = -5$$

Solve each equation.

B $9 = 6 - (x + 2)$

$9 = 6 + (-1)(x + 2)$ *Write subtraction as addition of the opposite.*

$9 = 6 + (-1)(x) + (-1)(2)$ *Distribute −1 on the right side.*

   Simplify.

$9 = 6 - x - 2$

   Use the Commutative Property of Addition.

$9 = 6 - 2 - x$

   Combine like terms.

$9 = \quad 4 - x$

$\underline{-4 \quad -4}$ *Since 4 is added to −x, subtract 4 from both*
   sides to undo the addition.

$5 = \quad -x$

$\dfrac{5}{-1} = \dfrac{-x}{-1}$ *Since x is multiplied by −1, divide both sides*
   by −1 to undo the multiplication.

$-5 = x$

Helpful Hint

You can think of an opposite sign as a coefficient of −1.
$-(x + 2) = -1(x + 2)$
and $-x = -1x$.

 CHECK IT OUT! Solve each equation. Check your answer.

3a. $2a + 3 - 8a = 8$

3b. $-2(3 - d) = 4$

3c. $4(x - 2) + 2x = 40$

EXAMPLE **4**

PROBLEM SOLVING

Problem-Solving Application

Alex belongs to a music club. In this club, students can buy a student discount card for $19.95. This card allows them to buy CDs for $3.95 each. After one year, Alex has spent $63.40. Write and solve an equation to find how many CDs Alex bought during the year.

 Understand the Problem

The **answer** will be the number of CDs that Alex bought during the year.

List the important information:

• Alex paid $19.95 for a student discount card.

• Alex pays $3.95 for each CD purchased.

• After one year, Alex has spent $63.40.

 Make a Plan

Let c represent the number of CDs that Alex purchased. That means Alex has spent $3.95c$. However, Alex must also add the amount spent on the card. Write an equation to represent this situation.

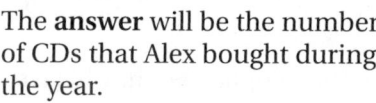

total cost	=	cost of compact discs	+	cost of discount card
63.40	=	3.95c	+	19.95

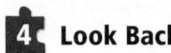 **Solve**

$$63.40 = 3.95c + 19.95$$
$$\underline{-19.95 \qquad\qquad -19.95}$$
$$43.45 = 3.95c$$
$$\frac{43.45}{3.95} = \frac{3.95c}{3.95}$$
$$11 = c$$

Since 19.95 is added to 3.95c, subtract 19.95 from both sides to undo the addition.

Since c is multiplied by 3.95, divide both sides by 3.95 to undo the multiplication.

Alex bought 11 CDs during the year.

 Look Back

Check that the answer is reasonable. The cost per CD is about $4, so if Alex bought 11 CDs, this amount is about $11(4) = 44.

Add the cost of the discount card, which is about $20: $44 + 20 = 64$. So the total cost was about $64, which is close to the amount given in the problem, $63.40.

CHECK IT OUT! **4.** Sara paid $15.95 to become a member at a gym. She then paid a monthly membership fee. Her total cost for 12 months was $735.95. How much was the monthly fee?

EXAMPLE 5 **Solving Equations to Find an Indicated Value**

If $3a + 12 = 30$, find the value of $a + 4$.

Step 1 Find the value of a.

$$3a + 12 = 30$$
$$\underline{-12 \quad -12}$$
$$3a \quad\;\; = 18$$
$$\frac{3a}{3} = \frac{18}{3}$$
$$a = 6$$

Since 12 is added to 3a, subtract 12 from both sides to undo the addition.

Since a is multiplied by 3, divide both sides by 3 to undo the multiplication.

Step 2 Find the value of $a + 4$.

$$a + 4$$
$$6 + 4$$
$$10$$

To find the value of a + 4, substitute 6 for a.

Simplify.

CHECK IT OUT! **5.** If $2x + 4 = -24$, find the value of $3x$.

THINK AND DISCUSS

1. Explain the steps you would follow to solve $2x + 1 = 7$. How is this procedure different from the one you would follow to solve $2x - 1 = 7$?

2. **GET ORGANIZED** Copy and complete the graphic organizer. In each box, write and solve a multi-step equation. Use addition, subtraction, multiplication, and division at least one time each.

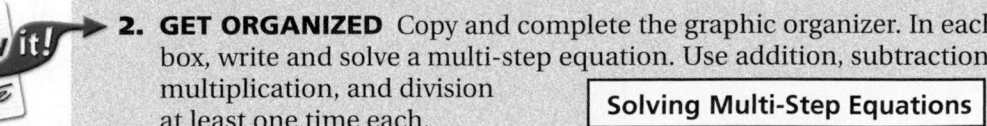

Solving Multi-Step Equations	

go.hrw.com
Homework Help Online
KEYWORD: MA7 2-3
Parent Resources Online
KEYWORD: MA7 Parent

GUIDED PRACTICE

Solve each equation. Check your answer.

SEE EXAMPLE **1**
p. 92

1. $4a + 3 = 11$ **2.** $8 = 3r - 1$ **3.** $42 = -2d + 6$

4. $x + 0.3 = 3.3$ **5.** $15y + 31 = 61$ **6.** $9 - c = -13$

SEE EXAMPLE **2**
p. 93

7. $\frac{x}{6} + 4 = 15$ **8.** $\frac{1}{3}y + \frac{1}{4} = \frac{5}{12}$ **9.** $\frac{2}{7}j - \frac{1}{7} = \frac{3}{14}$

10. $15 = \frac{a}{3} - 2$ **11.** $4 - \frac{m}{2} = 10$ **12.** $\frac{x}{8} - \frac{1}{2} = 6$

SEE EXAMPLE **3**
p. 93

13. $28 = 8x + 12 - 7x$ **14.** $2y - 7 + 5y = 0$ **15.** $2.4 = 3(m + 4)$

16. $3(x - 4) = 48$ **17.** $4t + 7 - t = 19$ **18.** $5(1 - 2w) + 8w = 15$

SEE EXAMPLE **4**
p. 94

19. Transportation Paul bought a student discount card for the bus. The card cost $7 and allows him to buy daily bus passes for $1.50. After one month, Paul spent $29.50. How many daily bus passes did Paul buy?

SEE EXAMPLE **5**
p. 95

20. If $3x - 13 = 8$, find the value of $x - 4$.   **21.** If $3(x + 1) = 7$, find the value of $3x$.

22. If $-3(y - 1) = 9$, find the value of $\frac{1}{2}y$.   **23.** If $4 - 7x = 39$, find the value of $x + 1$.

PRACTICE AND PROBLEM SOLVING

Independent Practice

For Exercises	See Example
24–29	1
30–35	2
36–41	3
42	4
43–46	5

Extra Practice
Skills Practice p. S6
Application Practice p. S29

Solve each equation. Check your answer.

24. $5 = 2g + 1$ **25.** $6h - 7 = 17$ **26.** $0.6v + 2.1 = 4.5$

27. $3x + 3 = 18$ **28.** $0.6g + 11 = 5$ **29.** $32 = 5 - 3t$

30. $2d + \frac{1}{5} = \frac{3}{5}$ **31.** $1 = 2x + \frac{1}{2}$ **32.** $\frac{z}{2} + 1 = \frac{3}{2}$

33. $\frac{2}{3} = \frac{4j}{6}$ **34.** $\frac{3}{4} = \frac{3}{8}x - \frac{3}{2}$ **35.** $\frac{1}{5} - \frac{x}{5} = -\frac{2}{5}$

36. $6 = -2(7 - c)$ **37.** $5(h - 4) = 8$ **38.** $-3x - 8 + 4x = 17$

39. $4x + 6x = 30$ **40.** $2(x + 3) = 10$ **41.** $17 = 3(p - 5) + 8$

42. Consumer Economics Jennifer is saving money to buy a bike. The bike costs $245. She has $125 saved, and each week she adds $15 to her savings. How long will it take her to save enough money to buy the bike?

43. If $2x + 13 = 17$, find the value of $3x + 1$.   **44.** If $-(x - 1) = 5$, find the value of $-4x$.

45. If $5(y + 10) = 40$, find the value of $\frac{1}{4}y$.   **46.** If $9 - 6x = 45$, find the value of $x - 4$.

Geometry Write and solve an equation to find the value of x for each triangle. (*Hint:* The sum of the angle measures in any triangle is 180°.)

47.

48.

49.

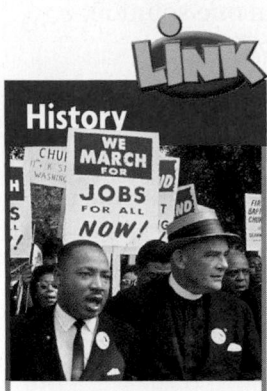

Write an equation to represent each relationship. Solve each equation.

50. Seven less than twice a number equals 19.

51. Eight decreased by 3 times a number equals 2.

52. The sum of two times a number and 5 is 11.

53. **History** In 1963, Dr. Martin Luther King Jr. began his famous "I have a dream" speech with the words "Five score years ago, a great American, in whose symbolic shadow we stand, signed the Emancipation Proclamation." The proclamation was signed by President Abraham Lincoln in 1863.

    a. Using the dates given, write and solve an equation that can be used to find the number of years in a score.

    b. How many score would represent 60?

Solve each equation. Check your answer.

54. $3t + 44 = 50$

55. $3(x - 2) = 18$

56. $15 = \dfrac{c}{3} - 2$

57. $2x + 6.5 = 15.5$

58. $3.9w - 17.9 = -2.3$

59. $17 = x - 3(x + 1)$

60. $5x + 9 = 39$

61. $15 + 5.5m = 70$

Biology Use the graph for Exercises 62 and 63.

62. The height of an ostrich is 20 inches more than 4 times the height of a kiwi. Write and solve an equation to find the height of a kiwi. Show that your answer is reasonable.

63. Five times the height of a kakapo minus 70 equals the height of an emu. Write and solve an equation to find the height of a kakapo. Show that your answer is reasonable.

64. The sum of two consecutive whole numbers is 57. What are the two numbers? (*Hint:* Let n represent the first number. Then $n + 1$ is the next consecutive whole number.)

65. Stan's, Mark's, and Wayne's ages are consecutive whole numbers. Stan is the youngest, and Wayne is the oldest. The sum of their ages is 111. Find their ages.

66. The sum of two consecutive even whole numbers is 206. What are the two numbers? (*Hint:* Let n represent the first number. What expression can you use to represent the second number?)

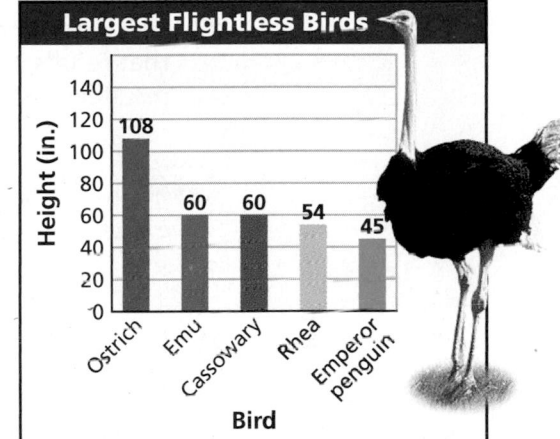

Largest Flightless Birds

Height (in.): 108, 60, 60, 54, 45
Birds: Ostrich, Emu, Cassowary, Rhea, Emperor penguin

Source: The Top Ten of Everything

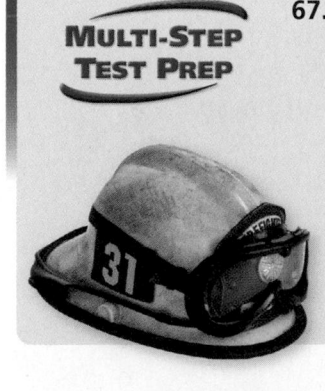

MULTI-STEP TEST PREP

67. This problem will prepare you for the Multi-Step Test Prep on page 118.

    a. The cost of fighting a certain forest fire is $225 per acre. Complete the table.

    b. Write an equation for the relationship between the cost c of fighting the fire and the number of acres n.

Cost of Fighting Fire	
Acres	**Cost ($)**
100	22,500
200	
500	
1000	
1500	
n	

68. Critical Thinking The equation $2(m - 8) + 3 = 17$ has more than one solution method. Give at least two different "first steps" to solve this equation.

69. Write About It Write a series of steps that you can use to solve any multi-step equation.

TEST PREP

70. Lin sold 4 more shirts than Greg. Fran sold 3 times as many shirts as Lin. In total, the three sold 51 shirts. Which represents the number of shirts Greg sold?

   Ⓐ $3g = 51$ Ⓑ $3 + g = 51$ Ⓒ $8 + 5g = 51$ Ⓓ $16 + 5g = 51$

71. If $\frac{4m - 3}{7} = 3$, what is the value of $7m - 5$?

   Ⓕ 6   Ⓖ 10.5   Ⓗ 37   Ⓙ 68.5

72. The equation $c = 48 + 0.06m$ represents the cost c of renting a car and driving m miles. Which statement best describes this cost?

   Ⓐ The cost is a flat rate of $0.06 per mile.

   Ⓑ The cost is $0.48 for the first mile and $0.06 for each additional mile.

   Ⓒ The cost is a $48 fee plus $0.06 per mile.

   Ⓓ The cost is a $6 fee plus $0.48 per mile.

73. Gridded Response A telemarketer earns $150 a week plus $2 for each call that results in a sale. Last week she earned a total of $204. How many of her calls resulted in sales?

CHALLENGE AND EXTEND

Solve each equation. Check your answer.

74. $\frac{9}{2}x + 18 + 3x = \frac{11}{2}$ **75.** $\frac{15}{4}x - 15 = \frac{33}{4}$

76. $(x + 6) - (2x + 7) - 3x = -9$ **77.** $(4x + 2) - (12x + 8) + 2(5x - 3) = 6 + 11$

78. Find a value for b so that the solution of $4x + 3b = -1$ is $x = 2$.

79. Find a value for b so that the solution of $2x - 3b = 0$ is $x = -9$.

80. Business The formula $p = nc - e$ gives the profit p when a number of items n are each sold at a cost c and expenses e are subtracted.

   a. If $p = 2500$, $n = 2000$, and $e = 800$, what is the value of c?

   b. If $p = 2500$, $n = 1000$, and $e = 800$, what is the value of c?

   c. What if...? If n is divided in half while p and e remain the same, what is the effect on c?

SPIRAL REVIEW

Write all classifications that apply to each real number. *(Lesson 1-5)*

81. $\sqrt{3}$ **82.** -58 **83.** $2\frac{1}{3}$ **84.** 0.17

Write each product using the Distributive Property. Then simplify. *(Lesson 1-7)*

85. $8(61)$ **86.** $9(28)$ **87.** $11(28)$ **88.** $13(21)$

Solve each equation. Check your answer. *(Lesson 2-1)*

89. $17 = k + 4$ **90.** $x - 18 = 3$ **91.** $a + 6 = -12$ **92.** $-7 = q - 7$

2-4 Algebra LAB

Model Equations with Variables on Both Sides

Algebra tile models can help you understand how to solve equations with variables on both sides.

Use with Lesson 2-4

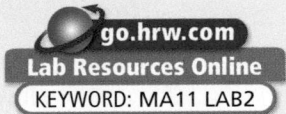

go.hrw.com
Lab Resources Online
KEYWORD: MA11 LAB2

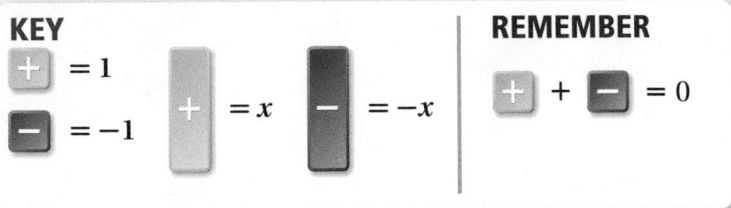

KEY

$\boxed{+}$ = 1

$\boxed{-}$ = −1

$\boxed{+}$ = x

$\boxed{-}$ = −x

REMEMBER

$\boxed{+}$ + $\boxed{-}$ = 0

Activity

Use algebra tiles to model and solve $5x - 2 = 2x + 10$.

MODEL		ALGEBRA
(algebra tile model)	Model $5x - 2$ on the left side of the mat and $2x + 10$ on the right side. Remember that $5x - 2$ is the same as $5x + (-2)$.	$5x - 2 = 2x + 10$
(algebra tile model)	Remove 2 x-tiles from both sides. This represents subtracting $2x$ from both sides of the equation.	$5x - 2 - 2x = 2x - 2x + 10$ $3x - 2 = 10$
(algebra tile model)	Place 2 yellow tiles on both sides. This represents adding 2 to both sides of the equation. Remove zero pairs.	$3x - 2 + 2 = 10 + 2$ $3x = 12$
(algebra tile model)	Separate each side into 3 equal groups. Each group is $\frac{1}{3}$ of the side. One x-tile is equivalent to 4 yellow tiles.	$\frac{1}{3}(3x) = \frac{1}{3}(12)$ $x = 4$

Try This

Use algebra tiles to model and solve each equation.

1. $3x + 2 = 2x + 5$ **2.** $5x + 12 = 2x + 3$ **3.** $9x - 5 = 6x + 13$ **4.** $x = -2x + 9$

2-4 Solving Equations with Variables on Both Sides

Objective
Solve equations in one variable that contain variable terms on both sides.

Vocabulary
identity

Why learn this?
You can compare prices and find the best value.

Many phone companies offer low rates for long-distance calls without requiring customers to sign up for their services. To compare rates, solve an equation with variables on both sides.

To solve an equation like this, use inverse operations to "collect" variable terms on one side of the equation.

Long-Distance Phone Plans

- Company A
- Company B
- Company C
- Company D
- Company E

EXAMPLE 1 Solving Equations with Variables on Both Sides

Solve each equation.

A $7k = 4k + 15$

$$7k = 4k + 15$$
$$\underline{-4k \quad -4k}$$
$$3k = \qquad 15$$
$$\frac{3k}{3} = \frac{15}{3}$$
$$k = 5$$

To collect the variable terms on one side, subtract 4k from both sides.

Since k is multiplied by 3, divide both sides by 3 to undo the multiplication.

B $5x - 2 = 3x + 4$

$$5x - 2 = 3x + 4$$
$$\underline{-3x \qquad -3x}$$
$$2x - 2 = \qquad 4$$
$$\underline{\quad +2 \qquad +2}$$
$$2x \quad = \qquad 6$$
$$\frac{2x}{2} = \frac{6}{2}$$
$$x = 3$$

To collect the variable terms on one side, subtract 3x from both sides.

Since 2 is subtracted from 2x, add 2 to both sides to undo the subtraction.

Since x is multiplied by 2, divide both sides by 2 to undo the multiplication.

Check $\quad 5x - 2 = 3x + 4$

$5(3) - 2$	$3(3) + 4$
$15 - 2$	$9 + 4$
13	$13 \checkmark$

To check your solution, substitute 3 for x in the original equation.

> **Helpful Hint**
> Equations are often easier to solve when the variable has a positive coefficient. Keep this in mind when deciding on which side to "collect" variable terms.

Solve each equation. Check your answer.
1a. $4b + 2 = 3b$ **1b.** $0.5 + 0.3y = 0.7y - 0.3$

To solve more complicated equations, you may need to first simplify by using the Distributive Property or combining like terms.

EXAMPLE 2 **Simplifying Each Side Before Solving Equations**

Solve each equation.

A $2(y + 6) = 3y$

$$2(y + 6) = 3y$$

$$2(y) + 2(6) = 3y$$

$$2y + 12 = 3y$$

$$\underline{-2y \qquad -2y}$$

$$12 = y$$

Distribute 2 to the expression in parentheses.

To collect the variable terms on one side, subtract 2y from both sides.

Check

$$2(y + 6) = 3y$$

$2(12 + 6)$	$3(12)$
$2(18)$	36
36	36 ✓

To check your solution, substitute 12 for y in the original equation.

B $2k - 5 = 3(1 - 2k)$

$$2k - 5 = 3(1 - 2k)$$

$$2k - 5 = 3(1) - 3(2k)$$

$$2k - 5 = 3 - 6k$$

$$\underline{+6k \qquad\qquad +6k}$$

$$8k - 5 = 3$$

$$\underline{\quad +5 \qquad +5}$$

$$8k = 8$$

$$\frac{8k}{8} = \frac{8}{8}$$

$$k = 1$$

Distribute 3 to the expression in parentheses.

To collect the variable terms on one side, add 6k to both sides.

Since 5 is subtracted from 8k, add 5 to both sides.

Since k is multiplied by 8, divide both sides by 8.

C $3 - 5b + 2b = -2 - 2(1 - b)$

$$3 - 5b + 2b = -2 - 2(1 - b)$$

$$3 - 5b + 2b = -2 - 2(1) - 2(-b)$$

$$3 - 5b + 2b = -2 - 2 + 2b$$

$$3 - 3b = -4 + 2b$$

$$\underline{\quad +3b \qquad\quad +3b}$$

$$3 = -4 + 5b$$

$$\underline{+4 \qquad\quad +4}$$

$$7 = 5b$$

$$\frac{7}{5} = \frac{5b}{5}$$

$$1.4 = b$$

Distribute −2 to the expression in parentheses.

Combine like terms.

Add 3b to both sides.

Since −4 is added to 5b, add 4 to both sides.

Since b is multiplied by 5, divide both sides by 5.

CHECK IT OUT! Solve each equation. Check your answer.

2a. $\frac{1}{2}(b + 6) = \frac{3}{2}b - 1$

2b. $3x + 15 - 9 = 2(x + 2)$

An **identity** is an equation that is always true, no matter what value is substituted for the variable. The solutions of an identity are all real numbers. Some equations are always false. These equations have no solutions.

EXAMPLE 3 Infinitely Many Solutions or No Solutions

Solve each equation.

A $x + 4 - 6x = 6 - 5x - 2$

$x + 4 - 6x = 6 - 5x - 2$	*Identify like terms.*
$4 - 5x = 4 - 5x$	*Combine like terms on the left and the right.*
$\underline{+5x \qquad +5x}$	*Add 5x to both sides.*
$4 \quad = 4 \checkmark$	*True statement*

The equation $x + 4 - 6x = 6 - 5x - 2$ is an identity. All values of x will make the equation true. All real numbers are solutions.

Writing Math

The solution set for Example 3B is an empty set—it contains no elements. The empty set can be written as ∅ or {}.

B $-8x + 6 + 9x = -17 + x$

$-8x + 6 + 9x = -17 + x$	*Identify like terms.*
$x + 6 = -17 + x$	*Combine like terms.*
$\underline{-x \qquad\qquad -x}$	*Subtract x from both sides.*
$6 = -17 ✗$	*False statement*

The equation $-8x + 6 + 9x = -17 + x$ is always false. There is no value of x that will make the equation true. There are no solutions.

 Solve each equation.

3a. $4y + 7 - y = 10 + 3y$ **3b.** $2c + 7 + c = -14 + 3c + 21$

EXAMPLE 4 *Consumer Application*

The long-distance rates of two phone companies are shown in the table. How long is a call that costs the same amount no matter which company is used? What is the cost of that call?

Phone Company	Charges
Company A	36¢ plus 3¢ per minute
Company B	6¢ per minute

Let m represent minutes, and write expressions for each company's cost.

When is	36¢	plus	3¢ per minute	times number of minutes	the same as	6¢ per minute	times number of minutes	?
	36	+	3	(m)	=	6	(m)	

$$36 + 3m = 6m$$

$\underline{-3m \quad -3m}$	*To collect the variable terms on one side,*
$36 \quad = 3m$	*subtract 3m from both sides.*
$\dfrac{36}{3} = \dfrac{3m}{3}$	*Since m is multiplied by 3, divide both sides by 3 to undo the multiplication.*
$12 = m$	

The charges will be the same for a 12-minute call using either phone service. To find the cost of this call, evaluate either expression for $m = 12$:

$$36 + 3m = 36 + 3(12) = 36 + 36 = 72 \qquad 6m = 6(12) = 72$$

The cost of a 12-minute call through either company is 72¢.

 4. Four times Greg's age, decreased by 3 is equal to 3 times Greg's age, increased by 7. How old is Greg?

THINK AND DISCUSS

1. Tell which of the following is an identity. Explain your answer.

    a. $4(a + 3) - 6 = 3(a + 3) - 6$ **b.** $8.3x - 9 + 0.7x = 2 + 9x - 11$

2. **GET ORGANIZED** Copy and complete the graphic organizer. In each box, write an example of an equation that has the indicated number of solutions.

An equation with variables on both sides can have...

one solution:	many solutions:	no solution:

2-4 Exercises

go.hrw.com
Homework Help Online
KEYWORD: MA7 2-4
Parent Resources Online
KEYWORD: MA7 Parent

GUIDED PRACTICE

1. **Vocabulary** How can you recognize an identity?

Solve each equation. Check your answer.

SEE EXAMPLE 1
p. 100

2. $2c - 5 = c + 4$ 3. $8r + 4 = 10 + 2r$

4. $2x - 1 = x + 11$ 5. $28 - 0.3y = 0.7y - 12$

SEE EXAMPLE 2
p. 101

6. $-2(x + 3) = 4x - 3$ 7. $3c - 4c + 1 = 5c + 2 + 3$

8. $5 + 3(q - 4) = 2(q + 1)$ 9. $5 - (t + 3) = -1 + 2(t - 3)$

SEE EXAMPLE 3
p. 102

10. $7x - 4 = -2x + 1 + 9x - 5$ 11. $8x + 6 - 9x = 2 - x - 15$

12. $6y = 8 - 9 + 6y$ 13. $6 - 2x - 1 = 4x + 8 - 6x - 3$

SEE EXAMPLE 4
p. 102

14. **Consumer Economics** A house-painting company charges $376 plus $12 per hour. Another painting company charges $280 plus $15 per hour.

    a. How long is a job for which both companies will charge the same amount?

    b. What will that cost be?

PRACTICE AND PROBLEM SOLVING

Solve each equation. Check your answer.

15. $7a - 17 = 4a + 1$ 16. $2b - 5 = 8b + 1$ 17. $4x - 2 = 3x + 4$

18. $2x - 5 = 4x - 1$ 19. $8x - 2 = 3x + 12.25$ 20. $5x + 2 = 3x$

21. $3c - 5 = 2c + 5$ 22. $-17 - 2x = 6 - x$ 23. $3(t - 1) = 9 + t$

24. $5 - x - 2 = 3 + 4x + 5$ 25. $2(x + 4) = 3(x - 2)$ 26. $3m - 10 = 2(4m - 5)$

27. $5 - (n - 4) = 3(n + 2)$ 28. $6(x + 7) - 20 = 6x$ 29. $8(x + 1) = 4x - 8$

30. $x - 4 - 3x = -2x - 3 - 1$ 31. $-2(x + 2) = -2x + 1$ 32. $2(x + 4) - 5 = 2x + 3$

<table>
<tr><td colspan="2">Independent Practice</td></tr>
<tr><td>For Exercises</td><td>See Example</td></tr>
<tr><td>15–22</td><td>1</td></tr>
<tr><td>23–29</td><td>2</td></tr>
<tr><td>30–32</td><td>3</td></tr>
<tr><td>33</td><td>4</td></tr>
</table>

Extra Practice
Skills Practice p. S6
Application Practice p. S29

33. Sports Justin and Tyson are beginning an exercise program to train for football season. Justin weighs 150 lb and hopes to gain 2 lb per week. Tyson weighs 195 lb and hopes to lose 1 lb per week.

    a. If the plan works, in how many weeks will the boys weigh the same amount?

    b. What will that weight be?

Write an equation to represent each relationship. Then solve the equation.

34. Three times the sum of a number and 4 is the same as 18 more than the number.

35. A number decreased by 30 is the same as 14 minus 3 times the number.

36. Two less than 2 times a number is the same as the number plus 64.

Solve each equation. Check your answer.

37. $2x - 2 = 4x + 6$

38. $3x + 5 = 2x + 2$

39. $4x + 3 = 5x - 4$

40. $-\frac{2}{5}p + 2 = \frac{1}{5}p + 11$

41. $5x + 24 = 2x + 15$

42. $5x - 10 = 14 - 3x$

43. $12 - 6x = 10 - 5x$

44. $5x - 7 = -6x - 29$

45. $1.8x + 2.8 = 2.5x + 2.1$

46. $2.6x + 18 = 2.4x + 22$

47. $1 - 3x = 2x + 8$

48. $\frac{1}{2}(8 - 6h) = h$

49. $3(x + 1) = 2x + 7$

50. $9x - 8 + 4x = 7x + 16$

51. $3(2x - 1) + 5 = 6(x + 1)$

52. Travel Rapid Rental Car company charges a $40 rental fee, $15 for gas, and $0.25 per mile driven. For the same car, Capital Cars charges $45 for rental and gas and $0.35 per mile.

    a. Find the number of miles for which the companies' charges will be the same. Then find that charge. Show that your answers are reasonable.

    b. The Barre family estimates that they will drive about 95 miles during their vacation to Hershey, Pennsylvania. Which company should they rent their car from? Explain.

    c. What if...? The Barres have extended their vacation and now estimate that they will drive about 120 miles. Should they still rent from the same company as in part **b**? Why or why not?

    d. Give a general rule for deciding which company to rent from.

53. Geometry The triangles shown have the same perimeter. What is the value of x?

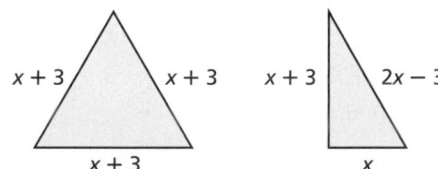

54. This problem will prepare you for the Multi-Step Test Prep on page 118.

    a. A fire currently covers 420 acres and continues to spread at a rate of 60 acres per day. How many total acres will be covered in the next 2 days? Show that your answer is reasonable.

    b. Write an expression for the total area covered by the fire in d days.

    c. The firefighters estimate that they can put out the fire at a rate of 80 acres per day. Write an expression for the total area that the firefighters can put out in d days.

    d. Set the expressions in parts **b** and **c** equal. Solve for d. What does d represent?

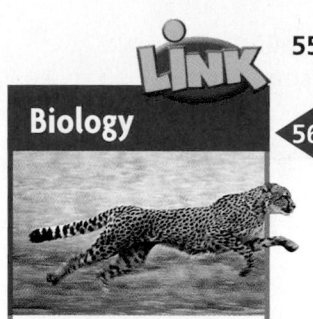

Biology

A cheetah's body is well designed for fast running. Its tail acts like a boat's rudder to help it make sharp turns. Its spine acts like a spring to propel it forward.

Source:
www.cheetahspot.com

55. **Critical Thinking** Write an equation with variables on both sides that has no solution.

56. **Biology** The graph shows the maximum recorded speeds of the four fastest mammals.

Top Speeds of the Fastest Mammals

Source: *The Top 10 of Everything*

a. Write an expression for the distance in miles that a Thompson's gazelle can run at top speed in *x* hours.

b. Write an expression for the distance in miles that a cheetah can run at top speed in *x* hours.

c. A cheetah and a Thompson's gazelle are running at their top speeds. The cheetah is one mile behind the gazelle. Write an expression for the distance the cheetah must run to catch up with the gazelle.

d. Write and solve an equation that represents how long the cheetah will have to run at top speed to catch up with the gazelle.

e. A cheetah can maintain its top speed for only 300 yards. Will the cheetah be able to catch the gazelle? Explain.

 57. **Write About It** Write a series of steps that you can use to solve any equation with variables on both sides.

 TEST PREP

58. Lindsey's monthly magazine subscription costs $1.25 per issue. Kenzie's monthly subscription costs $1.50 per issue, but she received her first 2 issues free. Which equation can be used to find the number of months after which the girls will have paid the same amount?

Ⓐ $1.25m = 1.50m - 2$ Ⓒ $1.25m = 1.50(m - 2)$

Ⓑ $1.25m = 1.50m - 2m$ Ⓓ $1.25m = 3m - 1.50$

59. What is the numerical solution of the equation *7 times a number equals 3 less than 5 times that number*?

Ⓕ -1.5 Ⓖ 0.25 Ⓗ $\frac{2}{3}$ Ⓙ 4

60. Three packs of markers cost $9.00 less than 5 packs of markers. Which equation best represents this situation?

Ⓐ $5x + 9 = 3x$ Ⓑ $3x + 9 = 5x$ Ⓒ $3x - 9 = 5x$ Ⓓ $9 - 3x = 5x$

61. Nicole has $120. If she saves $20 per week, in how many days will she have $500?

Ⓕ 19 Ⓖ 25 Ⓗ 133 Ⓙ 175

62. **Gridded Response** Solve $-2(x - 1) + 5x = 2(2x - 1)$.

CHALLENGE AND EXTEND

Solve each equation.

63. $4x + 2[4 - 2(x + 2)] = 2x - 4$

64. $\dfrac{x+5}{2} + \dfrac{x-1}{2} = \dfrac{x-1}{3}$

65. $\dfrac{2}{3}w - \dfrac{1}{4} = \dfrac{2}{3}\left(w - \dfrac{1}{4}\right)$

66. $-5 - 7 - 3f = -f - 2(f + 6)$

67. $\dfrac{2}{3}x + \dfrac{1}{2} = \dfrac{3}{5}x - \dfrac{5}{6}$

68. $x - \dfrac{1}{4} = \dfrac{x}{3} + 7\dfrac{3}{4}$

69. Find three consecutive integers such that twice the greatest integer is 2 less than 3 times the least integer.

70. Find three consecutive integers such that twice the least integer is 12 more than the greatest integer.

71. Rob had twice as much money as Sam. Then Sam gave Rob 1 quarter, 2 nickels, and 3 pennies. Rob then gave Sam 8 dimes. If they now have the same amount of money, how much money did Rob originally have? Check your answer.

SPIRAL REVIEW

Write an expression for the perimeter of each figure. *(Lesson 1-1)*

72. square with side x cm

73. equilateral triangle with side y cm

Multiply or divide. *(Lesson 1-3)*

74. $6.1 \div 0$

75. $3(-21)$

76. $0 \div \dfrac{7}{8}$

77. $\dfrac{2}{5} \div \dfrac{1}{10}$

78. $5 \div (-5)$

79. $\dfrac{-16}{-8}$

80. $-1000 \div (-0.001)$

81. $500(-0.25)$

Solve each equation. Check your answer. *(Lesson 2-3)*

82. $4x - 44 = 8$

83. $2(x - 3) = 24$

84. $-1 = \dfrac{x}{4} - 3$

85. $2x + 6 = 12$

2-5 Solving for a Variable

Objectives
Solve a formula for a given variable.

Solve an equation in two or more variables for one of the variables.

Vocabulary
formula
literal equation

Who uses this?
Athletes can "rearrange" the distance formula to calculate their average speed.

Many wheelchair athletes compete in marathons, which cover about 26.2 miles. Using the time t it took to complete the race, the distance d, and the *formula* $d = rt$, racers can find their average speed r.

A **formula** is an equation that states a rule for a relationship among quantities.

In the formula $d = rt$, d is isolated. You can "rearrange" a formula to isolate any variable by using inverse operations. This is called *solving for a variable*.

Solving for a Variable
Step 1 Locate the variable you are asked to solve for in the equation.
Step 2 Identify the operations on this variable and the order in which they are applied.
Step 3 Use inverse operations to undo operations and isolate the variable.

EXAMPLE 1 *Sports Application*

In 2004, Ernst Van Dyk won the wheelchair race of the Boston Marathon with a time of about 1.3 hours. The race was about 26.2 miles. What was his average speed? Use the formula $d = rt$ and round your answer to the nearest tenth.

The question asks for speed, so first solve the formula $d = rt$ for r.

$d = \mathbf{r}t$ *Locate r in the equation.*

$\dfrac{d}{t} = \dfrac{rt}{t}$ *Since r is multiplied by t, divide both sides by t to undo the multiplication.*

$\dfrac{d}{t} = r$, or $r = \dfrac{d}{t}$

Now use this formula and the information given in the problem.

$r = \dfrac{d}{t} \approx \dfrac{26.2}{1.3}$

≈ 20.2

Van Dyk's average speed was about 20.2 miles per hour.

Helpful Hint

A number divided by itself equals 1. For $t \neq 0$, $\frac{t}{t} = 1$.

1. Solve the formula $d = rt$ for t. Find the time in hours that it would take Van Dyk to travel 26.2 miles if his average speed was 18 miles per hour. Round to the nearest hundredth.

EXAMPLE 2 Solving Formulas for a Variable

A The formula for a Fahrenheit temperature in terms of degrees Celsius is $F = \frac{9}{5}C + 32$. Solve for C.

$$F = \frac{9}{5}\boxed{C} + 32$$ *Locate C in the equation.*

$$\underline{-32 \qquad\qquad -32}$$ *Since 32 is added to $\frac{9}{5}C$, subtract 32 from both sides to undo the addition.*

$$F - 32 = \frac{9}{5}C$$

$$\left(\frac{5}{9}\right)(F - 32) = \left(\frac{5}{9}\right)\frac{9}{5}C$$ *Since C is multiplied by $\frac{9}{5}$, divide both sides by $\frac{9}{5}$ (multiply by $\frac{5}{9}$) to undo the*

$$\frac{5}{9}(F - 32) = C$$ *multiplication.*

> **Remember!**
>
> Dividing by a fraction is the same as multiplying by the reciprocal.

B The formula for a person's typing speed is $s = \frac{w - 10e}{m}$, where s is speed in words per minute, w is number of words typed, e is number of errors, and m is number of minutes typing. Solve for w.

$$s = \frac{\boxed{w} - 10e}{m}$$ *Locate w in the equation.*

$$m(s) = m\left(\frac{w - 10e}{m}\right)$$ *Since w − 10e is divided by m, multiply both sides by m to undo the division.*

$$ms = w - 10e$$

$$\underline{+\,10e \qquad\quad +\,10e}$$ *Since 10e is subtracted from w, add 10e to both sides to undo the subtraction.*

$$ms + 10e = w$$

 2. The formula for an object's final velocity f is $f = i - gt$, where i is the object's initial velocity, g is acceleration due to gravity, and t is time. Solve for i.

A formula is a type of *literal equation*. A **literal equation** is an equation with two or more variables. To solve for one of the variables, use inverse operations.

EXAMPLE 3 Solving Literal Equations for a Variable

A Solve $m - n = 5$ for m.

$$\boxed{m} - n = 5$$ *Locate m in the equation.*

$$\underline{+\,n \quad\; +\,n}$$ *Since n is subtracted from m, add n to both sides to*

$$m = 5 + n$$ *undo the subtraction.*

B Solve $\frac{m}{k} = x$ for k.

$$\frac{m}{\boxed{k}} = x$$ *Locate k in the equation.*

$$k\left(\frac{m}{k}\right) = kx$$ *Since k appears in the denominator, multiply both sides by k.*

$$m = kx$$

$$\frac{m}{x} = \frac{kx}{x}$$ *Since k is multiplied by x, divide both sides by x to undo the multiplication.*

$$\frac{m}{x} = k$$

 3a. Solve $5 - b = 2t$ for t.   **3b.** Solve $D = \frac{m}{V}$ for V.

THINK AND DISCUSS

1. Describe a situation in which a formula could be used more easily if it were "rearranged." Include the formula in your description.

2. Explain how to solve $P = 2\ell + 2w$ for w.

3. **GET ORGANIZED** Copy and complete the graphic organizer. Write a formula that is used in each subject. Then solve the formula for each of its variables.

Common Formulas	
Subject	**Formula**
Geometry	
Physical science	
Earth science	

2-5 Exercises

go.hrw.com
Homework Help Online
KEYWORD: MA7 2-5
Parent Resources Online
KEYWORD: MA7 Parent

GUIDED PRACTICE

1. **Vocabulary** Explain why a *formula* is a type of *literal equation*.

SEE EXAMPLE 1
p. 107

2. **Construction** The formula $a = 46c$ gives the floor area a in square meters that can be wired using c circuits.

   a. Solve $a = 46c$ for c.

   b. If a room is 322 square meters, how many circuits are required to wire this room?

SEE EXAMPLE 2
p. 108

3. The formula for the volume of a rectangular prism with length ℓ, width w, and height h is $V = \ell wh$. Solve this formula for w.

SEE EXAMPLE 3
p. 108

4. Solve $st + 3t = 6$ for s.

5. Solve $m - 4n = 8$ for m.

6. Solve $\dfrac{f + 4}{g} = 6$ for f.

7. Solve $b + c = \dfrac{10}{a}$ for a.

PRACTICE AND PROBLEM SOLVING

Independent Practice

For Exercises	See Example
8	1
9	2
10–13	3

Extra Practice
Skills Practice p. S6
Application Practice p. S29

8. **Geometry** The formula $C = 2\pi r$ relates the circumference C of a circle to its radius r. (Recall that π is the constant ratio of circumference to diameter.)

   a. Solve $C = 2\pi r$ for r.

   b. If a circle's circumference is 15 inches, what is its radius? Leave the symbol π in your answer.

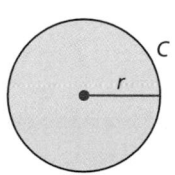

C is the distance around the circle.

r is the distance from the center of the circle to any point on the circle.

9. **Finance** The formula $A = P + I$ shows that the total amount of money A received from an investment equals the principal P (the original amount of money invested) plus the interest I. Solve this formula for I.

10. Solve $-2 = 4r + s$ for s.

11. Solve $xy - 5 = k$ for x.

12. Solve $\dfrac{m}{n} = p - 6$ for n.

13. Solve $\dfrac{x - 2}{y} = z$ for y.

Solve for the indicated variable.

14. $S = 180n - 360$ for n
15. $\frac{x}{5} - g = a$ for x
16. $A = \frac{1}{2}bh$ for b

17. $y = mx + b$ for x
18. $a = 3n + 1$ for n
19. $PV = nRT$ for T

20. $T + M = R$ for T
21. $M = T - R$ for T
22. $PV = nRT$ for R

23. $2a + 2b = c$ for b
24. $5p + 9c = p$ for c
25. $ax + r = 7$ for r

26. $3x + 7y = 2$ for y
27. $4y + 3x = 5$ for x
28. $y = 3x + 3b$ for b

29. Estimation The table shows the flying time and distance traveled for five flights on a certain airplane.

    a. Use the data in the table to write a rule that *estimates* the relationship between flying time t and distance traveled d.

    b. Use your rule from part **a** to estimate the time that it takes the airplane to fly 1300 miles.

    c. Solve your rule for d.

    d. Use your rule from part **c** to estimate the distance the airplane can fly in 8 hours.

Flying Times		
Flight	Time (h)	Distance (mi)
A	2	1018
B	3	1485
C	4	2103
D	5	2516
E	6	2886

30. Sports To find a baseball pitcher's earned run average (ERA), you can use the formula $Ei = 9r$, where E represents ERA, i represents number of innings pitched, and r represents number of earned runs allowed. Solve the equation for E. What is a pitcher's ERA if he allows 5 earned runs in 18 innings pitched?

31. Meteorology For altitudes up to 36,000 feet, the relationship between temperature and altitude can be described by the formula $t = -0.0035a + g$, where t is the temperature in degrees Fahrenheit, a is the altitude in feet, and g is the ground temperature in degrees Fahrenheit. Solve this formula for a.

 32. Write About It In your own words, explain how to solve a literal equation for one of the variables.

33. Critical Thinking How is solving $a - ab = c$ for a different from the problems in this lesson? How might you solve this equation for a?

MULTI-STEP TEST PREP

34. This problem will prepare you for the Multi-Step Test Prep on page 118.

    a. Suppose firefighters can extinguish a wildfire at a rate of 60 acres per day. Use this information to complete the table.

    b. Use the last row in the table to write an equation for acres A extinguished in terms of the number of days d.

    c. Graph the points in the table with *Days* on the horizontal axis and *Acres* on the vertical axis. Describe the graph.

Days	Acres
1	60
2	■
3	180
4	■
5	■
d	■

35. Which equation is the result of solving $9 + 3x = 2y$ for x?

(A) $\dfrac{9 + 3y}{2} = x$ (B) $\dfrac{2}{3}y - 9 = x$ (C) $x = \dfrac{2}{3}y - 3$ (D) $x = 2y - 3$

36. Which of the following is a correct method for solving $2a - 5b = 10$ for b?

(F) Add $5b$ to both sides, then divide both sides by 2.

(G) Subtract $5b$ from both sides, then divide both sides by 2.

(H) Divide both sides by 5, then add $2a$ to both sides.

(J) Subtract $2a$ from both sides, then divide both sides by -5.

37. The formula for the volume of a rectangular prism is $V = \ell wh$. Anna wants to make a cardboard box with a length of 7 inches, a width of 5 inches, and a volume of 210 cubic inches. Which variable does Anna need to solve for in order to build her box?

(A) V (B) ℓ (C) w (D) h

CHALLENGE AND EXTEND

Solve for the indicated variable.

38. $3.3x + r = 23.1$ for x **39.** $\dfrac{2}{5}a - \dfrac{3}{4}b = c$ for a **40.** $\dfrac{3}{5}x + 1.4y = \dfrac{2}{5}$ for y

41. $t = \dfrac{d}{500} + \dfrac{1}{2}$ for d **42.** $s = \dfrac{1}{2}gt^2$ for g **43.** $v^2 = u^2 + 2as$ for s

44. Solve $y = mx + 6$ for m. What can you say about y if $m = 0$?

45. Entertainment The formula $S = \dfrac{h \cdot w \cdot f \cdot t}{35,000}$ gives the approximate size in kilobytes (Kb) of a compressed video. The variables h and w represent the height and width of the frame measured in pixels, f is the number of frames per second (fps) the video plays, and t is the time the video plays in seconds. Estimate the time a movie trailer will play if it has a frame height of 320 pixels, has a frame width of 144 pixels, plays at 15 fps, and has a size of 2370 Kb.

SPIRAL REVIEW

46. Jill spent $\dfrac{1}{4}$ of the money she made baby-sitting. She made \$40 baby-sitting. How much did she spend? *(Previous course)*

47. In one class, $\dfrac{3}{5}$ of the students are boys. There are 30 students in the class. How many are girls? *(Previous course)*

Evaluate each expression for the given value of x. *(Lesson 1-6)*

48. $3 + 2 \cdot x + 4$ for $x = 3$ **49.** $24 \div 4 - x$ for $x = 12$ **50.** $43 - 62 + x$ for $x = 15$

Solve each equation. Check your answer. *(Lesson 2-1)*

51. $18 = -2 + w$ **52.** $2 = -3 + c$ **53.** $-8 + k = 4$ **54.** $-15 + a = -27$

Solving Absolute-Value Equations

Objective

Solve equations in one variable that contain absolute-value expressions.

Why learn this?

Engineers can solve absolute-value equations to calculate the length of the deck of a bridge. (See Example 3.)

Recall that the absolute value of a number is that number's distance from zero on a number line. For example, $|-5| = 5$ and $|5| = 5$.

For any nonzero absolute value, there are exactly two numbers with that absolute value. For example, both 5 and −5 have an absolute value of 5.

To write this statement using algebra, you would write $|x| = 5$. This equation asks, "What values of x have an absolute value of 5?" The solutions are 5 and −5. Notice that this equation has two solutions.

Absolute-Value Equations

WORDS	NUMBERS
The equation $|x| = a$ asks, "What values of x have an absolute value of a?" The solutions are a and the opposite of a.	$|x| = 5$ $x = 5$ or $x = -5$

GRAPH	ALGEBRA
←a units→←a units→ −a 0 a	$|x| = a$ $x = a$ or $x = -a$ $(a \geq 0)$

To solve absolute-value equations, perform inverse operations to isolate the absolute-value expression on one side of the equation. Then you must consider two cases.

EXAMPLE 1 Solving Absolute-Value Equations

Solve each equation.

A $|x| = 4$

$|x| = 4$ *Think: What numbers are 4 units from 0?*

Case 1	Case 2	*Rewrite the equation as two cases.*
$x = -4$	$x = 4$	

The solutions are −4 and 4.

Helpful Hint

Be sure to check both solutions when you solve an absolute-value equation.

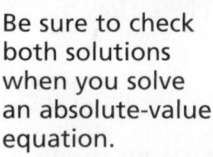

$$|x| = 4 \qquad |x| = 4$$
$$\frac{|-4|}{4} \quad \frac{4}{4}\checkmark \qquad \frac{|4|}{4} \quad \frac{4}{4}\checkmark$$

Solve each equation.

B $4|x + 2| = 24$

$$\frac{4|x + 2|}{4} = \frac{24}{4}$$

Since $|x + 2|$ is multiplied by 4, divide both sides by 4 to undo the multiplication.

$$|x + 2| = 6$$

Think: What numbers are 6 units from 0?

Case 1	Case 2
$x + 2 = -6$	$x + 2 = 6$
$\underline{-2 -2}$	$\underline{-2 -2}$
$x = -8$	$x = 4$

Rewrite the equation as two cases. Since 2 is added to x, subtract 2 from both sides of the equation.

The solutions are −8 and 4.

 Solve each equation. Check your answer.

1a. $|x| - 3 = 4$ **1b.** $8 = |x - 2.5|$

The table summarizes the steps for solving absolute-value equations.

Solving an Absolute-Value Equation
1. Use inverse operations to isolate the absolute-value expression.
2. Rewrite the resulting equation as two cases that do not involve absolute values.
3. Solve the equation in each of the two cases.

Not all absolute-value equations have two solutions. If the absolute-value expression equals 0, there is one solution. If an equation states that an absolute value is negative, there are no solutions.

EXAMPLE 2 **Special Cases of Absolute-Value Equations**

Solve each equation.

A $|x + 3| + 4 = 4$

$$|x + 3| + 4 = 4$$
$$\underline{ -4 -4}$$
$$|x + 3| = 0$$

Since 4 is added to $|x + 3|$, subtract 4 from both sides to undo the addition.

$$x + 3 = 0$$
$$\underline{ -3 -3}$$
$$x = -3$$

There is only one case. Since 3 is added to x, subtract 3 from both sides to undo the addition.

B $5 = |x + 2| + 8$

$$5 = |x + 2| + 8$$
$$\underline{-8 -8}$$
$$-3 = |x + 2| \; ✗$$

Since 8 is added to $|x + 2|$, subtract 8 from both sides to undo the addition.

Absolute value cannot be negative.

This equation has no solution.

Remember!

Absolute value must be nonnegative because it represents a distance.

 Solve each equation.

2a. $2 - |2x - 5| = 7$ **2b.** $-6 + |x - 4| = -6$

EXAMPLE 3 *Engineering Application*

Sydney Harbour Bridge in Australia is 1149 meters long. Because of changes in temperature, the bridge can expand or contract by as much as 420 millimeters. Write and solve an absolute-value equation to find the minimum and maximum lengths of the bridge.

First convert millimeters to meters.

420 mm = 0.4 2 0 m *Move the decimal point three places to the left.*

The length of the bridge can vary by 0.42 m, so find two numbers that are 0.42 units away from 1149 on a number line.

You can find these numbers by using the absolute-value equation $|x - 1149| = 0.42$. Solve the equation by rewriting it as two cases.

Case 1	Case 2	
$x - 1149 = -0.42$	$x - 1149 = 0.42$	*Since 1149 is subtracted*
$+1149 \quad +1149$	$+1149 \quad +1149$	*from x, add 1149 to*
$x \quad = 1148.58$	$x \quad = 1149.42$	*both sides of each equation.*

The minimum length of the bridge is 1148.58 m, and the maximum length is 1149.42 m.

 3. Sydney Harbour Bridge is 134 meters tall. The height of the bridge can rise or fall by 180 millimeters because of changes in temperature. Write and solve an absolute-value equation to find the minimum and maximum heights of the bridge.

THINK AND DISCUSS

1. Explain the steps you would use to solve the equation $\frac{1}{5}|x - 3| = 2$.

2. GET ORGANIZED Copy and complete the graphic organizer. In each box, write an example of an absolute-value equation that has the indicated number of solutions, and then solve.

2-6 **Exercises**

go.hrw.com
Homework Help Online
KEYWORD: MA11 2-6
Parent Resources Online
KEYWORD: MA7 Parent

GUIDED PRACTICE

Solve each equation.

SEE EXAMPLE **1**
p. 112

1. $|x| = 6$

2. $9 = |x + 5|$

3. $|3x| + 2 = 8$

4. $2|x| = 18$

5. $\left|x + \frac{1}{2}\right| = 1$

6. $|x - 3| - 6 = 2$

SEE EXAMPLE **2**
p. 113

7. $-8 = |x|$

8. $|x| = 0$

9. $|x + 4| = -7$

10. $7 = |3x + 9| + 7$

11. $|2.8 - x| + 1.5 = 1.5$

12. $5|x + 7| + 14 = 8$

SEE EXAMPLE **3**
p. 114

13. Communication Barry's walkie-talkie has a range of 2 mi. Barry is traveling on a straight highway and is at mile marker 207. Write and solve an absolute-value equation to find the minimum and maximum mile marker from 207 that Barry's walkie-talkie will reach.

PRACTICE AND PROBLEM SOLVING

Independent Practice

For Exercises	See Example
14–22	1
23–28	2
29	3

Extra Practice
Skills Practice p. S6
Application Practice p. S29

Solve each equation.

14. $|x| = \frac{1}{5}$

15. $|2x - 4| = 22$

16. $18 = 3|x - 1|$

17. $-2|x| = -4$

18. $3|x| - 12 = 18$

19. $|x - 42.04| = 23.24$

20. $\left|\frac{2}{3}x - \frac{2}{3}\right| = \frac{2}{3}$

21. $|3x + 1| = 13$

22. $|-2x + 3| = 5.8$

23. $|4x| + 9 = 9$

24. $8 = 7 - |x|$

25. $|x| + 6 = 12 - 6$

26. $|x - 3| + 14 = 5$

27. $0 = \left|\frac{2}{3} - x\right|$

28. $3 + |x - 1| = 3$

29. Space Shuttle The diameter of a valve for the space shuttle must be within 0.001 mm of 5 mm. Write and solve an absolute-value equation to find the boundary values for the acceptable diameters of the valve.

5 mm

30. The two numbers that are 5 units from 3 on the number line are represented by the equation $|n - 3| = 5$. What are these two numbers? Graph the solutions.

31. Write and solve an absolute-value equation that represents two numbers x that are 2 units from 7 on a number line. Graph the solutions.

32. Manufacturing A quality control inspector at a bolt factory examines random bolts that come off the assembly line. Any bolt whose diameter differs by more than 0.04 mm from 6.5 mm is sent back. Write and solve an absolute-value equation to find the maximum and minimum diameters of an acceptable bolt.

33. Construction A brick company guarantees to fill a contractor's order to within 5% accuracy. A contractor orders 1500 bricks. Write and solve an absolute-value equation to find the maximum and minimum number of bricks guaranteed.

34. Multi-Step A machine prints posters and then trims them to the correct size. The equation $|\ell - 65.1| = 0.2$ gives the maximum and minimum acceptable lengths for the posters in inches. Does a poster with a length of 64.8 inches fall within the acceptable range? Why or why not?

Write an absolute-value equation whose solutions are graphed on the number line.

35.
```
←+--+--●--+--+--+--+--+--●--+--+→
 −5 −4 −3 −2 −1  0  1  2  3  4  5
```

36.
```
←+--+--+--+--●--+--+--●--+--+--+→
 −5 −4 −3 −2 −1  0  1  2  3  4  5
```

37.
```
←+--+--+--●--+--+--+--+--+--●--+→
 −5 −4 −3 −2 −1  0  1  2  3  4  5
```

38.
```
←+--●--+--+--+--+--+--+--●--+--+→
 −5 −4 −3 −2 −1  0  1  2  3  4  5
```

Tell whether each statement is sometimes, always, or never true. Explain.

39. An absolute-value equation has two solutions.

40. The value of $|x + 4|$ is equal to the value of $|x| + 4$.

41. The absolute value of a number is nonnegative.

42. Temperature A thermostat is set so that the temperature in a laboratory freezer stays within 2.5 °F of 2 °F. Write and solve an absolute-value equation to find the maximum and minimum temperatures in the freezer.

43. Recreation To ensure safety, boaters must be aware of wind conditions while they are on the water. A particular anemometer gives a measurement of wind speed within a certain amount of the true wind speed, as shown in the table.

Measured Wind Speed (mi/h)	True Wind Speed (mi/h)
20	15–25
22	17–27
24	19–29
26	21–31
28	23–33
30	25–35

a. Use the table to write an absolute-value equation for the minimum and maximum possible true wind speeds *t* for the measured wind speed shown on the anemometer.

b. Solve your equation from part **a.** Check that the solution is correct by comparing it to the values given in the table when the measured wind speed is 24 mi/h.

c. Will your equation work for all of the values in the table? Explain.

d. Explain what your equation says about the instrument's measurements.

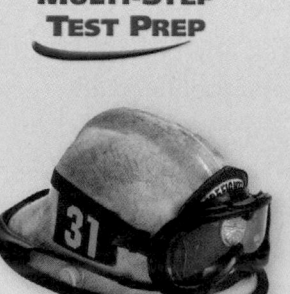

44. This problem will help prepare you for the Multi-Step Test Prep on page 118.

MULTI-STEP TEST PREP

The water pumps on a wildland fire apparatus can pump at various rates. The center of the acceptable range of pumping rates is 55 gallons per minute.

a. Write an absolute-value expression that gives the distance on the number line of a pump's rate *r* from 55.

b. The smallest and largest pumps have rates that differ by 45 gallons per minute from the rate at the center of the range. Write an absolute-value equation for the rates of these pumps.

c. Find the least and greatest rates that are acceptable for a wildland fire apparatus.

45. Write About It Do you agree with the following statement: "To solve an absolute-value equation, you need to solve two equations." Why or why not?

46. Critical Thinking Is there a value of a for which the equation $|x - a| = 1$ has exactly one solution? Explain.

47. Which situation could be modeled by the equation $|x - 65| = 3$?

    (A) Two numbers on the number line are 65 units away from 3.

    (B) The length of a carpet is 3 inches less than 65 inches.

    (C) The maximum and minimum weights of wrestlers on the team are within 3 kg of 65 kg.

    (D) The members of an exercise club for seniors are all between 63 and 67 years old.

48. For which of the following is $n = -3$ a solution?

    (F) $|n - 1| = 2$ (G) $|n + 2| = -1$ (H) $|n - 2| = 1$ (J) $|n + 1| = 2$

49. The minimum and maximum sound levels at a rock concert are 90 decibels and 95 decibels. Which equation models this situation?

    (A) $|x - 90| = 5$ (B) $|x - 92.5| = 2.5$ (C) $|x - 92.5| = 5$ (D) $|x - 95| = 2.5$

CHALLENGE AND EXTEND

50. The perimeter of a rectangle is 100 inches. The length of the rectangle is $|2x - 4|$ inches, and the width is x inches. What are the possible values of x? Explain.

51. Fill in the missing reasons to justify each step in solving the equation $3|2x + 1| = 21$.

Statements	Reasons
1. $3|2x + 1| = 21$	1. Given
2. $|2x + 1| = 7$	2. ?
3. $2x + 1 = -7$ or $2x + 1 = 7$	3. Definition of absolute value
4. $2x = -8$ or $2x = 6$	4. ?
5. $x = -4$ or $x = 3$	5. ?

52. Solve $|x| = |x + 1|$. (*Hint:* Consider two cases: $x \geq 0$ and $x < 0$.)

SPIRAL REVIEW

53. Sabrina is building a bookcase for her room. She has a piece of wood that is $4\frac{3}{8}$ ft long and estimates that she wants to use about $\frac{2}{5}$ of it. How much wood does she want to use? *(Lesson 1-3)*

Solve each equation. Check your answer. *(Lesson 2-1)*

54. $5 = p - 4.5$ **55.** $-2 = y + 6\frac{1}{2}$ **56.** $-12 + q = 3$ **57.** $y - 4.3 = -5.7$

Solve for the indicated variable. *(Lesson 2-5)*

58. $m + 5n = 7$ for m **59.** $S = T + R$ for T **60.** $2y + 3x = 1$ for y

61. $\frac{3 + w}{z} = x$ for w **62.** $c + d = \frac{5}{e}$ for e **63.** $6M - N = S$ for N

MULTI-STEP TEST PREP

Equations and Formulas

All Fired Up A large forest fire in the western United States burns for 14 days, spreading to cover approximately 3850 acres. Firefighters do their best to contain the fire, but hot temperatures and high winds may prompt them to request additional support.

1. The fire spreads at an average rate of how many acres per day?

2. Officials estimate that the fire will spread to cover 9075 acres before it is contained. At this rate, how many more days will it take for the fire to cover an area of 9075 acres? Answer this question using at least two different methods.

3. Additional help arrives, and the firefighters contain the fire in 7 more days. In total, how many acres does the fire cover before it is contained?

4. If the fire had spread to cover an area of 7000 acres, it would have reached Bowman Valley. Explain how the graph shows that firefighters stopped the spread of the fire before it reached Bowman Valley.

5. The total cost of fighting the fire for 21 days was approximately $1,440,000. What was the approximate cost per acre of fighting the fire?

READY TO GO ON?

Quiz for Lessons 2-1 Through 2-6

✓ **2-1** **Solving Equations by Adding or Subtracting**

Solve each equation.

1. $x - 32 = -18$ **2.** $1.1 = m - 0.9$ **3.** $j + 4 = -17$ **4.** $\dfrac{9}{8} = g + \dfrac{1}{2}$

5. When she first purchased it, Soledad's computer had 400 GB of hard drive space. After six months, there were only 313 GB available. Write and solve an equation to find the amount of hard drive space that Soledad used in the first six months.

✓ **2-2** **Solving Equations by Multiplying or Dividing**

Solve each equation.

6. $\dfrac{h}{3} = -12$ **7.** $-2.8 = \dfrac{w}{-3}$ **8.** $42 = 3c$ **9.** $-0.1b = 3.7$

10. A fund-raiser raised $2400, which was $\dfrac{3}{5}$ of the goal. Write and solve an equation to find the amount of the goal.

✓ **2-3** **Solving Two-Step and Multi-Step Equations**

Solve each equation.

11. $2r + 20 = 200$ **12.** $\dfrac{3}{5}k + 5 = 7$ **13.** $5n + 6 - 3n = -12$ **14.** $4(x - 7) = 2$

15. A taxicab company charges $2.10 plus $0.80 per mile. Carmen paid a fare of $11.70. Write and solve an equation to find the number of miles she traveled.

✓ **2-4** **Solving Equations with Variables on Both Sides**

Solve each equation.

16. $4x - 3 = 2x + 5$ **17.** $3(2x - 5) = 2(3x - 2)$

18. $2(2t - 3) = 6(t + 2)$ **19.** $7(x + 5) = -7(x + 5)$

20. On the first day of the year, Diego had $700 in his savings account and started spending $35 a week. His brother Juan had $450 and started saving $15 a week. After how many weeks will the brothers have the same amount? What will that amount be?

✓ **2-5** **Solving for a Variable**

21. Solve $2x + 3y = 12$ for x.   **22.** Solve $\dfrac{x}{r} = v$ for x.

23. Solve $5j + s = t - 2$ for t.   **24.** Solve $h + p = 3(k - 8)$ for k.

✓ **2-6** **Solving Absolute-Value Equations**

Solve each equation.

25. $|r| = 7$ **26.** $|h + 4| = 11$

27. $|2x + 4| = 0$ **28.** $16 = 7|p + 3| + 30$

2-7 Rates, Ratios, and Proportions

Objectives
Write and use ratios, rates, and unit rates.

Write and solve proportions.

Vocabulary
ratio   proportion
rate   cross products
scale   scale drawing
unit rate   scale model
conversion   dimensional
  factor   analysis

Why learn this?
Ratios and proportions are used to draw accurate maps. (See Example 5.)

A **ratio** is a comparison of two quantities by division. The ratio of a to b can be written $a{:}b$ or $\frac{a}{b}$, where $b \neq 0$. Ratios that name the same comparison are said to be *equivalent*.

A statement that two ratios are equivalent, such as $\frac{1}{12} = \frac{2}{24}$, is called a **proportion**.

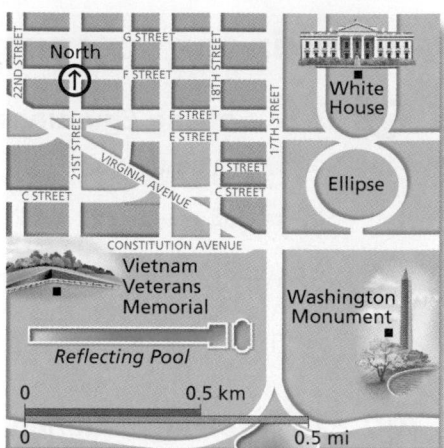

EXAMPLE 1   Using Ratios

The ratio of faculty members to students at a college is 1:15. There are 675 students. How many faculty members are there?

$$\frac{\text{faculty}}{\text{students}} \rightarrow \frac{1}{15}$$ *Write a ratio comparing faculty to students.*

$$\frac{1}{15} = \frac{x}{675}$$ *Write a proportion. Let x be the number of faculty members.*

$$675\left(\frac{x}{675}\right) = 675\left(\frac{1}{15}\right)$$ *Since x is divided by 675, multiply both sides of the equation by 675.*

$$x = 45$$

There are 45 faculty members.

Reading Math

Read the proportion $\frac{1}{15} = \frac{x}{675}$ as "1 is to 15 as x is to 675."

CHECK IT OUT!   **1.** The ratio of games won to games lost for a baseball team is 3:2. The team won 18 games. How many games did the team lose?

A **rate** is a ratio of two quantities with different units, such as $\frac{34 \text{ mi}}{2 \text{ gal}}$. Rates are usually written as *unit rates*. A **unit rate** is a rate with a second quantity of 1 unit, such as $\frac{17 \text{ mi}}{1 \text{ gal}}$, or 17 mi/gal. You can convert any rate to a unit rate.

EXAMPLE 2   Finding Unit Rates

Takeru Kobayashi of Japan ate 53.5 hot dogs in 12 minutes to win a contest. Find the unit rate in hot dogs per minute. Round to the nearest hundredth.

$$\frac{53.5}{12} = \frac{x}{1}$$ *Write a proportion to find an equivalent ratio with a second quantity of 1.*

$$4.46 \approx x$$ *Divide on the left side to find x.*

The unit rate is approximately 4.46 hot dogs per minute.

CHECK IT OUT!   **2.** Cory earns $52.50 in 7 hours. Find the unit rate in dollars per hour.

Dimensional analysis is a process that uses rates to convert measurements from one unit to another. A rate such as $\frac{12 \text{ in.}}{1 \text{ ft}}$, in which the two quantities are equal but use different units, is called a **conversion factor**. To convert from one set of units to another, multiply by a conversion factor.

EXAMPLE 3 Using Dimensional Analysis

A A large adult male human has about 12 pints of blood. Use dimensional analysis to convert this quantity to gallons.

Step 1 Convert pints to quarts.

$$12 \text{ pt} \cdot \frac{1 \text{ qt}}{2 \text{ pt}}$$

Multiply by a conversion factor whose first quantity is quarts and whose second quantity is pints.

6 qt

12 pints is 6 quarts.

Step 2 Convert quarts to gallons.

$$6 \text{ qt} \cdot \frac{1 \text{ gal}}{4 \text{ qt}}$$

$$\frac{6}{4} \text{ gal} = 1\frac{1}{2} \text{ gal}$$

Multiply by a conversion factor whose first quantity is gallons and whose second quantity is quarts.

A large adult male human has about $1\frac{1}{2}$ gallons of blood.

Hippocampus zosterae

B The dwarf sea horse *Hippocampus zosterae* swims at a rate of 52.68 feet per hour. Use dimensional analysis to convert this speed to inches per minute.

Use the conversion factor $\frac{12 \text{ in.}}{1 \text{ ft}}$ to convert feet to inches, and use the conversion factor $\frac{1 \text{ h}}{60 \text{ min}}$ to convert hours to minutes.

$$\frac{52.68 \text{ ft}}{1 \text{ h}} \cdot \frac{12 \text{ in.}}{1 \text{ ft}} \cdot \frac{1 \text{ h}}{60 \text{ min}} = \frac{10.536 \text{ in.}}{1 \text{ min}}$$

The speed is 10.536 inches per minute.

Check that the answer is reasonable. The answer is about 10 in./min.
- There are 60 min in 1 h, so 10 in./min is $60(10) = 600$ in./h.
- There are 12 in. in 1 ft, so 600 in./h is $\frac{600}{12} = 50$ ft/h. This is close to the rate given in the problem, 52.68 ft/h.

3. A cyclist travels 56 miles in 4 hours. Use dimensional analysis to convert the cyclist's speed to feet per second. Round your answer to the nearest tenth, and show that your answer is reasonable.

In the proportion $\frac{a}{b} = \frac{c}{d}$, the products $a \cdot d$ and $b \cdot c$ are called **cross products**. You can solve a proportion for a missing value by using the Cross Products Property.

Cross Products Property

WORDS	NUMBERS	ALGEBRA
In a proportion, cross products are equal.	$\frac{2}{3} \times \frac{4}{6}$ $2 \cdot 6 = 3 \cdot 4$	If $\frac{a}{b} \times \frac{c}{d}$ and $b \neq 0$ and $d \neq 0$, then $ad = bc$.

Helpful Hint

In Example 3A Step 1, "pt" appears to divide out, leaving "qt," as the unit. Use this strategy of "dividing out" units when using dimensional analysis.

EXAMPLE 4 Solving Proportions

Solve each proportion.

A $\dfrac{5}{9} = \dfrac{3}{w}$

$\dfrac{5}{9} \diagup\!\!\!\!\diagdown \dfrac{3}{w}$

$5(w) = 9(3)$ *Use cross*

$5w = 27$ *products.*

$\dfrac{5w}{5} = \dfrac{27}{5}$ *Divide both sides*
             by 5.

$w = \dfrac{27}{5}$

B $\dfrac{8}{x + 10} = \dfrac{1}{12}$

$\dfrac{8}{x + 10} \diagup\!\!\!\!\diagdown \dfrac{1}{12}$

$8(12) = 1(x + 10)$ *Use cross*

$96 = x + 10$ *products.*

$\underline{-10 \qquad -10}$ *Subtract 10 from*
                both sides.

$86 = x$

CHECK IT OUT! Solve each proportion.

4a. $\dfrac{-5}{2} = \dfrac{y}{8}$ **4b.** $\dfrac{g + 3}{5} = \dfrac{7}{4}$

A **scale** is a ratio between two sets of measurements, such as 1 in : 5 mi. A **scale drawing** or **scale model** uses a scale to represent an object as smaller or larger than the actual object. A map is an example of a scale drawing.

EXAMPLE 5 Scale Drawings and Scale Models

A On the map, the distance from Chicago to Evanston is 0.625 in. What is the actual distance?

$\dfrac{\text{map}}{\text{actual}} \rightarrow \dfrac{1 \text{ in.}}{18 \text{ mi}}$ *Write the scale as*
                    a fraction.

$\dfrac{1}{18} \diagup\!\!\!\!\diagdown \dfrac{0.625}{x}$ *Let x be the*
              actual distance.

$x \cdot 1 = 18(0.625)$ *Use cross products*

$x = 11.25$ *to solve.*

The actual distance is 11.25 mi.

Waukegan
North Chicago
Highland Park
Evanston
1 in : 18 mi
Chicago

B The actual distance between North Chicago and Waukegan is 4 mi. What is this distance on the map? Round to the nearest tenth.

$\dfrac{\text{map}}{\text{actual}} \rightarrow \dfrac{1 \text{ in.}}{18 \text{ mi}}$ *Write the scale as a fraction.*

$\dfrac{1}{18} \diagup\!\!\!\!\diagdown \dfrac{x}{4}$ *Let x be the distance on the map.*

$4 = 18x$ *Use cross products to solve the proportion.*

$\dfrac{4}{18} = \dfrac{18x}{18}$ *Since x is multiplied by 18, divide both sides by 18 to undo the multiplication.*

$0.2 \approx x$ *Round to the nearest tenth.*

The distance on the map is about 0.2 in.

Reading Math

A scale written without units, such as 32 : 1, means that 32 units of any measure correspond to 1 unit of that same measure.

CHECK IT OUT! **5.** A scale model of a human heart is 16 ft long. The scale is 32 : 1. How many inches long is the actual heart it represents?

THINK AND DISCUSS

1. Explain two ways to solve the proportion $\frac{t}{4} = \frac{3}{5}$.

2. How could you show that the answer to Example 5A is reasonable?

3. GET ORGANIZED Copy and complete the graphic organizer. In each box, write an example of each use of ratios.

Proportion — Uses of Ratios — Scale

Rate

Unit rate   Conversion factor

2-7 Exercises

go.hrw.com
Homework Help Online
KEYWORD: MA11 2-7
Parent Resources Online
KEYWORD: MA7 Parent

GUIDED PRACTICE

1. Vocabulary What does it mean when two ratios form a *proportion*?

SEE EXAMPLE **1**
p. 120

2. The ratio of the sale price of a jacket to the original price is $3:4$. The original price is $64. What is the sale price?

3. Chemistry The ratio of hydrogen atoms to oxygen atoms in water is $2:1$. If an amount of water contains 341 trillion atoms of oxygen, how many hydrogen atoms are there?

SEE EXAMPLE **2**
p. 120

4. A computer's fan rotates 2000 times in 40 seconds. Find the unit rate in rotations per second.

5. Twelve cows produce 224,988 pounds of milk. Find the unit rate in pounds per cow.

6. A yellow jacket can fly 4.5 meters in 9 seconds. Find the unit rate in meters per second.

SEE EXAMPLE **3**
p. 121

7. Lydia wrote $4\frac{1}{2}$ pages of her science report in one hour. What was her writing rate in pages per minute?

8. A model airplane flies 18 feet in 2 seconds. What is the airplane's speed in miles per hour? Round your answer to the nearest hundredth.

9. A vehicle uses 1 tablespoon of gasoline to drive 125 yards. How many miles can the vehicle travel per gallon? Round your answer to the nearest mile. (*Hint:* There are 256 tablespoons in a gallon.)

SEE EXAMPLE **4**
p. 122

Solve each proportion.

10. $\frac{3}{z} = \frac{1}{8}$

11. $\frac{x}{3} = \frac{1}{5}$

12. $\frac{b}{4} = \frac{3}{2}$

13. $\frac{f+3}{12} = \frac{7}{2}$

14. $\frac{-1}{5} = \frac{3}{2d}$

15. $\frac{3}{14} = \frac{s-2}{21}$

16. $\frac{-4}{9} = \frac{7}{x}$

17. $\frac{3}{s-2} = \frac{1}{7}$

18. $\frac{10}{h} = \frac{52}{13}$

SEE EXAMPLE 5
p. 122

19. **Archaeology** Stonehenge II in Hunt, Texas, is a scale model of the ancient construction in Wiltshire, England. The scale of the model to the original is 3:5. The Altar Stone of the original construction is 4.9 meters tall. Write and solve a proportion to find the height of the model of the Altar Stone.

Alfred Sheppard, one of the builders of Stonehenge II.

PRACTICE AND PROBLEM SOLVING

Independent Practice

For Exercises	See Example
20–21	1
22–23	2
24–25	3
26–37	4
38	5

Extra Practice
Skills Practice p. S7
Application Practice p. S29

20. **Gardening** The ratio of the height of a bonsai ficus tree to the height of a full-size ficus tree is 1:9. The bonsai ficus is 6 inches tall. What is the height of a full-size ficus?

21. **Manufacturing** At one factory, the ratio of defective light bulbs produced to total light bulbs produced is about 3:500. How many light bulbs are expected to be defective when 12,000 are produced?

22. Four gallons of gasoline weigh 25 pounds. Find the unit rate in pounds per gallon.

23. Fifteen ounces of gold cost $6058.50. Find the unit rate in dollars per ounce.

24. **Biology** The tropical giant bamboo can grow 11.9 feet in 3 days. What is this rate of growth in inches per hour? Round your answer to the nearest hundredth, and show that your answer is reasonable.

25. **Transportation** The maximum speed of the Tupolev Tu-144 airliner is 694 m/s. What is this speed in kilometers per hour?

Solve each proportion.

26. $\dfrac{v}{6} = \dfrac{1}{2}$

27. $\dfrac{2}{5} = \dfrac{4}{y}$

28. $\dfrac{2}{h} = \dfrac{-5}{6}$

29. $\dfrac{3}{10} = \dfrac{b+7}{20}$

30. $\dfrac{5t}{9} = \dfrac{1}{2}$

31. $\dfrac{2}{3} = \dfrac{6}{q-4}$

32. $\dfrac{x}{8} = \dfrac{7.5}{20}$

33. $\dfrac{3}{k} = \dfrac{45}{18}$

34. $\dfrac{6}{a} = \dfrac{15}{17}$

35. $\dfrac{9}{2} = \dfrac{5}{x+1}$

36. $\dfrac{3}{5} = \dfrac{x}{100}$

37. $\dfrac{38}{19} = \dfrac{n-5}{20}$

38. **Science** The image shows a dust mite as seen under a microscope. The scale of the drawing to the dust mite is 100:1. Use a ruler to measure the length of the dust mite in the image in millimeters. What is the actual length of the dust mite?

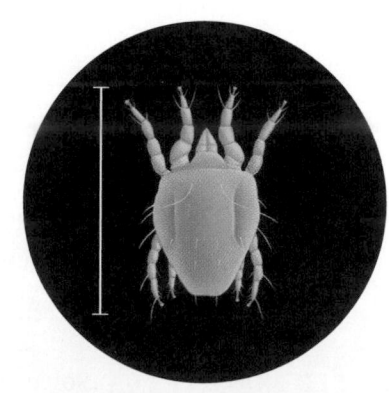

39. **Finance** On a certain day, the exchange rate was 60 U.S. dollars for 50 euro. How many U.S. dollars were 70 euro worth that day? Show that your answer is reasonable.

40. **Environmental Science** An environmental scientist wants to estimate the number of carp in a pond. He captures 100 carp, tags all of them, and releases them. A week later, he captures 85 carp and records how many have tags. His results are shown in the table. Write and solve a proportion to estimate the number of carp in the pond.

Status	Number Captured
Tagged	20
Not tagged	65

41. **///ERROR ANALYSIS///** Below is a bonus question that appeared on an algebra test and a student's response.

> The ratio of junior varsity members to varsity members on the track team is 3:5. There are 24 members on the team. Write a proportion to find the number of junior varsity members.
>
> $\dfrac{3}{5} = \dfrac{x}{24}$

The student did not receive the bonus points. Why is this proportion incorrect?

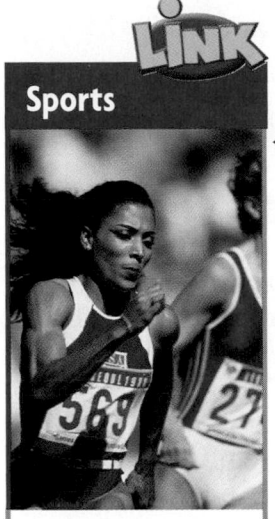
42. **Sports** The table shows world record times for women's races of different distances.

a. Find the speed in meters per second for each race. Round your answers to the nearest hundredth.

b. Which race has the fastest speed? the slowest?

c. **Critical Thinking** Give a possible reason why the speeds are different.

World Records (Women)	
Distance (m)	Time (s)
100	10.5
200	21.3
800	113.3
5000	864.7

43. **Entertainment** Lynn, Faith, and Jeremy are film animators. In one 8-hour day, Lynn rendered 203 frames, Faith rendered 216 frames, and Jeremy rendered 227 frames. How many more frames per hour did Faith render than Lynn did?

The records for the women's 100-meter dash and the women's 200-meter dash were set by Florence Griffith-Joyner, known as "Flo Jo." She is still referred to as the world's fastest woman.

Solve each proportion.

44. $\dfrac{x-1}{3} = \dfrac{x+1}{5}$

45. $\dfrac{m}{3} = \dfrac{m+4}{7}$

46. $\dfrac{1}{x-3} = \dfrac{3}{x-5}$

47. $\dfrac{a}{2} = \dfrac{a-4}{30}$

48. $\dfrac{3}{2y} = \dfrac{16}{y+2}$

49. $\dfrac{n+3}{5} = \dfrac{n-1}{2}$

50. $\dfrac{1}{y} = \dfrac{1}{6y-1}$

51. $\dfrac{2}{n} = \dfrac{4}{n+3}$

52. $\dfrac{5t-3}{2} = \dfrac{t+3}{2}$

53. $\dfrac{3}{d+3} = \dfrac{4}{d+12}$

54. $\dfrac{3x+5}{14} = \dfrac{x}{3}$

55. $\dfrac{5}{2n} = \dfrac{8}{3n-24}$

56. **Decorating** A particular shade of paint is made by mixing 5 parts red paint with 7 parts blue paint. To make this shade, Shannon mixed 12 quarts of blue paint with 8 quarts of red paint. Did Shannon mix the correct shade? Explain.

57. **Write About It** Give three examples of proportions. How do you know they are proportions? Then give three nonexamples of proportions. How do you know they are not proportions?

MULTI-STEP TEST PREP

58. This problem will prepare you for the Multi-Step Test Prep on page 152.

a. Marcus is shopping for a new jacket. He finds one with a price tag of $120. Above the rack is a sign that says that he can take off $\frac{1}{5}$. Find out how much Marcus can deduct from the price of the jacket.

b. What price will Marcus pay for the jacket?

c. Copy the model below. Complete it by placing numerical values on top and the corresponding fractional parts below.

$0	?	$48	?	?	$120
0	$\frac{1}{5}$	?	?	$\frac{4}{5}$	1

d. Explain how this model shows proportional relationships.

59. One day the U.S. dollar was worth approximately 100 yen. An exchange of 2500 yen was made that day. What was the value of the exchange in dollars?

Ⓐ $25   Ⓑ $400   Ⓒ $2500   Ⓓ $40,000

60. Brett walks at a speed of 4 miles per hour. He walks for 20 minutes in a straight line at this rate. Approximately what distance does Brett walk?

Ⓕ 0.06 miles   Ⓖ 1.3 miles   Ⓗ 5 miles   Ⓙ 80 miles

61. A shampoo company conducted a survey and found that 3 out of 8 people use their brand of shampoo. Which proportion could be used to find the expected number of users n in a city of 75,000 people?

Ⓐ $\dfrac{3}{8} = \dfrac{75{,}000}{n}$ Ⓑ $\dfrac{3}{75{,}000} = \dfrac{n}{8}$ Ⓒ $\dfrac{8}{3} = \dfrac{n}{75{,}000}$ Ⓓ $\dfrac{3}{8} = \dfrac{n}{75{,}000}$

62. A statue is 3 feet tall. The display case for a model of the statue can fit a model that is no more than 9 inches tall. Which of the scales below allows for the tallest model of the statue that will fit in the display case?

Ⓕ 2:1   Ⓖ 1:1   Ⓗ 1:3   Ⓙ 1:4

CHALLENGE AND EXTEND

63. Geometry Complementary angles are two angles whose measures add up to 90°. The ratio of the measures of two complementary angles is 4:5. What are the measures of the angles?

64. A customer wanted 24 feet of rope. The clerk at the hardware store used what she thought was a yardstick to measure the rope, but the yardstick was actually 2 inches too short. How many inches were missing from the customer's piece of rope?

65. Population The population density of Jackson, Mississippi, is 672.2 people per square kilometer. What is the population density in people per square meter? Show that your answer is reasonable. (*Hint:* There are 1000 meters in 1 kilometer. How many square meters are in 1 square kilometer?)

SPIRAL REVIEW

Evaluate each expression. *(Lesson 1-4)*

66. 8^2 **67.** $(-3)^3$ **68.** $(-3)^2$ **69.** $-\left(\dfrac{1}{2}\right)^5$

Write the power represented by each geometric model. *(Lesson 1-4)*

70.   **71.**   **72.**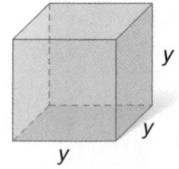

Solve each equation. Check your answer. *(Lesson 2-4)*

73. $2x - 12 = 5x + 3$ **74.** $3a - 4 = 6 - 7a$ **75.** $3x - 4 = 2x + 4$

Solve for the indicated variable. *(Lesson 2-5)*

76. $y = mx + b$ for b **77.** $PV = nRT$ for V **78.** $A = \dfrac{1}{2}bh$ for h

2-8 Applications of Proportions

Objectives
Use proportions to solve problems involving geometric figures.

Use proportions and similar figures to measure objects indirectly.

Vocabulary
similar
corresponding sides
corresponding angles
indirect measurement
scale factor

Why learn this?
Proportions can be used to find the heights of tall objects, such as totem poles, that would otherwise be difficult to measure. (See Example 2.)

Similar figures have exactly the same shape but not necessarily the same size.

Corresponding sides of two figures are in the same relative position, and **corresponding angles** are in the same relative position. Two figures are similar if and only if the lengths of corresponding sides are proportional and all pairs of corresponding angles have equal measures.

Reading Math

• $\overline{AB}$ means segment AB. AB means the length of $\overline{AB}$.
• ∠A means angle A. m∠A means the measure of angle A.

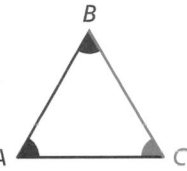

$$\frac{AB}{DE} = \frac{BC}{EF} = \frac{AC}{DF}$$

$$m\angle A = m\angle D$$
$$m\angle B = m\angle E$$
$$m\angle C = m\angle F$$

When stating that two figures are similar, use the symbol ~. For the triangles above, you can write $\triangle ABC \sim \triangle DEF$. Make sure corresponding vertices are in the same order. It would be incorrect to write $\triangle ABC \sim \triangle EFD$.

You can use proportions to find missing lengths in similar figures.

EXAMPLE 1 Finding Missing Measures in Similar Figures

Find the value of x in each diagram.

A $\triangle RST \sim \triangle BCD$

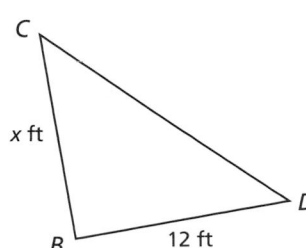

R corresponds to B, S corresponds to C, and T corresponds to D.

$$\frac{5}{12} = \frac{8}{x}$$ $\frac{RT}{BD} = \frac{RS}{BC}$
$$5x = 96$$ *Use cross products.*
$$\frac{5x}{5} = \frac{96}{5}$$ *Since x is multiplied by 5, divide both sides by 5 to undo the multiplication.*
$$x = 19.2$$

The length of $\overline{BC}$ is 19.2 ft.

Find the value of x in each diagram.

B **FGHJKL ~ MNPQRS**

$$\frac{6}{4} = \frac{x}{2} \qquad \frac{NP}{GH} = \frac{RQ}{KJ}$$

$4x = 12$ *Use cross products.*

$$\frac{4x}{4} = \frac{12}{4}$$ *Since x is multiplied by 4, divide both sides by 4 to*

$x = 3$ *undo the multiplication.*

The length of $\overline{QR}$ is 3 cm.

CHECK IT OUT!

1. Find the value of x in the diagram if $ABCD \sim WXYZ$.

You can solve a proportion involving similar triangles to find a length that is not easily measured. This method of measurement is called **indirect measurement**. If two objects form right angles with the ground, you can apply indirect measurement using their shadows.

EXAMPLE 2 *Measurement Application*

A totem pole casts a shadow 45 feet long at the same time that a 6-foot-tall man casts a shadow that is 3 feet long. Write and solve a proportion to find the height of the totem pole.

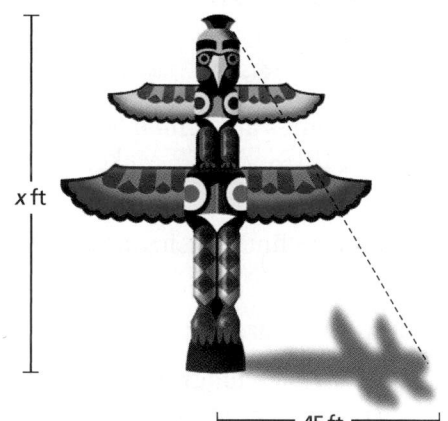

x ft

45 ft

Both the man and the totem pole form right angles with the ground, and their shadows are cast at the same angle. You can form two similar right triangles.

6 ft

3 ft

Helpful Hint

A height of 90 ft seems reasonable for a totem pole. If you got 900 or 9000 ft, that would not be reasonable, and you should check your work.

$$\frac{6}{x} = \frac{3}{45}$$

$3x = 270$

$$\frac{3x}{3} = \frac{270}{3}$$

$x = 90$

The totem pole is 90 feet tall.

$$\frac{\text{man's height}}{\text{pole's height}} = \frac{\text{man's shadow}}{\text{pole's shadow}}$$

Use cross products. Since x is multiplied by 3, divide both sides by 3 to undo the multiplication.

CHECK IT OUT!

2a. A forest ranger who is 150 cm tall casts a shadow 45 cm long. At the same time, a nearby tree casts a shadow 195 cm long. Write and solve a proportion to find the height of the tree.

2b. A woman who is 5.5 feet tall casts a shadow 3.5 feet long. At the same time, a building casts a shadow 28 feet long. Write and solve a proportion to find the height of the building.

If every dimension of a figure is multiplied by the same number, the result is a similar figure. The multiplier is called a **scale factor** .

EXAMPLE 3 **Changing Dimensions**

A Every dimension of a 2-by-4-inch rectangle is multiplied by 1.5 to form a similar rectangle. How is the ratio of the perimeters related to the ratio of corresponding sides? How is the ratio of the areas related to the ratio of corresponding sides?

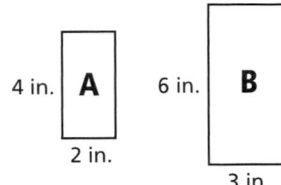

	Rectangle A	Rectangle B
$P = 2\ell + 2w$	$2(2) + 2(4) = 12$	$2(6) + 2(3) = 18$
$A = \ell w$	$4(2) = 8$	$6(3) = 18$

Sides: $\dfrac{4}{6} = \dfrac{2}{3}$ Perimeters: $\dfrac{12}{18} = \dfrac{2}{3}$ Areas: $\dfrac{8}{18} = \dfrac{4}{9} = \left(\dfrac{2}{3}\right)^2$

The ratio of the perimeters is equal to the ratio of corresponding sides. The ratio of the areas is the square of the ratio of corresponding sides.

Helpful Hint

A scale factor between 0 and 1 reduces a figure. A scale factor greater than 1 enlarges it.

B Every dimension of a cylinder with radius 4 cm and height 6 cm is multiplied by $\frac{1}{2}$ to form a similar cylinder. How is the ratio of the volumes related to the ratio of corresponding dimensions?

	Cylinder A	Cylinder B
$V = \pi r^2 h$	$\pi(4)^2(6) = 96\pi$	$\pi(2)^2(3) = 12\pi$

Radii: $\dfrac{4}{2} = \dfrac{2}{1} = 2$ Heights: $\dfrac{6}{3} = \dfrac{2}{1} = 2$ Volumes: $\dfrac{96\pi}{12\pi} = \dfrac{8}{1} = 8 = 2^3$

The ratio of the volumes is the cube of the ratio of corresponding dimensions.

 3. A rectangle has width 12 inches and length 3 inches. Every dimension of the rectangle is multiplied by $\frac{1}{3}$ to form a similar rectangle. How is the ratio of the perimeters related to the ratio of the corresponding sides?

THINK AND DISCUSS

1. Name some pairs of real-world items that appear to be similar figures.

2. GET ORGANIZED Copy and complete the graphic organizer. In the top box, sketch and label two similar triangles. Then list the corresponding sides and angles in the bottom boxes.

GUIDED PRACTICE

1. **Vocabulary** What does it mean for two figures to be *similar*?

SEE EXAMPLE **1**
p. 127

Find the value of *x* in each diagram.

2. $\triangle ABC \sim \triangle DEF$

3. $RSTV \sim WXYZ$

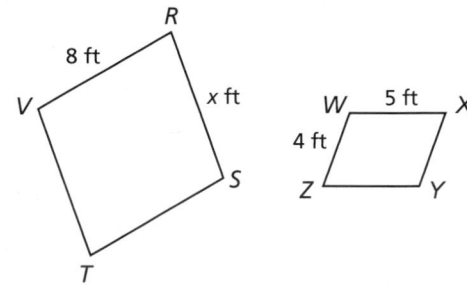

SEE EXAMPLE **2**
p. 128

4. Roger is 5 feet tall and casts a shadow 3.5 feet long. At the same time, the flagpole outside his school casts a shadow 14 feet long. Write and solve a proportion to find the height of the flagpole.

SEE EXAMPLE **3**
p. 129

5. A rectangle has length 12 feet and width 8 feet. Every dimension of the rectangle is multiplied by $\frac{3}{4}$ to form a similar rectangle. How is the ratio of the areas related to the ratio of corresponding sides?

PRACTICE AND PROBLEM SOLVING

Independent Practice

For Exercises	See Example
6–7	1
8	2
9	3

Extra Practice
Skills Practice p. S7
Application Practice p. S29

Find the value of *x* in each diagram.

6. $\triangle LMN \sim \triangle RST$

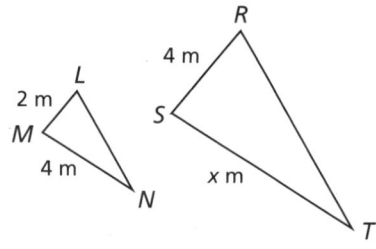

7. prism $A \sim$ prism B

8. Write and solve a proportion to find the height of the taller tree in the diagram at right.

9. A triangle has side lengths of 5 inches, 12 inches, and 15 inches. Every dimension is multiplied by $\frac{1}{5}$ to form a new triangle. How is the ratio of the perimeters related to the ratio of corresponding sides?

10. **Hobbies** For a baby shower gift, Heather crocheted a baby blanket whose length was $2\frac{1}{2}$ feet and whose width was 2 feet. She plans to crochet a proportionally larger similar blanket for the baby's mother. If she wants the length of the mother's blanket to be $6\frac{1}{4}$ feet, what should the width be? Show that your answer is reasonable.

11. **Real Estate** Refer to the home builder's advertisement. The family rooms in both models are rectangular. How much carpeting is needed to carpet the family room in the Weston model?

Our Homes Are Made for Families!

Our Easton model includes a 120-square-foot family room. In the new Weston model, we've doubled the dimensions of the family room!

120 ft² Family room

12. A rectangle has an area of 16 ft². Every dimension is multiplied by a scale factor, and the new rectangle has an area of 64 ft². What was the scale factor?

13. A cone has a volume of 98π cm³. Every dimension is multiplied by a scale factor, and the new cone has a volume of 6272π cm³. What was the scale factor?

Find the value of x in each diagram.

14. $FGHJK \sim MNPQR$

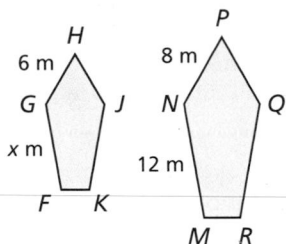

15. cylinder $A \sim$ cylinder B

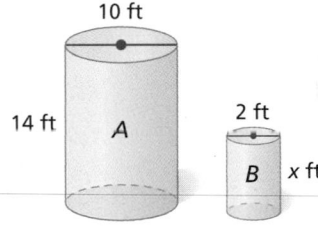

16. $\triangle BCD \sim \triangle FGD$

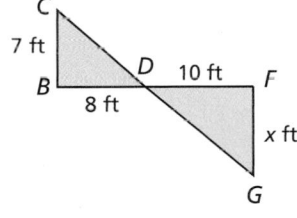

17. $\triangle RST \sim \triangle QSV$

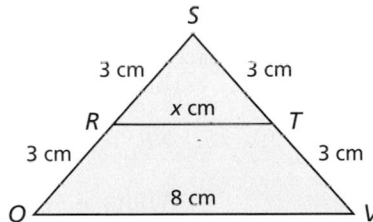

18. A tower casts a 450 ft shadow at the same time that a 4 ft child casts a 6 ft shadow. Write and solve a proportion to find the height of the tower.

19. **Write About It** At Pizza Palace, a pizza with a diameter of 8 inches costs $6.00. The restaurant manager says that a 16-inch pizza should be priced at $12.00 because it is twice as large. Do you agree? Explain why or why not.

20. This problem will prepare you for the Multi-Step Test Prep on page 152.

Another common application of proportion is *percents*. A percent is a ratio of a number to 100. For example, $80\% = \frac{80}{100}$.

   a. Write 12%, 18%, 25%, 67%, and 98% as ratios.

   b. Percents can also be written as decimals. Write each of your ratios from part **a** as a decimal.

   c. What do you notice about a percent and its decimal equivalent?

You will learn more about percents and their connections to proportions in upcoming lessons.

21. A lighthouse casts a shadow that is 36 meters long. At the same time, a person who is 1.5 meters tall casts a shadow that is 4.5 meters long. Write and solve a proportion to find the height of the lighthouse.

22. In the diagram, $\triangle ABC \sim \triangle DEC$. What is the distance across the river from A to B?

23. Critical Thinking If every dimension of a two-dimensional figure is multiplied by k, by what quantity is the area multiplied?

24. A beach ball holds 800 cubic inches of air. Another beach ball has a radius that is half that of the larger ball. How much air does the smaller ball hold?

Ⓐ 400 cubic inches   Ⓒ 100 cubic inches

Ⓑ 200 cubic inches   Ⓓ 80 cubic inches

25. For two similar triangles, $\dfrac{SG}{MW} = \dfrac{GT}{WR} = \dfrac{TS}{RM}$. Which statement below is NOT correct?

Ⓕ $\triangle SGT \sim \triangle MWR$ Ⓗ $\triangle TGS \sim \triangle RWM$

Ⓖ $\triangle GST \sim \triangle MRW$ Ⓙ $\triangle GTS \sim \triangle WRM$

26. Gridded Response A rectangle has length 5 centimeters and width 3 centimeters. A similar rectangle has length 7.25 centimeters. What is the width in centimeters of this rectangle?

CHALLENGE AND EXTEND

27. Find the values of w, x, and y given that $\triangle ABC \sim \triangle DEF \sim \triangle GHJ$.

28. $\triangle RST \sim \triangle VWX$ and $\dfrac{RT}{VX} = b$.

What is $\dfrac{\text{area of } \triangle RST}{\text{area of } \triangle VWX}$?

29. Multi-Step Rectangles A and B are similar. The area of A is 30.195 cm². The length of B is 6.1 cm. Each dimension of B is $\frac{2}{3}$ the corresponding dimension of A. What is the perimeter of B?

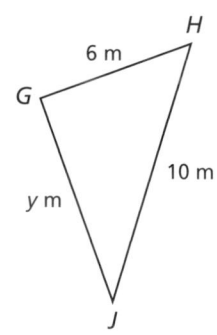

SPIRAL REVIEW

Add or subtract. *(Lesson 1-2)*

30. $-9 - 2$ **31.** $-7 + (-5)$ **32.** $12 - (-18)$ **33.** $19 - 65$

Generate ordered pairs for each function for $x = -2, -1, 0, 1, 2$. *(Lesson 1-8)*

34. $y = 2x$ **35.** $y = x^2$ **36.** $y = 6 - x$ **37.** $y = 3x - 1$

Solve each proportion. *(Lesson 2-7)*

38. $\dfrac{x}{8} = \dfrac{1}{4}$ **39.** $\dfrac{6}{x} = \dfrac{3}{16}$ **40.** $\dfrac{5}{12} = \dfrac{-4}{f}$ **41.** $\dfrac{3}{10} = \dfrac{x+1}{15}$

2-9 Percents

Objective
Solve problems involving percents.

Vocabulary
percent

Who uses this?
Jewelers use percents to determine the purity of precious metals. (See Example 4.)

A **percent** is a ratio that compares a number to 100. For example, $25\% = \frac{25}{100}$.

To find the fraction equivalent of a percent, write the percent as a ratio with a denominator of 100. Then simplify.

$$25\% = \frac{25}{100} = \frac{1}{4}$$

To find the decimal equivalent of a percent, divide by 100.

$$25\% = \frac{25}{100} = 0.25$$

Know it!
Note

Some Common Equivalents											
Percent	10%	20%	25%	$33\frac{1}{3}\%$	40%	50%	60%	$66\frac{2}{3}\%$	75%	80%	100%
Fraction	$\frac{1}{10}$	$\frac{1}{5}$	$\frac{1}{4}$	$\frac{1}{3}$	$\frac{2}{5}$	$\frac{1}{2}$	$\frac{3}{5}$	$\frac{2}{3}$	$\frac{3}{4}$	$\frac{4}{5}$	1
Decimal	0.1	0.2	0.25	$0.\overline{3}$	0.4	0.5	0.6	$0.\overline{6}$	0.75	0.8	1.0

The greatest percent shown in the table is 100%, or 1. But percents can be greater than 100%. For example, $120\% = \frac{120}{100} = 1.2$. You can also find percents that are less than 1%. For example, $0.5\% = \frac{0.5}{100} = 0.005$.

You can use the proportion $\frac{\text{part}}{\text{whole}} = \frac{\text{percent}}{100}$ to find unknown values.

EXAMPLE 1 Finding the Part

A Find 50% of 20.

Method 1 Use a proportion.

$$\frac{\text{part}}{\text{whole}} = \frac{\text{percent}}{100}$$ *Use the percent proportion.*

$$\frac{x}{20} = \frac{50}{100}$$ *Let x represent the part.*

$$100x = 1000$$ *Find the cross products.*

$$x = 10$$ *Since x is multiplied by 100, divide both sides by 100 to undo the multiplication.*

50% of 20 is 10.

Check   50% is the same as $\frac{1}{2}$, and $\frac{1}{2}$ of 20 is 10. ✓

B Find 105% of 72.

    Method 2 Use an equation.

$$x = 105\% \text{ of } 72$$ *Write an equation. Let x represent the part.*

$$x = 1.05(72)$$ *Write the percent as a decimal and multiply.*

$$x = 75.6$$

105% of 72 is 75.6.

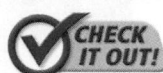 **1a.** Find 20% of 60.   **1b.** Find 210% of 8.   **1c.** Find 4% of 36.

EXAMPLE 2   **Finding the Percent**

A **What percent of 60 is 15?**

    Method 1 Use a proportion.

$$\frac{\text{part}}{\text{whole}} = \frac{\text{percent}}{100}$$ *Use the percent proportion.*

$$\frac{15}{60} = \frac{x}{100}$$ *Let x represent the percent.*

$$60x = 1500$$ *Find the cross products.*

$$\frac{60x}{60} = \frac{1500}{60}$$ *Since x is multiplied by 60, divide both sides by 60 to undo the multiplication.*

$$x = 25$$

15 is 25% of 60.

B **440 is what percent of 400?**

    Method 2 Use an equation.

$$440 = x \cdot 400$$ *Write an equation. Let x represent the percent.*

$$440 = 400x$$ *Since x is multiplied by 400, divide both sides by 400 to undo the multiplication.*

$$\frac{440}{400} = \frac{400x}{400}$$

$$1.1 = x$$ *The answer is a decimal.*

$$110\% = x$$ *Write the decimal as a percent. This answer is reasonable; 440 is more than 100% of 400.*

440 is 110% of 400.

 2a. What percent of 35 is 7?   **2b.** 27 is what percent of 9?

EXAMPLE 3   **Finding the Whole**

A **40% of what number is 14?**

    Method 1 Use a proportion.

$$\frac{\text{part}}{\text{whole}} = \frac{\text{percent}}{100}$$ *Use the percent proportion.*

$$\frac{14}{x} = \frac{40}{100}$$ *Let x represent the whole.*

$$40x = 1400$$ *Find the cross products.*

$$\frac{40x}{40} = \frac{1400}{40}$$ *Since x is multiplied by 40, divide both sides by 40 to undo the multiplication.*

$$x = 35$$

40% of 35 is 14.

B **40 is 0.8% of what number?**

Method 2 Use an equation.

$$40 = 0.8\% \text{ of } x \qquad \textit{Write an equation. Let x represent the whole.}$$

$$40 = 0.008 \cdot x \qquad \textit{Write the percent as a decimal.}$$

$$\frac{40}{0.008} = \frac{0.008x}{0.008} \qquad \begin{array}{l}\textit{Since x is multiplied by 0.008, divide both sides}\\ \textit{by 0.008 to undo the multiplication.}\end{array}$$

$$5000 = x$$

40 is 0.8% of 5000.

 3a. 120% of what number is 90?   **3b.** 48 is 15% of what number?

EXAMPLE **4**   *Career Application*

Jewelers use the karat system to determine the amount of pure gold in jewelry. Pure gold is 24 karat, meaning the item is 100% gold. A 14-karat gold ring contains 14 parts gold and 10 parts other metal. What percent of the ring is gold? Round your answer to the nearest percent.

$$\frac{\text{part}}{\text{whole}} = \frac{\text{percent}}{100} \qquad \textit{Use the percent proportion.}$$

$$\frac{14}{24} = \frac{x}{100} \qquad \textit{Let x represent the percent.}$$

$$24x = 1400 \qquad \textit{Find the cross products.}$$

$$\frac{24x}{24} = \frac{1400}{24} \qquad \begin{array}{l}\textit{Since x is multiplied by 24, divide both sides by 24 to}\\ \textit{undo the multiplication.}\end{array}$$

$$x = 58.\overline{3}$$

A 14-karat gold ring is approximately 58% gold.

 4. Use the information above to find the number of karats in a bracelet that is 42% gold. Round your answer to the nearest whole number.

THINK AND DISCUSS

1. Describe the numerical value of the percent when the part is greater than the whole. Give an example.

2. 64% of a number is 32. Is the number greater than or less than 32? Explain.

 3. GET ORGANIZED Copy and complete the graphic organizer. In each box, write and solve an example using the given method.

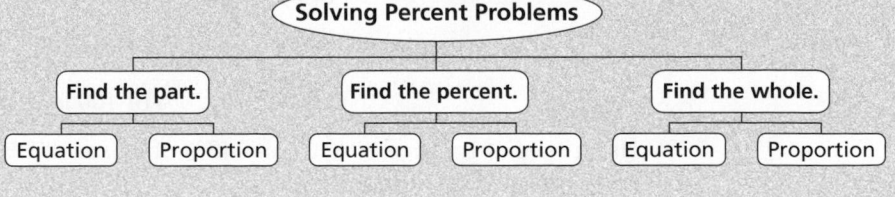

go.hrw.com
Homework Help Online
KEYWORD: MA11 2-9
Parent Resources Online
KEYWORD: MA7 Parent

GUIDED PRACTICE

1. **Vocabulary** In your own words, write a definition of *percent*.

SEE EXAMPLE **1**
p. 133

2. Find 75% of 40.
3. Find $12\frac{1}{2}$% of 168.
4. Find 115% of 57.
5. Find 70% of 8.

SEE EXAMPLE **2**
p. 134

6. What percent of 40 is 25?
7. What percent of 225 is 180?
8. 57 is what percent of 30?
9. 1 is what percent of 8?

SEE EXAMPLE **3**
p. 134

10. 28 is 32% of what number?
11. 4% of what number is 7?
12. 16 is 10% of what number?
13. 105% of what number is 37.8?

SEE EXAMPLE **4**
p. 135

14. **Nutrition** A certain granola bar has 2 grams of fiber. This is 8% of the recommended daily value. How many grams of fiber are recommended daily?

PRACTICE AND PROBLEM SOLVING

Independent Practice	
For Exercises	See Example
15–18	1
19–22	2
23–26	3
27	4

Extra Practice
Skills Practice p. S7
Application Practice p. S29

Find each value. Round to the nearest tenth if necessary.

15. 60% of 80
16. 35% of 90
17. $\frac{1}{2}$% of 500
18. 210% of 30
19. What percent of 52 is 13?
20. What percent of 9 is 27?
21. 11 is what percent of 22?
22. 5 is what percent of 67?
23. 36 is 90% of what number?
24. 8.2 is 2% of what number?
25. $4\frac{1}{2}$% of what number is 23?
26. 16% of what number is 94?

27. **Nutrition** A certain can of iced tea contains 4% of the recommended daily allowance of sodium. The recommended daily allowance is 2500 milligrams. How many milligrams of sodium are in the can of iced tea?

Write each decimal or fraction as a percent.

28. $\frac{5}{4}$
29. 0.02
30. 0.27
31. $\frac{2}{25}$
32. $\frac{7}{7}$

33. 0.64
34. $\frac{31}{100}$
35. 0.85
36. 0.003
37. $\frac{17}{20}$

Write each percent as a decimal and as a fraction.

38. 23%
39. 52%
40. 12.5%
41. 90%
42. 87.2%

43. 112%
44. 29%
45. 6%
46. 1.5%
47. $\frac{3}{5}$%

48. **Estimation** To estimate 26% of 400, think:

$$26\% \text{ is close to } 25\% \text{ and } 25\% = \frac{1}{4}$$

$$\frac{1}{4} \text{ of } 400 = 100.$$

Therefore, 26% of 400 is about 100.

Use a similar method to estimate 48% of 610 and 73% of 820. Then check your estimates by finding each percent.

49. Critical Thinking Which is greater, 0.5 or $\frac{1}{2}$%? Explain.

Write each list in order from least to greatest.

50. $\frac{1}{20}$, 5.3%, 5.1, 0.005, $\frac{1}{2}$

51. 1.1, 11%, $\frac{1}{10}$, 0.001, 1%

52. $\frac{3}{8}$, 29%, $\frac{2}{5}$, 0.25, 38%

53. 0.49, 82%, 0.94, $\frac{4}{5}$, $\frac{5}{9}$

54. Biology On average, sloths spend 16.5 hours per day sleeping. What percent of the day do sloths spend sleeping? Round your answer to the nearest percent.

55. Entertainment The numbers of various types of movies rented over a period of time are indicated in the graph.

   a. What percent of the movies rented were comedies?

   b. What type of movie made up 25% of the rentals?

   c. What percent of the movies rented were in the "other" category?

   d. What if...? If 25 of the comedy rentals had instead been action rentals, what percent of the movies rented would have been comedies? Round your answer to the nearest tenth.

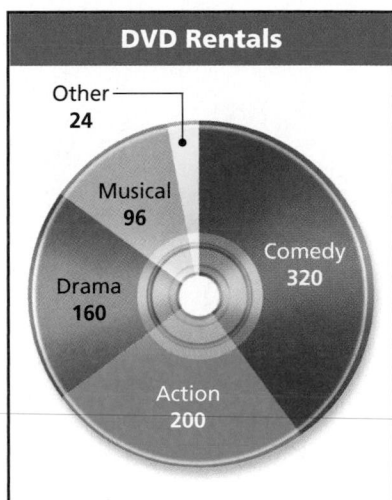

56. Multi-Step According to the 2000 U.S. Census, 138,053,563 Americans are male, and 143,368,343 Americans are female. About what percent of the population is male? female? Round your answers to the nearest percent.

57. Complete each statement in the table below. Describe any patterns you see in the completed table.

1% of 400 is 4.	100% of is 12.	% of 80 is 20.
2% of is 4.	50% of is 12.	% of 40 is 20.
4% of is 4.	25% of is 12.	% of 20 is 20.
8% of is 4.	12.5% of is 12.	% of 10 is 20.

58. Write About It Explain the advantages of using the proportion method to solve percent problems. Then, explain the advantages of using the equation method to solve percent problems.

MULTI-STEP TEST PREP

59. This problem will prepare you for the Multi-Step Test Prep on page 152.

Kathryn found a new dress at the mall. The price tag reads $90. The sign above the rack of dresses says that all items on the rack are 40% off.

   a. Set up a proportion to find 40% of $90. This is the amount of the discount.

   b. How much will Kathryn pay for the dress? Show that your answer is reasonable.

   c. Copy and complete the model below. Explain how this model can help you answer the above questions in another way.

60. Which proportion can be used to find 14% of 60?

(A) $\dfrac{x}{100} = \dfrac{60}{14}$ (B) $\dfrac{14}{100} = \dfrac{60}{x}$ (C) $\dfrac{x}{100} = \dfrac{14}{60}$ (D) $\dfrac{14}{100} = \dfrac{x}{60}$

61. Raul surveyed 35 students about their preferred lunch. Fourteen preferred chicken. Half of those students preferred chicken with barbecue sauce. What percent should Raul report as preferring chicken with barbecue sauce?

(F) 20%   (G) 40%   (H) 50%   (J) 80%

62. After an election in a small town, the newspaper reported that 42% of the registered voters actually voted. If 12,000 people voted, which equation can be used to find the number of registered voters?

(A) $v = 42 \cdot 12{,}000$ (B) $v = 0.42 \cdot 12{,}000$ (C) $42v = 12{,}000$ (D) $0.42v = 12{,}000$

63. Which list is in order from least to greatest?

(F) $\dfrac{1}{2}$, 20%, 33%, 0.625, $\dfrac{1}{8}$, 1   (H) $\dfrac{1}{8}$, $\dfrac{1}{2}$, 0.625, 1, 20%, 30%

(G) $\dfrac{1}{8}$, 20%, 33%, $\dfrac{1}{2}$, 0.625, 1   (J) 0.625, $\dfrac{1}{8}$, $\dfrac{1}{2}$, 1, 20%, 30%

64. Moises saves 8% of his weekly paycheck in his savings account. He deposited $18.80 from his last paycheck into his savings account. Which is the best estimate of the total amount of Moises's last paycheck?

(A) $26   (B) $100   (C) $160   (D) $200

CHALLENGE AND EXTEND

Find each value. Round to the nearest tenth if necessary.

65. What percent of 16 is 2.75?

66. 22 is 73.5% of what number?

67. 121.3% of 73 is what number?

68. What percent of 8000 is 6525?

69. Find 10% of 8 and 8% of 10. What do you notice? Try this with several other pairs of numbers. Do you think this relationship will be true for all pairs of numbers? Why or why not?

70. Chemistry A chemist has 20 milliliters of a solution that is 40% acid. She wants to increase the acid content of the solution to make it a 50%-acid solution. How many milliliters of pure acid should she add to the solution? (*Hint:* Begin by finding the number of milliliters of acid in the original solution.)

SPIRAL REVIEW

Simplify each expression. *(Lesson 1-7)*

71. $32 + 47 + 28 + 13$

72. $4 \cdot 23 \cdot 25$

73. $8 \cdot 4 \cdot 5$

74. $44 + 27 + 56$

75. A picture has a width of 4 in. and a length of 6 in. It is enlarged on a copier, and the new length is 9 in. What is the new width? *(Lesson 2-8)*

76. A picture has a width of 4 in. and a length of 6 in. It is reduced on a copier, and the new length is 4.8 in. What is the new width? *(Lesson 2-8)*

77. A rectangle has an area of 9 ft^2. Every dimension is multiplied by a scale factor, and the new rectangle has an area of 81 ft^2. What was the scale factor? *(Lesson 2-8)*

<table>
<tr><td>2-10</td><td>

Applications of Percents

</td></tr>
</table>

Objectives
Use common applications of percents.

Estimate with percents.

Vocabulary
commission   principal
interest   tip
sales tax

Who uses this?
Sales representatives use percents to calculate their total pay.

A **commission** is money paid to a person or a company for making a sale. Usually the commission is a percent of the sale amount.

EXAMPLE 1   *Business Application*

Caution! //////

You must convert a percent to a decimal or a fraction before doing any calculations with it.

Ms. Barns earns a base salary of $42,000 plus a 1.5% commission on sales. Her total sales one year were $700,000. Find her total pay for the year.

total pay = base salary + commission	*Write the formula for total pay.*
= base salary + % of total sales	*Write the formula for commission.*
= 42,000 + 1.5% of 700,000	*Substitute values given in the problem.*
= 42,000 + (0.015)(700,000)	*Write the percent as a decimal.*
= 42,000 + 10,500	*Multiply.*
= 52,500	*Add.*

Ms. Barns's total pay was $52,500.

 1. A telemarketer earns $350 per week plus a 12% commission on sales. Find her total pay for a week in which her sales are $940.

Interest is the amount of money charged for borrowing money, or the amount of money earned when saving or investing money. **Principal** is the amount borrowed or invested. Simple interest is interest paid only on the principal.

Simple Interest Paid Annually

Simple interest → $I = Prt$ ← Time in years

          Principal   Interest rate per year as a decimal

EXAMPLE 2   *Finance Application*

A Find the simple interest paid annually for 2 years on a $900 loan at 16% per year.

$I = Prt$	*Write the formula for simple interest.*
$I = (900)(0.16)(2)$	*Substitute known values. Write the interest rate as a decimal.*
$I = 288$	

The amount of interest is $288.

Helpful Hint

When you are using the formula $I = Prt$ to find simple interest paid annually, t represents time in years. One month is $\frac{1}{12}$ year. In Example 2B, $t = \frac{3}{12}$.

B After 3 months the simple interest earned annually on an investment of $7000 was $63. Find the interest rate.

$$I = Prt$$ *Write the formula for simple interest.*

$$63 = (7000)(r)\left(\frac{3}{12}\right)$$ *Substitute the given values.*

$$63 = 1750r$$ *Multiply $7000\left(\frac{3}{12}\right)$. Since r is multiplied by*

$$\frac{63}{1750} = \frac{1750r}{1750}$$ *1750, divide both sides by 1750 to undo the multiplication.*

$$0.036 = r$$

The interest rate is 3.6%.

2a. Find the simple interest earned after 2 years on an investment of $3000 at 4.5% interest earned annually.

2b. The simple interest paid on a loan after 6 months was $306. The annual interest rate was 8%. Find the principal.

A **tip** is an amount of money added to a bill for service. It is usually a percent of the bill before *sales tax* is added. **Sales tax** is a percent of an item's cost.

Sales tax and tips are sometimes estimated instead of calculated exactly. When estimating percents, use percents that you can calculate mentally.

- Find 10% of a number by moving the decimal point one place to the left.
- Find 1% of a number by moving the decimal point two places to the left.
- Find 5% of a number by finding $\frac{1}{2}$ of 10% of the number.

E X A M P L E   3   **Estimating with Percents**

A The dinner check for Maria's family is $67.95. Estimate a 15% tip.

     Step 1 First round $67.95 to $70.

     Step 2 Think: 15% = 10% + 5%

                   10% of $70 = $7.00   *Move the decimal point one place left.*

     Step 3 Think: 5% = 10% ÷ 2

                   = $7.00 ÷ 2 = $3.50

     Step 4 15% = 10% + 5%

                 = $7.00 + $3.50 = $10.50

     The tip should be about $10.50.

Helpful Hint

A 6.25% sales tax rate means that for every $100 you spend, you would pay $6.25 in sales tax.

B The sales tax rate is 6.25%. Estimate the sales tax on a shirt that costs $29.50.

     Step 1 First round 6.25% to 6% and $29.50 to $30.

     Step 2 Think: 6% = 6(1%)

               1% of $30 = $0.30   *Move the decimal point 2 places left.*

     Step 3 6% = 6(1%)

               = 6($0.30) = $1.80

     The sales tax is about $1.80.

3a. Estimate a 15% tip on a check for $21.98.

3b. Estimate the tax on shoes that cost $68.50 when the sales tax rate is 8.25%

THINK AND DISCUSS

1. Explain how commission, interest, sales tax, and tips are alike.

2. When the sales tax rate is 8.25%, the tax on a $10 purchase is $0.83. Is the tax on $20 twice as much? Explain.

3. **GET ORGANIZED** Copy and complete the graphic organizer. In each box, write an example of each type of application and find the answer.

```
                    Applications of Percents
        ┌──────────────┬──────────────┬──────────────┐
   Commission    Simple interest      Tips        Sales tax
```

2-10 Exercises

go.hrw.com
Homework Help Online
KEYWORD: MA11 2-10
Parent Resources Online
KEYWORD: MA7 Parent

GUIDED PRACTICE

1. **Vocabulary** How are *commission* and *tips* alike? How are they different?

SEE EXAMPLE 1
p. 139

2. A sales representative earns a 2.5% commission on sales. Find the commission earned when the total sales are $80,700.

3. Karen earns a salary of $28,600 per year plus a 4.25% commission on sales. Find her total earnings for a year when the sales are $310,000.

SEE EXAMPLE 2
p. 139

4. Find the amount of simple interest earned after 2 years on $480 invested at a 7% annual interest rate.

5. Find the number of years it would take for $1200 to earn simple interest of $324 at an annual interest rate of 6% per year.

6. Find the total amount owed after 6 months on a loan of $900 at an annual simple interest rate of 8.5%.

SEE EXAMPLE 3
p. 140

7. Estimate a 15% tip on a $42.65 check.

8. Estimate the tax on a $198 stereo when the sales tax is 5.25%.

PRACTICE AND PROBLEM SOLVING

Independent Practice

For Exercises	See Example
9–10	1
11–13	2
14–15	3

Extra Practice

Skills Practice p. S7
Application Practice p. S29

9. A boat salesperson earns a 2.5% commission on the sale of each boat. Find the commission earned on a boat that sells for $18,500.

10. A cell phone distributor earns a yearly salary of $28,000 plus a 17.5% commission on sales. Find the total earnings for a year when the sales are $38,000.

11. Find the simple interest paid after 3 months on a loan of $9700 borrowed at an annual interest rate of 11%.

12. After 8 months, $750 simple interest was owed on a loan of $9000. Find the annual interest rate.

13. How long will it take $680 to earn $102 in simple interest at an annual interest rate of 3%?

14. Estimate the tip on a $19.65 check using a tip rate of 15%.

15. Estimate the tax on tires that cost $498 with a 6.25% sales tax.

Use $I = Prt$ to complete the table. All interest rates are annual.

	I	$=$	P	$\times$	r	$\times$	t
16.			$8275		13%		3 years
17.	$3969				10.5%		9 months
18.	$23.75		$950				6 months
19.	$380		$4750		4%		

20. Chris has $21.50. He wants a book for $5.85 and a CD for $14.99. The sales tax is 6.25%.

    a. How could Chris estimate whether he has enough to buy the book and the CD?

    b. Does he have enough money to buy the book and the CD?

21. **Technology** An online auction company charges sellers a commission fee of 5.25% of an item's final selling price. If you sell an item for $55, what fee will you pay to the auction company? Show that your answer is reasonable.

22. **Business** Sometimes business partners do not share the ownership of a business equally. Instead, they each own a percent of the business, and each receives that percent of the profits. Alvarez, Brown, and Chow are partners in a business that earned $500,000. Alvarez owns 40% of the business. Chow received $175,000.

    a. How much money did Alvarez and Brown each receive?

    b. What percent of the business is owned by Brown? by Chow?

23. **Write About It** Lewis invested $1000 at 3% annual simple interest for 4 years. Lisa invested $1000 at 4% annual simple interest for 3 years. Explain why Lewis and Lisa earned the same amount of interest.

24. **Critical Thinking** To estimate a tip of 15%, Amy tips $1.00 for every $6.00 in the total bill. Is this method reasonable? Why or why not?

25. **///ERROR ANALYSIS///** Which solution is incorrect? Explain the error.

    (A)   4% of 240 / 0.4 • 240 / 96

    (B)   4% of 240 / 0.04 • 240 / 9.6

26. This problem will prepare you for the Multi-Step Test Prep on page 152.

    a. Juan is shopping for a new CD player. He finds one he likes for $225. The sales tax is 7.5%. What will be the total cost of the CD player?

    b. The salesperson tells Juan that a sale starts tomorrow, and the CD player will be reduced to $157.50. What is the total cost, including tax, that Juan will pay if he buys the CD player tomorrow?

    c. How much will Juan save if he buys the CD player tomorrow?

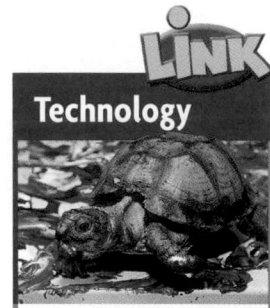

Technology

Koopa is a Gulf Coast box turtle from Hartford, Connecticut. His paintings have sold for hundreds of dollars at online auctions.

27. Which account earns the most simple interest after 1 year? Assume that interest is paid annually.

    Ⓐ $5000 at 8% per year   Ⓒ $8000 at 4.8% per year

    Ⓑ $10,000 at 4% per year   Ⓓ $4000 at 10.2% per year

28. Craig earns $200 per week plus 8% commission on sales. Joan earns $150 per week plus 12% commission on sales. Last week, both had sales of $1500. Who earned more money?

    Ⓕ Craig earned more than Joan.   Ⓗ Both earned the same amount.

    Ⓖ Joan earned more than Craig.   Ⓙ Cannot be determined

29. Short Response If 2% of a number is 300, what is 6% of the number? Explain how you got your answer.

CHALLENGE AND EXTEND

30. Multi-Step A lunch check for Mark and a friend was $19.50 before the 6% sales tax was added. Mark wants to leave a tip of at least 20%. He has no coins, and he does not want to wait for change. What is the least amount he should leave to pay the check, tax, and tip?

31. The final cost of an item was $50. This included 6% sales tax. What was the price of the item before tax?

Finance A stockbroker earns a commission based on the amount of a transaction according to the table below.

		Stockbroker's Commissions		
Transaction	$0–$10,000	For each additional dollar up to $20,000	For each additional dollar up to $40,000	For each additional dollar over $40,000
Commission	0.5%	0.4%	0.3%	0.2%

For example, the commission on a transaction of $11,000 is 0.5% of $10,000 plus 0.4% of $1000. Use the table for Exercises 32–34.

32. Find the amount of commission earned on a transaction of $15,000.

33. Find the amount of commission earned on a transaction of $21,000.

34. Find the amount of commission earned on a transaction of $100,000.

SPIRAL REVIEW

Compare. Write $<$, $>$, or $=$. *(Lesson 1-5)*

35. $\sqrt{65}$ ▨ 8   **36.** 7 ▨ $\sqrt{51}$ **37.** 9 ▨ $\sqrt{80}$ **38.** $\sqrt{196}$ ▨ 14

Solve each equation. Check your answer. *(Lesson 2-6)*

39. $|x - 7| = 5$ **40.** $|3x| + 5 = 14$ **41.** $8|3x - 10| - 12 = 20$

Find each value. Round to the nearest tenth if necessary. *(Lesson 2-9)*

42. 40% of 60 is what number?   **43.** What percent of 26 is 13?

44. 22 is what percent of 99?   **45.** 80% of what number is 64?

Percent Increase and Decrease

"May I suggest you read the sign again, Sir."

Objective
Find percent increase and decrease.

Vocabulary
percent change
percent increase
percent decrease
discount
markup

Who uses this?
Consumers can use percent change to determine how much money they can save. (See Example 3.)

A **percent change** is an increase or decrease given as a percent of the original amount. **Percent increase** describes an amount that has grown and **percent decrease** describes an amount that has been reduced.

Percent Change

$$\text{percent change} = \frac{\text{amount of increase or decrease}}{\text{original amount}}, \text{ expressed as a percent}$$

EXAMPLE 1 Finding Percent Increase or Decrease

Find each percent change. Tell whether it is a percent increase or decrease.

A from 25 to 49

$$\text{percent change} = \frac{\text{amount of increase}}{\text{original amount}}$$

$$= \frac{49 - 25}{25}$$

$$= \frac{24}{25} \qquad \textit{Simplify the numerator.}$$

$$= 0.96$$

$$= 96\% \qquad \textit{Write the answer as a percent.}$$

25 to 49 is an increase, so a change from 25 to 49 is a 96% increase.

B from 50 to 45

$$\text{percent change} = \frac{\text{amount of decrease}}{\text{original amount}}$$

$$= \frac{50 - 45}{50}$$

$$= \frac{5}{50} \qquad \textit{Simplify the numerator.}$$

$$= \frac{1}{10} \qquad \textit{Simplify the fraction.}$$

$$= 10\% \qquad \textit{Write the answer as a percent.}$$

50 to 45 is a decrease, so a change from 50 to 45 is a 10% decrease.

Helpful Hint

Before solving, decide what is a reasonable answer. For Example 1A, 25 to 50 would be a 100% increase. So 25 to 49 should be slightly less than 100%.

 CHECK IT OUT! Find each percent change. Tell whether it is a percent increase or decrease.

1a. from 200 to 110   **1b.** from 25 to 30   **1c.** from 80 to 115

EXAMPLE 2 Finding the Result of a Percent Increase or Decrease

A **Find the result when 30 is increased by 20%.**

$0.20(30) = 6$ *Find 20% of 30. This is the amount of the increase.*

$30 + 6 = 36$ *It is a percent increase, so add 6 to the original amount.*

30 increased by 20% is 36.

B **Find the result when 65 is decreased by 80%.**

$0.80(65) = 52$ *Find 80% of 65. This is the amount of the decrease.*

$65 - 52 = 13$ *It is a percent decrease, so subtract 52 from 65.*

65 decreased by 80% is 13.

 2a. Find the result when 72 is increased by 25%.

2b. Find the result when 10 is decreased by 40%.

Common applications of percent change are *discounts* and *markups*.

A **discount** is an amount by which an original price is reduced.

> **discount** = % of **original price**
>
> final price = **original price** − **discount**

A **markup** is an amount by which a wholesale cost is increased.

> **markup** = % of **wholesale cost**
>
> final price = **wholesale cost** + **markup**

EXAMPLE 3 Discounts

A **Admission to the museum is $8. Students receive a 15% discount. How much is the discount? How much do students pay?**

Method 1 A discount is a percent decrease. So find $8 decreased by 15%.

$0.15(8) = 1.20$ *Find 15% of 8. This is the amount of the discount.*

$8 - 1.20 = 6.80$ *Subtract 1.20 from 8. This is the student price.*

Method 2 Subtract percent discount from 100%.

$100\% - 15\% = 85\%$ *Students pay 85% of the regular price, $8.*

$0.85(8) = 6.80$ *Find 85% of 8. This is the student price.*

$8 - 6.80 = 1.20$ *Subtract 6.80 from 8. This is the amount of the discount.*

By either method, the discount is $1.20. Students pay $6.80.

> **Helpful Hint**
>
> Before solving, decide what is a reasonable answer. For Example 3A, a 25% discount is $2 off. So a 15% discount will be less than $2 off.

B **Christo used a coupon and paid $7.35 for a pizza that normally costs $10.50. Find the percent discount.**

$\$10.50 - \$7.35 = \$3.15$ *Think: 3.15 is what percent of 10.50? Let x represent the percent.*

$3.15 = x(10.50)$

$\dfrac{3.15}{10.50} = \dfrac{x \cdot 10.50}{10.50}$ *Since x is multiplied by 10.50, divide both sides by 10.50 to undo the multiplication.*

$0.3 = x$

$30\% = x$ *Write the answer as a percent.*

The discount is 30%.

 3a. A $220 bicycle was on sale for 60% off. Find the sale price.

3b. Ray paid $12 for a $15 T-shirt. What was the percent discount?

EXAMPLE 4   **Markups**

A   Kaleb buys necklaces at a wholesale cost of $48 each. He then marks up the price by 75% and sells the necklaces. What is the amount of the markup? What is the selling price?

Method 1
A markup is a percent increase. So find $48 increased by 75%.

$0.75(48) = 36$ *Find 75% of 48. This is the amount of the markup.*

$48 + 36 = 84$ *Add to 48. This is the selling price.*

Method 2
Add percent markup to 100%.

$100\% + 75\% = 175\%$ *The selling price is 175% of the wholesale price, $48.*

$1.75(48) = 84$ *Find 175% of 48. This is the selling price.*

$84 - 48 = 36$ *Subtract from 84. This is the amount of the markup.*

By either method, the amount of the markup is $36. The selling price is $84.

B   Lars purchased a daily planner for $32. The wholesale cost was $25. What was the percent markup?

$32 - 25 = 7$ *Find the amount of the markup.*

$7 = x(25)$ *Think: 7 is what percent of 25? Let x represent the percent.*

$\dfrac{7}{25} = \dfrac{25x}{25}$ *Since x is multiplied by 25, divide both sides by 25 to undo the multiplication.*

$0.28 = x$

$28\% = x$ *Write the answer as a percent.*

The markup was 28%.

 CHECK IT OUT!

4a. A video game has a 70% markup. The wholesale cost is $9. What is the selling price?

4b. What is the percent markup on a car selling for $21,850 that had a wholesale cost of $9500?

THINK AND DISCUSS

1. 80% of a number is the same as a ?% decrease from that number. A 30% increase from a number is the same as ?% of that number.

2. A markup of 200% will result in a final cost that is how many times the wholesale cost?

3. What information would you need to find the percent change in your school's population over the last ten years?

 4. GET ORGANIZED Copy and complete the graphic organizer. In each box, write and solve an example of the given type of problem.

Percent Increase	Percent Decrease	Discount	Markup

go.hrw.com

Homework Help Online
KEYWORD: MA11 2-11

Parent Resources Online
KEYWORD: MA7 Parent

GUIDED PRACTICE

1. **Vocabulary** Compare *percent increase* and *percent decrease*.

SEE EXAMPLE 1
p. 144

Find each percent change. Tell whether it is a percent increase or decrease

2. 25 to 45   3. 10 to 8   4. 400 to 300

5. 16 to 18   6. 40 to 50   7. 50 to 40

SEE EXAMPLE 2
p. 144

8. Find the result when 40 is increased by 85%.

9. Find the result when 60 is increased by 3%.

10. Find the result when 350 is decreased by 10%.

11. Find the result when 16 is decreased by 50%.

SEE EXAMPLE 3
p. 145

12. What is the final price on a $185 leather jacket that is on sale for 40% off?

13. Neal bought a book on sale for $3.60. It was originally priced at $12. What was Neal's discount as a percent?

SEE EXAMPLE 4
p. 146

14. Yolanda bought a video that was priced at a 65% markup over the manufacturer's cost of $12. What was Yolanda's cost?

15. Randy sells hats for $12.35. The wholesale cost of each hat is $6.50. What is Randy's markup as a percent?

PRACTICE AND PROBLEM SOLVING

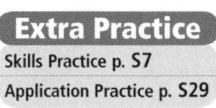

Independent Practice

For Exercises	See Example
16–27	1
28–31	2
32–33	3
34–35	4

Extra Practice
Skills Practice p. S7
Application Practice p. S29

Find each percent change. Tell whether it is a percent increase or decrease.

16. 50 to 60   17. 4 to 3   18. 96 to 84   19. 9 to 45

20. 32 to 30   21. 15 to 19.5   22. 150 to 180   23. 17 to 14.45

24. 20 to 15   25. 265 to 318   26. 35 to 105   27. 300 to 275

28. Find the result when 24 is increased by 75%.

29. Find the result when 240 is increased by 5%.

30. Find the result when 30 is decreased by 85%.

31. Find the result when 8 is decreased by 5%.

32. The cost of Hisako's school supplies was $49.80. She had a coupon for 30% off the entire purchase. What was the final price?

33. With the purchase of 10 greeting cards, Addie received a discount. She paid $26.35 for the cards that would normally have cost $31. What percent discount did Addie receive?

34. Irma sells boxing gloves in her sporting goods store for a 9% markup over the manufacturer's cost of $40. What is the selling price of the gloves?

35. Bottled water in a certain vending machine costs $1.50. This price is a markup from the wholesale cost of $0.20. What is the markup as a percent?

36. **Critical Thinking** Is the percent increase from 50 to 80 the same as the percent decrease from 80 to 50? Why or why not?

Multi-Step The graph shows the average height of a child from birth to age 4. Use the graph for Exercises 37–39.

37. By what percent does a child's height increase from birth to age 1 year?

38. By what percent does a child's height increase from birth to age 4 years?

39. **Estimation** Estimate the amount and percent of increase in a child's height from age 2 to age 3. Show that your estimate is reasonable.

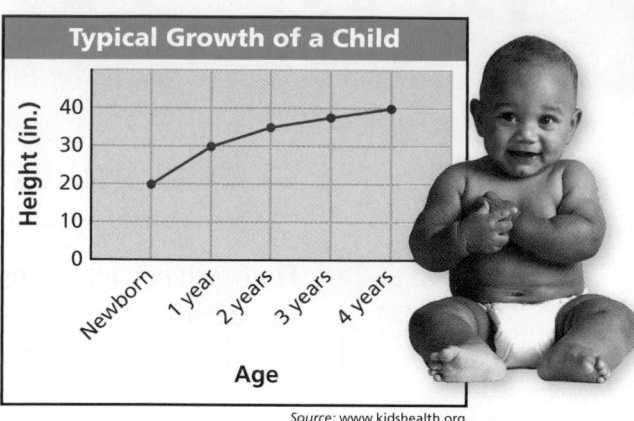

Typical Growth of a Child

Source: www.kidshealth.org

40. **Employment** Last summer, Duncan charged $20 to mow a lawn in his neighborhood. This summer, he'll charge $23. What is the percent increase in Duncan's price? Show that your answer is reasonable.

Copy and complete the table.

	Original Amount	New Amount	Percent Change
41.	12		50% increase
42.	$48	$42.24	
43.	$4\frac{1}{2}$	$13\frac{1}{2}$	
44.	8525		20% decrease

Find each missing number.

45. 20 increased by ▨% is 24.

46. 80 decreased by ▨% is 76.

47. 120 decreased by 50% is ▨.

48. 200 increased by ▨% is 210.

49. **Nutrition** A can of soup had 480 mg of sodium per serving. The sodium was reduced to 360 mg per serving so that the soup could be advertised as "low sodium." What was the percent change in sodium content?

 50. **Write About It** Dana is shopping for shoes at a store advertising "everything 45% off." Describe a method she could use to estimate the discount and final price on a pair of shoes.

MULTI-STEP TEST PREP

51. This problem will prepare you for the Multi-Step Test Prep on page 152.
   a. Robert finds a shirt on a sale rack. All items on the rack are 40% off. The price on his shirt is missing. When the clerk scans the bar code, he tells Robert that the sale price of the shirt is $18. What percent of the original price is $18?
   b. Set up a proportion to find the original price of the shirt.
   c. Copy and complete the model below and explain how it helps you to solve this problem in another way.

```
$0      ?      ?     $9     ?      ?     $18     ?      ?      ?      ?
|-------+------+------+------+------+------+------+------+------+------|
0%     10%    20%    30%     ?      ?    60%     ?      ?      ?     100%
```

52. Lucia gets film developed at Photo King, where 24 prints cost $7.80. This week, Photo King is having a sale, and 24 prints cost $6.63. What percent of the regular cost will Lucia save?

Ⓐ 15%   Ⓑ 17%   Ⓒ 25%   Ⓓ 85%

53. Which of these does NOT represent "200 decreased by 45%"?

Ⓕ 200(0.55)   Ⓖ 110   Ⓗ 200 − 0.45   Ⓙ 200(1 − 0.45)

54. Which of these represents a 15% increase?

Ⓐ A price is marked up from $12.50 to $15.

Ⓑ Joanna's bank account balance grew from $127.50 to $150.

Ⓒ A baseball card's value rose from $6 to $6.15.

Ⓓ Luis's hourly wage was raised from $8 to $9.20.

55. The original price of an item was $199. During a sale, the price was reduced by 45%. Then, during a clearance sale, the price was reduced an additional 20%. What was the final price?

Ⓕ $71.91   Ⓖ $87.56   Ⓗ $98.97   Ⓙ $101.89

56. Gridded Response A skateboard that sells for $65 is on sale for 15% off. What is the sale price in dollars?

CHALLENGE AND EXTEND

Find each missing number.

57. ▨ increased by 15% is 230.

58. ▨ increased by 50% is 48.

59. ▨ decreased by 20% is 500.

60. ▨ decreased by 70% is 4.35.

61. The label on a bottle of orange juice says "now 25% more." The bottle has 80 fluid ounces of juice. What was the original volume? Show that your answer is reasonable.

62. Angelina paid $21 for a backpack that was 30% off. What was the original price? Show that your answer is reasonable.

63. Multi-Step Mr. Hansen owns a bookstore. He buys used books at 25% of the cover price and sells them at a 45% markup of what he paid. Jerry sold Mr. Hansen three books with cover prices of $7.95, $5.95, and $12.10. If Jerry bought back his books, how much would he pay?

SPIRAL REVIEW

Find the complement and the supplement of each angle. *(Previous course)*

64. 65°   **65.** 10°   **66.** 45°   **67.** 30°

Solve each equation. Check your answer. *(Lessons 2-1 and 2-2)*

68. $-15 + x = -3$ **69.** $x + 16 = -4$ **70.** $r - 3 = 6$ **71.** $n - (-10) = 67$

72. $98 = 7z$ **73.** $\dfrac{x}{3} = 12$ **74.** $-x = 4$ **75.** $\dfrac{x}{5} = -20$

Estimate each amount. *(Lesson 2-10)*

76. the tip on a $60.65 check using a tip rate of 15%

77. the tax on a $70 DVD player when the sales tax is 6%

2-11

Algebra LAB

Explore Changes in Population

You can use percents to describe changes in populations. A population may grow by a certain percent or decrease by a certain percent. Explore changing populations in these activities.

Use with Lesson 2-11

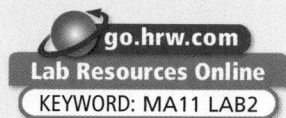

go.hrw.com
Lab Resources Online
KEYWORD: MA11 LAB2

Activity 1

A team of biologists is studying a population of deer. There are 32 deer in the first year of the study. Due to a lack of predators, the biologists find that the herd grows by 50% every year.

1 Copy and complete the table. The first two rows have been completed for you.

Year	Percent Increase	Amount of Increase	Population
1			32
2	50%	$0.50 \cdot 32 = 16$	$32 + 16 = 48$
3	50%	▓	▓
4	50%	▓	▓
5	50%	▓	▓
6	50%	▓	▓

Deer Population

2 Describe the percent increase from year to year.

3 Describe the amount of increase from year to year.

4 Copy the grid above onto graph paper. Plot the year and the population of deer on the graph as six ordered pairs (year, population). Connect the points with a smooth curve.

5 Describe the shape of your graph.

Try This

A researcher places 10 bacteria on a dish. This species increases by 100% every hour.

1. Copy and complete the table below.

Hour	0	1	2	3	4	5
Amount of Increase		▓	▓	▓	▓	▓
Bacteria	10	▓	▓	▓	▓	▓

2. Graph points from the table as (hour, bacteria). Connect the points with a smooth curve.

3. Compare this graph with the graph of the deer population.

4. Why does the amount of increase change when the percent of increase stays the same?

Activity 2

A second team of biologists is studying a population of wolves. There are 3125 wolves in the first year. The biologists find that this population decreases by 40% every year.

1 Make a Prediction Based on your results in Activity 1, what do you think will happen to the amount of decrease each year?

2 Copy and complete the table below. The first two rows have been completed for you.

Year	Percent Decrease	Amount of Decrease	Population
1			3125
2	40%	$0.40 \cdot 3125 = 1250$	$3125 - 1250 = 1875$
3	40%	▨	▨
4	40%	▨	▨
5	40%	▨	▨
6	40%	▨	▨

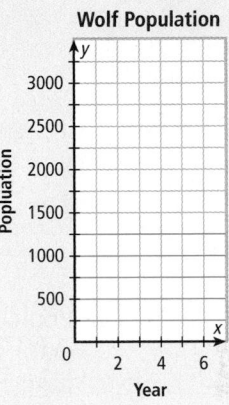

Wolf Population

3 What happens to the amount of decrease in the wolf population from year to year? Was your prediction from Problem 1 correct?

4 Make a Prediction Copy the grid above onto graph paper. Based on your results in Activity 1, what do you think the graph of ordered pairs (year, population) will look like?

5 Plot the year and the population of wolves on the graph as six ordered pairs (year, population). Connect the points with a smooth curve.

6 Describe the shape of your graph. Was your prediction from Problem 4 correct?

Try This

A half-life is the amount of time it takes half of an amount of radioactive substance to decay into another substance. Tritium is a radioactive form of hydrogen with a half-life of 12.3 years. In other words, after one half-life of 12.3 years, an amount of tritium will have decreased by 50%.

5. Suppose you start with 128 grams of tritium. Copy and complete the table below.

6. Make a graph that shows how much tritium is left after 0, 1, 2, 3, 4, and 5 half-lives.

Half-lives	0	1	2	3	4	5
Percent Decrease	0	50%	50%	50%	50%	50%
Amount of Decrease (g)		▨	▨	▨	▨	▨
Tritium Remaining (g)	128	▨	▨	▨	▨	▨

7. Compare this graph with the graph of the wolf population.

8. Describe the graph of a population that increases by a fixed percent. Why does the graph have this shape?

9. Describe the graph of a population that decreases by a fixed percent. Why does the graph have this shape?

MULTI-STEP TEST PREP

SALE PRICE
50% OFF

Percentages

Bargain Hunters Maria is on her high school's lacrosse team, and her friend Paula is on the softball team. The girls notice an advertisement in the newspaper for a clearance sale at their favorite sporting goods store. The ad shows an additional $\frac{1}{4}$ off the already reduced prices of 60% off. Maria and Paula head to the store to shop for bargains.

1. Maria finds a lacrosse stick with a regular price of $65. Find the sale price of the lacrosse stick prior to the additional $\frac{1}{4}$ off.

2. Find the sale price of Maria's lacrosse stick with the additional $\frac{1}{4}$ off.

3. Paula says that with the extra $\frac{1}{4}$ off, the total discount is 85% off. Maria thinks the discount is less than that. Who is correct? Explain your reasoning.

4. Paula finds a softball glove with a price tag that is not readable. The sales clerk scans the bar code and says the sale price, including the extra $\frac{1}{4}$ off, is $16.50. What was the original price of the softball glove? Show your reasoning.

5. Sales tax is 7.8%. Find the total amount that the girls will pay for the lacrosse stick and the softball glove together, including tax.

READY TO GO ON?

Quiz for Lessons 2-7 Through 2-11

☑ 2-7 Rates, Ratios, and Proportions

1. Last week, the ratio of laptops to desktops sold at a computer store was $2:3$. Eighteen desktop models were sold. How many laptop models were sold?

2. Anita read 150 pages in 5 hours. What is her reading rate in pages per minute?

3. Twenty-six crackers contain 156 Calories. Find the unit rate in Calories per cracker.

4. A store developed 1024 photographs in 8 hours. Find the unit rate in photographs per hour.

Solve each proportion.

5. $\dfrac{-18}{n} = \dfrac{9}{2}$ 6. $\dfrac{d}{5} = \dfrac{2}{4}$ 7. $\dfrac{4}{12} = \dfrac{r+2}{16}$ 8. $\dfrac{-3}{7} = \dfrac{6}{x+6}$

☑ 2-8 Applications of Proportions

Find the value of n in each diagram.

9. $\triangle RST \sim \triangle XYZ$

10. $ABCD \sim FGHJ$

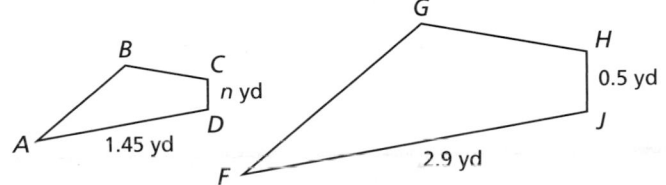

☑ 2-9 Percents

11. Find 40% of 25.

12. Find 130% of 9.

13. 35 is what percent of 70?

14. What percent of 400 is 640?

15. 16 is 80% of what number?

16. 200% of what number is 28?

17. A volunteer at the zoo is responsible for feeding the animals in 15 exhibits in the reptile house. This represents 20% of the total exhibits in the reptile house. How many exhibits are in the reptile house?

☑ 2-10 Applications of Percents

18. Peter earns $32,000 per year plus a 2.5% commission on his jewelry sales. Find Peter's total salary for the year when his sales are valued at $420,000.

19. Estimate the tax on a $21,899 car when the tax rate is 5%.

☑ 2-11 Percent Increase and Decrease

Find each percent change. Tell whether it is a percent increase or decrease.

20. from 60 to 66   21. from 48 to 12   22. from 200 to 80   23. from 9.8 to 14.7

24. Andrea purchased a picture frame for $14.56. This price was a 30% markup from the wholesale cost. What was the wholesale cost?

Study Guide: Review

Vocabulary

Complete the sentences below with vocabulary words from the list above.

1. A formula is a type of a(n) ___?___.

2. A(n) ___?___ is used to compare two quantities by division.

2-1 Solving Equations by Adding or Subtracting (pp. 77–82)

EXAMPLES

Solve each equation. Check your answer.

■ $x - 12 = -8.3$

$$\begin{array}{ccc} & +12 & +12 \\ \hline x & = & 3.7 \end{array}$$

■ $-7.8 = 5 + t$

$$\begin{array}{ccc} & -5 & -5 \\ \hline -12.8 = & & t \end{array}$$

Check $x - 12 = -8.3$

$$\begin{array}{c|c} 3.7 - 12 & -8.3 \\ -8.3 & -8.3 \checkmark \end{array}$$

Check $-7.8 = 5 + t$

$$\begin{array}{c|c} -7.8 & 5 + (-12.8) \\ -7.8 & -7.8 \checkmark \end{array}$$

EXERCISES

Solve each equation. Check your answer.

3. $b - 16 = 20$

4. $4 + x = 2$

5. $9 + a = -12$

6. $-7 + y = 11$

7. $z - \dfrac{1}{4} = \dfrac{7}{8}$

8. $w + \dfrac{2}{3} = 3$

9. Robin needs 108 signatures for her petition. So far, she has 27. Write and solve an equation to determine how many more signatures she needs.

2-2 Solving Equations by Multiplying or Dividing (pp. 84–90)

EXAMPLES

Solve each equation.

■ $\dfrac{z}{2.4} = 12$

$(2.4)\dfrac{z}{2.4} = (2.4)12$

$z = 28.8$

■ $-8x = 148$

$\dfrac{-8x}{-8} = \dfrac{148}{-8}$

$x = -18.5$

EXERCISES

Solve each equation. Check your answer.

10. $35 = 5x$

11. $-3n = 10$

12. $-30 = \dfrac{n}{3}$

13. $\dfrac{x}{-5} = -2.6$

14. $5y = 0$

15. $-4.6r = 9.2$

2-3 Solving Two-Step and Multi-Step Equations *(pp. 92–98)*

EXAMPLE

■ Solve $\dfrac{3x}{5} - \dfrac{x}{4} + \dfrac{1}{2} = \dfrac{6}{5}$.

$$\dfrac{3x}{5} - \dfrac{x}{4} + \dfrac{1}{2} = \dfrac{6}{5}$$

$$20\left(\dfrac{3x}{5} - \dfrac{x}{4} + \dfrac{1}{2}\right) = 20\left(\dfrac{6}{5}\right) \quad \text{Multiply by the LCD.}$$

$$12x - 5x + 10 = 24$$

$$7x + 10 = 24 \quad \text{Combine like terms.}$$

$$\dfrac{-10 \qquad -10}{7x \qquad = 14}$$

$$\dfrac{7x}{7} = \dfrac{14}{7}$$

$$x = 2$$

EXERCISES

Solve each equation. Check your answer.

16. $4t - 13 = 57$

17. $5 - 2y = 15$

18. $\dfrac{k}{5} - 6 = 2$

19. $\dfrac{5}{6}f - \dfrac{3}{4}f + \dfrac{3}{4} = \dfrac{1}{2}$

20. $7x - 19x = 6$

21. $4 + 3a - 6 = 43$

22. If $8n + 22 = 70$, find the value of $3n$.

23. If $0 = 6n - 36$, find the value of $n - 5$.

24. The sum of the measures of two angles is $180°$. One angle measures $3a$ and the other angle measures $2a - 25$ Find a. Then find the measure of each angle.

2-4 Solving Equations with Variables on Both Sides *(pp. 100–106)*

EXAMPLE

■ Solve $x + 7 = 12 + 3x - 7x$.

$$x + 7 = 12 + 3x - 7x$$

$$x + 7 = 12 - 4x \quad \text{Combine like terms.}$$

$$\dfrac{+4x \qquad\qquad +4x}{5x + 7 - 12}$$

$$\dfrac{-7 \quad -7}{5x \quad = 5}$$

$$\dfrac{5x}{5} = \dfrac{5}{5}$$

$$x = 1$$

EXERCISES

Solve each equation. Check your answer.

25. $4x + 2 = 3x$

26. $-3r - 8 = -5r - 12$

27. $-a - 3 + 7 = 3a$

28. $-(x - 4) = 2x + 6$

29. $\dfrac{2}{3}n = 4n - \dfrac{10}{3}n - \dfrac{1}{2}$

30. $0.2(7 + 2t) = 0.4t + 1.4$

31. One photo shop charges $0.36 per print. Another photo shop charges $2.52 plus $0.08 per print. Juan finds that the cost of printing his photos is the same at either shop. How many photos does Juan have to print?

2-5 Solving for a Variable *(pp. 107–111)*

EXAMPLE

■ Solve $A = P + Prt$ for r.

$$A = P + Prt$$

$$\dfrac{-P \quad -P}{A - P = \qquad Prt}$$

$$\dfrac{A - P}{Pt} = \dfrac{Prt}{Pt}$$

$$\dfrac{A - P}{Pt} = r$$

EXERCISES

Solve for the indicated variable.

32. $C = \dfrac{360}{n}$ for n

33. $S = \dfrac{n}{2}(a + \ell)$ for a

34. The formula $a = \dfrac{d}{g}$ gives the average gas mileage a of a vehicle that uses g gallons of gas to travel d miles. Use the formula to find how many gallons of gas a vehicle with an average gas mileage of 20.2 miles per gallon will use to travel 75 miles. Round your answer to the nearest tenth.

2-6 Solving Absolute-Value Equations (pp. 112–117)

EXAMPLES

■ Solve $3|y + 4| = 30$.

$$\frac{3|y + 4|}{3} = \frac{|30|}{3} \qquad \textit{Divide both sides by 3.}$$

$$|y + 4| = 10$$

Case 1

$$y + 4 = 10$$
$$\underline{ -4 \quad -4}$$
$$y = 6$$

Case 2

$$y + 4 = -10$$
$$\underline{ -4 \quad -4}$$
$$y = -14$$

EXERCISES

Solve each equation. Check your answer.

35. $|x + 6| = 21$ **36.** $7|y - 5| = 14$

37. $3|y| + 4 = 31$ **38.** $12 = |x - 5.4|$

39. $|g + 6| + 12 = 14$ **40.** $|x| = \dfrac{5}{7}$

41. Jason is driving his car at 55 mi/h. He needs to keep his car within 5 mi/h of his current speed. Write and solve an absolute-value equation to find Jason's maximum and minimum speeds.

2-7 Rates, Ratios, and Proportions (pp. 120–126)

■ The ratio of skateboarders to bikers in an extreme sports contest is 7 : 2. There are 91 skateboarders. How many bikers are there?

$$\frac{\text{skateboarders}}{\text{bikers}} \longrightarrow \frac{7}{2} \qquad \textit{Write a proportion.}$$

$$\frac{7}{2} \diagup\!\!\!\!\times \frac{91}{x} \qquad \textit{Let x be the number of bikers.}$$

$$7 \cdot x = 2 \cdot 91 \qquad \textit{Use cross products.}$$

$$7x = 182$$

$$\frac{7x}{7} = \frac{182}{7} \qquad \textit{Solve for x.}$$

$$x = 26$$

There are 26 bikers.

42. A recipe for a casserole calls for 2 cups of rice. The recipe makes 6 servings of casserole. How many cups of rice will you need to make 10 servings of casserole?

Use dimensional analysis to convert each rate. Round your answer to the nearest hundredth if necessary.

43. 30 cm/s to m/h   **44.** 75 ft/s to mi/min

Solve each proportion. Check your answer.

45. $\dfrac{n}{8} = \dfrac{2}{10}$ **46.** $\dfrac{2}{9} = \dfrac{12}{x}$

47. $\dfrac{3}{k} = \dfrac{9}{15}$ **48.** $\dfrac{1}{3} = \dfrac{x}{x - 6}$

2-8 Applications of Proportions (pp. 127–132)

■ When Janelle stood next to the Washington Monument, she cast a 1.2-foot-long shadow, and the monument cast a 111-foot-long shadow. Janelle is 6 feet tall. How tall is the monument?

$$\frac{x}{111} = \frac{6}{1.2} \qquad \textit{Write a proportion.}$$

$$1.2x = 666 \qquad \textit{Use cross products.}$$

$$\frac{1.2x}{1.2} = \frac{666}{1.2} \qquad \textit{Solve for x.}$$

The monument is 555 feet tall.

49. Find the value of x in the diagram.

$$\triangle ABC \sim \triangle DEF$$

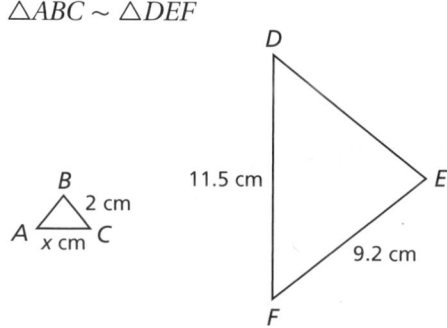

50. A tree casts a shadow that is 14 ft long at the same time that a nearby 2-foot-tall pole casts a shadow that is 1.75 ft long. How tall is the tree?

51. A circle has a radius of 9 inches. The radius is multiplied by $\dfrac{2}{3}$ to form a second circle. How is the ratio of the areas related to the ratio of the radii?

2-9 Percents (pp. 133–138)

EXAMPLES

- Earth's surface area is about 197 million square miles. About 58 million square miles is land. What percent is water?

  197 million − 58 million = 139 million

  $$\frac{\text{part}}{\text{whole}} = \frac{\text{percent}}{100}$$

  $$\frac{139}{197} = \frac{n}{100}$$

  $197n = 13{,}900$ *Use cross products.*

  $n = 70.56$ *Solve for n.*

  About 71% of Earth's surface area is water.

EXERCISES

52. Find 2.3% of 230.   **53.** Find 115% of 2700.

54. What percent of 18 is 12? Round your answer to the nearest tenth of a percent.

55. What percent of 14 is 56?

56. 90% of what number is 120? Round the number to the nearest tenth.

57. 90 is 37.5% of what number?

58. A student answered 32 questions correctly and 8 incorrectly. What percent of the questions were answered correctly?

2-10 Applications of Percents (pp. 139–143)

- After 10 months, the simple interest earned on $3000 was $52.50. Find the interest rate.

  197 million − 58 million = 139 million

  $$I = Prt$$

  $52.5 = 3000(r)\left(\dfrac{10}{12}\right)$ *Substitute.*

  $52.5 = 2500r$ *Multiply.*

  $\dfrac{52.5}{2500} = \dfrac{2500r}{2500}$ *Solve for r.*

  $0.021 = r$

  The interest rate is 2.1%.   *Write as a percent.*

59. A salesperson earns a base salary of $36,000 plus $2\frac{1}{2}$% commission on sales. His total sales for one year was $500,000. Find the salesperson's total pay for that year.

60. Find the simple interest paid for 10 years on a $10,000 loan at 9% per year.

61. The sales tax rate is 8%. Estimate the tax on a jacket that costs $69.95.

62. Estimate the tip on a $10.75 check using a tip rate of 20%.

2-11 Percent Increase and Decrease (pp. 144–149)

Find each percent change. Tell whether it is a percent increase or decrease.

- from 50 to 56

  $$\text{percent change} = \frac{\text{amount of increase}}{\text{original amount}}$$

  $$= \frac{56 - 50}{50} = \frac{6}{50} = 0.12 = 12\%$$

  The change is a 12% increase.

- from 120 to 72

  $$\text{percent change} = \frac{\text{amount of decrease}}{\text{original amount}}$$

  $$= \frac{120 - 72}{120} = \frac{48}{120} = 0.40 = 40\%$$

  The change is a 40% decrease.

Find each percent change. Tell whether it is a percent increase or decrease. Round your answer to the nearest percent.

63. from 19 to 26   **64.** from 42 to 28

65. Find the result when 65 is increased by 40%.

66. Find the result when 150 is decreased by 15%.

67. Tom sells sunglasses that he buys wholesale for $2.50 each. He then marks up the price 150%. What is the amount of the markup? What is the selling price?

68. The original price of a shirt was $79.99. It is on sale for $49.99. What is the percent discount? Round to the nearest tenth.

CHAPTER TEST

Solve each equation.

1. $y - 7 = 2$

2. $x + 12 = 19$

3. $-5 + z = 8$

4. $9x = 72$

5. $\dfrac{m}{-8} = -2.5$

6. $\dfrac{7}{8}a = 42$

7. $15 = 3 - 4x$

8. $\dfrac{2a}{3} + \dfrac{1}{5} = \dfrac{7}{6}$

9. $8 - (b - 2) = 11$

10. $-2x + 4 = 5 - 3x$

11. $3(q - 2) + 2 = 5q - 7 - 2q$

12. $5z = -3(z + 7)$

Solve for the indicated variable.

13. $r - 2s = 14$ for s

14. $V = \dfrac{1}{3}bh$ for b

15. $P = 2(\ell + w)$ for ℓ

Solve each equation.

16. $|x - 14| = 21$

17. $13 = |y + 2| - 3$

18. $4|z| = 20$

19. $3|x| + 5 = 8$

20. $3|g + 1| + 5 = 7$

21. $|2v| = 6$

22. A store sells 3 videotapes for $4.99. Find the unit rate in dollars per videotape. Round to the nearest cent.

23. Twenty-five students use 120 sheets of paper. Find the unit rate in sheets per student.

24. Nutritionists recommend that teenagers consume 1300 milligrams of calcium per day. Use dimensional analysis to convert this rate to grams per year.

Solve each proportion.

25. $\dfrac{5}{4} = \dfrac{x}{12}$

26. $\dfrac{8}{2z} = \dfrac{15}{60}$

27. $\dfrac{x + 10}{10} = \dfrac{18}{12}$

28. The scale on a map is 1 inch : 500 miles. If two cities are 875 miles apart, how far apart are they on the map?

Find the value of x in each diagram. Round your answer to the nearest tenth.

29. $\triangle EFG \sim \triangle RTS$

30. $HJKL \sim WXYZ$

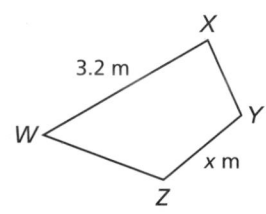

31. What is 23% of 46?

32. 37.5 is 60% of what number?

33. What percent of 175 is 35?

34. Find the simple interest earned after 5 years on an investment of $2000 at 3.2% per year.

35. A lunch check is $27.95. Estimate a 15% tip.

Find each percent change. Tell whether it is a percent increase or decrease.

36. from 180 to 234

37. from 12 to 48

38. from 56 to 21

COLLEGE ENTRANCE EXAM PRACTICE

FOCUS ON ACT

The ACT Mathematics Test is one of four tests in the ACT. You have 60 minutes to answer 60 multiple-choice questions. The questions cover material typically taught through the end of eleventh grade. You will need to know some basic formulas.

You may want to time yourself as you take this practice test. It should take you about 6 minutes to complete.

There is no penalty for incorrect answers on the ACT. If you are unsure of the correct answer, eliminate as many answer choices as possible. Then make your best guess. Be sure you have marked an answer for every question before time runs out.

---

1. At a certain high school, the ratio of left-handed to right-handed basketball players is $1:4$. If there are a total of 20 players on the team, how many players are right-handed?

    (A) 1

    (B) 4

    (C) 5

    (D) 12

    (E) 16

2. If $y - 3 = \frac{2}{5}(x + 1)$, then $x = $?

    (F) $\dfrac{5(y-3)-2}{2}$

    (G) $y - \dfrac{22}{5}$

    (H) $\dfrac{2(y-3)}{5} - 1$

    (J) $\dfrac{2(y+1)+15}{5}$

    (K) $\dfrac{5}{2}y - 4$

3. What is $\frac{1}{5}\%$ of 20?

    (A) 0.004

    (B) 0.04

    (C) 0.4

    (D) 4

    (E) 100

4. If $x - 3 = 4 - 2(x + 5)$, then $x = $?

    (F) -3

    (G) -1

    (H) 1

    (J) $\dfrac{3}{2}$

    (K) $\dfrac{11}{3}$

5. If $\triangle ABC \sim \triangle DEF$, what is the length of $\overline{AC}$?

    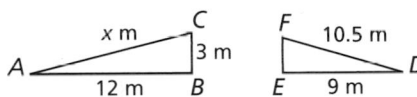

    (A) 2.6 meters

    (B) 3.5 meters

    (C) 7 meters

    (D) 14 meters

    (E) 15 meters

6. A movie theater makes 30% of its revenue from concession sales. If concession sales were $174,000, what was the total revenue?

    (F) $52,200

    (G) $121,800

    (H) $248,570

    (J) $580,000

    (K) $746,000

TEST TACKLER

Standardized Test Strategies

Multiple Choice: Eliminate Answer Choices

You can answer some problems without doing many calculations. Use logic to eliminate answer choices and save time.

EXAMPLE 1

Which number is the square of 123,765?

   (A) 15,317,775,225   **(C)** 15,317,775,230

   (B) 15,317,775,233   **(D)** 15,317,775,227

Your calculator will not help you on this question. Due to rounding, any of the answer choices are possible.

But you can use this fact to eliminate three of the answer choices:

The square of any number ending in 5 is also a number ending in 5.

$$\begin{array}{r} 5 \\ \times\ 5 \\ \hline 5 \end{array}$$

The only answer choice that ends in 5 is A, 15,317,775,225.

EXAMPLE 2

What is a possible area of the wooden triangle shown?

   (F) 11 square feet   **(H)** 14 square feet

   (G) 20 square feet   **(J)** 24 square feet

The triangle is inside a rectangle with an area of $7 \times 4 = 28$ square feet.

If the triangle had the same base and height as the rectangle, its area would be half the area of the rectangle, 14 square feet.

However, the triangle fits inside the rectangle, so its area must be less than 14 square feet.

4 ft

7 ft

The only answer choice that is less than 14 square feet is F, 11 square feet.

Try to eliminate unreasonable answer choices. Some choices may be too great or too small, have incorrect units, or not be divisible by a necessary number.

Read each test item and answer the questions that follow.

Item A
The top speed of a three-toed sloth is 0.12 miles per hour. About how many feet can a sloth travel in an hour?

(A) 0.12 feet

(C) 2.27 feet

(B) 600 feet

(D) 7500 inches

1. Are there any answer choices you can eliminate immediately? If so, which choices and why?

2. Describe how you can use estimation to find the correct answer.

Item B
A city park is shaped like a triangle. The Liberty Street side of the park is 120 feet long, and the First Avenue side is 50 feet long.

Liberty St.

First Ave.

Union St.

What is the approximate length of the side of the park that faces Union Street?

(F) 25 feet

(H) 65 feet

(G) 110 inches

(J) 130 feet

3. Can any of the answer choices be eliminated immediately? If so, which choices and why?

4. Are there any properties you can use to solve this problem? If so, what are they?

5. Describe how to find the correct answer without doing any calculations.

Item C
Approximately how long will the average 18-year-old have slept in his lifetime?

(A) 6 weeks

(C) 6 years

(B) 6 months

(D) 6 decades

6. Which answer choice can be eliminated immediately? Why?

7. Explain how to use mental math to solve this problem.

Item D
Sheila's paychecks for February and March were equal. If she worked every day during both months, for which month was her daily pay lower?

(F) February

(G) March

(H) Her daily pay did not change.

(J) Cannot be determined

8. What do you need to know to solve this problem?

9. Describe how you can find the correct answer.

Item E
Greg tripled the number of baseball cards he had last week. Which of these could be the number of cards Greg has now?

(A) 100

(C) 150

(B) 200

(D) 250

10. The number of cards that Greg has now must be divisible by what number? How can you tell if a number is divisible by this number?

11. Describe how to find the answer to this problem.

STANDARDIZED TEST PREP

CUMULATIVE ASSESSMENT, CHAPTERS 1–2

Multiple Choice

1. What operation does $\Diamond$ represent if $x \Diamond 2.2 = 4.5$ when $x = 9.9$?

- (A) Addition
- (B) Subtraction
- (C) Multiplication
- (D) Division

2. A couple earns $4819.25 a month. They pay 9.5% of their monthly income as the monthly payment on their car. To the nearest dollar, how much does the couple pay for their monthly car payment?

- (F) $458
- (H) $4578
- (G) $507
- (J) $4810

3. Every dimension of cylinder A is multiplied by 4 to make cylinder B. What is the ratio of the volume of cylinder A to the volume of cylinder B?

5 in. A
3 in.

- (A) $\frac{1}{64}$
- (C) $\frac{1}{4}$
- (B) $\frac{1}{16}$
- (D) $\frac{1}{3}$

4. A clock loses 5 minutes every day. How much time will it lose in 2 hours?

- (F) 0.417 second
- (H) 240 seconds
- (G) 25 seconds
- (J) 600 seconds

5. A statue is 8 feet tall. The display case for a model of the statue is 18 inches tall. Which scale allows for the tallest model of the statue that will fit in the display case?

- (A) 1 inch : 2 inches
- (C) 1 inch : 5 inches
- (B) 1 inch : 7 inches
- (D) 1 inch : 10 inches

6. What is the value of $-\left|6^2\right|$?

- (F) −36
- (H) −8
- (G) −12
- (J) −3

7. Mr. Phillips wants to install hardwood flooring in his den. The flooring costs $25.86 per square yard. The blueprint below shows his house. What other information do you need in order to find the total cost of the flooring?

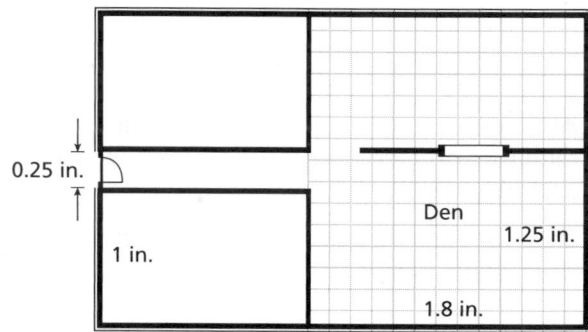

0.25 in.

1 in.

Den
1.25 in.

1.8 in.

- (A) The lengths and widths of the adjoining rooms in the blueprint
- (B) The total area of the blueprint
- (C) The scale of inches in the blueprint to yards in the house
- (D) The width of the den

8. What value of n makes the equation below have no solution?

$$2x + 2 = nx - 3$$

- (F) −2
- (G) 0
- (H) 2
- (J) 3

9. Which of the equations below represents the second step of the solution process?

Step 1: $3(5x - 2) + 27 = -24$
Step 2: ▭
Step 3: $15x + 21 = -24$
Step 4: $15x = -45$
Step 5: $x = -3$

- (A) $3(5x + 27) - 2 = -24$
- (B) $3(5x + 25) = -24$
- (C) $15x - 2 + 27 = -24$
- (D) $15x - 6 + 27 = -24$

HOT TIP! If you are stuck on a problem, skip it and come back later. Another problem might remind you of something that will help. If you feel yourself become tense, take a few deep breaths to relax.

10. Cass drove 3 miles to school, and then she drove m miles to a friend's house. The total mileage for these two trips was 8 miles. Which equation CANNOT be used to determine the number of miles Cass drove?

- (F) $3 + m = 8$
- (G) $3 - m = 8$
- (H) $8 - 3 = m$
- (J) $8 - m = 3$

11. If $\dfrac{20}{x} = \dfrac{4}{x-5}$, which of the following is a true statement?

- (A) $x(x - 5) = 80$
- (B) $20x = 4(x - 5)$
- (C) $20(x - 5) = 4x$
- (D) $24 = 2x - 5$

Gridded Response

12. Four times a number is two less than six times the same number minus ten. What is the number?

13. Melissa invested her savings in a retirement account that pays simple interest. A portion of her account record is shown below. What is the interest rate on Melissa's account? Write your answer as a decimal.

Date	Transaction	Amount	Balance
8/1	Beginning deposit	$6000.00	$6000.00
8/31	Interest payment	$192.00	$6192.00
9/1	Withdrawal	$1000.00	$5192.00
9/30	Interest payment	$166.14	$5358.14

14. At 2:45 P.M. you are 112 miles from Dallas. You want to be in Dallas at 4:30 P.M. What is the average number of miles per hour you must travel to be on time?

15. A cyclist travels 45 miles in 4 hours. How many feet does she travel in one second?

16. A bike rental shop charges a one-time charge of $8 plus an hourly fee to rent a bike. Dan paid $24.50 to rent a bike for $5\frac{1}{2}$ hours. Find the bike shop's hourly fee in dollars.

Short Response

17. Alex buys 5 calendars to give as gifts. Each calendar has the same price. When the cashier rings up Alex's calendars, the total cost before tax is $58.75.

- **a.** Write and solve an equation to find the cost of each calendar.
- **b.** The total cost of Alex's calendars after tax is $63.45. Find the percent sales tax. Show your work and explain in words how you found your answer.
- **c.** Alex's friend Keisha buys some calendars for the same price. She uses her 15% discount card. The total cost before tax is $39.95. How many calendars did Keisha buy? Show your work and explain in words how you found your answer.

18. Is the percent increase from 50 to 100 the same as the percent decrease from 100 to 50? Explain your reasoning in words.

Extended Response

19. Korena is putting a decorative border around her rectangular flower garden. The total perimeter of the garden is 200 feet.

- **a.** Draw three different rectangles that could represent Korena's flower garden. Label the dimensions of your rectangles.
- **b.** Use the table to show the lengths and widths of five different rectangles that could represent Korena's flower garden. Do not use any of your rectangles from part **a**.

Possible Dimensions of Korena's Garden		
Length (ℓ)	**Width (w)**	**Perimeter (P)**
▨	▨	▨
▨	▨	▨
▨	▨	▨
▨	▨	▨
▨	▨	▨

- **c.** The length of Korena's garden is 4 times its width. Explain how to use the perimeter formula $P = 2\ell + 2w$ to find the dimensions of Korena's garden.
- **d.** Find the dimensions of Korena's garden.

Real-World CONNECTIONS

Illinois

Shawnee National Forest

⭐ Bullfrogs

The bullfrog is the largest frog in Illinois. Adult bullfrogs are usually between $3\frac{1}{2}$ and 6 inches in length, but some have been known to grow even larger. The largest recorded bullfrog found in Illinois was 8 inches long and weighed more than a pound!

Choose one or more strategies to solve each problem.

1. A bullfrog jumping up a hill is 8 feet from the top. Each time it jumps, it moves forward 18 inches. However, mud on the hill causes it to slide backward 2 inches after each jump. How many jumps will it take the frog to reach the top of the hill?

2. A certain pond is home to 120 bullfrog tadpoles. This is 90 more than 3 times the number of adult bullfrogs that live in a second pond. How many adult bullfrogs live in the second pond?

For 3–5, use the table.

3. How far could the largest recorded bullfrog in Illinois jump?

4. If a bullfrog is $4\frac{1}{2}$ inches long, what is its maximum jumping distance?

5. A certain adult bullfrog can jump $8\frac{3}{4}$ feet. This bullfrog must be at least how long?

Jumping Distances of Bullfrogs	
Length of Bullfrog (in.)	Maximum Jumping Distance (in.)
4	60
5	75
6	90

⭐ The Great Snake Migration

When temperatures drop, large numbers of snakes leave the swamps of southern Illinois. Some travel just a few hundred feet, while others travel several miles, to Snake Road, a 3-mile-long road on the western edge of the Shawnee Forest. In this area, you can see as many as 40 to 50 snakes in a day, including cottonmouth water moccasins, rattlesnakes, and copperheads.

Choose one or more strategies to solve each problem.

1. In one hour, a researcher saw six snakes crossing Snake Road— three moccasins, a rattlesnake, a garter snake, and a diamondback water snake, though not in that order. The second snake to cross was a moccasin, and the other two moccasins crossed one after the other. The diamondback crossed before the garter snake. The first snake to cross was not the garter snake or the diamondback. A moccasin crossed last. In what order did the snakes cross Snake Road?

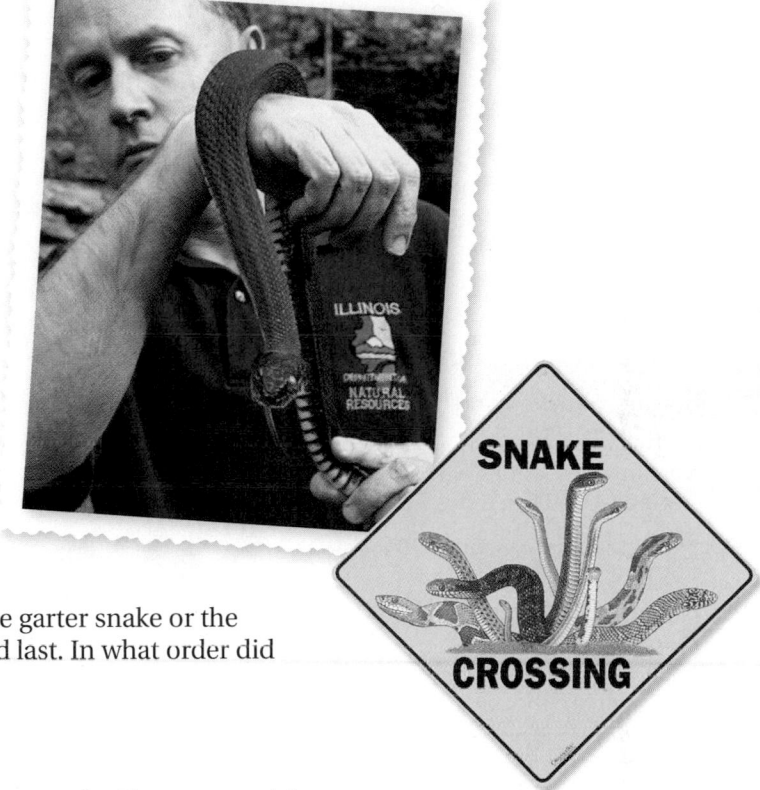

For 2, use the table.

In 2001–2002, several Illinois hospitals were asked how many vials of antivenom they had available to treat snake bites. The results are shown in the table. For example, 37 hospitals reported that they had between 1 and 4 vials of antivenom available.

Antivenom Survey Results						
Vials	0	1–4	5–9	10–14	15–19	20+
Hospitals		37	14	6	0	10

2. The number of hospitals with no antivenom available to treat snake bites was 6 less than 3 times the number of hospitals that had 1–4 vials. How many hospitals had no antivenom with which to treat snake bites? What percent of the total number of hospitals surveyed does this represent? Round your answer to the nearest percent.

Inequalities

Chapter Focus

- Solve multi-step inequalities.
- Write and solve inequalities to solve problems.

For a *Good* Cause

You can use the concepts in this chapter to plan for a fund-raising event. Inequalities help you determine how to reach your fund-raising goals.

go.hrw.com

Chapter Project Online

KEYWORD: MA7 ChProj

ARE YOU READY?

☑ Vocabulary

Match each term on the left with a definition on the right.

1. equation

2. evaluate

3. inverse operations

4. like terms

5. solution of an equation

A. mathematical phrase that contains operations, numbers, and/or variables

B. mathematical statement that two expressions are equivalent

C. value of a variable that makes a statement true

D. terms that contain the same variables raised to the same powers

E. to find the value of an expression

F. operations that undo each other

☑ Evaluate Expressions

Evaluate each expression for $a = 2$ and $b = 6$.

6. $b - a$ **7.** ab **8.** $b \div a$ **9.** $a + b$

☑ Compare and Order Real Numbers

Compare. Write $<$, $>$, or $=$.

10. $10 \ \blacksquare\ 21$ **11.** $5.27 \ \blacksquare\ 5.23$ **12.** $20\% \ \blacksquare\ 0.2$ **13.** $\frac{1}{3} \ \blacksquare\ \frac{2}{5}$

☑ Combine Like Terms

Simplify each expression by combining like terms.

14. $6x + x$ **15.** $-8a + 3a$

16. $9x^2 - 15x^2$ **17.** $2.1x + 4.3x$

☑ Distributive Property

Simplify each expression.

18. $2(x + 3)$ **19.** $(3 - d)5$

20. $4(r - 1)$ **21.** $3(4 + m)$

☑ Solve One-Step Equations

Solve.

22. $s - 3 = 8$ **23.** $-7x = 21$ **24.** $y + 11 = 2$ **25.** $\frac{h}{2} = 6$

26. $t + 2 = -2$ **27.** $6x = 42$ **28.** $r - 8 = -13$ **29.** $\frac{y}{3} = -12$

Study Guide: Preview

Where You've Been

Previously, you

- learned the properties of equality.
- solved equations by using inverse operations.
- solved equations with variables on both sides.

In This Chapter

You will study

- the properties of inequality.
- how to solve inequalities by using inverse operations.
- how to solve inequalities with variables on both sides.
- how to solve compound inequalities.

Where You're Going

You can use the skills in this chapter

- in all your future math classes, including Geometry.
- in other classes, such as Health, Chemistry, Physics, and Economics.
- in the real world to plan a budget, to find cost-efficient services, and to set financial goals.

Key Vocabulary/Vocabulario

compound inequality	desigualdad compuesta
inequality	desigualdad
intersection	intersección
solution of an inequality	solución de una desigualdad
union	unión

Vocabulary Connections

To become familiar with some of the vocabulary terms in the chapter, consider the following. You may refer to the chapter, the glossary, or a dictionary if you like.

1. The prefix *in-* means "not." An *equality* states that two things are equal. Use these meanings to write your own definition for the word **inequality** .

2. The word *compound* means "consisting of two or more parts." What do you think a **compound inequality** might be?

3. The **intersection** of two roads is the place where the two roads overlap. What do you think the *intersection* of two graphs would be?

4. The word **union** begins with the root *uni-*. List some other words that begin with *uni-*. What do all of these words have in common?

Reading and **Writing** **Math**

Study Strategy: Use Your Notes Effectively

Taking notes helps you arrange, organize, and process information from your textbook and class lectures. In addition to taking notes, you need to use your notes before and after class effectively.

Step 1: Before Class
- Review your notes from the last class.
- Then preview the next lesson and write down any questions you have.

Step 2: During Class
- Write down main ideas.
- If you miss something, leave a blank and keep taking notes. Fill in any holes later.
- Use diagrams and abbreviations. Make sure you will understand any abbreviations later.

Step 3: After Class
- Fill in the holes you left during class.
- Highlight or circle the most important ideas, such as vocabulary, formulas, or procedures.
- Use your notes to quiz yourself.

10/3   Lesson 2-8   Applications of Proportion

How do I know if figures are similar?

Similar figures—same shape, but maybe not same size

Corresponding sides and angles—same relative position.

Similar figures if corr. sides are <u>proportional</u> and corr. angles are same.

Use the symbol ~ to show figures are sim.

$$\frac{AB}{DE} = \frac{BC}{EF} = \frac{AC}{DF}$$

$$m\angle A \cong m\angle D$$
$$m\angle B \cong m\angle E$$
$$m\angle C \cong m\angle F$$

$\triangle ABC \sim \triangle DEF$

Try This

1. Look at the next lesson in your textbook. Write down some questions you have about the material in that lesson. Leave space between each question so that you can write the answers during the next class.

2. Look at the notes you took during the last class. List three ways you can improve your note-taking skills.

Graphing and Writing Inequalities

Objectives
Identify solutions of inequalities in one variable.

Write and graph inequalities in one variable.

Vocabulary
inequality
solution of an inequality

Who uses this?

Members of a crew team can use inequalities to be sure they fall within a range of weights. (See Example 4.)

The athletes on a lightweight crew team must weigh 165 pounds or less. The acceptable weights for these athletes can be described using an *inequality*.

An **inequality** is a statement that two quantities are not equal. The quantities are compared by using one of the following signs:

$<$	$>$	$\leq$	$\geq$	$\neq$
$A < B$	$A > B$	$A \leq B$	$A \geq B$	$A \neq B$
A **is less than** B.	A **is greater than** B.	A **is less than or equal to** B.	A **is greater than or equal to** B.	A **is not equal to** B.

A **solution of an inequality** is any value of the variable that makes the inequality true.

EXAMPLE 1 **Identifying Solutions of Inequalities**

Describe the solutions of $3 + x < 9$ in words.

Test values of x that are positive, negative, and 0.

Writing Math

The solutions of the inequality in Example 1 can be written in *set-builder notation* as $\{x \mid x < 6\}$, which is read as "the set of all real numbers x such that x is less than 6."

x	-2.75	0	5.99	6	6.01	6.1
$3 + x$	0.25	3	8.99	9	9.01	9.1
$3 + x \overset{?}{<} 9$	$0.25 \overset{?}{<} 9$	$3 \overset{?}{<} 9$	$8.99 \overset{?}{<} 9$	$9 \overset{?}{<} 9$	$9.01 \overset{?}{<} 9$	$9.1 \overset{?}{<} 9$
Solution?	Yes	Yes	Yes	No	No	No

When the value of x is a number less than 6, the value of $3 + x$ is less than 9.
When the value of x is 6, the value of $3 + x$ is equal to 9.
When the value of x is a number greater than 6, the value of $3 + x$ is greater than 9.

The solutions of $3 + x < 9$ are numbers less than 6.

 1. Describe the solutions of $2p > 8$ in words.

An inequality like $3 + x < 9$ has too many solutions to list. You can use a graph on a number line to show all the solutions.

The solutions are shaded and an arrow shows that the solutions continue past those shown on the graph. To show that an endpoint is a solution, draw a solid circle at the number. To show that an endpoint is not a solution, draw an empty circle.

Graphing Inequalities

WORDS	ALGEBRA	GRAPH
All real numbers less than 5	$x < 5$	
All real numbers greater than -1	$x > -1$	
All real numbers less than or equal to $\frac{1}{2}$	$x \leq \frac{1}{2}$	
All real numbers greater than or equal to 0	$x \geq 0$	

EXAMPLE 2 Graphing Inequalities

Graph each inequality.

A $b < -1.5$

Draw an empty circle at -1.5.
Shade all the numbers less than -1.5 and draw an arrow pointing to the left.

B $r \geq 2$

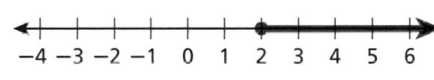

Draw a solid circle at 2.
Shade all the numbers greater than 2 and draw an arrow pointing to the right.

 Graph each inequality.

2a. $c > 2.5$ **2b.** $2^2 - 4 \geq w$ **2c.** $m \leq -3$

Student to Student

Graphing Inequalities

Victor Solomos
Palmer High School

To know which direction to shade a graph, I write inequalities with the variable on the left side of the inequality symbol. I know that the symbol has to point to the same number after I rewrite the inequality.

For example, I write $4 < y$ as $y > 4$.

Now the inequality symbol points in the direction that I should draw the shaded arrow on my graph.

EXAMPLE 3 **Writing an Inequality from a Graph**

Write the inequality shown by each graph.

A

4.5

-5 -4 -3 -2 -1 0 1 2 3 4 5

Use any variable. The arrow points to the right, so use either > or ≥.
The empty circle at 4.5 means that 4.5 is not a solution, so use >.

$h > 4.5$

B

-5 -4 -3 -2 -1 0 1 2 3 4 5

Use any variable. The arrow points to the left, so use either < or ≤.
The solid circle at −3 means that −3 is a solution, so use ≤.

$m \leq -3$

 3. Write the inequality shown by the graph.

2.5

-5 -4 -3 -2 -1 0 1 2 3 4 5

EXAMPLE 4 *Sports Application*

The members of a lightweight crew team can weigh no more than 165 pounds each. Define a variable and write an inequality for the acceptable weights of the team members. Graph the solutions.

Let w represent the weights that are allowed.

Athletes may weigh	no more than	165 pounds.
w	≤	165

$w \leq 165$

165

0 30 60 90 120 150 180

Stop the graph at 0 because a person's weight must be a positive number.

Reading Math

"No more than" means "less than or equal to."

"At least" means "greater than or equal to."

 4. A store's employees earn at least $8.25 per hour. Define a variable and write an inequality for the amount the employees may earn per hour. Graph the solutions.

THINK AND DISCUSS

1. Compare the solutions of $x > 2$ and $x \geq 2$.

 2. GET ORGANIZED Copy and complete the graphic organizer. Draw a graph in the first row and write the correct inequality in the second row.

Inequality	Graph
$x > 1$	
	-5 -4 -3 -2 -1 0 1

GUIDED PRACTICE

1. **Vocabulary** How is a *solution of an inequality* like a solution of an equation?

SEE EXAMPLE **1**
p. 170

Describe the solutions of each inequality in words.

2. $g - 5 \geq 6$ **3.** $-2 < h + 1$ **4.** $20 > 5t$ **5.** $5 - x \leq 2$

SEE EXAMPLE **2**
p. 171

Graph each inequality.

6. $x < -5$ **7.** $c \geq 3\frac{1}{2}$ **8.** $(4 - 2)^3 > m$ **9.** $p \geq \sqrt{17 + 8}$

SEE EXAMPLE **3**
p. 172

Write the inequality shown by each graph.

10. (number line from −6 to 4, closed dot at −2, shaded left)

11. $-8\frac{1}{2}$ (number line from −9 to 1, open dot at −8½, shaded right)

12. 5.5 (number line from −4 to 6, open dot at 5.5, shaded left)

13. −7 (number line from −12 to 0, open dot at −7, shaded left)

14. (number line from −4 to 6, closed dot at 3, shaded right)

15. (number line from −2 to 18, closed dot at 14, shaded left)

SEE EXAMPLE **4**
p. 172

Define a variable and write an inequality for each situation. Graph the solutions.

16. There must be at least 20 club members present in order to hold a meeting.

17. A trainer advises an athlete to keep his heart rate under 140 beats per minute.

PRACTICE AND PROBLEM SOLVING

Independent Practice	
For Exercises	See Example
18–21	1
22–25	2
26–31	3
32–33	4

Extra Practice
Skills Practice p. S8
Application Practice p. S30

Describe the solutions of each inequality in words.

18. $-2t > -8$ **19.** $0 > w - 2$ **20.** $3k > 9$ **21.** $\frac{1}{2}b \leq 6$

Graph each inequality.

22. $7 < x$ **23.** $t \leq -\frac{1}{2}$ **24.** $d > 4(5 - 8)$ **25.** $t \leq 3^2 - 2^2$

Write the inequality shown by each graph.

26. (number line from −4 to 6, closed dot at 5, shaded left)

27. −11 (number line from −16 to −4, open dot at −11, shaded left)

28. −3.5 (number line from −6 to 4, open dot at −3.5, shaded right)

29. −3.3 (number line from −5 to 5, open dot at −3.3, shaded right)

30. (number line from −5 to 5, open dot at 4, shaded left)

31. 9 (number line from −2 to 18, closed dot at 9, shaded right)

Define a variable and write an inequality for each situation. Graph the solutions.

32. The maximum speed allowed on Main Street is 25 miles per hour.

33. Applicants must have at least 5 years of experience.

Write each inequality in words.

34. $x > 7$ **35.** $h < -5$ **36.** $d \leq 23$ **37.** $r \geq -2$

Write each inequality with the variable on the left. Graph the solutions.

38. $19 < g$ **39.** $17 \geq p$ **40.** $10 < e$ **41.** $0 < f$

Define a variable and write an inequality for each situation. Graph the solutions.

42. The highest temperature ever recorded on Earth was 135.9 °F at Al Aziziyah, Libya, on September 13, 1922.

43. Businesses with profits less than $10,000 per year will be shut down.

44. You must be at least 46 inches tall to ride a roller coaster at an amusement park.

45. Due to a medical condition, a hiker can hike only in areas with an elevation no more than 5000 feet above sea level.

Write a real-world situation that could be described by each inequality.

46. $x \geq 0$ **47.** $x < 10$ **48.** $x \leq 12$ **49.** $x > 8.5$

Match each inequality with its graph.

50. $x \geq 5$ **A.**

51. $x < 5$ **B.**

52. $x > 5$ **C.**

53. $x \leq 5$ **D.**

54. ⫻**ERROR ANALYSIS**⫻ Two students graphed the inequality $4 > b$. Which graph is incorrect? Explain the error.

55. This problem will prepare you for the Multi-Step Test Prep on page 188.

   a. Mirna earned $125 baby-sitting during the spring break. She needs to save $90 for the German Club trip. She wants to spend the remainder of the money shopping. Write an inequality to show how much she can spend.

   b. Graph the inequality you wrote in part **a.**

   c. Mirna spends $15 on a bracelet. Write an inequality to show how much money she has left to spend.

56. Critical Thinking Graph all positive integer solutions of the inequality $x < 5$.

 57. Write About It Explain how to write an inequality that is modeled by a graph. What characteristics do you look for in the graph?

 58. Write About It You were told in the lesson that the phrase "no more than" means "less than or equal to" and the phrase "at least" means "greater than or equal to."

   a. What does the phrase "at most" mean?

   b. What does the phrase "no less than" mean?

TEST PREP

59. Which is NOT a solution of the inequality $5 - 2x \geq -3$?

   (A) 0   (B) 2   (C) 4   (D) 5

60. Which is NOT a solution of the inequality $3 - x < 2$?

   (F) 1   (G) 2   (H) 3   (J) 4

61. Which graph represents the solutions of $-2 \leq 1 - t$?

   (A)   (C)

   (B)   (D)

CHALLENGE AND EXTEND

Describe the values for x and y that make each inequality true.

62. $x + y \leq |x + y|$ **63.** $x^2 < xy$ **64.** $x - y \geq y - x$

Complete each statement. Write < or >.

65. If $a > b$, then $b \; \blacksquare \; a$.   **66.** If $x > y$ and $y > z$, then $x \; \blacksquare \; z$.

67. Name a value of x that makes the statement $0.35 < x < 1.27$ true.

68. Is $\frac{5}{6}$ a solution of $x < 1$? How many solutions of $x < 1$ are between 0 and 1?

 69. Write About It Explain how to graph all the solutions of $x \neq 5$.

SPIRAL REVIEW

Add or subtract. *(Lesson 1-2)*

70. $-7 + 5$ **71.** $6 - (-4)$ **72.** $8 - 13$ **73.** $12 + (-5)$

Simplify each expression. *(Lesson 1-7)*

74. $x + 3x$ **75.** $x + (x + 1) + (x + 2)$ **76.** $5 + (x + 3) + 5 + 2(x + 3)$

77. There are twice as many girls in Sally's class as boys. Write a rule for the number of girls in Sally's class. Find the number of girls if there are 8 boys. *(Lesson 1-8)*

78. A video club charges a \$12 membership fee plus \$2.00 for each movie rental. Write a rule for the cost of renting x videos. Find the cost of renting 3, 7, and 15 videos. *(Lesson 1-8)*

Solve each equation. Check your answer. *(Lesson 2-4)*

79. $2b - 6 = b + 3$ **80.** $-3(2 - x) = 5x + 2$ **81.** $2(y + 1) = 2y + 1$

Solving Inequalities by Adding or Subtracting

Objectives
Solve one-step inequalities by using addition.

Solve one-step inequalities by using subtraction.

Who uses this?
You can use inequalities to determine how many more photos you can take. (See Example 2.)

Tenea has a cell phone that also takes pictures. After taking some photos, Tenea can use a one-step inequality to determine how many more photos she can take.

Solving one-step inequalities is much like solving one-step equations. To solve an inequality, you need to isolate the variable using the properties of inequality and inverse operations.

Know it!
Note

Properties of Inequality

Addition and Subtraction

WORDS	NUMBERS	ALGEBRA
Addition You can add the same number to both sides of an inequality, and the statement will still be true.	$3 < 8$ $3 + 2 < 8 + 2$ $5 < 10$	$a < b$ $a + c < b + c$
Subtraction You can subtract the same number from both sides of an inequality, and the statement will still be true.	$9 < 12$ $9 - 5 < 12 - 5$ $4 < 7$	$a < b$ $a - c < b - c$

These properties are also true for inequalities that use the symbols $>$, $\geq$, and $\leq$.

EXAMPLE 1 **Using Addition and Subtraction to Solve Inequalities**

Solve each inequality and graph the solutions.

Helpful Hint

Use an inverse operation to "undo" the operation in an inequality. If the inequality contains addition, use subtraction to undo the addition.

A $x + 9 < 15$

$$
\begin{array}{r}
x + 9 < 15 \\
\underline{-9 \quad -9} \\
x \quad < \ 6
\end{array}
$$

Since 9 is added to x, subtract 9 from both sides to undo the addition.

B $d - 3 > -6$

$$
\begin{array}{r}
d - 3 > -6 \\
\underline{+3 \quad +3} \\
d \quad > -3
\end{array}
$$

Since 3 is subtracted from d, add 3 to both sides to undo the subtraction.

Solve each inequality and graph the solutions.

C $0.7 \geq n - 0.4$

$0.7 \geq n - 0.4$ *Since 0.4 is subtracted from n, add 0.4 to both sides to*
$\underline{+\,0.4 \qquad +\,0.4}$ *undo the subtraction.*
$1.1 \geq n$
$n \leq 1.1$

 CHECK IT OUT!   Solve each inequality and graph the solutions.

1a. $s + 1 \leq 10$ **1b.** $2\frac{1}{2} > -3 + t$ **1c.** $q - 3.5 < 7.5$

Since there can be an infinite number of solutions to an inequality, it is not possible to check all the solutions. You can check the endpoint and the direction of the inequality symbol.

The solutions of $x + 9 < 15$ are given by $x < 6$.

Step 1 Check the endpoint.

Substitute 6 for x in the related equation $x + 9 = 15$. The endpoint should be a solution of the equation.

$$x + 9 = 15$$
$$\begin{array}{c|c} 6 + 9 & 15 \\ \hline 15 & 15 \checkmark \end{array}$$

Step 2 Check the inequality symbol.

Substitute a number less than 6 for x in the original inequality. The number you choose should be a solution of the inequality.

$$x + 9 < 15$$
$$\begin{array}{c|c} 4 + 9 & < & 15 \\ \hline 13 & < & 15 \checkmark \end{array}$$

EXAMPLE 2   *Problem Solving Application*

PROBLEM
SOLVING

The memory in Tenea's camera phone allows her to take up to 20 pictures. Tenea has already taken 16 pictures. Write, solve, and graph an inequality to show how many more pictures Tenea could take.

1   **Understand the Problem**

The **answer** will be an inequality and a graph that show all the possible numbers of pictures that Tenea can take.

    List the important information:
- Tenea can take up to, or *at most*, 20 pictures.
- Tenea has taken 16 pictures already.

2   **Make a Plan**

Write an inequality.
Let p represent the remaining number of pictures Tenea can take.

Number taken	plus	number remaining	is at most	20 pictures.
16	+	p	$\leq$	20

3 Solve

$$16 + p \le 20 \qquad \text{Since 16 is added to p, subtract 16 from both sides to}$$
$$\underline{-16 \qquad -16} \qquad \text{undo the addition.}$$
$$p \le 4$$

It is not reasonable for Tenea to take a negative or fractional number of pictures, so graph the nonnegative integers less than or equal to 4.

Tenea could take 0, 1, 2, 3, or 4 more pictures.

4 Look Back

Check   Check the endpoint, 4.   Check a number less than 4.

$16 + p = 20$	
$16 + 4$	20
20	20 ✓

$16 + p \le 20$	
$16 + 2$	≤ 20
18	≤ 20 ✓

Adding 0, 1, 2, 3, or 4 more pictures will not exceed 20.

CHECK IT OUT!   **2.** The Recommended Dietary Allowance (RDA) of iron for a female in Sarah's age group (14–18 years) is 15 mg per day. Sarah has consumed 11 mg of iron today. Write and solve an inequality to show how many more milligrams of iron Sarah can consume without exceeding the RDA.

EXAMPLE 3   ***Sports Application***

Josh can bench press 220 pounds. He wants to bench press at least 250 pounds. Write and solve an inequality to determine how many more pounds Josh must lift to reach his goal. Check your answer.

Let p represent the number of additional pounds Josh must lift.

220 pounds	plus	additional pounds	is at least	250 pounds.
220	+	p	$\ge$	250

$$220 + p \ge 250 \qquad \text{Since 220 is added to p, subtract 220 from both}$$
$$\underline{-220 \qquad -220} \qquad \text{sides to undo the addition.}$$
$$p \ge 30$$

Check   Check the endpoint, 30.   Check a number greater than 30.

$220 + p = 250$	
$220 + 30$	250
250	250 ✓

$220 + p \ge 250$	
$220 + 40$	≥ 250
260	≥ 250 ✓

Josh must lift at least 30 additional pounds to reach his goal.

CHECK IT OUT!   **3. What if...?** Josh has reached his goal of 250 pounds and now wants to try to break the school record of 282 pounds. Write and solve an inequality to determine how many more pounds Josh needs to break the school record. Check your answer.

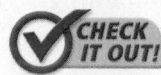

THINK AND DISCUSS

1. Show how to check your solution to Example 1B.

2. Explain how the Addition and Subtraction Properties of Inequality are like the Addition and Subtraction Properties of Equality.

3. **GET ORGANIZED** Copy and complete the graphic organizer. In each box, write an inequality that you must use the specified property to solve. Then solve and graph the inequality.

Properties of Inequality

Addition | Subtraction

3-2 Exercises

go.hrw.com
Homework Help Online
KEYWORD: MA7 3-2
Parent Resources Online
KEYWORD: MA7 Parent

GUIDED PRACTICE

SEE EXAMPLE **1**
p. 176

Solve each inequality and graph the solutions.

1. $12 < p + 6$
2. $w + 3 \geq 4$
3. $-5 + x \leq -20$
4. $z - 2 > -11$

SEE EXAMPLE **2**
p. 177

5. **Health** For adults, the maximum safe water temperature in a spa is 104 °F. The water temperature in Bill's spa is 102 °F. The temperature is increased by t °F. Write, solve, and graph an inequality to show the values of t for which the water temperature is still safe.

SEE EXAMPLE **3**
p. 178

6. **Consumer Economics** A local restaurant will deliver food to your house if the purchase amount of your order is at least $25.00. The total for part of your order is $17.95. Write and solve an inequality to determine how much more you must spend for the restaurant to deliver your order.

PRACTICE AND PROBLEM SOLVING

Independent Practice

For Exercises	See Example
7–10	1
11	2
12	3

Extra Practice
Skills Practice p. S8
Application Practice p. S30

Solve each inequality and graph the solutions.

7. $a - 3 \geq 2$
8. $2.5 > q - 0.8$
9. $-45 + x < -30$
10. $r + \frac{1}{4} \leq \frac{3}{4}$

11. **Engineering** The maximum load for a certain elevator is 2000 pounds. The total weight of the passengers on the elevator is 1400 pounds. A delivery man who weighs 243 pounds enters the elevator with a crate of weight w. Write, solve, and graph an inequality to show the values of w that will not exceed the weight limit of the elevator.

12. **Transportation** The gas tank in Mindy's car holds at most 15 gallons. She has already filled the tank with 7 gallons of gas. She will continue to fill the tank with g gallons more. Write and solve an inequality that shows all values of g that Mindy can add to the car's tank.

Write an inequality to represent each statement. Solve the inequality and graph the solutions.

13. Ten less than a number x is greater than 32.

14. A number n increased by 6 is less than or equal to 4.

15. A number r decreased by 13 is at most 15.

Solve each inequality and graph the solutions.

16. $x + 4 \leq 2$

17. $-12 + q > 39$

18. $x + \frac{3}{5} < 7$

19. $4.8 \geq p + 4$

20. $-12 \leq x - 12$

21. $4 < 206 + c$

22. $y - \frac{1}{3} > \frac{2}{3}$

23. $x + 1.4 \geq 1.4$

24. Use the inequality $s + 12 \geq 20$ to fill in the missing numbers.

    a. $s \geq$ ▮

    b. $s +$ ▮ ≥ 30

    c. $s - 8 \geq$ ▮

Health

Special-effects contact lenses are sometimes part of costumes for movies. All contact lenses should be worn under an eye doctor's supervision.

25. Health A particular type of contact lens can be worn up to 30 days in a row. Alex has been wearing these contact lenses for 21 days. Write, solve, and graph an inequality to show how many more days Alex could wear his contact lenses.

Solve each inequality and match the solutions to the correct graph.

26. $1 \leq x - 2$

A.

27. $8 > x - (-5)$

B.

28. $x + 6 > 9$

C.

29. $-4 \geq x - 7$

D.

30. Estimation Is $x < 10$ a reasonable estimate for the solutions to the inequality $11.879 + x < 21.709$? Explain your answer.

31. Sports At the Seattle Mariners baseball team's home games, there are 45,611 seats in the four areas listed in the table. Suppose all the suite level and club level seats during a game are filled. Write and solve an inequality to determine how many people p could be sitting in the other types of seats.

Mariners Home Game Seating	
Type of Seat	**Number of Seats**
Main bowl	24,399
Upper bowl	16,022
Club level	4,254
Suite level	936

32. Critical Thinking Recall that in Chapter 2 a balance scale was used to model solving equations. Describe how a balance scale could model solving inequalities.

33. Critical Thinking Explain why $x + 4 \geq 6$ and $x - 4 \geq -2$ have the same solutions.

34. Write About It How do the solutions of $x + 2 \geq 3$ differ from the solutions of $x + 2 > 3$? How do the graphs of the solutions differ?

MULTI-STEP TEST PREP

35. This problem will prepare you for the Multi-Step Test Prep on page 188.

    a. Daryl finds that the distance from Columbus, Ohio, to Washington, D.C., is 411 miles. What is the round-trip distance?

    b. Daryl can afford to drive a total of 1000 miles. Write an inequality to show the number of miles m he can drive while in Washington, D.C.

    c. Solve the inequality and graph the solutions on a number line. Show that your answer is reasonable.

36. Which is a reasonable solution of $4.7367 + p < 20.1784$?

    (A) 15   (B) 16   (C) 24   (D) 25

37. Which statement can be modeled by $x + 3 \leq 12$?

    (F) Sam has 3 bottles of water. Together, Sam and Dave have at most 12 bottles of water.

    (G) Jennie sold 3 cookbooks. To earn a prize, Jennie must sell at least 12 cookbooks.

    (H) Peter has 3 baseball hats. Peter and his brothers have fewer than 12 baseball hats.

    (J) Kathy swam 3 laps in the pool this week. She must swim more than 12 laps.

38. Which graph represents the solutions of $p + 3 < 1$?

39. Which inequality does NOT have the same solutions as $n + 12 \leq 26$?

    (F) $n \leq 14$ (G) $n + 6 \leq 20$ (H) $10 \geq n - 4$ (J) $n - 12 \leq 14$

CHALLENGE AND EXTEND

Solve each inequality and graph the solutions.

40. $6\frac{9}{10} \geq 4\frac{4}{5} + x$ **41.** $r - 1\frac{2}{5} \leq 3\frac{7}{10}$ **42.** $6\frac{2}{3} + m > 7\frac{1}{6}$

Determine whether each statement is sometimes, always, or never true. Explain.

43. $a + b > a - b$

44. If $a > c$, then $a + b > c + b$.

45. If $a > b$ and $c > d$, then $a + c > b + d$.

46. If $x + b > c$ and $x > 0$ have the same solutions, what is the relationship between b and c?

SPIRAL REVIEW

Solve each equation for the indicated variable. *(Lesson 2-5)*

47. $2x + 3y = 9$ for y **48.** $P = 4s$ for s **49.** $2 + ab = c$ for a

50. $p + e = f$ for e **51.** $2s - k = 11$ for k **52.** $5m + n = 0$ for m

Find the value of x in each diagram of similar figures. *(Lesson 2-8)*

53.   **54.**

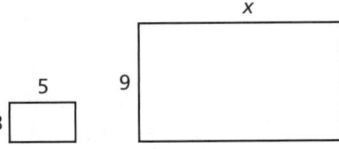

Write the inequality shown by each graph. *(Lesson 3-1)*

55.   **56.**

Solving Inequalities by Multiplying or Dividing

Objectives

Solve one-step inequalities by using multiplication.

Solve one-step inequalities by using division.

Who uses this?

You can solve an inequality to determine how much you can buy with a certain amount of money. (See Example 3.)

Remember, solving inequalities is similar to solving equations. To solve an inequality that contains multiplication or division, undo the operation by dividing or multiplying both sides of the inequality by the same number.

The rules below show the properties of inequality for multiplying or dividing by a positive number. The rules for multiplying or dividing by a negative number appear later in this lesson.

"This is all I have, so I'll take 3 pencils, 3 notebooks, a binder, and 0.9 calculators."

Jonny Hawkins/CartoonResource.com

Know it!
Note

Properties of Inequality

Multiplication and Division by Positive Numbers

WORDS	NUMBERS	ALGEBRA
Multiplication You can multiply both sides of an inequality by the same *positive* number, and the statement will still be true.	$7 < 12$ $7(3) < 12(3)$ $21 < 36$	If $a < b$ and $c > 0$, then $ac < bc$.
Division You can divide both sides of an inequality by the same *positive* number, and the statement will still be true.	$15 < 35$ $\dfrac{15}{5} < \dfrac{35}{5}$ $3 < 7$	If $a < b$ and $c > 0$, then $\dfrac{a}{c} < \dfrac{b}{c}$.

These properties are also true for inequalities that use the symbols $>$, $\geq$, and $\leq$.

EXAMPLE **1** **Multiplying or Dividing by a Positive Number**

Solve each inequality and graph the solutions.

A $3x > -27$

$3x > -27$ *Since x is multiplied by 3, divide both sides by 3 to*

$\dfrac{3x}{3} > \dfrac{-27}{3}$ *undo the multiplication.*

$x > -9$

Solve each inequality and graph the solutions.

B $\frac{2}{3}r < 6$

$$\frac{2}{3}r < 6$$

Since r is multiplied by $\frac{2}{3}$, multiply both sides by the reciprocal of $\frac{2}{3}$.

$$\frac{3}{2}\left(\frac{2}{3}r\right) < \frac{3}{2}(6)$$

$$r < 9$$

 Solve each inequality and graph the solutions.

1a. $4k > 24$ **1b.** $-50 \geq 5q$ **1c.** $\frac{3}{4}g > 27$

What happens when you multiply or divide both sides of an inequality by a negative number?

Look at the number line below.

$2 < 6$	$6 > -2$
$-2 \;\blacksquare\; -6$ *Multiply both sides by -1.*	$-6 \;\blacksquare\; 2$ *Multiply both sides by -1.*
$-2 > -6$ *Use the number line to determine the direction of the inequality.*	$-6 < 2$ *Use the number line to determine the direction of the inequality.*

Notice that when you multiply (or divide) both sides of an inequality by a negative number, you must reverse the inequality symbol. This means there is another set of properties of inequality for multiplying or dividing by a negative number.

Properties of Inequality

Multiplication and Division by Negative Numbers

WORDS	NUMBERS	ALGEBRA
Multiplication If you multiply both sides of an inequality by the same *negative* number, you must reverse the inequality symbol for the statement to still be true.	$8 > 4$ $8(-2) < 4(-2)$ $-16 < -8$	If $a > b$ and $c < 0$, then $ac < bc$.
Division If you divide both sides of an inequality by the same *negative* number, you must reverse the inequality symbol for the statement to still be true.	$12 > 4$ $\dfrac{12}{-4} < \dfrac{4}{-4}$ $-3 < -1$	If $a > b$ and $c < 0$, then $\dfrac{a}{c} < \dfrac{b}{c}$.

These properties are also true for inequalities that use the symbols $<$, $\geq$, and $\leq$.

EXAMPLE 2 **Multiplying or Dividing by a Negative Number**

Solve each inequality and graph the solutions.

A $-8x > 72$

$$\frac{-8x}{-8} < \frac{72}{-8}$$

$$x < -9$$

Since x is multiplied by −8, divide both sides by −8. Change > to <.

B $-3 \le \dfrac{x}{-5}$

$$-5(-3) \ge -5\left(\frac{x}{-5}\right)$$

$$15 \ge x \ (\text{or } x \le 15)$$

Since x is divided by −5, multiply both sides by −5. Change ≤ to ≥.

> **Caution!** ///////
>
> Do not change the direction of the inequality symbol just because you see a negative sign. For example, you do not change the symbol when solving $4x < -24$.

CHECK IT OUT! Solve each inequality and graph the solutions.

2a. $10 \ge -x$ **2b.** $4.25 > -0.25h$

EXAMPLE 3 *Consumer Application*

Ryan has a $16 gift card for a health store where a smoothie costs $2.50 with tax. What are the possible numbers of smoothies that Ryan can buy?

Let *s* represent the number of smoothies Ryan can buy.

$2.50	times	number of smoothies	is at most	$16.00.
2.50	•	s	≤	16.00

$$2.50s \le 16.00$$

$$\frac{2.50s}{2.50} \le \frac{16.00}{2.50}$$ *Since s is multiplied by 2.50, divide both sides by 2.50. The symbol does not change.*

$$s \le 6.4$$ *Ryan can buy only a whole number of smoothies.*

Ryan can buy 0, 1, 2, 3, 4, 5, or 6 smoothies.

CHECK IT OUT! **3.** A pitcher holds 128 ounces of juice. What are the possible numbers of 10-ounce servings that one pitcher can fill?

 Know it! Note

THINK AND DISCUSS

1. Compare the Multiplication and Division Properties of Inequality and the Multiplication and Division Properties of Equality.

2. **GET ORGANIZED** Copy and complete the graphic organizer. In each cell, write and solve an inequality.

Solving Inequalities by Using Multiplication and Division		
	By a Positive Number	**By a Negative Number**
Divide		
Multiply		

3-3

Exercises

go.hrw.com
Homework Help Online
KEYWORD: MA7 3-3
Parent Resources Online
KEYWORD: MA7 Parent

GUIDED PRACTICE

Solve each inequality and graph the solutions.

SEE EXAMPLE **1**
p. 182

1. $3b > 27$ **2.** $-40 \geq 8b$ **3.** $\dfrac{d}{3} > 6$ **4.** $24d \leq 6$

5. $1.1m \leq 1.21$ **6.** $\dfrac{2}{3}k > 6$ **7.** $9s > -18$ **8.** $\dfrac{4}{5} \geq \dfrac{r}{2}$

SEE EXAMPLE **2**
p. 184

9. $-2x < -10$ **10.** $\dfrac{b}{-2} \geq 8$ **11.** $-3.5n < 1.4$ **12.** $4 > -8g$

13. $\dfrac{d}{-6} < \dfrac{1}{2}$ **14.** $-10h \geq -6$ **15.** $12 > \dfrac{t}{-6}$ **16.** $-\dfrac{1}{2}m \geq -7$

SEE EXAMPLE **3**
p. 184

17. Travel Tom saved $550 to go on a school trip. The cost for a hotel room, including tax, is $80 per night. What are the possible numbers of nights Tom can stay at the hotel?

PRACTICE AND PROBLEM SOLVING

Independent Practice

For Exercises	See Example
18–29	1
30–41	2
42	3

Extra Practice
Skills Practice p. S8
Application Practice p. S30

Solve each inequality and graph the solutions.

18. $10 < 2t$ **19.** $\dfrac{1}{3}j \leq 4$ **20.** $-80 < 8c$ **21.** $21 > 3d$

22. $\dfrac{w}{4} \geq -2$ **23.** $\dfrac{h}{4} \leq \dfrac{2}{7}$ **24.** $6y < 4.2$ **25.** $12c \leq -144$

26. $\dfrac{4}{5}x \geq \dfrac{2}{5}$ **27.** $6b \geq \dfrac{3}{5}$ **28.** $-25 > 10p$ **29.** $\dfrac{b}{8} \leq -2$

30. $-9a > 81$ **31.** $\dfrac{1}{2} < \dfrac{r}{-3}$ **32.** $-6p > 0.6$ **33.** $\dfrac{y}{-4} > -\dfrac{1}{2}$

34. $-\dfrac{1}{6}f < 5$ **35.** $-2.25t < -9$ **36.** $24 \leq -10w$ **37.** $-11z > 121$

38. $\dfrac{3}{5} < \dfrac{f}{-5}$ **39.** $-k \geq 7$ **40.** $-2.2b < -7.7$ **41.** $16 \geq -\dfrac{4}{3}p$

42. Camping The rope Roz brought with her camping gear is 54 inches long. Roz needs to cut shorter pieces of rope that are each 18 inches long. What are the possible number of pieces Roz can cut?

Solve each inequality and graph the solutions.

43. $-8x < 24$ **44.** $3t \leq 24$ **45.** $\dfrac{1}{4}x < 5$ **46.** $\dfrac{4}{5}p \geq -24$

47. $54 \leq -9p$ **48.** $3t > -\dfrac{1}{2}$ **49.** $-\dfrac{3}{4}b > -\dfrac{3}{2}$ **50.** $216 > 3.6r$

Write an inequality for each statement. Solve the inequality and graph the solutions.

51. The product of a number and 7 is not less than 21.

52. The quotient of h and -6 is at least 5.

53. The product of $-\dfrac{4}{5}$ and b is at most -16.

54. Ten is no more than the quotient of t and 4.

55. Write About It Explain how you know whether to reverse the inequality symbol when solving an inequality.

56. Geometry The area of a rectangle is at most 21 square inches. The width of the rectangle is 3.5 inches. What are the possible measurements for the length of the rectangle?

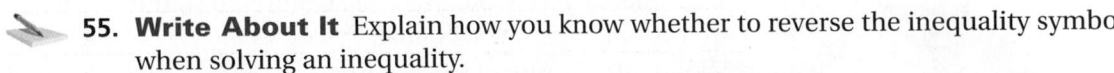

Solve each inequality and match the solution to the correct graph.

57. $-0.5t \geq 1.5$

A.

58. $\frac{1}{9}t \leq -3$

B.

59. $-13.5 \leq -4.5t$

C.

60. $\frac{t}{-6} \leq -\frac{1}{2}$

D.

61. **Animals** A wildlife shelter is home to birds, mammals, and reptiles. If cat chow is sold in 20 lb bags, what is the least number of bags of cat chow needed for one year at this shelter?

Food Consumed at a Wildlife Shelter per Week	
Type of Food	**Amount of Food (lb)**
Grapes	4
Mixed seed	10
Peanuts	5
Cat chow	10
Kitten chow	5

62. **Education** In order to earn an A in a college math class, a student must score no less than 90% of all possible points. One semester, students with at least 567 points earned an A in the class. Write an inequality to show the numbers of points possible.

63. **Critical Thinking** Explain why you cannot solve an inequality by multiplying both sides by zero.

64. **///ERROR ANALYSIS///** Two students have different answers for a homework problem. Which answer is incorrect? Explain the error.

Ⓐ
$9m \geq -27$
$\frac{9m}{9} \geq \frac{-27}{9}$
$m \leq -3$

Ⓑ
$9m \geq -27$
$\frac{9m}{9} \geq \frac{-27}{9}$
$m \geq -3$

65. Jan has a budget of $800 for catering. The catering company charges $12.50 per guest. Write and solve an inequality to show the numbers of guests Jan can invite.

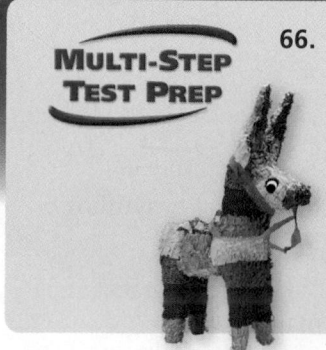

MULTI-STEP TEST PREP

66. This problem will prepare you for the Multi-Step Test Prep on page 188.
   a. The Swimming Club can spend a total of $250 for hotel rooms for its spring trip. One hotel costs $75 per night. Write an inequality to find the number of rooms the club can reserve at this hotel. Let n be the number of rooms.
   b. Solve the inequality you wrote in part a. Graph the solutions on a number line. Make sure your answer is reasonable.
   c. Another hotel offers a rate of $65 per night. Does this allow the club to reserve more rooms? Explain your reasoning.

67. Which inequality does NOT have the same solutions as $-\frac{2}{3}y > 4$?

   Ⓐ $12 < -2y$ Ⓒ $-\frac{3}{4}y > \frac{9}{2}$

   Ⓑ $\frac{y}{2} < -12$ Ⓓ $-3y > 18$

68. The solutions of which inequality are NOT represented by the following graph?

   Ⓕ $\frac{x}{2} \ge -2$ Ⓗ $3x \ge -12$

   Ⓖ $-5x \ge 20$ Ⓙ $-7x \le 28$

69. Which inequality can be used to find the number of 39-cent stamps you can purchase for $4.00?

   Ⓐ $0.39s \ge 4.00$ Ⓒ $\frac{s}{0.39} \le 4.00$

   Ⓑ $0.39s \le 4.00$ Ⓓ $\frac{4.00}{0.39} \le s$

70. Short Response Write three different inequalities that have the same solutions as $x > 4$. Show your work and explain each step.

CHALLENGE AND EXTEND

Solve each inequality.

71. $2\frac{1}{3} \le -\frac{5}{6}g$ **72.** $\frac{2x}{3} < 8.25$ **73.** $2\frac{5}{8}m > \frac{7}{10}$ **74.** $3\frac{3}{5}f \ge 14\frac{2}{5}$

75. Estimation What is the greatest possible integer solution of the inequality $3.806x < 19.902$?

76. Critical Thinking The Transitive Property of Equality states that if $a = b$ and $b = c$, then $a = c$. Is there a Transitive Property of Inequality using the symbol <? Give an example to support your answer.

77. Critical Thinking The Symmetric Property of Equality states that if $a = b$, then $b = a$. Is there a Symmetric Property of Inequality? Give an example to support your answer.

SPIRAL REVIEW

Write the power represented by each geometric model. *(Lesson 1-4)*

78.
• • •
• • •
• • •

79.

80.

Find each unit rate. *(Lesson 2-7)*

81. Twelve gallons of gas cost $22.68. Find the unit rate in dollars per gallon.

82. A tree grows four feet in six years. Find the unit rate in feet per year.

83. A student types 105 words in 3 minutes. Find the unit rate in words per minute.

Solve each inequality and graph the solutions. *(Lesson 3-2)*

84. $x + 5 \ge 3$ **85.** $t - \frac{1}{4} < \frac{3}{4}$ **86.** $4 > x - 1$ **87.** $6 > b - 8$

MULTI-STEP TEST PREP

Simple Inequalities

Remember the Alamo! The Spanish Club is planning a trip for next summer. They plan to travel from Fort Worth, Texas, to San Antonio, Texas. They can spend only $550 for the entire trip.

1. The treasurer of the club budgets $60 for gasoline. The current gas price is $1.95/gallon. The school van gets an average of 20 miles per gallon of gasoline. Determine how many miles they can drive on this budget. Round your answer to the nearest mile.

2. The distance from Fort Worth to San Antonio is 266 miles. Write an inequality that can be used to solve for the number of miles m that they can drive while in San Antonio. Solve your inequality and graph the solutions.

3. The treasurer budgeted $200 for hotel rooms for one night. The club chose a hotel that charges $58 per night. Write an inequality that can be used to solve for the number of rooms they can reserve n. What is the maximum number of rooms that they can reserve in the hotel?

4. Use the maximum number of rooms you found in part **3**. How much will the club spend on hotel rooms?

5. The club members plan to spend $80 on food. They also want to see attractions in San Antonio, such as SeaWorld and the Alamo.

   Write an inequality that can be solved to find the amount of money available for seeing attractions. What is the maximum amount the club can spend seeing attractions?

6. Write a summary of the budget for the Spanish Club trip. Include the amount they plan to spend on gasoline, hotel rooms, food, and attractions.

READY TO GO ON?

Quiz for Lessons 3-1 Through 3-3

3-1 Graphing and Writing Inequalities

Describe the solutions of each inequality in words.

1. $-2 < r$ **2.** $t - 1 \leq 7$ **3.** $2s \geq 6$ **4.** $4 > 5 - x$

Graph each inequality.

5. $x > -2$ **6.** $m \leq 1\frac{1}{2}$ **7.** $g < \sqrt{8 + 1}$ **8.** $h \geq 2^3$

Write the inequality shown by each graph.

9.
```
←+--+--●--+--+--+--+--+--+--+--+→
 -5 -4 -3 -2 -1  0  1  2  3  4  5
```

10.
```
←+--+--+--+--+--+--+--+--○--+→
 -4 -3 -2 -1  0  1  2  3  4  5  6
```

11.
```
         -1.5
←+--+--+--+--●--+--+--+--+--+--+→
 -6 -5 -4 -3 -2 -1  0  1  2  3  4
```

Write an inequality for each situation and graph the solutions.

12. You must purchase at least 5 tickets to receive a discount.

13. Children under 13 are not admitted to certain movies without an adult.

14. A cell phone plan allows up to 250 free minutes per month.

3-2 Solving One-Step Inequalities by Adding or Subtracting

Solve each inequality and graph the solutions.

15. $k + 5 \leq 7$ **16.** $4 > p - 3$ **17.** $r - 8 \geq -12$ **18.** $-3 + p < -6$

19. Allie must sell at least 50 gift baskets for the band fund-raiser. She already sold 36 baskets. Write and solve an inequality to determine how many more baskets Allie must sell for the fund-raiser.

20. Dante has at most $12 to spend on entertainment each week. So far this week, he spent $7.50. Write and solve an inequality to determine how much money Dante can spend on entertainment the rest of the week.

3-3 Solving One-Step Inequalities by Multiplying or Dividing

Solve each inequality and graph the solutions.

21. $-4x < 8$ **22.** $\frac{d}{3} \geq -3$ **23.** $\frac{3}{4}t \leq 12$ **24.** $8 > -16c$

25. A spool of ribbon is 80 inches long. Riley needs to cut strips of ribbon that are 14 inches long. What are the possible numbers of strips that Riley can cut?

3-4 Solving Two-Step and Multi-Step Inequalities

Objective
Solve inequalities that contain more than one operation.

Who uses this?
Contestants at a county fair can solve an inequality to find how many pounds a prize-winning pumpkin must weigh. (See Example 3.)

At the county fair, contestants can enter contests that judge animals, recipes, crops, art projects, and more. Sometimes an average score or average weight is used to determine the winner of the blue ribbon. A contestant can use a multi-step inequality to determine what score or weight is needed in order to win.

Inequalities that contain more than one operation require more than one step to solve. Use inverse operations to undo the operations in the inequality one at a time.

EXAMPLE 1 **Solving Multi-Step Inequalities**

Solve each inequality and graph the solutions.

A $160 + 4f \le 500$

$$160 + 4f \le 500$$
$$\underline{-160 \qquad\quad -160}$$
$$4f \le 340$$

Since 160 is added to 4f, subtract 160 from both sides to undo the addition.

$$\frac{4f}{4} \le \frac{340}{4}$$

Since f is multiplied by 4, divide both sides by 4 to undo the multiplication.

$$f \le 85$$

B $7 - 2t \le 21$

$$7 - 2t \le 21$$
$$\underline{-7 \qquad -7}$$
$$-2t \le 14$$

Since 7 is added to −2t, subtract 7 from both sides to undo the addition.

$$\frac{-2t}{-2} \ge \frac{14}{-2}$$

Since t is multiplied by −2, divide both sides by −2 to undo the multiplication. Change ≤ to ≥.

$$t \ge -7$$

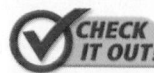

CHECK IT OUT! Solve each inequality and graph the solutions.

1a. $-12 \ge 3x + 6$ **1b.** $\frac{x + 5}{-2} > 3$ **1c.** $\frac{1 - 2n}{3} \ge 7$

To solve more complicated inequalities, you may first need to simplify the expressions on one or both sides by using the order of operations, combining like terms, or using the Distributive Property.

EXAMPLE **2** **Simplifying Before Solving Inequalities**

Solve each inequality and graph the solutions.

A $-4 + (-8) < -5c - 2$

$$-12 < -5c - 2$$ *Combine like terms. Since 2 is subtracted from $-5c$,*
$$\underline{+2 \qquad\quad +2}$$ *add 2 to both sides to undo the subtraction.*
$$-10 < -5c$$

$$\frac{-10}{-5} > \frac{-5c}{-5}$$ *Since c is multiplied by -5, divide both sides by -5*
to undo the multiplication. Change < to >.
$$2 > c \ (\text{or } c < 2)$$

B $-3(3 - x) < 4^2$

$$-3(3 - x) < 4^2$$ *Distribute -3 on the left side.*
$$-3(3) - (-3)x < 4^2$$
$$-9 + 3x < 4^2$$
$$-9 + 3x < 16$$ *Simplify the right side.*
$$-9 + 3x < 16$$ *Since -9 is added to $3x$, add 9 to both sides*
$$\underline{+9 \qquad\quad +9}$$ *to undo the addition.*
$$3x < 25$$ *Since x is multiplied by 3, divide both sides by*
$$\frac{3x}{3} < \frac{25}{3}$$ *3 to undo the multiplication.*
$$x < 8\frac{1}{3}$$

C $\frac{4}{5}x + \frac{1}{2} > \frac{3}{5}$

$$10\left(\frac{4}{5}x + \frac{1}{2}\right) > 10\left(\frac{3}{5}\right)$$ *Multiply both sides by 10, the LCD of the fractions.*
$$10\left(\frac{4}{5}x\right) + 10\left(\frac{1}{2}\right) > 10\left(\frac{3}{5}\right)$$ *Distribute 10 on the left side.*
$$8x + 5 > 6$$ *Since 5 is added to $8x$, subtract 5 from*
$$\underline{\quad -5 \quad -5}$$ *both sides to undo the addition.*
$$8x \quad > 1$$
$$\frac{8x}{8} > \frac{1}{8}$$ *Since x is multiplied by 8, divide both sides by 8 to undo the multiplication.*
$$x > \frac{1}{8}$$

CHECK IT OUT! Solve each inequality and graph the solutions.

2a. $2m + 5 > 5^2$ **2b.** $3 + 2(x + 4) > 3$ **2c.** $\frac{5}{8} < \frac{3}{8}x - \frac{1}{4}$

EXAMPLE 3 *Gardening Application*

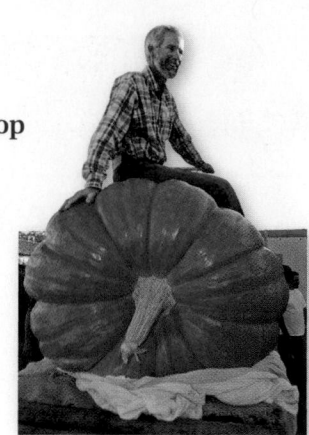

To win the blue ribbon for the Heaviest Pumpkin Crop at the county fair, the average weight of John's two pumpkins must be greater than 819 lb. One of his pumpkins weighs 887 lb. What is the least number of pounds the second pumpkin could weigh in order for John to win the blue ribbon?

Let *p* represent the weight of the second pumpkin. The average weight of the pumpkins is the sum of each weight divided by 2.

(887	plus	*p*)	divided by	2	must be greater than	819.
(887	+	*p*)	÷	2	>	819

$$\frac{887 + p}{2} > 819$$ *Since 887 + p is divided by 2, multiply both sides by 2 to undo the division.*

$$2\left(\frac{887 + p}{2}\right) > 2(819)$$

$$887 + p > 1638$$ *Since 887 is added to p, subtract 887 from both sides to undo the addition.*

$$\underline{-887 \qquad\quad -887}$$

$$p > \quad 751$$

The second pumpkin must weigh more than 751 pounds.

Check   Check the endpoint, 751.   Check a number greater than 751.

$\frac{887 + p}{2} = 819$		$\frac{887 + p}{2} > 819$	
$\frac{887 + 751}{2}$	819	$\frac{887 + 755}{2}$ >	819
$\frac{1638}{2}$	819	$\frac{1642}{2}$ >	819
819	819 ✓	821 >	819 ✓

 3. The average of Jim's two test scores must be at least 90 to make an A in the class. Jim got a 95 on his first test. What scores can Jim get on his second test to make an A in the class?

THINK AND DISCUSS

1. The inequality $v \geq 25$ states that 25 is the ___?___. (*value of v*, *minimum value of v*, or *maximum value of v*)

2. Describe two sets of steps for solving the inequality $\frac{x + 5}{3} > 7$.

3. GET ORGANIZED Copy and complete the graphic organizer.

> **Solving Multi-Step Equations and Inequalities**
>
> | How are they alike? | How are they different? |

Know it!
Note

GUIDED PRACTICE

Solve each inequality and graph the solutions.

SEE EXAMPLE **1**
p. 190

1. $2m + 1 > 13$

2. $2d + 21 \leq 11$

3. $6 \leq -2x + 2$

4. $4c - 7 > 5$

5. $\dfrac{4 + x}{3} > -4$

6. $1 < 0.2x - 0.7$

7. $\dfrac{3 - 2x}{3} \leq 7$

8. $2x + 5 \geq 2$

SEE EXAMPLE **2**
p. 191

9. $4(x + 2) > 6$

10. $\dfrac{1}{4}x + \dfrac{2}{3} < \dfrac{3}{4}$

11. $4 - x + 6^2 \geq 21$

12. $4 - x > 3(4 - 2)$

13. $0.2(x - 10) > -1.8$

14. $3(j + 41) \leq 35$

SEE EXAMPLE **3**
p. 192

15. Business A sales representative is given a choice of two paycheck plans. One choice includes a monthly base pay of $300 plus 10% commission on his sales. The second choice is a monthly salary of $1200. For what amount of sales would the representative make more money with the first plan?

PRACTICE AND PROBLEM SOLVING

Independent Practice

For Exercises	See Example
16–27	1
28–36	2
37	3

Extra Practice

Skills Practice p. S9

Application Practice p. S30

Solve each inequality and graph the solutions.

16. $4r - 9 > 7$

17. $3 \leq 5 - 2x$

18. $\dfrac{w + 3}{2} > 6$

19. $11w + 99 < 77$

20. $9 \geq \dfrac{1}{2}v + 3$

21. $-4x - 8 > 16$

22. $8 - \dfrac{2}{3}z \leq 2$

23. $f + 2\dfrac{1}{2} < -2$

24. $\dfrac{3n - 8}{5} \geq 2$

25. $-5 > -5 - 3w$

26. $10 > \dfrac{5 - 3p}{2}$

27. $2v + 1 > 2\dfrac{1}{3}$

28. $4(x + 3) > -24$

29. $4 > x - 3(x + 2)$

30. $-18 \geq 33 - 3h$

31. $-2 > 7x - 2(x - 4)$

32. $9 - (9)^2 > 10x - x$

33. $2a - (-3)^2 \geq 13$

34. $6 - \dfrac{x}{3} + 1 > \dfrac{2}{3}$

35. $12(x - 3) + 2x > 6$

36. $15 \geq 19 + 2(q - 18)$

37. Communications One cell phone company offers a plan that costs $29.99 and includes unlimited night and weekend minutes. Another company offers a plan that costs $19.99 and charges $0.35 per minute during nights and weekends. For what numbers of night and weekend minutes does the second company's plan cost more than the first company's plan?

Solve each inequality and graph the solutions.

38. $-12 > -4x - 8$

39. $5x + 4 \leq 14$

40. $\dfrac{2}{3}x - 5 > 7$

41. $x - 3x > 2 - 10$

42. $5 - x - 2 > 3$

43. $3 < 2x - 5(x + 3)$

44. $\dfrac{1}{6} - \dfrac{2}{3}m \geq \dfrac{1}{4}$

45. $4 - (r - 2) > 3 - 5$

46. $0.3 - 0.5n + 1 \geq 0.4$

47. $6^2 > 4(x + 2)$

48. $-4 - 2n + 4n > 7 - 2^2$

49. $\dfrac{1}{4}(p - 10) \geq 6 - 4$

50. Use the inequality $-4t - 8 \leq 12$ to fill in the missing numbers.

   a. $t \geq$ ▇

   b. $t + 4 \geq$ ▇

   c. $t -$ ▇ ≥ 0

   d. $t + 10 \geq$ ▇

   e. $3t \geq$ ▇

   f. $\dfrac{t}{▇} \geq -5$

Write an inequality for each statement. Solve the inequality and graph the solutions.

51. One-half of a number, increased by 9, is less than 33.

52. Six is less than or equal to the sum of 4 and $-2x$.

53. The product of 4 and the sum of a number and 12 is at most 16.

54. The sum of half a number and two-thirds of the number is less than 14.

Solve each inequality and match the solution to the correct graph.

55. $4x - 9 \geq 7$

A. ![number line from -5 to 5 with closed dot at -2 and arrow pointing left]

56. $-6 \geq 3(x - 2)$

B. ![number line from -5 to 5 with closed dot at 4 and arrow pointing right]

57. $-2x - 6 \geq -4 + 2$

C. ![number line from -5 to 5 with closed dot at $-\frac{3}{2}$ and arrow pointing left]

58. $\frac{1}{2} - \frac{1}{3}x \leq \left(\frac{2}{3} + \frac{1}{3}\right)^2$

D. ![number line from -5 to 5 with closed dot at 1 and arrow pointing left]

59. Entertainment A digital video recorder (DVR) records television shows on an internal hard drive. To use a DVR, you need a subscription with a DVR service company. Two companies advertise their charges for a DVR machine and subscription service.

EASY ELECTRONICS

$225 for DVR machine

$400 for lifetime subscription

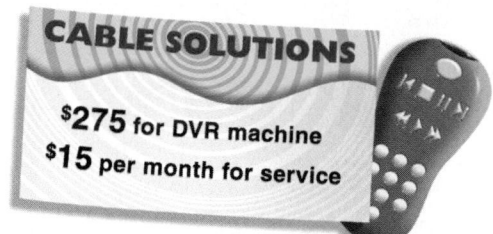

CABLE SOLUTIONS

$275 for DVR machine

$15 per month for service

For what numbers of months will a consumer pay less for the machine and subscription at Easy Electronics than at Cable Solutions?

60. Geometry The area of the triangle shown is less than 55 square inches.

a. Write an inequality that can be used to find x.

b. Solve the inequality you wrote in part **a.**

c. What is the maximum height of the triangle?

$(2x + 3)$ in.

5 in.

MULTI-STEP TEST PREP

61. This problem will prepare you for the Multi-Step Test Prep on page 218.

a. A band wants to create a CD of their last concert. They received a donation of $500 to cover the cost. The total cost is $350 plus $3 per CD. Complete the table to find a relationship between the number of CDs and the total cost.

b. Write an equation for the cost c of the CDs based on the number of CDs n.

c. Write an inequality that can be used to determine how many CDs can be made with the $500 donation. Solve the inequality and determine how many CDs the band can have made from the $500 donation.

Number	Process	Cost
1	350 + 3	353
2		
3		
10		
n		

62. Critical Thinking What is the least whole number that is a solution of $4r - 4.9 > 14.95$?

 63. Write About It Describe two sets of steps to solve $2(x + 3) > 10$.

64. What are the solutions of $3y > 2x + 4$ when $y = 6$?

   Ⓐ $7 > x$ Ⓑ $x > 7$ Ⓒ $x > 11$ Ⓓ $11 > x$

65. Cecilia has $30 to spend at a carnival. Admission costs $5.00, lunch will cost $6.00, and each ride ticket costs $1.25. Which inequality represents the number of ride tickets x that Cecilia can buy?

   Ⓕ $30 - (5 - 6) + 1.25x \le 30$ Ⓗ $30 - (5 + 6) \le 1.25x$

   Ⓖ $5 + 6 + 1.25x \le 30$ Ⓙ $30 + 1.25x \le 5 + 6$

66. Which statement is modeled by $2p + 5 < 11$?

   Ⓐ The sum of 5 and 2 times p is at least 11.

   Ⓑ Five added to the product of 2 and p is less than 11.

   Ⓒ Two times p plus 5 is at most 11.

   Ⓓ The product of 2 and p added to 5 is 11.

67. Gridded Response A basketball team scored 8 points more in its second game than in its first. In its third game, the team scored 42 points. The total number of points scored in the three games was more than 150. What is the least number of points the team might have scored in its *second* game?

CHALLENGE AND EXTEND

Solve each inequality and graph the solutions.

68. $3(x + 2) - 6x + 6 \le 0$ **69.** $-18 > -(2x + 9) - 4 + x$ **70.** $\dfrac{2 + x}{2} - (x - 1) > 1$

Write an inequality for each statement. Graph the solutions.

71. x is a positive number.   **72.** x is a negative number.

73. x is a nonnegative number.   **74.** x is not a positive number.

75. x times negative 3 is positive.   **76.** The opposite of x is greater than 2.

SPIRAL REVIEW

Find each root. *(Lesson 1-5)*

77. $\sqrt{49}$ **78.** $-\sqrt{144}$ **79.** $\sqrt{\dfrac{4}{9}}$

80. $\sqrt{196}$ **81.** $\sqrt[3]{-729}$ **82.** $\sqrt{10,000}$

83. Video rental store A charges a membership fee of $25 and $2 for each movie rental. Video rental store B charges a membership fee of $10 and $2.50 for each movie. Find the number of movie rentals for which both stores' charges are the same. *(Lesson 2-4)*

Solve each inequality and graph the solutions. *(Lesson 3-3)*

84. $2x < -8$ **85.** $\dfrac{a}{-2} \le -3$ **86.** $\dfrac{1}{4} < \dfrac{t}{12}$

3-5 Solving Inequalities with Variables on Both Sides

Objective
Solve inequalities that contain variable terms on both sides.

Who uses this?
Business owners can use inequalities to find the most cost-efficient services. (See Example 2.)

Some inequalities have variable terms on both sides of the inequality symbol. You can solve these inequalities like you solved equations with variables on both sides.

Use the properties of inequality to "collect" all the variable terms on one side and all the constant terms on the other side.

EXAMPLE 1 Solving Inequalities with Variables on Both Sides

Solve each inequality and graph the solutions.

A $x < 3x + 8$

$$x < 3x + 8$$

To collect the variable terms on one side, subtract x from both sides.

$$\underline{-x \quad\quad -x}$$
$$0 < 2x + 8$$

Since 8 is added to 2x, subtract 8 from both sides to undo the addition.

$$\underline{-8 \quad\quad -8}$$
$$-8 < 2x$$

$$\frac{-8}{2} < \frac{2x}{2}$$

Since x is multiplied by 2, divide both sides by 2 to undo the multiplication.

$$-4 < x \text{ (or } x > -4)$$

> **Helpful Hint**
>
> Your first step can also be to subtract 3x from both sides to get $-2x < 8$. When you divide by a negative number, remember to reverse the inequality symbol.

B $6x - 1 \le 3.5x + 4$

$$6x - 1 \le 3.5x + 4$$

Subtract 6x from both sides.

$$\underline{-6x \quad\quad -6x}$$
$$-1 \le -2.5x + 4$$

Since 4 is added to −2.5x, subtract 4 from both sides to undo the addition.

$$\underline{-4 \quad\quad\quad -4}$$
$$-5 \le -2.5x$$

$$\frac{-5}{-2.5} \ge \frac{-2.5x}{-2.5}$$

Since x is multiplied by −2.5, divide both sides by −2.5 to undo the multiplication. Reverse the inequality symbol.

$$2 \ge x$$

 CHECK IT OUT! Solve each inequality and graph the solutions.

1a. $4x \ge 7x + 6$ **1b.** $5t + 1 < -2t - 6$

EXAMPLE 2

Business Application

The *Daily Info* charges a fee of $650 plus $80 per week to run an ad. The *People's Paper* charges $145 per week. For how many weeks will the total cost at *Daily Info* be less expensive than the cost at *People's Paper*?

Let w be the number of weeks the ad runs in the paper.

Daily Info fee	plus	$80 per week	times	number of weeks	is less expensive than	People's Paper charge per week	times	number of weeks.
$650	+	$80	·	w	<	$145	·	w

$$650 + 80w < 145w$$

$$\underline{-80w \qquad -80w}$$

Subtract 80w from both sides.

$$650 \quad < \quad 65w$$

Since w is multiplied by 65, divide both sides by 65 to undo the multiplication.

$$\frac{650}{65} < \frac{65w}{65}$$

$$10 < w$$

The total cost at *Daily Info* is less than the cost at *People's Paper* if the ad runs for more than 10 weeks.

 2. A-Plus Advertising charges a fee of $24 plus $0.10 per flyer to print and deliver flyers. Print and More charges $0.25 per flyer. For how many flyers is the cost at A-Plus Advertising less than the cost at Print and More?

You may need to simplify one or both sides of an inequality before solving it. Look for like terms to combine and places to use Distributive Property.

EXAMPLE 3

Simplifying Each Side Before Solving

Solve each inequality and graph the solutions.

A $6(1 - x) < 3x$

$$6(1 - x) < 3x$$

Distribute 6 on the left side of the inequality.

$$6(1) - 6(x) < 3x$$

$$6 - 6x < 3x$$

Add 6x to both sides so that the coefficient of x is positive.

$$\underline{+6x \qquad +6x}$$

$$6 \quad < \quad 9x$$

$$\frac{6}{9} < \frac{9x}{9}$$

Since x is multiplied by 9, divide both sides by 9 to undo the multiplication.

$$\frac{2}{3} < x$$

Solve each inequality and graph the solutions.

B $1.6x \leq -0.2x + 0.9$

$$1.6x \leq -0.2x + 0.9$$

$$\underline{+\,0.2x \qquad +\,0.2x}$$

$$1.8x \leq \qquad\qquad 0.9$$

Since −0.2x is added to 0.9, subtract −0.2x from both sides. Subtracting −0.2x is the same as adding 0.2x.

$$\frac{1.8x}{1.8} \leq \frac{0.9}{1.8}$$

Since x is multiplied by 1.8, divide both sides by 1.8 to undo the multiplication.

$$x \leq \frac{1}{2}$$

A number line from −2 to 1 with marks at -2, $-1\frac{1}{2}$, -1, $-\frac{1}{2}$, 0, $\frac{1}{2}$, 1, shaded to the left of $\frac{1}{2}$.

CHECK IT OUT! Solve each inequality and graph the solutions. Check your answer.

3a. $5(2 - r) \geq 3(r - 2)$ **3b.** $0.5x - 0.3 + 1.9x < 0.3x + 6$

Some inequalities are true no matter what value is substituted for the variable. For these inequalities, all real numbers are solutions.

Some inequalities are false no matter what value is substituted for the variable. These inequalities have no solutions.

If both sides of an inequality are fully simplified and the same variable term appears on both sides, then the inequality has all real numbers as solutions or it has no solutions. Look at the other terms in the inequality to decide which is the case.

EXAMPLE 4 **All Real Numbers as Solutions or No Solutions**

Solve each inequality.

A $x + 5 \geq x + 3$

$$x + 5 \geq x + 3$$

The same variable term (x) appears on both sides. Look at the other terms.

For any number x, adding 5 will always result in a greater number than adding 3.

All values of x make the inequality true.
All real numbers are solutions.

B $2(x + 3) < 5 + 2x$

$$2x + 6 < 5 + 2x \qquad \textit{Distribute 2 on the left side.}$$

The same variable term ($2x$) appears on both sides. Look at the other terms.

For any number $2x$, adding 6 will never result in a lesser number than adding 5.

No values of x make the inequality true.
There are no solutions.

CHECK IT OUT! Solve each inequality.

4a. $4(y - 1) \geq 4y + 2$ **4b.** $x - 2 < x + 1$

THINK AND DISCUSS

1. Explain how you would collect the variable terms to solve the inequality $5c - 4 > 8c + 2$.

2. GET ORGANIZED Copy and complete the graphic organizer. In each box, give an example of an inequality of the indicated type.

Solutions of Inequalities with Variables on Both Sides

All real numbers | No solutions

3-5

Exercises

go.hrw.com
Homework Help Online
KEYWORD: MA7 3-5
Parent Resources Online
KEYWORD: MA7 Parent

GUIDED PRACTICE

SEE EXAMPLE 1
p. 196

Solve each inequality and graph the solutions.

1. $2x > 4x - 6$

2. $7y + 1 \le y - 5$

3. $27x + 33 > 58x - 29$

4. $-3r < 10 - r$

5. $5c - 4 > 8c + 2$

6. $4.5x - 3.8 \ge 1.5x - 2.3$

SEE EXAMPLE 2
p. 197

7. School The school band will sell pizzas to raise money for new uniforms. The supplier charges $100 plus $4 per pizza. If the band members sell the pizzas for $7 each, how many pizzas will they have to sell to make a profit?

SEE EXAMPLE 3
p. 197

Solve each inequality and graph the solutions.

8. $5(4 + x) \le 3(2 + x)$

9. $-4(3 - p) > 5(p + 1)$

10. $2(6 - x) < 4x$

11. $4x > 3(7 - x)$

12. $\frac{1}{2}f + \frac{3}{4} \ge \frac{1}{4}f$

13. $-36.72 + 5.65t < 0.25t$

SEE EXAMPLE 4
p. 198

Solve each inequality.

14. $2(x - 2) \le -2(1 - x)$

15. $4(y + 1) < 4y + 2$

16. $4v + 1 < 4v - 7$

17. $b - 4 \ge b - 6$

18. $3(x - 5) > 3x$

19. $2k + 7 \ge 2(k + 14)$

PRACTICE AND PROBLEM SOLVING

Solve each inequality and graph the solutions.

20. $3x \le 5x + 8$

21. $9y + 3 > 4y - 7$

22. $1.5x - 1.2 < 3.1x - 2.8$

23. $7 + 4b \ge 3b$

24. $7 - 5t < 4t - 2$

25. $2.8m - 5.2 > 0.8m + 4.8$

26. Geometry For what values of x is the area of the rectangle greater than the area of the triangle?

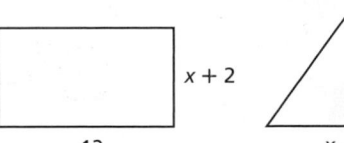

Solve each inequality and graph the solutions.

Independent Practice

For Exercises	See Example
20–25	1
26	2
27–32	3
33–38	4

Extra Practice

Skills Practice p. S9

Application Practice p. S30

27. $4(2 - x) \le 5(x - 2)$ **28.** $-3(n + 4) < 6(1 - n)$ **29.** $9(w + 2) \le 12w$

30. $4.5 + 1.3t > 3.8t - 3$ **31.** $\frac{1}{2}r + \frac{2}{3} \ge \frac{1}{3}r$ **32.** $2(4 - n) < 3n - 7$

Solve each inequality.

33. $3(2 - x) < -3(x - 1)$ **34.** $7 - y > 5 - y$ **35.** $3(10 + z) \le 3z + 36$

36. $-5(k - 1) \ge 5(2 - k)$ **37.** $4(x - 1) \le 4x$ **38.** $3(v - 9) \ge 15 + 3v$

Solve each inequality and graph the solutions.

39. $3t - 12 > 5t + 2$ **40.** $-5(y + 3) - 6 < y + 3$

41. $3x + 9 - 5x < x$ **42.** $18 + 9p > 12p - 31$

43. $2(x - 5) < -3x$ **44.** $-\frac{2}{5}x \le \frac{4}{5} - \frac{3}{5}x$

45. $-2(x - 7) - 4 - x < 8x + 32$ **46.** $-3(2r - 4) \ge 2(5 - 3r)$

47. $-7x - 10 + 5x \ge 3(x + 4) + 8$ **48.** $-\frac{1}{3}(n + 8) + \frac{1}{3}n \le 1 - n$

Recreation

49. **Recreation** A red kite is 100 feet off the ground and is rising at 8 feet per second. A blue kite is 180 feet off the ground and is rising at 5 feet per second. How long will it take for the red kite to be higher than the blue kite? Round your answer to the nearest second.

50. **Education** The table shows the enrollment in Howard High School and Phillips High School for three school years.

School Enrollment			
	Year 1	Year 2	Year 3
Howard High School	1192	1188	1184
Phillips High School	921	941	961

    a. How much did the enrollment change each year at Howard?

    b. Use the enrollment in year 1 and your answer from part **a** to write an expression for the enrollment at Howard in any year x.

    c. How much did the enrollment change each year at Phillips?

    d. Use the enrollment in year 1 and your answer from part **c** to write an expression for the enrollment at Phillips in any year x.

    e. Assume that the pattern in the table continues. Use your expressions from parts **b** and **d** to write an inequality that can be solved to find the year in which the enrollment at Phillips High School will be greater than the enrollment at Howard High School. Solve your inequality and graph the solutions.

The American Kitefliers Association has over 4000 members in 35 countries. Kitefliers participate in festivals, competitions, and kite-making workshops.

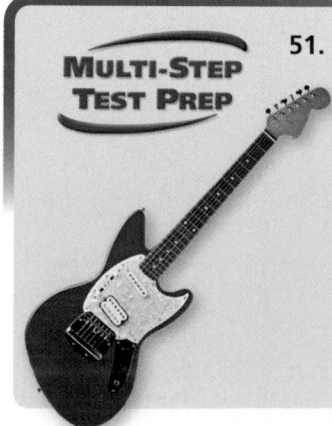

MULTI-STEP TEST PREP

51. This problem will prepare you for the Multi-Step Test Prep on page 218.

    a. The school orchestra is creating a CD of their last concert. The total cost is $400 + 4.50$ per CD. Write an expression for the cost of creating the CDs based on the number of CDs n.

    b. The orchestra plans to sell the CDs for $12. Write an expression for the amount the orchestra earns from the sale of n CDs.

    c. In order for the orchestra to make a profit, the amount they make selling the CDs must be greater than the cost of creating the CDs. Write an inequality that can be solved to find the number of CDs the orchestra must sell in order to make a profit. Solve your inequality.

Write an inequality to represent each relationship. Solve your inequality.

52. Four more than twice a number is greater than two-thirds of the number.

53. Ten less than five times a number is less than six times the number decreased by eight.

54. The sum of a number and twenty is less than four times the number decreased by one.

55. Three-fourths of a number is greater than or equal to five less than the number.

56. Entertainment Use the table to determine how many movies you would have to rent for Video View to be less expensive than Movie Place.

	Membership Fee ($)	Cost per Rental ($)
Movie Place	None	2.99
Video View	19.99	1.99

57. Geometry In an acute triangle, all angles measure less than 90°. Also, the sum of the measures of any two angles is greater than the measure of the third angle. Can the measures of an acute triangle be x, $x - 1$, and $2x$? Explain.

58. Write About It Compare the steps you would follow to solve an inequality to the steps you would follow to solve an equation.

59. Critical Thinking How can you tell just by looking at the inequality $x > x + 1$ that it has no solutions?

60. ///ERROR ANALYSIS/// Two students solved the inequality $5x < 3 - 4x$. Which is incorrect? Explain the error.

61. If $a - b > a + b$, which statement is true?

  A The value of a is positive.

  B The value of b is positive.

  C The value of a is negative.

  D The value of b is negative.

62. If $-a < b$, which statement is always true?

  F $a < b$ **G** $a > b$ **H** $a < -b$ **J** $a > -b$

63. Which is a solution of the inequality $7(2 - x) > 4(x - 2)$?

  A -2 **B** 2 **C** 4 **D** 7

64. Which is the graph of $-5x < -2x - 6$?

  F ... $-5 -4 -3 -2 -1\ 0\ 1\ 2\ 3\ 4\ 5$

  H ... $-5 -4 -3 -2 -1\ 0\ 1\ 2\ 3\ 4\ 5$

  G ... $-5 -4 -3 -2 -1\ 0\ 1\ 2\ 3\ 4\ 5$

  J ... $-5 -4 -3 -2 -1\ 0\ 1\ 2\ 3\ 4\ 5$

65. Short Response Write a real-world situation that could be modeled by the inequality $7x + 4 > 4x + 13$. Explain how the inequality relates to your situation.

CHALLENGE AND EXTEND

Solve each inequality.

66. $2\frac{1}{2} + 2x \geq 5\frac{1}{2} + 2\frac{1}{2}x$

67. $1.6x - 20.7 > 6.3x - (-2.2x)$

68. $1.3x - 7.5x < 8.5x - 29.4$

69. $-4w + \dfrac{-8 - 37}{9} \leq \dfrac{75 - 3}{9} + 3w$

70. Replace the square and circle with numbers so that the inequality has all real numbers as solutions. $\square - 2x < \bigcirc - 2x$

71. Replace the square and circle with numbers so that the inequality has no solutions. $\square - 2x < \bigcirc - 2x$

72. Critical Thinking Explain whether there are any numbers that can replace the square and circle so that the inequality has all real numbers as solutions. $\square + 2x < \bigcirc + x$

SPIRAL REVIEW

73. The ratio of the width of a rectangle to the length is $2:5$. The length is 65 inches. Find the width. *(Lesson 2-7)*

74. Find the simple interest paid after 6 months on a loan of $5000 borrowed at a rate of 9%. *(Lesson 2-10)*

Define a variable and write an inequality for each situation. Graph the solutions. *(Lesson 3-1)*

75. Participants must be at least 14 years old.

76. The maximum speed on a certain highway is 60 miles per hour.

Career Path

go.hrw.com
Career Resources Online
KEYWORD: MA7 Career

Katie Flannigan
Culinary Arts program

Q: What math classes did you take in high school?
A: Algebra 1, Geometry, and Algebra 2

Q: What math classes have you taken since high school?
A: I have taken a basic accounting class and a business math class.

Q: How do you use math?
A: I use math to estimate how much food I need to buy. I also use math when adjusting recipe amounts to feed large groups of people.

Q: What are your future plans?
A: I plan to start my own catering business. The math classes I took will help me manage the financial aspects of my business.

3-6 Algebra LAB

Truth Tables and Compound Statements

A compound statement is formed by combining two or more simple statements. A compound statement is either true or false depending on whether its simple statements are true or false.

Use with Lesson 3-6

Activity 1

• Let *P* be "Cindy is at least 17 years old."   • Let *Q* be "Cindy has a driver's license."

If...	then *P* is	and *Q* is	so *P* AND *Q* is
Cindy is 18 years old. Cindy has a driver's license.	True	True	True
Cindy is 17 years old. Cindy does not have a driver's license.	True	False	False
Cindy is 16 years old. Cindy has a driver's license.	False	True	False
Cindy is 15 years old. Cindy does not have a driver's license.	False	False	False

P **AND** *Q* is true when _____?_____.

Try This

For each pair of simple statements, tell whether *P* AND *Q* is true or false.

1. *P:* Many birds can fly; *Q:* A zebra is an animal.

Activity 2

• Let *P* be "Paul plays tennis."   • Let *Q* be "Paul has brown eyes."

If...	then *P* is	and *Q* is	so *P* OR *Q* is
Paul plays tennis. Paul has brown eyes.	True	True	True
Paul plays tennis. Paul has green eyes.	True	False	True
Paul does not play tennis. Paul has brown eyes.	False	True	True
Paul does not play tennis. Paul has green eyes.	False	False	False

P **OR** *Q* is true when _____?_____.

Try This

For each pair of simple statements, tell whether *P* OR *Q* is true or false.

2. *P:* The number 12 is even; *Q:* The number 12 is a composite number.

3-6 Solving Compound Inequalities

Objectives
Solve compound inequalities in one variable.

Graph solution sets of compound inequalities in one variable.

Vocabulary
compound inequality
intersection
union

Who uses this?
A lifeguard can use compound inequalities to describe the safe pH levels in a swimming pool. (See Example 1.)

The inequalities you have seen so far are simple inequalities. When two simple inequalities are combined into one statement by the words AND or OR, the result is called a **compound inequality**.

Know it! Note

Compound Inequalities

WORDS	ALGEBRA	GRAPH
All real numbers greater than 2 AND less than 6	$x > 2$ AND $x < 6$ $2 < x < 6$	
All real numbers greater than or equal to 2 AND less than or equal to 6	$x \geq 2$ AND $x \leq 6$ $2 \leq x \leq 6$	
All real numbers less than 2 OR greater than 6	$x < 2$ OR $x > 6$	
All real numbers less than or equal to 2 OR greater than or equal to 6	$x \leq 2$ OR $x \geq 6$	

EXAMPLE 1 Chemistry Application

A water analyst recommends that the pH level of swimming pool water be between 7.2 and 7.6 inclusive. Write a compound inequality to show the pH levels that are within the recommended range. Graph the solutions.

Let p be the pH level of swimming pool water.

Helpful Hint

The phrase "between 7.2 and 7.6 *inclusive*" means that the numbers 7.2 and 7.6 are included in the solutions. Use a solid circle for endpoints that are solutions.

7.2	is less than or equal to	pH level	is less than or equal to	7.6
7.2	$\leq$	p	$\leq$	7.6

$7.2 \leq p \leq 7.6$

1. The free chlorine level in a pool should be between 1.0 and 3.0 parts per million inclusive. Write a compound inequality to show the levels that are within this range. Graph the solutions.

In this diagram, oval *A* represents some integer solutions of $x < 10$, and oval *B* represents some integer solutions of $x > 0$. The overlapping region represents numbers that belong in both ovals. Those numbers are solutions of *both* $x < 10$ *and* $x > 0$.

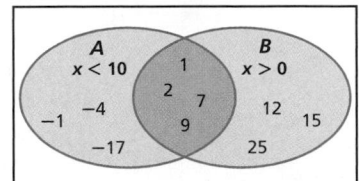

You can graph the solutions of a compound inequality involving AND by using the idea of an overlapping region. The overlapping region is called the **intersection** and shows the numbers that are solutions of both inequalities.

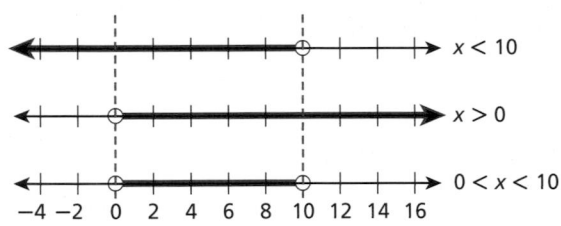

EXAMPLE 2 **Solving Compound Inequalities Involving AND**

Solve each compound inequality and graph the solutions.

A $4 \le x + 2 \le 8$

$$4 \le x + 2 \quad \text{AND} \quad x + 2 \le 8 \qquad \textit{Write the compound inequality using AND.}$$
$$\underline{-2 \qquad -2} \qquad \qquad \underline{-2 \quad -2} \qquad \textit{Solve each simple inequality.}$$
$$2 \le x \qquad \text{AND} \quad x \qquad \le 6$$

Graph $2 \le x$.

Graph $x \le 6$.

Graph the intersection by finding where the two graphs overlap.

Remember!

The statement $-5 \le 2x + 3 \le 9$ consists of two inequalities connected by AND. Example 2B shows a "shorthand" method for solving this type of inequality.

B $-5 \le 2x + 3 < 9$

$$-5 \le 2x + 3 < 9 \qquad \textit{Since 3 is added to 2x, subtract 3 from each part}$$
$$\underline{-3 \qquad -3 \quad -3} \qquad \textit{of the inequality.}$$
$$-8 \le 2x \qquad < 6$$

$$\frac{-8}{2} \le \frac{2x}{2} < \frac{6}{2} \qquad \textit{Since x is multiplied by 2, divide each part of the}$$
$$-4 \le x < 3 \qquad \textit{inequality by 2.}$$

Graph $-4 \le x$.

Graph $x < 3$.

Graph the intersection by finding where the two graphs overlap.

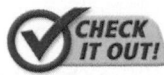

Solve each compound inequality and graph the solutions.

2a. $-9 < x - 10 < -5$ **2b.** $-4 \le 3n + 5 < 11$

In this diagram, circle A represents some integer solutions of $x < 0$, and circle B represents some integer solutions of $x > 10$. The combined shaded regions represent numbers that are solutions of *either* $x < 0$ *or* $x > 10$.

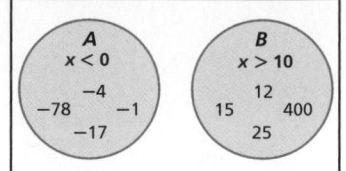

You can graph the solutions of a compound inequality involving OR by using the idea of combining regions. The combined regions are called the **union** and show the numbers that are solutions of either inequality.

EXAMPLE 3 **Solving Compound Inequalities Involving OR**

Solve each compound inequality and graph the solutions.

A $-4 + a > 1$ OR $-4 + a < -3$

$$-4 + a > \;\;\;1 \text{ OR } -4 + a < -3$$
$$\underline{+4 \qquad\quad +4 \quad\; +4 \qquad\quad +4} \qquad \textit{Solve each simple inequality.}$$
$$a > \;\;\;5 \text{ OR} \qquad a < \;\;1$$

Graph $a > 5$.

Graph $a < 1$.

Graph the union by combining the regions.

B $2x \le 6$ OR $3x > 12$

$$2x \le 6 \text{ OR } 3x > 12$$
$$\frac{2x}{2} \le \frac{6}{2} \qquad \frac{3x}{3} > \frac{12}{3} \qquad \textit{Solve each simple inequality.}$$
$$x \le 3 \text{ OR} \quad x > \;\;4$$

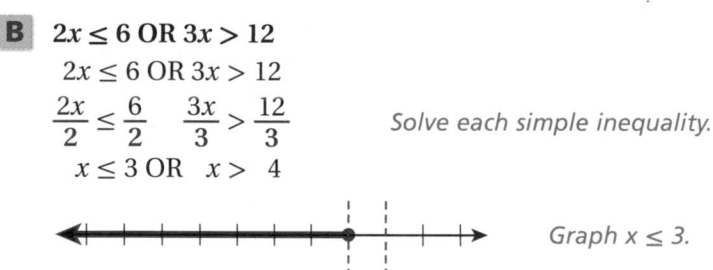

Graph $x \le 3$.

Graph $x > 4$.

Graph the union by combining the regions.

 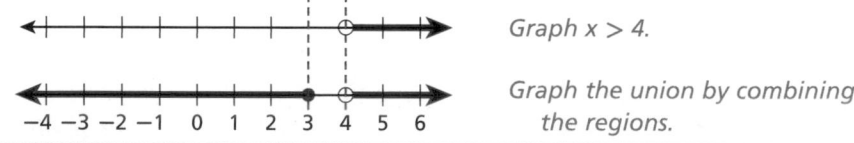 Solve each compound inequality and graph the solutions.

3a. $2 + r < 12$ OR $r + 5 > 19$

3b. $7x \ge 21$ OR $2x < -2$

Every solution of a compound inequality involving AND must be a solution of both parts of the compound inequality. If no numbers are solutions of *both* simple inequalities, then the compound inequality has no solutions.

The solutions of a compound inequality involving OR are not always two separate sets of numbers. There may be numbers that are solutions of both parts of the compound inequality.

EXAMPLE **4** **Writing a Compound Inequality from a Graph**

Write the compound inequality shown by each graph.

A

The shaded portion of the graph is not between two values, so the compound inequality involves OR.

> On the left, the graph shows an arrow pointing left, so use either < or ≤. The solid circle at −1 means −1 is a solution, so use ≤.

$x \le -1$

> On the right, the graph shows an arrow pointing right, so use either > or ≥. The solid circle at 7 means 7 is a solution, so use ≥.

$x \ge 7$

The compound inequality is $x \le -1$ OR $x \ge 7$.

B

The shaded portion of the graph is between the values 0 and 6, so the compound inequality involves AND.

> The shaded values are to the right of 0, so use > or ≥. The solid circle at 0 means 0 is a solution, so use ≥.

$x \ge 0$

> The shaded values are to the left of 6, so use < or ≤. The empty circle at 6 means 6 is not a solution, so use <.

$x < 6$

The compound inequality is $x \ge 0$ AND $x < 6$.

Writing Math

The compound inequality in Example 4B can also be written with the variable between the two endpoints.
$0 \le x < 6$

✓ **CHECK IT OUT!**

Write the compound inequality shown by the graph.

4a.

4b.

THINK AND DISCUSS

1. Describe how to write the compound inequality $y > 4$ AND $y \le 12$ without using the joining word AND.

2. GET ORGANIZED Copy and complete the graphic organizers. Write three solutions in each of the three sections of the diagram. Then write each of your nine solutions in the appropriate column or columns of the table.

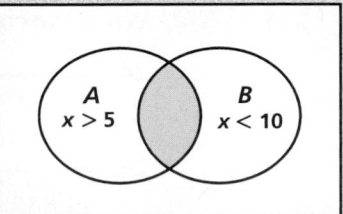

$x > 5$ AND $x < 10$	$x > 5$ OR $x < 10$

3-6

Exercises

go.hrw.com
Homework Help Online
KEYWORD: MA7 3-6
Parent Resources Online
KEYWORD: MA7 Parent

GUIDED PRACTICE

1. **Vocabulary** The graph of a(n) ___?___ shows all values that are solutions to both simple inequalities that make a compound inequality. (*union* or *intersection*)

SEE EXAMPLE **1**
p. 204

2. **Biology** An iguana needs to live in a warm environment. The temperature in a pet iguana's cage should be between 70 °F and 95 °F inclusive. Write a compound inequality to show the temperatures that are within the recommended range. Graph the solutions.

Solve each compound inequality and graph the solutions.

SEE EXAMPLE **2**
p. 205

3. $-3 < x + 2 < 7$

4. $5 \le 4x + 1 \le 13$

5. $2 < x + 2 < 5$

6. $11 < 2x + 3 < 21$

SEE EXAMPLE **3**
p. 206

7. $x + 2 < -6 \text{ OR } x + 2 > 6$

8. $r - 1 < 0 \text{ OR } r - 1 > 4$

9. $n + 2 < 3 \text{ OR } n + 3 > 7$

10. $x - 1 < -1 \text{ OR } x - 5 > -1$

SEE EXAMPLE **4**
p. 207

Write the compound inequality shown by each graph.

11.

12.

13.

14.

PRACTICE AND PROBLEM SOLVING

Independent Practice

For Exercises	See Example
15	1
16–19	2
20–23	3
24–27	4

Extra Practice

Skills Practice p. S9

Application Practice p. S30

15. **Meteorology** One layer of Earth's atmosphere is called the stratosphere. At one point above Earth's surface the stratosphere extends from an altitude of 16 km to an altitude of 50 km. Write a compound inequality to show the altitudes that are within the range of the stratosphere. Graph the solutions.

Solve each compound inequality and graph the solutions.

16. $-1 < x + 1 < 1$

17. $1 \le 2n - 5 \le 7$

18. $-2 < x - 2 < 2$

19. $5 < 3x - 1 < 17$

20. $x - 4 < -7 \text{ OR } x + 3 > 4$

21. $2x + 1 < 1 \text{ OR } x + 5 > 8$

22. $x + 1 < 2 \text{ OR } x + 5 > 8$

23. $x + 3 < 0 \text{ OR } x - 2 > 0$

Write the compound inequality shown by each graph.

24.

25.

26.

27.

28. **Music** A typical acoustic guitar has a range of three octaves. When the guitar is tuned to "concert pitch," the range of frequencies for those three octaves is between 82.4 Hz and 659.2 Hz inclusive. Write a compound inequality to show the frequencies that are within the range of a typical acoustic guitar. Graph the solutions.

MULTI-STEP TEST PREP

29. This problem will prepare you for the Multi-Step Test Prep on page 218.

Jenna's band is going to record a CD at a recording studio. They will pay $225 to use the studio for one day and $80 per hour for sound technicians. Jenna has $200 and can reasonably expect to raise up to an additional $350 by taking pre-orders for the CDs.

a. Explain how the inequality $200 \leq 225 + 80n \leq 550$ can be used to find the number of hours Jenna and her band can afford to use the studio and sound technicians.

b. Solve the inequality. Are there any numbers in the solution set that are not reasonable in this situation?

c. Suppose Jenna raises $350 in pre-orders. How much more money would she need to raise if she wanted to use the studio and sound technicians for 6 hours?

Write and graph a compound inequality for the numbers described.

30. all real numbers between −6 and 6

31. all real numbers less than or equal to 2 and greater than or equal to 1

32. all real numbers greater than 0 and less than 15

33. all real numbers between −10 and 10 inclusive

Chemistry

34. **Transportation** The cruise-control function on Georgina's car should keep the speed of the car within 3 mi/h of the set speed. Write a compound inequality to show the acceptable speeds s if the set speed is 55 mi/h. Graph the solutions.

35. **Chemistry** Water is not a liquid if its temperature is above 100 °C or below 0 °C. Write a compound inequality for the temperatures t when water is not a liquid.

Solve each compound inequality and graph the solutions.

The element gallium is in a solid state at room temperature but becomes a liquid at about 30 °C. Gallium stays in a liquid state until it reaches a temperature of about 2204 °C.

36. $5 \leq 4b - 3 \leq 9$

37. $-3 < x - 1 < 4$

38. $r + 2 < -2$ OR $r - 2 > 2$

39. $2a - 5 < -5$ OR $3a - 2 > 1$

40. $x - 4 \geq 5$ AND $x - 4 \leq 5$

41. $n - 4 < -2$ OR $n + 1 > 6$

42. **Sports** The ball used in a soccer game may not weigh more than 16 ounces or less than 14 ounces at the start of the match. After $1\frac{1}{2}$ ounces of air was added to a ball, the ball was approved for use in a game. Write and solve a compound inequality to show how much the ball might have weighed before the air was added.

43. **Meteorology** Tornado damage is rated using the Fujita scale shown in the table. A tornado has a wind speed of 200 miles per hour. Write and solve a compound inequality to show how many miles per hour the wind speed would need to increase for the tornado to be rated "devastating" but not "incredible."

Fujita Tornado Scale		
Category	Type	Wind Speed (mi/h)
F0	Weak	40 to 72
F1	Moderate	73 to 112
F2	Significant	113 to 157
F3	Severe	158 to 206
F4	Devastating	207 to 260
F5	Incredible	261 to 318

44. Give a real-world situation that can be described by a compound inequality. Write the inequality that describes your situation.

45. **Write About It** How are the graphs of the compound inequality $x < 3$ AND $x < 7$ and the compound inequality $x < 3$ OR $x < 7$ different? How are the graphs alike? Explain.

46. Critical Thinking If there is no solution to a compound inequality, does the compound inequality involve OR or AND? Explain.

47. Which of the following describes the solutions of $-x + 1 > 2$ OR $x - 1 > 2$?

  (A) all real numbers greater than 1 or less than 3

  (B) all real numbers greater than 3 or less than 1

  (C) all real numbers greater than -1 or less than 3

  (D) all real numbers greater than 3 or less than -1

48. Which of the following is a graph of the solutions of $x - 3 < 2$ AND $x + 3 > 2$?

  (F)   (H)

  (G)   (J)

49. Which compound inequality is shown by the graph?

  (A) $x \leq 2$ OR $x > 5$ (C) $x \leq 2$ OR $x \geq 5$

  (B) $x < 2$ OR $x \geq 5$ (D) $x \geq 2$ OR $x > 5$

50. Which of the following is a solution of $x + 1 \geq 3$ AND $x + 1 \leq 3$?

  (F) 0   (G) 1   (H) 2   (J) 3

CHALLENGE AND EXTEND

Solve and graph each compound inequality.

51. $2c - 10 < 5 - 3c < 7c$

52. $5p - 10 < p + 6 < 3p$

53. $2s \leq 18 - s$ OR $5s \geq s + 36$

54. $9 - x \geq 5x$ OR $20 - 3x \leq 17$

55. Write a compound inequality that represents all values of x that are NOT solutions to $x < -1$ OR $x > 3$.

56. For the compound inequality $x + 2 \geq a$ AND $x - 7 \leq b$, find values of a and b for which the only solution is $x = 1$.

SPIRAL REVIEW

Simplify each expression. Justify each step. *(Lesson 1-7)*

57. $4(x - 3) + 7$

58. $5x - 4y - x + 3y$

59. $6a - 3(a - 1)$

Generate ordered pairs for each function for $x = -2, -1, 0, 1,$ and 2. Graph the ordered pairs and describe the pattern. *(Lesson 1-8)*

60. $y = -2x + 2$

61. $y = x^2 - 1$

62. $y = x^2 + (-2)$

Solve each inequality and graph the solutions. *(Lesson 3-4)*

63. $3m - 5 < 1$

64. $2(x + 4) > 6$

65. $11 \leq 7 - 2x$

Connecting Algebra to Geometry

Triangle Inequality

For any triangle, the sum of the lengths of any two sides is greater than the length of the third side.

The sides of this triangle are labeled a, b, and c. You can use the Triangle Inequality to write three statements about the triangle.

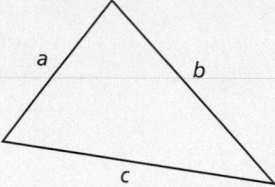

$$a + b > c \qquad a + c > b \qquad b + c > a$$

Unless all three of the inequalities are true, the lengths a, b, and c cannot form a triangle.

Example 1

Can three side lengths of 25 cm, 15 cm, and 5 cm form a triangle?

a. $25 + 15 > 5$
$40 > 5$ *True*

b. $25 + 5 > 15$
$30 > 15$ *True*

c. $15 + 5 > 25$
$20 > 25$ *False*

One of the inequalities is false, so the three lengths will not make a triangle. The situation is shown in the figure to the right.

Example 2

Two sides of a triangle measure 8 ft and 10 ft. What is the range of lengths of the third side?

Start by writing three statements about the triangle. Use x for the unknown side length.

a. $8 + 10 > x$
$18 > x$

The third side must be shorter than 18 ft.

b. $8 + x > 10$
$8 + x - 8 > 10 - 8$
$x > 2$

The third side must be longer than 2 ft.

c. $x + 10 > 8$
$x + 10 - 10 > 8 - 10$
$x > -2$

This provides no new useful information.

From part **a,** the third side must be shorter than 18 ft. And from part **b,** it must be longer than 2 ft. An inequality showing this is $2 < x < 18$.

Try This

Decide whether the three lengths given can form a triangle. If not, explain.

1. 14 ft, 30 ft, 10 ft

2. 11 cm, 8 cm, 17 cm

3. $6\frac{1}{2}$ yd, 3 yd, $2\frac{3}{4}$ yd

Write a compound inequality for the range of lengths of the third side of each triangle.

4.

5.

6.

3-7 Solving Absolute-Value Inequalities

Objective
Solve inequalities in one variable involving absolute-value expressions.

Why learn this?
You can solve an absolute-value inequality to determine the safe range for the pressure of a fire extinguisher. (See Example 3.)

When an inequality contains an absolute-value expression, it can be rewritten as a compound inequality. The inequality $|x| < 5$ describes all real numbers whose distance from 0 is less than 5 units. The solutions are all numbers between -5 and 5, so $|x| < 5$ can be rewritten as $-5 < x < 5$ or as $x > -5$ AND $x < 5$.

Absolute-Value Inequalities Involving <

WORDS	NUMBERS
The inequality $|x| < a$ (when $a > 0$) asks, "What values of x have an absolute value less than a?" The solutions are numbers between $-a$ and a.	$|x| < 5$ $-5 < x < 5$ $x > -5$ AND $x < 5$

GRAPH	ALGEBRA
	$|x| < a$ (when $a > 0$) $-a < x < a$ $x > -a$ AND $x < a$

The same properties are true for inequalities that use the symbol $\leq$.

EXAMPLE 1 Solving Absolute-Value Inequalities Involving <

Solve each inequality and graph the solutions.

A $|x| + 3 < 12$

$$|x| + 3 < 12$$
$$\underline{ -3 \quad -3}$$
$$|x| \quad < \quad 9$$

Since 3 is added to $|x|$, subtract 3 from both sides to undo the addition.

$x > -9$ AND $x < 9$ *Write as a compound inequality.*

Helpful Hint

Just as you do when solving absolute-value equations, you first isolate the absolute-value expression when solving absolute-value inequalities.

B $|x + 4| \leq 2$

$x + 4 \geq -2$ AND $x + 4 \leq 2$ *Write as a compound inequality.*
$$\underline{ -4 \quad -4} \qquad \underline{ -4 \quad -4}$$ *Solve each inequality.*
$x \qquad \geq -6$ AND $x \qquad \leq -2$ *Write as a compound inequality.*

CHECK IT OUT! Solve each inequality and graph the solutions.

1a. $2|x| \le 6$ **1b.** $|x + 3| - 4.5 \le 7.5$

The inequality $|x| > 5$ describes all real numbers whose distance from 0 is greater than 5 units. The solutions are all numbers less than -5 or greater than 5. The inequality $|x| > 5$ can be rewritten as the compound inequality $x < -5$ OR $x > 5$.

 Know it! Note

Absolute-Value Inequalities Involving >

WORDS	NUMBERS
The inequality $|x| > a$ (when $a > 0$) asks, "What values of x have an absolute value greater than a?" The solutions are numbers less than $-a$ or greater than a.	$|x| > 5$ $x < -5$ OR $x > 5$

GRAPH	ALGEBRA
	$|x| > a$ (when $a > 0$) $x < -a$ OR $x > a$

The same properties are true for inequalities that use the symbol $\ge$.

EXAMPLE **2** **Solving Absolute-Value Inequalities Involving >**

Solve each inequality and graph the solutions.

A $|x| - 20 > -13$

$$|x| - 20 > -13$$

$$\underline{+20 \qquad +20}$$

$$|x| \qquad > \quad 7$$ *Since 20 is subtracted from $|x|$, add 20 to both sides to undo the subtraction.*

$$x < -7 \text{ OR } x > 7$$ *Write as a compound inequality.*

|←—7 units —→|←—7 units —→|

$-10\ -8\ -6\ -4\ -2\ \ 0\ \ 2\ \ 4\ \ 6\ \ 8\ \ 10$

B $|x - 8| + 5 \ge 11$

$$|x - 8| + 5 \ge \quad 11$$

$$\underline{\qquad -5 \quad -5}$$

$$|x - 8| \quad \ge \quad 6$$ *Since 5 is added to $|x - 8|$, subtract 5 from both sides to undo the addition.*

$$x - 8 \le -6 \text{ OR } x - 8 \ge \quad 6$$ *Write as a compound inequality.*

$$\underline{+8 \quad +8 \qquad \quad +8 \quad +8}$$ *Solve each inequality.*

$$x \quad \le 2 \text{ OR } x \qquad \ge \ 14$$ *Write as a compound inequality.*

$-2\ \ 0\ \ 2\ \ 4\ \ 6\ \ 8\ \ 10\ 12\ 14\ 16\ 18$

 CHECK IT OUT! Solve each inequality and graph the solutions.

2a. $|x| + 10 \ge 12$ **2b.** $\left|x + 2\frac{1}{2}\right| + \frac{1}{2} \ge 4$

Safety Application

Some fire extinguishers contain pressurized water. The water pressure should be 162.5 psi (pounds per square inch), but it is acceptable for the pressure to differ from this value by at most 12.5 psi. Write and solve an absolute-value inequality to find the range of acceptable pressures. Graph the solutions.

Let p represent the actual water pressure of a fire extinguisher.

The difference between p and the ideal pressure	is at most	12.5 psi.
$\lvert p - 162.5 \rvert$	$\leq$	12.5

$\lvert p - 162.5 \rvert \leq 12.5$

$p - 162.5 \geq -12.5$ AND $p - 162.5 \leq 12.5$ *Solve the two inequalities.*

$\underline{+\,162.5 \quad +\,162.5} \qquad \underline{+\,162.5 \quad +\,162.5}$

$p \qquad \geq \qquad 150$ AND $p \qquad \leq \qquad 175$

140 145 150 155 160 165 170 175 180 185 190

The range of acceptable pressures is $150 \leq p \leq 175$.

CHECK IT OUT! **3.** A dry-chemical fire extinguisher should be pressurized to 125 psi, but it is acceptable for the pressure to differ from this value by at most 75 psi. Write and solve an absolute-value inequality to find the range of acceptable pressures. Graph the solutions.

When solving an absolute-value inequality, you may get a statement that is true for all values of the variable. In this case, all real numbers are solutions of the original inequality. If you get a false statement when solving an absolute-value inequality, the original inequality has no solutions.

E X A M P L E **4**

Special Cases of Absolute-Value Inequalities

Solve each inequality.

A $\lvert x - 6 \rvert + 7 > 2$

$\lvert x - 6 \rvert + 7 > 2$

$\underline{\qquad -7 \quad -7}$ *Subtract 7 from both sides.*

$\lvert x - 6 \rvert > -5$ *Absolute-value expressions are always nonnegative. Therefore, the statement is true for all values of x.*

All real numbers are solutions.

B $\lvert x + 12 \rvert - 5 \leq -6$

$\lvert x + 12 \rvert - 5 \leq -6$

$\underline{\qquad +5 \quad +5}$ *Add 5 to both sides.*

$\lvert x + 12 \rvert \leq -1$ *Absolute-value expressions are always nonnegative. Therefore, the statement is false for all values of x.*

The inequality has no solutions.

Remember!

An absolute value represents a distance, and distance cannot be less than 0.

CHECK IT OUT! Solve each inequality.

4a. $\lvert x \rvert - 9 \geq -11$ **4b.** $4\lvert x - 3.5 \rvert \leq -8$

THINK AND DISCUSS

1. Describe how the solutions of $7|x| \leq 21$ are different from the solutions of $7|x| < 21$.

2. GET ORGANIZED Copy and complete the graphic organizer. In each box, write an example of the indicated type of absolute-value inequality and then solve.

Absolute-Value Inequalities

AND   OR

3-7 Exercises

go.hrw.com
Homework Help Online
KEYWORD: MA11 3-7
Parent Resources Online
KEYWORD: MA7 Parent

GUIDED PRACTICE

Solve each inequality and graph the solutions.

SEE EXAMPLE 1
p. 212

1. $|x| - 5 \leq -2$

2. $|x + 1| - 7.8 < 6.2$

3. $|3x| + 2 < 8$

4. $4|x| \leq 20$

5. $|x - 5| + 1 < 2$

6. $\left|x + \dfrac{1}{2}\right| - \dfrac{1}{2} \leq 3\dfrac{1}{2}$

SEE EXAMPLE 2
p. 213

7. $|x| - 6 > 16$

8. $|x| + 2.9 > 8.6$

9. $2|x| \geq 8$

10. $|x + 2| > 7$

11. $|x - 3| + 2 \geq 4$

12. $|x + 5| - 4\dfrac{1}{2} \geq 7\dfrac{1}{2}$

SEE EXAMPLE 3
p. 214

13. Nutrition A nutritionist recommends that an adult male consume 55 grams of fat per day. It is acceptable for the fat intake to differ from this amount by at most 25 grams. Write and solve an absolute-value inequality to find the range of fat intake that is acceptable. Graph the solutions.

SEE EXAMPLE 4
p. 214

Solve each inequality.

14. $|x| + 8 \leq 2$

15. $|x + 3| < -5$

16. $|x + 4| \geq -8$

17. $|x - 5| + \dfrac{1}{3} > -1$

18. $|3x| + 7 > 2$

19. $|x - 7| + 3.5 \leq 2$

PRACTICE AND PROBLEM SOLVING

Independent Practice

For Exercises	See Example
20–25	1
26–31	2
32	3
33–38	4

Extra Practice
Skills Practice p. S9
Application Practice p. S30

Solve each inequality and graph the solutions.

20. $|x| + 6 \leq 10$

21. $|x - 3| < 1$

22. $|x - 2| - 8 \leq -3$

23. $|5x| < 15$

24. $|x - 2.4| + 4 \leq 6.4$

25. $4 + |x + 3| < 7$

26. $|x - 1| > 2$

27. $6|x| \geq 60$

28. $|x - 4| + 3 > 8$

29. $2|x + 2| \geq 16$

30. $3 + |x - 4| > 4$

31. $\left|x - \dfrac{1}{2}\right| + 9 > 10\dfrac{1}{2}$

32. The thermostat for a sauna is set to 175 °F, but the actual temperature of the sauna may vary by as much as 12 °F. Write and solve an absolute-value inequality to find the range of possible temperatures. Graph the solutions.

Solve each inequality.

33. $12 + |x| \leq 10$

34. $\left|x + \dfrac{3}{5}\right| - 2 > -4$

35. $|x + 1| + 5 \geq 4$

36. $|4x| - 3 < -6$

37. $3|x - 4| \leq -9$

38. $|2x| + 9 \geq 9$

Tell whether each statement is sometimes, always, or never true. Explain.

39. The value of $|x + 1|$ is greater than -5.

40. The value of $|x - 7|$ is less than 0.

41. An absolute-value inequality has all real numbers as solutions.

Write and solve an absolute-value inequality for each expression. Graph the solutions on a number line.

42. All numbers whose absolute value is less than or equal to 15

43. All numbers less than or equal to 3 units from 2 on the number line

44. All numbers at least 2 units from 8 on the number line

Write an absolute-value inequality for each graph.

45.

```
 ←+—+—+—●—+—+—+—+—●—+—+→
  -5 -4 -3 -2 -1  0  1  2  3  4  5
```

46.

```
 ←+—+—⊕—+—+—+—+—+—⊕—+—→
  -5 -4 -3 -2 -1  0  1  2  3  4  5
```

47.

```
            -6½                    6½
 ←—+—+—●—+—+—+—+—+—●—+—+—→
 -10 -8 -6 -4 -2  0  2  4  6  8  10
```

48.

```
       -7                          7
 ←+—+—⊖—+—+—+—+—+—+—⊖—+—+→
 -10 -8 -6 -4 -2  0  2  4  6  8  10
```

49. Multi-Step The frequency of a sound wave determines its pitch. The human ear can detect a wide range of frequencies, from 20 Hz (very low notes) to 20,000 Hz (very high notes).

   a. What frequency is at the middle of the range?

   b. Write an absolute-value inequality for the range of frequencies the human ear can detect.

50. Biology The diagram shows the temperature range at which several fish species can survive. For each species, write an absolute-value inequality that gives the range of temperatures at which it can survive.

Temperature Range of Fish

Sea Bass
Rainbow Trout
European Eel
Fish
Water Temperature (°C)
0 4 8 12 16 20 24 28 32 34 36

51. Entertainment On a game show, a contestant must guess a secret two-digit number. The secret number is 23. Write an absolute-value inequality that shows that the contestant's guess is more than 12 numbers away from the secret number.

MULTI-STEP TEST PREP

52. This problem will help prepare you for the Multi-Step Test Prep on page 218.

The manager of a band recommends that the band sell its CDs for $8.75. The band decides to sell the CDs for p dollars.

   a. Write an absolute-value expression that tells how far the band's price is from the recommended price.

   b. The band wants the price of its CD to be no more than $1.25 from the recommended price. Write an absolute-value inequality that gives the range of possible prices for the CD.

   c. Solve the inequality. Write the solution as a compound inequality.

53. **Critical Thinking** For which values of k does the inequality $|x| + 1 < k$ have no solutions? Explain.

54. **Write About It** Describe how to use an absolute-value inequality to find all the values on a number line that are within 5 units of -6.

55. What is the solution of the inequality $3 + |x + 4| < 6$?

    (A) $-13 < x < 5$ (C) $-6 < x < -2$

    (B) $-7 < x < -1$ (D) $1 < x < 7$

56. A thermometer gives temperature readings that may be inaccurate by at most 2 °F. The actual temperature is 75 °F. Which absolute-value inequality describes the range of temperatures that may be shown on the thermometer?

    (F) $|x - 75| \leq 2$ (G) $|x + 75| \leq 2$ (H) $|x - 75| \geq 2$ (J) $|x + 75| \geq 2$

57. The inequality $|w - 156| \leq 3$ describes the weights of members of a wrestling team. Which statement is NOT true?

    (A) All of the team members weigh no more than 159 pounds.

    (B) A team member may weigh 152 pounds.

    (C) Every member of the team is at most 3 pounds away from 156 pounds.

    (D) There are no team members who weigh 160 pounds.

CHALLENGE AND EXTEND

Write an absolute-value inequality for each graph.

58.

59.

60. **Critical Thinking** Fill in the missing reasons to justify each step in solving $|2x - 6| + 5 \leq 7$.

	Statements	Reasons
1.	$\|2x - 6\| + 5 \leq 7$	Given
2.	$\|2x - 6\| \leq 2$	?
3.	$2x - 6 \geq -2$ AND $2x - 6 \leq 2$	Definition of absolute value
4.	$2x \geq 4$ AND $2x \leq 8$	?
5.	$x \geq 2$ AND $x \leq 4$	?

SPIRAL REVIEW

Solve each proportion. Check your answer. *(Lesson 2-7)*

61. $\dfrac{x+1}{4} = \dfrac{5}{8}$ 62. $\dfrac{2}{15} = \dfrac{6}{y-5}$ 63. $\dfrac{12}{m+2} = \dfrac{8}{3}$ 64. $\dfrac{7+g}{10} = \dfrac{6}{8}$

Describe the solutions of each inequality in words. *(Lesson 3-1)*

65. $16 > 8m$ 66. $c + 4 < 11$ 67. $-4 \leq x + 2$ 68. $0 \geq x + 7$

Solve each compound inequality and graph the solutions. *(Lesson 3-6)*

69. $-3 < x - 3 < 1$ 70. $-3 \leq 2x + 1 \leq 9$

71. $x - 2 < -1$ OR $x - 2 > 2$ 72. $x + 4 \leq 3$ OR $x + 4 \geq 6$

MULTI-STEP TEST PREP

Multi-Step and Compound Inequalities

Guitar Picks Cullen and his band are interested in recording a CD of their music. The recording studio charges $450 to record the music and then charges $5 for each CD. The band is required to spend at least $1000 for the total of the recording and CD charges.

1. Write an equation for the cost c of the CDs based on the number of CDs n.

2. Write an inequality that can be used to determine the minimum number of CDs that must be burned at this studio to meet the $1000 total.

3. Solve your inequality from Problem 2.

4. The band orders the minimum number of CDs found in Problem 3. They want to sell the CDs and make at least as much money as they spent for the recording studio and making the CDs. Write an inequality that can be solved to determine the minimum amount the band should charge for their CDs.

5. Solve your inequality from Problem 4.

6. If the band has 30 more CDs made than the minimum number found in Problem 3 and charges the minimum price found in Problem 5, will they make a profit? If so, how much profit will the band make?

READY TO GO ON?

Quiz for Lessons 3-4 Through 3-7

3-4 Solving Two-Step and Multi-Step Inequalities

Solve each inequality and graph the solutions.

1. $2x + 3 < 9$

2. $3t - 2 > 10$

3. $7 \geq 1 - 6r$

Solve each inequality.

4. $2(x - 3) > -1$

5. $\frac{1}{3}a + \frac{1}{2} > \frac{2}{3}$

6. $15 < 5(m - 7)$

7. $2 + (-6) > 0.8p$

8. The average of Mindy's two test scores must be at least 92 to make an A in the class. Mindy got an 88 on her first test. What scores can she get on her second test to make an A in the class?

3-5 Solving Inequalities with Variables on Both Sides

Solve each inequality and graph the solutions.

9. $5x < 3x + 8$

10. $6p - 3 > 9p$

11. $r - 8 \geq 3r - 12$

Solve each inequality.

12. $3(y + 6) > 2(y + 4)$

13. $4(5 - g) \geq g$

14. $4x < 4(x - 1)$

15. $3(1 - x) \geq -3(x + 2)$

16. Phillip has \$100 in the bank and deposits \$18 per month. Gil has \$145 in the bank and deposits \$15 per month. For how many months will Gil have a larger bank balance than Phillip?

3-6 Solving Compound Inequalities

Solve each compound inequality and graph the solutions.

17. $-2 \leq x + 3 < 9$

18. $m + 2 < -1$ OR $m - 2 > 6$

19. $-3 \geq x - 1 > 2$

20. $-2 > r + 2$ OR $r + 4 < 5$

21. It is recommended that a certain medicine be stored in temperatures above 32 °F and below 70 °F. Write a compound inequality to show the acceptable storage temperatures for this medicine.

3-7 Solving Absolute-Value Inequalities

Solve each inequality and graph the solutions.

22. $|x| + 9 \leq 12$

23. $|x + 7| - 15 < 6$

24. $4.5|x| \geq 31.5$

Solve each inequality.

25. $|x - 2| \leq 14$

26. $|x| - 9.2 < -5.7$

27. $\frac{1}{2} + 2|x| > -4$

28. $7 + |3x| > 13$

29. Eli attended a concert. The decibel level of the music averaged 110 decibels but varied by 22 decibels from the average. Write and solve an absolute-value inequality to find the decibel range. Graph the solutions.

Vocabulary

Complete the sentences below with vocabulary words from the list above.

1. A(n) ___?___ is a mathematical statement that two quantities are not equal.

2. The numbers that are solutions to either inequality of a compound inequality is the ___?___ .

3. A statement formed by combining two simple inequalities with the words AND or OR is a(n) ___?___ .

4. The numbers that are solutions to both inequalities of a compound inequality is the ___?___ .

5. Any value that makes the inequality true is a(n) ___?___ .

3-1 Graphing and Writing Inequalities (pp. 170–175)

EXAMPLES

■ Graph the inequality $y > -1$.

Draw an empty circle at −1.

Shade all the numbers greater than −1.

■ Write the inequality shown by the graph.

$n \leq 3.5$ *Use the variable n.*
The arrow points left, so use either
$<$ or $\leq$. The solid circle means 3.5
is a solution, so use $\leq$.

■ Write an inequality for the situation and graph the solutions.

Applicants for a driver's permit must be at least 16 years old.

age	must be at least	16 years
a	$\geq$	16

EXERCISES

Graph each inequality.

6. $x > -3$

7. $p \leq 4$

8. $-1 > t$

9. $r \geq 9.5$

10. $2(3 - 5) < k$

11. $w < 3$

Write the inequality shown by each graph.

12.

13.

14.

Define a variable and write an inequality for each situation. Graph the solutions.

15. The temperature must be at least 72 °F.

16. No more than 12 students were present.

17. It takes less than 30 minutes to complete the lab activity.

3-2 Solving Inequalities by Adding or Subtracting (pp. 176–181)

EXAMPLES

Solve each inequality and graph the solutions.

■ $x + 6 > 2$

$$\begin{array}{rl} x + 6 > & 2 \\ \underline{-6 \quad -6} & \\ x \quad > & -4 \end{array}$$ *Since 6 is added to x, subtract 6 from both sides.*

$$\begin{array}{c} \\ \leftarrow\!\!+\!\!\!\;\!\!\ominus\!\!+\!\!+\!\!+\!\!+\!\!+\!\!+\!\!+\!\!+\!\!+\!\!+\!\!\rightarrow \\ -5\;-4\;-3\;-2\;-1\;\;0\;\;1\;\;2\;\;3\;\;4\;\;5 \end{array}$$

■ $n - 1.3 < 3.2$

$$\begin{array}{rl} n - 1.3 < & 3.2 \\ \underline{+1.3 \quad +1.3} & \\ n \quad < & 4.5 \end{array}$$ *Since 1.3 is subtracted from x, add 1.3 to both sides.*

$$\begin{array}{c} \\ \leftarrow\!\!+\!\!+\!\!+\!\!+\!\!+\!\!+\!\!+\!\!+\!\!+\!\!\ominus\!\!+\!\!\rightarrow \\ 0\;\;0.5\;\;1\;\;1.5\;\;2\;\;2.5\;\;3\;\;3.5\;\;4\;\;4.5\;\;5 \end{array}$$

EXERCISES

Solve each inequality and graph the solutions.

18. $t + 3 < 10$ **19.** $k - 7 \le -5$

20. $-1 < m + 4$ **21.** $x + 2.3 \ge 6.8$

22. $w - 3 < 6.5$ **23.** $4 > a - 1$

24. $h - \dfrac{1}{4} < \dfrac{3}{4}$ **25.** $5 > 7 + v$

26. Tammy wants to run at least 10 miles per week. So far this week, she ran 4.5 miles. Write and solve an inequality to determine how many more miles Tammy must run this week to reach her goal.

27. Rob has a gift card for $50. So far, he has selected a shirt that costs $32. Write and solve an inequality to determine the additional amount Rob could spend without exceeding the gift card limit.

3-3 Solving Inequalities by Multiplying or Dividing (pp. 182–187)

EXAMPLES

■ Solve $\dfrac{p}{-3} \le 6$ and graph the solutions.

$$\dfrac{p}{-3} \le 6$$ *Since p is divided by −3, multiply both sides by −3.*

$$-3 \cdot \dfrac{p}{-3} \ge -3 \cdot 6$$

$$p \ge -18$$ *Change ≤ to ≥.*

$$\begin{array}{c} \\ \leftarrow\!\!+\!\!\bullet\!\!+\!\!+\!\!+\!\!+\!\!+\!\!+\!\!\rightarrow \\ -21\;-18\;-15\;-12\;-9\;-6\;-3 \end{array}$$

■ Pizzas cost $5.50 each. What are the possible numbers of pizzas that can be purchased with $30?

Let n represent the number of pizzas that can be purchased.

$5.50	times	number of pizzas	is at most	$30.
5.50	•	n	≤	30

$$5.50n \le 30$$

$$\dfrac{5.50n}{5.50} \le \dfrac{30}{5.50}$$ *Since n is multiplied by 5.50, divide both sides by 5.50.*

$$n \le 5\dfrac{5}{11}$$

Only a whole number of pizzas can be purchased, so 0, 1, 2, 3, 4, or 5 pizzas can be purchased.

EXERCISES

Solve each inequality and graph the solutions.

28. $3a \le 15$

29. $-18 < 6t$

30. $\dfrac{p}{4} > 2$

31. $\dfrac{2}{5}x \le -10$

32. $-3n < -18$

33. $\dfrac{g}{-2} > 6$

34. $-2k < 14$

35. $-3 > \dfrac{1}{3}r$

36. $27 < -9h$

37. $-0.4g > -1$

38. Notebooks cost $1.39 each. What are the possible numbers of notebooks that can be purchased with $10?

39. A senior class is selling lanyards as a fundraiser. The profit for each lanyard is $0.75. Write and solve an inequality to determine the number of lanyards the class must sell to make a profit of at least $250.

3-4 Solving Two-Step and Multi-Step Inequalities (pp. 190–195)

EXAMPLES

Solve each inequality and graph the solutions.

■ $18 + 3t > -12$

$$\begin{aligned} 18 + 3t &> -12 \\ \underline{-18 \qquad -18} \\ 3t &> -30 \end{aligned}$$ *Since 18 is added to 3t, subtract 18 from both sides.*

$$\frac{3t}{3} > \frac{-30}{3}$$ *Since t is multiplied by 3, divide both sides by 3.*

$$t > -10$$

■ $3^2 - 5 \le 2(1 + x)$

$$3^2 - 5 \le 2(1 + x)$$ *Simplify the left side using order of operations.*

$$9 - 5 \le 2(1 + x)$$

$$4 \le 2(1 + x)$$ *Distribute 2 on the right side.*

$$4 \le 2(1) + 2(x)$$

$$\begin{aligned} 4 &\le \quad 2 + 2x \\ \underline{-2 \qquad -2} \\ 2 &\le \qquad 2x \end{aligned}$$ *Since 2 is added to 2x, subtract 2 from both sides*

$$\frac{2}{2} \le \frac{2x}{2}$$ *Since x is multiplied by 2, divide both sides by 2.*

$$1 \le x$$

EXERCISES

Solve each inequality and graph the solutions.

40. $3x + 4 < 19$

41. $7 \le 2t - 5$

42. $\dfrac{m + 3}{2} > -4$

43. $2(x + 5) < 8$

44. $-4(2 - 5) > (-3)^2 - h$

45. $\dfrac{1}{5}x + \dfrac{1}{2} > \dfrac{4}{5}$

46. $0.5(b - 2) \le 4$

47. $\dfrac{1}{3}y - \dfrac{1}{2} > \dfrac{2}{3}$

48. $6 - 0.2n < 9$

49. Carl's Cable Company charges \$55 for monthly service plus \$4 for each pay-per-view movie. Teleview Cable Company charges \$110 per month with no fee for movies. For what number of movies is the cost of Carl's Cable Company less than the cost of Teleview?

3-5 Solving Inequalities with Variables on Both Sides (pp. 196–202)

EXAMPLES

■ Solve $b + 16 < 3b$ and graph the solutions.

$$\begin{aligned} b + 16 &> 3b \\ \underline{-b \qquad -b} \\ 16 &> 2b \end{aligned}$$ *Subtract b from both sides so that the coefficient of b is positive.*

$$\frac{16}{2} > \frac{2b}{2}$$ *Since b is multiplied by 2, divide both sides by 2.*

$$8 > b$$

■ Solve the inequality $3(1 + k) > 4 + 3k$.

$3 + 3k > 4 + 3k$ *Distribute 3 on the left side.*

The same variable term ($3k$) appears on both sides.

For any number $3k$, adding 3 will never result in a greater number than adding 4.

There are no solutions.

EXERCISES

Solve each inequality and graph the solutions.

50. $5 + 2m < -3m$ **51.** $y \le 6 + 4y$

52. $4c - 7 > 9c + 8$ **53.** $-3(2 - q) \ge 6(q + 1)$

54. $2(5 - x) < 3x$ **55.** $3.5t - 1.8 < 1.6t + 3.9$

Solve each inequality.

56. $d - 2 < d - 4$ **57.** $2(1 - x) > -2(1 + x)$

58. $4(1 - p) < 4(2 + p)$ **59.** $3w + 1 > 3(w - 1)$

60. $5(4 - k) < 5k$ **61.** $3(c + 1) > 3c + 5$

62. Hanna has a savings account with a balance of \$210 and deposits \$16 per month. Faith has a savings account with a balance of \$175 and deposits \$20 per month. Write and solve an inequality to determine the number of months Hanna's account balance will be greater than Faith's account balance.

3-6 Solving Compound Inequalities (pp. 204–210)

EXAMPLES

Solve each compound inequality and graph the solutions.

■ $-3 < c + 5 \le 11$ *Since 5 is added to c, subtract*
   $\underline{-5 \quad\quad -5 \quad -5}$ *5 from each part of the*
   $-8 < c \quad\quad\ \le 6$ *inequality.*

Graph $c > -8$
and $c \le 6$.

Graph the
intersection.

■ $-2 + t \ge \quad 2$ OR $t + 3 < \quad 1$
  $\underline{+2 \quad\quad +2}$ OR $\underline{\quad -3 \quad -3}$ *Solve the simple*
   $t \ge \quad 4$ OR $\quad\quad t < -2$ *inequalities.*

Graph $t \ge 4$
and $t < -2$.
Graph the
union.

EXERCISES

Solve each compound inequality and graph the solutions.

63. $-4 < t + 6 < 10$ **64.** $-8 < k - 2 \le 5$

65. $-3 + r > 4$ OR $r + 1 < -1$

66. $2 > n + 3 > 5$

67. $12 \ge p + 7 > 5$

68. $3 < s + 9$ OR $1 > s - 4$

69. One day, the high temperature was 84 °F and the low temperature was 68 °F. Write a compound inequality to represent the day's temperatures.

70. The table shows formulas for the recommended heart rates during exercise for a person who is a years old. Write and solve a compound inequality to determine the heart rate range for a 16-year-old person.

Recommended Heart Rate Range	
Lower Limit	$0.5 \times (220 - a)$
Upper Limit	$0.9 \times (220 - a)$

3-7 Solving Absolute-Value Inequalities (pp. 212–217)

EXAMPLES

Solve each inequality and graph the solutions.

■ $|x| + 4 < 9$
   $|x| + 4 < \quad 9$
   $\underline{\quad -4 \quad -4}$ *Subtract 4 from both sides.*
   $|x| \quad\quad < \ 5$

   $x > -5$ AND $x < 5$ *Write as a compound*
                       inequality.

$$\xleftarrow{\quad} \underset{-7}{\bullet} \underset{-5}{\circ} \underset{-3}{} \underset{-1}{} \underset{1}{} \underset{3}{} \underset{5}{\circ} \xrightarrow{\quad}$$

■ $|x - 3| + 7 \ge 13$
   $\underline{\quad\quad\ -7 \quad -7}$ *Subtract 7 from both sides.*
   $|x - 3| \quad\quad \ge 6$
   $x - 3 \le -6$ OR $x - 3 \ge \ 6$ *Solve the two*
   $\underline{+3 \quad +3}$ $\underline{+3 \quad +3}$ *inequalities.*
   $x \quad\quad \le -3$ OR $x \quad\quad \ge 9$

$$\xleftarrow{\quad} \underset{-6}{} \underset{-3}{\bullet} \underset{0}{} \underset{3}{} \underset{6}{} \underset{9}{\bullet} \xrightarrow{\quad}$$

EXERCISES

Solve each inequality and graph the solutions.

71. $|x| - 7 \le 15$ **72.** $|x + 4| > 8$

73. $6|x| \le 24$ **74.** $|x + 9| + 11 < 20$

75. $3|x| \ge 9$ **76.** $4|2x| < 24$

Solve the inequality.

77. $|x| - 5.4 > 8.5$ **78.** $|5.2 + x| < 7.3$

79. $|x - 7| + 10 \ge 12$ **80.** $14|x| - 15 \ge 41$

81. $\left|x - \dfrac{1}{2}\right| + 4 \le \dfrac{5}{2}$ **82.** $|x + 5.5| - 6.4 \le 4.9$

83. The water depth for a pool is set to 6 ft, but the actual depth of the pool may vary by as much as 4 in. Write and solve an absolute-value inequality to find the range of possible water depths in inches. Graph the solutions.

CHAPTER TEST

Describe the solutions of each inequality in words.

1. $-6 \le m$ **2.** $3t > 12$ **3.** $-x \ge 2$ **4.** $2 + b \le 10$

Graph each inequality.

5. $b > -3$ **6.** $2.5 < c$ **7.** $y \le -\sqrt{25}$ **8.** $3 - (4 + 7) \ge h$

Write the inequality shown by each graph.

9.

```
<----+----+----+----+----+---o----+----+----+----+---->
    -5   -4   -3   -2   -1    0    1    2    3    4    5
```

10.

```
        -4.5
<---+---•---+----+----+----+----+----+----+----+--->
   -5      -4      -3      -2      -1       0
```

Write an inequality for the situation and graph the solutions.

11. Madison must run a mile in no more than 9 minutes to qualify for the race.

Solve each inequality and graph the solutions.

12. $d - 5 > -7$ **13.** $f + 4 < -3$ **14.** $4.5 \ge s + 3.2$ **15.** $g + (-2) \le 9$

16. Students need at least 75 hours of volunteer service to meet their graduation requirement. Samir has already completed 48 hours. Write and solve an inequality to determine how many more hours he needs to complete.

Solve each inequality and graph the solutions.

17. $-2c \le 2$ **18.** $3 > \dfrac{k}{2}$ **19.** $\dfrac{4}{5}x \le -8$ **20.** $\dfrac{b}{3} > -7$

21. Marco needs to buy premium gasoline for his car. He has \$20 in his wallet. Write and solve an inequality to determine how many gallons of gas Marco can buy.

Gasoline Prices (\$)		
Regular	Plus	Premium
2.05	2.12	2.25

Solve each inequality and graph the solutions.

22. $3x - 8 < 4$ **23.** $-2(c - 3) > 4$ **24.** $5 \le \dfrac{3}{4}n - 2^4$ **25.** $3 - 2a \le -15 + (-9)$

Solve each inequality.

26. $2k - 6 > 3k + 2$ **27.** $2(5 - f) \le f + 12$ **28.** $\dfrac{3}{2}d \le -\dfrac{1}{2}d + 6$

Solve each compound inequality and graph the solutions.

29. $-1 \le x - 3 < 3$ **30.** $t + 7 < 3 \text{ OR } t - 1 > 4$ **31.** $4 \le d - 2 < 5$

32. The driving school instructor has asked Lina to stay within 2 miles of the posted speed limits. The current road has a speed limit of 45 mi/h. Write a compound inequality to show Lina's acceptable speeds s.

Solve each inequality.

33. $|x - 3| + 7 < 17$ **34.** $6|x| + 4 \ge 16$ **35.** $|x + 12| \le 23$

COLLEGE ENTRANCE EXAM PRACTICE

FOCUS ON SAT STUDENT-PRODUCED RESPONSES

Ten questions on the SAT require you to enter your answer in a special grid like the one shown. You do not have to write your answer in the boxes at the top of the grid, but doing this may help you avoid errors when filling in the grid. The circles must be filled in correctly for you to receive credit.

You cannot enter a zero in the first column of the grid. This is to encourage you to give a more accurate answer when you need to round. For example, $\frac{1}{16}$ written as a decimal is 0.0625. This should be entered in the grid as .063 instead of 0.06.

You may want to time yourself as you take this practice test. It should take you about 9 minutes to complete.

1. Mailing a standard-sized letter in 2005 by first-class mail cost $0.37 for a letter weighing 1 ounce or less and $0.23 for each additional ounce. How much did it cost, in dollars, to send a standard-sized letter that weighed 3 ounces?

2. If $p = q - 2$ and $\frac{q}{3} = 9$, what is the value of p?

3. Give the maximum value of x if $12 - 3(x + 1) \geq \frac{1}{2}(3 - 5)$.

4. Give the minimum value of x if $2x + y \leq 7x - 9$ and $y = -3$.

5. For what integer value of x is $2x - 9 < 5$ and $x - 1 > 4$?

6. What is the minimum value of z that satisfies the inequality $z - 7.3 \geq 4.1$?

7. To be eligible for financial aid, Alisa must work at least 15 hours per week in a work-study program. She wants to spend at least 5 more hours studying than working each week. What is the minimum number of hours per day (Monday through Friday) that she must study to meet this goal and be eligible for financial aid?

8. For all real numbers a and b, define the operation # as follows:
$$a \# b = 2a - b$$
Given $a = 3$ and $a \# b = 1$, what is the value of b?

TEST TACKLER
Standardized Test Strategies

Short Response: Understand Short Response Scores

To answer a short-response question completely, you must show how you solved the problem and explain your answer. Short response questions are scored using a 2-point scoring rubric. A sample scoring rubric is provided below.

EXAMPLE 1

Short Response An online company offers free shipping if the cost of the order is at least $35. Your order currently totals $26.50. Write an inequality to show how much more you need to spend to qualify for free shipping. Solve the inequality and explain what your answer means.

2-point response:

Let c be the amount I must add to my order.
c plus the amount I already ordered must be at least $35.
c +   26.50 $\geq$ 35

$c + 26.50 \geq 35$
$c + 26.50 - 26.50 \geq 35 - 26.50$
$c \geq 8.50$

Check:
$8.50 + 26.50 \geq 35$ ✓

To get free shipping on the order, I must spend at least $8.50 more since $8.50 + $26.50 is at least $35.

The student wrote and solved an inequality correctly. The student showed all work and explained the meaning of the solution to the inequality.

1-point response:

$c + 26.50 > 35$
$c > 8.50$
$ 8.50$

The student gave a correct answer, but the inequality symbol shown in the student's work is incorrect. No explanation was given.

0-point response:

$ 9.25$

The student gave an answer that satisfies the problem but did not show any work or give an explanation.

Scoring Rubric:

2 points: The student writes and correctly solves an inequality, showing all work. Student defines the variable, answers the question in a complete sentence, and provides an explanation.

1 point: The student writes and correctly solves an inequality but does not show all work, does not define the variable, or does not provide an explanation.

1 point: The student writes and solves an inequality but gives an incorrect answer. The student shows all work and provides an explanation for the answer.

0 points: The student gives no response or provides a solution without showing any work or explanation.

Read short-response test items carefully. If you are allowed to write in the test booklet, underline or circle the parts of the question that tell you what your answer must include. Be sure to explain how you get your answer in complete sentences.

Read each sample and answer the questions that follow by using the scoring rubric below.

Scoring Rubric:

2 points: The student demonstrates a thorough understanding of the concept, correctly answers the question, and provides a complete explanation.

1 point: The student correctly answers the question but does not show all work or does not provide an explanation.

1 point: The student makes minor errors resulting in an incorrect solution but shows and explains understanding of the concept.

0 points: The student gives a response but shows no work or explanation, or the student gives no response.

Sample A

Short Response Write a real-world situation that can be modeled by the inequality $25s - 75 \geq 250$. Solve for s and explain how the value of s relates to your situation.

Student's Answer

A painter rents a booth at the county fair for $75. The artist sells his paintings for $25 each. If he makes at least $250 in profit, he can buy a new easel.

The artist has to sell at least 13 paintings.

1. What score should the student's answer receive? Explain your reasoning.

2. What additional information, if any, should the student's answer include in order to receive full credit?

Sample B

Short Response How do the solutions of $3s - 10 < 15 - 2s$ and $-34 + 9s \leq 4s - 9$ differ? How are the solutions alike? Include a graph in your explanation.

Student's Answer

Solve both inequalities.

$$3s - 10 < 15 - 2s$$
$$+2s \qquad +2s$$
$$5s - 10 < 15$$
$$+10 \quad +10$$
$$5s < 25$$
$$\frac{5s}{5} < \frac{25}{5}$$
$$s < 5$$

$$-34 + 9s \leq 4s - 9$$
$$-4s \quad -4s$$
$$-34 + 5s \leq -9$$
$$+34 \qquad +34$$
$$5s \leq 25$$
$$\frac{5s}{5} \leq \frac{25}{5}$$
$$s \leq 5$$

Blue graph: $s < 5$ Red graph: $s \leq 5$

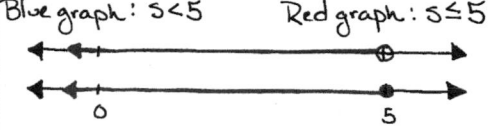

3. What score should the student's answer receive? Explain your reasoning.

4. What additional information, if any, should the student's answer include in order to receive full credit?

Sample C

Short Response Explain the difference between the solution of the equation $x - 6 = 2x + 9$ and the solutions of the inequality $x - 6 < 2x + 9$.

Student's Answer

The equation has a solution of $x = -15$, and the inequality has a solution of $x > -15$. The equation is true only when x equals –15. The inequality is true for all values greater than –15.

5. What score should the student's answer receive? Explain your reasoning.

6. What additional information, if any, should the student's answer include in order to receive full credit?

CHAPTER
3

STANDARDIZED
TEST PREP

go.hrw.com
State Test Practice Online
KEYWORD: MA7 TestPrep

CUMULATIVE ASSESSMENT, CHAPTERS 1–3

Multiple Choice

1. Which algebraic expression means "5 less than *y*"?

   (A) $5 - y$

   (B) $y - 5$

   (C) $5 < y$

   (D) $5 \div y$

2. Which expression is equivalent to $5 + 2(x - 5)$?

   (F) $2x$

   (G) $2x + 5$

   (H) $2x - 5$

   (J) $7x - 35$

3. If $t + 8 = 2$, find the value of $2t$.

   (A) -12

   (B) -6

   (C) 12

   (D) 20

4. The length of the rectangle is $2(x + 1)$ meters and the perimeter is 60 meters. What is the length of the rectangle?

   (F) 12 meters

   (G) 26 meters

   (H) 28 meters

   (J) 56 meters

5. Samantha opened a bank account in June and deposited some money. She deposited twice that amount in August. At the end of August, Samantha had less than $600 in her account. If she made no other withdrawals or deposits, which inequality could be used to determine the maximum amount Samantha could have deposited in June?

   (A) $2x < 600$

   (B) $2x > 600$

   (C) $3x < 600$

   (D) $3x > 600$

6. Which proportion could be used to determine the ratio of the areas of these similar rectangles?

   (F) $\dfrac{2}{3}$

   (G) $\dfrac{2}{5}$

   (H) $\dfrac{4}{9}$

   (J) $\dfrac{4}{25}$

7. For which inequality is -2 a solution?

   (A) $2x < -4$

   (B) $-2x < 4$

   (C) $-2x > -4$

   (D) $-2x < -4$

8. Which graph shows the solutions of $-2(1 - x) < 3(x - 2)$?

   (F)
```
←——┼——┼——┼——┼——┼——┼——┼——┼——┼——⊕——┼——→
   -5  -4  -3  -2  -1   0   1   2   3   4   5
```

   (G)
```
←——┼——┼——┼——┼——┼——┼——┼——┼——┼——⊕——●——→
   -5  -4  -3  -2  -1   0   1   2   3   4   5
```

   (H)
```
←——┼——┼——┼——┼——┼——┼——┼——⊕——●——●——●——→
   -5  -4  -3  -2  -1   0   1   2   3   4   5
```

   (J)
```
←——●——⊕——┼——┼——┼——┼——┼——┼——┼——┼——┼——→
   -5  -4  -3  -2  -1   0   1   2   3   4   5
```

9. Which compound inequality has no solution?

   (A) $x > 1$ OR $x < -2$

   (B) $x < 1$ AND $x > -2$

   (C) $x < 1$ OR $x < -2$

   (D) $x > 1$ AND $x < -2$

To check your answer, use a different method to solve the problem from the one you originally used. If you made a mistake the first time, you are unlikely to make the same mistake when you solve the problem a different way.

10. Which inequality has the same solutions as $p < -2$?

  (F) $p + 1 < -2$

  (G) $p + 4 < 2$

  (H) $2p + 1 < -4$

  (J) $3p < -12$

11. What is the greatest integer solution of $5 - 3m > 11$?

  (A) 0

  (B) -1

  (C) -2

  (D) -3

Gridded Response

12. The sum of the measures of any two sides of a triangle must be greater than the measure of the third side. What is the greatest possible integer value for x?

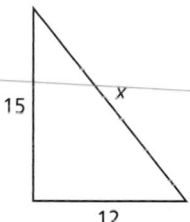

13. After 2 years, the simple interest paid on an investment of $2500 was $175. What percent was the interest rate?

14. Amy's bowling score in her third game was 10 points less than her score in the first game and 5 points more than her score in the second game. The total points for all three games was no more than 275. What is the greatest number of points Amy could have scored in her first game?

15. Trevor needs a 93 on his second quiz to have a quiz average of 90. What score did Trevor receive on his first quiz?

16. The radius of a circle can be determined by the formula $r = \sqrt{\frac{A}{\pi}}$. What is the length in meters of the radius of a circle that has an area of 314 square meters? (Use 3.14 for π.)

Short Response

17. Write 2 different inequalities that have the same solution as $n > 3$ such that

  a. the first inequality uses the symbol $>$ and requires addition or subtraction to solve.

  b. the second inequality uses the symbol $<$ and requires multiplication or division to solve.

18. Alison has twice as many video games as Kyle. Maurice has 5 more video games than Alison. The total number of video games is less than 40.

  a. Write an inequality to represent this situation.

  b. Solve the inequality to determine the greatest number of video games Maurice could have. Justify each step in your solution.

19. Donna's Deli delivers lunches for $7 per person plus a $35 delivery fee. Larry's Lunches delivers lunches for $11 per person.

  a. Write an expression to represent the cost of x lunches from Donna's Deli. Write an expression to represent the cost of ordering x lunches from Larry's Lunches.

  b. Write an inequality to determine the number of lunches for which the cost of Larry's Lunches is less than the cost of Donna's Deli.

  c. Solve the inequality and explain what the answer means. Which restaurant charges less for an order of 10 lunches?

Extended Response

20. Aleya has two employment opportunities. Company A offered her a yearly salary of $31,000. Company B offered her a similar position with a yearly salary of $27,000 plus 2.5% commission on her total sales for the year.

  a. Let x represent Aleya's total sales for the year at company B. Write an expression to represent the total income after one year at company B.

  b. Use your expression from part **a** to write an inequality that could be solved to determine the amount of sales for which the yearly income at company A would be greater than that at company B.

  c. Solve the inequality from part **b** and explain the meaning of the solution in relation to Aleya's decision to work for company A or company B.

  d. How much more than the salary at company A would Aleya make after one year at company B if her total sales for the year were $200,000?

Functions

Chapter

- Use tables, diagrams, graphs, and equations to describe functions.
- Translate among representations of functions.
- Use functions to represent, analyze, and solve problems.

Is That *Your* Foot?

Criminologists use measurements, such as the size of footprints, and functions to help them identify criminals.

go.hrw.com
Chapter Project Online
KEYWORD: MA7 ChProj

ARE YOU READY?

✓ Vocabulary

Match each term on the left with a definition on the right.

1. absolute value
2. algebraic expression
3. input
4. output
5. x-axis

A. a letter used to represent a value that can change

B. the value generated for y

C. a group of numbers, symbols, and variables with one or more operations

D. the distance of a number from zero on the number line

E. the horizontal number line in the coordinate plane

F. a value substituted for x

✓ Ordered Pairs

Graph each point on the same coordinate plane.

6. $(-2, 4)$ 7. $(0, -5)$ 8. $(1, -3)$ 9. $(4, 2)$

10. $(3, -2)$ 11. $(-1, -2)$ 12. $(-1, 3)$ 13. $(-4, 0)$

✓ Function Tables

Generate ordered pairs for each function for $x = -2, -1, 0, 1, 2.$

14. $y = -2x - 1$ 15. $y = x + 1$ 16. $y = x^2$

17. $y = \frac{1}{2}x + 2$ 18. $y = (x + 1)^2$ 19. $y = (x - 1)^2$

✓ Solve Multi-Step Equations

Solve each equation. Check your answer.

20. $17x - 15 = 12$ 21. $-7 + 2t = 7$ 22. $-6 = \frac{p}{3} + 9$

23. $5n - 10 = 35$ 24. $3r - 14 = 7$ 25. $9 = \frac{x}{2} + 1$

26. $-2.4 + 1.6g = 5.6$ 27. $34 - 2x = 12$ 28. $2(x + 5) = -8$

✓ Solve for a Variable

Solve each equation for the indicated variable.

29. $A = \ell w$ for w 30. $V = \ell w h$ for w 31. $A = bh$ for h

32. $C = 2\pi r$ for r 33. $I = Prt$ for P 34. $V = \frac{1}{3}\ell w h$ for h

Where You've Been

Previously, you

- were introduced to functions when you generated and graphed ordered pairs.
- stated rules for relationships among values.
- represented and interpreted data using bar graphs and circle graphs.

In This Chapter

You will study

- relationships between variables and determine whether a relation is a function.
- relationships in function notation.
- how trend lines on scatter plots can help you make predictions.

Where You're Going

You can use the skills in this chapter

- to find values of a function from a graph.
- to analyze data and make predictions in other courses, such as Chemistry.
- to calculate total earnings for a certain hourly rate.

Key Vocabulary/Vocabulario

arithmetic sequence	sucesión aritmética
common difference	diferencia común
correlation	correlación
dependent variable	variable dependiente
domain	dominio
function	función
function notation	notación de función
independent variable	variable independiente
no correlation	sin correlación
range	rango
relation	relación
scatter plot	diagrama de dispersión
sequence	sucesión

Vocabulary Connections

To become familiar with some of the vocabulary terms in the chapter, consider the following. You may refer to the chapter, the glossary, or a dictionary if you like.

1. What does the word *dependent* mean? What do you think is true about the value of a **dependent variable**?

2. A *function* is a special type of relation and *notation* is a method of writing. What do you suppose is meant by **function notation**?

3. The word *correlation* means "relationship." What might it mean if two sets of data have **no correlation**?

4. What does it mean when someone says that two people have something in *common*? If *difference* is the answer to a subtraction problem, what might it mean for a list of numbers to have a **common difference**?

Reading Strategy: Read and Interpret Math Symbols

It is essential that as you read through each lesson of the textbook, you can interpret mathematical symbols.

Common Math Symbols

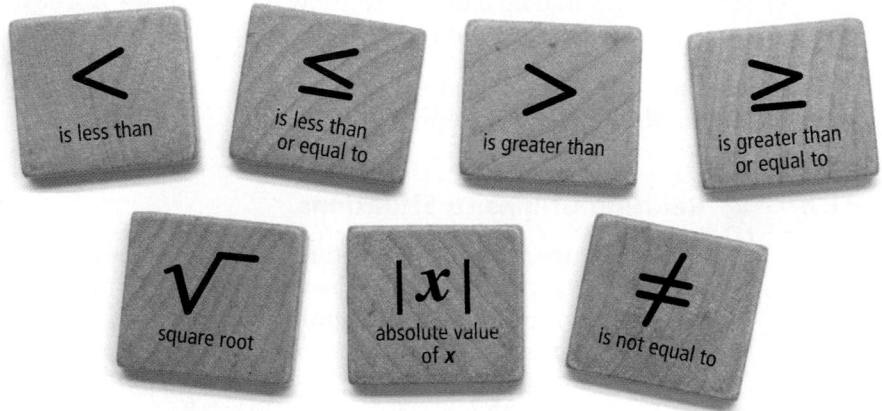

You must be able to translate symbols into words . . .

Using Symbols	Using Words
$3\left(\dfrac{x}{12}\right) - 1 = 21$	Three times the quotient of x and 12, minus 1 **equals** 21.
$25x + 6 \geq 17$	Twenty-five times x plus 6 **is greater than or equal to** 17.
$\lvert x \rvert > 14$	The **absolute value** of x **is greater than** 14.
$\sqrt{60 + x} \leq 40$	The **square root** of the sum of 60 and x **is less than or equal to** 40.

. . . and words into symbols.

Using Words	Using Symbols
The height of the shed **is at least** 9 feet.	$h \geq 9$ ft
The distance **is at most** one tenth of a mile.	$d \leq 0.1$ mi
The silo contains **more than** 600 cubic feet of corn.	$c > 600$ ft^3

Try This

Translate the symbols into words.

1. $x \leq \sqrt{10}$ **2.** $\lvert x \rvert + 2 > 45$ **3.** $-5 \leq x < 8$ **4.** $-6 - \dfrac{1}{5}x = -32$

Translate the words into symbols.

5. There are less than 15 seconds remaining. **6.** The tax rate is 8.25 percent of the cost.

7. Ann counted over 100 pennies. **8.** Joe can spend at least $22 but no more than $30.

Graphing Relationships

Objectives
Match simple graphs with situations.

Graph a relationship.

Vocabulary
continuous graph
discrete graph

Who uses this?
Cardiologists can use graphs to analyze their patients' heartbeats. (See Example 2.)

Graphs can be used to illustrate many different situations. For example, trends shown on a cardiograph can help a doctor see how the patient's heart is functioning.

To relate a graph to a given situation, use key words in the description.

EXAMPLE 1 Relating Graphs to Situations

The air temperature was constant for several hours at the beginning of the day and then rose steadily for several hours. It stayed the same temperature for most of the day before dropping sharply at sundown. Choose the graph that best represents this situation.

Step 1 Read the graphs from left to right to show time passing.

Step 2 List key words in order and decide which graph shows them.

Key Words	Segment Description	Graphs
Was constant	Horizontal	Graphs A and B
Rose steadily	Slanting upward	Graphs A and B
Stayed the same	Horizontal	Graph B
Dropped sharply	Slanting downward	Graph B

Step 3 Pick the graph that shows all the key phrases in order.

horizontal, slanting upward, horizontal, slanting downward

The correct graph is B.

 1. The air temperature increased steadily for several hours and then remained constant. At the end of the day, the temperature increased slightly again before dropping sharply. Choose the graph above that best represents this situation.

As seen in Example 1, some graphs are connected lines or curves called **continuous graphs**. Some graphs are only distinct points. These are called **discrete graphs**.

The graph on theme-park attendance is an example of a discrete graph. It consists of distinct points because each year is distinct and people are counted in whole numbers only. The values between the whole numbers are not included, since they have no meaning for the situation.

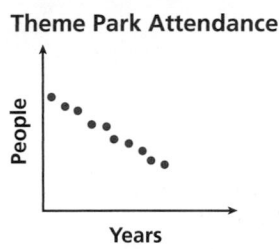

Theme Park Attendance

EXAMPLE **2** **Sketching Graphs for Situations**

Sketch a graph for each situation. Tell whether the graph is continuous or discrete.

A Simon is selling candles to raise money for the school dance. For each candle he sells, the school will get $2.50. He has 10 candles that he can sell.

Simon's Earnings

The amount earned (y-axis) increases by $2.50 for each candle Simon sells (x-axis).

Since Simon can only sell whole numbers of candles, the graph is 11 distinct points.

The graph is discrete.

B Angelique's heart rate is being monitored while she exercises on a treadmill. While walking, her heart rate remains the same. As she increases her pace, her heart rate rises at a steady rate. When she begins to run, her heart rate increases more rapidly and then remains high while she runs. As she decreases her pace, her heart rate slows down and returns to her normal rate.

As time passes during her workout (moving left to right along the *x*-axis), her heart rate (*y*-axis) does the following:

- remains the same,
- rises at a steady rate,
- increases **more rapidly** (**steeper** than previous segment),
- **remains high**,
- slows down,
- and then returns to her normal rate.

The graph is continuous.

Angelique's Heart Rate

Sketch a graph for each situation. Tell whether the graph is continuous or discrete.

2a. Jamie is taking an 8-week keyboarding class. At the end of each week, she takes a test to find the number of words she can type per minute. She improves each week.

2b. Henry begins to drain a water tank by opening a valve. Then he opens another valve. Then he closes the first valve. He leaves the second valve open until the tank is empty.

When sketching or interpreting a graph, pay close attention to the labels on each axis. Both graphs below show a relationship about a child going down a slide. **Graph A** represents the child's *distance from the ground* over time. **Graph B** represents the child's *speed* over time.

EXAMPLE 3 **Writing Situations for Graphs**

Write a possible situation for the given graph.

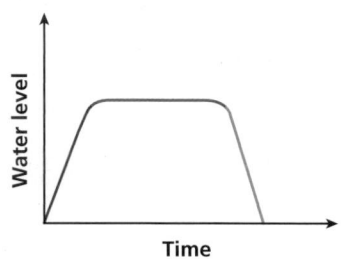

Step 1 Identify labels.
    x-axis: time   *y*-axis: water level

Step 2 Analyze sections.
    Over time, the water level
- **increases steadily,**
- **remains unchanged,**
- and then decreases steadily.

Possible Situation: A watering can is **filled with water**. It **sits for a while** until some flowers are planted. The water is then emptied on top of the planted flowers.

 3. Write a possible situation for the given graph.

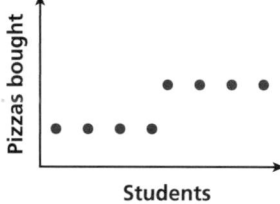

THINK AND DISCUSS

1. Should a graph of age related to height be a continuous graph or a discrete graph? Explain.

2. Give an example of a situation that, when graphed, would include a horizontal segment.

3. GET ORGANIZED Copy and complete the graphic organizer. Write an example of key words that suggest the given segments on a graph. One example for each segment is given for you.

go.hrw.com
Homework Help Online
KEYWORD: MA7 4-1
Parent Resources Online
KEYWORD: MA7 Parent

GUIDED PRACTICE

Vocabulary Apply the vocabulary from this lesson to answer each question.

1. A ____?____ graph is made of connected lines or curves. (*continuous* or *discrete*)

2. A ____?____ graph is made of only distinct points. (*continuous* or *discrete*)

SEE EXAMPLE 1
p. 234

Choose the graph that best represents each situation.

3. A person alternates between running and walking.

4. A person gradually speeds up to a constant running pace.

5. A person walks, gradually speeds up to a run, and then slows back down to a walk.

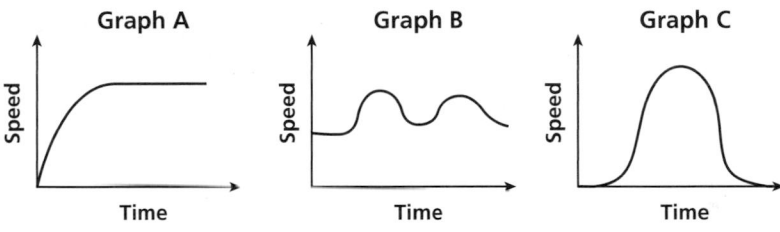

SEE EXAMPLE 2
p. 235

6. Maxine is buying extra pages for her photo album. Each page holds exactly 8 photos. Sketch a graph to show the maximum number of photos she can add to her album if she buys 1, 2, 3, or 4 extra pages. Tell whether the graph is continuous or discrete.

SEE EXAMPLE 3
p. 236

Write a possible situation for each graph.

7.
8.
9.

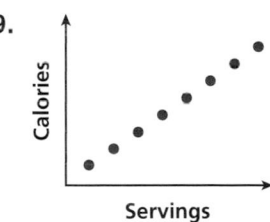

PRACTICE AND PROBLEM SOLVING

Independent Practice

For Exercises	See Example
10–12	1
13	2
14–16	3

Extra Practice
Skills Practice p. S10
Application Practice p. S31

Choose the graph that best represents each situation.

10. A flag is raised up a flagpole quickly at the beginning and then more slowly near the top.

11. A flag is raised up a flagpole in a jerky motion, using a hand-over-hand method.

12. A flag is raised up a flagpole at a constant rate of speed.

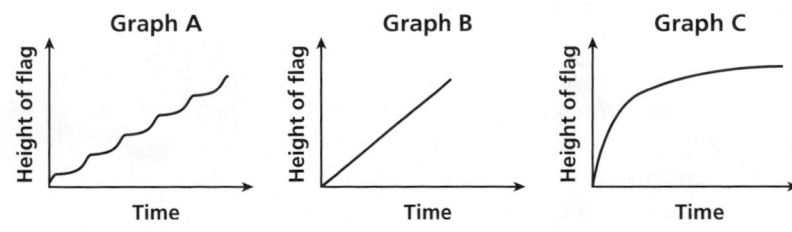

13. For six months, a puppy gained weight at a steady rate. Sketch a graph to illustrate the weight of the puppy during that time period. Tell whether the graph is continuous or discrete.

Write a possible situation for each graph.

14.

15.

16.

17. Data Collection Use a graphing calculator and motion detector for the following.

    a. On a coordinate plane, draw a graph relating distance from a starting point walking at various speeds and time.

    b. Using the motion detector as the starting point, walk away from the motion detector to make a graph on the graphing calculator that matches the one you drew.

    c. Compare your walking speeds to each change in steepness on the graph.

18. Sports The graph shows the speed of a horse during and after a race. Use it to describe the changing pace of the horse during the race.

19. Recreation You hike up a mountain path starting at 10 A.M. You camp overnight and then walk back down the same path at the same pace at 10 A.M. the next morning. On the same set of axes, graph the relationship between distance from the top of the mountain and the time of day for both the hike up and the hike down. What does the point of intersection of the graphs represent?

20. Critical Thinking Suppose that you sketched a graph of speed related to time for a brick that fell from the top of a building. Then you sketched a graph for speed related to time for a ball that was rolled down a hill and then came to rest. How would the graphs be the same? How would they be different?

 21. Write About It Describe a real-life situation that could be represented by a distinct graph. Then describe a real-life situation that could be represented by a continuous graph.

MULTI-STEP TEST PREP

22. This problem will prepare you for the Multi-Step Test Prep on page 264.

A rectangular pool that is 4 feet deep at all places is being filled at a constant rate.

    a. Sketch a graph to show the depth of the water as it increases over time.

    b. The side view of another swimming pool is shown. If the pool is being filled at a constant rate, sketch a graph to show the depth of the water as it increases over time.

23. Which situation would NOT be represented by a distinct graph?

   Ⓐ   Amount of money earned based on the number of cereal bars sold

   Ⓑ   Number of visitors to a grocery store per day for one week

   Ⓒ   The amount of iced tea in a pitcher at a restaurant during the lunch hour

   Ⓓ   The total cost of buying 1, 2, or 3 CDs at the music store

24. Which situation is best represented by the graph?

   Ⓕ   A snowboarder starts at the bottom of the hill and takes a ski lift to the top.

   Ⓖ   A cruise boat travels at a steady pace from the port to its destination.

   Ⓗ   An object falls from the top of a building and gains speed at a rapid pace before hitting the ground.

   Ⓙ   A marathon runner starts at a steady pace and then runs faster at the end of the race before stopping at the finish line.

25. Short Response Marla participates in a triathlon consisting of swimming, biking, and running. Would a graph of Marla's speed during the triathlon be a continuous graph or a distinct graph? Explain.

CHALLENGE AND EXTEND

Pictured are three vases and graphs representing the height of water as it is poured into each of the vases at a constant rate. Match each vase with the correct graph.

A   **B**   **C**

26.   **27.**   **28.**

SPIRAL REVIEW

Evaluate each expression. *(Lesson 1-4)*

29. -2^3 **30.** 4^4 **31.** $\left(\dfrac{1}{3}\right)^2$

Generate ordered pairs for each function for $x = -2, -1, 0, 1,$ and 2. Graph the ordered pairs and describe the pattern. *(Lesson 1-8)*

32. $y = x - 2$ **33.** $2x + y = 1$ **34.** $y = |x - 1|$ **35.** $y = x^2 + 2$

Write and solve an equation to represent each relationship. *(Lesson 2-1)*

36. A number increased by 11 is equal to 3.   **37.** Five less than a number is equal to -2.

Relations and Functions

Objectives
Identify functions.

Find the domain and range of relations and functions.

Vocabulary
relation
domain
range
function

Why learn this?
You can use a relation to show finishing positions and scores in a track meet.

In Lesson 4-1, you saw relationships represented by graphs. Relationships can also be represented by a set of ordered pairs, called a **relation**.

In the scoring system of some track meets, **first place** is worth **5** points, **second place** is worth **3** points, third place is worth **2** points, and **fourth place** is worth **1** point. This scoring system is a relation, so it can be shown as ordered pairs, $\{(1, 5), (2, 3), (3, 2), (4, 1)\}$. You can also show relations in other ways, such as tables, graphs, or *mapping diagrams*.

E X A M P L E **1** **Showing Multiple Representations of Relations**

Express the relation for the track meet scoring system, $\{(1, 5), (2, 3), (3, 2), (4, 1)\}$, as a table, as a graph, and as a mapping diagram.

Table	Graph	Mapping Diagram
Track Scoring	**Track Scoring**	**Place** **Points**

Place	Points
1	5
2	3
3	2
4	1

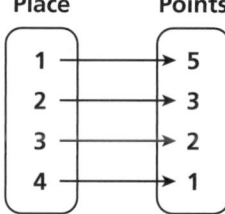

Write all x-values under "Place" and all y-values under "Points."

Use the x- and y-values to plot the ordered pairs.

Write all x-values under "Place" and all y-values under "Points." Draw an arrow from each x-value to its corresponding y-value.

 1. Express the relation $\{(1, 3) (2, 4), (3, 5)\}$ as a table, as a graph, and as a mapping diagram.

The **domain** of a relation is the set of first coordinates (or *x*-values) of the ordered pairs. The **range** of a relation is the set of second coordinates (or *y*-values) of the ordered pairs. The domain of the track meet scoring system is $\{1, 2, 3, 4\}$. The range is $\{5, 3, 2, 1\}$.

EXAMPLE 2 Finding the Domain and Range of a Relation

Give the domain and range of the relation.

The domain is all *x*-values from 1 through 3, inclusive.

The range is all *y*-values from 2 through 4, inclusive.

D: $1 \leq x \leq 3$ R: $2 \leq y \leq 4$

 Give the domain and range of each relation.

2a.
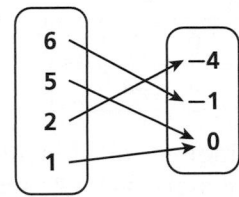

2b.

x	y
1	1
4	4
8	1

A **function** is a special type of relation that pairs each domain value with exactly one range value.

EXAMPLE 3 Identifying Functions

Give the domain and range of each relation. Tell whether the relation is a function. Explain.

A

Field Trip	
Students *x*	Buses *y*
75	2
68	2
125	3

D: $\{75, 68, 125\}$ *Even though 2 appears twice in the table, it is written only once when writing the range.*
R: $\{2, 3\}$

This relation is a function. Each domain value is paired with exactly one range value.

Writing Math

When there is a finite number of values in a domain or range, list the values inside braces.

B

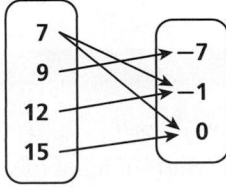

Use the arrows to determine which domain values correspond to each range value.

D: $\{7, 9, 12, 15\}$

R: $\{-7, -1, 0\}$

This relation is not a function. Each domain value does not have exactly one range value. The domain value 7 is paired with the range values −1 and 0.

Give the domain and range of each relation. Tell whether the relation is a function. Explain.

C

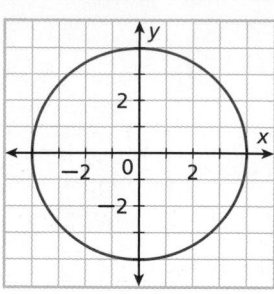

Draw lines to see the domain and range values.

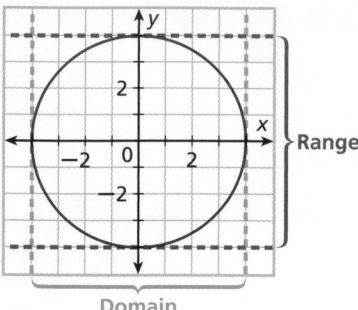

Range

Domain

D: $-4 \leq x \leq 4$ R: $-4 \leq y \leq 4$

x	4	0	0	−4
y	0	4	−4	0

To compare domain and range values, make a table using points from the graph.

This relation is not a function because there are several domain values that have more than one range value. For example, the domain value 0 is paired with both 4 and −4.

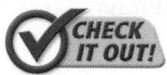 Give the domain and range of each relation. Tell whether the relation is a function. Explain.

3a. $\{(8, 2), (-4, 1), (-6, 2), (1, 9)\}$ **3b.**

THINK AND DISCUSS

1. Describe how to tell whether a set of ordered pairs is a function.

2. Can the graph of a vertical line segment represent a function? Explain.

3. GET ORGANIZED Copy and complete the graphic organizer by explaining when a relation is a function and when it is not a function.

A relation is...	
A function if...	Not a function if...

GUIDED PRACTICE

Vocabulary Apply the vocabulary from this lesson to answer each question.

1. Use a mapping diagram to show a relation that is not a *function*.

2. The set of *x*-values for a relation is also called the ___?___. (*domain* or *range*)

SEE EXAMPLE 1
p. 240

Express each relation as a table, as a graph, and as a mapping diagram.

3. $\{(1, 1), (1, 2)\}$

4. $\left\{(-1, 1), \left(-2, \frac{1}{2}\right), \left(-3, \frac{1}{3}\right), \left(-4, \frac{1}{4}\right)\right\}$

5. $\{(-1, 1), (-3, 3), (5, -5), (-7, 7)\}$

6. $\{(0, 0), (2, -4), (2, -2)\}$

SEE EXAMPLE 2
p. 241

Give the domain and range of each relation.

7. $\{(-5, 7), (0, 0), (2, -8), (5, -20)\}$

8. $\{(1, 2), (2, 4), (3, 6), (4, 8), (5, 10)\}$

9.

x	3	5	2	8	6
y	9	25	4	81	36

10.
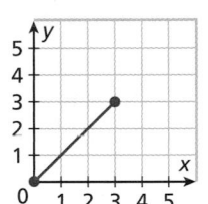

SEE EXAMPLE 3
p. 241

Multi-Step Give the domain and range of each relation. Tell whether the relation is a function. Explain.

11. $\{(1, 3), (1, 0), (1, -2), (1, 8)\}$

12. $\{(-2, 1), (-1, 2), (0, 3), (1, 4)\}$

13.

x	−2	−1	0	1	2
y	1	1	1	1	1

14.
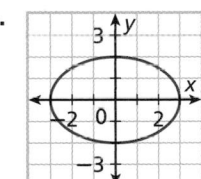

PRACTICE AND PROBLEM SOLVING

Extra Practice
Skills Practice p. S10
Application Practice p. S31

Express each relation as a table, as a graph, and as a mapping diagram.

15. $\{(-2, -4), (-1, -1), (0, 0), (1, -1), (2, -4)\}$

16. $\left\{(2, 1), \left(2, \frac{1}{2}\right), (2, 2), \left(2, 2\frac{1}{2}\right)\right\}$

Give the domain and range of each relation.

17.

18.

x	y
4	4
5	5
6	6
7	7
8	8

Multi-Step Give the domain and range of each relation. Tell whether the relation is a function. Explain.

19.

20.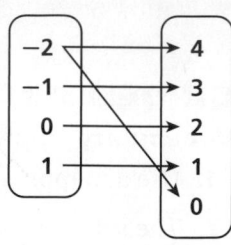

21. **Consumer Application** An electrician charges a base fee of $75 plus $50 for each hour of work. Create a table that shows the amount the electrician charges for 1, 2, 3, and 4 hours of work. Let *x* represent the number of hours and *y* represent the amount charged for *x* hours. Is this relation a function? Explain.

22. **Geometry** Write a relation as a set of ordered pairs in which the *x*-value represents the side length of a square and the *y*-value represents the area of that square. Use a domain of 2, 4, 6, 9, and 11.

23. **Multi-Step** Create a mapping diagram to display the numbers of days in 1, 2, 3, and 4 weeks. Is this relation a function? Explain.

24. **Nutrition** The illustrations list the number of grams of fat and the number of Calories from fat for selected foods.

   a. Create a graph for the relation between grams of fat and Calories from fat.

   b. Is this relation a function? Explain.

Hamburger
Fat (g):   14
Fat (Cal): 126

Cheeseburger
Fat (g):   18
Fat (Cal): 162

Grilled chicken filet
Fat (g):   3.5
Fat (Cal): 31.5

Breaded chicken filet
Fat (g):   11
Fat (Cal): 99

Taco salad
Fat (g):   19
Fat (Cal): 171

25. **Recreation** A shop rents canoes for a $7 equipment fee plus $2 per hour, with a maximum cost of $15 per day. Express the number of hours *x* and the cost *y* as a relation in table form, and find the cost to rent a canoe for 1, 2, 3, 4, and 5 hours. Is this relation a function? Explain.

26. **Health** You can burn about 6 Calories per minute bicycling. Let *x* represent the number of minutes bicycled, and let *y* represent the number of Calories burned.

   a. Write ordered pairs to show the number of Calories burned by bicycling for 60, 120, 180, 240, or 300 minutes. Graph the ordered pairs.

   b. Find the domain and range of the relation.

   c. Does this graph represent a function? Explain.

27. **Critical Thinking** For a function, can the number of elements in the range be greater than the number of elements in the domain? Explain.

28. **Critical Thinking** Tell whether each statement is true or false. If false, explain why.

   a. All relations are functions.   b. All functions are relations.

MULTI-STEP TEST PREP

29. This problem will prepare you for the Multi-Step Test Prep on page 264.

   a. The graph shows the amount of water being pumped into a pool over a 5-hour time period. Find the domain and range.

   b. Does the graph represent a function? Explain.

   c. Give the time and volume as ordered pairs at 2 hours and at 3 hours 30 minutes.

Filling Pool with Water

30. ///ERROR ANALYSIS/// When asked whether the relation $\{(-4, 16), (-2, 4), (0, 0), (2, 4)\}$ is a function, a student stated that the relation is not a function because 4 appears twice. What error did the student make? How would you explain to the student why this relation is a function?

31. **Write About It** Describe a real-world situation for a relation that is NOT a function. Create a mapping diagram to show why the relation is not a function.

TEST PREP

32. Which of the following relations is NOT a function?

   Ⓐ $\{(6, 2), (-1, 2), (-3, 2), (-5, 2)\}$

   Ⓒ
x	3	5	7
y	1	15	30

   Ⓑ

   Ⓓ

33. Which is NOT a correct way to describe the function $\{(-3, 2), (1, 8), (-1, 5), (3, 11)\}$?

   Ⓕ
   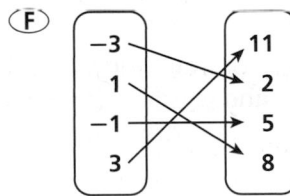

   Ⓗ Domain: $\{-3, 1, -1, 3\}$

   Range: $\{2, 8, 5, 11\}$

   Ⓖ
   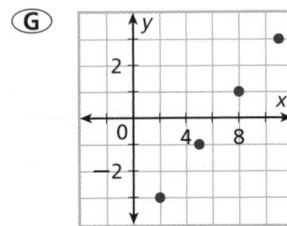

   Ⓙ
x	y
-3	2
-1	5
1	8
3	11

34. Which graph represents a function?

35. Extended Response Use the table for the following.

x	−3	−1	0	1	3
y	5	7	9	11	13

    a. Express the relation as ordered pairs.

    b. Give the domain and range of the relation.

    c. Does the relation represent a function? Explain your answer.

CHALLENGE AND EXTEND

36. What values of a make the relation $\{(a, 1), (2, 3), (4, 5)\}$ a function? Explain.

37. What values of b make the relation $\{(5, 6), (7, 8), (9, b)\}$ a function? Explain.

38. The *inverse* of a relation is created by interchanging the x- and y- coordinates of each ordered pair in the relation.

    a. Find the inverse of the following relation: $\{(-2, 5), (0, 4), (3, -8), (7, 5)\}$.

    b. Is the original relation a function? Why or why not? Is the inverse of the relation a function? Why or why not?

    c. The statement "If a relation is a function, then the inverse of the relation is also a function" is sometimes true. Give an example of a relation and its inverse that are both functions. Then give an example of a relation and its inverse that are both not functions.

SPIRAL REVIEW

39. The ratio of a rectangle's width to its length is $3:4$. The length of the rectangle is 36 cm. Write and solve a proportion to find the rectangle's width. *(Lesson 2-7)*

40. A scale drawing of a house is drawn with a scale of 1 in.: 16 ft. Find the actual length of a hallway that is $\frac{5}{8}$ in. on the scale drawing. *(Lesson 2-7)*

41. Penny wants to drink at least 64 ounces of water today. She has consumed 45 ounces of water so far. Write, solve, and graph an inequality to determine how many more ounces of water Penny must drink to reach her goal. *(Lesson 3-2)*

42. The local pizza parlor sold the following number of pizzas over 10 days. Sketch a graph for the situation. Tell whether the graph is continuous or discrete. *(Lesson 4-1)*

Time (days)	1	2	3	4	5	6	7	8	9	10
Pizzas Sold	5	11	2	4	8	10	3	6	12	1

4-2

Algebra LAB

The Vertical-Line Test

The *vertical-line test* can be used to visually determine whether a graphed relation is a function.

Use with Lesson 4-2

Activity

1 Look at the values in Table 1. Is every *x*-value paired with exactly one *y*-value? If not, what *x*-value(s) are paired with more than one *y*-value?

2 Is the relation a function? Explain.

3 Graph the points from the Table 1. Draw a vertical line through each point of the graph. Does any vertical line touch more than one point?

Table 1	
x	*y*
−2	−5
−1	−3
0	−1
1	1
2	3
3	5

4 Look at the values in Table 2. Is every *x*-value paired with exactly one *y*-value? If not, what *x*-value(s) are paired with more than one *y*-value?

5 Is the relation a function? Explain.

6 Graph the points from the Table 2. Draw a vertical line through each point of the graph. Does any vertical line touch more than one point?

7 What is the *x*-value of the two points that are on the same vertical line? Is that *x*-value paired with more than one *y*-value?

Table 2	
x	*y*
−2	−3
1	4
0	5
1	2
2	3
3	5

8 Write a statement describing how to use a vertical line to tell if a relation is a function. This is called the vertical-line test.

9 Why does the vertical-line test work?

Try This

Use the vertical-line test to determine whether each relation is a function. If a relation is not a function, list two ordered pairs that show the same *x*-value with two different *y*-values.

1.

2.

3.

Model Variable Relationships

You can use models to represent an algebraic relationship. Using these models, you can write an algebraic expression to help describe and extend patterns.

Use with Lesson 4-3

The diagrams below represent the side views of tables. Each has a tabletop and a base. Copy and complete the chart using the pattern shown in the diagrams.

Tabletop →
Base →

TERM NUMBER	FIGURE	DESCRIPTION OF FIGURE	EXPRESSION FOR NUMBER OF BLOCKS	VALUE OF TERM (NUMBER OF BLOCKS)	ORDERED PAIR
1		length of tabletop = 4 height of base = 1	$4 + (2)1$	6	$(1, 6)$
2		length of tabletop = 4 height of base = 2	▪	8	▪
3		length of tabletop = 4 height of base = 3	▪	10	▪
4	▪	▪	▪	▪	▪
5	▪	▪	▪	▪	▪
n	✕	▪	▪	✕	▪

Try This

1. Explain why you must multiply the height of the base by 2.

2. What does the ordered pair (1, 6) mean?

3. Does the ordered pair (10, 24) belong in this pattern? Why or why not?

4. Which expression from the table describes how you would find the total number of blocks for any term number n?

5. Use your rule to find the 25th term in this pattern.

4-3 Writing Functions

Objectives
Identify independent and dependent variables.

Write an equation in function notation and evaluate a function for given input values.

Vocabulary
independent variable
dependent variable
function rule
function notation

Why learn this?
You can use a function rule to calculate how much money you will earn for working specific amounts of time.

Suppose Tasha baby-sits and charges $5 per hour.

Time Worked (h) *x*	1	2	3	4
Amount Earned ($) *y*	5	10	15	20

The amount of money Tasha earns is $5 times the number of hours she works. Write an equation using two different variables to show this relationship.

Amount earned is $5 times the number of hours worked.

$$y = 5 \cdot x$$

Tasha can use this equation to find how much money she will earn for any number of hours she works.

EXAMPLE 1 **Using a Table to Write an Equation**

Determine a relationship between the *x*- and *y*-values. Write an equation.

x	1	2	3	4
y	−2	−1	0	1

Step 1 List possible relationships between the first *x*- and *y*-values.

$$1 - 3 = -2 \text{ or } 1(-2) = -2$$

Step 2 Determine if one relationship works for the remaining values.

$2 - 3 = -1$ ✓ $\qquad 2(-2) \neq -1$ ✗

$3 - 3 = 0$ ✓ $\qquad 3(-2) \neq 0$ ✗

$4 - 3 = 1$ ✓ $\qquad 4(-2) \neq 1$ ✗

The first relationship works. The value of *y* is 3 less than *x*.

Step 3 Write an equation.

$$y = x - 3 \qquad \textit{The value of y is 3 less than x.}$$

 1. Determine a relationship between the *x*- and *y*-values in the relation $\{(1, 3), (2, 6), (3, 9), (4, 12)\}$. Write an equation.

The equation in Example 1 describes a function because for each *x*-value (input), there is only one *y*-value (output).

The input of a function is the **independent variable** . The output of a function is the **dependent variable** . The value of the dependent variable *depends* on, or is a function of, the value of the independent variable. For Tasha, the amount she earns depends on, or is a function of, the amount of time she works.

EXAMPLE 2 **Identifying Independent and Dependent Variables**

Identify the independent and dependent variables in each situation.

A In the winter, more electricity is used when the temperature goes down, and less is used when the temperature rises.

The **amount of electricity** used *depends on* the temperature.

Dependent: **amount of electricity**   Independent: temperature

Helpful Hint

There are several different ways to describe the variables of a function.

Independent Variable	Dependent Variable
x-values	*y*-values
Domain	Range
Input	Output
x	*f*(*x*)

B The cost of shipping a package is based on its weight.

The **cost** of shipping a package *depends on* its weight.

Dependent: **cost**   Independent: weight

C The faster Ron walks, the quicker he gets home.

The **time** it takes Ron to get home *depends on* the speed he walks.

Dependent: **time**   Independent: speed

CHECK IT OUT! Identify the independent and dependent variables in each situation.

2a. A company charges $10 per hour to rent a jackhammer.

2b. Apples cost $0.99 per pound.

An algebraic expression that defines a function is a **function rule** . $5 \cdot x$ in the equation about Tasha's earnings is a function rule.

If x is the independent variable and y is the dependent variable, then **function notation** for y is $f(x)$, read "*f* of *x*," where *f* names the function. When an equation in two variables describes a function, you can use function notation to write it.

The dependent variable	is	a function of	the independent variable .
y	is	a function of	x .
y	=	f	(x)

Since $y = f(x)$, Tasha's earnings, $y = 5x$, can be rewritten in function notation by substituting $f(x)$ for y: $f(x) = 5x$. Sometimes functions are written using y, and sometimes functions are written using $f(x)$.

EXAMPLE 3 **Writing Functions**

Identify the independent and dependent variables. Write an equation in function notation for each situation.

A A lawyer's fee is $200 per hour for her services.

The **fee** for the lawyer depends on how many hours she works.

Dependent: **fee**   Independent: hours

Let h represent the number of hours the lawyer works.

The function for the lawyer's fee is $f(h) = 200h$.

Identify the independent and dependent variables. Write an equation in function notation for each situation.

B The admission fee to a local carnival is $8. Each ride costs $1.50.

The **total cost** depends on the number of rides ridden, plus $8.

Dependent: **total cost**   Independent: number of rides

Let r represent the number of rides ridden.

The function for the total cost of the carnival is $f(r) = 1.50r + 8$.

 CHECK IT OUT! Identify the independent and dependent variables. Write an equation in function notation for each situation.

3a. Steven buys lettuce that costs $1.69/lb.

3b. An amusement park charges a $6.00 parking fee plus $29.99 per person.

You can think of a function as an **input**-**output** machine. For Tasha's earnings, $f(x) = 5x$, if you input a value x, the output is $5x$.

If Tasha wanted to know how much money she would earn by working 6 hours, she could input 6 for x and find the output. This is called *evaluating the function.*

Input

x 6 2

Function

$f(x) = 5x$

30 5x 10

Output

EXAMPLE **4** **Evaluating Functions**

Evaluate each function for the given input values.

A For $f(x) = 5x$, find $f(x)$ when $x = 6$ and when $x = 7.5$.

$f(x) = 5x$ $f(x) = 5x$

$f(6) = 5(6)$ *Substitute 6 for x.* $f(7.5) = 5(7.5)$ *Substitute 7.5 for x.*

     $= 30$ *Simplify.* $= 37.5$ *Simplify.*

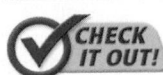 **Reading Math**

Functions can be named with any letter; f, g, and h are the most common. You read $f(6)$ as "f of 6," and $g(2)$ as "g of 2."

B For $g(t) = 2.30t + 10$, find $g(t)$ when $t = 2$ and when $t = -5$.

$g(t) = 2.30t + 10$ $g(t) = 2.30t + 10$

$g(2) = 2.30(2) + 10$ $g(-5) = 2.30(-5) + 10$

     $= 4.6 + 10$ $= -11.5 + 10$

     $= 14.6$ $= -1.5$

C For $h(x) = \frac{1}{2}x - 3$, find $h(x)$ when $x = 12$ and when $x = -8$.

$h(x) = \frac{1}{2}x - 3$ $h(x) = \frac{1}{2}x - 3$

$h(12) = \frac{1}{2}(12) - 3$ $h(-8) = \frac{1}{2}(-8) - 3$

     $= 6 - 3$ $= -4 - 3$

     $= 3$ $= -7$

CHECK IT OUT! Evaluate each function for the given input values.

4a. For $h(c) = 2c - 1$, find $h(c)$ when $c = 1$ and $c = -3$.

4b. For $g(t) = \frac{1}{4}t + 1$, find $g(t)$ when $t = -24$ and $t = 400$.

When a function describes a real-world situation, every real number is not always reasonable for the domain and range. For example, a number representing the length of an object cannot be negative, and only whole numbers can represent a number of people.

EXAMPLE 5 **Finding the Reasonable Domain and Range of a Function**

Manuel has already sold $20 worth of tickets to the school play. He has 4 tickets left to sell at $2.50 per ticket. Write a function to describe how much money Manuel can collect from selling tickets. Find the reasonable domain and range for the function.

Money collected from ticket sales	is	$2.50	per	ticket	plus	the $20 already sold.
$f(x)$	=	$2.50	·	x	+	20

If he sells x more tickets, he will have collected $f(x) = 2.50x + 20$ dollars.

Manuel has only 4 tickets left to sell, so he could sell 0, 1, 2, 3, or 4 tickets. A reasonable domain is {0, 1, 2, 3, 4}.

Substitute these values into the function rule to find the range values.

x	0	1	2	3	4
$f(x)$	2.50(0) + 20 = 20	2.50(1) + 20 = 22.50	2.50(2) + 20 = 25	2.50(3) + 20 = 27.50	2.50(4) + 20 = 30

The reasonable range for this situation is {$20, $22.50, $25, $27.50, $30}.

 CHECK IT OUT! 5. The settings on a space heater are the whole numbers from 0 to 3. The total number of watts used for each setting is 500 times the setting number. Write a function to describe the number of watts used for each setting. Find the reasonable domain and range for the function.

THINK AND DISCUSS

1. When you input water into an ice machine, the output is ice cubes. Name another real-world object that has an input and an output.

2. How do you identify the independent and dependent variables in a situation?

3. Explain how to find reasonable domain values for a function.

 4. **GET ORGANIZED** Copy and complete the graphic organizer. Use the function $y = x + 3$ and the domain {−2, −1, 0, 1, 2}.

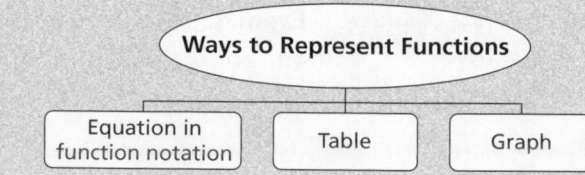

Ways to Represent Functions

Equation in function notation | Table | Graph

go.hrw.com
Homework Help Online
KEYWORD: MA7 4-3
Parent Resources Online
KEYWORD: MA7 Parent

GUIDED PRACTICE

Vocabulary Apply the vocabulary from this lesson to answer each question.

1. The output of a function is the ___?___ variable. (*independent* or *dependent*)

2. An algebraic expression that defines a function is a ___?___. (*function rule* or *function notation*)

SEE EXAMPLE **1**
p. 249

Determine a relationship between the *x*- and *y*-values. Write an equation.

3.

x	1	2	3	4
y	−1	0	1	2

4. $\{(1, 4), (2, 7), (3, 10), (4, 13)\}$

SEE EXAMPLE **2**
p. 250

Identify the independent and dependent variables in each situation.

5. A small-size bottle of water costs $1.99 and a large-size bottle of water costs $3.49.

6. An employee receives 2 vacation days for every month worked.

SEE EXAMPLE **3**
p. 250

Identify the independent and dependent variables. Write an equation in function notation for each situation.

7. An air-conditioning technician charges customers $75 per hour.

8. An ice rink charges $3.50 for skates and $1.25 per hour.

SEE EXAMPLE **4**
p. 251

Evaluate each function for the given input values.

9. For $f(x) = 7x + 2$, find $f(x)$ when $x = 0$ and when $x = 1$.

10. For $g(x) = 4x - 9$, find $g(x)$ when $x = 3$ and when $x = 5$.

11. For $h(t) = \frac{1}{3}t - 10$, find $h(t)$ when $t = 27$ and when $t = -15$.

SEE EXAMPLE **5**
p. 252

12. A construction company uses beams that are 2, 3, or 4 meters long. The measure of each beam must be converted to centimeters. Write a function to describe the situation. Find the reasonable domain and range for the function. (*Hint*: 1 m = 100 cm)

PRACTICE AND PROBLEM SOLVING

Independent Practice

For Exercises	See Example
13–14	1
15–16	2
17–19	3
20–22	4
23	5

Extra Practice

Skills Practice p. S10
Application Practice p. S31

Determine a relationship between the *x*- and *y*-values. Write an equation.

13.

x	1	2	3	4
y	−2	−4	−6	−8

14. $\{(1, -1), (2, -2), (3, -3), (4, -4)\}$

Identify the independent and dependent variables in each situation.

15. Gardeners buy fertilizer according to the size of a lawn.

16. The cost to gift wrap an order is $3 plus $1 per item wrapped.

Identify the independent and dependent variables. Write an equation in function notation for each situation.

17. To rent a DVD, a customer must pay $3.99 plus $0.99 for every day that it is late.

18. Stephen charges $25 for each lawn he mows.

19. A car can travel 28 miles per gallon of gas.

Evaluate each function for the given input values.

20. For $f(x) = x^2 - 5$, find $f(x)$ when $x = 0$ and when $x = 3$.

21. For $g(x) = x^2 + 6$, find $g(x)$ when $x = 1$ and when $x = 2$.

22. For $f(x) = \frac{2}{3}x + 3$, find $f(x)$ when $x = 9$ and when $x = -3$.

23. A mail-order company charges \$5 per order plus \$2 per item in the order, up to a maximum of 4 items. Write a function to describe the situation. Find the reasonable domain and range for the function.

24. Transportation Air Force One can travel 630 miles per hour. Let h be the number of hours traveled. The function $d = 630h$ gives the distance d in miles that Air Force One travels in h hours.

 a. Identify the independent and dependent variables. Write $d = 630h$ using function notation.

 b. What are reasonable values for the domain and range in the situation described?

 c. How far can Air Force One travel in 12 hours?

25. Complete the table for $g(z) = 2z - 5$.

z	1	2	3	4
g(z)				

26. Complete the table for $h(x) = x^2 + x$.

x	0	1	2	3
h(x)				

27. Estimation For $f(x) = 3x + 5$, estimate the output when $x = -6.89$, $x = 1.01$, and $x = 4.67$.

28. Transportation A car can travel 30 miles on a gallon of gas and has a 20-gallon gas tank. Let g be the number of gallons of gas the car has in its tank. The function $d = 30g$ gives the distance d in miles that the car travels on g gallons.

 a. What are reasonable values for the domain and range in the situation described?

 b. How far can the car travel on 12 gallons of gas?

29. Critical Thinking Give an example of a real-life situation for which the reasonable domain consists of 1, 2, 3, and 4 and the reasonable range consists of 2, 4, 6, and 8.

30. /// ERROR ANALYSIS /// Rashid saves \$150 each month. He wants to know how much he will have saved in 2 years. He writes the rule $s = m + 150$ to help him figure out how much he will save, where s is the amount saved and m is the number of months he saves. Explain why his rule is incorrect.

31. Write About It Give a real-life situation that can be described by a function. Identify the independent variable and the dependent variable.

MULTI-STEP TEST PREP

32. This problem will prepare you for the Multi-Step Test Prep on page 264.

The table shows the volume v of water pumped into a pool after t hours.

 a. Determine a relationship between the time and the volume of water and write an equation.

 b. Identify the independent and dependent variables.

 c. If the pool holds 10,000 gallons, how long will it take to fill?

Amount of Water in Pool	
Time (h)	Volume (gal)
0	0
1	1250
2	2500
3	3750
4	5000

33. Marsha buys x pens at \$0.70 per pen and one pencil for \$0.10. Which function gives the total amount Marsha spends?

   Ⓐ $c(x) = 0.70x + 0.10x$ Ⓒ $c(x) = (0.70 + 0.10)x$

   Ⓑ $c(x) = 0.70x + 1$ Ⓓ $c(x) = 0.70x + 0.10$

34. Belle is buying pizzas for her daughter's birthday party, using the prices in the table. Which equation best describes the relationship between the total cost c and the number of pizzas p?

Pizzas	Total Cost ($)
5	26.25
10	52.50
15	78.75

   Ⓕ $c = 26.25p$ Ⓗ $c = p + 26.25$

   Ⓖ $c = 5.25p$ Ⓙ $c = 6p - 3.75$

35. Gridded Response What is the value of $f(x) = 5 - \frac{1}{2}x$ when $x = 3$?

CHALLENGE AND EXTEND

36. The formula to convert a temperature that is in degrees Celsius x to degrees Fahrenheit $f(x)$ is $f(x) = \frac{9}{5}x + 32$. What are reasonable values for the domain and range when you convert to Fahrenheit the temperature of water as it rises from 0° to 100° Celsius?

37. Math History In his studies of the motion of free-falling objects, Galileo Galilei found that regardless of its mass, an object will fall a distance d that is related to the square of its travel time t in seconds. The modern formula that describes free-fall motion is $d = \frac{1}{2}gt^2$, where g is the acceleration due to gravity and t is the length of time in seconds the object falls. Find the distance an object falls in 3 seconds. (*Hint:* Research to find acceleration due to gravity in meters per second squared.)

SPIRAL REVIEW

Solve each equation. Check your answer. *(Lesson 2-3)*

38. $5x + 2 - 7x = -10$ **39.** $3(2 - y) = 15$ **40.** $\frac{2}{3}p - \frac{1}{2} = \frac{1}{6}$

Find the value of x in each diagram. *(Lesson 2-8)*

41. $\triangle ABC \sim \triangle DEF$ **42.** $QRST \sim LMNP$

   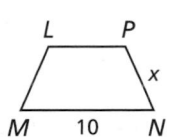

Give the domain and range of each relation. Tell whether the relation is a function. Explain. *(Lesson 4-2)*

43. 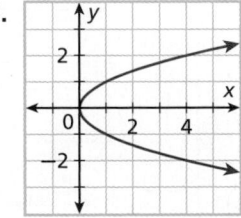   **44.**

x	y
−3	4
−1	2
0	0
1	2
3	−4

Graphing Functions

Objectives

Graph functions given a limited domain.

Graph functions given a domain of all real numbers.

Who uses this?

Scientists can use a function to make conclusions about rising sea level.

Sea level is rising at an approximate rate of 2.5 millimeters per year. If this rate continues, the function $y = 2.5x$ can describe how many millimeters y sea level will rise in the next x years.

One way to understand functions such as the one above is to graph them. You can graph a function by finding ordered pairs that satisfy the function.

Current Florida coastline.

Possible Florida coastline in 2400 years.

EXAMPLE 1 Graphing Solutions Given a Domain

Graph each function for the given domain.

A $-x + 2y = 6$; D: $\{-4, -2, 0, 2\}$

Step 1 Solve for y since you are given values of the domain, or x.

$$-x + 2y = 6$$

$$\underline{+x \qquad \qquad +x} \qquad \text{Add } x \text{ to both sides.}$$

$$2y = x + 6$$

$$\frac{2y}{2} = \frac{x + 6}{2} \qquad \text{Since } y \text{ is multiplied by 2, divide both sides by 2.}$$

$$y = \frac{x}{2} + \frac{6}{2} \qquad \text{Rewrite } \frac{x + 6}{2} \text{ as two separate fractions.}$$

$$y = \frac{1}{2}x + 3 \qquad \text{Simplify.}$$

> **Helpful Hint**
>
> Sometimes solving for y first makes it easier to substitute values of x and find an ordered pair.
>
> To review solving for a variable, see Lesson 2-5.

Step 2 Substitute the given values of the domain for x and find values of y.

Step 3 Graph the ordered pairs.

x	$y = \frac{1}{2}x + 3$	(x, y)
-4	$y = \frac{1}{2}(-4) + 3 = 1$	$(-4, 1)$
-2	$y = \frac{1}{2}(-2) + 3 = 2$	$(-2, 2)$
0	$y = \frac{1}{2}(0) + 3 = 3$	$(0, 3)$
2	$y = \frac{1}{2}(2) + 3 = 4$	$(2, 4)$

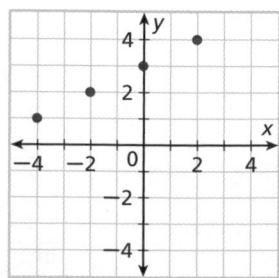

Graph each function for the given domain.

B $f(x) = |x|$; D: $\{-2, -1, 0, 1, 2\}$

Step 1 Use the given values of the domain to find values of $f(x)$.

x	f(x) = |x|	(x, f(x))
−2	$f(x) = \|-2\| = 2$	(−2, 2)
−1	$f(x) = \|-1\| = 1$	(−1, 1)
0	$f(x) = \|0\| = 0$	(0, 0)
1	$f(x) = \|1\| = 1$	(1, 1)
2	$f(x) = \|2\| = 2$	(2, 2)

Step 2 Graph the ordered pairs.

 Graph each function for the given domain.

1a. $-2x + y = 3$; D: $\{-5, -3, 1, 4\}$

1b. $f(x) = x^2 + 2$; D: $\{-3, -1, 0, 1, 3\}$

If the domain of a function is all real numbers, any number can be used as an input value. This process will produce an infinite number of ordered pairs that satisfy the function. Therefore, arrowheads are drawn at both "ends" of a smooth line or curve to represent the infinite number of ordered pairs. If a domain is not given, assume that the domain is all real numbers.

Graphing Functions Using a Domain of All Real Numbers	
Step 1	Use the function to generate ordered pairs by choosing several values for x.
Step 2	Plot enough points to see a pattern for the graph.
Step 3	Connect the points with a line or smooth curve.

EXAMPLE 2 **Graphing Functions**

Graph each function.

A $2x + 1 = y$

Step 1 Choose several values of x and generate ordered pairs.

Helpful Hint

When choosing values of x, be sure to choose both positive and negative values. You may not need to graph all the points to see the pattern.

x	2x + 1 = y	(x, y)
−3	$2(-3) + 1 = -5$	(−3, −5)
−2	$2(-2) + 1 = -3$	(−2, −3)
−1	$2(-1) + 1 = -1$	(−1, −1)
0	$2(0) + 1 = 1$	(0, 1)
1	$2(1) + 1 = 3$	(1, 3)
2	$2(2) + 1 = 5$	(2, 5)
3	$2(3) + 1 = 7$	(3, 7)

Step 2 Plot enough points to see a pattern.

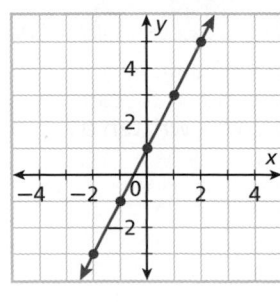

Step 3 The ordered pairs appear to form a line. **Draw a line** through all the points to show all the ordered pairs that satisfy the function. Draw arrowheads on both "ends" of the line.

Graph each function.

B $y = x^2$

Step 1 Choose several values of x and generate ordered pairs.

Step 2 Plot enough points to see a pattern.

x	$y = x^2$	(x, y)
-3	$y = (-3)^2 = 9$	$(-3, 9)$
-2	$y = (-2)^2 = 4$	$(-2, 4)$
-1	$y = (-1)^2 = 1$	$(-1, 1)$
0	$y = (0)^2 = 0$	$(0, 0)$
1	$y = (1)^2 = 1$	$(1, 1)$
2	$y = (2)^2 = 4$	$(2, 4)$

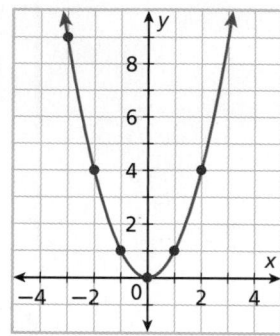

Step 3 The ordered pairs appear to form an almost U-shaped graph. **Draw a smooth curve** through the points to show all the ordered pairs that satisfy the function. Draw arrowheads on the "ends" of the curve.

Check If the graph is correct, any point on it will satisfy the function. Choose an ordered pair on the graph that was not in your table, such as $(3, 9)$. Check whether it satisfies $y = x^2$.

$$\begin{array}{c|c} y = x^2 \\ \hline 9 & 3^2 \\ 9 & 9 ✓ \end{array}$$

Substitute the values for x and y into the function. Simplify.

The ordered pair (3, 9) satisfies the function.

 Graph each function.

2a. $f(x) = 3x - 2$ **2b.** $y = |x - 1|$

EXAMPLE 3 **Finding Values Using Graphs**

Use a graph of the function $f(x) = \frac{1}{3}x + 2$ to find the value of $f(x)$ when $x = 6$. Check your answer.

Locate 6 on the x-axis. Move **up** to the graph of the function. Then move **left** to the y-axis to find the corresponding value of y.

$f(x) = 4$

Check Use substitution.

$$\begin{array}{c|c} f(x) = \frac{1}{3}x + 2 \\ \hline 4 & \frac{1}{3}(6) + 2 \\ 4 & 2 + 2 \\ 4 & 4 ✓ \end{array}$$

Substitute the values for x and y into the function.

Simplify.

The ordered pair (4, 6) satisfies the function.

 3. Use the graph above to find the value of x when $f(x) = 3$. Check your answer.

Recall that in real-world situations you may have to limit the domain to make answers reasonable. For example, quantities such as time, distance, and number of people can be represented using only nonnegative values. When both the domain and the range are limited to nonnegative values, the function is graphed only in Quadrant I.

Problem-Solving Application

The function $y = 2.5x$ describes how many millimeters sea level y rises in x years. Graph the function. Use the graph to estimate how many millimeters sea level will rise in 3.5 years.

1 **Understand the Problem**

The **answer** is a graph that can be used to find the value of y when x is 3.5.

List the important information:
• The function $y = 2.5x$ describes how many millimeters sea level rises.

2 **Make a Plan**

Think: What values should I use to graph this function? Both, the number of years sea level has risen and the distance sea level rises, cannot be negative. Use only nonnegative values for both the domain and the range. The function will be graphed in Quadrant I.

3 **Solve**

Choose several nonnegative values of x to find values of y. Then graph the ordered pairs.

x	$y = 2.5x$	(x, y)
0	$y = 2.5(0) = 0$	$(0, 0)$
1	$y = 2.5(1) = 2.5$	$(1, 2.5)$
2	$y = 2.5(2) = 5$	$(2, 5)$
3	$y = 2.5(3) = 7.5$	$(3, 7.5)$
4	$y = 2.5(4) = 10$	$(4, 10)$

Draw a line through the points to show all the ordered pairs that satisfy this function.

Use the graph to estimate the y-value when x is 3.5.
Sea level will rise about 8.75 millimeters in 3.5 years.

4 **Look Back**

As the number of years increases, sea level also increases, so the graph is reasonable. When x is between 3 and 4, y is between 7.5 and 10. Since 3.5 is between 3 and 4, it is reasonable to estimate y to be 8.75 when x is 3.5.

 4. The fastest recorded Hawaiian lava flow moved at an average speed of 6 miles per hour. The function $y = 6x$ describes the distance y the lava moved on average in x hours. Graph the function. Use the graph to estimate how many miles the lava moved after 5.5 hours.

THINK AND DISCUSS

1. How do you find the range of a function if the domain is all real numbers?

2. Explain how to use a graph to find the value of a function for a given value of x.

3. **GET ORGANIZED** Copy and complete the graphic organizer. Explain how to graph a function for each situation.

```
        Graphing a Function
        ┌──────────┴──────────┐
  Not a real-world      Real-world
    situation            situation
```

4-4 Exercises

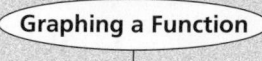

go.hrw.com
Homework Help Online
KEYWORD: MA7 4-4

Parent Resources Online
KEYWORD: MA7 Parent

GUIDED PRACTICE

SEE EXAMPLE 1
p. 256

Graph each function for the given domain.

1. $3x - y = 1$; D: $\{-3, -1, 0, 4\}$

2. $f(x) = -|x|$; D: $\{-5, -3, 0, 3, 5\}$

3. $f(x) = x + 4$; D: $\{-5, -3, 0, 4\}$

4. $y = x^2 - 1$; D: $\{-3, -1, 0, 1, 3\}$

SEE EXAMPLE 2
p. 257

Graph each function.

5. $f(x) = 6x + 4$

6. $y = \frac{1}{2}x + 4$

7. $x + y = 0$

8. $y = |x| - 4$

9. $f(x) = 2x^2 - 7$

10. $y = -x^2 + 5$

SEE EXAMPLE 3
p. 258

11. Use a graph of the function $f(x) = \frac{1}{2}x - 2$ to find the value of y when $x = 2$. Check your answer.

SEE EXAMPLE 4
p. 259

12. **Oceanography** The floor of the Atlantic Ocean is spreading at an average rate of 1 inch per year. The function $y = x$ describes the number of inches y the ocean floor spreads in x years. Graph the function. Use the graph to estimate the number of inches the ocean floor will spread in $10\frac{1}{2}$ years.

PRACTICE AND PROBLEM SOLVING

Independent Practice

For Exercises	See Example
13–16	1
17–24	2
25–26	3
27	4

Extra Practice
Skills Practice p. S12
Application Practice p. S31

Graph each function for the given domain.

13. $2x + y = 4$; D: $\{-3, -1, 4, 7\}$

14. $y = |x| - 1$; D: $\{-4, -2, 0, 2, 4\}$

15. $f(x) = -7x$; D: $\{-2, -1, 0, 1\}$

16. $y = (x + 1)^2$; D: $\{-2, -1, 0, 1, 2\}$

Graph each function.

17. $y = -3x + 5$

18. $f(x) = 3x$

19. $x + y = 8$

20. $f(x) = 2x + 2$

21. $y = -|x| + 10$

22. $f(x) = -5 + x^2$

23. $y = |x + 1| + 1$

24. $y = (x - 2)^2 - 1$

25. Use a graph of the function $f(x) = -2x - 3$ to find the value of y when $x = -4$. Check your answer.

26. Use a graph of the function $f(x) = \frac{1}{3}x + 1$ to find the value of y when $x = 6$. Check your answer.

27. **Transportation** An electric motor scooter can travel at 0.25 miles per minute. The function $y = 0.25x$ describes the number of miles y the scooter can travel in x minutes. Graph the function. Use the graph to estimate the number of miles an electric motor scooter travels in 15 minutes.

Graph each function.

28. $f(x) = x - 1$

29. $12 - x - 2y = 0$

30. $3x - y = 13$

31. $y = x^2 - 2$

32. $x^2 - y = -4$

33. $2x^2 = f(x)$

34. $f(x) = |2x| - 2$

35. $y = |-x|$

36. $-|2x + 1| = y$

37. Find the value of x so that $(x, 12)$ satisfies $y = 4x + 8$.

38. Find the value of x so that $(x, 6)$ satisfies $y = -x - 4$.

39. Find the value of y so that $(-2, y)$ satisfies $y = -2x^2$.

For each function, determine whether the given points are on the graph.

40. $y = 7x - 2$; $(1, 5)$ and $(2, 10)$

41. $y = |x| + 2$; $(3, 5)$ and $(-1, 3)$

42. $y = x^2$; $(1, 1)$ and $(-3, -9)$

43. $y = \dfrac{1}{4}x - 2$; $\left(1, -\dfrac{3}{4}\right)$ and $(4, -1)$

44. **/// ERROR ANALYSIS ///** Student A says that $(3, 2)$ is on the graph of $y = 4x - 5$, but student B says that it is not. Who is incorrect? Explain the error.

Determine whether $(0, -7)$, $\left(-6, -\dfrac{5}{3}\right)$, **and** $(-2, -3)$ **lie on the graph of each function.**

45. $x + 3y = -11$

46. $y + |x| = -1$

47. $x^2 - y = 7$

For each function, find three ordered pairs that lie on the graph of the function.

48. $-6 = 3x + 2y$

49. $y = 1.1x + 2$

50. $y = \dfrac{4}{5}x$

51. $y = 3x - 1$

52. $y = |x| + 6$

53. $y = x^2 - 5$

54. **Critical Thinking** Graph the functions $y = |x|$ and $y = -|x|$. Describe how they are alike. How are they different?

MULTI-STEP TEST PREP

55. This problem will prepare you for the Multi-Step Test Prep on page 264.

A pool containing 10,000 gallons of water is being drained. Every hour, the volume of the water in the pool decreases by 1500 gallons.

a. Write an equation to describe the volume v of water in the pool after h hours.

b. How much water is in the pool after 1 hour?

c. Create a table of values showing the volume of the water in gallons in the pool as a function of the time in hours and graph the function.

56. Estimation Use the graph to estimate the value of y when $x = 2.117$.

57. Write About It Why is a graph a convenient way to show the ordered pairs that satisfy a function?

58. Which function is graphed?

Ⓐ $2y - 3x = 2$ Ⓒ $y = 2x - 1$

Ⓑ $5x + y = 1$ Ⓓ $y = 5x + 8$

59. Which ordered pair is NOT on the graph of $y = 4 - |x|$?

Ⓕ $(0, 4)$ Ⓗ $(-1, 3)$

Ⓖ $(4, 0)$ Ⓙ $(3, -1)$

60. Which function has $(3, 2)$ on its graph?

Ⓐ $2x - 3y = 12$ Ⓒ $y = -\dfrac{2}{3}x + 4$

Ⓑ $-2x - 3y = 12$ Ⓓ $y = -\dfrac{3}{2}x + 4$

61. Which statement(s) is true about the function $y = x^2 + 1$?

I.   All points on the graph are above the origin.

II. All ordered pairs have positive x-values.

III. All ordered pairs have positive y-values.

Ⓕ I Only   Ⓖ II Only   Ⓗ I and II   Ⓙ I and III

CHALLENGE AND EXTEND

62. Graph the function $y = x^3$. Make sure you have enough ordered pairs to see the shape of the graph.

63. The temperature of a liquid that started at 64 °F is increasing by 4 °F per hour. Write a function that describes the temperature of the liquid over time. Graph the function to show the temperatures over the first 10 hours.

SPIRAL REVIEW

Write the power represented by each geometric model. *(Lesson 1-4)*

64.

65.

66.

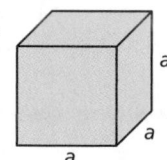

Solve each inequality and graph the solutions. *(Lesson 3-3)*

67. $5p < -20$ **68.** $18 > -9k$ **69.** $\dfrac{3}{4}b \geq 15$

Evaluate each function for the given input values. *(Lesson 4-3)*

70. For $f(x) = -2x - 3$, find $f(x)$ when $x = -4$ and when $x = 2$.

71. For $h(t) = \dfrac{2}{3}t + 1$, find $h(t)$ when $t = -6$ and when $t = 9$.

4-4
Technology LAB

Connect Function Rules, Tables, and Graphs

You can use a graphing calculator to understand the connections among function rules, tables, and graphs.

Use with Lesson 4-4

go.hrw.com
Lab Resources Online
KEYWORD: MA7 Lab4

Activity

Make a table of values for the function $f(x) = 4x + 3$.
Then graph the function.

1 Press **Y=** and enter the function rule **4x + 3**.

2 Press **2nd** **WINDOW** (TBLSET). Make sure **Indpnt: Auto** and **Depend: Auto** are selected.

3 To view the table, press **2nd** **GRAPH** (TABLE). The *x*-values and the corresponding *y*-values appear in table form. Use the up and down arrow keys to scroll through the table.

4 To view the table with the graph, press **MODE** and select **G-T** view. Press **ENTER**. Be sure to use the standard window.

5 Press **TRACE** to see both the graph and a table of values.

6 Press the left arrow key several times to move the cursor. Notice that the point on the graph and the values in the table correspond.

Try This

Make a table of values for each function. Then graph the function.

1. $f(x) = 2x - 1$

2. $f(x) = 1.5x$

3. $f(x) = \frac{1}{2}x + 2$

4. Explain the relationship between a function, its table of values, and the graph of the function.

MULTI-STEP TEST PREP

Function Concepts

Down the Drain The graph shows the relationship between the number of hours that have passed since a pool began to drain and the amount of water in the pool.

Pool Draining

1. Describe in words the relationship between the amount of water in the pool and the number of hours that have passed since the pool began to drain.

2. What are the domain and range for the graph?

3. Use the graph to determine how much water is in the pool after 3 hours. How much water is in the pool after $4\frac{1}{2}$ hours?

4. Copy and complete the table.

Draining Pool	
Time (h)	**Volume (gal)**
0	1400
1	▨
2	▨
3	▨
4	▨
5	▨
6	▨
7	▨

5. Write an equation to describe the relationship between the volume v and the time t. Use the equation to find how much water is in the pool after 5.2 hours.

READY TO GO ON?

Quiz for Lessons 4-1 Through 4-4

4-1 Graphing Relationships

Choose the graph that best represents each situation.

1. A person bungee jumps from a high platform.

2. A person jumps on a trampoline in a steady motion.

3. Xander takes a quiz worth 100 points. Each question is worth 20 points. Sketch a graph to show his score if he misses 1, 2, 3, 4, or 5 questions.

4-2 Relations and Functions

Give the domain and range of each relation. Tell whether the relation is a function. Explain.

4.
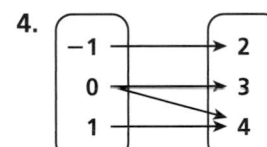

5.

x	−2	−2	0	2	2
y	3	3	3	3	3

6.
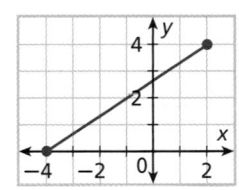

4-3 Writing Functions

Determine a relationship between the *x*- and *y*-values. Write an equation.

7.

x	1	2	3	4
y	−6	−5	−4	−3

8.

x	1	2	3	4
y	−3	−6	−9	−12

9. A printer can print 8 pages per minute. Identify the dependent and independent variables for the situation. Write an equation in function notation.

Evaluate each function for the given input values.

10. For $f(x) = 3x - 1$, find $f(x)$ when $x = 2$.   11. For $g(x) = x^2 - x$, find $g(x)$ when $x = -2$.

12. A photographer charges a sitting fee of $15 plus $3 for each pose. Write a function to describe the situation. Find a reasonable domain and range for up to 5 poses.

4-4 Graphing Functions

Graph each function for the given domain.

13. $2x - y = 3$; D: $\left\{-2, 0, 1, 3\right\}$ 14. $y = 4 - x^2$; D: $\left\{-1, 0, 1, 2\right\}$ 15. $y = 3 - 2x$; D: $\left\{-1, 0, 1, 3\right\}$

Graph each function.

16. $x + y = 6$ 17. $y = |x| - 3$ 18. $y = x^2 + 1$

19. The function $y = 8x$ represents how many miles *y* a certain storm travels in *x* hours. Graph the function and estimate the number of miles the storm travels in 10.5 h.

Scatter Plots and Trend Lines

Objectives
Create and interpret scatter plots.

Use trend lines to make predictions.

Vocabulary
scatter plot
correlation
positive correlation
negative correlation
no correlation
trend line

Who uses this?
Ecologists can use scatter plots to help them analyze data about endangered species, such as ocelots. (See Example 1.)

In this chapter, you have examined relationships between sets of ordered pairs, or data. Displaying data visually can help you see relationships.
A **scatter plot** is a graph with points plotted to show a possible relationship between two sets of data. A scatter plot is an effective way to display some types of data.

EXAMPLE 1 Graphing a Scatter Plot from Given Data

The table shows the number of species added to the list of endangered and threatened species in the United States during the given years. Graph a scatter plot using the given data.

Increase in List							
Calendar Year	1996	1997	1998	1999	2000	2001	2002
Species	91	79	62	11	39	10	9

Source: U.S. Fish and Wildlife Service

Helpful Hint

The point (2000, 39) tells you that in the year 2000, the list increased by 39 species.

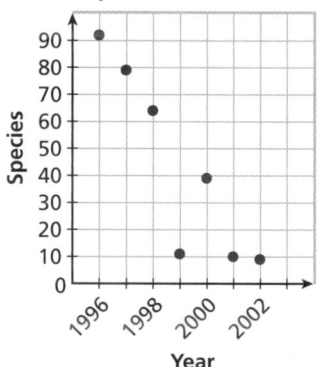

Use the table to make ordered pairs for the scatter plot.

The x-value represents the calendar year and the y-value represents the number of species added.

Plot the ordered pairs.

 1. The table shows the number of points scored by a high school football team in the first four games of a season. Graph a scatter plot using the given data.

Game	1	2	3	4
Score	6	21	46	34

A **correlation** describes a relationship between two data sets. A graph may show the correlation between data. The correlation can help you analyze trends and make predictions. There are three types of correlations between data.

Correlations

Positive Correlation	Negative Correlation	No Correlation
Both sets of data values increase.	One set of data values increases as the other set decreases.	There is no relationship between the data sets.

In the endangered species graph, as time increases, the number of new species added decreases. So the correlation between the data is negative.

EXAMPLE 2 **Describing Correlations from Scatter Plots**

Describe the correlation illustrated by the scatter plot.

TV Watching and Test Scores

As the number of hours spent watching TV increased, test scores decreased.

There is a negative correlation between the two data sets.

CHECK IT OUT!

2. Describe the correlation illustrated by the scatter plot.

EXAMPLE 3 **Identifying Correlations**

Identify the correlation you would expect to see between each pair of data sets. Explain.

A the number of empty seats in a classroom and the number of students seated in the class

You would expect to see a negative correlation. As the number of students increases, the number of empty seats decreases.

B the number of pets a person owns and the number of books that person read last year

You would expect to see no correlation. The number of pets a person owns has nothing to do with how many books the person has read.

Identify the correlation you would expect to see between each pair of data sets. Explain.

C the monthly rainfall and the depth of water in a reservoir

You would expect to see a positive correlation. As more rain falls, there is more water in the reservoir.

 Identify the correlation you would expect to see between each pair of data sets. Explain.

3a. the temperature in Houston and the number of cars sold in Boston

3b. the number of members in a family and the size of the family's grocery bill

3c. the number of times you sharpen your pencil and the length of your pencil

EXAMPLE 4 Matching Scatter Plots to Situations

Choose the scatter plot that best represents the relationship between the number of days since a sunflower seed was planted and the height of the plant. Explain.

There will be a positive correlation between the number of days and the height because the plant will grow each day.

Graph A has a negative correlation, so it is incorrect.

Neither the number of days nor the plant heights can be negative.

Graph B shows negative values, so it is incorrect.

This graph shows all positive coordinates and a positive correlation, so it could represent the data sets.

Graph C is the correct scatter plot.

 4. Choose the scatter plot that best represents the relationship between the number of minutes since a pie has been taken out of the oven and the temperature of the oven. Explain.

You can graph a line on a scatter plot to help show a relationship in the data. This line, called a **trend line,** helps show the correlation between data sets more clearly. It can also be helpful when making predictions based on the data.

EXAMPLE 5 *Fund-raising Application*

The scatter plot shows a relationship between the total amount of money collected and the total number of rolls of wrapping paper sold as a school fund-raiser. Based on this relationship, predict how much money will be collected when 175 rolls have been sold.

Draw a trend line and use it to make a prediction.

Draw a line that has about the same number of points above and below it. Your line may or may not go through data points.

Find the point on the line whose x-value is 175. The corresponding y-value is 1200.

Based on the data, $1200 is a reasonable prediction of how much money will be collected when 175 rolls have been sold.

 5. Based on the trend line above, predict how many wrapping paper rolls need to be sold to raise $500.

THINK AND DISCUSS

1. Is it possible to make a prediction based on a scatter plot with no correlation? Explain your answer.

2. GET ORGANIZED Copy and complete the graphic organizer with either a scatter plot, a real-world example, or both.

	Graph	Example
Positive Correlation		
Negative Correlation		The amount of water in a watering can and the number of flowers watered
No Correlation		

GUIDED PRACTICE

Vocabulary Apply the vocabulary from this lesson to answer each question.

1. Give an example of a graph that is not a *scatter plot*.

2. How is a scatter plot that shows *no correlation* different from a scatter plot that shows a *negative correlation*?

3. Does a *trend line* always pass through every point on a scatter plot? Explain.

SEE EXAMPLE **1**
p. 266

4. Graph a scatter plot using the given data.

Garden Statue	Cupid	Gnome	Lion	Flamingo	Wishing well
Height (in.)	32	18	35	28	40
Price ($)	50	25	80	15	75

SEE EXAMPLE **2**
p. 267

Describe the correlation illustrated by each scatter plot.

5.

6.

SEE EXAMPLE **3**
p. 267

Identify the correlation you would expect to see between each pair of data sets. Explain.

7. the volume of water poured into a container and the amount of empty space left in the container

8. a person's shoe size and the length of the person's hair

9. the outside temperature and the number of people at the beach

SEE EXAMPLE **4**
p. 268

Choose the scatter plot that best represents the described relationship. Explain.

10. age of car and number of miles traveled

11. age of car and sales price of car

12. age of car and number of states traveled to

Graph A

Graph B

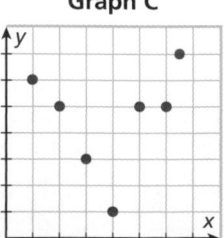

Graph C

SEE EXAMPLE 5
p. 270

13. **Transportation** The scatter plot shows the total number of miles passengers flew on U.S. domestic flights in the month of April for the years 1997–2004. Based on this relationship, predict how many miles passengers flew in April 2008.

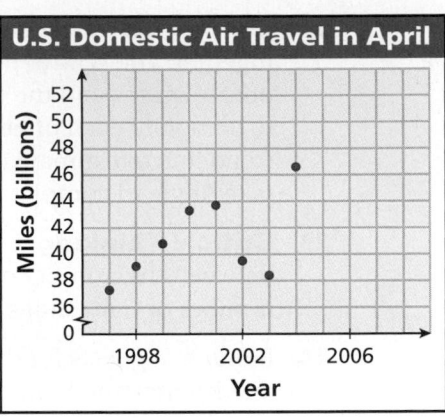
U.S. Domestic Air Travel in April

PRACTICE AND PROBLEM SOLVING

Independent Practice

For Exercises	See Example
14	1
15–16	2
17–18	3
19–20	4
21	5

Extra Practice
Skills Practice p. S12
Application Practice p. S31

14. Graph a scatter plot using the given data.

Train Arrival Time	6:45 A.M.	7:30 A.M.	8:15 A.M.	9:45 A.M.	10:30 A.M.
Passengers	160	148	194	152	64

Describe the correlation illustrated by each scatter plot.

15.
Nascar

16.
Concert Ticket Costs

Identify the correlation you would expect to see between each pair of data sets. Explain.

17. the speed of a runner and the distance she can cover in 10 minutes

18. the year a car was made and the total mileage

Choose the scatter plot that best represents the described relationship. Explain.

19. the number of college classes taken and the number of roommates

20. the number of college classes taken and the hours of free time.

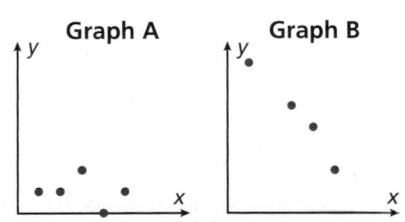
Graph A   Graph B

21. **Ecology** The scatter plot shows a projection of the average ocelot population living in Laguna Atascosa National Wildlife Refuge near Brownsville, Texas. Based on this relationship, predict the number of ocelots living at the wildlife refuge in 2014 if nothing is done to help manage the ocelot population.

Ocelot Population

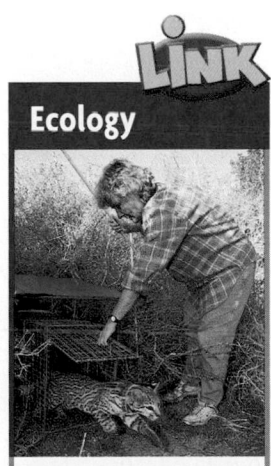
Ecology

The ocelot population in Texas is dwindling due in part to their habitat being destroyed. The ocelot population at Laguna Atascosa National Wildlife Refuge is monitored by following 5–10 ocelots yearly by radio telemetry.

22. **Estimation** Angie enjoys putting jigsaw puzzles together. The scatter plot shows the number of puzzle pieces and the time in minutes it took her to complete each of her last six puzzles. Use the trend line to estimate the time in minutes it will take Angie to complete a 1200-piece puzzle.

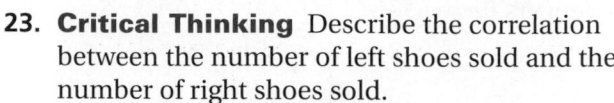

Puzzle Completion

23. **Critical Thinking** Describe the correlation between the number of left shoes sold and the number of right shoes sold.

24. Roma had guests for dinner at her house eight times and has recorded the number of guests and the total cost for each meal in the table.

Guests	3	4	4	6	6	7	8	8
Cost ($)	30	65	88	90	115	160	150	162

a. Graph a scatter plot of the data.

b. Describe the correlation.

c. Draw a trend line.

d. Based on the trend line you drew, predict the cost of dinner for 11 guests.

e. **What if...?** Suppose that each cost in the table increased by $5. How will this affect the cost of dinner for 11 guests?

25. **///ERROR ANALYSIS///** Students graphed a scatter plot for the temperature of hot bath water and time if no new water is added. Which graph is incorrect? Explain the error.

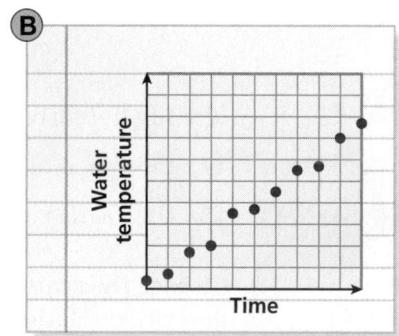

26. **Critical Thinking** Will more people or fewer people buy an item if the price goes up? Explain the relationship and describe the correlation.

MULTI-STEP TEST PREP

27. This problem will prepare you for the Multi-Step Test Prep on page 282.

Juan and his parents are visiting a university 205 miles from their home. As they travel, Juan uses the car odometer and his watch to keep track of the distance.

a. Make a scatter plot for this data set.

b. Describe the correlation. Explain.

c. Draw a trend line for the data and predict the distance Juan would have traveled going to a university 4 hours away.

Time (min)	Distance (mi)
0	0
30	28
60	58
90	87
120	117
150	148
180	178
210	205

28. **Write About It** Conduct a survey of your classmates to find the number of siblings they have and the number of pets they have. Predict whether there will be a positive, negative, or no correlation. Then graph the data in a scatter plot. What is the relationship between the two data sets? Was your prediction correct?

29. Which graph is the best example of a negative correlation?

30. Which situation best describes a positive correlation?
    F The amount of rainfall on Fridays
    G The height of a candle and the amount of time it stays lit
    H The price of a pizza and the number of toppings added
    J The temperature of a cup of hot chocolate and the length of time it sits

31. **Short Response** Write a real-world situation for the graph. Explain your answer.

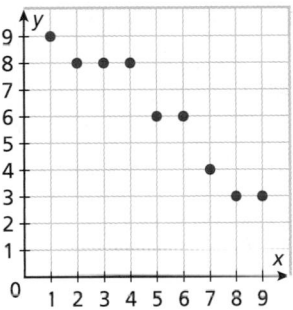

CHALLENGE AND EXTEND

32. Describe a situation that involves a positive correlation. Gather data on the situation. Make a scatter plot showing the correlation. Use the scatter plot to make a prediction. Repeat for a negative correlation and for no correlation.

33. Research an endangered or threatened species in your state. Gather information on its population for several years. Make a scatter plot using the data you gather. Is there a positive or negative correlation? Explain. Draw a trend line and make a prediction about the species population over the next 5 years.

SPIRAL REVIEW

Write an equation to represent each relationship. Then solve the equation. *(Lesson 2-4)*

34. Five times a number increased by 2 is equal to twice the number decreased by 4.

35. Five times the sum of a number and 2 is equal to 8 less than twice the number.

Solve each inequality. *(Lesson 3-5)*

36. $4(6 + x) \geq -2x$ 37. $3(x - 1) > 3x$ 38. $2(3 - x) < 2(1 + x)$

Graph each function. *(Lesson 4-4)*

39. $y = 2x - 3$ 40. $y = -|x| + 3$ 41. $y = x^2 - 4$

4-5 Technology LAB

Interpret Scatter Plots and Trend Lines

You can use a graphing calculator to graph a trend line on a scatter plot.

Use with Lesson 4-5

go.hrw.com
Lab Resources Online
KEYWORD: MA7 Lab 4

Activity

The table shows the recommended dosage of a particular medicine as related to a person's weight. Graph a scatter plot of the given data. Draw the trend line. Then predict the dosage for a person weighing 240 pounds.

Weight (lb)	90	100	110	125	140	155	170	180	200
Dosage (mg)	20	25	30	35	40	53	60	66	75

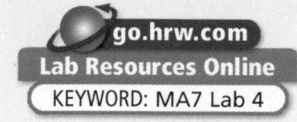

1 First enter the data. Press STAT and select **1: Edit**. In **L1**, enter the first weight. Press ENTER. Continue entering all weights. Use ▶ to move to **L2**. Enter the first dosage. Press ENTER. Continue entering all dosages.

2 To view the scatter plot, press 2nd Y=. Select **Plot 1**. Select **On**, the first plot type, and the plot mark +. Press ZOOM. Select **9: ZoomStat**. You should see a scatter plot of the data.

3 To find the trend line, press STAT and select the **CALC** menu. Select **LinReg (ax+b)**. Press ENTER. This gives you the values of *a* and *b* in the trend line.

4 To enter the equation for the trend line, press Y=, and then input **.5079441502x − 26.78767453**. Press GRAPH.

5 Now predict the dosage for a weight of 240 pounds. Press VARS. Select **Y-VARS** menu and select **1:Function**. Select **1:Y1**. Enter **(240)**. Press ENTER. The dosage is about 95 milligrams.

Try This

1. The table shows the price of a stock over an 8-month period. Graph a scatter plot of the given data. Draw the trend line. Then predict what the price of one share of stock will be in the twelfth month.

Month	1	2	3	4	5	6	7	8
Price ($)	32	35	37	41	46	50	54	59

Median-Fit Line

You have learned about trend lines. Now you will learn about another line of fit called the *median-fit line*.

Example

At a water raft rental shop, a group of up to four people can rent a single raft. The table shows the number of rafts rented to different groups of people one morning. Graph the median-fit line for the data.

People x	1	2	4	5	5	5	7	9	10	11	12	15
Rafts Rented y	1	1	1	3	4	5	4	7	5	3	4	6

1 Plot the points on a coordinate plane.

2 Divide the data into three sections of equal size. Find the medians of the x-values and the y-values for each section. Plot the three median points with an X.

1	2	4	5	5	5	7	9	10	11	12	15
1	1	1	3	4	5	4	7	5	3	4	6

Median point: (3, 1)   Median point: (6, 4.5)   Median point: (11.5, 4.5)

3 Connect the outside, or first and third, median points with a line.

4 Lightly draw a dashed line straight down from the middle median point to the line just drawn. Mark the dashed line to create three equal segments.

5 Keeping your ruler parallel to the first line you drew, move your ruler to the mark closest to the line. Draw the line. This is the median-fit line.

Canoe Rentals

Canoe Rentals

Try This

1. A manager at a restaurant kept track one afternoon of the number of people in a party and the time it took to seat them. Graph the median-fit line for the data.

2. Use your median-fit line to predict the time it would take to seat a party of 6.

People x	3	7	8	8	10	12
Wait Time y (min)	1	5	3	9	6	6

Arithmetic Sequences

Why learn this?

The distance between you and a lightning strike can be approximated by using an arithmetic sequence.

During a thunderstorm, you can estimate your distance from a lightning strike by counting the number of seconds from the time you see the lightning until the time you hear the thunder.

Time (s)	Distance (mi)
1	0.2
2	0.4
3	0.6
4	0.8
5	1.0
6	1.2
7	1.4
8	1.6

+ 0.2
+ 0.2
+ 0.2
+ 0.2
+ 0.2
+ 0.2
+ 0.2

When you list the times and distances in order, each list forms a *sequence*. A **sequence** is a list of numbers that may form a pattern. Each number in a sequence is a **term**.

In the distance sequence, each distance is 0.2 mi greater than the previous distance. When the terms of a sequence differ by the same nonzero number d, the sequence is an **arithmetic sequence** and d is the **common difference**. The distances in the table form an arithmetic sequence with $d = 0.2$.

The variable a is often used to represent terms in a sequence. The variable a_9, read "a sub 9," is the ninth term in a sequence. To designate any term, or the nth term, in a sequence, you write a_n, where n can be any number.

To find a term in an arithmetic sequence, add d to the previous term.

Finding a Term of an Arithmetic Sequence

The nth term of an arithmetic sequence with **common difference** d is

$$a_n = a_{n-1} + d.$$

EXAMPLE 1   Identifying Arithmetic Sequences

Determine whether each sequence appears to be an arithmetic sequence. If so, find the common difference and the next three terms in the sequence.

A $12, 8, 4, 0, \ldots$

Step 1 Find the difference between successive terms.

$12, \quad 8, \quad 4, \quad 0, \ldots$

$-4 \quad -4 \quad -4$

Add -4 to each term to find the next term. The common difference is -4.

Step 2 Use the common difference to find the next 3 terms.

$12, 8, 4, 0, \quad -4, \quad -8, \quad -12$

$-4 \quad -4 \quad -4$

$a_n = a_{n-1} + d$

The sequence appears to be an arithmetic sequence with a common difference of -4. The next 3 terms are $-4, -8, -12$.

Reading Math

The three dots at the end of a sequence are called an ellipsis. They mean that the sequence continues and can be read as "and so on."

B 1, 4, 9, 16, …

Find the difference between successive terms.

1,   4,   9,   16, …   *The difference between successive terms is*
+3 +5 +7   *not the same.*

This sequence is not an arithmetic sequence.

 Determine whether each sequence appears to be an arithmetic sequence. If so, find the common difference and the next three terms.

1a. $-\frac{3}{4}, -\frac{1}{4}, \frac{1}{4}, \frac{3}{4}, \ldots$ **1b.** $-4, -2, 1, 5, \ldots$

To find the *n*th term of an arithmetic sequence when *n* is a large number, you need an equation or rule. Look for a pattern to find a rule for the sequence below.

1	2	3	4…		*n*	← Position
↓	↓	↓	↓			
3,	5,	7,	9…			← Term
a_1	a_2	a_3	a_4	a_n		

The sequence starts with 3. The common difference *d* is 2. You can use the first term and the common difference to write a rule for finding a_n.

Words	Numbers	Algebra
1st term	3	a_1
2nd term = 1st term plus common difference	$3 + (1)2 = 5$	$a_1 + 1d$
3nd term = 1st term plus 2 common differences	$3 + (2)2 = 7$	$a_1 + 2d$
4th term = 1st term plus 3 common differences	$3 + (3)2 = 9$	$a_1 + 3d$
⋮	⋮	⋮
*n*th term = 1st term plus $(n-1)$ common differences	$3 + (n-1)2$	$a_1 + (n-1)d$

The pattern in the table shows that to find the *n*th term, add the first term to the product of $(n-1)$ and the common difference.

Finding the *n*th Term of an Arithmetic Sequence

The *n*th term of an arithmetic sequence with **common difference *d*** and **first term a_1** is

$$a_n = a_1 + (n-1)d.$$

EXAMPLE 2 Finding the *n*th Term of an Arithmetic Sequence

Find the indicated term of each arithmetic sequence.

A 22nd term: 5, 2, −1, −4, …

Step 1 Find the common difference.

5,   2,   −1,   −4, …   *The common difference is −3.*
−3 −3 −3

Step 2 Find the 22nd term.

$$a_n = a_1 + (n-1)d$$ *Write the rule to find the nth term.*

$$a_{22} = 5 + (22-1)(-3)$$ *Substitute 5 for a_1, 22 for n, and −3 for d.*

$$= 5 + (21)(-3)$$ *Simplify the expression in parentheses.*

$$= 5 - 63$$ *Multiply.*

$$= -58$$ *Subtract.*

B   15th term: $a_1 = 7$; $d = 3$

$$a_n = a_1 + (n-1)d$$ *Write the rule to find the nth term.*

$$a_{15} = 7 + (15-1)3$$ *Substitute 7 for a_1, 15 for n, and 3 for d.*

$$= 7 + (14)3$$ *Simplify the expression in parentheses.*

$$= 7 + 42$$ *Multiply.*

$$= 49$$ *Add.*

 Find the indicated term of each arithmetic sequence.

2a. 60th term: 11, 5, −1, −7, …   **2b.** 12th term: $a_1 = 4.2$; $d = 1.4$

EXAMPLE 3   *Travel Application*

The odometer on a car reads 60,473 on day 1. Every day, the car is driven 54 miles. If this pattern continues, what is the odometer reading on day 20?

Notice that the sequence for the situation is arithmetic with $d = 54$ because the odometer reading will increase by **54** miles per day.

Since the odometer reading on day 1 is **60,473** miles, $a_1 = 60,473$.

Since you want to find the odometer reading on day 20, you will need to find the **20th term** of the sequence, so $n = 20$.

$$a_n = a_1 + (n-1)d$$ *Write the rule to find the nth term.*

$$a_{20} = 60,473 + (20-1)54$$ *Substitute 60,473 for a_1, 54 for d, and 21 for n.*

$$= 60,473 + (19)54$$ *Simplify the expression in parentheses.*

$$= 60,473 + 1026$$ *Multiply.*

$$= 61,499$$ *Add.*

The odometer will read 61,499 miles on day 20.

 3. Each time a truck stops, it drops off 250 pounds of cargo. After stop 1, its cargo weighed 2000 pounds. How much does the load weigh after stop 6?

THINK AND DISCUSS

1. Explain how to determine if a sequence appears to be arithmetic.

2. GET ORGANIZED Copy and complete the graphic organizer with steps for finding the *n*th term of an arithmetic sequence.

4-6 Exercises

go.hrw.com
Homework Help Online
KEYWORD: MA7 4-6
Parent Resources Online
KEYWORD: MA7 Parent

GUIDED PRACTICE

1. **Vocabulary** When trying to find the *n*th term of an arithmetic sequence you must first know the _____?_____. (*common difference* or *sequence*)

SEE EXAMPLE **1**
p. 276

Multi-Step Determine whether each sequence appears to be an arithmetic sequence. If so, find the common difference and the next three terms.

2. 2, 8, 14, 20, …

3. 2.1, 1.4, 0.7, 0, …

4. 1, 1, 2, 3, …

5. 0.1, 0.3, 0.9, 2.7, …

SEE EXAMPLE **2**
p. 277

Find the indicated term of each arithmetic sequence.

6. 21st term: 3, 8, 13, 18, …

7. 18th term: $a_1 = -2$; $d = -3$

SEE EXAMPLE **3**
p. 278

8. **Shipping** To package and ship an item, it costs $5.75 for the first pound and $0.75 for each additional pound. What is the cost of shipping a 12-pound package?

PRACTICE AND PROBLEM SOLVING

Independent Practice

For Exercises	See Example
9–12	1
13–14	2
15	3

Extra Practice
Skills Practice p. S12
Application Practice p. S31

Multi-Step Determine whether each sequence appears to be an arithmetic sequence. If so, find the common difference and the next three terms.

9. −1, 10, −100, 1,100, …

10. 0, −2, −4, −6, …

11. −22, −31, −40, −49, …

12. 0.2, 0.5, 0.9, 1.1, …

Find the indicated term of each arithmetic sequence.

13. 31st term: 1.40, 1.55, 1.70, …

14. 50th term: $a_1 = 2.2$; $d = 1.1$

15. **Travel** Rachel signed up for a frequent-flier program. She receives 4300 frequent-flier miles for her first round trip and 1300 frequent-flier miles for each additional round-trip. How many frequent-flier miles will she have after 5 round-trips?

Find the common difference for each arithmetic sequence.

16. 0, 6, 12, 18, …

17. $\frac{1}{2}, \frac{3}{4}, 1, \frac{5}{4}, …$

18. 107, 105, 103, 101, …

19. 7.9, 5.7, 3.5, 1.3, …

20. $\frac{1}{5}, \frac{2}{5}, \frac{3}{5}, \frac{4}{5}, …$

21. 4.25, 4.32, 4.39, 4.46, …

Find the next four terms in each arithmetic sequence.

22. −4, −7, −10, −13, …

23. $\frac{1}{8}, 0, -\frac{1}{8}, -\frac{1}{4}, …$

24. 505, 512, 519, 526, …

25. 1.8, 1.3, 0.8, 0.3, …

26. $\frac{2}{3}, \frac{4}{3}, 2, \frac{8}{3}, …$

27. −1.1, −0.9, −0.7, −0.5

Find the given term of each arithmetic sequence.

28. 5, 10, 15, 20, …; 17th term

29. 121, 110, 99, 88, …; 10th term

30. −2, −5, −8, −11, …; 41st term

31. −30, −22, −14, −6, …; 20th term

32. **Critical Thinking** Is the sequence $5a - 1, 3a - 1, a - 1, -a - 1, …$ arithmetic? If not, explain why not. If so, find the common difference and the next three terms.

33. **Recreation** The rates for a go-cart course are shown.

a. Explain why the relationship described on the flyer could be represented by an arithmetic sequence.

b. Find the cost for 1, 2, 3, and 4 laps. Write a rule to find the nth term of the sequence.

c. How much would 15 laps cost?

d. **What if...?** After 9 laps, you get the 10th one free. Will the sequence still be arithmetic? Explain.

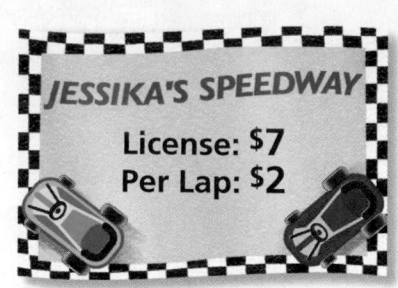

JESSIKA'S SPEEDWAY
License: $7
Per Lap: $2

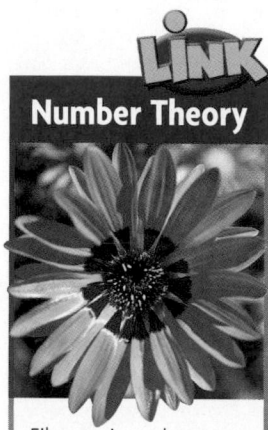

Number Theory

Fibonacci numbers occur frequently throughout nature. The number of petals on many flowers are numbers of the Fibonacci sequence. Two petals on a flower are rare but 3, 5, and even 34 petals are common.

Find the given term of each arithmetic sequence.

34. 2.5, 8.5, 14.5, 20.5, …; 30th term

35. 189.6, 172.3, 155, 137.7, …; 18th term

36. $\frac{1}{4}, \frac{3}{4}, \frac{5}{4}, \frac{7}{4}$, …; 15th term

37. $\frac{2}{3}, \frac{11}{12}, \frac{7}{6}, \frac{17}{12}$, …; 25th term

38. **Number Theory** The sequence 1, 1, 2, 3, 5, 8, 13, … is a famous sequence called the Fibonacci sequence. After the first two terms, each term is the sum of the previous two terms.

a. Write the first 10 terms of the Fibonacci sequence. Is the Fibonacci sequence arithmetic? Explain.

b. Notice that the third term is divisible by 2. Are the 6th and 9th terms also divisible by 2? What conclusion can you draw about every third term? Why is this true?

c. Can you find any other patterns? (*Hint:* Look at every 4th and 5th term.)

39. **Entertainment** Seats in a concert hall are arranged in the pattern shown.

a. The numbers of seats in the rows form an arithmetic sequence. Write a rule for the arithmetic sequence.

b. How many seats are in the 15th row?

c. A ticket costs $40. Suppose every seat in the first 10 rows is filled. What is the total revenue from those seats?

Row 1
Row 2
Row 3
Row 4

d. **What if...?** An extra chair is added to each row. Write the new rule for the arithmetic sequence and find the new total revenue from the first 10 rows.

40. **Write About It** Explain how to find the common difference of an arithmetic sequence. How can you determine whether the arithmetic sequence has a positive common difference or a negative common difference?

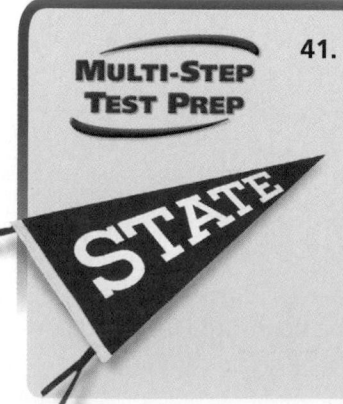

MULTI-STEP TEST PREP

STATE

41. This problem will prepare you for the Multi-Step Test Prep on page 282.

Juan is traveling to visit universities. He notices mile markers along the road. He records the mile marker every 10 minutes. His father is driving at a constant speed.

a. Copy and complete the table.

b. Write the rule for the sequence.

c. What does the common difference represent?

d. If this sequence continues, find the mile marker for time interval 10.

Time Interval	Mile Marker
1	520
2	509
3	498
4	■
5	■
6	■

42. What are the next three terms in the arithmetic sequence −21, −12, −3, 6, … ?

Ⓐ 9, 12, 15　　Ⓑ 15, 24, 33　　Ⓒ 12, 21, 27　　Ⓓ 13, 20, 27

43. What is the common difference for the data listed in the second column?

Ⓕ −1.8　　　Ⓗ 2.8

Ⓖ 1.8　　　Ⓙ −3.6

Altitude (ft)	Boiling Point of Water (°F)
1000	210.2
2000	208.4
3000	206.6

44. Which of the following sequences is NOT arithmetic?

Ⓐ −4, 2, 8, 14, …　　Ⓑ 9, 4, −1, −6, …　　Ⓒ 2, 4, 8, 16, …　　Ⓓ $\frac{1}{3}$, $1\frac{1}{3}$, $2\frac{1}{3}$, $3\frac{1}{3}$, …

CHALLENGE AND EXTEND

45. The first term of an arithmetic sequence is 2, and the common difference is 9. Find two consecutive terms of the sequence that have a sum of 355. What positions in the sequence are the terms?

46. The 60th term of an arithmetic sequence is 106.5, and the common difference is 1.5. What is the first term of the sequence?

47. **Athletics** Verona is training for a marathon. The first part of her training schedule is shown below.

Session	1	2	3	4	5	6
Distance Run (mi)	3.5	5	6.5	8	9.5	11

a. If Verona continues this pattern, during which training session will she run 26 miles? Is her training schedule an arithmetic sequence? Explain.

b. If Verona's training schedule starts on a Monday and she runs every third day, on which day will she run 26 miles?

SPIRAL REVIEW

48. Three sides of a triangle are represented by x, $x + 3$ and $x + 5$. The perimeter of the triangle is 35 units. Solve for x. *(Lesson 2-3)*

49. The length of a rectangle is 2 and the width is represented by $x + 4$. The area of the rectangle is 40 square units. Find the width of the rectangle. *(Lesson 2-3)*

Solve each compound inequality and graph the solutions. *(Lesson 3-6)*

50. $4 < 2n + 6 \le 20$

51. $t + 5 > 7$ OR $2t − 8 < −12$

Describe the correlation illustrated by each scatter plot. *(Lesson 4-5)*

52. **Household Televisions**

53. **Safe Heart Rate**

MULTI-STEP TEST PREP

Applying Functions

College Knowledge Myra is helping her brother plan a college visit 10 hours away from their home. She creates a table listing approximate travel times and distances from their home.

1. Create a scatter plot for the data.

2. Draw a trend line through the data.

3. Based on the trend line, how many miles will they have traveled after 5 hours?

4. If Myra's brother decided to visit a college 13 hours away from their home, approximately how many miles will they travel?

5. To find the average speed for the entire trip, find $\frac{\text{change in distance}}{\text{change in time}}$ between the initial ordered pair and the final ordered pair. Include the units.

Time (h)	Distance (mi)
0	0
2	123
3	190
4	207
6	355
8	472
10	657

READY TO GO ON?

Quiz for Lessons 4-5 Through 4-6

✅ **4-5** **Scatter Plots and Trend Lines**

The table shows the time it takes different people to read a given number of pages.

Pages Read	2	6	6	8	8	10	10
Time (min)	10	15	20	15	30	25	30

1. Graph a scatter plot using the given data.

2. Describe the correlation illustrated by the scatter plot.

Choose the scatter plot that best represents the described relationship. Explain.

3. number of movie tickets sold and number of available seats

4. number of movie tickets sold and amount of concession sales

5. number of movie tickets sold and length of movie

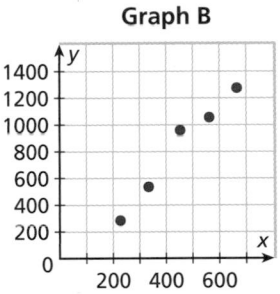

6. The scatter plot shows the estimated annual sales for an electronics and appliance chain of stores for the years 2004–2009. Based on this relationship, predict the annual sales in 2012.

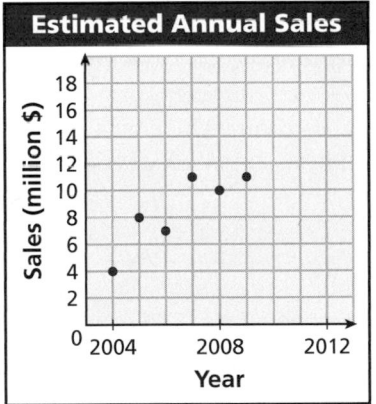

✅ **4-6** **Arithmetic Sequences**

Determine whether each sequence appears to be an arithmetic sequence. If so, find the common difference and the next three terms.

7. $7, 3, -1, -5, \ldots$ 8. $3, 6, 12, 24, \ldots$ 9. $-3.5, -2, -0.5, 1, \ldots$

Find the indicated term of the arithmetic sequence.

10. 31st term: $12, 7, 2, -3, \ldots$ 11. 22nd term: $a_1 = 6; d = 4$

12. With no air resistance, an object would fall 16 feet during the first second, 48 feet during the second second, 80 feet during the third second, 112 feet during the fourth second, and so on. How many feet will the object fall during the ninth second?

Vocabulary

Complete the sentences below with vocabulary words from the list above.

1. The set of *x*-coordinates of the ordered pairs of a relation is called the ___?___ .

2. If one set of data values increases as another set of data values decreases, the relationship can be described as having a(n) ___?___ .

3. A sequence is an ordered list of numbers where each number is a(n) ___?___ .

4-1 Graphing Relationships *(pp. 234–239)*

EXAMPLES

Sketch a graph for each situation. Tell whether the graph is continuous or discrete.

■ A parking meter has a limit of 1 hour. The cost is $0.25 per 15 minutes and the meter accepts quarters only.

Since only quarters are accepted, the points are not connected.

The graph is discrete.

■ Ian bought a cup of coffee. At first, he sipped slowly. As it cooled, he drank more quickly. The last bit was cold, and he dumped it out.

As time passes the coffee was **sipped slowly**, **drank more quickly**, and then **dumped out**.

The graph is continuous.

EXERCISES

Sketch a graph for each situation. Tell whether the graph is continuous or discrete.

4. A girl was walking home at a steady pace. Then she stopped to talk to a friend. After her friend left, she jogged the rest of the way home.

5. A ball is dropped from a second story window and bounces to a stop on the patio below.

6. Jason was on the second floor when he got a call to attend a meeting on the sixth floor. He took the stairs. After the meeting, he took the elevator to the first floor.

Write a possible situation for each graph.

4-2 Relations and Functions (pp. 240–246)

EXAMPLES

- Express the relation $\{(2, 15), (4, 12), (5, 7), (7, 2)\}$ as a table, as a graph, and as a mapping diagram.

Table

x	y
2	15
4	12
5	7
7	2

Graph

Mapping Diagram

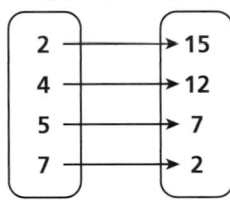

Give the domain and range of each relation. Tell whether the relation is a function. Explain.

■

x	y
−3	0
−2	0
−1	1

D: $\{-3, -2, -1\}$

R: $\{0, 1\}$

The relation is a function because each domain value is paired with exactly one range value.

■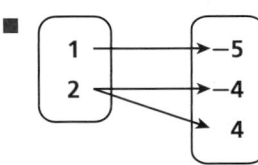

D: $\{1, 2\}$

R: $\{-5, -4, 4\}$

The relation is not a function because one domain value is paired with two range values.

■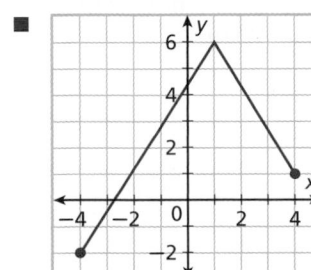

D: $-4 \leq x \leq 4$

R: $-2 \leq y \leq 6$

The relation is a function because every x-value is paired with exactly one y-value.

EXERCISES

Express each relation as a table, as a graph, and as a mapping diagram.

9. $\{(-1, 0), (0, 1), (2, 1)\}$

10. $\{(-2, -1), (-1, 1), (2, 3), (3, 4)\}$

Give the domain and range of each relation.

11. $\{(-4, 5), (-2, 3), (0, 1), (2, -1)\}$

12. $\{(-2, -1) \ (-1, 0), (0, -1), (1, 0), (2, -1)\}$

13.

x	0	1	4	1	4
y	0	−1	−2	1	2

14.

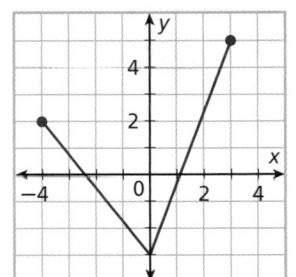

Give the domain and range of each relation. Tell whether the relation is a function. Explain.

15. $\{(-5, -3), (-3, -2), (-1, -1), (1, 0)\}$

16.

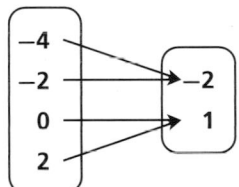

17.

x	1	2	3	4	1
y	3	2	1	0	−1

18. A local parking garage charges $5.00 for the first hour plus $1.50 for each additional hour or part of an hour. Write a relation as a set of ordered pairs in which the x-value represents the number of hours and the y-value represents the cost for x hours. Use a domain of 1, 2, 3, 4, 5. Is this relation a function? Explain.

19. A baseball coach is taking the team for ice cream. Four students can ride in each car. Create a mapping diagram to show the number of cars needed to transport 8, 10, 14, and 16 students. Is this relation a function? Explain.

Writing Functions *(pp. 249–255)*

EXAMPLES

- Determine a relationship between the *x*- and *y*-values in the table. Write an equation.

What are possible relationships between the x-values and the y-values?

x	1	2	3	4
y	−3	−6	−9	−12

$1 - 4 = -3$ $1(-3) = -3$

$2 - 4 \neq -6$ ✗ $2(-3) = -6$ ✓

$3(-3) = -9$ ✓

$4(-3) = -12$ ✓

$y = -3x$ *Write an equation.*

- **Nia earns $5.25 per hour. Identify the independent and dependent variables. Write an equation in function notation for the situation.**

  Nia's **pay** depends on the **number of hours** she works.
  Dependent: **pay**
  Independent: **hours**
  Let *h* represent the number of hours Nia works.
  The function for Nia's pay is $f(h) = 5.25h$.

EXERCISES

Determine the relationship between the *x*- and *y*-values. Write an equation.

20.

x	1	2	3	4
y	−6	−5	−4	−3

21. $\{(1, 9), (2, 18), (3, 27), (4, 36)\}$

Identify the independent and dependent variables. Write an equation in function notation for the situation.

22. A baker spends $6 on ingredients for each cake he bakes.

23. Tim will buy twice as many CDs as Raul.

Evaluate each function for the given input values.

24. For $f(x) = -2x + 4$, find $f(x)$ when $x = -5$.

25. For $g(n) = -n^2 - 2$, find $g(n)$ when $n = -3$.

26. For $h(t) = 7 - |t + 3|$, find $h(t)$ when $t = -4$ and when $t = 5$.

Graphing Functions *(pp. 256–262)*

EXAMPLE

- Graph the function $y = 3x - 1$.

  Step 1 Choose several values of *x* to generate ordered pairs.

x	$y = 3x - 1$	*y*
−1	$y = 3(-1) - 1 = -4$	−4
0	$y = 3(0) - 1 = -1$	−1
1	$y = 3(1) - 1 = 2$	2
2	$y = 3(2) - 1 = 5$	5

  Step 2 Plot enough points to see a pattern.

  Step 3 Draw a line through the points to show all the ordered pairs that satisfy this function.

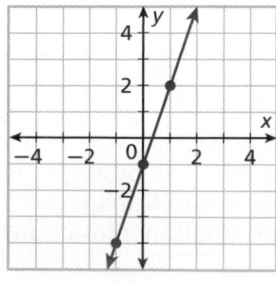

EXERCISES

Graph each function for the domain $\{-2, -1, 1, 2\}$.

27. $4x + y = 2$ **28.** $y = (1 - x)^2$

Graph each function.

29. $3x - y = 1$ **30.** $y = 2 - |x|$

31. $y = x^2 - 6$ **32.** $y = |x + 5| + 1$

33. The function $y = 6.25x$ describes the amount of money *y* Peter gets paid after *x* hours. Graph the function. Use the graph to estimate how much money Peter gets paid after 7 hours.

4-5 Scatter Plots and Trend Lines (pp. 266–273)

EXAMPLE

■ The graph shows the amount of money in a savings account. Based on this relationship, predict how much money will be in the account in month 7.

Monthly Savings

Draw a line that has about the same number of points above and below it. Your line may or may not go through data points.

Find the point on the line whose x-value is 7.

Based on the data, $90 is a reasonable prediction.

EXERCISES

34. The table shows the value of a car for the given years. Graph a scatter plot using the given data. Describe the correlation illustrated by the scatter plot.

Year	2000	2001	2002	2003
Value (thousand $)	28	25	23	20

35. The graph shows the results of a 2003–2004 survey on class size at the given grade levels. Based on this relationship, predict the class size for the 9th grade.

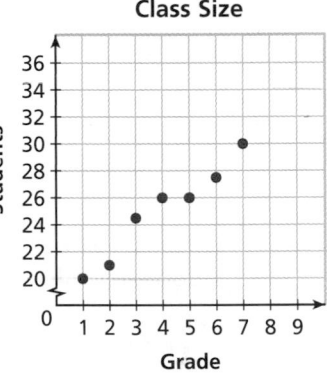

Class Size

4-6 Arithmetic Sequences (pp. 276–281)

EXAMPLES

■ Determine whether the sequence appears to be arithmetic. If so, find the common difference and the next three terms.

$-8, -5, -2, 1,\ldots$

Step 1 Find the difference between successive terms.

$-8, -5, -2, 1,\ldots$ *The common difference is 3.*
$+3 \ +3 \ +3$

Step 2 Use the common difference to find the next 3 terms.

$-8, -5, -2, 1, \ 4, \ 7, \ 10$
$+3 \ +3 \ +3$

■ Find the 18th term of the arithmetic sequence for which $a_1 = -4$ and $d = 6$.

$a_n = a_1 + (n-1)d$ *Write the rule.*
$a_{18} = -4 + (18-1)6$ *Substitute.*
$= -4 + (17)6$ *Simplify.*
$= -4 + 102$ *Simplify.*
$= 98$

The 18th term is 98.

EXERCISES

Determine whether each sequence appears to be arithmetic. If so, find the common difference and the next three terms.

36. $20, 14, 8, 2,\ldots$

37. $-15, -12, -9, -4,\ldots$

38. $5, 4, 2, -1,\ldots$

39. $-8, -5.5, -3, -0.5,\ldots$

Find the indicated term of each arithmetic sequence.

40. 31st term: $-15, -11, -7, -3,\ldots$

41. 24th term: $a_1 = 7; d = -3$

42. 17th term: $a_1 = -20; d = 2.5$

43. Marie has $180 in a savings account in week 1. She plans to deposit $12 each following week. Assuming that she does not withdraw any money from her account, what will her balance be in week 20?

44. The table shows the temperature at the given heights above sea level. Use an arithmetic sequence to find the temperature at 8000 feet above sea level.

Height Above Sea Level (thousand feet)	1	2	3	4
Temperature (°C)	30	23.5	17	10.5

CHAPTER TEST

Choose the graph that best represents each situation.

1. A person walks leisurely, stops, and then continues walking.

2. A person jogs, then runs, and then jogs again.

Give the domain and range for each relation.
Tell whether the relation is a function. Explain.

3.

x	−2	1	0	1	3
y	3	2	1	0	−1

4.

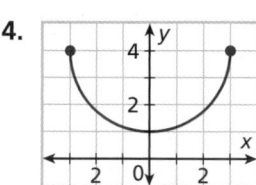

5. Bowling costs $3 per game plus $2.50 for shoe rental. Identify the independent and dependent variables. Write an equation in function notation for the situation.

Evaluate each function for the given input values.

6. For $f(x) = -3x + 4$, find $f(x)$ when $x = -2$.

7. For $f(x) = 2x^2$, find $f(x)$ when $x = -3$.

8. An engraver charges a $10 fee plus $6 for each line of engraving. Write a function to describe the situation. Find a reasonable domain and range for the function for up to 8 lines.

Graph each function for the given domain.

9. $3x + y = 4$; D: $\{-2, -1, 0, 1, 2\}$ 10. $y = |x - 1|$; D: $\{-3, 0, 1, 3, 5\}$ 11. $y = x^2 - 1$; D: $\{-2, -1, 0, 1, 2\}$

Graph each function.

12. $y = x - 5$ 13. $y = x^2 - 5$ 14. $y = |x| + 3$

15. The function $y = 30x$ describes the amount of interest y earned in a savings account in x years. Graph the function. Use the graph to estimate the total amount of interest earned in 7 years.

The table shows possible recommendations for the amount of sleep that children should get every day.

16. Graph a scatter plot of the given data.

17. Describe the correlation illustrated by the scatter plot.

18. Predict how many hours of sleep a 16-year-old needs.

Age (yr)	1	2	3	4	5	14
Sleep Needed (h)	14	13	12	12	11	9

Determine whether each sequence appears to be an arithmetic sequence. If so, find the common difference and the next three terms.

19. 11, 6, 1, −4,...   20. −4, −3, −1, 2,...   21. 7, 21, 30, 45,...

Find the indicated term of the arithmetic sequence.

22. 32nd term: 18, 11, 4, −3,...   23. 24th term: $a_1 = 4$; $d = 6$

24. Mandy's new job has a starting salary of $16,000 and annual increases of $800. How much will she earn during her fifth year?

COLLEGE ENTRANCE EXAM PRACTICE

FOCUS ON ACT

Questions on the ACT Mathematics Test do not require the use of a calculator, but you may bring one to use with the test. Make sure that it is a calculator that is on the approved list for the ACT.

You may want to time yourself as you take this practice test. It should take you about 6 minutes to complete.

When taking the test, you will be more comfortable using a calculator that you are used to. If you already have a calculator, make sure it is one of the permitted calculators. If you plan to use a new one, make sure to practice using it before the test.

---

1. The soccer team is ordering new uniforms. There is a one-time setup charge of $50.00, and each uniform costs $23.50. Which of the following best describes the total cost C for ordering uniforms for p players?

   (A) $C = 23.50p$

   (B) $C = 50p$

   (C) $C = 73.50p$

   (D) $C = 23.50p + 50$

   (E) $C = 50p + 23.50$

---

2. In the given relation, what domain value corresponds to the range value -2?
   $\{(-1, 2), (-2, 4), (2, 5), (0, -2), (2, 0)\}$

   (F) -2

   (G) 0

   (H) 2

   (J) 4

   (K) 5

---

3. Evaluate $h(x) = \frac{1}{2}(5 - 6x) + 9x$ when $x = \frac{2}{3}$.

   (A) $\frac{9}{2}$

   (B) $\frac{13}{2}$

   (C) 7

   (D) $\frac{19}{2}$

   (E) $\frac{23}{2}$

---

4. What is the seventh term of the arithmetic sequence $-4, -1, 2 \ldots$?

   (F) 5

   (G) 10

   (H) 11

   (J) 14

   (K) 17

---

5. The graph of which function is shown below?

   (A) $y = -3x - 5$

   (B) $y = -\frac{1}{3}x - \frac{5}{3}$

   (C) $y = -5x - 3$

   (D) $y = 3x - 5$

   (E) $y = 5x + 3$

---

6. Which of the following relations is NOT a function?

   (F) $\{(0, 1), (1, 2), (2, 3), (3, 4)\}$

   (G) $\{(1, 2), (2, 2), (3, 3), (4, 3)\}$

   (H) $\{(0, 2), (2, 4), (4, 1), (1, 3)\}$

   (J) $\{(1, 3), (4, 2), (2, 0), (3, 4)\}$

   (K) $\{(0, 2), (1, 3), (4, 3), (1, 2)\}$

TEST TACKLER

Standardized Test Strategies

Extended Response: Understand the Scores

Extended response test items are typically multipart questions that require a high level of thinking. The responses are scored using a 4-point rubric. To receive full credit, you must correctly answer all parts of the question and provide a clear explanation. A partial answer is worth 2 or 3 points, an incorrect solution is worth 1 point, and no response is worth 0 points.

EXAMPLE 1

Extended Response A train traveling from Boston, Massachusetts, to Richmond, Virginia, averages about 55 miles per hour. Define variables, write an equation, make a table, and draw a graph to show the distance the train travels in 5 hours.

Here are examples of four different responses and their scores using the rubric shown.

4-point response:

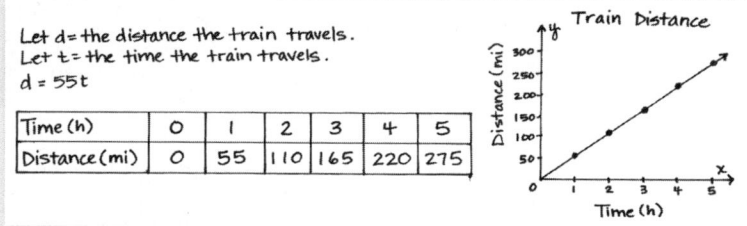

Let d = the distance the train travels.
Let t = the time the train travels.
d = 55t

Time (h)	0	1	2	3	4	5
Distance (mi)	0	55	110	165	220	275

3-point response:

Let d = the distance the train travels
Let t = the time the train travels

d = 55t

Time (h)	0	1	2	3	4	5
Distance (mi)	0	55	110	165	200	250

The student shows all of the work, but there are two minor computation errors when t = 4 and t = 5.

2-point response:

d = 55 + t

Time (h)	0	1	2	3	4	5
Distance (mi)	55	56	57	58	59	60

The student writes an incorrect equation and uses it to create an incorrect table and graph.

1-point response:

d = 55t

The student does not answer two parts of the question.

Read each test item and answer the questions that follow using the rubric below.

Scoring Rubric:

4 points: The student shows all of the work, correctly answers all parts of the question, and provides a clear explanation.

3 points: The student shows most of the work and provides a clear explanation but has a minor computation error, or the student shows all of the work and arrives at a correct solution but does not provide a clear explanation.

2 points: The student makes major errors resulting in an incorrect solution, or the student gives a correct solution but does not show any work nor provide an explanation.

1 point: The student shows no work and gives an incorrect solution.

0 points: The student gives no response.

Item A
Extended Response Draw a graph that is a function. Explain why it is a function. Then draw a graph that is NOT a function. Explain why it is not a function.

1. What should be included in a 4-point response?

2. Explain how would you score the response below.

Function   Not a function

The first graph is a function because each x-value has exactly one y-value. When x=1, y=1. The second graph is not a function because there is more than one y-value for each x-value. When x=1, y=1, and y=-1. Therefore, the second graph is not a function.

Item B
Extended Response A car travels at a steady rate of 60 miles per hour. Identify the independent and dependent variables. Describe the domain and range. Write an equation to describe the situation.

3. Ana wrote the response below.

The equation is $y = 60x$. The independent variable is time and the dependent variable is distance. The domain and range are all real numbers.

Explain how would you score Ana's response.

4. If you did not give Ana full credit, what should be added to Ana's response, if anything, so that it receives full credit?

Item C
Extended Response Lara bought 8 notebooks and 4 binders. She spent $14 total without tax. How much did each notebook cost if each binder cost $2.50? Write an equation and find the solution.

5. Explain how would you score the response below.

Let s = the cost of each notebook.
Let b = the cost of each binder.
$8s + 4b = 14$
$8s + 4(2.50) = 14$
$8s + 10 = 14$
$8s = 4$
$s = 2$ The notebooks cost $2 each

6. If you did not give the response full credit, what should be added to the response, if anything, so that it receives full credit?

STANDARDIZED TEST PREP

CUMULATIVE ASSESSMENT, CHAPTERS 1–4

Multiple Choice

1. Find the value of $|a| - b^2$ when $a = -3$ and $b = -5$.

(A) −28   (C) −7

(B) −22   (D) 4

2. Benito has x apples. He cuts each apple in half and gives each half to a different horse. Which expression represents the number of horses Benito feeds?

(F) $x \cdot \frac{1}{2}$ (H) $x \cdot 1\frac{1}{2}$

(G) $x \div \frac{1}{2}$ (J) $x \div 1\frac{1}{2}$

3. If the value of a^5 is positive, then which is true?

(A) a is positive.

(B) a is negative.

(C) a^5 is odd.

(D) a^5 is even.

4. Find the value of $\frac{2a}{a^3}$ if $4 - a = -6$.

(F) $\frac{1}{50}$ (H) 8

(G) $\frac{1}{2}$ (J) 10

5. There are 36 flowers in a bouquet. Two-thirds of the flowers are roses. One-fourth of the roses are red. What percent of the bouquet is made up of red roses?

(A) 9%   (C) 25%

(B) $16\frac{2}{3}\%$ (D) $66\frac{2}{3}\%$

6. A large tree should be planted at least 70 feet away from a power line. Which inequality shows the acceptable number of feet x between a large tree and a power line?

(F) $x < 70$ (H) $x > 70$

(G) $x \le 70$ (J) $x \ge 70$

7. Which statement is modeled by $3f + 2 > -16$?

(A) Two added to 3 times f is at least −16.

(B) Three times the sum of f and 2 is at most −16.

(C) The sum of 2 and 3 times f is more than −16.

(D) The product of $3f$ and 2 is no more than −16.

8. Jo Ann needs at least 3 pounds of peaches for a recipe. At the market, she calculates that she has enough money to buy 5 pounds at most. Which graph shows all possible numbers of pounds of peaches Jo Ann can buy so that she has enough for the recipe?

(F)

(G)

(H)

(J)

9. A bird flies from the ground to the top of a tree, sits there and sings for a while, flies down to the top of a picnic table to eat crumbs, and then flies back to the top of the tree to sing some more. Which graph best represents this situation?

(A)   (C)

(B)   (D)

10. Which relation is NOT a function?

(F) $\{(1, -5), (3, 1), (-5, 4), (4, -2)\}$

(G) $\{(2, 7), (3, 7), (4, 7), (5, 8)\}$

(H) $\{(1, -5), (-1, 6), (1, 5), (6, -3)\}$

(J) $\{(3, -2), (5, -6), (7, 7), (8, 8)\}$

11. The graph below shows a function.

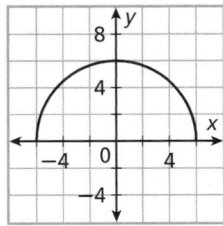

What is the domain of the function?

Ⓐ $x \geq 0$

Ⓑ $x \geq -6$

Ⓒ $0 \leq x \leq 6$

Ⓓ $-6 \leq x \leq 6$

12. Which situation best describes a negative correlation?

Ⓕ The speed of a runner and the time it takes to run a race

Ⓖ The number of apples in a bag and the weight of the bag of apples

Ⓗ The time it takes to repair a car and the amount of the bill

Ⓙ The number of people in a household and the amount of mail in their mailbox

13. Which of the following is a solution of $x + 1 \leq \frac{3}{2}$ AND $x - 1 \geq -\frac{5}{4}$?

Ⓐ $\frac{3}{2}$ Ⓒ $-\frac{1}{3}$

Ⓑ $\frac{1}{3}$ Ⓓ $-\frac{3}{2}$

Gridded Response

14. What is the value of x when $3(x + 7) - 6x = 4 - (x + 1)$?

15. For $h(x) = x^3 + 2x$, find $h(4)$.

16. WalkieTalkie phone company charges $18.00 for basic phone service per month and $0.15 per minute for long distance calls. Arena Calls charges $80.00 per month with no fee for long distance calls. What is the minimum number of minutes of long distance calls for which the cost of WalkieTalkie is more than the cost of Arena Calls?

Short Response

17. A function is graphed below.

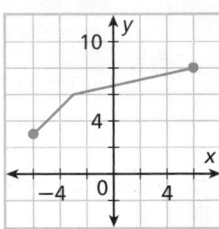

What is the domain and range of the function?

18. Rory made a pentagon by cutting two triangles from a square piece of cardboard as shown.

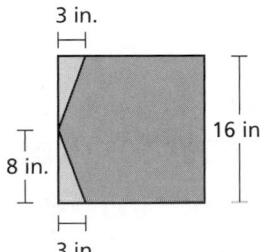

What is the area of the pentagon? Show your work or explain how you got your answer.

19. The manager of a new restaurant needs at most 12 servers. He has already hired 7 servers.

a. Write and solve an inequality to determine how many more servers the manager could hire.

b. Graph the solutions to the inequality you solved in part **a.**

20. Study the sequence below.

18, 24.5, 31, 37.5, 44,...

a. Could this sequence be arithmetic? Explain.

b. Find the 100th term of the sequence. Show your work.

Extended Response

21. A relation is shown in the table.

a. Express the relation as a mapping diagram.

b. Is the relation a function? Explain why or why not.

c. Write a possible real-life situation for the relation.

x	y
2	12
3	15
3	18
5	40
6	64

Real-World CONNECTIONS

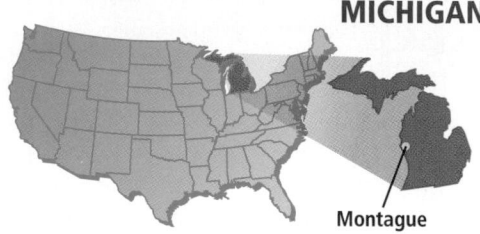

MICHIGAN

Montague

★ The World's Largest Weather Vane

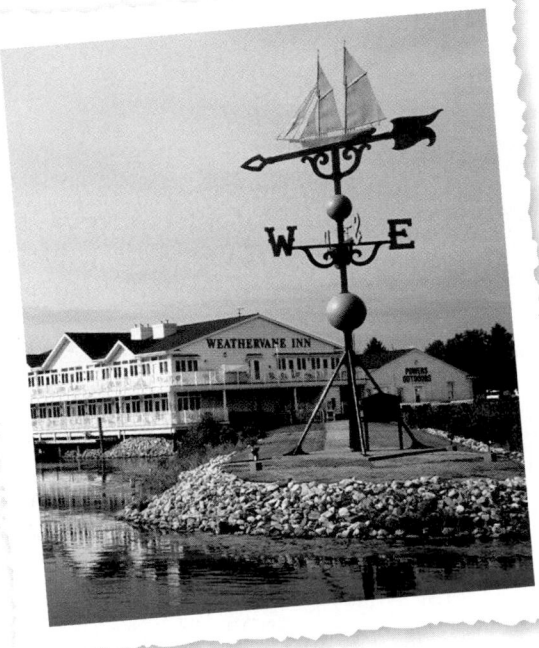

The world's largest working weather vane weighs approximately 4300 pounds and is located in Montague, Michigan. Weather vanes are used to indicate the direction of the wind. When the wind blows, the vane points in the direction from which the wind is coming.

Choose one or more strategies to solve each problem.

1. The arrow on the world's largest weather vane has a length of 26 feet. The height of the weather vane is 4 feet shorter than twice its length. What is the height of the world's largest weather vane?

At the base of the weather vane is a working weather station. Weather stations include instruments such as thermometers, rain gauges, and wind gauges that measure different characteristics of the weather. The data gathered from weather stations are used to make predictions about future weather.

For 2 and 3, use the graph.

2. The data in the graph represent the average snowfall for each month, measured over a 30-year time period. The average amount of snowfall received in April is less than $\frac{1}{4}$ of the average snowfall in March. What is the greatest possible average snowfall for April? Round to the nearest tenth of an inch.

3. Which month do you predict will get the most snowfall next year? Explain your reasoning.

Average Snowfall in Montague, MI

Snowfall (in.)

Oct	Nov	Dec	Jan	Feb	Mar
0.3	5.1	22.6	31.2	15.9	7.7

Month

⭐ Maple Syrup

Michigan produces about 90,000 gallons of maple syrup each year. This places the state among the top ten states in U.S. production of maple syrup. Maple syrup is made from the sap of maple trees, but only about 1% of Michigan's maple trees are used in maple syrup production.

Choose one or more strategies to solve each problem.

1. The standard sugar concentration level of maple syrup is 66%. At certain levels above 66%, the product develops into maple cream, soft maple sugar, or hard maple sugar. The sugar concentration never reaches 100%, even in hard maple sugar. What is the range of sugar concentration levels in the various maple products? Show your answer on a number line.

For 2 and 3, use the table.

2. How many Calories are in 1 cup of maple syrup? (*Hint*: 4 tbsp = $\frac{1}{4}$ c)

3. Approximately how many tablespoons of maple syrup would you need to have the same number of Calories that are in 7 tablespoons of honey? Round to the nearest tablespoon.

4. It takes 40 gallons of maple sap to make 1 gallon of maple syrup. Each tap hole in a maple tree will produce about 10 gallons of sap in an average year. How many gallons of maple syrup could be made with the sap from 20 tap holes?

Sweetener	Calories (per tbsp)
Blackstrap molasses	43
Granulated sugar	46
Maple syrup	50
Corn syrup	57
Honey	64

5. It is recommended that maple trees be at least 10 inches in diameter before they are tapped. Only one tap should be placed in trees that are 10 to 18 inches in diameter, while 2 taps can be placed in trees greater than 18 inches in diameter. An orchard has 130 trees that are less than 10 inches in diameter, 104 trees that are 10–18 inches in diameter, and 48 trees that are greater than 18 inches in diameter. What is the maximum number of tap holes this orchard should have?

Linear Functions

Chapter Focus

- Translate among different representations of linear functions.
- Find and interpret slopes and intercepts of linear equations that model real-world problems
- Solve real-world problems involving linear equations.

Take *Flight*

You can use linear functions to describe patterns and relationships in flight times.

go.hrw.com
Chapter Project Online
KEYWORD: MA7 ChProj

ARE YOU READY?

✓ Vocabulary

Match each term on the left with a definition on the right.

1. coefficient
2. coordinate plane
3. transformation
4. perpendicular

A. a change in the size or position of a figure

B. forming right angles

C. a two-dimensional system formed by the intersection of a horizontal number line and a vertical number line

D. an ordered pair of numbers that gives the location of a point

E. a number that is multiplied by a variable

✓ Ordered Pairs

Graph each point on the same coordinate plane.

5. $A(2, 5)$
6. $B(-1, -3)$
7. $C(-5, 2)$
8. $D(4, -4)$
9. $E(-2, 0)$
10. $F(0, 3)$
11. $G(8, 7)$
12. $H(-8, -7)$

✓ Solve for a Variable

Solve each equation for the indicated variable.

13. $2x + y = 8; y$
14. $5y = 5x - 10; y$
15. $2y = 6x - 8; y$
16. $10x + 25 = 5y; y$

✓ Evaluate Expressions

Evaluate each expression for the given value of the variable.

17. $4g - 3; g = -2$
18. $8p - 12; p = 4$
19. $4x + 8; x = -2$
20. $-5t - 15; t = 1$

✓ Connect Words and Algebra

21. The value of a stock begins at $0.05 and increases by $0.01 each month. Write an equation representing the value of the stock v in any month m.

22. Write a situation that could be modeled by the equation $b = 100 - s$.

✓ Rates and Unit Rates

Find each unit rate.

23. 322 miles on 14 gallons of gas
24. $14.25 for 3 pounds of deli meat
25. 32 grams of fat in 4 servings
26. 120 pictures on 5 rolls of film

Where You've Been

Previously, you

- wrote equations in function notation.
- graphed functions.
- identified the domain and range of functions.
- identified independent and dependent variables.

In This Chapter

You will study

- writing and graphing linear functions.
- identifying and interpreting the components of linear graphs, including the *x*-intercept, *y*-intercept, and slope.
- graphing and analyzing families of functions.

Where You're Going

You can use the skills in this chapter

- to solve systems of linear equations in Chapter 6.
- to identify rates of change in linear data in biology and economics.
- to make calculations and comparisons in your personal finances.

Key Vocabulary/Vocabulario

constant of variation	constante de variación
direct variation	variación directa
family of functions	familia de funciones
linear function	función lineal
parallel lines	líneas paralelas
perpendicular lines	líneas perpendiculares
slope	pendiente
transformation	transformación
x-intercept	intersección con el eje *x*
y-intercept	intersección con el eje *y*

Vocabulary Connections

To become familiar with some of the vocabulary terms in the chapter, consider the following. You may refer to the chapter, the glossary, or a dictionary if you like.

1. What shape do you think is formed when a **linear function** is graphed on a coordinate plane?

2. The meaning of *intercept* is similar to the meaning of *intersection*. What do you think an **x-intercept** might be?

3. **Slope** is a word used in everyday life, as well as in mathematics. What is your understanding of the word *slope*?

4. A family is a group of related people. Use this concept to define **family of functions**.

Reading and *Writing* Math

Study Strategy: Use Multiple Representations

Representing a math concept in more than one way can help you understand it more clearly. As you read the explanations and example problems in your text, note the use of tables, lists, graphs, diagrams, and symbols, as well as words to explain a concept.

From Lesson 4-4:

In this example from Chapter 4, the given function is described using an equation, a table, ordered pairs, and a graph.

Graphing Functions

Graph each function.

A $2x + 1 = y$ — **Equation**

Step 1 Choose several values of x and generate ordered pairs.

Step 2 Plot enough points to see a pattern.

Table

x	$2x + 1 = y$	(x, y)
-3	$2(-3) + 1 = -5$	$(-3, -5)$
-2	$2(-2) + 1 = -3$	$(-2, -3)$
-1	$2(-1) + 1 = -1$	$(-1, -1)$
0	$2(0) + 1 = 1$	$(0, 1)$
1	$2(1) + 1 = 3$	$(1, 3)$
2	$2(2) + 1 = 5$	$(2, 5)$
3	$2(3) + 1 = 7$	$(3, 7)$

Graph

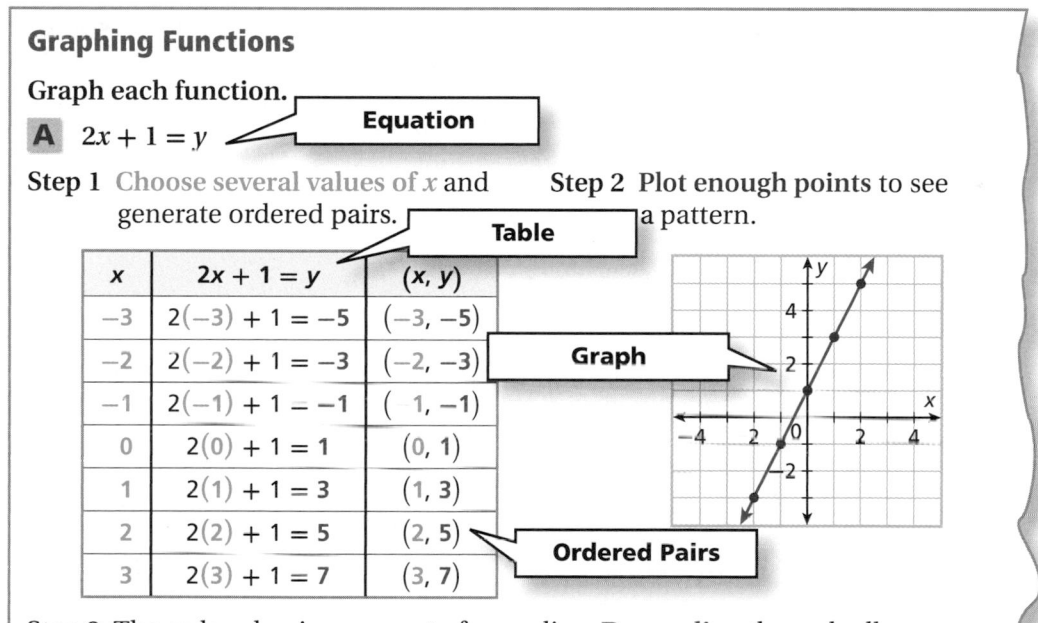

Ordered Pairs

Step 3 The ordered pairs appear to form a line. **Draw a line** through all the points to show all the ordered pairs that satisfy the function. Draw arrowheads on both "ends" of the line.

Try This

1. If an employee earns $8.00 an hour, $y = 8x$ gives the total pay y the employee will earn for working x hours. For this equation, make a table of ordered pairs and a graph. Explain the relationships between the equation, the table, and the graph. How does each one describe the situation?

2. What situations might make one representation more useful than another?

5-1 Identifying Linear Functions

Why learn this?
Linear functions can describe many real-world situations, such as distances traveled at a constant speed.

Most people believe that there is no speed limit on the German autobahn. However, many stretches have a speed limit of 120 km/h. If a car travels continuously at this speed, $y = 120x$ gives the number of kilometers y that the car would travel in x hours. Solutions are shown in the graph.

The graph represents a function because each domain value (x-value) is paired with exactly one range value (y-value). Notice that the graph is a straight line. A function whose graph forms a straight line is called a **linear function**.

Distance Traveled

EXAMPLE 1 Identifying a Linear Function by Its Graph

Identify whether each graph represents a function. Explain. If the graph does represent a function, is the function linear?

A

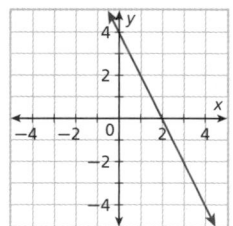

Each domain value is paired with exactly one range value. The graph forms a line.

linear function

B

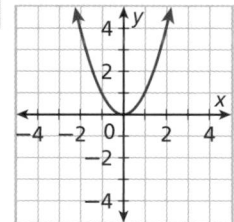

Each domain value is paired with exactly one range value. The graph is not a line.

not a linear function

C

The only domain value, 3, is paired with many different range values.

not a function

Identify whether each graph represents a function. Explain. If the graph does represent a function, is the function linear?

1a.

1b.

1c.

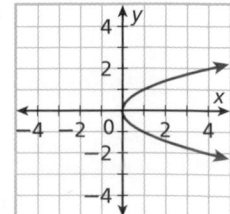

You can sometimes identify a linear function by looking at a table or a list of ordered pairs. In a linear function, a constant change in x corresponds to a constant change in y.

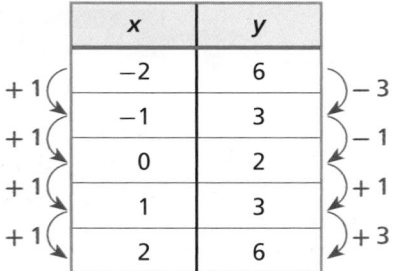

In this table, a constant change of $+1$ in x corresponds to a constant change of -3 in y. These points satisfy a linear function.

The points from this table lie on a line.

In this table, a constant change of $+1$ in x does *not* correspond to a constant change in y. These points do *not* satisfy a linear function.

The points from this table do not lie on a line.

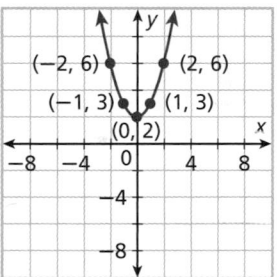

EXAMPLE 2 **Identifying a Linear Function by Using Ordered Pairs**

Tell whether each set of ordered pairs satisfies a linear function. Explain.

A $\{(2, 4), (5, 3), (8, 2), (11, 1)\}$

x	y
2	4
5	3
8	2
11	1

$+3$ ... -1
$+3$ ... -1
$+3$ ... -1

Write the ordered pairs in a table. Look for a pattern.

A constant change of $+3$ in x corresponds to a constant change of -1 in y.

These points satisfy a linear function.

B $\{(-10, 10), (-5, 4), (0, 2), (5, 0)\}$

x	y
-10	10
-5	4
0	2
5	0

$+5$ ... -6
$+5$ ... -2
$+5$ ... -2

Write the ordered pairs in a table. Look for a pattern.

A constant change of $+5$ in x corresponds to different changes in y.

These points do not satisfy a linear function.

2. Tell whether the set of ordered pairs $\{(3, 5), (5, 4), (7, 3), (9, 2), (11, 1)\}$ satisfies a linear function. Explain.

Another way to determine whether a function is linear is to look at its equation. A function is linear if it is described by a *linear equation*. A **linear equation** is any equation that can be written in the *standard form* shown below.

Standard Form of a Linear Equation

$Ax + By = C$ where A, B, and C are real numbers and A and B are not both 0

Notice that when a linear equation is written in standard form
- x and y both have exponents of 1.
- x and y are not multiplied together.
- x and y do not appear in denominators, exponents, or radical signs.

Linear		Not Linear	
$3x + 2y = 10$	*Standard form*	$3xy + x = 1$	*x and y are multiplied.*
$y - 2 = 3x$	*Can be written as* $3x - y = -2$	$x^3 + y = -1$	*x has an exponent other than 1.*
$-y = 5x$	*Can be written as* $5x + y = 0$	$x + \dfrac{6}{y} = 12$	*y is in a denominator.*

For any two points, there is exactly one line that contains them both. This means you need only two ordered pairs to graph a line.

EXAMPLE 3 Graphing Linear Functions

Tell whether each function is linear. If so, graph the function.

A $y = x + 3$

$$\begin{aligned} y &= x + 3 & &\text{\textit{Write the equation in standard form.}} \\ \underline{-x} &\underline{-x} & &\text{\textit{Subtraction Property of Equality}} \\ y - x &= 3 \\ -x + y &= 3 & &\text{\textit{The equation is in standard form (A = −1, B = 1, C = 3).}} \end{aligned}$$

The equation can be written in standard form, so the function is linear.

To graph, choose three values of x, and use them to generate ordered pairs. (You only need two, but graphing three points is a good check.)

Plot the points and connect them with a straight line.

x	$y = x + 3$	(x, y)
0	$y = 0 + 3 = 3$	$(0, 3)$
1	$y = 1 + 3 = 4$	$(1, 4)$
2	$y = 2 + 3 = 5$	$(2, 5)$

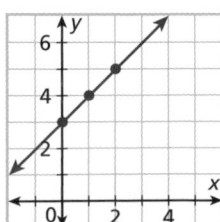

B $y = x^2$

This is not linear, because x has an exponent other than 1.

CHECK IT OUT! Tell whether each function is linear. If so, graph the function.

3a. $y = 5x - 9$ **3b.** $y = 12$ **3c.** $y = 2^x$

For linear functions whose graphs are not horizontal, the domain and range are all real numbers. However, in many real-world situations, the domain and range must be restricted. For example, some quantities cannot be negative, such as time.

Sometimes domain and range are restricted even further to a set of points. For example, a quantity such as number of people can only be whole numbers. When this happens, the graph is not actually connected because every point on the line is not a solution. However, you may see these graphs shown connected to indicate that the linear pattern, or trend, continues.

EXAMPLE 4 *Career Application*

Sue rents a manicure station in a salon and pays the salon owner $5.50 for each manicure she gives. The amount Sue pays each day is given by $f(x) = 5.50x$, where x is the number of manicures. Graph this function and give its domain and range.

Choose several values of x and make a table of ordered pairs.

x	$f(x) = 5.50x$
0	$f(0) = 5.50(0) = 0$
1	$f(1) = 5.50(1) = 5.50$
2	$f(2) = 5.50(2) = 11.00$
3	$f(3) = 5.50(3) = 16.50$
4	$f(4) = 5.50(4) = 22.00$
5	$f(5) = 5.50(5) = 27.50$

Graph the ordered pairs.

The individual points are solutions in this situation. The line shows that the trend continues.

The number of manicures must be a whole number, so the domain is $\{0, 1, 2, 3, ...\}$. The range is $\{0, 5.50, 11.00, 16.50, ...\}$.

4. **What if...?** At another salon, Sue can rent a station for $10.00 per day plus $3.00 per manicure. The amount she would pay each day is given by $f(x) = 3x + 10$, where x is the number of manicures. Graph this function and give its domain and range.

THINK AND DISCUSS

1. Suppose you are given five ordered pairs that satisfy a function. When you graph them, four lie on a straight line, but the fifth does not. Is the function linear? Why or why not?

2. In Example 4, why is every point on the line not a solution?

3. **GET ORGANIZED** Copy and complete the graphic organizer. In each box, describe how to use the information to identify a linear function. Include an example.

Determining Whether a Function Is Linear

| From its graph | From its equation | From a list of ordered pairs |

GUIDED PRACTICE

1. **Vocabulary** Is the *linear equation* $3x - 2 = y$ in standard form? Explain.

SEE EXAMPLE **1**
p. 300

Identify whether each graph represents a function. Explain. If the graph does represent a function, is the function linear?

2.

3.

4.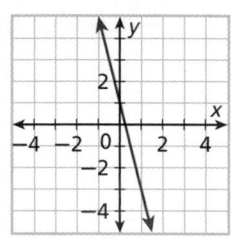

SEE EXAMPLE **2**
p. 301

Tell whether the given ordered pairs satisfy a linear function. Explain.

5.

x	5	4	3	2	1
y	0	2	4	6	8

6.

x	1	4	9	16	25
y	1	2	3	4	5

7. $\{(0, 5), (-2, 3), (-4, 1), (-6, -1), (-8, -3)\}$

8. $\{(2, -2), (-1, 0), (-4, 1), (-7, 3), (-10, 6)\}$

SEE EXAMPLE **3**
p. 302

Tell whether each function is linear. If so, graph the function.

9. $2x + 3y = 5$ 10. $2y = 8$ 11. $\dfrac{x^2 + 3}{5} = y$ 12. $\dfrac{x}{5} = \dfrac{y}{3}$

SEE EXAMPLE **4**
p. 303

13. **Transportation** A train travels at a constant speed of 75 mi/h. The function $f(x) = 75x$ gives the distance that the train travels in x hours. Graph this function and give its domain and range.

14. **Entertainment** A movie rental store charges a $6.00 membership fee plus $2.50 for each movie rented. The function $f(x) = 2.50x + 6$ gives the cost of renting x movies. Graph this function and give its domain and range.

PRACTICE AND PROBLEM SOLVING

Independent Practice

For Exercises	See Example
15–17	1
18–20	2
21–24	3
25	4

Extra Practice

Skills Practice p. S12
Application Practice p. S32

Identify whether each graph represents a function. Explain. If the graph does represent a function, is the function linear?

15.

16.

17.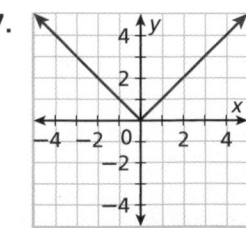

Tell whether the given ordered pairs satisfy a linear function. Explain.

18.

x	−3	0	3	6	9
y	−2	−1	0	2	4

19.

x	−1	0	1	2	3
y	−3	−2	−1	0	1

20. $\{(3, 4), (0, 2), (-3, 0), (-6, -2), (-9, -4)\}$

Tell whether each function is linear. If so, graph the function.

21. $y = 5$ **22.** $4y - 2x = 0$ **23.** $\dfrac{3}{x} + 4y = 10$ **24.** $5 + 3y = 8$

25. Transportation The gas tank in Tony's car holds 15 gallons, and the car can travel 25 miles for each gallon of gas. When Tony begins with a full tank of gas, the function $f(x) = -\dfrac{1}{25}x + 15$ gives the amount of gas $f(x)$ that will be left in the tank after traveling x miles (if he does not buy more gas). Graph this function and give its domain and range.

Tell whether the given ordered pairs satisfy a function. If so, is it a linear function?

26. $\{(2, 5), (2, 4), (2, 3), (2, 2), (2, 1)\}$ **27.** $\{(-8, 2), (-6, 0), (-4, -2), (-2, -4), (0, -6)\}$

28.

x	−10	−6	−2	2	4
y	0	0.25	0.50	0.75	1

29.

x	−5	−1	3	7	11
y	1	1	1	1	1

Tell whether each equation is linear. If so, write the equation in standard form and give the values of A, B, and C.

30. $2x - 8y = 16$ **31.** $y = 4x + 2$ **32.** $2x = \dfrac{y}{3} - 4$ **33.** $\dfrac{4}{x} = y$

34. $\dfrac{x + 4}{2} = \dfrac{y - 4}{3}$ **35.** $x = 7$ **36.** $xy = 6$ **37.** $3x - 5 + y = 2y - 4$

38. $y = -x + 2$ **39.** $5x = 2y - 3$ **40.** $2y = -6$ **41.** $y = \sqrt{x}$

Graph each linear function.

42. $y = 3x + 7$ **43.** $y = x + 25$ **44.** $y = 8 - x$ **45.** $y = 2x$

46. $-2y = -3x + 6$ **47.** $y - x = 4$ **48.** $y - 2x = -3$ **49.** $x = 5 + y$

50. Measurement One inch is equal to approximately 2.5 centimeters. Let x represent inches and y represent centimeters. Write an equation in standard form relating x and y. Give the values of A, B, and C.

51. Wages Molly earns $8.00 an hour at her job.

     a. Let x represent the number of hours that Molly works. Write a function using x and $f(x)$ that describes Molly's pay for working x hours.

     b. Graph this function and give its domain and range.

 52. Write About It For $y = 2x - 1$, make a table of ordered pairs and a graph. Describe the relationships between the equation, the table, and the graph.

53. Critical Thinking Describe a real-world situation that can be represented by a linear function whose domain and range must be limited. Give your function and its domain and range.

MULTI-STEP TEST PREP

54. This problem will prepare you for the Multi-Step Test Prep on page 342.

     a. Juan is running on a treadmill. The table shows the number of Calories Juan burns as a function of time. Explain how you can tell that this relationship is linear by using the table.

     b. Create a graph of the data.

     c. How can you tell from the graph that the relationship is linear?

Time (min)	Calories
3	27
6	54
9	81
12	108
15	135
18	162
21	189

55. Physical Science A ball was dropped from a height of 100 meters. Its height above the ground in meters at different times after its release is given in the table. Do these ordered pairs satisfy a linear function? Explain.

Time (s)	0	1	2	3
Height (m)	100	90.2	60.8	11.8

56. Critical Thinking Is the equation $x = 9$ a linear equation? Does it describe a linear function? Explain.

57. Which is NOT a linear function?

Ⓐ $y = 8x$　　　Ⓑ $y = x + 8$　　　Ⓒ $y = \dfrac{8}{x}$　　　Ⓓ $y = 8 - x$

58. The speed of sound in 0 °C air is about 331 feet per second. Which function could be used to describe the distance in feet d that sound will travel in air in s seconds?

Ⓕ $d = s + 331$　　　Ⓖ $d = 331s$　　　Ⓗ $s = 331d$　　　Ⓙ $s = 331 - d$

59. Extended Response Write your own linear function. Show that it is a linear function in at least three different ways. Explain any connections you see between your three methods.

CHALLENGE AND EXTEND

60. What equation describes the x-axis? the y-axis? Do these equations represent linear functions?

Geometry Copy and complete each table below. Then tell whether the table shows a linear relationship.

61.

Perimeter of a Square	
Side Length	Perimeter
1	
2	
3	
4	

62.

Area of a Square	
Side Length	Area
1	
2	
3	
4	

63.

Volume of a Cube	
Side Length	Volume
1	
2	
3	
4	

SPIRAL REVIEW

Simplify each expression. *(Lesson 1-4)*

64. 8^2　　　　**65.** $(-1)^3$　　　　**66.** $(-4)^4$　　　　**67.** $\left(\dfrac{1}{3}\right)^2$

Solve each equation. Check your answer. *(Lesson 2-4)*

68. $6m + 5 = 3m - 4$　　　**69.** $2(t - 4) = 3 - (3t + 1)$　　　**70.** $9y + 5 - 2y = 2y + 5 - y + 3$

Find the value of x in each diagram. *(Lesson 2-8)*

71. $\triangle ABC \sim \triangle DEF$

72. $ABCD \sim QRST$

5-2 Using Intercepts

Objectives
Find *x*- and *y*-intercepts and interpret their meanings in real-world situations.

Use *x*- and *y*-intercepts to graph lines.

Vocabulary
y-intercept
x-intercept

Who uses this?
Divers can use intercepts to determine the time a safe ascent will take.

A diver explored the ocean floor 120 feet below the surface and then ascended at a rate of 30 feet per minute. The graph shows the diver's elevation below sea level during the ascent.

The **y-intercept** is the *y*-coordinate of the point where the graph intersects the *y*-axis. The *x*-coordinate of this point is always 0.

The **x-intercept** is the *x*-coordinate of the point where the graph intersects the *x*-axis. The *y*-coordinate of this point is always 0.

The *x*-intercept is 4. It represents the time that the diver reaches the surface, or when depth = 0.

The *y*-intercept is −120. It represents the diver's elevation at the start of the ascent, when time = 0.

EXAMPLE 1 · Finding Intercepts

Find the *x*- and *y*-intercepts.

A

The graph intersects the x-axis at (−4, 0).
The *x*-intercept is −4.

The graph intersects the y-axis at (0, −3).
The *y*-intercept is −3.

B $3x - 2y = 12$

To find the *x*-intercept, replace *y* with 0 and solve for *x*.	To find the *y*-intercept, replace *x* with 0 and solve for *y*.
$3x - 2y = 12$	$3x - 2y = 12$
$3x - 2(0) = 12$	$3(0) - 2y = 12$
$3x - 0 = 12$	$0 - 2y = 12$
$3x = 12$	$-2y = 12$
$\dfrac{3x}{3} = \dfrac{12}{3}$	$\dfrac{-2y}{-2} = \dfrac{12}{-2}$
$x = 4$	$y = -6$
The *x*-intercept is 4.	The *y*-intercept is −6.

✓ CHECK IT OUT!

Find the *x*- and *y*-intercepts.

1a.

1b. $-3x + 5y = 30$

1c. $4x + 2y = 16$

Finding Intercepts

I use the "cover-up" method to find intercepts. To use this method, make sure the equation is in standard form first.

If I have 4x − 3y = 12:

First, I cover 4x with my finger and solve the equation I can still see.

$$\text{🖐} - 3y = 12$$
$$y = -4$$

The y-intercept is −4.

Then I cover −3y with my finger and do the same thing.

$$4x\ \text{🖐} = 12$$
$$x = 3$$

The x-intercept is 3.

EXAMPLE 2   *Travel Application*

The Sandia Peak Tramway in Albuquerque, New Mexico, travels a distance of about 4500 meters to the top of Sandia Peak. Its speed is 300 meters per minute. The function $f(x) = 4500 - 300x$ gives the tram's distance in meters from the top of the peak after x minutes. Graph this function and find the intercepts. What does each intercept represent?

Neither time nor distance can be negative, so choose several nonnegative values for x. Use the function to generate ordered pairs.

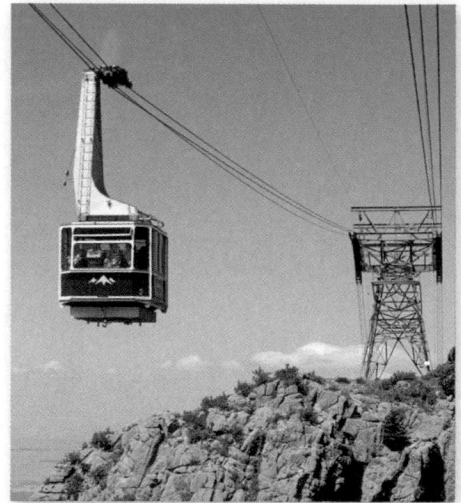

x	0	2	5	10	15
f(x) = 4500 − 300x	4500	3900	3000	1500	0

Graph the ordered pairs. Connect the points with a line.

Sandia Peak Tramway

- *y*-intercept: 4500. This is the starting distance from the top (time = 0).
- *x*-intercept: 15. This the time when the tram reaches the peak (distance = 0).

Caution!

The graph is not the path of the tram. Even though the line is descending, the graph describes the distance from the peak as the tram goes *up* the mountain.

CHECK IT OUT!   **2.** The school store sells pens for $2.00 and notebooks for $3.00. The equation $2x + 3y = 60$ describes the number of pens x and notebooks y that you can buy for $60.

  a. Graph the function and find its intercepts.

  b. What does each intercept represent?

Remember, to graph a linear function, you need to plot only two ordered pairs. It is often simplest to find the ordered pairs that contain the intercepts.

EXAMPLE 3 **Graphing Linear Equations by Using Intercepts**

Use intercepts to graph the line described by each equation.

A $2x - 4y = 8$

Step 1 Find the intercepts.

x-intercept:	y-intercept:
$2x - 4y = 8$	$2x - 4y = 8$
$2x - 4(0) = 8$	$2(0) - 4y = 8$
$2x = 8$	$-4y = 8$
$\dfrac{2x}{2} = \dfrac{8}{2}$	$\dfrac{-4y}{-4} = \dfrac{8}{-4}$
$x = 4$	$y = -2$

Step 2 Graph the line.

Plot (4, 0) and (0, −2).
Connect with a straight line.

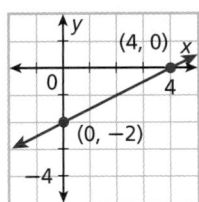

> **Helpful Hint**
> You can use a third point to check your line. Either choose a point from your graph and check it in the equation, or use the equation to generate a point and check that it is on your graph.

B $\dfrac{2}{3}y = 4 - \dfrac{1}{2}x$

Step 1 Write the equation in standard form.

$$6\left(\dfrac{2}{3}y\right) = 6\left(4 - \dfrac{1}{2}x\right)$$ *Multiply both sides by 6, the LCD of the fractions, to clear the fractions.*

$$4y = 24 - 3x$$

$$3x + 4y = 24$$ *Write the equation in standard form.*

Step 2 Find the intercepts.

x-intercept:	y-intercept:
$3x + 4y = 24$	$3x + 4y = 24$
$3x + 4(0) = 24$	$3(0) + 4y = 24$
$3x = 24$	$4y = 24$
$\dfrac{3x}{3} = \dfrac{24}{3}$	$\dfrac{4y}{4} = \dfrac{24}{4}$
$x = 8$	$y = 6$

Step 3 Graph the line.

Plot (8, 0) and (0, 6).
Connect with a straight line.

 Use intercepts to graph the line described by each equation.

3a. $-3x + 4y = -12$ **3b.** $y = \dfrac{1}{3}x - 2$

THINK AND DISCUSS

1. A function has x-intercept 4 and y-intercept 2. Name two points on the graph of this function.

2. What is the y-intercept of $2.304x + y = 4.318$? What is the x-intercept of $x - 92.4920y = -21.5489$?

3. GET ORGANIZED Copy and complete the graphic organizer.

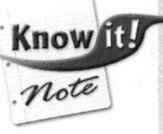

> Graphing $Ax + By = C$ Using Intercepts
>
> 1. Find the x-intercept by __?__.
> 2. Find the y-intercept by __?__.
> 3. Graph the line by __?__.

go.hrw.com
Homework Help Online
KEYWORD: MA7 5-2
Parent Resources Online
KEYWORD: MA7 Parent

GUIDED PRACTICE

1. **Vocabulary** The ____?____ is the y-coordinate of the point where a graph crosses the y-axis. (*x-intercept* or *y-intercept*)

SEE EXAMPLE **1**
p. 307

Find the x- and y-intercepts.

2.

3.

4.

5. $2x - 4y = 4$ 6. $-2y = 3x - 6$ 7. $4y + 5x = 2y - 3x + 16$

SEE EXAMPLE **2**
p. 308

8. **Biology** To thaw a specimen stored at $-25\ °C$, the temperature of a refrigeration tank is raised $5\ °C$ every hour. The temperature in the tank after x hours can be described by the function $f(x) = -25 + 5x$.

   a. Graph the function and find its intercepts.

   b. What does each intercept represent?

SEE EXAMPLE **3**
p. 309

Use intercepts to graph the line described by each equation.

9. $4x - 5y = 20$ 10. $y = 2x + 4$ 11. $\frac{1}{3}x - \frac{1}{4}y = 2$ 12. $-5y + 2x = -10$

PRACTICE AND PROBLEM SOLVING

Independent Practice

For Exercises	See Example
13–21	1
22–23	2
24–29	3

Extra Practice

Skills Practice p. S12

Application Practice p. S32

Find the x- and y-intercepts.

13.

14.

15.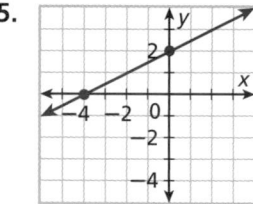

16. $6x + 3y = 12$ 17. $4y - 8 = 2x$ 18. $-2y + x = 2y - 8$

19. $4x + y = 8$ 20. $y - 3x = -15$ 21. $2x + y = 10x - 1$

22. **Environmental Science** A fishing lake was stocked with 300 bass. Each year, the population decreases by 25. The population of bass in the lake after x years is represented by the function $f(x) = 300 - 25x$.

   a. Graph the function and find its intercepts.

   b. What does each intercept represent?

23. **Sports** Julie is running a 5-kilometer race. She runs 1 kilometer every 5 minutes. Julie's distance from the finish line after x minutes is represented by the function $f(x) = 5 - \frac{1}{5}x$.

   a. Graph the function and find its intercepts.

   b. What does each intercept represent?

Use intercepts to graph the line described by each equation.

24. $4x - 6y = 12$

25. $2x + 3y = 18$

26. $\frac{1}{2}x - 4y = 4$

27. $y - x = -1$

28. $5x + 3y = 15$

29. $x - 3y = -1$

Biology

Bamboo is the world's fastest-growing woody plant. Some varieties can grow more than 30 centimeters a day and up to 40 meters tall.

30. Biology A bamboo plant is growing 1 foot per day. When you first measure it, it is 4 feet tall.

   a. Write an equation to describe the height y, in feet, of the bamboo plant x days after you measure it.

   b. What is the y-intercept?

   c. What is the meaning of the y-intercept in this problem?

31. Estimation Look at the scatter plot and trend line.

   a. Estimate the x- and y-intercepts.

   b. What is the real-world meaning of each intercept?

32. Personal Finance A bank employee notices an abandoned checking account with a balance of $412. If the bank charges a $4 monthly fee for the account, the function $b = 412 - 4m$ shows the balance b in the account after m months.

   a. Graph the function and give its domain and range. (*Hint:* The bank will keep charging the monthly fee even after the account is empty.)

   b. Find the intercepts. What does each intercept represent?

   c. When will the bank account balance be 0?

33. Critical Thinking Complete the following to learn about intercepts and horizontal and vertical lines.

   a. Graph $x = -6$, $x = 1$, and $x = 5$. Find the intercepts.

   b. Graph $y = -3$, $y = 2$, and $y = 7$. Find the intercepts.

   c. Write a rule describing the intercepts of linear equations whose graphs are horizontal and vertical lines.

Match each equation with a graph.

34. $-2x - y = 4$

35. $y = 4 - 2x$

36. $2y + 4x = 8$

37. $4x - 2y = 8$

A.

B.

C.

D.

38. This problem will prepare you for the Multi-Step Test Prep on page 342.

MULTI-STEP TEST PREP

Kristyn rode a stationary bike at the gym. She programmed the timer for 20 minutes. The display counted backward to show how much time remained in her workout. It also showed her mileage.

a. What are the intercepts?

b. What do the intercepts represent?

Time Remaining (min)	Distance Covered (mi)
20	0
16	0.35
12	0.70
8	1.05
4	1.40
0	1.75

39. Write About It Write a real-world problem that could be modeled by a linear function whose *x*-intercept is 5 and whose *y*-intercept is 60.

TEST PREP

40. Which is the *x*-intercept of $-2x = 9y - 18$?

(A) -9 (B) -2 (C) 2 (D) 9

41. Which of the following situations could be represented by the graph?

(F) Jamie owed her uncle $200. Each week for 40 weeks she paid him $5.

(G) Jamie owed her uncle $200. Each week for 5 weeks she paid him $40.

(H) Jamie owed her uncle $40. Each week for 5 weeks she paid him $200.

(J) Jamie owed her uncle $40. Each week for 200 weeks she paid him $5.

42. Gridded Response What is the *y*-intercept of $60x + 55y = 660$?

CHALLENGE AND EXTEND

Use intercepts to graph the line described by each equation.

43. $\frac{1}{2}x + \frac{1}{5}y = 1$ **44.** $0.5x - 0.2y = 0.75$ **45.** $y = \frac{3}{8}x + 6$

46. For any linear equation $Ax + By = C$, what are the intercepts?

47. Find the intercepts of $22x - 380y = 20,900$. Explain how to use the intercepts to determine appropriate scales for the graph.

SPIRAL REVIEW

48. Marlon's fish tank is 80% filled with water. Based on the measurements shown, what volume of the tank is NOT filled with water? *(Lesson 2-9)*

Solve each inequality and graph the solutions. *(Lesson 3-3)*

49. $3c > 12$ **50.** $-4 \geq \frac{t}{2}$ **51.** $\frac{1}{2}m \geq -3$ **52.** $-2w > 14$

Tell whether the given ordered pairs satisfy a linear function. Explain. *(Lesson 5-1)*

53. $\{(-2, 0), (0, 3), (2, 6), (4, 9), (6, 12)\}$ **54.** $\{(0, 0), (1, 1), (4, 2), (9, 3), (16, 4)\}$

**Connecting
Algebra to**

Geometry

Area in the Coordinate Plane

Lines in the coordinate plane can form the sides of polygons.
You can use points on these lines to help you find the areas
of these polygons.

Example

Find the area of the triangle formed by the x-axis, the y-axis, and the line
described by $3x + 2y = 18$.

Step 1 Find the intercepts of $3x + 2y = 18$.

x-intercept:	y-intercept:
$3x + 2y = 18$	$3x + 2y = 18$
$3x + 2(0) = 18$	$3(0) + 2y = 18$
$3x = 18$	$2y = 18$
$x = 6$	$y = 9$

Step 2 Use the intercepts to graph the line. The x-intercept is 6,
so plot $(6, 0)$. The y-intercept is 9, so plot $(0, 9)$. Connect
with a straight line. Then shade the triangle formed by the
line and the axes, as described.

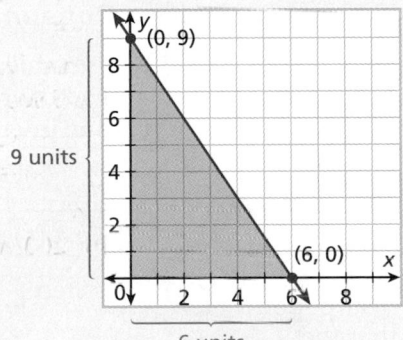

Step 3 Recall that the area of a triangle is given by $A = \frac{1}{2}bh$.

• The length of the base is 6.

• The height is 9.

Step 4 Substitute these values into the formula.

$A = \frac{1}{2}bh$

$A = \frac{1}{2}(6)(9)$ *Substitute into the area formula.*

$\quad = \frac{1}{2}(54)$ *Simplify.*

$\quad = 27$

The area of the triangle is 27 square units.

Try This

1. Find the area of the triangle formed by the x-axis, the y-axis, and the line
   described by $3x + 2y = 12$.

2. Find the area of the triangle formed by the x-axis, the y-axis, and the line
   described by $y = 6 - x$.

3. Find the area of the polygon formed by the x-axis, the y-axis, the line described by
   $y = 6$, and the line described by $x = 4$.

5-3 Rate of Change and Slope

Objectives
Find rates of change and slopes.

Relate a constant rate of change to the slope of a line.

Vocabulary
rate of change
rise
run
slope

Why learn this?

Rates of change can be used to find how quickly costs have increased.

In 1985, the cost of sending a 1-ounce letter was 22 cents. In 1988, the cost was 25 cents. How fast did the cost change from 1985 to 1988? In other words, at what *rate* did the cost change?

A **rate of change** is a ratio that compares the amount of change in a dependent variable to the amount of change in an independent variable.

$$\text{rate of change} = \frac{\text{change in dependent variable}}{\text{change in independent variable}}$$

EXAMPLE 1 Consumer Application

The table shows the cost of mailing a 1-ounce letter in different years. Find the rate of change in cost for each time interval. During which time interval did the cost increase at the greatest rate?

Year	1988	1990	1991	2004	2008
Cost (¢)	25	25	29	37	42

Caution!

A rate of change of 1.25 cents per year for a 4-year period means that the *average* change was 1.25 cents per year. The *actual* change in each year may have been different.

Step 1 Identify the dependent and independent variables.

> dependent: cost   independent: year

Step 2 Find the rates of change.

1988 to 1990 $\dfrac{\text{change in cost}}{\text{change in years}} = \dfrac{25 - 25}{1990 - 1988} = \dfrac{0}{2} = 0$ *0 cents / year*

1990 to 1991 $\dfrac{\text{change in cost}}{\text{change in years}} = \dfrac{29 - 25}{1991 - 1990} = \dfrac{4}{1} = 4$ *4 cents / year*

1991 to 2004 $\dfrac{\text{change in cost}}{\text{change in years}} = \dfrac{37 - 29}{2004 - 1991} = \dfrac{8}{13} \approx 0.62 \approx$ *0.62 cents / year*

2004 to 2008 $\dfrac{\text{change in cost}}{\text{change in years}} = \dfrac{42 - 37}{2008 - 2004} = \dfrac{5}{4} = 1.25$ *1.25 cents / year*

The cost increased at the greatest rate from 1990 to 1991.

 CHECK IT OUT!

1. The table shows the balance of a bank account on different days of the month. Find the rate of change for each time interval. During which time interval did the balance decrease at the greatest rate?

Day	1	6	16	22	30
Balance ($)	550	285	210	210	175

EXAMPLE 2 Finding Rates of Change from a Graph

Graph the data from Example 1 and show the rates of change.

Postage Costs

Graph the ordered pairs. The vertical blue segments show the changes in the dependent variable, and the horizontal green segments show the changes in the independent variable.

Notice that the greatest rate of change is represented by the steepest of the red line segments.

Also notice that between 1988 and 1990, when the cost did not change, the red line segment is horizontal.

2. Graph the data from Check It Out Problem 1 and show the rates of change.

If all of the connected segments have the same rate of change, then they all have the same steepness and together form a straight line. The constant rate of change of a nonvertical line is called the *slope* of the line.

Slope of a Line

The **rise** is the difference in the *y*-values of two points on a line.

The **run** is the difference in the *x*-values of two points on a line.

The **slope** of a line is the ratio of rise to run for any two points on the line.

$$\text{slope} = \frac{\text{rise}}{\text{run}} = \frac{\text{change in } y}{\text{change in } x}$$

(Remember that *y* is the **dependent variable** and *x* is the **independent variable**.)

EXAMPLE 3 Finding Slope

Find the slope of the line.

Caution!

Pay attention to the scales on the axes. One square on the grid may not represent 1 unit. In Example 3, each square represents $\frac{1}{2}$ unit.

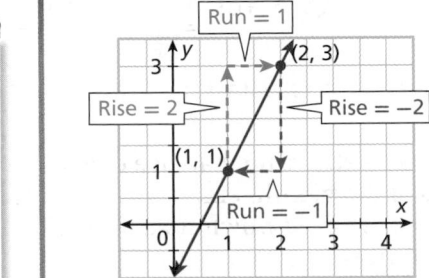

Begin at one point and count vertically to find the rise.

Then count horizontally to the second point to find the run.

It does not matter which point you start with. The slope is the same.

$$\text{slope} = \frac{2}{1} = 2$$

$$\text{slope} = \frac{-2}{-1} = 2$$

3. Find the slope of the line that contains $(0, -3)$ and $(5, -5)$.

EXAMPLE 4 **Finding Slopes of Horizontal and Vertical Lines**

Find the slope of each line.

A
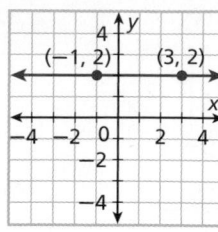

$$\frac{\text{rise}}{\text{run}} = \frac{0}{4} = 0$$

The slope is 0.

B

$$\frac{\text{rise}}{\text{run}} = \frac{2}{0}$$ *You cannot divide by 0.*

The slope is undefined.

 Find the slope of each line.

4a.

4b.
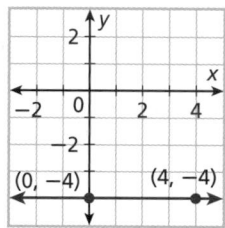

As shown in the previous examples, slope can be positive, negative, zero, or undefined. You can tell which of these is the case by looking at the graph of a line—you do not need to calculate the slope.

Positive Slope	Negative Slope	Zero Slope	Undefined Slope
Line rises from left to right.	Line falls from left to right.	Horizontal line	Vertical line

EXAMPLE 5 **Describing Slope**

Tell whether the slope of each line is positive, negative, zero, or undefined.

A
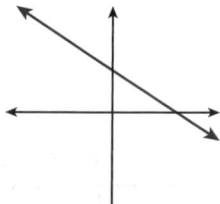

The line falls from left to right.

The slope is negative.

B
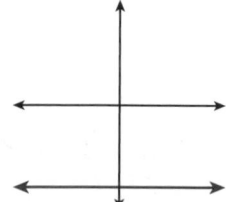

The line is horizontal.

The slope is 0.

Tell whether the slope of each line is positive, negative, zero, or undefined.

5a.

5b.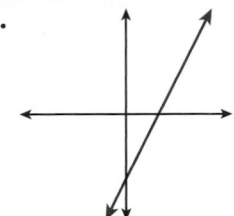

A line's slope is a measure of its steepness. Some lines are steeper than others. As the absolute value of the slope increases, the line becomes steeper.
As the absolute value of the slope decreases, the line becomes less steep.

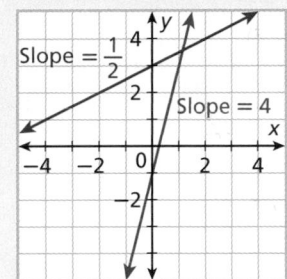

Comparing Slopes		
The line with slope **4** is steeper than the line with slope $\frac{1}{2}$. $\left|4\right| > \left|\frac{1}{2}\right|$	The line with slope **−2** is steeper than the line with slope **−1**. $\left|-2\right| > \left|-1\right|$	The line with slope **−3** is steeper than the line with slope $\frac{3}{4}$. $\left|-3\right| > \left|\frac{3}{4}\right|$

THINK AND DISCUSS

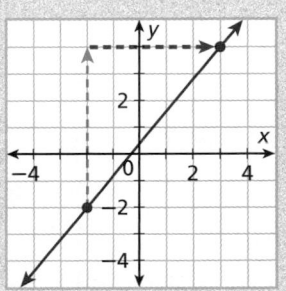

1. What is the rise shown in the graph? What is the run? What is the slope?

2. The rate of change of the profits of a company over one year is negative. How have the profits of the company changed over that year?

3. Would you rather climb a hill with a slope of 4 or a hill with a slope of $\frac{5}{2}$? Explain your answer.

4. **GET ORGANIZED** Copy and complete the graphic organizer. In each box, sketch a line whose slope matches the given description.

go.hrw.com
Homework Help Online
KEYWORD: MA7 5-3
Parent Resources Online
KEYWORD: MA7 Parent

GUIDED PRACTICE

1. **Vocabulary** The *slope* of any nonvertical line is ___?___. (*positive* or *constant*)

SEE EXAMPLE **1**
p. 314

2. The table shows the volume of gasoline in a gas tank at different times. Find the rate of change for each time interval. During which time interval did the volume decrease at the greatest rate?

Time (h)	0	1	3	6	7
Volume (gal)	12	9	5	1	1

SEE EXAMPLE **2**
p. 315

3. The table shows a person's heart rate over time. Graph the data and show the rates of change.

Time (min)	0	2	5	7	10
Heart Rate (beats/min)	64	92	146	84	64

Find the slope of each line.

SEE EXAMPLE **3**
p. 315

4.

5.

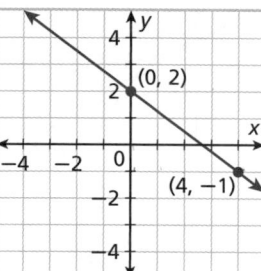

SEE EXAMPLE **4**
p. 316

6.

7.

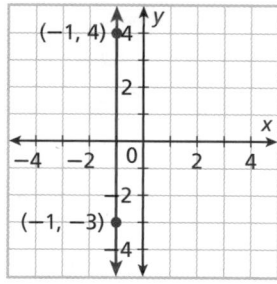

SEE EXAMPLE **5**
p. 316

Tell whether the slope of each line is positive, negative, zero, or undefined.

8.

9.

10.

11.

PRACTICE AND PROBLEM SOLVING

Independent Practice

For Exercises	See Example
12	1
13	2
14–15	3
16–17	4
18–19	5

Extra Practice

Skills Practice p. S12

Application Practice p. S32

12. The table shows the length of a baby at different ages. Find the rate of change for each time interval. Round your answers to the nearest tenth. During which time interval did the baby have the greatest growth rate?

Age (mo)	3	9	18	26	33
Length (in.)	23.5	27.5	31.6	34.5	36.7

13. The table shows the distance of an elevator from the ground floor at different times. Graph the data and show the rates of change.

Time (s)	0	15	23	30	35
Distance (m)	30	70	0	45	60

Find the slope of each line.

14.

15.

16.

17.
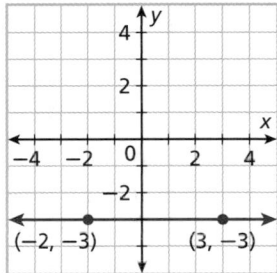

Tell whether the slope of each line is positive, negative, zero, or undefined.

18.

19.
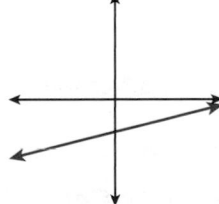

20. **Travel** The Lookout Mountain Incline Railway in Chattanooga, Tennessee, is the steepest passenger railway in the world. A section of the railway has a slope of about 0.73. In this section, a vertical change of 1 unit corresponds to a horizontal change of what length? Round your answer to the nearest hundredth.

21. **Critical Thinking** In Lesson 5-1, you learned that in a linear function, a constant change in x corresponds to a constant change in y. How is this related to slope?

22. This problem will prepare you for the Multi-Step Test Prep on page 342.

    a. The graph shows a relationship between a person's age and his or her estimated maximum heart rate in beats per minute. Find the slope.

    b. Describe the rate of change in this situation.

Estimated Maximum Heart Rate

(20, 200)

(60, 160)

Maximum heart rate (beats/min): 240, 200, 160, 120, 80, 40

Age (yr): 10 20 30 40 50 60 70 80 90

23. **Construction** Most staircases in use today have 9-inch treads and $8\frac{1}{2}$-inch risers. What is the slope of a staircase with these measurements?

24. A ladder is leaned against a building. The bottom of the ladder is 9 feet from the building. The top of the ladder is 16 feet above the ground.

    a. Draw a diagram to represent this situation.

    b. What is the slope of the ladder?

Tread

Riser

25. **Write About It** Why will the slope of any horizontal line be 0? Why will the slope of any vertical line be undefined?

26. The table shows the distance traveled by a car during a five-hour road trip.

Time (h)	0	1	2	3	4	5
Distance (mi)	0	40	80	80	110	160

    a. Graph the data and show the rates of change.

    b. The rate of change represents the average speed. During which hour was the car's average speed the greatest?

27. **Estimation** The graph shows the number of files scanned by a computer virus detection program over time.

    a. Estimate the coordinates of point A.

    b. Estimate the coordinates of point B.

    c. Use your answers from parts **a** and **b** to estimate the rate of change (in files per second) between points A and B.

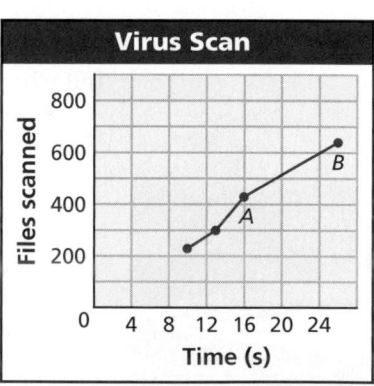

Virus Scan

Files scanned: 800, 600, 400, 200

B

A

Time (s): 4 8 12 16 20 24

28. **Data Collection** Use a graphing calculator and a motion detector for the following. Set the equipment so that the graph shows distance on the y-axis and time on the x-axis.

    a. Experiment with walking in front of the motion detector. How must you walk to graph a straight line? Explain.

    b. Describe what you must do differently to graph a line with a positive slope vs. a line with a negative slope.

    c. How can you graph a line with slope 0? Explain.

29. The slope of which line has the greatest absolute value?

    Ⓐ line *A*   Ⓒ line *C*

    Ⓑ line *B*   Ⓓ line *D*

30. For which line is the run equal to 0?

    Ⓐ line *A*   Ⓒ line *C*

    Ⓑ line *B*   Ⓓ line *D*

31. Which line has a slope of 4?

    Ⓕ   Ⓗ

    Ⓖ   Ⓙ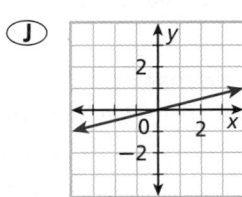

CHALLENGE AND EXTEND

32. **Recreation** Tara and Jade are hiking up a hill. Each has a different stride. The run for Tara's stride is 32 inches, and the rise is 8 inches. The run for Jade's stride is 36 inches. What is the rise of Jade's stride?

33. **Economics** The table shows cost in dollars charged by an electric company for various amounts of energy in kilowatt-hours.

Energy (kWh)	0	200	400	600	1000	2000
Cost ($)	3	3	31	59	115	150

    a. Graph the data and show the rates of change.

    b. Compare the rates of change for each interval. Are they all the same? Explain.

    c. What do the rates of change represent?

    d. Describe in words the electric company's billing plan.

SPIRAL REVIEW

Add or subtract. *(Lesson 1-2)*

34. $-5 + 15$ 35. $9 - 11$ 36. $-5 - (-25)$

Find the domain and range of each relation, and tell whether the relation is a function. *(Lesson 4-2)*

37. $\{(3, 4), (3, 2), (3, 0), (3, -2)\}$ 38.

x	0	2	4	−2	−4
y	0	2	4	2	4

Find the *x*- and *y*-intercepts. *(Lesson 5-2)*

39. $2x + y = 6$ 40. $y = -3x - 9$ 41. $2y = -4x + 1$

5-3
Algebra LAB

Explore Constant Changes

There are many real-life situations in which the amount of change is constant. In these activities, you will explore what happens when

• a quantity increases by a constant amount.

• a quantity decreases by a constant amount.

Use with Lesson 5-3

Activity 1

Janice has read 7 books for her summer reading club. She plans to read 2 books each week for the rest of the summer. The table shows the total number of books that Janice will have read after different numbers of weeks have passed.

1 What number is added to the number of books in each row to get the number of books in the next row?

2 What does your answer to Problem 1 represent in Janice's situation? Describe the meaning of the constant change.

3 Graph the ordered pairs from the table. Describe how the points are related.

4 Look again at your answer to Problem 1. Explain how this number affects your graph.

Janice's Summer Reading	
Week	Total Books Read
0	7
1	9
2	11
3	13
4	15
5	17

Try This

At a particular college, a full-time student must take at least 12 credit hours per semester and may take up to 18 credit hours per semester. Tuition costs $200 per credit hour.

1. Copy and complete the table by using the information above.

2. What number is added to the cost in each row to get the cost in the next row?

3. What does your answer to Problem 2 above represent in the situation? Describe the meaning of the constant change.

4. Graph the ordered pairs from the table. Describe how the points are related.

5. Look again at your answer to Problem 2. Explain how this number affects your graph.

6. Compare your graphs from Activity 1 and Problem 4. How are they alike? How are they different?

7. **Make a Conjecture** Describe the graph of any situation that involves repeated addition of a positive number. Why do you think your description is correct?

Tuition Costs	
Credit Hours	Cost ($)
12	▨
13	▨
14	▨
15	▨
16	▨
17	▨
18	▨

Activity 2

An airplane is 3000 miles from its destination. The plane is traveling at a rate of 540 miles per hour. The table shows how far the plane is from its destination after various amounts of time have passed.

1 What number is subtracted from the distance in each row to get the distance in the next row?

2 What does your answer to Problem 1 represent in the situation? Describe the meaning of the constant change.

3 Graph the ordered pairs from the table. Describe how the points are related.

4 Look again at your answer to Problem 1. Explain how this number affects your graph.

Airplane's Distance	
Time (h)	**Distance to Destination (mi)**
0	3000
1	2460
2	1920
3	1380
4	840

Try This

A television game show begins with 20 contestants. Each week, the players vote 2 contestants off the show.

8. Copy and complete the table by using the information above.

9. What number is subtracted from the number of contestants in each row to get the number of contestants in the next row?

10. What does your answer to Problem 9 represent in the situation? Describe the meaning of the constant change.

11. Graph the ordered pairs from the table. Describe how the points are related.

12. Look again at your answer to Problem 9. Explain how this number affects your graph.

13. Compare your graphs from Activity 2 and Problem 11. How are they alike? How are they different?

14. **Make a Conjecture** Describe the graph of any situation that involves repeated subtraction of a positive number. Why do you think your description is correct?

15. Compare your two graphs from Activity 1 with your two graphs from Activity 2. How are they alike? How are they different?

16. **Make a Conjecture** How are graphs of situations involving repeated subtraction different from graphs of situations involving repeated addition? Explain your answer.

Game Show	
Week	**Contestants Remaining**
0	20
1	▨
2	▨
3	▨
4	▨
5	▨
6	▨

5-4 The Slope Formula

Objective
Find slope by using the slope formula.

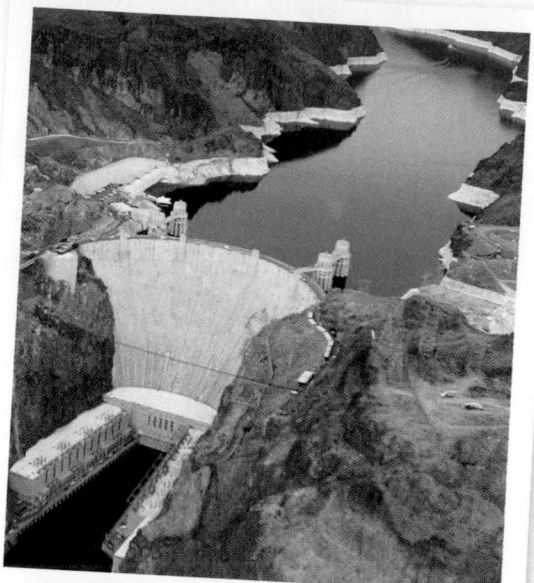

Why learn this?

You can use the slope formula to find how quickly a quantity, such as the amount of water in a reservoir, is changing. (See Example 3.)

In Lesson 5-3, slope was described as the constant rate of change of a line. You saw how to find the slope of a line by using its graph.

There is also a formula you can use to find the slope of a line, which is usually represented by the letter m. To use this formula, you need the coordinates of two different points on the line.

Slope Formula

WORDS	FORMULA	EXAMPLE
The slope of a line is the ratio of the difference in y-values to the difference in x-values between any two different points on the line.	If (x_1, y_1) and (x_2, y_2) are any two different points on a line, the slope of the line is $m = \frac{y_2 - y_1}{x_2 - x_1}$.	If $(2, -3)$ and $(1, 4)$ are two points on a line, the slope of the line is $m = \frac{4 - (-3)}{1 - 2} = \frac{7}{-1} = -7.$

EXAMPLE 1 Finding Slope by Using the Slope Formula

Find the slope of the line that contains $(4, -2)$ and $(-1, 2)$.

$m = \dfrac{y_2 - y_1}{x_2 - x_1}$ *Use the slope formula.*

$= \dfrac{2 - (-2)}{-1 - 4}$ *Substitute $(4, -2)$ for (x_1, y_1) and $(-1, 2)$ for (x_2, y_2).*

$= \dfrac{4}{-5}$ *Simplify.*

$= -\dfrac{4}{5}$

The slope of the line that contains $(4, -2)$ and $(-1, 2)$ is $-\dfrac{4}{5}$.

CHECK IT OUT!

1a. Find the slope of the line that contains $(-2, -2)$ and $(7, -2)$.

1b. Find the slope of the line that contains $(5, -7)$ and $(6, -4)$.

1c. Find the slope of the line that contains $\left(\dfrac{3}{4}, \dfrac{7}{5}\right)$ and $\left(\dfrac{1}{4}, \dfrac{2}{5}\right)$.

Reading Math

The small numbers to the bottom right of the variables are called subscripts. Read x_1 as "x sub one" and y_2 as "y sub two."

Sometimes you are not given two points to use in the formula. You might have to choose two points from a graph or a table.

EXAMPLE **Finding Slope from Graphs and Tables**

Each graph or table shows a linear relationship. Find the slope.

A

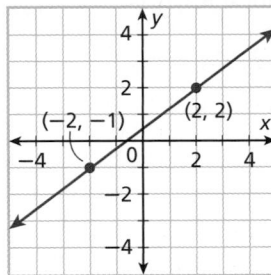

Let $(2, 2)$ be (x_1, y_1) and $(-2, -1)$ be (x_2, y_2).

$m = \dfrac{y_2 - y_1}{x_2 - x_1}$ *Use the slope formula.*

$= \dfrac{-1 - 2}{-2 - 2}$ *Substitute $(2, 2)$ for (x_1, y_1) and $(-2, -1)$ for (x_2, y_2).*

$= \dfrac{-3}{-4}$ *Simplify.*

$= \dfrac{3}{4}$

B

x	2	2	2	2
y	0	1	3	5

Step 1 Choose any two points from the table. Let $(2, 0)$ be (x_1, y_1) and $(2, 3)$ be (x_2, y_2).

Step 2 Use the slope formula.

$m = \dfrac{y_2 - y_1}{x_2 - x_1}$ *Use the slope formula.*

$= \dfrac{3 - 0}{2 - 2}$ *Substitute $(2, 0)$ for (x_1, y_1) and $(2, 3)$ for (x_2, y_2).*

$= \dfrac{3}{0}$ *Simplify.*

The slope is undefined.

CHECK IT OUT! Each graph or table shows a linear relationship. Find the slope.

2a.

2b.

2c.

x	0	2	5	6
y	1	5	11	13

2d.

x	−2	0	2	4
y	3	0	−3	−6

Remember that slope is a rate of change. In real-world problems, finding the slope can give you information about how a quantity is changing.

EXAMPLE 3 *Environmental Science Application*

The graph shows how much water is in a reservoir at different times. Find the slope of the line. Then tell what the slope represents.

Step 1 Use the slope formula.

$$m = \frac{y_2 - y_1}{x_2 - x_1}$$

$$= \frac{2000 - 3000}{60 - 20}$$

$$= \frac{-1000}{40} = -25$$

Step 2 Tell what the slope represents.

In this situation, y represents **volume of water** and x represents **time**.

So slope represents $\frac{\text{change in volume}}{\text{change in time}}$ in units of $\frac{\text{thousands of cubic feet}}{\text{hours}}$.

A slope of -25 means the amount of water in the reservoir is decreasing (negative change) at a rate of 25 thousand cubic feet each hour.

 3. The graph shows the height of a plant over a period of days. Find the slope of the line. Then tell what the slope represents.

If you know the equation that describes a line, you can find its slope by using any two ordered-pair solutions. It is often easiest to use the ordered pairs that contain the intercepts.

EXAMPLE 4 **Finding Slope from an Equation**

Find the slope of the line described by $6x - 5y = 30$.

Step 1 Find the x-intercept.

$6x - 5y = 30$

$6x - 5(0) = 30$ *Let y = 0.*

$6x = 30$

$\dfrac{6x}{6} = \dfrac{30}{6}$

$x = 5$

Step 2 Find the y-intercept.

$6x - 5y = 30$

$6(0) - 5y = 30$ *Let x = 0.*

$-5y = 30$

$\dfrac{-5y}{-5} = \dfrac{30}{-5}$

$y = -6$

Step 3 The line contains $(5, 0)$ and $(0, -6)$. Use the slope formula.

$$m = \frac{y_2 - y_1}{x_2 - x_1} = \frac{-6 - 0}{0 - 5} = \frac{-6}{-5} = \frac{6}{5}$$

 4. Find the slope of the line described by $2x + 3y = 12$.

THINK AND DISCUSS

1. The slope of a line is the difference of the ____?____ divided by the difference of the ____?____ for any two points on the line.

2. Two points lie on a line. When you substitute their coordinates into the slope formula, the value of the denominator is 0. Describe this line.

3. GET ORGANIZED Copy and complete the graphic organizer. In each box, describe how to find slope using the given method.

Finding Slope

From a graph | From a table | From an equation

5-4 Exercises

go.hrw.com
Homework Help Online
KEYWORD: MA7 5-4
Parent Resources Online
KEYWORD: MA7 Parent

GUIDED PRACTICE

SEE EXAMPLE 1
p. 324

Find the slope of the line that contains each pair of points.

1. $(3, 6)$ and $(6, 9)$ **2.** $(2, 7)$ and $(4, 4)$ **3.** $(-1, -5)$ and $(-9, -1)$

SEE EXAMPLE 2
p. 325

Each graph or table shows a linear relationship. Find the slope.

4.

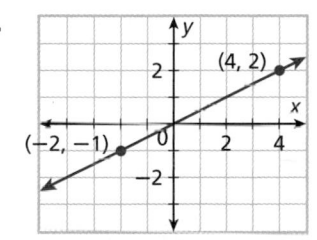

5.

x	y
0	25
2	45
4	65
6	85

SEE EXAMPLE 3
p. 326

Find the slope of each line. Then tell what the slope represents.

6.

7.

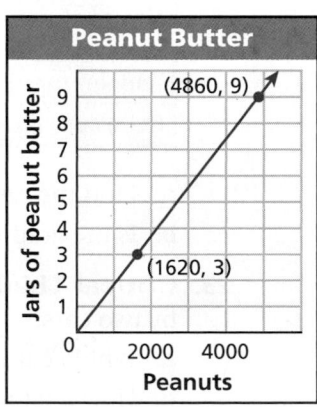

SEE EXAMPLE 4
p. 326

Find the slope of the line described by each equation.

8. $8x + 2y = 96$ **9.** $5x = 90 - 9y$ **10.** $5y = 160 + 9x$

PRACTICE AND PROBLEM SOLVING

Independent Practice

For Exercises	See Example
11–13	1
14–15	2
16–17	3
18–20	4

Extra Practice

Skills Practice p. S12
Application Practice p. S32

Find the slope of the line that contains each pair of points.

11. (2, 5) and (3, 1) **12.** (−9, −5) and (6, −5) **13.** (3, 4) and (3, −1)

Each graph or table shows a linear relationship. Find the slope.

14.

x	y
1	18.5
2	22
3	25.5
4	29

15.

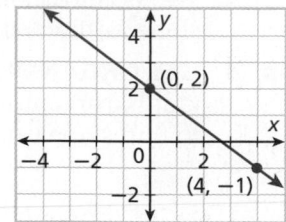

Find the slope of each line. Then tell what the slope represents.

16.

17.

Find the slope of the line described by each equation.

18. $7x + 13y = 91$ **19.** $5y = 130 − 13x$ **20.** $7 − 3y = 9x$

21. **///ERROR ANALYSIS///** Two students found the slope of the line that contains (−6, 3) and (2, −1). Who is incorrect? Explain the error.

Ⓐ $m = \dfrac{-1-3}{2-(-6)} = \dfrac{-4}{8} = -\dfrac{1}{2}$

Ⓑ $m = \dfrac{-1-3}{-6-2} = \dfrac{-4}{-8} = \dfrac{1}{2}$

22. **Environmental Science** The table shows how the number of cricket chirps per minute changes with the air temperature.

Temperature (°F)	40	50	60	70	80	90
Chirps per minute	0	40	80	120	160	200

a. Find the rates of change.

b. Is the graph of the data a line? If so, what is the slope? If not, explain why not.

23. **Critical Thinking** The graph shows the distance traveled by two cars.

a. Which car is going faster? How much faster?

b. How are the speeds related to slope?

c. At what rate is the distance between the cars changing?

24. **Write About It** You are given the coordinates of two points on a line. Describe two different ways to find the slope of that line.

25. This problem will prepare you for the Multi-Step Test Prep on page 342.

    a. One way to estimate your maximum heart rate is to subtract your age from 220. Write a function to describe the relationship between maximum heart rate y and age x.

    b. The graph of this function is a line. Find its slope. Then tell what the slope represents.

TEST PREP

26. The equation $2y + 3x = -6$ describes a line with what slope?

    Ⓐ $\dfrac{3}{2}$ Ⓑ 0   Ⓒ $\dfrac{1}{2}$ Ⓓ $-\dfrac{3}{2}$

27. A line with slope $-\dfrac{1}{3}$ could pass through which of the following pairs of points?

    Ⓕ $\left(0, -\dfrac{1}{3}\right)$ and $(1, 1)$ Ⓗ $(0, 0)$ and $\left(-\dfrac{1}{3}, -\dfrac{1}{3}\right)$

    Ⓖ $(-6, 5)$ and $(-3, 4)$ Ⓙ $(5, -6)$ and $(4, 3)$

28. **Gridded Response** Find the slope of the line that contains $(-1, 2)$ and $(5, 5)$.

CHALLENGE AND EXTEND

Find the slope of the line that contains each pair of points.

29. $(a, 0)$ and $(0, b)$ 30. $(2x, y)$ and $(x, 3y)$ 31. (x, y) and $(x + 2, 3 - y)$

Find the value of x so that the points lie on a line with the given slope.

32. $(x, 2)$ and $(-5, 8)$, $m = -1$ 33. $(4, x)$ and $(6, 3x)$, $m = \dfrac{1}{2}$

34. $(1, -3)$ and $(3, x)$, $m = -1$ 35. $(-10, -4)$ and (x, x), $m = \dfrac{1}{7}$

36. A line contains the point $(1, 2)$ and has a slope of $\dfrac{1}{2}$. Use the slope formula to find another point on this line.

37. The points $(-2, 4)$, $(0, 2)$, and $(3, x - 1)$ all lie on the same line. What is the value of x? (*Hint:* Remember that the slope of a line is constant for any two points on the line.)

SPIRAL REVIEW

Solve each inequality and graph the solutions. *(Lesson 3-7)*

38. $|x| + 5 < 16$ 39. $|x + 8| < 3$ 40. $3|x| \le 12$

41. $|x| - 11 \ge -4$ 42. $|x - 6| > 10$ 43. $|x + 1| \ge 7$

Tell whether the given ordered pairs satisfy a linear function. *(Lesson 5-1)*

44. $\{(1, 1), (2, 4), (3, 9), (4, 16)\}$ 45. $\{(9, 0), (8, -5), (5, -20), (3, -30)\}$

Use the intercepts to graph the line described by each equation. *(Lesson 5-2)*

46. $x - y = 5$ 47. $3x + y = 9$ 48. $y = 5x + 10$

The Midpoint and Distance Formulas

Objectives
Apply the formula for midpoint.

Use the Distance Formula to find the distance between two points.

Vocabulary
midpoint

Why learn this?
You can use the coordinate plane to model and solve problems involving distances, such as the distance across a lake. (See Example 4.)

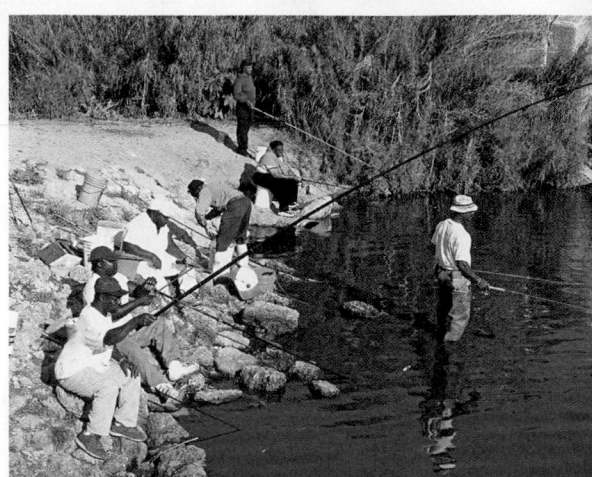

In Lesson 5-4, you used the coordinates of points to determine the slope of lines. You can also use coordinates to determine the *midpoint* of a line segment on the coordinate plane.

The **midpoint** of a line segment is the point that divides the segment into two congruent segments. *Congruent segments* are segments that have the same length.

You can find the midpoint of a segment by using the coordinates of its endpoints. Calculate the average of the *x*-coordinates and the average of the *y*-coordinates of the endpoints.

Midpoint Formula

The midpoint M of $\overline{AB}$ with endpoints $A(x_1, y_1)$ and $B(x_2, y_2)$ is

$$M\left(\frac{x_1 + x_2}{2}, \frac{y_1 + y_2}{2}\right).$$

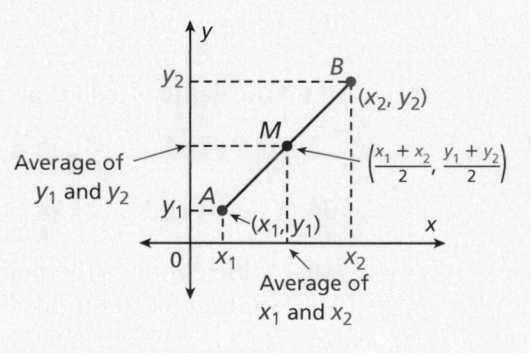

EXAMPLE 1 Finding the Coordinates of a Midpoint

Find the coordinates of the midpoint of $\overline{CD}$ with endpoints $C(-2, -1)$ and $D(4, 2)$.

$M\left(\dfrac{x_1 + x_2}{2}, \dfrac{y_1 + y_2}{2}\right)$ *Write the formula.*

$M\left(\dfrac{-2 + 4}{2}, \dfrac{-1 + 2}{2}\right)$ *Substitute.*

$M\left(\dfrac{2}{2}, \dfrac{1}{2}\right) = M\left(1, \dfrac{1}{2}\right)$ *Simplify.*

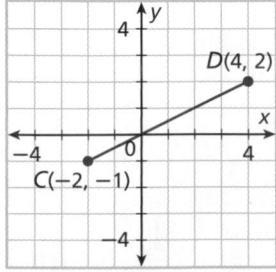

Remember!

A segment is named by its endpoints. The notation $\overline{CD}$ is read "segment *CD*."

1. Find the coordinates of the midpoint of $\overline{EF}$ with endpoints $E(-2, 3)$ and $F(5, -3)$.

EXAMPLE **2**   **Finding the Coordinates of an Endpoint**

M is the midpoint of $\overline{AB}$. *A* has coordinates $(2, 2)$, and *M* has coordinates $(4, -3)$. Find the coordinates of *B*.

Step 1 Let the coordinates of *B* equal (x, y).

Step 2 Use the Midpoint Formula.

$$(4, -3) = \left(\frac{2 + x}{2}, \frac{2 + y}{2} \right)$$

Step 3 Find the *x*-coordinate.   Find the *y*-coordinate.

$4 = \dfrac{2 + x}{2}$	*Set the coordinates equal.*	$-3 = \dfrac{2 + y}{2}$
$2(4) = 2\left(\dfrac{2 + x}{2}\right)$	*Multiply both sides by 2.*	$2(-3) = 2\left(\dfrac{2 + y}{2}\right)$
$8 = \ \ 2 + x$	*Simplify.*	$-6 = \ \ 2 + y$
$\underline{-2 \quad -2}$	*Subtract 2 from both sides.*	$\underline{-2 \quad -2}$
$6 = \qquad x$	*Simplify.*	$-8 = \qquad y$

The coordinates of *B* are $(6, -8)$.

Check   Graph points *A* and *B* and midpoint *M*.

Point M appears to be the midpoint of $\overline{AB}$.

 2. *S* is the midpoint of $\overline{RT}$. *R* has coordinates $(-6, -1)$, and *S* has coordinates $(-1, 1)$. Find the coordinates of *T*.

You can also use coordinates to find the distance between two points or the length of a line segment. To find the length of segment *PQ*, draw a horizontal segment from *P* and a vertical segment from *Q* to form a right triangle.

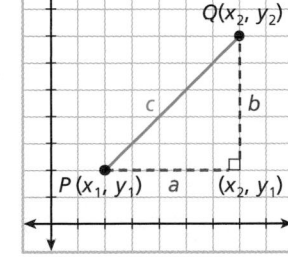

$c^2 = a^2 + b^2$	*Pythagorean Theorem*
$c = \sqrt{a^2 + b^2}$	*Solve for c. Use the positive square root to represent distance.*

$$PQ = \sqrt{\underbrace{(x_2 - x_1)^2}_{} + \underbrace{(y_2 - y_1)^2}_{}}$$

Length of   Length of
horizontal segment   vertical segment

This equation represents the Distance Formula.

Remember!

The *Pythagorean Theorem* states that if a right triangle has legs of lengths *a* and *b* and a hypotenuse of length *c*, then $a^2 + b^2 = c^2$.

Distance Formula

In a coordinate plane, the distance *d* between two points (x_1, y_1) and (x_2, y_2) is
$$d = \sqrt{(x_2 - x_1)^2 + (y_2 - y_1)^2}.$$

EXAMPLE 3 — Finding Distance in the Coordinate Plane

Use the Distance Formula to find the distance, to the nearest hundredth, from $A(-2, 3)$ to $B(2, -2)$.

$d = \sqrt{(x_2 - x_1)^2 + (y_2 - y_1)^2}$ *Distance Formula*

$d = \sqrt{[2 - (-2)]^2 + (-2 - 3)^2}$ *Substitute $(-2, 3)$ for (x_1, y_1) and $(2, -2)$ for (x_2, y_2).*

$d = \sqrt{4^2 + (-5)^2}$ *Subtract.*

$d = \sqrt{16 + 25}$ *Simplify powers.*

$d = \sqrt{41}$ *Add.*

$d \approx 6.40$ *Find the square root to the nearest hundredth.*

CHECK IT OUT!
3. Use the Distance Formula to find the distance, to the nearest hundredth, from $R(3, 2)$ to $S(-3, -1)$.

EXAMPLE 4 — *Geography Application*

Each unit on the map of Lake Okeechobee represents 1 mile. Delia and her father plan to travel from point A near the town of Okeechobee to point B at Pahokee. To the nearest tenth of a mile, how far do Delia and her father plan to travel?

$d = \sqrt{(x_2 - x_1)^2 + (y_2 - y_1)^2}$

$d = \sqrt{(33 - 22)^2 + (13 - 39)^2}$ *Substitute.*

$d = \sqrt{11^2 + (-26)^2}$ *Subtract.*

$d = \sqrt{121 + 676}$ *Simplify powers.*

$d = \sqrt{797}$ *Add.*

$d \approx 28.2$ *Find the square root to the nearest tenth.*

Delia and her father plan to travel about 28.2 miles.

CHECK IT OUT!
4. Jacob takes a boat from Pahokee to Clewiston. To the nearest tenth of a mile, how far does he travel?

THINK AND DISCUSS

1. If you use the formula $M\left(\dfrac{x_2 + x_1}{2}, \dfrac{y_2 + y_1}{2}\right)$ to find the midpoint of a segment, will you get the correct coordinates for the midpoint? Explain.

2. GET ORGANIZED Copy and complete the graphic organizer. In each box, write a formula. Then make a sketch that will illustrate the formula.

go.hrw.com
Homework Help Online
KEYWORD: MA11 5-5
Parent Resources Online
KEYWORD: MA7 Parent

GUIDED PRACTICE

1. **Vocabulary** In your own words, describe the *midpoint* of a line segment.

SEE EXAMPLE 1
p. 330

Find the coordinates of the midpoint of each segment.

2. $\overline{AB}$ with endpoints $A(4, -6)$ and $B(-4, 2)$

3. $\overline{CD}$ with endpoints $C(0, -8)$ and $D(3, 0)$

4. $\overline{EF}$ with endpoints $E(-8, 17)$ and $F(-12, -16)$

SEE EXAMPLE 2
p. 331

5. M is the midpoint of $\overline{LN}$. L has coordinates $(-3, -1)$, and M has coordinates $(0, 1)$. Find the coordinates of N.

6. B is the midpoint of $\overline{AC}$. A has coordinates $(-3, 4)$, and B has coordinates $\left(-1\frac{1}{2}, 1\right)$. Find the coordinates of C.

SEE EXAMPLE 3
p. 332

Use the Distance Formula to find the distance, to the nearest hundredth, between each pair of points.

7. $A(1, -2)$ and $B(-4, -4)$

8. $X(-2, 7)$ and $Y(-2, -8)$

9. $V(2, -1)$ and $W(-4, 8)$

SEE EXAMPLE 4
p. 332

10. **Recreation** Each unit on the map of a public park represents 1 kilometer. To the nearest tenth of a kilometer, what is the distance from the campground to the waterfall?

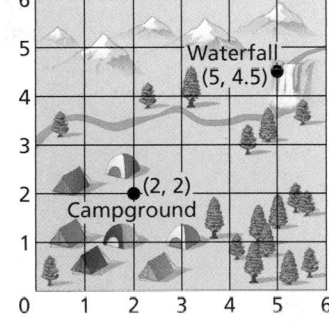

PRACTICE AND PROBLEM SOLVING

Independent Practice

For Exercises	See Example
11–12	1
13–15	2
16–19	3
20	4

Extra Practice

Skills Practice p. S12
Application Practice p. S32

Find the coordinates of the midpoint of each segment.

11. $\overline{XY}$ with endpoints $X(-3, -7)$ and $Y(-1, 1)$

12. $\overline{MN}$ with endpoints $M(12, -7)$ and $N(-5, -2)$

13. M is the midpoint of $\overline{QR}$. Q has coordinates $(-3, 5)$, and M has coordinates $(7, -9)$. Find the coordinates of R.

14. D is the midpoint of $\overline{CE}$. E has coordinates $(-3, -2)$, and D has coordinates $\left(2\frac{1}{2}, 1\right)$. Find the coordinates of C.

15. Y is the midpoint of $\overline{XZ}$. X has coordinates $(0, -1)$, and Y has coordinates $\left(1, -4\frac{1}{2}\right)$. Find the coordinates of Z.

Use the Distance Formula to find the distance, to the nearest hundredth, between each pair of points.

16. $U(0, 1)$ and $V(-3, -9)$

17. $M(10, -1)$ and $N(2, -5)$

18. $P(-10, 1)$ and $Q(5, 5)$

19. $F(6, 15)$ and $G(4, 24)$

20. **Astronomy** Each unit on the map of a section of a moon represents 1 kilometer. To the nearest tenth of a kilometer, what is the distance between the two craters?

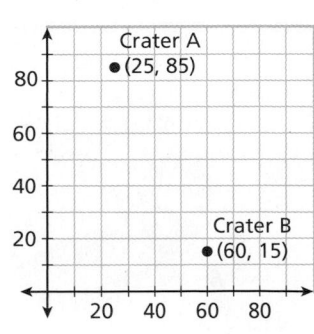

For Exercises 21 and 22, use the map, and round your answers to the nearest tenth of a mile. Each unit on the map represents 1 mile.

21. How far is it from Cedar City to Milltown along Highway 201?

22. A car breaks down on Route 1 halfway between Jefferson and Milltown. A tow truck is sent out from Jefferson. How far does the truck travel to reach the car?

23. Estimation Estimate the distance between the points $(-5.21, 1.84)$ and $(16.62, -23.19)$. Explain how you determined your answer.

24. Geometry The coordinates of the vertices of $\triangle ABC$ are $A(1, 4)$, $B(-2, -1)$, and $C(3, -2)$. Find the perimeter of $\triangle ABC$ to the nearest whole number.

Find the distance, to the nearest hundredth, between each pair of points.

25. $J(0, 3)$ and $K(-6, -9)$ **26.** $L(-5, 2)$ and $M(-8, 10)$ **27.** $N(4, -6)$ and $P(-2, 7)$

28. Aviation A Coast Guard helicopter receives a distress signal from a boat. The units on the map represent miles. To the nearest minute, how long will it take the helicopter to reach the boat if the helicopter travels at an average speed of 75 miles per hour?

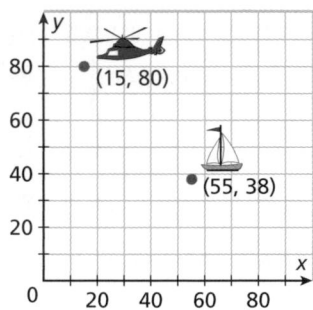

29. Geometry A diameter of a circle has endpoints $(-2, -5)$ and $(2, 1)$.

  a. Find the length of the diameter to the nearest tenth.

  b. Find the coordinates of the center of the circle.

  c. Find the circumference of the circle to the nearest whole number.

30. Travel A group of tourists is traveling by camel in the desert. They are following a straight path from point $(2, 4)$ to point $(8, 12)$ on a map. Each unit on the map represents 1 mile. An oasis lies at the midpoint of the path. The group has already traveled 3.2 miles. How much farther do they need to go to reach the oasis?

31. Multi-Step Use the Distance Formula to order $\overline{AB}$, $\overline{CD}$, and $\overline{EF}$ from shortest to longest.

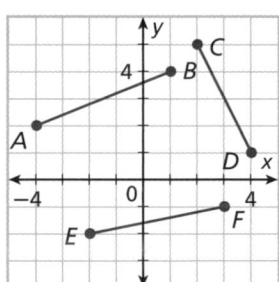

32. Critical Thinking Rebecca found the x-coordinate of the midpoint of $\overline{AB}$ with endpoints $A(x_1, y_1)$ and $B(x_2, y_2)$ by dividing the difference between x_2 and x_1 by 2 and then adding the quotient to x_1. Did this method give the correct x-coordinate for the midpoint? Explain.

33. Write About It Explain why the Distance Formula is not needed to find the distance between two points that lie on a horizontal or vertical line.

MULTI-STEP TEST PREP

34. This problem will help you prepare for the Multi-Step Test Prep on page 342.

On a map of a city park, the ordered pairs $(3, 5)$ and $(8, 17)$ mark the starting and ending points of a straight jogging trail. Each unit on the map represents 0.1 mile.

  a. What is the length of the trail in miles?

  b. How many back-and-forth trips would Marisol need to make on the trail in order to run at least 7 miles?

35. Which segment has a length closest to 4 units?

    (A) $\overline{EF}$ (C) $\overline{JK}$

    (B) $\overline{GH}$ (D) $\overline{LM}$

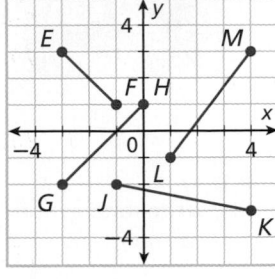

36. What is the distance between the points $(7, -3)$ and $(-5, 6)$?

    (F) 4   (H) 15

    (G) 9   (J) 21

37. A coordinate plane is placed over the map of a town. A library is located at $(-5, 1)$, and a museum is located at $(3, 5)$. What is the distance, to the nearest tenth, from the library to the museum?

    (A) 4.5 units   (B) 5.7 units   (C) 6.3 units   (D) 8.9 units

38. Short Response Brian is driving along a straight highway. His truck can travel 22 miles per gallon of gasoline, and it has 2 gallons of gas remaining. On a map, the truck's current location is $(7, 12)$, and the nearest gas station on the highway is located at $(16, 52)$. Each unit on the map represents 1 mile. Will the truck reach the gas station before running out of gas? Support your answer.

CHALLENGE AND EXTEND

39. Geometry Find the area of a trapezoid with vertices $A(-4, 2)$, $B(0, 4)$, $C(3, 3)$, and $D(-3, 0)$. (*Hint*: The formula for the area of a trapezoid is $A = \frac{1}{2}h(b_1 + b_2)$.)

40. X has coordinates $(a, 3a)$, and Y has coordinates $(-5a, 0)$. Find the coordinates of the midpoint of $\overline{XY}$.

41. The coordinates of P are $(a - 5, 0)$. The coordinates of Q are $(a + 1, a)$. The distance between P and Q is 10 units. Find the value of a.

42. Find two points on the y-axis that are a distance of 5 units from $(4, 2)$.

43. The coordinates of S are $(4, 5)$. The coordinates of the midpoint of $\overline{ST}$ are $(-1, -7)$. Find the length of $\overline{ST}$.

SPIRAL REVIEW

44. In the 2007–2008 season, the Orlando Magic won 52 games and lost 30 games. What percent of its games did the team win? Round your answer to the nearest percent. *(Lesson 2-9)*

Solve each inequality and graph the solutions. *(Lesson 3-5)*

45. $4x < 7x + 6$ **46.** $4y + 3 \geq 5y - 8$ **47.** $6(z + 2) > 3z$

Find the slope of each line. *(Lesson 5-3)*

48.

49.

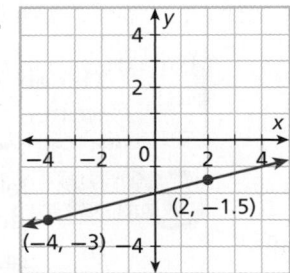

5-6 Direct Variation

Objective
Identify, write, and graph direct variation.

Vocabulary
direct variation
constant of variation

Who uses this?
Chefs can use direct variation to determine ingredients needed for a certain number of servings.

A recipe for paella calls for 1 cup of rice to make 5 servings. In other words, a chef needs 1 cup of rice for every 5 servings.

Rice (c) x	1	2	3	4
Servings y	5	10	15	20

Paella is a rice dish that originated in Valencia, Spain.

The equation $y = 5x$ describes this relationship. In this relationship, the number of servings *varies directly* with the number of cups of rice.

A **direct variation** is a special type of linear relationship that can be written in the form $y = kx$, where k is a nonzero constant called the **constant of variation**.

EXAMPLE 1 **Identifying Direct Variations from Equations**

Tell whether each equation represents a direct variation. If so, identify the constant of variation.

A $y = 4x$

This equation represents a direct variation because it is in the form $y = kx$. The constant of variation is 4.

B $-3x + 5y = 0$

$$-3x + 5y = \quad 0 \qquad \textit{Solve the equation for y.}$$
$$\underline{+ 3x \qquad\qquad + 3x} \qquad \textit{Since } -3x \textit{ is added to } 5y, \textit{ add } 3x \textit{ to both sides.}$$
$$5y = \quad 3x$$
$$\frac{5y}{5} = \frac{3x}{5} \qquad \textit{Since y is multiplied by 5, divide both sides by 5.}$$
$$y = \frac{3}{5}x$$

This equation represents a direct variation because it can be written in the form $y = kx$. The constant of variation is $\frac{3}{5}$.

C $2x + y = 10$

$$2x + y = \quad 10 \qquad \textit{Solve the equation for y.}$$
$$\underline{- 2x \qquad\qquad - 2x} \qquad \textit{Since 2x is added to y, subtract 2x from both sides.}$$
$$y = -2x + 10$$

This equation does not represent a direct variation because it cannot be written in the form $y = kx$.

 CHECK IT OUT! Tell whether each equation represents a direct variation. If so, identify the constant of variation.

1a. $3y = 4x + 1$ **1b.** $3x = -4y$ **1c.** $y + 3x = 0$

What happens if you solve $y = kx$ for k?

$$y = kx$$

$$\frac{y}{x} = \frac{kx}{x} \qquad \text{\textit{Divide both sides by x (x ≠ 0).}}$$

$$\frac{y}{x} = k$$

So, in a direct variation, the ratio $\frac{y}{x}$ is equal to the constant of variation. Another way to identify a direct variation is to check whether $\frac{y}{x}$ is the same for each ordered pair (except where $x = 0$).

EXAMPLE 2 **Identifying Direct Variations from Ordered Pairs**

Tell whether each relationship is a direct variation. Explain.

A

x	1	3	5
y	6	18	30

Method 1 Write an equation.

$y = 6x$ \qquad *Each y-value is 6 times the corresponding x-value.*

This is a direct variation because it can be written as $y = kx$, where $k = 6$.

Method 2 Find $\frac{y}{x}$ for each ordered pair.

$$\frac{6}{1} = 6 \qquad\qquad \frac{18}{3} = 6 \qquad\qquad \frac{30}{5} = 6$$

This is a direct variation because $\frac{y}{x}$ is the same for each ordered pair.

B

x	2	4	8
y	−2	0	4

Method 1 Write an equation.

$y = x - 4$ \qquad *Each y-value is 4 less than the corresponding x-value.*

This is not a direct variation because it cannot be written as $y = kx$.

Method 2 Find $\frac{y}{x}$ for each ordered pair.

$$\frac{-2}{2} = -1 \qquad\qquad \frac{0}{4} = 0 \qquad\qquad \frac{4}{8} = \frac{1}{2}$$

This is not a direct variation because $\frac{y}{x}$ is not the same for all ordered pairs.

CHECK IT OUT! Tell whether each relationship is a direct variation. Explain.

2a.
x	y
−3	0
1	3
3	6

2b.
x	y
2.5	−10
5	−20
7.5	−30

2c.
x	y
−2	5
1	3
4	1

If you know one ordered pair that satisfies a direct variation, you can write the equation. You can also find other ordered pairs that satisfy the direct variation.

EXAMPLE 3 **Writing and Solving Direct Variation Equations**

The value of y varies directly with x, and $y = 6$ when $x = 12$.
Find y when $x = 27$.

Method 1 Find the value of k and then write the equation.

$y = kx$	*Write the equation for a direct variation.*
$6 = k(12)$	*Substitute 6 for y and 12 for x. Solve for k.*
$\frac{1}{2} = k$	*Since k is multiplied by 12, divide both sides by 12.*

The equation is $y = \frac{1}{2}x$. When $x = 27$, $y = \frac{1}{2}(27) = 13.5$.

Method 2 Use a proportion.

$\frac{6}{12} \times \frac{y}{27}$	*In a direct variation, $\frac{y}{x}$ is the same for all values of x and y.*
$12y = 162$	*Use cross products.*
$y = 13.5$	*Since y is multiplied by 12, divide both sides by 12.*

 3. The value of y varies directly with x, and $y = 4.5$ when $x = 0.5$.
Find y when $x = 10$.

EXAMPLE 4 **Graphing Direct Variations**

The three-toed sloth is an extremely slow animal. On the ground, it travels at a speed of about 6 feet per minute. Write a direct variation equation for the distance y a sloth will travel in x minutes. Then graph.

Step 1 Write a direct variation equation.

distance =	**6 feet per minute**	**times**	**number of minutes**
y =	6	•	x

Step 2 Choose values of x and generate ordered pairs.

Step 3 Graph the points and connect.

x	$y = 6x$	(x, y)
0	$y = 6(0) = 0$	$(0, 0)$
1	$y = 6(1) = 6$	$(1, 6)$
2	$y = 6(2) = 12$	$(2, 12)$

Speed of a Sloth

 4. The perimeter y of a square varies directly with its side length x.
Write a direct variation equation for this relationship. Then graph.

Look at the graph in Example 4. It passes through $(0, 0)$ and has a slope of 6.
The graph of any direct variation $y = kx$
   • is a line through $(0, 0)$.   • has a slope of k.

THINK AND DISCUSS

1. How do you know that a direct variation is linear?

2. How does the graph of a direct variation differ from the graphs of other types of linear relationships?

3. **GET ORGANIZED** Copy and complete the graphic organizer. In each box, describe how you can use the given information to identify a direct variation.

Recognizing a Direct Variation		
From an Equation	From Ordered Pairs	From a Graph

5-6 Exercises

go.hrw.com
Homework Help Online
KEYWORD: MA11 5-6
Parent Resources Online
KEYWORD: MA7 Parent

GUIDED PRACTICE

1. Vocabulary If x varies directly with y, then the relationship between the two variables is said to be a ___?___. (*direct variation* or *constant of variation*)

SEE EXAMPLE 1
p. 336

Tell whether each equation represents a direct variation. If so, identify the constant of variation.

2. $y = 4x + 9$ **3.** $2y = -8x$ **4.** $x + y = 0$

SEE EXAMPLE 2
p. 337

Tell whether each relationship is a direct variation. Explain.

5.

x	10	5	2
y	12	7	4

6.

x	3	−1	−4
y	−6	2	8

SEE EXAMPLE 3
p. 338

7. The value of y varies directly with x, and $y = -3$ when $x = 1$. Find y when $x = -6$.

8. The value of y varies directly with x, and $y = 6$ when $x = 18$. Find y when $x = 12$.

SEE EXAMPLE 4
p. 338

9. Wages Cameron earns $7 per hour at her after-school job. The total amount of her paycheck varies directly with the amount of time she works. Write a direct variation equation for the amount of money y that she earns for working x hours. Then graph.

PRACTICE AND PROBLEM SOLVING

Tell whether each equation represents a direct variation. If so, identify the constant of variation.

10. $y = \frac{1}{6}x$ **11.** $4y = x$ **12.** $x = 2y - 12$

Tell whether each relationship is a direct variation. Explain.

13.

x	6	9	17
y	13.2	19.8	37.4

14.

x	−6	3	12
y	4	−2	−8

Independent Practice

For Exercises	See Example
10–12	1
13–14	2
15–16	3
17	4

Extra Practice

Skills Practice p. S13

Application Practice p. S32

15. The value of y varies directly with x, and $y = 8$ when $x = -32$. Find y when $x = 64$.

16. The value of y varies directly with x, and $y = \frac{1}{2}$ when $x = 3$. Find y when $x = 1$.

17. While on his way to school, Norman saw that the cost of gasoline was $2.50 per gallon. Write a direct variation equation to describe the cost y of x gallons of gas. Then graph.

Tell whether each relationship is a direct variation. Explain your answer.

18. The equation $-15x + 4y = 0$ relates the length of a videotape in inches x to its approximate playing time in seconds y.

19. The equation $y - 2.00x = 2.50$ relates the cost y of a taxicab ride to distance x of the cab ride in miles.

Each ordered pair is a solution of a direct variation. Write the equation of direct variation. Then graph your equation and show that the slope of the line is equal to the constant of variation.

20. $(2, 10)$ **21.** $(-3, 9)$ **22.** $(8, 2)$ **23.** $(1.5, 6)$

24. $(7, 21)$ **25.** $(1, 2)$ **26.** $(2, -16)$ **27.** $\left(\frac{1}{7}, 1\right)$

28. $(-2, 9)$ **29.** $(9, -2)$ **30.** $(4, 6)$ **31.** $(3, 4)$

32. $(5, 1)$ **33.** $(1, -6)$ **34.** $\left(-1, \frac{1}{2}\right)$ **35.** $(7, 2)$

Astronomy

36. **Astronomy** Weight varies directly with gravity. A Mars lander weighed 767 pounds on Earth but only 291 pounds on Mars. Its accompanying Mars rover weighed 155 pounds on Mars. How much did it weigh on Earth? Round your answer to the nearest pound.

37. **Environment** Mischa bought an energy-efficient washing machine. She will save about 15 gallons of water per wash load.

  a. Write an equation of direct variation to describe how many gallons of water y Mischa saves for x loads of laundry she washes.

  b. Graph your direct variation from part **a.** Is every point on the graph a solution in this situation? Why or why not?

  c. If Mischa does 2 loads of laundry per week, how many gallons of water will she have saved at the end of a year?

The Mars rover *Spirit* landed on Mars in January 2004 and immediately began sending photos of the planet's surface back to Earth.

38. **Critical Thinking** If you double an x-value in a direct variation, will the corresponding y-value double? Explain.

 39. **Write About It** In a direct variation $y = kx$, k is sometimes called the "constant of proportionality." How are proportions related to direct variations?

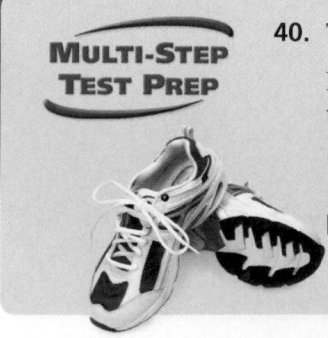

MULTI-STEP TEST PREP

40. This problem will prepare you for the Multi-Step Test Prep on page 342.

Rhea exercised on a treadmill at the gym. When she was finished, the display showed that she had walked at an average speed of 3 miles per hour.

  a. Write an equation that gives the number of miles y that Rhea would cover in x hours if she walked at this speed.

  b. Explain why this is a direct variation and find the value of k. What does this value represent in Rhea's situation?

41. Which equation does NOT represent a direct variation?

(A) $y = \frac{1}{3}x$ (B) $y = -2x$ (C) $y = 4x + 1$ (D) $6x - y = 0$

42. Identify which set of data represents a direct variation.

(F)
x	1	2	3
y	1	2	3

(H)
x	1	2	3
y	3	5	7

(G)
x	1	2	3
y	0	1	2

(J)
x	1	2	3
y	3	4	5

43. Two yards of fabric cost $13, and 5 yards of fabric cost $32.50. Which equation relates the cost of the fabric c to its length ℓ?

(A) $c = 2.6\ell$ (B) $c = 6.5\ell$ (C) $c = 13\ell$ (D) $c = 32.5\ell$

44. Gridded Response A car is traveling at a constant speed. After 3 hours, the car has traveled 180 miles. If the car continues to travel at the same constant speed, how many hours will it take to travel a total of 270 miles?

CHALLENGE AND EXTEND

45. Transportation The function $y = 20x$ gives the number of miles y that a sport-utility vehicle (SUV) can travel on x gallons of gas. The function $y = 60x$ gives the number of miles y that a hybrid car can travel on x gallons of gas.

   a. If you drive 120 miles, how much gas will you save by driving the hybrid instead of the SUV?

   b. Graph both functions on the same coordinate plane. Will the lines ever meet other than at the origin? Explain.

   c. What if...? Shannon drives 15,000 miles in one year. How many gallons of gas will she use if she drives the SUV? the hybrid?

46. Suppose the equation $ax + by = c$, where a, b, and c are real numbers, describes a direct variation. What do you know about the value of c?

SPIRAL REVIEW

Solve for the indicated variable. *(Lesson 2-5)*

47. $p + 4q = 7; p$ **48.** $\frac{s-5}{t} = 2; s$ **49.** $xy + 2y = 4; x$

Determine a relationship between the x- and y-values and write an equation.
(Lesson 4-3)

50.
x	y
1	−5
2	−4
3	−3
4	−2

51.
x	y
1	−2
2	−4
3	−6
4	−8

52.
x	y
−3	9
−2	6
−1	3
0	0

Find the slope of the line described by each equation. *(Lesson 5-4)*

53. $4x + y = -9$ **54.** $6x - 3y = -9$ **55.** $5x = 10y - 5$

MULTI-STEP TEST PREP

Characteristics of Linear Functions

Heart Health People who exercise need to be aware of their maximum heart rate.

1. One way to estimate your maximum heart rate m is to subtract 85% of your age in years from 217. Create a table of values that shows the maximum heart rates for people ages 13 to 18. Then write an equation to describe the data in the table.

2. Use your table from Problem 1 to graph the relationship between age and maximum heart rate. What are the intercepts? What is the slope?

3. What do the intercepts represent in this situation?

4. What does the slope represent? Explain why the slope is negative.

5. Another formula for estimating maximum heart rate is $m = 206.3 - 0.711a$, where a represents age in years. Describe how this equation is different from your equation in Problem 1. Include slope and intercepts in your description.

6. Which equation gives a higher maximum heart rate for people ages 75 and younger?

7. To be exercising in your *aerobic training zone* means that your heart rate is 70% to 80% of your maximum heart rate. Write two equations that someone could use to estimate the range of heart rates that are within his or her aerobic training zone. Use your equation for maximum heart rate from Problem 1.

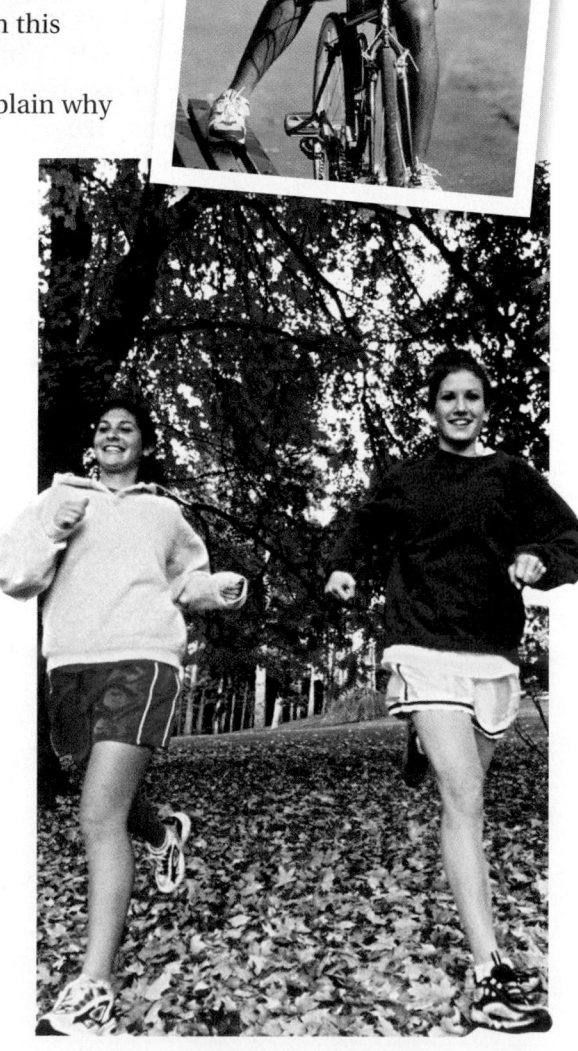

READY TO GO ON?

Quiz for Lessons 5-1 Through 5-6

✓ **5-1 Identifying Linear Functions**

Tell whether the given ordered pairs satisfy a linear function. Explain.

1.

x	−2	−1	0	1	2
y	1	0	1	4	9

2. $\{(-3, 8), (-2, 6), (-1, 4), (0, 2), (1, 0)\}$

✓ **5-2 Using Intercepts**

Use intercepts to graph the line described by each equation.

3. $2x - 4y = 16$ **4.** $-3y + 6x = -18$ **5.** $y = -3x + 3$

✓ **5-3 Rate of Change and Slope**

6. The chart gives the amount of water in a rain gauge in inches at various times. Graph the data and show the rates of change.

Time (h)	1	2	3	4	5
Rain (in.)	0.2	0.4	0.7	0.8	1.0

✓ **5-4 The Slope Formula**

Find the slope of each line. Then tell what the slope represents.

7.

8.

9.

✓ **5-5 The Midpoint and Distance Formulas**

10. Find the coordinates of the midpoint of $\overline{XY}$ with endpoints $X(-4, 6)$ and $Y(3, 8)$.

11. On a treasure map, the coordinates of a crooked palm tree are (3, 6), and the coordinates of a buried treasure chest are (12, 18). Each unit on the map represents 10 feet. What is the distance in feet between the palm tree and the treasure chest?

✓ **5-6 Direct Variation**

Tell whether each relationship is a direct variation. If so, identify the constant of variation.

12.

x	1	4	8	12
y	3	6	10	14

13.

x	−6	−2	0	3
y	−3	−1	0	1.5

5-7 Slope-Intercept Form

Objectives

Write a linear equation in slope-intercept form.

Graph a line using slope-intercept form.

Who uses this?

Consumers can use slope-intercept form to model and calculate costs, such as the cost of renting a moving van. (See Example 4.)

You have seen that you can graph a line if you know two points on the line. Another way is to use the slope of the line and the point that contains the *y*-intercept.

EXAMPLE 1 **Graphing by Using Slope and *y*-intercept**

Graph the line with slope −2 and *y*-intercept 4.

Step 1 The *y*-intercept is 4, so the line contains (0, 4). Plot (0, 4).

Step 2 Slope = $\dfrac{\text{change in } y}{\text{change in } x} = \dfrac{-2}{1}$

Count **2 units down** and **1 unit right** from (0, 4) and plot another point.

Step 3 Draw the line through the two points.

Writing Math

Any integer can be written as a fraction with 1 in the denominator.

$-2 = \dfrac{-2}{1}$

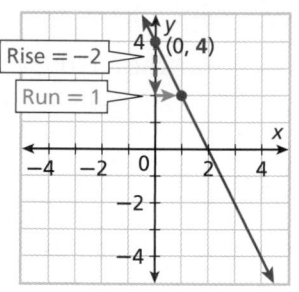

CHECK IT OUT! Graph each line given the slope and *y*-intercept.

1a. slope = 2, *y*-intercept = −3 **1b.** slope = $-\dfrac{2}{3}$, *y*-intercept = 1

If you know the slope of a line and the *y*-intercept, you can write an equation that describes the line.

Step 1 If a line has slope 2 and the *y*-intercept is 3, then $m = 2$ and $(0, 3)$ is on the line. Substitute these values into the slope formula.

$$\text{Slope formula} \rightarrow m = \frac{y_2 - y_1}{x_2 - x_1} \qquad 2 = \frac{y - 3}{x - 0} \quad \leftarrow \text{Since you don't know } (x_2, y_2), \text{ use } (x, y).$$

Step 2 Solve for *y*:

$2 = \dfrac{y - 3}{x - 0}$

$2 = \dfrac{y - 3}{x}$ *Simplify the denominator.*

$2 \cdot x = \left(\dfrac{y - 3}{x}\right) \cdot x$ *Multiply both sides by x.*

$2x = y - 3$

$\underline{+3 \qquad +3}$ *Add 3 to both sides.*

$2x + 3 = y$, or $y = 2x + 3$

Slope-Intercept Form of a Linear Equation

If a line has **slope** m and the **y-intercept** is b, then the line is described by the equation $y = mx + b$.

Any linear equation can be written in slope-intercept form by solving for y and simplifying. In this form, you can immediately see the slope and y-intercept. Also, you can quickly graph a line when the equation is written in slope-intercept form.

EXAMPLE **2** **Writing Linear Equations in Slope-Intercept Form**

Write the equation that describes each line in slope-intercept form.

A slope $= \dfrac{1}{3}$, y-intercept $= 6$ **B** slope $= 0$, y-intercept $= -5$

$y = mx + b$ *Substitute the given* $y = mx + b$

$y = \dfrac{1}{3}x + 6$ *values for m and b.* $y = 0x + (-5)$

        Simplify if necessary. $y = -5$

C

Step 1 Find the y-intercept. The graph crosses the y-axis at $(0, 1)$, so $b = 1$.

Step 2 Find the slope. The line contains the points $(0, 1)$ and $(1, 3)$.

$m = \dfrac{y_2 - y_1}{x_2 - x_1}$ *Use the slope formula.*

$m = \dfrac{3 - 1}{1 - 0} = \dfrac{2}{1} = 2$ *Substitute (0, 1) for (x₁, y₁) and (1, 3) for (x₂, y₂).*

Step 3 Write the equation.

$y = mx + b$ *Write the slope-intercept form.*

$y = 2x + 1$ *Substitute 2 for m and 1 for b.*

D slope $= 4$, $(2, 5)$ is on the line

Step 1 Find the y-intercept.

$y = mx + b$ *Write the slope-intercept form.*

$5 = 4(2) + b$ *Substitute 4 for m, 2 for x, and 5 for y.*

$5 = 8 + b$ *Solve for b. Since 8 is added to b, subtract 8 from both*

$\underline{-8 \quad -8}$ *sides to undo the addition.*

$-3 = b$

Step 2 Write the equation.

$y = mx + b$ *Write the slope-intercept form.*

$y = 4x + (-3)$ *Substitute 4 for m and −3 for b.*

$y = 4x - 3$

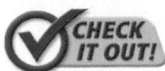 Write the equation that describes each line in slope-intercept form.

2a. slope $= -12$, y-intercept $= -\dfrac{1}{2}$

2b. slope $= 1$, y-intercept $= 0$

2c. slope $= 8$, $(-3, 1)$ is on the line.

EXAMPLE 3 **Using Slope-Intercept Form to Graph**

Write each equation in slope-intercept form. Then graph the line described by the equation.

A $y = 4x - 3$

$y = 4x - 3$ is in the form $y = mx + b$.

slope: $m = 4 = \dfrac{4}{1}$

y-intercept: $b = -3$

Step 1 Plot $(0, -3)$.

Step 2 Count **4 units up** and **1 unit right** and plot another point.

Step 3 Draw the line connecting the two points.

B $y = -\dfrac{2}{3}x + 2$

$y = -\dfrac{2}{3}x + 2$ is in the form $y = mx + b$.

slope: $m = -\dfrac{2}{3} = \dfrac{-2}{3}$

y-intercept: $b = 2$

Step 1 Plot $(0, 2)$

Step 2 Count **2 units down** and **3 units right** and plot another point.

Step 3 Draw the line connecting the two points.

C $3x + 2y = 8$

Step 1 Write the equation in slope-intercept form by solving for y.

$$3x + 2y = 8$$
$$\underline{-3x \qquad\qquad -3x}$$ *Subtract 3x from both sides.*
$$2y = 8 - 3x$$
$$\dfrac{2y}{2} = \dfrac{8 - 3x}{2}$$ *Since y is multiplied by 2, divide both sides by 2.*
$$y = 4 - \dfrac{3}{2}x \qquad \dfrac{3x}{2} = \dfrac{3}{2}x$$
$$y = -\dfrac{3}{2}x + 4 \qquad \text{Write the equation in the form } y = mx + b.$$

Step 2 Graph the line.

$y = -\dfrac{3}{2}x + 4$ is in the form $y = mx + b$.

slope: $m = -\dfrac{3}{2} = \dfrac{-3}{2}$

y-intercept: $b = 4$

• Plot $(0, 4)$.

• Then count **3 units down** and **2 units right** and plot another point.

• Draw the line connecting the two points.

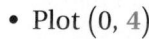
Helpful Hint

To divide $(8 - 3x)$ by 2, you can multiply by $\frac{1}{2}$ and use the Distributive Property.

$\dfrac{8 - 3x}{2} = \dfrac{1}{2}(8 - 3x)$

$= \dfrac{1}{2}(8) + \dfrac{1}{2}(-3x)$

$= 4 - \dfrac{3}{2}x$

CHECK IT OUT! Write each equation in slope-intercept form. Then graph the line described by the equation.

3a. $y = \dfrac{2}{3}x$ **3b.** $6x + 2y = 10$ **3c.** $y = -4$

EXAMPLE 4 *Consumer Application*

To rent a van, a moving company charges $30.00 plus $0.50 per mile. The cost as a function of the number of miles driven is shown in the graph.

Moving Van Costs

a. Write an equation that represents the cost as a function of the number of miles.

Cost	is	$0.50 per mile	times	miles	plus	$30.00
y	=	0.5	•	x	+	30

An equation is $y = 0.5x + 30$.

b. Identify the slope and y-intercept and describe their meanings.

The y-intercept is 30. This is the cost for 0 miles, or the initial fee of $30.00.

The slope is 0.5. This is the rate of change of the cost: $0.50 per mile.

c. Find the cost of the van for 150 miles.

$y = 0.5x + 30$

$= 0.5(150) + 30 = 105$ *Substitute 150 for x in the equation.*

The cost of the van for 150 miles is $105.

 4. A caterer charges a $200 fee plus $18 per person served. The cost as a function of the number of guests is shown in the graph.

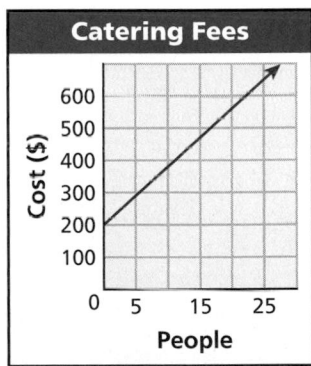

Catering Fees

a. Write an equation that represents the cost as a function of the number of guests.

b. Identify the slope and y-intercept and describe their meanings.

c. Find the cost of catering an event for 200 guests.

THINK AND DISCUSS

1. If a linear function has a y-intercept of b, at what point does its graph cross the y-axis?

2. Where does the line described by $y = 4.395x - 23.75$ cross the y-axis?

3. GET ORGANIZED Copy and complete the graphic organizer.

Graphing the Line Described by $y = mx + b$

| 1. Plot the point ?. | 2. Find a second point on the line by ?. | 3. Draw ?. |

go.hrw.com
Homework Help Online
KEYWORD: MA11 5-7
Parent Resources Online
KEYWORD: MA7 Parent

GUIDED PRACTICE

SEE EXAMPLE 1
p. 344

Graph each line given the slope and y-intercept.

1. slope $= \frac{1}{3}$, y-intercept $= -3$

2. slope $= 0.5$, y-intercept $= 3.5$

3. slope $= 5$, y-intercept $= -1$

4. slope $= -2$, y-intercept $= 2$

SEE EXAMPLE 2
p. 345

Write the equation that describes each line in slope-intercept form.

5.

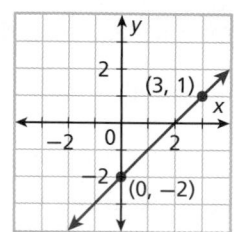

6. slope $= 8$, y-intercept $= 2$

7. slope $= 0$, y-intercept $= -3$

8. slope $= 5$, $(2, 7)$ is on the line.

9. slope $= -2$, $(1, -3)$ is on the line.

SEE EXAMPLE 3
p. 346

Write each equation in slope-intercept form. Then graph the line described by the equation.

10. $y = \frac{2}{5}x - 6$

11. $3x - y = 1$

12. $2x + y = 4$

SEE EXAMPLE 4
p. 347

13. Helen is in a bicycle race. She has already biked 10 miles and is now biking at a rate of 18 miles per hour. Her distance as a function of time is shown in the graph.

  a. Write an equation that represents the distance Helen has biked as a function of time.

  b. Identify the slope and y-intercept and describe their meanings.

  c. How far will Helen have biked after 2 hours?

Distance Biked

Distance (mi) vs Time (h)

PRACTICE AND PROBLEM SOLVING

Independent Practice

For Exercises	See Example
14–17	1
19–22	2
23–25	3
26	4

Graph each line given the slope and y-intercept.

14. slope $= \frac{1}{4}$, y-intercept $= 7$

15. slope $= -6$, y-intercept $= -3$

16. slope $= 1$, y-intercept $= -4$

17. slope $= -\frac{4}{5}$, y-intercept $= 6$

Write the equation that describes each line in slope-intercept form.

Extra Practice
Skills Practice p. S13
Application Practice p. S32

18.

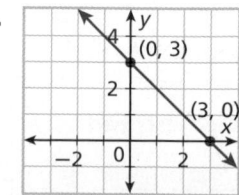

19. slope $= 5$, y-intercept $= -9$

20. slope $= -\frac{2}{3}$, y-intercept $= 2$

21. slope $= -\frac{1}{2}$, $(6, 4)$ is on the line.

22. slope $= 0$, $(6, -8)$ is on the line.

Write each equation in slope-intercept form. Then graph the line described by the equation.

23. $-\frac{1}{2}x + y = 4$ **24.** $\frac{2}{3}x + y = 2$ **25.** $2x + y = 8$

26. Fitness Pauline's health club has an enrollment fee of $175 and costs $35 per month. Total cost as a function of number of membership months is shown in the graph.

   a. Write an equation that represents the total cost as a function of months.

   b. Identify the slope and *y*-intercept and describe their meanings.

   c. Find the cost of one year of membership.

Health Club Membership Costs

27. A company rents video games. The table shows the linear relationship between the number of games a customer can rent at one time and the monthly cost of the service.

   a. Graph the relationship.

   b. Write an equation that represents the monthly cost as a function of games rented at one time.

Games Rented at One Time	1	2	3
Monthly Cost ($)	14	18	22

Critical Thinking Tell whether each situation is possible or impossible. If possible, draw a sketch of the graphs. If impossible, explain.

28. Two different lines have the same slope.

29. Two different linear functions have the same *y*-intercept.

30. Two intersecting lines have the same slope.

31. A linear function does not have a *y*-intercept.

Match each equation with its corresponding graph.

32.   **33.**   **34.**

   A. $y = 2x - 1$ **B.** $y = \frac{1}{2}x - 1$ **C.** $y = -\frac{1}{2}x + 1$

 35. Write About It Write an equation that describes a vertical line. Can you write this equation in slope-intercept form? Why or why not?

36. This problem will prepare you for the Multi-Step Test Prep on page 376.

   a. Ricardo and Sam walk from Sam's house to school. Sam lives 3 blocks from Ricardo's house. The graph shows their distance from Ricardo's house as they walk to school. Create a table of these values.

   b. Find an equation for the distance as a function of time.

   c. What are the slope and *y*-intercept? What do they represent in this situation?

Walk to School

37. Which function has the same y-intercept as $y = \frac{1}{2}x - 2$?

     Ⓐ $2x + 3y = 6$ Ⓑ $x + 4y = -8$ Ⓒ $-\frac{1}{2}x + y = 4$ Ⓓ $\frac{1}{2}x - 2y = -2$

38. What is the slope-intercept form of $x - y = -8$?

     Ⓕ $y = -x - 8$ Ⓖ $y = x - 8$ Ⓗ $y = -x + 8$ Ⓙ $y = x + 8$

39. Which function has a y-intercept of 3?

     Ⓐ $2x - y = 3$ Ⓑ $2x + y = 3$ Ⓒ $2x + y = 6$ Ⓓ $y = 3x$

40. Gridded Response What is the slope of the line described by $-6x = -2y + 5$?

41. Short Response Write a function whose graph has the same slope as the line described by $3x - 9y = 9$ and the same y-intercept as $8x - 2y = 6$. Show your work.

CHALLENGE AND EXTEND

42. The standard form of a linear equation is $Ax + By = C$. Rewrite this equation in slope-intercept form. What is the slope? What is the y-intercept?

43. What value of n in the equation $nx + 5 = 3y$ would give a line with slope -2?

44. If b is the y-intercept of a linear function whose graph has slope m, then $y = mx + b$ describes the line. Below is an incomplete justification of this statement. Fill in the missing information.

Statements	Reasons
1. $m = \dfrac{y_2 - y_1}{x_2 - x_1}$	1. Slope formula
2. $m = \dfrac{y - b}{x - 0}$	2. By definition, if b is the y-intercept, then $\left(\boxed{}, b\right)$ is a point on the line. (x, y) is any other point on the line.
3. $m = \dfrac{y - b}{x}$	3. _____ ?
4. $m\boxed{} = y - b$	4. Multiplication Property of Equality (Multiply both sides of the equation by x.)
5. $mx + b = y$, or $y = mx + b$	5. _____ ?

SPIRAL REVIEW

Define a variable and write an inequality for each situation. Graph the solutions. *(Lesson 3-1)*

45. Molly has, at most, 2 hours to work out at the gym today.

46. Mishenko is hoping to save at least $300 this month.

Solve each inequality. *(Lesson 3-5)*

47. $3n \le 2n + 8$ **48.** $4x - 4 > 2(x + 5)$ **49.** $2(2t + 1) > 6t + 8$

50. The amount of water conditioner needed for an aquarium varies directly with the capacity of the aquarium. For every 10 gallons of water, you need 1 teaspoon of conditioner. Write a direct variation equation for the amount of water conditioner y needed for an aquarium that holds x gallons of water. Then graph. *(Lesson 5-6)*

5-8 Point-Slope Form

Objectives
Graph a line and write a linear equation using point-slope form.

Write a linear equation given two points.

Why learn this?
You can use point-slope form to represent a cost function, such as the cost of placing a newspaper ad. (See Example 5.)

> PIES
> old,
> ded.
> yful!
> teer.

> **KITTENS AVAILABLE**
> to good home. 2 mo.
> old, litter trained. Very
> cute and playful! $10
> adoption fee.

> DOG
> 8 mo
> shots
> Very
> happ

If you know the slope and any point on the line, you can write an equation of the line by using the slope formula. For example, suppose a line has a slope of 3 and contains $(2, 1)$. Let (x, y) be any other point on the line.

$$m = \frac{y_2 - y_1}{x_2 - x_1} \longrightarrow 3 = \frac{y - 1}{x - 2} \qquad \text{Substitute into the slope formula.}$$

Slope formula

$$3(x - 2) = \left(\frac{y - 1}{x - 2}\right)(x - 2) \qquad \text{Multiplication Property of Equality}$$

$$3(x - 2) = y - 1 \qquad \text{Simplify.}$$

$$y - 1 = 3(x - 2)$$

Know it!
Note

Point-Slope Form of a Linear Equation

The line with slope m that contains the point (x_1, y_1) can be described by the equation $y - y_1 = m(x - x_1)$.

EXAMPLE 1 | **Writing Linear Equations in Point-Slope Form**

Write an equation in point-slope form for the line with the given slope that contains the given point.

A slope $= \frac{5}{2}$; $(-3, 0)$

$$y - y_1 = m(x - x_1) \qquad \text{Write the point-slope form.}$$

$$y - 0 = \frac{5}{2}[x - (-3)] \qquad \text{Substitute } \frac{5}{2} \text{ for } m, -3 \text{ for } x_1, \text{ and } 0 \text{ for } y_1.$$

$$y - 0 = \frac{5}{2}(x + 3) \qquad \text{Rewrite subtraction of negative numbers as addition.}$$

B slope $= -7$; $(4, 2)$

$$y - y_1 = m(x - x_1)$$

$$y - 2 = -7(x - 4)$$

C slope $= 0$; $(-2, -3)$

$$y - y_1 = m(x - x_1)$$

$$y - (-3) = 0[x - (-2)]$$

$$y + 3 = 0(x + 2)$$

CHECK IT OUT! Write an equation in point-slope form for the line with the given slope that contains the given point.

1a. slope $= 2$; $\left(\frac{1}{2}, 1\right)$

1b. slope $= 0$; $(3, -4)$

In Lesson 5-7, you graphed a line given its equation in slope-intercept form. You can also graph a line when given its equation in point-slope form. Start by using the equation to identify a point on the line. Then use the slope of the line to identify a second point.

EXAMPLE 2 **Using Point-Slope Form to Graph**

Graph the line described by each equation.

A $y - 1 = 3(x - 1)$

$y - 1 = 3(x - 1)$ is in the form $y - y_1 = m(x - x_1)$.

The line contains the point $(1, 1)$.

slope: $m = 3 = \dfrac{3}{1}$

Step 1 Plot $(1, 1)$.

Step 2 Count **3 units up** and **1 unit right** and plot another point.

Step 3 Draw the line connecting the two points.

B $y + 2 = -\dfrac{1}{2}(x - 3)$

Step 1 Write the equation in point-slope form: $y - y_1 = m(x - x_1)$.

$y - (-2) = -\dfrac{1}{2}(x - 3)$ *Rewrite addition of 2 as subtraction of −2.*

Step 2 Graph the line.

The line contains the point $(3, -2)$.

slope: $m = -\dfrac{1}{2} = \dfrac{1}{-2}$

• Plot $(3, -2)$.

• Count 1 unit up and 2 units left and plot another point.

• Draw the line connecting the two points.

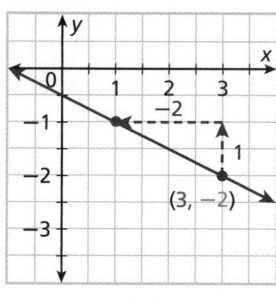

Helpful Hint

For a negative fraction, you can write the negative sign in one of three places.

$-\dfrac{1}{2} = \dfrac{-1}{2} = \dfrac{1}{-2}$

CHECK IT OUT!   **Graph the line described by each equation.**

2a. $y + 2 = -(x - 2)$ **2b.** $y + 3 = -2(x - 1)$

EXAMPLE 3 **Writing Linear Equations in Slope-Intercept Form**

Write the equation that describes each line in slope-intercept form.

A slope $= -4$, $(-1, -2)$ is on the line.

Step 1 Write the equation in point-slope form: $y - y_1 = m(x - x_1)$.

$y - (-2) = -4[x - (-1)]$

Step 2 Write the equation in slope-intercept form by solving for y.

$y - (-2) = -4[x - (-1)]$

$y + 2 = -4(x + 1)$ *Rewrite subtraction of negative numbers as*

$y + 2 = -4x - 4$ *addition. Distribute −4 on the right side.*

$\underline{ -2 \qquad\quad -2}$ *Subtract 2 from both sides.*

$y \qquad = -4x - 6$

B $(1, -4)$ and $(3, 2)$ are on the line.

Step 1 Find the slope.

$$m = \frac{y_2 - y_1}{x_2 - x_1} = \frac{2 - (-4)}{3 - 1} = \frac{6}{2} = 3$$

Step 2 Substitute the slope and one of the points into the point-slope form. Then write the equation in slope-intercept form.

$y - y_1 = m(x - x_1)$

$y - 2 = 3(x - 3)$ *Use (3, 2).*

$y - 2 = 3x - 9$ *Distribute 3 on the right side.*

$y = 3x - 7$ *Add 2 to both sides.*

C *x*-intercept $= -2$, *y*-intercept $= 4$

Step 1 Use the intercepts to find two points: $(-2, 0)$ and $(0, 4)$.

Step 2 Find the slope.

$$m = \frac{y_2 - y_1}{x_2 - x_1} = \frac{4 - 0}{0 - (-2)} = \frac{4}{2} = 2$$

Step 3 Write the equation in slope-intercept form.

$y = mx + b$ *Write the slope-intercept form.*

$y = 2x + 4$ *Substitute 2 for m and 4 for b.*

 Write the equation that describes each line in slope-intercept form.

3a. slope $= \frac{1}{3}$, $(-3, 1)$ is on the line.

3b. $(1, -2)$ and $(3, 10)$ are on the line.

EXAMPLE **4** **Using Two Points to Find Intercepts**

The points $(4, 8)$ and $(-1, -12)$ are on a line. Find the intercepts.

Step 1 Find the slope.

$$m = \frac{y_2 - y_1}{x_2 - x_1} = \frac{-12 - 8}{-1 - 4} = \frac{-20}{-5} = 4$$

Step 2 Write the equation in slope-intercept form.

$y - y_1 = m(x - x_1)$ *Write the point-slope form.*

$y - 8 = 4(x - 4)$ *Substitute (4, 8) for (x_1, y_1) and 4 for m.*

$y - 8 = 4x - 16$ *Distribute 4 on the right side.*

$y = 4x - 8$ *Add 8 to both sides.*

Step 3 Find the intercepts.

x-intercept:

$y = 4x - 8$ *Replace y with*

$0 = 4x - 8$ *0 and solve*

$8 = 4x$ *for x.*

$2 = x$

y-intercept:

$y = 4x - 8$ *Use the slope-*

$b = -8$ *intercept form to identify the y-intercept.*

The *x*-intercept is 2, and the *y*-intercept is -8.

 4. The points $(2, 15)$ and $(-4, -3)$ are on a line. Find the intercepts.

EXAMPLE 5

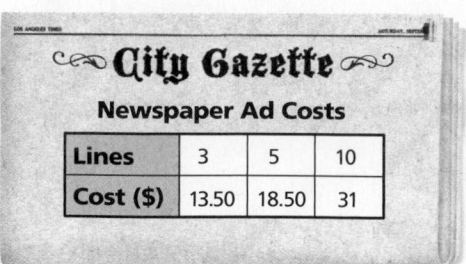

PROBLEM SOLVING

Problem-Solving Application

The cost to place an ad in a newspaper for one week is a linear function of the number of lines in the ad. The costs for 3, 5, and 10 lines are shown. Write an equation in slope-intercept form that represents the function. Then find the cost of an ad that is 18 lines long.

City Gazette
Newspaper Ad Costs

Lines	3	5	10
Cost ($)	13.50	18.50	31

1 Understand the Problem

- The **answer** will have two parts—an equation in slope-intercept form and the cost of an ad that is 18 lines long.
- The ordered pairs given in the table satisfy the equation.

2 Make a Plan

First, find the slope. Then use point-slope form to write the equation. Finally, write the equation in slope-intercept form.

3 Solve

Step 1 Choose any two ordered pairs from the table to find the slope.

$$m = \frac{y_2 - y_1}{x_2 - x_1} = \frac{18.50 - 13.50}{5 - 3} = \frac{5}{2} = 2.5 \quad \text{Use (3, 13.50) and (5, 18.50).}$$

Step 2 Substitute the slope and any ordered pair from the table into the point-slope form.

$$y - y_1 = m(x - x_1)$$
$$y - 31 = 2.5(x - 10) \qquad \text{Use (10, 31).}$$

Step 3 Write the equation in slope-intercept form by solving for y.

$$y - 31 = 2.5(x - 10)$$
$$y - 31 = 2.5x - 25 \qquad \text{Distribute 2.5.}$$
$$y = 2.5x + 6 \qquad \text{Add 31 to both sides.}$$

Step 4 Find the cost of an ad containing 18 lines by substituting 18 for x.

$$y = 2.5x + 6$$
$$y = 2.5(18) + 6 = 51$$

The cost of an ad containing 18 lines is $51.

4 Look Back

Check the equation by substituting the ordered pairs (3, 13.50) and (5, 18.50).

$y = 2.5x + 6$	
13.50	$2.5(3) + 6$
13.5	$7.5 + 6$
13.5	$13.5 ✓$

$y = 2.5x + 6$	
18.50	$2.5(5) + 6$
18.5	$12.5 + 6$
18.5	$18.5 ✓$

 CHECK IT OUT!

5. What if...? At a different newspaper, the costs to place an ad for one week are shown. Write an equation in slope-intercept form that represents this linear function. Then find the cost of an ad that is 21 lines long.

Lines	Cost ($)
3	12.75
5	17.25
10	28.50

THINK AND DISCUSS

1. How are point-slope form and slope-intercept form alike? different?

2. When is point-slope form useful? When is slope-intercept form useful?

3. **GET ORGANIZED** Copy and complete the graphic organizer. In each box, describe how to find the equation of a line by using the given method.

```
                    Writing the Equation of a Line
        ┌──────────────────────┼──────────────────────┐
  If you know two      If you know the        If you know the
  points on the line   slope and              slope and a
                       y-intercept            point on the line
```

5-8 Exercises

go.hrw.com
Homework Help Online
KEYWORD: MA11 5-8
Parent Resources Online
KEYWORD: MA7 Parent

GUIDED PRACTICE

SEE EXAMPLE 1
p. 351

Write an equation in point-slope form for the line with the given slope that contains the given point.

1. slope $= \frac{1}{5}$; $(2, -6)$ 2. slope $= -4$; $(1, 5)$ 3. slope $= 0$; $(3, -7)$

SEE EXAMPLE 2
p. 352

Graph the line described by each equation.

4. $y - 1 = -(x - 3)$ 5. $y + 2 = -2(x + 4)$ 6. $y + 1 = -\frac{1}{2}(x + 4)$

SEE EXAMPLE 3
p. 352

Write the equation that describes each line in slope-intercept form.

7. slope $= -\frac{1}{3}$, $(-3, 8)$ is on the line.   8. slope $= 2$; $(1, 1)$ is on the line.

9. $(-2, 2)$ and $(2, -2)$ are on the line.   10. $(1, 1)$ and $(-5, 3)$ are on the line.

11. x-intercept $= 8$, y-intercept $= 4$ 12. x-intercept $= -2$, y-intercept $= 3$

SEE EXAMPLE 4
p. 353

Each pair of points is on a line. Find the intercepts.

13. $(5, 2)$ and $(7, 4)$ 14. $(-1, 5)$ and $(-3, -5)$ 15. $(2, 9)$ and $(-4, -9)$

SEE EXAMPLE 5
p. 354

16. **Measurement** An oil tank is being filled at a constant rate. The depth of the oil is a function of the number of minutes the tank has been filling, as shown in the table. Write an equation in slope-intercept form that represents this linear function. Then find the depth of the oil after one-half hour.

Time (min)	Depth (ft)
0	3
10	5
15	6

PRACTICE AND PROBLEM SOLVING

Write an equation in point-slope form for the line with the given slope that contains the given point.

17. slope $= \frac{2}{9}$; $(-1, 5)$ 18. slope $= 0$; $(4, -2)$ 19. slope $= 8$; $(1, 8)$

Independent Practice

For Exercises	See Example
17–19	1
20–22	2
23–30	3
31–33	4
34	5

Extra Practice

Skills Practice p. S13

Application Practice p. S32

Graph the line described by each equation.

20. $y - 4 = -\frac{1}{2}(x + 3)$

21. $y + 2 = \frac{3}{5}(x - 1)$

22. $y - 0 = 4(x - 1)$

Write the equation that describes each line in slope-intercept form.

23. slope $= -\frac{2}{7}$, $(14, -3)$ is on the line.

24. slope $= \frac{4}{5}$, $(-15, 1)$ is on the line.

25. slope $= -6$, $(9, 3)$ is on the line.

26. $(7, 8)$ and $(-7, 6)$ are on the line.

27. $(2, 7)$ and $(4, -4)$ are on the line.

28. $(-1, 2)$ and $(4, -23)$ are on the line.

29. x-intercept $= 3$, y-intercept $= -6$

30. x-intercept $= 4$, y-intercept $= -1$

Each pair of points is on a line. Find the intercepts.

31. $(-1, -4)$ and $(6, 10)$

32. $(3, 4)$ and $(-6, 16)$

33. $(4, 15)$ and $(-2, 6)$

34. **History** The amount of fresh water left in the tanks of a 19th-century clipper ship is a linear function of the time since the ship left port, as shown in the table. Write an equation in slope-intercept form that represents the function. Then find the amount of water that will be left in the ship's tanks 50 days after leaving port.

Fresh Water Aboard Ship	
Time (days)	Amount (gal)
1	3555
8	3240
15	2925

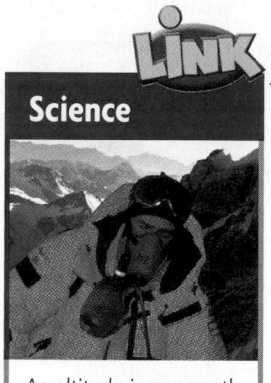

Science

35. **Science** At higher altitudes, water boils at lower temperatures. This relationship between altitude and boiling point is linear. At an altitude of 1000 feet, water boils at 210 °F. At an altitude of 3000 feet, water boils at 206 °F. Write an equation in slope-intercept form that represents this linear function. Then find the boiling point at 6000 feet.

36. **Consumer Economics** Lora has a gift card from an online music store where all downloads cost the same amount. After downloading 2 songs, the balance on her card was $18.10. After downloading a total of 5 songs, the balance was $15.25.

   a. Write an equation in slope-intercept form that represents the amount in dollars remaining on the card as a function of songs downloaded.

   b. Identify the slope of the line and tell what the slope represents.

   c. Identify the y-intercept of the line and tell what it represents.

   d. How many additional songs can Lora download when there is $15.25 left on the card?

As altitude increases, the amount of breathable oxygen decreases. At elevations above 8000 feet, this can cause altitude sickness. To prevent this, mountain climbers often use tanks containing a mixture of air and pure oxygen.

Graph the line with the given slope that contains the given point.

37. slope $= -3$; $(2, 4)$

38. slope $= -\frac{1}{4}$; $(0, 0)$

39. slope $= \frac{1}{2}$; $(-2, -1)$

Tell whether each statement is sometimes, always, or never true.

40. A line described by the equation $y = mx + b$ contains the point $(0, b)$.

41. The slope of the line that contains the points $(0, 0)$ and (c, d) is negative if both c and d are negative.

42. The y-intercept of the graph of $y - y_1 = m(x - x_1)$ is negative if y_1 is negative.

43. **Meteorology** Snowfall accumulates at an average rate of 2.5 inches per hour during a snowstorm. Two hours after the snowstorm begins, the average depth of snow on the ground is 11 inches.

   a. Write an equation in point-slope form that represents the depth of the snow in inches as a function of hours since the snowstorm began.

   b. How much snow is on the ground when the snowstorm starts?

   c. The snowstorm begins at 2:15 P.M. and continues until 6:30 P.M. How much snow is on the ground at the end of the storm?

Write an equation in point-slope form that describes each graph.

44.

45.

46.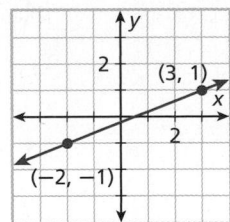

The tables show linear relationships between *x* and *y*. Copy and complete the tables.

47.

x	−2	0		7
y	−18		12	27

48.

x	−4	1	0	
y	14	4		−6

49. ///**ERROR ANALYSIS**/// Two students used point-slope form to find an equation that describes the line with slope −3 through $(-5, 2)$. Who is incorrect? Explain the error.

Ⓐ
$$y - y_1 = m(x - x_1)$$
$$y - 2 = -3(x - 5)$$

Ⓑ
$$y - y_1 = m(x - x_1)$$
$$y - 2 = -3[x - (-5)]$$
$$y - 2 = -3(x + 5)$$

50. Critical Thinking Compare the methods for finding the equation that describes a line when you know

- a point on the line and the slope of the line.
- two points on the line.

How are the methods alike? How are they different?

 51. Write About It Explain why the first statement is false but the second is true.

- All linear equations can be written in point-slope form.
- All linear equations that describe functions can be written in point-slope form.

52. Multi-Step The table shows the mean scores on a standardized test for several different years.

Years Since 1985	0	5	10	17	21
Mean Combined Score	994	1009	1001	1016	1020

a. Make a scatter plot of the data and add a trend line to your graph.

b. Use your trend line to estimate the slope and *y*-intercept, and write an equation in slope-intercept form.

c. What do the slope and *y*-intercept represent in this situation?

53. This problem will prepare you for the Multi-Step Test Prep on page 376.

a. Stephen is walking from his house to his friend Sharon's house. When he is 12 blocks away, he looks at his watch. He looks again when he is 8 blocks away and finds that 6 minutes have passed. Write two ordered pairs for these data in the form (time, blocks).

b. Write a linear equation for these two points.

c. What is the total amount of time it takes Stephen to reach Sharon's house? Explain how you found your answer.

TEST PREP

54. Which equation describes the line through $(-5, 1)$ with slope of 1?

   Ⓐ $y + 1 = x - 5$ Ⓒ $y - 1 = -5(x - 1)$

   Ⓑ $y + 5 = x - 1$ Ⓓ $y - 1 = x + 5$

55. A line contains $(4, 4)$ and $(5, 2)$. What are the slope and y-intercept?

   Ⓕ slope $= -2$; y-intercept $= 2$ Ⓗ slope $= -2$; y-intercept $= 12$

   Ⓖ slope $= 1.2$; y-intercept $= -2$ Ⓙ slope $= 12$; y-intercept $= 1.2$

CHALLENGE AND EXTEND

56. A linear function has the same y-intercept as $x + 4y = 8$ and its graph contains the point $(2, 7)$. Find the slope and y-intercept.

57. Write the equation of a line in slope-intercept form that contains $\left(\frac{3}{4}, \frac{1}{2}\right)$ and has the same slope as the line described by $y + 3x = 6$.

58. Write the equation of a line in slope-intercept form that contains $\left(-\frac{1}{2}, -\frac{1}{3}\right)$ and $\left(1\frac{1}{2}, 1\right)$.

SPIRAL REVIEW

Solve each compound inequality and graph the solutions. *(Lesson 3-6)*

59. $-4 \le x + 2 \le 1$ 60. $m - 5 > -7$ AND $m + 1 < 2$

61. A group of hikers is walking the Appalachian Trail. The function $y = 12x$ describes how many miles y the group has traveled in x days. Graph the function. Then use the graph to estimate how many miles the group will hike in 18 days. *(Lesson 4-4)*

Write the equation that describes each line in slope-intercept form. *(Lesson 5-7)*

62. slope $= 3$, y-intercept $= -5$ 63. slope $= -2$, $(2, 4)$ is on the line

---

Career Path

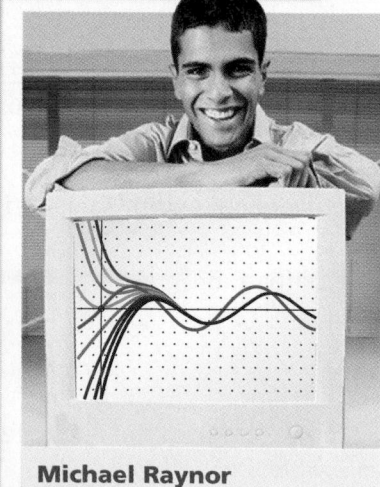

Michael Raynor
Data mining major

Q: What math classes did you take in high school?
A: Algebra 1 and 2, Geometry, and Statistics

Q: What math classes have you taken in college?
A: Applied Statistics, Data Mining Methods, Web Mining, and Artificial Intelligence

Q: How do you use math?
A: Once for a class, I used software to analyze basketball statistics. What I learned helped me develop strategies for our school team.

Q: What are your future plans?
A: There are many options for people with data mining skills. I could work in banking, pharmaceuticals, or even the military. But my dream job is to develop game strategies for an NBA team.

5-8

Technology LAB

Graph Linear Functions

You can use a graphing calculator to quickly graph lines whose equations are in point-slope form. To enter an equation into your calculator, it must be solved for y, but it does not necessarily have to be in slope-intercept form.

Use with Lesson 5-8

go.hrw.com
Lab Resources Online
KEYWORD: MA11 LAB5

Activity

Graph the line with slope 2 that contains the point $(2, 6.09)$.

1. Use point-slope form.
$$y - y_1 = m(x - x_1)$$
$$y - 6.09 = 2(x - 2)$$

2. Solve for y by adding 6.09 to both sides of the equation.
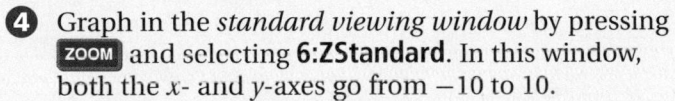
$$y - 6.09 = 2(x - 2)$$
$$\underline{+6.09 \qquad +6.09}$$
$$y \qquad = 2(x - 2) + 6.09$$

3. Enter this equation into your calculator.

[Y=] 2 [(] [X,T,θ,n] [−] 2 [)] [+] 6.09 [ENTER]

4. Graph in the *standard viewing window* by pressing [ZOOM] and selecting **6:ZStandard**. In this window, both the x- and y-axes go from -10 to 10.

5. Notice that the scale on the y-axis is smaller than the scale on the x-axis. This is because the width of the calculator screen is about 50% greater than its height. To see a more accurate graph of this line, use the *square viewing window*. Press [ZOOM] and select **5:ZSquare**.

Try This

1. Graph the function represented by the line with slope -1.5 that contains the point $(2.25, -3)$. View the graph in the standard viewing window.

2. Now view the graph in the square viewing window. Press [WINDOW] and write down the minimum and maximum values on the x- and y-axes.

3. In which graph does the line appear steeper? Why?

4. Explain why it might sometimes be useful to look at a graph in a square window.

Interpreting Trend Lines

In Chapter 4 you learned how to draw trend lines on scatter plots. Now you will learn how to find the equations of trend lines and write them in slope-intercept form.

Example

Write an equation for the trend line on the scatter plot.

Two points on the trend line are (30, 75) and (60, 90).

To find the slope of the line that contains (30, 75) and (60, 90), use the slope formula.

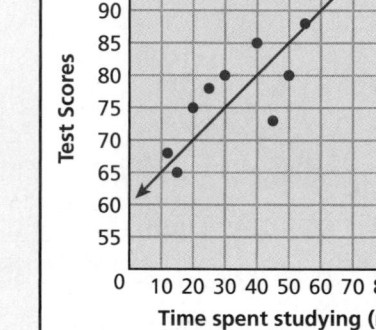

Test Scores vs. Study Time

$$m = \frac{y_2 - y_1}{x_2 - x_1} \qquad \text{Use the slope formula.}$$

$$m = \frac{90 - 75}{60 - 30} \qquad \begin{array}{l} \textit{Substitute (30, 75) for } (x_1, y_1) \textit{ and} \\ \textit{(60, 90) for } (x_2, y_2). \end{array}$$

$$m = \frac{15}{30} \qquad \textit{Simplify.}$$

$$m = \frac{1}{2}$$

Use the slope and the point (30, 75) to find the y-intercept of the line.

$$y = mx + b \qquad \textit{Slope-intercept form}$$

$$75 = \frac{1}{2}(30) + b \qquad \textit{Substitute } \tfrac{1}{2} \textit{ for m, 30 for x, and 75 for y.}$$

$$75 = 15 + b \qquad \textit{Solve for b.}$$

$$60 = b$$

Write the equation.

$$y = \frac{1}{2}x + 60 \qquad \textit{Substitute } \tfrac{1}{2} \textit{ for m and 60 for b.}$$

Try This

1. In the example above, what is the meaning of the slope?

2. What does the y-intercept represent?

3. Use the equation to predict the test score of a student who spent 25 minutes studying.

4. Use the table to create a scatter plot. Draw a trend line and find the equation of your trend line. Tell the meaning of the slope and y-intercept. Then use your equation to predict the race time of a runner who ran 40 miles in training.

Distance Run in Training (mi)	12	15	16	18	21	23	24	25	33
Race Time (min)	65	64	55	58	55	50	50	47	36

5-9 Slopes of Parallel and Perpendicular Lines

Objectives
Identify and graph parallel and perpendicular lines.

Write equations to describe lines parallel or perpendicular to a given line.

Vocabulary
parallel lines
perpendicular lines

Why learn this?
Parallel lines and their equations can be used to model costs, such as the cost of a booth at a farmers' market.

To sell at a particular farmers' market for a year, there is a $100 membership fee. Then you pay $3 for each hour that you sell at the market. However, if you were a member the previous year, the membership fee is reduced to $50.

- The **red** line shows the total cost if you are a new member.

- The **blue** line shows the total cost if you are a returning member.

These two lines are *parallel*. **Parallel lines** are lines in the same plane that have no points in common. In other words, they do not intersect.

Farmers' Market Fees

Know it! Note

Parallel Lines		
WORDS	Two different nonvertical lines are parallel if and only if they have the same slope.	All different vertical lines are parallel.
GRAPH	$y = \frac{1}{2}x + 5$ $y = \frac{1}{2}x + 1$	$x = -2$ $x = 4$

EXAMPLE 1   Identifying Parallel Lines

Identify which lines are parallel.

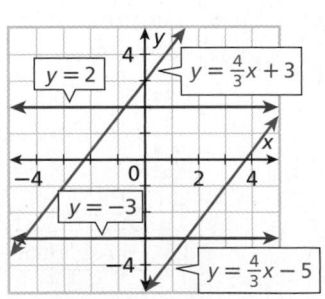

A $y = \frac{4}{3}x + 3$; $y = 2$; $y = \frac{4}{3}x - 5$; $y = -3$

The lines described by $y = \frac{4}{3}x + 3$ and $y = \frac{4}{3}x - 5$ both have slope $\frac{4}{3}$. These lines are parallel. The lines described by $y = 2$ and $y = -3$ both have slope 0. These lines are parallel.

Identify which lines are parallel.

B $y = 3x + 2$; $y = -\dfrac{1}{2}x + 4$; $x + 2y = -4$; $y - 5 = 3(x - 1)$

Write all equations in slope-intercept form to determine the slopes.

$y = 3x + 2$	$y = -\dfrac{1}{2}x + 4$
slope-intercept form ✓	slope-intercept form ✓
$x + 2y = -4$	$y - 5 = 3(x - 1)$
$\dfrac{-x \qquad\qquad -x}{\quad}$	$y - 5 = 3x - 3$
$2y = -x - 4$	$\dfrac{+5 \qquad\qquad +5}{\quad}$
$\dfrac{2y}{2} = \dfrac{-x - 4}{2}$	$y \qquad = 3x + 2$
$y = -\dfrac{1}{2}x - 2$	

The lines described by $y = 3x + 2$ and $y - 5 = 3(x - 1)$ have the same slope, but they are not parallel lines. They are the same line.

The lines described by $y = -\dfrac{1}{2}x + 4$ and $x + 2y = -4$ represent parallel lines. They each have slope $-\dfrac{1}{2}$.

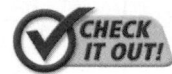

Identify which lines are parallel.

1a. $y = 2x + 2$; $y = 2x + 1$; $y = -4$; $x = 1$

1b. $y = \dfrac{3}{4}x + 8$; $-3x + 4y = 32$; $y = 3x$; $y - 1 = 3(x + 2)$

EXAMPLE **2**

□**I**O **Geometry**

Geometry Application

Show that $ABCD$ is a parallelogram.

Use the ordered pairs and the slope formula to find the slopes of $\overline{AB}$ and $\overline{CD}$.

$$\text{slope of } \overline{AB} = \frac{7 - 5}{4 - (-1)} = \frac{2}{5}$$

$$\text{slope of } \overline{CD} = \frac{3 - 1}{4 - (-1)} = \frac{2}{5}$$

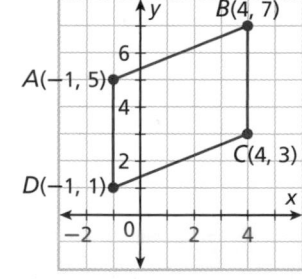

> **Remember!**
>
> In a parallelogram, opposite sides are parallel.

$\overline{AB}$ is parallel to $\overline{CD}$ because they have the same slope.

$\overline{AD}$ is parallel to $\overline{BC}$ because they are both vertical.

Therefore, $ABCD$ is a parallelogram because both pairs of opposite sides are parallel.

2. Show that the points $A(0, 2)$, $B(4, 2)$, $C(1, -3)$, and $D(-3, -3)$ are the vertices of a parallelogram.

Perpendicular lines are lines that intersect to form right angles (90°).

Know it!
Note

Perpendicular Lines

WORDS	Two nonvertical lines are perpendicular if and only if the product of their slopes is −1.	Vertical lines are perpendicular to horizontal lines.
GRAPH	$y = -\frac{2}{3}x + 3$ $y = \frac{3}{2}x - 2$	$y = 3$ $x = 2$

EXAMPLE 3 **Identifying Perpendicular Lines**

Identify which lines are perpendicular: $x = -2$; $y = 1$; $y = -4x$;
$y + 2 = \frac{1}{4}(x + 1)$.

The graph described by $x = -2$ is a vertical line, and the graph described by $y = 1$ is a horizontal line. These lines are perpendicular.

The slope of the line described by $y = -4x$ is -4. The slope of the line described by $y + 2 = \frac{1}{4}(x - 1)$ is $\frac{1}{4}$.

$$(-4)\left(\frac{1}{4}\right) = -1$$

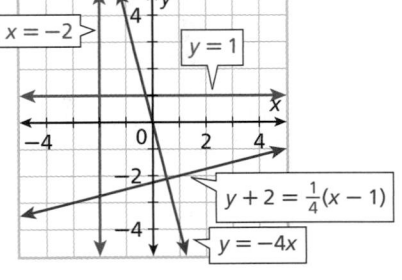

These lines are perpendicular because the product of their slopes is −1.

CHECK IT OUT! **3.** Identify which lines are perpendicular: $y = -4$; $y - 6 = 5(x + 4)$; $x = 3$; $y = -\frac{1}{5}x + 2$.

EXAMPLE 4 *Geometry Application*

Geometry

Show that PQR is a right triangle.

If PQR is a right triangle, $\overline{PQ}$ will be perpendicular to $\overline{QR}$.

$$\text{slope of } \overline{PQ} = \frac{3 - 1}{3 - 0} = \frac{2}{3}$$

$$\text{slope of } \overline{QR} = \frac{3 - 0}{3 - 5} = \frac{3}{-2} = -\frac{3}{2}$$

$\overline{PQ}$ is perpendicular to $\overline{QR}$ because $\frac{2}{3}\left(-\frac{3}{2}\right) = -1$.

Therefore, PQR is a right triangle because it contains a right angle.

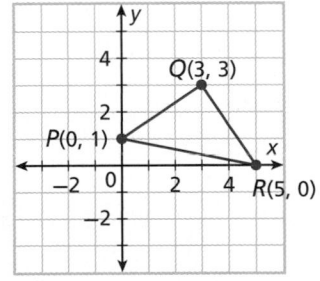

Helpful Hint

A right triangle contains one right angle. In Example 4, $\angle P$ and $\angle R$ are clearly not right angles, so the only possibility is $\angle Q$.

CHECK IT OUT! **4.** Show that $P(1, 4)$, $Q(2, 6)$, and $R(7, 1)$ are the vertices of a right triangle.

EXAMPLE 5 **Writing Equations of Parallel and Perpendicular Lines**

A Write an equation in slope-intercept form for the line that passes through $(4, 5)$ and is parallel to the line described by $y = 5x + 10$.

Step 1 Find the slope of the line.

$y = 5x + 10$ *The slope is 5.*

The parallel line also has a slope of 5.

Step 2 Write the equation in point-slope form.

$y - y_1 = m(x - x_1)$ *Use point-slope form.*

$y - 5 = 5(x - 4)$ *Substitute 5 for m, 4 for x_1, and 5 for y_1.*

Step 3 Write the equation in slope-intercept form.

$y - 5 = 5(x - 4)$

$y - 5 = 5x - 20$ *Distributive Property*

$y = 5x - 15$ *Addition Property of Equality*

B Write an equation in slope-intercept form for the line that passes through $(3, 2)$ and is perpendicular to the line described by $y = 3x - 1$.

Step 1 Find the slope of the line.

$y = 3x - 1$ *The slope is 3.*

The perpendicular line has a slope of $-\frac{1}{3}$, because $3\left(-\frac{1}{3}\right) = -1$.

Step 2 Write the equation in point-slope form.

$y - y_1 = m(x - x_1)$ *Use point-slope form.*

$y - 2 = -\frac{1}{3}(x - 3)$ *Substitute $-\frac{1}{3}$ for m, 3 for x_1, and 2 for y_1.*

Step 3 Write the equation in slope-intercept form.

$y - 2 = -\frac{1}{3}(x - 3)$

$y - 2 = -\frac{1}{3}x + 1$ *Distributive Property*

$y = -\frac{1}{3}x + 3$ *Addition Property of Equality*

> **Helpful Hint**
>
> If you know the slope of a line, the slope of a perpendicular line will be the "opposite reciprocal."
>
> $\frac{2}{3} \rightarrow -\frac{3}{2}$
>
> $\frac{1}{5} \rightarrow -5$
>
> $-7 \rightarrow \frac{1}{7}$

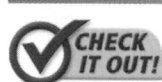 **5a.** Write an equation in slope-intercept form for the line that passes through $(5, 7)$ and is parallel to the line described by $y = \frac{4}{5}x - 6$.

5b. Write an equation in slope-intercept form for the line that passes through $(-5, 3)$ and is perpendicular to the line described by $y = 5x$.

THINK AND DISCUSS

1. Are the lines described by $y = \frac{1}{2}x$ and $y = 2x$ perpendicular? Explain.

2. Describe the slopes and y-intercepts when two nonvertical lines are parallel.

 3. **GET ORGANIZED** Copy and complete the graphic organizer. In each box, sketch an example and describe the slopes.

Parallel lines	Perpendicular lines

go.hrw.com
Homework Help Online
KEYWORD: MA11 5-9
Parent Resources Online
KEYWORD: MA7 Parent

GUIDED PRACTICE

1. **Vocabulary** ___?___ lines have the same slope. (*Parallel* or *Perpendicular*)

SEE EXAMPLE **1**
p. 361

Identify which lines are parallel.

2. $y = 6$; $y = 6x + 5$; $y = 6x - 7$; $y = -8$

3. $y = \frac{3}{4}x - 1$; $y = -2x$; $y - 3 = \frac{3}{4}(x - 5)$; $y - 4 = -2(x + 2)$

SEE EXAMPLE **2**
p. 362

4. **Geometry** Show that *ABCD* is a trapezoid.
(*Hint:* In a trapezoid, exactly one pair of opposite sides is parallel.)

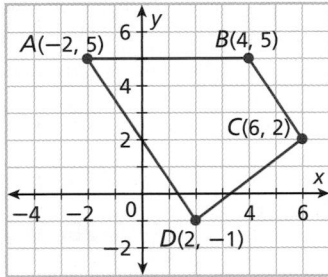

SEE EXAMPLE **3**
p. 363

Identify which lines are perpendicular.

5. $y = \frac{2}{3}x - 4$; $y = -\frac{3}{2}x + 2$; $y = -1$; $x = 3$

6. $y = -\frac{3}{7}x - 4$; $y - 4 = -7(x + 2)$;

   $y - 1 = \frac{1}{7}(x - 4)$; $y - 7 = \frac{7}{3}(x - 3)$

SEE EXAMPLE **4**
p. 363

7. **Geometry** Show that *PQRS* is a rectangle. (*Hint:* In a rectangle, all four angles are right angles.)

SEE EXAMPLE **5**
p. 364

8. Write an equation in slope-intercept form for the line that passes through (5, 0) and is perpendicular to the line described by $y = -\frac{5}{2}x + 6$.

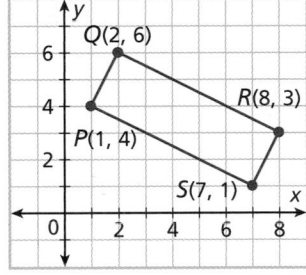

PRACTICE AND PROBLEM SOLVING

Independent Practice

For Exercises	See Example
9–11	1
12	2
13–15	3
16	4
17	5

Extra Practice

Skills Practice p. S13

Application Practice p. S32

Identify which lines are parallel.

9. $x = 7$; $y = -\frac{5}{6}x + 8$; $y = -\frac{5}{6}x - 4$; $x = -9$

10. $y = -x$; $y - 3 = -1(x + 9)$; $y - 6 = \frac{1}{2}(x - 14)$; $y + 1 = \frac{1}{2}x$

11. $y = -3x + 2$; $y = \frac{1}{2}x - 1$; $-x + 2y = 17$; $3x + y = 27$

12. **Geometry** Show that *LMNP* is a parallelogram.

Identify which lines are perpendicular.

13. $y = 6x$; $y = \frac{1}{6}x$; $y = -\frac{1}{6}x$; $y = -6x$

14. $y - 9 = 3(x + 1)$; $y = -\frac{1}{3}x + 5$; $y = 0$; $x = 6$

15. $x - 6y = 15$; $y = 3x - 2$; $y = -3x - 3$; $y = -6x - 8$; $3y = -x - 11$

16. Geometry Show that *ABC* is a right triangle.

17. Write an equation in slope-intercept form for the line that passes through $(0, 0)$ and is parallel to the line described by $y = -\frac{6}{7}x + 1$.

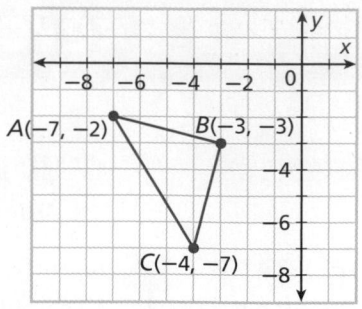

Without graphing, tell whether each pair of lines is parallel, perpendicular, or neither.

18. $x = 2$ and $y = -5$

19. $y = 7x$ and $y - 28 = 7(x - 4)$

20. $y = 2x - 1$ and $y = \frac{1}{2}x + 2$

21. $y - 3 = \frac{1}{4}(x - 3)$ and $y + 13 = \frac{1}{4}(x + 1)$

Write an equation in slope-intercept form for the line that is parallel to the given line and that passes through the given point.

22. $y = 3x - 7; (0, 4)$

23. $y = \frac{1}{2}x + 5; (4, -3)$

24. $4y = x; (4, 0)$

25. $y = 2x + 3; (1, 7)$

26. $5x - 2y = 10; (3, -5)$

27. $y = 3x - 4; (-2, 7)$

28. $y = 7; (2, 4)$

29. $x + y = 1; (2, 3)$

30. $2x + 3y = 7; (4, 5)$

31. $y = 4x + 2; (5, -3)$

32. $y = \frac{1}{2}x - 1; (0, -4)$

33. $3x + 4y = 8; (4, -3)$

Write an equation in slope-intercept form for the line that is perpendicular to the given line and that passes through the given point.

34. $y = -3x + 4; (6, -2)$

35. $y = x - 6; (-1, 2)$

36. $3x - 4y = 8; (-6, 5)$

37. $5x + 2y = 10; (3, -5)$

38. $y = 5 - 3x; (2, -4)$

39. $-10x + 2y = 8; (4, -3)$

40. $2x + 3y = 7; (4, 5)$

41. $4x - 2y = -6; (3, -2)$

42. $-2x - 8y = 16; (4, 5)$

43. $y = -2x + 4; (-2, 5)$

44. $y = x - 5; (0, 5)$

45. $x + y = 2; (8, 5)$

46. Write an equation describing the line that is parallel to the *y*-axis and that is 6 units to the right of the *y*-axis.

47. Write an equation describing the line that is perpendicular to the *y*-axis and that is 4 units below the *x*-axis.

48. Critical Thinking Is it possible for two linear functions whose graphs are parallel lines to have the same *y*-intercept? Explain.

49. Estimation Estimate the slope of a line that is perpendicular to the line through $(2.07, 8.95)$ and $(-1.9, 25.07)$.

 50. Write About It Explain in words how to write an equation in slope-intercept form that describes a line parallel to $y - 3 = -6(x - 3)$.

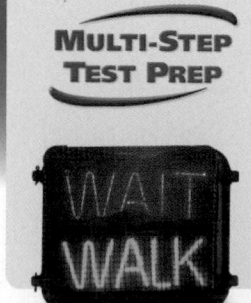

MULTI-STEP TEST PREP

51. This problem will prepare you for the Multi-Step Test Prep on page 376.

   a. Flora walks from her home to the bus stop at a rate of 50 steps per minute. Write a rule that gives her distance from home (in steps) as a function of time.

   b. Flora's neighbor Dan lives 30 steps closer to the bus stop. He begins walking at the same time and at the same pace as Flora. Write a rule that gives Dan's distance from *Flora's* house as a function of time.

   c. Will Flora meet Dan along the walk? Use a graph to help explain your answer.

52. Which describes a line parallel to the line described by $y = -3x + 2$?

Ⓐ $y = -3x$ Ⓑ $y = \frac{1}{3}x$ Ⓒ $y = 2 - 3x$ Ⓓ $y = \frac{1}{3}x + 2$

53. Which describes a line passing through $(3, 3)$ that is perpendicular to the line described by $y = \frac{3}{5}x + 2$?

Ⓕ

Ⓗ
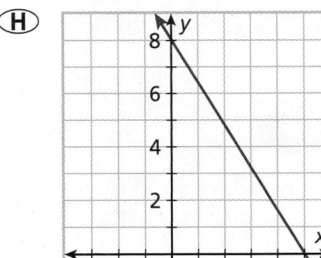

Ⓖ $y = \frac{5}{3}x - 2$ Ⓙ $y = \frac{3}{5}x + \frac{6}{5}$

54. **Gridded Response** The graph of a linear function $f(x)$ is parallel to the line described by $2x + y = 5$ and contains the point $(6, -2)$. What is the y-intercept of $f(x)$?

CHALLENGE AND EXTEND

55. Three or more points that lie on the same line are called *collinear points*. Explain why the points A, B, and C must be collinear if the line containing A and B has the same slope as the line containing B and C.

56. The lines described by $y = (a + 12)x + 3$ and $y = 4ax$ are parallel. What is the value of a?

57. The lines described by $y = (5a + 3)x$ and $y = -\frac{1}{2}x$ are perpendicular. What is the value of a?

 58. **Geometry** The diagram shows a square in the coordinate plane. Use the diagram to show that the diagonals of a square are perpendicular.

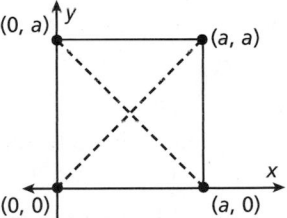

SPIRAL REVIEW

59. The record high temperature for a given city is 112 °F. The morning temperature today was 94 °F and the temperature will increase t degrees. Write and solve an inequality to find all values of t that would break the record for the high temperature. *(Lesson 3-2)*

Graph each function. *(Lesson 4-4)*

60. $y = -3x + 5$ **61.** $y = x - 1$ **62.** $y = x^2 - 3$

Write an equation in slope-intercept form for the line with the given slope that contains the given point. *(Lesson 5-8)*

63. slope $= \frac{2}{3}$; $(6, -1)$ **64.** slope $= -5$; $(2, 4)$ **65.** slope $= -\frac{1}{2}$; $(-1, 0)$

66. slope $= -\frac{1}{3}$; $(2, 7)$ **67.** slope $= 0$; $(-3, 3)$ **68.** slope $= \frac{1}{5}$; $(-4, -2)$

Technology LAB

Use with Lesson 5-10

The Family of Linear Functions

A *family of functions* is a set of functions whose graphs have basic characteristics in common. For example, all linear functions form a family. You can use a graphing calculator to explore families of functions.

go.hrw.com
Lab Resources Online
KEYWORD: MA11 LAB5

Activity

Graph the lines described by $y = x - 2$, $y = x - 1$, $y = x$, $y = x + 1$, $y = x + 2$, $y = x + 3$, and $y = x + 4$. How does the value of b affect the graph described by $y = x + b$?

1 All of the functions are in the form $y = x + b$. Enter them into the **Y=** editor.

[Y=] [X,T,θ,n] [−] 2 [ENTER]
[X,T,θ,n] [−] 1 [ENTER]

and so on.

2 Press [ZOOM] and select **6:Zstandard**. Think about the different values of b as you watch the graphs being drawn. Notice that the lines are all parallel.

3 It appears that the value of b in $y = x + b$ shifts the graph up or down—up if b is positive and down if b is negative.

Try This

1. Make a prediction about the lines described by $y = 2x - 3$, $y = 2x - 2$, $y = 2x - 1$, $y = 2x$, $y = 2x + 1$, $y = 2x + 2$, and $y = 2x + 3$. Then graph. Was your prediction correct?

2. Now use your calculator to explore what happens to the graph of $y = mx$ when you change the value of m.

   a. Make a Prediction How do you think the lines described by $y = -2x$, $y = -x$, $y = x$, and $y = 2x$ will be related? How will they be alike? How will they be different?

   b. Graph the functions given in part **a**. Was your prediction correct?

   c. How is the effect of m different when m is positive from when m is negative?

Transforming Linear Functions

Objective
Describe how changing slope and *y*-intercept affect the graph of a linear function.

Vocabulary
family of functions
parent function
transformation
translation
rotation
reflection

Who uses this?
Business owners can use transformations to show the effects of price changes, such as the price of trophy engraving. (See Example 5.)

A **family of functions** is a set of functions whose graphs have basic characteristics in common. For example, all linear functions form a family because all of their graphs are the same basic shape.

A **parent function** is the most basic function in a family. For linear functions, the parent function is $f(x) = x$.

The graphs of all other linear functions are *transformations* of the graph of the parent function, $f(x) = x$. A **transformation** is a change in position or size of a figure.

There are three types of transformations—*translations, rotations, and reflections.*

Look at the four functions and their graphs below.

Remember!
Function notation—$f(x)$, $g(x)$, and so on—can be used in place of *y*.
$$y = f(x)$$

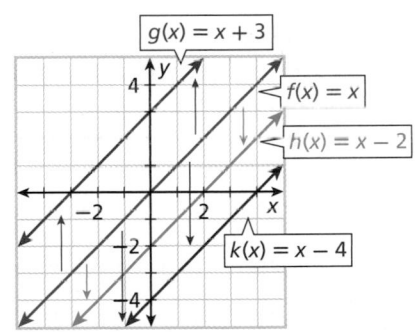

Notice that all of the lines above are parallel. The slopes are the same but the *y*-intercepts are different.

The graphs of $g(x) = x + 3$, $h(x) = x - 2$, and $k(x) = x - 4$ are vertical *translations* of the graph of the parent function, $f(x) = x$. A **translation** is a type of transformation that moves every point the same distance in the same direction. You can think of a translation as a "slide."

Know it! Note

Vertical Translation of a Linear Function

When the *y*-intercept *b* is changed in the function $f(x) = mx + b$, the graph is translated vertically.

- If *b* increases, the graph is translated up.
- If *b* decreases, the graph is translated down.

EXAMPLE 1 **Translating Linear Functions**

Graph $f(x) = x$ and $g(x) = x - 5$. Then describe the transformation from the graph of $f(x)$ to the graph of $g(x)$.

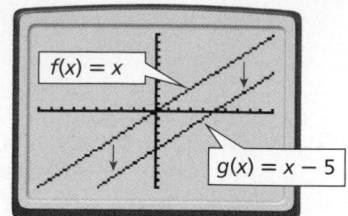

The graph of $g(x) = x - 5$ is the result of translating the graph of $f(x) = x$ 5 units down.

CHECK IT OUT! **1.** Graph $f(x) = x + 4$ and $g(x) = x - 2$. Then describe the transformation from the graph of $f(x)$ to the graph of $g(x)$.

The graphs of $g(x) = 3x$, $h(x) = 5x$, and $k(x) = \frac{1}{2}x$ are *rotations* of the graph of $f(x) = x$. A **rotation** is a transformation about a point. You can think of a rotation as a "turn." The y-intercepts are the same, but the slopes are different.

Know it! Note **Rotation of a Linear Function**

When the slope m is changed in the function $f(x) = mx + b$ it causes a rotation of the graph about the point $(0, b)$, which changes the line's steepness.

EXAMPLE 2 **Rotating Linear Functions**

Graph $f(x) = x + 2$ and $g(x) = 2x + 2$. Then describe the transformation from the graph of $f(x)$ to the graph of $g(x)$.

The graph of $g(x) = 2x + 2$ is the result of rotating the graph of $f(x) = x + 2$ about $(0, 2)$. The graph of $g(x)$ is steeper than the graph of $f(x)$.

CHECK IT OUT! **2.** Graph $f(x) = 3x - 1$ and $g(x) = \frac{1}{2}x - 1$. Then describe the transformation from the graph of $f(x)$ to the graph of $g(x)$.

The diagram shows the *reflection* of the graph of $f(x) = 2x$ across the y-axis, producing the graph of $g(x) = -2x$. A **reflection** is a transformation across a line that produces a mirror image. You can think of a reflection as a "flip" over a line.

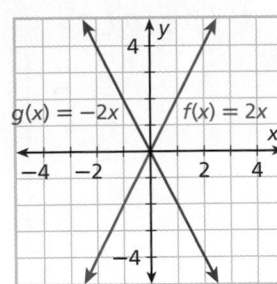

Know it!
Note

Reflection of a Linear Function

When the slope m is multiplied by -1 in $f(x) = mx + b$, the graph is reflected across the y-axis.

EXAMPLE 3 **Reflecting Linear Functions**

Graph $f(x)$. Then reflect the graph of $f(x)$ across the y-axis. Write a function $g(x)$ to describe the new graph.

A $f(x) = x$

 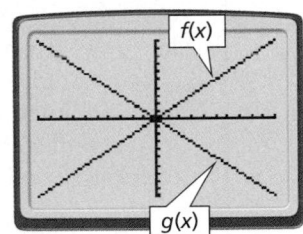

To find $g(x)$, multiply the value of m by -1.
In $f(x) = x$, $m = 1$.
$1(-1) = -1$ *This is the value of m for g(x).*
$g(x) = -x$

B $f(x) = -4x - 1$

 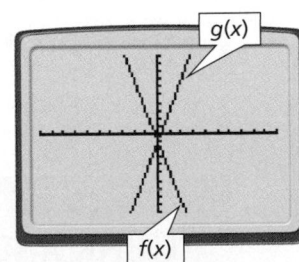

To find $g(x)$, multiply the value of m by -1.
In $f(x) = -4x - 1$, $m = -4$.
$-4(-1) = 4$ *This is the value of m for g(x).*
$g(x) = 4x - 1$

 3. Graph $f(x) = \frac{2}{3}x + 2$. Then reflect the graph of $f(x)$ across the y-axis. Write a function $g(x)$ to describe the new graph.

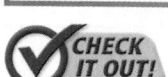

EXAMPLE **4** **Multiple Transformations of Linear Functions**

Graph $f(x) = x$ and $g(x) = 3x + 1$. Then describe the transformations from the graph of $f(x)$ to the graph of $g(x)$.

Find transformations of $f(x) = x$ that will result in $g(x) = 3x + 1$:

- Multiply $f(x)$ by 3 to get $h(x) = 3x$. This rotates the graph about $(0, 0)$ and makes it steeper.

- Then add 1 to $h(x)$ to get $g(x) = 3x + 1$. This translates the graph 1 unit up.

The transformations are a rotation and a translation.

CHECK IT OUT! **4.** Graph $f(x) = x$ and $g(x) = -x + 2$. Then describe the transformations from the graph of $f(x)$ to the graph of $g(x)$.

EXAMPLE **5** *Business Application*

A trophy company charges $175 for a trophy plus $0.20 per letter for the engraving. The total charge for a trophy with x letters is given by the function $f(x) = 0.20x + 175$. How will the graph change if the trophy's cost is lowered to $172? if the charge per letter is raised to $0.50?

$f(x) = 0.20x + 175$ is graphed in blue.

If the trophy's cost is lowered to $172, the new function is $g(x) = 0.20x + 172$. The original graph will be translated 3 units down.

If the charge per letter is raised to $0.50, the new function is $h(x) = 0.50x + 175$. The original graph will be rotated about $(0, 175)$ and become steeper.

CHECK IT OUT! **5.** **What if...?** How will the graph change if the charge per letter is lowered to $0.15? if the trophy's cost is raised to $180?

THINK AND DISCUSS

1. Describe the graph of $f(x) = x + 3.45$

2. Look at the graphs in Example 5. For each line, is every point on the line a solution in this situation? Explain.

3. **GET ORGANIZED** Copy and complete the graphic organizer. In each box, sketch a graph of the given transformation of $f(x) = x$, and label it with a possible equation.

5-10

Exercises

go.hrw.com
Homework Help Online
KEYWORD: MA11 5-10
Parent Resources Online
KEYWORD: MA7 Parent

GUIDED PRACTICE

Vocabulary Apply the vocabulary from this lesson to answer each question.

1. Changing the value of b in $f(x) = mx + b$ results in a ___?___ of the graph. (*translation* or *reflection*)

2. Changing the value of m in $f(x) = mx + b$ results in a ___?___ of the graph. (*translation* or *rotation*)

Graph $f(x)$ and $g(x)$. Then describe the transformation from the graph of $f(x)$ to the graph of $g(x)$.

SEE EXAMPLE **1**
p. 370

3. $f(x) = x, g(x) = x - 4$

4. $f(x) = x, g(x) = x + 1$

5. $f(x) = x, g(x) = x + 2$

6. $f(x) = x, g(x) = x - 6.5$

SEE EXAMPLE **2**
p. 370

7. $f(x) = x, g(x) = \frac{1}{4}x$

8. $f(x) = \frac{1}{5}x + 3, g(x) = x + 3$

9. $f(x) = 2x - 2, g(x) = 4x - 2$

10. $f(x) = x + 1, g(x) = \frac{1}{2}x + 1$

Graph $f(x)$. Then reflect the graph of $f(x)$ across the y-axis. Write a function $g(x)$ to describe the new graph.

SEE EXAMPLE **3**
p. 371

11. $f(x) = -\frac{1}{5}x$

12. $f(x) = 2x + 4$

13. $f(x) = \frac{1}{3}x - 6$

14. $f(x) = 5x - 1$

Graph $f(x)$ and $g(x)$. Then describe the transformations from the graph of $f(x)$ to the graph of $g(x)$.

SEE EXAMPLE **4**
p. 372

15. $f(x) = x, g(x) = 2x - 2$

16. $f(x) = x, g(x) = \frac{1}{3}x + 1$

17. $f(x) = -x - 1, g(x) = -4x$

18. $f(x) - -x, g(x) = -\frac{1}{2}x - 3$

SEE EXAMPLE **5**
p. 372

19. **Entertainment** For large parties, a restaurant charges a reservation fee of $25, plus $15 per person. The total charge for a party of x people is $f(x) = 15x + 25$. How will the graph of this function change if the reservation fee is raised to $50? if the per-person charge is lowered to $12?

PRACTICE AND PROBLEM SOLVING

Extra Practice
Skills Practice p. S13
Application Practice p. S32

Graph $f(x)$ and $g(x)$. Then describe the transformation(s) from the graph of $f(x)$ to the graph of $g(x)$.

20. $f(x) = x, g(x) = x + \frac{1}{2}$

21. $f(x) = x, g(x) = x - 4$

22. $f(x) = \frac{1}{5}x - 1, g(x) = \frac{1}{10}x - 1$

23. $f(x) = x + 2, g(x) = \frac{2}{3}x + 2$

Graph $f(x)$. Then reflect the graph of $f(x)$ across the y-axis. Write a function $g(x)$ to describe the new graph.

24. $f(x) = 6x$

25. $f(x) = -3x - 2$

Graph $f(x)$ and $g(x)$. Then describe the transformations from the graph of $f(x)$ to the graph of $g(x)$.

26. $f(x) = 2x, g(x) = 4x - 1$

27. $f(x) = -7x + 5, g(x) = -14x$

28. School The number of chaperones on a field trip must include 1 teacher for every 4 students, plus 2 parents total. The function describing the number of chaperones for a trip of x students is $f(x) = \frac{1}{4}x + 2$. How will the graph change if the number of parents is reduced to 0? if the number of teachers is raised to 1 for every 3 students?

Describe the transformation(s) on the graph of $f(x) = x$ that result in the graph of $g(x)$. Graph $f(x)$ and $g(x)$, and compare the slopes and intercepts.

29. $g(x) = -x$ **30.** $g(x) = x + 8$ **31.** $g(x) = 3x$

32. $g(x) = -\frac{2}{7}x$ **33.** $g(x) = 6x - 3$ **34.** $g(x) = -2x + 1$

Sketch the transformed graph. Then write a function to describe your graph.

35. Rotate the graph of $f(x) = -x + 2$ until it has the same steepness in the opposite direction.

36. Reflect the graph of $f(x) = x - 1$ across the y-axis, and then translate it 4 units down.

37. Translate the graph of $f(x) = \frac{1}{6}x - 10$ six units up.

38. Hobbies A book club charges a membership fee of $20 and then $12 for each book purchased.

     a. Write and graph a function to represent the cost y of membership in the club based on the number of books purchased x.

     b. What if...? Write and graph a second function to represent the cost of membership if the club raises its membership fee to $30.

     c. Describe the relationship between your graphs from parts **a** and **b**.

Describe the transformation(s) on the graph of $f(x) = x$ that result in the graph of $g(x)$.

39. $g(x) = x - 9$ **40.** $g(x) = -x$ **41.** $g(x) = 5x$

42. $g(x) = -\frac{2}{3}x + 1$ **43.** $g(x) = -2x$ **44.** $g(x) = \frac{1}{5}x$

45. Careers Kelly works as a salesperson. She earns a weekly base salary plus a commission that is a percent of her total sales. Her total weekly pay is described by $f(x) = 0.20x + 300$, where x is total sales in dollars.

     a. What is Kelly's weekly base salary?

     b. What percent of total sales does Kelly receive as commission?

     c. What if...? What is the change in Kelly's salary plan if the weekly pay function changes to $g(x) = 0.25x + 300$? to $h(x) = 0.2x + 400$?

46. Critical Thinking To transform the graph of $f(x) = x$ into the graph of $g(x) = -x$, you can reflect the graph of $f(x)$ across the y-axis. Find another transformation that will have the same result.

47. Write About It Describe how a reflection across the y-axis affects each point on a graph. Give an example to illustrate your answer.

48. This problem will prepare you for the Multi-Step Test Prep on page 376.

     a. Maria is walking from school to the softball field at a rate of 3 feet per second. Write a rule that gives her distance from school (in feet) as a function of time (in seconds). Then graph.

     b. Give a real-world situation that could be described by a line parallel to the one in part **a.**

     c. What does the y-intercept represent in each of these situations?

Hobbies

Seattle librarian Nancy Pearl started the first citywide reading program, "If All Seattle Reads the Same Book," in 1998. Many cities have since emulated this program, attempting to unite communities by having everyone read the same book at the same time.

49. Which best describes the effect on $f(x) = 2x - 5$ if the slope changes to 10?

    Ⓐ Its graph becomes less steep.

    Ⓑ Its graph moves 15 units up.

    Ⓒ Its graph makes 10 complete rotations.

    Ⓓ The x-intercept becomes $\frac{1}{2}$.

50. Given $f(x) = 22x - 182$, which does NOT describe the effect of increasing the y-intercept by 182?

    Ⓕ The new line passes through the origin.

    Ⓖ The new x-intercept is 0.

    Ⓗ The new line is parallel to the original.

    Ⓙ The new line is steeper than the original.

CHALLENGE AND EXTEND

51. You have seen that the graph of $g(x) = x + 3$ is the result of translating the graph of $f(x) = x$ three units up. However, you can also think of this as a *horizontal* translation—that is, a translation left or right. Graph $g(x) = x + 3$. Describe the horizontal translation of the graph of $f(x) = x$ to get the graph of $g(x) = x + 3$.

52. If $c > 0$, how can you describe the translation that transforms the graph of $f(x) = x$ into the graph of $g(x) = x + c$ as a horizontal translation? $g(x) = x - c$ as a horizontal translation?

SPIRAL REVIEW

Give an expression in simplest form for the perimeter of each figure. *(Lesson 1-7)*

53.

54.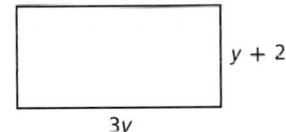

Identify the correlation you would expect to see between each pair of data sets. Explain. *(Lesson 4-5)*

55. the temperature and the number of people at the local ice cream parlor

56. the amount of electricity used and the total electric bill

57. the number of miles driven after a fill-up and the amount of gasoline in the tank

Identify which lines are parallel. *(Lesson 5-9)*

58. $y = -2x + 3; y = 2x; y = -2; y = -2x - 4; y = \frac{1}{2}x; y - 1 = -\frac{1}{2}(x + 6)$

59. $y = \frac{3}{5}x + 8; y = -\frac{3}{5}x; y + 1 = -\frac{3}{5}(x - 2); y = \frac{5}{3}x + 9; y = 3x + 5$

Identify which lines are perpendicular. *(Lesson 5-9)*

60. $3x - 5y = 5; 5y = -2x - 15; y = 3x + 5; 5x + 3y = -21; y = \frac{5}{2}x - 2$

61. $x = 4; 2y + x = 6; 3x - y = 12; y = 2x + 3; y = -3$

MULTI-STEP TEST PREP

Using Linear Functions

Take a Walk! All intersections in Durango, Colorado, have crossing signals with timers. Once the signal changes to walk, the timer begins at 28 seconds and counts down to show how much time pedestrians have to cross the street.

1. Pauline counted her steps as she crossed the street. She counted 15 steps with 19 seconds remaining. When she reached the opposite side of the street, she had counted a total of 30 steps and had 10 seconds remaining. Copy and complete the table below using these values.

Time Remaining (s)	28		
Steps	0		

2. Find the average rate of change for Pauline's walk.

3. Sketch a graph of the points in the table, or plot them on your graphing calculator.

4. Find an equation that describes the line through the points.

5. How would the graph change if Pauline increased her speed? What if she decreased her speed?

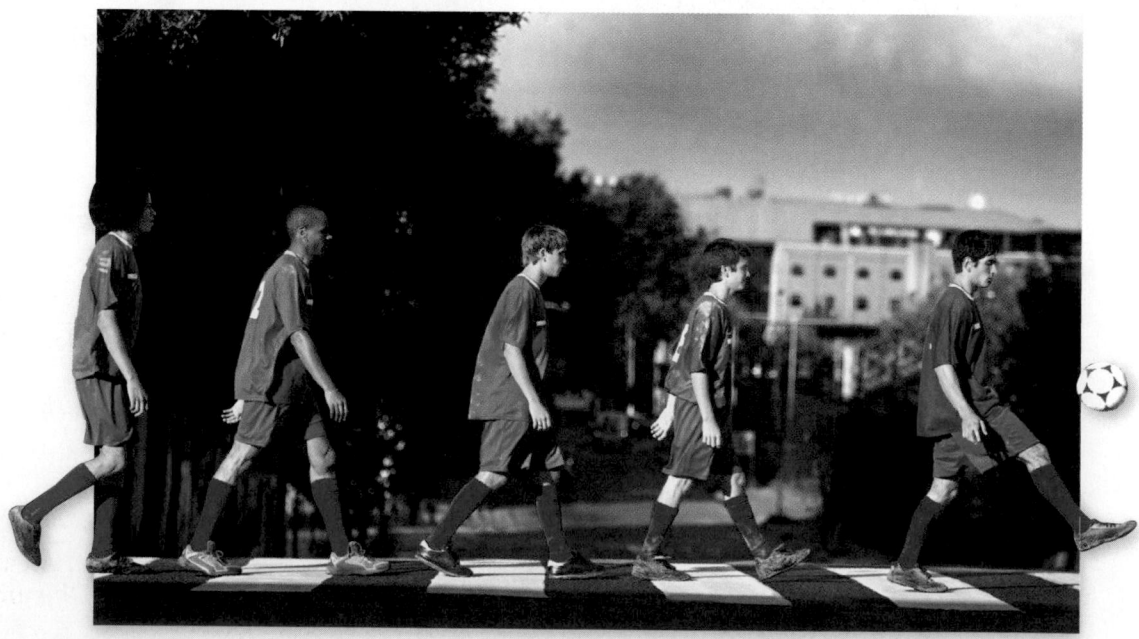

READY TO GO ON?

CHAPTER 5

SECTION 5B

Quiz for Lessons 5-7 Through 5-10

5-7 Slope-Intercept Form

Graph each line given the slope and y-intercept.

1. slope $= \frac{1}{4}$; y-intercept $= 2$
2. slope $= -3$; y-intercept $= 5$
3. slope $= -1$; y-intercept $= -6$

Write each equation in slope-intercept form. Then graph the line described by the equation.

4. $2x + y = 5$
5. $2x - 6y = 6$
6. $3x + y = 3x - 4$

7. Entertainment At a chili cook-off, people pay a $3.00 entrance fee and $0.50 for each bowl of chili they taste. The graph shows the total cost per person as a function of the number of bowls of chili tasted.

a. Write an equation that represents the total cost per person as a function of the number of bowls of chili tasted.

b. Identify the slope and y-intercept and describe their meanings.

5-8 Point-Slope Form

Graph the line with the given slope that contains the given point.

8. slope $= -3$; $(0, 3)$
9. slope $= -\frac{2}{3}$; $(-3, 5)$
10. slope $= 2$; $(-3, -1)$

Write an equation in slope-intercept form for the line through the two points.

11. $(3, 1)$ and $(4, 3)$
12. $(-1, -1)$ and $(1, 7)$
13. $(1, -4)$ and $(-2, 5)$

5-9 Slopes of Parallel and Perpendicular Lines

Identify which lines are parallel.

14. $y = -2x$; $y = 2x + 1$; $y = 2x$; $y = 2(x + 5)$
15. $-3y = x$; $y = -\frac{1}{3}x + 1$; $y = -3x$; $y + 2 = x + 4$

Identify which lines are perpendicular.

16. $y = -4x - 1$; $y = \frac{1}{4}x$; $y = 4x - 6$; $x = -4$
17. $y = -\frac{3}{4}x$; $y = \frac{3}{4}x - 3$; $y = \frac{4}{3}x$; $y = 4$; $x = 3$

18. Write an equation in slope-intercept form for the line that passes through $(5, 2)$ and is parallel to the line described by $3x - 5y = 15$.

19. Write an equation in slope-intercept form for the line that passes through $(3, 5)$ and is perpendicular to the line described by $y = -\frac{3}{2}x - 2$.

5-10 Transforming Linear Functions

Graph $f(x)$ and $g(x)$. Then describe the transformation(s) from the graph of $f(x)$ to the graph of $g(x)$.

20. $f(x) = 5x$, $g(x) = -5x$
21. $f(x) = \frac{1}{2}x - 1$, $g(x) = \frac{1}{2}x + 4$

22. An attorney charges an initial fee of $250 and then $150 per hour. The total bill after x hours is $f(x) = 150x + 250$. How will the graph of this function change if the initial fee is reduced to $200? if the hourly rate is increased to $175?

Absolute-Value Functions

Objectives
Graph absolute-value functions.

Identify characteristics of absolute-value functions and their graphs.

Vocabulary
absolute-value function
axis of symmetry
vertex

An **absolute-value function** is a function whose rule contains an absolute-value expression. To graph an absolute-value function, choose several values of x and generate some ordered pairs.

x	$f(x) = |x|$
−2	2
−1	1
0	0
1	1
2	2

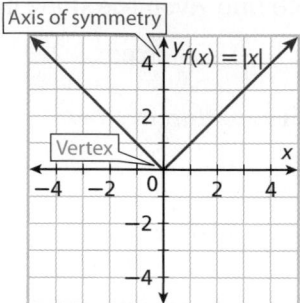

Absolute-value graphs are composed of two linear pieces. The **axis of symmetry** is the line that divides the graph into two congruent halves. The **vertex** is the "corner" point on the graph.

From the table and the graph of $f(x) = |x|$, you can tell that
- the **axis of symmetry** is the y-axis $(x = 0)$.
- the **vertex** is $(0, 0)$.
- the domain $(x\text{-values})$ is the set of all real numbers.
- the range $(y\text{-values})$ is described by $y \geq 0$.
- the x-intercept and the y-intercept are both 0.
- the slope of the left linear piece is −1 and the slope of the right linear piece is 1.

E X A M P L E   1   Absolute-Value Functions

Graph $f(x) = |2x| - 1$ and label the axis of symmetry and the vertex. Identify the intercepts, give the domain and range, and find the slope of each piece.

Choose positive, negative, and zero values for x, and find ordered pairs.

x	−2	−1	0	1	2
$f(x) = |2x| - 1$	3	1	−1	1	3

Plot the ordered pairs and connect them.

From the table and the graph, you can tell that
- the **axis of symmetry** is the y-axis $(x = 0)$.
- the **vertex** is $(0, -1)$.
- the x-intercepts are $\frac{1}{2}$ and $-\frac{1}{2}$.
- the y-intercept is −1.
- the domain is all real numbers.
- the range is described by $y \geq -1$.
- the slope of the left piece is −2 and the slope of the right piece is 2.

1. Graph $f(x) = 3|x|$ and label the axis of symmetry and the vertex. Identify the intercepts, give the domain and range, and find the slope of each piece.

The parent function for absolute-value functions is $f(x) = |x|$. The graphs of all other absolute-value functions are transformations of the graph of $f(x) = |x|$.

For $f(x) = a|x - b| + c$

WORDS	EXAMPLES	WORDS	EXAMPLES
Opening Direction • If $a > 0$, the graph opens upward. • If $a < 0$, the graph opens downward.	*(graph showing $f(x) = |x|$ and $g(x) = -|x|$)*	**Horizontal Translation** • If $b > 0$, the graph is translated b units right from $f(x) = |x|$. • If $b < 0$, the graph is translated b units left from $f(x) = |x|$.	*(graph showing $h(x) = |x + 2|$, $f(x) = |x|$, and $g(x) = |x - 2|$)*
Width • If $|a| > 1$, the graph is narrower than the graph of $f(x) = |x|$. • If $|a| < 1$, the graph is wider than the graph of $f(x) = |x|$. The slopes of the two linear pieces are a and $-a$.	*(graph showing $g(x) = 3|x|$, $f(x) = |x|$, and $h(x) = \frac{1}{2}|x|$)*	**Vertical Translation** • If $c > 0$, the graph is translated c units up from $f(x) = |x|$. • If $c < 0$, the graph is translated c units down from $f(x) = |x|$.	*(graph showing $g(x) = |x| + 2$, $f(x) = |x|$, and $h(x) = |x| - 2$)*

EXAMPLE **Transforming Absolute-Value Functions**

Describe the transformations from the graph of $f(x) = |x|$ to the graph of $g(x)$. Then graph both functions.

A $g(x) = 2|x + 1|$

Identify a, b, and c.

$g(x) = 2|x + 1| = 2|x - (-1)| + 0$

• $a = 2$: graph is narrower
• $b = -1$: translated 1 unit left
• $c = 0$: no vertical translation

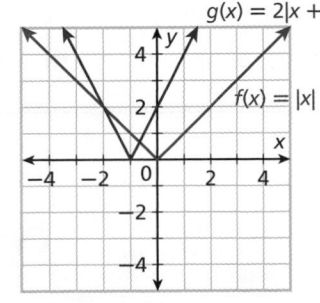

Describe the transformations from the graph of $f(x) = |x|$ to the graph of $g(x)$. Then graph both functions.

B $g(x) = -|x - 3| + 2$

Identify a, b, and c.

$g(x) = -|x - 3| + 2 = -1|x - 3| + 2$

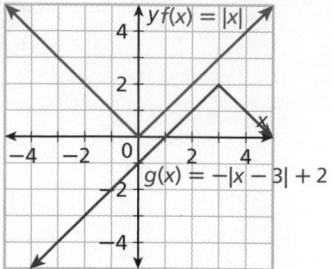

- $a = -1$: graph opens downward and width is unchanged
- $b = 3$: translated 3 units right
- $c = 2$: translated 2 units up

CHECK IT OUT! Describe the transformations from the graph of $f(x) = |x|$ to the graph of $g(x)$. Then graph both functions.

2a. $g(x) = |x - 4| - 2$ **2b.** $g(x) = \frac{1}{3}|x| + 1$

Minimum and Maximum Values of Absolute-Value Functions

WORDS	If the graph of an absolute-value function opens upward, the *y*-value of the vertex is the **minimum** value of the function.	If the graph of an absolute-value function opens downward, the *y*-value of the vertex is the **maximum** value of the function.
EXAMPLES	$f(x) = 2\,|x| - 2$	$f(x) = -|x - 1|$

EXAMPLE 3   **Identifying the Minimum or Maximum**

Graph $f(x) = |x + 3| - 5$. Identify the vertex and give the minimum or maximum value of the function.

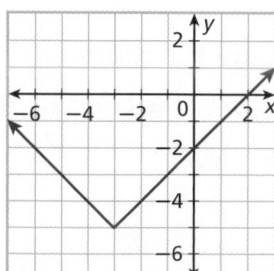

The vertex is $(-3, -5)$.

The graph opens upward, so the function has a minimum.

The minimum is -5.

CHECK IT OUT! Graph each absolute-value function. Identify the vertex and give the minimum or maximum value of the function.

3a. $f(x) = -|x| + 5$ **3b.** $f(x) = |x + 1| - 6$

EXAMPLE 4 *Sports Application*

Distance From Water Stand

In a charity race, a water stand for the runners is halfway between the start and finish lines. The function $y = \left| \frac{x}{8} - 3 \right|$ models Riley's distance y in miles from the water stand x minutes into the race.

A How long is the race?

$y = \left| \frac{x}{8} - 3 \right|$ is graphed in blue.

At the start of the race ($x = 0$), Riley is 3 mi from the water stand. The water stand is halfway between the start and finish lines, so the race is 6 mi.

B How much time does it take Riley to reach the water stand?

When Riley reaches the water stand, $y = 0$. This happens when $x = 24$. It takes Riley 24 min to reach the water stand.

C The function $y = \left| \frac{x}{10} - 3 \right|$ models Dean's distance from the water stand during the same race. Compare Dean's graph to Riley's graph. What can you conclude about Dean's speed?

$y = \left| \frac{x}{10} - 3 \right|$ is graphed in red. Both graphs start at the same point, but Dean's graph is translated to the right. It takes him more time to reach the water stand and to finish the race. Therefore, he is running more slowly than Riley.

CHECK IT OUT!

4. How would the graph be different for someone who runs faster than Riley?

EXTENSION

Exercises

Graph each absolute-value function and label the axis of symmetry and the vertex. Identify the intercepts, give the domain and range, and find the slope of each piece. Identify the maximum or minimum.

1. $f(x) = |x| + 3$ **2.** $f(x) = |x + 3|$ **3.** $f(x) = \frac{1}{2}|x|$ **4.** $f(x) = |x - 3|$

Tell whether each statement is sometimes, always, or never true.

5. The absolute value of a number is negative.

6. An absolute-value function has an x-intercept.

7. An absolute-value function has two y-intercepts.

Write a function to describe each of the following.

8. The graph of $f(x) = |x|$ is translated 2 units right.

9. The graph of $f(x) = |x|$ is narrowed and reflected across the x-axis.

10. **Critical Thinking** Suppose that an absolute-value function has no x-intercepts. What can you say about the function rule?

Vocabulary

Complete the sentences below with vocabulary words from the list above. Words may be used more than once.

1. A(n) ___?___ is a "slide," a(n) ___?___ is a "turn," and a(n) ___?___ is a "flip."

2. The x-coordinate of the point that contains the ___?___ is always 0.

3. In the equation $y = mx + b$, the value of m is the ___?___ , and the value of b is the ___?___ .

5-1 Identifying Linear Functions (pp. 300–306)

EXAMPLES

Tell whether each function is linear. If so, graph the function.

■ $y = -3x + 2$

$$
\begin{array}{ll}
y = -3x + 2 & \text{\textit{Write the equation in}} \\
\underline{+\,3x \quad +3x} & \text{\textit{standard form.}} \\
3x + y = \quad\quad 2 & \text{This is a linear function.}
\end{array}
$$

Generate ordered pairs.

x	y = -3x + 2	(x, y)
-2	y = -3(-2) + 2 = 8	(-2, 8)
0	y = -3(0) + 2 = 2	(0, 2)
2	y = -3(2) + 2 = -4	(2, -4)

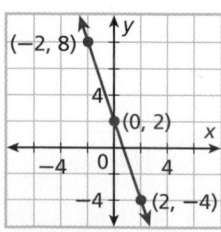

Plot the points and connect them with a straight line.

■ $y = 2x^3$

This is not a linear function because x has an exponent other than 1.

EXERCISES

Tell whether the given ordered pairs satisfy a linear function. Explain.

4.

x	y
-3	3
-1	1
1	1
3	3

5.

x	y
0	-3
1	-1
2	1
3	3

6. $\{(-2, 5), (-1, 3), (0, 1), (1, -1), (2, -3)\}$

7. $\{(1, 7), (3, 6), (6, 5), (9, 4), (13, 3)\}$

Each equation below is linear. Write each equation in standard form and give the values of A, B, and C.

8. $y = -5x + 1$

9. $\dfrac{x + 2}{2} = -3y$

10. $4y = 7x$

11. $9 = y$

12. Helene is selling cupcakes for $0.50 each. The function $f(x) = 0.5x$ gives the total amount of money Helene makes after selling x cupcakes. Graph this function and give its domain and range.

5-2 Using Intercepts (pp. 307–312)

EXAMPLE

- Find the x- and y-intercepts of $2x + 5y = 10$.

Let $y = 0$.	Let $x = 0$.
$2x + 5(0) = 10$	$2(0) + 5y = 10$
$2x + 0 = 10$	$0 + 5y = 10$
$2x = 10$	$5y = 10$
$\dfrac{2x}{2} = \dfrac{10}{2}$	$\dfrac{5y}{5} = \dfrac{10}{5}$
$x = 5$	$y = 2$

The x-intercept is 5.   The y-intercept is 2.

EXERCISES

Find the x- and y-intercepts.

13.

14.

15. $3x - y = 9$

16. $-2x + y = 1$

17. $-x + 6y = 18$

18. $3x - 4y = 1$

5-3 Rate of Change and Slope (pp. 314–321)

EXAMPLE

- Find the slope of the line.

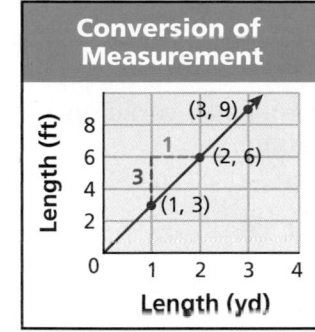

$$\text{slope} = \frac{\text{change in } y}{\text{change in } x}$$

$$= \frac{3}{1} = 3$$

EXERCISES

19. Graph the data and show the rates of change.

Time (s)	Distance (ft)
0	0
1	16
2	64
3	144
4	256

20. Find the slope of the line graphed below.

5-4 The Slope Formula (pp. 324–329)

EXAMPLE

- Find the slope of the line described by $2x - 3y = 6$.

Step 1 Find the x- and y-intercepts.

Let $y = 0$.	Let $x = 0$.
$2x - 3(0) = 6$	$2(0) - 3y = 6$
$2x = 6$	$-3y = 6$
$x = 3$	$y = -2$

The line contains $(3, 0)$ and $(0, -2)$.

Step 2 Use the slope formula.

$$m = \frac{y_2 - y_1}{x_2 - x_1} = \frac{-2 - 0}{0 - 3} = \frac{-2}{-3} = \frac{2}{3}$$

EXERCISES

Find the slope of the line described by each equation.

21. $4x + 3y = 24$

22. $y = -3x + 6$

23. $x + 2y = 10$

24. $3x = y + 3$

25. $y + 2 = 7x$

26. $16x = 4y + 1$

Find the slope of the line that contains each pair of points.

27. $(1, 2)$ and $(2, -3)$

28. $(4, -2)$ and $(-5, 7)$

29. $(-3, -6)$ and $(4, 1)$

30. $\left(\dfrac{1}{2}, 2\right)$ and $\left(\dfrac{3}{4}, \dfrac{5}{2}\right)$

31. $(2, 2)$ and $(2, 7)$

32. $(1, -3)$ and $(5, -3)$

5-5 The Midpoint and Distance Formulas (pp. 330–335)

EXAMPLE

■ Find the coordinates of the midpoint of $\overline{AB}$ with endpoints $A(-4, 3)$ and $B(5, -6)$

$M\left(\dfrac{x_1 + x_2}{2}, \dfrac{y_1 + y_2}{2}\right)$ *Write the formula.*

$M\left(\dfrac{-4 + 5}{2}, \dfrac{3 + (-6)}{2}\right) = M\left(\dfrac{1}{2}, -\dfrac{3}{2}\right)$

■ Use the Distance Formula to find the distance, to the nearest hundredth, from $C(-4, 1)$ to $D(5, -3)$.

$d = \sqrt{(x_2 - x_1)^2 + (y_2 - y_1)^2}$

$d = \sqrt{\left[5 - (-4)\right]^2 + (-3 - 1)^2}$

$d = \sqrt{9^2 + (-4)^2}$ *Subtract within grouping symbols.*

$d = \sqrt{97} \approx 9.85$ *Simplify and estimate.*

EXERCISES

Find the coordinates of the midpoint of each segment.

33. $\overline{EF}$ with endpoints $E(9, 12)$ and $F(21, 18)$

34. $\overline{GH}$ with endpoints $G(-5, -7)$ and $H(4, -11)$

Use the Distance Formula to find the distance, to the nearest hundredth, between each pair of points.

35. $J(3, 10)$ and $K(-2, 4)$

36. $L(-6, 0)$ and $M(8, -7)$

37. Each unit on a map of a forest represents 1 mile. To the nearest tenth of a mile, what is the distance from a ranger station at $(1, 2)$ on the map to a river crossing at $(2, 4)$?

5-6 Direct Variation (pp. 336–341)

EXAMPLE

■ Tell whether $6x = -4y$ represents a direct variation. If so, identify the constant of variation.

$6x = -4y$

$\dfrac{6x}{-4} = \dfrac{-4y}{-4}$ *Solve the equation for y.*

$-\dfrac{6}{4}x = y$

$y = -\dfrac{3}{2}x$ *Simplify.*

This equation represents a direct variation because it can be written in the form $y = kx$, where $k = -\dfrac{3}{2}$.

EXERCISES

Tell whether each equation is a direct variation. If so, identify the constant of variation.

38. $y = -6x$ **39.** $x - y = 0$

40. $y + 4x = 3$ **41.** $2x = -4y$

42. The value of y varies directly with x, and $y = -8$ when $x = 2$. Find y when $x = 3$.

43. Maleka charges $8 per hour for baby-sitting. The amount of money she makes varies directly with the number of hours she baby-sits. Write a direct variation equation for the amount y Maleka earns for baby-sitting x hours. Then graph.

5-7 Slope-Intercept Form (pp. 344–350)

EXAMPLE

■ Graph the line with slope $= -\dfrac{4}{5}$ and y-intercept $= 8$.

Step 1 Plot $(0, 8)$.

Step 2 For a slope of $\dfrac{-4}{5}$, count **4 down** and **5 right** from $(0, 8)$. Plot another point.

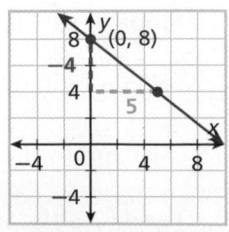

Step 3 Connect the two points with a line.

EXERCISES

Graph each line given the slope and y-intercept.

44. slope $= -\dfrac{1}{2}$; y-intercept $= 4$

45. slope $= 3$; y-intercept $= -7$

Write the equation that describes each line in slope-intercept form.

46. slope $= \dfrac{1}{3}$, y-intercept $= 5$

47. slope $= 4$, $(1, -5)$ is on the line.

5-8 Point-Slope Form (pp. 351–358)

EXAMPLE

■ Write an equation in slope-intercept form for the line through $(4, -1)$ and $(-2, 8)$.

Step 1 Find the slope.

$$m = \frac{y_2 - y_1}{x_2 - x_1} = \frac{8 - (-1)}{-2 - 4} = \frac{9}{-6} = -\frac{3}{2}$$

Step 2 Write the point-slope form.

$$y - 8 = -\frac{3}{2}[x - (-2)] \quad \textit{Substitute into the}$$
$$\textit{point-slope form.}$$

$$y - 8 = -\frac{3}{2}(x + 2)$$

Step 3 Write the slope-intercept form.

$$y = -\frac{3}{2}x + 5 \quad \textit{Solve for y.}$$

EXERCISES

Graph the line described by each equation.

48. $y + 3 = \frac{1}{2}(x - 4)$ **49.** $y - 1 = -(x + 3)$

Write the equation that describes each line in slope-intercept form.

50. slope $= 2$, $(1, 3)$ is on the line.

51. slope $= -5$, $(-6, 4)$ is on the line.

52. $(1, 4)$ and $(3, 8)$ are on the line.

53. $(-2, 4)$ and $(-1, 6)$ are on the line.

5-9 Slopes of Parallel and Perpendicular Lines (pp. 361–367)

EXAMPLE

■ Write an equation in slope-intercept form for the line that passes through $(4, -2)$ and is perpendicular to the line described by $y = -4x + 3$.

The slope of $y = -4x + 3$ is -4.

The perpendicular line has a slope of $\frac{1}{4}$ and contains $(4, -2)$.

$$y + 2 = \frac{1}{4}(x - 4) \quad \textit{Substitute into the}$$
$$\textit{point-slope form.}$$

$$y = \frac{1}{4}x - 3 \quad \textit{Solve for y.}$$

EXERCISES

Identify which lines are parallel.

54. $y = -\frac{1}{3}x$; $y = 3x + 2$; $y = -\frac{1}{3}x - 6$; $y = 3$

55. $y - 2 = -4(x - 1)$; $y = 4x - 4$; $y = \frac{1}{4}x$; $y = -4x - 2$

Identify which lines are perpendicular.

56. $y - 1 = -5(x - 6)$; $y = \frac{1}{5}x + 2$; $y = 5$; $y = 5x + 8$

57. $y = 2x$; $y - 2 = 3(x + 1)$; $y = \frac{2}{3}x - 4$; $y = -\frac{1}{3}x$

58. Write an equation in slope-intercept form for the line that passes through $(1, -1)$ and is parallel to the line described by $y = 2x - 4$.

5-10 Transforming Linear Functions (pp. 369–375)

EXAMPLE

■ Graph $f(x) = \frac{1}{2}x$ and $g(x) = 4x + 2$. Then describe the transformation(s) from the graph of $f(x)$ to the graph of $g(x)$.

- Multiply $f(x) = \frac{1}{2}x$ by 8 to get $h(x) = 4x$. This rotates the graph about $(0, 0)$, making it steeper.

- Then add 2 to $h(x) = 4x$ to get $g(x) = 4x + 2$. This translates the graph 2 units up.

EXERCISES

Graph $f(x)$ and $g(x)$. Then describe the transformation(s) from the graph of $f(x)$ to the graph of $g(x)$.

59. $f(x) = x$, $g(x) = x + 4$

60. $f(x) = 4x$, $g(x) = -4x$

61. $f(x) = \frac{1}{3}x - 2$, $g(x) = -\frac{1}{3}x - 2$

62. The entrance fee at a carnival is $3 and each ride costs $1. The total cost for x rides is $f(x) = x + 3$. How will the graph of this function change if the entrance fee is increased to $5? if the cost per ride is increased to $2?

CHAPTER TEST

Tell whether each function is linear. If so, graph the function.

1. $3y = 2x + 3$

2. $y = x(4 + x)$

3. Lily plans to volunteer at the tutoring center for 45 hours. She can tutor 3 hours per week. The function $f(x) = 45 - 3x$ gives the number of hours she will have left to tutor after x weeks. Graph the function and find its intercepts. What does each intercept represent?

4. The table shows the number of guppies in an aquarium over time. Graph the data and show the rates of change.

Time (mo)	0	1	2	5	8
Guppies	4	4	10	25	31

Find the slope of each line. Then tell what the slope represents.

5.

6.

7.

8. Each unit on a map of a bay represents 1 kilometer. Two buoys are located at $(1, 5)$ and $(3, 6)$ on the map. To the nearest tenth of a kilometer, what is the distance between the two buoys?

9. In orbit around Earth, a space shuttle travels at a speed of about 5 miles per second. Write a direct variation equation for the distance y the space shuttle will travel in x seconds. Then graph.

10. Write the equation $2x - 2y = 4$ in slope-intercept form. Then graph the line described by the equation.

Write the equation that describes each line in slope-intercept form.

11. slope $= -2$, y-intercept $= 7$

12. slope $= 4$, $(-3, 3)$ is on the line.

13. $(1, 5)$ and $(-2, 8)$ are on the line.

14. x-intercept $= 3$, y-intercept $= -3$

Write an equation in point-slope form for the line with the given slope that contains the given point.

15. slope $= -1$; $(1, 3)$

16. slope $= 5$; $(-3, 2)$

17. Write an equation in slope-intercept form for the line that passes through $(0, 6)$ and is parallel to the line described by $y = 2x + 3$.

Graph $f(x)$ and $g(x)$. Then describe the transformation(s) from the graph of $f(x)$ to the graph of $g(x)$.

18. $f(x) = 8x$, $g(x) = 4x$

19. $f(x) = -x + 2$, $g(x) = -x - 1$

20. $f(x) = 3x$, $g(x) = 6x - 1$

COLLEGE ENTRANCE EXAM PRACTICE

FOCUS ON SAT

SAT scores are based on the total number of items answered correctly minus a fraction of the number of multiple-choice questions answered incorrectly. No points are subtracted for questions unanswered.

On the SAT, there is a penalty for incorrect answers on multiple-choice items. Guess only when you can eliminate at least one of the answer choices.

You may want to time yourself as you take this practice test. It should take you about 7 minutes to complete.

---

1. The line through $A(1, -3)$ and $B(-2, d)$ has slope -2. What is the value of d?

   (A) $-\dfrac{3}{2}$

   (B) -1

   (C) $\dfrac{1}{2}$

   (D) 3

   (E) 5

---

2. The ordered pairs $\{(0, -3), (4, -1), (6, 0), (10, 2)\}$ satisfy a pattern. Which is NOT true?

   (A) The pattern is linear.

   (B) The pattern can be described by $2x - 4y = 12$.

   (C) The ordered pairs lie on a line.

   (D) $(-4, 1)$ satisfies the same pattern.

   (E) The set of ordered pairs is a function.

---

3. If y varies directly as x, what is the value of x when $y = 72$?

x	7	12	
y	28	48	72

   (A) 17

   (B) 18

   (C) 24

   (D) 28

   (E) 36

---

4. The line segment between the points $(4, 0)$ and $(2, -2)$ forms one side of a rectangle. Which of the following coordinates could determine another vertex of that rectangle?

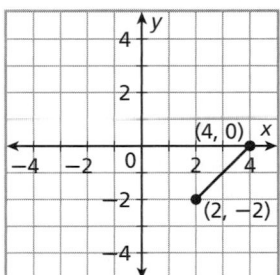

   (A) $(-2, 6)$

   (B) $(-2, -2)$

   (C) $(0, 6)$

   (D) $(1, 2)$

   (E) $(4, 6)$

---

5. Which of the following has the same slope as the line described by $2x - 3y = 3$?

   (A) $3x - 2y = 2$

   (B) $\dfrac{2}{3}x - y = -2$

   (C) $2x - 2y = 3$

   (D) $\dfrac{1}{3}x - 2y = -2$

   (E) $-2x - 3y = 2$

TEST TACKLER

Standardized Test Strategies

Multiple Choice: Recognize Distracters

In multiple-choice items, the options that are incorrect are called *distracters*. This is an appropriate name, because these incorrect options can distract you from the correct answer.

Test writers create distracters by using common student errors. Beware! Even if the answer you get when you work the problem is one of the options, it may not be the correct answer.

EXAMPLE 1

What is the *y*-intercept of $4x + 10 = -2y$?

   (A) 10   (C) -2.5

   (B) 5   (D) -5

Look at each option carefully.

  (A) This is a distracter. The *y*-intercept would be 10 if the function was $4x + 10 = y$. A common error is to ignore the coefficient of *y*.

  (B) This is a distracter. Another common error is to divide by 2 instead of -2 when solving for *y*.

  (C) This is a distracter. One of the most common errors students make is confusing the *x*-intercept and the *y*-intercept. This distracter is actually the *x-intercept* of the given line.

  (D) This is the correct answer.

EXAMPLE 2

What is the equation of a line with a slope of -4 that contains $(2, -3)$?

   (F) $y - 3 = -4(x - 2)$ (H) $y + 3 = -4(x - 2)$

   (G) $y - 2 = -4(x + 3)$ (J) $y + 4 = -3(x - 2)$

Look at each option carefully.

  (F) This is a distracter. Students often make errors with positive and negative signs. You would get this answer if you simplified $y - (-3)$ as $y - 3$.

  (G) This is a distracter. You would get this answer if you switched the *x*-coordinate and the *y*-coordinate.

  (H) This is the correct answer.

  (J) This is a distracter. You would get this answer if you substituted the given values incorrectly in the point-slope equation.

Read each test item and answer the questions that follow.

Item A
A line contains $(1, 2)$ and $(-2, 14)$. What are the slope and y-intercept?

Ⓐ Slope $= -4$; y-intercept $= -2$

Ⓑ Slope $= 4$; y-intercept $= 6$

Ⓒ Slope $= -\frac{1}{4}$; y-intercept $= 1$

Ⓓ Slope $= -4$; y-intercept $= 6$

1. What common error does the slope in choice B represent?

2. The slope given in choice A is correct, but the y-intercept is not. What error was made when finding the y-intercept?

3. What formula can you use to find the slope of a line? How was this formula used incorrectly to get the slope in choice C?

Item B
Which of these functions has a graph that is NOT parallel to the line described by $y = \frac{1}{2}x + 4$?

Ⓕ $y = 6 - \frac{1}{2}x$

Ⓖ $y = \frac{1}{2}x + 6$

Ⓗ $-2y = -x + 1$

Ⓙ $2y = x$

4. When given two linear functions, describe how to determine whether their graphs are parallel.

5. Which is the correct answer? Describe the errors a student might make to get each of the distracters.

Item C
Which of these lines has a slope of -3?

Ⓐ   Ⓒ

Ⓑ   Ⓓ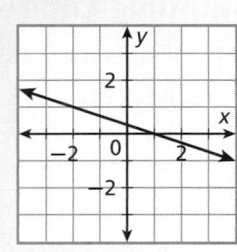

6. Which two answer choices can be eliminated immediately? Why?

7. Describe how to find the slope of a line from its graph.

8. What common error does choice A represent?

9. What common error does choice D represent?

10. Which is the correct answer?

Item D
Which is NOT a linear function?

Ⓕ $f(x) = 4 + x$

Ⓖ $f(x) = -x - 4$

Ⓗ $f(x) = 4x^2$

Ⓙ $f(x) = \frac{1}{4}x$

11. When given a function rule, how can you tell if the function is linear?

12. What part of the function given in choice G might make someone think it is not linear?

13. What part of the function given in choice J might make someone think it is not linear?

14. What part of the function given in choice H makes it NOT linear?

CHAPTER
5

STANDARDIZED
TEST PREP

go.hrw.com
State Test Practice Online
KEYWORD: MA7 TestPrep

CUMULATIVE ASSESSMENT, CHAPTERS 1–5

Multiple Choice

1. What is the value of $2 - \left[1 - (2 - 1)\right]$?

 (A) −2

 (B) 0

 (C) 2

 (D) 4

2. Frank borrowed $5000 with an annual simple interest rate. The amount of interest he owed after 6 months was $300. What is the interest rate of the loan?

 (F) 1%

 (G) 6%

 (H) 10%

 (J) 12%

3. Patty's Pizza charges $5.50 for a large pizza plus $0.30 for each topping. Pizza Town charges $5.00 for a large pizza plus $0.40 for each topping. Which inequality can you use to find the number of toppings x so that the cost of a pizza at Pizza Town is greater than the cost of a pizza at Patty's Pizza?

 (A) $(5 + 0.4)x > (5.5 + 0.3)x$

 (B) $5.5x + 0.3 > 5x + 0.4$

 (C) $5.5 + 0.3x > 5 + 0.4x$

 (D) $5 + 0.4x > 5.5 + 0.3x$

4. The side length of a square s can be determined by the formula $s = \sqrt{A}$ where A represents the area of the square. What is the side length of a square with area 0.09 square meter?

 (F) 0.0081 meters

 (G) 0.81 meters

 (H) 0.03 meters

 (J) 0.3 meters

5. What is the value of $f(x) = -3 - x$ when $x = -7$?

 (A) −10

 (B) −4

 (C) 4

 (D) 10

6. Which relationship is a direct variation?

 (F)

x	1	2	3	4
y	−1	0	1	2

 (G)

x	1	2	3	4
y	0	−1	−2	−3

 (H)

x	1	2	3	4
y	3	5	7	9

 (J)

x	1	2	3	4
y	3	6	9	12

7. Which function has x-intercept −2 and y-intercept 4?

 (A) $2x - y = 4$

 (B) $2y - x = 4$

 (C) $y - 2x = 4$

 (D) $x - 2y = 4$

8. Which equation describes the relationship between x and y in the table below?

x	−8	−4	0	4	8
y	2	1	0	−1	−2

 (F) $y = -4x$ (H) $y = 4x$

 (G) $y = -\dfrac{1}{4}x$ (J) $y = \dfrac{1}{4}x$

9. Which graph is described by $x - 3y = -3$?

 (A)   (C)

 (B)   (D)

10. Which steps could you use to graph the line that has slope 2 and contains the point $(-1, 3)$?

(F) Plot $(-1, 3)$. Move 1 unit up and 2 units right and plot another point.

(G) Plot $(-1, 3)$. Move 2 units up and 1 unit right and plot another point.

(H) Plot $(-1, 3)$. Move 1 unit up and 2 units left and plot another point.

(J) Plot $(-1, 3)$. Move 2 units up and 1 unit left and plot another point.

11. Which line is parallel to the line described by $2x + 3y = 6$?

(A) $3x + 2y = 6$ (C) $2x + 3y = -6$

(B) $3x - 2y = -6$ (D) $2x - 3y = 6$

12. Which function's graph is NOT perpendicular to the line described by $4x - y = -2$?

(F) $y + \frac{1}{4}x = 0$ (H) $3y = \frac{3}{4}x + 3$

(G) $\frac{1}{2}x = 10 - 2y$ (J) $y = -\frac{1}{4}x + \frac{3}{2}$

13. Company A charges $30 plus $0.40 per mile for a car rental. The total charge for m miles is given by $f(m) = 30 + 0.4m$. For a similar car, company B charges $30 plus $0.30 per mile. The total charge for m miles is given by $g(m) = 30 + 0.3m$. Which best describes the transformation from the graph of $f(m)$ to the graph of $g(m)$?

(A) Translation up

(B) Translation down

(C) Rotation

(D) Reflection

Gridded Response

14. What is the value of x in the diagram below?

$$\triangle ABC \sim \triangle DEF$$

15. What is the 46th term in the arithmetic sequence $-1.5, -1.3, -1.1, -0.9, \ldots$?

16. What is the y-intercept of $y - 2 = 3(x + 4)$?

Short Response

17. A video store charges a $10 membership fee plus $2 for each movie rental. The total cost for x movie rentals is given by $f(x) = 2x + 10$.

a. Graph this function.

b. Give a reasonable domain and range.

18. The table below shows the federal minimum wage in different years.

Year	1960	1970	1980	1990	2000
Minimum Wage ($)	1.00	1.60	3.10	3.80	5.15

a. Find the rate of change for each ten-year time period. Show your work.

b. During which time period did the minimum wage increase the fastest? Explain what the rate of change for this time period means.

19. a. Find the slope of the line below.

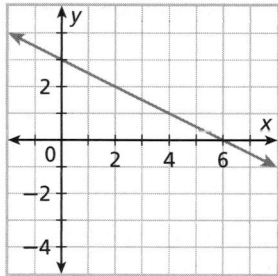

b. Write an equation in slope-intercept form for a line that is perpendicular to the line in part **a** and has the same y-intercept as the function in part **a**. Show your work and explain how you found your answer.

Extended Response

20. The relationship between the wind speed at a given temperature and the apparent temperature is approximately linear. The table shows the apparent temperature at various wind speeds when the actual temperature is t °F.

Wind Speed (mi/h)	5	10	15
Apparent Temperature (°F)	36	34	32

a. Write an equation in slope-intercept form that describes the data in the table. Explain how you found your answer.

b. What does the slope mean in this situation?

c. What is the actual temperature t? Explain.

d. Determine the apparent temperature when the wind speed is 12 miles per hour. Show your work.

Systems of Equations and Inequalities

Chapter

- Solve real-world problems involving systems of linear equations and inequalities.

Where's *the* Money?

You can solve a system of equations to determine how many basketball game tickets you can buy at different price levels.

go.hrw.com
Chapter Project Online
KEYWORD: MA7 ChProj

ARE YOU READY?

✓ Vocabulary

Match each term on the left with a definition on the right.

1. inequality
2. linear equation
3. ordered pair
4. slope
5. solution of an equation

A. a pair of numbers (x, y) that represent the coordinates of a point

B. a statement that two quantities are not equal

C. the y-value of the point at which the graph of an equation crosses the y-axis

D. a value of the variable that makes the equation true

E. the ratio of the vertical change to the horizontal change for a nonvertical line

F. an equation whose graph is a straight line

✓ Graph Linear Functions

Graph each function.

6. $y = \frac{3}{4}x + 1$

7. $y = -3x + 5$

8. $y = x - 6$

9. $x + y = 4$

10. $y = -\frac{2}{3}x + 4$

11. $y = -5$

✓ Solve Multi-Step Equations

Solve each equation.

12. $-7x - 18 = 3$

13. $12 = -3n + 6$

14. $\frac{1}{2}d + 30 = 32$

15. $-2p + 9 = -3$

16. $33 = 5y + 8$

17. $-3 + 3x = 27$

✓ Solve for a Variable

Solve each equation for y.

18. $7x + y = 4$

19. $y + 2 = -4x$

20. $8 = x - y$

21. $x + 2 = y - 5$

22. $2y - 3 = 12x$

23. $y + \frac{3}{4}x = 4$

✓ Evaluate Expressions

Evaluate each expression for the given value of the variable.

24. $t - 5$ for $t = 7$

25. $9 - 2a$ for $a = 4$

26. $\frac{1}{2}x - 2$ for $x = 14$

27. $n + 15$ for $n = 37$

28. $9c + 4$ for $c = \frac{1}{3}$

29. $16 + 3d$ for $d = 5$

✓ Solve and Graph Inequalities

Solve and graph each inequality.

30. $b - 9 \geq 1$

31. $-2x < 10$

32. $3y \leq -3$

33. $\frac{1}{3}y \leq 5$

Where You've Been

Previously, you

- solved one-step and multi-step equations.
- solved one-step and multi-step inequalities.
- graphed linear equations on a coordinate plane.

In This Chapter

You will study

- how to find a solution that satisfies two linear equations.
- how to find solutions that satisfy two linear inequalities.
- how to graph one or more linear inequalities on a coordinate plane.

Where You're Going

You can use the skills in this chapter

- to determine which purchases are better deals.
- in other classes, such as Economics and Chemistry.
- to solve linear equations that involve three or more variables in future math classes.

Key Vocabulary/Vocabulario

consistent system	sistema consistente
dependent system	sistema dependiente
inconsistent system	sistema inconsistente
independent system	sistema independiente
linear inequality	desigualdad lineal
solution of a linear inequality	solución de una desigualdad lineal
system of linear equations	sistema de ecuaciones lineales

Vocabulary Connections

To become familiar with some of the vocabulary terms in the chapter, consider the following. You may refer to the chapter, the glossary, or a dictionary if you like.

1. The word *system* means "a group." How do you think a **system of linear equations** is different from a linear equation?

2. A **consistent system** has *at least one* solution. How many solutions do you think an **inconsistent system** has?

3. A **dependent system** has infinitely many solutions. Which vocabulary term above means a system with *exactly one* solution?

4. In Chapter 5, you saw that a solution of a linear equation was an ordered pair that made the equation true. Modify this to define **solution of a linear inequality**.

Writing Strategy: Write a Convincing Argument/Explanation

The Write About It icon appears throughout the book. These icons identify questions that require you to write a complete argument or explanation. Writing a convincing argument or explanation shows that you have a solid understanding of a concept.

To be effective, an argument or explanation should include

- evidence, work, or facts.
- a complete response that will answer or explain.

From Lesson 2-10

23. Write About It Lewis invested $1000 at 3% simple interest for 4 years. Lisa invested $1000 at 4% simple interest for 3 years. Explain why Lewis and Lisa earned the same amount of interest.

Step 1 Identify what you need to answer or explain.
Explain why Lewis and Lisa earned the same amount of interest.

Step 2 Give evidence, work, or facts that are needed to answer the question.
Use the formula for simple interest to find the amount of interest earned: $I = Prt$.

Lewis: $P = 1000$, $r = 0.03$, $t = 4$ **Lisa:** $P = 1000$, $r = 0.04$, $t = 3$

$$I = Prt = 1000(0.03)(4) = 120$$ $$I = Prt = 1000(0.04)(3) = 120$$

$$I = 1000(0.12) = \$120$$ $$I = 1000(0.12) = \$120$$

Step 3 Write a complete response that answers or explains.
Lewis and Lisa both invested the same amount of money, $1000. They earned the same amount of interest because 0.04×3 and 0.03×4 both equal 0.12. They both earned $0.12 \times \$1000$, or $120.

Try This

Write a convincing argument or explanation.

1. What is the least whole number that is a solution of $12x + 15.4 > 118.92$? Explain.

2. Which equation has an error? Explain the error.

    A. $4(6 \cdot 5) = (4)6 \cdot (4)5$ **B.** $4(6 \cdot 5) = (4 \cdot 6)5$

6-1 Technology LAB

Solve Linear Equations by Using a Spreadsheet

You can use a spreadsheet to answer "What if...?" questions. By changing one or more values, you can quickly model different scenarios.

Use with Lesson 6-1

go.hrw.com
Lab Resources Online
KEYWORD: MA7 Lab6

Activity

Company Z makes DVD players. The company's costs are $400 per week plus $20 per DVD player. Each DVD player sells for $45. How many DVD players must company Z sell in one week to make a profit?

Let n represent the number of DVD players company Z sells in one week.

$c = 400 + 20n$ *The total cost is $400 plus $20 times the number of DVD players made.*

$s = 45n$ *The total sales income is $45 times the number of DVD players sold.*

$p = s - c$ *The total profit is the sales income minus the total cost.*

1 Set up your spreadsheet with columns for number of DVD players, total cost, total income, and profit.

2 Under Number of DVD Players, enter 1 in cell A2.

3 Use the equations above to enter the formulas for total cost, total sales, and total profit in row 2.

• In cell B2, enter the formula for total cost.

• In cell C2, enter the formula for total sales income.

• In cell D2, enter the formula for total profit.

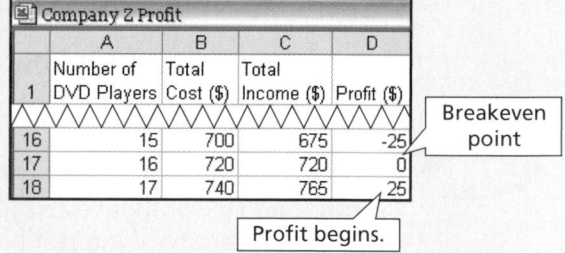

Company Z Profit

	A	B	C	D
1	Number of DVD Players	Total Cost ($)	Total Income ($)	Profit ($)
2	1	420	45	-375

= 400 + 20*A2   = 45*A2   = C2 – B2

4 Fill columns A, B, C, and D by selecting cells A1 through D1, clicking the small box at the bottom right corner of cell D2, and dragging the box down through several rows.

Company Z Profit

	A	B	C	D
1	Number of DVD Players	Total Cost ($)	Total Income ($)	Profit ($)
16	15	700	675	-25
17	16	720	720	0
18	17	740	765	25

Breakeven point

Profit begins.

5 Find the point where the profit is $0. This is known as the breakeven point, where total cost and total income are the same.

Company Z must sell 17 DVD players to make a profit. The profit is $25.

Try This

For Exercises 1 and 2, use the spreadsheet from the activity.

1. If company Z sells 10 DVD players, will they make a profit? Explain. What if they sell 16?

2. Company Z makes a profit of $225 dollars. How many DVD players did they sell?

For Exercise 3, make a spreadsheet.

3. Company Y's costs are $400 per week plus $20 per DVD player. They want the breakeven point to occur with sales of 8 DVD players. What should the sales price be?

<table>
<tr><td>6-1</td></tr>
</table>

Solving Systems by Graphing

Objectives
Identify solutions of systems of linear equations in two variables.

Solve systems of linear equations in two variables by graphing.

Vocabulary
system of linear equations
solution of a system of linear equations

Why learn this?
You can compare costs by graphing a system of linear equations. (See Example 3.)

Sometimes there are different charges for the same service or product at different places. For example, Bowl-o-Rama charges $2.50 per game plus $2 for shoe rental while Bowling Pinz charges $2 per game plus $4 for shoe rental. A *system of linear equations* can be used to compare these charges.

A **system of linear equations** is a set of two or more linear equations containing two or more variables. A **solution of a system of linear equations** with two variables is an ordered pair that satisfies each equation in the system. So, if an ordered pair is a solution, it will make both equations true.

EXAMPLE 1 **Identifying Solutions of Systems**

Tell whether the ordered pair is a solution of the given system.

A $(4, 1); \begin{cases} x + 2y = 6 \\ x - y = 3 \end{cases}$

$x + 2y = 6$	
$4 + 2(1)$	6
$4 + 2$	6
	6 ∣ 6 ✓

$x - y = 3$	
$4 - 1$	3
	3 ∣ 3 ✓

Substitute 4 for x and 1 for y in each equation in the system.

The ordered pair $(4, 1)$ makes both equations true.

$(4, 1)$ is a solution of the system.

Helpful Hint
If an ordered pair does not satisfy the first equation in the system, there is no need to check the other equations.

B $(-1, 2); \begin{cases} 2x + 5y = 8 \\ 3x - 2y = 5 \end{cases}$

$2x + 5y = 8$	
$2(-1) + 5(2)$	8
$-2 + 10$	8
	8 ∣ 8 ✓

$3x - 2y = 5$	
$3(-1) - 2(2)$	5
$-3 - 4$	5
	-7 ∣ 5 ✗

Substitute −1 for x and 2 for y in each equation in the system.

The ordered pair $(-1, 2)$ makes one equation true, but not the other.

$(-1, 2)$ is not a solution of the system.

 CHECK IT OUT! Tell whether the ordered pair is a solution of the given system.

1a. $(1, 3); \begin{cases} 2x + y = 5 \\ -2x + y = 1 \end{cases}$

1b. $(2, -1); \begin{cases} x - 2y = 4 \\ 3x + y = 6 \end{cases}$

All solutions of a linear equation are on its graph. To find a solution of a system of linear equations, you need a point that each line has in common. In other words, you need their point of intersection.

$$\begin{cases} y = 2x - 1 \\ y = -x + 5 \end{cases}$$

The point $(2, 3)$ is where the two lines intersect and is a solution of both equations, so $(2, 3)$ is the solution of the system.

EXAMPLE 2 Solving a System of Linear Equations by Graphing

Solve each system by graphing. Check your answer.

A $\begin{cases} y = x - 3 \\ y = -x - 1 \end{cases}$

Graph the system.

The solution appears to be at $(1, -2)$.

Check
Substitute $(1, -2)$ into the system.

$y = x - 3$	
-2	$1 - 3$
-2	-2 ✓

$y = -x - 1$	
-2	$-1 - 1$
-2	-2 ✓

The solution is $(1, -2)$.

B $\begin{cases} x + y = 0 \\ y = -\dfrac{1}{2}x + 1 \end{cases}$

$$\begin{array}{r} x + y = 0 \\ \underline{-x \qquad -x} \\ y = -x \end{array}$$

Rewrite the first equation in slope-intercept form.

Graph using a calculator and then use the intersection command.

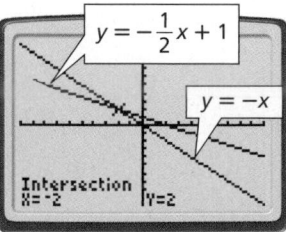

Check Substitute $(-2, 2)$ into the system.

$x + y = 0$	
$-2 + 2$	0
	0 0 ✓

$y = -\dfrac{1}{2}x + 1$	
2	$-\dfrac{1}{2}(-2) + 1$
2	$1 + 1$
2	2 ✓

The solution is $(-2, 2)$.

 Solve each system by graphing. Check your answer.

2a. $\begin{cases} y = -2x - 1 \\ y = x + 5 \end{cases}$

2b. $\begin{cases} y = \dfrac{1}{3}x - 3 \\ 2x + y = 4 \end{cases}$

EXAMPLE 3 *Problem-Solving Application*

Bowl-o-Rama charges $2.50 per game plus $2 for shoe rental, and Bowling Pinz charges $2 per game plus $4 for shoe rental. For how many games will the cost to bowl be the same at both places? What is that cost?

1. **Understand the Problem**

The **answer** will be the number of games played for which the total cost is the same at both bowling alleys. **List the important information:**
- Game price: Bowl-o-Rama $2.50   Bowling Pinz: $2
- Shoe-rental fee: Bowl-o-Rama $2   Bowling Pinz: $4

2 **Make a Plan**

Write a system of equations, one equation to represent the price at each company. Let x be the number of games played and y be the total cost.

	Total cost	is	price per game	times	games	plus	shoe rental.
Bowl-o-Rama	y	$=$	2.5	$\cdot$	x	$+$	2
Bowling Pinz	y	$=$	2	$\cdot$	x	$+$	4

3 **Solve**

Graph $y = 2.5x + 2$ and $y = 2x + 4$. The lines appear to intersect at $(4, 12)$. So, the cost at both places will be the same for 4 games bowled and that cost will be $12.

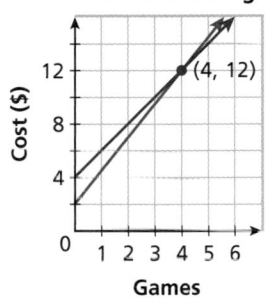

Cost of Bowling

4 **Look Back**

Check $(4, 12)$ using both equations.
Cost of bowling 4 games at Bowl-o-Rama:
$2.5(4) + \$2 = 10 + 2 = 12$ ✓
Cost of bowling 4 games at Bowling Pinz:
$2(4) + \$4 = 8 + 4 = 12$ ✓

CHECK IT OUT!

3. Video club A charges $10 for membership and $3 per movie rental. Video club B charges $15 for membership and $2 per movie rental. For how many movie rentals will the cost be the same at both video clubs? What is that cost?

THINK AND DISCUSS

1. Explain how to use a graph to solve a system of linear equations.

2. Explain how to check a solution of a system of linear equations.

3. **GET ORGANIZED** Copy and complete the graphic organizer. In each box, write a step for solving a linear system by graphing. More boxes may be added.

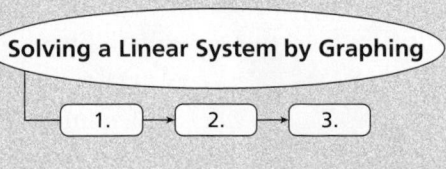

Solving a Linear System by Graphing

1. → 2. → 3.

go.hrw.com
Homework Help Online
KEYWORD: MA7 6-1
Parent Resources Online
KEYWORD: MA7 Parent

GUIDED PRACTICE

1. **Vocabulary** Describe a *solution of a system of linear equations*.

SEE EXAMPLE 1
p. 397

Tell whether the ordered pair is a solution of the given system.

2. $(2, -2)$; $\begin{cases} 3x + y = 4 \\ x - 3y = -4 \end{cases}$ 3. $(3, -1)$; $\begin{cases} x - 2y = 5 \\ 2x - y = 7 \end{cases}$ 4. $(-1, 5)$; $\begin{cases} -x + y = 6 \\ 2x + 3y = 13 \end{cases}$

SEE EXAMPLE 2
p. 398

Solve each system by graphing. Check your answer.

5. $\begin{cases} y = \frac{1}{2}x \\ y = -x + 3 \end{cases}$ 6. $\begin{cases} y = x - 2 \\ 2x + y = 1 \end{cases}$ 7. $\begin{cases} -2x - 1 = y \\ x + y = 3 \end{cases}$

SEE EXAMPLE 3
p. 399

8. To deliver mulch, Lawn and Garden charges $30 per cubic yard of mulch plus a $30 delivery fee. Yard Depot charges $25 per cubic yard of mulch plus a $55 delivery fee. For how many cubic yards will the cost be the same? What will that cost be?

PRACTICE AND PROBLEM SOLVING

Independent Practice

For Exercises	See Example
9–11	1
12–15	2
16	3

Tell whether the ordered pair is a solution of the given system.

9. $(1, -4)$; $\begin{cases} x - 2y = 8 \\ 4x - y = 8 \end{cases}$ 10. $(-2, 1)$; $\begin{cases} 2x - 3y = -7 \\ 3x + y = -5 \end{cases}$ 11. $(5, 2)$; $\begin{cases} 2x + y = 12 \\ -3y - x = -11 \end{cases}$

Solve each system by graphing. Check your answer.

Extra Practice
Skills Practice p. S14
Application Practice p. S33

12. $\begin{cases} y = \frac{1}{2}x + 2 \\ y = -x - 1 \end{cases}$ 13. $\begin{cases} y = x \\ y = -x + 6 \end{cases}$ 14. $\begin{cases} -2x - 1 = y \\ x = -y + 3 \end{cases}$ 15. $\begin{cases} x + y = 2 \\ y = x - 4 \end{cases}$

16. **Multi-Step** Angelo runs 7 miles per week and increases his distance by 1 mile each week. Marc runs 4 miles per week and increases his distance by 2 miles each week. In how many weeks will Angelo and Marc be running the same distance? What will that distance be?

17. **School** The school band sells carnations on Valentine's Day for $2 each. They buy the carnations from a florist for $0.50 each, plus a $16 delivery charge.

   a. Write a system of equations to describe the situation.

   b. Graph the system. What does the solution represent?

   c. Explain whether the solution shown on the graph makes sense in this situation. If not, give a reasonable solution.

MULTI-STEP TEST PREP

18. This problem will prepare you for the Multi-Step Test Prep on page 426.

   a. The Warrior baseball team is selling hats as a fund-raiser. They contacted two companies. Hats Off charges a $50 design fee and $5 per hat. Top Stuff charges a $25 design fee and $6 per hat. Write an equation for each company's pricing.

   b. Graph the system of equations from part **a**. For how many hats will the cost be the same? What is that cost?

   c. Explain when it is cheaper for the baseball team to use Top Stuff and when it is cheaper to use Hats Off.

Graphing Calculator Use a graphing calculator to graph and solve the systems of equations in Exercises 19–22. Round your answer to the nearest tenth.

19. $\begin{cases} y = 4.7x + 2.1 \\ y = 1.6x - 5.4 \end{cases}$

20. $\begin{cases} 4.8x + 0.6y = 4 \\ y = -3.2x + 2.7 \end{cases}$

21. $\begin{cases} y = \dfrac{5}{4}x - \dfrac{2}{3} \\ \dfrac{8}{3}x + y = \dfrac{5}{9} \end{cases}$

22. $\begin{cases} y = 6.9x + 12.4 \\ y = -4.1x - 5.3 \end{cases}$

Landscaping

 23. Landscaping The gardeners at Middleton Place Gardens want to plant a total of 45 white and pink hydrangeas in one flower bed. In another flower bed, they want to plant 120 hydrangeas. In this bed, they want 2 times the number of white hydrangeas and 3 times the number of pink hydrangeas as in the first bed. Use a system of equations to find how many white and how many pink hydrangeas the gardeners should buy altogether.

24. Fitness Rusty burns 5 Calories per minute swimming and 11 Calories per minute jogging. In the morning, Rusty burns 200 Calories walking and swims for x minutes. In the afternoon, Rusty will jog for x minutes. How many minutes must he jog to burn at least as many Calories y in the afternoon as he did in the morning? Round your answer up to the next whole number of minutes.

Middleton Place Gardens, South Carolina, are the United States' oldest landscaped gardens. The gardens were established in 1741 and opened to the public in the 1920s.

25. A tree that is 2 feet tall is growing at a rate of 1 foot per year. A 6-foot tall tree is growing at a rate of 0.5 foot per year. In how many years will the trees be the same height?

26. Critical Thinking Write a real-world situation that could be represented by the system $\begin{cases} y = 3x + 10 \\ y = 5x + 20 \end{cases}$.

 27. Write About It When you graph a system of linear equations, why does the intersection of the two lines represent the solution of the system?

 TEST PREP

28. Taxi company A charges \$4 plus \$0.50 per mile. Taxi company B charges \$5 plus \$0.25 per mile. Which system best represents this problem?

Ⓐ $\begin{cases} y = 4x + 0.5 \\ y = 5x + 0.25 \end{cases}$

Ⓒ $\begin{cases} y = -4x + 0.5 \\ y = -5x + 0.25 \end{cases}$

Ⓑ $\begin{cases} y = 0.5x + 4 \\ y = 0.25x + 5 \end{cases}$

Ⓓ $\begin{cases} y = -0.5x + 4 \\ y = -0.25x + 5 \end{cases}$

29. Which system of equations represents the given graph?

Ⓕ $\begin{cases} y = 2x - 1 \\ y = \dfrac{1}{3}x + 3 \end{cases}$

Ⓗ $\begin{cases} y = 2x + 1 \\ y = \dfrac{1}{3}x - 3 \end{cases}$

Ⓖ $\begin{cases} y = -2x + 1 \\ y = 2x - 3 \end{cases}$

Ⓙ $\begin{cases} y = -2x - 1 \\ y = 3x - 3 \end{cases}$

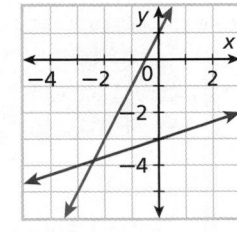

30. Gridded Response Which value of b will make the system $y = 2x + 2$ and $y = 2.5x + b$ intersect at the point $(2, 6)$?

CHALLENGE AND EXTEND

31. Entertainment If the pattern in the table continues, in what month will the number of sales of VCRs and DVD players be the same? What will that number be?

Total Number Sold				
Month	1	2	3	4
VCRs	500	490	480	470
DVD Players	250	265	280	295

32. Long Distance Inc. charges a $1.45 connection charge and $0.03 per minute. Far Away Calls charges a $1.52 connection charge and $0.02 per minute.

  a. For how many minutes will a call cost the same from both companies? What is that cost?

  b. When is it better to call using Long Distance Inc.? Far Away Calls? Explain.

  c. What if...? Long Distance Inc. raised its connection charge to $1.50 and Far Away Calls decreased its connection charge by 2 cents. How will this affect the graphs? Now which company is better to use for calling long distance? Why?

SPIRAL REVIEW

Solve each equation. *(Lesson 2-2)*

33. $18 = \frac{3}{7}x$

34. $-\frac{x}{5} = 12$

35. $-6y = -13.2$

36. $\frac{2}{5} = \frac{y}{12}$

Describe the solutions of each inequality in words. *(Lesson 3-1)*

37. $3c < 15$

38. $\frac{1}{3}x \geq 9$

39. $5 + a > 11$

Solve each inequality and graph the solutions. *(Lesson 3-4)*

40. $4(2x + 1) > 28$

41. $3^3 + 9 \leq -4c$

42. $\frac{1}{8}x + \frac{3}{5} \leq \frac{3}{8}$

Career Path

Ethan Reynolds
Applied Sciences major

go.hrw.com
Career Resources Online
KEYWORD: MA7 Career

Q: What math classes did you take in high school?
A: Career Math, Algebra, and Geometry

Q: What are you studying and what math classes have you taken?
A: I am really interested in aviation. I am taking Statistics and Trigonometry. Next year I will take Calculus.

Q: How is math used in aviation?
A: I use math to interpret aeronautical charts. I also perform calculations involving wind movements, aircraft weight and balance, and fuel consumption. These skills are necessary for planning and executing safe air flights.

Q: What are your future plans?
A: I could work as a commercial or corporate pilot or even as a flight instructor. I could also work toward a bachelor's degree in aviation management, air traffic control, aviation electronics, aviation maintenance, or aviation computer science.

6-2 Algebra LAB

Model Systems of Linear Equations

You can use algebra tiles to model and solve some systems of linear equations.

Use with Lesson 6-2

KEY

 $= 1$

 $= -1$

$= x$ $= -x$

REMEMBER
When two expressions are equal, you can substitute one for the other in any expression or equation.

Activity

Use algebra tiles to model and solve $\begin{cases} y = 2x - 3 \\ x + y = 9 \end{cases}$.

MODEL		ALGEBRA
	The first equation is solved for y. Model the second equation, x + y = 9, by substituting 2x − 3 for y.	$\begin{aligned} x + y &= 9 \\ x + (2x - 3) &= 9 \\ 3x - 3 &= 9 \end{aligned}$
	Add 3 yellow tiles on both sides of the mat. This represents adding 3 to both sides of the equation. Remove zero pairs.	$\begin{aligned} 3x - 3 &= 9 \\ +3 & +3 \\ \hline 3x &= 12 \end{aligned}$
	Divide each side into 3 equal groups. Align one x-tile with each group on the right side. One x-tile is equivalent to 4 yellow tiles. x = 4	$\dfrac{3x}{3} = \dfrac{12}{3}$ $x = 4$

To solve for *y*, substitute 4 for *x* in one of the equations:

$\begin{aligned} y &= 2x - 3 \\ &= 2(4) - 3 \\ &= 5 \end{aligned}$

The solution is (4, 5).

Try This

Model and solve each system of equations.

1. $\begin{cases} y = x + 3 \\ 2x + y = 6 \end{cases}$

2. $\begin{cases} 2x + 3 = y \\ x + y = 6 \end{cases}$

3. $\begin{cases} 2x + 3y = 1 \\ x = -1 - y \end{cases}$

4. $\begin{cases} y = x + 1 \\ 2x - y = -5 \end{cases}$

Solving Systems by Substitution

CAMPING OUT FOR THE BEST TICKETS ISN'T WHAT IT USED TO BE...

Off the Mark by Mark Parisi. Cartoon copyrighted by Mark Parisi, printed with permission.

Objective
Solve systems of linear equations in two variables by substitution.

Why learn this?
You can solve systems of equations to help select the best value among high-speed Internet providers. (See Example 3.)

Sometimes it is difficult to identify the exact solution to a system by graphing. In this case, you can use a method called *substitution*.

The goal when using substitution is to reduce the system to one equation that has only one variable. Then you can solve this equation by the methods taught in Chapter 2.

Know it! Note

Solving Systems of Equations by Substitution
Step 1 Solve for one variable in at least one equation, if necessary.
Step 2 Substitute the resulting expression into the other equation.
Step 3 Solve that equation to get the value of the first variable.
Step 4 Substitute that value into one of the original equations and solve.
Step 5 Write the values from Steps 3 and 4 as an ordered pair, (x, y), and check.

EXAMPLE 1 Solving a System of Linear Equations by Substitution

Solve each system by substitution.

A $\begin{cases} y = 2x \\ y = x + 5 \end{cases}$

Step 1 $y = 2x$ *Both equations are solved for y.*
$ y = x + 5$

Step 2 $ y = x + 5$ *Substitute 2x for y in the second equation.*
$ 2x = x + 5$

Step 3 $\dfrac{-x -x}{x = 5}$ *Solve for x.*

Step 4 $y = 2x$ *Write one of the original equations.*
$ y = 2(5)$ *Substitute 5 for x.*
$ y = \mathbf{10}$

Step 5 $(5, 10)$ *Write the solution as an ordered pair.*

Check   Substitute $(5, 10)$ into both equations in the system.

$y = 2x$	
10	$2(5)$
10	10 ✓

$y = x + 5$	
10	$5 + 5$
10	10 ✓

Helpful Hint
You can substitute the value of one variable into *either* of the original equations to find the value of the other variable.

Solve each system by substitution.

 $\begin{cases} 2x + y = 5 \\ y = x - 4 \end{cases}$

Step 1 $y = x - 4$ *The second equation is solved for y.*

Step 2 $2x + y = 5$
$2x + (x - 4) = 5$ *Substitute x − 4 for y in the first equation.*

Step 3 $3x - 4 = 5$ *Simplify. Then solve for x.*
$$\underline{+4 \quad +4}$$ *Add 4 to both sides.*
$$3x \quad = \quad 9$$
$$\frac{3x}{3} = \frac{9}{3}$$ *Divide both sides by 3.*
$$x = 3$$

Step 4 $y = x - 4$ *Write one of the original equations.*
$y = 3 - 4$ *Substitute 3 for x.*
$y = -1$

Step 5 $(3, -1)$ *Write the solution as an ordered pair.*

C $\begin{cases} x + 4y = 6 \\ x + y = 3 \end{cases}$

Step 1 $x + 4y = 6$ *Solve the first equation for x by subtracting*
$$\underline{-4y \quad -4y}$$ *4y from both sides.*
$$x \quad = \quad 6 - 4y$$

Step 2 $x + y = 3$
$(6 - 4y) + y = 3$ *Substitute 6 − 4y for x in the second equation.*

Step 3 $6 - 3y = 3$ *Simplify. Then solve for y.*
$$\underline{-6 \qquad -6}$$ *Subtract 6 from both sides.*
$$-3y = -3$$
$$\frac{-3y}{-3} = \frac{-3}{-3}$$ *Divide both sides by −3.*
$$y = 1$$

Step 4 $x + y = 3$ *Write one of the original equations.*
$x + 1 = 3$ *Substitute 1 for y.*
$$\underline{-1 \quad -1}$$ *Subtract 1 from both sides.*
$$x \quad = \quad 2$$

Step 5 $(2, 1)$ *Write the solution as an ordered pair.*

Helpful Hint

Sometimes neither equation is solved for a variable. You can begin by solving either equation for either *x* or *y*.

 Solve each system by substitution.

1a. $\begin{cases} y = x + 3 \\ y = 2x + 5 \end{cases}$ **1b.** $\begin{cases} x = 2y - 4 \\ x + 8y = 16 \end{cases}$ **1c.** $\begin{cases} 2x + y = -4 \\ x + y = -7 \end{cases}$

Sometimes you substitute an expression for a variable that has a coefficient. When solving for the second variable in this situation, you can use the Distributive Property.

EXAMPLE 2 **Using the Distributive Property**

Solve $\begin{cases} 4y - 5x = 9 \\ x - 4y = 11 \end{cases}$ by substitution.

Step 1 $\quad x - 4y = \quad 11$

$\qquad\qquad \underline{+ 4y \quad + 4y}$

$\qquad\qquad x \quad = \quad 4y + 11$

Solve the second equation for x by adding 4y to each side.

Step 2 $\qquad\qquad 4y - 5x = 9$

$\qquad\qquad 4y - 5(4y + 11) = 9$

Substitute 4y + 11 for x in the first equation.

Step 3 $\quad 4y - 5(4y) - 5(11) = 9$

$\qquad\qquad 4y - 20y - 55 = 9$

$\qquad\qquad\quad -16y - 55 = \quad 9$

$\qquad\qquad\qquad\quad \underline{+ 55 \quad + 55}$

$\qquad\qquad\qquad -16y \quad = \quad 64$

$\qquad\qquad\qquad \dfrac{-16y}{-16} = \dfrac{64}{-16}$

$\qquad\qquad\qquad\qquad y = -4$

Distribute −5 to the expression in parentheses. Simplify. Solve for y.

Add 55 to both sides.

Divide both sides by −16.

Step 4 $\qquad x - 4y = 11$

$\qquad\qquad x - 4(-4) = 11$

$\qquad\qquad\quad x + 16 = \quad 11$

$\qquad\qquad\qquad \underline{- 16 \quad - 16}$

$\qquad\qquad\quad x \qquad = \quad -5$

Write one of the original equations.

Substitute −4 for y.

Simplify.

Subtract 16 from both sides.

Step 5 $(-5, -4)$

Write the solution as an ordered pair.

> **Caution!**
>
> When you solve one equation for a variable, you must substitute the value or expression into the *other* original equation, not the one that has just been solved.

 CHECK IT OUT! **2.** Solve $\begin{cases} -2x + y = 8 \\ 3x + 2y = 9 \end{cases}$ by substitution.

Student to Student

Solving Systems by Substitution

Erika Chu
Terrell High School

I always look for a variable with a coefficient of 1 or −1 when deciding which equation to solve for x or y.

For the system

$\begin{cases} 2x + y = 14 \\ -3x + 4y = -10 \end{cases}$

I would solve the first equation for y because it has a coefficient of 1.

$2x + y = 14$

$\qquad y = -2x + 14$

Then I use substitution to find the values of x and y.

$-3x + 4y = -10$

$-3x + 4(-2x + 14) = -10$

$-3x + (-8x) + 56 = -10$

$-11x + 56 = -10$

$-11x = -66$

$x = 6$

$y = -2x + 14$

$y = -2(6) + 14 = 2$

The solution is (6, 2).

EXAMPLE 3 *Consumer Economics Application*

One high-speed Internet provider has a $50 setup fee and costs $30 per month. Another provider has no setup fee and costs $40 per month.

a. In how many months will both providers cost the same? What will that cost be?

Write an equation for each option. Let t represent the total amount paid and m represent the number of months.

	Total paid	is	setup fee	plus	cost per month	times	months.
Option 1	t	$=$	50	$+$	30	$\cdot$	m
Option 2	t	$=$	0	$+$	40	$\cdot$	m

Step 1 $t = 50 + 30m$ *Both equations are solved for t.*
$ t = 40m$

Step 2 $50 + 30m = 40m$ *Substitute $50 + 30m$ for t in the second equation.*

Step 3 $\dfrac{-30m -30m}{50 = 10m}$ *Solve for m. Subtract 30m from both sides.*

$\dfrac{50}{10} = \dfrac{10m}{10}$ *Divide both sides by 10.*

$5 = m$

Step 4 $t = 40m$ *Write one of the original equations.*
$ = 40(5)$ *Substitute 5 for m.*
$ = 200$

Step 5 $(5, 200)$ *Write the solution as an ordered pair.*

In 5 months, the total cost for each option will be the same—$200.

b. If you plan to cancel in 1 year, which is the cheaper provider? Explain.

Option 1: $t = 50 + 30(12) = 410$ Option 2: $t = 40(12) = 480$
Option 1 is cheaper.

3. One cable television provider has a $60 setup fee and charges $80 per month, and another provider has a $160 equipment fee and charges $70 per month.

a. In how many months will the cost be the same? What will that cost be?

b. If you plan to move in 6 months, which is the cheaper option? Explain.

THINK AND DISCUSS

1. If you graphed the equations in Example 1A, where would the lines intersect?

$$\begin{cases} x + y = 8 \\ x - y = 2 \end{cases}$$

2. **GET ORGANIZED** Copy and complete the graphic organizer. In each box, solve the system by substitution using the first step given. Show that each method gives the same solution.

Solve $x + y = 8$ for x.	Solve $x + y = 8$ for y.
Solve $x - y = 2$ for x.	Solve $x - y = 2$ for y.

Exercises

go.hrw.com
Homework Help Online
KEYWORD: MA7 6-2
Parent Resources Online
KEYWORD: MA7 Parent

GUIDED PRACTICE

Solve each system by substitution.

SEE EXAMPLE **1**
p. 404

1. $\begin{cases} y = 5x - 10 \\ y = 3x + 8 \end{cases}$

2. $\begin{cases} 3x + y = 2 \\ 4x + y = 20 \end{cases}$

3. $\begin{cases} y = x + 5 \\ 4x + y = 20 \end{cases}$

SEE EXAMPLE **2**
p. 406

4. $\begin{cases} x - 2y = 10 \\ \frac{1}{2}x - 2y = 4 \end{cases}$

5. $\begin{cases} y - 4x = 3 \\ 2x - 3y = 21 \end{cases}$

6. $\begin{cases} x = y - 8 \\ -x - y = 0 \end{cases}$

SEE EXAMPLE **3**
p. 407

7. **Consumer Economics** The Strauss family is deciding between two lawn-care services. Green Lawn charges a $49 startup fee, plus $29 per month. Grass Team charges a $25 startup fee, plus $37 per month.

   a. In how many months will both lawn-care services cost the same? What will that cost be?

   b. If the family will use the service for only 6 months, which is the better option? Explain.

PRACTICE AND PROBLEM SOLVING

Independent Practice

For Exercises	See Example
8–10	1
11–16	2
17	3

Extra Practice
Skills Practice p. S14
Application Practice p. S33

Solve each system by substitution.

8. $\begin{cases} y = x + 3 \\ y = 2x + 4 \end{cases}$

9. $\begin{cases} y = 2x + 10 \\ y = -2x - 6 \end{cases}$

10. $\begin{cases} x + 2y = 8 \\ x + 3y = 12 \end{cases}$

11. $\begin{cases} 2x + 2y = 2 \\ -4x + 4y = 12 \end{cases}$

12. $\begin{cases} y = 0.5x + 2 \\ -y = -2x + 4 \end{cases}$

13. $\begin{cases} -x + y = 4 \\ 3x - 2y = -7 \end{cases}$

14. $\begin{cases} 3x + y = -8 \\ -2x - y = 6 \end{cases}$

15. $\begin{cases} x + 2y = -1 \\ 4x - 4y = 20 \end{cases}$

16. $\begin{cases} 4x = y - 1 \\ 6x - 2y = -3 \end{cases}$

17. **Recreation** Casey wants to buy a gym membership. One gym has a $150 joining fee and costs $35 per month. Another gym has no joining fee and costs $60 per month.

    a. In how many months will both gym memberships cost the same? What will that cost be?

    b. If Casey plans to cancel in 5 months, which is the better option for him? Explain.

Solve each system by substitution. Check your answer.

18. $\begin{cases} x = 5 \\ x + y = 8 \end{cases}$

19. $\begin{cases} y = -3x + 4 \\ x = 2y + 6 \end{cases}$

20. $\begin{cases} 3x - y = 11 \\ 5y - 7x = 1 \end{cases}$

21. $\begin{cases} \frac{1}{2}x + \frac{1}{3}y = 6 \\ x - y = 2 \end{cases}$

22. $\begin{cases} x = 7 - 2y \\ 2x + y = 5 \end{cases}$

23. $\begin{cases} y = 1.2x - 4 \\ 2.2x + 5 = y \end{cases}$

24. The sum of two numbers is 50. The first number is 43 less than twice the second number. Write and solve a system of equations to find the two numbers.

25. **Money** A jar contains n nickels and d dimes. There are 20 coins in the jar, and the total value of the coins is $1.40. How many nickels and how many dimes are in the jar? (*Hint:* Nickels are worth $0.05 and dimes are worth $0.10.)

26. **Multi-Step** Use the receipts below to write and solve a system of equations to find the cost of a large popcorn and the cost of a small drink.

CINEMA SNAKSHAK

Customer #3598

3 large popcorn buckets
2 small drinks

Total due: $21.00

CUSTOMER COPY

CINEMA SNAKSHAK

Customer #3599

2 large popcorn buckets
4 small drinks

Total due: $22.00

CUSTOMER COPY

27. **Finance** Helene invested a total of $1000 in two simple-interest bank accounts. One account paid 5% annual interest; the other paid 6% annual interest. The total amount of interest she earned after one year was $58. Write and solve a system of equations to find the amount invested in each account. (*Hint:* Change the interest rates into decimals first.)

Geometry Two angles whose measures have a sum of 90° are called complementary angles. For Exercises 28–30, x and y represent the measures of complementary angles. Use this information and the equation given in each exercise to find the measure of each angle.

28. $y = 4x - 10$

29. $x = 2y$

30. $y = 2(x - 15)$

31. **Aviation** With a headwind, a small plane can fly 240 miles in 3 hours. With a tailwind, the plane can fly the same distance in 2 hours. Follow the steps below to find the rates of the plane and wind.

   a. Copy and complete the table. Let p be the rate of the plane and w be the rate of the wind.

	Rate	•	Time	=	Distance
With Headwind	$p - w$	•	▓	=	240
With Tailwind	▓	•	2	=	▓

   b. Use the information in each row to write a system of equations.

   c. Solve the system of equations to find the rates of the plane and wind.

32. **Write About It** Explain how to solve a system of equations by substitution.

33. **Critical Thinking** Explain the connection between the solution of a system solved by graphing and the solution of the same system solved by substitution.

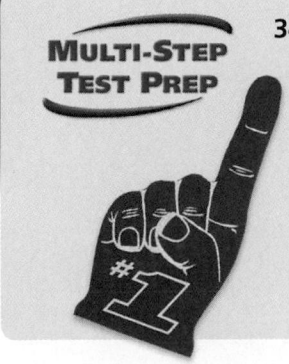

MULTI-STEP TEST PREP

34. This problem will prepare you for the Multi-Step Test Prep on page 426.

At the school store, Juanita bought 2 books and a backpack for a total of $26 before tax. Each book cost $8 less than the backpack.

   a. Write a system of equations that can be used to find the price of each book and the price of the backpack.

   b. Solve this system by substitution.

   c. Solve this system by graphing. Discuss advantages and disadvantages of solving by substitution and solving by graphing.

35. Estimation Use the graph to estimate the solution to $\begin{cases} 2x - y = 6 \\ x + y = -0.6 \end{cases}$. Round your answer to the nearest tenth. Then solve the system by substitution.

36. Elizabeth met 24 of her cousins at a family reunion. The number of male cousins m was 6 less than twice the number of female cousins f. Which system can be used to find the number of male cousins and female cousins?

Ⓐ $\begin{cases} m + f = 24 \\ f = 2m - 6 \end{cases}$ Ⓑ $\begin{cases} m + f = 24 \\ f = 2m \end{cases}$ Ⓒ $\begin{cases} m = 24 + f \\ m = f - 6 \end{cases}$ Ⓓ $\begin{cases} f = 24 - m \\ m = 2f - 6 \end{cases}$

37. Which problem is best represented by the system $\begin{cases} d = n + 5 \\ d + n = 12 \end{cases}$?

Ⓕ Roger has 12 coins in dimes and nickels. There are 5 more dimes than nickels.

Ⓖ Roger has 5 coins in dimes and nickels. There are 12 more dimes than nickels.

Ⓗ Roger has 12 coins in dimes and nickels. There are 5 more nickels than dimes.

Ⓙ Roger has 5 coins in dimes and nickels. There are 12 more nickels than dimes.

CHALLENGE AND EXTEND

38. A car dealership has 378 cars on its lot. The ratio of new cars to used cars is 5:4. Write and solve a system of equations to find the number of new and used cars on the lot.

Solve each system by substitution.

39. $\begin{cases} 2r - 3s - t = 12 \\ s + 3t = 10 \\ t = 4 \end{cases}$ **40.** $\begin{cases} x + y + z = 7 \\ y + z = 5 \\ 2y - 4z = -14 \end{cases}$ **41.** $\begin{cases} a + 2b + c = 19 \\ -b + c = -5 \\ 3b + 2c = 15 \end{cases}$

SPIRAL REVIEW

Write a possible situation for the given graph. *(Lesson 4-1)*

42.   **43.**   **44.**

Find the *x*- and *y*-intercepts. *(Lesson 5-2)*

45. $6x - 2y = 12$ **46.** $-3y + x = 15$ **47.** $4y - 40 = -5x$

Tell whether each ordered pair is a solution of the given system. *(Lesson 6-1)*

48. $(3, 0)$; $\begin{cases} 2x - y = -6 \\ x + y = 3 \end{cases}$ **49.** $(-1, 4)$; $\begin{cases} y - 2x = 6 \\ x + 4y = 15 \end{cases}$ **50.** $(5, 6)$; $\begin{cases} \frac{1}{3}y + x = 7 \\ 2x = 12 \end{cases}$

Solving Systems by Elimination

Objectives

Solve systems of linear equations in two variables by elimination.

Compare and choose an appropriate method for solving systems of linear equations.

Why learn this?

You can solve a system of linear equations to determine how many flowers of each type you can buy to make a bouquet. (See Example 4.)

Another method for solving systems of equations is *elimination*. Like substitution, the goal of elimination is to get one equation that has only one variable.

Remember that an equation stays balanced if you add equal amounts to both sides. Consider the system $\begin{cases} x - 2y = 19 \\ 5x + 2y = 1 \end{cases}$. Since $5x + 2y = 1$, you can add $5x + 2y$ to one side of the first equation and 1 to the other side and the balance is maintained.

Since $-2y$ and $2y$ have **opposite coefficients**, you can eliminate the y by adding the two equations. The result is one equation that has only one variable: $6x = -18$.

When you use the elimination method to solve a system of linear equations, align all like terms in the equations. Then determine whether any like terms can be eliminated because they have opposite coefficients.

Solving Systems of Equations by Elimination
Step 1 Write the system so that like terms are aligned.
Step 2 Eliminate one of the variables and solve for the other variable.
Step 3 Substitute the value of the variable into one of the original equations and solve for the other variable.
Step 4 Write the answers from Steps 2 and 3 as an ordered pair, (x, y), and check.

Later in this lesson you will learn how to multiply one or more equations by a number in order to produce opposites that can be eliminated.

EXAMPLE **1** **Elimination Using Addition**

Solve $\begin{cases} x - 2y = -19 \\ 5x + 2y = 1 \end{cases}$ by elimination.

Step 1 $\quad x - 2y = -19$ *Write the system so that like terms are aligned.*

$\underline{+\; 5x + 2y = \quad 1}$ *Notice that −2y and 2y are opposites.*

Step 2 $\quad 6x\; + 0 = -18$ *Add the equations to eliminate y.*

$6x = -18$ *Simplify and solve for x.*

$\dfrac{6x}{6} = \dfrac{-18}{6}$ *Divide both sides by 6.*

$x = -3$

Step 3 $\; x - 2y = -19$ *Write one of the original equations.*

$-3 - 2y = -19$ *Substitute −3 for x.*

$\underline{+3 \qquad\quad +3}$ *Add 3 to both sides.*

$-2y = -16$

$\dfrac{-2y}{-2} = \dfrac{-16}{-2}$ *Divide both sides by −2.*

$y = 8$

Step 4 $(-3, 8)$ *Write the solution as an ordered pair.*

Helpful Hint

Check your answer.

$x - 2y = -19$	
$-3 - 2(8)$	-19
$-3 - 16$	-19
-19	$-19\;✓$

$5x + 2y = 1$	
$5(-3) + 2(8)$	1
$-15 + 16$	1
1	$1\;✓$

 1. Solve $\begin{cases} y + 3x = -2 \\ 2y - 3x = 14 \end{cases}$ by elimination. Check your answer.

When two equations each contain the same term, you can subtract one equation from the other to solve the system. To subtract an equation, add the opposite of *each* term.

EXAMPLE **2** **Elimination Using Subtraction**

Solve $\begin{cases} 3x + 4y = 18 \\ -2x + 4y = 8 \end{cases}$ by elimination.

Step 1 $\quad 3x + 4y = 18$

$- \left(-2x + 4y = \;8 \right)$ *Notice that both equations contain 4y.*

$3x + 4y = \;18$ *Add the opposite of each term*

$\underline{+\; 2x - 4y = -8}$ *in the second equation.*

Step 2 $\quad 5x + \;\;0 = 10$ *Eliminate y.*

$5x = 10$ *Simplify and solve for x.*

$x = 2$

Step 3 $\;-2x + 4y = \;\;8$ *Write one of the original equations.*

$-2(2) + 4y = \;\;8$ *Substitute 2 for x.*

$-4 + 4y = \;\;8$

$\underline{+4 \qquad\quad +4}$ *Add 4 to both sides.*

$4y = 12$ *Simplify and solve for y.*

$y = 3$

Step 4 $(2, 3)$ *Write the solution as an ordered pair.*

Remember!

Remember to check by substituting your answer into both original equations.

2. Solve $\begin{cases} 3x + 3y = 15 \\ -2x + 3y = -5 \end{cases}$ by elimination. Check your answer.

In some cases, you will first need to multiply one or both of the equations by a number so that one variable has opposite coefficients.

EXAMPLE 3 **Elimination Using Multiplication First**

Solve each system by elimination.

A $\begin{cases} 2x + y = 3 \\ -x + 3y = -12 \end{cases}$

Helpful Hint

In Example 3A, you could have also multiplied the first equation by -3 to eliminate y.

Step 1
$$\begin{array}{r} 2x + y = 3 \\ + 2(-x + 3y = -12) \\ \hline 2x + y = 3 \end{array}$$

Multiply each term in the second equation by 2 to get opposite x-coefficients.

$$+(-2x + 6y = -24)$$

Add the new equation to the first equation to eliminate x.

Step 2
$$7y = -21$$
$$y = -3$$

Solve for y.

Step 3
$$\begin{array}{r} 2x + y = 3 \\ 2x + (-3) = 3 \\ +\ 3 \quad +3 \\ \hline 2x = 6 \\ x = 3 \end{array}$$

Write one of the original equations.
Substitute −3 for y.
Add 3 to both sides.
Solve for x.

Step 4 $(3, -3)$

Write the solution as an ordered pair.

B $\begin{cases} 7x - 12y = -22 \\ 5x - 8y = -14 \end{cases}$

Step 1
$$\begin{array}{r} 2(7x - 12y = -22) \\ + (-3)(5x - 8y = -14) \\ \hline 14x - 24y = -44 \end{array}$$

Multiply the first equation by 2 and the second equation by −3 to get opposite y-coefficients.

$$+(-15x + 24y = 42)$$

Add the new equations to eliminate y.

Step 2
$$-x = -2$$
$$x = 2$$

Solve for x.

Step 3
$$\begin{array}{r} 7x - 12y = -22 \\ 7(2) - 12y = -22 \\ 14 - 12y = -22 \\ -14 \quad\quad -14 \\ \hline -12y = -36 \\ y = 3 \end{array}$$

Write one of the original equations.
Substitute 2 for x.

Subtract 14 from both sides.
Solve for y.

Step 4 $(2, 3)$

Write the solution as an ordered pair.

 Solve each system by elimination. Check your answer.

3a. $\begin{cases} 3x + 2y = 6 \\ -x + y = -2 \end{cases}$

3b. $\begin{cases} 2x + 5y = 26 \\ -3x - 4y = -25 \end{cases}$

Consumer Economics Application

ROSES
$2.50 each

DAISIES
$1.75 each

Sam spent $24.75 to buy 12 flowers for his mother. The bouquet contained roses and daisies. How many of each type of flower did Sam buy?

Write a system. Use r for the number of roses and d for the number of daisies.

$$2.50r + 1.75d = 24.75 \qquad \textit{The cost of roses and daisies totals \$24.75.}$$

$$r + d = 12 \qquad \textit{The total number of roses and daisies is 12.}$$

Step 1

$$2.50r + 1.75d = 24.75$$
$$+ (-2.50)(r + d = 12) \qquad \textit{Multiply the second equation}$$

$$2.50r + 1.75d = \quad 24.75 \qquad \begin{array}{l}\textit{by } -2.50 \textit{ to get opposite}\\ \textit{r-coefficients.}\end{array}$$

$$+ (-2.50r - 2.50d = -30.00) \qquad \begin{array}{l}\textit{Add this equation to the first}\\ \textit{equation to eliminate r.}\end{array}$$

Step 2

$$-0.75d = \quad -5.25$$

$$d = \quad 7 \qquad \textit{Solve for d.}$$

Step 3

$$r + d = 12 \qquad \textit{Write one of the original equations.}$$

$$r + 7 = \quad 12 \qquad \textit{Substitute 7 for d.}$$

$$\underline{-7 \qquad -7} \qquad \textit{Subtract 7 from both sides.}$$

$$r \quad = \quad 5$$

Step 4

$$(5, 7) \qquad \textit{Write the solution as an ordered pair.}$$

Sam can buy 5 roses and 7 daisies.

CHECK IT OUT!

4. What if...? Sally spent $14.85 to buy 13 flowers. She bought lilies, which cost $1.25 each, and tulips, which cost $0.90 each. How many of each flower did Sally buy?

All systems can be solved in more than one way. For some systems, some methods may be better than others.

Know it!
·Note

Systems of Linear Equations

METHOD	USE WHEN...	EXAMPLE
Graphing	• Both equations are solved for y. • You want to estimate a solution.	$\begin{cases} y = 3x + 2 \\ y = -2x + 6 \end{cases}$
Substitution	• A variable in either equation has a coefficient of 1 or -1. • Both equations are solved for the same variable. • Either equation is solved for a variable.	$\begin{cases} x + 2y = 7 \\ x = 10 - 5y \end{cases}$ or $\begin{cases} x = 2y + 10 \\ x = 3y + 5 \end{cases}$
Elimination	• Both equations have the same variable with the same or opposite coefficients. • A variable term in one equation is a multiple of the corresponding variable term in the other equation.	$\begin{cases} 3x + 2y = 8 \\ 5x + 2y = 12 \end{cases}$ or $\begin{cases} 6x + 5y = 10 \\ 3x + 2y = 15 \end{cases}$

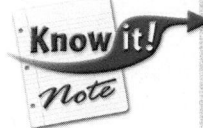
6-3 Exercises

go.hrw.com
Homework Help Online
KEYWORD: MA7 6-3
Parent Resources Online
KEYWORD: MA7 Parent

GUIDED PRACTICE

Solve each system by elimination. Check your answer.

SEE EXAMPLE 1 p. 412

1. $\begin{cases} -x + y = 5 \\ x - 5y = -9 \end{cases}$

2. $\begin{cases} x + y = 12 \\ x - y = 2 \end{cases}$

3. $\begin{cases} 2x + 5y = -24 \\ 3x - 5y = 14 \end{cases}$

SEE EXAMPLE 2 p. 412

4. $\begin{cases} x - 10y = 60 \\ x + 14y = 12 \end{cases}$

5. $\begin{cases} 5x + y = 0 \\ 5x + 2y = 30 \end{cases}$

6. $\begin{cases} -5x + 7y = 11 \\ -5x + 3y = 19 \end{cases}$

SEE EXAMPLE 3 p. 413

7. $\begin{cases} 2x + 3y = 12 \\ 5x - y = 13 \end{cases}$

8. $\begin{cases} -3x + 4y = 12 \\ 2x + y = -8 \end{cases}$

9. $\begin{cases} 2x + 4y = -4 \\ 3x + 5y = -3 \end{cases}$

SEE EXAMPLE 4 p. 414

10. **Consumer Economics** Each family in a neighborhood is contributing $20 worth of food to the neighborhood picnic. The Harlin family is bringing 12 packages of buns. The hamburger buns cost $2.00 per package. The hot-dog buns cost $1.50 per package. How many packages of each type of bun did they buy?

PRACTICE AND PROBLEM SOLVING

Independent Practice

For Exercises	See Example
11–13	1
14–16	2
17–19	3
20	4

Extra Practice

Skills Practice p. S14

Application Practice p. S33

Solve each system by elimination. Check your answer.

11. $\begin{cases} -x + y = -1 \\ 2x - y = 0 \end{cases}$

12. $\begin{cases} -2x + y = -20 \\ 2x + y = 48 \end{cases}$

13. $\begin{cases} 3x - y = -2 \\ -2x + y = 3 \end{cases}$

14. $\begin{cases} x - y = 4 \\ x - 2y = 10 \end{cases}$

15. $\begin{cases} x + 2y = 5 \\ 3x + 2y = 17 \end{cases}$

16. $\begin{cases} 3x - 2y = -1 \\ 3x - 4y = 9 \end{cases}$

17. $\begin{cases} x - y = -3 \\ 5x + 3y = 1 \end{cases}$

18. $\begin{cases} 9x - 3y = 3 \\ 3x + 8y = -17 \end{cases}$

19. $\begin{cases} 5x + 2y = -1 \\ 3x + 7y = 11 \end{cases}$

20. **Multi-Step** Mrs. Gonzalez bought centerpieces to put on each table at a graduation party. She spent $31.50. There are 8 tables each requiring either a candle or vase. Candles cost $3 and vases cost $4.25. How many of each type did she buy?

21. **Geometry** The difference between the length and width of a rectangle is 2 units. The perimeter is 40 units. Write and solve a system of equations to determine the length and width of the rectangle. (*Hint:* The perimeter of a rectangle is $2\ell + 2w$.)

22. ///**ERROR ANALYSIS**/// Which is incorrect? Explain the error.

Ⓐ
$$\begin{cases} x + y = -3 \\ 3x + y = 3 \end{cases} \quad \begin{aligned} x + y = -3 \\ -(3x + y = 3) \\ \hline -2x = 0 \\ x = 0 \end{aligned}$$

Ⓑ
$$\begin{cases} x + y = -3 \\ 3x + y = 3 \end{cases} \quad \begin{aligned} x + y = -3 \\ -(3x + y = 3) \\ \hline -2x = -6 \\ x = 3 \end{aligned}$$

23. **Chemistry** A chemist has a bottle of a 1% acid solution and a bottle of a 5% acid solution. She wants to mix the two solutions to get 100 mL of a 4% acid solution. Follow the steps below to find how much of each solution she should use.

	1% Solution	+	5% Solution	=	4% Solution
Amount of Solution (mL)	x	+	y	=	▮
Amount of Acid (mL)	$0.01x$	+	▮	=	$0.04(100)$

a. Copy and complete the table.

b. Use the information in the table to write a system of equations.

c. Solve the system of equations to find how much she will use from each bottle to get 100 mL of a 4% acid solution.

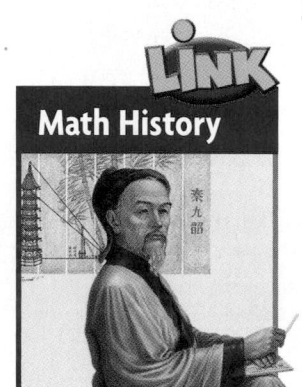

Math History

In 1247, Qin Jiushao wrote *Mathematical Treatise in Nine Sections*. Its contents included solving systems of equations and the Chinese Remainder Theorem.

Critical Thinking Which method would you use to solve each system? Explain.

24. $\begin{cases} \dfrac{1}{2}x - 5y = 30 \\ \dfrac{1}{2}x + 7y = 6 \end{cases}$

25. $\begin{cases} -x + 2y = 3 \\ 4x - 5y = -3 \end{cases}$

26. $\begin{cases} 3x - y = 10 \\ 2x - y = 7 \end{cases}$

27. $\begin{cases} 3y + x = 10 \\ x = 4y + 2 \end{cases}$

28. $\begin{cases} y = -4x \\ y = 2x + 3 \end{cases}$

29. $\begin{cases} 2x + 6y = 12 \\ 4x + 5y = 15 \end{cases}$

30. **Business** A local boys club sold 176 bags of mulch and made a total of $520. They did not sell any of the expensive cocoa mulch. Use the table to determine how many bags of each type of mulch they sold.

Mulch Prices ($)	
Cocoa	4.75
Hardwood	3.50
Pine Bark	2.75

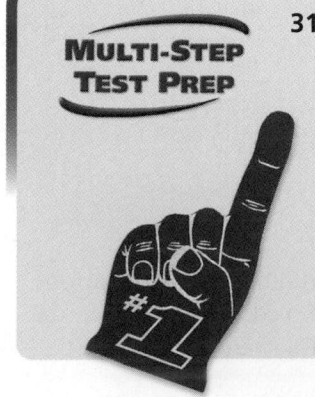

MULTI-STEP TEST PREP

31. This problem will prepare you for the Multi-Step Test Prep on page 426.

a. The school store is running a promotion on school supplies. Different supplies are placed on two shelves. You can purchase 3 items from shelf A and 2 from shelf B for $16. Or you can purchase 2 items from shelf A and 3 from shelf B for $14. Write a system of equations that can be used to find the individual prices for the supplies on shelf A and on shelf B.

b. Solve the system of equations by elimination.

c. If the supplies on shelf A are normally $6 each and the supplies on shelf B are normally $3 each, how much will you save on each package plan from part **a**?

32. Write About It Solve the system $\begin{cases} 3x + y = 1 \\ 2x + 4y = -6 \end{cases}$. Explain how you can check your solution algebraically and graphically.

33. A math test has 25 problems. Some are worth 2 points, and some are worth 3 points. The test is worth 60 points total. Which system can be used to determine the number of 2-point problems and the number of 3-point problems on the test?

Ⓐ $\begin{cases} x + y = 25 \\ 2x + 3y = 60 \end{cases}$ Ⓑ $\begin{cases} x + y = 60 \\ 2x + 3y = 25 \end{cases}$ Ⓒ $\begin{cases} x - y = 25 \\ 2x + 3y = 60 \end{cases}$ Ⓓ $\begin{cases} x - y = 60 \\ 2x - 3y = 25 \end{cases}$

34. An electrician charges $15 plus $11 per hour. Another electrician charges $10 plus $15 per hour. For what amount of time will the cost be the same? What is that cost?

Ⓕ 1 hour; $25

Ⓖ $1\frac{1}{4}$ hours; $28.75

Ⓗ $1\frac{1}{2}$ hours; $30

Ⓙ $1\frac{3}{4}$ hours; $32.50

35. Short Response Three hundred fifty-eight tickets to the school basketball game on Friday were sold. Student tickets were $1.50, and nonstudent tickets were $3.25. The school made $752.25.

a. Write a system of linear equations that could be used to determine how many student and how many nonstudent tickets were sold. Define the variables you use.

b. Solve the system you wrote in part a. How many student and how many nonstudent tickets were sold?

CHALLENGE AND EXTEND

Solve each system by any method.

36. $\begin{cases} x + 16\frac{1}{2} = -\frac{3}{4}y \\ y = \frac{1}{2}x \end{cases}$

37. $\begin{cases} 2x + y + z = 17 \\ \frac{1}{2}z = 5 \\ x - y = 5 \end{cases}$

38. $\begin{cases} x - 2y - z = -1 \\ -x + 2y + 4z = -11 \\ 2x + y + z = 1 \end{cases}$

39. The sum of the digits of a two-digit number is 5. If the number is multiplied by 3, the result is 42. Write and solve a system of equations to find the number. (*Hint:* One equation involves the digits in the number. The other equation involves the values of the digits.)

SPIRAL REVIEW

Determine a relationship between the *x*- and *y*-values. Write an equation. *(Lesson 4-3)*

40.

x	1	2	3	4
y	6	7	8	9

41.

x	1	2	3	4
y	3	6	9	12

42.

x	1	2	3	4
y	-9	-8	-7	-6

Tell whether each equation is a direct variation. If so, identify the constant of variation. *(Lesson 5-6)*

43. $x = 2y$

44. $y = -6x$

45. $y - 1 = x$

Solve each system by substitution. *(Lesson 6-2)*

46. $\begin{cases} y = x - 1 \\ x + y = 10 \end{cases}$

47. $\begin{cases} x = y - 5 \\ 2x + 1 = y \end{cases}$

48. $\begin{cases} y = 2x - 1 \\ x - y = 3 \end{cases}$

Solving Classic Problems

You can use systems of linear equations to solve some "classic" math problems that are common in textbooks and puzzle books.

Example 1

Yuri is twice as old as Zack. Four years from now, the sum of their ages will be 23. How old is Yuri?

Step 1 Write a system. Let y represent Yuri's age. Let z represent Zack's age.

Yuri is twice as old as Zack.

$$y = 2z$$

In 4 years, the sum of their ages will be 23.

$$(y + 4) + (z + 4) = 23$$
$$y + z + 8 = 23$$
$$y + z = 15$$

Step 2 Solve the equations for y.

$$\begin{cases} y = 2z \\ y + z = 15 \end{cases} \rightarrow \begin{cases} y = 2z \\ y = -z + 15 \end{cases}$$

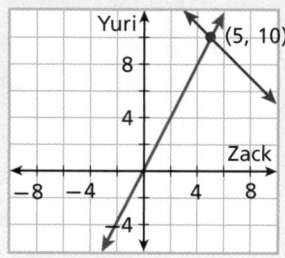

Step 3 Graph $y = 2z$ and $y = -z + 15$.

The lines appear to intersect at $(5, 10)$.

The solution $(5, 10)$ means that Yuri is 10 years old.

Example 2

Mandy has 11 coins in dimes and quarters. The value of her coins is $2.15. How many dimes does she have?

Step 1 Write a system. Let d be the number of dimes. Let q be the number of quarters.

The total number of coins is 11.

$$q + d = 11$$

The value of the coins is $2.15.

$$0.25q + 0.10d = 2.15$$
$$100(0.25q + 0.10d = 2.15)$$
$$25q + 10d = 215$$
$$5q + 2d = 43$$

Step 2 Solve the first equation for d.

$$d = 11 - q$$

Step 3 Substitute $11 - q$ for d in the second equation.

$$5q + 2(11 - q) = 43$$
$$3q + 22 = 43 \qquad \textit{Distribute 2 and then combine like terms.}$$
$$3q = 21$$
$$q = 7 \qquad \textit{Solve for q.}$$

Step 4 Substitute 7 for q in one of the original equations.

$$q + d = 11$$
$$7 + d = 11$$
$$d = 4$$

The solution $(4, 7)$ means that there are 4 dimes and 7 quarters. Mandy has 4 dimes.

Example 3

When the digits of a two-digit number are reversed, the new number is 45 less than the original number. The sum of the digits is 7. What is the original number?

Step 1 Write expressions for the original number and the new number. Let a represent the tens digit. Let b represent the ones digit.

The original number: The new number:
$$10a + b$$ $$10b + a$$

Step 2 Write a system.

The new number is 45 less
than the original number.   The sum of the digits is 7.

$$10b + a = (10a + b) - 45$$ $$a + b = 7$$
$$9b - 9a = -45$$
$$b - a = -5 \longrightarrow a - b = 5$$

Step 3 Add the equations to eliminate b. Solve for a.

$$\begin{array}{r} a - b = 5 \\ + (a + b = 7) \\ \hline 2a \phantom{{}- b} = 12 \\ a = 6 \end{array}$$

Step 4 Substitute 6 for a in one of the original equations.

$$a + b = 7$$
$$6 + b = 7$$
$$b = 1$$

The solution is $(6, 1)$. This means that 6 is the tens digit and 1 is the ones digit. The original number is 61.

Check Check your solution using the original problem.
The sum of the digits is 7: $6 + 1 = 7$ ✓
When the digits are reversed, the new number is 45 less than the original number: $16 = 61 - 45$ ✓

Try This

1. The sum of the digits of a two-digit number is 17. When the digits are reversed, the new number is 9 more than the original number. What is the original number?

2. Vic has 14 coins in nickels and quarters. The value of his coins is $1.70. How many quarters does he have?

3. Grace is 8 years older than her brother Sam. The sum of their ages is 24. How old is Grace?

6-4 Solving Special Systems

Objectives
Solve special systems of linear equations in two variables.

Classify systems of linear equations and determine the number of solutions.

Vocabulary
consistent system
inconsistent system
independent system
dependent system

Why learn this?

Linear systems can be used to analyze business growth, such as comic book sales. (See Example 4.)

In Lesson 6-1, you saw that when two lines intersect at a point, there is exactly one solution to the system. A system with at least one solution is a **consistent system**.

When the two lines in a system do not intersect, they are parallel lines. There are no ordered pairs that satisfy both equations, so there is no solution. A system that has no solution is an **inconsistent system**.

EXAMPLE 1 **Systems with No Solution**

Show that $\begin{cases} y = x - 1 \\ -x + y = 2 \end{cases}$ has no solution.

Method 1 Compare slopes and y-intercepts.

$y = x - 1 \rightarrow y = 1x - 1$ *Write both equations in slope-intercept form.*
$-x + y = 2 \rightarrow y = 1x + 2$ *The lines are parallel because they have the same slope and different y-intercepts.*

This system has no solution.

Method 2 Graph the system.
  The lines are parallel.

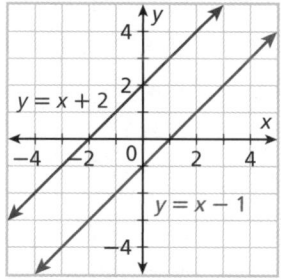

This system has no solution.

Method 3 Solve the system algebraically. Use the substitution method.

$-x + (x - 1) = 2$ *Substitute $x - 1$ for y in the second equation, and solve.*
$-1 = 2$ ✗ *False*

This system has no solution.

 1. Show that $\begin{cases} y = -2x + 5 \\ 2x + y = 1 \end{cases}$ has no solution.

If two linear equations in a system have the same graph, the graphs are coincident lines, or the same line. There are infinitely many solutions of the system because every point on the line represents a solution of both equations.

EXAMPLE 2 **Systems with Infinitely Many Solutions**

Show that $\begin{cases} y = 2x + 1 \\ 2x - y + 1 = 0 \end{cases}$ has infinitely many solutions.

Method 1 Compare slopes and y-intercepts.

$$y = 2x + 1 \rightarrow y = 2x + 1$$
$$2x - y + 1 = 0 \rightarrow y = 2x + 1$$

Write both equations in slope-intercept form. The lines have the same slope and the same y-intercept.

If this system were graphed, the graphs would be the same line. There are infinitely many solutions.

Method 2 Solve the system algebraically. Use the elimination method.

$$y = 2x + 1 \rightarrow -2x + y = 1 \quad \text{Write equations to line up like terms.}$$
$$2x - y + 1 = 0 \rightarrow \underline{+2x - y = -1} \quad \text{Add the equations.}$$
$$0 = 0 \checkmark \quad \text{True. The equation is an identity.}$$

Caution!

$0 = 0$ is a true statement. It does not mean the system has zero solutions or no solution.

There are infinitely many solutions.

 2. Show that $\begin{cases} y = x - 3 \\ x - y - 3 = 0 \end{cases}$ has infinitely many solutions.

Consistent systems can either be independent or dependent.

- An **independent system** has exactly one solution. The graph of an independent system consists of two intersecting lines.
- A **dependent system** has infinitely many solutions. The graph of a dependent system consists of two coincident lines.

Know it! *Note*

Classification of Systems of Linear Equations

CLASSIFICATION	CONSISTENT AND INDEPENDENT	CONSISTENT AND DEPENDENT	INCONSISTENT
Number of Solutions	Exactly one	Infinitely many	None
Description	Different slopes	Same slope, same y-intercept	Same slope, different y-intercepts
Graph	Intersecting lines	Coincident lines	Parallel lines

EXAMPLE 3 **Classifying Systems of Linear Equations**

Classify each system. Give the number of solutions.

A $\begin{cases} 2y = x + 2 \\ -\dfrac{1}{2}x + y = 1 \end{cases}$

$2y = x + 2 \rightarrow y = \dfrac{1}{2}x + 1$ *Write both equations in slope-intercept form.*

$-\dfrac{1}{2}x + y = 1 \rightarrow y = \dfrac{1}{2}x + 1$ *The lines have the same slope and the same y-intercepts. They are the same.*

The system is consistent and dependent. It has infinitely many solutions.

B $\begin{cases} y = 2(x - 1) \\ y = x + 1 \end{cases}$

$y = 2(x - 1) \rightarrow y = 2x - 2$ *Write both equations in slope-intercept form.*

$y = x + 1 \rightarrow y = 1x + 1$ *The lines have different slopes. They intersect.*

The system is consistent and independent. It has one solution.

 Classify each system. Give the number of solutions.

3a. $\begin{cases} x + 2y = -4 \\ -2(y + 2) = x \end{cases}$ **3b.** $\begin{cases} y = -2(x - 1) \\ y = -x + 3 \end{cases}$ **3c.** $\begin{cases} 2x - 3y = 6 \\ y = \dfrac{2}{3}x \end{cases}$

EXAMPLE 4   *Business Application*

The sales manager at Comics Now is comparing its sales with the sales of its competitor, Dynamo Comics. If the sales patterns continue, will the sales for Comics Now ever equal the sales for Dynamo Comics? Explain.

Comic Books Sold per Year (thousands)	POW!			
	2005	2006	2007	2008
Comics Now	130	170	210	250
Dynamo Comics	180	220	260	300

Use the table to write a system of linear equations. Let y represent the sales total and x represent the number of years since 2005.

	Sales total	equals	increase in sales per year	times	years	plus	beginning sales.
Comics Now	y	$=$	40	$\cdot$	x	$+$	130
Dynamo Comics	y	$=$	40	$\cdot$	x	$+$	180

$\begin{cases} y = 40x + 130 \\ y = 40x + 180 \end{cases}$

$y = 40x + 130$ *Both equations are in slope-intercept form.*

$y = 40x + 180$ *The lines have the same slope, but different y-intercepts.*

The graphs of the two equations are parallel lines, so there is no solution. If the patterns continue, sales for the two companies will never be equal.

> **Helpful Hint**
>
> The increase in sales is the difference between sales each year.

 4. Matt has $100 in a checking account and deposits $20 per month. Ben has $80 in a checking account and deposits $30 per month. Will the accounts ever have the same balance? Explain.

THINK AND DISCUSS

1. What methods can be used to determine the number of solutions of a system of linear equations?

2. **GET ORGANIZED** Copy and complete the graphic organizer. In each box, write the word or words that describes a system with that number of solutions and sketch a graph.

Linear System of Equations
- No solution
- Exactly one
- Infinitely many

go.hrw.com
Homework Help Online
KEYWORD: MA7 6-4
Parent Resources Online
KEYWORD: MA7 Parent

GUIDED PRACTICE

1. **Vocabulary** A _____?_____ system can be independent or dependent. (*consistent* or *inconsistent*)

SEE EXAMPLE 1
p. 420

Show that each system has no solution.

2. $\begin{cases} y = x + 1 \\ -x + y = 3 \end{cases}$

3. $\begin{cases} 3x + y = 6 \\ y = -3x + 2 \end{cases}$

4. $\begin{cases} -y = 4x + 1 \\ 4x + y = 2 \end{cases}$

SEE EXAMPLE 2
p. 421

Show that each system has infinitely many solutions.

5. $\begin{cases} y = -x + 3 \\ x + y - 3 = 0 \end{cases}$

6. $\begin{cases} y = 2x - 4 \\ 2x - y - 4 = 0 \end{cases}$

7. $\begin{cases} -7x + y = -2 \\ 7x - y = 2 \end{cases}$

SEE EXAMPLE 3
p. 422

Classify each system. Give the number of solutions.

8. $\begin{cases} y = 2x + 3 \\ -2y = 2x + 6 \end{cases}$

9. $\begin{cases} y = -3x - 1 \\ 3x + y = 1 \end{cases}$

10. $\begin{cases} 9y = 3x + 18 \\ \frac{1}{3}x - y = -2 \end{cases}$

SEE EXAMPLE 4
p. 422

11. **Athletics** Micah walks on a treadmill at 4 miles per hour. He has walked 2 miles when Luke starts running at 6 miles per hour on the treadmill next to him. If their rates continue, will Luke's distance ever equal Micah's distance? Explain.

PRACTICE AND PROBLEM SOLVING

Show that each system has no solution.

12. $\begin{cases} y = 2x - 2 \\ -2x + y = 1 \end{cases}$

13. $\begin{cases} x + y = 3 \\ y = -x - 1 \end{cases}$

14. $\begin{cases} x + 2y = -4 \\ y = -\frac{1}{2}x - 4 \end{cases}$

15. $\begin{cases} -6 + y = 2x \\ y = 2x - 36 \end{cases}$

Show that each system has infinitely many solutions.

16. $\begin{cases} y = -2x + 3 \\ 2x + y - 3 = 0 \end{cases}$

17. $\begin{cases} y = x - 2 \\ x - y - 2 = 0 \end{cases}$

18. $\begin{cases} x + y = -4 \\ y = -x - 4 \end{cases}$

19. $\begin{cases} -9x - 3y = -18 \\ 3x + y = 6 \end{cases}$

Independent Practice

For Exercises	See Example
12–15	1
16–19	2
20–22	3
23	4

Extra Practice

Skills Practice p. S15

Application Practice p. S33

Classify each system. Give the number of solutions.

20. $\begin{cases} y = -x + 5 \\ x + y = 5 \end{cases}$

21. $\begin{cases} y = -3x + 2 \\ y = 3x \end{cases}$

22. $\begin{cases} y - 1 = 2x \\ y = 2x - 1 \end{cases}$

23. **Sports** Mandy is skating at 5 miles per hour. Nikki is skating at 6 miles per hour and started 1 mile behind Mandy. If their rates stay the same, will Mandy catch up with Nikki? Explain.

24. **Multi-Step** Photocopier A can print 35 copies per minute. Photocopier B can print 35 copies per minute. Copier B is started and makes 10 copies. Copier A is then started. If the copiers continue, will the number of copies from machine A ever equal the number of copies from machine B? Explain.

25. **Entertainment** One week Trey rented 4 DVDs and 2 video games for $18. The next week he rented 2 DVDs and 1 video game for $9. Find the rental costs for each video game and DVD. Explain your answer.

26. Rosa bought 1 pound of cashews and 2 pounds of peanuts for $10. At the same store, Sabrina bought 2 pounds of cashews and 1 pound of peanuts for $11. Find the cost per pound for cashews and peanuts.

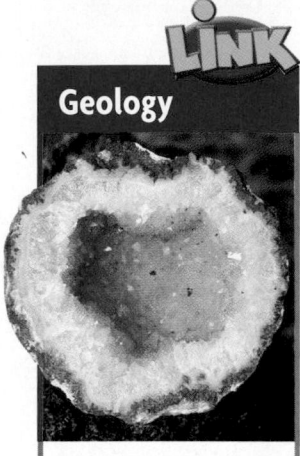

Geology

27. **Geology** Pam and Tommy collect geodes. Pam's parents gave her 2 geodes to start her collection, and she buys 4 every year. Tommy has 2 geodes that were given to him for his birthday. He buys 4 every year. If Pam and Tommy continue to buy the same amount of geodes per year, when will Tommy have as many geodes as Pam? Explain your answer.

Geodes are rounded, hollow rock formations. Most are partially or completely filled with layers of colored quartz crystals. The world's largest geode was discovered in Spain in 2000. It is 26 feet long and 5.6 feet high.

28. Use the data given in the tables.

x	3	4	5	6
y	6	8	10	12

x	12	13	14	15
y	24	26	28	30

a. Write an equation to describe the data in each table.

b. Graph the system of equations from part **a**. Describe the graph.

c. How could you have predicted the graph by looking at the equations?

d. **What if...?** Each y-value in the second table increases by 1. How does this affect the graphs of the two equations? How can you tell how the graphs would be affected without actually graphing?

29. **Critical Thinking** Describe the graphs of two equations if the result of solving the system by substitution or elimination is the statement $1 = 3$.

30. This problem will prepare you for the Multi-Step Test Prep on page 426.

The Crusader pep club is selling team buttons that support the sports teams. They contacted Buttons, Etc. which charges $50 plus $1.10 per button, and Logos, which charges $40 plus $1.10 per button.

a. Write an equation for each company's cost.

b. Use the system from part **a** to find when the price for both companies is the same. Explain.

c. What part of the equation should the pep club negotiate to change so that the cost of Buttons, Etc. is the same as Logos? What part of the equation should change in order to get a better price?

31. **///ERROR ANALYSIS///** Student A says there is no solution to the graphed system of equations. Student B says there is one solution. Which student is incorrect? Explain the error.

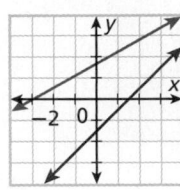

32. **Write About It** Compare the graph of a system that is consistent and independent with the graph of a system that is consistent and dependent.

TEST PREP

33. Which of the following classifications fit the following system?

$$\begin{cases} 2x - y = 3 \\ 6x - 3y = 9 \end{cases}$$

Ⓐ Inconsistent and independent   Ⓒ Inconsistent and dependent

Ⓑ Consistent and independent   Ⓓ Consistent and dependent

34. Which of the following would be enough information to classify a system of two linear equations?

Ⓕ The graphs have the same slope.

Ⓖ The y-intercepts are the same.

Ⓗ The graphs have different slopes.

Ⓙ The y-intercepts are different.

CHALLENGE AND EXTEND

35. What conditions are necessary for the system $\begin{cases} y = 2x + p \\ y = 2x + q \end{cases}$ to have infinitely many solutions? no solution?

36. Solve the systems in parts **a** and **b**. Use this information to make a conjecture about all solutions that exist for the system in part **c**.

a. $\begin{cases} 3x + 4y = 0 \\ 4x + 3y = 0 \end{cases}$ b. $\begin{cases} 2x + 5y = 0 \\ 5x + 2y = 0 \end{cases}$ c. $\begin{cases} ax + by = 0 \\ bx + ay = 0 \end{cases}$, for $a > 0, b > 0, a \neq b$

SPIRAL REVIEW

Use the map to find the actual distances between each pair of cities. *(Lesson 2-7)*

37. from Hon to Averly

38. from Averly to Lewers

Determine if each sequence appears to be an arithmetic sequence. If so, find the common difference and the next three terms. *(Lesson 4-6)*

39. 1, 3, 5, 9, ...

40. 1, 5, 9, 13, ...

41. $0, -1\frac{1}{2}, -3, -4\frac{1}{2}, ...$

Solve each system by graphing. *(Lesson 6-1)*

42. $\begin{cases} y = x - 2 \\ y = -x + 4 \end{cases}$ 43. $\begin{cases} y = 2x \\ x + y = -6 \end{cases}$ 44. $\begin{cases} y = -\frac{1}{2}x \\ y - x = 9 \end{cases}$

MULTI-STEP TEST PREP

Systems of Equations

We've Got Spirit Some cheerleaders are going to sell spirit bracelets and foam fingers to raise money for traveling to away games.

1. Two companies, Spirit for You and Go Team, are interested in providing the foam fingers. The cheerleaders plan to sell 100 foam fingers. Based on this information, which company should they choose? Explain your reasoning.

Company	Design fee	Cost per item
Spirit for You	$35	$2.50
Go Team	$20	$3.00

2. The cheerleaders sold foam fingers for $5 and spirit bracelets for $4. They sold 40 more foam fingers than bracelets, and they earned $965. Write a system of equations to describe this situation.

3. Solve this system using at least two different methods. Explain each method.

4. Using the company you chose in Problem 1, how much profit did the cheerleaders make from the foam fingers alone? (*Hint:* profit = amount earned − expenses)

5. What is the maximum price the cheerleaders could pay for each spirit bracelet in order to make a total profit of $500?

READY TO GO ON?

Quiz for Lessons 6-1 Through 6-4

6-1 Solving Systems by Graphing

Tell whether the ordered pair is a solution of the given system.

1. $(-2, 1);$ $\begin{cases} y = -2x - 3 \\ y = x + 3 \end{cases}$

2. $(9, 2);$ $\begin{cases} x - 4y = 1 \\ 2x - 3y = 3 \end{cases}$

3. $(3, -1);$ $\begin{cases} y = -\frac{1}{3}x \\ y + 2x = 5 \end{cases}$

Solve each system by graphing.

4. $\begin{cases} y = x + 5 \\ y = \frac{1}{2}x + 4 \end{cases}$

5. $\begin{cases} y = -x - 2 \\ 2x - y = 2 \end{cases}$

6. $\begin{cases} \frac{2}{3}x + y = -3 \\ 4x + y = 7 \end{cases}$

7. Banking Christiana and Marlena opened their first savings accounts on the same day. Christiana opened her account with $50 and plans to deposit $10 every month. Marlena opened her account with $30 and plans to deposit $15 every month. After how many months will their two accounts have the same amount of money? What will that amount be?

6-2 Solving Systems by Substitution

Solve each system by substitution.

8. $\begin{cases} y = -x + 5 \\ 2x + y = 11 \end{cases}$

9. $\begin{cases} 4x - 3y = -1 \\ 3x - y = -2 \end{cases}$

10. $\begin{cases} y = -x \\ y = -2x - 5 \end{cases}$

6-3 Solving Systems by Elimination

Solve each system by elimination.

11. $\begin{cases} x + 3y = 15 \\ 2x - 3y = -6 \end{cases}$

12. $\begin{cases} x + y = 2 \\ 2x + y = -1 \end{cases}$

13. $\begin{cases} -2x + 5y = -1 \\ 3x + 2y = 11 \end{cases}$

14. It takes Akira 10 minutes to make a black and white drawing and 25 minutes for a color drawing. On Saturday he made a total of 9 drawings in 2 hours. Write and solve a system of equations to determine how many drawings of each type Akira made.

6-4 Solving Special Systems

Solve each system of linear equations.

15. $\begin{cases} y = -2x - 6 \\ 2x + y = 5 \end{cases}$

16. $\begin{cases} x + y = 2 \\ 2x + 2y = -6 \end{cases}$

17. $\begin{cases} y = -2x + 4 \\ 2x + y = 4 \end{cases}$

Classify each system. Give the number of solutions.

18. $\begin{cases} 3x = -6y + 3 \\ 2y = -x + 1 \end{cases}$

19. $\begin{cases} y = -4x + 2 \\ 4x + y = -2 \end{cases}$

20. $\begin{cases} 4x - 3y = 8 \\ y = 4(x + 2) \end{cases}$

6-5 Solving Linear Inequalities

Objective
Graph and solve linear inequalities in two variables.

Vocabulary
linear inequality
solution of a linear
    inequality

Who uses this?
Consumers can use linear inequalities to determine how much food they can buy for an event. (See Example 3.)

A **linear inequality** is similar to a linear equation, but the equal sign is replaced with an inequality symbol. A **solution of a linear inequality** is any ordered pair that makes the inequality true.

EXAMPLE 1 Identifying Solutions of Inequalities

Tell whether the ordered pair is a solution of the inequality.

A $(7, 3); y < x - 1$

$$\begin{array}{c|c} y & < & x - 1 \\ \hline 3 & & 7 - 1 \\ 3 & < & 6 \checkmark \end{array}$$

Substitute (7, 3) for (x, y).

$(7, 3)$ is a solution.

B $(4, 5); y > 3x + 2$

$$\begin{array}{c|c} y & > & 3x + 2 \\ \hline 5 & & 3(4) + 2 \\ 5 & & 12 + 2 \\ 5 & > & 14 \ ✗ \end{array}$$

Substitute (4, 5) for (x, y).

$(4, 5)$ is not a solution.

 CHECK IT OUT! Tell whether the ordered pair is a solution of the inequality.

1a. $(4, 5); y < x + 1$ **1b.** $(1, 1); y > x - 7$

A linear inequality describes a region of a coordinate plane called a *half-plane*. All points in the region are solutions of the linear inequality. The boundary line of the region is the graph of the related equation.

When the inequality is written as $y \le$ or $y \ge$, the points on the boundary line are solutions of the inequality, and the line is **solid**.

When the inequality is written as $y <$ or $y >$, the points on the boundary line are not solutions of the inequality, and the line is **dashed**.

When the inequality is written as $y >$ or $y \ge$, the points **above** the boundary line are solutions of the inequality.

When the inequality is written as $y <$ or $y \le$, the points **below** the boundary line are solutions of the inequality.

	Graphing Linear Inequalities	
Step 1	Solve the inequality for y.	
Step 2	Graph the boundary line. Use a solid line for $\leq$ or $\geq$. Use a dashed line for $<$ or $>$.	
Step 3	Shade the half-plane above the line for $y >$ or $y \geq$. Shade the half-plane below the line for $y <$ or $y \leq$. Check your answer.	

EXAMPLE 2 **Graphing Linear Inequalities in Two Variables**

Graph the solutions of each linear inequality.

A $y < 3x + 4$

Step 1 The inequality is already solved for y.

Step 2 Graph the boundary line $y = 3x + 4$. Use a dashed line for $<$.

Step 3 The inequality is $<$, so shade below the line.

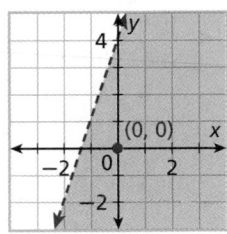

Helpful Hint

The point (0, 0) is a good test point to use if it does not lie on the boundary line.

Check $y < 3x + 4$

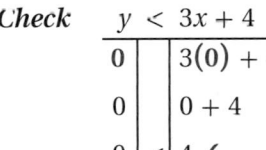

0	3(0) + 4
0	0 + 4
0 $<$	4 ✓

Substitute (0, 0) for (x, y) because it is not on the boundary line.

The point (0, 0) satisfies the inequality, so the graph is shaded correctly.

B $3x + 2y \geq 6$

Step 1 Solve the inequality for y.

$$3x + 2y \geq 6$$
$$\underline{-3x \qquad\qquad -3x}$$
$$2y \geq -3x + 6$$
$$y \geq -\frac{3}{2}x + 3$$

Step 2 Graph the boundary line $y = -\frac{3}{2}x + 3$. Use a solid line for $\geq$.

Step 3 The inequality is $\geq$, so shade above the line.

Check $y \geq \frac{3}{2}x + 3$

0	$\frac{3}{2}(0) + 3$
0	0 + 3
0 $\geq$	3 ✗

A false statement means that the half-plane containing (0, 0) should NOT be shaded. (0, 0) is not one of the solutions, so the graph is shaded correctly.

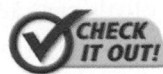 Graph the solutions of each linear inequality.

2a. $4x - 3y > 12$ **2b.** $2x - y - 4 > 0$ **2c.** $y \geq -\frac{2}{3}x + 1$

EXAMPLE 3 *Consumer Economics Application*

Sarah can spend at most $7.50 on vegetables for a party. Broccoli costs $1.25 per bunch and carrots cost $0.75 per package.

a. Write a linear inequality to describe the situation.

Let x represent the number of bunches of broccoli and let y represent the number of packages of carrots.

Write an inequality. Use $\leq$ for "at most."

Cost of broccoli	plus	cost of carrots	is at most	$7.50.
1.25x	+	0.75y	$\leq$	7.50

Solve the inequality for y.

$$1.25x + 0.75y \leq 7.50$$

$$100(1.25x + 0.75y) \leq 100(7.50)$$

$$125x + 75y \leq 750$$

$$\underline{-125x \qquad\qquad -125x}$$

$$75y \leq 750 - 125x$$

$$\frac{75y}{75} \leq \frac{750 - 125x}{75}$$

$$y \leq 10 - \frac{5}{3}x$$

You can multiply both sides of the inequality by 100 to eliminate the decimals.
Subtraction Property of Inequality

Division Property of Inequality

b. Graph the solutions.

Step 1 Since Sarah cannot buy a negative amount of vegetables, the system is graphed only in Quadrant I. Graph the boundary line $y = -\frac{5}{3}x + 10$. Use a solid line for $\leq$.

Step 2 Shade below the line. Sarah must buy whole numbers of bunches or packages. All points on or below the line with whole-number coordinates represent combinations of broccoli and carrots that Sarah can buy.

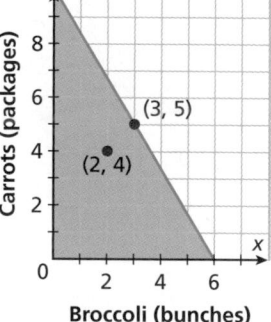

Vegetable Combinations

Carrots (packages) — vertical axis

(3, 5)

(2, 4)

Broccoli (bunches) — horizontal axis

c. Give two combinations of vegetables that Sarah can buy.

Two different combinations that Sarah could buy for $7.50 or less are 2 bunches of broccoli and 4 packages of carrots, or 3 bunches of broccoli and 5 packages of carrots.

CHECK IT OUT!

3. Dirk is going to bring two types of olives to the Honor Society induction and can spend no more than $6. Green olives cost $2 per pound and black olives cost $2.50 per pound.

    a. Write a linear inequality to describe the situation.

    b. Graph the solutions.

    c. Give two combinations of olives that Dirk could buy.

EXAMPLE 4 **Writing an Inequality from a Graph**

Write an inequality to represent each graph.

A

y-intercept: **2**; slope: $-\dfrac{1}{3}$

Write an equation in slope-intercept form.

$$y = mx + b \longrightarrow y = -\dfrac{1}{3}x + 2$$

The graph is shaded *below* a *dashed* boundary line.

Replace = with < to write the inequality $y < -\dfrac{1}{3}x + 2$.

B

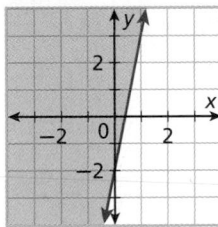

y-intercept: **−2**; slope: **5**

Write an equation in slope-intercept form.

$$y = mx + b \longrightarrow y = 5x + (-2)$$

The graph is shaded *above* a *solid* boundary line.

Replace = with ≥ to write the inequality $y \geq 5x - 2$.

C

y-intercept: **none**; slope: **undefined**

The graph is a vertical line at $x = -2$.

The graph is shaded on the *right* side of a *solid* boundary line.

Replace = with ≥ to write the inequality $x \geq -2$.

CHECK IT OUT! Write an inequality to represent each graph.

4a.   4b.

THINK AND DISCUSS

1. Tell how graphing a linear inequality is the same as graphing a linear equation. Tell how it is different.

2. Explain how you would write a linear inequality from a graph.

3. GET ORGANIZED Copy and complete the graphic organizer.

Inequality	$y < 5x + 2$	$y > 7x - 3$	$y \leq 9x + 1$	$y \geq -3x - 2$
Symbol	<			
Boundary Line	Dashed			
Shading	Below			

go.hrw.com
Homework Help Online
KEYWORD: MA7 6-5
Parent Resources Online
KEYWORD: MA7 Parent

GUIDED PRACTICE

1. **Vocabulary** Can a *solution of a linear inequality* lie on a dashed boundary line? Explain.

SEE EXAMPLE **1**
p. 428

Tell whether the ordered pair is a solution of the given inequality.

2. $(0, 3); y \le -x + 3$ 3. $(2, 0); y > -2x - 2$ 4. $(-2, 1); y < 2x + 4$

SEE EXAMPLE **2**
p. 429

Graph the solutions of each linear inequality.

5. $y \le -x$ 6. $y > 3x + 1$ 7. $-y < -x + 4$ 8. $-y \ge x + 1$

SEE EXAMPLE **3**
p. 430

9. **Multi-Step** Jack is making punch with orange juice and pineapple juice. He can make at most 16 cups of punch.

   a. Write an inequality to describe the situation.

   b. Graph the solutions.

   c. Give two combinations of cups of orange juice and pineapple juice that Jack can use in his punch.

SEE EXAMPLE **4**
p. 431

Write an inequality to represent each graph.

10.   11.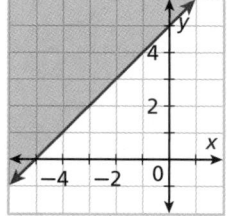

PRACTICE AND PROBLEM SOLVING

Tell whether the ordered pair is a solution of the given inequality.

12. $(2, 3); y \ge 2x + 3$ 13. $(1, -1); y < 3x - 3$ 14. $(0, 7); y > 4x + 7$

Graph the solutions of each linear inequality.

15. $y > -2x + 6$ 16. $-y \ge 2x$ 17. $x + y \le 2$ 18. $x - y \ge 0$

19. **Multi-Step** Beverly is serving hamburgers and hot dogs at her cookout. Hamburger meat costs $3 per pound, and hot dogs cost $2 per pound. She wants to spend no more than $30.

    a. Write an inequality to describe the situation.

    b. Graph the solutions.

    c. Give two combinations of pounds of hamburger and hot dogs that Beverly can buy.

Write an inequality to represent each graph.

20.   21.

22. **Business** An electronics store makes $125 profit on every DVD player it sells and $100 on every CD player it sells. The store owner wants to make a profit of at least $500 a day selling DVD players and CD players.

    a. Write a linear inequality to determine the number of DVD players x and the number of CD players y that the owner needs to sell to meet his goal.

    b. Graph the linear inequality.

    c. Describe the possible values of x. Describe the possible values of y.

    d. List three combinations of DVD players and CD players that the owner could sell to meet his goal.

Graph the solutions of each linear inequality.

23. $y \leq 2 - 3x$ 24. $-y < 7 + x$ 25. $2x - y \leq 4$ 26. $3x - 2y > 6$

 27. **Geometry** Marvin has 18 yards of fencing that he can use to put around a rectangular garden.

    a. Write an inequality to describe the possible lengths and widths of the garden.

    b. Graph the inequality and list three possible solutions to the problem.

    c. What are the dimensions of the largest *square* garden that can be fenced in with whole-number dimensions?

28. **Hobbies** Stephen wants to buy yellow tangs and clown fish for his saltwater aquarium. He wants to spend no more than $77 on fish. At the store, yellow tangs cost $15 each and clown fish cost $11 each. Write and graph a linear inequality to find the number of yellow tangs x and the number of clown fish y that Stephen could purchase. Name a solution of your inequality that is not reasonable for the situation. Explain.

Graph each inequality on a coordinate plane.

29. $y > 1$ 30. $-2 < x$ 31. $x \geq -3$ 32. $y \leq 0$

33. $0 \geq x$ 34. $-12 + y > 0$ 35. $x + 7 < 7$ 36. $-4 \geq x - y$

37. **School** At a high school football game, tickets at the gate cost $7 per adult and $4 per student. Write a linear inequality to determine the number of adult and student tickets that need to be sold so that the amount of money taken in at the gate is at least $280. Graph the inequality and list three possible solutions.

38. **Critical Thinking** Why must a region of a coordinate plane be shaded to show all solutions of a linear inequality?

39. **Write About It** Give a real-world situation that can be described by a linear inequality. Then graph the inequality and give two solutions.

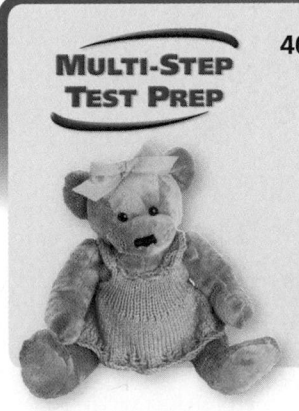

MULTI-STEP TEST PREP

40. This problem will prepare you for the Multi-Step Test Prep on page 442.

    Gloria is making teddy bears. She is making boy and girl bears. She has enough stuffing to create 50 bears. Let x represent the number of girl bears and y represent the number of boy bears.

    a. Write an inequality that shows the possible number of boy and girl bears Gloria can make.

    b. Graph the inequality.

    c. Give three possible solutions for the numbers of boy and girl bears that can be made.

41. ///ERROR ANALYSIS/// Student A wrote $y < 2x - 1$ as the inequality represented by the graph. Student B wrote $y \leq 2x - 1$ as the inequality represented by the graph. Which student is incorrect? Explain the error.

42. Write About It How do you decide to shade above or below a boundary line? What does this shading represent?

43. Which point is a solution of the inequality $y > -x + 3$?

Ⓐ $(0, 3)$ Ⓑ $(1, 4)$ Ⓒ $(-1, 4)$ Ⓓ $(0, -3)$

44. Which inequality is represented by the graph at right?

Ⓕ $2x + y \geq 3$ Ⓗ $2x + y \leq 3$

Ⓖ $2x + y > 3$ Ⓙ $2x + y < 3$

45. Which of the following describes the graph of $3 \leq x$?

Ⓐ The boundary line is dashed, and the shading is to the right.

Ⓑ The boundary line is dashed, and the shading is to the left.

Ⓒ The boundary line is solid, and the shading is to the right.

Ⓓ The boundary line is solid, and the shading is to the left.

CHALLENGE AND EXTEND

Graph each inequality.

46. $0 \geq -6 - 2x - 5y$ **47.** $y > |x|$ **48.** $y \geq |x - 3|$

49. A linear inequality has the points $(0, 3)$ and $(-3, 1.5)$ as solutions on the boundary line. Also, the point $(1, 1)$ is not a solution. Write the linear inequality.

50. Two linear inequalities are graphed on the same coordinate plane. The point $(0, 0)$ is a solution of both inequalities. The entire coordinate plane is shaded except for Quadrant I. What are the two inequalities?

SPIRAL REVIEW

Tell whether each function is linear. If so, graph the function. *(Lesson 5-1)*

51. $y = 2x - 4$ **52.** $y = x^2 + 2$ **53.** $y = 3$

Write an equation in slope-intercept form for the line through the two points. *(Lesson 5-8)*

54. $(0, 9)$ and $(5, 2)$ **55.** $(-5, -2)$ and $(7, 7)$ **56.** $(0, 0)$ and $(-8, -10)$

57. $(-1, -2)$ and $(1, 4)$ **58.** $(2, 2)$ and $(6, 5)$ **59.** $(-3, 2)$ and $(3, -1)$

Solve each system by elimination. *(Lesson 6-3)*

60. $\begin{cases} x + 6y = 14 \\ x - 6y = -10 \end{cases}$ **61.** $\begin{cases} x + y = 13 \\ 3x + y = 9 \end{cases}$ **62.** $\begin{cases} 2x - 4y = 18 \\ 5x - y = 36 \end{cases}$

63. $\begin{cases} 2y + x = 12 \\ y - 2x = 1 \end{cases}$ **64.** $\begin{cases} 2y - 6x = -8 \\ y = -5x + 12 \end{cases}$ **65.** $\begin{cases} 2x + 3y = 33 \\ y = \frac{1}{4}x \end{cases}$

Solving Systems of Linear Inequalities

Objective
Graph and solve systems of linear inequalities in two variables.

Vocabulary
system of linear inequalities
solutions of a system of linear inequalities

Who uses this?
The owner of a surf shop can use systems of linear inequalities to determine how many surfboards and wakeboards need to be sold to make a certain profit. (See Example 4.)

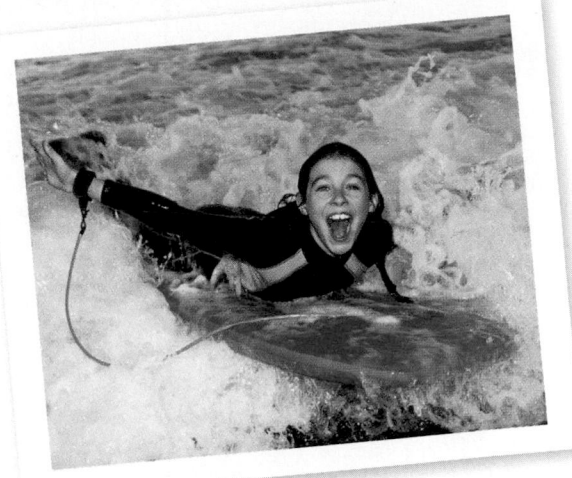

A **system of linear inequalities** is a set of two or more linear inequalities containing two or more variables. The **solutions of a system of linear inequalities** are all of the ordered pairs that satisfy all the linear inequalities in the system.

E X A M P L E 1 Identifying Solutions of Systems of Linear Inequalities

Tell whether the ordered pair is a solution of the given system.

> **Remember!**
> An ordered pair must be a solution of all inequalities to be a solution of the system.

A $(2, 1)$; $\begin{cases} y < -x + 4 \\ y \le x + 1 \end{cases}$

$(2, 1)$
$$\begin{array}{c|c} y < -x + 4 \\ \hline 1 & -2 + 4 \\ 1 & < 2 \checkmark \end{array}$$

$(2, 1)$
$$\begin{array}{c|c} y \le x + 1 \\ \hline 1 & 2 + 1 \\ 1 & \le 3 \checkmark \end{array}$$

$(2, 1)$ is a solution to the system because it satisfies both inequalities.

B $(2, 0)$; $\begin{cases} y \ge 2x \\ y < x + 1 \end{cases}$

$(2, 0)$
$$\begin{array}{c|c} y \ge 2x \\ \hline 0 & 2(2) \\ 0 & \ge 4 ✗ \end{array}$$

$(2, 0)$
$$\begin{array}{c|c} y < x + 1 \\ \hline 0 & 2 + 1 \\ 0 & < 3 \checkmark \end{array}$$

$(2, 0)$ is not a solution to the system because it does not satisfy both inequalities.

 Tell whether the ordered pair is a solution of the given system.

1a. $(0, 1)$; $\begin{cases} y < -3x + 2 \\ y \ge x - 1 \end{cases}$

1b. $(0, 0)$; $\begin{cases} y > -x + 1 \\ y > x - 1 \end{cases}$

To show all the solutions of a system of linear inequalities, graph the solutions of each inequality. The solutions of the system are represented by the overlapping shaded regions. Below are graphs of Examples 1A and 1B.

Example 1A

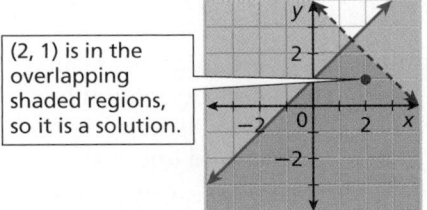

(2, 1) is in the overlapping shaded regions, so it is a solution.

Example 1B

(2, 0) is not in the overlapping shaded regions, so it is not a solution.

EXAMPLE **2** **Solving a System of Linear Inequalities by Graphing**

Graph the system of linear inequalities. Give two ordered pairs that are solutions and two that are not solutions.

$$\begin{cases} 8x + 4y \le 12 \\ y > \dfrac{1}{2}x - 2 \end{cases}$$

$8x + 4y \le 12$ *Solve the first inequality for y.*
       $4y \le -8x + 12$
         $y \le -2x + 3$

Graph the system.

$$\begin{cases} y \le -2x + 3 \\ y > \dfrac{1}{2}x - 2 \end{cases}$$

$(-1, 1)$ and $(-3, 4)$ are solutions.
$(2, -1)$ and $(2, -4)$ are not solutions.

CHECK IT OUT! Graph each system of linear inequalities. Give two ordered pairs that are solutions and two that are not solutions.

2a. $\begin{cases} y \le x + 1 \\ y > 2 \end{cases}$

2b. $\begin{cases} y > x - 7 \\ 3x + 6y \le 12 \end{cases}$

In Lesson 6-4, you saw that in systems of linear equations, if the lines are parallel, there are no solutions. With systems of linear inequalities, that is not always true.

EXAMPLE **3** **Graphing Systems with Parallel Boundary Lines**

Graph each system of linear inequalities. Describe the solutions.

A $\begin{cases} y < 2x - 3 \\ y > 2x + 2 \end{cases}$

B $\begin{cases} y > x - 3 \\ y \le x + 1 \end{cases}$

C $\begin{cases} y \le -3x - 2 \\ y \le -3x + 4 \end{cases}$

This system has no solution.

The solutions are all points between the parallel lines and on the solid line.

The solutions are the same as the solutions of $y \le -3x - 2$.

436 *Chapter 6 Systems of Equations and Inequalities*

Graph each system of linear inequalities. Describe the solutions.

3a. $\begin{cases} y > x + 1 \\ y \leq x - 3 \end{cases}$ 　　**3b.** $\begin{cases} y \geq 4x - 2 \\ y \leq 4x + 2 \end{cases}$ 　　**3c.** $\begin{cases} y > -2x + 3 \\ y > -2x \end{cases}$

EXAMPLE 4 　*Business Application*

A surf shop makes the profits given in the table. The shop owner sells at least 10 surfboards and at least 20 wakeboards per month. He wants to earn at least $2000 a month. Show and describe all possible combinations of surfboards and wakeboards that the store owner needs to sell to meet his goals. List two possible combinations.

Profit per Board Sold ($)	
Surfboard	150
Wakeboard	100

Step 1 Write a system of inequalities.
Let x represent the number of surfboards and y represent the number of wakeboards.

$x \geq 10$ 　　　　*He sells at least 10 surfboards.*

$y \geq 20$ 　　　　*He sells at least 20 wakeboards.*

$150x + 100y \geq 2000$ 　　*He wants to earn a total of at least $2000.*

Step 2 Graph the system.
The graph should be in only the first quadrant because sales are not negative.

Step 3 Describe all possible combinations.
To meet the sales goals, the shop could sell any combination represented by an ordered pair of whole numbers in the solution region. Answers must be whole numbers because the shop cannot sell part of a surfboard or wakeboard.

Sales Goals

Step 4 List two possible combinations.
Two possible combinations are:
15 surfboards and 25 wakeboards
25 surfboards and 20 wakeboards

4. At her party, Alice is serving pepper jack cheese and cheddar cheese. She wants to have at least 2 pounds of each. Alice wants to spend at most $20 on cheese. Show and describe all possible combinations of the two cheeses Alice could buy. List two possible combinations.

Price per Pound ($)	
Pepper Jack	4
Cheddar	2

THINK AND DISCUSS

1. How would you write a system of linear inequalities from a graph?

2. GET ORGANIZED Copy and complete each part of the graphic organizer. In each box, draw a graph and list one solution.

$\begin{cases} y \geq 2x + 1 \\ y > \frac{1}{2}x - 2 \end{cases}$ 　　 $\begin{cases} y < 2x + 1 \\ y \geq \frac{1}{2}x - 2 \end{cases}$

| Graph | Solution | | Graph | Solution |

go.hrw.com
Homework Help Online
KEYWORD: MA7 6-6
Parent Resources Online
KEYWORD: MA7 Parent

GUIDED PRACTICE

1. **Vocabulary** A solution of a system of inequalities is a solution of _____?_____ of the inequalities in the system. (*at least one* or *all*)

SEE EXAMPLE 1
p. 435

Tell whether the ordered pair is a solution of the given system.

2. $(0, 0);$ $\begin{cases} y < -x + 3 \\ y < x + 2 \end{cases}$

3. $(0, 0);$ $\begin{cases} y < 3 \\ y > x - 2 \end{cases}$

4. $(1, 0);$ $\begin{cases} y > 3x \\ y \le x + 1 \end{cases}$

SEE EXAMPLE 2
p. 436

Graph each system of linear inequalities. Give two ordered pairs that are solutions and two that are not solutions.

5. $\begin{cases} y < 2x - 1 \\ y > 2 \end{cases}$

6. $\begin{cases} x < 3 \\ y > x - 2 \end{cases}$

7. $\begin{cases} y \ge 3x \\ 3x + y \ge 3 \end{cases}$

8. $\begin{cases} 2x - 4y \le 8 \\ y > x - 2 \end{cases}$

SEE EXAMPLE 3
p. 436

Graph each system of linear inequalities. Describe the solutions.

9. $\begin{cases} y > 2x + 3 \\ y < 2x \end{cases}$

10. $\begin{cases} y \le -3x - 1 \\ y \ge -3x + 1 \end{cases}$

11. $\begin{cases} y > 4x - 1 \\ y \le 4x + 1 \end{cases}$

12. $\begin{cases} y < -x + 3 \\ y > -x + 2 \end{cases}$

13. $\begin{cases} y > 2x - 1 \\ y > 2x - 4 \end{cases}$

14. $\begin{cases} y \le -3x + 4 \\ y \le -3x - 3 \end{cases}$

SEE EXAMPLE 4
p. 437

15. **Business** Sandy makes $2 profit on every cup of lemonade that she sells and $1 on every cupcake that she sells. Sandy wants to sell at least 5 cups of lemonade and at least 5 cupcakes per day. She wants to earn at least $25 per day. Show and describe all the possible combinations of lemonade and cupcakes that Sandy needs to sell to meet her goals. List two possible combinations.

PRACTICE AND PROBLEM SOLVING

Independent Practice	
For Exercises	See Example
16–18	1
19–22	2
23–28	3
29	4

Extra Practice
Skills Practice p. S15
Application Practice p. S33

Tell whether the ordered pair is a solution of the given system.

16. $(0, 0);$ $\begin{cases} y > -x - 1 \\ y < 2x + 4 \end{cases}$

17. $(0, 0);$ $\begin{cases} x + y < 3 \\ y > 3x - 4 \end{cases}$

18. $(1, 0);$ $\begin{cases} y > 3x \\ y > 3x + 1 \end{cases}$

Graph each system of linear inequalities. Give two ordered pairs that are solutions and two that are not solutions.

19. $\begin{cases} y < -3x - 3 \\ y \ge 0 \end{cases}$

20. $\begin{cases} y < -1 \\ y > 2x - 1 \end{cases}$

21. $\begin{cases} y > 2x + 4 \\ 6x + 2y \ge -2 \end{cases}$

22. $\begin{cases} 9x + 3y \le 6 \\ y > x \end{cases}$

Graph each system of linear inequalities. Describe the solutions.

23. $\begin{cases} y < 3 \\ y > 5 \end{cases}$

24. $\begin{cases} y < x - 1 \\ y > x - 2 \end{cases}$

25. $\begin{cases} x \ge 2 \\ x \le 2 \end{cases}$

26. $\begin{cases} y > -4x - 3 \\ y < -4x + 2 \end{cases}$

27. $\begin{cases} y > -1 \\ y > 2 \end{cases}$

28. $\begin{cases} y \le 2x + 1 \\ y \le 2x - 4 \end{cases}$

29. **Multi-Step** Linda works at a pharmacy for $15 an hour. She also baby-sits for $10 an hour. Linda needs to earn at least $90 per week, but she does not want to work more than 20 hours per week. Show and describe the number of hours Linda could work at each job to meet her goals. List two possible solutions.

30. **Farming** Tony wants to plant at least 40 acres of corn and at least 50 acres of soybeans. He wants no more than 200 acres of corn and soybeans. Show and describe all the possible combinations of the number of acres of corn and of soybeans Tony could plant. List two possible combinations.

Graph each system of linear inequalities.

31. $\begin{cases} y \geq -3 \\ y \geq 2 \end{cases}$　　32. $\begin{cases} y > -2x - 1 \\ y > -2x - 3 \end{cases}$　　33. $\begin{cases} x \leq -3 \\ x \geq 1 \end{cases}$　　34. $\begin{cases} y < 4 \\ y > 0 \end{cases}$

Write a system of linear inequalities to represent each graph.

35. 　　36. 　　37.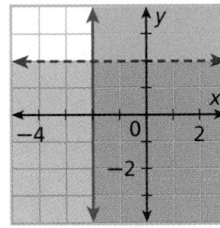

38. **Military** For males to enter the United States Air Force Academy, located in Colorado Springs, CO, they must be at least 17 but less than 23 years of age. Their standing height must be not less than 60 inches and not greater than 80 inches. Graph all possible heights and ages for eligible male candidates. Give three possible combinations.

39. **///ERROR ANALYSIS///** Two students wrote a system of linear inequalities to describe the graph. Which student is incorrect? Explain the error.

A 　　B

40. **Recreation** Vance wants to fence in a rectangular area for his dog. He wants the length of the rectangle to be at least 30 feet and the perimeter to be no more than 150 feet. Graph all possible dimensions of the rectangle.

41. **Critical Thinking** Can the solutions of a system of linear inequalities be the points on a line? Explain.

MULTI-STEP TEST PREP

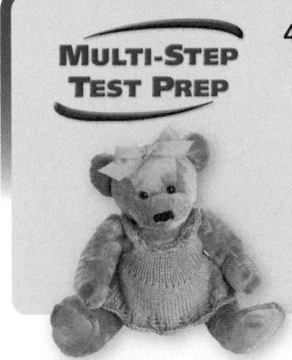

42. This problem will prepare you for the Multi-Step Test Prep on page 442.

Gloria is starting her own company making teddy bears. She has enough bear bodies to create 40 bears. She will make girl bears and boy bears.

a. Write an inequality to show this situation.

b. Gloria will charge $15 for girl bears and $12 for boy bears. She wants to earn at least $540 a week. Write an inequality to describe this situation.

c. Graph this situation and locate the solution region.

43. **Write About It** What must be true of the boundary lines in a system of two linear inequalities if there is no solution of the system? Explain.

44. Which point is a solution of $\begin{cases} 2x + y \geq 3 \\ y \geq -2x + 1 \end{cases}$?

  (A) $(0, 0)$ (B) $(0, 1)$ (C) $(1, 0)$ (D) $(1, 1)$

45. Which system of inequalities best describes the graph?

  (F) $\begin{cases} y < 2x - 3 \\ y > 2x + 1 \end{cases}$ (H) $\begin{cases} y < 2x - 3 \\ y < 2x + 1 \end{cases}$

  (G) $\begin{cases} y > 2x - 3 \\ y < 2x + 1 \end{cases}$ (J) $\begin{cases} y > 2x - 3 \\ y > 2x + 1 \end{cases}$

46. **Short Response** Graph and describe $\begin{cases} y + x > 2 \\ y \leq -3x + 4 \end{cases}$. Give two possible solutions of the system.

CHALLENGE AND EXTEND

47. **Estimation** Graph the given system of inequalities. Estimate the area of the overlapping solution regions.
$$\begin{cases} y \geq 0 \\ y \leq x + 3.5 \\ y \leq -x + 3.5 \end{cases}$$

48. Write a system of linear inequalities for which $(-1, 1)$ and $(1, 4)$ are solutions and $(0, 0)$ and $(2, -1)$ are not solutions.

49. Graph $|y| < 1$.

50. Write a system of linear inequalities for which the solutions are all the points in the third quadrant.

SPIRAL REVIEW

Use the diagram to find each of the following. *(Lesson 1-6)*

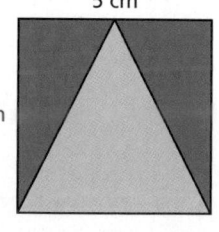

51. area of the square

52. area of the yellow triangle

53. combined area of the blue triangles

Tell whether the given ordered pairs satisfy a linear function. *(Lesson 5-1)*

54. $\{(3, 8), (4, 6), (5, 4), (6, 2), (7, 0)\}$ 55. $\{(6, 1), (7, 2), (8, 4), (9, 7), (10, 11)\}$

56. $\{(2, 10), (7, 9), (12, 8), (17, 7), (22, 6)\}$ 57. $\{(1, -9), (3, -7), (5, -5), (7, -3), (9, -1)\}$

Graph the solutions of each linear inequality. *(Lesson 6-5)*

58. $y \leq 2x - 1$ 59. $-\frac{1}{4}x + y > 6$ 60. $5 - x \geq 0$

Solve Systems of Linear Inequalities

A graphing calculator gives a visual solution to a system of linear inequalities.

Use with Lesson 6-6

Activity

Graph the system $\begin{cases} y > 2x - 4 \\ 2.75y - x < 6 \end{cases}$. Give two ordered pairs that are solutions.

1 The first inequality is solved for y.

2 Graph the first inequality. First graph the boundary line $y = 2x - 4$. Press **Y=** and enter $2x - 4$ for **Y1.**

The inequality contains the symbol >. The solution region is above the boundary line. Press ◀ to move the cursor to the left of **Y1**. Press **ENTER** until the icon that looks like a region above a line appears. Press **GRAPH**.

3 Solve the second inequality for y.

$$2.75y - x < 6$$
$$2.75y < x + 6$$
$$y < \frac{x + 6}{2.75}$$

4 Graph the second inequality. First graph the boundary line $y = \frac{x + 6}{2.75}$. Press **Y=** and enter $(x + 6)/2.75$ for **Y2.**

The inequality contains the symbol <. The solution region is below the boundary line. Press ◀ to move the cursor to the left of **Y2**. Press **ENTER** until the icon that looks like a region below a line appears. Press **GRAPH**.

5 The solutions of the system are represented by the overlapping shaded regions. The points $(0, 0)$ and $(-1, 0)$ are in the shaded region.

Check   Test $(0, 0)$ in both inequalities.

$y > 2x - 4$	
0	$2(0) - 4$
0	> −4 ✓

$2.75y - x < 6$	
$2.75(0) - 0$	6
0	< 6 ✓

Test $(-1, 0)$ in both inequalities.

$y > 2x - 4$	
0	$2(-1) - 4$
0	> −6 ✓

$2.75y - x < 6$	
$2.75(0) - (-1)$	6
1	< 6 ✓

Try This

Graph each system. Give two ordered pairs that are solutions.

1. $\begin{cases} x + 5y > -10 \\ x - y < 4 \end{cases}$

2. $\begin{cases} y > x - 2 \\ y \le x + 2 \end{cases}$

3. $\begin{cases} y > x - 2 \\ y \le 3 \end{cases}$

4. $\begin{cases} y < x - 3 \\ y - 3 > x \end{cases}$

MULTI-STEP TEST PREP

Equations and Formulas

Bearable Sales Gloria makes teddy bears. She dresses some as girl bears with dresses and bows and some as boy bears with bow ties. She is running low on supplies. She has only 100 eyes, 30 dresses, and 60 ties that can be used as bows on the girls and bow ties on the boys.

1. Write the inequalities that describe this situation. Let x represent the number of boy bears and y represent the number of girl bears.

2. Graph the inequalities and locate the region showing the number of boy and girl bears Gloria can make.

3. List at least three combinations of girl and boy bears that Gloria can make.

For 4 and 5, use the table.

4. Using the boundary line in your graph from Problem 2, copy and complete the table with the corresponding number of girl bears.

5. Gloria sells the bears for profit. She makes a profit of $8 for the girl bears and $5 for the boy bears. Use the table from Problem 4 to find the profit she makes for each given combination.

6. Which combination is the most profitable? Explain. Where does it lie on the graph?

Bear Combinations	
Boy	**Girl**
0	
10	
20	
30	
40	
50	

READY TO GO ON?

Quiz for Lessons 6-5 Through 6-6

✓ **6-5** **Solving Linear Inequalities**

Tell whether the ordered pair is a solution of the inequality.

1. $(3, -2)$; $y < -2x + 1$ **2.** $(2, 1)$; $y \geq 3x - 5$ **3.** $(1, -6)$; $y \leq 4x - 10$

Graph the solutions of each linear inequality.

4. $y \geq 4x - 3$ **5.** $3x - y < 5$ **6.** $2x + 3y < 9$ **7.** $y \leq -\frac{1}{2}x$

8. Theo's mother has given him at most $150 to buy clothes for school. The pants cost $30 each and the shirts cost $15 each. Write a linear inequality to describe the situation. Graph the solutions and give three combinations of pants and shirts that Theo could buy.

Write an inequality to represent each graph.

9.   **10.**   **11.**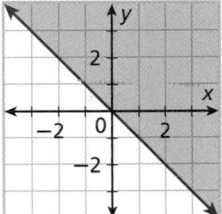

✓ **6-6** **Solving Systems of Linear Inequalities**

Tell whether the ordered pair is a solution of the given system.

12. $(-3, -1)$; $\begin{cases} y > -2 \\ y < x + 4 \end{cases}$ **13.** $(-3, 0)$; $\begin{cases} y \leq x + 4 \\ y \geq -2x - 6 \end{cases}$ **14.** $(0, 0)$; $\begin{cases} y \geq 3x \\ 2x + y < -1 \end{cases}$

Graph each system of linear inequalities. Give two ordered pairs that are solutions and two that are not solutions.

15. $\begin{cases} y > -2 \\ y < x + 3 \end{cases}$ **16.** $\begin{cases} x + y \leq 2 \\ 2x + y \geq -1 \end{cases}$ **17.** $\begin{cases} 2x - 5y \leq -5 \\ 3x + 2y < 10 \end{cases}$

Graph each system of linear inequalities. Describe the solutions.

18. $\begin{cases} y \geq x + 1 \\ y \geq x - 4 \end{cases}$ **19.** $\begin{cases} y \geq 2x - 1 \\ y < 2x - 3 \end{cases}$ **20.** $\begin{cases} y < -3x + 5 \\ y > -3x - 2 \end{cases}$

21. A grocer sells mangos for $4/lb and apples for $3/lb. The grocer starts with 45 lb of mangos and 50 lb of apples each day. The grocer's goal is to make at least $300 by selling mangos and apples each day. Show and describe all possible combinations of mangos and apples that could be sold to meet the goal. List two possible combinations.

Vocabulary

Complete the sentences below with vocabulary words from the list above.

1. A(n) ___?___ is a system that has exactly one solution.

2. A set of two or more linear equations that contain the same variable(s) is
a(n) ___?___ .

3. The ___?___ consists of all the ordered pairs that satisfy all the inequalities
in the system.

4. A system consisting of equations of parallel lines with different y-intercepts
is a(n) ___?___ .

5. A(n) ___?___ consists of two intersecting lines.

6-1 Solving Systems by Graphing (pp. 397–402)

EXAMPLE

■ Solve $\begin{cases} y = 2x - 2 \\ x + 2y = 16 \end{cases}$ by graphing.

Check your answer.

$\begin{cases} y = 2x - 2 \\ y = -\dfrac{1}{2}x + 8 \end{cases}$ *Write the second equation in slope-intercept form.*

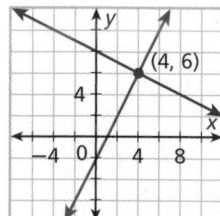

The solution appears to be at $(4, 6)$.

$y = 2x - 2$			$x + 2y = 16$	
6	$2(4) - 2$		$4 + 2(6)$	16
6	6 ✓		16	16 ✓

The ordered pair $(4, 6)$ makes both equations
true, so it is a solution of the system.

EXERCISES

Tell whether the ordered pair is a solution of the
given system.

6. $(0, -5); \begin{cases} y = -6x + 5 \\ x - y = 5 \end{cases}$ **7.** $(4, 3); \begin{cases} x - 2y = -2 \\ y = \dfrac{1}{2}x + 1 \end{cases}$

8. $\left(1\dfrac{3}{4}, 7\dfrac{1}{4}\right); \begin{cases} x + y = 9 \\ 2y = 6x + 4 \end{cases}$ **9.** $(-1, -1); \begin{cases} y = -2x + 5 \\ 3y = 6x + 3 \end{cases}$

Solve each system by graphing. Check your answer.

10. $\begin{cases} y = 3x + 2 \\ y = -2x - 3 \end{cases}$ **11.** $\begin{cases} y = -\dfrac{1}{3}x + 5 \\ 2x - 2y = -2 \end{cases}$

12. Raheel is comparing the cost of two parking
garages. Garage A charges a flat fee of $6 per car
plus $0.50 per hour. Garage B charges a flat fee of
$2 per car plus $1 per hour. After how many hours
will the cost at garage A be the same as the cost at
garage B? What will that cost be?

6-2 Solving Systems by Substitution (pp. 404–410)

EXAMPLE

■ Solve $\begin{cases} 2x - 3y = -2 \\ y - 3x = 10 \end{cases}$ by substitution.

Step 1 $y - 3x = 10$ — *Solve the second*
$\qquad\quad y = 3x + 10$ — *equation for y.*

Step 2 $\qquad\quad 2x - 3y = -2$ — *Substitute 3x + 10*
$\qquad 2x - 3(3x + 10) = -2$ — *for y in the first equation.*

Step 3 $2x - 9x - 30 = -2$ — *Solve for x.*
$\qquad\quad -7x - 30 = -2$
$\qquad\qquad\quad -7x = 28$
$\qquad\qquad\qquad x = -4$

Step 4 $\qquad y - 3x = 10$ — *Substitute −4 for x.*
$\qquad\quad y - 3(-4) = 10$
$\qquad\quad\; y + 12 = 10$ — *Find the value of y.*
$\qquad\qquad\quad y = -2$

Step 5 $(-4, -2)$ — *Write the solution as an ordered pair.*

To check the solution, substitute $(-4, -2)$ into both equations in the system.

EXERCISES

Solve each system by substitution.

13. $\begin{cases} y = x + 3 \\ y = 2x + 12 \end{cases}$ **14.** $\begin{cases} y = -4x \\ y = 2x - 3 \end{cases}$

15. $\begin{cases} 2x + y = 4 \\ 3x + y = 3 \end{cases}$ **16.** $\begin{cases} x + y = -1 \\ y = -2x + 3 \end{cases}$

17. $\begin{cases} x = y - 7 \\ -y - 2x = 8 \end{cases}$ **18.** $\begin{cases} \frac{1}{2}x + y = 9 \\ 3x - 4y = -6 \end{cases}$

19. The Nash family's car needs repairs. Estimates for parts and labor from two garages are shown below.

Garage	Parts ($)	Labor ($ per hour)
Motor Works	650	70
Jim's Car Care	800	55

For how many hours of labor will the total cost of fixing the car be the same at both garages? What will that cost be? Which garage will be cheaper if the repairs require 8 hours of labor? Explain.

6-3 Solving Systems by Elimination (pp. 411–417)

EXAMPLE

■ Solve $\begin{cases} 2x - 3y = -8 \\ x + 4y = 7 \end{cases}$ by elimination.

Step 1 $\qquad 2x - 3y = -8$ — *Multiply the*
$\qquad +(-2)(x + 4y = 7)$ — *second equation by −2.*
$\qquad\quad\; 2x - 3y = -8$ — *Eliminate x.*
$\qquad +(-2x - 8y = -14)$

Step 2 $\qquad -11y = -22$ — *Solve for y.*
$\qquad\qquad\quad\; y = 2$

Step 3 $\quad 2x - 3y = -8$
$\qquad 2x - 3(2) = -8$ — *Substitute 2 for y.*
$\qquad\; 2x - 6 = -8$ — *Simplify and solve*
$\qquad\qquad 2x = -2$ — *for x.*
$\qquad\qquad\; x = -1$

Step 4 $(-1, 2)$ — *Write the solution as an ordered pair.*

To check the solution, substitute $(-1, 2)$ into both equations in the system.

EXERCISES

Solve each system by elimination.

20. $\begin{cases} 4x + y = -1 \\ 2x - y = -5 \end{cases}$ **21.** $\begin{cases} x + 2y = -1 \\ x + y = 2 \end{cases}$

22. $\begin{cases} x + y = 12 \\ 2x + 5y = 27 \end{cases}$ **23.** $\begin{cases} 3x - 2y = -6 \\ \frac{1}{3}x + 3y = 9 \end{cases}$

Solve each system by any method. Explain why you chose each method. Check your answer.

24. $\begin{cases} 3x + y = 2 \\ y = -4x \end{cases}$ **25.** $\begin{cases} y = \frac{1}{3}x - 6 \\ y = -2x + 1 \end{cases}$

26. $\begin{cases} 2y = -3x \\ y = -2x + 2 \end{cases}$ **27.** $\begin{cases} x - y = 0 \\ 3x + y = 8 \end{cases}$

EXAMPLES

Classify each system. Give the number of solutions.

■ $\begin{cases} y = 3x + 4 \\ 6x - 2y = -8 \end{cases}$

Use the substitution method because the first equation is solved for y.

$6x - 2(3x + 4) = -8$ *Substitute $3x + 4$ for y in*
$6x - 6x - 8 = -8$ *the second equation.*
$-8 = -8$ ✓   *True*

The equation is an identity. There are infinitely many solutions.

This system is **consistent** and **dependent**. When graphed, the two lines are coincident (the same line)—they have identical slopes and y-intercepts.

■ $\begin{cases} y = 2x - 1 \\ 2x - y = -2 \end{cases}$

Compare slopes and y-intercepts. Write both equations in slope-intercept form.

$\begin{cases} y = 2x - 1 & \Rightarrow y = 2x - 1 \\ 2x - y = -2 & \Rightarrow y = 2x + 2 \end{cases}$

The lines have the same slope and different y-intercepts. The lines are parallel.

The lines never intersect, so this system is **inconsistent**. It has **no solution.**

■ $\begin{cases} 2x - y = 6 \\ y = x - 1 \end{cases}$

Write both equations in slope-intercept form.

$\begin{cases} 2x - y = 6 & \Rightarrow y = 2x - 6 \\ y = x - 1 & \Rightarrow y = 1x - 1 \end{cases}$

The lines intersect because they have different slopes.

The system is **consistent** and **independent**. There is **one solution:** $(5, 4)$.

EXERCISES

Solve each system of linear equations.

28. $\begin{cases} y = \dfrac{1}{4}x - 3 \\ y = \dfrac{1}{4}x + 5 \end{cases}$

29. $\begin{cases} y = -x + 4 \\ x + y = 4 \end{cases}$

30. $\begin{cases} y = 3x + 2 \\ y = 2x \end{cases}$

31. $\begin{cases} -4x - y = 6 \\ \dfrac{1}{2}y = -2x - 3 \end{cases}$

32. $\begin{cases} x + 2y = 8 \\ y = -\dfrac{1}{2}x + 4 \end{cases}$

33. $\begin{cases} y - 2x = -1 \\ y + 2x = -5 \end{cases}$

34. Tristan and his friend Marco just started DVD collections. They continue to get DVDs at the rate shown in the table below. Will Tristan ever have the same number of DVDs as Marco? Explain.

DVD Collections			
	Month 1	Month 2	Month 3
Tristan	2	7	12
Marco	8	12	16

Classify each system. Give the number of solutions.

35. $\begin{cases} y = \dfrac{1}{2}x + 2 \\ y = \dfrac{1}{4}x - 8 \end{cases}$

36. $\begin{cases} y = 3x - 7 \\ y = 3x + 2 \end{cases}$

37. $\begin{cases} 2x + y = 2 \\ y - 2 = -2x \end{cases}$

38. $\begin{cases} -3x - y = -5 \\ y = -3x - 5 \end{cases}$

39. $\begin{cases} 2x + 3y = 1 \\ 3x + 2y = 1 \end{cases}$

40. $\begin{cases} x + \dfrac{1}{2}y = 3 \\ 2x = 6 - y \end{cases}$

41. The two parallel lines graphed below represent a system of equations. Classify the system and give the number of solutions.

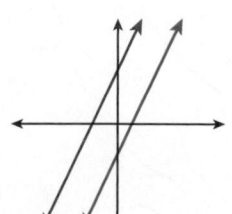

6-5 Solving Linear Inequalities (pp. 428–434)

EXAMPLE

■ Graph the solutions of $x - 2y < 6$.

Step 1 Solve the inequality for y.

$$x - 2y < 6$$
$$-2y < -x + 6$$
$$y > \frac{1}{2}x - 3$$

Step 2 Graph $y = \frac{1}{2}x - 3$.
Use a dashed line for >.

Step 3 The inequality is
>, so shade above the
boundary line.

Check Substitute $(0, 0)$ for (x, y).

$$\frac{x - 2y \quad < 6}{0 - 2(0) \quad | \quad 6}$$
$$0 \quad < 6 \checkmark$$

*(0, 0) satisfies the
inequality, so the
graph is shaded
correctly.*

EXERCISES

Tell whether the ordered pair is a solution of the inequality.

42. $(0, -3); y < 2x - 3$

43. $(2, -1); y \geq x - 3$

44. $(6, 0); y > -3x + 4$

45. $(10, 10); y \leq x - 3$

Graph the solutions of each linear inequality.

46. $y < -2x + 5$ **47.** $x - y \geq 2$

48. $-x + 2y \geq 6$ **49.** $y > -4x$

50. $x + y + 4 > 0$ **51.** $5 - y \geq 2x$

52. The Mathematics Club is selling pizza and
lemonade to raise money for a trip. They estimate
that the trip will cost at least $450. They earn $2
on each slice of pizza and $1 on each bottle of
lemonade. Write an inequality to describe the
situation. Graph the solutions and then give two
combinations of the number of pizza slices and
number of lemonade bottles they could sell to
meet their goal.

6-6 Solving Systems of Linear Inequalities (pp. 435–440)

EXAMPLES

■ Graph $\begin{cases} y < -x + 5 \\ y \geq 2x - 3 \end{cases}$. Give two ordered pairs
that are solutions and two that are not
solutions.

Graph both inequalities.

The solutions of the system are represented by
the overlapping shaded regions.

The points $(0, 0)$ and
$(-2, 2)$ are solutions of
the system.

The points $(3, -2)$ and
$(4, 4)$ are not solutions.

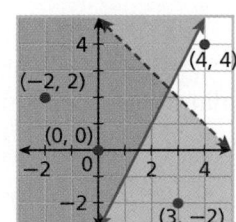

EXERCISES

Tell whether the ordered pair is a solution of the
given system.

53. $(3, 3); \begin{cases} y > -2x + 9 \\ y \geq x \end{cases}$ **54.** $(-1, 0); \begin{cases} 2x - y > -5 \\ y \leq -3x - 3 \end{cases}$

Graph each system of linear inequalities. Give two
ordered pairs that are solutions and two that are not
solutions.

55. $\begin{cases} y \geq x + 4 \\ y > 6x - 3 \end{cases}$ **56.** $\begin{cases} y \leq -2x + 8 \\ y > 3x - 5 \end{cases}$

57. $\begin{cases} -x + 2y > 6 \\ x + y < 4 \end{cases}$ **58.** $\begin{cases} x - y > 7 \\ x + 3y \leq 15 \end{cases}$

Graph each system of linear inequalities.

59. $\begin{cases} y > -x - 6 \\ y < -x + 5 \end{cases}$ **60.** $\begin{cases} 4x + 2y \geq 10 \\ 6x + 3y < -9 \end{cases}$

CHAPTER TEST

Tell whether the ordered pair is a solution of the given system.

1. $(1, -4);$ $\begin{cases} y = -4x \\ y = 2x - 2 \end{cases}$

2. $(0, -1);$ $\begin{cases} 3x - y = 1 \\ x + 5y = -5 \end{cases}$

3. $(3, 2);$ $\begin{cases} x - 2y = -1 \\ -3x + 2y = 5 \end{cases}$

Solve each system by graphing.

4. $\begin{cases} y = x - 3 \\ y = -2x - 3 \end{cases}$

5. $\begin{cases} 2x + y = -8 \\ y = \frac{1}{3}x - 1 \end{cases}$

6. $\begin{cases} y = -x + 4 \\ x = y + 2 \end{cases}$

Solve each system by substitution.

7. $\begin{cases} y = -6 \\ y = -2x - 2 \end{cases}$

8. $\begin{cases} -x + y = -4 \\ y = 2x - 11 \end{cases}$

9. $\begin{cases} x - 3y = 3 \\ 2x = 3y \end{cases}$

10. The costs for services at two kennels are shown in the table. Joslyn plans to board her dog and have him bathed once during his stay. For what number of days will the cost for boarding and bathing her dog at each kennel be the same? What will that cost be? If Joslyn plans a week-long vacation, which is the cheaper service? Explain.

Kennel Costs		
	Boarding ($ per day)	Bathing ($)
Pet Care	30	15
Fido's	28	27

Solve each system by elimination.

11. $\begin{cases} 3x - y = 7 \\ 2x + y = 3 \end{cases}$

12. $\begin{cases} 4x + y = 0 \\ x + y = -3 \end{cases}$

13. $\begin{cases} 2x + y = 3 \\ x - 2y = -1 \end{cases}$

Classify each system. Give the number of solutions.

14. $\begin{cases} y = 6x - 1 \\ 6x - y = 1 \end{cases}$

15. $\begin{cases} y = -3x - 3 \\ 3x + y = 3 \end{cases}$

16. $\begin{cases} 2x - y = 1 \\ -4x + y = 1 \end{cases}$

Graph the solutions of each linear inequality.

17. $y < 2x - 5$

18. $-y \geq 8$

19. $y > \frac{1}{3}x$

Graph each system of linear inequalities. Give two ordered pairs that are solutions and two that are not solutions.

20. $\begin{cases} y > \frac{1}{2}x - 5 \\ y \leq 4x - 1 \end{cases}$

21. $\begin{cases} y > -x + 4 \\ 3x - y > 3 \end{cases}$

22. $\begin{cases} y \geq 2x \\ y - 2x < 6 \end{cases}$

23. Ezra and Tava sold at least 150 coupon books. Ezra sold at most 30 books more than twice the number Tava sold. Show and describe all possible combinations of the numbers of coupon books Ezra and Tava sold. List two possible combinations.

COLLEGE ENTRANCE EXAM PRACTICE

FOCUS ON ACT

Four scores are reported for the ACT Mathematics Test: one score based on all 60 problems and one for each content area. The three content areas are: Pre-Algebra/ Elementary Algebra, Intermediate Algebra/Coordinate Geometry, and Plane Geometry/Trigonometry.

Taking classes that cover the content areas on the ACT is a good idea. This way you will have skills from each area of the test. Preparation over a long term is better than cramming at the last minute.

You may want to time yourself as you take this practice test. It should take you about 5 minutes to complete.

1. Which system of inequalities is represented by the graph?

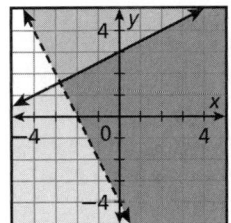

(A) $\begin{cases} -x + 2y < 6 \\ 2x + y > -4 \end{cases}$

(B) $\begin{cases} x - 2y \leq 6 \\ 2x - y \geq 4 \end{cases}$

(C) $\begin{cases} -x + 2y \leq 6 \\ 2x + y \geq 4 \end{cases}$

(D) $\begin{cases} -x + 2y \leq 6 \\ 2x + y > -4 \end{cases}$

(E) $\begin{cases} x - 2y \leq 6 \\ 2x - y > 4 \end{cases}$

2. What is the y-value of the solution of the given system?
$$\begin{cases} 4x + 3y = 1 \\ -4x + 3y = -7 \end{cases}$$

(F) -1

(G) 0

(H) 1

(J) 2

(K) 6

3. Wireless phone company A charges $20 per month plus $0.12 per minute. Wireless phone company B charges $50 per month plus $0.06 per minute. For how many minutes of calls will the monthly bills be the same?

(A) 80 minutes

(B) 100 minutes

(C) 160 minutes

(D) 250 minutes

(E) 500 minutes

4. Which of the following systems of equations does NOT have a solution?

(F) $\begin{cases} x + 5y = 30 \\ -4x + 5y = 10 \end{cases}$

(G) $\begin{cases} x + 5y = -30 \\ -4x + 5y = 10 \end{cases}$

(H) $\begin{cases} x + 5y = -30 \\ -4x + 5y = -10 \end{cases}$

(J) $\begin{cases} -4x + 5y = -10 \\ -8x + 10y = -20 \end{cases}$

(K) $\begin{cases} -4x + 5y = -10 \\ -4x + 5y = -30 \end{cases}$

TEST TACKLER

Any Question Type: Read the Problem for Understanding

Standardized test questions may vary in format including multiple choice, gridded response, and short or extended response. No matter what format the test uses, read each question carefully and critically. Do not rush. Be sure you completely understand what you are asked to do and what your response should include.

EXAMPLE

Extended Response

An interior decorator charges a consultation fee of $50 plus $12 per hour. Another interior decorator charges a consultation fee of $5 plus $22 per hour. Write a system of equations to find the amount of time for which the cost of both decorators will be the same. Graph the system. After how many hours will the cost be the same for both decorators? What will the cost be?

Read the problem again.

  What information are you given?

  the consultation fees and hourly rates of two decorators

  What are you asked to do?

  1. Write a system of equations.

  2. Graph the system.

  3. Interpret the solution to the system.

  What should your response include?

  1. a system of equations with variables defined

  2. a graph of the system

  3. the time when the cost is the same for both decorators

  4. the cost at that time

Read each test item and answer the questions that follow.

After you answer each item, read the item again to be sure your response includes everything that is asked for.

Item A
Short Response Which value of b will make the lines intersect at the point $(-2, 14)$?

$$\begin{cases} y = -6x + 2 \\ y = 4x + b \end{cases}$$

1. What information are you given?

2. What are you asked to do?

3. Ming's answer to this test problem was $y = 4x + 22$. Did Ming answer correctly? Explain.

Item B
Extended Response Solve the system by using elimination. Explain how you can check your solution algebraically and graphically.

$$\begin{cases} 4x + 10y = -48 \\ 6x - 10y = 28 \end{cases}$$

4. What method does the problem ask you to use to solve the system of equations?

5. What methods does the problem ask you to use to check your solution?

6. How many parts are there to this problem? List what needs to be included in your response.

Item C
Gridded Response What is the x-coordinate of the solution to this system? $\begin{cases} y = 6x + 9 \\ y = 12x - 15 \end{cases}$

7. What question is being asked?

8. A student correctly found the solution of the system to be $(4, 33)$. What should the student mark on the grid so that the answer is correct?

Item D
Short Response Write an inequality to represent the graph below. Give a real-world situation that this inequality could describe.

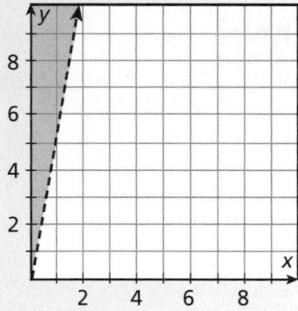

9. As part of his answer, a student wrote the following response:

   The point $(1, 5)$ is not a solution to the inequality because it lies on the line, but $(2, 12)$ is a solution because it lies above the line.

   Is his response appropriate? Explain.

10. What should the response include so that it answers all parts of the problem?

Item E
Multiple Choice Taylor bikes 50 miles per week and increases her distance by 2 miles each week. Josie bikes 30 miles per week and increases her distance by 10 miles each week. In how many weeks will Taylor and Josie be biking the same distance?

Ⓐ 2.5 weeks   Ⓒ 55 weeks

Ⓑ 7.5 weeks   Ⓓ 110 weeks

11. What question is being asked?

12. Carson incorrectly selected option C as his answer. What question did he most likely answer?

STANDARDIZED TEST PREP

CUMULATIVE ASSESSMENT, CHAPTERS 1–6

Multiple Choice

1. If $a > 0$ and $b < 0$, which of the following must be true?

   A $ab > 0$ **C** $a + b > 0$

   B $ab < 0$ **D** $a + b < 0$

2. Which of the problems below could be solved by finding the solution of this system?

$$\begin{cases} 2x + 2y = 56 \\ y = \dfrac{1}{3}x \end{cases}$$

   F The area of a rectangle is 56 square units. The width is one-third the length. Find the length of the rectangle.

   G The area of a rectangle is 56 square units. The length is one-third the perimeter. Find the length of the rectangle.

   H The perimeter of a rectangle is 56 units. The length is one-third more than the width. Find the length of the rectangle.

   J The perimeter of a rectangle is 56 units. The width is one-third the length. Find the length of the rectangle.

3. What is the slope of a line perpendicular to a line that passes through $(3, 8)$ and $(1, -4)$?

   A $-\dfrac{1}{6}$ **C** 2

   B $-\dfrac{1}{2}$ **D** 6

4. Which inequality is graphed below?

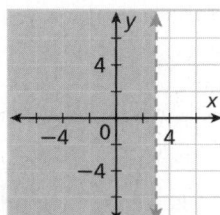

   F $-x > -3$ **H** $2x < -6$

   G $-y > -3$ **J** $3y < 9$

5. A chemist has a bottle of a 10% acid solution and a bottle of a 30% acid solution. He mixes the solutions together to get 500 mL of a 25% acid solution. How much of the 30% solution did he use?

   A 125 mL   **C** 375 mL

   B 150 mL   **D** 450 mL

6. Which ordered pair is NOT a solution of the system graphed below?

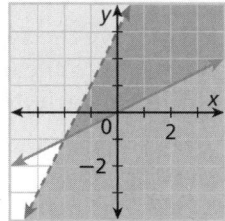

   F $(0, 0)$ **H** $(1, 1)$

   G $(0, 3)$ **J** $(2, 1)$

7. Which of the following best classifies a system of linear equations whose graph is two intersecting lines?

   A inconsistent and dependent

   B inconsistent and independent

   C consistent and dependent

   D consistent and independent

8. Which ordered pair is a solution of this system?

$$\begin{cases} 2x - y = -2 \\ \dfrac{1}{3}y = x \end{cases}$$

   F $(0, 2)$ **H** $(2, 6)$

   G $(1, 3)$ **J** $(3, 8)$

9. Where does the graph of $5x - 10y = 30$ cross the y-axis?

   A $(0, -3)$ **C** $(6, 0)$

   B $\left(0, \dfrac{1}{2}\right)$ **D** $(0, -6)$

10. Hillary needs markers and poster board for a project. The markers are $0.79 each and the poster board is $1.89 per sheet. She needs at least 4 sheets of poster board. Hillary has $15 to spend on project materials. Which system models this information?

(F) $\begin{cases} p \geq 4 \\ 0.79m + 1.89p \leq 15 \end{cases}$

(G) $\begin{cases} 0.79m \geq 1.89p \\ 4p \leq 15 \end{cases}$

(H) $\begin{cases} 4p \geq 1.89 \\ m + 4p \leq 15 \end{cases}$

(J) $\begin{cases} p + m \leq 15 \\ 0.79m + 1.89p \geq 4 \end{cases}$

11. Find the slope of the line described by $4x - 2y = -8$.

(A) -2 (C) 2

(B) $-\frac{1}{2}$ (D) 4

Gridded Response

12. The floor in the entranceway of Kendra's house is square and measures 6.5 feet on each side. Colored tiles have been set in the center of the floor in a square measuring 4 feet on each side. The remaining floor consists of white tiles.

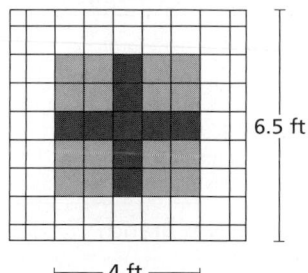

6.5 ft

4 ft

How many square feet of the entranceway floor consists of white tiles?

13. What value of y will make the line passing through $(4, -4)$ and $(-8, y)$ have a slope of $-\frac{1}{2}$?

14. What value of k will make the system $y - 5x = -1$ and $y = kx + 3$ inconsistent?

Short Response

15. The data in the table represents a linear relationship between x and y. Find the missing y-value. Explain your answer.

x	y
−3	−15
−1	−7
0	−3
2	▒
5	17

16. Graph $y > \frac{-x}{3} - 1$ on a coordinate plane. Name one point that is a solution of the inequality.

17. Marc and his brother Ty start saving money at the same time. Marc has $145 and will add $10 to his savings every week. Ty has $20 and will add $15 to his savings every week. After how many weeks will Marc and Ty have the same amount saved? What is that amount? Show your work.

18. A movie producer is looking for extras to act as office employees in his next movie. The producer needs extras that are at least 40 years old but less than 70 years old. They should be at least 60 inches tall but less than 75 inches tall. Graph all the possible combinations of ages and heights for extras that match the producer's needs. Let x represent age and y represent height. Show your work.

19. Graph the system $\begin{cases} y < -2x + 3 \\ y \geq 6x + 6 \end{cases}$.

a. Is $(0, 0)$ a solution of the system you graphed? Explain why or why not.

b. Is $(-4, 5)$ a solution of the system you graphed? Explain why or why not.

Extended Response

20. Every year, Erin knits scarves and sells them at the craft fair. This year she used $6 worth of yarn for each scarf. She also paid $50 to rent a table at the fair. She sold every scarf for $10.

a. Write a system of linear equations to represent the amount Erin spent and the amount she collected. Tell what your variables represent. Tell what each equation in the system represents.

b. Use any method to solve the system you wrote in part **a**. Show your work. How many scarves did Erin need to sell to make a profit? Explain.

c. Describe two ways you could check your solution to part **b**. Check your solution by using one of those ways. Show your work.

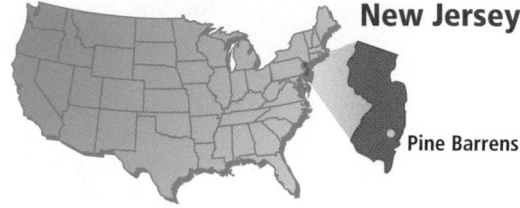

New Jersey

Pine Barrens

⭐ Kayaking and Canoeing in the Pine Barrens

The Pine Barrens, or Pinelands, of New Jersey cover over 1 million acres in southern and central New Jersey. Kayaking on the Wading and Oswego Rivers is a popular summertime activity. There are several campgrounds and canoe and kayak rentals located along the rivers.

Choose one or more strategies to solve each problem.

1. A group of kayakers starts at Evans Bridge and kayaks to Beaver Branch. Two other groups of kayakers start at Oswego Lake. One of these groups heads toward Harrisville, and the other heads toward Bodine Field. A fourth group starts at Speedwell and kayaks to Chips Folly. Draw a mapping diagram to represent the starting and ending points of the trips. Tell whether the relation is a function. Explain.

For 2 and 3, use the table.

2. If the average speed of canoes on the river is $1\frac{1}{2}$ miles per hour, about how far is it from Oswego Lake to Beaver Branch?

3. All river trips must be completed by 4:30 P.M. What is the latest time a canoetrip can start in order to make it from Speedwell to Evans Bridge?

| Approximate Canoe Trip Times on the Wading and Oswego Rivers ||
Trip	Time (h)
Evans Bridge to Beaver Branch	2
Hawkins Bridge to Evans Bridge	3
Oswego Lake to Harrisville	4
Oswego Lake to Beaver Branch	$4\frac{1}{2}$
Hawkins Bridge to Beaver Branch	5
Speedwell to Evans Bridge	6
Speedwell to Beaver Branch	8

American Black Bear

American black bears are the most common bears in the United States. They can be found in 11 of the 21 counties in New Jersey. Most wild male black bears weigh between 125 and 600 pounds, while females generally weigh between 90 and 300 pounds. Their weight depends upon their age, the season of the year, and how much food is available.

Choose one or more strategies to solve each problem.

1. Black bears hibernate for about 5 months in the winter. They must store 50 to 60 pounds of fat to survive hibernation. During the month before hibernation, a black bear may consume up to 20,000 Calories per day. If a bear consumes an average of 18,500 Calories per day in the month of August, about how many total Calories will he consume that month?

For 2, use the graph.

Male Black Bear Weight

2. A male bear weighed $\frac{2}{3}$ pound at birth. When he died at 20 years of age, he weighed 400 pounds. Use the graph to estimate how much the bear weighed when he was 7 years old.

3. A white-tailed deer is running from a black bear at 20 miles per hour. It is $\frac{1}{3}$ mile in front of the bear. The bear is running at 30 miles per hour. How long will it take the bear to catch the deer? Assume both continue running at that same pace.

4. During the hibernation months, the bear's heart rate slows to about 10 beats per minute. If the bear hibernates for 155 days, how many times will his heart beat?

Chapter

- Use exponents and scientific notation to describe numbers.
- Use laws of exponents to simplify monomials.
- Perform operations with polynomials.

Every Second *Counts*

How many seconds until you graduate? The concepts in this chapter will help you find and use large numbers such as this one.

go.hrw.com
Chapter Project Online
KEYWORD: MA7 ChProj

ARE YOU READY?

✓ Vocabulary

Match each term on the left with a definition on the right.

1. Associative Property
2. coefficient
3. Commutative Property
4. exponent
5. like terms

A. a number that is raised to a power

B. a number that is multiplied by a variable

C. a property of addition and multiplication that states you can add or multiply numbers in any order

D. the number of times a base is used as a factor

E. terms that contain the same variables raised to the same powers

F. a property of addition and multiplication that states you can group the numbers in any order

✓ Exponents

Write each expression using a base and an exponent.

6. $4 \cdot 4 \cdot 4 \cdot 4 \cdot 4 \cdot 4 \cdot 4$
7. $5 \cdot 5$
8. $(-10)(-10)(-10)(-10)$
9. $x \cdot x \cdot x$
10. $k \cdot k \cdot k \cdot k \cdot k$
11. 9

✓ Evaluate Powers

Evaluate each expression.

12. 3^4
13. -12^2
14. 5^3
15. 2^5
16. 4^3
17. $(-1)^6$

✓ Multiply Decimals

Multiply.

18. 0.006×10
19. 25.25×100
20. 2.4×6.5

✓ Combine Like Terms

Simplify each expression.

21. $6 + 3p + 14 + 9p$
22. $8y - 4x + 2y + 7x - x$
23. $(12 + 3w - 5) + 6w - 3 - 5w$
24. $6n - 14 + 5n$

✓ Squares and Square Roots

Tell whether each number is a perfect square. If so, identify its positive square root.

25. 42
26. 81
27. 36
28. 50
29. 100
30. 4
31. 1
32. 12

Study Guide: Preview

Where You've Been

Previously, you

- wrote and evaluated exponential expressions.
- simplified algebraic expressions by combining like terms.

In This Chapter

You will study

- properties of exponents.
- powers of 10 and scientific notation.
- how to add, subtract, and multiply polynomials by using properties of exponents and combining like terms.

Where You're Going

You can use the skills in this chapter

- to model area, perimeter, and volume in geometry.
- to express very small or very large quantities in science classes such as Chemistry, Physics, and Biology.
- in the real world to model business profits and population growth or decline.

Key Vocabulary/Vocabulario

binomial	binomio
degree of a monomial	grado de un monomio
degree of a polynomial	grado de un polinomio
leading coefficient	coeficiente principal
monomial	monomio
perfect-square trinomial	trinomio cuadrado perfecto
polynomial	polinomio
scientific notation	notación científica
standard form of a polynomial	forma estándar de un polinomio
trinomial	trinomio

Vocabulary Connections

To become familiar with some of the vocabulary terms in the chapter, consider the following. You may refer to the chapter, the glossary, or a dictionary if you like.

1. Very large and very small numbers are often encountered in the sciences. If *notation* means a method of writing something, what might **scientific notation** mean?

2. A **polynomial** written in standard form may have more than one algebraic term. What do you think the **leading coefficient** of a polynomial is?

3. A simple definition of **monomial** is "an expression with exactly one term." If the prefix *mono-* means "one" and the prefix *bi-* means "two," define the word **binomial**.

4. What words do you know that begin with the prefix *tri-*? What do they all have in common? Define the word **trinomial** based on the prefix *tri-* and the information given in Problem 3.

Reading and Writing Math

Reading Strategy: Read and Understand the Problem

Follow this strategy when solving word problems.

• Read the problem through once.

• Identify exactly what the problem asks you to do.

• Read the problem again, slowly and carefully, to break it into parts.

• Highlight or underline the key information.

• Make a plan to solve the problem.

From Lesson 6-6

29. Multi-Step Linda works at a pharmacy for $15 an hour. She also baby-sits for $10 an hour. Linda needs to earn at least $90 per week, but she does not want to work more than 20 hours per week. Show and describe the number of hours Linda could work at each job to meet her goals. List two possible solutions.

Step 1	Identify exactly what the problem asks you to do.	• Show and describe the number of hours Linda can work at each job and earn at least $90 per week, without working more than 20 hours per week. • List two possible solutions of the system.
Step 2	Break the problem into parts. Highlight or underline the key information.	• Linda has two jobs. She makes **$15 per hour** at one job and **$10 per hour** at the other job. • She wants to earn **at least $90 per week**. • She does **not** want to work **more than 20 hours per week.**
Step 3	Make a plan to solve the problem.	• Write a system of inequalities. • Solve the system. • Identify two possible solutions of the system.

 Try This

For the problem below,

    a. identify exactly what the problem asks you to do.

    b. break the problem into parts. Highlight or underline the key information.

    c. make a plan to solve the problem.

1. The difference between the length and the width of a rectangle is 14 units. The area is 120 square units. Write and solve a system of equations to determine the length and the width of the rectangle. (*Hint:* The formula for the area of a rectangle is $A = \ell w$.)

7-1 Integer Exponents

Objectives

Evaluate expressions containing zero and integer exponents.

Simplify expressions containing zero and integer exponents.

Who uses this?

Manufacturers can use negative exponents to express very small measurements.

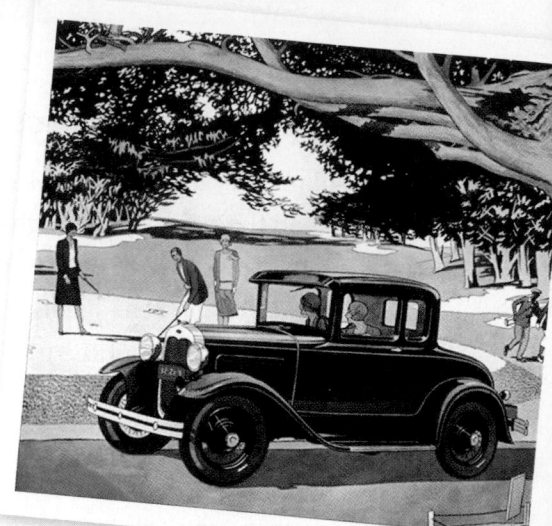

In 1930, the Model A Ford was one of the first cars to boast precise craftsmanship in mass production. The car's pistons had a diameter of $3\frac{7}{8}$ inches; this measurement could vary by at most 10^{-3} inch.

You have seen positive exponents. Recall that to simplify 3^2, use 3 as a factor 2 times: $3^2 = 3 \cdot 3 = 9$.

But what does it mean for an exponent to be negative or 0? You can use a table and look for a pattern to figure it out.

Remember!

Base $\searrow$ x^4 $\nearrow$ Exponent

Power	5^5	5^4	5^3	5^2	5^1	5^0	5^{-1}	5^{-2}
Value	3125	625	125	25	5			

$\div 5 \qquad \div 5 \qquad \div 5 \qquad \div 5$

When the exponent decreases by one, the value of the power is divided by 5. Continue the pattern of dividing by 5:

$$5^0 = \frac{5}{5} = 1 \qquad\qquad 5^{-1} = \frac{1}{5} = \frac{1}{5^1} \qquad\qquad 5^{-2} = \frac{1}{5} \div 5 = \frac{1}{25} = \frac{1}{5^2}$$

Know it! Note

Integer Exponents

WORDS	NUMBERS	ALGEBRA
Zero exponent—Any nonzero number raised to the zero power is 1.	$3^0 = 1 \quad 123^0 = 1$ $(-16)^0 = 1 \quad \left(\frac{3}{7}\right)^0 = 1$	If $x \neq 0$, then $x^0 = 1$.
Negative exponent—A nonzero number raised to a negative exponent is equal to 1 divided by that number raised to the opposite (positive) exponent.	$3^{-2} = \frac{1}{3^2} = \frac{1}{9}$ $2^{-4} = \frac{1}{2^4} = \frac{1}{16}$	If $x \neq 0$ and n is an integer, then $x^{-n} = \frac{1}{x^n}$.

Reading Math

2^{-4} is read "2 to the negative fourth power."

Notice the phrase "nonzero number" in the table above. This is because 0^0 and 0 raised to a negative power are both undefined. For example, if you use the pattern given above the table with a base of 0 instead of 5, you would get $0^0 = \frac{0}{0}$. Also, 0^{-6} would be $\frac{1}{0^6} = \frac{1}{0}$. Since division by 0 is undefined, neither value exists.

EXAMPLE 1 *Manufacturing Application*

The diameter for the Model A Ford piston could vary by at most 10^{-3} inch. Simplify this expression.

$$10^{-3} = \frac{1}{10^3} = \frac{1}{10 \cdot 10 \cdot 10} = \frac{1}{1000}$$

10^{-3} inch is equal to $\frac{1}{1000}$ inch, or 0.001 inch.

 1. A sand fly may have a wingspan up to 5^{-3} m. Simplify this expression.

EXAMPLE 2 **Zero and Negative Exponents**

Simplify.

A 2^{-3}

$$2^{-3} = \frac{1}{2^3} = \frac{1}{2 \cdot 2 \cdot 2} = \frac{1}{8}$$

B 5^0

$5^0 = 1$ *Any nonzero number raised to the zero power is 1.*

Caution!

In $(-3)^{-4}$, the base is negative because the negative sign is inside the parentheses.

In -3^{-4} the base (3) is positive.

C $(-3)^{-4}$

$$(-3)^{-4} = \frac{1}{(-3)^4} = \frac{1}{(-3)(-3)(-3)(-3)} = \frac{1}{81}$$

D -3^{-4}

$$-3^{-4} = -\frac{1}{3^4} = -\frac{1}{3 \cdot 3 \cdot 3 \cdot 3} = -\frac{1}{81}$$

 Simplify.

2a. 10^{-4} **2b.** $(-2)^{-4}$ **2c.** $(-2)^{-5}$ **2d.** -2^{-5}

EXAMPLE 3 **Evaluating Expressions with Zero and Negative Exponents**

Evaluate each expression for the given value(s) of the variable(s).

A x^{-1} for $x = 2$

2^{-1} *Substitute 2 for x.*

$2^{-1} = \frac{1}{2^1} = \frac{1}{2}$ *Use the definition $x^{-n} = \frac{1}{x^n}$.*

B $a^0 b^{-3}$ for $a = 8$ and $b = -2$

$8^0 \cdot (-2)^{-3}$ *Substitute 8 for a and −2 for b.*

$1 \cdot \dfrac{1}{(-2)^3}$ *Simplify expressions with exponents.*

$1 \cdot \dfrac{1}{(-2)(-2)(-2)}$ *Write the power in the denominator as a product.*

$1 \cdot \dfrac{1}{-8}$ *Simplify the power in the denominator.*

$-\dfrac{1}{8}$ *Simplify.*

 Evaluate each expression for the given value(s) of the variable(s).

3a. p^{-3} for $p = 4$ **3b.** $8a^{-2}b^0$ for $a = -2$ and $b = 6$

What if you have an expression with a negative exponent in a denominator, such as $\frac{1}{x^{-8}}$?

$$x^{-n} = \frac{1}{x^n}, \text{ or } \frac{1}{x^n} = x^{-n} \qquad \textit{Definition of negative exponent}$$

$$\frac{1}{x^{-8}} = x^{-(-8)} \qquad \textit{Substitute } -8 \textit{ for } n.$$

$$= x^8 \qquad \textit{Simplify the exponent on the right side.}$$

So if a base with a negative exponent is in a denominator, it is equivalent to the same base with the opposite (positive) exponent in the numerator.

An expression that contains negative or zero exponents is not considered to be simplified. Expressions should be rewritten with only positive exponents.

EXAMPLE **4** **Simplifying Expressions with Zero and Negative Exponents**

Simplify.

A $3y^{-2}$

$$3y^{-2} = 3 \cdot y^{-2}$$

$$= 3 \cdot \frac{1}{y^2}$$

$$= \frac{3}{y^2}$$

B $\frac{-4}{k^{-4}}$

$$\frac{-4}{k^{-4}} = -4 \cdot \frac{1}{k^{-4}}$$

$$= -4 \cdot k^4$$

$$= -4k^4$$

C $\frac{x^{-3}}{a^0 y^5}$

$$\frac{x^{-3}}{a^0 y^5} = \frac{1}{x^3 \cdot 1 \cdot y^5} \qquad a^0 = 1 \text{ and } x^{-3} = \frac{1}{x^3}.$$

$$= \frac{1}{x^3 y^5}$$

 Simplify.

4a. $2r^0 m^{-3}$ **4b.** $\frac{r^{-3}}{7}$ **4c.** $\frac{g^4}{h^{-6}}$

THINK AND DISCUSS

1. Complete each equation: $2b^? = \frac{2}{b^2}$, $\frac{s^{-3}}{k^?} = \frac{1}{s^3}$, $?^{-2} = \frac{1}{t^2}$

2. **GET ORGANIZED** Copy and complete the graphic organizer. In each box, describe how to simplify, and give an example.

Simplifying Expressions with Negative Exponents

For a negative exponent in the numerator . . .   For a negative exponent in the denominator . . .

7-1

Exercises

go.hrw.com
Homework Help Online
KEYWORD: MA7 7-1
Parent Resources Online
KEYWORD: MA7 Parent

GUIDED PRACTICE

SEE EXAMPLE **1**
p. 461

1. **Medicine** A typical virus is about 10^{-7} m in size. Simplify this expression.

SEE EXAMPLE **2**
p. 461

Simplify.

2. 6^{-2} 3. 3^0 4. -5^{-2} 5. 3^{-3} 6. 1^{-8}

7. -8^{-3} 8. 10^{-2} 9. $(4.2)^0$ 10. $(-3)^{-3}$ 11. 4^{-2}

SEE EXAMPLE **3**
p. 461

Evaluate each expression for the given value(s) of the variable(s).

12. b^{-2} for $b = -3$ 13. $(2t)^{-4}$ for $t = 2$

14. $(m - 4)^{-5}$ for $m = 6$ 15. $2x^0y^{-3}$ for $x = 7$ and $y = -4$

SEE EXAMPLE **4**
p. 462

Simplify.

16. $4m^0$ 17. $3k^{-4}$ 18. $\dfrac{7}{r^{-7}}$ 19. $\dfrac{x^{10}}{d^{-3}}$

20. $2x^0y^{-4}$ 21. $\dfrac{f^{-4}}{g^{-6}}$ 22. $\dfrac{c^4}{d^{-3}}$ 23. p^7q^{-1}

PRACTICE AND PROBLEM SOLVING

Independent Practice	
For Exercises	See Example
24	1
25–36	2
37–42	3
43–57	4

Extra Practice
Skills Practice p. S16
Application Practice p. S34

24. **Biology** One of the smallest bats is the northern blossom bat, which is found from Southeast Asia to Australia. This bat weighs about 2^{-1} ounce. Simplify this expression.

Simplify.

25. 8^0 26. 5^{-4} 27. 3^{-4} 28. -9^{-2}

29. -6^{-2} 30. 7^{-2} 31. $\left(\dfrac{2}{5}\right)^0$ 32. 13^{-2}

33. $(-3)^{-1}$ 34. $(-4)^2$ 35. $\left(\dfrac{1}{2}\right)^{-2}$ 36. -7^{-1}

Evaluate each expression for the given value(s) of the variable(s).

37. x^{-4} for $x = 4$ 38. $\left(\dfrac{2}{3}v\right)^{-3}$ for $v = 9$

39. $(10 - d)^0$ for $d - 11$ 40. $10m^{-1}n^{-5}$ for $m = 10$ and $n = -2$

41. $(3ab)^{-2}$ for $a = \dfrac{1}{2}$ and $b = 8$ 42. $4w^vx^v$ for $w = 3$, $v = 0$, and $x = -5$

Simplify.

43. k^{-4} 44. $2z^{-8}$ 45. $\dfrac{1}{2b^{-3}}$ 46. $c^{-2}d$ 47. $-5x^{-3}$

48. $4x^{-6}y^{-2}$ 49. $\dfrac{2f^0}{7g^{-10}}$ 50. $\dfrac{r^{-5}}{s^{-1}}$ 51. $\dfrac{s^5}{t^{-12}}$ 52. $\dfrac{3w^{-5}}{x^{-6}}$

53. b^0c^0 54. $\dfrac{2}{3}m^{-1}n^5$ 55. $\dfrac{q^{-2}r^0}{s^0}$ 56. $\dfrac{a^{-7}b^2}{c^3d^{-4}}$ 57. $\dfrac{h^3k^{-1}}{6m^2}$

Evaluate each expression for $x = 3$, $y = -1$, and $z = 2$.

58. z^{-5} **59.** $(x + y)^{-4}$ **60.** $(yz)^0$ **61.** $(xyz)^{-1}$

62. $(xy - 3)^{-2}$ **63.** x^{-y} **64.** $(yz)^{-x}$ **65.** xy^{-4}

66. **///ERROR ANALYSIS///** Look at the two equations below. Which is incorrect? Explain the error.

Ⓐ $5x^{-3} = \dfrac{1}{5x^3}$

Ⓑ $5x^{-3} = \dfrac{5}{x^3}$

Simplify.

67. a^3b^{-2} **68.** $c^{-4}d^3$ **69.** $v^0w^2y^{-1}$ **70.** $(a^2b^{-7})^0$ **71.** $-5y^{-6}$

72. $\dfrac{2a^{-5}}{b^{-6}}$ **73.** $\dfrac{2a^3}{b^{-1}}$ **74.** $\dfrac{m^2}{n^{-3}}$ **75.** $\dfrac{x^{-8}}{3y^{12}}$ **76.** $-\dfrac{20p^{-1}}{5q^{-3}}$

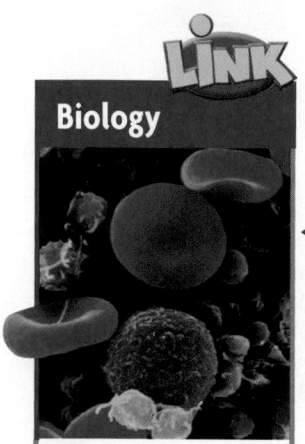
77. **Biology** Human blood contains red blood cells, white blood cells, and platelets. The table shows the sizes of these components. Simplify each expression.

Blood Components	
Part	Size (m)
Red blood cell	$125,000^{-1}$
White blood cell	$3(500)^{-2}$
Platelet	$3(1000)^{-2}$

Tell whether each statement is sometimes, always, or never true.

78. If n is a positive integer, then $x^{-n} = \dfrac{1}{x^n}$.

79. If x is positive, then x^{-n} is negative.

80. If n is zero, then x^{-n} is 1.

81. If n is a negative integer, then $x^{-n} = 1$.

82. If x is zero, then x^{-n} is 1.

83. If n is an integer, then $x^{-n} > 1$.

84. **Critical Thinking** Find the value of $2^3 \cdot 2^{-3}$. Then find the value of $3^2 \cdot 3^{-2}$. Make a conjecture about the value of $a^n \cdot a^{-n}$.

85. **Write About It** Explain in your own words why 2^{-3} is the same as $\dfrac{1}{2^3}$.

Find the missing value.

86. $\dfrac{1}{4} = 2^{\blacksquare}$ **87.** $9^{-2} = \dfrac{1}{\blacksquare}$ **88.** $\dfrac{1}{64} = \blacksquare^{-2}$ **89.** $\dfrac{\blacksquare}{3} = 3^{-1}$

90. $7^{-2} = \dfrac{1}{\blacksquare}$ **91.** $10^{\blacksquare} = \dfrac{1}{1000}$ **92.** $3 \cdot 4^{-2} = \dfrac{3}{\blacksquare}$ **93.** $2 \cdot \dfrac{1}{5} = 2 \cdot 5^{\blacksquare}$

94. This problem will prepare you for the Multi-Step Test Prep on page 494.

  a. The product of the frequency f and the wavelength w of light in air is a constant v. Write an equation for this relationship.

  b. Solve this equation for wavelength. Then write this equation as an equation with f raised to a negative exponent.

  c. The units for frequency are hertz (Hz). One hertz is one cycle per second, which is often written as $\dfrac{1}{s}$. Rewrite this expression using a negative exponent.

95. Which is NOT equivalent to the other three?

Ⓐ $\frac{1}{25}$ Ⓑ 5^{-2} Ⓒ 0.04 Ⓓ -25

96. Which is equal to 6^{-2}?

Ⓕ $6(-2)$ Ⓖ $(-6)(-6)$ Ⓗ $-\frac{1}{6 \cdot 6}$ Ⓙ $\frac{1}{6 \cdot 6}$

97. Simplify $\frac{a^3b^{-2}}{c^{-1}}$.

Ⓐ $\frac{a^3c}{b^2}$ Ⓑ $\frac{a^3b^2}{-c}$ Ⓒ $\frac{a^3}{-b^2c}$ Ⓓ $\frac{c}{a^3b^2}$

98. Gridded Response Simplify $\left[2^{-2} + (6+2)^0\right]$.

99. Short Response If a and b are real numbers and n is a positive integer, write a simplified expression for the product $a^{-n} \cdot b^0$ that contains only positive exponents. Explain your answer.

CHALLENGE AND EXTEND

100. Multi-Step Copy and complete the table of values below. Then graph the ordered pairs and describe the shape of the graph.

x	−4	−3	−2	−1	0	1	2	3	4
$y = 2^x$									

101. Multi-Step Copy and complete the table. Then write a rule for the values of 1^n and $(-1)^n$ when n is any negative integer.

n	−1	−2	−3	−4	−5
1^n					
$(-1)^n$					

SPIRAL REVIEW

Solve each equation. *(Lesson 2-3)*

102. $6x - 4 = 8$

103. $-9 = 3(p - 1)$

104. $\frac{y}{5} - 8 = -12$

105. $1.5h - 5 = 1$

106. $2w + 6 - 3w = -10$

107. $-12 = \frac{1}{2}n + 2 - n$

Identify the independent and dependent variables. Write a rule in function notation for each situation. *(Lesson 4-3)*

108. Pink roses cost $1.50 per stem.

109. For dog-sitting, Beth charges a $30 flat fee plus $10 a day.

Write the equation that describes each line in slope-intercept form. *(Lesson 5-7)*

110. slope = 3, y-intercept = −4

111. slope = $\frac{1}{3}$, y-intercept = 5

112. slope = 0, y-intercept = $\frac{2}{3}$

113. slope = −4, the point $(1, 5)$ is on the line.

Powers of 10 and Scientific Notation

Nucleus of a silicon atom

Evaluate and multiply by powers of 10.

Convert between standard notation and scientific notation.

Vocabulary
scientific notation

Why learn this?
Powers of 10 can be used to read and write very large and very small numbers, such as the masses of atomic particles. (See Exercise 44.)

The table shows relationships between several powers of 10.

	$\div 10$	$\div 10$	$\div 10$	$\div 10$	$\div 10$	$\div 10$	
Power	10^3	10^2	10^1	10^0	10^{-1}	10^{-2}	10^{-3}
Value	1000	100	10	1	$\frac{1}{10} = 0.1$	$\frac{1}{100} = 0.01$	$\frac{1}{1000} = 0.001$
	$\times 10$	$\times 10$	$\times 10$	$\times 10$	$\times 10$	$\times 10$	

- Each time you **divide by 10**, the exponent decreases by 1 and the decimal point moves one place to the left.
- Each time you **multiply by 10**, the exponent increases by 1 and the decimal point moves one place to the right.

Know it! Note

Powers of 10

WORDS	NUMBERS
Positive Integer Exponent If n is a positive integer, find the value of 10^n by starting with 1 and moving the decimal point n places to the right.	$10^4 = 1\,0,0\,0\,0$ 4 places
Negative Integer Exponent If n is a positive integer, find the value of 10^{-n} by starting with 1 and moving the decimal point n places to the left.	$10^{-6} = \dfrac{1}{10^6} = 0.0\,0\,0\,0\,0\,1$ 6 places

EXAMPLE 1 **Evaluating Powers of 10**

Find the value of each power of 10.

Writing Math

You may need to add zeros to the right or left of a number in order to move the decimal point in that direction.

A 10^{-3}

Start with 1 and move the decimal point three places to the left.

0.001

B 10^2

Start with 1 and move the decimal point two places to the right.

100

C 10^0

Start with 1 and move the decimal point zero places.

1

CHECK IT OUT! Find the value of each power of 10.

1a. 10^{-2} **1b.** 10^5 **1c.** 10^{10}

EXAMPLE 2   **Writing Powers of 10**

Reading Math

If you do not see a decimal point in a number, it is understood to be at the end of the number.

Write each number as a power of 10.

A 10,000,000	**B** 0.001	**C** 10
The decimal point is seven places to the right of 1, so the exponent is 7.	*The decimal point is three places to the left of 1, so the exponent is −3.*	*The decimal point is one place to the right of 1, so the exponent is 1.*
10^7	10^{-3}	10^1

CHECK IT OUT! Write each number as a power of 10.

2a. 100,000,000   **2b.** 0.0001   **2c.** 0.1

You can also move the decimal point to find the product of any number and a power of 10. You start with the number instead of starting with 1.

Know it! Note

Multiplying by Powers of 10	
If the exponent is a positive integer, move the decimal point to the right.	$125 \times 10^5 = 12,5\,0\,0,\,0\,0\,0$ 5 places
If the exponent is a negative integer, move the decimal point to the left.	$36.2 \times 10^{-3} = 0.0\,3\,6\,2$ 3 places

EXAMPLE 3   **Multiplying by Powers of 10**

Find the value of each expression.

A 97.86×10^6

   $97.8\,6\,0\,0\,0\,0$ *Move the decimal point 6 places to the right.*

   $97,860,000$

B 19.5×10^{-4}

   $0\,0\,1\,9.5$ *Move the decimal point 4 places to the left.*

   0.00195

CHECK IT OUT! Find the value of each expression.

3a. 853.4×10^5 **3b.** 0.163×10^{-2}

Scientific notation is a method of writing numbers that are very large or very small. A number written in scientific notation has two parts that are multiplied.

The first part is a number that is greater than or equal to 1 and less than 10.

$$3.5 \times 10^{11} \qquad 9.98 \times 10^{-2}$$

The second part is a power of 10.

EXAMPLE 4 *Astronomy Application*

Jupiter has a diameter of about 143,000 km. Its shortest distance from Earth is about 5.91×10^8 km, and its average distance from the Sun is about 778,400,000 km. Jupiter's orbital speed is approximately 1.3×10^4 m/s.

—143,000 km—

A Write Jupiter's shortest distance from Earth in standard form.

5.91×10^8

5.9 1 0 0 0 0 0 0   *Move the decimal point 8 places to the right.*

591,000,000 km

B Write Jupiter's average distance from the Sun in scientific notation.

778,400,000

7 7 8, 4 0 0, 0 0 0   *Count the number of places you need to move the decimal point to get a number between 1 and 10.*

8 places

7.784×10^8 km   *Use that number as the exponent of 10.*

 CHECK IT OUT! **4a.** Use the information above to write Jupiter's diameter in scientific notation.

4b. Use the information above to write Jupiter's orbital speed in standard form.

EXAMPLE 5 Comparing and Ordering Numbers in Scientific Notation

Order the list of numbers from least to greatest.

$1.2 \times 10^{-1}, 8.2 \times 10^4, 6.2 \times 10^5, 2.4 \times 10^5, 1 \times 10^{-1}, 9.9 \times 10^{-4}$

Step 1 List the numbers in order by powers of 10.

$9.9 \times 10^{-4}, 1.2 \times 10^{-1}, 1 \times 10^{-1}, 8.2 \times 10^4, 6.2 \times 10^5, 2.4 \times 10^5$

Step 2 Order the numbers that have the same power of 10.

$9.9 \times 10^{-4}, 1 \times 10^{-1}, \mathbf{1.2 \times 10^{-1}}, 8.2 \times 10^4, \mathbf{2.4 \times 10^5}, \mathbf{6.2 \times 10^5}$

 CHECK IT OUT! **5.** Order the list of numbers from least to greatest.
$5.2 \times 10^{-3}, 3 \times 10^{14}, 4 \times 10^{-3}, 2 \times 10^{-12}, 4.5 \times 10^{30}, 4.5 \times 10^{14}$

THINK AND DISCUSS

1. Tell why 34.56×10^4 is not correctly written in scientific notation.

 **2. GET ORGANIZED** Copy and complete the graphic organizer.

> **Powers of 10 and Scientific Notation**
>
> | A negative exponent corresponds to moving the decimal point ___?___. | A positive exponent corresponds to moving the decimal point ___?___. |

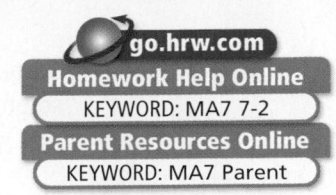

go.hrw.com
Homework Help Online
KEYWORD: MA7 7-2
Parent Resources Online
KEYWORD: MA7 Parent

GUIDED PRACTICE

1. **Vocabulary** Explain how you can tell whether a number is written in *scientific notation*.

SEE EXAMPLE **1**
p. 466

Find the value of each power of 10.

2. 10^6
3. 10^{-5}
4. 10^{-4}
5. 10^8

SEE EXAMPLE **2**
p. 467

Write each number as a power of 10.

6. 10,000
7. 0.000001
8. 100,000,000,000,000,000

SEE EXAMPLE **3**
p. 467

Find the value of each expression.

9. 650.3×10^6
10. 48.3×10^{-4}
11. 92×10^{-3}

SEE EXAMPLE **4**
p. 468

12. **Astronomy** A light-year is the distance that light travels in a year and is equivalent to 9.461×10^{12} km. Write this distance in standard form.

SEE EXAMPLE **5**
p. 468

13. Order the list of numbers from least to greatest.
$8.5 \times 10^{-1}, 3.6 \times 10^8, 5.85 \times 10^{-3}, 2.5 \times 10^{-1}, 8.5 \times 10^8$

PRACTICE AND PROBLEM SOLVING

Independent Practice

For Exercises	See Example
14–17	1
18–20	2
21–24	3
25–26	4
27	5

Extra Practice
Skills Practice p. S16
Application Practice p. S34

Find the value of each power of 10.

14. 10^3
15. 10^{-9}
16. 10^{-12}
17. 10^{14}

Write each number as a power of 10.

18. 0.01
19. 1,000,000
20. 0.000000000000001

Find the value of each expression.

21. 9.2×10^4
22. 1.25×10^{-7}
23. 42×10^{-5}
24. 0.05×10^7

25. **Biology** The human body is made of about 1×10^{13} cells. Write this number in standard form.

26. **Statistics** At the beginning of the twenty-first century, the population of China was about 1,287,000,000. Write this number in scientific notation.

27. Order the list of numbers from least to greatest.
$2.13 \times 10^{-1}, 3.12 \times 10^2, 1.23 \times 10^{-3}, 2.13 \times 10^1, 1.32 \times 10^{-3}, 3.12 \times 10^{-3}$

28. **Health** Donnell is allergic to pollen. The diameter of a grain of pollen is between 1.2×10^{-5} m and 9×10^{-5} m. Donnell's air conditioner has a filter that removes particles larger than 3×10^{-7} m. Will the filter remove pollen? Explain.

29. **Entertainment** In the United States, a CD is certified platinum if it sells 1,000,000 copies. A CD that has gone 2 times platinum has sold 2,000,000 copies. How many copies has a CD sold if it has gone 27 times platinum? Write your answer in scientific notation.

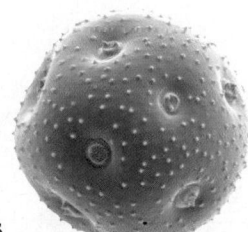

Grain of pollen, enlarged 1300 times

Write each number in scientific notation.

30. 40,080,000
31. 235,000
32. 170,000,000,000
33. 0.0000006
34. 0.000077
35. 0.0412

State whether each number is written in scientific notation. If not, write it in scientific notation.

36. 50×10^{-5} **37.** 8.1×10^{-2} **38.** $1{,}200{,}000$ **39.** 0.25×10^{3}

40. 0.1 **41.** 7×10^{8} **42.** $48{,}000$ **43.** 3.5×10^{-6}

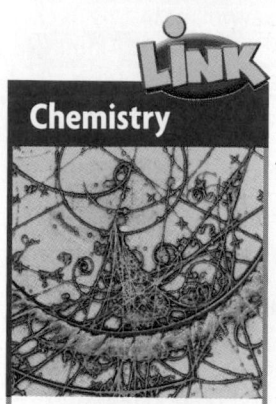

Chemistry

The image above is a colored bubble-chamber photograph. It shows the tracks left by subatomic particles in a particle accelerator.

44. Chemistry Atoms are made of three elementary particles: protons, electrons, and neutrons. The mass of a proton is about 1.67×10^{-27} kg. The mass of an electron is about $0.000000000000000000000000000000911$ kg. The mass of a neutron is about 1.68×10^{-27} kg. Which particle has the least mass? (*Hint:* Compare the numbers after they are written in scientific notation.)

45. Communication This bar graph shows the increase of cellular telephone subscribers worldwide.

a. Write the number of subscribers for the following years in standard form: 1999, 2000, and 2003.

b. Zorah looks at the bar graph and says, "It looks like the number of cell phone subscribers nearly doubled from 2000 to 2003." Do you agree with Zorah? Use scientific notation to explain your answer.

Worldwide Cell Phone Subscribers

Subscribers: 1.4×10^9, 1.2×10^9, 1×10^9, 8×10^8, 6×10^8, 4×10^8, 2×10^8

1999: 4.9×10^8
2000: 7.4×10^8
2001: 9.5×10^8
2002: 1.155×10^9
2003: 1.329×10^9

Year

46. Measurement In the metric system, the basic unit for measuring length is the meter (m). Other units for measuring length are based on the meter and powers of 10, as shown in the table.

Selected Metric Lengths	
1 millimeter (mm) = 10^{-3} m	1 dekameter (dam) = 10^{1} m
1 centimeter (cm) = 10^{-2} m	1 hectometer (hm) = 10^{2} m
1 decimeter (dm) = 10^{-1} m	1 kilometer (km) = 10^{3} m

a. Which lengths in the table are longer than a meter? Which are shorter than a meter? How do you know?

b. Evaluate each power of 10 in the table to check your answers to part **a**.

47. Critical Thinking Recall that $\frac{1}{10^3} = 10^{-3}$. Based on this information, complete the following statement: Dividing a number by 10^3 is equivalent to multiplying by ▒.

48. Write About It When you change a number from scientific notation to standard form, explain how you know which way to move the decimal point and how many places to move it.

MULTI-STEP TEST PREP

49. This problem will prepare you for the Multi-Step Test Prep on page 494.

a. The speed of light is approximately 3×10^{8} m/s. Write this number in standard form.

b. Why do you think it would be better to express this number in scientific notation rather than standard form?

c. The wavelength of a shade of red light is 0.00000068 meters. Write this number in scientific notation.

50. There are about 3.2×10^7 seconds in one year. What is this number in standard form?
   Ⓐ 0.000000032
   Ⓑ 0.00000032
   Ⓒ 32,000,000
   Ⓓ 320,000,000

51. Which expression is the scientific notation for 82.35?
   Ⓕ 8.235×10^1 Ⓖ 823.5×10^{-1} Ⓗ 8.235×10^{-1} Ⓙ 0.8235×10^2

52. Which statement is correct for the list of numbers below?
   2.35×10^{-8}, 0.000000029, 1.82×10^8, 1,290,000,000, 1.05×10^9
   Ⓐ The list is in increasing order.
   Ⓑ If 0.000000029 is removed, the list will be in increasing order.
   Ⓒ If 1,290,000,000 is removed, the list will be in increasing order.
   Ⓓ The list is in decreasing order.

CHALLENGE AND EXTEND

53. **Technology** The table shows estimates of computer storage. A CD-ROM holds 700 MB. A DVD-ROM holds 4.7 GB. Estimate how many times more storage a DVD has than a CD. Explain how you found your answer.

Computer Storage
1 kilobyte (KB) ≈ 1000 bytes
1 megabyte (MB) ≈ 1 million bytes
1 gigabyte (GB) ≈ 1 billion bytes

54. For parts **a–d**, use what you know about multiplying by powers of 10 and the Commutative and Associative Properties of Multiplication to find each product. Write each answer in scientific notation.
   a. $(3 \times 10^2)(2 \times 10^3)$
   b. $(5 \times 10^8)(1.5 \times 10^{-6})$
   c. $(2.2 \times 10^{-8})(4 \times 10^{-3})$
   d. $(2.5 \times 10^{-12})(2 \times 10^6)$
   e. Based on your answers to parts **a–d**, write a rule for multiplying numbers in scientific notation.
   f. Does your rule work when you multiply $(6 \times 10^3)(8 \times 10^5)$? Explain.

SPIRAL REVIEW

Define a variable and write an inequality for each situation. Graph the solutions. *(Lesson 3-1)*

55. Melanie must wait at least 45 minutes for the results of her test.

56. Ulee's dog can lose no more than 8 pounds to stay within a healthy weight range.

57. Charlene must spend more than $50 to get the advertised discount.

Solve each system by elimination. *(Lesson 6-3)*

58. $\begin{cases} x + y = 8 \\ x - y = 2 \end{cases}$

59. $\begin{cases} 2x + y = -3 \\ 2x + 3y = -1 \end{cases}$

60. $\begin{cases} x - 6y = -3 \\ 3x + 4y = 13 \end{cases}$

Evaluate each expression for the given value(s) of the variable(s). *(Lesson 7-1)*

61. t^{-4} for $t = 2$

62. $(-8m)^0$ for $m = -5$

63. $3a^{-3}b^0$ for $a = 5$ and $b = 6$

7-3

Algebra LAB

Explore Properties of Exponents

You can use patterns to find some properties of exponents.

Use with Lesson 7-3

Activity 1

1 Copy and complete the table below.

$$3^2 \cdot 3^3 = (3 \cdot 3)(3 \cdot 3 \cdot 3) = 3^{\blacksquare}$$

$$5^4 \cdot 5^2 = (\blacksquare \cdot \blacksquare \cdot \blacksquare \cdot \blacksquare)(\blacksquare \cdot \blacksquare) = 5^{\blacksquare}$$

$$4^3 \cdot 4^3 = (\blacksquare \cdot \blacksquare \cdot \blacksquare)(\blacksquare \cdot \blacksquare \cdot \blacksquare) = \blacksquare^{\blacksquare}$$

$$2^3 \cdot 2^2 = (\blacksquare \cdot \blacksquare \cdot \blacksquare)(\blacksquare \cdot \blacksquare) = \blacksquare^{\blacksquare}$$

$$6^3 \cdot 6^4 = (\quad)(\quad) =$$

2 Examine your completed table. Look at the two exponents in each factor and the exponent in the final answer. What pattern do you notice?

3 Use your pattern to make a conjecture: $a^m \cdot a^n = a^{\blacksquare}$.

Try This

Use your conjecture to write each product below as a single power.

1. $5^3 \cdot 5^5$ **2.** $7^2 \cdot 7^2$ **3.** $10^8 \cdot 10^4$ **4.** $8^7 \cdot 8^3$

5. Make a table similar to the one above to explore what happens when you multiply more than two powers that have the same base. Then write a conjecture in words to summarize what you find.

Activity 2

1 Copy and complete the table below.

$$(2^3)^2 = 2^3 \cdot 2^3 = (\blacksquare \cdot \blacksquare \cdot \blacksquare)(\blacksquare \cdot \blacksquare \cdot \blacksquare) = 2^{\blacksquare}$$

$$(2^2)^3 = \blacksquare \cdot \blacksquare \cdot \blacksquare = (\blacksquare \cdot \blacksquare)(\blacksquare \cdot \blacksquare)(\blacksquare \cdot \blacksquare) = \blacksquare^{\blacksquare}$$

$$(4^2)^4 = \blacksquare \cdot \blacksquare \cdot \blacksquare \cdot \blacksquare = (\blacksquare \cdot \blacksquare)(\blacksquare \cdot \blacksquare)(\blacksquare \cdot \blacksquare)(\blacksquare \cdot \blacksquare) = \blacksquare^{\blacksquare}$$

$$(3^4)^2 = \blacksquare \cdot \blacksquare = (\blacksquare \cdot \blacksquare \cdot \blacksquare \cdot \blacksquare)(\blacksquare \cdot \blacksquare \cdot \blacksquare \cdot \blacksquare) = \blacksquare^{\blacksquare}$$

$$(6^3)^4 =$$

2 Examine your completed table. Look at the two exponents in the original expression and the exponent in the final answer. What pattern do you notice?

3 Use your pattern to make a conjecture: $(a^m)^n = a^{\blacksquare}$.

Try This

Use your conjecture to write each product below as a single power.

6. $\left(5^3\right)^2$ **7.** $\left(7^2\right)^2$ **8.** $\left(3^3\right)^4$ **9.** $\left(9^7\right)^3$

10. Make a table similar to the one in Activity 2 to explore what happens when you raise a power to two powers, for example, $\left[\left(4^2\right)^3\right]^3$. Then write a conjecture in words to summarize what you find.

Activity 3

1 Copy and complete the table below.

$(ab)^3 = (ab)(ab)(ab) = (a \cdot a \cdot a)(b \cdot b \cdot b) = a^{\blacksquare} b^{\blacksquare}$

$(mn)^4 = (\blacksquare)(\blacksquare)(\blacksquare)(\blacksquare) = (\blacksquare \cdot \blacksquare \cdot \blacksquare \cdot \blacksquare)(\blacksquare \cdot \blacksquare \cdot \blacksquare \cdot \blacksquare) = \blacksquare^{\blacksquare} \blacksquare^{\blacksquare}$

$(xy)^2 = (\blacksquare)(\blacksquare) = (\blacksquare \cdot \blacksquare)(\blacksquare \cdot \blacksquare) = \blacksquare^{\blacksquare} \blacksquare^{\blacksquare}$

$(cd)^5 = (\blacksquare)(\blacksquare)(\blacksquare)(\blacksquare)(\blacksquare) = (\blacksquare \cdot \blacksquare \cdot \blacksquare \cdot \blacksquare \cdot \blacksquare)(\blacksquare \cdot \blacksquare \cdot \blacksquare \cdot \blacksquare \cdot \blacksquare) = \blacksquare^{\blacksquare} \blacksquare^{\blacksquare}$

$(pq)^6 =$

2 Examine your completed table. Look at the original expression and the final answer. What pattern do you notice?

3 Use your pattern to make a conjecture: $(ab)^n = a^{\blacksquare} b^{\blacksquare}$.

Try This

Use your conjecture to write each power below as a product.

11. $(rs)^8$ **12.** $(yz)^9$ **13.** $(ab)^7$ **14.** $(xz)^{12}$

15. Look at the first row of your table. What property or properties allow you to write $(ab)(ab)(ab)$ as $(a \cdot a \cdot a)(b \cdot b \cdot b)$?

16. Make a table similar to the one above to explore what happens when you raise a product containing more than two factors to a power, for example, $(xyz)^7$. Then write a conjecture in words to summarize what you find.

Multiplication Properties of Exponents

Objective
Use multiplication properties of exponents to evaluate and simplify expressions.

Who uses this?
Astronomers can multiply expressions with exponents to find the distance between objects in space. (See Example 2.)

You have seen that exponential expressions are useful when writing very small or very large numbers. To perform operations on these numbers, you can use properties of exponents. You can also use these properties to simplify your answer.

In this lesson, you will learn some properties that will help you simplify exponential expressions containing multiplication.

Know it! Note

Simplifying Exponential Expressions

An exponential expression is completely simplified if...
- There are no negative exponents.
- The same base does not appear more than once in a product or quotient.
- No powers are raised to powers.
- No products are raised to powers.
- No quotients are raised to powers.
- Numerical coefficients in a quotient do not have any common factor other than 1.

Examples	Nonexamples
$\dfrac{b}{a}$ x^3 z^{12} a^4b^4 $\dfrac{s^5}{t^5}$ $\dfrac{5a^2}{2b}$	$a^{-2}ba$ $x \cdot x^2$ $\left(z^3\right)^4$ $(ab)^4$ $\left(\dfrac{s}{t}\right)^5$ $\dfrac{10a^2}{4b}$

Products of powers with the same base can be found by writing each power as repeated multiplication.

$$3^5 \cdot 3^2 = (3\cdot3\cdot3\cdot3\cdot3) \cdot (3\cdot3) = 3^7$$

Notice the relationship between the exponents in the factors and the exponent in the product: $5 + 2 = 7$.

Know it! Note

Product of Powers Property

WORDS	NUMBERS	ALGEBRA
The product of two powers with the same base equals that base raised to the sum of the exponents.	$6^7 \cdot 6^4 = 6^{7+4} = 6^{11}$	If a is any nonzero real number and m and n are integers, then $a^m \cdot a^n = a^{m+n}$.

EXAMPLE 1 **Finding Products of Powers**

Simplify.

A $2^5 \cdot 2^6$

$2^5 \cdot 2^6$

2^{5+6} *Since the powers have the same base, keep the*

2^{11} *base and add the exponents.*

B $4^2 \cdot 3^{-2} \cdot 4^5 \cdot 3^6$

$4^2 \cdot 3^{-2} \cdot 4^5 \cdot 3^6$ *Group powers with the same base together.*

$\left(4^2 \cdot 4^5\right) \cdot \left(3^{-2} \cdot 3^6\right)$

$4^{2+5} \cdot 3^{-2+6}$ *Add the exponents of powers with the same base.*

$4^7 \cdot 3^4$

C $a^4 \cdot b^5 \cdot a^2$

$a^4 \cdot b^5 \cdot a^2$

$\left(a^4 \cdot a^2\right) \cdot b^5$ *Group powers with the same base together.*

$a^6 \cdot b^5$ *Add the exponents of powers with the same base.*

$a^6 b^5$

D $y^2 \cdot y \cdot y^{-4}$

$\left(y^2 \cdot y^1\right) \cdot y^{-4}$ *Group the first two powers.*

$y^3 \cdot y^{-4}$ *The first two powers have the same base, so add the exponents.*

y^{-1} *The two remaining powers have the same base, so add the exponents.*

$\dfrac{1}{y}$ *Write with a positive exponent.*

> **Remember!**
>
> A number or variable written without an exponent actually has an exponent of 1.
>
> $10 = 10^1$
>
> $y = y^1$

 Simplify.

1a. $7^8 \cdot 7^4$ **1b.** $3^{-3} \cdot 5^8 \cdot 3^4 \cdot 5^2$

1c. $m \cdot n^{-4} \cdot m^4$ **1d.** $x \cdot x^{-1} \cdot x^{-3} \cdot x^{-4}$

EXAMPLE 2 ***Astronomy Application***

Light from the Sun travels at about 1.86×10^5 miles per second. It takes about 500 seconds for the light to reach Earth. Find the approximate distance from the Sun to Earth. Write your answer in scientific notation.

distance = rate × time

$= \left(1.86 \times 10^5\right) \times 500$

$= \left(1.86 \times 10^5\right) \times \left(5 \times 10^2\right)$ *Write 500 in scientific notation.*

$= \left(1.86 \times 5\right) \times \left(10^5 \times 10^2\right)$ *Use the Commutative and Associative Properties to group.*

$= 9.3 \times 10^7$ *Multiply within each group.*

The Sun is about 9.3×10^7 miles from Earth.

 2. Light travels at about 1.86×10^5 miles per second. Find the approximate distance that light travels in one hour. Write your answer in scientific notation.

To find a power of a power, you can use the meaning of exponents.

$$\left(4^3\right)^2 = 4^3 \cdot 4^3 = \left(4\cdot4\cdot4\right)\cdot\left(4\cdot4\cdot4\right) = 4^6$$

Notice the relationship between the exponents in the original power and the exponent in the final power: $3 \cdot 2 = 6$.

Power of a Power Property

WORDS	NUMBERS	ALGEBRA
A power raised to another power equals that base raised to the product of the exponents.	$\left(6^7\right)^4 = 6^{7\cdot4} = 6^{28}$	If a is any nonzero real number and m and n are integers, then $\left(a^m\right)^n = a^{mn}$.

E X A M P L E 3 Finding Powers of Powers

Simplify.

A $\left(7^4\right)^3$

$7^{4\cdot3}$ *Use the Power of a Power Property.*

7^{12} *Simplify.*

B $\left(3^6\right)^0$

$3^{6\cdot0}$ *Use the Power of a Power Property.*

3^0 *Zero multiplied by any number is zero.*

1 *Any number raised to the zero power is 1.*

C $\left(x^2\right)^{-4} \cdot x^5$

$x^{2\cdot(-4)} \cdot x^5$ *Use the Power of a Power Property.*

$x^{-8} \cdot x^5$ *Simplify the exponent of the first term.*

x^{-8+5} *Since the powers have the same base, add the*

x^{-3} *   exponents.*

$\dfrac{1}{x^3}$ *Write with a positive exponent.*

 Simplify.

3a. $\left(3^4\right)^5$ **3b.** $\left(6^0\right)^3$ **3c.** $\left(a^3\right)^4 \cdot \left(a^{-2}\right)^{-3}$

Student to Student   *Multiplication Properties of Exponents*

Briana Tyler
Memorial High School

Sometimes I can't remember when to add exponents and when to multiply them. When this happens, I write everything in expanded form.

For example, I would write $x^2 \cdot x^3$ as $(x \cdot x)(x \cdot x \cdot x) = x^5$. Then $x^2 \cdot x^3 = x^{2+3} = x^5$.

I would write $\left(x^2\right)^3$ as $x^2 \cdot x^2 \cdot x^2$, which is $(x \cdot x)(x \cdot x)(x \cdot x) = x^6$.

Then $\left(x^2\right)^3 = x^{2\cdot3} = x^6$.

This way I get the right answer even if I forget the properties.

Powers of products can be found by using the meaning of an exponent.

$$(8x)^3 = 8x \cdot 8x \cdot 8x = 8 \cdot 8 \cdot 8 \cdot x \cdot x \cdot x = 8^3 x^3 = 512x^3$$

 Know it! Note

Power of a Product Property

WORDS	NUMBERS	ALGEBRA
A product raised to a power equals the product of each factor raised to that power.	$(2 \cdot 4)^3 = 2^3 \cdot 4^3$ $= 8 \cdot 64$ $= 512$	If a and b are any nonzero real numbers and n is any integer, then $(ab)^n = a^n b^n$.

EXAMPLE 4 **Finding Powers of Products**

Simplify.

A $(-3x)^2$

$(-3)^2 \cdot x^2$ *Use the Power of a Product Property.*

$9x^2$ *Simplify.*

Caution!

In Example 4B, the negative sign is not part of the base.
$-(3x)^2 = -1 \cdot (3x)^2$

B $-(3x)^2$

$-(3^2 \cdot x^2)$ *Use the Power of a Product Property.*

$-(9 \cdot x^2)$ *Simplify.*

$-9x^2$

C $\left(x^{-2} \cdot y^0\right)^3$

$\left(x^{-2}\right)^3 \cdot \left(y^0\right)^3$ *Use the Power of a Product Property.*

$x^{-2 \cdot 3} \cdot y^{0 \cdot 3}$ *Use the Power of a Power Property.*

$x^{-6} \cdot y^0$ *Simplify.*

$x^{-6} \cdot 1$ *Write y^0 as 1.*

$\dfrac{1}{x^6}$ *Write with a positive exponent.*

 CHECK IT OUT! **Simplify.**

4a. $(4p)^3$ **4b.** $\left(-5t^2\right)^2$ **4c.** $\left(x^2 y^3\right)^4 \cdot \left(x^2 y^4\right)^{-4}$

THINK AND DISCUSS

1. Explain why $\left(a^2\right)^3$ and $a^2 \cdot a^3$ are not equivalent expressions.

 Know it! Note

2. **GET ORGANIZED** Copy and complete the graphic organizer. In each box, supply the missing exponents. Then give an example for each property.

Multiplication Properties of Exponents		
Product of Powers Property	**Power of a Power Property**	**Power of a Product Property**
$a^m \cdot a^n = a^{\blacksquare}$	$(a^m)^n = a^{\blacksquare}$	$(ab)^n = a^{\blacksquare} b^{\blacksquare}$

7-3

Exercises

go.hrw.com
Homework Help Online
KEYWORD: MA7 7-3
Parent Resources Online
KEYWORD: MA7 Parent

GUIDED PRACTICE

SEE EXAMPLE **1**
p. 475

Simplify.

1. $2^2 \cdot 2^3$ 2. $5^3 \cdot 5^3$ 3. $n^6 \cdot n^2$ 4. $x^2 \cdot x^{-3} \cdot x^4$

SEE EXAMPLE **2**
p. 475

5. **Science** If you traveled in space at a speed of 1000 miles per hour, how far would you travel in 7.5×10^5 hours? Write your answer in scientific notation.

Simplify.

SEE EXAMPLE **3**
p. 476

6. $\left(x^2\right)^5$ 7. $\left(y^4\right)^8$ 8. $\left(p^3\right)^3$

9. $\left(3^{-2}\right)^2$ 10. $\left(a^{-3}\right)^4 \cdot \left(a^7\right)^2$ 11. $xy \cdot \left(x^2\right)^3 \cdot \left(y^3\right)^4$

SEE EXAMPLE **4**
p. 477

12. $(2t)^5$ 13. $(6k)^2$ 14. $\left(r^2s\right)^7$

15. $\left(-2x^5\right)^3$ 16. $-\left(2x^5\right)^3$ 17. $\left(a^2b^2\right)^5 \cdot \left(a^{-5}\right)^2$

PRACTICE AND PROBLEM SOLVING

Independent Practice	
For Exercises	See Example
18–21	1
22	2
23–28	3
29–34	4

Extra Practice
Skills Practice p. S16
Application Practice p. S34

Simplify.

18. $3^3 \cdot 2^3 \cdot 3$ 19. $6 \cdot 6^2 \cdot 6^3 \cdot 6^2$ 20. $a^5 \cdot a^0 \cdot a^{-5}$ 21. $x^7 \cdot x^{-6} \cdot y^{-3}$

22. **Geography** Rhode Island is the smallest state in the United States. Its land area is about 2.9×10^{10} square feet. Alaska, the largest state, is about 5.5×10^2 times as large as Rhode Island. What is the land area of Alaska in square feet? Write your answer in scientific notation.

Simplify.

23. $\left(2^3\right)^3$ 24. $\left(3^6\right)^0$ 25. $\left(x^2\right)^{-1}$

26. $\left(b^4\right)^6 \cdot b$ 27. $b \cdot \left(a^3\right)^4 \cdot \left(b^{-2}\right)^3$ 28. $\left(x^4\right)^2 \cdot \left(x^{-1}\right)^{-4}$

29. $(3x)^3$ 30. $\left(5w^8\right)^2$ 31. $\left(p^4q^2\right)^7$

32. $\left(-4x^3\right)^4$ 33. $-\left(4x^3\right)^4$ 34. $\left(x^3y^4\right)^3 \cdot \left(xy^3\right)^{-2}$

Find the missing exponent in each expression.

35. $a^{\blacksquare}a^4 = a^{10}$ 36. $\left(a^{\blacksquare}\right)^4 = a^{12}$ 37. $\left(a^2b^{\blacksquare}\right)^4 = a^8b^{12}$

38. $\left(a^3b^6\right)^{\blacksquare} = \dfrac{1}{a^9b^{18}}$ 39. $\left(b^2\right)^{-4} = \dfrac{1}{b^{\blacksquare}}$ 40. $a^{\blacksquare} \cdot a^6 = a^6$

 Geometry Write an expression for the area of each figure.

41.

42.

43.

Simplify, if possible.

44. x^6y^5 45. $\left(2x^2\right)^2 \cdot \left(3x^3\right)^3$ 46. $x^2 \cdot y^{-3} \cdot x^{-2} \cdot y^{-3}$

47. $\left(5x^2\right)\left(5x^2\right)^2$ 48. $-\left(x^2\right)^4\left(-x^2\right)^4$ 49. $a^3 \cdot a^0 \cdot 3a^3$

50. $(ab)^3(ab)^{-2}$ 51. $10^2 \cdot 10^{-4} \cdot 10^5$ 52. $\left(x^2y^2\right)^2\left(x^2y\right)^{-2}$

53. **Astronomy** The graph shows the approximate time it takes light from the Sun, which travels at a speed of 1.86×10^5 miles per second, to reach several planets. Find the approximate distance from the Sun to each planet in the graph. Write your answers in scientific notation. (*Hint:* Remember $d = rt$.)

Sunlight Travel Time to Planets

Planet	Time (s)
Earth	500
Mars	760
Jupiter	2600
Saturn	4800

 54. **Geometry** The volume of a rectangular prism can be found by using the formula $V = \ell wh$ where ℓ, w, and h represent the length, width, and height of the prism. Find the volume of a rectangular prism whose dimensions are $3a^2$, $4a^5$, and $4a^2b^2$.

55. **///ERROR ANALYSIS///** Explain the error in each simplification below. What is the correct answer in each case?

  a. $x^2 \cdot x^4 = x^8$　　　**b.** $\left(x^4\right)^5 = x^9$　　　**c.** $\left(x^2\right)^3 = x^{2^3} = x^8$

Simplify.

56. $\left(-3x^2\right)\left(5x^{-3}\right)$　　57. $\left(a^4b\right)\left(a^3b^{-6}\right)$　　58. $\left(6w^5\right)\left(2v^2\right)\left(w^6\right)$

59. $\left(3m^7\right)\left(m^2n\right)\left(5m^3n^8\right)$　　60. $\left(b^2\right)^{-2}\left(b^4\right)^5$　　61. $\left(3st\right)^2t^5$

62. $\left(2^2\right)^2\left(x^5y\right)^3$　　63. $(-t)(-t)^2\left(-t^4\right)$　　64. $\left(2m^2\right)\left(4m^4\right)(8n)^2$

65. **Estimation** Estimate the value of each expression. Explain how you estimated.

  a. $\left[(-3.031)^2\right]^3$　　　**b.** $\left(6.2085 \times 10^2\right) \times \left(3.819 \times 10^{-5}\right)$

66. **Physical Science** The speed of sound at sea level is about 344 meters per second. The speed of light is about 8.7×10^5 times faster than the speed of sound. What is the speed of light in meters per second? Write your answer in scientific notation and in standard form.

 67. **Write About It** Is $\left(x^2\right)^3$ equal to $\left(x^3\right)^2$? Explain.

68. **Biology** A newborn baby has about 26,000,000,000 cells. An adult has about 1.9×10^3 times as many cells as a baby. About how many cells does an adult have? Write your answer in scientific notation.

Simplify.

69. $(-4k)^2 + k^2$　　70. $-3z^3 + (-3z)^3$　　71. $\left(2x^2\right)^2 + 2\left(x^2\right)^2$

72. $(2r)^2s^2 + 6(rs)^2 + 1$　　73. $(3a)^2b^3 + 3(ab)^2(2b)$　　74. $\left(x^2\right)\left(x^2\right)\left(x^2\right) + 3x^2$

MULTI-STEP TEST PREP

75. This problem will prepare you for the Multi-Step Test Prep on page 494.

  a. The speed of light v is the product of the frequency f and the wavelength w ($v = fw$). Wavelengths are often measured in *nanometers*. *Nano* means 10^{-9}, so 1 nanometer $= 10^{-9}$ meters. What is 600 nanometers in meters? Write your answer in scientific notation.

  b. Use your answer from part **a** to find the speed of light in meters per second if $f = 5 \times 10^{14}$ Hz.

  c. Explain why you can rewrite $\left(6 \times 10^{-7}\right)\left(5 \times 10^{14}\right)$ as $(6 \times 5)\left(10^{-7}\right)\left(10^{14}\right)$.

Critical Thinking Rewrite each expression so that it has only one exponent. (*Hint:* You may use parentheses.)

76. c^3d^3

77. $36a^2b^2$

78. $\dfrac{8a^3}{b^3}$

79. $\dfrac{k^{-2}}{4m^2n^2}$

80. Which of the following is equivalent to $x^2 \cdot x^0$?

   Ⓐ 0   Ⓑ 1   Ⓒ x^2 Ⓓ x^{20}

81. Which of the following is equivalent to $(3 \times 10^5)^2$?

   Ⓕ 9×10^7 Ⓖ 9×10^{10} Ⓗ 6×10^7 Ⓙ 6×10^{10}

82. What is the value of n^3 when $n = 4 \times 10^5$?

   Ⓐ 1.2×10^9 Ⓑ 1.2×10^{16} Ⓒ 6.4×10^9 Ⓓ 6.4×10^{16}

83. Which represents the area of the triangle?

   Ⓕ $6x^2$ Ⓗ $7x^2$

   Ⓖ $12x^2$ Ⓙ $24x^2$

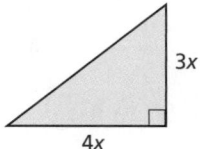

CHALLENGE AND EXTEND

Simplify.

84. $3^2 \cdot 3^x$

85. $(3^2)^x$

86. $(x^yz)^2$

87. $(x+1)^{-2}(x+1)^3$

88. $(x+1)^2(x+1)^{-3}$

89. $(x^y \cdot x^z)^3$

90. $(4^x)^x$

91. $(x^x)^x$

92. $(3x)^{2y}$

Find the value of x.

93. $5^x \cdot 5^4 = 5^8$

94. $7^3 \cdot 7^x = 7^{12}$

95. $(4^x)^3 = 4^{12}$

96. $(6^2)^x = 6^{16}$

97. Multi-Step The edge of a cube measures 1.2×10^{-2} m. What is the volume of the cube in cubic centimeters?

SPIRAL REVIEW

Find the value of x in each diagram. *(Lesson 2-8)*

98. $\square ABCD \sim \square WXYZ$

99. $\triangle ABC \sim \triangle RST$

Determine whether each sequence appears to be an arithmetic sequence. If so, find the common difference and the next three terms. *(Lesson 4-6)*

100. $5, 1, -3, -7, \ldots$

101. $-3, -2, 0, 3, \ldots$

102. $0.4, 1.0, 1.6, 2.2, \ldots$

Write each number in standard form. *(Lesson 7-2)*

103. 7.8×10^6

104. 4.95×10^{-4}

105. 983×10^{-1}

106. 0.06×10^8

Division Properties of Exponents

Objective
Use division properties of exponents to evaluate and simplify expressions.

Who uses this?
Economists can use expressions with exponents to calculate national debt statistics. (See Example 3.)

A quotient of powers with the same base can be found by writing the powers in factored form and dividing out common factors.

$$\frac{3^5}{3^3} = \frac{\cancel{3}\cdot\cancel{3}\cdot\cancel{3}\cdot 3\cdot 3}{\cancel{3}\cdot\cancel{3}\cdot\cancel{3}} = 3\cdot 3 = 3^2$$

Notice the relationship between the exponents in the original quotient and the exponent in the final answer: $5 - 3 = 2$.

Know it! Note

Quotient of Powers Property

WORDS	NUMBERS	ALGEBRA
The quotient of two nonzero powers with the same base equals the base raised to the difference of the exponents.	$\frac{6^7}{6^4} = 6^{7-4} = 6^3$	If a is a nonzero real number and m and n are integers, then $\frac{a^m}{a^n} = a^{m-n}$.

EXAMPLE 1 **Finding Quotients of Powers**

Simplify.

A $\dfrac{3^8}{3^2}$

$$\frac{3^8}{3^2} = 3^{8-2}$$
$$= 3^6 = 729$$

B $\dfrac{x^5}{x^5}$

$$\frac{x^5}{x^5} = x^{5-5}$$
$$= x^0 = 1$$

Helpful Hint

$3^6 = 729$
Both 3^6 and 729 are considered to be simplified.

C $\dfrac{a^5b^9}{(ab)^4}$

$$\frac{a^5b^9}{(ab)^4} = \frac{a^5b^9}{a^4b^4}$$
$$= a^{5-4}\cdot b^{9-4}$$
$$= a^1\cdot b^5$$
$$= ab^5$$

D $\dfrac{2^3\cdot 3^2\cdot 5^7}{2\cdot 3^4\cdot 5^5}$

$$\frac{2^3\cdot 3^2\cdot 5^7}{2\cdot 3^4\cdot 5^5} = 2^{3-1}\cdot 3^{2-4}\cdot 5^{7-5}$$
$$= 2^2\cdot 3^{-2}\cdot 5^2$$
$$= \frac{2^2\cdot 5^2}{3^2}$$
$$= \frac{4\cdot 25}{9} = \frac{100}{9}$$

 CHECK IT OUT! Simplify.

1a. $\dfrac{2^9}{2^7}$ 1b. $\dfrac{y}{y^4}$ 1c. $\dfrac{m^5n^4}{(m^5)^2 n}$ 1d. $\dfrac{3^5\cdot 2^4\cdot 4^3}{3^4\cdot 2^2\cdot 4^6}$

EXAMPLE 2 **Dividing Numbers in Scientific Notation**

Simplify $(2 \times 10^8) \div (8 \times 10^5)$ and write the answer in scientific notation.

$$(2 \times 10^8) \div (8 \times 10^5) = \frac{2 \times 10^8}{8 \times 10^5}$$

$$= \frac{2}{8} \times \frac{10^8}{10^5} \qquad \textit{Write as a product of quotients.}$$

$$= 0.25 \times 10^{8-5} \qquad \textit{Simplify each quotient.}$$

$$= 0.25 \times 10^3 \qquad \textit{Simplify the exponent.}$$

$$= 2.5 \times 10^{-1} \times 10^3 \qquad \textit{Write 0.25 in scientific notation as}$$
$$\textit{2.5} \times 10^{-1}.$$

$$= 2.5 \times 10^{-1+3} \qquad \textit{The second two terms have the}$$
$$\textit{same base, so add the exponents.}$$

$$= 2.5 \times 10^2 \qquad \textit{Simplify the exponent.}$$

 2. Simplify $(3.3 \times 10^6) \div (3 \times 10^8)$ and write the answer in scientific notation.

Writing Math

You can "split up" a quotient of products into a product of quotients:

$$\frac{a \times c}{b \times d} = \frac{a}{b} \times \frac{c}{d}$$

Example:

$$\frac{3 \times 4}{5 \times 7} = \frac{3}{5} \times \frac{4}{7} = \frac{12}{35}$$

EXAMPLE 3 *Economics Application*

In the year 2000, the United States public debt was about 5.6×10^{12} dollars. The population of the United States in that year was about 2.8×10^8 people. What was the average debt per person? Give your answer in standard form.

To find the average debt per person, divide the total debt by the number of people.

$$\frac{\text{total debt}}{\text{number of people}} = \frac{5.6 \times 10^{12}}{2.8 \times 10^8}$$

$$= \frac{5.6}{2.8} \times \frac{10^{12}}{10^8} \qquad \textit{Write as a product of quotients.}$$

$$= 2 \times 10^{12-8} \qquad \textit{Simplify each quotient.}$$

$$= 2 \times 10^4 \qquad \textit{Simplify the exponent.}$$

$$= 20,000 \qquad \textit{Write in standard form.}$$

The average debt per person was about $20,000.

 3. In 1990, the United States public debt was about 3.2×10^{12} dollars. The population of the United States in 1990 was about 2.5×10^8 people. What was the average debt per person? Write your answer in standard form.

A power of a quotient can be found by first writing factors and then writing the numerator and denominator as powers.

$$\left(\frac{2}{3}\right)^3 = \frac{2}{3} \cdot \frac{2}{3} \cdot \frac{2}{3} = \frac{2 \cdot 2 \cdot 2}{3 \cdot 3 \cdot 3} = \frac{2^3}{3^3}$$

Notice that the exponents in the final answer are the same as the exponent in the original expression.

Know it!
Note

Positive Power of a Quotient Property

WORDS	NUMBERS	ALGEBRA
A quotient raised to a positive power equals the quotient of each base raised to that power.	$\left(\dfrac{3}{5}\right)^4 = \dfrac{3}{5} \cdot \dfrac{3}{5} \cdot \dfrac{3}{5} \cdot \dfrac{3}{5} = \dfrac{3 \cdot 3 \cdot 3 \cdot 3}{5 \cdot 5 \cdot 5 \cdot 5} = \dfrac{3^4}{5^4}$	If a and b are nonzero real numbers and n is a positive integer, then $\left(\dfrac{a}{b}\right)^n = \dfrac{a^n}{b^n}$.

EXAMPLE 4 **Finding Positive Powers of Quotients**

Simplify.

A $\left(\dfrac{3}{4}\right)^3$

$\left(\dfrac{3}{4}\right)^3 = \dfrac{3^3}{4^3}$ *Use the Power of a Quotient Property.*

$\qquad = \dfrac{27}{64}$ *Simplify.*

B $\left(\dfrac{2x^3}{yz}\right)^3$

$\left(\dfrac{2x^3}{yz}\right)^3 = \dfrac{\left(2x^3\right)^3}{\left(yz\right)^3}$ *Use the Power of a Quotient Property.*

$\qquad = \dfrac{2^3\left(x^3\right)^3}{y^3z^3}$ *Use the Power of a Product Property:*
$\qquad\qquad\qquad\qquad\qquad \left(2x^3\right)^3 = 2^3\left(x^3\right)^3 \text{ and } (yz)^3 = y^3z^3.$

$\qquad = \dfrac{8x^9}{y^3z^3}$ *Simplify 2^3 and use the Power of a Power Property: $\left(x^3\right)^3 = x^{3\cdot3} = x^9$.*

CHECK IT OUT! Simplify.

4a. $\left(\dfrac{2^3}{3^2}\right)^2$ **4b.** $\left(\dfrac{ab^4}{c^2d^3}\right)^5$ **4c.** $\left(\dfrac{a^3b}{a^2b^2}\right)^3$

Remember that $x^{-n} = \dfrac{1}{x^n}$. What if x is a fraction?

$\left(\dfrac{a}{b}\right)^{-n} = \dfrac{1}{\left(\dfrac{a}{b}\right)^n} = 1 \div \left(\dfrac{a}{b}\right)^n$ *Write the fraction as division.*

$\qquad\qquad = 1 \div \dfrac{a^n}{b^n}$ *Use the Power of a Quotient Property.*

$\qquad\qquad = 1 \cdot \dfrac{b^n}{a^n}$ *Multiply by the reciprocal.*

$\qquad\qquad = \dfrac{b^n}{a^n}$ *Simplify.*

$\qquad\qquad = \left(\dfrac{b}{a}\right)^n$ *Use the Power of a Quotient Property.*

Therefore, $\left(\dfrac{a}{b}\right)^{-n} = \left(\dfrac{b}{a}\right)^n$.

Know it! Note

Negative Power of a Quotient Property

WORDS	NUMBERS	ALGEBRA
A quotient raised to a negative power equals the reciprocal of the quotient raised to the opposite (positive) power.	$\left(\frac{2}{3}\right)^{-4} = \left(\frac{3}{2}\right)^{4} = \frac{3^4}{2^4}$	If a and b are nonzero real numbers and n is a positive integer, then $\left(\frac{a}{b}\right)^{-n} = \left(\frac{b}{a}\right)^{n} = \frac{b^n}{a^n}$.

EXAMPLE 5 **Finding Negative Powers of Quotients**

Simplify.

A $\left(\frac{2}{5}\right)^{-3}$

$\left(\frac{2}{5}\right)^{-3} = \left(\frac{5}{2}\right)^{3}$ *Rewrite with a positive exponent.*

$= \frac{5^3}{2^3}$ *Use the Power of a Quotient Property.*

$= \frac{125}{8}$ $5^3 = 125$ and $2^3 = 8$.

B $\left(\frac{3x}{y^2}\right)^{-3}$

$\left(\frac{3x}{y^2}\right)^{-3} = \left(\frac{y^2}{3x}\right)^{3}$ *Rewrite with a positive exponent.*

$= \frac{\left(y^2\right)^3}{(3x)^3}$ *Use the Power of a Quotient Property.*

     Use the Power of a Power Property:
     $\left(y^2\right)^3 = y^{2\cdot3} = y^6.$

$= \frac{y^6}{3^3 x^3}$ *Use the Power of a Product Property:*
     $(3x)^3 = 3^3 x^3.$

$= \frac{y^6}{27x^3}$ *Simplify the denominator.*

C $\left(\frac{3}{4}\right)^{-1}\left(\frac{2x}{3y}\right)^{-2}$

$\left(\frac{3}{4}\right)^{-1}\left(\frac{2x}{3y}\right)^{-2} = \left(\frac{4}{3}\right)^{1}\left(\frac{3y}{2x}\right)^{2}$ *Rewrite each fraction with a positive exponent.*

$= \frac{4}{3} \cdot \frac{(3y)^2}{(2x)^2}$ *Use the Power of a Quotient Property.*

$= \frac{4}{3} \cdot \frac{3^2 y^2}{2^2 x^2}$ *Use the Power of a Product Property:*
     $(3y)^2 = 3^2 y^2$ and $(2x)^2 = 2^2 x^2.$

$= \frac{{}^1\cancel{4}}{{}_1\cancel{3}} \cdot \frac{\cancel{9}^3 y^2}{{}_1\cancel{4}x^2}$ *Divide out common factors.*

$= \frac{3y^2}{x^2}$

Helpful Hint

Whenever all of the factors in the numerator or the denominator divide out, replace them with 1.

 CHECK IT OUT! Simplify.

5a. $\left(\frac{4}{3^2}\right)^{-3}$ **5b.** $\left(\frac{2a}{b^2c^3}\right)^{-4}$ **5c.** $\left(\frac{s}{3}\right)^{-2}\left(\frac{9s^2}{t}\right)^{-1}$

7-4 Exercises

GUIDED PRACTICE

SEE EXAMPLE **1**
p. 481

Simplify.

1. $\dfrac{5^8}{5^6}$

2. $\dfrac{2^2 \cdot 3^4 \cdot 4^4}{2^9 \cdot 3^5}$

3. $\dfrac{15x^6}{5x^6}$

4. $\dfrac{a^5 b^6}{a^3 b^7}$

SEE EXAMPLE **2**
p. 482

Simplify each quotient and write the answer in scientific notation.

5. $(2.8 \times 10^{11}) \div (4 \times 10^8)$
6. $(5.5 \times 10^3) \div (5 \times 10^8)$
7. $(1.9 \times 10^4) \div (1.9 \times 10^4)$

SEE EXAMPLE **3**
p. 482

8. **Sports** A star baseball player earns an annual salary of 8.1×10^6. There are 162 games in a baseball season. How much does this player earn per game? Write your answer in standard form.

Simplify.

SEE EXAMPLE **4**
p. 483

9. $\left(\dfrac{2}{5}\right)^2$

10. $\left(\dfrac{x^2}{xy^3}\right)^3$

11. $\left(\dfrac{a^3}{(a^3 b)^2}\right)^2$

12. $\dfrac{y^{10}}{y}$

SEE EXAMPLE **5**
p. 484

13. $\left(\dfrac{3}{4}\right)^{-2}$

14. $\left(\dfrac{2x}{y^3}\right)^{-4}$

15. $\left(\dfrac{2}{3}\right)^{-1}\left(\dfrac{3a}{2h}\right)^{-2}$

16. $\left(\dfrac{x^3}{y^2}\right)^{-4}$

PRACTICE AND PROBLEM SOLVING

Simplify.

17. $\dfrac{3^9}{3^6}$

18. $\dfrac{5^4 \cdot 3^3}{5^2 \cdot 3^2}$

19. $\dfrac{x^8 y^3}{x^3 y^3}$

20. $\dfrac{x^8 y^4}{x^9 yz}$

Simplify each quotient and write the answer in scientific notation.

21. $(4.7 \times 10^{-3}) \div (9.4 \times 10^3)$

22. $(8.4 \times 10^9) \div (4 \times 10^{-5})$

23. $(4.2 \times 10^{-5}) \div (6 \times 10^{-3})$

24. $(2.1 \times 10^2) \div (8.4 \times 10^5)$

Independent Practice

For Exercises	See Example
17–20	1
21–24	2
25	3
26–29	4
30–33	5

Extra Practice

Skills Practice p. S16
Application Practice p. S34

25. Astronomy The mass of Earth is about 3×10^{-3} times the mass of Jupiter. The mass of Earth is about 6×10^{24} kg. What is the mass of Jupiter? Give your answer in scientific notation.

Simplify.

26. $\left(\dfrac{2}{3}\right)^4$

27. $\left(\dfrac{a^4}{b^2}\right)^3$

28. $\left(\dfrac{a^3b^2}{ab^3}\right)^6$

29. $\left(\dfrac{xy^2}{x^3y}\right)^3$

30. $\left(\dfrac{1}{7}\right)^{-3}$

31. $\left(\dfrac{x^2}{y^5}\right)^{-5}$

32. $\left(\dfrac{8w^7}{16}\right)^{-1}$

33. $\left(\dfrac{1}{4}\right)^{-2}\left(\dfrac{6x}{7}\right)^{-2}$

Simplify, if possible.

34. $\dfrac{x^6}{x^5}$

35. $\dfrac{8d^5}{4d^3}$

36. $\dfrac{x^2y^3}{a^2b^3}$

37. $\dfrac{(3x^3)^3}{(6x^2)^2}$

38. $\dfrac{(5x^2)^3}{5x^2}$

39. $\left(\dfrac{c^2a^3}{a^5}\right)^2$

40. $\left(\dfrac{3a}{a^3 \cdot a^0}\right)^3$

41. $\left(\dfrac{-p^4}{-5p^3}\right)^{-2}$

42. $\left(\dfrac{b^{-2}}{b^3}\right)^2$

43. $\left(\dfrac{10^2}{10^{-5} \cdot 10^5}\right)^{-1}$

44. $\left(\dfrac{x^2y^2}{x^2y}\right)^{-3}$

45. $\dfrac{(-x^2)^4}{-(x^2)^4}$

46. Critical Thinking How can you use the Quotient of a Power Property to explain the definition of x^{-n}? $\left(\text{Hint: Think of }\dfrac{1}{x^n}\text{ as }\dfrac{x^0}{x^n}.\right)$

47. Geography *Population density* is the number of people per unit of area. The area of the United States is approximately 9.37×10^6 square kilometers. The table shows population data from the U. S. Census Bureau.

United States Population	
Year	Population (to nearest million)
2000	2.81×10^8
1995	2.66×10^8
1990	2.48×10^8

Write the approximate population density (people per square kilometer) for each of the given years in scientific notation. Round decimals to the nearest hundredth.

48. Chemistry The pH of a solution is a number that describes the concentration of hydrogen ions in that solution. For example, if the concentration of hydrogen ions in a solution is 10^{-4}, that solution has a pH of 4.

Lemon juice
pH 2

Apples
pH 3

Water
pH 7

Ammonia
pH 11

 a. What is the concentration of hydrogen ions in lemon juice?

 b. What is the concentration of hydrogen ions in water?

 c. How many times more concentrated are the hydrogen ions in lemon juice than in water?

49. Write About It Explain how to simplify $\dfrac{4^5}{4^2}$. How is it different from simplifying $\dfrac{4^2}{4^5}$?

Find the missing exponent(s).

50. $\dfrac{x^{\blacksquare}}{x^4} = x^2$

51. $\dfrac{x^7}{x^{\blacksquare}} = x^4$

52. $\left(\dfrac{a^2}{b^{\blacksquare}}\right)^4 = \dfrac{a^8}{b^{12}}$

53. $\left(\dfrac{x^4}{y}\right)^{-1} = \dfrac{y^3}{x^{\blacksquare}}$

54. This problem will prepare you for the Multi-Step Test Prep on page 494.

   a. Yellow light has a wavelength of 589 nm. A nanometer (nm) is 10^{-9} m. What is 589 nm in meters? Write your answer in scientific notation.

   b. The speed of light in air, v, is 3×10^8 m/s, and $v = fw$, where f represents the frequency in hertz (Hz) and w represents the wavelength in meters. What is the frequency of yellow light?

TEST PREP

55. Which of the following is equivalent to $(8 \times 10^6) \div (4 \times 10^2)$?

   Ⓐ 2×10^3 Ⓑ 2×10^4 Ⓒ 4×10^3 Ⓓ 4×10^4

56. Which of the following is equivalent to $\left(\dfrac{x^{12}}{3xy^4}\right)^{-2}$?

   Ⓕ $\dfrac{9y^8}{x^{22}}$ Ⓖ $\dfrac{3y^8}{x^{22}}$ Ⓗ $\dfrac{3y^6}{x^{12}}$ Ⓙ $\dfrac{6y^8}{x^{26}}$

57. Which of the following is equivalent to $\dfrac{(-3x)^4}{-(3x)^4}$?

   Ⓐ -1 Ⓑ 1 Ⓒ $-81x^4$ Ⓓ $\dfrac{1}{81x^4}$

CHALLENGE AND EXTEND

58. **Geometry** The volume of the prism at right is $V = 30x^4y^3$. Write and simplify an expression for the prism's height in terms of x and y.

59. Simplify $\dfrac{3^{2x}}{3^{2x-1}}$.   **60.** Simplify $\dfrac{(x+1)^2}{(x+1)^3}$.

61. Copy and complete the table below to show how the Quotient of Powers Property can be found by using the Product of Powers Property.

Statements	Reasons
1. $a^{m-n} = a^{\blacksquare + \blacksquare}$	1. Subtraction is addition of the opposite.
2. $\quad = a^{\blacksquare} \cdot a^{\blacksquare}$	2. Product of Powers Property
3. $\quad = a^m \cdot \dfrac{1}{a^n}$	3. _____ ?
4. $\quad = \dfrac{a^m}{\blacksquare}$	4. Multiplication can be written as division.

SPIRAL REVIEW

Find each square root. *(Lesson 1-5)*

62. $\sqrt{36}$ **63.** $\sqrt{1}$ **64.** $-\sqrt{49}$ **65.** $\sqrt{144}$

Solve each equation. *(Lesson 2-4)*

66. $-2(x-1) + 4x = 5x + 3$ **67.** $x - 1 - (4x + 3) = 5x$

Simplify. *(Lesson 7-3)*

68. $3^2 \cdot 3^3$ **69.** $k^5 \cdot k^{-2} \cdot k^{-3}$ **70.** $(4t^5)^2$ **71.** $-(5x^4)^3$

7-5 Rational Exponents

Objective
Evaluate and simplify expressions containing rational exponents.

Vocabulary
index

Why learn this?
You can use rational exponents to find the number of Calories animals need to consume each day to maintain health. (See Example 3.)

Recall that the radical symbol $\sqrt{}$ is used to indicate roots. The **index** is the small number to the left of the radical symbol that tells which root to take. For example, $\sqrt[3]{}$ represents a cube root. Since $2^3 = 2 \cdot 2 \cdot 2 = 8$, $\sqrt[3]{8} = 2$.

Another way to write nth roots is by using exponents that are fractions. For example, for $b > 1$, suppose $\sqrt{b} = b^k$.

$$\sqrt{b} = b^k$$
$$\left(\sqrt{b}\right)^2 = \left(b^k\right)^2 \quad \text{\textit{Square both sides.}}$$
$$b^1 = b^{2k} \quad \text{\textit{Power of a Power Property}}$$
$$1 = 2k \quad \text{\textit{If } } b^m = b^n \text{\textit{, then } } m = n.$$
$$\frac{1}{2} = k \quad \text{\textit{Divide both sides by 2.}}$$

Helpful Hint
When $b = 0$, $\sqrt[n]{b} = 0$.
When $b = 1$, $\sqrt[n]{b} = 1$.

So for all $b > 1$, $\sqrt{b} = b^{\frac{1}{2}}$.

Definition of $b^{\frac{1}{n}}$

WORDS	NUMBERS	ALGEBRA
A number raised to the power of $\frac{1}{n}$ is equal to the nth root of that number.	$3^{\frac{1}{2}} = \sqrt{3}$ $5^{\frac{1}{4}} = \sqrt[4]{5}$ $2^{\frac{1}{7}} = \sqrt[7]{2}$	If $b > 1$ and n is an integer, where $n \geq 2$, then $b^{\frac{1}{n}} = \sqrt[n]{b}$. $b^{\frac{1}{2}} = \sqrt{b}$, $b^{\frac{1}{3}} = \sqrt[3]{b}$, $b^{\frac{1}{4}} = \sqrt[4]{b}$, and so on.

EXAMPLE 1 Simplifying $b^{\frac{1}{n}}$

Simplify each expression.

A $125^{\frac{1}{3}}$

$125^{\frac{1}{3}} = \sqrt[3]{125} = \sqrt[3]{5^3}$ *Use the definition of $b^{\frac{1}{n}}$.*

$= 5$

Remember!
$\sqrt{}$ is equivalent to $\sqrt[2]{}$. See Lesson 1-5.

B $64^{\frac{1}{6}} + 25^{\frac{1}{2}}$

$64^{\frac{1}{6}} + 25^{\frac{1}{2}} = \sqrt[6]{64} + \sqrt{25}$ *Use the definition of $b^{\frac{1}{n}}$.*

$= \sqrt[6]{2^6} + \sqrt{5^2}$

$= 2 + 5 = 7$

Simplify each expression.

1a. $81^{\frac{1}{4}}$ **1b.** $121^{\frac{1}{2}} + 256^{\frac{1}{4}}$

A fractional exponent can have a numerator other than 1, as in the expression $b^{\frac{2}{3}}$. You can write the exponent as a product in two different ways.

$$b^{\frac{2}{3}} = b^{\frac{1}{3} \cdot 2}$$
$$= \left(b^{\frac{1}{3}}\right)^2 \qquad \textit{Power of a Power Property}$$
$$= \left(\sqrt[3]{b}\right)^2 \qquad \textit{Definition of } b^{\frac{1}{n}}$$

$$b^{\frac{2}{3}} = b^{2 \cdot \frac{1}{3}}$$
$$= \left(b^2\right)^{\frac{1}{3}}$$
$$= \sqrt[3]{b^2}$$

Definition of $b^{\frac{m}{n}}$

WORDS	NUMBERS	ALGEBRA
A number raised to the power of $\frac{m}{n}$ is equal to the nth root of the number raised to the mth power.	$8^{\frac{2}{3}} = \left(\sqrt[3]{8}\right)^2 = 2^2 = 4$ $8^{\frac{2}{3}} = \sqrt[3]{8^2} = \sqrt[3]{64} = 4$	If $b > 1$ and m and n are integers, where $m \geq 1$ and $n \geq 2$, then $b^{\frac{m}{n}} = \left(\sqrt[n]{b}\right)^m = \sqrt[n]{b^m}$.

EXAMPLE 2 **Simplifying Expressions with Fractional Exponents**

Simplify each expression.

A $216^{\frac{2}{3}}$

$216^{\frac{2}{3}} = \left(\sqrt[3]{216}\right)^2 \qquad \textit{Definition of } b^{\frac{m}{n}}$
$= \left(\sqrt[3]{6^3}\right)^2$
$= (6)^2 = 36$

B $32^{\frac{4}{5}}$

$32^{\frac{4}{5}} = \left(\sqrt[5]{32}\right)^4$
$= \left(\sqrt[5]{2^5}\right)^4$
$= (2)^4 = 16$

 Simplify each expression.

2a. $16^{\frac{3}{4}}$ **2b.** $1^{\frac{2}{5}}$ **2c.** $27^{\frac{4}{3}}$

EXAMPLE 3 **Biology Application**

The approximate number of Calories C that an animal needs each day is given by $C = 72m^{\frac{3}{4}}$, where m is the animal's mass in kilograms. Find the number of Calories that a 16 kg dog needs each day.

$C = 72m^{\frac{3}{4}}$
$= 72(16)^{\frac{3}{4}} \qquad \textit{Substitute 16 for m.}$
$= 72 \cdot \left(\sqrt[4]{16}\right)^3 \qquad \textit{Definition of } b^{\frac{m}{n}}$
$= 72 \cdot \left(\sqrt[4]{2^4}\right)^3$
$= 72 \cdot (2)^3$
$= 72 \cdot 8 = 576$

The dog needs 576 Calories per day to maintain health.

 **3.** Find the number of Calories that an 81 kg panda needs each day.

Remember that $\sqrt{}$ always indicates a nonnegative square root. When you simplify variable expressions that contain $\sqrt{}$, such as $\sqrt{x^2}$, the answer cannot be negative. But x may be negative. Therefore you simplify $\sqrt{x^2}$ as $|x|$ to ensure the answer is nonnegative.

When x is...	and n is...	x^n is...	and $\sqrt[n]{x^n}$ is...
Positive	Even	Positive	Positive
Negative	Even	Positive	Positive
Positive	Odd	Positive	Positive
Negative	Odd	Negative	Negative

When n is even, you must simplify $\sqrt[n]{x^n}$ to $|x|$, because you do not know whether x is positive or negative. When n is odd, simplify $\sqrt[n]{x^n}$ to x.

EXAMPLE **4** **Using Properties of Exponents to Simplify Expressions**

Simplify. All variables represent nonnegative numbers.

A $\sqrt[3]{x^9 y^3}$

$$\sqrt[3]{x^9 y^3} = \left(x^9 y^3\right)^{\frac{1}{3}} \qquad \textit{Definition of } b^{\frac{1}{n}}$$

$$= \left(x^9\right)^{\frac{1}{3}} \cdot \left(y^3\right)^{\frac{1}{3}} \qquad \textit{Power of a Product Property}$$

$$= \left(x^{9 \cdot \frac{1}{3}}\right) \cdot \left(y^{3 \cdot \frac{1}{3}}\right) \qquad \textit{Power of a Power Property}$$

$$= \left(x^3\right) \cdot \left(y^1\right) = x^3 y \qquad \textit{Simplify exponents.}$$

> **Helpful Hint**
>
> When you are told that all variables represent non-negative numbers, you do not need to use absolute values in your answers.

B $\left(x^2 y^{\frac{1}{2}}\right)^4 \sqrt[3]{y^3}$

$$\left(x^2 y^{\frac{1}{2}}\right)^4 \sqrt[3]{y^3} = \left(x^2 y^{\frac{1}{2}}\right)^4 \cdot y \qquad \sqrt[3]{y^3} = y$$

$$= \left(x^{2 \cdot 4}\right) \cdot \left(y^{\frac{1}{2} \cdot 4}\right) \cdot y \qquad \textit{Power of a Product Property}$$

$$= \left(x^8\right) \cdot \left(y^2\right) \cdot y \qquad \textit{Simplify exponents.}$$

$$= x^8 \cdot y^{2+1} = x^8 y^3 \qquad \textit{Product of Powers Property}$$

 Simplify. All variables represent nonnegative numbers.

4a. $\sqrt[4]{x^4 y^{12}}$

4b. $\dfrac{\left(xy^{\frac{1}{2}}\right)^2}{\sqrt[5]{x^5}}$

THINK AND DISCUSS

1. Explain how to find the value of $\left(\sqrt[10]{25}\right)^5$.

2. GET ORGANIZED Copy and complete the graphic organizer. In each cell, provide the definition and a numerical example of each type of exponent.

Exponent	Definition	Numerical Example
$b^{\frac{1}{n}}$		
$b^{\frac{m}{n}}$		

7-5

Exercises

go.hrw.com
Homework Help Online
KEYWORD: MA11 7-5
Parent Resources Online
KEYWORD: MA7 Parent

GUIDED PRACTICE

1. **Vocabulary** In the expression $\sqrt[5]{3x}$, what is the *index*?

Simplify each expression.

SEE EXAMPLE **1**
p. 488

2. $8^{\frac{1}{3}}$

3. $16^{\frac{1}{2}}$

4. $0^{\frac{1}{6}}$

5. $27^{\frac{1}{3}}$

6. $81^{\frac{1}{2}}$

7. $216^{\frac{1}{3}}$

8. $1^{\frac{1}{9}}$

9. $625^{\frac{1}{4}}$

10. $36^{\frac{1}{2}} + 1^{\frac{1}{3}}$

11. $8^{\frac{1}{3}} + 64^{\frac{1}{2}}$

12. $81^{\frac{1}{4}} + 8^{\frac{1}{3}}$

13. $25^{\frac{1}{2}} - 1^{\frac{1}{4}}$

SEE EXAMPLE **2**
p. 489

14. $81^{\frac{3}{4}}$

15. $8^{\frac{5}{3}}$

16. $125^{\frac{2}{3}}$

17. $25^{\frac{3}{2}}$

18. $36^{\frac{3}{2}}$

19. $64^{\frac{4}{3}}$

20. $1^{\frac{3}{4}}$

21. $0^{\frac{2}{3}}$

SEE EXAMPLE **3**
p. 489

22. **Geometry** Given a square with area a, you can use the formula $P = 4a^{\frac{1}{2}}$ to find the perimeter P of the square. Find the perimeter of a square that has an area of 64 m².

SEE EXAMPLE **4**
p. 490

Simplify. All variables represent nonnegative numbers.

23. $\sqrt{x^4 y^2}$

24. $\sqrt[4]{z^4}$

25. $\sqrt{x^6 y^6}$

26. $\sqrt[3]{a^{12} b^6}$

27. $\left(a^{\frac{1}{2}}\right)^2 \sqrt{a^2}$

28. $\left(x^{\frac{1}{3}}\right)^6 \sqrt[4]{y^4}$

29. $\dfrac{\left(z^{\frac{1}{3}}\right)^3}{\sqrt{z^2}}$

30. $\dfrac{\sqrt[3]{x^6 y^9}}{x^2}$

PRACTICE AND PROBLEM SOLVING

Independent Practice

For Exercises	See Example
31–42	1
43–50	2
51	3
52–59	4

Extra Practice
Skills Practice p. S17
Application Practice p. S34

Simplify each expression.

31. $100^{\frac{1}{2}}$

32. $1^{\frac{1}{5}}$

33. $512^{\frac{1}{3}}$

34. $729^{\frac{1}{2}}$

35. $32^{\frac{1}{5}}$

36. $196^{\frac{1}{2}}$

37. $256^{\frac{1}{8}}$

38. $400^{\frac{1}{2}}$

39. $125^{\frac{1}{3}} + 81^{\frac{1}{2}}$

40. $25^{\frac{1}{2}} - 81^{\frac{1}{4}}$

41. $121^{\frac{1}{2}} - 243^{\frac{1}{5}}$

42. $256^{\frac{1}{4}} + 0^{\frac{1}{3}}$

43. $4^{\frac{3}{2}}$

44. $27^{\frac{2}{3}}$

45. $256^{\frac{3}{4}}$

46. $64^{\frac{5}{6}}$

47. $100^{\frac{3}{2}}$

48. $1^{\frac{5}{3}}$

49. $9^{\frac{5}{2}}$

50. $243^{\frac{2}{5}}$

51. **Biology** Biologists use a formula to estimate the mass of a mammal's brain. For a mammal with a mass of m grams, the approximate mass B of the brain, also in grams, is given by $B = \frac{1}{8} m^{\frac{2}{3}}$. Find the approximate mass of the brain of a mouse that has a mass of 64 grams.

Simplify. All variables represent nonnegative numbers.

52. $\sqrt[3]{a^6 c^9}$

53. $\sqrt[3]{8m^3}$

54. $\sqrt[4]{x^{16} y^4}$

55. $\sqrt[3]{27x^6}$

56. $\left(x^{\frac{1}{2}} y^3\right)^2 \sqrt{x^2}$

57. $\left(a^2 b^4\right)^{\frac{1}{2}} \sqrt[3]{b^6}$

58. $\dfrac{\sqrt[3]{x^6 y^6}}{yx^2}$

59. $\dfrac{\left(a^2 b^{\frac{1}{2}}\right)^4}{\sqrt{b^2}}$

Fill in the boxes to make each statement true.

60. $256^{\frac{\blacksquare}{4}} = 4$

61. $\blacksquare^{\frac{1}{5}} = 1$

62. $225^{\frac{1}{\blacksquare}} = 15$

63. $\blacksquare^{\frac{1}{6}} = 0$

64. $64^{\frac{3}{\blacksquare}} = 16$

65. $\blacksquare^{\frac{3}{4}} = 125$

66. $27^{\frac{4}{\blacksquare}} = 81$

67. $36^{\frac{\blacksquare}{2}} = 216$

Simplify each expression.

68. $\left(\dfrac{81}{169}\right)^{\frac{1}{2}}$

69. $\left(\dfrac{8}{27}\right)^{\frac{1}{3}}$

70. $\left(\dfrac{256}{81}\right)^{\frac{1}{4}}$

71. $\left(\dfrac{1}{16}\right)^{\frac{1}{2}}$

72. $\left(\dfrac{9}{16}\right)^{\frac{3}{2}}$

73. $\left(\dfrac{8}{27}\right)^{\frac{2}{3}}$

74. $\left(\dfrac{16}{81}\right)^{\frac{3}{4}}$

75. $\left(\dfrac{4}{49}\right)^{\frac{3}{2}}$

76. $\left(\dfrac{4}{25}\right)^{\frac{3}{2}}$

77. $\left(\dfrac{1}{81}\right)^{\frac{3}{4}}$

78. $\left(\dfrac{27}{64}\right)^{\frac{2}{3}}$

79. $\left(\dfrac{8}{125}\right)^{\frac{4}{3}}$

80. **Multi-Step** Scientists have found that the life span of a mammal living in captivity is related to the mammal's mass. The life span in years L can be approximated by the formula $L = 12m^{\frac{1}{5}}$, where m is the mammal's mass in kilograms. How much longer is the life span of a lion compared with that of a wolf?

Typical Mass of Mammals	
Mammal	Mass (kg)
Koala	8
Wolf	32
Lion	243
Giraffe	1024

81. **Geometry** Given a sphere with volume V, the formula $r = 0.62V^{\frac{1}{3}}$ may be used to approximate the sphere's radius r. Find the approximate radius of a sphere that has a volume of 27 in³.

82. **Critical Thinking** Show that a number raised to the power $\frac{1}{3}$ is the same as the cube root of that number. (*Hint:* Use properties of exponents to find the cube of $b^{\frac{1}{3}}$. Then compare this with the cube of $\sqrt[3]{b}$. Use the fact that if two numbers have the same cube, then they are equal.)

83. **Critical Thinking** Compare $n^{\frac{2}{3}}$ and $n^{\frac{3}{2}}$ for values of n greater than 1. When simplifying each of these expressions, will the result be greater than n or less than n? Explain.

84. **/// ERROR ANALYSIS ///** Two students simplified $64^{\frac{3}{2}}$. Which solution is incorrect? Explain the error.

A
$64^{\frac{3}{2}} = \left(\sqrt[3]{64}\right)^2$
  $= (4)^2$
  $= 16$

B
$64^{\frac{3}{2}} = \left(\sqrt{64}\right)^3$
  $= (8)^3$
  $= 512$

MULTI-STEP TEST PREP

85. This problem will prepare you for the Multi-Step Test Prep on page 494.
You can estimate an object's distance in inches from a light source by using the formula $d = \left(0.8\dfrac{L}{B}\right)^{\frac{1}{2}}$, where L is the light's luminosity in lumens and B is the light's brightness in lumens per square inch.

a. Find an object's distance to a light source with a luminosity of 4000 lumens and a brightness of 32 lumens per square inch.

b. Suppose the brightness of this light source decreases to 8 lumens per square inch. How does the object's distance from the source change?

86. **Write About It** You can write $4^{\frac{3}{2}}$ as $4^{3 \cdot \frac{1}{2}}$ or as $4^{\frac{1}{2} \cdot 3}$. Use the Power of a Power Property to show that both expressions are equal. Is one method easier than the other? Explain.

87. What is $9^{\frac{1}{2}} + 8^{\frac{1}{3}}$?

    (A) 4   (B) 5   (C) 6   (D) 10

88. Which expression is equal to 8?

    (F) $4^{\frac{3}{2}}$ (G) $16^{\frac{1}{2}}$ (H) $32^{\frac{4}{5}}$ (J) $64^{\frac{3}{2}}$

89. Which expression is equivalent to $\sqrt[3]{a^9 b^3}$?

    (A) $a^2 b$ (B) a^3 (C) $a^3 b$ (D) $a^3 b^3$

90. Which of the following is NOT equal to $16^{\frac{3}{2}}$?

    (F) $\left(\sqrt{16}\right)^3$ (G) 4^3 (H) $\left(\sqrt[3]{16}\right)^2$ (J) $\sqrt{16^3}$

CHALLENGE AND EXTEND

Use properties of exponents to simplify each expression.

91. $\left(a^{\frac{1}{3}}\right)\left(a^{\frac{1}{3}}\right)\left(a^{\frac{1}{3}}\right)$

92. $\left(x^{\frac{1}{2}}\right)^5 \left(x^{\frac{3}{2}}\right)$

93. $\left(x^{\frac{1}{3}}\right)^4 \left(x^5\right)^{\frac{1}{3}}$

You can use properties of exponents to help you solve equations. For example, to solve $x^3 = 64$, raise both sides to the $\frac{1}{3}$ power to get $\left(x^3\right)^{\frac{1}{3}} = 64^{\frac{1}{3}}$. Simplifying both sides gives $x = 4$. Use this method to solve each equation. Check your answer.

94. $y^5 = 32$

95. $27x^3 = 729$

96. $1 = \frac{1}{8}x^3$

 97. **Geometry** The formula for the surface area of a sphere S in terms of its volume V is $S = (4\pi)^{\frac{1}{3}} (3V)^{\frac{2}{3}}$. What is the surface area of a sphere that has a volume of 36π cm^3? Leave the symbol π in your answer. What do you notice?

SPIRAL REVIEW

Solve each equation. *(Lesson 2-6)*

98. $|x + 6| = 2$

99. $|5x + 5| = 0$

100. $|2x - 1| = 3$

Solve each inequality and graph the solutions. *(Lesson 3-4)*

101. $3n + 5 < 14$

102. $4 \leq \frac{1}{2}x + 3$

103. $7 \geq 2y + 11$

Give the domain and range of each relation. Tell whether the relation is a function. Explain. *(Lesson 4-2)*

104. $\{(2, 3), (2, 4), (2, 5), (2, 6)\}$

105. $\{(-2, 0), (-1, 1), (0, 2), (1, 3)\}$

106.

x	y
5	2
7	2
9	2
11	2

107.

MULTI-STEP TEST PREP

Exponents

I See the Light! The speed of light is the product of its frequency f and its wavelength w. In air, the speed of light is 3×10^8 m/s.

1. Write an equation for the relationship described above, and then solve this equation for frequency. Write this equation as an equation with w raised to a negative exponent.

2. Wavelengths of visible light range from 400 to 700 nanometers (10^{-9} meters). Use a graphing calculator and the relationship you found in Problem 1 to graph frequency as a function of wavelength. Sketch the graph with the axes clearly labeled. Describe your graph.

3. The speed of light in water is $\frac{3}{4}$ of its speed in air. Find the speed of light in water.

4. When light enters water, some colors bend more than others. How much the light bends depends on its wavelength. This is what creates a rainbow. The frequency of green light is about 5.9×10^{14} cycles per second. Find the wavelength of green light in water.

5. When light enters water, colors with shorter wavelengths bend more than colors with longer wavelengths. Violet light has a frequency of 7.5×10^{14} cycles per second, and red light has a frequency of 4.6×10^{14} cycles per second. Which of these colors of light will bend more when it enters water? Justify your answer.

READY TO GO ON?

Quiz for Lessons 7-1 Through 7-5

7-1 Integer Exponents

Evaluate each expression for the given value(s) of the variable(s).

1. t^{-6} for $t = 2$ **2.** n^{-3} for $n = -5$ **3.** $r^0 s^{-2}$ for $r = 8$ and $s = 10$

Simplify.

4. $5k^{-3}$ **5.** $\dfrac{x^4}{y^{-6}}$ **6.** $8f^{-4} g^0$ **7.** $\dfrac{a^{-3}}{b^{-2}}$

8. Measurement Metric units can be written in terms of a base unit. The table shows some of these equivalencies. Simplify each expression.

Selected Metric Prefixes					
Milli-	Centi-	Deci-	Deka-	Hecto-	Kilo-
10^{-3}	10^{-2}	10^{-1}	10^1	10^2	10^3

7-2 Powers of 10 and Scientific Notation

9. Find the value of 10^4.

10. Write 0.0000001 as a power of 10.

11. Write 100,000,000,000 as a power of 10.

12. Find the value of 82.1×10^4.

13. Measurement The lead in a mechanical pencil has a diameter of 0.5 mm. Write this number in scientific notation.

7-3 Multiplication Properties of Exponents

Simplify.

14. $2^2 \cdot 2^5$ **15.** $3^5 \cdot 3^{-3}$ **16.** $p^4 \cdot p^5$ **17.** $a^3 \cdot a^{-6} \cdot a^{-2}$

18. Biology A swarm of locusts was estimated to contain 2.8×10^{10} individual insects. If each locust weighs about 2.5 grams, how much did this entire swarm weigh? Write your answer in scientific notation.

Simplify.

19. $\left(3x^4\right)^3$ **20.** $\left(m^3 n^2\right)^5$ **21.** $\left(-4d^7\right)^2$ **22.** $\left(cd^6\right)^3 \cdot \left(c^5 d^2\right)^2$

7-4 Division Properties of Exponents

Simplify.

23. $\dfrac{6^9}{6^7}$ **24.** $\dfrac{12a^5}{3a^2}$ **25.** $\left(\dfrac{3}{5}\right)^3$ **26.** $\left(\dfrac{4p^3}{2pq^4}\right)^2$

Simplify each quotient and write the answer in scientific notation.

27. $\left(8 \times 10^9\right) \div \left(2 \times 10^6\right)$ **28.** $\left(3.5 \times 10^5\right) \div \left(7 \times 10^8\right)$ **29.** $\left(1 \times 10^4\right) \div \left(4 \times 10^4\right)$

7-5 Rational Exponents

Simplify each expression. All variables represent nonnegative numbers.

30. $81^{\frac{1}{2}}$ **31.** $125^{\frac{1}{3}}$ **32.** $4^{\frac{3}{2}}$ **33.** $0^{\frac{2}{9}}$

34. $\sqrt{x^8 y^4}$ **35.** $\sqrt[3]{r^9}$ **36.** $\sqrt[6]{z^{12}}$ **37.** $\sqrt[3]{p^3 q^{12}}$

7-6 Polynomials

Objectives

Classify polynomials and write polynomials in standard form.

Evaluate polynomial expressions.

Vocabulary

monomial
degree of a monomial
polynomial
degree of a polynomial
standard form of a polynomial
leading coefficient
quadratic
cubic
binomial
trinomial

Who uses this?

Pyrotechnicians can use polynomials to plan complex fireworks displays. (See Example 5.)

A **monomial** is a number, a variable, or a product of numbers and variables with whole-number exponents.

Monomials	Not Monomials
$5 \quad x \quad -7xy \quad 0.5x^4$	$-0.3x^{-2} \quad 4x - y \quad \dfrac{2}{x^3}$

The **degree of a monomial** is the sum of the exponents of the variables. A constant has degree 0.

EXAMPLE 1 **Finding the Degree of a Monomial**

Find the degree of each monomial.

A $-2a^2b^4$

The degree is 6.   *Add the exponents of the variables: 2 + 4 = 6*

B 4

$4x^0$ *There is no variable, but you can write 4 as $4x^0$.*

The degree is 0.

C $8y$

$8y^1$ *A variable written without an exponent has exponent 1.*

The degree is 1.

Remember!

The *terms* of an expression are the parts being added or subtracted. See Lesson 1-7.

 CHECK IT OUT! Find the degree of each monomial.

1a. $1.5k^2m$ **1b.** $4x$ **1c.** $2c^3$

A **polynomial** is a monomial or a sum or difference of monomials. The **degree of a polynomial** is the degree of the term with the greatest degree.

EXAMPLE 2 **Finding the Degree of a Polynomial**

Find the degree of each polynomial.

A $4x - 18x^5$

$4x$: degree 1 $-18x^5$: degree 5   *Find the degree of each term.*

The degree of the polynomial is the greatest degree, 5.

Find the degree of each polynomial.

B $0.5x^2y + 0.25xy + 0.75$

$0.5x^2y$: degree 3 $0.25xy$: degree 2 0.75: degree 0

The degree of the polynomial is the greatest degree, 3.

C $6x^4 + 9x^2 - x + 3$

$6x^4$: degree 4 $9x^2$: degree 2 $-x$: degree 1   3: degree 0

The degree of the polynomial is the greatest degree, 4.

CHECK IT OUT! Find the degree of each polynomial.

2a. $5x - 6$ **2b.** $x^3y^2 + x^2y^3 - x^4 + 2$

The terms of a polynomial may be written in any order. However, polynomials that contain only one variable are usually written in *standard form*.

The **standard form of a polynomial** that contains one variable is written with the terms in order from greatest degree to least degree. When written in standard form, the coefficient of the first term is called the **leading coefficient**.

EXAMPLE 3 **Writing Polynomials in Standard Form**

Write each polynomial in standard form. Then give the leading coefficient.

A $20x - 4x^3 + 2 - x^2$

Find the degree of each term. Then arrange them in descending order.

$$\underbrace{20x}_{} \; \underbrace{-4x^3}_{} \; \underbrace{+2}_{} \; \underbrace{-x^2}_{} \longrightarrow \underbrace{-4x^3}_{} \; \underbrace{-x^2}_{} \; \underbrace{+20x}_{} \; \underbrace{+2}_{}$$
Degree: 1   3   0   2   3   2   1   0

The standard form is $-4x^3 - x^2 + 20x + 2$. The leading coefficient is -4.

B $y^3 + y^5 + 4y$

Find the degree of each term. Then arrange them in descending order.

$$\underbrace{y^3}_{} \; \underbrace{+y^5}_{} \; \underbrace{+4y}_{} \longrightarrow \underbrace{y^5}_{} \; \underbrace{+y^3}_{} \; \underbrace{+4y}_{}$$
Degree: 3   5   1   5   3   1

The standard form is $y^5 + y^3 + 4y$. The leading coefficient is 1.

> **Remember!**
>
> A variable written without a coefficient has a coefficient of 1.
>
> $y^5 = 1y^5$

CHECK IT OUT! Write each polynomial in standard form. Then give the leading coefficient.

3a. $16 - 4x^2 + x^5 + 9x^3$ **3b.** $18y^5 - 3y^8 + 14y$

Some polynomials have special names based on their degree and the number of terms they have.

Degree	Name
0	Constant
1	Linear
2	**Quadratic**
3	**Cubic**
4	Quartic
5	Quintic
6 or more	6th degree, 7th degree, and so on

Terms	Name
1	Monomial
2	**Binomial**
3	**Trinomial**
4 or more	Polynomial

EXAMPLE 4 **Classifying Polynomials**

Classify each polynomial according to its degree and number of terms.

A $5x - 6$

Degree: 1   Terms: 2 $5x - 6$ is a linear binomial.

B $y^2 + y + 4$

Degree: 2   Terms: 3 $y^2 + y + 4$ is a quadratic trinomial.

C $6x^7 + 9x^2 - x + 3$

Degree: 7   Terms: 4 $6x^7 + 9x^2 - x + 3$ is a 7th-degree polynomial.

 Classify each polynomial according to its degree and number of terms.

4a. $x^3 + x^2 - x + 2$ **4b.** 6   **4c.** $-3y^8 + 18y^5 + 14y$

EXAMPLE 5 *Physics Application*

A firework is launched from a platform 6 feet above the ground at a speed of 200 feet per second. The firework has a 5-second fuse. The height of the firework in feet is given by the polynomial $-16t^2 + 200t + 6$, where t is the time in seconds. How high will the firework be when it explodes?

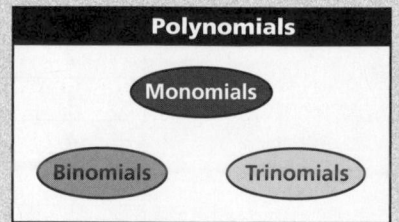

Substitute the time for t to find the firework's height.

$$-16t^2 + 200t + 6$$
$$-16(5)^2 + 200(5) + 6 \qquad \textit{The time is}$$
$$-16(25) + 200(5) + 6 \qquad \textit{5 seconds.}$$
$$-400 + 1000 + 6 \qquad \textit{Evaluate the polynomial by using the}$$
$$606 \qquad\qquad \textit{order of operations.}$$

When the firework explodes, it will be 606 feet above the ground.

 5. What if...? Another firework with a 5-second fuse is launched from the same platform at a speed of 400 feet per second. Its height is given by $-16t^2 + 400t + 6$. How high will this firework be when it explodes?

THINK AND DISCUSS

1. Explain why each expression is not a polynomial: $2x^2 + 3x^{-3}$; $1 - \frac{a}{b}$.

2. GET ORGANIZED Copy and complete the graphic organizer. In each oval, write an example of the given type of polynomial.

Know it!
Note

Polynomials

Monomials

Binomials   Trinomials

go.hrw.com
Homework Help Online
KEYWORD: MA11 7-6
Parent Resources Online
KEYWORD: MA7 Parent

GUIDED PRACTICE

Vocabulary Match each polynomial on the left with its classification on the right.

1. $2x^3 + 6$

2. $3x^3 + 4x^2 - 7$

3. $5x^2 - 2x + 3x^4 - 6$

a. quartic polynomial

b. quadratic polynomial

c. cubic trinomial

d. cubic binomial

SEE EXAMPLE **1**
p. 496

Find the degree of each monomial.

4. 10^6 **5.** $-7xy^2$ **6.** $0.4n^8$ **7.** 2

SEE EXAMPLE **2**
p. 496

Find the degree of each polynomial.

8. $x^2 - 2x + 1$ **9.** $0.75a^2b - 2a^3b^5$ **10.** $15y - 84y^3 + 100 - 3y^2$

11. $r^3 + r^2 - 5$ **12.** $a^3 + a^2 - 2a$ **13.** $3k^4 + k^3 - 2k^2 + k$

SEE EXAMPLE **3**
p. 497

Write each polynomial in standard form. Then give the leading coefficient.

14. $-2b + 5 + b^2$ **15.** $9a^8 - 8a^9$ **16.** $5s^2 - 3s + 3 - s^7$

17. $2x + 3x^2 - 1$ **18.** $5g - 7 + g^2$ **19.** $3c^2 + 5c^4 + 5c^3 - 4$

SEE EXAMPLE **4**
p. 498

Classify each polynomial according to its degree and number of terms.

20. $x^2 + 2x + 3$ **21.** $x - 7$ **22.** $8 + k + 5k^4$

23. $q^2 + 6 - q^3 + 3q^4$ **24.** $5k^2 + 7k^3$ **25.** $2a^3 + 4a^2 - a^4$

SEE EXAMPLE **5**
p. 498

26. Geometry The surface area of a cone is approximated by the polynomial $3.14r^2 + 3.14r\ell$, where r is the radius and ℓ is the slant height. Find the approximate surface area of this cone.

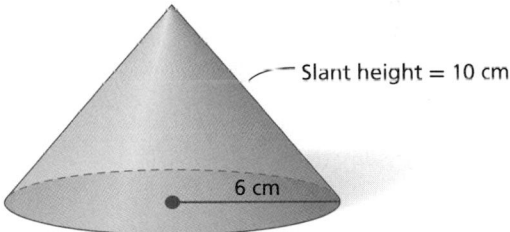

Slant height = 10 cm

6 cm

PRACTICE AND PROBLEM SOLVING

Independent Practice

For Exercises	See Example
27–34	1
35–40	2
41–49	3
50–57	4
58	5

Extra Practice

Skills Practice p. S17

Application Practice p. S34

Find the degree of each monomial.

27. $3y^4$ **28.** $6k$ **29.** $2a^3b^2c$ **30.** 325

31. $2y^4z^3$ **32.** $9m^5$ **33.** p **34.** 5

Find the degree of each polynomial.

35. $a^2 + a^4 - 6a$ **36.** $3^2b - 5$ **37.** $3.5y^2 - 4.1y - 6$

38. $-5f^4 + 2f^6 + 10f^8$ **39.** $4n^3 - 2n$ **40.** $4r^3 + 4r^6$

Write each polynomial in standard form. Then give the leading coefficient.

41. $2.5 + 4.9t^3 - 4t^2 + t$ **42.** $8a - 10a^2 + 2$ **43.** $x^7 - x + x^3 - x^5 + x^{10}$

44. $-m + 7 - 3m^2$ **45.** $3x^2 + 5x - 4 + 5x^3$ **46.** $-2n + 1 - n^2$

47. $4d + 3d^2 - d^3 + 5$ **48.** $3s^2 + 12s^3 + 6$ **49.** $4x^2 - x^5 - x^3 + 1$

Transportation

Hybrid III is the crash test dummy used by the Insurance Institute for Highway Safety. During a crash test, sensors in the dummy's head, neck, chest, legs, and feet measure and record forces. Engineers study this data to help design safer cars.

Classify each polynomial according to its degree and number of terms.

50. 12

51. $6k$

52. $3.5x^3 - 4.1x - 6$

53. $4g + 2g^2 - 3$

54. $2x^2 - 6x$

55. $6 - s^3 - 3s^4$

56. $c^2 + 7 - 2c^3$

57. $-y^2$

58. Transportation The polynomial $3.675v + 0.096v^2$ is used by transportation officials to estimate the stopping distance in feet for a car whose speed is v miles per hour on flat, dry pavement. What is the stopping distance for a car traveling at 30 miles per hour?

Tell whether each statement is sometimes, always, or never true.

59. A monomial is a polynomial.

60. A trinomial is a 3rd-degree polynomial.

61. A binomial is a trinomial.

62. A polynomial has two or more terms.

63. Geometry A piece of 8.5-by-11-inch cardboard has identical squares cut from its corners. It is then folded into a box with no lid. The volume of the box in cubic inches is $4c^3 - 39c^2 + 93.5c$, where c is the side length of the missing squares in inches.

   a. What is the volume of the box if $c = 1$ in.?

   b. What is the volume of the box if $c = 1.5$ in.?

   c. What is the volume of the box if $c = 4.25$ in.?

   d. Critical Thinking Does your answer to part **c** make sense? Explain why or why not.

Copy and complete the table by evaluating each polynomial for the given values of x.

	Polynomial	$x = -2$	$x = 0$	$x = 5$
64.	$5x - 6$	$5(-2) - 6 = -16$	$5(0) - 6 = -6$	▨
65.	$x^5 + x^3 + 4x$	▨	▨	▨
66.	$-10x^2$	▨	▨	▨

Give one example of each type of polynomial.

67. quadratic trinomial

68. linear binomial

69. constant monomial

70. cubic monomial

71. quintic binomial

72. 12th-degree trinomial

73. Write About It Explain the steps you would follow to write the polynomial $4x^3 - 3 + 5x^2 - 2x^4 - x$ in standard form.

MULTI-STEP TEST PREP

74. This problem will prepare you for the Multi-Step Test Prep on page 528.

   a. The perimeter of the rectangle shown is $12x + 6$. What is the degree of this polynomial?

   b. The area of the rectangle is $8x^2 + 12x$. What is the degree of this polynomial?

$2x + 3$

$4x$

75. **///ERROR ANALYSIS///** Two students evaluated $4x - 3x^5$ for $x = -2$. Which is incorrect? Explain the error.

A

$4(-2) - 3(-2)^5$
$-8 + 6^5$
$-8 + 7776$
7768

B

$4(-2) - 3(-2)^5$
$-8 - 3(-32)$
$-8 + 96$
88

TEST PREP

76. Which polynomial has the highest degree?
- Ⓐ $3x^8 - 2x^7 + x^6$
- Ⓑ $5x - 100$
- Ⓒ $25x^{10} + 3x^5 - 15$
- Ⓓ $134x^2$

77. What is the value of $-3x^3 + 4x^2 - 5x + 7$ when $x = -1$?
- Ⓕ 3
- Ⓖ 13
- Ⓗ 9
- Ⓙ 19

78. **Short Response** A toy rocket is launched from the ground at 75 feet per second. The polynomial $-16t^2 + 75t$ gives the rocket's height in feet after t seconds. Make a table showing the rocket's height after 1 second, 2 seconds, 3 seconds, and 4 seconds. At which of these times will the rocket be the highest?

CHALLENGE AND EXTEND

79. **Medicine** Doctors and nurses use growth charts and formulas to tell whether a baby is developing normally. The polynomial $0.016m^3 - 0.390m^2 + 4.562m + 50.310$ gives the average length in centimeters of a baby boy between 0 and 10 months of age, where m is the baby's age in months.

   a. What is the average length of a 2-month-old baby boy? a 5-month-old baby boy? Round your answers to the nearest centimeter.

   b. What is the average length of a newborn (0-month-old) baby boy?

   c. How could you find the answer to part **b** without doing any calculations?

80. Consider the binomials $4x^5 + x$, $4x^4 + x$, and $4x^3 + x$.

   a. Without calculating, which binomial has the greatest value for $x = 5$?

   b. Are there any values of x for $4x^3 + x$ which will have the greatest value? Explain.

SPIRAL REVIEW

81. Jordan is allowed 90 minutes of screen time per day. Today, he has already used m minutes. Write an expression for the remaining number of minutes Jordan has today. *(Lesson 1-1)*

82. Pens cost $0.50 each. Giselle bought p pens. Write an expression for the total cost of Giselle's pens. *(Lesson 1-1)*

Classify each system. Give the number of solutions. *(Lesson 6-4)*

83. $\begin{cases} y = -4x + 5 \\ 4x + y = 2 \end{cases}$

84. $\begin{cases} 2x + 8y = 10 \\ 4y = -x + 5 \end{cases}$

85. $\begin{cases} y = 3x + 2 \\ y = -5x - 6 \end{cases}$

Simplify. *(Lesson 7-4)*

86. $\dfrac{4^7}{4^4}$

87. $\dfrac{x^6 y^4}{x^4 y^9}$

88. $\left(\dfrac{2v^4}{vw^5}\right)^2$

89. $\left(\dfrac{2p}{p^3}\right)^{-4}$

7-7

Algebra LAB

Model Polynomial Addition and Subtraction

You can use algebra tiles to model polynomial addition and subtraction.

Use with Lesson 7-7

go.hrw.com
Lab Resources Online
KEYWORD: MA11 LAB7

KEY

 $= 1$

 $= -1$

 $= x$ $= -x$ $= x^2$ $= -x^2$

Activity 1

Use algebra tiles to find $(2x^2 - x) + (x^2 + 3x - 1)$.

MODEL		ALGEBRA
	Use tiles to represent all terms from both expressions.	$(2x^2 - x) + (x^2 + 3x - 1)$
	Rearrange tiles so that like tiles are together. Like tiles are the same size and shape.	$(2x^2 + x^2) + (-x + 3x) - 1$
	Remove any zero pairs.	$3x^2 - x + x + 2x - 1$
	The remaining tiles represent the sum.	$3x^2 + 2x - 1$

Try This

Use algebra tiles to find each sum.

1. $(-2x^2 + 1) + (-x^2)$

2. $(3x^2 + 2x + 5) + (x^2 - x - 4)$

3. $(x - 3) + (2x - 2)$

4. $(5x^2 - 3x - 6) + (x^2 + 3x + 6)$

5. $-5x^2 + (2x^2 + 5x)$

6. $(x^2 - x - 1) + (6x - 3)$

Activity 2

Use algebra tiles to find $(2x^2 + 6) - 4x^2$.

MODEL		ALGEBRA
	Use tiles to represent the terms in the first expression.	$2x^2 + 6$

To subtract $4x^2$, you would remove 4 yellow x^2-tiles, but there are not enough to do this. Remember that subtraction is the same as adding the opposite, so rewrite $(2x^2 + 6) - 4x^2$ as $(2x^2 + 6) + (-4x^2)$.

MODEL		ALGEBRA
	Add 4 red x^2-tiles.	$2x^2 + 6 + (-4x^2)$
	Rearrange tiles so that like tiles are together.	$2x^2 + (-4x^2) + 6$
	Remove zero pairs.	$2x^2 + (-2x^2) + (-2x^2) + 6$
	The remaining tiles represent the difference.	$-2x^2 + 6$

Try This

Use algebra tiles to find each difference.

7. $(6x^2 + 4x) - 3x^2$ **8.** $(2x^2 + x - 7) - 5x$ **9.** $(3x + 6) - 6$

10. $(8x + 5) - (-2x)$ **11.** $(x^2 + 2x) - (-4x^2 + x)$ **12.** $(3x^2 - 4) - (x^2 + 6x)$

13. represents a zero pair. Use algebra tiles to model two other zero pairs.

14. When is it not necessary to "add the opposite" for polynomial subtraction using algebra tiles?

Adding and Subtracting Polynomials

Objective
Add and subtract polynomials.

Who uses this?
Business owners can add and subtract polynomials that model profit. (See Example 4.)

"This one pretty much sums it up."

Just as you can perform operations on numbers, you can perform operations on polynomials. To add or subtract polynomials, combine like terms.

E X A M P L E **1** **Adding and Subtracting Monomials**

Add or subtract.

A $15m^3 + 6m^2 + 2m^3$

$15m^3 + 6m^2 + 2m^3$	*Identify like terms.*
$15m^3 + 2m^3 + 6m^2$	*Rearrange terms so that like terms are together.*
$17m^3 + 6m^2$	*Combine like terms.*

Remember!

Like terms are constants or terms with the same variable(s) raised to the same power(s). To review combining like terms, see Lesson 1-7.

B $3x^2 + 5 - 7x^2 + 12$

$3x^2 + 5 - 7x^2 + 12$	*Identify like terms.*
$3x^2 - 7x^2 + 5 + 12$	*Rearrange terms so that like terms are together.*
$-4x^2 + 17$	*Combine like terms.*

C $0.9y^5 - 0.4y^5 + 0.5x^5 + y^5$

$0.9y^5 - 0.4y^5 + 0.5x^5 + y^5$	*Identify like terms.*
$0.9y^5 - 0.4y^5 + y^5 + 0.5x^5$	*Rearrange terms so that like terms are together.*
$1.5y^5 + 0.5x^5$	*Combine like terms.*

D $2x^2y - x^2y - x^2y$

$2x^2y - x^2y - x^2y$	*All terms are like terms.*
0	*Combine.*

Add or subtract.

1a. $2s^2 + 3s^2 + s$

1b. $4z^4 - 8 + 16z^4 + 2$

1c. $2x^8 + 7y^8 - x^8 - y^8$

1d. $9b^3c^2 + 5b^3c^2 - 13b^3c^2$

Polynomials can be added in either vertical or horizontal form.

In vertical form, align the like terms and add:

$$
\begin{array}{r}
5x^2 + 4x + 1 \\
+\ 2x^2 + 5x + 2 \\
\hline
7x^2 + 9x + 3
\end{array}
$$

In horizontal form, use the Associative and Commutative Properties to regroup and combine like terms:

$$(5x^2 + 4x + 1) + (2x^2 + 5x + 2)$$
$$= (5x^2 + 2x^2) + (4x + 5x) + (1 + 2)$$
$$= 7x^2 + 9x + 3$$

EXAMPLE 2 Adding Polynomials

Add.

A $(2x^2 - x) + (x^2 + 3x - 1)$

$(2x^2 - x) + (x^2 + 3x - 1)$ *Identify like terms.*

$(2x^2 + x^2) + (-x + 3x) + (-1)$ *Group like terms together.*
   Combine like terms.

$3x^2 + 2x - 1$

B $(-2ab + b) + (2ab + a)$

$(-2ab + b) + (2ab + a)$ *Identify like terms.*

$(-2ab + 2ab) + b + a$ *Group like terms together.*

$0 + b + a$ *Combine like terms.*

$b + a$ *Simplify.*

C $(4b^5 + 8b) + (3b^5 + 6b - 7b^5 + b)$

$(4b^5 + 8b) + (3b^5 + 6b - 7b^5 + b)$ *Identify like terms.*

$(4b^5 + 8b) + (-4b^5 + 7b)$ *Combine like terms in the second*
   polynomial.

$\quad 4b^5 + 8b$ *Use the vertical method.*

$\underline{+ \; -4b^5 + 7b}$

$\quad\quad 0 \;\; + 15b$ *Combine like terms.*

$15b$ *Simplify.*

D $(20.2y^2 + 6y + 5) + (1.7y^2 - 8)$

$(20.2y^2 + 6y + 5) + (1.7y^2 - 8)$ *Identify like terms.*

$\quad 20.2y^2 + 6y + 5$ *Use the vertical method.*

$\underline{+ \; 1.7y^2 + 0y - 8}$ *Write 0y as a placeholder in the*
   second polynomial.

$\quad 21.9y^2 + 6y - 3$ *Combine like terms.*

 2. Add $(5a^3 + 3a^2 - 6a + 12a^2) + (7a^3 - 10a)$.

To subtract polynomials, remember that subtracting is the same as adding the opposite. To find the opposite of a polynomial, you must write the opposite of *each* term in the polynomial:

$$-(2x^3 - 3x + 7) = -2x^3 + 3x - 7$$

EXAMPLE 3 Subtracting Polynomials

Subtract.

A $(2x^2 + 6) - (4x^2)$

$(2x^2 + 6) + (-4x^2)$ *Rewrite subtraction as addition of the opposite.*

$(2x^2 + 6) + (-4x^2)$ *Identify like terms.*

$(2x^2 - 4x^2) + 6$ *Group like terms together.*

$-2x^2 + 6$ *Combine like terms.*

B $(a^4 - 2a) - (3a^4 - 3a + 1)$

$(a^4 - 2a) + (-3a^4 + 3a - 1)$ *Rewrite subtraction as addition of the opposite.*

$(a^4 - 2a) + (-3a^4 + 3a - 1)$ *Identify like terms.*

$(a^4 - 3a^4) + (-2a + 3a) - 1$ *Group like terms together.*

$-2a^4 + a - 1$ *Combine like terms.*

Subtract.

C $(3x^2 - 2x + 8) - (x^2 - 4)$

$(3x^2 - 2x + 8) + (-x^2 + 4)$ *Rewrite subtraction as addition of the opposite.*

$(3x^2 - 2x + 8) + (-x^2 + 4)$ *Identify like terms.*

$$\begin{array}{r} 3x^2 - 2x \;\; + 8 \\ + \;\; -x^2 + 0x \;\; + 4 \\ \hline 2x^2 - 2x + 12 \end{array}$$

Use the vertical method.
Write 0x as a placeholder.
Combine like terms.

D $(11z^3 - 2z) - (z^3 - 5)$

$(11z^3 - 2z) + (-z^3 + 5)$ *Rewrite subtraction as addition of the opposite.*

$(11z^3 - 2z) + (-z^3 + 5)$ *Identify like terms.*

$$\begin{array}{r} 11z^3 - 2z + 0 \\ + \;\; -z^3 + 0z + 5 \\ \hline 10z^3 - 2z + 5 \end{array}$$

Use the vertical method.
Write 0 and 0z as placeholders.
Combine like terms.

 3. Subtract $(2x^2 - 3x^2 + 1) - (x^2 + x + 1)$.

EXAMPLE 4   *Business Application*

The profits of two different manufacturing plants can be modeled as shown, where x is the number of units produced at each plant.

Eastern:
$-0.03x^2 + 25x - 1500$

Southern:
$-0.02x^2 + 21x - 1700$

Write a polynomial that represents the difference of the profits at the eastern plant and the profits at the southern plant.

$$\begin{array}{l} (-0.03x^2 + 25x - 1500) \\ - (-0.02x^2 + 21x - 1700) \end{array}$$

Eastern plant profits
Southern plant profits

$$\begin{array}{r} -0.03x^2 + 25x - 1500 \\ + (+0.02x^2 - 21x + 1700) \\ \hline -0.01x^2 + \;\; 4x + \;\; 200 \end{array}$$

Write subtraction as addition of the opposite.
Combine like terms.

 4. Use the information above to write a polynomial that represents the total profits from both plants.

THINK AND DISCUSS

1. Identify the like terms in the following list: $-12x^2$, $-4.7y$, $\frac{1}{5}x^2y$, y, $3xy^2$, $-9x^2$, $5x^2y$, $-12x$

2. Describe how to find the opposite of $9t^2 - 5t + 8$.

 **3. GET ORGANIZED** Copy and complete the graphic organizer. In each box, write an example that shows how to perform the given operation.

7-7

Exercises

go.hrw.com
Homework Help Online
KEYWORD: MA11 7-7
Parent Resources Online
KEYWORD: MA7 Parent

GUIDED PRACTICE

SEE EXAMPLE 1
p. 504

Add or subtract.

1. $7a^2 - 10a^2 + 9a$

2. $13x^2 + 9y^2 - 6x^2$

3. $0.07r^4 + 0.32r^3 + 0.19r^4$

4. $\frac{1}{4}p^3 + \frac{2}{3}p^3$

5. $5b^3c + b^3c - 3b^3c$

6. $-8m + 5 - 16 + 11m$

SEE EXAMPLE 2
p. 505

Add.

7. $\left(5n^3 + 3n + 6\right) + \left(18n^3 + 9\right)$

8. $\left(3.7q^2 - 8q + 3.7\right) + \left(4.3q^2 - 2.9q + 1.6\right)$

9. $\left(-3x + 12\right) + \left(9x^2 + 2x - 18\right)$

10. $\left(9x^4 + x^3\right) + \left(2x^4 + 6x^3 - 8x^4 + x^3\right)$

SEE EXAMPLE 3
p. 505

Subtract.

11. $\left(6c^4 + 8c + 6\right) - \left(2c^4\right)$

12. $\left(16y^2 - 8y + 9\right) - \left(6y^2 - 2y + 7y\right)$

13. $\left(2r + 5\right) - \left(5r - 6\right)$

14. $\left(-7k^2 + 3\right) - \left(2k^2 + 5k - 1\right)$

SEE EXAMPLE 4
p. 506

15. Geometry Write a polynomial that represents the measure of angle ABD.

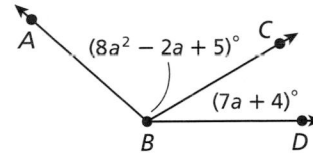

PRACTICE AND PROBLEM SOLVING

Independent Practice

For Exercises	See Example
16–24	1
25–28	2
29–32	3
33–34	4

Extra Practice

Skills Practice p. S17

Application Practice p. S34

Add or subtract.

16. $4k^3 + 6k^2 + 9k^3$

17. $5m + 12n^2 + 6n - 8m$

18. $2.5a^4 - 8.1b^4 - 3.6b^4$

19. $2d^5 + 1 - d^5$

20. $7xy - 4x^2y - 2xy$

21. $-6x^3 + 5x + 2x^3 + 4x^3$

22. $x^2 + x + 3x + 2x^2$

23. $3x^3 - 4 - x^3 - 1$

24. $3b^3 - 2b - 1 - b^3 - b$

Add.

25. $\left(2t^2 - 8t\right) + \left(8t^2 + 9t\right)$

26. $\left(-7x^2 - 2x + 3\right) + \left(4x^2 - 9x\right)$

27. $\left(x^5 - x\right) + \left(x^4 + x\right)$

28. $\left(-2z^3 + z + 2z^3 + z\right) + \left(3z^3 - 5z^2\right)$

Subtract.

29. $\left(t^3 + 8t^2\right) - \left(3t^3\right)$

30. $\left(3x^2 - x\right) - \left(x^2 + 3x - x\right)$

31. $\left(5m + 3\right) - \left(6m^3 - 2m^2\right)$

32. $\left(3s^2 + 4s\right) - \left(-10s^2 + 6s\right)$

33. Photography The measurements of a photo and its frame are shown in the diagram. Write a polynomial that represents the width of the photo.

34. Geometry The length of a rectangle is represented by $4a + 3b$, and its width is represented by $7a - 2b$. Write a polynomial for the perimeter of the rectangle.

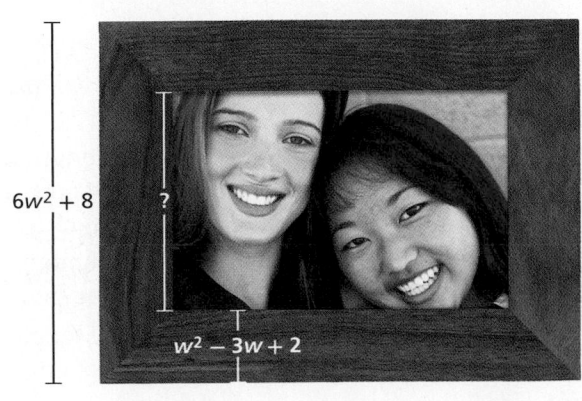

$6w^2 + 8$

?

$w^2 - 3w + 2$

Add or subtract.

35. $(2t - 7) + (-t + 2)$

36. $(4m^2 + 3m) + (-2m^2)$

37. $(4n - 2) - 2n$

38. $(-v - 7) - (-2v)$

39. $(4x^2 + 3x - 6) + (2x^2 - 4x + 5)$

40. $(2z^2 - 3z - 3) + (2z^2 - 7z - 1)$

41. $(5u^2 + 3u + 7) - (u^3 + 2u^2 + 1)$

42. $(-7h^2 - 4h + 7) - (7h^2 - 4h + 11)$

 43. Geometry The length of a rectangle is represented by $2x + 3$, and its width is represented by $3x + 7$. The perimeter of the rectangle is 35 units. Find the value of x.

44. Write About It If the parentheses are removed from $(3m^2 - 5m) + (12m^2 + 7m - 10)$, is the new expression equivalent to the original? If the parentheses are removed from $(3m^2 - 5m) - (12m^2 + 7m - 10)$, is the new expression equivalent to the original? Explain.

45. ///ERROR ANALYSIS/// Two students found the sum of the polynomials $(-3n^4 + 6n^3 + 4n^2)$ and $(8n^4 - 3n^2 + 9n)$. Which is incorrect? Explain the error.

A

$$-3n^4 + 6n^3 + 4n^2 + 0n$$
$$+8n^4 + 0n^3 - 3n^2 + 9n$$
$$5n^4 + 6n^3 + n^2 + 9n$$

B

$$-3n^4 + 6n^3 + 4n^2$$
$$+8n^4 - 3n^2 + 9n$$
$$5n^4 + 3n^3 + 13n^2$$

Copy and complete the table by finding the missing polynomials.

	Polynomial 1	Polynomial 2	Sum
46.	$x^2 - 6$	$3x^2 - 10x + 2$	▨
47.	$12x + 5$	▨	$15x + 11$
48.	▨	$5x^4 + 8$	$6x^4 - 3x^2 - 1$
49.	$7x^3 - 6x - 3$	▨	$7x^3 + 11$
50.	$2x^3 + 5x^2$	$7x^3 - 5x^2 + 1$	▨
51.	▨	$x + x^2 + 6$	$3x^2 + 2x + 1$

52. Critical Thinking Does the order in which you add polynomials affect the sum? Does the order in which you subtract polynomials affect the difference? Explain.

MULTI-STEP TEST PREP

53. This problem will prepare you for the Multi-Step Test Prep on page 528.

a. Ian plans to build a fenced dog pen. At first, he planned for the pen to be a square of length x feet on each side, but then he decided that a square may not be best. He added 4 feet to the length and subtracted 3 feet from the width. Draw a diagram to show the dimensions of the new pen.

b. Write a polynomial that represents the amount of fencing that Ian will need for the new dog pen.

c. How much fencing will Ian need if $x = 15$?

54. What is the missing term?

$$\left(-14y^2 + 9y^2 - 12y + 3\right) + \left(2y^2 + \blacksquare - 6y - 2\right) = \left(-3y^2 - 15y + 1\right)$$

(A) $-6y$ (B) $-3y$ (C) $3y$ (D) $6y$

55. Which is NOT equivalent to $-5t^3 - t$?

(F) $-\left(5t^3 + t\right)$ (H) $\left(t^3 + 6t\right) - \left(6t^3 + 7t\right)$

(G) $\left(2t^3 - 4t\right) - \left(-7t - 3t\right)$ (J) $\left(2t^3 - 3t^2 + t\right) - \left(7t^3 - 3t^2 + 2t\right)$

56. Extended Response Tammy plans to put a wallpaper border around the perimeter of her room. She will not put the border across the doorway, which is 3 feet wide.

Door

$(x + 4)$ ft

$(2x - 1)$ ft

  a. Write a polynomial that represents the number of feet of wallpaper border that Tammy will need.

  b. A local store has 50 feet of the border that Tammy has chosen. What is the greatest whole-number value of x for which this amount would be enough for Tammy's room? Justify your answer.

  c. Determine the dimensions of Tammy's room for the value of x that you found in part **b.**

CHALLENGE AND EXTEND

57. Geometry The legs of the isosceles triangle at right measure $\left(x^3 + 5\right)$ units. The perimeter of the triangle is $\left(2x^3 + 3x^2 + 8\right)$ units. Write a polynomial that represents the measure of the base of the triangle.

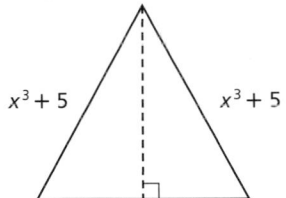

$x^3 + 5$ $x^3 + 5$

58. Write two polynomials whose sum is $4m^3 + 3m$.

59. Write two polynomials whose difference is $4m^3 + 3m$.

60. Write three polynomials whose sum is $4m^3 + 3m$.

61. Write two monomials whose sum is $4m^3 + 3m$.

62. Write three trinomials whose sum is $4m^3 + 3m$.

SPIRAL REVIEW

Solve each inequality and graph the solutions. *(Lesson 3-2)*

63. $d + 5 \geq -2$ **64.** $15 < m - 11$ **65.** $-6 + t < -6$

Write each equation in slope-intercept form. Then graph the line described by each equation. *(Lesson 5-7)*

66. $3x + y = 8$ **67.** $2y = \frac{1}{2}x + 6$ **68.** $y = 4\left(-x + 1\right)$

Simplify. *(Lesson 7-3)*

69. $b^4 \cdot b^7$ **70.** $cd^4 \cdot \left(c^{-5}\right)^3$ **71.** $\left(-3z^6\right)^2$ **72.** $\left(j^3 k^{-5}\right)^3 \cdot \left(k^2\right)^4$

Model Polynomial Multiplication

You can use algebra tiles to multiply polynomials. Use the length and width of a rectangle to represent the factors. The area of the rectangle represents the product.

Use with Lesson 7-8

KEY

 $= 1$

 $= -1$

 $= x$

 $= -x$

 $= x^2$

REMEMBER
- The product of two values with the same sign is positive.
- The product of two values with different signs is negative.

Activity 1

Use algebra tiles to find $2(x + 1)$.

MODEL		ALGEBRA
	Place the first factor in a column along the left side of the grid. This will be the width of the rectangle. Place the second factor across the top of the grid. This will be the length of the rectangle.	$2(x + 1)$
	Fill in the grid with tiles that have the same width as the tiles in the left column and the same length as the tiles in the top row.	
	The area of the rectangle inside the grid represents the product.	$x + x + 1 + 1$ $2x + 2$

The rectangle has an area of $2x + 2$, so $2(x + 1) = 2x + 2$. Notice that this is the same product you would get by using the Distributive Property to multiply $2(x + 1)$.

Try This

Use algebra tiles to find each product.

1. $3(x + 2)$ **2.** $2(2x + 1)$ **3.** $3(x + 1)$ **4.** $3(2x + 2)$

Activity 2

Use algebra tiles to find $2x(x - 3)$.

MODEL		ALGEBRA
	Place tiles to form the length and width of a rectangle and fill in the rectangle. The product of two values with the same sign (same color) is positive (yellow). The product of two values with different signs (different colors) is negative (red).	$2x(x - 3)$
	The area of the rectangle inside the grid represents the product. The rectangle has an area of $2x^2 - 6x$, so $2x(x - 3) = 2x^2 - 6x$.	$x^2 + x^2 - x - x - x - x - x - x$ $2x^2 - 6x$

Try This

Use algebra tiles to find each product.

5. $3x(x - 2)$ **6.** $x(2x - 1)$ **7.** $x(x + 1)$ **8.** $(8x + 5)(-2x)$

Activity 3

Use algebra tiles to find $(x + 1)(x - 2)$.

MODEL		ALGEBRA
	Place tiles for each factor to form the length and width of a rectangle. Fill in the grid and remove any zero pairs.	$(x + 1)(x - 2)$ $x^2 - x - x + x - 1 - 1$
	The area inside the grid represents the product. The remaining area is $x^2 - x - 2$, so $(x + 1)(x - 2) = x^2 - x - 2$.	$x^2 - x - 1 - 1$ $x^2 - x - 2$

Try This

Use algebra tiles to find each product.

9. $(x + 2)(x - 3)$ **10.** $(x - 1)(x + 3)$ **11.** $(x - 2)(x - 3)$ **12.** $(x + 1)(x + 2)$

7-8 Multiplying Polynomials

Objective
Multiply polynomials.

Why learn this?
You can multiply polynomials to write expressions for areas, such as the area of a dulcimer. (See Example 5.)

To multiply monomials and polynomials, you will use some of the properties of exponents that you learned earlier in this chapter.

EXAMPLE 1 | **Multiplying Monomials**

Multiply.

A $(5x^2)(4x^3)$

$(5x^2)(4x^3)$

$(5 \cdot 4)(x^2 \cdot x^3)$ *Group factors with like bases together.*

$20x^5$ *Multiply.*

B $(-3x^3y^2)(4xy^5)$

$(-3x^3y^2)(4xy^5)$

$(-3 \cdot 4)(x^3 \cdot x)(y^2 \cdot y^5)$ *Group factors with like bases together.*

$-12x^4y^7$ *Multiply.*

C $\left(\frac{1}{2}a^3b\right)(a^2c^2)(6b^2)$

$\left(\frac{1}{2}a^3b\right)(a^2c^2)(6b^2)$

$\left(\frac{1}{2} \cdot 6\right)(a^3 \cdot a^2)(b \cdot b^2)(c^2)$ *Group factors with like bases together.*

$3a^5b^3c^2$ *Multiply.*

> **Remember!**
> When multiplying powers with the same base, keep the base and add the exponents.
> $x^2 \cdot x^3 = x^{2+3} = x^5$

 CHECK IT OUT! Multiply.

1a. $(3x^3)(6x^2)$ **1b.** $(2r^2t)(5t^3)$ **1c.** $\left(\frac{1}{3}x^2y\right)(12x^3z^2)(y^4z^5)$

To multiply a polynomial by a monomial, use the Distributive Property.

EXAMPLE 2 | **Multiplying a Polynomial by a Monomial**

Multiply.

A $5(2x^2 + x + 4)$

$5\,(2x^2 + x + 4)$

$(5)2x^2 + (5)x + (5)4$ *Distribute 5.*

$10x^2 + 5x + 20$ *Multiply.*

Multiply.

B $2x^2y(3x - y)$

$(2x^2y)(3x - y)$

$(2x^2y)3x + (2x^2y)(-y)$ — *Distribute $2x^2y$.*

$(2 \cdot 3)(x^2 \cdot x)y + 2(-1)(x^2)(y \cdot y)$ — *Group like bases together.*

$6x^3y - 2x^2y^2$ — *Multiply.*

C $4a(a^2b + 2b^2)$

$4a(a^2b + 2b^2)$

$(4a)a^2b + (4a)2b^2$ — *Distribute $4a$.*

$(4)(a \cdot a^2)(b) + (4 \cdot 2)(a)(b^2)$ — *Group like bases together.*

$4a^3b + 8ab^2$ — *Multiply.*

CHECK IT OUT! **Multiply.**

2a. $2(4x^2 + x + 3)$ **2b.** $3ab(5a^2 + b)$ **2c.** $5r^2s^2(r - 3s)$

To multiply a binomial by a binomial, you can apply the Distributive Property more than once:

$(x + 3)(x + 2) = x(x + 2) + 3(x + 2)$ — *Distribute.*

$= x(x + 2) + 3(x + 2)$

$= x(x) + x(2) + 3(x) + 3(2)$ — *Distribute again.*

$= x^2 + 2x + 3x + 6$ — *Multiply.*

$= x^2 + 5x + 6$ — *Combine like terms.*

Another method for multiplying binomials is called the FOIL method.

1. Multiply the **F**irst terms. $\overset{F}{(x+3)(x+2)} \rightarrow x \cdot x = x^2$

2. Multiply the **O**uter terms. $\overset{O}{(x+3)(x+2)} \rightarrow x \cdot 2 = 2x$

3. Multiply the **I**nner terms. $\overset{I}{(x+3)(x+2)} \rightarrow 3 \cdot x = 3x$

4. Multiply the **L**ast terms. $\overset{L}{(x+3)(x+2)} \rightarrow 3 \cdot 2 = 6$

$(x+3)(x+2) = x^2 + 2x + 3x + 6 = x^2 + 5x + 6$

$$\uparrow \quad \uparrow \quad \uparrow \quad \uparrow$$
$$F \quad O \quad I \quad L$$

EXAMPLE **3** **Multiplying Binomials**

Multiply.

A $(x + 2)(x - 5)$

$(x + 2)(x - 5)$

$x(x - 5) + 2(x - 5)$ *Distribute.*

$x(x) + x(-5) + 2(x) + 2(-5)$ *Distribute again.*

$x^2 - 5x + 2x - 10$ *Multiply.*

$x^2 - 3x - 10$ *Combine like terms.*

B $(x + 5)^2$

$(x + 5)(x + 5)$ *Write as a product of two binomials.*

$(x \cdot x) + (x \cdot 5) + (5 \cdot x) + (5 \cdot 5)$ *Use the FOIL method.*

$x^2 + 5x + 5x + 25$ *Multiply.*

$x^2 + 10x + 25$ *Combine like terms.*

C $(3a^2 - b)(a^2 - 2b)$

$3a^2(a^2) + 3a^2(-2b) - b(a^2) - b(-2b)$ *Use the FOIL method.*

$3a^4 - 6a^2b - a^2b + 2b^2$ *Multiply.*

$3a^4 - 7a^2b + 2b^2$ *Combine like terms.*

> **Helpful Hint**
>
> In the expression $(x + 5)^2$, the base is $(x + 5)$.
> $(x + 5)^2 =$
> $(x + 5)(x + 5)$

 3a. $(a + 3)(a - 4)$ **3b.** $(x - 3)^2$ **3c.** $(2a - b^2)(a + 4b^2)$

To multiply polynomials with more than two terms, you can use the Distributive Property several times. Multiply $(5x + 3)$ by $(2x^2 + 10x - 6)$:

$$(5x + 3)(2x^2 + 10x - 6) = 5x(2x^2 + 10x - 6) + 3(2x^2 + 10x - 6)$$

$$= 5x(2x^2 + 10x - 6) + 3(2x^2 + 10x - 6)$$

$$= 5x(2x^2) + 5x(10x) + 5x(-6) + 3(2x^2) + 3(10x) + 3(-6)$$

$$= 10x^3 + 50x^2 - 30x + 6x^2 + 30x - 18$$

$$= 10x^3 + 56x^2 - 18$$

You can also use a rectangle model to multiply polynomials with more than two terms. This is similar to finding the area of a rectangle with length $(2x^2 + 10x - 6)$ and width $(5x + 3)$:

	$2x^2$	$+ 10x$	$- 6$
$5x$	$10x^3$	$50x^2$	$-30x$
$+ 3$	$6x^2$	$30x$	-18

Write the product of the monomials in each row and column.

To find the product, add all of the terms inside the rectangle by combining like terms and simplifying if necessary.

$$10x^3 + 6x^2 + 50x^2 + 30x - 30x - 18$$

$$10x^3 + 56x^2 - 18$$

Another method that can be used to multiply polynomials with more than two terms is the vertical method. This is similar to methods used to multiply whole numbers.

$$2x^2 + 10x - 6$$

$$\times \qquad 5x + 3$$

$$6x^2 + 30x - 18 \qquad \textit{Multiply each term in the top polynomial by 3.}$$

$$+ \; 10x^3 + 50x^2 - 30x \qquad \textit{Multiply each term in the top polynomial by 5x, and align like terms.}$$

$$10x^3 + 56x^2 \; + 0x - 18 \qquad \textit{Combine like terms by adding vertically.}$$

$$10x^3 + 56x^2 \qquad\quad - 18 \qquad \textit{Simplify.}$$

EXAMPLE 4 **Multiplying Polynomials**

Multiply.

A $(x + 2)(x^2 - 5x + 4)$

$(x + 2)(x^2 - 5x + 4)$

$x(x^2 - 5x + 4) + 2(x^2 - 5x + 4)$ *Distribute.*

$x(x^2) + x(-5x) + x(4) + 2(x^2) + 2(-5x) + 2(4)$ *Distribute again.*

$x^3 + 2x^2 - 5x^2 - 10x + 4x + 8$ *Simplify.*

$x^3 - 3x^2 - 6x + 8$ *Combine like terms.*

Helpful Hint

A polynomial with *m* terms multiplied by a polynomial with *n* terms has a product that, before simplifying, has *mn* terms. In Example 4A, there are 2 · 3, or 6, terms before simplifying.

B $(3x - 4)(-2x^3 + 5x - 6)$

$(3x - 4)(-2x^3 + 5x - 6)$

$$-2x^3 + \; 0x^2 + \; 5x - \; 6 \qquad \textit{Add 0x}^2 \textit{ as a placeholder.}$$

$$\times \qquad\qquad\qquad 3x - \; 4$$

$$8x^3 + \; 0x^2 - 20x + 24 \qquad \textit{Multiply each term in the top polynomial by } -4.$$

$$+ \; -6x^4 + 0x^3 + 15x^2 - 18x \qquad \textit{Multiply each term in the top polynomial by 3x, and align like terms.}$$

$$-6x^4 + 8x^3 + 15x^2 - 38x + 24 \qquad \textit{Combine like terms by adding vertically.}$$

C $(x - 2)^3$

$[(x - 2)(x - 2)](x - 2)$ *Write as the product of three binomials.*

$[x \cdot x + x(-2) + (-2)x + (-2)(-2)](x - 2)$ *Use the FOIL method on the first two factors.*

$(x^2 - 2x - 2x + 4)(x - 2)$ *Multiply.*

$(x^2 - 4x + 4)(x - 2)$ *Combine like terms.*

$(x - 2)(x^2 - 4x + 4)$ *Use the Commutative Property of Multiplication.*

$x(x^2 - 4x + 4) + (-2)(x^2 - 4x + 4)$ *Distribute.*

$x(x^2) + x(-4x) + x(4) + (-2)(x^2) + (-2)(-4x) + (-2)(4)$ *Distribute again.*

$x^3 - 4x^2 + 4x - 2x^2 + 8x - 8$ *Simplify.*

$x^3 - 6x^2 + 12x - 8$ *Combine like terms.*

Multiply.

D $(2x + 3)(x^2 - 6x + 5)$

	x^2	$-6x$	$+5$
$2x$	$2x^3$	$-12x^2$	$10x$
$+3$	$3x^2$	$-18x$	15

Write the product of the monomials in each row and column.

$2x^3 + 3x^2 - 12x^2 - 18x + 10x + 15$ *Add all terms inside the rectangle.*

$2x^3 - 9x^2 - 8x + 15$ *Combine like terms.*

 Multiply.

4a. $(x + 3)(x^2 - 4x + 6)$

4b. $(3x + 2)(x^2 - 2x + 5)$

$b_2 = h + 1$

h

$b_1 = 2h - 1$

EXAMPLE 5   *Music Application*

A dulcimer is a musical instrument that is sometimes shaped like a trapezoid.

A Write a polynomial that represents the area of the dulcimer shown.

$$A = \frac{1}{2}h(b_1 + b_2)$$ *Write the formula for area of a trapezoid.*

$$= \frac{1}{2}h[(2h - 1) + (h + 1)]$$ *Substitute $2h - 1$ for b_1 and $h + 1$ for b_2.*

$$= \frac{1}{2}h(3h)$$ *Combine like terms.*

$$= \frac{3}{2}h^2$$ *Simplify.*

The area is represented by $\frac{3}{2}h^2$.

B Find the area of the dulcimer when the height is 22 inches.

$$A = \frac{3}{2}h^2$$ *Use the polynomial from part a.*

$$= \frac{3}{2}(22)^2$$ *Substitute 22 for h.*

$$= \frac{3}{2}(484) = 726$$

The area is 726 square inches.

 5. The length of a rectangle is 4 meters shorter than its width.

   a. Write a polynomial that represents the area of the rectangle.

   b. Find the area of the rectangle when the width is 6 meters.

THINK AND DISCUSS

1. Compare the vertical method for multiplying polynomials with the vertical method for multiplying whole numbers.

2. GET ORGANIZED Copy and complete the graphic organizer. In each box, multiply two polynomials using the given method.

7-8

Exercises

go.hrw.com
Homework Help Online
KEYWORD: MA11 7-8
Parent Resources Online
KEYWORD: MA7 Parent

GUIDED PRACTICE

Multiply.

SEE EXAMPLE **1**
p. 512

1. $(2x^2)(7x^4)$

2. $(-5mn^3)(4m^2n^2)$

3. $(6rs^2)(s^3t^2)(\frac{1}{2}r^4t^3)$

4. $(\frac{1}{3}a^5)(12a)$

5. $(-3x^4y^2)(-7x^3y)$

6. $(-2pq^3)(5p^2q^2)(-3q^4)$

SEE EXAMPLE **2**
p. 512

7. $4(x^2 + 2x + 1)$

8. $3ab(2a^2 + 3b^3)$

9. $2a^3b(3a^2b + ab^2)$

10. $-3x(x^2 - 4x + 6)$

11. $5x^2y(2xy^3 - y)$

12. $5m^2n^3 \cdot mn^2(4m - n)$

SEE EXAMPLE **3**
p. 514

13. $(x + 1)(x - 2)$

14. $(x + 1)^2$

15. $(x - 2)^2$

16. $(y - 3)(y - 5)$

17. $(4a^3 - 2b)(a - 3b^2)$

18. $(m^2 - 2mn)(3mn + n^2)$

SEE EXAMPLE **4**
p. 515

19. $(x + 5)(x^2 - 2x + 3)$

20. $(3x + 4)(x^2 - 5x + 2)$

21. $(2x - 4)(-3x^3 + 2x - 5)$

22. $(-4x + 6)(2x^3 - x^2 + 1)$

23. $(x - 5)(x^2 + x + 1)$

24. $(a + b)(a - b)(b - a)$

SEE EXAMPLE **5**
p. 516

25. **Photography** The length of a rectangular photograph is 3 inches less than twice the width.

a. Write a polynomial that represents the area of the photograph.

b. Find the area of the photograph when the width is 4 inches.

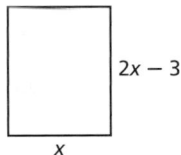
$2x - 3$
x

PRACTICE AND PROBLEM SOLVING

Independent Practice

For Exercises	See Example
26–34	1
35–43	2
44–52	3
53–61	4
62	5

Extra Practice

Skills Practice p. S17
Application Practice p. S34

Multiply.

26. $(3x^2)(8x^5)$

27. $(-2r^3s^4)(6r^2s)$

28. $(15xy^2)(\frac{1}{3}x^2z^3)(y^3z^4)$

29. $(-2a^3)(-5a)$

30. $(6x^3y^2)(-2x^2y)$

31. $(-3a^2b)(-2b^3)(-a^3b^2)$

32. $(7x^2)(xy^5)(2x^3y^2)$

33. $(-4a^3bc^2)(a^3b^2c)(3ab^4c^5)$

34. $(12mn^2)(2m^2n)(mn)$

35. $9s(s + 6)$

36. $9(2x^2 - 5x)$

37. $3x(9x^2 - 4x)$

38. $3(2x^2 + 5x + 4)$

39. $5s^2t^3(2s - 3t^2)$

40. $x^2y^3 \cdot 5x^2y(6x + y^2)$

41. $-5x(2x^2 - 3x - 1)$

42. $-2a^2b^3(3ab^2 - a^2b)$

43. $-7x^3y \cdot x^2y^2(2x - y)$

44. $(x + 5)(x - 3)$

45. $(x + 4)^2$

46. $(m - 5)^2$

47. $(5x - 2)(x + 3)$

48. $(3x - 4)^2$

49. $(5x + 2)(2x - 1)$

50. $(x - 1)(x - 2)$

51. $(x - 8)(7x + 4)$

52. $(2x + 7)(3x + 7)$

53. $(x + 2)(x^2 - 3x + 5)$

54. $(2x + 5)(x^2 - 4x + 3)$

55. $(5x - 1)(-2x^3 + 4x - 3)$

56. $(x - 3)(x^2 - 5x + 6)$

57. $(2x^2 - 3)(4x^3 - x^2 + 7)$

58. $(x - 4)^3$

59. $(x - 2)(x^2 + 2x + 1)$

60. $(2x + 10)(4 - x + 6x^3)$

61. $(1 - x)^3$

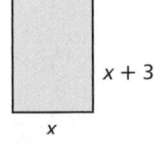

62. **Geometry** The length of the rectangle at right is 3 feet longer than its width.

a. Write a polynomial that represents the area of the rectangle.

b. Find the area of the rectangle when the width is 5 feet.

$x + 3$
x

63. A square tabletop has side lengths of $(4x - 6)$ units. Write a polynomial that represents the area of the tabletop.

64. This problem will prepare you for the Multi-Step Test Prep on page 528.

   a. Marie is creating a garden. She designs a rectangular garden with a length of $(x + 4)$ feet and a width of $(x + 1)$ feet. Draw a diagram of Marie's garden with the length and width labeled.

   b. Write a polynomial that represents the area of Marie's garden.

   c. What is the area when $x = 4$?

65. Copy and complete the table below.

	A	Degree of A	B	Degree of B	A · B	Degree of A · B
	$2x^2$	2	$3x^5$	5	$6x^7$	7
a.	$5x^3$	▨	$2x^2 + 1$	▨	▨	▨
b.	$x^2 + 2$	▨	$x^2 - x$	▨	▨	▨
c.	$x - 3$	▨	$x^3 - 2x^2 + 1$	▨	▨	▨

   d. Use the results from the table to complete the following: The product of a polynomial of degree m and a polynomial of degree n has a degree of ▨.

Geometry Write a polynomial that represents the area of each rectangle.

66.

67.

68.

Sports

69. **Sports** The length of a regulation team handball court is twice its width.

   a. Write a polynomial that represents the area of the court.

   b. The width of a team handball court is 20 meters. Find the area of the court.

Team handball is a game with elements of soccer and basketball. It originated in Europe in the 1900s and was first played at the Olympics in 1936 with teams of 11 players. Today, a handball team consists of seven players—six court players and one goalie.

Multiply.

70. $(1.5a^3)(4a^6)$

71. $(2x + 5)(x - 6)$

72. $(3g - 1)(g + 5)$

73. $(4x - 2y)(2x - 3y)$

74. $(x + 3)(x - 3)$

75. $(1.5x - 3)(4x + 2)$

76. $(x - 10)(x + 4)$

77. $x^2(x + 3)$

78. $(x + 1)(x^2 + 2x)$

79. $(x - 4)(2x^2 + x - 6)$

80. $(a + b)(a - b)^2$

81. $(2p - 3q)^3$

82. **Multi-Step** A rectangular swimming pool is 25 feet long and 10 feet wide. It is surrounded by a fence that is x feet from each side of the pool.

   a. Draw a diagram of this situation.

   b. Write expressions for the length and width of the fenced region. (*Hint:* How much longer is one side of the fenced region than the corresponding side of the pool?)

   c. Write an expression for the area of the fenced region.

 83. **Write About It** Explain why the FOIL method can be used to multiply only two binomials at a time.

84. Geometry Write a polynomial that represents the volume of the rectangular prism.

$x + 2$

$x + 5$

x

85. Critical Thinking Is there any value for x that would make the statement $(x + 3)^3 = x^3 + 3^3$ true? Give an example to justify your answer.

86. Estimation The length of a rectangle is 1 foot more than its width. Write a polynomial that represents the area of the rectangle. Estimate the width of the rectangle if its area is 25 square feet.

87. Which of the following products is equal to $a^2 - 5a - 6$?

Ⓐ $(a - 1)(a - 5)$ Ⓑ $(a - 2)(a - 3)$ Ⓒ $(a + 1)(a - 6)$ Ⓓ $(a + 2)(a - 3)$

88. Which of the following is equal to $2a(a^2 - 1)$?

Ⓕ $2a^2 - 2a$ Ⓖ $2a^3 - 1$ Ⓗ $2a^3 - 2a$ Ⓙ $2a^2 - 1$

89. What is the degree of the product of $3x^3y^2z$ and x^2yz?

Ⓐ 5 Ⓑ 6 Ⓒ 7 Ⓓ 10

CHALLENGE AND EXTEND

Simplify.

90. $6x^2 - 2(3x^2 - 2x + 4)$ **91.** $x^2 - 2x(x + 3)$ **92.** $x(4x - 2) + 3x(x + 1)$

93. The diagram shows a sandbox and the frame that surrounds it.

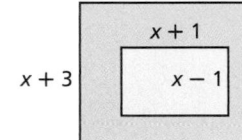

$x + 5$

$x + 1$

$x + 3$

$x - 1$

   a. Write a polynomial that represents the area of the sandbox.

   b. Write a polynomial that represents the area of the frame that surrounds the sandbox.

94. Geometry The side length of a square is $(8 + 2x)$ units. The area of this square is the same as the perimeter of another square with a side length of $(x^2 + 48)$ units. Find the value of x.

95. Write a polynomial that represents the product of three consecutive integers. Let x represent the first integer.

96. Find m and n so that $x^m(x^n + x^{n-2}) = x^5 + x^3$.

97. Find a so that $2x^a(5x^{2a-3} + 2x^{2a+2}) = 10x^3 + 4x^8$

SPIRAL REVIEW

98. A stop sign is 2.5 meters tall and casts a shadow that is 3.5 meters long. At the same time, a flagpole casts a shadow that is 28 meters long. How tall is the flagpole? *(Lesson 2-8)*

Find the distance, to the nearest hundredth, between each pair of points. *(Lesson 5-5)*

99. $(2, 3)$ and $(4, 6)$ **100.** $(-1, 4)$ and $(0, 8)$ **101.** $(-3, 7)$ and $(-6, -2)$

Graph the solutions of each linear inequality. *(Lesson 6-5)*

102. $y \leq x - 2$ **103.** $4x - 2y < 10$ **104.** $-y \geq -3x + 1$

Volume and Surface Area

The volume V of a three-dimensional figure is the amount of space it occupies. The surface area S is the total area of the two-dimensional surfaces that make up the figure.

Rectangular Prism

$V = \ell wh$
$S = 2(\ell w + \ell h + wh)$

Cylinder

$V = \pi r^2 h$
$S = 2\pi r^2 + 2\pi rh$

Cone

$V = \frac{1}{3}\pi r^2 h$

Pyramid

$V = \frac{1}{3}\ell wh$

Example

Write and simplify a polynomial expression for the volume of the cone. Leave the symbol π in your answer.

$V = \frac{1}{3}\pi r^2 h$ Choose the correct formula.

$= \frac{1}{3}\pi(6p)^2(p+1)$ Substitute $6p$ for r and $p + 1$ for h.

$= \frac{1}{3}\pi(36p^2)(p+1)$ Use the Power of a Product Property.

$= \frac{1}{3}(36)\pi[p^2(p+1)]$ Use the Associative and Commutative Properties of Multiplication.

$= 12\pi p^2(p+1)$ Distribute $12\pi p^2$.

$= 12\pi p^3 + 12\pi p^2$

Try This

Write and simplify a polynomial expression for the volume of each figure.

1.

2.

3.

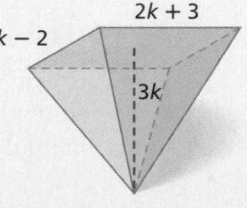

Write and simplify a polynomial expression for the surface area of each figure.

4.

5.

6.

7-9 Special Products of Binomials

Objective
Find special products of binomials.

Vocabulary
perfect-square trinomial
difference of two squares

Why learn this?

You can use special products to find areas, such as the area of a deck around a pond. (See Example 4.)

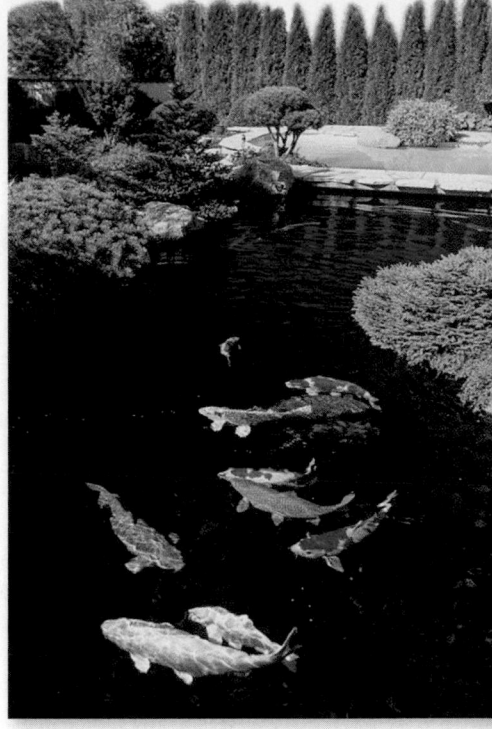

Imagine a square with sides of length $(a + b)$:

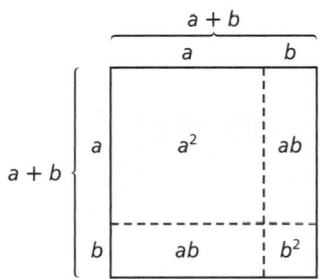

The area of this square is $(a + b)(a + b)$, or $(a + b)^2$. The area of this square can also be found by adding the areas of the smaller squares and rectangles inside. The sum of the areas inside is $a^2 + ab + ab + b^2$.

This means that $(a + b)^2 = a^2 + 2ab + b^2$.

You can use the FOIL method to verify this:

$$(a + b)^2 = (a + b)(a + b) = a^2 + ab + ab + b^2$$
$$= a^2 + 2ab + b^2$$

A trinomial of the form $a^2 + 2ab + b^2$ is called a *perfect-square trinomial*. A **perfect-square trinomial** is a trinomial that is the result of squaring a binomial.

EXAMPLE 1 Finding Products in the Form $(a + b)^2$

Multiply.

A $(x + 4)^2$

$(a + b)^2 = a^2 + 2ab + b^2$ *Use the rule for $(a + b)^2$.*

$(x + 4)^2 = x^2 + 2(x)(4) + 4^2$ *Identify a and b: a = x and b = 4.*

$\quad\quad\quad = x^2 + 8x + 16$ *Simplify.*

B $(3x + 2y)^2$

$(a + b)^2 = a^2 + 2ab + b^2$ *Use the rule for $(a + b)^2$.*

$(3x + 2y)^2 = (3x)^2 + 2(3x)(2y) + (2y)^2$ *Identify a and b: a = 3x and b = 2y.*

$\quad\quad\quad\quad = 9x^2 + 12xy + 4y^2$ *Simplify.*

Multiply.

C $(4 + s^2)^2$

$(a + b)^2 = a^2 + 2ab + b^2$ *Use the rule for $(a + b)^2$.*

$(4 + s^2)^2 = (4)^2 + 2(4)(s^2) + (s^2)^2$ *Identify a and b: a = 4 and b = s^2.*

$= 16 + 8s^2 + s^4$ *Simplify.*

D $(-m + 3)^2$

$(a + b)^2 = a^2 + 2ab + b^2$ *Use the rule for $(a + b)^2$.*

$(-m + 3)^2 = (-m)^2 + 2(-m)(3) + 3^2$ *Identify a and b: a = −m and b = 3.*

$= m^2 - 6m + 9$ *Simplify.*

 Multiply.

1a. $(x + 6)^2$ **1b.** $(5a + b)^2$ **1c.** $(1 + c^3)^2$

You can use the FOIL method to find products in the form $(a - b)^2$:

$$(a - b)^2 = (a - b)(a - b) = a^2 - ab - ab + b^2$$

$$= a^2 - 2ab + b^2$$

A trinomial of the form $a^2 - 2ab + b^2$ is also a perfect-square trinomial because it is the result of squaring the binomial $(a - b)$.

EXAMPLE **2** **Finding Products in the Form $(a - b)^2$**

Multiply.

A $(x - 5)^2$

$(a - b)^2 = a^2 - 2ab + b^2$ *Use the rule for $(a - b)^2$.*

$(x - 5)^2 = x^2 - 2(x)(5) + 5^2$ *Identify a and b: a = x and b = 5.*

$= x^2 - 10x + 25$ *Simplify.*

B $(6a - 1)^2$

$(a - b)^2 = a^2 - 2ab + b^2$ *Use the rule for $(a - b)^2$.*

$(6a - 1)^2 = (6a)^2 - 2(6a)(1) + (1)^2$ *Identify a and b: a = 6a and b = 1.*

$= 36a^2 - 12a + 1$ *Simplify.*

C $(4c - 3d)^2$

$(a - b)^2 = a^2 - 2ab + b^2$ *Use the rule for $(a - b)^2$.*

$(4c - 3d)^2 = (4c)^2 - 2(4c)(3d) + (3d)^2$ *Identify a and b: a = 4c and b = 3d.*

$= 16c^2 - 24cd + 9d^2$ *Simplify.*

D $(3 - x^2)^2$

$(a - b)^2 = (a)^2 - 2ab + b^2$ *Use the rule for $(a - b)^2$.*

$(3 - x^2)^2 = (3)^2 - 2(3)(x^2) + (x^2)^2$ *Identify a and b: a = 3 and b = x^2.*

$= 9 - 6x^2 + x^4$ *Simplify.*

 Multiply.

2a. $(x - 7)^2$ **2b.** $(3b - 2c)^2$ **2c.** $(a^2 - 4)^2$

You can use an area model to see that $(a + b)(a - b) = a^2 - b^2$.

 Begin with a square with area a^2. Remove a square with area b^2. The area of the new figure is $a^2 - b^2$.

 Then remove the smaller rectangle on the bottom. Turn it and slide it up next to the top rectangle.

 The new arrangement is a rectangle with length $a + b$ and width $a - b$. Its area is $(a + b)(a - b)$.

So $(a + b)(a - b) = a^2 - b^2$. A binomial of the form $a^2 - b^2$ is called a **difference of two squares**.

EXAMPLE 3 **Finding Products in the Form $(a + b)(a - b)$**

Multiply.

A $(x + 6)(x - 6)$

$(a + b)(a - b) = a^2 - b^2$ *Use the rule for $(a + b)(a - b)$.*

$(x + 6)(x - 6) = x^2 - 6^2$ *Identify a and b: $a = x$ and $b = 6$.*

$ = x^2 - 36$ *Simplify.*

B $\left(x^2 + 2y\right)\left(x^2 - 2y\right)$

$(a + b)(a - b) = a^2 - b^2$ *Use the rule for $(a + b)(a - b)$.*

$\left(x^2 + 2y\right)\left(x^2 - 2y\right) = \left(x^2\right)^2 - \left(2y\right)^2$ *Identify a and b: $a = x^2$ and $b = 2y$.*

$ = x^4 - 4y^2$ *Simplify.*

C $(7 + n)(7 - n)$

$(a + b)(a - b) = a^2 - b^2$ *Use the rule for $(a + b)(a - b)$.*

$(7 + n)(7 - n) = 7^2 - n^2$ *Identify a and b: $a = 7$ and $b = n$.*

$ = 49 - n^2$ *Simplify.*

 Multiply.

3a. $(x + 8)(x - 8)$ **3b.** $\left(3 + 2y^2\right)\left(3 - 2y^2\right)$ **3c.** $(9 + r)(9 - r)$

EXAMPLE 4 *Problem-Solving Application*

 PROBLEM SOLVING

A square koi pond is surrounded by a gravel path. Write an expression that represents the area of the path.

1. Understand the Problem

The **answer** will be an expression that represents the area of the path.

List the important information:

- The pond is a square with a side length of $x - 2$.

- The path has a side length of $x + 2$.

Make a Plan

The area of the pond is $(x - 2)^2$. The total area of the path plus the pond is $(x + 2)^2$. You can subtract the area of the pond from the total area to find the area of the path.

 Solve

Step 1 Find the total area.

$$(x + 2)^2 = x^2 + 2(x)(2) + 2^2$$ *Use the rule for $(a + b)^2$: $a = x$ and $b = 2$.*

$$= \boxed{x^2 + 4x + 4}$$

Step 2 Find the area of the pond.

$$(x - 2)^2 = x^2 - 2(x)(2) + 2^2$$ *Use the rule for $(a - b)^2$: $a = x$ and $b = 2$.*

$$= \boxed{x^2 - 4x + 4}$$

Step 3 Find the area of the path.

area of path	=	total area	−	area of pond

$$a \;\;\; = \;\; \boxed{x^2 + 4x + 4} \; - \; \left(\boxed{x^2 - 4x + 4} \right)$$

$$= x^2 + 4x + 4 - x^2 + 4x - 4 \qquad \textit{Identify like terms.}$$

$$= (x^2 - x^2) + (4x + 4x) + (4 - 4) \; \textit{Group like terms together.}$$

$$= 8x$$

The area of the path is $8x$.   *Combine like terms.*

 Look Back

Suppose that $x = 10$. Then one side of the path is 12, and the total area is 12^2, or 144. Also, if $x = 10$, one side of the pond is 8, and the area of the pond is 8^2, or 64. This means the area of the path is $144 - 64 = 80$.

According to the solution above, the area of the path is $8x$. If $x = 10$, then $8x = 8(10) = 80$. ✓

Remember!

To subtract a polynomial, add the opposite of *each* term.

✓ **CHECK IT OUT!**

4. Write an expression that represents the area of the swimming pool at right.

Special Products of Binomials

Perfect-Square Trinomials

$$(a + b)^2 = (a + b)(a + b) = a^2 + 2ab + b^2$$

$$(a - b)^2 = (a - b)(a - b) = a^2 - 2ab + b^2$$

Difference of Two Squares

$$(a + b)(a - b) = a^2 - b^2$$

THINK AND DISCUSS

1. Use the FOIL method to verify that $(a + b)(a - b) = a^2 - b^2$.

2. When a binomial is squared, the middle term of the resulting trinomial is twice the _____?_____ of the first and last terms.

3. **GET ORGANIZED** Copy and complete the graphic organizer. Complete the special product rules and give an example of each.

Special Products of Binomials		
Perfect-Square Trinomials		Difference of Two Squares
$(a + b)^2 = ?$	$(a - b)^2 = ?$	$(a + b)(a - b) = ?$

7-9 Exercises

go.hrw.com
Homework Help Online
KEYWORD: MA11 7-9
Parent Resources Online
KEYWORD: MA7 Parent

GUIDED PRACTICE

1. Vocabulary In your own words, describe a *perfect-square trinomial*.

Multiply.

SEE EXAMPLE **1**
p. 521

2. $(x + 7)^2$

3. $(2 + x)^2$

4. $(x + 1)^2$

5. $(2x + 6)^2$

6. $(5x + 9)^2$

7. $(2a + 7b)^2$

SEE EXAMPLE **2**
p. 522

8. $(x - 6)^2$

9. $(x - 2)^2$

10. $(2x - 1)^2$

11. $(8 - x)^2$

12. $(6p - q)^2$

13. $(7a - 2b)^2$

SEE EXAMPLE **3**
p. 523

14. $(x + 5)(x - 5)$

15. $(x + 6)(x - 6)$

16. $(5x + 1)(5x - 1)$

17. $(2x^2 + 3)(2x^2 - 3)$

18. $(9 - x^3)(9 + x^3)$

19. $(2x - 5y)(2x + 5y)$

SEE EXAMPLE **4**
p. 523

20. Geometry Write a polynomial that represents the area of the figure.

PRACTICE AND PROBLEM SOLVING

Independent Practice

For Exercises	See Example
21–26	1
27–32	2
33–38	3
39	4

Extra Practice

Skills Practice p. S17

Application Practice p. S34

Multiply.

21. $(x + 3)^2$

22. $(4 + z)^2$

23. $(x^2 + y^2)^2$

24. $(p + 2q^3)^2$

25. $(2 + 3x)^2$

26. $(r^2 + 5t)^2$

27. $(s^2 - 7)^2$

28. $(2c - d^3)^2$

29. $(a - 8)^2$

30. $(5 - w)^2$

31. $(3x - 4)^2$

32. $(1 - x^2)^2$

33. $(a - 10)(a + 10)$

34. $(y + 4)(y - 4)$

35. $(7x + 3)(7x - 3)$

36. $(x^2 - 2)(x^2 + 2)$

37. $(5a^2 + 9)(5a^2 - 9)$

38. $(x^3 + y^2)(x^3 - y^2)$

39. Entertainment Write a polynomial that represents the area of the circular puzzle. Remember that the formula for area of a circle is $A = \pi r^2$, where r is the radius of the circle. Leave the symbol π in your answer.

$r = x + 4$

40. Multi-Step A square has sides that are $(x - 1)$ units long and a rectangle has a length of x units and a width of $(x - 2)$ units.

  a. What are the possible values of x? Explain.

  b. Which has the greater area, the square or the rectangle?

  c. What is the difference in the areas?

Multiply.

41. $(x + y)^2$ **42.** $(x - y)^2$ **43.** $(x^2 + 4)(x^2 - 4)$

44. $(x^2 + 4)^2$ **45.** $(x^2 - 4)^2$ **46.** $(1 - x)^2$

47. $(1 + x)^2$ **48.** $(1 - x)(1 + x)$ **49.** $(x^3 - a^3)(x^3 - a^3)$

50. $(5 + n)(5 + n)$ **51.** $(6a - 5b)(6a + 5b)$ **52.** $(r - 4t^4)(r - 4t^4)$

Copy and complete the tables to verify the special products of binomials.

	a	b	$(a - b)^2$	$a^2 - 2ab + b^2$
	1	4	$(1 - 4)^2 = 9$	$1^2 - 2(1)(4) + 4^2 = 9$
53.	2	4	▨	▨
54.	3	2	▨	▨

	a	b	$(a + b)^2$	$a^2 + 2ab + b^2$
55.	1	4	▨	▨
56.	2	5	▨	▨
57.	3	0	▨	▨

	a	b	$(a + b)(a - b)$	$a^2 - b^2$
58.	1	4	▨	▨
59.	2	3	▨	▨
60.	3	2	▨	▨

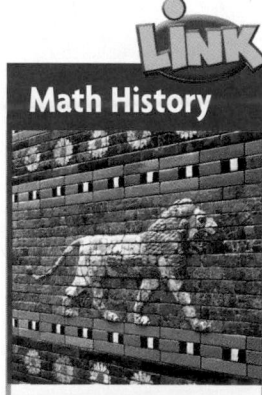

Math History

Beginning about 3000 B.C.E., the Babylonians lived in what is now Iraq and Turkey. Around 575 B.C.E., they built the Ishtar Gate to serve as one of eight main entrances into the city of Babylon. The image above is a relief sculpture from a restoration of the Ishtar Gate.

61. Math History The Babylonians used tables of squares and the formula $ab = \dfrac{(a + b)^2 - (a - b)^2}{4}$ to multiply two numbers. Use this formula to find the product $35 \cdot 24$.

62. Critical Thinking Find a value of c that makes $16x^2 - 24x + c$ a perfect-square trinomial.

63. ///ERROR ANALYSIS/// Explain the error below. What is the correct product?
$(a - b)^2 = a^2 - b^2$

64. This problem will prepare you for the Multi-Step Test Prep on page 528.
   a. Michael is fencing part of his yard. He started with a square of length x on each side. He then added 3 feet to the length and subtracted 3 feet from the width. Make a sketch to show the fenced area with the length and width labeled.
   b. Write a polynomial that represents the area of the fenced region.
   c. Michael bought a total of 48 feet of fencing. What is the area of his fenced region?

65. **Critical Thinking** The polynomial $ax^2 - 49$ is a difference of two squares. Find all possible values of a between 1 and 100 inclusive.

66. **Write About It** When is the product of two binomials also a binomial? Explain and give an example.

 TEST PREP

67. What is $(5x - 6y)(5x - 6y)$?
   (A) $25x^2 - 22xy + 36y^2$
   (B) $25x^2 - 60xy + 36y^2$
   (C) $25x^2 + 22xy + 36y^2$
   (D) $25x^2 + 60xy + 36y^2$

68. Which product is represented by the model?
   (F) $(2x + 5)(2x + 5)$
   (G) $(5x - 2)(5x - 2)$
   (H) $(5x + 2)(5x - 2)$
   (J) $(5x + 2)(5x + 2)$

$25x^2$	$10x$
$10x$	4

69. If $a + b = 12$ and $a^2 - b^2 = 96$ what is the value of a?
   (A) 2   (B) 4   (C) 8   (D) 10

70. If $rs = 15$ and $(r + s)^2 = 64$, what is the value of $r^2 + s^2$?
   (F) 25   (G) 30   (H) 34   (J) 49

CHALLENGE AND EXTEND

71. Multiply $(x + 4)(x + 4)(x - 4)$.   72. Multiply $(x + 4)(x - 4)(x - 4)$.

73. If $x^2 + bx + c$ is a perfect-square trinomial, what is the relationship between b and c?

74. You can multiply two numbers by rewriting the numbers as the difference of two squares. For example:

$$36 \cdot 24 = (30 + 6)(30 - 6) = 30^2 - 6^2 = 900 - 36 = 864$$

Use this method to multiply $27 \cdot 19$. Explain how you rewrote the numbers.

SPIRAL REVIEW

75. The square paper that Yuki is using to make an origami frog has an area of 165 cm². Find the side length of the paper to the nearest centimeter. *(Lesson 1-5)*

Use intercepts to graph the line described by each equation. *(Lesson 5-2)*

76. $2x + 3y = 6$ 77. $y = -3x + 9$ 78. $\frac{1}{2}x + y = 4$

Add or subtract. *(Lesson 7-7)*

79. $3x^2 + 8x - 2x + 9x^2$ 80. $(8m^4 + 2n - 3m^3 + 6) + (9m^3 + 5 - 4m^4)$
81. $(2p^3 + p) - (5p^3 + 9p)$ 82. $(12t - 3t^2 + 10) - (-5t^2 - 7 - 4t)$

MULTI-STEP TEST PREP

Polynomials

Don't Fence Me In James has 500 feet of fencing to enclose a rectangular region on his farm for some sheep.

1. Make a sketch of three possible regions that James could enclose and give the corresponding areas.

2. If the length of the region is x, find an expression for the width.

3. Use your answer to Problem 2 to write an equation for the area of the region.

4. Graph your equation from Problem 3 on your calculator. Sketch the graph.

5. James wants his fenced region to have the largest area possible using 500 feet of fencing. Find this area using the graph or a table of values.

6. What are the length and width of the region with the area from Problem 5? Describe this region.

READY TO GO ON?

Quiz for Lessons 7-6 Through 7-9

✓ 7-6 Polynomials

Write each polynomial in standard form and give the leading coefficient.

1. $4r^2 + 2r^6 - 3r$ **2.** $y^2 + 7 - 8y^3 + 2y$ **3.** $-12t^3 - 4t + t^4$

4. $n + 3 + 3n^2$ **5.** $2 + 3x^3$ **6.** $-3a^2 + 16 + a^7 + a$

Classify each polynomial according to its degree and number of terms.

7. $2x^3 + 5x - 4$ **8.** $5b^2$ **9.** $6p^2 + 3p - p^4 + 2p^3$

10. $x^2 + 12 - x$ **11.** $-2x^3 - 5 + x - 2x^7$ **12.** $5 - 6b^2 + b - 4b^4$

13. Business The function $C(x) = x^3 - 15x + 14$ gives the cost to manufacture x units of a product. What is the cost to manufacture 900 units?

✓ 7-7 Adding and Subtracting Polynomials

Add or subtract.

14. $\left(10m^3 + 4m^2\right) + \left(7m^2 + 3m\right)$ **15.** $\left(3t^2 - 2t\right) + \left(9t^2 + 4t - 6\right)$

16. $\left(12d^6 - 3d^2\right) + \left(2d^4 + 1\right)$ **17.** $\left(6y^3 + 4y^2\right) - \left(2y^2 + 3y\right)$

18. $\left(7n^2 - 3n\right) - \left(5n^2 + 5n\right)$ **19.** $\left(b^2 - 10\right) - \left(-5b^3 + 4b\right)$

20. Geometry The measures of the sides of a triangle are shown as polynomials. Write a simplified polynomial to represent the perimeter of the triangle.

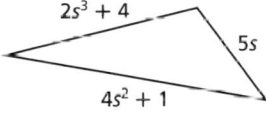

$2s^3 + 4$ $5s$ $4s^2 + 1$

✓ 7-8 Multiplying Polynomials

Multiply.

21. $2h^3 \cdot 5h^5$ **22.** $\left(s^8 t^4\right)\left(-6st^3\right)$ **23.** $2ab\left(5a^3 + 3a^2 b\right)$

24. $(3k + 5)^2$ **25.** $\left(2x^3 + 3y\right)\left(4x^2 + y\right)$ **26.** $\left(p^2 + 3p\right)\left(9p^2 - 6p - 5\right)$

27. Geometry Write a simplified polynomial expression for the area of a parallelogram whose base is $(x + 7)$ units and whose height is $(x - 3)$ units.

✓ 7-9 Special Products of Binomials

Multiply.

28. $(d + 9)^2$ **29.** $(3 + 2t)^2$ **30.** $(2x + 5y)^2$ **31.** $(m - 4)^2$

32. $(a - b)^2$ **33.** $(3w - 1)^2$ **34.** $(c + 2)(c - 2)$ **35.** $(5r + 6)(5r - 6)$

36. Sports A child's basketball has a radius of $(x - 5)$ inches. Write a polynomial that represents the surface area of the basketball. (The formula for the surface area of a sphere is $S = 4\pi r^2$, where r represents the radius of the sphere.) Leave the symbol π in your answer.

Study Guide: Review

Vocabulary

Complete the sentences below with vocabulary words from the list above.

1. A(n) ___?___ polynomial is a polynomial of degree 3.

2. When a polynomial is written with the terms in order from highest to lowest degree, it is in ___?___ .

3. A(n) ___?___ is a number, a variable, or a product of numbers and variables with whole-number exponents.

4. A(n) ___?___ is a polynomial with three terms.

5. ___?___ is a method of writing numbers that are very large or very small.

7-1 Integer Exponents (pp. 460–465)

EXAMPLES

Simplify.

- -2^{-4}

  $-2^{-4} = -\dfrac{1}{2^4} = -\dfrac{1}{2 \cdot 2 \cdot 2 \cdot 2} = -\dfrac{1}{16}$

- 3^0

  $3^0 = 1$ *Any nonzero number raised to the zero power is 1.*

- Evaluate $r^3 s^{-4}$ for $r = -3$ and $s = 2$.

  $r^3 s^{-4}$

  $(-3)^3 (2)^{-4} = \dfrac{(-3)(-3)(-3)}{2 \cdot 2 \cdot 2 \cdot 2} = -\dfrac{27}{16}$

- Simplify $\dfrac{a^{-3} b^4}{c^{-2}}$.

  $\dfrac{a^{-3} b^4}{c^{-2}} = \dfrac{b^4 c^2}{a^3}$

EXERCISES

6. The diameter of a certain bearing is 2^{-5} in. Simplify this expression.

Simplify.

7. $(3.6)^0$

8. $(-1)^{-4}$

9. 5^{-3}

10. 10^{-4}

Evaluate each expression for the given value(s) of the variable(s).

11. b^{-4} for $b = 2$

12. $\left(\dfrac{2}{5} b\right)^{-4}$ for $b = 10$

13. $-2 p^3 q^{-3}$ for $p = 3$ and $q = -2$

Simplify.

14. m^{-2}

15. bc^0

16. $-\dfrac{1}{2} x^{-2} y^{-4}$

17. $\dfrac{2b^6}{c^{-4}}$

18. $\dfrac{3a^2 c^{-2}}{4b^0}$

19. $\dfrac{q^{-1} r^{-2}}{s^{-3}}$

7-2 Powers of 10 and Scientific Notation (pp. 466–471)

EXAMPLES

■ Write 1,000,000 as a power of 10.

1,000,000   *The decimal point is 6 places*
1,000,000 $= 10^6$ *to the right of 1.*

■ Find the value of 386.21×10^5.

386.2 1 0 0 0   *Move the decimal point 5*
           places to the right.
38,621,000

■ Write 0.000000041 in scientific notation.

0.0 0 0 0 0 0 0 4 1   *Move the decimal*
         point 8 places to the
4.1×10^{-8} *right to get a number*
         between 1 and 10.

EXERCISES

Find the value of each power of 10.

20. 10^7 21. 10^{-5}

Write each number as a power of 10.

22. 100   23. 0.00000000001

Find the value of each expression.

24. 3.25×10^5 25. 0.18×10^4

26. 17×10^{-2} 27. 299×10^{-6}

28. Order the list of numbers from least to greatest.
$6.3 \times 10^{-3}, 1.2 \times 10^4, 5.8 \times 10^{-7}, 2.2 \times 10^2$

29. In 2003, the average daily value of shares traded on the New York Stock Exchange was about $\$3.85 \times 10^{10}$. Write this amount in standard form.

7-3 Multiplication Properties of Exponents (pp. 474–480)

EXAMPLES

Simplify.

■ $5^3 \cdot 5^{-2}$
$5^3 \cdot 5^{-2}$ *The powers have the*
          same base.
$5^{3+(-2)}$ *Add the exponents.*
5^1
5

■ $a^4 \cdot b^{-3} \cdot b \cdot a^{-2}$
$a^4 \cdot b^{-3} \cdot b \cdot a^{-2}$
$\left(a^4 \cdot a^{-2}\right) \cdot \left(b^{-3} \cdot b\right)$ *Use properties to group*
             factors.
$a^2 \cdot b^{-2}$ *Add the exponents of powers*
           with the same base.
$\dfrac{a^2}{b^2}$ *Write with a positive*
          exponent.

■ $\left(a^{-3}b^2\right)^{-2}$
$\left(a^{-3}\right)^{-2} \cdot \left(b^2\right)^{-2}$ *Power of a Product Property*
$a^6 \cdot b^{-4}$ *Power of a Power Property*
$\dfrac{a^6}{b^4}$ *Write with a positive*
         exponent.

EXERCISES

Simplify.

30. $5^3 \cdot 5^6$ 31. $2^6 \cdot 3 \cdot 2^{-3} \cdot 3^3$

32. $b^2 \cdot b^8$ 33. $r^4 \cdot r$

34. $\left(x^3\right)^4$ 35. $\left(s^3\right)^0$

36. $\left(2^3\right)^{-1}$ 37. $\left(5^2\right)^{-2}$

38. $\left(4b^3\right)^{-2}$ 39. $\left(g^3h^2\right)^4$

40. $\left(-x^2y\right)^2$ 41. $-\left(x^2y\right)^2$

42. $\left(x^2y^3\right)\left(xy^3\right)^4$ 43. $\left(j^2k^3\right)\left(j^4k^6\right)$

44. $\left(5^3 \cdot 5^{-2}\right)^{-1}$ 45. $\left(mn^3\right)^5\left(mn^5\right)^3$

46. $\left(4 \times 10^8\right)\left(2 \times 10^3\right)$ 47. $\left(3 \times 10^2\right)\left(3 \times 10^5\right)$

48. $\left(5 \times 10^3\right)\left(2 \times 10^6\right)$ 49. $\left(7 \times 10^5\right)\left(4 \times 10^9\right)$

50. $\left(3 \times 10^{-4}\right)\left(2 \times 10^5\right)$ 51. $\left(3 \times 10^{-8}\right)\left(6 \times 10^{-1}\right)$

52. In 2003, Wyoming's population was about 5.0×10^5. California's population was about 7.1×10 times as large as Wyoming's. What was the approximate population of California? Write your answer in scientific notation.

7-4 Division Properties of Exponents *(pp. 481–487)*

EXAMPLES

■ Simplify $\dfrac{x^9}{x^2}$.

$$\frac{x^9}{x^2} = x^{9-2} = x^7 \qquad \text{\textit{Subtract the exponents.}}$$

EXERCISES

Simplify.

53. $\dfrac{2^8}{2^2}$ **54.** $\dfrac{m^6}{m}$ **55.** $\dfrac{2^6 \cdot 4 \cdot 7^3}{2^5 \cdot 4^4 \cdot 7^2}$

56. $\dfrac{24b^6}{4b^5}$ **57.** $\dfrac{t^4 v^5}{tv}$ **58.** $\left(\dfrac{1}{2}\right)^{-4}$

Simplify each quotient and write the answer in scientific notation.

59. $(2.5 \times 10^8) \div (0.5 \times 10^7)$

60. $(2 \times 10^{10}) \div (8 \times 10^2)$

7-5 Rational Exponents *(pp. 488–493)*

EXAMPLES

■ Simplify $\sqrt[3]{r^6 s^{12}}$.

$$\sqrt[3]{r^6 s^{12}} = \left(r^6 s^{12}\right)^{\frac{1}{3}} \qquad \text{\textit{Definition of }} b^{\frac{1}{n}}$$

$$= \left(r^6\right)^{\frac{1}{3}} \cdot \left(s^{12}\right)^{\frac{1}{3}} \qquad \begin{array}{l}\text{\textit{Power of a Product}}\\\text{\textit{Property}}\end{array}$$

$$= \left(r^{6 \cdot \frac{1}{3}}\right) \cdot \left(s^{12 \cdot \frac{1}{3}}\right) \qquad \begin{array}{l}\text{\textit{Power of a Power}}\\\text{\textit{Property}}\end{array}$$

$$= \left(r^2\right) \cdot \left(s^4\right) \qquad \text{\textit{Simplify exponents.}}$$

$$= r^2 s^4$$

EXERCISES

Simplify each expression.

61. $81^{\frac{1}{2}}$ **62.** $343^{\frac{1}{3}}$

63. $64^{\frac{2}{3}}$ **64.** $\left(2^6\right)^{\frac{1}{2}}$

Simplify each expression. All variables represent nonnegative numbers.

65. $\sqrt[5]{z^{10}}$ **66.** $\sqrt[3]{125x^6}$

67. $\sqrt{x^8 y^6}$ **68.** $\sqrt[3]{m^6 n^{12}}$

7-6 Polynomials *(pp. 496–501)*

EXAMPLES

■ Find the degree of the polynomial $3x^2 + 8x^5$.

$3x^2 + 8x^5$ *$8x^5$ has the highest degree.*

The degree is 5.

■ Classify the polynomial $y^3 - 2y$ according to its degree and number of terms.

Degree: 3
Terms: 2

The polynomial $y^3 - 2y$ is a **cubic binomial**.

EXERCISES

Find the degree of each polynomial.

69. 5   **70.** $8st^3$

71. $3z^6$ **72.** $6h$

Write each polynomial in standard form. Then give the leading coefficient.

73. $2n - 4 + 3n^2$ **74.** $2a - a^4 - a^6 + 3a^3$

Classify each polynomial according to its degree and number of terms.

75. $2s - 6$ **76.** $-8p^5$

77. $-m^4 - m^2 - 1$ **78.** 2

7-7 Adding and Subtracting Polynomials (pp. 504–509)

EXAMPLES

Add.

■ $(h^3 - 2h) + (3h^2 + 4h) - 2h^3$
  $(h^3 - 2h) + (3h^2 + 4h) - 2h^3$
  $(h^3 - 2h^3) + (3h^2) + (4h - 2h)$
  $-h^3 + 3h^2 + 2h$

Subtract.

■ $(n^3 + 5 - 6n^2) - (3n^2 - 7)$
  $(n^3 + 5 - 6n^2) + (-3n^2 + 7)$
  $(n^3 + 5 - 6n^2) + (-3n^2 + 7)$
  $n^3 + (-6n^2 - 3n^2) + (5 + 7)$
  $n^3 - 9n^2 + 12$

EXERCISES

Add or subtract.

79. $3t + 5 - 7t - 2$

80. $4x^5 - 6x^6 + 2x^5 - 7x^5$

81. $-h^3 - 2h^2 + 4h^3 - h^2 + 5$

82. $(3m - 7) + (2m^2 - 8m + 6)$

83. $(12 + 6p) - (p - p^2 + 4)$

84. $(3z - 9z^2 + 2) + (2z^2 - 4z + 8)$

85. $(10g - g^2 + 3) - (-4g^2 + 8g - 1)$

92. $(-5x^3 + 2x^2 - x + 5) - (-5x^3 + 3x^2 - 5x - 3)$

7-8 Multiplying Polynomials (pp. 512–519)

EXAMPLES

Multiply.

■ $(2x - 4)(3x + 5)$
  $2x(3x) + 2x(5) - 4(3x) - 4(5)$
  $6x^2 + 10x - 12x - 20$
  $6x^2 - 2x - 20$

■ $(b - 2)(b^2 + 4b - 5)$
  $b(b^2) + b(4b) - b(5) - 2(b^2) - 2(4b) - 2(-5)$
  $b^3 + 4b^2 - 5b - 2b^2 - 8b + 10$
  $b^3 + 2b^2 - 13b + 10$

EXERCISES

Multiply.

87. $(2r)(4r)$

88. $(3a^5)(2ab)$

89. $(-3xy)(-6x^2y)$

90. $(3s^3t^2)(2st^4)\left(\frac{1}{2}s^2t^8\right)$

91. $2(x^2 - 4x + 6)$

92. $-3ab(ab - 2a^2b + 5a)$

93. $(a + 3)(a - 6)$

94. $(b - 9)(b + 3)$

95. $(x - 10)(x - 2)$

96. $(t - 1)(t + 1)$

97. $(2q + 6)(4q + 5)$

98. $(5g - 8)(4g - 1)$

7-9 Special Products of Binomials (pp. 521–527)

EXAMPLES

Multiply.

■ $(2h - 6)^2$
  $(2h - 6)^2 = (2h)^2 + 2(2h)(-6) + (-6)^2$
  $4h^2 - 24h + 36$

■ $(4x - 3)(4x + 3)$
  $(4x - 3)(4x + 3) = (4x)^2 - 3^2$
  $16x^2 - 9$

EXERCISES

Multiply.

99. $(p - 4)^2$

100. $(x + 12)^2$

101. $(m + 6)^2$

102. $(3c + 7)^2$

103. $(2r - 1)^2$

104. $(3a - b)^2$

105. $(2n - 5)^2$

106. $(h - 13)^2$

107. $(x - 1)(x + 1)$

108. $(z + 15)(z - 15)$

109. $(c^2 - d)(c^2 + d)$

110. $(3k^2 + 7)(3k^2 - 7)$

Evaluate each expression for the given value(s) of the variable(s).

1. $\left(\frac{1}{3}b\right)^{-2}$ for $b = 12$

2. $\left(14 - a^0 b^2\right)^{-3}$ for $a = -2$ and $b = 4$

Simplify.

3. $2r^{-3}$

4. $-3f^0 g^{-1}$

5. $m^2 n^{-3}$

6. $\frac{1}{2}s^{-5}t^3$

Write each number as a power of 10.

7. 0.0000001

8. 10,000,000,000,000

9. 1

Find the value of each expression.

10. 1.25×10^{-5}

11. $10^8 \times 10^{-11}$

12. 325×10^{-2}

13. Technology In 2002, there were approximately 544,000,000 Internet users worldwide. Write this number in scientific notation.

Simplify.

14. $\left(f^4\right)^3$

15. $\left(4b^2\right)^0$

16. $\left(a^3 b^6\right)^6$

17. $-\left(x^3\right)^5 \cdot \left(x^2\right)^6$

Simplify each quotient and write the answer in scientific notation.

18. $\left(3.6 \times 10^9\right) \div \left(6 \times 10^4\right)$

19. $\left(3 \times 10^{12}\right) \div \left(9.6 \times 10^{16}\right)$

Simplify.

20. $\dfrac{y^4}{y}$

21. $\dfrac{d^2 f^5}{\left(d^3\right)^2 f^{-4}}$

22. $\dfrac{2^5 \cdot 3^3 \cdot 5^4}{2^8 \cdot 3^2 \cdot 5^4}$

23. $\left(\dfrac{4s}{3t}\right)^{-2} \cdot \left(\dfrac{2s}{6t}\right)^2$

24. Geometry The surface area of a cone is approximated by the polynomial $3.14r^2 + 3.14r\ell$, where r is the radius and ℓ is the slant height. Find the approximate surface area of a cone when $\ell = 5$ cm and $r = 3$ cm.

Simplify each expression. All variables represent nonnegative numbers.

25. $\left(\dfrac{27}{125}\right)^{\frac{1}{3}}$

26. $\sqrt[3]{43^3}$

27. $\sqrt{25y^8}$

28. $\sqrt[5]{3^5 t^{10}}$

Add or subtract.

29. $3a - 4b + 2a$

30. $\left(2b^2 - 4b^3\right) - \left(6b^3 + 8b^2\right)$

31. $-9g^2 + 3g - 4g^3 - 2g + 3g^2 - 4$

Multiply.

32. $-5\left(r^2 s - 6\right)$

33. $(2t - 7)(t + 4)$

34. $\left(4g - 1\right)\left(4g^2 - 5g - 3\right)$

35. $(m + 6)^2$

36. $(3t - 7)(3t + 7)$

37. $\left(3x^2 - 7\right)^2$

38. Carpentry Carpenters use a tool called a *speed square* to help them mark right angles. A speed square is a right triangle.

  a. Write a polynomial that represents the area of the speed square shown.

  b. Find the area when $x = 4.5$ in.

$x - 4$

$A = \frac{1}{2}bh$

$2x + 6$

COLLEGE ENTRANCE EXAM PRACTICE

FOCUS ON SAT

When you receive your SAT scores, you will find a percentile for each score. The percentile tells you what percent of students scored lower than you on the same test. Your percentile at the national and state levels may differ because of the different groups being compared.

You may use some types of calculators on the math section of the SAT. For about 40% of the test items, a graphing calculator is recommended. Bring a calculator that you are comfortable using. You won't have time to figure out how a new calculator works.

You may want to time yourself as you take this practice test. It should take you about 7 minutes to complete.

1. If $(x + 1)(x + 4) - (x - 1)(x - 2) = 0$, what is the value of x?

(A) -1

(B) $-\dfrac{1}{4}$

(C) 0

(D) $\dfrac{1}{4}$

(E) 1

2. Which of the following is equal to 4^5?

   I. $3^5 \times 1^5$

   II. 2^{10}

   III. $4^0 \times 4^5$

(A) I only

(B) II only

(C) I and II only

(D) II and III only

(E) I, II, and III

3. If $x^{-4} = 81$, then $x =$

(A) -3

(B) $\dfrac{1}{4}$

(C) $\dfrac{1}{3}$

(D) 3

(E) 9

4. What is the value of $2x^3 - 4x^2 + 3x + 1$ when $x = -2$?

(A) -37

(B) -25

(C) -5

(D) 7

(E) 27

5. What is the area of a rectangle with a length of $x - a$ and a width of $x + b$?

(A) $x^2 - a^2$

(B) $x^2 + b^2$

(C) $x^2 - abx + ab$

(D) $x^2 - ax - bx - ab$

(E) $x^2 + bx - ax - ab$

6. For integers greater than 0, define the following operations.

$$a \square b = 2a^2 + 3b$$

$$a \triangle b = 5a^2 - 2b$$

What is $(a \square b) + (a \triangle b)$?

(A) $7a^2 + b$

(B) $-3a^2 + 5b$

(C) $7a^2 - b$

(D) $3a^2 - 5b$

(E) $-3a^2 - b$

TEST TACKLER

Standardized Test Strategies

Any Question Type: Use a Diagram

When a test item includes a diagram, use it to help solve the problem. Gather as much information from the drawing as possible. However, keep in mind that diagrams are not always drawn to scale and can be misleading.

EXAMPLE 1

Multiple Choice What is the height of the triangle when $x = 4$ and $y = 1$?

    (A) 2   (C) 8

    (B) 4   (D) 16

In the diagram, the height appears to be less than 6, so you might eliminate choices C and D. However, doing the math shows that the height is actually greater than 6. Do not rely solely on visual information. Always use the numbers given in the problem.

The height of the triangle is $(xy)^2$.

When $x = 4$ and $y = 1$, $(xy)^2 = (4 \cdot 1)^2 = (4)^2 = 16$.

Choice D is the correct answer.

If a test item does not have a diagram, draw a quick sketch of the problem situation. Label your diagram with the data given in the problem.

EXAMPLE 2

Short Response A square placemat is lying in the middle of a rectangular table. The side length of the placemat is $\left(\frac{x}{2}\right)$. The length of the table is $12x$, and the width is $8x$. Write a polynomial to represent the area of the placemat. Then write a polynomial to represent the area of the table that surrounds the placemat.

Use the information in the problem to draw and label a diagram. Then write the polynomials.

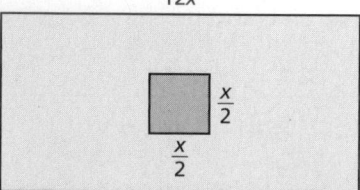

area of placemat $= s^2 = \left(\frac{x}{2}\right)^2 = \left(\frac{x}{2}\right)\left(\frac{x}{2}\right) = \frac{x^2}{4}$

area of table $= \ell w = (12x)(8x) = 96x^2$

area of table $-$ area of placemat $= 96x^2 - \frac{x^2}{4} = \frac{384x^2 - x^2}{4} = \frac{383x^2}{4}$

The area of the placemat is $\frac{x^2}{4}$.

The area of the table that surrounds the placemat is $\frac{383x^2}{4}$.

If a given diagram does not reflect the problem, draw a sketch that is more accurate. If a test item does not have a diagram, use the given information to sketch your own. Try to make your sketch as accurate as possible.

Read each test item and answer the questions that follow.

1. What is the unknown measure in this problem?

2. How will drawing a diagram help you solve the problem?

3. Draw and label a sketch of the situation.

4. Look at the dimensions in the diagram. Do you think that the length of rectangle *ABDC* is greater or less than the length of rectangle *MNPO*?

5. Do you think the drawings reflect the information in the problem accurately? Why or why not?

6. Draw your own sketch to match the information in the problem.

7. Describe how redrawing the figure can help you better understand the information in the problem.

8. After reading this test item, a student redrew the figure as shown below. Is this a correct interpretation of the original figure? Explain.

9. What information does the diagram provide that the problem does not?

10. Will the measure of angle *XYW* be less than or greater than the measure of angle *XYZ*? Explain.

STANDARDIZED TEST PREP

CUMULATIVE ASSESSMENT, CHAPTERS 1–7

Multiple Choice

1. A negative number is raised to a power. The result is a negative number. What do you know about the power?

   (A) It is an even number.

   (B) It is an odd number.

   (C) It is zero.

   (D) It is a whole number.

2. Which expression represents the phrase *eight less than the product of a number and two*?

   (F) $2 - 8x$

   (G) $8 - 2x$

   (H) $2x - 8$

   (J) $\dfrac{x}{2} - 8$

3. An Internet service provider charges a $20 set-up fee plus $12 per month. A competitor charges $15 per month. Which equation can you use to find x, the number of months when the total charge will be the same for both companies?

   (A) $15 = 20 + 12x$

   (B) $20 + 12x = 15x$

   (C) $20x + 12 = 15x$

   (D) $20 = 15x + 12x$

4. Which is a solution of the inequality $7 - 3(x - 3) > 2(x + 3)$?

   (F) 0

   (G) 2

   (H) 5

   (J) 12

5. One dose of Ted's medication contains 0.625 milligram, or $\dfrac{5}{8}$ milligram, of a drug. Which expression is equivalent to 0.625?

   (A) $5(4)^{-2}$

   (B) $5(2)^{-4}$

   (C) $5(-2)^3$

   (D) $5(2)^{-3}$

6. A restaurant claims to have served 352×10^6 hamburgers. What is this number in scientific notation?

   (F) 3.52×10^6

   (G) 3.52×10^8

   (H) 3.52×10^4

   (J) 352×10^6

7. Janet is ordering game cartridges from an online retailer. The retailer's prices, including shipping and handling, are given in the table below.

Game Cartridges	Total Cost ($)
1	54.95
2	104.95
3	154.95
4	204.95

   Which equation best describes the relationship between the total cost c and the number of game cartridges g?

   (A) $c = 54.95g$

   (B) $c = 51g + 0.95$

   (C) $c = 50g + 4.95$

   (D) $c = 51.65g$

8. Which equation describes a line parallel to $y = 5 - 2x$?

   (F) $y = -2x + 8$ (H) $y = 5 + \dfrac{1}{2}x$

   (G) $y = 2x - 5$ (J) $y = 5 - \dfrac{1}{2}x$

9. A square has sides of length $x - 4$. A rectangle has a length of $x + 2$ and a width of $2x - 1$. What is the total combined area of the square and the rectangle?

   (A) $10x - 14$

   (B) $4x - 3$

   (C) $3x^2 - 5x + 14$

   (D) $3x^2 + 3x - 18$

10. Jennifer has a pocketful of change, all in nickels and quarters. There are 11 coins with a total value of $1.15. Which system of equations can you use to find the number of each type of coin?

(F) $\begin{cases} n + q = 11 \\ n + q = 1.15 \end{cases}$

(G) $\begin{cases} n + q = 11 \\ 5n + 25q = 1.15 \end{cases}$

(H) $\begin{cases} 5n + 25q = 11 \\ n + q = 1.15 \end{cases}$

(J) $\begin{cases} n + q = 11 \\ 0.05n + 0.25q = 1.15 \end{cases}$

11. Which of the following is a true statement?

(A) $\left[(a^m)^n\right]^p = a^{m+n+p}$

(B) $\left[(a^m)^n\right]^p = a^{mn+p}$

(C) $\left[(a^m)^n\right]^p = a^{mnp}$

(D) $\left[(a^m)^n\right]^p = (a^{m+n})^p$

12. In 1867, the United States purchased the Alaska Territory from Russia for 7.2×10^6. The total area was about 6×10^5 square miles. What was the price per square mile?

(F) About $0.12 per square mile

(G) About $1.20 per square mile

(H) About $12.00 per square mile

(J) About $120.00 per square mile

Gridded Response

13. Evaluate the expression $3b^{-2}c^0$ for $b = 2$ and $c = -3$.

14. What is the slope of the line described by $-3y = 6x - 12$?

15. The quotient $(5.6 \times 10^8) \div (8 \times 10^3)$ is written in scientific notation as (7×10^n). What is the value of n?

16. The volume of a plastic cylinder is 64 cubic centimeters. A glass cylinder has the same height and a radius that is half that of the plastic cylinder. What is the volume in cubic centimeters of the glass cylinder?

Short Response

17. A sweater that normally sells for $35 was marked down 20% and placed on the sale rack. Later, the sweater was marked down an additional 30% and placed on the clearance rack.

a. Find the price of the sweater while on the sale rack. Show your work.

b. Find the price of the sweater while on the clearance rack. Show your work.

18. A set of positive integers (a, b, c) is called a *Pythagorean triple* if $a^2 + b^2 = c^2$.

a. Find a^2, b^2, and c^2 when $a = 2x$, $b = x^2 - 1$, and $c = x^2 + 1$. Show your work.

b. Is $(2x, x^2 - 1, x^2 + 1)$ a Pythagorean triple? Explain your reasoning.

19. Ron is making an ice sculpture. The block of ice is in the shape of a rectangular prism with a length of $(x + 2)$ inches, a width of $(x - 2)$ inches, and a height of $2x$ inches.

a. Write and simplify a polynomial expression for the volume of the block of ice. Show your work.

b. The final volume of the ice sculpture is $(x^3 + 4x^2 - 10x + 1)$ cubic inches. Write an expression for the volume of ice that Ron carved away. Show your work.

20. Simplify the expression $(3 \cdot a^2 \cdot b^{-4} \cdot a \cdot b^{-3})^{-3}$ using two different methods. Show that the results are the same.

Extended Response

21. Look at the pentagon below.

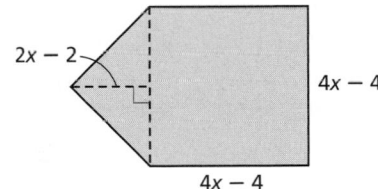

a. Write and simplify an expression that represents the area of the pentagon. Show your work or explain your answer.

b. Show one method of checking that your expression in part **a** is correct.

c. The triangular part of the pentagon can be rearranged to form a square. Write the area of this square as the square of a binomial.

d. Expand the product that you wrote in part **c**. What type of polynomial is this?

e. Is the square of a binomial ever a binomial? Explain your reasoning.

8A Factoring Methods

8B Applying Factoring Methods

Chapter Focus

- Factor polynomials.
- Apply factoring techniques to solve problems involving area and volume.

High Fliers

You can use polynomials to model area. When given the area of a kite as a polynomial, you can factor to find the kite's dimensions.

go.hrw.com
Chapter Project Online
KEYWORD: MA7 ChProj

ARE YOU READY?

✓ Vocabulary

Match each term on the left with a definition on the right.

1. binomial
2. composite number
3. factor
4. multiple
5. prime number

A. a whole number greater than 1 that has more than two positive factors

B. a polynomial with two terms

C. the product of any number and a whole number

D. a number that is written as the product of its prime factors

E. a whole number greater than 1 that has exactly two positive factors, itself and 1

F. a number that is multiplied by another number to get a product

✓ Multiples

Write the first four multiples of each number.

6. 3　　　　7. 4　　　　8. 8　　　　9. 15

✓ Factors

Tell whether the second number is a factor of the first number.

10. 20, 5　　　11. 50, 6　　　12. 120, 8　　　13. 245, 7

✓ Prime and Composite Numbers

Tell whether each number is prime or composite. If the number is composite, write it as the product of two numbers.

14. 2　　　　15. 7　　　　16. 10　　　　17. 38

18. 115　　　19. 147　　　20. 151　　　21. 93

✓ Multiply Monomials and Polynomials

Multiply.

22. $2(x + 5)$　　　23. $3h(h + 1)$　　　24. $xy(x^2 - xy^3)$　　　25. $6m(m^2 - 4m - 1)$

✓ Multiply Binomials

Find each product.

26. $(x + 3)(x + 8)$　　　　27. $(b - 7)(b + 1)$

28. $(2p - 5)(p - 1)$　　　　29. $(3n + 4)(2n + 3)$

Study Guide: Preview

Where You've Been

Previously, you

- used properties of exponents to evaluate and simplify expressions.
- added and subtracted polynomials by combining like terms.
- multiplied polynomials.

In This Chapter

You will study

- greatest common factors.
- how to factor polynomials.
- how to factor special products.
- how to choose a factoring method.

Where You're Going

You can use the skills in this chapter

- in Geometry to solve area problems.
- in Physics to solve quadratic equations.
- in the real world to calculate dimensions in landscaping, construction, or design work.

Key Vocabulary/Vocabulario

greatest common factor	máximo común divisor
prime factorization	factorización prima

Vocabulary Connections

To become familiar with the vocabulary terms in the chapter, consider the following. You may refer to the chapter, the glossary, or a dictionary if you like.

1. The word *factor* refers to a number or polynomial that is multiplied by another number or polynomial to form a product. What do you think the word *factor* means when it is used as a verb (action word)?

2. List some words that end with the suffixes *-ize* or *-ization*. What does the ending *-ization* seem to mean? What do you think *factorization* means?

3. The words *prime, primer, primary,* and *primitive* all come from the same root word. What are the meanings of these words? How can their meanings help you understand what a *prime factor* is?

4. What is a prime number? How might the **prime factorization** of a number differ from another factorization?

5. What does the word *common* mean? How can you use this meaning to understand the term **greatest common factor**?

Reading and *Writing* Math

Reading Strategy: Read a Lesson for Understanding

To help you learn new concepts, you should read each lesson with a purpose. As you read a lesson, make notes. Include the main ideas of the lesson and any questions you have. In class, listen for explanations of the vocabulary, clarification of the examples, and answers to your questions.

Reading Tips

Objectives
Evaluate and multiply by powers of 10.

Convert between standard notation and scientific notation.

> The objectives tell you the main idea of the lesson.

If a power of 10 has a negative integer exponent, does that make the number negative?
How do I enter numbers written in scientific notation into my calculator?

> Write down questions you have as you read the lesson.

EXAMPLE 1 Evaluating Powers of 10

Find the value of each power of 10.

A 10^{-3}

Start with 1 and move the decimal point three places to the left.

0. 0 0 1

0.001

> Work through the examples and write down any questions you have.

✓ **CHECK IT OUT!**

> Practice what you've learned in the Check It Out sections.

Try This

Read Lesson 8-1 prior to your next class. Then answer the questions below.

1. What are the lesson objectives?

2. What vocabulary, formulas, and symbols are new?

3. Which examples, if any, are unclear?

4. What questions do you have about the lesson?

8-1 Factors and Greatest Common Factors

Objectives
Write the prime factorization of numbers.

Find the GCF of monomials.

Vocabulary
prime factorization
greatest common factor

Who uses this?
Web site designers who sell electronic greeting cards can use the greatest common factor of numbers to design their Web sites. (See Example 4.)

The numbers that are multiplied to find a product are called *factors* of that product. A number is divisible by its factors.

You can use the factors of a number to write the number as a product. The number 12 can be factored several ways.

Factorizations of 12

1 · 12   2 · 6   3 · 4   1 · 4 · 3   (2 · 2 · 3)

The order of the factors does not change the product, but there is only one example above that cannot be factored further. The circled factorization is the **prime factorization** because all the factors are prime numbers. The prime factors can be written in any order, and, except for changes in the order, there is only one way to write the prime factorization of a number.

EXAMPLE 1 **Writing Prime Factorizations**

Write the prime factorization of 60.

Method 1 Factor tree
Choose any two factors of 60 to begin. Keep finding factors until each branch ends in a prime factor.

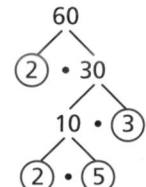

$$60 = 2 \cdot 2 \cdot 5 \cdot 3$$

Method 2 Ladder diagram
Choose a prime factor of 60 to begin. Keep dividing by prime factors until the quotient is 1.

$$
\begin{array}{r|r}
2 & 60 \\
3 & 30 \\
2 & 10 \\
5 & 5 \\
& 1
\end{array}
$$

$$60 = 2 \cdot 3 \cdot 2 \cdot 5$$

The prime factorization of 60 is $2 \cdot 2 \cdot 3 \cdot 5$ or $2^2 \cdot 3 \cdot 5$.

 Write the prime factorization of each number.

1a. 40   **1b.** 33   **1c.** 49   **1d.** 19

Factors that are shared by two or more whole numbers are called *common factors*. The greatest of these common factors is called the **greatest common factor**, or GCF.

Factors of 12: 1, 2, 3, 4, 6, 12

Factors of 32: 1, 2, 4, 8, 16, 32

Common factors: 1, 2, ④

The greatest of the common factors is 4.

EXAMPLE 2 **Finding the GCF of Numbers**

Find the GCF of each pair of numbers.

A **24 and 60**
Method 1 List the factors.

factors of 24: 1, 2, 3, 4, 6, 8, ⑫, 24   *List all the factors.*
factors of 60: 1, 2, 3, 4, 5, 6, 10, ⑫, 15, 20, 30, 60   *Circle the GCF.*

The GCF of 24 and 60 is 12.

B **18 and 27**
Method 2 Use prime factorization.

$18 = 2 \cdot \boxed{3} \cdot \boxed{3}$ *Write the prime factorization of each number.*
$27 = \quad \boxed{3} \cdot \boxed{3} \cdot 3$ *Align the common factors.*

$3 \cdot 3 = 9$

The GCF of 18 and 27 is 9.

 Find the GCF of each pair of numbers.
    2a. 12 and 16   **2b.** 15 and 25

You can also find the GCF of monomials that include variables. To find the GCF of monomials, write the prime factorization of each coefficient and write all powers of variables as products. Then find the product of the common factors.

EXAMPLE 3 **Finding the GCF of Monomials**

Find the GCF of each pair of monomials.

A $3x^3$ and $6x^2$
$3x^3 = \quad \boxed{3} \cdot \boxed{x} \cdot \boxed{x} \cdot x$ *Write the prime factorization of each coefficient and write powers as products.*
$6x^2 = 2 \cdot \boxed{3} \cdot \boxed{x} \cdot \boxed{x}$ *Align the common factors.*

$3 \cdot x \cdot x = 3x^2$ *Find the product of the common factors.*
The GCF of $3x^3$ and $6x^2$ is $3x^2$.

B $4x^2$ and $5y^3$
$4x^2 = 2 \cdot 2 \cdot \quad x \cdot x$ *Write the prime factorization of each coefficient and write powers as products.*
$5y^3 = \quad\quad 5 \cdot \quad y \cdot y \cdot y$ *Align the common factors.*
                                             There are no common factors other than 1.

The GCF of $4x^2$ and $5y^3$ is 1.

Helpful Hint

If two terms contain the same variable raised to different powers, the GCF will contain that variable raised to the lower power.

 Find the GCF of each pair of monomials.
    3a. $18g^2$ and $27g^3$ **3b.** $16a^6$ and $9b$ **3c.** $8x$ and $7v^2$

EXAMPLE 4 *Technology Application*

Garrison is creating a Web page that offers electronic greeting cards. He has 24 special occasion designs and 42 birthday designs. The cards will be displayed with the same number of designs in each row. Special occasion and birthday designs will not appear in the same row. How many rows will there be if Garrison puts the greatest possible number of designs in each row?

The 24 special occasion designs and 42 birthday designs must be divided into groups of equal size. The number of designs in each row must be a common factor of 24 and 42.

factors of 24: **1, 2, 3, 4,**⑥**8, 12, 24**   *Find the common factors of*
factors of 42: **1, 2, 3,**⑥**7, 14, 21, 42**   *24 and 42.*

The GCF of 24 and 42 is 6.

The greatest possible number of designs in each row is 6. Find the number of rows of each group of designs when there are 6 designs in each row.

$$\frac{24 \text{ special occasion designs}}{6 \text{ designs per row}} = 4 \text{ rows}$$

$$\frac{42 \text{ birthday designs}}{6 \text{ designs per row}} = 7 \text{ rows}$$

When the greatest possible number of designs is in each row, there are 11 rows in total.

 4. Adrianne is shopping for a CD storage unit. She has 36 CDs by pop music artists and 48 CDs by country music artists. She wants to put the same number of CDs on each shelf without putting pop music and country music CDs on the same shelf. If Adrianne puts the greatest possible number of CDs on each shelf, how many shelves does her storage unit need?

THINK AND DISCUSS

1. Describe two ways you can find the prime factorization of a number.

2. GET ORGANIZED Copy and complete the graphic organizer. Show how to write the prime factorization of $100x^2$ by filling in each box.

GUIDED PRACTICE

1. **Vocabulary** Define the term *greatest common factor* in your own words.

SEE EXAMPLE **1**
p. 544

Write the prime factorization of each number.

2. 20   **3.** 36   **4.** 27   **5.** 54

6. 96   **7.** 7   **8.** 100   **9.** 75

SEE EXAMPLE **2**
p. 545

Find the GCF of each pair of numbers.

10. 12 and 60   **11.** 14 and 49   **12.** 55 and 121

SEE EXAMPLE **3**
p. 545

Find the GCF of each pair of monomials.

13. $6x^2$ and $5x^2$ **14.** $15y^3$ and $-20y$ **15.** $13q^4$ and $2p^2$

SEE EXAMPLE **4**
p. 546

16. Samantha is making beaded necklaces using 54 glass beads and 18 clay beads. She wants each necklace to have the same number of beads, but each necklace will have only one type of bead. If she puts the greatest possible number of beads on each necklace, how many necklaces can she make?

PRACTICE AND PROBLEM SOLVING

Independent Practice

For Exercises	See Example
17–24	1
25–27	2
28–30	3
31	4

Extra Practice
Skills Practice p. S18
Application Practice p. S35

Write the prime factorization of each number.

17. 18   **18.** 64   **19.** 12   **20.** 150

21. 17   **22.** 226   **23.** 49   **24.** 63

Find the GCF of each pair of numbers.

25. 36 and 63   **26.** 14 and 15   **27.** 30 and 40

Find the GCF of each pair of monomials.

28. $8a^2$ and 11   **29.** $9s$ and $63s^3$ **30.** $-64n^4$ and $24n^2$

31. José is making fruit-filled tart shells for a party. He has 72 raspberries and 108 blueberries. The tarts will each have the same number of berries. Raspberries and blueberries will not be in the same tart. If he puts the greatest possible number of fruits in each tart, how many tarts can he make?

Find the GCF of each pair of products.

32. $3 \cdot 5 \cdot t$ and $2 \cdot 2 \cdot 5 \cdot t \cdot t$ **33.** $-1 \cdot 2 \cdot 2 \cdot x \cdot x$ and $2 \cdot 2 \cdot 7 \cdot x \cdot x \cdot x$

34. $2 \cdot 2 \cdot 2 \cdot 11 \cdot x \cdot x \cdot x$ and $3 \cdot 11$ **35.** $2 \cdot 5 \cdot n \cdot n \cdot n$ and $-1 \cdot 2 \cdot 3 \cdot n$

 36. Write About It The number 2 is even and is prime. Explain why all other prime numbers are odd numbers.

37. Critical Thinking The GCF of two numbers is 1. Explain whether this means the two numbers must be prime.

38. Multi-Step Angelo is making a rectangular floor for a clubhouse with an area of 84 square feet. The length of each side of the floor is a whole number of feet.

  a. What are the possible lengths and widths for Angelo's clubhouse floor?

  b. What is the minimum perimeter for the clubhouse floor?

  c. What is the maximum perimeter for the clubhouse floor?

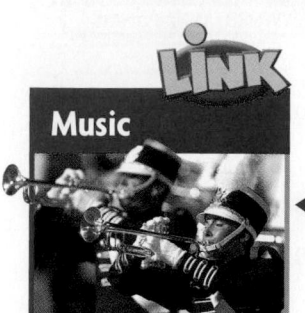

39. Music The Cavaliers and the Blue Devils are two of the marching bands that are members of Drum Corps International (DCI). DCI bands are made up of percussionists, brass players, and color guard members who use flags and other props.

In 2004, there were 35 color guard members in the Cavaliers and 40 in the Blue Devils. The two color guards will march in rows with the same number of people in each row without mixing the guards together. If the greatest possible number of people are in each row, how many rows will there be?

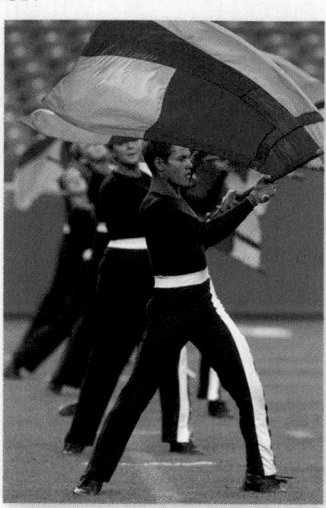

For each set of numbers, determine which two numbers have a GCF greater than 1, and find that GCF.

40. 11, 12, 14

41. 8, 20, 63

42. 16, 21, 27

43. 32, 63, 105

44. 25, 35, 54

45. 35, 54, 72

46. Number Sense The prime factorization of 24 is $2^3 \cdot 3$. Without using a diagram, write the prime factorization of 48. Explain your reasoning.

Fill in each diagram. Then write the prime factorization of the number.

47.

48.

49.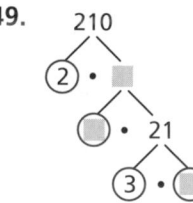

50.

☐	56
2	28
2	☐
☐	7
	1

51.

☐	108
☐	54
3	☐
☐	9
3	3
	1

52.

2	136
☐	68
2	☐
☐	17
	1

53.

2	48
2	☐
☐	12
2	☐
☐	3
	1

54.

☐	140
2	☐
☐	35
7	7
	1

55.

2	40
☐	20
☐	☐
5	☐
	1

56. This problem will prepare you for the Multi-Step Test Prep on page 576.

The equation for the motion of an object with constant acceleration is $d = vt + \frac{1}{2}at^2$ where d is distance traveled in feet, v is starting velocity in ft/s, a is acceleration in ft/s², and t is time in seconds.

a. A toy car begins with a velocity of 2 ft/s and accelerates at 2 ft/s². Write an expression for the distance the toy car travels after t seconds.

b. What is the GCF of the terms in your expression from part **a**?

TEST PREP

57. Which set of numbers has a GCF greater than 6?

(A) 18, 24, 36   (B) 30, 35, 40   (C) 11, 29, 37   (D) 16, 24, 48

58. The slope of a line is the GCF of 48 and 12. The y-intercept is the GCF of the slope and 8. Which equation describes the line?

(F) $y = 12x + 4$ (G) $y = 6x + 2$ (H) $y = 4x + 4$ (J) $y = 3x + 1$

59. Extended Response Patricia is making a dog pen in her back yard. The pen will be rectangular and have an area of 24 square feet. Draw and label a diagram that shows all possible whole-number dimensions for the pen. Find the perimeter of each rectangle you drew. Which dimensions should Patricia use in order to spend the least amount of money on fencing materials? Explain your reasoning.

CHALLENGE AND EXTEND

Find the GCF of each set.

60. $4n^3, 16n^2, 8n$

61. $27y^3, 18y^2, 81y$

62. $100, 25s^5, 50s$

63. $2p^4r, 8p^3r^2, 16p^2r^3$

64. $2x^3y, 8x^2y^2, 17xy^3$

65. $8a^4b^3, 4a^3b^3, 12a^2b^3$

66. Geometry The area of a triangle is 10 in². What are the possible whole-number dimensions for the base and height of the triangle?

67. Number Sense The GCF of three different numbers is 7. The sum of the three numbers is 105. What are the three numbers?

68. Critical Thinking Find three different *composite* numbers whose GCF is 1. (*Hint: A composite number has factors other than 1 and itself.*)

SPIRAL REVIEW

Use dimensional analysis to convert each measure. *(Lesson 2-7)*

69. 11,232 s to h

70. 9 gal to pt

71. 18 in./day to mi/yr

Find each value. Round to the nearest tenth if necessary. *(Lesson 2-9)*

72. 40% of 60

73. 250% of 16

74. What percent of 80 is 20?

75. Write a simplified polynomial expression for the perimeter of the triangle. *(Lesson 7-7)*

$x^2 + 3x$

$6x - 2$

$2x^2 + 5x - 1$

Model Factoring

You can use algebra tiles to write a polynomial as the product of its factors. This process is called *factoring*. Factoring is the reverse of multiplying.

Use with Lesson 8-2

KEY

Activity

Use algebra tiles to factor $4x + 8$.

MODEL		ALGEBRA
	Model $4x + 8$.	$4x + 8$
	Arrange the tiles into a rectangle. The total area represents $4x + 8$. The length and width represent the factors. The rectangle has a width of $x + 2$ and a length of 4.	$4x + 8 = 4(x + 2)$

Use algebra tiles to factor $x^2 - 2x$.

MODEL		ALGEBRA
	Model $x^2 - 2x$.	$x^2 - 2x$
	Arrange the tiles into a rectangle. The total area represents $x^2 - 2x$. The length and width represent the factors. The rectangle has a width of $x - 2$ and a length of x.	$x^2 - 2x = x(x - 2)$

Try This

Use algebra tiles to factor each polynomial.

1. $3x + 9$ **2.** $2x + 8$ **3.** $4x - 12$ **4.** $3x - 12$

5. $2x^2 + 2x$ **6.** $x^2 + 4x$ **7.** $x^2 - 3x$ **8.** $2x^2 - 4x$

8-2 Factoring by GCF

Objective
Factor polynomials by using the greatest common factor.

Why learn this?
You can determine the dimensions of a solar panel by factoring an expression representing the panel's area. (See Example 2.)

Recall that the Distributive Property states that $ab + ac = a(b + c)$. The Distributive Property allows you to factor out the GCF of the terms in a polynomial to write a factored form of the polynomial.

A polynomial is in its factored form when it is written as a product of monomials and polynomials that cannot be factored further. The expression $2(3x - 4x)$ is not fully factored because the terms in the parentheses have a common factor of x.

EXAMPLE 1 Factoring by Using the GCF

Factor each polynomial. Check your answer.

Writing Math
Aligning common factors can help you find the greatest common factor of two or more terms.

A $4x^2 - 3x$

$$4x^2 = 2 \cdot 2 \cdot \boxed{x} \cdot x$$
$$3x = \quad\quad 3 \cdot \boxed{x}$$
$$\downarrow$$
$$x$$

Find the GCF.

The GCF of $4x^2$ and $3x$ is x.

$4x(x) - 3(x)$

Write terms as products using the GCF as a factor.

$x(4x - 3)$

Use the Distributive Property to factor out the GCF.

Check $x(4x - 3)$

$4x^2 - 3x$ ✓

Multiply to check your answer.
The product is the original polynomial.

B $10y^3 + 20y^2 - 5y$

$$10y^3 = \quad 2 \cdot \boxed{5} \cdot \boxed{y} \cdot y \cdot y$$
$$20y^2 = 2 \cdot 2 \cdot 5 \cdot y \cdot y$$
$$5y = \quad\quad\quad 5 \cdot y$$
$$\downarrow \quad \downarrow$$
$$5 \cdot y = 5y$$

Find the GCF.

The GCF of $10y^3$, $20y^2$, and $5y$ is $5y$.

$2y^2(5y) + 4y(5y) - 1(5y)$

Write terms as products using the GCF as a factor.

$5y(2y^2 + 4y - 1)$

Use the Distributive Property to factor out the GCF.

Check $5y(2y^2 + 4y - 1)$

$10y^3 + 20y^2 - 5y$ ✓

Multiply to check your answer.
The product is the original polynomial.

Factor each polynomial. Check your answer.

C $-12x - 8x^2$

$-1(12x + 8x^2)$ *Both coefficients are negative. Factor out −1.*

$12x = \boxed{2} \cdot \boxed{2} \cdot 3 \cdot \boxed{x}$ *Find the GCF.*
$8x^2 = \boxed{2} \cdot \boxed{2} \cdot 2 \cdot \boxed{x} \cdot x$

$2 \cdot 2 \cdot \quad x = 4x$ *The GCF of 12x and $8x^2$ is 4x.*

$-1[3(4x) + 2x(4x)]$ *Write each term as a product using the GCF.*

$-1[4x(3 + 2x)]$ *Use the Distributive Property to factor out*
$-1(4x)(3 + 2x)$ *the GCF.*

$-4x(3 + 2x)$

Check

$-4x(3 + 2x) = -12x - 8x^2$ ✓ *Multiply to check your answer.*

D $5x^2 + 7$

$5x^2 = 5 \quad \cdot x \cdot x$ *Find the GCF.*
$7 = \quad 7$

$5x^2 + 7$ *There are no common factors other than 1.*

The polynomial cannot be factored.

 Factor each polynomial. Check your answer.

1a. $5b + 9b^3$ **1b.** $9d^2 - 8^2$

1c. $-18y^3 - 7y^2$ **1d.** $8x^4 + 4x^3 - 2x^2$

To write expressions for the length and width of a rectangle whose area is expressed as a polynomial, you need to write the polynomial as a product. You can write a polynomial as a product by factoring it.

EXAMPLE 2 **Science Application**

Mandy's calculator is powered by solar energy. The area of the solar panel is $(7x^2 + x)$ cm². Factor this polynomial to find possible expressions for the dimensions of the solar panel.

$A = 7x^2 + x$ *The GCF of $7x^2$ and x is x.*

$= 7x(x) + 1(x)$ *Write each term as a product using the GCF as a factor.*

$= x(7x + 1)$ *Use the Distributive Property to factor out the GCF.*

Possible expressions for the dimensions of the solar panel are x cm and $(7x + 1)$ cm.

 2. What if...? The area of the solar panel on another calculator is $(2x^2 + 4x)$ cm². Factor this polynomial to find possible expressions for the dimensions of the solar panel.

Sometimes the GCF of terms is a binomial. This GCF is called a *common binomial factor*. You factor out a common binomial factor the same way you factor out a monomial factor.

EXAMPLE 3 | **Factoring Out a Common Binomial Factor**

Factor each expression.

A $7(x-3) - 2x(x-3)$

$7(x-3) - 2x(x-3)$ *(x − 3) is a common binomial factor.*

$(x-3)(7-2x)$ *Factor out (x − 3).*

B $-t(t^2+4) + (t^2+4)$

$-t(t^2+4) + (t^2+4)$ *(t² + 4) is a common binomial factor.*

$-t(t^2+4) + 1(t^2+4)$ *(t² + 4) = 1(t² + 4)*

$(t^2+4)(-t+1)$ *Factor out (t² + 4).*

C $9x(x+4) - 5(4+x)$

$9x(x+4) - 5(4+x)$ *(x + 4) = (4 + x), so (x + 4) is a common binomial factor.*

$9x(x+4) - 5(x+4)$

$(x+4)(9x-5)$ *Factor out (x + 4).*

D $-3x^2(x+2) + 4(x-7)$

$-3x^2(x+2) + 4(x-7)$ *There are no common factors.*

The expression cannot be factored.

CHECK IT OUT!

Factor each expression.

3a. $4s(s+6) - 5(s+6)$ **3b.** $7x(2x+3) + (2x+3)$

3c. $3x(y+4) - 2y(x+4)$ **3d.** $5x(5x-2) - 2(5x-2)$

You may be able to factor a polynomial by grouping. When a polynomial has four terms, you can make two groups and factor out the GCF from each group.

EXAMPLE 4 | **Factoring by Grouping**

Factor each polynomial by grouping. Check your answer.

A $12a^3 - 9a^2 + 20a - 15$

$(12a^3 - 9a^2) + (20a - 15)$ *Group terms that have a common number or variable as a factor.*

$3a^2(4a-3) + 5(4a-3)$ *Factor out the GCF of each group.*

$3a^2(4a-3) + 5(4a-3)$ *(4a − 3) is a common factor.*

$(4a-3)(3a^2+5)$ *Factor out (4a − 3).*

Check   *Multiply to check your solution.*

$4a(3a^2) + 4a(5) - 3(3a^2) - 3(5)$

$12a^3 + 20a - 9a^2 - 15$

$12a^3 - 9a^2 + 20a - 15 ✓$ *The product is the original polynomial.*

Factor each polynomial by grouping. Check your answer.

B $9x^3 + 18x^2 + x + 2$

$(9x^3 + 18x^2) + (x + 2)$ *Group terms.*

$9x^2(x + 2) + 1(x + 2)$ *Factor out the GCF of each group.*

$9x^2(x + 2) + 1(x + 2)$ *(x + 2) is a common factor.*

$(x + 2)(9x^2 + 1)$ *Factor out (x + 2).*

Check $(x + 2)(9x^2 + 1)$ *Multiply to check your solution.*

$x(9x^2) + x(1) + 2(9x^2) + 2(1)$

$9x^3 + x + 18x^2 + 2$

$9x^3 + 18x^2 + x + 2 ✓$ *The product is the original polynomial.*

 Factor each polynomial by grouping. Check your answer.

4a. $6b^3 + 8b^2 + 9b + 12$ **4b.** $4r^3 + 24r + r^2 + 6$

Helpful Hint

If two quantities are opposites, their sum is 0.

$(5 - x) + (x - 5)$
$5 - x + x - 5$
$(-x + x) + (5 - 5)$
$0 + 0$
0

Recognizing opposite binomials can help you factor polynomials. The binomials $(5 - x)$ and $(x - 5)$ are opposites. Notice $(5 - x)$ can be written as $-1(x - 5)$.

$-1(x - 5) = (-1)(x) + (-1)(-5)$ *Distributive Property*

$= -x + 5$ *Simplify.*

$= 5 - x$ *Commutative Property of Addition*

So, $(5 - x) = -1(x - 5)$.

EXAMPLE 5   **Factoring with Opposites**

Factor $3x^3 - 15x^2 + 10 - 2x$ by grouping.

$3x^3 - 15x^2 + 10 - 2x$

$(3x^3 - 15x^2) + (10 - 2x)$ *Group terms.*

$3x^2(x - 5) + 2(5 - x)$ *Factor out the GCF of each group.*

$3x^2(x - 5) + 2(-1)(x - 5)$ *Write (5 − x) as −1(x − 5).*

$3x^2(x - 5) - 2(x - 5)$ *Simplify. (x − 5) is a common factor.*

$(x - 5)(3x^2 - 2)$ *Factor out (x − 5).*

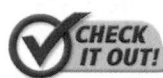 Factor each polynomial by grouping. Check your answer.

5a. $15x^2 - 10x^3 + 8x - 12$ **5b.** $8y - 8 - x + xy$

THINK AND DISCUSS

1. Explain how finding the GCF of monomials helps you factor a polynomial.

2. GET ORGANIZED Copy and complete the graphic organizer.

Factoring by GCF

1. Find the __?__ common factor.

2. Write each term as a __?__ using the GCF.

3. Use the __?__ to factor out the GCF.

4. Check by __?__.

go.hrw.com
Homework Help Online
KEYWORD: MA7 8-2
Parent Resources Online
KEYWORD: MA7 Parent

GUIDED PRACTICE

SEE EXAMPLE 1
p. 551

Factor each polynomial. Check your answer.

1. $15a - 5a^2$ **2.** $10g^3 - 3g$

3. $-35x + 42$ **4.** $-4x^2 - 6x$

5. $12h^4 + 8h^2 - 6h$ **6.** $3x^2 - 9x + 3$

7. $9m^2 + m$ **8.** $14n^3 + 7n + 7n^2$

9. $36f + 18f^2 + 3$ **10.** $-15b^2 + 7b$

SEE EXAMPLE 2
p. 552

11. Physics A model rocket is fired vertically into the air at 320 ft/s. The expression $-16t^2 + 320t$ gives the rocket's height after t seconds. Factor this expression.

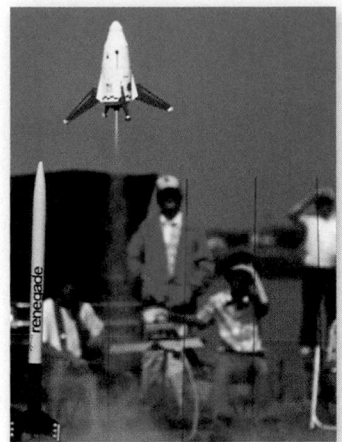

SEE EXAMPLE 3
p. 553

Factor each expression.

12. $5(m - 2) - m(m - 2)$ **13.** $2b(b + 3) + 5(b + 3)$ **14.** $4(x - 3) - x(y + 2)$

Factor each polynomial by grouping. Check your answer.

SEE EXAMPLE 4
p. 553

15. $x^3 + 4x^2 + 2x + 8$ **16.** $6x^3 + 4x^2 + 3x + 2$ **17.** $4b^3 - 6b^2 + 10b - 15$

18. $2m^3 + 4m^2 + 6m + 12$ **19.** $7r^3 - 35r^2 + 6r - 30$ **20.** $10a^3 + 4a^2 + 5a + 2$

SEE EXAMPLE 5
p. 554

21. $2r^2 - 6r + 12 - 4r$ **22.** $6b^2 - 3b + 4 - 8b$ **23.** $14q^2 - 21q + 6 - 4q$

24. $3r - r^2 + 2r - 6$ **25.** $2m^3 - 6m^2 + 9 - 3m$ **26.** $6a^3 - 9a^2 - 12 + 8a$

PRACTICE AND PROBLEM SOLVING

Independent Practice	
For Exercises	See Example
27–35	1
36	2
37–42	3
43–48	4
49–54	5

Extra Practice
Skills Practice p. S18
Application Practice p. S35

Factor each polynomial. Check your answer.

27. $9y^2 + 45y$ **28.** $36d^3 + 24$ **29.** $-14x^4 + 5x^2$

30. $-15f - 10f^2$ **31.** $-4d^4 + d^3 - 3d^2$ **32.** $14x^3 + 63x^2 - 7x$

33. $21c^2 + 14c$ **34.** $33d^3 + 22d + 11$ **35.** $-5g^3 - 15g^2$

36. Finance After t years, the amount of money in a savings account that earns simple interest is $P + Prt$, where P is the starting amount and r is the yearly interest rate. Factor this expression.

Factor each expression.

37. $6a(a - 2) - 5b(b + 4)$ **38.** $-4x(x + 2) + 9(x + 2)$ **39.** $6y(y - 7) + (y - 7)$

40. $a(x - 3) + 2b(x - 3)$ **41.** $-3(2 + b) + 4b(b + 2)$ **42.** $5(3x - 2) + x(3x - 2)$

Factor each polynomial by grouping. Check your answer.

43. $2a^3 - 8a^2 + 3a - 12$ **44.** $x^3 + 3x^2 + 5x + 15$ **45.** $6x^3 + 18x^2 + x + 3$

46. $7x^3 + 2x^2 + 28x + 8$ **47.** $n^3 - 2n^2 + 5n - 10$ **48.** $10b^3 - 16b^2 + 25b - 40$

49. $2m^3 - 2m^2 + 3 - 3m$ **50.** $2d^3 - d^2 - 3 + 6d$ **51.** $6f^3 - 8f^2 + 20 - 15f$

52. $5k^2 - k^3 + 3k - 15$ **53.** $b^3 - 2b - 8 + 4b^2$ **54.** $20 - 15x - 6x^2 + 8x$

Fill in the missing part of each factorization.

55. $16v + 12v^2 = 4v(4 + \blacksquare)$

56. $15x - 25x^2 = 5x(3 - \blacksquare)$

57. $-16k^3 - 24k^2 = -8k^2(\blacksquare + 3)$

58. $-x - 10 = -1(\blacksquare + 10)$

Copy and complete the table.

	Polynomial	Number of Terms	Name	Completely Factored Form
	$3y + 3x + 9$	3	trinomial	$3(y + x + 3)$
59.	$x^2 + 5x$	■	■	■
60.	$28c^2 - 49c$	■	■	■
61.	$a^4 + a^3 + a^2$	■	■	■
62.	$36 + 99r - 40r^2 - 110r^3$	■	■	■

63. Personal Finance The final amount of money earned by a certificate of deposit (CD) after n years is $P(1 + r)^n$, where P is the original amount contributed and r is the interest rate as a decimal.

Year	Amount of CD
2004	$100.00
2005	$200.00
2006	$400.00

Justin's aunt purchased three CDs with the same interest rate to help him pay for college. The table shows the amount of the CD she purchased each year. In 2007, she paid $800.00 directly to the college.

a. Let $x = 1 + r$. Write expressions in terms of x for the value of the CDs purchased in 2004, 2005, and 2006 when Justin started college in 2007.

b. Write a polynomial in terms of x to represent the total value of the CDs purchased in 2004, 2005, and 2006 plus the amount paid to the college in 2007.

c. Factor the polynomial in part **b** by grouping. Evaluate the factored form of the polynomial when the interest rate is 9%. (*Hint*: Remember that $x = 1 +$ the interest rate expressed as a decimal.)

 64. Write About It Describe how to find the area of the figure shown. Show each step and write your answer in factored form.

65. Critical Thinking Show two methods of factoring the expression $3a - 3b - 4a + 4b$.

66. Geometry The area of a triangle is $\frac{1}{2}(x^3 - 2x + 2x^2 - 4)$. The height h is $x + 2$. Write an expression for the base b of the triangle. $\left(Hint:\text{ Area of a triangle} = \frac{1}{2}bh\right)$

 67. Write About It Explain how you know when two binomials are opposites.

MULTI-STEP TEST PREP

68. This problem will prepare you for the Multi-Step Test Prep on page 576.

a. The Multiplication Property of Zero states that the product of any number and 0 is 0. What must be true about either a or b to make $ab = 0$?

b. A toy car's distance in feet from the starting point is given by the equation $d = t(3 - t)$. Explain why $t(3 - t) = 0$ means that either $t = 0$ or $3 - t = 0$.

c. When $d = 0$, the car is at the starting point. Use the fact that $t = 0$ or $3 - t = 0$ when $d = 0$ to find the two times when the car is at the starting point.

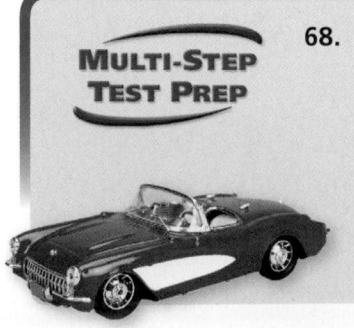

Fill in each blank with a property or definition that justifies the step.

69. $7x^3 + 2x + 21x^2 + 6 = 7x^3 + 21x^2 + 2x + 6$ **a.** _____?_____

$\quad\quad = (7x^3 + 21x^2) + (2x + 6)$ **b.** _____?_____

$\quad\quad = 7x^2(x + 3) + 2(x + 3)$ **c.** _____?_____

$\quad\quad = (x + 3)(7x^2 + 2)$ **d.** _____?_____

70. ///**ERROR ANALYSIS**/// Which factorization of $3n^3 - n^2$ is incorrect? Explain.

$3n^3 - n^2$
$n^2(3n) - n^2(0)$
$n^2(3n - 0)$

$3n^3 - n^2$
$n^2(3n) - n^2(1)$
$n^2(3n - 1)$

71. Which is the complete factorization of $24x^3 - 12x^2$?

Ⓐ $6(4x^3 - 2x^2)$ Ⓑ $12(2x^3 - x^2)$ Ⓒ $12x(2x^2 - x)$ Ⓓ $12x^2(2x - 1)$

72. Which is NOT a factor of $18x^2 + 36x$?

Ⓕ 1   Ⓖ $4x$ Ⓗ $x + 2$ Ⓙ $18x$

73. The area of a rectangle is represented by the polynomial $x^2 + 3x - 6x - 18$. Which of the following could represent the length and width of the rectangle?

Ⓐ Length: $x + 3$; width: $x + 6$ Ⓒ Length: $x + 3$; width: $x - 6$

Ⓑ Length: $x - 3$; width: $x - 6$ Ⓓ Length: $x - 3$; width: $x + 6$

CHALLENGE AND EXTEND

Factor each polynomial.

74. $6ab^2 - 24a^2$ **75.** $-72a^2b^2 - 45ab$ **76.** $-18a^2b^2 + 21ab$

77. $ab + bc + ad + cd$ **78.** $4y^2 + 8ay - y - 2a$ **79.** $x^3 - 4x^2 + 3x - 12$

 80. Geometry The area between two concentric circles is called an *annulus*. The formula for area of an annulus is $A = \pi R^2 - \pi r^2$, where R is the radius of the larger circle and r is the radius of the smaller circle.

  a. Factor the GCF from the formula for area of an annulus.

  b. Use your answer from part **a** to find the area of an annulus with $R = 12$ cm and $r = 5$ cm.

SPIRAL REVIEW

Solve each equation. *(Lesson 2-4)*

81. $4(x + 1) = 3(2x - 6)$ **82.** $-20 + 8n = n + 29$ **83.** $8\left(n + \frac{3}{4}\right) = 10n - 4$

84. The coordinates of the vertices of a quadrilateral are $A(-2, 5)$, $B(6, 5)$, $C(4, -3)$, and $D(-4, -3)$. Use slope to show that $ABCD$ is a parallelogram. *(Lesson 5-9)*

85. Graph the data in the table and show the rates of change. *(Lesson 5-3)*

Time (yr)	1998	1999	2002	2004	2005
Profit (million $)	0.6	0.8	1.3	1.9	2.4

Algebra LAB

Model Factorization of Trinomials

You can use algebra tiles to write a trinomial as a product of two binomials. This is called *factoring a trinomial*.

Use with Lesson 8-3

KEY

$\boxed{+} = 1$

$\boxed{-} = -1$

$\boxed{+} = x$ $\boxed{-} = -x$ $\boxed{+} = x^2$

Activity 1

Use algebra tiles to factor $x^2 + 7x + 6$.

MODEL		ALGEBRA
	Model $x^2 + 7x + 6$.	$x^2 + 7x + 6$
	Try to arrange all of the tiles in a rectangle. Start by placing the x^2-tile in the upper left corner.	
	Arrange the unit tiles in a rectangle so that the top left corner of this rectangle touches the bottom right corner of the x^2-tile.	$x^2 + 7x + 6 \neq (x + 2)(x + 3)$
	Arrange the x-tiles so that all the tiles together make one large rectangle.	
	This arrangement does not work because two x-tiles are left over.	
	Rearrange the unit tiles to form another rectangle.	
	Fill in the empty spaces with x-tiles. All 7 x-tiles fit. This is the correct arrangement.	$x^2 + 7x + 6 = (x + 1)(x + 6)$
	The total area represents the trinomial. The length and width represent the factors.	

The rectangle has width $x + 1$ and length $x + 6$. So $x^2 + 7x + 6 = (x + 1)(x + 6)$.

Use algebra tiles to factor each trinomial.

1. $x^2 + 2x + 1$ **2.** $x^2 + 3x + 2$ **3.** $x^2 + 6x + 5$ **4.** $x^2 + 6x + 9$

5. $x^2 + 5x + 4$ **6.** $x^2 + 6x + 8$ **7.** $x^2 + 5x + 6$ **8.** $x^2 + 8x + 12$

Activity 2

Use algebra tiles to factor $x^2 + x - 2$.

MODEL		ALGEBRA
	Model $x^2 + x - 2$.	$x^2 + x - 2$
	Start by placing the x^2-tile in the upper left corner. Arrange the unit tiles in a rectangle so that the top left corner of this rectangle touches the bottom right corner of the x^2-tile. To make a rectangle, you need to fill in the empty spaces, but there aren't enough x-tiles to fill in the empty spaces.	
	Add a zero pair. Arrange the x-tiles to complete the rectangle. Remember that the product of two positive values is positive and the product of a positive and a negative value is negative.	
	The total area represents the trinomial. The length and width represent the factors.	$x^2 + x - 2 = (x - 1)(x + 2)$

The rectangle has width $x - 1$ and length $x + 2$. So, $x^2 + x - 2 = (x - 1)(x + 2)$.

Try This

9. Why can you add one red $-x$-tile and one yellow x-tile?

Use algebra tiles to factor each trinomial.

10. $x^2 - x - 2$ **11.** $x^2 - 2x - 3$ **12.** $x^2 - 5x + 4$ **13.** $x^2 - 7x + 10$

14. $x^2 - 2x + 1$ **15.** $x^2 - 6x + 5$ **16.** $x^2 + 5x - 6$ **17.** $x^2 + 3x - 4$

18. $x^2 - x - 6$ **19.** $x^2 + 3x - 10$ **20.** $x^2 - 2x - 8$ **21.** $x^2 + x - 12$

8-3 Factoring $x^2 + bx + c$

Objective
Factor quadratic trinomials of the form $x^2 + bx + c$.

Why learn this?
Factoring polynomials will help you find the dimensions of rectangular shapes, such as a fountain. (See Exercise 71.)

In Chapter 7, you learned how to multiply two binomials using the Distributive Property or the FOIL method. In this lesson, you will learn how to factor a trinomial into two binomials.

Notice that when you multiply $(x + 2)(x + 5)$, the constant term in the trinomial is the product of the constants in the binomials.

$$(x + 2)(x + 5) = x^2 + 7x + 10$$

You can use this fact to factor a trinomial into its binomial factors. Look for two numbers that are factors of the constant term in the trinomial. Write two binomials with those numbers, and then multiply to see if you are correct.

EXAMPLE 1 **Factoring Trinomials by Guess and Check**

Factor $x^2 + 19x + 60$ by guess and check.

$(\blacksquare + \blacksquare)(\blacksquare + \blacksquare)$ *Write two sets of parentheses.*

$(x + \blacksquare)(x + \blacksquare)$ *The first term is x^2, so the variable terms have a coefficient of 1.*

> **Remember!**
> When you multiply two binomials, multiply:
> **First terms**
> **Outer terms**
> **Inner terms**
> **Last terms**

The constant term in the trinomial is 60.

$(x + 1)(x + 60) = x^2 + 61x + 60$ ✗   *Try factors of 60 for the constant*
$(x + 2)(x + 30) = x^2 + 32x + 60$ ✗   *terms in the binomials.*
$(x + 3)(x + 20) = x^2 + 23x + 60$ ✗
$(x + 4)(x + 15) = x^2 + 19x + 60$ ✓

The factors of $x^2 + 19x + 60$ are $(x + 4)$ and $(x + 15)$.

$x^2 + 19x + 60 = (x + 4)(x + 15)$

 CHECK IT OUT! Factor each trinomial by guess and check.

1a. $x^2 + 10x + 24$ **1b.** $x^2 + 7x + 12$

The guess and check method is usually not the most efficient method of factoring a trinomial. Look at the product of $(x + 3)$ and $(x + 4)$.

$$(x+3)(x+4) = x^2 + 7x + 12$$

The coefficient of the middle term is the sum of 3 and 4. The third term is the product of 3 and 4.

Know it! Note

Factoring $x^2 + bx + c$	
WORDS	**EXAMPLE**
To factor a quadratic trinomial of the form $x^2 + bx + c$, find two factors of c whose sum is b. If no such integers exist, the trinomial is not factorable.	To factor $x^2 + 9x + 18$, look for factors of 18 whose sum is 9. Factors of 18 | Sum 1 and 18 | 19 ✗ 2 and 9 | 11 ✗ 3 and 6 | 9 ✓ $x^2 + 9x + 18 = (x + 3)(x + 6)$

When c is positive, its factors have the same sign. The sign of b tells you whether the factors are positive or negative. When b is positive, the factors are positive, and when b is negative, the factors are negative.

EXAMPLE **2** **Factoring $x^2 + bx + c$ When c Is Positive**

Factor each trinomial. Check your answer.

A $x^2 + 6x + 8$

$(x + \blacksquare)(x + \blacksquare)$ *$b = 6$ and $c = 8$; look for factors of 8 whose sum is 6.*

Factors of 8	Sum	
1 and 8	9	✗
2 and 4	6	✓

The factors needed are 2 and 4.

$(x + 2)(x + 4)$

Check $(x + 2)(x + 4) = x^2 + 4x + 2x + 8$ *Use the FOIL method.*
$$= x^2 + 6x + 8 ✓$$ *The product is the original polynomial.*

B $x^2 + 5x + 6$

$(x + \blacksquare)(x + \blacksquare)$ *$b = 5$ and $c = 6$; look for factors of 6 whose sum is 5.*

Factors of 6	Sum	
1 and 6	7	✗
2 and 3	5	✓

The factors needed are 2 and 3.

$(x + 2)(x + 3)$

Use the FOIL method.

Check $(x + 2)(x + 3) = x^2 + 3x + 2x + 6$
$$= x^2 + 5x + 6 ✓$$

The product is the original polynomial.

Factor each trinomial. Check your answer.

C $x^2 - 10x + 16$

$(x + \blacksquare)(x + \blacksquare)$

$b = -10$ and $c = 16$; look for factors of 16 whose sum is -10.

Factors of 16	Sum	
-1 and -16	-17	✗
-2 and -8	-10	✓

The factors needed are -2 and -8.

$(x - 2)(x - 8)$

Check $(x - 2)(x - 8) = x^2 - 8x - 2x + 16$ *Use the FOIL method.*

$= x^2 - 10x + 16$ ✓   *The product is the original polynomial.*

 Factor each trinomial. Check your answer.

2a. $x^2 + 8x + 12$ **2b.** $x^2 - 5x + 6$

2c. $x^2 + 13x + 42$ **2d.** $x^2 - 13x + 40$

When c is negative, its factors have opposite signs. The sign of b tells you which factor is positive and which is negative. The factor with the greater absolute value has the same sign as b.

EXAMPLE 3   **Factoring $x^2 + bx + c$ When c Is Negative**

Factor each trinomial.

A $x^2 + 7x - 18$

$(x + \blacksquare)(x + \blacksquare)$

$b = 7$ and $c = -18$; look for factors of -18 whose sum is 7. The factor with the greater absolute value is positive.

Factors of -18	Sum	
-1 and 18	17	✗
-2 and 9	7	✓

The factors needed are -2 and 9.

$(x - 2)(x + 9)$

B $x^2 - 5x - 24$

$(x + \blacksquare)(x + \blacksquare)$

$b = -5$ and $c = -24$; look for factors of -24 whose sum is -5. The factor with the greater absolute value is negative.

Factors of -24	Sum	
1 and -24	-23	✗
2 and -12	-10	✗
3 and -8	-5	✓

The factors needed are 3 and -8.

$(x + 3)(x - 8)$

> **Helpful Hint**
>
> If you have trouble remembering the rules for which factor is positive and which is negative, you can try all the factor pairs and check their sums.

 Factor each trinomial. Check your answer.

3a. $x^2 + 2x - 15$ **3b.** $x^2 - 6x + 8$ **3c.** $x^2 - 8x - 20$

A polynomial and the factored form of the polynomial are equivalent expressions. When you evaluate these two expressions for the same value of the variable, the results are the same.

EXAMPLE 4 **Evaluating Polynomials**

Factor $n^2 + 11n + 24$. Show that the original polynomial and the factored form have the same value for $n = 0, 1, 2, 3,$ and 4.

$$n^2 + 11n + 24$$
$$(n + \blacksquare)(n + \blacksquare)$$ *b = 11 and c = 24; look for factors of 24 whose sum is 11.*

Factors of 24	Sum	
1 and 24	25	✗
2 and 12	14	✗
3 and 8	11	✓

The factors needed are 3 and 8.

$$(n + 3)(n + 8)$$

Evaluate the original polynomial and the factored form for $n = 0, 1, 2, 3,$ and 4.

n	$n^2 + 11n + 24$
0	$0^2 + 11(0) + 24 = 24$
1	$1^2 + 11(1) + 24 = 36$
2	$2^2 + 11(2) + 24 = 50$
3	$3^2 + 11(3) + 24 = 66$
4	$4^2 + 11(4) + 24 = 84$

n	$(n + 3)(n + 8)$
0	$(0 + 3)(0 + 8) = 24$
1	$(1 + 3)(1 + 8) = 36$
2	$(2 + 3)(2 + 8) = 50$
3	$(3 + 3)(3 + 8) = 66$
4	$(4 + 3)(4 + 8) = 84$

The original polynomial and the factored form have the same value for the given values of n.

CHECK IT OUT! 4. Factor $n^2 - 7n + 10$. Show that the original polynomial and the factored form have the same value for $n = 0, 1, 2, 3,$ and 4.

THINK AND DISCUSS

1. Explain in your own words how to factor $x^2 + 9x + 14$. Show how to check your answer.

2. Explain how you can determine the signs of the factors of c when factoring a trinomial of the form $x^2 + bx + c$.

3. **GET ORGANIZED** Copy and complete the graphic organizer. In each box, write an example of a trinomial with the given properties and factor it.

go.hrw.com
Homework Help Online
KEYWORD: MA7 8-3
Parent Resources Online
KEYWORD: MA7 Parent

GUIDED PRACTICE

SEE EXAMPLE **1**
p. 560

Factor each trinomial by guess and check.

1. $x^2 + 13x + 36$ **2.** $x^2 + 11x + 24$ **3.** $x^2 + 14x + 40$

SEE EXAMPLE **2**
p. 561

Factor each trinomial. Check your answer.

4. $x^2 + 4x + 3$ **5.** $x^2 + 10x + 16$ **6.** $x^2 + 15x + 44$

7. $x^2 - 7x + 6$ **8.** $x^2 - 9x + 14$ **9.** $x^2 - 11x + 24$

SEE EXAMPLE **3**
p. 562

10. $x^2 - 6x - 7$ **11.** $x^2 + 6x - 27$ **12.** $x^2 + x - 30$

13. $x^2 - x - 2$ **14.** $x^2 - 3x - 18$ **15.** $x^2 - 4x - 45$

SEE EXAMPLE **4**
p. 563

16. Factor $n^2 + 6n - 7$. Show that the original polynomial and the factored form have the same value for $n = 0, 1, 2, 3,$ and 4.

PRACTICE AND PROBLEM SOLVING

Independent Practice

For Exercises	See Example
17–19	1
20–25	2
26–31	3
32	4

Extra Practice
Skills Practice p. S18
Application Practice p. S35

Factor each trinomial by guess and check.

17. $x^2 + 13x + 30$ **18.** $x^2 + 11x + 28$ **19.** $x^2 + 16x + 48$

Factor each trinomial. Check your answer.

20. $x^2 + 12x + 11$ **21.** $x^2 + 16x + 28$ **22.** $x^2 + 15x + 36$

23. $x^2 - 6x + 5$ **24.** $x^2 - 9x + 18$ **25.** $x^2 - 12x + 32$

26. $x^2 + x - 12$ **27.** $x^2 + 4x - 21$ **28.** $x^2 + 9x - 36$

29. $x^2 - 12x - 13$ **30.** $x^2 - 10x - 24$ **31.** $x^2 - 2x - 35$

32. Factor $n^2 - 12n - 45$. Show that the original polynomial and the factored form have the same value for $n = 0, 1, 2, 3,$ and 4.

Match each trinomial with its correct factorization.

33. $x^2 + 3x - 10$ **A.** $(x - 2)(x - 5)$

34. $x^2 - 7x + 10$ **B.** $(x + 1)(x + 10)$

35. $x^2 - 9x - 10$ **C.** $(x - 2)(x + 5)$

36. $x^2 + 11x + 10$ **D.** $(x + 1)(x - 10)$

 37. Write About It Compare multiplying binomials with factoring polynomials into binomial factors.

Factor each trinomial. Check your answer.

38. $x^2 + x - 20$ **39.** $x^2 - 11x + 18$ **40.** $x^2 - 4x - 21$

41. $x^2 + 10x + 9$ **42.** $x^2 - 12x + 32$ **43.** $x^2 + 13x + 42$

44. $x^2 - 7x + 12$ **45.** $x^2 + 11x + 18$ **46.** $x^2 - 6x - 27$

47. $x^2 + 5x - 24$ **48.** $x^2 - 10x + 21$ **49.** $x^2 + 4x - 45$

50. Factor $n^2 + 11n + 28$. Show that the original polynomial and the factored form have the same value for $n = 0, 1, 2, 3,$ and 4.

51. Estimation The graph shows the areas of rectangles with dimensions $(x + 1)$ yards and $(x + 2)$ yards. Estimate the value of x for a rectangle with area 9 square yards.

52. Geometry The area of a rectangle in square feet can be represented by $x^2 + 8x + 12$. The length is $(x + 6)$ ft. What is the width of the rectangle?

Area (yd²) vs x-values graph

53. Remodeling A homeowner wants to enlarge a rectangular closet that has an area of $(x^2 + 3x + 2)$ ft². The length is $(x + 2)$ ft. After construction, the area will be $(x^2 + 8x + 15)$ ft² with a length of $(x + 3)$ ft.

  a. Find the dimensions of the closet before construction.

  b. Find the dimensions of the closet after construction.

  c. By how many feet will the length and width increase after construction?

Art Write the polynomial modeled and then factor.

54.
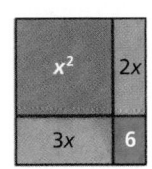
x^2 | $2x$
$3x$ | 6

55.

x^2 | $2x$
$4x$ | 8

56.

x^2 | $-2x$
$4x$ | -8

Copy and complete the table.

	$x^2 + bx + c$	Sign of c	Binomial Factors	Signs of Numbers in Binomials
	$x^2 + 4x + 3$	Positive	$(x + 1)(x + 3)$	Both positive
57.	$x^2 - 4x + 3$	▨	$(x \;▨\; 1)(x \;▨\; 3)$	▨
58.	$x^2 + 2x - 3$	▨	$(x \;▨\; 1)(x \;▨\; 3)$	▨
59.	$x^2 - 2x - 3$	▨	$(x \;▨\; 1)(x \;▨\; 3)$	▨

60. Geometry A rectangle has area $x^2 + 6x + 8$. The length is $x + 4$. Find the width of the rectangle. Could the rectangle be a square? Explain why or why not.

61. This problem will prepare you for the Multi-Step Test Prep on page 576.

The equation for the motion of an object with constant acceleration is $d = vt + \frac{1}{2}at^2$ where d is distance traveled in feet, v is starting velocity in feet per second, a is acceleration in feet per second squared, and t is time in seconds.

  a. Janna has two toy race cars on a track. One starts with a velocity of 0 ft/s and accelerates at 2 ft/s². Write an equation for the distance the car travels in time t.

  b. The second car travels at a constant speed of 4 ft/s. Write an equation for the distance the second car travels in time t. (*Hint:* When speed is constant, the acceleration is 0 ft/s².)

  c. By setting the equations equal to each other you can determine when the cars have traveled the same distance: $t^2 = 4t$. This can be written as $t^2 - 4t = 0$. Factor the left side of the equation.

Art

The Dutch painter Theo van Doesburg (1883–1931) is most famous for his paintings composed of lines and rectangles, such as the one shown above.

62. Construction The length of a rectangular porch is $(x + 7)$ ft. The area of the porch is $(x^2 + 9x + 14)$ ft^2. Find the width of the porch.

$(x + 7)$ ft

Tell whether each statement is true or false. If false, explain.

63. The third term in a factorable trinomial is equal to the product of the constants in its binomial factors.

64. The constants in the binomial factors of $x^2 + x - 2$ are both negative.

65. The correct factorization of $x^2 - 3x - 4$ is $(x + 4)(x - 1)$.

66. All trinomials of the form $x^2 + bx + c$ can be factored.

Fill in the missing part of each factorization.

67. $x^2 - 6x + 8 = (x - 2)(x - \blacksquare)$

68. $x^2 - 2x - 8 = (x + 2)(x - \blacksquare)$

69. $x^2 + 2x - 8 = (x - 2)(x + \blacksquare)$

70. $x^2 + 6x + 8 = (x + 2)(x + \blacksquare)$

71. Construction The area of a rectangular fountain is $(x^2 + 12x + 20)$ ft^2. The width is $(x + 2)$ ft.
   a. Find the length of the fountain.
   b. A 2-foot walkway is built around the fountain. Find the dimensions of the outside border of the walkway.
   c. Find the total area covered by the fountain and walkway.

$(x + 2)$ ft

72. Critical Thinking Find all possible values of b so that $x^2 + bx + 6$ can be factored into binomial factors.

TEST PREP

73. Which is the correct factorization of $x^2 - 10x - 24$?
   Ⓐ $(x - 4)(x - 6)$ Ⓒ $(x - 2)(x + 12)$
   Ⓑ $(x + 4)(x - 6)$ Ⓓ $(x + 2)(x - 12)$

74. Which value of b would make $x^2 + bx - 20$ factorable?
   Ⓕ 9   Ⓖ 12   Ⓗ 19   Ⓙ 21

75. Which value of b would NOT make $x^2 + bx - 36$ factorable?
   Ⓐ 5   Ⓑ 9   Ⓒ 15   Ⓓ 16

76. Short Response What are the factors of $x^2 + 2x - 24$? Show and explain each step of factoring the polynomial.

CHALLENGE AND EXTEND

Factor each expression.

77. $x^4 + 18x^2 + 81$ **78.** $y^4 - 5y^2 - 24$ **79.** $d^4 + 22d^2 + 21$

80. $(u + v)^2 + 2(u + v) - 3$ **81.** $(de)^2 - (de) - 20$ **82.** $(m - n)^2 - 4(m - n) - 45$

83. Find all possible values of b such that, when $x^2 + bx + 28$ is factored, both constants in the binomials are positive.

84. Find all possible values of b such that, when $x^2 + bx + 32$ is factored, both constants in the binomials are negative.

85. The area of Beth's rectangular garden is $(x^2 + 13x + 42)$ ft². The width is $(x + 6)$ ft.

Item	Cost
Fertilizer	0.28 ($/ft²)
Fencing	2.00 ($/ft)

   a. What is the length of the garden?

   b. Find the perimeter in terms of x.

   c. Find the cost to fence the garden when x is 5.

   d. Find the cost of fertilizer when x is 5.

   e. Find the total cost to fence and fertilize Beth's garden when x is 5.

SPIRAL REVIEW

86. Choose the situation that best describes the graph. *(Lesson 4-1)*

   A. An object increases speed, stops, and then moves in reverse.

   B. An object starts at rest, increases speed steadily, maintains constant speed, and then comes to an immediate stop.

   C. An object increases speed quickly, then increases speed slowly, and then comes to an immediate stop.

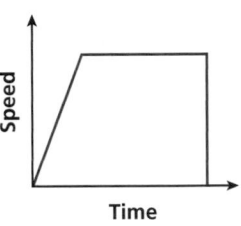

Simplify. *(Lesson 7-3)*

87. $x^3 x^2$ **88.** $m^8 n^3 m^{-12}$ **89.** $\left(t^4\right)^3$ **90.** $\left(-2xy^3\right)^5$

Factor each polynomial by grouping. *(Lesson 8-2)*

91. $x^3 + 2x^2 + 5x + 10$ **92.** $2n^3 - 8n^2 - 3n + 12$

93. $2p^4 - 4p^3 + 7p - 14$ **94.** $x^3 - 4x^2 + x - 4$

Career Path

Jessica Rubino
Environmental Sciences major

Q: What math classes did you take in high school?

A: Algebra 1, Algebra 2, and Geometry

Q: What college math classes have you taken?

A: I took several computer modeling and programming classes as well as Statistics and Probability.

Q: How is math used in some of your projects?

A: Computer applications help me analyze data collected from a local waste disposal site. I used my mathematical knowledge to make recommendations on how to preserve surrounding water supplies.

Q: What plans do you have for the future?

A: I enjoy my studies in the area of water pollution. I would also like to research more efficient uses of natural energy resources.

Factoring $ax^2 + bx + c$

Objective
Factor quadratic trinomials of the form $ax^2 + bx + c$.

Why learn this?
The height of a football that has been kicked can be modeled by a factored polynomial. (See Exercise 69.)

In the previous lesson you factored trinomials of the form $x^2 + bx + c$. Now you will factor trinomials of the form $ax^2 + bx + c$, where $a \neq 0$ or 1.

When you multiply $(3x + 2)(2x + 5)$, the coefficient of the x^2-term is the product of the coefficients of the x-terms. Also, the constant term in the trinomial is the product of the constants in the binomials.

$$(3x + 2)(2x + 5) = 6x^2 + 19x + 10$$

To factor a trinomial like $ax^2 + bx + c$ into its binomial factors, write two sets of parentheses: $(\blacksquare x + \blacksquare)(\blacksquare x + \blacksquare)$.

Write two numbers that are factors of a next to the x's and two numbers that are factors of c in the other blanks. Then multiply to see if the product is the original trinomial. If there are not two such integers, the trinomial is unfactorable.

EXAMPLE 1 **Factoring $ax^2 + bx + c$ by Guess and Check**

Factor $4x^2 + 16x + 15$ by guess and check.

$(\blacksquare + \blacksquare)(\blacksquare + \blacksquare)$ *Write two sets of parentheses.*

$(\blacksquare x + \blacksquare)(\blacksquare x + \blacksquare)$ *The first term is $4x^2$, so at least one variable term has a coefficient other than 1.*

The coefficient of the x^2-term is 4. The constant term in the trinomial is 15.

$(1x + 15)(4x + 1) = 4x^2 + 61x + 15$ ✗   *Try factors of 4 for the coefficients and factors of 15 for the constant terms.*

$(1x + 5)(4x + 3) = 4x^2 + 23x + 15$ ✗

$(1x + 3)(4x + 5) = 4x^2 + 17x + 15$ ✗

$(1x + 1)(4x + 15) = 4x^2 + 19x + 15$ ✗

$(2x + 15)(2x + 1) = 4x^2 + 32x + 15$ ✗

$(2x + 5)(2x + 3) = 4x^2 + 16x + 15$ ✓

The factors of $4x^2 + 16x + 15$ are $(2x + 5)$ and $(2x + 3)$.

$4x^2 + 16x + 15 = (2x + 5)(2x + 3)$

 CHECK IT OUT! Factor each trinomial by guess and check.

1a. $6x^2 + 11x + 3$ **1b.** $3x^2 - 2x - 8$

So, to factor $ax^2 + bx + c$, check the factors of a and the factors of c in the binomials. The sum of the products of the outer and inner terms should be b.

Product = a — — Product = c

$$(\boxed{}x + \boxed{})(\boxed{}x + \boxed{}) = ax^2 + bx + c$$

Sum of outer and inner products = b

Since you need to check all the factors of a and all the factors of c, it may be helpful to make a table. Then check the products of the outer and inner terms to see if the sum is b. You can multiply the binomials to check your answer.

EXAMPLE 2 **Factoring $ax^2 + bx + c$ When c Is Positive**

Factor each trinomial. Check your answer.

A $2x^2 + 11x + 12$

$(\boxed{}x + \boxed{})(\boxed{}x + \boxed{})$ $a = 2$ and $c = 12$; Outer + Inner = 11

Factors of 2	Factors of 12	Outer + Inner	
1 and 2	1 and 12	$1(12) + 2(1) = 14$	✗
1 and 2	12 and 1	$1(1) + 2(12) = 25$	✗
1 and 2	2 and 6	$1(6) + 2(2) = 10$	✗
1 and 2	6 and 2	$1(2) + 2(6) = 14$	✗
1 and 2	3 and 4	$1(4) + 2(3) = 10$	✗
1 and 2	4 and 3	$1(3) + 2(4) = 11$	✓

$$(x + 4)(2x + 3)$$

Check $(x + 4)(2x + 3) = 2x^2 + 3x + 8x + 12$ *Use the FOIL method.*
$$= 2x^2 + 11x + 12 \checkmark$$

B $5x^2 - 14x + 8$

$(\boxed{}x + \boxed{})(\boxed{}x + \boxed{})$ $a = 5$ and $c = 8$; Outer + Inner = -14

Factors of 5	Factors of 8	Outer + Inner	
1 and 5	-1 and -8	$1(-8) + 5(-1) = -13$	✗
1 and 5	-8 and -1	$1(-1) + 5(-8) = -41$	✗
1 and 5	-2 and -4	$1(-4) + 5(-2) = -14$	✓

$$(x - 2)(5x - 4)$$

Check $(x - 2)(5x - 4) = 5x^2 - 4x - 10x + 8$ *Use the FOIL method.*
$$= 5x^2 - 14x + 8 \checkmark$$

> **Remember!**
>
> When b is negative and c is positive, the factors of c are both negative.

CHECK IT OUT! Factor each trinomial. Check your answer.

2a. $6x^2 + 17x + 5$ **2b.** $9x^2 - 15x + 4$ **2c.** $3x^2 + 13x + 12$

When c is negative, one factor of c will be positive and the other factor will be negative. Only some of the factors are shown in the examples, but you may need to check all of the possibilities.

EXAMPLE 3 **Factoring $ax^2 + bx + c$ When c Is Negative**

Factor each trinomial. Check your answer.

A $4y^2 + 7y - 2$

$$\left(\blacksquare y + \blacksquare\right)\left(\blacksquare y + \blacksquare\right)$$ *a = 4 and c = −2; Outer + Inner = 7*

Factors of 4	Factors of −2	Outer + Inner
1 and 4	1 and −2	$1(-2) + 4(1) = 2$ ✗
1 and 4	−1 and 2	$1(2) + 4(-1) = -2$ ✗
1 and 4	2 and −1	$1(-1) + 4(2) = 7$ ✓

$$(y + 2)(4y - 1)$$

Check $(y + 2)(4y - 1) = 4y^2 - y + 8y - 2$ *Use the FOIL method.*
$$= 4y^2 + 7y - 2 ✓$$

B $4x^2 + 19x - 5$

$$\left(\blacksquare x + \blacksquare\right)\left(\blacksquare x + \blacksquare\right)$$ *a = 4 and c = −5; Outer + Inner = 19*

Factors of 4	Factors of −5	Outer + Inner
1 and 4	1 and −5	$1(-5) + 4(1) = -1$ ✗
1 and 4	−1 and 5	$1(5) + 4(-1) = 1$ ✗
1 and 4	5 and −1	$1(-1) + 4(5) = 19$ ✓

$$(x + 5)(4x - 1)$$

Check $(x + 5)(4x - 1) = 4x^2 - x + 20x - 5$ *Use the FOIL method.*
$$= 4x^2 + 19x - 5 ✓$$

C $2x^2 - 7x - 15$

$$\left(\blacksquare x + \blacksquare\right)\left(\blacksquare x + \blacksquare\right)$$ *a = 2 and c = −15; Outer + Inner = −7*

Factors of 2	Factors of −15	Outer + Inner
1 and 2	1 and −15	$1(-15) + 2(1) = -13$ ✗
1 and 2	−1 and 15	$1(15) + 2(-1) = 13$ ✗
1 and 2	3 and −5	$1(-5) + 2(3) = 1$ ✗
1 and 2	−3 and 5	$1(5) + 2(-3) = -1$ ✗
1 and 2	5 and −3	$1(-3) + 2(5) = 7$ ✗
1 and 2	−5 and 3	$1(3) + 2(-5) = -7$ ✓

$$(x - 5)(2x + 3)$$

Check $(x - 5)(2x + 3) = 2x^2 + 3x - 10x - 15$ *Use the FOIL method.*
$$= 2x^2 - 7x - 15 ✓$$

CHECK IT OUT! Factor each trinomial. Check your answer.

3a. $6x^2 + 7x - 3$ **3b.** $4n^2 - n - 3$

Factoring $ax^2 + bx + c$

When a, b, and c are positive, I like to use a box to help me factor. I look for factors of ac that add to b. Then I arrange the terms in a box and factor.

To factor $6x^2 + 7x + 2$, first I find the factors I need.

$$ac = 2(6) = 12 \quad b = 7$$

Factors of 12	Sum
1 and 12	13
2 and 6	8
3 and 4	7

Then I rewrite the trinomial as $6x^2 + 3x + 4x + 2$.

Now I arrange $6x^2 + 3x + 4x + 2$ in a box and factor out the common factors from each row and column.

The factors are $(2x + 1)$ and $(3x + 2)$.

When the leading coefficient is negative, factor out -1 from each term before using other factoring methods.

EXAMPLE 4 **Factoring $ax^2 + bx + c$ When a Is Negative**

Factor $-2x^2 - 15x - 7$.

$$-1(2x^2 + 15x + 7) \qquad \text{Factor out } -1.$$

$$-1(\blacksquare x + \blacksquare)(\blacksquare x + \blacksquare) \qquad a = 2 \text{, and } c = 7; \text{ Outer + Inner} = 15$$

Caution!

When you factor out -1 in an early step, you must carry it through the rest of the steps.

Factors of 2	Factors of 7	Outer + Inner	
1 and 2	1 and 7	$1(7) + 2(1) = 9$	✗
1 and 2	7 and 1	$1(1) + 2(7) = 15$	✓

$$(x + 7)(2x + 1)$$

$$-1(x + 7)(2x + 1)$$

CHECK IT OUT! Factor each trinomial. Check your answer.

4a. $-6x^2 - 17x - 12$ **4b.** $-3x^2 - 17x - 10$

THINK AND DISCUSS

1. Let a, b, and c be positive. If $ax^2 + bx + c$ is the product of two binomials, what do you know about the signs of the numbers in the binomials?

2. GET ORGANIZED Copy and complete the graphic organizer. Write each of the following trinomials in the appropriate box and factor each one.

$3x^2 + 10x - 8$ $3x^2 + 10x + 8$
$3x^2 - 10x + 8$ $3x^2 - 10x - 8$

Factoring $ax^2 + bx + c$	
$c > 0$	
$b > 0$	$b < 0$
$c < 0$	
$b < 0$	$b > 0$

go.hrw.com
Homework Help Online
KEYWORD: MA7 8-4
Parent Resources Online
KEYWORD: MA7 Parent

GUIDED PRACTICE

SEE EXAMPLE 1
p. 568

Factor each trinomial by guess and check.

1. $2x^2 + 9x + 10$ **2.** $5x^2 + 31x + 6$ **3.** $5x^2 + 7x - 6$

4. $6x^2 + 37x + 6$ **5.** $3x^2 - 14x - 24$ **6.** $6x^2 + x - 2$

Factor each trinomial. Check your answer.

SEE EXAMPLE 2
p. 569

7. $5x^2 + 11x + 2$ **8.** $2x^2 + 11x + 5$ **9.** $4x^2 - 9x + 5$

10. $2y^2 - 11y + 14$ **11.** $5x^2 + 9x + 4$ **12.** $3x^2 + 7x + 2$

SEE EXAMPLE 3
p. 570

13. $4a^2 + 8a - 5$ **14.** $15x^2 + 4x - 3$ **15.** $2x^2 + x - 6$

16. $6n^2 - 11n - 10$ **17.** $10x^2 - 9x - 1$ **18.** $7x^2 - 3x - 10$

SEE EXAMPLE 4
p. 571

19. $-2x^2 + 5x + 12$ **20.** $-4n^2 - 16n + 9$ **21.** $-5x^2 + 7x + 6$

22. $-6x^2 + 13x - 2$ **23.** $-4x^2 - 8x + 5$ **24.** $-5x^2 + x + 18$

PRACTICE AND PROBLEM SOLVING

Independent Practice	
For Exercises	See Example
25–33	1
34–42	2
43–48	3
49–51	4

Extra Practice
Skills Practice p. S19
Application Practice p. S35

Factor each trinomial by guess and check.

25. $9x^2 + 9x + 2$ **26.** $2x^2 + 7x + 5$ **27.** $3n^2 + 8n + 4$

28. $10d^2 + 17d + 7$ **29.** $4c^2 - 17c + 15$ **30.** $6x^2 + 14x + 4$

31. $8x^2 + 22x + 5$ **32.** $6x^2 - 13x + 6$ **33.** $5x^2 + 9x - 18$

Factor each trinomial. Check your answer.

34. $6x^2 + 23x + 7$ **35.** $10n^2 - 17n + 7$ **36.** $3x^2 + 11x + 6$

37. $7x^2 + 15x + 2$ **38.** $3n^2 + 4n + 1$ **39.** $3x^2 - 19x + 20$

40. $6x^2 + 11x + 4$ **41.** $4x^2 - 31x + 21$ **42.** $10x^2 + 31x + 15$

43. $12y^2 + 17y - 5$ **44.** $3x^2 + 10x - 8$ **45.** $4x^2 + 4x - 3$

46. $2n^2 - 7n - 4$ **47.** $3x^2 - 4x - 15$ **48.** $3n^2 - n - 4$

49. $-4x^2 - 4x + 15$ **50.** $-3x^2 + 16x - 16$ **51.** $-3x^2 - x + 2$

Geometry For Exercises 52–54, write the polynomial modeled and then factor.

52.

53.

$2x^2$	$-x$
$-4x$	2

54.

$5x^2$	$-4x$
$35x$	-28

Factor each trinomial, if possible.

55. $9n^2 + 17n + 8$ **56.** $2x^2 - 7x - 4$ **57.** $4x^2 - 12x + 5$

58. $5x^2 - 4x + 12$ **59.** $3x^2 + 14x + 16$ **60.** $-3x^2 - 11x + 4$

61. $6x^2 - x - 12$ **62.** $10a^2 + 11a + 3$ **63.** $4x^2 - 12x + 9$

64. **Geometry** The area of a rectangle is $(6x^2 + 11x + 5)$ cm^2. The width is $(x + 1)$ cm. What is the length of the rectangle?

$(x + 1)$ cm

65. **Write About It** Write a paragraph describing how to factor $6x^2 + 13x + 6$. Show each step you would take and explain your steps.

Complete each factorization.

66. $8x^2 + 18x - 5$
$8x^2 + 20x - 2x - 5$
$(8x^2 + 20x) - (2x + 5)$
$\blacksquare(\blacksquare + \blacksquare) - \blacksquare(2x + 5)$
$(\blacksquare - \blacksquare)(2x + 5)$

67. $4x^2 + 9x + 2$
$4x^2 + 8x + x + 2$
$(4x^2 + 8x) + (x + 2)$
$\blacksquare(\blacksquare + \blacksquare) + \blacksquare(x + 2)$
$(\blacksquare + \blacksquare)(x + 2)$

68. **Gardening** The length of Rebecca's rectangular garden was two times the width w. Rebecca increased the length and width of the garden so that the area of the new garden is $(2w^2 + 7w + 6)$ square yards. By how much did Rebecca increase the length and the width?

69. **Physics** The height of a football that has been thrown or kicked can be described by the expression $-16t^2 + vt + h$ where t is the time in seconds, v is the initial upward velocity, and h is the initial height in feet.

   a. Write an expression for the height of a football at time t when the initial upward velocity is 20 feet per second and the initial height is 6 feet.

   b. Factor your expression from part **a**.

   c. Find the height of the football after 1 second.

70. **///ERROR ANALYSIS///** A student attempted to factor $2x^2 + 11x + 12$ as shown. Find and explain the error.

$2x^2 + 11x + 12$

Factors of 12	Sum	
1 and 12	13	✓
2 and 6	8	✗
3 and 4	7	✗

$(2x + 1)(x + 12)$

71. This problem will prepare you for the Multi-Step Test Prep on page 576.

The equation $d = 2t^2$ gives the distance from the start point of a toy boat that starts at rest and accelerates at 4 cm/s^2. The equation $d = 10t - 8$ gives the distance from the start point of a second boat that starts at rest 8 cm behind the first boat and travels at a constant rate of 10 cm/s.

   a. By setting the equations equal to each other, you can determine when the cars are the same distance from the start point: $2t^2 = 10t - 8$. Use properties of algebra to collect all terms on the left side of the equation, leaving 0 on the right side.

   b. Factor the expression on the left side of the equation.

   c. The boats are the same distance from the start point at $t = 1$ and $t = 4$. Explain how the factors you found in part **b** were used to find these two times.

MULTI-STEP TEST PREP

Match each trinomial with its correct factorization.

72. $6x^2 - 29x - 5$ **A.** $(x + 5)(6x + 1)$

73. $6x^2 - 31x + 5$ **B.** $(x - 5)(6x - 1)$

74. $6x^2 + 31x + 5$ **C.** $(x + 5)(6x - 1)$

75. $6x^2 + 29x - 5$ **D.** $(x - 5)(6x + 1)$

76. Critical Thinking The quadratic trinomial $ax^2 + bx + c$ has $a > 0$ and can be factored into the product of two binomials.

   a. Explain what you know about the signs of the constants in the factors if $c > 0$.

   b. Explain what you know about the signs of the constants in the factors if $c < 0$.

 TEST PREP

77. What value of b would make $3x^2 + bx - 8$ factorable?

   Ⓐ 3   Ⓑ 10   Ⓒ 11   Ⓓ 25

78. Which product of binomials is represented by the model?

$5x^2$	$4x$
$15x$	12

   Ⓕ $(x + 4)(3x + 5)$ Ⓗ $(x + 3)(5x + 4)$

   Ⓖ $(x + 4)(5x + 3)$ Ⓙ $(x + 5)(3x + 4)$

79. Which binomial is a factor of $24x^2 - 49x + 2$?

   Ⓐ $x - 2$ Ⓑ $x - 1$ Ⓒ $x + 1$ Ⓓ $x + 2$

80. Which value of c would make $2x^2 + x + c$ NOT factorable?

   Ⓕ -15 Ⓖ -9 Ⓗ -6 Ⓙ -1

CHALLENGE AND EXTEND

Factor each trinomial. Check your answer.

81. $1 + 4x + 4x^2$ **82.** $1 - 14x + 49x^2$ **83.** $1 + 18x + 81x^2$

84. $25 + 30x + 9x^2$ **85.** $4 + 20x + 25x^2$ **86.** $4 - 12x + 9x^2$

87. Find all possible values of b such that $3x^2 + bx + 2$ can be factored.

88. Find all possible values of b such that $3x^2 + bx - 2$ can be factored.

89. Find all possible values of b such that $5x^2 + bx + 1$ can be factored.

SPIRAL REVIEW

90. Archie makes $12 per hour. The function $f(x) = 12x$ gives the amount of money that Archie makes in x hours. Graph this function and give its domain and range. *(Lesson 5-1)*

Graph each system of linear inequalities. Give two ordered pairs that are solutions and two that are not solutions. *(Lesson 6-6)*

91. $\begin{cases} y < -2x + 1 \\ y > 3x - 5 \end{cases}$ **92.** $\begin{cases} y \geq -x + 2 \\ y \leq x - 3 \end{cases}$ **93.** $\begin{cases} y \leq -4x \\ y > 2x - 6 \end{cases}$

Factor each trinomial. Check your answer. *(Lesson 8-3)*

94. $x^2 + 6x + 8$ **95.** $x^2 - 8x - 9$ **96.** $x^2 - 8x + 12$

8-4 Technology Lab

Use a Graph to Factor Polynomials

You can use a graphing calculator to help factor polynomials.

Use with Lesson 8-4

go.hrw.com
Lab Resources Online
KEYWORD: MA7 Lab8

Activity

Factor $x^2 - 3x - 4$ using algebra and check your factorization using a graphing calculator.

1 $x^2 - 3x - 4$

$(x + \boxed{})(x + \boxed{})$ *b = −3 and c = −4; look for factors of −4 whose sum is −3.*

$(x - 4)(x + 1)$ *−4(1) = −4; −4 + 1 = −3*

2 Press [Y=] and enter $x^2 - 3x - 4$ for **Y1**.

3 Press [GRAPH] to view the graph of the equation.

4 Press [TRACE] and use the left and right buttons to move the cursor along the graph. The graph appears to cross the *x*-axis at $x = -1$ and $x = 4$.

5 To find the value of *y* at $x = -1$, enter -1 and press [ENTER] while in *Trace* mode. The calculator gives you a value for *y*. Then enter 4 to find the value of *y* at $x = 4$.

The calculator tells you that $y = 0$ at $x = -1$ and at $x = 4$.

Notice that for a function with a binomial factor of the form $(x - a)$, it appears that *a* is an *x*-intercept.

Try This

Graph each trinomial and use the graph to predict the factors. Then factor each trinomial using algebra.

1. $x^2 - x - 2$ **2.** $x^2 + 5x + 6$ **3.** $x^2 + x - 12$

4. $x^2 + 12x - 64$ **5.** $x^2 - 4x - 5$ **6.** $3x^2 + 16x - 12$

MULTI-STEP TEST PREP

Factoring

Red Light, Green Light The equation for the motion of an object with constant acceleration is $d = vt + \frac{1}{2}at^2$ where d is distance traveled in meters, v is starting velocity in m/s, a is acceleration in m/s², and t is time in seconds.

1. A car is stopped at a traffic light. The light changes to green and the driver starts to drive, accelerating at a rate of 4 m/s². Write an equation for the distance the car travels in time t.

Speed = 15 m/s

Acceleration = 4 m/s²

2. A bus is traveling at a speed of 15 m/s. The driver approaches the same traffic light in another traffic lane. He does not brake, and continues at the same speed. Write an equation for the distance the bus travels in time t. (*Hint:* At a constant speed, the acceleration is 0 m/s².)

3. Set the equations equal to each other so you can determine when the car and bus are the same distance from the intersection. Collect all the terms on the left side of this new equation, leaving 0 on the right side. Factor the expression on the left side of the equation.

4. Let $t = 0$ be the point at which the car is just starting to drive and the bus is even with the car. Find the other time when the vehicles will be the same distance from the intersection.

5. What distance will the two vehicles have traveled when they are again at the same distance from the intersection?

6. A truck traveling at 16 m/s is 24 meters behind the bus at $t = 0$. The equation $d = -24 + 16t$ gives the position of the truck. At what time will the truck be the same distance from the intersection as the bus? What will that distance be?

READY TO GO ON?

Quiz for Lessons 8-1 Through 8-4

8-1 Factors and Greatest Common Factors

Write the prime factorization of each number.

1. 54   **2.** 42   **3.** 50   **4.** 120   **5.** 44   **6.** 78

Find the GCF of each pair of monomials.

7. $6p^3$ and $2p$ **8.** $12x^3$ and $18x^4$

9. -15 and $20s^4$ **10.** $3a$ and $4b^2$

11. Brent is making a wooden display case for his baseball collection. He has 24 balls from American League games and 30 balls from National League games. He wants to display the same number of baseballs in each row and does not want to put American League baseballs in the same row as National League baseballs. How many rows will Brent need in the display case to put the greatest number of baseballs possible in each row?

8-2 Factoring by GCF

Factor each polynomial. Check your answer.

12. $2d^3 + 4d$ **13.** $m^2 - 8m^5$

14. $12x^4 - 8x^3 - 4x^2$ **15.** $3k^2 + 6k - 3$

16. The surface area of a cone can be found using the expression $s\pi r + \pi r^2$, where s represents the slant height and r represents the radius of the base. Factor this expression.

Factor each polynomial by grouping. Check your answer.

17. $w^3 - 4w^2 + w - 4$ **18.** $3x^3 + 6x^2 - 4x - 8$

19. $2p^3 - 6p^2 + 15 - 5p$ **20.** $n^3 - 6n^2 + 5n - 30$

8-3 Factoring $x^2 + bx + c$

Factor each trinomial. Check your answer.

21. $n^2 + 9n + 20$ **22.** $d^2 - 6d - 7$ **23.** $x^2 - 6x + 8$

24. $y^2 + 7y - 30$ **25.** $k^2 - 6k + 5$ **26.** $c^2 - 10c + 24$

27. Simplify and factor the expression $n(n + 3) - 4$. Show that the original expression and the factored form have the same value for $n = 0, 1, 2, 3,$ and 4.

8-4 Factoring $ax^2 + bx + c$

Factor each trinomial. Check your answer.

28. $2x^2 + 11x + 5$ **29.** $3n^2 + 16n + 21$ **30.** $5y^2 - 7y - 6$

31. $4g^2 - 10g + 6$ **32.** $6p^2 - 18p - 24$ **33.** $12d^2 + 7d - 12$

34. The area of a rectangle is $(8x^2 + 8x + 2)$ cm². The width is $(2x + 1)$ cm. What is the length of the rectangle?

Factoring Special Products

Objectives

Factor perfect-square trinomials.

Factor the difference of two squares.

Who uses this?

Urban planners can use the area of a square park to find its length and width. (See Example 2.)

You studied the patterns of some special products of binomials in Chapter 7. You can use those patterns to factor certain polynomials.

A trinomial is a perfect square if:
- The **first** and **last** terms are perfect squares.
- The **middle** term is two times one factor from the first term and one factor from the last term.

$$9x^2 \ + \ 12x \ + \ 4$$
$$3x \cdot 3x \quad 2(3x \cdot 2) \quad 2 \cdot 2$$

Know it!
Note

Perfect-Square Trinomials

PERFECT-SQUARE TRINOMIAL	EXAMPLES
$a^2 + 2ab + b^2 = (a + b)(a + b) = (a + b)^2$	$x^2 + 6x + 9 = (x + 3)(x + 3) = (x + 3)^2$
$a^2 - 2ab + b^2 = (a - b)(a - b) = (a - b)^2$	$x^2 - 2x + 1 = (x - 1)(x - 1) = (x - 1)^2$

EXAMPLE 1 **Recognizing and Factoring Perfect-Square Trinomials**

Determine whether each trinomial is a perfect square. If so, factor. If not, explain.

A $x^2 + 12x + 36$

$$x^2 + 12x + 36$$
$$x \cdot x \quad 2(x \cdot 6) \quad 6 \cdot 6$$

The trinomial is a perfect square. Factor.

Method 1 Factor.

$x^2 + 12x + 36$

Factors of 36	Sum	
1 and 36	37	✗
2 and 18	20	✗
3 and 12	15	✗
4 and 9	13	✗
6 and 6	12	✓

$(x + 6)(x + 6)$

Method 2 Use the rule.

$x^2 + 12x + 36 \quad a = x, b = 6$

$x^2 + 2(x)(6) + 6^2$ *Write the trinomial as $a^2 + 2ab + b^2$.*

$(x + 6)^2$ *Write the trinomial as $(a + b)^2$.*

You can check your answer by using the FOIL method.

For Example 1B,
$(2x - 3)^2 =$
$(2x - 3)(2x - 3) =$
$4x^2 - 6x - 6x + 9 =$
$4x^2 - 12x + 9$

Determine whether each trinomial is a perfect square. If so, factor. If not, explain.

B $4x^2 - 12x + 9$

$2x \cdot 2x \qquad 2(2x \cdot 3) \qquad 3 \cdot 3$ *The trinomial is a perfect square. Factor.*

$$4x^2 - 12x + 9 \qquad\qquad a = 2x,\ b = 3$$
$$(2x)^2 - 2(2x)(3) + 3^2 \qquad a^2 - 2ab + b^2$$
$$(2x - 3)^2 \qquad\qquad (a - b)^2$$

C $x^2 + 9x + 16$

$x \cdot x \qquad 2(x \cdot 4) \qquad 4 \cdot 4$ *$2(x \cdot 4) \neq 9x$*

$x^2 + 9x + 16$ is not a perfect-square trinomial because $9x \neq 2(x \cdot 4)$.

CHECK IT OUT! Determine whether each trinomial is a perfect square. If so, factor. If not, explain.

1a. $x^2 + 4x + 4$ **1b.** $x^2 - 14x + 49$ **1c.** $9x^2 - 6x + 4$

EXAMPLE 2   *Problem-Solving Application*

PROBLEM SOLVING

The park in the center of the Place des Vosges in Paris, France, is in the shape of a square. The area of the park is $(25x^2 + 70x + 49)$ ft². The side length of the park is in the form $cx + d$, where c and d are whole numbers. Find an expression in terms of x for the perimeter of the park. Find the perimeter when $x = 8$ ft.

1 Understand the Problem

The **answer** will be an expression for the perimeter of the park and the value of the expression when $x = 8$.

List the **important information:**
- The park is a square with area $(25x^2 + 70x + 49)$ ft².
- The side length of the park is in the form $cx + d$, where c and d are whole numbers.

2 Make a Plan

The formula for the area of a square is area $= (\text{side})^2$.

Factor $25x^2 + 70x + 49$ to find the side length of the park. Write a formula for the perimeter of the park, and evaluate the expression for $x = 8$.

Solve

$$25x^2 + 70x + 49 \qquad a = 5x, \, b = 7$$
$$(5x)^2 + 2(5x)(7) + 7^2 \qquad \text{Write the trinomial as } a^2 + 2ab + b^2.$$
$$(5x + 7)^2 \qquad \text{Write the trinomial as } (a + b)^2.$$
$$25x^2 + 70x + 49 = (5x + 7)(5x + 7)$$

The side length of the park is $(5x + 7)$ ft.

Write a formula for the perimeter of the park.
$$P = 4s \qquad \text{Write the formula for the perimeter of a square.}$$
$$= 4(5x + 7) \qquad \text{Substitute the side length for s.}$$
$$= 20x + 28 \qquad \text{Distribute 4.}$$

An expression for the perimeter of the park in feet is $20x + 28$.

Evaluate the expression when $x = 8$.
$$P = 20x + 28$$
$$= 20(8) + 28 \qquad \text{Substitute 8 for x.}$$
$$= 188$$

When $x = 8$ ft, the perimeter of the park is 188 ft.

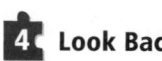 **Look Back**

For a square with a perimeter of 188 ft, the side length is $\frac{188}{4} = 47$ ft and the area is $47^2 = 2209$ ft^2.

Evaluate $25x^2 + 70x + 49$ for $x = 8$:
$$25(8)^2 + 70(8) + 49$$
$$1600 + 560 + 49$$
$$2209 \checkmark$$

 2. What if...? A company produces square sheets of aluminum, each of which has an area of $(9x^2 + 6x + 1)$ m^2. The side length of each sheet is in the form $cx + d$, where c and d are whole numbers. Find an expression in terms of x for the perimeter of a sheet. Find the perimeter when $x = 3$ m.

In Chapter 7 you learned that the difference of two squares has the form $a^2 - b^2$. The difference of two squares can be written as the product $(a + b)(a - b)$. You can use this pattern to factor some polynomials.

A polynomial is a difference of two squares if:
- There are two terms, one subtracted from the other.
- Both terms are perfect squares.

$$\begin{array}{c} 4x^2 - 9 \\ \overbrace{2x \cdot 2x} \quad \overbrace{3 \cdot 3} \end{array}$$

Difference of Two Squares

DIFFERENCE OF TWO SQUARES	EXAMPLE
$a^2 - b^2 = (a + b)(a - b)$	$x^2 - 9 = (x + 3)(x - 3)$

EXAMPLE **3** **Recognizing and Factoring the Difference of Two Squares**

Determine whether each binomial is a difference of two squares. If so, factor. If not, explain.

A $x^2 - 81$

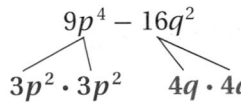

$$x^2 - 81$$
$$x \cdot x \qquad 9 \cdot 9$$

The polynomial is a difference of two squares.

$$x^2 - 9^2 \qquad \qquad a = x, b = 9$$
$$(x + 9)(x - 9) \qquad \textit{Write the polynomial as } (a + b)(a - b).$$
$$x^2 - 81 = (x + 9)(x - 9)$$

B $9p^4 - 16q^2$

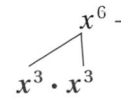

$$9p^4 - 16q^2$$
$$3p^2 \cdot 3p^2 \qquad 4q \cdot 4q$$

The polynomial is a difference of two squares.

$$\left(3p^2\right)^2 - \left(4q\right)^2 \qquad a = 3p^2, b = 4q$$
$$\left(3p^2 + 4q\right)\left(3p^2 - 4q\right) \qquad \textit{Write the polynomial as } (a + b)(a - b).$$
$$9p^4 - 16q^2 = \left(3p^2 + 4q\right)\left(3p^2 - 4q\right)$$

C $x^6 - 7y^2$

$$x^6 - 7y^2$$
$$x^3 \cdot x^3$$

$7y^2$ is not a perfect square.

$x^6 - 7y^2$ is not the difference of two squares because $7y^2$ is not a perfect square.

CHECK IT OUT! Determine whether the binomial is a difference of two squares. If so, factor. If not, explain.

3a. $1 - 4x^2$ **3b.** $p^8 - 49q^6$ **3c.** $16x^2 - 4y^5$

THINK AND DISCUSS

1. The binomial $1 - x^4$ is a difference of two squares. Use the rule to identify a and b in $1 - x^4$.

2. The polynomial $x^2 + 8x + 16$ is a perfect-square trinomial. Use the rule to identify a and b in $x^2 + 8x + 16$.

3. GET ORGANIZED Copy and complete the graphic organizer. Write an example of each type of special product and factor it.

Special Product	Factored Form
Perfect-square trinomial with positive coefficient of middle term	
Perfect-square trinomial with negative coefficient of middle term	
Difference of two squares	

go.hrw.com
Homework Help Online
KEYWORD: MA7 8-5
Parent Resources Online
KEYWORD: MA7 Parent

GUIDED PRACTICE

SEE EXAMPLE 1
p. 578

Determine whether each trinomial is a perfect square. If so, factor. If not, explain.

1. $x^2 - 4x + 4$

2. $x^2 - 4x - 4$

3. $9x^2 - 12x + 4$

4. $x^2 + 2x + 1$

5. $x^2 - 6x + 9$

6. $x^2 - 6x - 9$

SEE EXAMPLE 2
p. 579

7. City Planning A city purchases a square plot of land with an area of $(x^2 + 24x + 144)$ yd^2 for a park. The dimensions of the plot are of the form $ax + b$, where a and b are whole numbers. Find an expression for the perimeter of the park. Find the perimeter when $x = 10$ yd.

SEE EXAMPLE 3
p. 581

Determine whether each binomial is a difference of two squares. If so, factor. If not, explain.

8. $1 - 4x^2$

9. $s^2 - 4^2$

10. $81x^2 - 1$

11. $4x^4 - 9y^2$

12. $x^8 - 50$

13. $x^6 - 9$

PRACTICE AND PROBLEM SOLVING

Independent Practice	
For Exercises	See Example
14–19	1
20	2
21–26	3

Extra Practice
Skills Practice p. S19
Application Practice p. S35

Determine whether the trinomial is a perfect square. If so, factor. If not, explain.

14. $4x^2 - 4x + 1$

15. $4x^2 - 4x - 1$

16. $36x^2 - 12x + 1$

17. $25x^2 + 10x + 4$

18. $9x^2 + 18x + 9$

19. $16x^2 - 40x + 25$

20. Measurement You are given a sheet of paper and told to cut out a square piece with an area of $(4x^2 - 44x + 121)$ mm^2. The dimensions of the square have the form $ax - b$, where a and b are whole numbers. Find an expression for the perimeter of the square you cut out. Find the perimeter when $x = 41$ mm.

Determine whether each binomial is a difference of two squares. If so, factor. If not, explain.

21. $1^2 - 4x^2$

22. $25m^2 - 16n^2$

23. $4x - 9y$

24. $49p^{12} - 9q^6$

25. $9^2 - 100x^4$

26. $x^3 - y^3$

Find the missing term in each perfect-square trinomial.

27. $x^2 + 14x + \blacksquare$

28. $9x^2 + \blacksquare + 25$

29. $\blacksquare - 36y + 81$

Factor each polynomial using the rule for perfect-square trinomials or the rule for a difference of two squares. Tell which rule you used.

30. $x^2 - 8x + 16$

31. $100x^2 - 81y^2$

32. $36x^2 + 24x + 4$

33. $4r^6 - 25s^6$

34. $49x^2 - 70x + 25$

35. $x^{14} - 144$

36. Write About It What is similar about a perfect-square trinomial and a difference of two squares? What is different?

37. Critical Thinking Describe two ways to create a perfect-square trinomial.

38. For what value of b would $(x + b)(x + b)$ be the factored form of $x^2 - 22x + 121$?

39. For what value of c are the factors of $x^2 + cx + 256$ the same?

40. This problem will prepare you for the Multi-Step Test Prep on page 592.

This problem will prepare you for the Multi-Step Test Prep on page 592.

Juanita designed a vegetable garden in the shape of a square and purchased fencing for that design. Then she decided to change the design to a rectangle.

a. The square garden had an area of x^2 ft^2. The area of the rectangular garden is $(x^2 - 25)$ ft^2. Factor this expression.

b. The rectangular garden must have the same perimeter as the square garden, so Juanita added a number of feet to the length and subtracted the same number of feet from the width. Use your factors from part **a** to determine how many feet were added to the length and subtracted from the width.

c. If the original length of the square garden was 8 feet, what are the length and width of the new garden?

41. Multi-Step The area of a square is represented by $25z^2 - 40z + 16$.

a. What expression represents the length of a side of the square?

b. What expression represents the perimeter of the square?

c. What are the length of a side, the perimeter, and the area of the square when $z = 3$?

42. Multi-Step A small rectangle is drawn inside a larger rectangle as shown.

a. What is the area of each rectangle?

b. What is the area of the green region?

c. Factor the expression for the area of the green region. (*Hint:* First factor out the common factor of 3 and then factor the binomial.)

43. Evaluate each expression for the values of x.

	x	$x^2 + 10x + 25$	$(x + 5)^2$	$(x - 5)^2$	$x^2 - 10x + 25$	$x^2 - 25$
a.	-5					
b.	-1					
c.	0					
d.	1					
e.	5					

44. In the table above, which columns have equivalent values? Explain why.

45. Geometry A model for the difference of two squares is shown below. Copy and complete the second figure by writing the missing labels.

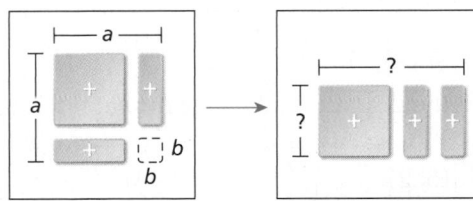

46. ///ERROR ANALYSIS/// Two students factored $25x^4 - 9y^2$. Which is incorrect? Explain the error.

Ⓐ

$25x^4 - 9y^2$
$(5x - 3)(5x + 3)$

Ⓑ

$25x^4 - 9y^2$
$(5x^2 - 3y)(5x^2 + 3y)$

47. A polynomial expression is evaluated for the x- and y-values shown in the table. Which expression could have been evaluated to give the values shown in the third column?

x	y	Value of Expression
0	0	0
−1	−1	0
1	1	0
1	−1	4

  Ⓐ $x^2 - y^2$
  Ⓑ $x^2 + 2xy + y^2$
  Ⓒ $x^2 - 2xy + y^2$
  Ⓓ None of the above

48. The area of a square is $4x^2 + 20x + 25$. Which expression can also be used to model the area of the square?
  Ⓕ $(2x - 5)(5 - 2x)$
  Ⓖ $(2x + 5)(2x - 5)$
  Ⓗ $(2x - 5)^2$
  Ⓙ $(2x + 5)^2$

49. Gridded Response Evaluate the polynomial expression $x^2 - 18x + 81$ for $x = 10$.

CHALLENGE AND EXTEND

50. The binomial $81x^4 - 16$ can be factored using the rule for a difference of two squares.

  a. Fill in the factorization: $81x^4 - 16$
  $$\left(9x^2 + \blacksquare\right)\left(\blacksquare - \blacksquare\right)$$

  b. One binomial from part **a** can be further factored. Identify the binomial and factor it.

  c. Write your own binomial that can be factored twice as the difference of two squares.

51. The expression $4 - (v + 2)^2$ is the difference of two squares, because it fits the rule $a^2 - b^2$.

  a. Identify a and b in the expression.
  b. Factor and simplify $4 - (v + 2)^2$.

The *difference of cubes* is an expression of the form $a^3 - b^3$. It can be factored according to the rule $a^3 - b^3 = (a - b)(a^2 + ab + b^2)$. For each binomial, identify a and b, and factor using the rule.

52. $x^3 - 1$ **53.** $27y^3 - 64$ **54.** $n^6 - 8$

SPIRAL REVIEW

Find the domain and range for each relation and tell whether the relation is a function. *(Lesson 4-2)*

55. $\{(5, 2), (4, 1), (3, 0), (2, -1)\}$ **56.** $\{(-3, 6), (-1, 6), (1, 6), (3, 6)\}$
57. $\{(2, -8), (2, -2), (2, 4), (2, 10)\}$ **58.** $\{(-2, 4), (-1, 1), (0, 0), (1, 1)\}$

Multiply. *(Lesson 7-8)*

59. $2a(3a^2 + 7a - 5)$ **60.** $(x + 3)(x - 8)$ **61.** $(t - 4)^2$

Find the GCF of each pair of monomials. *(Lesson 8-1)*

62. $9m^2$ and $3m^2$ **63.** $8c^2$ and $8d^2$ **64.** $-12x^3y$ and $16y^2$

Connecting
Algebra to

Number Theory

Mental Math

Recognizing patterns of special products can help you perform multiplication mentally.

Remember these special products that you studied in Chapters 7 and 8.

Patterns of Special Products	
Difference of Two Squares	$(a + b)(a - b) = a^2 - b^2$
Perfect-Square Trinomial	$(a + b)^2 = a^2 + 2ab + b^2$ $(a - b)^2 = a^2 - 2ab + b^2$

Example 1

Simplify $17^2 - 7^2$.

This expression is a difference of two squares with $a = 17$ and $b = 7$.

$a^2 - b^2 = (a + b)(a - b)$ *Write the rule for a difference of two squares.*

$17^2 - 7^2 = (17 + 7)(17 - 7)$ *Substitute 17 for a and 7 for b.*

$= (24)(10)$ *Simplify.*

$= 240$

Example 2

Simplify $14^2 + 2(14)(6) + 6^2$.

This expression is a perfect-square trinomial with $a = 14$ and $b = 6$.

$a^2 + 2ab + b^2 = (a + b)^2$ *Write the rule for a perfect-square trinomial.*

$14^2 + 2(14)(6) + 6^2 = (14 + 6)^2$ *Substitute 14 for a and 6 for b.*

$= (20)^2$ *Simplify.*

$= 400$

Try This

Simplify each expression using the rules for special products.

1. $18^2 - 12^2$
2. $11^2 + 2(11)(14) + 14^2$
3. $22^2 - 18^2$
4. $38^2 - 2(38)(27) + 27^2$
5. $29^2 - 2(29)(17) + 17^2$
6. $55^2 + 2(55)(45) + 45^2$
7. $14^2 - 9^2$
8. $13^2 - 12^2$
9. $14^2 + 2(14)(16) + 16^2$

Choosing a Factoring Method

Objectives

Choose an appropriate method for factoring a polynomial.

Combine methods for factoring a polynomial.

Why learn this?

You will need to factor polynomials to solve quadratic equations, which have many applications in physics. (See Exercise 42.)

The height of a leaping ballet dancer can be modeled by a quadratic polynomial. Solving an equation that contains that polynomial may require factoring the polynomial.

Recall that a polynomial is in its fully factored form when it is written as a product that cannot be factored further.

EXAMPLE 1 **Determining Whether an Expression Is Completely Factored**

Tell whether each expression is completely factored. If not, factor it.

A $2x(x^2 + 4)$

$2x(x^2 + 4)$ *Neither 2x nor $x^2 + 4$ can be factored further.*

$2x(x^2 + 4)$ is completely factored.

> **Caution!**
>
> $x^2 + 4$ is a *sum* of squares, and cannot be factored.

B $(2x + 6)(x + 5)$

$(2x + 6)(x + 5)$ *2x + 6 can be further factored.*

$2(x + 3)(x + 5)$ *Factor out 2, the GCF of 2x and 6.*

$2(x + 3)(x + 5)$ is completely factored.

CHECK IT OUT! Tell whether each expression is completely factored. If not, factor it.

1a. $5x^2(x - 1)$ **1b.** $(4x + 4)(x + 1)$

To factor a polynomial completely, you may need to use more than one factoring method. Use the steps below to factor a polynomial completely.

Factoring Polynomials
Step 1   Check for a greatest common factor.
Step 2   Check for a pattern that fits the difference of two squares or a perfect-square trinomial.
Step 3   To factor $x^2 + bx + c$, look for two numbers whose sum is b and whose product is c. To factor $ax^2 + bx + c$, check factors of a and factors of c in the binomial factors. The sum of the products of the outer and inner terms should be b.
Step 4   Check for common factors.

EXAMPLE 2
Factoring by GCF and Recognizing Patterns

Factor $-2xy^2 + 16xy - 32x$ completely. Check your answer.

$$-2xy^2 + 16xy - 32x$$
$$-2x(y^2 - 8y + 16)$$ *Factor out the GCF. $y^2 - 8y + 16$ is a perfect-square trinomial of the form $a^2 - 2ab + b^2$.*
$$-2x(y - 4)^2$$ *$a = y$, $b = 4$*

Check $-2x(y - 4)^2 = -2x(y^2 - 8y + 16)$
$$= -2xy^2 + 16xy - 32x \checkmark$$

CHECK IT OUT! Factor each polynomial completely. Check your answer.
2a. $4x^3 + 16x^2 + 16x$ **2b.** $2x^2y - 2y^3$

If none of the factoring methods work, the polynomial is unfactorable.

EXAMPLE 3
Factoring by Multiple Methods

Factor each polynomial completely.

A $2x^2 + 5x + 4$

$$2x^2 + 5x + 4$$ *The GCF is 1 and there is no pattern.*
$$(\blacksquare x + \blacksquare)(\blacksquare x + \blacksquare)$$ *$a = 2$ and $c = 4$; Outer + Inner = 5*

Factors of 2	Factors of 4	Outer + Inner	
1 and 2	1 and 4	$1(4) + 2(1) = 6$	✗
1 and 2	4 and 1	$1(1) + 2(4) = 9$	✗
1 and 2	2 and 2	$1(2) + 2(2) = 6$	✗

$2x^2 + 5x + 4$ is unfactorable.

Remember!

For a polynomial of the form $ax^2 + bx + c$, if there are no integers whose sum is b and whose product is ac, then the polynomial is unfactorable.

B $3n^4 - 15n^3 + 12n^2$

$$3n^2(n^2 - 5n + 4)$$ *Factor out the GCF. There is no pattern.*
$$(n + \blacksquare)(n + \blacksquare)$$ *$b = -5$ and $c = 4$; look for factors of 4 whose sum is -5.*

Factors of 4	Sum	
-1 and -4	-5	✓

The factors needed are -1 and -4.

$$3n^2(n - 1)(n - 4)$$

C $4x^3 + 18x^2 + 20x$

$$2x(2x^2 + 9x + 10)$$ *Factor out the GCF. There is no pattern.*
$$(\blacksquare x + \blacksquare)(\blacksquare x + \blacksquare)$$ *$a = 2$ and $c = 10$; Outer + Inner = 9*

Factors of 2	Factors of 10	Outer + Inner	
1 and 2	1 and 10	$1(10) + 2(1) = 12$	✗
1 and 2	10 and 1	$1(11) + 2(10) = 21$	✗
1 and 2	2 and 5	$1(5) + 2(2) = 9$	✓

$$(x + 2)(2x + 5)$$

$$2x(x + 2)(2x + 5)$$

D $p^5 - p$

$p(p^4 - 1)$ *Factor out the GCF.*

$p(p^2 + 1)(p^2 - 1)$ *$p^4 - 1$ is a difference of two squares.*

$p(p^2 + 1)(p + 1)(p - 1)$ *$p^2 - 1$ is a difference of two squares.*

 CHECK IT OUT!   **Factor each polynomial completely. Check your answer.**

3a. $3x^2 + 7x + 4$ **3b.** $2p^5 + 10p^4 - 12p^3$

3c. $9q^6 + 30q^5 + 24q^4$ **3d.** $2x^4 + 18$

Methods to Factor Polynomials

Any Polynomial—Look for the greatest common factor.

$ab - ac = a(b - c)$	$6x^2y + 10xy^2 = 2xy(3x + 5y)$

Binomials—Look for a difference of two squares.

$a^2 - b^2 = (a + b)(a - b)$	$x^2 - 9y^2 = (x + 3y)(x - 3y)$

Trinomials—Look for perfect-square trinomials and other factorable trinomials.

$a^2 + 2ab + b^2 = (a + b)^2$	$x^2 + 4x + 4 = (x + 2)^2$
$a^2 - 2ab + b^2 = (a - b)^2$	$x^2 - 2x + 1 = (x - 1)^2$
$x^2 + bx + c = (x + \blacksquare)(x + \blacksquare)$	$x^2 + 3x + 2 = (x + 1)(x + 2)$
$ax^2 + bx + c = (\blacksquare x + \blacksquare)(\blacksquare x + \blacksquare)$	$6x^2 + 7x + 2 = (2x + 1)(3x + 2)$

Polynomials of Four or More Terms—Factor by grouping.

$ax + bx + ay + by = x(a + b) + y(a + b)$ $= (x + y)(a + b)$	$2x^3 + 4x^2 + x + 2 = (2x^3 + 4x^2) + (x + 2)$ $= 2x^2(x + 2) + 1(x + 2)$ $= (x + 2)(2x^2 + 1)$

THINK AND DISCUSS

1. Give an expression that includes a polynomial that is not completely factored.

2. Give an example of an unfactorable binomial and an unfactorable trinomial.

 3. GET ORGANIZED Copy the graphic organizer. Draw an arrow from each expression to the method you would use to factor it.

Factoring Methods	
Polynomial	**Method**
1. $16x^4 - 25y^8$	**A.** Factoring out the GCF
2. $x^2 + 10x + 25$	**B.** Factoring by grouping
3. $9t^2 + 27t + 18t^4$	**C.** Unfactorable
4. $a^2 + 3a - 7a - 21$	**D.** Difference of two squares
5. $100b^2 + 81$	**E.** Perfect-square trinomial

8-6

Exercises

go.hrw.com
Homework Help Online
KEYWORD: MA7 8-6
Parent Resources Online
KEYWORD: MA7 Parent

GUIDED PRACTICE

SEE EXAMPLE 1
p. 586

Tell whether each expression is completely factored. If not, factor it.

1. $3x(9x^2 + 1)$ **2.** $2(4x^3 - 3x^2 - 8x)$ **3.** $2k^2(4 - k^3)$

4. $(2x + 3)(3x - 5)$ **5.** $4(4p^4 - 1)$ **6.** $a(a^3 + 2ab + b^2)$

Factor each polynomial completely. Check your answer.

SEE EXAMPLE 2
p. 587

7. $3x^5 - 12x^3$ **8.** $4x^3 + 8x^2 + 4x$ **9.** $8pq^2 + 8pq + 2p$

10. $18rs^2 - 2r$ **11.** $mn^5 - m^3n$ **12.** $2x^2y - 20xy + 50y$

SEE EXAMPLE 3
p. 587

13. $6x^4 - 3x^3 - 9x^2$ **14.** $3y^2 + 14y + 4$ **15.** $p^5 + 3p^3 + p^2 + 3$

16. $7x^5 + 21x^4 - 28x^3$ **17.** $2z^2 + 11z + 6$ **18.** $9p^2 - q^2 + 3p$

PRACTICE AND PROBLEM SOLVING

Independent Practice

For Exercises	See Example
19–24	1
25–30	2
31–36	3

Extra Practice

Skills Practice p. S19
Application Practice p. S35

Tell whether each expression is completely factored. If not, factor it.

19. $2x(y^3 - 4y^2 + 5y)$ **20.** $2r(25r^6 - 36)$ **21.** $3n^2(n^2 - 25)$

22. $2m(m + 1)(m + 4)$ **23.** $2y^2(4x^2 + 9)$ **24.** $4(7g + 9h^2)$

Factor each polynomial completely. Check your answer.

25. $-4x^3 + 24x^2 - 36x$ **26.** $24r^2 - 6r^4$ **27.** $5d^2 - 60d + 135$

28. $4y^8 + 36y^7 + 81y^6$ **29.** $98x^3 - 50xy^2$ **30.** $4x^3y - 4x^2y - 8xy$

31. $5x^2 - 10x + 14$ **32.** $121x^2 + 36y^2$ **33.** $p^4 - 16$

34. $4m^6 - 30m^5 + 36m^4$ **35.** $2k^3 + 3k^2 + 6k + 9$ **36.** $ab^4 - 16a$

Write an expression for each situation. Factor your expression.

37. the square of Ella's age plus 12 times Ella's age plus 36

38. the square of the distance from point A to point B minus 81

39. the square of the number of seconds Bob can hold his breath minus 16 times the number of seconds plus 28

40. three times the square of the number of apples on a tree minus 22 times the number of apples plus 35

41. the square of Beth's score minus 49

42. **Physics** The height in meters of a ballet dancer's center of mass when she leaps can be modeled by the polynomial $-5t^2 + 30t + 1$, where t is time in seconds after the jump. Tell whether the polynomial is fully factored when written as $-1(5t^2 - 30t - 1)$. Explain.

 43. **Write About It** When asked to factor a polynomial completely, you first determine that the terms in the polynomial do not share any common factors. What would be your next step?

Factor and simplify each expression.

44. $12(x + 1)^2 + 60(x + 1) + 75$ **45.** $(2x + 3)^2 - (x - 4)^2$

46. $45x(x - 2)^2 + 60x(x - 2) + 20x$ **47.** $(3x - 5)^2 - (y + 2)^2$

MULTI-STEP TEST PREP

48. This problem will prepare you for the Multi-Step Test Prep on page 588.
    a. The area of a Marci's rectangular flower garden is $(x^2 + 2x - 15)$ ft². Factor this expression.
    b. Draw a diagram of the garden and label the length and width with your factors from part **a**.
    c. Find the length and width of the flower garden if $x = 7$ ft.

49. **Critical Thinking** Show two methods of factoring $4x^2 - 100$.

50. **Estimation** Estimate the value of $2x^2 + 5xy + 3y^2$ when $x = -10.1$ and $y = 10.05$. (*Hint:* Factor the expression first.)

51. ///**ERROR ANALYSIS**/// Examine the factorization shown. Explain why the factorization is incorrect.

> $12x^2 - 12x - 3$
> $3(4x^2 - 4x - 1)$
> $3(2x - 1)(2x - 1)$

Math History Use the following information for Exercises 52–54.

The triangle at right is called *Pascal's Triangle*. The triangle starts with 1 and each of the other numbers in the triangle is the sum of the two numbers in the row above it.

0					1				
1				1		1			
2			1		2		1		
3		1		3		3		1	
4	1		4		6		4		1
5	1	5		10		10		5	1

Pascal's Triangle can be used to write the product of a binomial raised to an integer power. The numbers in each row give you the coefficients of each term in the product.

$$(a + b)^3 = a^3 + 3a^2b + 3ab^2 + b^3$$

The numbers in row 3 are 1, 3, 3, 1. These are the coefficients of the terms in the product $(a + b)^3$. The power of *a* decreases in each term and the power of *b* increases in each term.

Use the patterns you see in Pascal's Triangle to write the power of the binomial $a + b$ given by each polynomial.

52. $a^6 + 6a^5b + 15a^4b^2 + 20a^3b^3 + 15a^2b^4 + 6ab^5 + b^6 = (a + b)^\blacksquare$

53. $a^8 + 8a^7b + 28a^6b^2 + 56a^5b^3 + 70a^4b^4 + 56a^3b^5 + 28a^2b^6 + 8ab^7 + b^8 = (a + b)^\blacksquare$

54. $a^7 + 7a^6b + 21a^5b^2 + 35a^4b^3 + 35a^3b^4 + 21a^2b^5 + 7ab^6 + b^7 = (a + b)^\blacksquare$

 TEST PREP

55. Which expression equals $6x^2 + 7x - 10$?
    Ⓐ $(6x + 2)(x - 5)$ Ⓒ $(x + 2)(6x - 5)$
    Ⓑ $(2x + 5)(3x - 2)$ Ⓓ $(3x + 2)(2x - 5)$

56. What is the complete factorization of $16x^{12} - 256$?
    Ⓕ $16(x^6 + 4)(x^6 - 4)$ Ⓗ $16(x^6 + 4)(x^3 + 2)(x^3 - 2)$
    Ⓖ $(4x^6 + 16)(4x^6 - 16)$ Ⓙ $(4x^6 + 16)(2x^3 + 4)(2x^3 - 4)$

57. Which of the expressions below represents the fifth step of the factorization?

> **Step 1:** $40a^3 - 60a^2 - 10a + 15$
>
> **Step 2:** $5(8a^3 - 12a^2 - 2a + 3)$
>
> **Step 3:** $5\left[(8a^3 - 12a^2) - (2a - 3)\right]$
>
> **Step 4:** $5\left[4a^2(2a - 3) - 1(2a - 3)\right]$
>
> **Step 5:** �_____
>
> **Step 6:** $5(2a - 3)(2a + 1)(2a - 1)$

(A) $5(2a - 3)(2a + 3)(4a^2 - 1)$ (C) $5(2a - 3)(4a^2 - 1)$
(B) $5(2a - 3)(4a^2 + 1)$ (D) $5(2a - 3)(2a - 3)(4a^2 - 1)$

58. Short Response Use the polynomial $8x^3 + 24x^2 + 18x$ for the following.

a. Factor the polynomial. Explain each step and tell whether you used any rules for special products.

b. Explain another set of steps that could be used to factor the polynomial.

CHALLENGE AND EXTEND

59. Geometry The volume of the cylinder shown is represented by the expression $72\pi p^3 + 48\pi p^2 + 8\pi p$. The height of the cylinder is $8p$.

a. Factor the expression for volume.

b. What expression represents the radius of the cylinder?

c. If the radius is 4 cm, what are the height and volume of the cylinder?

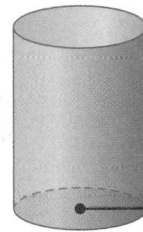

$V = \pi r^2 h$

Factor.

60. $g^7 + g^3 + g^5 + g^4$

61. $h^2 + h^8 + h^6 + h^4$

62. $x^{n+2} + x^{n+1} + x^n$

63. $x^{n+5} + x^{n+4} + x^{n+3}$

64. Geometry The rectangular prism has the dimensions shown.

a. Write expressions for the height and length of the prism using w.

b. Write a polynomial that represents the volume of the prism using w.

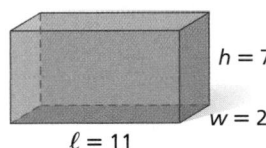

$h = 7$
$w = 2$
$\ell = 11$

SPIRAL REVIEW

Simplify each expression by combining like terms. *(Lesson 1-7)*

65. $-6n + 4n$ **66.** $5x^2 - 8x + 4x^2$ **67.** $2.6r + 9.7r$

Write and solve a proportion to answer each question. *(Lesson 2-7)*

68. The ratio of fiction to nonfiction books on Jessika's shelf is 3 to 4. Jessika has 12 nonfiction books. How many fiction books does she have?

69. The scale of a model car is 23:2. The steering wheel on the model car has a diameter of 3 cm. What is the diameter of the steering wheel on the actual car?

Factor each trinomial. *(Lesson 8-4)*

70. $2x^2 + 13x + 15$ **71.** $4x^2 + 4x - 3$ **72.** $6x^2 - 11x - 10$

MULTI-STEP TEST PREP

Factoring

Shaping the Environment The Environmental Awareness Club is going to plant a garden on the front lawn of the school. Henry suggests a garden in the shape of a square. Theona suggests a rectangular shape.

1. Henry's plans include a square garden with an area of $(x^2 + 12x + 36)$ m². Write expressions for the length and width of the square garden.

2. A drawing of the square garden shows a length of 12 m. What is the width of the square garden? What is the value of x? What is the total area of the square garden?

3. Theona's plans include a rectangular garden with an area of $(x^2 + 14x + 24)$ m². Write expressions for the length and width of the rectangular garden.

4. A drawing of the rectangular garden shows that the length is 6 m longer than the length of the square garden. What is the width of the rectangular garden? How much shorter is the width of the rectangular garden than the square garden?

5. Find the perimeter of each garden in terms of x.

6. Which plan should the club choose if they want the garden that covers the most area? Which plan should the club choose if they want the garden that requires the least fencing around it? Explain your reasoning.

Width = ?

Length = 12 m

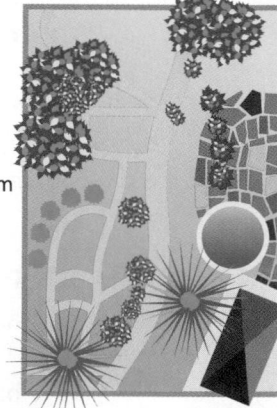

Width = ?

Length = (12 + 6) m

READY TO GO ON?

Quiz for Lessons 8-5 Through 8-6

✔ **8-5** **Factoring Special Products**

Determine whether each trinomial is a perfect square. If so, factor. If not, explain.

1. $x^2 + 8x + 16$

2. $4x^2 - 20x + 25$

3. $x^2 + 3x + 9$

4. $2x^2 - 4x + 4$

5. $9x^2 - 12x + 4$

6. $x^2 - 12x - 36$

7. An architect is designing square windows with an area of $(x^2 + 20x + 100)$ ft². The dimensions of the windows are of the form $ax + b$, where a and b are whole numbers. Find an expression for the perimeter of the windows. Find the perimeter of a window when $x = 4$ ft.

Determine whether each trinomial is a difference of two squares. If so, factor. If not, explain.

8. $x^2 - 121$

9. $4t^2 - 20$

10. $1 - 9y^4$

11. $25m^2 - 4m^6$

12. $16x^2 + 49$

13. $r^4 - t^2$

14. The area of a square is $(36d^2 - 36d + 9)$ in².

 a. What expression represents the length of a side of the square?

 b. What expression represents the perimeter of the square?

 c. What are the length of a side, the perimeter, and the area of the square when $d = 2$ in.?

✔ **8-6** **Choosing a Factoring Method**

Tell whether each expression is completely factored. If not, factor it.

15. $5(x^2 + 3x + 1)$

16. $6x(5x^2 - x)$

17. $3t(t^4 - 9)$

18. $2(m^2 - 10m + 25)$

19. $3(2y^2 - 5)(y + 1)$

20. $(2n + 6)(n - 4)$

Factor each polynomial completely. Check your answer.

21. $3x^3 - 12x^2 + 12x$

22. $16m^3 - 4m$

23. $5x^3y - 45xy$

24. $3t^2 + 5t - 1$

25. $3c^2 + 12c - 63$

26. $x^5 - 81x$

Write an expression for each situation. Then factor your expression.

27. the difference of the square of a board's length and 36

28. the square of Michael's age minus 8 times Michael's age plus 16

29. two times the square of a car's speed plus 2 times the car's speed minus 12

30. three times the cube of Jessie's height plus 3 times the square of Jessie's height minus 6 times Jessie's height

31. Write an expression for the area of the shaded region. Then factor the expression.

Study Guide: Review

Vocabulary

greatest common factor 544   prime factorization 544

Complete the sentences below with vocabulary words from the list above.

1. A number written as a product so that each of its factors has no factors other than 1 and itself is the ___?___ .

2. The ___?___ of two monomials is the greatest of the factors that the monomials share.

8-1 Factors and Greatest Common Factors (pp. 544–549)

EXAMPLES

■ Write the prime factorization of 84.

84

4 · 21

②·②·③·⑦

Write as a product. Continue until all factors are prime.

■ Write the prime factorization of 75.

$$\begin{array}{r|r} 3 & 75 \\ 5 & 25 \\ 5 & 5 \\ \hline & 1 \end{array}$$

Keep dividing by prime factors until the quotient is 1.

$75 = 3 \cdot 5 \cdot 5 = 3 \cdot 5^2$

■ Find the GCF of 36 and 90.

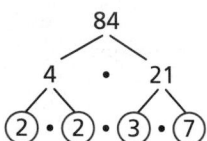
$36 = 2 \cdot 2 \cdot 3 \cdot 3$
$90 = 2 \cdot 3 \cdot 3 \cdot 5$

$2 \cdot 3 \cdot 3 = 18$

The GCF of 36 and 90 is 18.

Write the prime factorization of each number. Find the product of the common factors.

■ Find the GCF of $10x^5$ and $4x^2$.

$10x^5 = 2 \cdot 5 \cdot x \cdot x \cdot x \cdot x \cdot x$
$4x^2 = 2 \cdot 2 \cdot x \cdot x$

$2 \cdot x \cdot x = 2x^2$

The GCF of $10x^5$ and $4x^2$ is $2x^2$.

Write the prime factorization of each coefficient. Write powers as products. Find the product of the common factors.

EXERCISES

Write the prime factorization of each number.

3. 12   **4.** 20

5. 32   **6.** 23

7. 40   **8.** 64

9. 66   **10.** 114

Find the GCF of each pair of numbers.

11. 15 and 50

12. 36 and 132

13. 29 and 30

14. 54 and 81

15. 20 and 48

Find the GCF of each pair of monomials.

16. $9m$ and 3

17. $4x$ and $2x^2$

18. $-18b^4$ and $27b^2$

19. $100r$ and $25r^5$

20. A hardware store carries 42 types of boxed nails and 36 types of boxed screws. The store manager wants to build a rack so that he can display the hardware in rows. He wants to put the same number of boxes in each row, but he wants no row to contain both nails and screws. What is the greatest number of boxes that he can display in one row? How many rows will there be if the manager puts the greatest number of boxes in each row?

8-2 Factoring by GCF (pp. 551–557)

EXAMPLES

■ Factor $3t^3 - 9t^2$. Check your answer.

$3t^3 = 3 \cdot t \cdot t \cdot t$
$9t^2 = 3 \cdot 3 \cdot t \cdot t$ *Find the GCF.*

GCF: $3 \cdot t \cdot t = 3t^2$

$3t^3 - 9t^2 = 3t^2(t) - 3t^2(3)$
$\qquad\quad = 3t^2(t - 3)$ *Factor out the GCF.*

Check $3t^2(t - 3) = 3t^3 - 9t^2$ ✓

■ Factor $-12s - 6s^3$. Check your answer.

$-1(12s + 6s^3)$ *Factor out −1.*

$12s = 2 \cdot 2 \cdot 3 \cdot s$
$6s^3 = 2 \cdot \quad 3 \cdot s \cdot s \cdot s$ *Find the GCF.*

GCF: $2 \cdot 3 \cdot s = 6s$

$-1(12s + 6s^3)$
$-1[(6s)(2) + (6s)(s^2)]$
$-1[(6s)(2 + s^2)]$
$-6s(2 + s^2)$ *Factor out the GCF.*

Check $-6s(2 + s^2) = -12s - 6s^3$ ✓

■ Factor $5(x - 7) + 3x(x - 7)$ by grouping.

$5(x - 7) + 3x(x - 7)$ *(x − 7) is a*
                                 common factor.

$(x - 7)(5 + 3x)$ *Factor out (x − 7).*

■ Factor $6b^3 + 8b + 15b^2 + 20$ by grouping.

$(6b^3 + 8b) + (15b^2 + 20)$ *Group terms that*
                                  have a common
                                  factor.

$2b(3b^2 + 4) + 5(3b^2 + 4)$ *Factor each group.*

$(3b^2 + 4)(2b + 5)$ *Factor out*
                              $(3b^2 + 4)$.

■ Factor $2m^3 - 6m^2 + 15 - 5m$. Check your answer.

$(2m^3 - 6m^2) + (15 - 5m)$ *Group terms.*
$2m^2(m - 3) + 5(3 - m)$ *Factor each*
                               group.

$2m^2(m - 3) + 5(-1)(m - 3)$ *Rewrite (3 − m)*
                                  as (−1)(m − 3).

$2m^2(m - 3) - 5(m - 3)$ *Simplify.*
$(m - 3)(2m^2 - 5)$ *Factor out*
                              (m − 3).

Check $(m - 3)(2m^2 - 5)$

$\qquad\qquad 2m^3 - 5m - 6m^2 + 15$
$\qquad\qquad 2m^3 - 6m^2 + 15 - 5m$ ✓

EXERCISES

Factor each polynomial. Check your answer.

21. $5x - 15x^3$ **22.** $-16b + 32$

23. $-14v - 21$ **24.** $4a^2 - 12a - 8$

25. $5g^5 - 10g^3 - 15g$ **26.** $40p^2 - 10p + 30$

27. A civil engineer needs the area of a rectangular lot to be $(6x^2 + 5x)$ ft^2. Factor this polynomial to find possible expressions for the dimensions of the lot.

Factor each expression.

28. $2x(x - 4) + 9(x - 4)$

29. $t(3t + 5) - 6(3t + 5)$

30. $5(6 - n) - 3n(6 - n)$

31. $b(b + 4) + 2(b + 4)$

32. $x^2(x - 3) + 7(x - 3)$

Factor each polynomial. Check your answer.

33. $n^3 + n - 4n^2 - 4$

34. $6b^2 - 8b + 15b - 20$

35. $2h^3 - 7h + 14h^2 - 49$

36. $3t^2 + 18t + t + 6$

37. $10m^3 + 15m^2 - 2m - 3$

38. $8p^3 + 4p - 6p^2 - 3$

39. $5r - 10 + 2r - r^2$

40. $b^3 - 5b + 15 - 3b^2$

41. $6t - t^3 - 4t^2 + 24$

42. $12h - 3h^2 + h - 4$

43. $d - d^2 + d - 1$

44. $6b - 5b^2 + 10b - 12$

45. $5t - t^2 - t + 5$

46. $8b^2 - 2b^3 - 5b + 20$

47. $3r - 3r^2 - 1 + r$

48. Write an expression for the area of each of the two rectangles shown. Then write and factor an expression for the combined area.

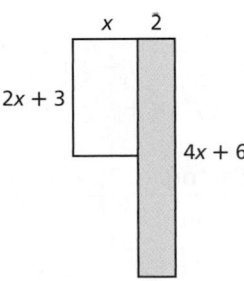

8-3 Factoring $x^2 + bx + c$ (pp. 560–567)

EXAMPLES

Factor each trinomial. Check your answer.

■ $x^2 + 14x + 45$

$(x + \boxed{})(x + \boxed{})$ *Look for factors of 45*

$(x + 9)(x + 5)$ *whose sum is 14.*

Check $(x + 9)(x + 5) = x^2 + 5x + 9x + 45$

$= x^2 + 14x + 45$ ✓

■ $x^2 + 6x - 27$

$(x + \boxed{})(x - \boxed{})$ *Look for factors of −27*

$(x + 9)(x - 3)$ *whose sum is 6.*

Check $(x + 9)(x - 3) = x^2 - 3x + 9x - 27$

$= x^2 + 6x - 27$ ✓

EXERCISES

Factor each trinomial. Check your answer.

49. $x^2 + 6x + 5$ **50.** $x^2 + 6x + 8$

51. $x^2 + 8x + 15$ **52.** $x^2 - 8x + 12$

53. $x^2 + 10x + 25$ **54.** $x^2 - 13x + 22$

55. $x^2 + 24x + 80$ **56.** $x^2 - 26x + 120$

57. $x^2 + 5x - 84$ **58.** $x^2 - 5x - 24$

59. $x^2 - 3x - 28$ **60.** $x^2 + 4x - 5$

61. $x^2 + x - 6$ **62.** $x^2 + x - 20$

63. $x^2 - 2x - 48$ **64.** $x^2 - 5x - 36$

65. $x^2 - 6x - 72$ **66.** $x^2 - 3x - 70$

67. $x^2 + 14x - 120$ **68.** $x^2 + 6x - 7$

69. The rectangle shown has an area of $\left(y^2 + 8y + 15\right)$ m². What is the width of the rectangle?

8-4 Factoring $ax^2 + bx + c$ (pp. 568–574)

EXAMPLES

Factor each trinomial.

■ $6x^2 + 17x + 5$

$\left(\boxed{}x + \boxed{}\right)\left(\boxed{}x + \boxed{}\right)$ *a = 6 and c = 5;*

Outer + Inner = 17

Factors of 6	Factors of 5	Outer + Inner	
1 and 6	5 and 1	$1(1) + 6(5) = 31$	✗
2 and 3	1 and 5	$2(5) + 3(1) = 13$	✗
2 and 3	5 and 1	$1(1) + 3(5) = 17$	✓

$(2x + 5)(3x + 1)$

■ $2n^2 - n - 10$

$\left(\boxed{}n + \boxed{}\right)\left(\boxed{}n + \boxed{}\right)$ *a = 2 and c = −10;*

Outer + Inner = −1

Factors of 2	Factors of −10	Outer + Inner	
1 and 2	1 and −10	$1(-10) + 2(1) = -8$	✗
1 and 2	−1 and 10	$1(10) + 2(-1) = 8$	✗
1 and 2	2 and −5	$1(-5) + 2(2) = -1$	✓

$(1n + 2)(2n - 5) = (n + 2)(2n - 5)$

EXERCISES

Factor each trinomial. Check your answer.

70. $2x^2 + 11x + 5$ **71.** $3x^2 + 10x + 7$

72. $2x^2 - 3x + 1$ **73.** $3x^2 + 8x + 4$

74. $5x^2 + 28x + 15$ **75.** $6x^2 - 19x + 15$

76. $4x^2 + 13x + 10$ **77.** $3x^2 + 10x + 8$

78. $7x^2 - 37x + 10$ **79.** $9x^2 + 18x + 8$

80. $2x^2 - x - 1$ **81.** $3x^2 - 11x - 4$

82. $2x^2 - 11x + 5$ **83.** $7x^2 - 19x - 6$

84. $5x^2 - 9x - 2$ **85.** $-6x^2 - x + 2$

86. $6x^2 - x - 5$ **87.** $6x^2 + 17x - 14$

88. $-4x^2 + 8x + 5$ **89.** $-10x^2 + 11x + 6$

90. Write the polynomial modeled and then factor.

8-5 Factoring Special Products (pp. 578–584)

EXAMPLES

■ Determine whether $x^2 + 18x + 81$ is a perfect square. If so, factor. If not, explain.

The trinomial is of the form $a^2 + 2ab + b^2$, so it is a perfect-square trinomial.

$x^2 + 18x + 81 = (x + 9)^2$

■ Determine whether $49x^4 - 25y^6$ is a difference of two squares. If so, factor. If not, explain.

$$49x^4 - 25y^6$$

$7x^2 \cdot 7x^2 \quad 5y^3 \cdot 5y^3$

The binomial is a difference of two squares.

$$\left(7x^2\right)^2 - \left(5y^3\right)^2$$

$a = 7x^2$, $b = 5x^3$

$$\left(7x^2 + 5y^3\right)\left(7x^2 - 5y^3\right)$$

Write the binomial as $(a + b)(a - b)$.

$$49x^4 - 25y^6 = \left(7x^2 + 5y^3\right)\left(7x^2 - 5y^3\right)$$

EXERCISES

Determine whether each trinomial is a perfect square. If so, factor. If not, explain.

91. $x^2 + 12x + 36$ **92.** $x^2 + 5x + 25$

93. $4x^2 - 2x + 1$ **94.** $9x^2 + 12x + 4$

95. $16x^2 + 8x + 4$ **96.** $x^2 + 14x + 49$

Determine whether each binomial is a difference of two squares. If so, factor. If not, explain.

97. $100x^2 - 81$ **98.** $x^2 - 2$

99. $5x^4 - 10y^6$ **100.** $(-12)^2 - \left(x^3\right)^2$

101. $121b^2 + 9c^8$ **102.** $100p^2 - 25q^2$

Factor each polynomial using the rule for perfect-square trinomials or the rule for a difference of two squares. Tell which rule you used.

103. $x^2 - 25$ **104.** $x^2 + 20x + 100$

105. $j^2 - k^4$ **106.** $9x^2 - 42x + 49$

107. $81x^2 + 144x + 64$ **108.** $16b^4 - 121c^6$

8-6 Choosing a Factoring Method (pp. 586–591)

EXAMPLES

■ Tell whether $(3x - 9)(x + 4)$ is completely factored. If not, factor it.

$(3x - 9)(x + 4)$ *$3x - 9$ can be factored.*

$3(x - 3)(x + 4)$ *Factor out 3, the GCF of $3x$ and 9.*

■ $3ab^2 - 48a$

$3a\left(b^2 - 16\right)$ *Factor out the GCF.*

$3a(b + 4)(b - 4)$ *Factor the difference of two squares.*

Check $3a(b + 4)(b - 4) = 3a\left(b^2 - 16\right)$

$= 3ab^2 - 48a$ ✓

■ $2m^3 + 4m^2 - 48m$

$2m\left(m^2 + 2m - 24\right)$ *Factor out the GCF.*

$2m(m - 4)(m + 6)$ *Factor the trinomial.*

Check $2m(m - 4)(m + 6)$

$2m\left(m^2 + 2m - 24\right)$

$2m^3 + 4m^2 - 48m$ ✓

EXERCISES

Tell whether each polynomial is completely factored. If not, factor it.

109. $4x^2 + 10x + 6 = (4x + 6)(x + 1)$

110. $3y^2 + 75 = 3\left(y^2 + 25\right)$

111. $b^4 - 81 = \left(b^2 + 9\right)\left(b^2 - 9\right)$

112. $x^2 - 6x + 9 = (x - 3)^2$

Factor each polynomial completely. Check your answer.

113. $4x^2 - 64$ **114.** $3b^5 - 6b^4 - 24b^3$

115. $a^4b^3 - a^2b^5$ **116.** $t^{20} - t^4$

117. $5x^2 + 20x + 15$ **118.** $2x^4 - 50x^2$

119. $8t + 32 + 2st + 8s$

120. $25m^3 - 90m^2 - 40m$

121. $32x^4 - 48x^3 + 8x^2 - 12x$

122. $6s^4t + 12s^3t^2 + 6s^2t^3$

123. $10m^3 + 4m^2 - 90m - 36$

CHAPTER TEST

Find the GCF of each pair of monomials.

1. $3t^4$ and $8t^2$

2. $2y^3$ and $-12y$

3. $15n^5$ and $9n^4$

4. Write the prime factorization of 360.

5. A coin collector is arranging a display of three types of nickels. The types of nickels and number of each type are shown in the table. The collector wants to arrange them in rows with the same number in each row without having different types in the same row. How many rows will she need if she puts the greatest possible number of nickels in each row?

Type of Nickel	Number of Nickels
Liberty	16
Buffalo	24
Jefferson	40

Factor each expression.

6. $24m^2 + 4m^3$

7. $9x^5 - 12x$

8. $-2r^4 - 6$

9. $3(c - 5) + 4c(c - 5)$

10. $10x^3 + 4x - 25x^2 - 10$

11. $4y^3 - 4y^2 - 3 + 3y$

12. A model rocket is shot vertically from a deck into the air at a speed of 50 m/s. The expression $-5t^2 + 50t + 5$ gives the approximate height of the rocket after t seconds. Factor this expression.

Factor each trinomial.

13. $x^2 + 6x + 5$

14. $x^2 - 4x - 21$

15. $x^2 - 8x + 15$

16. $2x^2 + 9x + 7$

17. $2x^2 + 9x - 18$

18. $-3x^2 - 2x + 8$

Determine whether each trinomial is a perfect square. If so, factor. If not, explain.

19. $a^2 + 14a + 49$

20. $2x^2 + 10x + 25$

21. $9t^2 - 6t + 1$

Determine whether each binomial is a difference of two squares. If so, factor. If not, explain.

22. $b^2 - 16$

23. $25y^2 - 10$

24. $9a^2 - b^{10}$

25. A company is producing square sheets of plastic. Each has an area of $(9x^2 + 30x + 25)$ ft^2. The dimensions of each sheet are of the form $ax + b$, where a and b are whole numbers. Find an expression for the perimeter of a sheet. Find the perimeter when $x = 4$ ft.

Tell whether each expression is completely factored. If not, factor it.

26. $(6x - 3)(x + 5)$

27. $(v^5 + 10)(v^5 - 10)$

28. $(2b + 3)(3b - 2)$

Factor each polynomial completely.

29. $8x^3 + 72x^2 + 160x$

30. $3x^5 - 27x^3$

31. $8x^3 + 64x^2 - 20x - 160$

32. $cd^4 - c^7d^6$

33. $100x^2 - 80x + 16$

34. $7m^8 - 7$

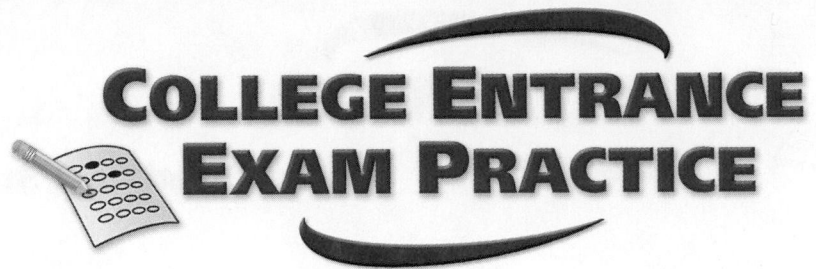

FOCUS ON ACT

The ACT Mathematics test booklet usually has writing space for scratch work. You may not bring your own scratch paper to the testing center. Remember that any scratch work done in the test booklet is for your use only and will not be scored. Be sure to transfer your final answer to the answer sheet.

If you are unsure how to solve a problem, look through the answer choices. They may provide you with a clue to the solution method. It may take longer to work backward from the answer choices, so make sure you monitor your time.

You may want to time yourself as you take this practice test. It should take you about 6 minutes to complete.

1. What is the value of $c^2 - d^2$ if $c + d = 7$ and $c - d = -2$?

   (A) -14

   (B) -5

   (C) 5

   (D) 14

   (E) 45

2. Which of the following is the complete factorization of $6a^3b + 3a^2b^3$?

   (F) $6a^3b^3$

   (G) $9a^5b^4$

   (H) $3ab(2a^2 + ab^2)$

   (J) $3a^2b(2a + b^2)$

   (K) $(6a^3b)(3a^2b^3)$

3. Which of the following is a factor of $x^2 + 3x - 18$?

   (A) $x + 2$

   (B) $x + 3$

   (C) $x + 6$

   (D) $x + 9$

   (E) $x + 18$

4. The binomial $x - 3$ is NOT a factor of which of the following trinomials?

   (F) $2x^2 - x - 3$

   (G) $2x^2 - 5x - 3$

   (H) $2x^2 - 8x + 6$

   (J) $3x^2 - 6x - 9$

   (K) $3x^2 - 10x + 3$

5. For what value of n is $4x^2 + 20x + n^2 = (2x + n)^2$ true for any real number x?

   (A) 4

   (B) 5

   (C) 8

   (D) 10

   (E) 25

6. What is the factored form of $x^2 + \frac{2x}{3} + \frac{x}{2} + \frac{2}{6}$?

   (F) $\left(x + \frac{1}{3}\right)\left(x + \frac{1}{2}\right)$

   (G) $\left(x + \frac{1}{2}\right)\left(x + \frac{2}{3}\right)$

   (H) $\left(x + \frac{2}{3}\right)\left(x + \frac{1}{6}\right)$

   (J) $(x + 2)\left(x + \frac{1}{3}\right)$

   (K) $\left(x + \frac{1}{3}\right)\left(x + \frac{2}{3}\right)$

TEST TACKLER

Any Question Type: Translate Words to Math

When reading a word problem, look for key words and context clues to help you translate the words into a mathematical equation or expression.

Some key words, such as those shown in this table, represent certain mathematical operations.

Action	Math Operation
Combining, increasing	Addition
Decreasing, reducing	Subtraction
Increasing or decreasing by a factor	Multiplication
Separating	Division

EXAMPLE

Short Response The polynomial $x^2 + 7x + 12$ represents the area of a rectangle in square meters. The width is $(x + 3)$ meters. Find the combined measure of the length and the width.

Use action words and context clues to translate the words into equations.

$x^2 + 7x + 12$ represents the area of a rectangle in square meters.
$x^2 + 7x + 12 \quad = \quad A$
The width is $(x + 3)$ meters.
$\quad w \quad = (x + 3)$
Find the combined measure of the length and the width.
$\quad m \quad = \quad \ell \quad + \quad w$

Now use the equations to solve the problem.

$A = \ell w$	*Write the formula for area of a rectangle.*
$x^2 + 7x + 12 = \ell(x + 3)$	*Substitute $x^2 + 7x + 12$ for A and $(x + 3)$ for w.*
$(x + \boxed{?})(x + 3)$	*Factor $x^2 + 7x + 12$ to find an expression for the length.*
$(x + 4)(x + 3)$	*$3(4) = 12; 3 + 4 = 7$*

The length is $(x + 4)$.

$m = \ell + w$	*Write the equation for the combined measure of the length and width.*
$m = (x + 4) + (x + 3)$	*Substitute $(x + 4)$ for ℓ and $(x + 3)$ for w.*
$m = 2x + 7$	*Combine like terms.*

The combined measure of the length and width is $(2x + 7)$ meters.

Sometimes you cannot write an expression or equation in the order that the key words appear. For example, the expression "4 years younger than Maria" is written mathematically as $m - 4$.

Read each test item and answer the questions that follow.

Item A
Short Response The width of Alvin's rectangular mural is 6 times the length x. Alvin plans to make a new mural with an area of $(6x^2 - 24x + 24)$ square meters. By how much did Alvin decrease the area of the mural? Show your work.

1. What key words or context clues are in the first sentence of the test item? Use these clues to write an expression that represents the width of the rectangle.

2. Write an equation to represent the area of Alvin's first mural.

3. What math operation does the key word *decrease* represent?

Item B
Multiple Choice Which factored expression represents the phrase shown below?

the square of the number of hours it takes to empty a cistern minus 20 times the number of hours plus 64

Ⓐ $(h - 16)(h - 4)$ Ⓒ $(h - 8)(h - 8)$

Ⓑ $(h^2 - 20)(h - 64)$ Ⓓ $(h - 16)(h + 4)$

4. Which word in the phrase tells you to use an exponent in your expression?

5. What is the unknown value in the expression? Define a variable to represent this value.

6. Identify other key words and the mathematical operation phrase each one represents.

Item C
Multiple Choice A company owns two packaging plants. The polynomial $0.05x^2 + 16x - 9400$ models one plant's profit, where x is the number of units packaged. The polynomial $-0.01x^2 + 17x - 5400$ models the other plant's profit. If x is 25,000, what is the total profit of both plants?

Ⓐ $-\$5,830,300$

Ⓑ $\$25,810,200$

Ⓒ $\$31,640,500$

Ⓓ $\$37,471,000$

7. What mathematical symbol does the word *models* represent?

8. Write an equation for each plant that can be used to determine its profit P.

9. What mathematical operation does the term "total profit" represent?

Item D
Gridded Response One of the bases of a trapezoid is 12 meters greater than its height. The other base is 4 meters less than its height. Find the area of the trapezoid when the height is 6 meters.

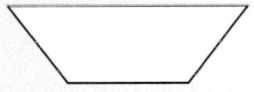

10. Identify the unknown dimension, and assign it a variable.

11. A student is unsure how many bases a trapezoid has. Identify the context clues that can help this student.

12. Make a list of the key words in the problem, and link each word to its mathematical meaning.

13. Write an expression for each base of the trapezoid.

CUMULATIVE ASSESSMENT, CHAPTERS 1–8

Multiple Choice

1. A rectangle has an area of $(x^2 + 5x - 24)$ square units. Which of the following are possible expressions for the length and the width of the rectangle?

- Ⓐ Length: $(x - 24)$ units; width: $(x + 1)$ units
- Ⓑ Length: $(x - 4)$ units; width: $(x + 6)$ units
- Ⓒ Length: $(x - 3)$ units; width: $(x + 8)$ units
- Ⓓ Length: $(x + 12)$ units; width: $(x - 2)$ units

2. Which property of real numbers is used to transform the equation in Step 1 into the equation in Step 2?

Step 1: $4(x - 5) + 8 = 88$
Step 2: $4x - 20 + 8 = 88$
Step 3: $4x - 12 = 88$
Step 4: $4x = 100$
Step 5: $4x = 25$

- Ⓕ Commutative Property of Multiplication
- Ⓖ Associative Property of Multiplication
- Ⓗ Multiplication Property
- Ⓙ Distributive Property

3. If $\frac{2}{3}x - 9 = 3$, what is the value of the expression $8x - 3$?

- Ⓐ -75
- Ⓒ 61
- Ⓑ -35
- Ⓓ 141

4. Carlos and Bonita were just hired at a manufacturing plant. Carlos will earn $12.50 per hour. He will receive a hiring bonus of $300. Bonita will not get a hiring bonus, but she will earn $14.50 per hour. Which equation can you use to determine the number of hours h when both employees will have earned the same total amount?

- Ⓕ $300 + 14.50h = 12.50h$
- Ⓖ $14.50h + 300 = 12.50h$
- Ⓗ $14.50h + 12.50h = 300$
- Ⓙ $300 + 12.50h = 14.50h$

5. Which of the following expressions is equivalent to $x^2 - 8x + 16$?

- Ⓐ $(x + 4)^2$
- Ⓒ $(x + 8)(x + 2)$
- Ⓑ $(x + 4)(x - 4)$
- Ⓓ $(x - 4)^2$

6. An amusement park has two jumping attractions called moonbounces in the shape of similar cubes. The larger moonbounce has a volume of 4800 cubic feet. The smaller moonbounce is half the length of the larger one. What is the volume of the smaller moonbounce?

- Ⓕ 300 cubic feet
- Ⓖ 600 cubic feet
- Ⓗ 1200 cubic feet
- Ⓙ 2400 cubic feet

7. What is the value of y if the line through $(1, -1)$ and $(2, 2)$ is parallel to the line through $(-2, 1)$ and $(-1, y)$?

- Ⓐ -8
- Ⓒ 3
- Ⓑ -2
- Ⓓ 4

8. Which of the following shows the complete factorization of $2x^3 + 4x^2 - 6x$?

- Ⓕ $(2x^2 - 2x)(x + 3)$
- Ⓖ $2x(x^2 + 2x - 3)$
- Ⓗ $2x(x - 1)(x + 3)$
- Ⓙ $2(x^3 + 2x^2 - 3x)$

9. Which graph shows the solution set of the compound inequality $-9 \le 5 - 2x \le 13$?

Ⓐ

Ⓑ

Ⓒ

Ⓓ

10. Which point lies on the graph of both functions?

$f(x) = 2x - 10$
$g(x) = 10 - 2x$

 (F) (5, 0)   (H) (0, 0)

 (G) (1, −8)   (J) (2, 6)

11. Hayley plans to solve the system of equations below.

$$\begin{cases} x + 3y = 8 \\ 5x - y = 8 \end{cases}$$

Which of the following does NOT show an equation Hayley can use to solve the system of equations?

 (A) $x + 3(5x - 8) = 8$

 (B) $5(8 - 3y) - y = 8$

 (C) $x = 8 - 3y$

 (D) $5x - (-x + 8) = 8$

12. Which value of b would make $x^2 + bx - 2$ factorable?

 (F) −2   (H) 0

 (G) −1   (J) 3

13. Which expression is equivalent to $5(x - 2) + 4x$?

 (A) $5x - 10$ (C) $9x - 10$

 (B) $9x - 2$ (D) $20x - 2$

Gridded Response

14. The complete factorization of $-12x^3 + 14x^2 + 6x$ is $-2x(ax + 1)(2x - 3)$. What is the value of a?

15. The expression $x^2 + x + b$ is a perfect-square trinomial. What is the value of b?

16. Margaret is buying a $35 sweater that is on sale for 20% off. What is the total price of the sweater, in dollars, when 5% sales tax is added?

17. A car is traveling at a constant speed. In 4 hours, the car travels 220 miles. How many hours will it take the car to travel 550 miles?

Short Response

18. The area of a certain circle is $\pi(9x^2 + 6x + 1)$ square centimeters. Find an expression for the length of the circle's radius. Explain how you found your answer.

19. A rectangle has an area of $(x^2 - 25)$ square feet.

 a. Use factoring to write possible expressions for the length and width of the rectangle.

 b. Use your expressions from part **a** to write an expression for the perimeter of the rectangle. Simplify the expression.

 c. Use your expressions from parts **a** and **b** to find the perimeter and the area of the rectangle when $x = 10$ feet. Show your work.

20. Write the numbers 57,000,000,000 and 19,000 in scientific notation. Then show how to divide 57,000,000,000 by 19,000 using properties of exponents.

21. Show that you can factor the expression $x^2y - 12 + 3y - 4x^2$ by grouping in two different ways.

Extended Response

22. The diagram below can be used to show that the expression $(a + b)^2$ is equivalent to the expression $a^2 + 2ab + b^2$.

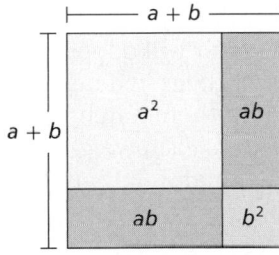

 a. Make a diagram similar to the one above to model the expression $(a + b + c)^2$. Label each distinct area.

 b. Use the labels from your diagram to write an expression equivalent to $(a + b + c)^2$.

 c. Show that your expression in part **b** is equivalent to $(a + b + c)^2$ by evaluating each expression for $a = 4$, $b = 2$, and $c = 1$.

 d. Factor $x^2 + y^2 + 9 + 2xy + 6x + 6y$. Show or explain how you found your answer.

Real-World CONNECTIONS

South Carolina

Columbia

Myrtle Beach

⭐ Alligator Adventure

Alligator Adventure is a tourist attraction in North Myrtle Beach, South Carolina. Its exhibits feature alligators, snakes, Galapagos tortoises, bears, frogs, lizards, tropical birds, and crocodiles.

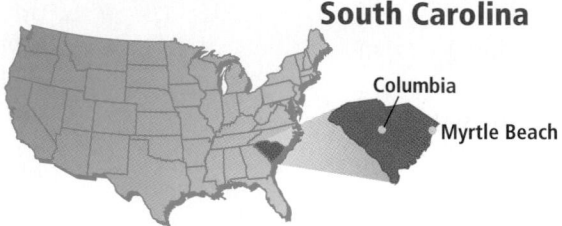

Choose one or more strategies to solve each problem.

1. At birth, alligators are about 8 inches long. Adult male alligators can grow up to 18 feet long. How many times as long as a newborn alligator is an alligator that measures 18 feet?

2. Alligators build their nests out of dirt, grass, and leaves. The female alligator will deposit 40 to 50 eggs in her nest. Suppose there were 40 eggs in a nest and 80 percent of them hatched. The baby alligators each weigh 3 ounces. What is the total weight of the hatched alligators?

3. Most alligators have U-shaped snouts while most crocodiles have V-shaped snouts. Which of the equations below has a graph that could model the shape of an alligator's snout? Explain.

$$y = 3x - 4$$
$$y = x^2 - 12$$
$$y = |x^2 - 4|$$

★ Melton Memorial Observatory

Melton Memorial Observatory is run by the University of South Carolina in Columbia, South Carolina. The table lists some of the stars that can be seen from the observatory.

A light-year is the distance light can travel in one year, which is 9,500,000,000,000 kilometers.

Eight of the Brightest Stars as Seen from Earth				
Name	Rank	Apparent Magnitude	Distance from Earth (light-years)	Temperature (kelvins)
Sirius	1	−1.46	8.6	9,400
Arcturus	4	−0.04	34	4,290
Vega	5	0.03	25	9,600
Procyon	8	0.38	11.4	6,500
Altair	12	0.77	16	7,550
Spica	14	0.98	220	22,400
Deneb	20	1.25	1500	8,400
Regulus	25	1.35	69	12,000

Choose one or more strategies and use the table to solve each problem.

1. Write 1 light-year as a distance in kilometers in scientific notation. Write the distance in kilometers of each star from Earth in scientific notation.

2. Order the stars from closest to Earth to farthest from Earth.

3. Identify which star is farthest from and which is closest to Earth. Approximate how many times as far as the closest star the farthest star is.

Apparent magnitude is a measure of how bright a star (or other object) appears from Earth. The lower the apparent magnitude of a star, the brighter the star appears.

4. Describe the correlation between apparent magnitude and distance from Earth in light-years. Make a scatter plot to support your answer.

Chapter

- Graph quadratic functions.
- Solve quadratic equations.
- Use quadratic functions and equations to solve real-world problems.

FREE *Falling*

Physicists use quadratic equations to describe the motion of falling objects, such as water over a waterfall.

go.hrw.com
Chapter Project Online
KEYWORD: MA7 ChProj

ARE YOU READY?

✓ Vocabulary

Match each term on the left with a definition on the right.

1. factoring

2. quadratic

3. trinomial

4. x-intercept

A. the process of writing a number or an algebraic expression as a product

B. the x-coordinate(s) of the point(s) where a graph intersects the x-axis

C. a polynomial with three terms

D. a polynomial with degree 2

E. the first number of an ordered pair of numbers that describes the location of a point on the coordinate plane

✓ Graph Functions

Graph each function for the given domain.

5. $y = -2x + 8$; D: $\{-4, -2, 0, 2, 4\}$

6. $y = (x + 1)^2$; D: $\{-3, -2, -1, 0, 1\}$

7. $y = x^2 + 3$; D: $\{-2, -1, 0, 1, 2\}$

8. $y = 2x^2$; D: all real numbers

✓ Multiply Binomials

Find each product.

9. $(m + 2)(m + 5)$

10. $(y - 7)(y + 2)$

11. $(2a + 4)(5a + 6)$

12. $(x + 1)(x + 1)$

13. $(t + 5)(t + 5)$

14. $(3n - 8)(3n - 8)$

✓ Factor Trinomials

Factor each polynomial completely.

15. $x^2 - 2x + 1$

16. $x^2 - x - 2$

17. $x^2 - 6x + 5$

18. $x^2 - x - 12$

19. $x^2 - 9x + 18$

20. $x^2 - 7x - 18$

✓ Squares and Square Roots

Find each square root.

21. $\sqrt{36}$

22. $\sqrt{121}$

23. $-\sqrt{64}$

24. $\sqrt{16}\sqrt{81}$

25. $\sqrt{\dfrac{9}{25}}$

26. $-\sqrt{6(24)}$

✓ Solve Multi-Step Equations

Solve each equation.

27. $3m + 5 = 11$

28. $3t + 4 = 10$

29. $5n + 13 = 28$

30. $2(k - 4) + k = 7$

31. $10 = \dfrac{r}{3} + 8$

32. $2(y - 6) = 8.6$

Study Guide: Preview

Where You've Been

Previously, you

- identified and graphed linear functions.
- transformed linear functions.
- solved linear equations.
- factored quadratic polynomials, including perfect-square trinomials.

In This Chapter

You will study

- identifying and graphing quadratic functions.
- transforming quadratic equations.
- solving quadratic equations.
- using factoring to graph quadratic functions and solve quadratic equations.

Where You're Going

You can use the skills in this chapter

- to determine the maximum height of a ball thrown into the air.
- to graph higher-degree polynomials in future math classes, including Algebra 2.
- to solve problems about the height of launched or thrown objects in Physics.

Key Vocabulary/Vocabulario

axis of symmetry	eje de simetría
completing the square	completar el cuadrado
maximum	máximo
minimum	mínimo
parabola	parábola
quadratic equation	ecuación cuadrática
quadratic function	función cuadrática
vertex	vértice
zero of a function	cero de una función

Vocabulary Connections

To become familiar with some of the vocabulary terms in the chapter, consider the following. You may refer to the chapter, the glossary, or a dictionary if you like.

1. The value of a function is determined by its rule. The rule is an algebraic expression. What is true about the algebraic expression that determines a **quadratic function**?

2. The shape of a **parabola** is similar to the shape of an open parachute. Predict the shape of a *parabola*.

3. A **minimum** is a point on the graph of a curve with the least *y*-coordinate. How might a **maximum** be described?

4. An axis is an imaginary line. Use this information and your understanding of symmetry to define the term **axis of symmetry**.

Study Strategy: Learn Vocabulary

Mathematics has a vocabulary all its own. Many new terms appear on the pages of your textbook. Learn these new terms as they are introduced. They will give you the necessary tools to understand new concepts.

Some tips to learning new vocabulary include:

• Look at the **context** in which a new word appears.

• Use **prefixes** or **suffixes** to figure out the word's meaning.

• Relate the new term to familiar **everyday words.** Keep in mind that a word's mathematical meaning may not exactly match its everyday meaning.

polynomial = many

intersection = overlap

conversion = change

Vocabulary Word	Study Tip	Definition
Polynomial	The prefix "poly-" means many.	One monomial or the sum or the difference of monomials
Intersection	Relate it to the meaning of the "intersection of two roads".	The overlapping region that shows the solution to a system of inequalities
Conversion Factor	Relate it to the word "convert", which means change or alter.	Used to convert a measurement to different units

Complete the chart.

	Vocabulary Word	Study Tips	Definition
1.	Trinomial		
2.	Independent system		
3.	Variable		

Use the context of each sentence to define the underlined word. Then relate the word to everyday words.

4. If two linear equations in a system have the same graph, the graphs are called <u>coincident</u> lines, or simply the same line.

5. In the formula $d = rt$, d is <u>isolated</u>.

Identifying Quadratic Functions

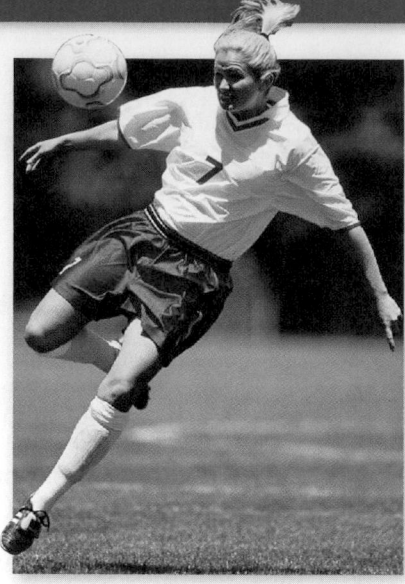

Objectives
Identify quadratic functions and determine whether they have a minimum or maximum.

Graph a quadratic function and give its domain and range.

Vocabulary
quadratic function
parabola
vertex
minimum
maximum

Why learn this?
The height of a soccer ball after it is kicked into the air can be described by a quadratic function. (See Exercise 51.)

The function $y = x^2$ is shown in the graph. Notice that the graph is not linear. This function is a *quadratic function*. A **quadratic function** is any function that can be written in the standard form $y = ax^2 + bx + c$, where a, b, and c are real numbers and $a \neq 0$. The function $y = x^2$ can be written as $y = 1x^2 + 0x + 0$, where $a = 1$, $b = 0$, and $c = 0$.

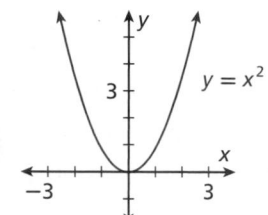

In Lesson 5-1, you identified linear functions by finding that a constant change in x corresponded to a constant change in y. The differences between y-values for a **constant change in x-values** are called *first differences*.

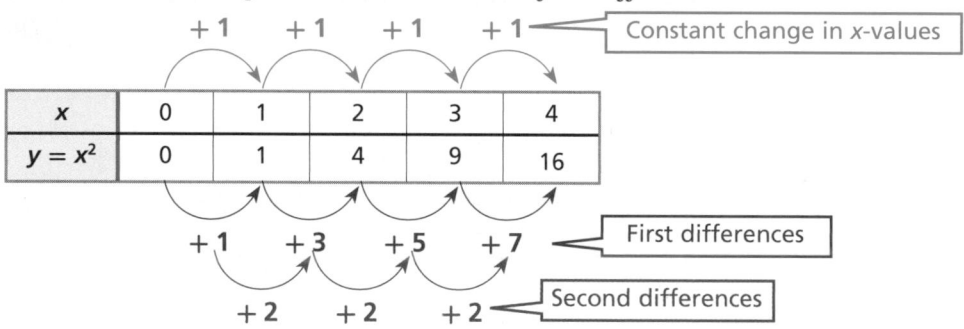

x	0	1	2	3	4
$y = x^2$	0	1	4	9	16

Notice that the quadratic function $y = x^2$ does not have constant first differences. It has constant *second differences*. This is true for all quadratic functions.

EXAMPLE **1** **Identifying Quadratic Functions**

Tell whether each function is quadratic. Explain.

A

x	y
−4	8
−2	2
0	0
2	2
4	8

Since you are given a table of ordered pairs with a constant change in x-values, see if the second differences are constant.

Find the first differences, then find the second differences.

The function is quadratic. The second differences are constant.

Caution!
Be sure there is a constant change in x-values before you try to find first or second differences.

B $y = -3x + 20$ *Since you are given an equation, use $y = ax^2 + bx + c$.*

This is not a quadratic function because the value of a is 0.

Helpful Hint

In a quadratic function, only *a* cannot equal 0. It is okay for the values of *b* and *c* to be 0.

Tell whether each function is quadratic. Explain.

 $y + 3x^2 = -4$

$$\underline{\quad -3x^2 \quad\quad -3x^2\quad}$$
$$y = -3x^2 - 4$$

Try to write the function in the form $y = ax^2 + bx + c$ by solving for y. Subtract $3x^2$ from both sides.

This is a quadratic function because it can be written in the form $y = ax^2 + bx + c$ where $a = -3$, $b = 0$, and $c = -4$.

CHECK IT OUT! Tell whether each function is quadratic. Explain.

1a. $\{(-2, 4), (-1, 1), (0, 0), (1, 1), (2, 4)\}$ **1b.** $y + x = 2x^2$

The graph of a quadratic function is a curve called a **parabola**. To graph a quadratic function, generate enough ordered pairs to see the shape of the parabola. Then connect the points with a smooth curve.

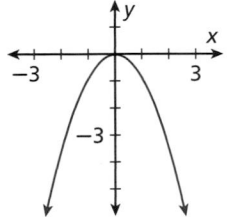

EXAMPLE 2 **Graphing Quadratic Functions by Using a Table of Values**

Use a table of values to graph each quadratic function.

A $y = 2x^2$

x	$y = 2x^2$
-2	8
-1	2
0	0
1	2
2	8

Make a table of values. Choose values of x and use them to find values of y.

Graph the points. Then connect the points with a smooth curve.

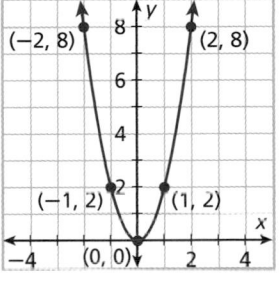

B $y = -2x^2$

x	$y = -2x^2$
-2	-8
-1	-2
0	0
1	-2
2	-8

Make a table of values. Choose values of x and use them to find values of y.

Graph the points. Then connect the points with a smooth curve.

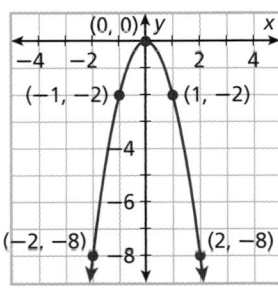

CHECK IT OUT! Use a table of values to graph each quadratic function.

2a. $y = x^2 + 2$ **2b.** $y = -3x^2 + 1$

As shown in the graphs in Examples 2A and 2B, some parabolas open upward and some open downward. Notice that the only difference between the two equations is the value of *a*. When a quadratic function is written in the form $y = ax^2 + bx + c$, the value of *a* determines the direction a parabola opens.

• A parabola opens **upward** when $a > 0$.
• A parabola opens **downward** when $a < 0$.

EXAMPLE **3** **Identifying the Direction of a Parabola**

Tell whether the graph of each quadratic function opens upward or downward. Explain.

A $y = 4x^2$

$y = 4x^2$

$a = 4$ — *Identify the value of a.*

Since $a > 0$, the parabola opens **upward**.

B $2x^2 + y = 5$

$2x^2 + y = 5$

$\underline{-2x^2 \qquad -2x^2}$ — *Write the function in the form $y = ax^2 + bx + c$*

$y = -2x^2 + 5$ — *by solving for y. Subtract $2x^2$ from both sides.*

$a = -2$ — *Identify the value of a.*

Since $a < 0$, the parabola opens **downward**.

 CHECK IT OUT! Tell whether the graph of each quadratic function opens upward or downward. Explain.

3a. $f(x) = -4x^2 - x + 1$ **3b.** $y - 5x^2 = 2x - 6$

The highest or lowest point on a parabola is the **vertex**. If a parabola opens upward, the vertex is the lowest point. If a parabola opens downward, the vertex is the highest point.

Know it! Note

Minimum and Maximum Values		
WORDS	If $a > 0$, the parabola opens upward, and the y-value of the vertex is the **minimum** value of the function.	If $a < 0$, the parabola opens downward, and the y-value of the vertex is the **maximum** value of the function.
GRAPHS	$y = x^2 + 6x + 9$ Vertex: $(-3, 0)$ Minimum: 0	$y = -x^2 + 6x - 4$ Vertex: $(3, 5)$ Maximum: 5

EXAMPLE **4** **Identifying the Vertex and the Minimum or Maximum**

Identify the vertex of each parabola. Then give the minimum or maximum value of the function.

A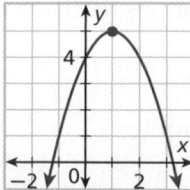

The vertex is $(1, 5)$, and the maximum is 5.

B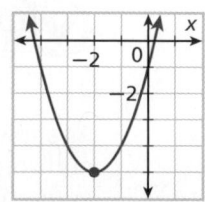

The vertex is $(-2, -5)$, and the minimum is -5.

CHECK IT OUT! Identify the vertex of each parabola. Then give the minimum or maximum value of the function.

4a.

4b.
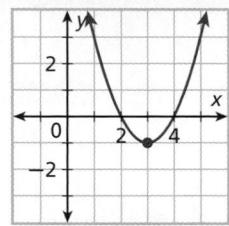

Unless a specific domain is given, you may assume that the domain of a quadratic function is all real numbers. You can find the range of a quadratic function by looking at its graph.

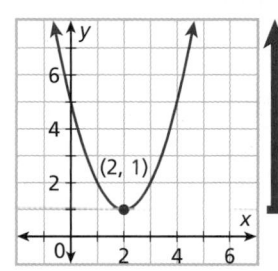

For the graph of $y = x^2 - 4x + 5$, the **range** begins at the minimum value of the function, where $y = 1$. All the y-values of the function are greater than or equal to 1. So the range is $y \geq 1$.

EXAMPLE 5 **Finding Domain and Range**

Find the domain and range.

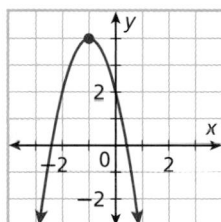

Step 1 The graph opens downward, so identify the maximum.

The vertex is $(-1, 4)$, so the maximum is 4.

Step 2 Find the domain and range.

D: all real numbers
R: $y \leq 4$

 CHECK IT OUT! Find the domain and range.

5a.

5b.

THINK AND DISCUSS

1. How can you identify a quadratic function from ordered pairs? from looking at the function rule?

 2. **GET ORGANIZED** Copy and complete the graphic organizer below. In each box, describe a way of identifying quadratic functions.

go.hrw.com
Homework Help Online
KEYWORD: MA7 9-1
Parent Resources Online
KEYWORD: MA7 Parent

GUIDED PRACTICE

1. **Vocabulary** The y-value of the vertex of a parabola that opens upward is the _____?_____ value of the function. (*maximum* or *minimum*)

SEE EXAMPLE 1
p. 610

Tell whether each function is quadratic. Explain.

2. $y + 6x = -14$

3. $2x^2 + y = 3x - 1$

4.

x	−4	−3	−2	−1	0
y	39	18	3	−6	−9

5. $\{(-10, 15), (-9, 17), (-8, 19), (-7, 21), (-6, 23)\}$

SEE EXAMPLE 2
p. 611

Use a table of values to graph each quadratic function.

6. $y = 4x^2$

7. $y = \frac{1}{2}x^2$

8. $y = -x^2 + 1$

9. $y = -5x^2$

SEE EXAMPLE 3
p. 612

Tell whether the graph of each quadratic function opens upward or downward. Explain.

10. $y = -3x^2 + 4x$

11. $y = 1 - 2x + 6x^2$

12. $y + x^2 = -x - 2$

13. $y + 2 = x^2$

14. $y - 2x^2 = -3$

15. $y + 2 + 3x^2 = 1$

SEE EXAMPLE 4
p. 612

Identify the vertex of each parabola. Then give the minimum or maximum value of the function.

16.

17.
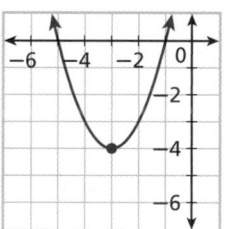

SEE EXAMPLE 5
p. 613

Find the domain and range.

18.

19.

20.

21.
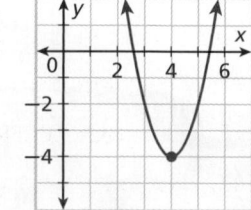

PRACTICE AND PROBLEM SOLVING

Independent Practice

For Exercises	See Example
22–25	1
26–29	2
30–32	3
33–34	4
35–38	5

Extra Practice

Skills Practice p. S20

Application Practice p. S36

Tell whether each function is quadratic. Explain.

22.

x	−2	−1	0	1	2
y	−1	0	4	9	15

23. $-3x^2 + x = y - 11$

24. $\{(0, -3), (1, -2), (2, 1), (3, 6), (4, 13)\}$ **25.** $y = \frac{2}{3}x - \frac{4}{9} + \frac{1}{6}x^2$

Use a table of values to graph each quadratic function.

26. $y = x^2 - 5$ **27.** $y = -\frac{1}{2}x^2$ **28.** $y = -2x^2 + 2$ **29.** $y = 3x^2 - 2$

Tell whether the graph of each quadratic function opens upward or downward. Explain.

30. $y = 7x^2 - 4x$ **31.** $x - 3x^2 + y = 5$ **32.** $y = -\frac{2}{3}x^2$

Identify the vertex of each parabola. Then give the minimum or maximum value of the function.

33.   **34.**

Find the domain and range.

35.   **36.**

37.   **38.**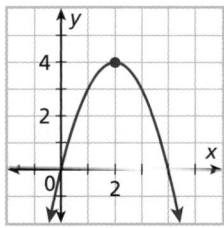

Tell whether each statement is sometimes, always, or never true.

39. The graph of a quadratic function is a straight line.

40. The range of a quadratic function is the set of all real numbers.

41. The highest power of the independent variable in a quadratic function is 2.

42. The graph of a quadratic function contains the point $(0, 0)$.

43. The vertex of a parabola occurs at the minimum value of the function.

44. The graph of a quadratic function that has a minimum opens upward.

Tell whether each function is quadratic. If it is, write the function in standard form. If not, explain why not.

45. $y = 3x - 1$ **46.** $y = 2x^2 - 5 + 3x$ **47.** $y = (x + 1)^2$

48. $y = 5 - (x - 1)^2$ **49.** $y = 3x^2 - 9$ **50.** $y = (x + 1)^3 - x^2$

51. Estimation The graph shows the approximate height y in meters of a volleyball x seconds after it is served.

  a. Estimate the time it takes for the volleyball to reach its greatest height.

  b. Estimate the greatest height that the volleyball reaches.

  c. Critical Thinking If the domain of a quadratic function is all real numbers, why is the domain of this function limited to nonnegative numbers?

Volleyball's Height

Height (m) / Time (s)

52. Sports The height in feet of a soccer ball x seconds after it is kicked into the air is modeled by the function $y = 48x - 16x^2$.

  a. Graph the function.

  b. In this situation, what values make sense for the domain?

  c. Does the soccer ball ever reach a height of 50 ft? How do you know?

Tell whether each function is linear, quadratic, or neither.

53. $y = \frac{1}{2}x - x^2$ **54.** $y = \frac{1}{2}x - 3$ **55.** $y + 3 = -x^2$ **56.** $y - 2x^2 = 0$

57. $y = \frac{1}{2}x(x^2)$ **58.** $y = \frac{3}{x^2}$ **59.** $y = \frac{3}{2}x$ **60.** $x^2 + 2x + 1 = y$

61. Marine Biology A scientist records the motion of a dolphin as it jumps from the water. The function $h(t) = -16t^2 + 32t$ models the dolphin's height in feet above the water after t seconds.

  a. Graph the function.

  b. What domain makes sense for this situation?

  c. What is the dolphin's maximum height above the water?

  d. How long is the dolphin out of the water?

 62. Write About It Explain how to tell the difference between a linear function and a quadratic function when given each of the following:

  a. ordered pairs **b.** the function rule **c.** the graph

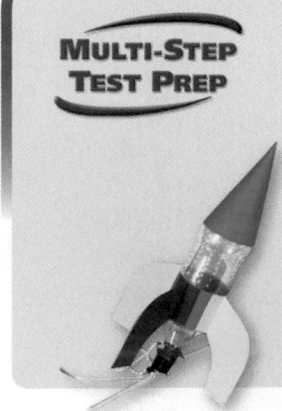

MULTI-STEP TEST PREP

63. This problem will prepare you for the Multi-Step Test Prep on page 640.

A rocket team is using simulation software to create and study water bottle rockets. The team begins by simulating the launch of a rocket without a parachute. The table gives data for one rocket design.

  a. Show that the data represent a quadratic function.

  b. Graph the function.

  c. The acceleration due to gravity is 9.8 m/s². How is this number related to the data for this water bottle rocket?

Time (s)	Height (m)
0	0
1	34.3
2	58.8
3	73.5
4	78.4
5	73.5
6	58.8
7	34.3
8	0

64. Critical Thinking Given the function $-3 - y = x^2 + x$, why is it incorrect to state that the parabola opens upward and has a minimum?

65. Which of the following is the graph of a quadratic function?

Ⓐ

Ⓒ

Ⓑ

Ⓓ
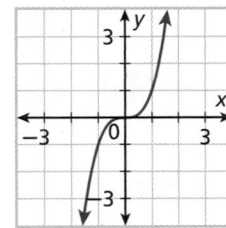

66. Which of the following quadratic functions has a maximum?

Ⓕ $2x^2 - y = 3x - 2$

Ⓖ $y = x^2 + 4x + 16$

Ⓗ $y - x^2 + 6 = 9x$

Ⓙ $y + 3x^2 = 9$

67. Short Response Is the function $f(x) = 5 - 2x^2 + 3x$ quadratic? Explain your answer by using two different methods of identification.

CHALLENGE AND EXTEND

68. Multi-Step A rectangular picture measuring 6 in. by 10 in. is surrounded by a frame with uniform width x. Write a quadratic function to show the combined area of the picture and frame.

 69. Graphing Calculator Use a graphing calculator to find the domain and range of the quadratic functions $y = x^2 - 4$ and $y = -(x + 2)^2$.

SPIRAL REVIEW

Write each number as a power of the given base. *(Lesson 1-4)*

70. 10,000; base 10   **71.** 16; base -2 **72.** $\frac{8}{27}$; base $\frac{2}{3}$

73. A map shows a scale of 1 inch:3 miles. On the map, the distance from Lin's home to the park is $14\frac{1}{4}$ inches. What is the actual distance? *(Lesson 2-7)*

Write a function to describe the situation. Find the reasonable domain and range for the function. *(Lesson 4-3)*

74. Camp Wildwood has collected $400 in registration fees. It can enroll another 3 campers for $25 each.

75. Sal works between 30 and 35 hours per week. He earns $9 per hour.

9-2 Algebra LAB

Use with Lesson 9-2

Explore the Axis of Symmetry

Every graph of a quadratic function is a parabola that is symmetric about a vertical line through its vertex called the *axis of symmetry*.

There is a relationship between a and b in the quadratic function and the equation of the axis of symmetry.

Axis of symmetry

Activity

1 Copy and complete the table.

Function	$y = 1x^2 - 2x - 3$	$y = -2x^2 - 8x - 6$	$y = -1x^2 + 4x$
Graph			
a	1	▦	▦
b	−2	▦	▦
$\dfrac{b}{a}$	▦	▦	▦
Axis of Symmetry (from graph)	$x = 1$	▦	▦

2 Compare the axis of symmetry with $\frac{b}{a}$ in your chart. What can you multiply $\frac{b}{a}$ by to get the number in the equation of the axis of symmetry? (*Hint:* Write and solve an equation to find the value.) Check your answer for each function.

3 Use your answer from Problem 2 to complete the equation of the axis of symmetry of a quadratic function. $x = $ _____?_____

Try This

For the graph of each quadratic function, find the equation of the axis of symmetry.

1. $y = 2x^2 + 12x - 7$ **2.** $y = 4x^2 + 8x - 12$ **3.** $y = 5x^2 - 20x + 10$

4. $y = -3x^2 + 9x + 1$ **5.** $y = x^2 - 7$ **6.** $y = 3x^2 + x + 4$

9-2 Characteristics of Quadratic Functions

Objectives
Find the zeros of a quadratic function from its graph.

Find the axis of symmetry and the vertex of a parabola.

Vocabulary
zero of a function
axis of symmetry

Who uses this?
Engineers can use characteristics of quadratic functions to find the height of the arch supports of bridges. (See Example 5.)

Recall that an x-intercept of a function is a value of x when $y = 0$. A **zero of a function** is an x-value that makes the function equal to 0. So a zero of a function is the same as an x-intercept of a function. Since a graph intersects the x-axis at the point or points containing an x-intercept these intersections are also at the zeros of the function. A quadratic function may have one, two, or no zeros.

EXAMPLE 1 **Finding Zeros of Quadratic Functions From Graphs**

Find the zeros of each quadratic function from its graph. Check your answer.

A $y = x^2 - x - 2$

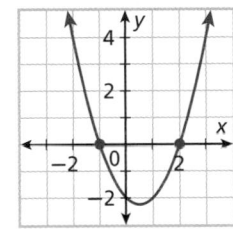

The zeros appear to be -1 and 2.
Check
$y = x^2 - x - 2$
$y = (-1)^2 - (-1) - 2$
$\quad = 1 + 1 - 2 = 0 ✓$
$y = 2^2 - 2 - 2$
$\quad = 4 - 2 - 2 = 0 ✓$

B $y = -2x^2 + 4x - 2$

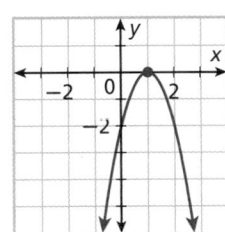

The only zero appears to be 1.
Check
$y = -2x^2 + 4x - 2$
$y = -2(1)^2 + 4(1) - 2$
$\quad = -2(1) + 4 - 2$
$\quad = -2 + 4 - 2$
$\quad = 0 ✓$

C $y = \frac{1}{4}x^2 + 1$

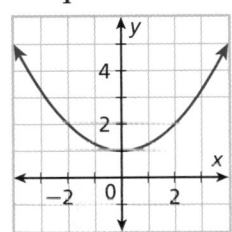

The graph does not cross the x-axis, so there are no zeros of this function.

> **Helpful Hint**
> Notice that if a parabola has only one zero, the zero is the x-coordinate of the vertex.

CHECK IT OUT! Find the zeros of each quadratic function from its graph. Check your answer.

1a. $y = -4x^2 - 2$

1b. $y = x^2 - 6x + 9$

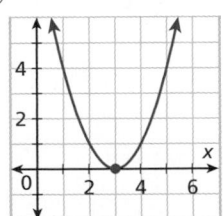

A vertical line that divides a parabola into two symmetrical halves is the **axis of symmetry**. The axis of symmetry always passes through the vertex of the parabola. You can use the zeros to find the axis of symmetry.

Know it! Note

Finding the Axis of Symmetry by Using Zeros

WORDS	NUMBERS	GRAPH
One Zero If a function has one zero, use the x-coordinate of the vertex to find the axis of symmetry.	Vertex: $(3, 0)$ Axis of symmetry: $x = 3$	
Two Zeros If a function has two zeros, use the average of the two zeros to find the axis of symmetry.	$\dfrac{-4 + 0}{2} = \dfrac{-4}{2} = -2$ Axis of symmetry: $x = -2$	

EXAMPLE 2 **Finding the Axis of Symmetry by Using Zeros**

Find the axis of symmetry of each parabola.

A

$(2, 0)$ *Identify the x-coordinate of the vertex.*

The axis of symmetry is $x = 2$.

B

$\dfrac{1 + 5}{2} = \dfrac{6}{2} = 3$ *Find the average of the zeros.*

The axis of symmetry is $x = 3$.

CHECK IT OUT! Find the axis of symmetry of each parabola.

2a.   **2b.**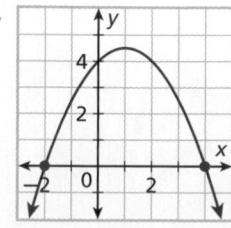

If a function has no zeros or they are difficult to identify from a graph, you can use a formula to find the axis of symmetry. The formula works for all quadratic functions.

Finding the Axis of Symmetry by Using the Formula

FORMULA	EXAMPLE
For a quadratic function $y = ax^2 + bx + c$, the axis of symmetry is the vertical line $$x = -\frac{b}{2a}.$$	$y = 2x^2 + 4x + 5$ $$x = -\frac{b}{2a}$$ $$= -\frac{4}{2(2)} = -1$$ The axis of symmetry is $x = -1$.

E X A M P L E 3 **Finding the Axis of Symmetry by Using the Formula**

Find the axis of symmetry of the graph of $y = x^2 + 3x + 4$.

Step 1 Find the values of a and b.
$$y = 1x^2 + 3x + 4$$
$$a = 1, b = 3$$

Step 2 Use the formula $x = -\dfrac{b}{2a}$.
$$x = -\frac{3}{2(1)} = -\frac{3}{2} = -1.5$$

The axis of symmetry is $x = -1.5$.

 3. Find the axis of symmetry of the graph of $y = 2x^2 + x + 3$.

Once you have found the axis of symmetry, you can use it to identify the vertex.

Finding the Vertex of a Parabola

Step 1 To find the x-coordinate of the vertex, find the axis of symmetry by using zeros or the formula.
Step 2 To find the corresponding y-coordinate, substitute the x-coordinate of the vertex into the function.
Step 3 Write the vertex as an ordered pair.

E X A M P L E 4 **Finding the Vertex of a Parabola**

Find the vertex.

A $y = -x^2 - 2x$

Caution!

In Example 4A Step 2, use the order of operations to simplify.
$$-(-1)^2 = -(1) = -1$$

Step 1 Find the x-coordinate.
The zeros are -2 and 0.
$$x = \frac{-2 + 0}{2} = \frac{-2}{2} = -1$$

Step 2 Find the corresponding y-coordinate.
$$y = -x^2 - 2x \qquad \textit{Use the function rule.}$$
$$= -(-1)^2 - 2(-1) = 1 \qquad \textit{Substitute } -1 \textit{ for } x.$$

Step 3 Write the ordered pair.
$$(-1, 1)$$

The vertex is $(-1, 1)$.

Find the vertex.

B $y = 5x^2 - 10x + 3$

Step 1 Find the x-coordinate.

$a = 5, b = -10$ *Identify a and b.*

$x = -\dfrac{b}{2a}$

$= -\dfrac{-10}{2(5)} = -\dfrac{-10}{10} = 1$ *Substitute 5 for a and −10 for b.*

The x-coordinate of the vertex is 1.

Step 2 Find the corresponding y-coordinate.

$y = 5x^2 - 10x + 3$ *Use the function rule.*

$= 5(1)^2 - 10(1) + 3$ *Substitute 1 for x.*

$= 5 - 10 + 3$

$= -2$

Step 3 Write the ordered pair.

The vertex is $(1, -2)$.

 4. Find the vertex of the graph of $y = x^2 - 4x - 10$.

EXAMPLE 5 *Architecture Application*

The height above water level of a curved arch support for a bridge can be modeled by $f(x) = -0.007x^2 + 0.84x + 0.8$, where x is the distance in feet from where the arch support enters the water. Can a sailboat that is 24 feet tall pass under the bridge? Explain.

The vertex represents the highest point of the arch support.

Step 1 Find the x-coordinate.

$a = -0.007, b = 0.84$ *Identify a and b.*

$x = -\dfrac{b}{2a}$

$= -\dfrac{0.84}{2(-0.007)} = 60$ *Substitute −0.007 for a and 0.84 for b.*

Step 2 Find the corresponding y-coordinate.

$f(x) = -0.007x^2 + 0.84x + 0.8$ *Use the function rule.*

$= -0.007(60)^2 + 0.84(60) + 0.8$ *Substitute 60 for x.*

$= 26$

Since the height of the arch support is 26 feet, the sailboat can pass under the bridge.

 5. The height of a small rise in a roller coaster track is modeled by $f(x) = -0.07x^2 + 0.42x + 6.37$, where x is the horizontal distance in feet from a support pole at ground level. Find the greatest height of the rise.

THINK AND DISCUSS

1. How do you find the zeros of a function from its graph?

2. Describe how to find the axis of symmetry of a quadratic function if its graph does not cross the *x*-axis

3. **GET ORGANIZED** Copy and complete the graphic organizer. In each box, sketch a graph that fits the given description.

```
            Graphs of Quadratic Functions
            ┌──────────────┴──────────────┐
      Opens Upward                  Opens Downward
    ┌──────┼──────┐              ┌──────┼──────┐
Two zeros│One zero│No zeros  Two zeros│One zero│No zeros
```

Exercises

go.hrw.com
Homework Help Online
KEYWORD: MA7 9-2
Parent Resources Online
KEYWORD: MA7 Parent

GUIDED PRACTICE

Vocabulary Apply the vocabulary from this lesson to answer each question.

1. Why is the *zero of a function* the same as an *x*-intercept of a function?

2. Where is the *axis of symmetry* of a parabola located?

SEE EXAMPLE 1
p. 619

Find the zeros of each quadratic function from its graph. Check your answer.

3. $y = x^2 + 2x + 1$

4. $y = 9 - x^2$

5. $y = -x^2 - x - 4$

 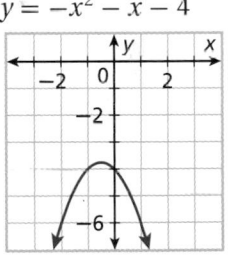

SEE EXAMPLE 2
p. 620

Find the axis of symmetry of each parabola.

6.

7.

8.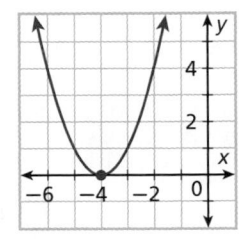

SEE EXAMPLE 3
p. 621

For each quadratic function, find the axis of symmetry of its graph.

9. $y = x^2 + 4x - 7$

10. $y = 3x^2 - 18x + 1$

11. $y = 2x^2 + 3x - 4$

12. $y = -3x^2 + x + 5$

SEE EXAMPLE 4
p. 621

Find the vertex.

13. $y = -5x^2 + 10x + 3$

14. $y = x^2 + 4x - 7$

15. $y = \frac{1}{2}x^2 + 2x$

16. $y = -x^2 + 6x + 1$

17.

$y = x^2 + 4x - 5$

SEE EXAMPLE 5
p. 622

18. **Archery** The height in feet above the ground of an arrow after it is shot can be modeled by $y = -16t^2 + 63t + 4$. Can the arrow pass over a tree that is 68 feet tall? Explain.

PRACTICE AND PROBLEM SOLVING

Independent Practice

For Exercises	See Example
19–21	1
22–24	2
25–28	3
29–33	4
34	5

Extra Practice

Skills Practice p. S20

Application Practice p. S36

Find the zeros of each quadratic function from its graph. Check your answer.

19. $y = \frac{1}{4}x^2 - x + 3$

20. $y = -\frac{1}{3}x^2$

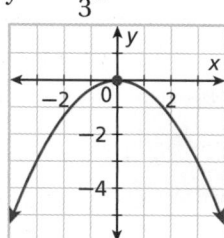

21. $y = x^2 + 10x + 16$

Find the axis of symmetry of each parabola.

22.

23.

24.

For each quadratic function, find the axis of symmetry of its graph.

25. $y = x^2 + x + 2$

26. $y = 3x^2 - 2x - 6$

27. $y = \frac{1}{2}x^2 - 5x + 4$

28. $y = -2x^2 + \frac{1}{3}x - \frac{3}{4}$

Find the vertex.

29. $y = x^2 + 7x$

30. $y = -x^2 + 8x + 16$

31. $y = -2x^2 - 8x - 3$

32. $y = -x^2 + \frac{1}{2}x + 2$

33.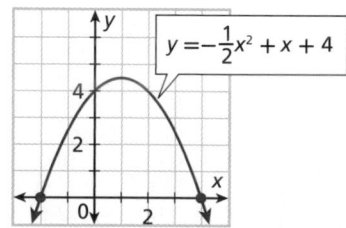

$y = -\frac{1}{2}x^2 + x + 4$

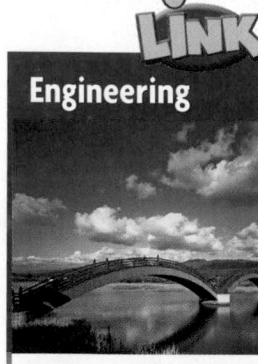

34. **Engineering** The height in feet of the curved arch support for a bridge over a creek can be modeled by $f(x) = -0.628x^2 + 4.5x$, where x is the horizontal distance in feet from where the arch support enters the water. If there is a flood that raises the level of the creek by 5.5 feet, will the top of the arch support be above the water? Explain.

35. **Critical Thinking** What conclusion can be drawn about the axis of symmetry of any quadratic function for which $b = 0$?

36. This problem will prepare you for the Multi-Step Test Prep on page 640.

Height of Rocket

a. Use the graph of the height of a water bottle rocket to estimate the coordinates of the parabola's vertex.

b. What does the vertex represent?

c. Find the zeros of the function. What do they represent?

d. Find the axis of symmetry. How is it related to the vertex and the zeros?

Graphing Calculator Tell how many zeros each quadratic function has.

37. $y = 8x^2 - 4x + 2$

38. $0 = y + 16x^2$

39. $\frac{1}{4}x^2 - 7x - 12 = y - 4$

40. Write About It If you are given the axis of symmetry of a quadratic function and know that the function has two zeros, how would you describe the location of the two zeros?

TEST PREP

41. Which function has the zeros shown in the graph?

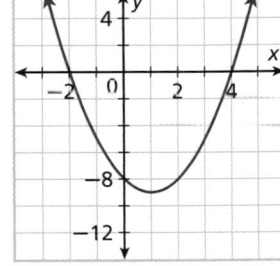

ⓐ $y = x^2 + 2x + 8$ ⓒ $y = x^2 + 2x - 8$

ⓑ $y = x^2 - 2x - 8$ ⓓ $y = 2x^2 - 2x + 8$

42. Which of the following functions has a graph with an axis of symmetry of $x = -\frac{1}{2}$?

ⓕ $y = 2x^2 - 2x + 5$ ⓗ $2x^2 + y = 2x + 5$

ⓖ $2x + 5 = 2x^2 - y$ ⓙ $2x - y = 5 - 2x^2$

43. Gridded Response For the graph of $f(x) = -3 + 20x - 5x^2$, what is the x-coordinate of its vertex?

CHALLENGE AND EXTEND

44. Describe the domain and range of a quadratic function that has exactly one zero and whose graph opens downward.

45. Graphing Calculator The height in feet of a parabolic bridge support is modeled by $f(x) = -0.01x^2 + 20$, where $y = -5$ represents ground level and the x-axis represents the middle of the bridge. Find the height and the width of the bridge support.

SPIRAL REVIEW

46. The value of y varies directly with x, and $y = -4$ when $x = 2$. Find y when $x = 6$. *(Lesson 5-6)*

Write each equation in slope-intercept form. *(Lesson 5-7)*

47. $2x + y = 3$

48. $4y = 12x - 8$

49. $10 - 5y = 20x$

Tell whether each function is quadratic. Explain. *(Lesson 9-1)*

50. $y = 5x - 7$

51. $x^2 - 5x = 2 + y$

52. $y = -x^2 - 6x$

9-3 Graphing Quadratic Functions

Objective
Graph a quadratic function in the form $y = ax^2 + bx + c$.

Why use this?
Graphs of quadratic functions can help you determine how high an object is tossed or kicked. (See Exercise 14.)

Recall that a *y*-intercept is the *y*-coordinate of the point where a graph intersects the *y*-axis. The *x*-coordinate of this point is always 0. For a quadratic function written in the form $y = ax^2 + bx + c$, when $x = 0$, $y = c$. So the *y*-intercept of a quadratic function is *c*.

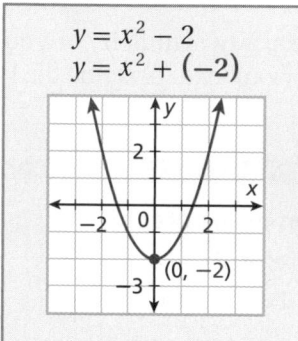
$y = x^2 - 2$
$y = x^2 + (-2)$

$y = x^2 - 4x + 4$

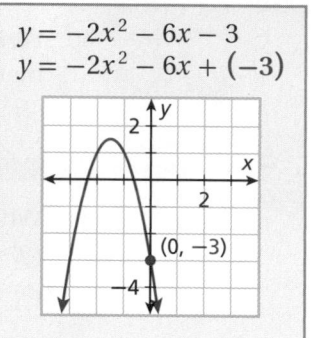
$y = -2x^2 - 6x - 3$
$y = -2x^2 - 6x + (-3)$

In the previous lesson, you found the axis of symmetry and vertex of a parabola. You can use these characteristics, the *y*-intercept, and symmetry to graph a quadratic function.

EXAMPLE 1   Graphing a Quadratic Function

Graph $y = x^2 - 4x - 5$.

Step 1 Find the axis of symmetry.

$$x = -\frac{-4}{2(1)}$$ *Use $x = -\dfrac{b}{2a}$. Substitute 1 for a and −4 for b.*

$$= 2$$ *Simplify.*

The axis of symmetry is $x = 2$.

Step 2 Find the vertex.

$$y = x^2 - 4x - 5$$
$$= 2^2 - 4(2) - 5$$ *The x-coordinate of the vertex is 2. Substitute 2 for x.*
$$= 4 - 8 - 5$$ *Simplify.*
$$= -9$$ *The y-coordinate is −9.*

The vertex is $(2, -9)$.

Step 3 Find the *y*-intercept.

$$y = x^2 - 4x - 5$$
$$y = x^2 - 4x + (-5)$$ *Identify c.*

The *y*-intercept is −5; the graph passes through $(0, -5)$.

Step 4 Find two more points on the same side of the axis of symmetry as the point containing the y-intercept.

Since the axis of symmetry is $x = 2$, choose x-values less than 2.

Let $x = 1$.

$y = 1^2 - 4(1) - 5$ *Substitute x-coordinates.*

$= 1 - 4 - 5$ *Simplify.*

$= -8$

Let $x = -1$.

$y = (-1)^2 - 4(-1) - 5$

$= 1 + 4 - 5$

$= 0$

Two other points are $(1, -8)$ and $(-1, 0)$.

Step 5 Graph the axis of symmetry, the vertex, the point containing the y-intercept, and **two other points**.

Step 6 Reflect the points across the axis of symmetry. Connect the points with a smooth curve.

 CHECK IT OUT! Graph each quadratic function.

1a. $y = 2x^2 + 6x + 2$

1b. $y + 6x = x^2 + 9$

EXAMPLE **2** **Problem-Solving Application**

The height in feet of a football that is kicked can be modeled by the function $f(x) = -16x^2 + 64x$, where x is the time in seconds after it is kicked. Find the football's maximum height and the time it takes the football to reach this height. Then find how long the football is in the air.

1 **Understand the Problem**

The **answer** includes three parts: the maximum height, the time to reach the maximum height, and the time to reach the ground.

List the important information:

• The function $f(x) = -16x^2 + 64x$ models the approximate height of the football after x seconds.

2 **Make a Plan**

Find the vertex of the graph because the maximum height of the football and the time it takes to reach it are the coordinates of the vertex. The football will hit the ground when its height is 0, so find the zeros of the function. You can do this by graphing.

3 Solve

Step 1 Find the axis of symmetry.

$$x = -\frac{64}{2(-16)}$$ *Use $x = -\frac{b}{2a}$. Substitute -16 for a and 64 for b.*

$$= -\frac{64}{-32} = 2$$ *Simplify.*

The axis of symmetry is $x = 2$.

Step 2 Find the vertex.

$$y = -16x^2 + 64x$$
$$= -16(2)^2 + 64(2)$$ *The x-coordinate of the vertex is 2. Substitute 2 for x.*
$$= -16(4) + 128$$ *Simplify.*
$$= -64 + 128$$
$$= 64$$ *The y-coordinate is 64.*

The vertex is $(2, 64)$.

Step 3 Find the y-intercept.

$$y = -16x^2 + 64x + \mathbf{0}$$ *Identify c.*

The y-intercept is $\mathbf{0}$; the graph passes through $(0, 0)$.

Step 4 Find another point on the same side of the axis of symmetry as the point containing the y-intercept.

Since the axis of symmetry is $x = 2$, choose an x-value that is less than 2. Let $x = 1$.

$$y = -16(1)^2 + 64(1)$$ *Substitute 1 for x.*
$$= -16 + 64$$ *Simplify.*
$$= 48$$

Another point is $(1, 48)$.

Step 5 Graph the axis of symmetry, the vertex, the point containing the y-intercept, and the other point. Then reflect the points across the axis of symmetry. Connect the points with a smooth curve.

The vertex is $(2, 64)$. So at 2 seconds, the football has reached its maximum height of 64 feet. The graph shows the zeros of the function are 0 and 4. At 0 seconds the football has not yet been kicked, and at 4 seconds it reaches the ground. The football is in the air for 4 seconds.

4 Look Back

Check by substituting $(2, 64)$ and $(4, 0)$ into the function.

$64 = -16(2)^2 + 64(2)$	$0 = -16(4)^2 + 64(4)$
$64 = -64 + 128$	$0 = -256 + 256$
$64 = 64 \checkmark$	$0 = 0 \checkmark$

2. As Molly dives into her pool, her height in feet above the water can be modeled by the function $f(x) = -16x^2 + 16x + 12$ where x is the time in seconds after she begins diving. Find the maximum height of her dive and the time it takes Molly to reach this height. Then find how long it takes her to reach the pool.

THINK AND DISCUSS

1. Explain how to find the y-intercept of a quadratic function that is written in the form $ax^2 - y = bx + c$.

2. Explain how to graph a quadratic function.

3. What do the vertex and zeros of the function represent in the situation in the Check It Out for Example 2?

 4. GET ORGANIZED Copy and complete the graphic organizer using your own quadratic function.

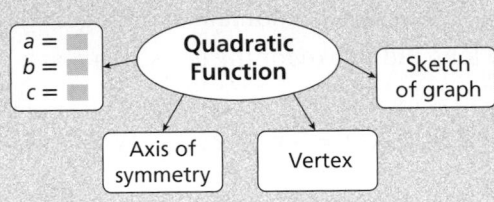

9-3 Exercises

go.hrw.com
Homework Help Online
KEYWORD: MA7 9-3
Parent Resources Online
KEYWORD: MA7 Parent

GUIDED PRACTICE

SEE EXAMPLE **1**
p. 626

Graph each quadratic function.

1. $y = x^2 - 2x - 3$

2. $-y - 3x^2 = -3$

3. $y = 2x^2 + 2x - 4$

4. $y = x^2 + 4x - 8$

5. $y + x^2 + 5x + 2 = 0$

6. $y = 4x^2 + 2$

SEE EXAMPLE **2**
p. 627

7. Multi-Step The height in feet of a golf ball that is hit from the ground can be modeled by the function $f(x) = -16x^2 + 96x$, where x is the time in seconds after the ball is hit. Find the ball's maximum height and the time it takes the ball to reach this height. Then find how long the ball is in the air.

PRACTICE AND PROBLEM SOLVING

Independent Practice

For Exercises	See Example
8–13	1
14	2

Extra Practice

Skills Practice p. S20
Application Practice p. S36

Graph each quadratic function.

8. $y = -4x^2 + 12x - 5$

9. $y = 3x^2 + 12x + 9$

10. $y - 7x^2 - 14x = 3$

11. $y = -x^2 + 2x$

12. $y - 1 = 4x^2 + 8x$

13. $y = -2x^2 - 3x + 4$

14. Multi-Step A juggler tosses a ring into the air. The height of the ring in feet above the juggler's hands can be modeled by the function $f(x) = -16x^2 + 16x$, where x is the time in seconds after the ring is tossed. Find the ring's maximum height above the juggler's hands and the time it takes the ring to reach this height. Then find how long the ring is in the air.

For each quadratic function, find the axis of symmetry and the vertex of its graph.

15. $y = x^2 - 8x$

16. $y = -x^2 + 6x - 4$

17. $y = 4 - 3x^2$

18. $y = -2x^2 - 4$

19. $y = -x^2 - x - 4$

20. $y = x^2 + 8x + 16$

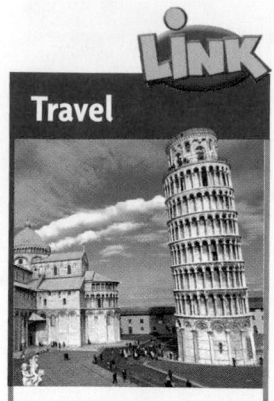
Graph each quadratic function. On your graph, label the coordinates of the vertex. Draw and label the axis of symmetry.

21. $y = -x^2$

22. $y = -x^2 + 4x$

23. $y = x^2 - 6x + 4$

24. $y = x^2 - x$

25. $y = 3x^2 - 4$

26. $y = -2x^2 - 16x - 25$

27. Travel While on a vacation in Italy, Rudy visited the Leaning Tower of Pisa. When he leaned over the railing to look down from the tower, his sunglasses fell off. The height in meters of the sunglasses as they fell can be approximated by the function $y = -5x^2 + 50$, where x is the time in seconds.

   a. Graph the function. (*Hint:* Use a graphing calculator.)

   b. What is a reasonable domain and range?

   c. How long did it take for the glasses to reach the ground?

28. ///**ERROR ANALYSIS**/// Two students found the equation of the axis of symmetry for the graph of $f(x) = -x^2 - 2x + 1$. Who is incorrect? Explain the error.

Ⓐ
$$x = -\frac{b}{2a}$$
$$x = -\frac{-1}{2(-2)} = -\frac{1}{4}$$
Axis of symmetry is $x = -\frac{1}{4}$.

Ⓑ
$$x = -\frac{b}{2a}$$
$$x = -\frac{-2}{2(-1)} = -\frac{-2}{-2} = -1$$
Axis of symmetry is $x = -1$.

29. Critical Thinking The point $(5, 4)$ lies on the graph of a quadratic function whose axis of symmetry is $x = 2$. Find another point on the graph. Explain how you found the point.

Engineering Use the graph for Exercises 30–32. The velocity v in centimeters per second of a fluid flowing in a pipe varies according to the radius r of the pipe.

30. Find the radius of the pipe when the velocity is 7 cm/s.

31. Find the velocity of the fluid when the radius is 2 cm.

32. What is a reasonable domain for this function? Explain.

33. Critical Thinking The graph of a quadratic function has the vertex $(0, 5)$. One point on the graph is $(1, 6)$. Find another point on the graph. Explain how you found the point.

Velocity of a Fluid Through a Pipe

Velocity (cm/s) axis: 0, 4, 8, 12, 16
Radius (cm) axis: 0, 2, 4, 6, 8

34. Write About It Explain how the vertex and the range can help you graph a quadratic function.

MULTI-STEP TEST PREP

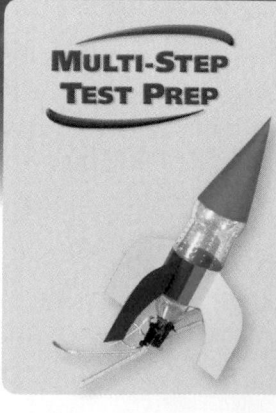

35. This problem will prepare you for the Multi-Step Test Prep on page 640.

A water bottle rocket is shot upward with an initial velocity of $v_i = 45$ ft/s from the roof of a school, which is at h_i, 50 ft above the ground. The equation $h = -\frac{1}{2}at^2 + v_i t + h_i$ models the rocket's height as a function of time. The acceleration due to gravity a is 32 ft/s^2.

   a. Write the equation for height as a function of time for this situation.

   b. Find the vertex of this parabola.

   c. Sketch the graph of this parabola and label the vertex.

   d. What do the coordinates of the vertex represent in terms of time and height?

36. Copy and complete the table for each function.

Function	Graph Opens	Axis of Symmetry	Vertex	Zeros	Domain and Range
$y = x^2 + 4$	▨	$x =$ ▨	(▨, ▨)	▨	D: ▨ R: ▨
$y = -x^2 + 4$	▨	$x =$ ▨	(▨, ▨)	▨	D: ▨ R: ▨
$y + 8 - x^2 = -2x$	▨	$x =$ ▨	(▨, ▨)	▨	D: ▨ R: ▨

 TEST PREP

37. Which is the axis of symmetry for the graph of $f(x) = 6 - 5x + \frac{1}{2}x^2$?

   Ⓐ $x = 5$ Ⓑ $x = \frac{1}{20}$ Ⓒ $x = -5$ Ⓓ $x = -\frac{1}{20}$

38. What are the coordinates of the vertex for the graph of $f(x) = x^2 - 5x + 6$?

   Ⓕ $\left(-\frac{5}{2}, -\frac{1}{4}\right)$ Ⓖ $\left(-\frac{5}{2}, \frac{1}{4}\right)$ Ⓗ $\left(\frac{5}{2}, \frac{1}{4}\right)$ Ⓙ $\left(\frac{5}{2}, -\frac{1}{4}\right)$

39. Which function's graph has an axis of symmetry of $x = 1$ and a vertex of $(1, 8)$?

   Ⓐ $y = -x^2 + x + 8$ Ⓒ $y = 2x^2 - 4x - 8$

   Ⓑ $y = x^2 + 8x + 1$ Ⓓ $y = -3x^2 + 6x + 5$

40. Short Response Graph $y = x^2 + 3x + 2$. What are the zeros, the axis of symmetry, and the coordinates of the vertex? Show your work.

CHALLENGE AND EXTEND

41. The graph of a quadratic function has its vertex at $(1, -4)$ and one zero of the function is 3. Find the other zero. Explain how you found the other zero.

42. The x-intercepts of a quadratic function are 3 and -3. The y-intercept is 6. What are the coordinates of the vertex? Does the function have a maximum or a minimum? Explain.

SPIRAL REVIEW

Find the x- and y-intercepts. *(Lesson 5-2)*

43.   **44.**   **45.**

Solve each system by using any method. *(Lessons 6-1, 6-2, and 6-3)*

46. $\begin{cases} 3x - y = 2 \\ x + 4y = 18 \end{cases}$ **47.** $\begin{cases} 2x + 3y = 3 \\ 4x - y = 13 \end{cases}$ **48.** $\begin{cases} -2x + 3y = 12 \\ 6x + y = 4 \end{cases}$

Find the vertex. *(Lesson 9-2)*

49. $y = x^2 + 2x - 15$ **50.** $y = -3x^2 + 12x - 4$ **51.** $y = -2x - x^2 + 3$

9-4 Technology LAB

Use with Lesson 9-4

The Family of Quadratic Functions

In Chapter 5, you learned that functions whose graphs share the same basic characteristics form a *family of functions*. All quadratic functions form a family because their graphs are all parabolas. You can use a graphing calculator to explore the family of quadratic functions.

go.hrw.com
Lab Resources Online
KEYWORD: MA7 Lab9

Activity

Describe how the value of a affects the graph of $y = ax^2$.

1 Press Y= . Enter Y_1 through Y_4 as shown.

Notice that Y_2 represents the parent function $y = x^2$. To make it stand out from the other functions, change its line style. When you enter Y_2, move the cursor to the line style indicator by pressing ◀. Then press ENTER to cycle through the choices until a thicker line appears.

Line style indicator

2 Press GRAPH .

Keep in mind the values of a as the functions are graphed. The graphing calculator will graph the functions in order.

Notice that the graph of $y = \frac{1}{2}x^2$ is wider than the graph of the parent function. The graphs of $y = 2x^2$ and $y = 3x^2$ are narrower than the graph of the parent function.

$y = 3x^2$
$y = 2x^2$
$y = x^2$
$y = \frac{1}{2}x^2$

Try This

1. How would the graph of $y = 6x^2$ compare with the graph of the parent function?

2. How would the graph of $y = \frac{1}{5}x^2$ compare with the graph of the parent function?

3. **Make a Conjecture** Make a conjecture about the effect of a on the graph of $y = ax^2$.

Consider the graphs of $y = -\frac{1}{2}x^2$, $y = -x^2$, $y = -2x^2$, and $y = -3x^2$.

4. Describe the differences in the graphs.

5. How would the graph of $y = -8x^2$ compare with the graph of $y = -x^2$?

6. How do these results affect your conjecture from Problem 3?

Consider the graphs of $y = x^2 - 1$, $y = x^2$, $y = x^2 + 2$, and $y = x^2 + 4$.

7. Describe the differences in the graphs.

8. How would the graph of $y = x^2 - 7$ compare with the graph of the parent function?

9. **Make a Conjecture** Make a conjecture about the effect of c on the graph of $y = x^2 + c$.

9-4 Transforming Quadratic Functions

Why learn this?

You can compare how long it takes raindrops to reach the ground from different heights. (See Exercise 18.)

Objective
Graph and transform quadratic functions.

Remember!

You saw in Lesson 5-10 that the graphs of all linear functions are transformations of the linear parent function, $f(x) = x$.

The quadratic parent function is $f(x) = x^2$. The graph of all other quadratic functions are transformations of the graph of $f(x) = x^2$.

For the parent function $f(x) = x^2$:
- The axis of symmetry is $x = 0$, or the y-axis.
- The vertex is $(0, 0)$.
- The function has only one zero, 0.

$f(x) = x^2$

Vertex: (0, 0)   Axis of symmetry: $x = 0$

Compare the coefficients in the following functions.

$$f(x) = x^2 \qquad g(x) = \frac{1}{2}x^2$$

$$h(x) = -3x^2$$

$$f(x) = 1x^2 + 0x + 0$$
$$g(x) = \frac{1}{2}x^2 + 0x + 0$$
$$h(x) = -3x^2 + 0x + 0$$

Same	Different
• $b = 0$	• Value of a
• $c = 0$	

Compare the graphs of the same functions.

$f(x) = x^2$ $g(x) = \frac{1}{2}x^2$

$h(x) = -3x^2$

Same	Different
• Axis of symmetry is $x = 0$.	• Widths of parabolas
• Vertex is $(0, 0)$.	

The value of a in a quadratic function determines not only the direction a parabola opens, but also the width of the parabola.

Know it!
Note

Width of a Parabola

WORDS	EXAMPLES
The graph of $f(x) = ax^2$ is narrower than the graph of $f(x) = x^2$ if $\lvert a\rvert > 1$ and wider if $\lvert a\rvert < 1$.	Compare the graphs of $g(x)$ and $h(x)$ with the graph of $f(x)$. $\lvert -2\rvert\ ?\ 1 \qquad \lvert\frac{1}{4}\rvert\ ?\ 1$ $2 > 1 \qquad \frac{1}{4} < 1$ narrower $\qquad$ wider 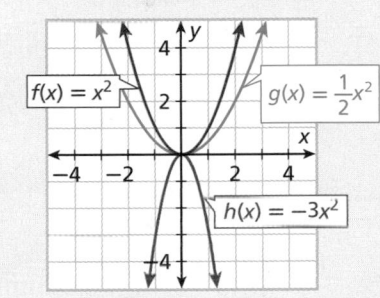 $f(x) = x^2$ $\quad h(x) = \frac{1}{4}x^2$ $\quad g(x) = -2x^2$

EXAMPLE 1 **Comparing Widths of Parabolas**

Order the functions from narrowest graph to widest.

A $f(x) = -2x^2, g(x) = \frac{1}{3}x^2, h(x) = 4x^2$

Step 1 Find $|a|$ for each function.

$$|-2| = 2 \qquad \left|\frac{1}{3}\right| = \frac{1}{3} \qquad |4| = 4$$

Step 2 Order the functions.

$h(x) = 4x^2$

$f(x) = -2x^2$ *The function with the narrowest graph has the greatest value for |a|.*

$g(x) = \frac{1}{3}x^2$

Check Use a graphing calculator to compare the graphs.

$h(x) = 4x^2$ has the narrowest graph, and $g(x) = \frac{1}{3}x^2$ has the widest graph. ✓

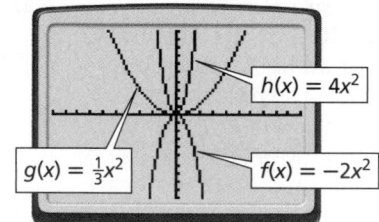

B $f(x) = 2x^2, g(x) = -2x^2$

Step 1 Find $|a|$ for each function.
$$|2| = 2 \qquad |-2| = 2$$

Step 2 Order the functions from narrowest graph to widest.
Since the absolute values are equal, the graphs are the same width.

 CHECK IT OUT! Order the functions from narrowest graph to widest.

1a. $f(x) = -x^2, g(x) = \frac{2}{3}x^2$

1b. $f(x) = -4x^2, g(x) = 6x^2, h(x) = 0.2x^2$

Compare the coefficients in the following functions.

$f(x) = x^2 \qquad g(x) = x^2 - 4$

$h(x) = x^2 + 3$

$f(x) = 1x^2 + 0x + 0$

$g(x) = 1x^2 + 0x + (-4)$

$h(x) = 1x^2 + 0x + 3$

Same	Different
• $a = 1$ • $b = 0$	• Value of c

Compare the graphs of the same functions.

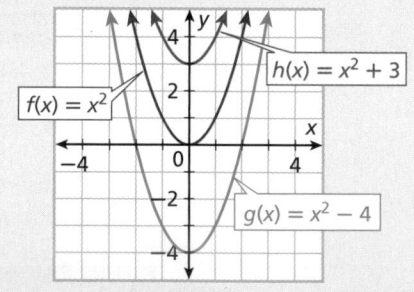

Same	Different
• Axis of symmetry is $x = 0$. • Width of parabola	• Vertex of parabola

The value of c makes these graphs look different. The value of c in a quadratic function determines not only the value of the y-intercept but also a vertical translation of the graph of $f(x) = ax^2$ up or down the y-axis.

Know it!
Note

Vertical Translations of a Parabola

The graph of the function $f(x) = x^2 + c$ is the graph of $f(x) = x^2$ translated vertically.

- If $c > 0$, the graph of $f(x) = x^2$ is translated c units **up**.
- If $c < 0$, the graph of $f(x) = x^2$ is translated c units **down**.

EXAMPLE 2 **Comparing Graphs of Quadratic Functions**

Compare the graph of each function with the graph of $f(x) = x^2$.

A $g(x) = -\dfrac{1}{3}x^2 + 2$

Helpful Hint

When comparing graphs, it is helpful to draw them on the same coordinate plane.

Method 1 Compare the graphs.

- The graph of $g(x) = -\dfrac{1}{3}x^2 + 2$ is **wider** than the graph of $f(x) = x^2$.

- The graph of $g(x) = -\dfrac{1}{3}x^2 + 2$ opens **downward**, and the graph of $f(x) = x^2$ opens **upward**.

- The axis of symmetry is the same.

- The vertex of $f(x) = x^2$ is $(0, 0)$.

  The vertex of $g(x) = -\dfrac{1}{3}x^2 + 2$ is translated **2 units up** to $(0, 2)$.

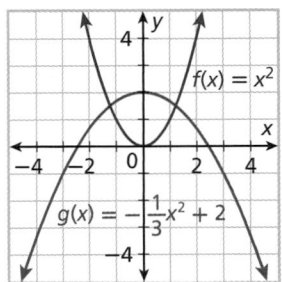

B $g(x) = 2x^2 - 3$

Method 2 Use the functions.

- Since $|2| > |1|$, the graph of $g(x) = 2x^2 - 3$ is **narrower** than the graph of $f(x) = x^2$.

- Since $-\dfrac{b}{2a} = 0$ for both functions, the axis of symmetry is the same.

- The vertex of $f(x) = x^2$ is $(0, 0)$. The vertex of $g(x) = 2x^2 - 3$ is translated **3 units down** to $(0, -3)$.

Check Use a graph to verify all comparisons.

CHECK IT OUT! Compare the graph of each function with the graph of $f(x) = x^2$.

2a. $g(x) = -x^2 - 4$ **2b.** $g(x) = 3x^2 + 9$ **2c.** $g(x) = \dfrac{1}{2}x^2 + 2$

The quadratic function $h(t) = -16t^2 + c$ can be used to approximate the height h in feet above the ground of a falling object t seconds after it is dropped from a height of c feet. This model is used only to approximate the height of falling objects because it does not account for air resistance, wind, and other real-world factors.

EXAMPLE 3 Physics Application

Two identical water balloons are dropped from different heights as shown in the diagram.

a. Write the two height functions and compare their graphs.

Step 1 Write the height functions.
The y-intercept c represents the original height.

$h_1(t) = -16t^2 + 64$ *Dropped from 64 feet*
$h_2(t) = -16t^2 + 144$ *Dropped from 144 feet*

Step 2 Use a graphing calculator.
Since time and height cannot be negative, set the window for nonnegative values.

The graph of h_2 is a vertical translation of the graph of h_1. Since the balloon in h_2 is dropped from 80 feet higher than the one in h_1, the y-intercept of h_2 is 80 units higher.

b. Use the graphs to tell when each water balloon reaches the ground.

The zeros of each function are when the water balloons reach the ground.

The water balloon dropped from 64 feet reaches the ground in 2 seconds. The water balloon dropped from 144 feet reaches the ground in 3 seconds.

Check These answers seem reasonable because the water balloon dropped from a greater height should take longer to reach the ground.

3. Two tennis balls are dropped, one from a height of 16 feet and the other from a height of 100 feet.

a. Write the two height functions and compare their graphs.

b. Use the graphs to tell when each tennis ball reaches the ground.

THINK AND DISCUSS

1. Describe how the graph of $f(x) = x^2 + c$ differs from the graph of $f(x) = x^2$ when the value of c is positive and when the value of c is negative.

2. Tell how to determine whether a graph of a function is wider or narrower than the graph of $f(x) = x^2$.

3. GET ORGANIZED Copy and complete the graphic organizer by explaining how each change affects the graph $f(x) = ax^2 + c$.

> **Caution!**
>
> Remember that the graphs shown here represent the *height* of the objects over time, not the *paths* of the objects.

9-4 Exercises

go.hrw.com
Homework Help Online
KEYWORD: MA7 9-4
Parent Resources Online
KEYWORD: MA7 Parent

GUIDED PRACTICE

SEE EXAMPLE 1
p. 634

Order the functions from narrowest graph to widest.

1. $f(x) = 3x^2, g(x) = 2x^2$

2. $f(x) = 5x^2, g(x) = -5x^2$

3. $f(x) = \frac{3}{4}x^2, g(x) = -2x^2,$
$h(x) = -8x^2$

4. $f(x) = x^2, g(x) = -\frac{4}{5}x^2,$
$h(x) = 3x^2$

SEE EXAMPLE 2
p. 635

Compare the graph of each function with the graph of $f(x) = x^2$.

5. $g(x) = x^2 + 6$

6. $g(x) = -2x^2 + 5$

7. $g(x) = \frac{1}{3}x^2$

8. $g(x) = -\frac{1}{4}x^2 - 2$

SEE EXAMPLE 3
p. 636

9. Multi-Step Two baseballs are dropped, one from a height of 16 feet and the other from a height of 256 feet.

a. Write the two height functions and compare their graphs.

b. Use the graphs to tell when each baseball reaches the ground.

PRACTICE AND PROBLEM SOLVING

Independent Practice

For Exercises	See Example
10–13	1
14–17	2
18	3

Order the functions from narrowest graph to widest.

10. $f(x) = x^2, g(x) = 4x^2$

11. $f(x) = -2x^2, g(x) = \frac{1}{2}x^2$

12. $f(x) = -x^2, g(x) = -\frac{5}{8}x^2, h(x) = \frac{1}{2}x^2$

13. $f(x) = -5x^2, g(x) = -\frac{3}{8}x^2, h(x) = 3x^2$

Extra Practice
Skills Practice p. S20
Application Practice p. S36

Compare the graph of each function with the graph of $f(x) = x^2$.

14. $g(x) = \frac{1}{2}x^2 - 10$

15. $g(x) = -4x^2 - 2$

16. $g(x) = \frac{2}{3}x^2 - 9$

17. $g(x) = -\frac{1}{5}x^2 + 1$

18. Multi-Step A raindrop falls from a cloud at an altitude of 10,000 ft. Another raindrop falls from a cloud at an altitude of 14,400 ft.

a. Write the two height functions and compare their graphs.

b. Use the graphs to tell when each raindrop reaches the ground.

Tell whether each statement is sometimes, always, or never true.

19. The graphs of $f(x) = ax^2$ and $g(x) = -ax^2$ have the same width.

20. The function $f(x) = ax^2 + c$ has three zeros.

21. The graph of $y = ax^2 + 1$ has its vertex at the origin.

22. The graph of $y = -x^2 + c$ intersects the x-axis.

23. Data Collection Use a graphing calculator and a motion detector to graph the height of a falling object over time.

a. Find a function to model the height of the object while it is in motion.

b. **Critical Thinking** Explain why the value of a in your function is not -16.

Write a function to describe each of the following.

24. The graph of $f(x) = x^2 + 10$ is translated 10 units down.

25. The graph of $f(x) = 3x^2 - 2$ is translated 4 units down.

26. The graph of $f(x) = 0.5x^2$ is narrowed.

27. The graph of $f(x) = -5x^2$ is narrowed and translated 2 units up.

28. The graph of $f(x) = x^2 - 7$ is widened and has no x-intercept.

Match each function to its graph.

29. $f(x) = 4x^2 - 3$ **30.** $f(x) = \frac{1}{4}x^2 - 3$ **31.** $f(x) = 4x^2 + 3$ **32.** $f(x) = -\frac{1}{4}x^2 - 3$

A.   **B.**   **C.**   **D.**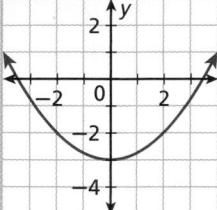

33. Critical Thinking For what values of a and c will $f(x) = ax^2 + c$ have one zero?

34. Physics The graph compares the heights of two identical coconuts that fell from different trees.

   a. What are the starting heights of each coconut?

   b. What is a possible function for the blue graph?

   c. Estimate the time for each coconut to reach the ground.

35. Give an example of a quadratic function for each description.

   a. Its graph opens upward.

   b. Its graph has the same width as in part **a,** but the graph opens downward.

   c. Its graph is narrower than the graph in part **a.**

36. Critical Thinking Describe how the effect that the value of c has on the graph of $y = x^2 + c$ is similar to the effect that the value of b has on the graph of $y = x + b$.

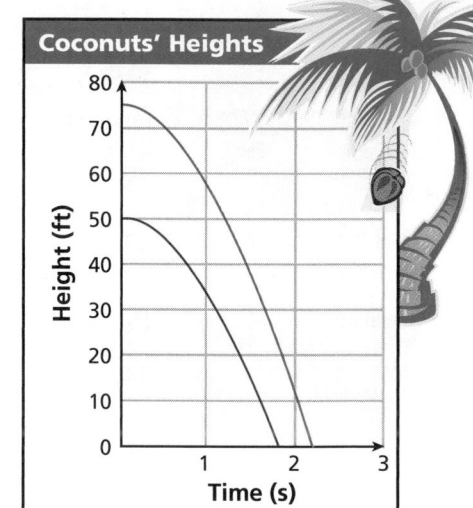

37. Write About It Explain how you know, without graphing, what the graph of $f(x) = \frac{1}{10}x^2 - 5$ looks like.

MULTI-STEP TEST PREP

38. This problem will prepare you for the Multi-Step Test Prep on page 640.

   a. Use a graphing calculator to graph $y = (x - 3)^2$. Compare this graph to the graph of $y = x^2$. How does this differ from $y = x^2 - 3$?

   b. The equation $h = -16(x - 2)^2 + 64$ describes the height in feet of a water bottle rocket as a function of time. What is the highest point that the rocket will reach? When will it return to the ground?

   c. How can the vertex be located from the equation? from the graph?

39. Which function's graph is the result of shifting the graph of $f(x) = -x^2 - 4$ 3 units down?

    Ⓐ $g(x) = -x^2 - 1$ Ⓒ $g(x) = -4x^2 - 4$

    Ⓑ $g(x) = -\frac{1}{3}x^2 - 4$ Ⓓ $g(x) = -x^2 - 7$

40. Which of the following is true when the graph of $f(x) = x^2 + 4$ is transformed into the graph of $g(x) = 2x^2 + 4$?

    Ⓕ The new function has more zeroes than the old function.

    Ⓖ Both functions have the same vertex.

    Ⓗ The function is translated up.

    Ⓙ The axis of symmetry changes.

41. Gridded Response For what value of c will $f(x) = x^2 + c$ have one zero?

CHALLENGE AND EXTEND

42. Graphing Calculator Graph the functions $f(x) = (x + 1)^2$, $g(x) = (x + 4)^2$, $h(x) = (x - 2)^2$, and $k(x) = (x - 5)^2$. Make a conjecture about the result of transforming the graph of $f(x) = x^2$ into the graph of $f(x) = (x - h)^2$.

43. Using the function $f(x) = x^2$, write each new function:

    a. The graph is translated 7 units down.

    b. The graph is reflected across the x-axis and translated 2 units up.

    c. Each y-value is halved, and then the graph is translated 1 unit up.

SPIRAL REVIEW

44. Justify each step. *(Lesson 1-7)*

Procedure	Justification
$5x - 2(4 - x)$	
$5x - 2(4 - x) = 5x - 8 + 2x$	**a.** _____?_____
$\quad\quad\quad\quad\quad = 5x + 2x - 8$	**b.** _____?_____
$\quad\quad\quad\quad\quad = (5x + 2x) - 8$	**c.** _____?_____
$\quad\quad\quad\quad\quad = 7x - 8$	**d.** _____?_____

Describe the correlation illustrated by each scatter plot. *(Lesson 4-5)*

45.

46.

Graph each quadratic function. *(Lesson 9-3)*

47. $y = 2x^2 - 1$ **48.** $y = x^2 - 2x - 2$ **49.** $y = -3x^2 - x + 6$

MULTI-STEP TEST PREP

Quadratic Functions

The Sky's the Limit The Physics Club is using computer simulation software to design a water bottle rocket that doesn't have a parachute. The data for their current design are shown in the table.

1. Tell whether the data satisfy a quadratic function.

2. Graph the function from Problem 1.

3. Find and label the zeros, axis of symmetry, and vertex.

Time (s)	Height (ft)
0	0
1	80
2	128
3	144
4	128
5	80

4. Explain what the x- and y-coordinates of the vertex represent in the context of the problem.

5. Estimate how many seconds it will take the rocket to reach 110 feet. Explain.

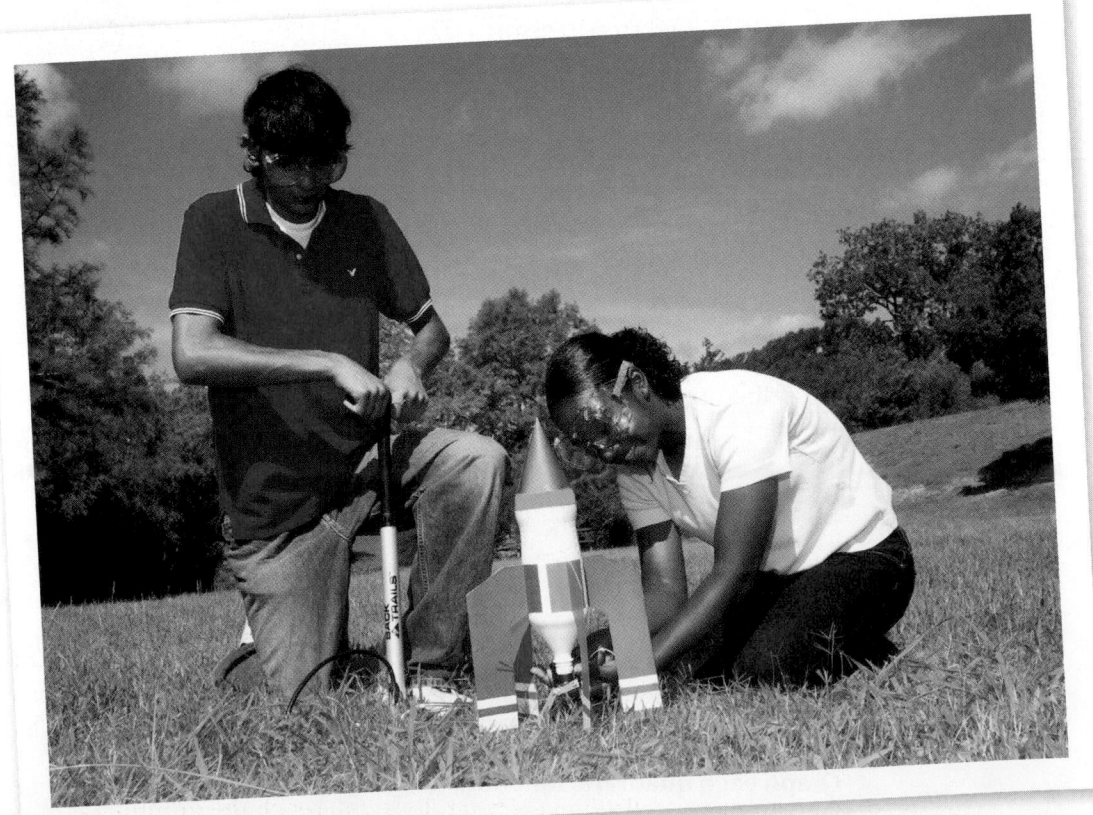

Quiz for Lessons 9-1 Through 9-4

9-1 Identifying Quadratic Functions

Tell whether each function is quadratic. Explain.

1. $y + 2x^2 = 3x$

2. $x^2 + y = 4 + x^2$

3. $\{(2, 12), (-1, 3), (0, 0), (1, 3)\}$

Tell whether the graph of each quadratic function opens upward or downward and whether the parabola has a maximum or a minimum.

4. $y = -x^2 - 7x + 18$

5. $y - 2x^2 = 4x + 3$

6. $y = 5x - 0.5x^2$

7. Graph the function $y = \frac{1}{2}x^2 - 2$ and give the domain and range.

9-2 Characteristics of Quadratic Functions

Find the zeros of each quadratic function from its graph. Then find the axis of symmetry.

8.

9.

10.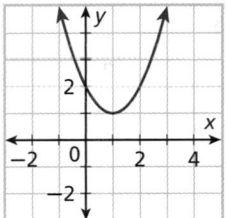

Fnd the vertex.

11. $y = x^2 + 6x + 2$

12. $y = 3 + 4x - 2x^2$

13. $y = 3x^2 + 12x - 12$

14. The height in feet of the curved roof of an aircraft hangar can be modeled by $y = -0.02x^2 + 1.6x$, where x is the horizontal distance in feet from one wall at ground level. What is the greatest height of the hangar?

9-3 Graphing Quadratic Functions

Graph each quadratic function.

15. $y = x^2 + 3x + 9$

16. $y = x^2 - 2x - 15$

17. $y = x^2 - 2x - 8$

18. $y = 2x^2 - 6$

19. $y = 4x^2 + 8x - 2$

20. $y = 2x^2 + 10x + 1$

9-4 Transforming Quadratic Functions

Compare the graph of each function with the graph of $f(x) = x^2$.

21. $g(x) = x^2 - 2$

22. $g(x) = \frac{2}{3}x^2$

23. $g(x) = 5x^2 + 3$

24. $g(x) = -x^2 + 4$

25. The pilot of a hot-air balloon drops a sandbag onto a target from a height of 196 feet. Later, he drops an identical sandbag from a height of 676 feet.

   a. Write the two height functions and compare their graphs. Use $h(t) = -16t^2 + c$, where c is the height of the balloon.

   b. Use the graphs to tell when each sandbag will reach the ground.

Solving Quadratic Equations by Graphing

Objective
Solve quadratic equations by graphing.

Vocabulary
quadratic equation

Who uses this?
Dolphin trainers can use solutions of quadratic equations to plan the choreography for their shows. (See Example 2.)

Every quadratic function has a related *quadratic equation*. A **quadratic equation** is an equation that can be written in the standard form $ax^2 + bx + c = 0$, where a, b, and c are real numbers and $a \neq 0$.

When writing a quadratic function as its related quadratic equation, you replace y with 0.

$$y = ax^2 + bx + c$$
$$0 = ax^2 + bx + c$$
$$ax^2 + bx + c = 0$$

One way to solve a quadratic equation in standard form is to graph the related function and find the x-values where $y = 0$. In other words, find the zeros of the related function. Recall that a quadratic function may have two, one, or no zeros.

Solving Quadratic Equations by Graphing
Step 1 Write the related function.
Step 2 Graph the related function.
Step 3 Find the zeros of the related function.

EXAMPLE 1 **Solving Quadratic Equations by Graphing**

Solve each equation by graphing the related function.

A $2x^2 - 2 = 0$

Step 1 Write the related function.
$2x^2 - 2 = y$, or $y = 2x^2 + 0x - 2$

Step 2 Graph the function.
- The axis of symmetry is $x = 0$.
- The vertex is $(0, -2)$.
- Two other points are $(1, 0)$ and $(2, 6)$.
- Graph the points and **reflect** them across the axis of symmetry.

Step 3 Find the zeros.
The zeros appear to be -1 and 1.

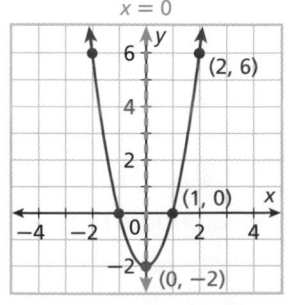

Check

$2x^2 - 2 = 0$	
$2(-1)^2 - 2$	0
$2(1) - 2$	0
$2 - 2$	0
0	0 ✓

Substitute -1 and 1 for x in the quadratic equation.

$2x^2 - 2 = 0$	
$2(1)^2 - 2$	0
$2(1) - 2$	0
$2 - 2$	0
0	0 ✓

Solve each equation by graphing the related function.

B $-x^2 - 4x - 4 = 0$

Step 1 Write the related function.

$$y = -x^2 - 4x - 4$$

Step 2 Graph the function.

- The axis of symmetry is $x = -2$.
- The vertex is $(-2, 0)$.
- The y-intercept is -4.
- Another point is $(-1, -1)$.
- Graph the points and **reflect** them across the axis of symmetry.

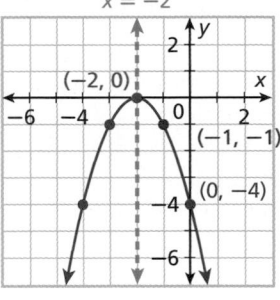

Step 3 Find the zeros.

The only zero appears to be -2.

Check

$$
\begin{array}{r|l}
\multicolumn{2}{c}{-x^2 - 4x - 4 = 0} \\
\hline
-(-2)^2 - 4(-2) - 4 & 0 \\
-(4) + 8 - 4 & 0 \\
4 - 4 & 0 \\
0 & 0 ✓
\end{array}
$$

You can also confirm the solution by using the **Table** function. Enter the equation and press **2nd** **GRAPH** (TABLE). When $y = 0$, $x = -2$. The x-intercept is -2.

C $x^2 + 5 = 4x$

Step 1 Write the related function.

$$x^2 - 4x + 5 = 0$$
$$y = x^2 - 4x + 5$$

Step 2 Graph the function.

Use a graphing calculator.

Step 3 Find the zeros.

The function appears to have no zeros.

The equation has no real-number solutions.

Check reasonableness Use the table function.

There are no zeros in the Y1 column. Also, the signs of the values in this column do not change. The function appears to have no zeros.

 Solve each equation by graphing the related function.

1a. $x^2 - 8x - 16 = 2x^2$

1b. $6x + 10 = -x^2$

1c. $-x^2 + 4 = 0$

EXAMPLE 2 *Aquatics Application*

A dolphin jumps out of the water. The quadratic function $y = -16x^2 + 20x$ models the dolphin's height above the water after x seconds. How long is the dolphin out of the water?

When the dolphin leaves the water, its height is 0, and when the dolphin reenters the water, its height is 0. So solve $0 = -16x^2 + 20x$ to find the times when the dolphin leaves and reenters the water.

Step 1 Write the related function.

$$0 = -16x^2 + 20x$$
$$y = -16x^2 + 20x$$

Step 2 Graph the function.

Use a graphing calculator.

Step 3 Use **TRACE** to estimate the zeros.

The zeros appear to be 0 and 1.25.

The dolphin leaves the water at 0 seconds and reenters the water at 1.25 seconds.

The dolphin is out of the water for 1.25 seconds.

Check $0 = -16x^2 + 20x$

0	$-16(1.25)^2 + 20(1.25)$	*Substitute 1.25 for x in the*
0	$-16(1.5625) + 25$	*quadratic equation.*
0	$-25 + 25$	
0	$0 \checkmark$	

2. What if...? Another dolphin jumps out of the water. The quadratic function $y = -16x^2 + 32x$ models the dolphin's height above the water after x seconds. How long is the dolphin out of the water?

THINK AND DISCUSS

1. Describe the graph of a quadratic function whose related quadratic equation has only one solution.

2. Describe the graph of a quadratic function whose related quadratic equation has no real solutions.

3. Describe the graph of a quadratic function whose related quadratic equation has two solutions.

4. GET ORGANIZED Copy and complete the graphic organizer. In each of the boxes, write the steps for solving quadratic equations by graphing.

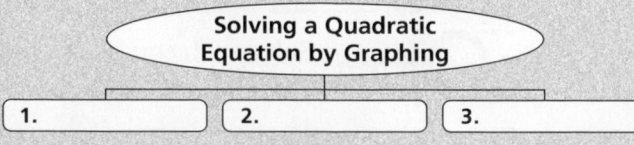

Solving a Quadratic Equation by Graphing

| 1. | 2. | 3. |

9-5
Exercises

go.hrw.com
Homework Help Online
KEYWORD: MA7 9-5
Parent Resources Online
KEYWORD: MA7 Parent

GUIDED PRACTICE

1. **Vocabulary** Write two words related to the graph of a quadratic function that can be used to find the solution of the related *quadratic equation*.

SEE EXAMPLE **1**
p. 642

Solve each equation by graphing the related function.

2. $x^2 - 4 = 0$

3. $x^2 = 16$

4. $-2x^2 - 6 = 0$

5. $-x^2 + 12x - 36 = 0$

6. $-x^2 = -9$

7. $2x^2 = 3x^2 - 2x - 8$

8. $x^2 - 6x + 9 = 0$

9. $8x = -4x^2 - 4$

10. $x^2 + 5x + 4 = 0$

11. $x^2 + 2 = 0$

12. $x^2 - 6x = 7$

13. $x^2 + 5x = -8$

SEE EXAMPLE **2**
p. 644

14. **Sports** A baseball coach uses a pitching machine to simulate pop flies during practice. The quadratic function $y = -16x^2 + 80x$ models the height of the baseball after x seconds. How long is the baseball in the air?

PRACTICE AND PROBLEM SOLVING

Independent Practice

For Exercises	See Example
15–23	1
24	2

Solve each equation by graphing the related function.

15. $-x^2 + 16 = 0$

16. $3x^2 = -7$

17. $5x^2 - 12x + 10 = x^2 + 10x$

18. $x^2 + 10x + 25 = 0$

19. $-4x^2 - 24x = 36$

20. $-9x^2 + 10x - 9 = -8x$

21. $-x^2 - 1 = 0$

22. $3x^2 - 27 = 0$

23. $4x^2 - 4x + 5 = 2x^2$

Extra Practice
Skills Practice p. S21
Application Practice p. S36

24. **Geography** Yosemite Falls in California is made of three smaller falls. The upper fall drops 1450 feet. The height h in feet of a water droplet falling from the upper fall to the next fall is modeled by $h(t) = -16t^2 + 1450$, where t is the time in seconds after the initial fall. Estimate the time it takes for the droplet to reach the next cascade.

Tell whether each statement is always, sometimes, or never true.

25. If the graph of a quadratic function has its vertex at the origin, then the related quadratic equation has exactly one solution.

26. If the graph of a quadratic function opens upward, then the related quadratic equation has two solutions.

27. If the graph of a quadratic function has its vertex on the x-axis, then the related quadratic equation has exactly one solution.

28. If the graph of a quadratic function has its vertex in the first quadrant, then the related quadratic equation has two solutions.

29. A quadratic equation in the form $ax^2 - c = 0$, where $a < 0$ and $c > 0$, has two solutions.

30. **Graphing Calculator** A fireworks shell is fired from a mortar. Its height is modeled by the function $h(t) = -16(t - 7)^2 + 784$, where t is the time in seconds and h is the height in feet.

a. Graph the function.

b. If the shell is supposed to explode at its maximum height, at what height should it explode?

c. If the shell does not explode, how long will it take to return to the ground?

31. **Athletics** The graph shows the height y in feet of a gymnast jumping off a vault after x seconds.

   a. How long does the gymnast stay in the air?

   b. What is the maximum height that the gymnast reaches?

   c. Explain why the function $y = -5x^2 + 10x$ cannot accurately model the gymnast's motion.

Height of Gymnast

32. **Graphing Calculator** Use a graphing calculator to solve the equation $x^2 = x + 12$ by graphing $y_1 = x^2$ and $y_2 = x + 12$ and finding the x-coordinates of the points of intersection. (*Hint:* Find the points of intersection by using the [2nd] [TRACE] function after graphing.)

33. **Biology** The quadratic function $y = -5x^2 + 7x$ approximates the height y in meters of a kangaroo x seconds after it has jumped. How long does it take the kangaroo to return to the ground?

For Exercises 34–36, use the table to determine the solutions of the related quadratic equation.

34.

x	y
−2	−1
−1	0
0	−1
1	−4
2	−9

35.

x	y
−2	−6
−1	0
0	2
1	0
2	−6

36.

x	y
−2	6
−1	3
0	2
1	3
2	6

37. **Geometry** The hypotenuse of a right triangle is 4 cm longer than one leg and 8 cm longer than the other leg. Let x represent the length of the hypotenuse.

   a. Write an expression for the length of each leg in terms of x.

   b. Use the Pythagorean Theorem to write an equation that can be solved for x.

   c. Find the solutions of your equation from part **b.**

   d. **Critical Thinking** What do the solutions of your equation represent? Are both solutions reasonable? Explain.

38. **Write About It** Explain how to find solutions of a quadratic equation by analyzing a table of values.

39. **Critical Thinking** Explain why a quadratic equation in the form $ax^2 - c = 0$, where $a > 0$ and $c > 0$, will always have two solutions. Explain why a quadratic equation in the form $ax^2 + c = 0$, where $a > 0$ and $c > 0$, will never have any real-number solutions.

Biology

Some species of kangaroos are able to jump 30 feet in distance and 6 feet in height.

MULTI-STEP TEST PREP

40. This problem will prepare you for the Multi-Step Test Prep on page 640. The quadratic equation $0 = -16t^2 + 80t$ gives the time t in seconds when a golf ball is at height 0 feet.

   a. How long is the golf ball in the air?

   b. What is the maximum height of the golf ball?

   c. After how many seconds is the ball at its maximum height?

   d. What is the height of the ball after 3.5 seconds? Is there another time when the ball reaches that height? Explain.

41. Use the graph to find the number of solutions of $-2x^2 + 2 = 0$.

   Ⓐ 0   Ⓒ 2

   Ⓑ 1   Ⓓ 3

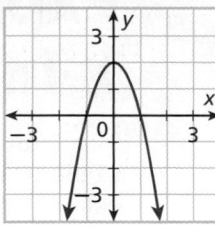

42. Which graph could be used to find the solutions of $x^2 = -4x + 12$?

Ⓕ

Ⓗ

Ⓖ

Ⓙ
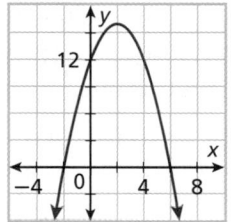

43. Short Response Find the solutions of $2x^2 + x - 1 = 0$ by graphing. Explain how the graph of the related function shows the solutions of the equation.

CHALLENGE AND EXTEND

 Graphing Calculator Use a graphing calculator to approximate the solutions of each quadratic equation.

44. $\dfrac{5}{16}x + \dfrac{1}{4}x^2 = \dfrac{3}{5}$ **45.** $1200x^2 - 650x - 100 = -200x - 175$

46. $\dfrac{1}{5}x + \dfrac{3}{4}x^2 = \dfrac{7}{12}$ **47.** $400x^2 - 100 = -300x + 456$

SPIRAL REVIEW

Write an equation in point-slope form for the line with the given slope that contains the given point. *(Lesson 5-8)*

48. slope $-\dfrac{1}{2}$; $(2, 3)$ **49.** slope $= -3$; $(-2, 4)$ **50.** slope $= 0$; $(2, 1)$

Simplify. *(Lesson 7-4)*

51. $\dfrac{3^4}{3}$ **52.** $\dfrac{5^2 \cdot 2^4}{5 \cdot 2^2}$ **53.** $\dfrac{(x^4)^5}{(x^3)^3}$ **54.** $\left(\dfrac{x^3}{y^2}\right)^{-3}$

55. $\left(\dfrac{a^2 b^3}{ab^2}\right)^3$ **56.** $\left(\dfrac{4s}{3t}\right)^{-2}$ **57.** $\left(\dfrac{2}{3}\right)^{-3} \cdot \left(\dfrac{a^3}{b}\right)^{-2}$ **58.** $\left(\dfrac{-k^2}{5k^3}\right)^{-3}$

Compare the graph of each function with the graph of $f(x) = x^2$. *(Lesson 9-4)*

59. $g(x) = 3x^2$ **60.** $g(x) = x^2 - 8$ **61.** $g(x) = \dfrac{3}{4}x^2 + 2$

9-5
Technology LAB

Use with Lesson 9-5

Explore Roots, Zeros, and *x*-Intercepts

The solutions, or *roots*, of a quadratic equation are the *x*-intercepts, or zeros, of the related quadratic function. You can use tables or graphs on a graphing calculator to understand the connections between zeros, roots, and *x*-intercepts.

go.hrw.com
Lab Resources Online
KEYWORD: MA7 Lab9

Activity 1

Solve $5x^2 + 8x - 4 = 0$ by using a table.

1 Enter the related function in Y_1.

2 Press `2nd` `GRAPH` (TABLE) to use the **TABLE** function.

3 Scroll through the values by using ▲ and ▼. Look for values of 0 in the Y_1 column. The corresponding *x*-value is a zero of the function. There is one zero at −2.

Also look for places where the signs of nonzero *y*-values change. There is a zero between the corresponding *x*-values. So there is another zero somewhere between 0 and 1.

The signs of the *y*-values change.

4 To get a better estimate of the zero, change the table settings. Press `2nd` `WINDOW` (TBLSET) to view the **TABLE SETUP** screen. Set **TblStart = 0** and the step value △**Tbl = .1**. Press `2nd` `GRAPH` (TABLE) to see the table again. The table will show you more *x*-values between 0 and 1.

5 Scroll through the values by using ▲ and ▼. The second zero is at 0.4.

The zeros of the function, −2 and 0.4, are the solutions, or roots, of the equation $5x^2 + 8x - 4 = 0$. Check the solutions algebraically.

Check

$5x^2 + 8x - 4 = 0$		$5x^2 + 8x - 4 = 0$	
$5(-2)^2 + 8(-2) - 4$	0	$5(0.4)^2 + 8(0.4) - 4$	0
$5(4) - 16 - 4$	0	$5(0.16) + 3.2 - 4$	0
$20 - 16 - 4$	0	$0.8 + 3.2 - 4$	0
0	0 ✓	0	0 ✓

Try This

Solve each equation by using a table.

1. $x^2 - 4x - 5 = 0$ **2.** $x^2 - x - 6 = 0$ **3.** $2x^2 + x - 1 = 0$ **4.** $5x^2 - 6x - 8 = 0$

5. Critical Thinking How would you find the zero of a function that showed a sign change in the *y*-values between the *x*-values 1.2 and 1.3?

6. Make a Conjecture If you scrolled up and down the list and found only positive *y*-values, what might you conclude?

Activity 2

Solve $5x^2 + x - 8.4 = 0$ by using a table and a graph.

1 Enter the related function in Y_1.

2 To view both the table and the graph at the same time, set your calculator to the Graph-Table mode. Press MODE and select **G-T**.

3 Press GRAPH. You should see the graph and the table. Notice that the function appears to have one negative zero and one positive zero near the *y*-axis.

4 To get a closer view of the graph, press ZOOM and select **4:ZDecimal**.

5 Press TRACE. Use ◄ to scroll to find the negative zero. The graph and the table show that the zero is −1.4.

6 Use ► to scroll and find the positive zero. The graph and the table show that the zero is 1.2.

The solutions are −1.4 and 1.2. Check the solutions algebraically.

$5x^2 + x - 8.4 = 0$		$5x^2 + x - 8.4 = 0$	
$5(-1.4)^2 + (-1.4) - 8.4$	0	$5(1.2)^2 + (1.2) - 8.4$	0
$5(1.96) - 1.4 - 8.4$	0	$5(1.44) + 1.2 - 8.4$	0
$9.8 - 1.4 - 8.4$	0	$7.2 + 1.2 - 8.4$	0
0	0 ✓	0	0 ✓

Try This

Solve each equation by using a table and a graph.

7. $2x^2 - x - 3 = 0$ **8.** $5x^2 + 13x + 6 = 0$ **9.** $10x^2 - 3x - 4 = 0$ **10.** $x^2 - 2x - 0.96 = 0$

11. Critical Thinking Suppose that when you graphed a quadratic function, you could see only one side of the graph and one zero. What methods would you use to try to find the other zero?

Solving Quadratic Equations by Factoring

Objective
Solve quadratic equations by factoring.

Who uses this?

In order to determine how many seconds she will be in the air, a high diver can use a quadratic equation. (See Example 3.)

You have solved quadratic equations by graphing. Another method used to solve quadratic equations is to factor and use the Zero Product Property.

Zero Product Property

For all real numbers a and b,

WORDS	NUMBERS	ALGEBRA
If the product of two quantities equals zero, at least one of the quantities equals zero.	$3(0) = 0$ $0(4) = 0$	If $ab = 0$, then $a = 0$ or $b = 0$.

EXAMPLE **1** **Using the Zero Product Property**

Use the Zero Product Property to solve each equation. Check your answer.

A $(x - 3)(x + 7) = 0$

$x - 3 = 0$ or $x + 7 = 0$ *Use the Zero Product Property.*

$x = 3$ or $x = -7$ *Solve each equation.*

The solutions are 3 and −7.

Check

$(x - 3)(x + 7) = 0$	
$(3 - 3)(3 + 7)$	0
$(0)(10)$	0
0	0 ✓

Substitute each solution for x into the original equation.

$(x - 3)(x + 7) = 0$	
$(-7 - 3)(-7 + 7)$	0
$(-10)(0)$	0
0	0 ✓

B $(x)(x - 5) = 0$

$x = 0$ or $x - 5 = 0$ *Use the Zero Product Property.*

$x = 5$ *Solve the second equation.*

The solutions are 0 and 5.

Check

$(x)(x - 5) = 0$	
$(0)(0 - 5)$	0
$(0)(-5)$	0
0	0 ✓

Substitute each solution for x into the original equation.

$(x)(x - 5) = 0$	
$(5)(5 - 5)$	0
$(5)(0)$	0
0	0 ✓

 Use the Zero Product Property to solve each equation. Check your answer.

1a. $(x)(x + 4) = 0$ **1b.** $(x + 4)(x - 3) = 0$

If a quadratic equation is written in standard form, $ax^2 + bx + c = 0$, you may need to factor before using the Zero Product Property to solve the equation.

EXAMPLE **2** **Solving Quadratic Equations by Factoring**

Solve each quadratic equation by factoring. Check your answer.

A $x^2 + 7x + 10 = 0$

$(x + 5)(x + 2) = 0$ *Factor the trinomial.*

$x + 5 = 0$ or $x + 2 = 0$ *Use the Zero Product Property.*

$x = -5$ or $x = -2$ *Solve each equation.*

The solutions are -5 and -2.

> **Helpful Hint**
>
> To review factoring techniques, see Lessons 8-3 through 8-5.

Check

$x^2 + 7x + 10 = 0$	
$(-5)^2 + 7(-5) + 10$	0
$25 - 35 + 10$	0
0	0 ✓

$x^2 + 7x + 10 = 0$	
$(-2)^2 + 7(-2) + 10$	0
$4 - 14 + 10$	0
0	0 ✓

B $x^2 + 2x = 8$

$$x^2 + 2x = 8$$
$$\underline{-8 \quad -8}$$
$$x^2 + 2x - 8 = 0$$

The equation must be written in standard form. So subtract 8 from both sides.

$(x + 4)(x - 2) = 0$ *Factor the trinomial.*

$x + 4 = 0$ or $x - 2 = 0$ *Use the Zero Product Property.*

$x = -4$ or $x = 2$ *Solve each equation.*

The solutions are -4 and 2.

Check   Graph the related quadratic function. The zeros of the related function should be the same as the solutions from factoring.

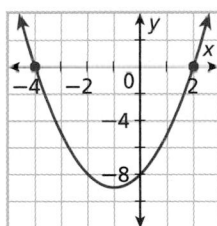

The graph of $y = x^2 + 2x - 8$ shows two zeros that appear to be -4 and 2, the same as the solutions from factoring. ✓

C $x^2 + 2x + 1 = 0$

$(x + 1)(x + 1) = 0$ *Factor the trinomial.*

$x + 1 = 0$ or $x + 1 = 0$ *Use the Zero Product property.*

$x = -1$ or $x = -1$ *Solve each equation.*

Both factors result in the same solution, so there is one solution, -1.

Check   Use a graphing calculator to graph the related function.

The graph of $y = x^2 + 2x + 1$ shows one zero that appears to be -1, the same as the solution from factoring. ✓

Solve each quadratic equation by factoring. Check your answer.

D $-2x^2 = 18 - 12x$

$$-2x^2 + 12x - 18 = 0 \qquad \textit{Write the equation in standard form.}$$
$$-2(x^2 - 6x + 9) = 0 \qquad \textit{Factor out the GCF, } -2.$$
$$-2(x - 3)(x - 3) = 0 \qquad \textit{Factor the trinomial.}$$
$$-2 \neq 0 \ \text{ or } \ x - 3 = 0 \qquad \textit{Use the Zero Product Property. } -2 \textit{ cannot equal } 0.$$
$$x = 3 \qquad \textit{Solve the remaining equation.}$$

The only solution is 3.

Helpful Hint

$(x - 3)(x - 3)$ is a perfect square. Since both factors are the same, you solve only one of them.

Check $\quad -2x^2 = 18 - 12x$

$-2(3)^2$	$18 - 12(3)$	*Substitute 3 into the original equation.*
-18	$18 - 36$	
-18	-18 ✓	

 CHECK IT OUT! Solve each quadratic equation by factoring. Check your answer.

2a. $x^2 - 6x + 9 = 0$ **2b.** $x^2 + 4x = 5$

2c. $30x = -9x^2 - 25$ **2d.** $3x^2 - 4x + 1 = 0$

E X A M P L E 3 **Sports Application**

The height of a diver above the water during a dive can be modeled by $h = -16t^2 + 8t + 48$, where h is height in feet and t is time in seconds. Find the time it takes for the diver to reach the water.

48 ft

$$h = -16t^2 + 8t + 48$$
$$0 = -16t^2 + 8t + 48 \qquad \textit{The diver reaches the water when } h = 0.$$
$$0 = -8(2t^2 - t - 6) \qquad \textit{Factor out the GCF, } -8.$$
$$0 = -8(2t + 3)(t - 2) \qquad \textit{Factor the trinomial.}$$
$$-8 \neq 0, \ 2t + 3 = 0 \ \text{ or } t - 2 = 0 \qquad \textit{Use the Zero Product Property.}$$
$$2t = -3 \text{ or } \qquad t = 2 \qquad \textit{Solve each equation.}$$
$$t = -\frac{3}{2} \ \text{✗} \qquad \textit{Since time cannot be negative, } -\frac{3}{2} \textit{ does not make sense in this situation.}$$

It takes the diver 2 seconds to reach the water.

Check $\quad 0 = -16t^2 + 8t + 48$

0	$-16(2)^2 + 8(2) + 48$	*Substitute 2 into the original equation.*
0	$-64 + 16 + 48$	
0	0 ✓	

CHECK IT OUT! **3. What if...?** The equation for the height above the water for another diver can be modeled by $h = -16t^2 + 8t + 24$. Find the time it takes this diver to reach the water.

THINK AND DISCUSS

1. Explain two ways to solve $x^2 + x - 6 = 0$. How are these two methods similar?

2. Describe the relationships among the solutions of $x^2 - 4x - 12 = 0$, the zeros and x-intercepts of $y = x^2 - 4x - 12$, and the factors of $x^2 - 4x - 12$.

3. **GET ORGANIZED** Copy and complete the graphic organizer. In each box, write a step used to solve a quadratic equation by factoring.

```
        Solving Quadratic Equations
               by Factoring

   ┌──────────┐   ┌──────┐   ┌──────┐
   │ 1. Factor│ → │  2.  │ → │  3.  │
   └──────────┘   └──────┘   └──────┘
```

9-6 Exercises

go.hrw.com
Homework Help Online
KEYWORD: MA11 9-6
Parent Resources Online
KEYWORD: MA7 Parent

GUIDED PRACTICE

SEE EXAMPLE 1
p. 650

Use the Zero Product Property to solve each equation. Check your answer.

1. $(x + 2)(x - 8) = 0$
2. $(x - 6)(x - 5) = 0$
3. $(x + 7)(x + 9) = 0$
4. $(x)(x - 1) = 0$
5. $(x)(x + 11) = 0$
6. $(3x + 2)(4x - 1) = 0$

SEE EXAMPLE 2
p. 651

Solve each quadratic equation by factoring. Check your answer.

7. $x^2 + 4x - 12 = 0$
8. $x^2 - 8x - 9 = 0$
9. $x^2 - 5x + 6 = 0$
10. $x^2 - 3x = 10$
11. $x^2 + 10x = -16$
12. $x^2 + 2x = 15$
13. $x^2 - 8x + 16 = 0$
14. $-3x^2 = 18x + 27$
15. $x^2 + 36 = 12x$
16. $2x^2 + 5x - 3 = 0$
17. $2x^2 + 7x + 6 = 0$
18. $2x^2 + 6x = -18$

SEE EXAMPLE 3
p. 652

19. **Games** A group of friends tries to keep a beanbag from touching the ground. On one kick, the beanbag's height can be modeled by $h = -16t^2 + 14t + 2$, where h is the height in feet above the ground and t is the time in seconds. Find the time it takes the beanbag to reach the ground.

PRACTICE AND PROBLEM SOLVING

Independent Practice

For Exercises	See Example
20–25	1
26–31	2
32	3

Extra Practice

Skills Practice p. S21
Application Practice p. S36

Use the Zero Product Property to solve each equation. Check your answer.

20. $(x - 8)(x + 6) = 0$
21. $(x + 4)(x + 7) = 0$
22. $(x - 2)(x - 5) = 0$
23. $(x - 9)(x) = 0$
24. $(x)(x + 25) = 0$
25. $(2x + 1)(3x - 1) = 0$

Solve each quadratic equation by factoring. Check your answer.

26. $x^2 + 8x + 15 = 0$
27. $x^2 - 2x - 8 = 0$
28. $x^2 - 4x + 3 = 0$
29. $3x^2 - 2x - 1 = 0$
30. $4x^2 - 9x + 2 = 0$
31. $-x^2 = 4x + 4$

32. Multi-Step The height of a flare can be approximated by the function $h = -16t^2 + 95t + 6$, where h is the height in feet and t is the time in seconds. Find the time it takes the flare to hit the ground.

Determine the number of solutions of each equation.

33. $(x + 8)(x + 8) = 0$ 　　**34.** $(x - 3)(x + 3) = 0$ 　　**35.** $(x + 7)^2 = 0$

36. $3x^2 + 12x + 9 = 0$ 　　**37.** $x^2 + 12x + 40 = 4$ 　　**38.** $(x - 2)^2 = 9$

39. /// **ERROR ANALYSIS** /// Which solution is incorrect? Explain the error.

A
$x^2 + x - 2 = 0$
$(x - 1)(x + 2) = 0$
$x = 1$ or $x = -2$

B
$x^2 + x - 2 = 0$
$(x - 1)(x + 2) = 0$
$x = -1$ or $x = 2$

40. Number Theory Write an equation that could be used to find two consecutive even integers whose product is 24. Let x represent the first integer. Solve the equation and give the two integers.

41. Geometry The photo shows a traditional thatched house as found in Santana, Madeira, in Portugal. The front of the house is in the shape of a triangle. Suppose the base of the triangle is 1 m less than its height and the area of the triangle is 15 m². Find the height of the triangle. $\left(\text{Hint: Use } A = \frac{1}{2}bh.\right)$

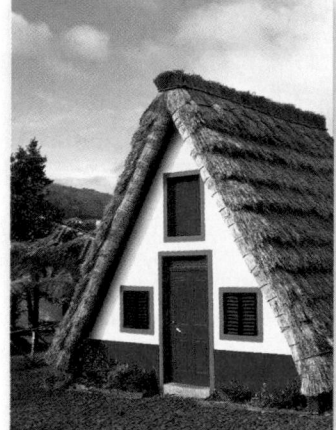

42. Multi-Step The length of a rectangle is 1 ft less than 3 times the width. The area is 310 ft². Find the dimensions of the rectangle.

43. Physics The height of a fireworks rocket in meters can be approximated by $h = -5t^2 + 30t$, where h is the height in meters and t is time in seconds. Find the time it takes the rocket to reach the ground after it has been launched.

44. Geometry One base of a trapezoid is the same length as the height of the trapezoid. The other base is 4 cm more than the height. The area of the trapezoid is 48 cm². Find the length of the shorter base. $\left(\text{Hint: Use } A = \frac{1}{2}h(b_1 + b_2).\right)$

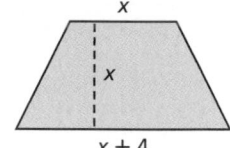

45. Critical Thinking Can you solve $(x - 2)(x + 3) = 5$ by solving $x - 2 = 5$ and $x + 3 = 5$? Why or why not?

46. Write About It Explain why you set each factor equal to zero when solving a quadratic equation by factoring.

MULTI-STEP TEST PREP

47. This problem will prepare you for the Multi-Step Test Prep on page 678.

A tee box is 48 feet above its fairway. When a golf ball is hit from the tee box with an initial vertical velocity of 32 ft/s, the quadratic equation $0 = -16t^2 + 32t + 48$ gives the time t in seconds when a golf ball is at height 0 feet on the fairway.

　a. Solve the quadratic equation by factoring to see how long the ball is in the air.

　b. What is the height of the ball at 1 second?

　c. Is the ball at its maximum height at 1 second? Explain.

48. What are the solutions to $(x - 1)(2x + 5) = 0$?

    Ⓐ -1 and $\dfrac{5}{2}$ Ⓒ 1 and $-\dfrac{5}{2}$

    Ⓑ -1 and $\dfrac{2}{5}$ Ⓓ 1 and $-\dfrac{2}{5}$

49. Which graph could be used to solve the equation $(x - 3)(x - 2) = 0$?

Ⓕ

Ⓗ

Ⓖ

Ⓙ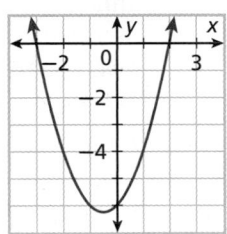

CHALLENGE AND EXTEND

Solve each equation by factoring.

50. $6x^2 + 11x = 10$ **51.** $0.2x^2 + 1 = -1.2x$ **52.** $\dfrac{1}{3}x^2 = 2x - 3$

53. $75x - 45 = -30x^2$ **54.** $x^2 = -4(2x + 3)$ **55.** $\dfrac{x(x - 3)}{2} = 5$

56. $x(x - 10)(x - 3) = 0$ **57.** $x^3 + 2x^2 + x = 0$ **58.** $x^3 + 4x^2 = 0$

🖳🔾 **Geometry** Use the diagram for Exercises 59–61.

59. Write a polynomial to represent the area of the larger rectangle.

60. Write a polynomial to represent the area of the smaller rectangle.

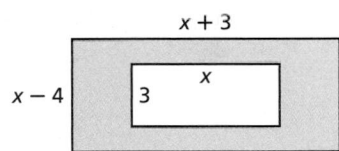

61. Write a polynomial to represent the area of the shaded region. Then solve for x given that the area of the shaded region is 48 square units.

SPIRAL REVIEW

Find each root. *(Lesson 1-5)*

62. $\sqrt{121}$ **63.** $-\sqrt{64}$ **64.** $-\sqrt{100}$ **65.** $\sqrt[4]{16}$

Solve each system by using substitution. *(Lesson 6-2)*

66. $\begin{cases} 2x + 2y = 10 \\ y = x - 3 \end{cases}$ **67.** $\begin{cases} 4x - 3y = 12 \\ x - y = 7 \end{cases}$ **68.** $\begin{cases} x - 2y = 6 \\ 10x + y = 18 \end{cases}$

Solve each equation by graphing the related function. *(Lesson 9-5)*

69. $x^2 - 49 = 0$ **70.** $x^2 = x + 12$ **71.** $-x^2 + 8x = 15$

Solving Quadratic Equations by Using Square Roots

Objective
Solve quadratic equations by using square roots.

Why learn this?
Square roots can be used to find how much fencing is needed for a pen at a zoo. (See Example 4.)

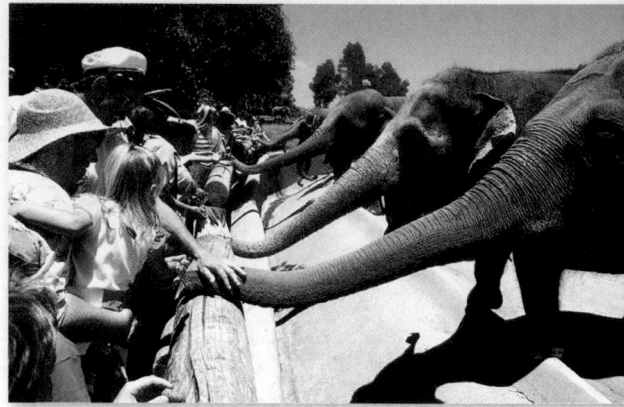

Some quadratic equations cannot be easily solved by factoring. Square roots can be used to solve some of these quadratic equations. Recall from Lesson 1-5 that every positive real number has two square roots, one positive and one negative.

$$3(3) = 3^2 = 9 \rightarrow \sqrt{9} = 3 \leftarrow \text{Positive square root of 9}$$

$$(-3)(-3) = (-3)^2 = 9 \rightarrow -\sqrt{9} = -3 \leftarrow \text{Negative square root of 9}$$

Reading Math

The expression ± 3 is read "plus or minus three."

When you take the square root of a positive real number and the sign of the square root is not indicated, you must find both the positive and negative square root. This is indicated by $\pm\sqrt{}$.

$$\pm\sqrt{9} = \pm 3 \leftarrow \text{Positive and negative square roots of 9}$$

Know it!
Note

Square-Root Property

WORDS	NUMBERS	ALGEBRA
To solve a quadratic equation in the form $x^2 = a$, take the square root of both sides.	$x^2 = 15$ $x = \pm\sqrt{15}$	If $x^2 = a$ and a is a positive real number, then $x = \pm\sqrt{a}$.

EXAMPLE 1 Using Square Roots to Solve $x^2 = a$

Solve using square roots.

A $x^2 = 16$

$x = \pm\sqrt{16}$ *Solve for x by taking the square root of both*
$x = \pm 4$ *sides. Use $\pm$ to show both square roots.*

The solutions are 4 and -4.

Check

$x^2 = 16$			$x^2 = 16$	
$(4)^2$	16	*Substitute 4 and -4 into*	$(-4)^2$	16
	16 ∣ 16 ✓	*the original equation.*		16 ∣ 16 ✓

Solve using square roots.

B $x^2 = -4$

$x = \pm\sqrt{-4}$ *There is no real number whose square is negative.*
There is no real solution.

 Solve using square roots. Check your answer.

1a. $x^2 = 121$ **1b.** $x^2 = 0$ **1c.** $x^2 = -16$

If necessary, use inverse operations to isolate the squared part of a quadratic equation before taking the square root of both sides.

EXAMPLE 2   **Using Square Roots to Solve Quadratic Equations**

Solve using square roots.

A $x^2 + 5 = 5$

$$x^2 + 5 = 5$$
$$\underline{-5 \quad -5}$$ *Subtract 5 from both sides.*
$$x^2 = 0$$
$$x = \pm\sqrt{0} = 0$$ *Take the square root of both sides.*

The solution is 0.

Helpful Hint

0 is neither positive nor negative.

B $4x^2 - 25 = 0$

$$4x^2 - 25 = 0$$
$$\underline{+25 \quad +25}$$ *Add 25 to both sides.*
$$\frac{4x^2}{4} = \frac{25}{4}$$ *Divide both sides by 4.*
$$x^2 = \frac{25}{4}$$
$$x = \pm\sqrt{\frac{25}{4}} = \pm\frac{5}{2}$$ *Take the square root of both sides. Use $\pm$ to show both square roots.*

The solutions are $\frac{5}{2}$ and $-\frac{5}{2}$.

C $(x + 2)^2 = 9$

$$(x + 2)^2 = 9$$
$$x + 2 = \pm\sqrt{9}$$ *Take the square root of both sides. Use $\pm$ to show both square roots.*
$$x + 2 = \pm 3$$
$$x + 2 = 3 \text{ or } x + 2 = -3$$ *Write two equations, using both the positive and negative square roots, and solve each equation.*
$$\underline{-2 \quad -2} \qquad \underline{-2 \quad -2}$$
$$x = 1 \text{ or } x = -5$$

The solutions are 1 and -5.

Check

$(x + 2)^2 = 9$	
$(1 + 2)^2$	9
3^2	9
9	9 ✓

$(x + 2)^2 = 9$	
$(-5 + 2)^2$	9
$(-3)^2$	9
9	9 ✓

 Solve by using square roots. Check your answer.

2a. $100x^2 + 49 = 0$ **2b.** $(x - 5)^2 = 16$

When solving quadratic equations by using square roots, you may need to find the square root of a number that is not a perfect square. In this case, the answer is an irrational number. You can approximate the solutions.

EXAMPLE 3 Solve the equation $0 = -2x^2 + 80$. Round to the nearest hundredth.

$$0 = -2x^2 + 80$$

$$\underline{-80 \qquad -80} \qquad \text{Subtract 80 from both sides.}$$

$$\frac{-80}{-2} = \frac{-2x^2}{-2} \qquad \text{Divide both sides by } -2.$$

$$40 = x^2$$

$$\pm\sqrt{40} = x \qquad \text{Take the square root of both sides.}$$

$$x \approx \pm 6.32 \qquad \text{Find } \sqrt{40} \text{ on a calculator.}$$

The approximate solutions are 6.32 and −6.32.

Check Use a graphing calculator to support your answer.

Use the zero function.
The approximate solutions
are 6.32 and −6.32. ✓

 Solve. Round to the nearest hundredth.

3a. $0 = 90 - x^2$ **3b.** $2x^2 - 64 = 0$ **3c.** $x^2 + 45 = 0$

EXAMPLE 4 *Career Application*

A zookeeper is buying fencing to enclose a pen at the zoo. The pen is an isosceles right triangle. There is already a fence on the side that borders a path. The area of the pen will be 4500 square feet. The zookeeper can buy the fencing in whole feet only. How many feet of fencing should he buy?

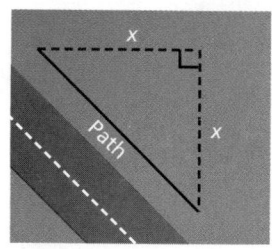

Let x represent the length of one of the sides.

$$\frac{1}{2}bh = A \qquad \text{Use the formula for area of a triangle.}$$

$$\frac{1}{2}x(x) = 4500 \qquad \text{Substitute } x \text{ for both } b \text{ and } h \text{ and 4500 for } A.$$

$$(2)\frac{1}{2}x^2 = 4500(2) \qquad \text{Simplify. Multiply both sides by 2.}$$

$$x^2 = 9000$$

$$x = \pm\sqrt{9000} \qquad \text{Take the square root of both sides.}$$

$$x \approx \pm 94.9 \qquad \text{Find } \sqrt{9000} \text{ on a calculator.}$$

Negative numbers are not reasonable for length, so $x \approx 94.9$ is the only solution that makes sense. Therefore, the zookeeper needs 95 + 95, or 190, feet of fencing.

> **Remember!**
>
> An isosceles triangle has at least two sides of the same length.

 4. A house is on a lot that is shaped like a trapezoid. The solid lines show the boundaries, where x represents the width of the front yard. Find the width of the front yard, given that the area is 6000 square feet. Round to the nearest foot. (*Hint:* Use $A = \frac{1}{2}h(b_1 + b_2)$.)

THINK AND DISCUSS

1. Explain why there are no solutions to the quadratic equation $x^2 = -9$.

2. Describe how to estimate the solutions of $4 = x^2 - 16$. What are the approximate solutions?

3. **GET ORGANIZED** Copy and complete the graphic organizer. In each box, write an example of a quadratic equation with the given number of solutions. Solve each equation.

```
        Solving Quadratic Equations by Using
        Square Roots When the Equation Has...

   No real solutions      One solution      Two solutions
```

Exercises

go.hrw.com
Homework Help Online
KEYWORD: MA7 9-7
Parent Resources Online
KEYWORD: MA7 Parent

GUIDED PRACTICE

Solve using square roots. Check your answer.

SEE EXAMPLE 1
p. 656

1. $x^2 = 225$
2. $x^2 = 49$
3. $x^2 = -100$
4. $x^2 = 400$
5. $-25 = x^2$
6. $36 = x^2$

SEE EXAMPLE 2
p. 657

7. $3x^2 - 75 = 0$
8. $0 = 81x^2 - 25$
9. $49x^2 + 64 = 0$
10. $16x^2 + 10 = 131$
11. $(x - 3)^2 = 64$
12. $(x - 9)^2 = 25$

SEE EXAMPLE 3
p. 658

Solve. Round to the nearest hundredth.

13. $3x^2 = 81$
14. $0 = x^2 - 60$
15. $100 - 5x^2 = 0$

SEE EXAMPLE 4
p. 658

16. **Geometry** The length of a rectangle is 3 times its width. The area of the rectangle is 170 square meters. Find the width. Round to the nearest tenth of a meter. (*Hint:* Use $A = \ell w$.)

PRACTICE AND PROBLEM SOLVING

Independent Practice

For Exercises	See Example
17–22	1
23–28	2
29–34	3
35	4

Solve using square roots. Check your answer.

17. $x^2 = 169$
18. $x^2 = 25$
19. $x^2 = -36$
20. $x^2 = 10,000$
21. $-121 = x^2$
22. $625 = x^2$
23. $4 - 81x^2 = 0$
24. $(2x + 1)^2 = 25$
25. $64x^2 - 5 = 20$
26. $(x - 7)^2 = 1$
27. $49x^2 + 1 = 170$
28. $81x^2 + 17 = 81$

Extra Practice
Skills Practice p. S21
Application Practice p. S36

Solve. Round to the nearest hundredth.

29. $4x^2 = 88$
30. $x^2 - 29 = 0$
31. $x^2 + 40 = 144$
32. $3x^2 - 84 = 0$
33. $50 - x^2 = 0$
34. $2x^2 - 10 = 64$

35. **Entertainment** For a scene in a movie, a sack of money is dropped from the roof of a 600 ft skyscraper. The height of the sack above the ground is given by $h = -16t^2 + 600$, where t is the time in seconds. How long will it take the sack to reach the ground? Round to the nearest tenth of a second.

Solve for the indicated variable. Assume all values are positive.

36. $A = \pi r^2$ for r

37. $d = \frac{1}{2}at^2$ for t

38. $F = \frac{mv^2}{r}$ for v

39. **Number Theory** If $a = 2b$ and $2ab = 36$, find all possible solutions for a and b.

40. **Geometry** The geometric mean of two positive numbers a and b is the positive number x such that $\frac{a}{x} = \frac{x}{b}$. Find the geometric mean of 2 and 18.

41. **Estimation** The area y of any rectangle with side length x and one side twice as long as the other is represented by $y = 2x^2$. Use the graph to estimate the dimensions of such a rectangle whose area is 35 square feet.

42. **Physics** The period of a pendulum is the amount of time it takes to swing back and forth one time. The relationship between the length of the pendulum L in inches and the length of the period t in seconds can be approximated by $L = 9.78t^2$. Find the period of a pendulum whose length is 60 inches. Round to the nearest tenth of a second.

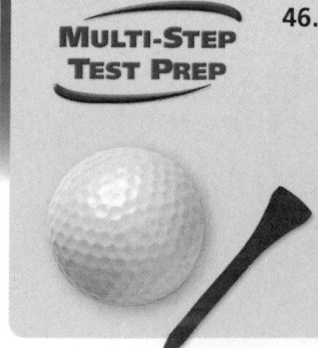

The first pendulum clock was invented by Christian Huygens, a Dutch physicist and mathematician, around 1656. Early pendulum clocks swung about 50° to the left and right. Modern pendulum clocks swing only 10° to 15°.

Physics

43. **/// ERROR ANALYSIS ///** Which solution is incorrect? Explain the error.

A
$$x^2 + 100 = 0$$
$$x^2 = 100$$
$$x = 10 \text{ or } x = -10$$

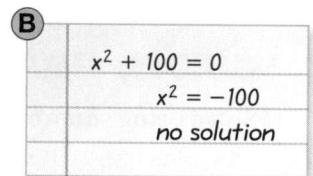

B
$$x^2 + 100 = 0$$
$$x^2 = -100$$
no solution

Determine whether each statement is always, sometimes, or never true.

44. There are two solutions to $x^2 = n$ when n is positive.

45. If n is a rational number, then the solutions to $x^2 = n$ are rational numbers.

46. **Multi-Step** The height in feet of a soccer ball kicked upward from the ground with initial velocity 60 feet per second is modeled by $h = -16t^2 + 60t$, where t is the time in seconds. Find the time it takes for the ball to return to the ground.

47. **Critical Thinking** For the equation $x^2 = a$, describe the values of a that will result in each of the following.

a. two solutions

b. one solution

c. no solution

MULTI-STEP TEST PREP

46. This problem will prepare you for the Multi-Step Test Prep on page 678.

The equation $d = 16t^2$ describes the distance d in feet that a golf ball falls in relation to the number of seconds t that it falls.

a. How many seconds will it take a golf ball to drop to the ground from a height of 4 feet?

b. Make a table and graph the function.

c. How far will the golf ball drop in 1 second?

d. How many seconds will it take the golf ball to drop 64 feet?

For the quadratic equation $x^2 + a = 0$, determine whether each value of a will result in two rational solutions. Explain.

49. $-\dfrac{1}{2}$ **50.** $\dfrac{1}{2}$ **51.** $-\dfrac{1}{4}$ **52.** $\dfrac{1}{4}$

 53. Write About It Explain why the quadratic equation $x^2 + 4 = 0$ has no real solutions but the quadratic equation $x^2 - 4 = 0$ has two solutions.

54. The formula for finding the approximate volume of a cylinder is $V = 3.14r^2 h$, where r is the radius and h is the height. The height of a cylinder is 100 cm, and the approximate volume is 1256 cm^3. Find the radius of the cylinder.

100 cm

   Ⓐ 400 cm   Ⓒ 4 cm

   Ⓑ 20 cm   Ⓓ 2 cm

55. Which best describes the positive solution of $\frac{1}{2}x^2 = 20$?

   Ⓕ Between 4 and 5   Ⓗ Between 6 and 7

   Ⓖ Between 5 and 6   Ⓙ Between 7 and 8

56. Which best describes the solutions of $81x^2 - 169 = 0$?

   Ⓐ Two rational solutions   Ⓒ No solution

   Ⓑ Two irrational solutions   Ⓓ One solution

CHALLENGE AND EXTEND

Find the solutions of each equation without using a calculator.

57. $288x^2 - 19 = -1$ **58.** $-75x^2 = -48$ **59.** $x^2 = \dfrac{128}{242}$

60. Geometry The Pythagorean Theorem states that $a^2 + b^2 = c^2$ if a and b represent the lengths of the legs of a right triangle and c represents the length of the hypotenuse.

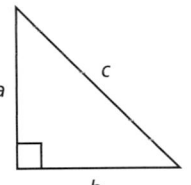

   a. Find the length of the hypotenuse if the lengths of the legs are 9 cm and 12 cm.

   b. Find the length of each leg of an isosceles right triangle whose hypotenuse is 10 cm. Round to the nearest tenth of a centimeter.

SPIRAL REVIEW

61. The figures shown have the same perimeter. What is the value of x? *(Lesson 2-4)*

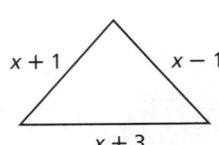

62. Identify which of the following lines are parallel:

   $y = -2x + 3$, $2x - y = 8$, $6x - 2y = 10$, and $y + 4 = 2(3 - x)$. *(Lesson 5-9)*

Solve each quadratic equation by factoring. Check your answer. *(Lesson 9-6)*

63. $x^2 - 6x + 8 = 0$ **64.** $x^2 + 5x - 6 = 0$ **65.** $x^2 - 5x = 14$

Model Completing the Square

One way to solve a quadratic equation is by using a procedure called *completing the square*. In this procedure, you add something to a quadratic expression to make it a perfect-square trinomial. This procedure can be modeled with algebra tiles.

Use with Lesson 9-8

KEY

☐ = 1   ▮ = x   ■ = x^2

Activity

Use algebra tiles to model $x^2 + 6x$. Add unit tiles to complete a perfect-square trinomial. Then write the new expression in factored form.

MODEL		ALGEBRA
	Arrange the tiles to form part of a large square. Part of the square is missing. How many one-tiles do you need to complete it?	$x^2 + 6x$
	Complete the square by placing 9 one-tiles on the mat. $x^2 + 6x + 9$ is a perfect-square trinomial.	$x^2 + 6x + 9$
	Use the length and the width of the square to rewrite the area expression in factored form.	$(x + 3)^2$

Try This

Use algebra tiles to model each expression. Add unit tiles to complete a perfect-square trinomial. Then write the new expression in factored form.

1. $x^2 + 4x$ **2.** $x^2 + 2x$ **3.** $x^2 + 10x$ **4.** $x^2 + 8x$

5. Make a Conjecture Examine the pattern in Problems 1–4. How many unit tiles would you have to add to make $x^2 + 12x$ a perfect-square trinomial?

Completing the Square

Objective
Solve quadratic equations by completing the square.

Vocabulary
completing the square

Who uses this?
Landscapers can solve quadratic equations to find dimensions of patios. (See Example 4.)

In the previous lesson, you solved quadratic equations by isolating x^2 and then using square roots. This method works if the quadratic equation, when written in standard form, is a perfect square.

When a trinomial is a perfect square, there is a relationship between the **coefficient of the x-term** and the **constant term**.

$$x^2 + 6x + 9 \qquad x^2 - 8x + 16$$
$$\left(\frac{6}{2}\right)^2 = 9 \qquad \left(\frac{-8}{2}\right)^2 = 16$$

Divide the coefficient of the x-term by 2, then square the result to get the constant term.

An expression in the form $x^2 + bx$ is not a perfect square. However, you can use the relationship shown above to add a term to $x^2 + bx$ to form a trinomial that is a perfect square. This is called **completing the square**.

Know it! Note

Completing the Square

WORDS	NUMBERS	ALGEBRA
To complete the square of $x^2 + bx$, add $\left(\frac{b}{2}\right)^2$ to the expression. This will form a perfect-square trinomial.	$x^2 + 6x + \blacksquare$ $x^2 + 6x + \left(\frac{6}{2}\right)^2$ $x^2 + 6x + 9$ $(x + 3)^2$	$x^2 + bx + \blacksquare$ $x^2 + bx + \left(\frac{b}{2}\right)^2$ $\left(x + \frac{b}{2}\right)^2$

EXAMPLE 1 Completing the Square

Complete the square to form a perfect-square trinomial.

A $x^2 + 10x + \blacksquare$
$x^2 + 10x$ *Identify b.*
$\left(\frac{10}{2}\right)^2 = 5^2 = 25$ *Find $\left(\frac{b}{2}\right)^2$.*
$x^2 + 10x + 25$ *Add $\left(\frac{b}{2}\right)^2$ to the expression.*

B $x^2 - 9x + \blacksquare$
$x^2 + -9x$
$\left(\frac{-9}{2}\right)^2 = \frac{81}{4}$
$x^2 - 9x + \frac{81}{4}$

CHECK IT OUT! Complete the square to form a perfect-square trinomial.
1a. $x^2 + 12x + \blacksquare$ **1b.** $x^2 - 5x + \blacksquare$ **1c.** $8x + x^2 + \blacksquare$

To solve a quadratic equation in the form $x^2 + bx = c$, first complete the square of $x^2 + bx$. Then you can solve using square roots.

Know it!
Note

Solving a Quadratic Equation by Completing the Square
Step 1 Write the equation in the form $x^2 + bx = c$.
Step 2 Find $\left(\frac{b}{2}\right)^2$.
Step 3 Complete the square by adding $\left(\frac{b}{2}\right)^2$ to both sides of the equation.
Step 4 Factor the perfect-square trinomial.
Step 5 Take the square root of both sides.
Step 6 Write two equations, using both the positive and negative square root, and solve each equation.

EXAMPLE 2 **Solving $x^2 + bx = c$ by Completing the Square**

Solve by completing the square. Check your answer.

A $x^2 + 14x = 15$

Step 1 $x^2 + 14x = 15$ *The equation is in the form $x^2 + bx = c$.*

Step 2 $\left(\dfrac{14}{2}\right)^2 = 7^2 = 49$ *Find $\left(\frac{b}{2}\right)^2$.*

Step 3 $x^2 + 14x + 49 = 15 + 49$ *Complete the square.*

Step 4 $(x + 7)^2 = 64$ *Factor and simplify.*

Step 5 $x + 7 = \pm 8$ *Take the square root of both sides.*

Step 6 $x + 7 = 8$ or $x + 7 = -8$ *Write and solve two equations.*
        $x = 1$ or $x = -15$

> **Helpful Hint**
>
> $(x + 7)(x + 7) =$ $(x + 7)^2$. So the square root of $(x + 7)^2$ is $x + 7$.

The solutions are 1 and -15.

Check

$x^2 + 14x = 15$	
$(1)^2 + 14(1)$	15
$1 + 14$	15
15	15 ✓

$x^2 + 14x = 15$	
$(-15)^2 + 14(-15)$	15
$225 - 210$	15
15	15 ✓

B $x^2 - 2x - 2 = 0$

Step 1 $x^2 + (-2)x = 2$ *Write in the form $x^2 + bx = c$.*

Step 2 $\left(\dfrac{-2}{2}\right)^2 = (-1)^2 = 1$ *Find $\left(\frac{b}{2}\right)^2$.*

Step 3 $x^2 - 2x + 1 = 2 + 1$ *Complete the square.*

Step 4 $(x - 1)^2 = 3$ *Factor and simplify.*

Step 5 $x - 1 = \pm\sqrt{3}$ *Take the square root of both sides.*

Step 6 $x - 1 = \sqrt{3}$ or $x - 1 = -\sqrt{3}$ *Write and solve*
       $x = 1 + \sqrt{3}$ or $x = 1 - \sqrt{3}$ *two equations.*

The solutions are $1 + \sqrt{3}$ and $1 - \sqrt{3}$.

> **Writing Math**
>
> The expressions $1 + \sqrt{3}$ and $1 - \sqrt{3}$ can be written as one expression: $1 \pm \sqrt{3}$, which is read as "1 plus or minus the square root of 3."

Check Use a graphing calculator to check your answer.

CHECK IT OUT!

Solve by completing the square. Check your answer.

2a. $x^2 + 10x = -9$ **2b.** $t^2 - 8t - 5 = 0$

EXAMPLE 3 **Solving $ax^2 + bx = c$ by Completing the Square**

Solve by completing the square.

A $-2x^2 + 12x - 20 = 0$

Step 1 $\dfrac{-2x^2}{-2} + \dfrac{12x}{-2} - \dfrac{20}{-2} = \dfrac{0}{-2}$ *Divide by −2 to make a = 1.*

$x^2 - 6x + 10 = 0$ *Write in the form x² + bx = c.*

$x^2 - 6x = -10$

$x^2 + (-6)x = -10$

Step 2 $\left(\dfrac{-6}{2}\right)^2 = (-3)^2 = 9$ *Find $\left(\frac{b}{2}\right)^2$.*

Step 3 $x^2 - 6x + 9 = -10 + 9$ *Complete the square.*

Step 4 $(x - 3)^2 = -1$ *Factor and simplify.*

There is no real number whose square is negative, so there are no real solutions.

B $3x^2 - 10x = -3$

Step 1 $\dfrac{3x^2}{3} - \dfrac{10}{3}x = \dfrac{-3}{3}$ *Divide by 3 to make a = 1.*

$x^2 - \dfrac{10}{3}x = -1$

$x^2 + \left(-\dfrac{10}{3}\right)x = -1$ *Write in the form x² + bx = c.*

Step 2 $\left(-\dfrac{10}{3} \cdot \dfrac{1}{2}\right)^2 = \left(-\dfrac{10}{6}\right)^2 = \dfrac{100}{36} = \dfrac{25}{9}$ *Find $\left(\frac{b}{2}\right)^2$.*

Step 3 $x^2 - \dfrac{10}{3}x + \dfrac{25}{9} = -1 + \dfrac{25}{9}$ *Complete the square.*

$x^2 - \dfrac{10}{3}x + \dfrac{25}{9} = -\dfrac{9}{9} + \dfrac{25}{9}$ *Rewrite using like denominators.*

Step 4 $\left(x - \dfrac{5}{3}\right)^2 = \dfrac{16}{9}$ *Factor and simplify.*

Step 5 $x - \dfrac{5}{3} = \pm\dfrac{4}{3}$ *Take the square root of both sides.*

Step 6 $x - \dfrac{5}{3} = \dfrac{4}{3}$ or $x - \dfrac{5}{3} = -\dfrac{4}{3}$ *Write and solve two equations.*

$x = 3$ or $x = \dfrac{1}{3}$

The solutions are 3 and $\frac{1}{3}$.

> **Remember!**
>
> Dividing by 2 is the same as multiplying by $\frac{1}{2}$.

Solve by completing the square.

3a. $3x^2 - 5x - 2 = 0$ **3b.** $4t^2 - 4t + 9 = 0$

EXAMPLE 4 ***Problem-Solving Application***

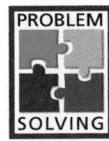

A landscaper is designing a rectangular brick patio. She has enough bricks to cover 144 square feet. She wants the length of the patio to be 10 feet greater than the width. What dimensions should she use for the patio?

1 **Understand the Problem**

The **answer** will be the length and width of the patio.

List the important information:
- There are enough bricks to cover 144 square feet.
- One edge of the patio is to be 10 feet longer than the other edge.

2 Make a Plan

Set the formula for the area of a rectangle equal to 144, the area of the patio. Solve the equation.

3 Solve

Let x be the width.

Then $x + 10$ is the length.

Use the formula for area of a rectangle.

ℓ	$\cdot$	w	$=$	A
length	times	width	=	area of patio
$(x + 10)$	$\cdot$	x	=	144

Step 1 $x^2 + 10x = 144$ *Simplify.*

Step 2 $\left(\dfrac{10}{2}\right)^2 = 5^2 = 25$ *Find $\left(\dfrac{b}{2}\right)^2$.*

Step 3 $x^2 + 10x + 25 = 144 + 25$ *Complete the square by adding 25 to both sides.*

Step 4 $(x + 5)^2 = 169$ *Factor the perfect-square trinomial.*

Step 5 $x + 5 = \pm 13$ *Take the square root of both sides.*

Step 6 $x + 5 = 13$ or $x + 5 = -13$ *Write and solve two equations.*

$x = 8$ or $x = -18$

Negative numbers are not reasonable for length, so $x = 8$ is the only solution that makes sense.

The width is 8 feet, and the length is $8 + 10$, or 18, feet.

4 Look Back

The length of the patio is 10 feet greater than the width. Also, $8(18) = 144$.

 4. An architect designs a rectangular room with an area of 400 ft². The length is to be 8 ft longer than the width. Find the dimensions of the room. Round your answers to the nearest tenth of a foot.

THINK AND DISCUSS

1. Tell how to solve a quadratic equation in the form $x^2 + bx + c = 0$ by completing the square.

 2. GET ORGANIZED Copy and complete the graphic organizer. In each box, write and solve an example of the given type of quadratic equation.

Solving Quadratic Equations by Completing the Square

| $x^2 + bx = c$ | $ax^2 + bx = c$ | $x^2 + bx + c = 0$ |

9-8

Exercises

go.hrw.com
Homework Help Online
KEYWORD: MA7 9-8
Parent Resources Online
KEYWORD: MA7 Parent

GUIDED PRACTICE

1. **Vocabulary** Describe in your own words how to *complete the square* for the equation $1 = x^2 + 4x$.

SEE EXAMPLE 1
p. 663

Complete the square to form a perfect-square trinomial.

2. $x^2 + 14x + \blacksquare$

3. $x^2 - 4x + \blacksquare$

4. $x^2 - 3x + \blacksquare$

Solve by completing the square.

SEE EXAMPLE 2
p. 664

5. $x^2 + 6x = -5$

6. $x^2 - 8x = 9$

7. $x^2 + x = 30$

8. $x^2 + 2x = 21$

9. $x^2 - 10x = -9$

10. $x^2 + 16x = 91$

SEE EXAMPLE 3
p. 665

11. $-x^2 - 5x = -5$

12. $-x^2 - 3x + 2 = 0$

13. $-6x = 3x^2 + 9$

14. $2x^2 - 6x = -10$

15. $-x^2 + 8x - 6 = 0$

16. $4x^2 + 16 = -24x$

SEE EXAMPLE 4
p. 665

17. **Multi-Step** The length of a rectangle is 4 meters longer than the width. The area of the rectangle is 80 square meters. Find the length and width. Round your answers to the nearest tenth of a meter.

PRACTICE AND PROBLEM SOLVING

Complete the square to form a perfect-square trinomial.

18. $x^2 - 16x + \blacksquare$

19. $x^2 - 2x + \blacksquare$

20. $x^2 + 11x + \blacksquare$

Solve by completing the square.

21. $x^2 - 10x = 24$

22. $x^2 - 6x = -9$

23. $x^2 + 15x = -26$

24. $x^2 + 6x = 16$

25. $x^2 - 2x = 48$

26. $x^2 + 12x = -36$

27. $-x^2 + x + 6 = 0$

28. $2x^2 = -7x - 29$

29. $-x^2 - x + 1 = 0$

30. $3x^2 - 6x - 9 = 0$

31. $-x^2 = 15x + 30$

32. $2x^2 + 20x - 10 = 0$

33. **Geometry** The base of a parallelogram is 8 inches longer than twice the height. The area of the parallelogram is 64 square inches. What is the height?

Solve each equation by completing the square.

34. $3x^2 + x = 10$

35. $x^2 = 2x + 6$

36. $2a^2 = 5a + 12$

37. $2x^2 + 5x = 3$

38. $4x = 7 - x^2$

39. $8x = -x^2 + 20$

40. **Hobbies** The height in feet h of a water bottle rocket launched from a rooftop is given by the equation $h = -16t^2 + 320t + 32$, where t is the time in seconds. After the rocket is fired, how long will it take to return to the ground? Solve by completing the square. Round your answer to the nearest tenth of a second.

Complete each trinomial so that it is a perfect square.

41. $x^2 + 18x + \blacksquare$

42. $x^2 - 100x + \blacksquare$

43. $x^2 - 7x + \blacksquare$

44. $x^2 + \blacksquare x + 4$

45. $x^2 - \blacksquare x + \dfrac{81}{4}$

46. $x^2 + \blacksquare x + \dfrac{1}{36}$

47. **Multi-Step** A roped-off area of width x is created around a 34-by-10-foot rectangular museum display of Egyptian artifacts, as shown. The combined area of the display and the roped-off area is 640 square feet.

   a. Write an equation for the combined area.

   b. Find the width of the roped-off area.

48. **Graphing Calculator** Compare solving a quadratic equation by completing the square with finding the solutions on a graphing calculator.

   a. Complete the square to solve $2x^2 - 3x - 2 = 0$.

   b. Use your graphing calculator to graph $y = 2x^2 - 3x - 2$.

   c. Explain how to use this graph to find the solutions of $2x^2 - 3x - 2 = 0$.

   d. Compare the two methods of solving the equation. What are the advantages and disadvantages of each?

49. **///ERROR ANALYSIS///** Explain the error below. What is the correct answer?

$$x^2 + 4x = 77$$
$$x^2 + 4x + 4 = 77 + 4$$
$$(x + 2)^2 = 81$$
$$x + 2 = 9$$
$$x = 7$$

Solve each equation by completing the square.

50. $5x^2 - 50x = 55$

51. $3x^2 + 36x = -30$

52. $28x - 2x^2 = 26$

53. $-36x = 3x^2 + 108$

54. $0 = 4x^2 + 32x + 44$

55. $16x + 40 = -2x^2$

56. $x^2 + 5x + 6 = 10x$

57. $x^2 + 3x + 18 = -3x$

58. $4x^2 + x + 1 = 3x^2$

59. **Write About It** Jamal prefers to solve $x^2 + 20x - 21 = 0$ by completing the square. Heather prefers to solve $x^2 + 11x + 18 = 0$ by factoring. Explain their reasoning.

60. **Critical Thinking** What should be done to the binomial $x^2 + y^2$ to make it a perfect-square trinomial? Explain.

MULTI-STEP TEST PREP

61. This problem will prepare you for the Multi-Step Test Prep on page 678.

   The function $h(t) = -16t^2 + vt + c$ models the height in feet of a golf ball after t seconds when it is hit with initial vertical velocity v from initial height c feet. A golfer stands on a tee box that is 32 feet above the fairway. He hits the golf ball from the tee at an initial vertical velocity of 64 feet per second.

   a. Write an equation that gives the time t when the golf ball lands on the fairway at height 0.

   b. What number would be added to both sides of the equation in part **a** to complete the square while solving for t?

   c. Solve the equation from part **a** by completing the square to find the time it takes the ball to reach the fairway. Round to the nearest tenth of a second.

62. **Write About It** Compare solving an equation of the form $x^2 + bx + c = 0$ by completing the square and solving an equation of the form $ax^2 + bx + c = 0$ by completing the square.

63. What value of c will make $x^2 + 16x + c$ a perfect-square trinomial?

  Ⓐ 32   Ⓑ 64   Ⓒ 128   Ⓓ 256

64. What value of b will make $x^2 + b + 25$ a perfect-square trinomial?

  Ⓕ 5   Ⓖ 5x   Ⓗ 10   Ⓙ 10x

65. Which of the following is closest to a solution of $3x^2 + 2x - 4 = 0$?

  Ⓐ 0   Ⓑ 1   Ⓒ 2   Ⓓ 3

66. **Short Response** Solve $x^2 - 8x - 20 = 0$ by completing the square. Explain each step in your solution.

CHALLENGE AND EXTEND

Solve each equation by completing the square.

67. $6x^2 + 5x = 6$ 68. $7x + 3 = 6x^2$ 69. $4x = 1 - 3x^2$

70. What should be done to the binomial $ax^2 + bx$ to obtain a perfect-square trinomial?

71. Solve $ax^2 + bx = 0$ for x.

72. **Geometry** The hypotenuse of a right triangle is 20 cm. One of the legs is 4 cm longer than the other leg. Find the area of the triangle. (*Hint:* Use the Pythagorean Theorem.)

SPIRAL REVIEW

Graph the line with the given slope and y-intercept. *(Lesson 5-7)*

73. slope $= 4$, y-intercept $= -3$ 74. slope $= -\dfrac{2}{3}$, y-intercept $= 4$

75. slope $= -2$, y-intercept $= -2$ 76. slope $= -\dfrac{4}{3}$, y-intercept $= 0$

Multiply. *(Lesson 7-9)*

77. $(x - 4)^2$ 78. $(x - 4)(x + 4)$ 79. $(4 - t)^2$

80. $(2z + 3)^2$ 81. $(8b^2 - 2)(8b^2 + 2)$ 82. $(2x - 6)(2x + 6)$

Solve using square roots. *(Lesson 9-7)*

83. $5x^2 = 5$ 84. $x^2 + 3 = 12$ 85. $5x^2 = 80$

86. $9x^2 = 64$ 87. $25 + x^2 = 250$ 88. $64x^2 + 3 = 147$

Solve. Round to the nearest hundredth. *(Lesson 9-7)*

89. $12 = 5x^2$ 90. $3x^2 - 4 = 15$ 91. $x^2 - 7 = 19$

92. $6 + x^2 = 72$ 93. $10x^2 - 10 = 12$ 94. $2x^2 + 2 = 33$

The Quadratic Formula and the Discriminant

Objectives

Solve quadratic equations by using the Quadratic Formula.

Determine the number of solutions of a quadratic equation by using the discriminant.

Vocabulary

discriminant

Why learn this?

You can use the discriminant to determine whether the weight in a carnival strength test will reach a certain height. (See Exercise 4.)

In the previous lesson, you completed the square to solve quadratic equations. If you complete the square of $ax^2 + bx + c = 0$, you can derive the *Quadratic Formula*. The Quadratic Formula can be used to solve *any* quadratic equation.

Numbers		Algebra
$2x^2 + 6x + 1 = 0$		$ax^2 + bx + c = 0, a \neq 0$
$\frac{2}{2}x^2 + \frac{6}{2}x + \frac{1}{2} = \frac{0}{2}$	Divide both sides by a.	$\frac{a}{a}x^2 + \frac{b}{a}x + \frac{c}{a} = \frac{0}{a}$
$x^2 + 3x + \frac{1}{2} = 0$		$x^2 + \frac{b}{a}x + \frac{c}{a} = 0$
$x^2 + 3x = -\frac{1}{2}$	Subtract $\frac{c}{a}$ from both sides.	$x^2 + \frac{b}{a}x = -\frac{c}{a}$
$x^2 + 3x + \left(\frac{3}{2}\right)^2 = -\frac{1}{2} + \left(\frac{3}{2}\right)^2$	Complete the square.	$x^2 + \frac{b}{a}x + \left(\frac{b}{2a}\right)^2 = -\frac{c}{a} + \left(\frac{b}{2a}\right)^2$
$\left(x + \frac{3}{2}\right)^2 = \frac{9}{4} - \frac{1}{2}$	Factor and simplify.	$\left(x + \frac{b}{2a}\right)^2 = \frac{b^2}{4a^2} - \frac{c}{a}$
$\left(x + \frac{3}{2}\right)^2 = \frac{9}{4} - \frac{2}{4}$	Use common denominators.	$\left(x + \frac{b}{2a}\right)^2 = \frac{b^2}{4a^2} - \frac{4ac}{4a^2}$
$\left(x + \frac{3}{2}\right)^2 = \frac{7}{4}$	Simplify.	$\left(x + \frac{b}{2a}\right)^2 = \frac{b^2 - 4ac}{4a^2}$
$x + \frac{3}{2} = \pm\frac{\sqrt{7}}{2}$	Take square roots.	$x + \frac{b}{2a} = \pm\frac{\sqrt{b^2 - 4ac}}{2a}$
$x = -\frac{3}{2} \pm \frac{\sqrt{7}}{2}$	Subtract $\frac{b}{2a}$ from both sides.	$x = -\frac{b}{2a} \pm \frac{\sqrt{b^2 - 4ac}}{2a}$
$x = \frac{-3 \pm \sqrt{7}}{2}$	Simplify.	$x = \frac{-b \pm \sqrt{b^2 - 4ac}}{2a}$

Remember!

To add fractions, you need a common denominator.

$$\frac{b^2}{4a^2} - \frac{c}{a} = \frac{b^2}{4a^2} - \frac{c}{a}\left(\frac{4a}{4a}\right)$$

$$= \frac{b^2}{4a^2} - \frac{4ac}{4a^2}$$

$$= \frac{b^2 - 4ac}{4a^2}$$

Know it! Note

The Quadratic Formula

The solutions of $ax^2 + bx + c = 0$, where $a \neq 0$, are $x = \frac{-b \pm \sqrt{b^2 - 4ac}}{2a}$.

EXAMPLE 1 Using the Quadratic Formula

Solve using the Quadratic Formula.

A $2x^2 + 3x - 5 = 0$

$$2x^2 + 3x + (-5) = 0$$ *Identify a, b, and c.*

$$x = \frac{-b \pm \sqrt{b^2 - 4ac}}{2a}$$ *Use the Quadratic Formula.*

$$x = \frac{-3 \pm \sqrt{3^2 - 4(2)(-5)}}{2(2)}$$ *Substitute 2 for a, 3 for b, and −5 for c.*

$$x = \frac{-3 \pm \sqrt{9 - (-40)}}{4}$$ *Simplify.*

$$x = \frac{-3 \pm \sqrt{49}}{4} = \frac{-3 \pm 7}{4}$$ *Simplify.*

$$x = \frac{-3 + 7}{4} \text{ or } x = \frac{-3 - 7}{4}$$ *Write as two equations.*

$$x = 1 \quad \text{or} \quad x = -\frac{5}{2}$$ *Simplify.*

B $2x = x^2 - 3$

$$1x^2 + (-2)x + (-3) = 0$$ *Write in standard form. Identify a, b, and c. Substitute 1 for a, −2 for b, and −3 for c.*

$$x = \frac{-(-2) \pm \sqrt{(-2)^2 - 4(1)(-3)}}{2(1)}$$

$$x = \frac{2 \pm \sqrt{4 - (-12)}}{2}$$ *Simplify.*

$$x = \frac{2 \pm \sqrt{16}}{2} = \frac{2 \pm 4}{2}$$ *Simplify.*

$$x = \frac{2 + 4}{2} \text{ or } x = \frac{2 - 4}{2}$$ *Write as two equations.*

$$x = 3 \quad \text{or} \quad x = -1$$ *Simplify.*

 Solve using the Quadratic Formula.

1a. $-3x^2 + 5x + 2 = 0$ **1b.** $2 - 5x^2 = -9x$

Many quadratic equations can be solved by graphing, factoring, taking the square root, or completing the square. Some cannot be easily solved by any of these methods, but you can use the Quadratic Formula to solve any quadratic equation.

EXAMPLE 2 Using the Quadratic Formula to Estimate Solutions

Solve $x^2 - 2x - 4 = 0$ using the Quadratic Formula.

$$x = \frac{-(-2) \pm \sqrt{(-2)^2 - 4(1)(-4)}}{2(1)}$$

$$x = \frac{2 \pm \sqrt{4 - (-16)}}{2} = \frac{2 \pm \sqrt{20}}{2}$$

$$x = \frac{2 + \sqrt{20}}{2} \quad \text{or} \quad x = \frac{2 - \sqrt{20}}{2}$$

Use a calculator: $x \approx 3.24$ or $x \approx -1.24$.

Check reasonableness

 2. Solve $2x^2 - 8x + 1 = 0$ using the Quadratic Formula.

If the quadratic equation is in standard form, the **discriminant** of a quadratic equation is $b^2 - 4ac$, the part of the equation under the radical sign. Recall that quadratic equations can have two, one, or no real solutions. You can determine the number of solutions of a quadratic equation by evaluating its discriminant.

Equation	$x^2 - 4x + 3 = 0$	$x^2 + 2x + 1 = 0$	$x^2 - 2x + 2 = 0$
Discriminant	$a = 1, b = -4, c = 3$ $b^2 - 4ac$ $(-4)^2 - 4(1)(3)$ $16 - 12$ 4 The discriminant is **positive**.	$a = 1, b = 2, c = 1$ $b^2 - 4ac$ $2^2 - 4(1)(1)$ $4 - 4$ 0 The discriminant is **zero**.	$a = 1, b = -2, c = 2$ $b^2 - 4ac$ $(-2)^2 - 4(1)(2)$ $4 - 8$ -4 The discriminant is negative.
Graph of Related Function	Notice that the related function has **two** *x*-intercepts.	Notice that the related function has **one** *x*-intercept.	Notice that the related function has no *x*-intercepts.
Number of Solutions	**two** real solutions	**one** real solution	no real solutions

Know it! Note

The Discriminant of Quadratic Equation $ax^2 + bx + c = 0$

If $b^2 - 4ac > 0$, the equation has **two** real solutions.

If $b^2 - 4ac = 0$, the equation has **one** real solution.

If $b^2 - 4ac < 0$, the equation has **no** real solutions.

EXAMPLE 3 Using the Discriminant

Find the number of real solutions of each equation using the discriminant.

A $3x^2 + 10x + 2 = 0$
$a = 3, b = 10, c = 2$
$b^2 - 4ac$
$10^2 - 4(3)(2)$
$100 - 24$
76
$b^2 - 4ac$ is positive.
There are two real solutions.

B $9x^2 - 6x + 1 = 0$
$a = 9, b = -6, c = 1$
$b^2 - 4ac$
$(-6)^2 - 4(9)(1)$
$36 - 36$
0
$b^2 - 4ac$ is zero.
There is one real solution.

C $x^2 + x + 1 = 0$
$a = 1, b = 1, c = 1$
$b^2 - 4ac$
$1^2 - 4(1)(1)$
$1 - 4$
-3
$b^2 - 4ac$ is negative.
There are no real solutions.

 CHECK IT OUT! Find the number of real solutions of each equation using the discriminant.

3a. $2x^2 - 2x + 3 = 0$ **3b.** $x^2 + 4x + 4 = 0$ **3c.** $x^2 - 9x + 4 = 0$

The height h in feet of an object shot straight up with initial velocity v in feet per second is given by $h = -16t^2 + vt + c$, where c is the beginning height of the object above the ground.

EXAMPLE 4 *Physics Application*

A weight 1 foot above the ground on a carnival strength test is shot straight up with an initial velocity of 35 feet per second. Will it ring the bell at the top of the pole? Use the discriminant to explain your answer.

$$h = -16t^2 + vt + c$$
$$20 = -16t^2 + 35t + 1 \qquad \textit{Substitute 20 for h, 35 for v, and 1 for c.}$$
$$0 = -16t^2 + 35t + (-19) \qquad \textit{Subtract 20 from both sides.}$$
$$b^2 - 4ac \qquad \textit{Evaluate the discriminant.}$$
$$35^2 - 4(-16)(-19) = 9 \qquad \textit{Substitute −16 for a, 35 for b, and −19 for c.}$$

The discriminant is positive, so the equation has two solutions. The weight will reach a height of 20 feet so it will ring the bell.

CHECK IT OUT!

4. What if...? Suppose the weight is shot straight up with an initial velocity of 20 feet per second. Will it ring the bell? Use the discriminant to explain your answer.

There is no one correct way to solve a quadratic equation. Many quadratic equations can be solved using several different methods.

EXAMPLE 5 **Solving Using Different Methods**

Solve $x^2 + 7x + 6 = 0$.

Method 1 Solve by graphing.

$$y = x^2 + 7x + 6 \qquad \textit{Write the related quadratic function and graph it.}$$

The solutions are the x-intercepts, -6 and -1.

Method 2 Solve by factoring.

$$x^2 + 7x + 6 = 0$$
$$(x + 6)(x + 1) = 0 \qquad \textit{Factor.}$$
$$x + 6 = 0 \text{ or } x - 1 = 0 \qquad \textit{Use the Zero Product Property.}$$
$$x = -6 \quad \text{or} \quad x = -1 \qquad \textit{Solve each equation.}$$

Method 3 Solve by completing the square.

$$x^2 + 7x + 6 = 0$$
$$x^2 + 7x = -6$$
$$x^2 + 7x + \frac{49}{4} = -6 + \frac{49}{4} \qquad \textit{Add } \left(\frac{b}{2}\right)^2 \textit{ to both sides.}$$
$$\left(x + \frac{7}{2}\right)^2 = \frac{25}{4} \qquad \textit{Factor and simplify.}$$
$$x + \frac{7}{2} = \pm\frac{5}{2} \qquad \textit{Take the square root of both sides.}$$
$$x + \frac{7}{2} = \frac{5}{2} \text{ or } x + \frac{7}{2} = -\frac{5}{2} \qquad \textit{Solve each equation.}$$
$$x = -1 \quad \text{or} \quad x = -6$$

Method 4 Solve using the Quadratic Formula.

$1x^2 + 7x + 6 = 0$ *Identify a, b, and c.*

$x = \dfrac{-7 \pm \sqrt{7^2 - 4(1)(6)}}{2(1)}$ *Substitute 1 for a, 7 for b, and 6 for c.*

$x = \dfrac{-7 \pm \sqrt{49 - 24}}{2} = \dfrac{-7 \pm \sqrt{25}}{2} = \dfrac{-7 \pm 5}{2}$ *Simplify.*

$x = \dfrac{-7 + 5}{2}$ or $x = \dfrac{-7 - 5}{2}$ *Write as two equations.*

$x = -1$ or $x = -6$ *Solve each equation.*

 Solve.

5a. $x^2 + 7x + 10 = 0$ **5b.** $-14 + x^2 = 5x$ **5c.** $2x^2 + 4x - 21 = 0$

Notice that all of the methods in Example 5 produce the same solutions, -1 and -6. The only method you cannot use to solve $x^2 + 7x + 6 = 0$ is using square roots. Sometimes one method is better for solving certain types of equations. The table below gives some advantages and disadvantages of the different methods.

Methods of Solving Quadratic Equations

METHOD	ADVANTAGES	DISADVANTAGES
Graphing	• Always works to give approximate solutions • Can quickly see the number of solutions	• Cannot always get an exact solution
Factoring	• Good method to try first • Straightforward if the equation is factorable	• Complicated if the equation is not easily factorable • Not all quadratic equations are factorable.
Using square roots	• Quick when the equation has no *x*-term	• Cannot easily use when there is an *x*-term
Completing the square	• Always works	• Sometimes involves difficult calculations
Using the Quadratic Formula	• Always works • Can always find exact solutions	• Other methods may be easier or less time consuming.

Student to Student   *Solving Quadratic Equations*

Binh Pham
Johnson High School

No matter what method I use, I like to check my answers for reasonableness by graphing.

I used the Quadratic Formula to solve $2x^2 - 7x - 10 = 0$. I found that $x \approx -1.09$ and $x \approx 4.59$. Then I graphed $y = 2x^2 - 7x - 10$. The x-intercepts appeared to be close to -1 and 4.5, so I knew my solutions were reasonable.

THINK AND DISCUSS

1. Describe how to use the discriminant to find the number of real solutions to a quadratic equation.

2. Choose a method to solve $x^2 + 5x + 4 = 0$ and explain why you chose that method.

3. Describe how the discriminant can be used to determine if an object will reach a given height.

4. **GET ORGANIZED** Copy and complete the graphic organizer. In each box, write the number of real solutions.

The number of real solutions of $ax^2 + bx + c = 0$ when...

$b^2 - 4ac > 0$ is ▇. | $b^2 - 4ac < 0$ is ▇. | $b^2 - 4ac = 0$ is ▇.

9-9 Exercises

go.hrw.com
Homework Help Online
KEYWORD: MA7 9-9
Parent Resources Online
KEYWORD: MA7 Parent

GUIDED PRACTICE

1. **Vocabulary** If the *discriminant* is negative, the quadratic equation has _____?_____ real solution(s). (*no*, *one*, or *two*)

SEE EXAMPLE 1
p. 671

Solve using the Quadratic Formula.

2. $x^2 - 5x + 4 = 0$
3. $2x^2 = 7x - 3$
4. $x^2 - 6x - 7 = 0$
5. $x^2 = -14x - 40$
6. $3x^2 - 2x = 8$
7. $4x^2 - 4x - 3 = 0$

SEE EXAMPLE 2
p. 671

8. $2x^2 - 6 = 0$
9. $x^2 + 6x + 3 = 0$
10. $x^2 - 7x + 2 = 0$
11. $3x^2 = -x + 5$
12. $x^2 - 4x - 7 = 0$
13. $2x^2 + x - 5 = 0$

SEE EXAMPLE 3
p. 672

Find the number of real solutions of each equation using the discriminant.

14. $2x^2 + 4x + 3 = 0$
15. $x^2 + 4x + 4 = 0$
16. $2x^2 - 11x + 6 = 0$
17. $x^2 + x + 1 = 0$
18. $3x^2 = 5x - 1$
19. $-2x + 3 = 2x^2$
20. $2x^2 + 12x = -18$
21. $5x^2 + 3x = -4$
22. $8x = 1 - x^2$

SEE EXAMPLE 4
p. 673

23. **Hobbies** The height above the ground in meters of a model rocket on a particular launch can be modeled by the equation $h = -4.9t^2 + 102t + 100$, where t is the time in seconds after its engine burns out 100 m above the ground. Will the rocket reach a height of 600 m? Use the discriminant to explain your answer.

SEE EXAMPLE 5
p. 673

Solve.

24. $x^2 + x - 12 = 0$
25. $x^2 + 6x + 9 = 0$
26. $2x^2 - x - 1 = 0$
27. $4x^2 + 4x + 1 = 0$
28. $2x^2 + x - 7 = 0$
29. $9 = 2x^2 + 3x$

PRACTICE AND PROBLEM SOLVING

Independent Practice

For Exercises	See Example
30–32	1
33–35	2
36–38	3
39	4
40–42	5

Extra Practice

Skills Practice p. S21

Application Practice p. S36

Solve using the Quadratic Formula.

30. $3x^2 = 13x - 4$ **31.** $x^2 - 10x + 9 = 0$ **32.** $1 = 3x^2 + 2x$

33. $x^2 - 4x + 1 = 0$ **34.** $3x^2 - 5 = 0$ **35.** $2x^2 + 7x = -4$

Find the number of real solutions of each equation using the discriminant.

36. $3x^2 - 6x + 3 = 0$ **37.** $x^2 - 3x - 8 = 0$ **38.** $7x^2 + 6x + 2 = 0$

39. Multi-Step A gymnast who can stretch her arms up to reach 6 feet jumps straight up on a trampoline. The height of her feet above the trampoline can be modeled by the equation $h = -16x^2 + 12x$, where x is the time in seconds after her jump. Do the gymnast's hands reach a height of 10 feet above the trampoline? Use the discriminant to explain. (*Hint:* Let $h = 10 - 6$, or 4.)

10 ft

Solve.

40. $x^2 + 4x + 3 = 0$ **41.** $x^2 + 2x = 15$ **42.** $x^2 - 12 = -x$

Write each equation in standard form. Use the discriminant to determine the number of solutions. Then find any real solutions.

43. $2x = 3 + 2x^2$ **44.** $x^2 = 2x + 9$ **45.** $2 = 7x + 4x^2$

46. $-7 = x^2$ **47.** $-12x = -9x^2 - 4$ **48.** $x^2 - 14 = 0$

Multi-Step Use the discriminant to determine the number of x-intercepts. Then find them.

49. $y = 2x^2 - x - 21$ **50.** $y = 5x^2 + 12x + 8$ **51.** $y = x^2 - 10x + 25$

52. Copy and complete the table.

Quadratic Equation	Discriminant	Number of Real Solutions
$x^2 + 12x - 20 = 0$	▦	▦
$8x + x^2 = -16$	▦	▦
$0.5x^2 + x - 3 = 0$	▦	▦
$-3x^2 - 2x = 1$	▦	▦

53. Sports A diver begins on a platform 10 meters above the surface of the water. The diver's height is given by the equation $h(t) = -4.9t^2 + 3.5t + 10$, where t is the time in seconds after the diver jumps.

    a. How long does it take the diver to reach a point 1 meter above the water?

    b. How many solutions does the equation you used in part **a** have?

    c. Do all of the solutions to the equation make sense in the situation? Explain.

54. Critical Thinking How many real solutions does the equation $x^2 = k$ have when $k > 0$, when $k < 0$, and when $k = 0$? Use the discriminant to explain.

55. Write About It How can you use the discriminant to save time?

56. This problem will prepare you for the Multi-Step Test Prep on page 678.

The equation $0 = -16t^2 + 80t + 20$ gives the time t in seconds when a golf ball is at height 0 feet.

a. Will the height of the ball reach 130 feet? Explain.

b. Will the golf ball reach a height of 116 feet? If so, when?

c. Solve the given quadratic equation using the Quadratic Formula.

TEST PREP

57. How many real solutions does $4x^2 - 3x + 1 = 0$ have?

    (A) 0   (B) 1   (C) 2   (D) 4

58. For which of the following conditions does $ax^2 + bx + c = 0$ have two real solutions?

  I. $b^2 = 4ac$

  II. $b^2 > 4ac$

  III. $a = b, c = b$

    (F) I only   (G) II only   (H) III only   (J) II and III

59. Extended Response Use the equation $0 = x^2 + 2x + 1$ to answer the following.

a. How many solutions does the equation have?

b. Solve the equation by graphing.

c. Solve the equation by factoring.

d. Solve the equation by using the Quadratic Formula.

e. Explain which method was easiest for you. Why?

CHALLENGE AND EXTEND

60. Agriculture A rancher has 80 yards of fencing to build a rectangular pen. Let w be the width of the pen. Write an equation giving the area of the pen. Find the dimensions of the pen when the area is 400 square yards.

61. Agriculture A farmer wants to fence a four-sided field using an existing fence along the south side of the field. He has 1000 feet of fencing. He makes the northern boundary perpendicular to and twice as long as the western boundary. The eastern and western boundaries have to be parallel, but the northern and southern ones do not.

a. Can the farmer enclose an area of 125,000 square feet? Explain why or why not. $\left(\text{Hint: Use the formula for the area of a trapezoid, } A = \frac{1}{2} h(b_1 + b_2).\right)$

b. What geometric shape will the field be?

SPIRAL REVIEW

Solve each equation by completing the square. *(Lesson 9-8)*

62. $x^2 - 2x - 24 = 0$ **63.** $x^2 + 6x = 40$ **64.** $-3x^2 + 12x = 15$

Factor each polynomial by grouping. *(Lesson 8-2)*

65. $s^2 r^3 + 5r^3 + 5t + s^2 t$ **66.** $b^3 - 4b^2 + 2b - 8$ **67.** $n^5 - 6n^4 - 2n + 12$

Order the functions from narrowest graph to widest. *(Lesson 9-4)*

68. $f(x) = 0.2x^2, g(x) = 1.5x^2 + 4, h(x) = x^2 - 8$ **69.** $f(x) = -\frac{1}{5}x^2 + 5, g(x) = \frac{1}{6}x^2$

MULTI-STEP TEST PREP

Solving Quadratic Equations

Seeing Green A golf player hits a golf ball from a tee with an initial vertical velocity of 80 feet per second. The height of the golf ball t seconds after it is hit is given by $h = -16t^2 + 80t$.

1. How long is the golf ball in the air?

2. What is the maximum height of the golf ball?

3. How long after the golf ball is hit does it reach its maximum height?

4. What is the height of the golf ball after 3.5 seconds?

5. At what times is the golf ball 64 feet in the air? Explain.

READY TO GO ON?

Quiz for Lessons 9-5 Through 9-9

✓ **9-5** **Solving Quadratic Equations by Graphing**

Solve each equation by graphing the related function.

1. $x^2 - 9 = 0$ **2.** $x^2 + 3x - 4 = 0$ **3.** $4x^2 + 8x = 32$

4. The height of a fireworks rocket launched from a platform 35 meters above the ground can be approximated by $h = -5t^2 + 30t + 35$, where h is the height in meters and t is the time in seconds. Find the time it takes the rocket to reach the ground after it is launched.

✓ **9-6** **Solving Quadratic Equations by Factoring**

Use the Zero Product Property to solve each equation.

5. $(x + 1)(x + 3) = 0$ **6.** $(x - 6)(x - 3) = 0$ **7.** $(x + 6)(x - 3) = 0$ **8.** $(x + 7)(x - 10) = 0$

Solve each quadratic equation by factoring.

9. $x^2 - 4x - 32 = 0$ **10.** $x^2 - 8x + 15 = 0$ **11.** $x^2 + x = 6$ **12.** $-8x - 33 = -x^2$

13. The height of a soccer ball kicked from the ground can be approximated by the function $h = -16t^2 + 64t$, where h is the height in feet and t is the time in seconds. Find the time it takes for the ball to return to the ground.

✓ **9-7** **Solving Quadratic Equations by Using Square Roots**

Solve using square roots.

14. $3x^2 = 48$ **15.** $36x^2 - 49 = 0$ **16.** $-12 = x^2 - 21$

17. Solve $3x^2 + 5 = 21$. Round to the nearest hundredth.

✓ **9-8** **Completing the Square**

Complete the square to form a perfect-square trinomial.

18. $x^2 - 12x + \blacksquare$ **19.** $x^2 + 4x + \blacksquare$ **20.** $x^2 + 9x + \blacksquare$

Solve by completing the square.

21. $x^2 + 2x = 3$ **22.** $x^2 - 5 = 2x$ **23.** $x^2 + 7x = 8$

24. The width of a rectangle is 4 feet shorter than its length. The area of the rectangle is 42 square feet. Find the length and width. Round your answer to the nearest tenth of a foot.

✓ **9-9** **Using the Quadratic Formula and the Discriminant**

Solve using the Quadratic Formula. Round your answer to the nearest hundredth.

25. $x^2 + 5x + 1 = 0$ **26.** $3x^2 + 1 = 2x$ **27.** $5x + 8 = 3x^2$

Find the number of real solutions of each equation using the discriminant.

28. $2x^2 - 3x + 4 = 0$ **29.** $x^2 + 1 + 2x = 0$ **30.** $x^2 - 5 + 4x = 0$

Cubic Functions and Equations

Objectives
Recognize and graph cubic functions.

Solve cubic equations.

Vocabulary
cubic function
cubic equation

A **cubic function** is a function that can be written in the form $f(x) = ax^3 + bx^2 + cx + d$, where $a \neq 0$. The parent cubic function is $f(x) = x^3$. To graph this function, choose several values of x and find ordered pairs.

x	$f(x)$
2	8
1	1
0	0
−1	−1
−2	−8

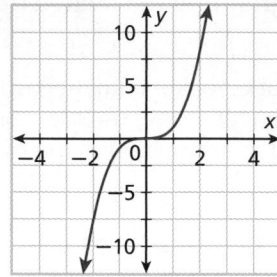

From the graph of $f(x) = x^3$, you can see
- the general shape of a cubic function.
- that the domain and the range are all real numbers.
- that the x-intercept and the y-intercept are both 0.

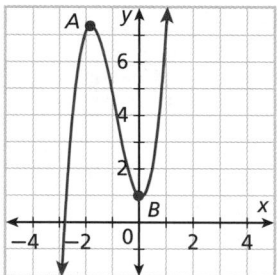

The graph of $f(x) = 2x^3 + 5x^2 - x + 1$ illustrates another characteristic of the graphs of cubic functions. Points A and B are called *turning points*. In general, the graph of a cubic function will have two turning points.

EXAMPLE 1 **Graphing Cubic Functions**

Graph $f(x) = -2x^3 + 3x^2 + x - 4$. Identify the intercepts and give the domain and range.

x	$f(x) = -2x^3 + 3x^2 + x - 4$	$f(x)$
−1	$-2(-1)^3 + 3(-1)^2 - 1 - 4$	0
0	$-2(0)^3 + 3(0)^2 + 0 - 4$	−4
1	$-2(1)^3 + 3(1)^2 + 1 - 4$	−2
2	$-2(2)^3 + 3(2)^2 + 2 - 4$	−6

Choose positive, negative, and zero values for x, and find ordered pairs.

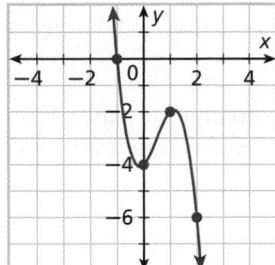

Plot the ordered pairs and connect them with a smooth curve.

Notice that, in general, this graph falls from left to right. This is because the value of a is negative.

The x-intercept is -1. The y-intercept is -4. The domain and range are all real numbers.

 Graph each cubic function. Identify the intercepts and give the domain and range.

1a. $f(x) = (x - 1)^3$ **1b.** $f(x) = 2x^3 - 12x^2 + 18x$

Previously, you saw that every quadratic function has a related quadratic equation. Cubic functions also have related *cubic equations*. A **cubic equation** is an equation that can be written in the form $ax^3 + bx^2 + cx + d = 0$, where $a \neq 0$.

One way to solve a cubic equation is by graphing the related function and finding its zeros.

EXAMPLE 2   **Solving Cubic Equations by Graphing**

Solve $x^3 - 2x^2 - x = -2$ by graphing. Check your answer.

Step 1 Rewrite the equation in the form $ax^3 + bx^2 + cx + d = 0$.

$x^3 - 2x^2 - x = -2$

$x^3 - 2x^2 - x + 2 = 0$ *Add 2 to both sides of the equation.*

Step 2 Write and graph the related function: $f(x) = x^3 - 2x^2 - x + 2$

x	$f(x) = x^3 - 2x^2 - x + 2$	$f(x)$
-1	$(-1)^3 - 2(-1)^2 - (\ 1) + 2$	0
0	$(0)^3 - 2(0)^2 - 0 + 2$	2
1	$(1)^3 - 2(1)^2 - 1 + 2$	0
2	$(2)^3 - 2(2)^2 - 2 + 2$	0
3	$(3)^3 - 2(3)^2 - 3 + 2$	8

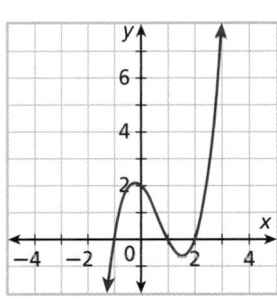

Step 3 Find the zeros.

The zeros appear to be -1, 1, and 2. Check these values in the original equation.

$$x^3 - 2x^2 - x = -2$$
$$\begin{array}{r|l} (-1)^3 - 2(-1)^2 - (-1) & -2 \\ \hline (-1) - 2 + 1 & -2 \\ \hline -2 & -2 \checkmark \end{array}$$

$$x^3 - 2x^2 - x = -2$$
$$\begin{array}{r|l} 1^3 - 2(1)^2 - 1 & -2 \\ \hline 1 - 2 - 1 & -2 \\ \hline -2 & -2 \checkmark \end{array}$$

$$x^3 - 2x^2 - x = -2$$
$$\begin{array}{r|l} 2^3 - 2(2)^2 - 2 & -2 \\ \hline 8 - 8 - 2 & -2 \\ \hline -2 & -2 \checkmark \end{array}$$

Solve each equation by graphing. Check your answer.

2a. $x^3 - 2x^2 - 25x = -50$ **2b.** $2x^3 + 12x^2 = 30x + 200$

Cubic equations can also be solved algebraically. Many of the methods used to solve quadratic equations can be applied to cubic equations as well.

EXAMPLE 3

Solving Cubic Equations Algebraically

Solve each equation. Check your answer.

A $(x + 5)^3 = 27$

$$\sqrt[3]{(x + 5)^3} = \sqrt[3]{27}$$ *Take the cube root of both sides.*

$$x + 5 = 3$$

$$x = -2$$ *Subtract 5 from both sides.*

Check

$(x + 5)^3 = 27$	
$(-2 + 5)^3$	27
3^3	27
27	27 ✓

Substitute –2 for x in the original equation.

B $x^3 + 3x^2 = -2x$

$$x^3 + 3x^2 + 2x = 0$$ *Add 2x to both sides.*

$$x(x^2 + 3x + 2) = 0$$ *Factor out x on the left side.*

$$x(x + 1)(x + 2) = 0$$ *Factor the quadratic trinomial.*

$$x = 0 \text{ or } x + 1 = 0 \text{ or } x + 2 = 0$$ *Zero Product Property*

$$x = -1 \text{ or } \quad x = -2$$ *Solve each equation.*

The solutions are 0, –1, and –2.

> **Remember!**
> The factored expression must equal zero to use the Zero Product Property.

Check

$x^3 + 3x^2 = -2x$	
$0^3 + 3(0)^2$	$-2(0)$
$0 + 0$	0
0	0 ✓

$x^3 + 3x^2 = -2x$	
$(-1)^3 + 3(-1)^2$	$-2(-1)$
$-1 + 3(1)$	2
$-1 + 3$	2
2	2 ✓

$x^3 + 3x^2 = -2x$	
$(-2)^3 + 3(-2)^2$	$-2(-2)$
$-8 + 3(4)$	4
$-8 + 12$	4
4	4 ✓

C $x^3 - 3.125x = -1.25x^2$

$$x^3 + 1.25x^2 - 3.125x = 0$$ *Add $1.25x^2$ to both sides.*

$$x(x^2 + 1.25x - 3.125) = 0$$ *Factor out x on the left side.*

$$x = 0 \text{ or } x^2 + 1.25x - 3.125 = 0$$ *Zero Product Property*

$$x = \frac{-1.25 \pm \sqrt{(1.25)^2 - 4(1)(-3.125)}}{2(1)}$$ *Quadratic Formula*

$$x = \frac{-1.25 \pm 3.75}{2}$$ *Simplify.*

$$x = -2.5 \text{ or } x = 1.25$$

The solutions are –2.5, 0, and 1.25.

Check   Use a graphing calculator.

Graph the related function and look for the zeros.

The solutions look reasonable.

 Solve each equation. Check your answer.

3a. $(x + 2)^3 = 64$ **3b.** $4x^3 - 12x^2 + 4x = 0$ **3c.** $x^3 + 3x^2 = 10x$

EXTENSION Exercises

Graph each cubic function. Identify the intercepts and give the domain and range.

1. $f(x) = x^3 - 2x^2 + 3x + 6$ **2.** $g(x) = -4x^3 + 2x - 2$

Solve each equation by graphing. Check your answer.

3. $2x^3 - 6x = -4x^2$ **4.** $-3x^3 + 12x^2 + 12x = 48$

Solve each equation. Check your answer.

5. $(x - 9)^3 = 64$ **6.** $8x + 4x^2 = 4x^3$ **7.** $5x^3 + 3x^2 = 4x$

8. The Send-It Store uses shipping labels that are x in. tall and $2x$ in. wide. Six labels fit on the front of the store's standard shipping box with an area of $3x$ in^2 left over. Three labels fit on the side of the box. The volume of the box is $108x$ in^3. What is the area of one label?

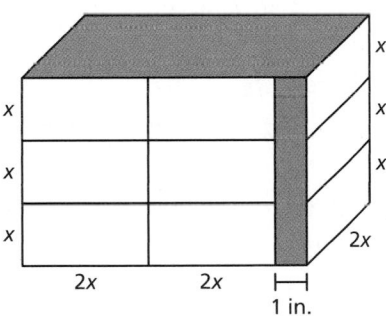

9. a. Graph the functions $f(x) = x^3$, $f(x) = x^3 + 1$, and $f(x) = x^3 + 2$ on the same coordinate plane. Describe any patterns you observe. Predict the shape of the graph of $f(x) = x^3 + c$.

    b. Graph the functions $g(x) = x^3$, $g(x) = (x - 1)^3$, and $g(x) = (x - 2)^3$ on the same coordinate plane. Describe any patterns you observe. Predict the shape of the graph of $g(x) = (x - c)^3$.

Use a graphing calculator to find the approximate solution(s) of each cubic equation. Round to the nearest hundredth.

10. $100x^3 - 40x^2 = 6x$ **11.** $2x^3 - 5x^2 + 4x = -3$

12. $-1.32x^3 - 3.65x^2 = -0.43x$ **13.** $\frac{3}{5}x^3 + x^2 - \frac{1}{2}x = 9$

14. Critical Thinking How many zeros can a cubic function have? What does this tell you about the number of real solutions possible for a cubic equation?

Study Guide: Review

Vocabulary

Complete the sentences below with vocabulary words from the list above.

1. The ___?___ is the highest or lowest point on a parabola.

2. A quadratic function has a ___?___ if its graph opens upward and a ___?___ if its graph opens downward.

3. A ___?___ can also be called an *x*-intercept of the function.

4. Finding the ___?___ can tell you how many real-number solutions a quadratic equation has.

5. ___?___ is a process that results in a perfect-square trinomial.

9-1 Identifying Quadratic Functions (pp. 610–617)

EXAMPLE

■ Use a table of values to graph $y = -5x^2 + 40x$.

Step 1 Make a table of values.
Choose values of x and use them to find values of y.

x	0	1	3	4	6	7	8
y	0	35	75	80	60	35	0

Step 2 Plot the points and connect them with a smooth curve.

EXERCISES

Tell whether each function is quadratic. Explain.

6. $y = 2x^2 + 9x - 5$

7. $y = -4x + 3$

8. $y = -\dfrac{1}{2}x^2$

9. $y = 5x^3 + 8$

Use a table of values to graph each quadratic function.

10. $y = 6x^2$

11. $y = -4x^2$

12. $y = \dfrac{1}{4}x^2$

13. $y = -3x^2$

Tell whether the graph of each function opens upward or downward. Explain.

14. $y = 5x^2 - 12$

15. $y = -x^2 + 3x - 7$

16. Identify the vertex of the parabola. Then give the minimum or maximum value of the function.

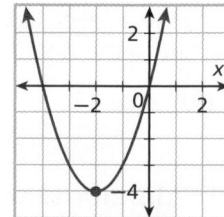

9-2 Characteristics of Quadratic Functions (pp. 619–625)

EXAMPLE

■ Find the zeros of $y = 2x^2 - 4x - 6$ from its graph. Then find the axis of symmetry and the vertex.

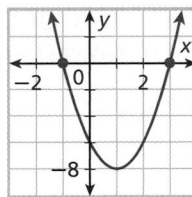

Step 1 Use the graph to find the zeros. The zeros are -1 and 3.

Step 2 Find the axis of symmetry.
$$x = \frac{-1 + 3}{2} = \frac{2}{2} = 1$$
Find the average of the zeros.

The axis of symmetry is the vertical line $x = 1$.

Step 3 Find the vertex.
$$y = 2x^2 - 4x - 6$$
$$y = 2(1)^2 - 4(1) - 6$$
$$y = -8$$
Substitute 1 for x to find the y-value of the vertex.

The vertex is $(1, -8)$.

EXERCISES

Find the zeros of each quadratic function from its graph. Check your answer.

17. $y = x^2 + 3x - 10$

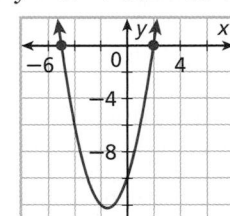

18. $y = x^2 - x - 2$

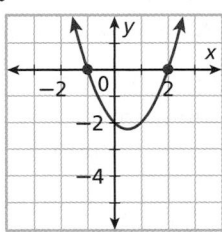

Find the axis of symmetry and vertex of each parabola.

19. $y = -x^2 + 12x - 32$

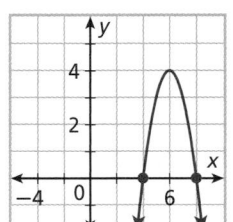

20. $y = 2x^2 + 4x - 16$

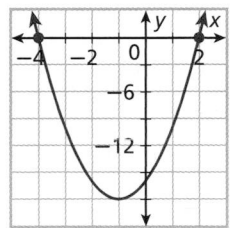

9-3 Graphing Quadratic Functions (pp. 626–631)

EXAMPLE

■ Graph $y = 2x^2 - 8x - 10$.

Step 1 Find the axis of symmetry.
$$x = \frac{-b}{2a} = \frac{-(-8)}{2(2)} = \frac{8}{4} = 2$$
The axis of symmetry is $x = 2$.

Step 2 Find the vertex.
$$y = 2x^2 - 8x - 10$$
$$y = 2(2)^2 - 8(2) - 10$$
$$y = -18$$
The vertex is $(2, -18)$.

Step 3 Find the y-intercept.
$$c = -10$$

Step 4 Find one more point on the graph.
$$y = 2(-1)^2 - 8(-1) - 10 = 0 \qquad Let\ x = -1.$$
Use $(-1, 0)$.

Step 5 Graph the axis of symmetry and the points. **Reflect** the points and connect with a smooth curve.

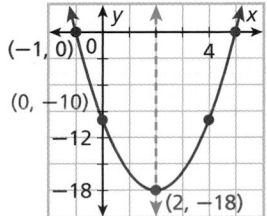

EXERCISES

Graph each quadratic function.

21. $y = x^2 + 6x + 6$

22. $y = x^2 - 4x - 12$

23. $y = x^2 - 8x + 7$

24. $y = 2x^2 - 6x - 8$

25. $3x^2 + 6x = y - 3$

26. $2 - 4x^2 + y = 8x - 10$

27. Water that is sprayed upward from a sprinkler with an initial velocity of 20 m/s can be approximated by the function $y = -5x^2 + 20x$, where y is the height of a drop of water x seconds after it is released. Graph this function. Find the time it takes a drop of water to reach its maximum height, the water's maximum height, and the time it takes the water to reach the ground.

9-4 Transforming Quadratic Functions (pp. 633–639)

EXAMPLE

■ Compare the graph of $g(x) = 3x^2 - 4$ with the graph of $f(x) = x^2$. Use the functions.

- Both graphs open upward because $a > 0$.

- The axis of symmetry is the same, $x = 0$, because $b = 0$ in both functions.

- The graph of $g(x)$ is narrower than the graph of $f(x)$ because $|3| > |1|$.

- The vertex of $f(x)$ is $(0, 0)$. The vertex of $g(x)$ is translated 4 units down to $(0, -4)$.

- $f(x)$ has one zero at the origin. $g(x)$ has two zeros because the vertex is below the origin and the parabola opens upward.

EXERCISES

Compare the widths of the graphs of the given quadratic functions. Order functions with different widths from narrowest graph to widest.

28. $f(x) = 2x^2$, $g(x) = 4x^2$

29. $f(x) = 6x^2$, $g(x) = -6x^2$

30. $f(x) = x^2$, $g(x) = \frac{1}{3}x^2$, $h(x) = 3x^2$

Compare the graph of each function with the graph of $f(x) = x^2$.

31. $g(x) = x^2 + 5$

32. $g(x) = 3x^2 - 1$

33. $g(x) = 2x^2 + 3$

9-5 Solving Quadratic Equations by Graphing (pp. 642–647)

EXAMPLE

■ Solve $-4 = 4x^2 - 8x$ by graphing the related function.

Step 1 Write the equation in standard form.

$$0 = 4x^2 - 8x + 4$$

Step 2 Graph the related function.

$$y = 4x^2 - 8x + 4$$

Step 3 Find the zeros.
The only zero is 1. The solution is $x = 1$.

EXERCISES

Solve each equation by graphing the related function.

34. $0 = x^2 + 4x + 3$

35. $0 = x^2 + 6x + 9$

36. $-4x^2 = 3$

37. $x^2 + 5 = 6x$

38. $-4x^2 = 64 - 32x$

39. $9 = 9x^2$

40. $-3x^2 + 2x = 5$

9-6 Solving Quadratic Equations by Factoring (pp. 650–655)

EXAMPLE

■ Solve $3x^2 - 6x = 24$ by factoring.

$3x^2 - 6x = 24$	*Write the equation in*
$3x^2 - 6x - 24 = 0$	*standard form.*
$3(x^2 - 2x - 8) = 0$	*Factor out 3.*
$3(x + 2)(x - 4) = 0$	*Factor the trinomial.*
	Zero Product
$3 \neq 0, x + 2 = 0$ or $x - 4 = 0$	*Property*
$x = -2$ or $x = 4$	*Solve each equation.*

EXERCISES

Solve each quadratic equation by factoring.

41. $x^2 + 6x + 5 = 0$ **42.** $x^2 + 9x + 14 = 0$

43. $x^2 - 2x - 15 = 0$ **44.** $2x^2 - 2x - 4 = 0$

45. $x^2 + 10x + 25 = 0$ **46.** $4x^2 - 36x = -81$

47. A rectangle is 2 feet longer than it is wide. The area of the rectangle is 48 square feet. Write and solve an equation that can be used to find the width of the rectangle.

9-7 Solving Quadratic Equations by Using Square Roots (pp. 656–661)

EXAMPLE

■ Solve $2x^2 = 98$ using square roots.

$$\frac{2x^2}{2} = \frac{98}{2}$$ *Divide both sides of the equation by 2 to isolate x^2.*

$$x^2 = 49$$

$$x = \pm\sqrt{49}$$ *Take the square root of both sides.*

$$x = \pm 7$$ *Use $\pm$ to show both roots.*

The solutions are -7 and 7.

EXERCISES

Solve using square roots.

48. $5x^2 = 320$

49. $-x^2 + 144 = 0$

50. $x^2 = -16$

51. $x^2 + 7 = 7$

52. $2x^2 = 50$

53. $4x^2 = 25$

54. A rectangle is twice as long as it is wide. The area of the rectangle is 32 square feet. Find the rectangle's width.

9-8 Completing the Square (pp. 663–669)

EXAMPLE

■ Solve $x^2 - 6x = -5$ by completing the square.

$$\left(\frac{-6}{2}\right)^2 = 9$$ *Find $\left(\frac{b}{2}\right)^2$.*

$$x^2 - 6x + 9 = -5 + 9$$ *Complete the square by*

$$x^2 - 6x + 9 = 4$$ *adding $\left(\frac{b}{2}\right)^2$ to both sides.*

$$(x - 3)^2 = 4$$ *Factor the trinomial.*

$$x - 3 = \pm\sqrt{4}$$ *Take the square root of both sides.*

$$x - 3 = \pm 2$$ *Use the $\pm$ symbol.*

$$x - 3 = 2 \text{ or } x - 3 = -2$$ *Solve each*

$$x = 5 \quad \text{or} \quad x = 1$$ *equation.*

The solutions are 5 and 1.

EXERCISES

Solve by completing the square.

55. $x^2 + 2x = 48$

56. $x^2 + 4x = 21$

57. $2x^2 - 12x + 10 = 0$

58. $x^2 - 10x = -20$

59. A homeowner is planning an addition to her house. She wants the new family room to be a rectangle with an area of 192 square feet. The contractor says that the length needs to be 4 more feet than the width. What will the dimensions of the new room be?

9-9 The Quadratic Formula and the Discriminant (pp. 670–677)

EXAMPLE

■ Solve $x^2 + 4x + 4 = 0$ using the Quadratic Formula.

The equation $x^2 + 4x + 4 = 0$ is in standard form with $a = 1$, $b = 4$, and $c = 4$.

$$x = \frac{-b \pm \sqrt{b^2 - 4ac}}{2a}$$ *Write the Quadratic Formula.*

$$= \frac{-4 \pm \sqrt{4^2 - 4(1)(4)}}{2(1)}$$ *Substitute for a, b, and c.*

$$= \frac{-4 \pm \sqrt{16 - 16}}{2}$$ *Simplify.*

$$= \frac{-4 \pm \sqrt{0}}{2} = \frac{-4}{2} = -2$$

The solution is $x = -2$.

EXERCISES

Solve using the Quadratic Formula.

60. $x^2 - 5x - 6 = 0$

61. $2x^2 - 9x - 5 = 0$

62. $4x^2 - 8x + 4 = 0$

63. $x^2 - 6x = -7$

Find the number of real solutions of each equation using the discriminant.

64. $x^2 - 12x + 36 = 0$

65. $3x^2 + 5 = 0$

66. $2x^2 - 13x = -20$

67. $6x^2 - 20 = 15x + 1$

CHAPTER TEST

Tell whether each function is quadratic. Explain.

1. $\{(10, 50), (11, 71), (12, 94), (13, 119), (14, 146)\}$ 2. $3x^2 + y = 4 + 3x^2$

3. Tell whether the graph of $y = -2x^2 + 7x - 5$ opens upward or downward and whether the parabola has a maximum or a minimum.

4. Estimate the zeros of the quadratic function.   5. Find the axis of symmetry of the parabola.

6. Find the vertex of the graph of $y = x^2 + 6x + 8$.

7. Graph the quadratic function $y = x^2 - 4x + 2$.

Compare the graph of each function with the graph of $f(x) = x^2$.

8. $g(x) = -x^2 - 2$ 9. $h(x) = \frac{1}{3}x^2 + 1$ 10. $g(x) = 3x^2 - 4$

11. A hammer is dropped from a 40-foot scaffold. Another one is dropped from a 60-foot scaffold.

   a. Write the two height functions and compare their graphs. Use $h(t) = -16t^2 + c$, where c is the height of the scaffold.

   b. Use the graphs to estimate when each hammer will reach the ground.

12. A rocket is launched with an initial vertical velocity of 110 m/s. The height of the rocket in meters is approximated by the quadratic equation $h = -5t^2 + 110t$ where t is the time after launch in seconds. About how long does it take for the rocket to return to the ground?

Solve each quadratic equation by factoring.

13. $x^2 + 6x + 5 = 0$ 14. $x^2 - 12x = -36$ 15. $x^2 - 81 = 0$

Solve by using square roots.

16. $-2x^2 = -72$ 17. $9x^2 - 49 = 0$ 18. $3x^2 + 12 = 0$

Solve by completing the square.

19. $x^2 + 10x = -21$ 20. $x^2 - 6x + 4 = 0$ 21. $2x^2 + 16x = 0$

22. A landscaper has enough cement to make a rectangular patio with an area of 150 square feet. The homeowner wants the length to be 6 feet longer than the width. What dimensions should be used for the patio? Round to the nearest tenth of a foot.

Solve each quadratic equation. Round to the nearest hundredth if necessary.

23. $x^2 + 3x - 40 = 0$ 24. $2x^2 + 7x = -5$ 25. $8x^2 + 3x - 1 = 0$

Find the number of real solutions of each equation using the discriminant.

26. $4x^2 - 4x + 1 = 0$ 27. $2x^2 + 5x - 25 = 0$ 28. $\frac{1}{2}x^2 + 8 = 0$

COLLEGE ENTRANCE EXAM PRACTICE

FOCUS ON SAT SUBJECT TESTS

In addition to the SAT, some colleges require the SAT Subject Tests for admission. Colleges that don't require the SAT Subject Tests may still use the scores to learn about your academic background and to place you in the appropriate college math class.

Take the SAT Subject Test in mathematics while the material is still fresh in your mind. You are not expected to be familiar with all of the test content, but you should have completed at least three years of college-prep math.

You may want to time yourself as you take this practice test. It should take you about 6 minutes to complete.

1. The graph below corresponds to which of the following quadratic functions?

(A) $f(x) = x^2 + 4x - 5$

(B) $f(x) = -x^2 - 4x + 3$

(C) $f(x) = -x^2 + 5x - 4$

(D) $f(x) = -x^2 - 4x + 5$

(E) $f(x) = -x^2 - 3x + 5$

2. What is the sum of the solutions to the equation $9x^2 - 6x = 8$?

(A) $\frac{4}{3}$

(B) $\frac{2}{3}$

(C) $\frac{1}{3}$

(D) $-\frac{2}{3}$

(E) $-\frac{8}{3}$

3. If $h(x) = ax^2 + bx + c$, where $b^2 - 4ac < 0$ and $a < 0$, which of the following statements must be true?

I. The graph of $h(x)$ has no points in the first or second quadrants.

II. The graph of $h(x)$ has no points in the third or fourth quadrants.

III. The graph of $h(x)$ has points in all quadrants.

(A) I only

(B) II only

(C) III only

(D) I and II only

(E) None of the statements are true.

4. What is the axis of symmetry for the graph of a quadratic function whose zeros are −2 and 4?

(A) $x = -2$

(B) $x = 0$

(C) $x = 1$

(D) $x = 2$

(E) $x = 6$

5. How many real-number solutions does $0 = x^2 - 7x + 1$ have?

(A) None

(B) One

(C) Two

(D) All real numbers

(E) It is impossible to determine.

TEST TACKLER

Standardized Test Strategies

Extended Response: Explain Your Reasoning

Extended response test items often include multipart questions that evaluate your understanding of a math concept. To receive full credit, you must answer the problem correctly, show all of your work, and explain your reasoning. Use complete sentences and show your problem-solving method clearly.

EXAMPLE 1

Extended Response Given $\frac{1}{2}x^2 + y = 4x - 3$ and $y = 2x - 12x$, identify which is a quadratic function. Provide an explanation for your decision. For the quadratic function, tell whether the graph of the function opens upward or downward and whether the parabola has a maximum or a minimum. Explain your reasoning.

Read the solutions provided by two different students.

Student A   *Excellent explanation*

> The quadratic function is $\frac{1}{2}x^2 + y = 4x - 3$ because it can be written in standard form, $y = -\frac{1}{2}x^2 + 4x - 3$, where a, b, and c are real numbers and $a \neq 0$. The other function, $y = 2x - 12x$, is not quadratic because there is no x^2-term.
>
> The graph of this function will open downward because a, which is equal to $-\frac{1}{2}$, is less than 0. Because the parabola opens downward, the graph will have a maximum.

The response includes the correct answers along with a detailed explanation for each part of the problem. The explanation is written using complete sentences and is presented in an order that is easy to follow and to understand. It is obvious that this student knows how to determine and interpret a quadratic function.

Student B   *Poor explanation*

> $\frac{1}{2}x^2 + y = 4x - 3$ There is an x^2.
>
> When I graphed the function on my calculator, I saw a parabola that opened downward.
>
> It had a maximum.

The response includes the correct answers, but the explanation does not include details. The reason for defining the function as quadratic does not show knowledge of the concept. The student shows a lack of understanding of how to write and interpret a quadratic function in standard form.

Include as many details as possible to support your reasoning. This increases the chance of getting full credit for your response.

Read each test item and answer the questions that follow.

Item A

The height y in feet of a tennis ball x seconds after it is ejected from a serving machine is given by the ordered pairs $\{(0, 10), (0.5, 9), (1, 7), (1.5, 4), (2, 0)\}$. Determine whether the function is quadratic. Find its domain and range. Explain your answers.

1. What should a student include in the explanation to receive full credit?

2. Read the two explanations below. Which explanation is better? Why?

Student A

Range: $0 \le y \le 10$ Domain: $0 \le x \le 2$
Second differences are -1: quadratic

Student B

The function is quadratic because the second differences are constant: -1. The domain and range are determined by the points $(0, 10)$ and $(2, 0)$. The range is $0 \le y \le 10$, and the domain is $0 \le x \le 2$.

Item B

The height of a golf ball can be approximated by the function $y = -5x^2 + 20x + 8$, where y is the height in meters above the ground and x is the time in seconds after the ball is hit. What is the maximum height of the ball? How long does it take for the ball to reach its maximum height? Explain.

3. A student correctly found the following answers. Use this information to write a clear and concise explanation.

Axis of symmetry is the vertical line at $x = 2$.
Vertex is at $(2, 28)$.
28 meters; 2 seconds

Item C

A science teacher set off a bottle rocket as part of a lab experiment. The function $h = -16t^2 + 96t$ represents the height in feet of a rocket that is shot out of a bottle with an initial vertical velocity of 96 feet per second. Find the time that the rocket is in the air. Explain how you found your answer.

4. Read the two responses below.

   a. Which student provided the better explanation? Why?

   b. What advice would you give the other student to improve his or her explanation?

Student C

Graph the function $h = -16t^2 + 96t$, and then find the zeros. The first zero is when $t = 0$, when the rocket is launched. The second zero is when the rocket hits the ground: $t = 6$. The difference between 6 and 0 is the time that the rocket is in the air: 6 seconds.

Student D

6 seconds.
Graph the function to find how long the rocket is in the air, and find the values where it crosses the x-axis.

Item D

The base of a parallelogram is 12 centimeters more than its height. The area of the parallelogram is 13 square centimeters. Explain how to determine the height and base of the figure. What is the height? What is the base?

5. Read the following response. Identify any areas that need improvement. Rewrite the response so that it will receive full credit.

$x^2 + 12x + 36 = 49$ Complete the square.
$(x+6)^2 = 49$
$x + 6 = \sqrt{49}$
$x + 6 = \pm 7$; $x = 1$ or -13

base = 13, height = 1

CHAPTER
9

STANDARDIZED
TEST PREP

go.hrw.com
State Test Practice Online
KEYWORD: MA7 TestPrep

CUMULATIVE ASSESSMENT, CHAPTERS 1–9

Multiple Choice

1. Which expression is NOT equal to the other three?

(A) 0^1 (C) 1^0

(B) 1^1 (D) $(-1)^0$

2. Which function's graph is a translation of the graph of $f(x) = 3x^2 + 4$ seven units down?

(F) $f(x) = -4x^2 + 4$

(G) $f(x) = 10x^2 + 4$

(H) $f(x) = 3x^2 - 3$

(J) $f(x) = 3x^2 + 11$

3. The area of a circle in square units is $\pi(9x^2 + 42x + 49)$. Which expression represents the circumference of the circle in units?

(A) $\pi(3x + 7)$

(B) $2\pi(3x + 7)$

(C) $2\pi(3x + 7)^2$

(D) $6x + 14$

4. CyberCafe charges a computer station rental fee of \$5, plus \$0.20 for each quarter-hour spent surfing. Which expression represents the total amount Carl will pay to use a computer station for three and a half hours?

(F) $5 + 0.20(3.5)$

(G) $5 + 0.20(3.5)(4)$

(H) $5 + \dfrac{0.20}{3.5 \div 4}$

(J) $5 + \dfrac{1}{4} \cdot \dfrac{0.20}{3.5}$

5. What is the numerical solution to the equation *five less than three times a number equals four more than eight times the number?*

(A) $-\dfrac{9}{5}$ (C) $\dfrac{1}{11}$

(B) $-\dfrac{1}{5}$ (D) $\dfrac{1}{5}$

6. Which is a possible situation for the graph?

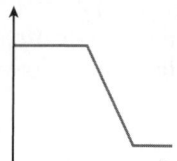

(F) A car travels at a steady speed, slows down in a school zone, and then resumes its previous speed.

(G) A child climbs the ladder of a slide and then slides down.

(H) A person flies in an airplane for a while, parachutes out, and gets stuck in a tree.

(J) The number of visitors increases in the summer, declines in the fall, and levels off in the winter.

7. Which of the following is the graph of $f(x) = -x^2 + 2$?

(A)

(C)

(B)

(D)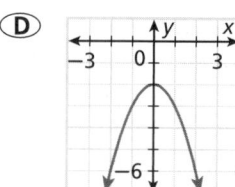

8. The value of y varies directly with x, and $y = 40$ when $x = -5$. Find y when $x = 8$.

(F) 25   (H) -8

(G) -1 (J) -64

9. What is the slope of the line that passes through the points $(4, 7)$ and $(5, 3)$?

(A) 4   (C) $-\dfrac{1}{4}$

(B) $\dfrac{1}{4}$ (D) -4

10. Putting Green Mini Golf charges a $4 golf club rental fee plus $1.25 per game. Good Times Golf charges a $1.25 golf club rental fee plus $3.75 per game. Which system of equations could be solved to determine for how many games the cost is the same at both places?

F $\begin{cases} y = 4x + 1.25 \\ y = 3.75 + 1.25x \end{cases}$

G $\begin{cases} y = 4 - 1.25x \\ y = -3.75 + 1.25x \end{cases}$

H $\begin{cases} y = 1.25x + 4 \\ y = 3.75x + 1.25 \end{cases}$

J $\begin{cases} y = 1.25x - 4 \\ y = 1.25x + 3.75 \end{cases}$

11. The graph of which quadratic function has an axis of symmetry of $x = -2$?

A $y = 2x^2 - x + 3$

B $y = 4x^2 + 2x + 3$

C $y = x^2 - 2x + 3$

D $y = x^2 + 4x + 3$

12. Which polynomial is the product of $x - 4$ and $x^2 - 4x + 1$?

F $-4x^2 + 17x - 4$

G $x^3 - 8x^2 + 17x - 4$

H $x^3 + 17x - 4$

J $x^3 - 15x + 4$

Gridded Response

13. The length of a rectangle is 2 units greater than the width. The area of the rectangle is 24 square units. What is its width in units?

14. Find the value of the discriminant of the equation $0 = -2x^2 + 3x + 4$.

15. What is the positive solution of $4x^2 = 10x + 2$? Round your answer to the nearest hundredth if necessary.

Short Response

16. The data in the table shows ordered pair solutions to a linear function. Find the missing y-value. Show your work.

x	y
−2	−7
−1	−3
0	▮
1	5
2	9

17. Answer the following questions using the function $f(x) = 2x^2 + 4x - 1$.

a. Make a table of values and give five points on the graph.

b. Find the axis of symmetry and vertex. Show all calculations.

18. a. Show how to solve $x^2 - 2x - 8 = 0$ by graphing the related function. Show all your work.

b. Show another way to solve the equation in part a. Show all your work.

19. What can you say about the value of a if the graph of $y = ax^2 - 8$ has no x-intercepts? Explain.

Extended Response

20. The graph shows the quadratic function $f(x) = ax^2 + bx + c$.

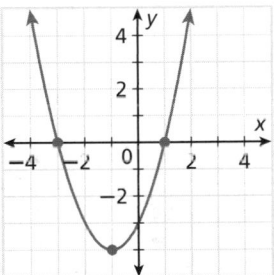

a. What are the solutions of the equation $0 = ax^2 + bx + c$? Explain how you know.

b. If the point $(-5, 12)$ lies on the graph of $f(x)$, the point $(a, 12)$ also lies on the graph. Find the value of a.

c. What do you know about the relationship between the values of a and b? Use the coordinates of the vertex in your explanation.

d. Use what you know about solving quadratic equations by factoring to make a conjecture about the values of a, b, and c in the function $f(x) = ax^2 + bx + c$.

10 Data Analysis and Probability

Chapter

- Organize and display data to answer questions.
- Use descriptive statistics to summarize data sets.
- Understand experimental probability and theoretical probability.
- Use probability to make appropriate predictions.

You're *the Designer*

Research studies are designed to gather and analyze data in order to answer questions. The results are displayed in tables and graphs.

go.hrw.com
Chapter Project Online
KEYWORD: MA7 ChProj

ARE YOU READY?

✅ Vocabulary
Match each term on the left with a definition on the right.

1. difference
2. factor
3. natural numbers
4. ratio
5. sum

A. the result of an addition

B. a whole number that is multiplied by another whole number to get a product

C. numbers that can be expressed in the form $\frac{a}{b}$, where a and b are both integers and $b \neq 0$

D. the result of a subtraction

E. a comparison of two quantities by division

F. the counting numbers: 1, 2, 3, …

✅ Solve Proportions
Solve each proportion.

6. $\frac{3}{4} = \frac{x}{12}$

7. $\frac{15}{9} = \frac{3}{x}$

8. $\frac{10}{20} = \frac{x}{100}$

9. $\frac{250}{1500} = \frac{x}{100}$

✅ Compare and Order Real Numbers
Compare. Write <, >, or =.

10. 20 ▦ 13

11. $\frac{2}{3}$ ▦ $\frac{1}{2}$

12. $\frac{3}{4}$ ▦ $\frac{7}{9}$

13. 0.75 ▦ $\frac{9}{12}$

Order the numbers from least to greatest.

14. $\frac{1}{2}, \frac{4}{5}, \frac{1}{8}, \frac{3}{4}, \frac{2}{3}$

15. $0.12, \frac{2}{5}, \frac{3}{4}, 0.3, \frac{1}{3}$

✅ Multiply Decimals
Multiply.

16. 0.25×300

17. 0.5×4000

18. 0.05×200

19. 0.125×9600

✅ Divide Decimals
Divide.

20. $435 \div 10$

21. $32 \div 100$

22. $777 \div 1000$

23. $295 \div 10{,}000$

✅ Fractions, Decimals, and Percents
Write the equivalent decimal.

24. $\frac{3}{5}$

25. 45%

26. $\frac{3}{4}$

27. 8%

Write the equivalent percent.

28. $\frac{1}{4}$

29. 0.2

30. 0.36

31. $\frac{1}{10}$

Study Guide: Preview

Where You've Been

Previously, you

- read information from tables and graphs.
- added, subtracted, multiplied, and divided real numbers.
- worked with ratios and percents.

In This Chapter

You will study

- how to organize data in tables, graphs, and plots.
- how to find the central tendency of a data set by calculating mean, median, and mode.
- writing experimental and theoretical probability as ratios, percents, and decimals.
- combinations, permutations, and factorials as extensions of multiplication.

Where You're Going

You can use the skills in this chapter

- to present your findings from science laboratory experiments in an appropriate and accurate graphical form.
- to be more informed about statistical information in the news and not to be misled by how it is presented.

Key Vocabulary/Vocabulario

combination	combinación
compound event	suceso compuesto
dependent events	sucesos dependientes
experimental probability	probabilidad experimental
frequency	frecuencia
independent events	sucesos independientes
median	mediana
outlier	valor extremo
permutation	permutación
probability	probabilidad
quartile	cuartil
theoretical probability	probabilidad teórica

Vocabulary Connections

To become familiar with some of the vocabulary terms in the chapter, consider the following. You may refer to the chapter, the glossary, or a dictionary if you like.

1. The *median strip* is the middle region that divides a highway in half. Use this knowledge to define **median** as it relates to a set of data.

2. The word **quartile** starts with the prefix *quart-*. What are some other words that start with the prefix *quart-*? What do they all have in common?

3. **Probability** is the chance something will happen. Based on your understanding of the words *experiment* and *theory*, compare and contrast the terms **experimental probability** and **theoretical probability**.

4. A *compound word* is made up of two or more words. What do you think makes up a **compound event**?

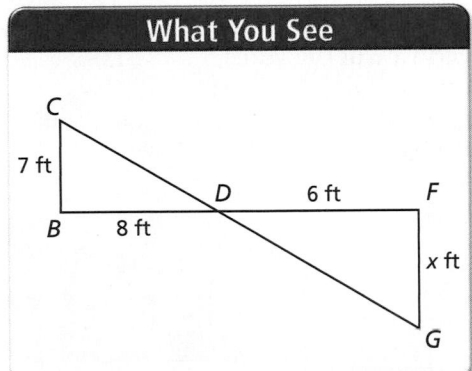

Reading and Writing Math

Reading Strategy: Read and Interpret Graphics

Knowing how to interpret figures, diagrams, charts, and graphs will help you gather the information you need to get the correct answer.

What You See	How to Interpret
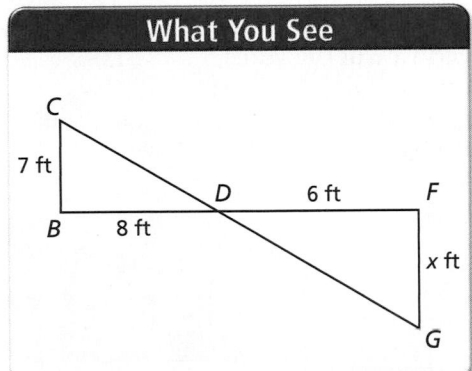	✔ **Read all labels.** $CB = 7$ ft; $BD = 8$ ft; $DF = 6$ ft; $FG = x$ ft ✗ **Do not assume anything.** It appears that $\overline{DF}$ is longer than $\overline{BD}$, but the labels indicate that it is shorter. $\angle B$ and $\angle F$ appear to be 90°, but the diagram does not indicate this.

What You See	How to Interpret
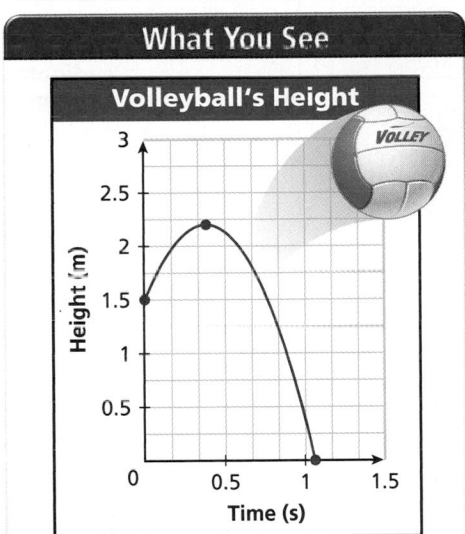	✔ **Read the title.** "Volleyball's Height" ✔ **Read each axis label.** *x*-axis Indicates **time** measured in seconds *y*-axis Indicates **height** measured in meters ✔ **Determine what information is represented.** Each point on the graph gives the **height** of the ball at that **time**.

Try This

Look up each exercise in the text and answer the corresponding questions.

1. Lesson 2-7 Exercise 42: What is the title of the table? What is the record for the 200-meter run?

2. Lesson 7-8 Exercise 69: What does *x* represent in the diagram? Make a list of the information you know from the diagram.

3. Lesson 8-3 Exercise 51: What is represented by the *y*-axis? What is the *y*-value when *x* equals 3.5? Is the graph linear? How do you know?

4. Lesson 9-8 Exercise 33: What does the dashed line represent? What facts about the parallelogram are given from the diagram?

Bar and Circle Graphs

Data displayed in bar graphs and circle graphs can be used to solve equations. In these problems, parts of the graphs are missing.

Example 1

The top part of this graph was torn off. If Warren received 15% of the votes, how many votes did Adams receive?

Step 1 Find the total number of votes. Let t represent the total.

15%	of	the total votes	is	42 votes.
0.15	•	t	=	42

$$0.15t = 42$$

$$t = 280 \text{ votes}$$

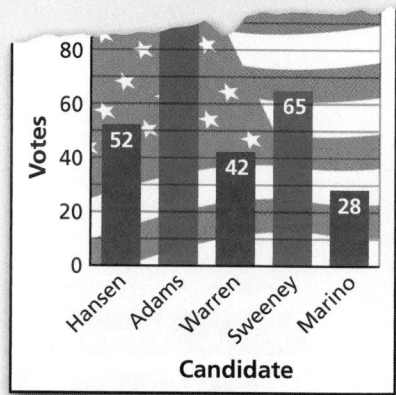

Step 2 Find the number of votes Adams received.

Let a represent the number of votes received by Adams. Let h, w, s, and m represent the number of votes received by Hansen, Warren, Sweeney, and Marino.

$$t = a + h + w + s + m$$
$$280 = a + 52 + 42 + 65 + 28$$ *Substitute the numbers shown on the graph.*
$$280 = a + 187$$ *Simplify the right side of the equation.*
$$\underline{-187 \qquad -187}$$ *Subtract 187 from both sides.*
$$93 = a$$

Adams received 93 votes.

Try This

1. The missing bar is twice as tall as the bar for week 2. How many total miles did Kim bike in these five weeks?

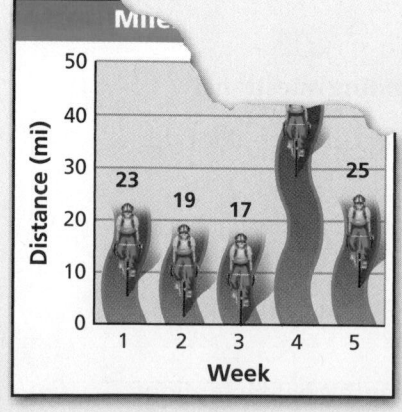

2. People aged 20–29 years walked 275 more miles than the oldest age group. Find the total miles walked by all age groups.

Remember that a circle graph represents all the data in a data set. The percent represented by each section is a part of the whole data set, so the sum of all the percents must be 100%.

Example 2

A survey asked people in a neighborhood to agree or disagree with the following statement:

   "We need a traffic light at Jefferson Avenue and Third Street."

If 35% of the people disagreed with the statement, how many people had no opinion?

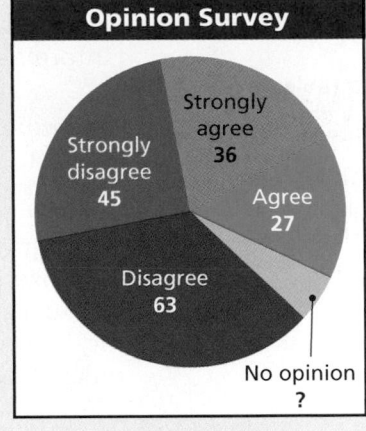

Opinion Survey

The number of people who answered "no opinion" is missing from the graph.

> **Step 1** Find the total number of people who answered the survey. Let t represent the total number of people.
>
> | 35% | of | the total number of people | is | 63 people. |
> |---|---|---|---|---|
> | 0.35 | • | t | = | 63 |
>
> $$0.35t = 63$$
> $$t = 180 \text{ people}$$

> **Step 2** Find the number of people who answered "no opinion."
>
> Let n represent the number of "no opinion" answers. Let d, s, g, and a represent the number of "disagree," "strongly disagree," "strongly agree," and "agree" answers.
>
> $$t = n + d + s + g + a$$
> $180 = n + 63 + 45 + 36 + 27$ *Substitute the numbers shown on the graph.*
> $180 = n + 171$ *Simplify the right side of the equation.*
> $\underline{-171 \qquad -171}$ *Subtract 171 from both sides.*
> $\qquad 9 = n$

There were 9 people who had no opinion.

Try This

3. The students in a junior high school voted on their choice for a field trip. Sixteen students voted for the natural history museum. How many students voted for the winning choice?

Field Trip Vote

Aquarium 25% | Zoo 20%
Planetarium ? | Museum 20%

4. At the fall dance recital, 40% of the tickets were sold to adults. What percent of the sales were to seniors?

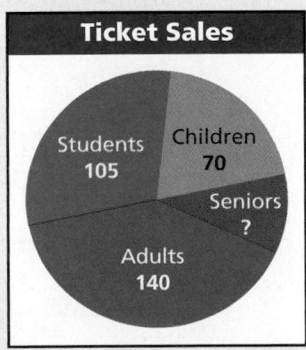

Ticket Sales

Students 105 | Children 70
Adults 140 | Seniors ?

10-1 Organizing and Displaying Data

Objectives
Organize data in tables and graphs.

Choose a table or graph to display data.

Vocabulary
bar graph
line graph
circle graph

Who uses this?
Nutritionists can display health information about food in bar graphs.

Bar graphs, line graphs, and *circle graphs* can be used to present data in a visual way.

A **bar graph** displays data with vertical or horizontal bars. Bar graphs are a good way to display data that can be organized into categories. Using a bar graph, you can quickly compare the categories.

EXAMPLE 1 **Reading and Interpreting Bar Graphs**

Use the graph to answer each question.

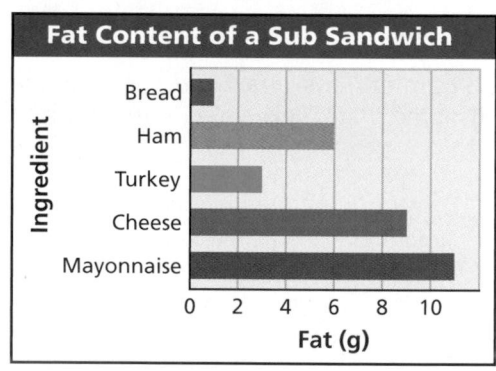

A Which ingredient contains the most fat?

mayonnaise   *The bar for mayonnaise is the longest.*

B How many more grams of fat are in ham than in turkey?

$6 - 3 = 3$ *There are 6 grams of fat in ham and 3 grams of fat in turkey.*

C How many total fat grams are in this sandwich?

$1 + 6 + 3 + 9 + 11 = 30$ *Add the number of fat grams for each ingredient.*

D What percent of the total fat grams in this sandwich are from turkey?

$\frac{3}{30} = \frac{1}{10} = 10\%$ *Out of 30 total fat grams, 3 fat grams are from turkey.*

 Use the graph to answer each question.

1a. Which ingredient contains the least amount of fat?

1b. Which ingredients contain at least 8 grams of fat?

A double-bar graph can be used to compare two data sets. A double-bar graph has a key to distinguish between the two sets of data.

EXAMPLE **2** **Reading and Interpreting Double Bar Graphs**

Use the graph to answer each question.

A In which year did State College have the greatest average attendance for basketball?

2003

Find the tallest orange bar.

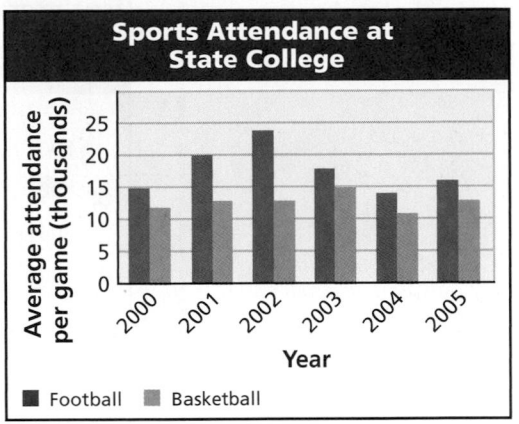

B On average, how many more people attended a football game than a basketball game in 2001?

$20,000 - 13,000 = 7000$

Find the height of each bar for 2001 and subtract.

2. Use the graph to determine which years had the same average basketball attendance. What was the average attendance for those years?

A **line graph** displays data using line segments. Line graphs are a good way to display data that changes over a period of time.

EXAMPLE **3** **Reading and Interpreting Line Graphs**

Use the graph to answer each question.

A At what time was the temperature the warmest?

4:00 P.M.   *Identify the highest point.*

B During which 4-hour time period did the temperature increase the most?

From 8:00 A.M. to noon   *Look for the segment with the greatest positive slope.*

3. Use the graph to estimate the difference in temperature between 4:00 A.M. and noon.

A double-line graph can be used to compare how two related data sets change over time. A double-line graph has a key to distinguish between the two sets of data.

EXAMPLE 4 **Reading and Interpreting Double-Line Graphs**

Use the graph to answer each question.

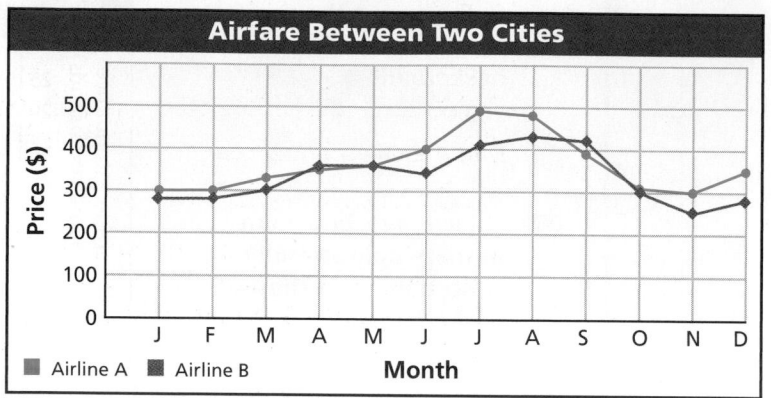

A In which month(s) did airline B charge more than airline A?

April and September   *Identify the points when the purple line is higher than the blue line.*

B During which month(s) did the airlines charge the same airfare?

May   *Look for the point where the data points overlap.*

 **4.** Use the graph to describe the general trend of the data.

A **circle graph** shows parts of a whole. The entire circle represents 100% of the data and each sector represents a percent of the total. Circle graphs are good for comparing each category of data to the whole set.

EXAMPLE 5 **Reading and Interpreting Circle Graphs**

Use the graph to answer each question.

A Which two fruits together make up half of the fruit salad?

bananas and strawberries

Look for two fruits that together make up half of the circle.

B Which fruit is used more than any other?

cantaloupe

Look for the largest sector of the graph.

Reading Math

The sections of a circle graph are called *sectors*.

 5. Use the graph to determine what percent of the fruit salad is cantaloupe.

EXAMPLE **6** **Choosing and Creating an Appropriate Display**

Use the given data to make a graph. Explain why you chose that type of graph.

A

Livestock Show Entries	
Animal	Number
Chicken	38
Goat	10
Horse	32
Pig	12
Sheep	25

A bar graph is appropriate for this data because it will be a good way to compare categories.

Step 1 Determine an appropriate scale and interval. The scale must include all of the data values. The scale is separated into equal parts, called intervals.

Step 2 Use the data to determine the lengths of the bars. Draw bars of equal width. The bars should not touch.

Step 3 Title the graph and label the horizontal and vertical scales.

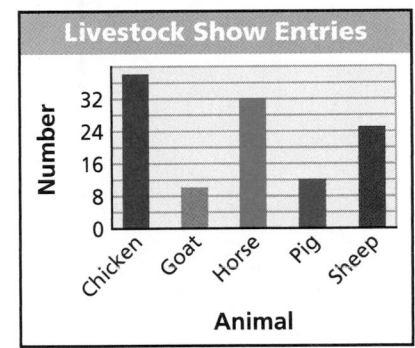

B

Division of Crops	
Crop	Area (acres)
Corn	70
Fallow	50
Mixed vegetables	10
Soybeans	40
Wheat	30

A circle graph is appropriate for this data because it shows categories as parts of a whole.

Step 1 Calculate the percent of the total represented by each category.

Corn: $\frac{70}{200} = 0.35 = 35\%$

Soybeans: $\frac{40}{200} = 0.2 = 20\%$

Fallow: $\frac{50}{200} = 0.25 = 25\%$

Wheat: $\frac{30}{200} = 0.15 = 15\%$

Mixed vegetables: $\frac{10}{200} = 0.05 = 5\%$

Step 2 Find the angle measure for each sector of the graph. Since there are 360° in a circle, multiply each percent by 360°.

Corn: $0.35 \times 360° = 126°$

Fallow: $0.25 \times 360° = 90°$

Mixed vegetables: $0.05 \times 360° = 18°$

Soybeans: $0.2 \times 360° = 72°$

Wheat: $0.15 \times 360° = 54°$

Step 3 Use a compass to draw a circle. Mark the center and use a straightedge to draw one radius. Then use a protractor to draw each central angle.

Step 4 Title the graph and label each sector.

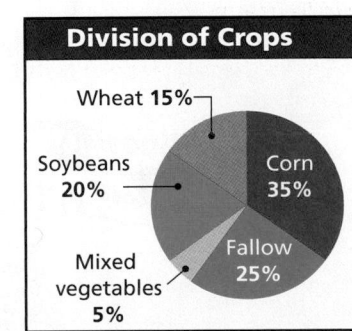

Use the given data to make a graph. Explain why you chose that type of graph.

C

Chinnick College Enrollment	
Year	Students
1930	586
1955	2,361
1980	15,897
2005	21,650

A line graph is appropriate for this data because it will show the change in enrollment over a period of time.

Step 1 Determine the scale and interval for each set of data. Time should be plotted on the horizontal axis because it is independent.

Step 2 Plot a point for each pair of values. Connect the points using line segments.

Step 3 Title the graph and label the horizontal and vertical scales.

CHECK IT OUT!

6. Use the given data to make a graph. Explain why you chose that type of graph.

The data below shows how Vera spends her time during a typical 5-day week during the school year.

Vera's Schedule						
Activity	Sleeping	Eating	School	Sports	Homework	Other
Time (h)	45	8	30	10	10	17

THINK AND DISCUSS

1. What are some comparisons you can make by looking at a bar graph?

2. Name some key components of a good line graph.

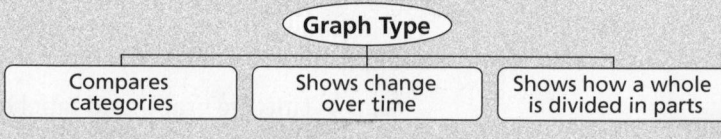

3. GET ORGANIZED Copy and complete the graphic organizer. In each box, tell which kind of graph is described.

Graph Type

| Compares categories | Shows change over time | Shows how a whole is divided in parts |

go.hrw.com
Homework Help Online
KEYWORD: MA7 10-1
Parent Resources Online
KEYWORD: MA7 Parent

GUIDED PRACTICE

Vocabulary Use the vocabulary from this lesson to answer the following questions.

1. In a *circle graph*, what does each sector represent?

2. In a *line graph*, how does the slope of a line segment relate to the rate of change?

SEE EXAMPLE **1**
p. 700

Use the bar graph for Exercises 3 and 4.

3. Estimate the total number of animals at the shelter.

4. There are 3 times as many ___?___ as ___?___ at the animal shelter.

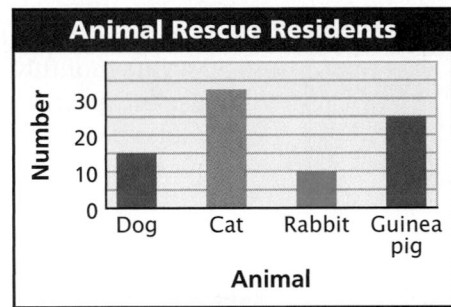

SEE EXAMPLE **2**
p. 701

Use the double-bar graph for Exercises 5–7.

5. About how much more is a club level seat at stadium A than at stadium B?

6. Which type of seat is the closest in price at the two stadiums?

7. Describe one relationship between the ticket prices at stadium A and stadium B.

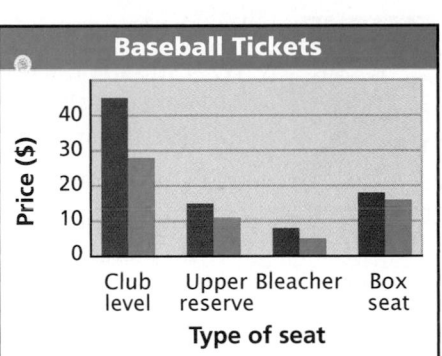

SEE EXAMPLE **3**
p. 701

Use the line graph for Exercises 8 and 9.

8. Estimate the number of tickets sold during the week of the greatest sales.

9. Which one-week period of time saw the greatest change in sales?

SEE EXAMPLE **4**
p. 702

Use the double-line graph for Exercises 10–12.

10. When was the support for the two candidates closest?

11. Estimate the difference in voter support for the two candidates five weeks before the election.

12. Describe the general trend(s) of voter support for the two candidates.

SEE EXAMPLE **5**
p. 702

Use the circle graph for Exercises 13–15.

13. Which color is least represented in the ball playpen?

14. There are 500 balls in the playpen. How many are yellow?

15. Which two colors are approximately equally represented in the ball playpen?

Colors in Ball Playpen

SEE EXAMPLE **6**
p. 703

16. The table shows the breakdown of Karim's monthly budget of $100. Use the given data to make a graph. Explain why you chose that type of graph.

Item/Activity	Spending ($)
Clothing	35
Food	25
Entertainment	25
Other	15

PRACTICE AND PROBLEM SOLVING

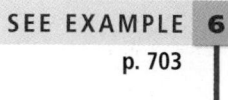

Independent Practice

For Exercises	See Example
17–18	1
19–21	2
22–23	3
24–26	4
27–28	5
29	6

Extra Practice

Skills Practice p. S22

Application Practice p. S37

Use the bar graph for Exercises 17 and 18.

17. Estimate the difference in population between the tribes with the largest and the smallest population.

18. Approximately what percent of the total population shown in the table is Cherokee?

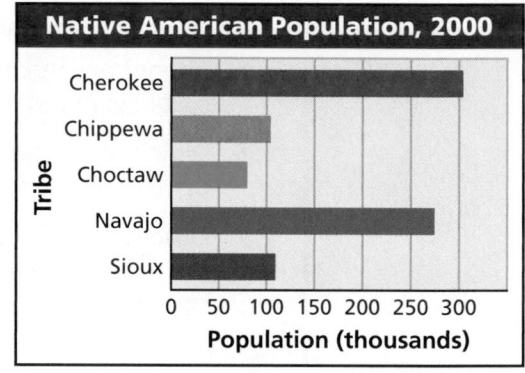

Native American Population, 2000

Source: U.S. Census Bureau

Use the double bar graph for Exercises 19–21.

19. On what day did Ray do the most overall business?

20. On what day did Ray have the busiest lunch?

21. On Sunday, about how many times as great was the number of dinner customers as the number of lunch customers?

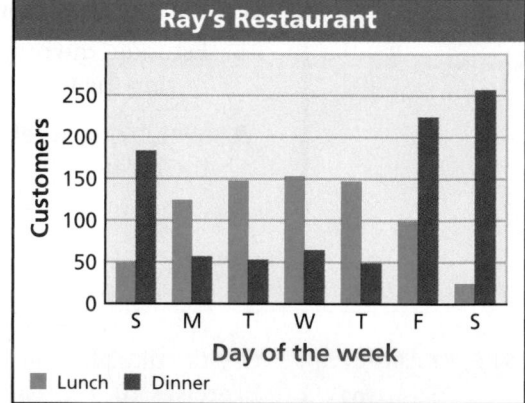

Ray's Restaurant

Use the line graph for Exercises 22 and 23.

22. Between which two games did Marlon's score increase the most?

23. Between which three games did Marlon's score increase by about the same amount?

Marlon's Video Game Scores

Use the double-line graph for Exercises 24–26.

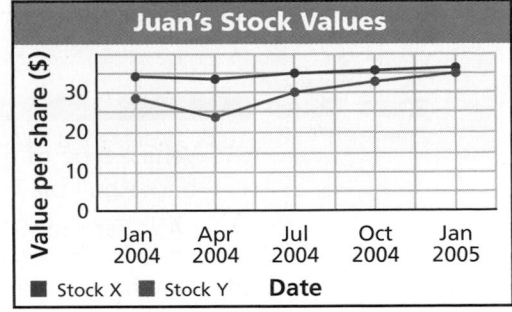

Juan's Stock Values

24. What was the average value per share of Juan's two stocks in July 2004?

25. Which stock's value changed the most over any time period?

26. Describe the trend of the values of both stocks.

Use the circle graph for Exercises 27 and 28.

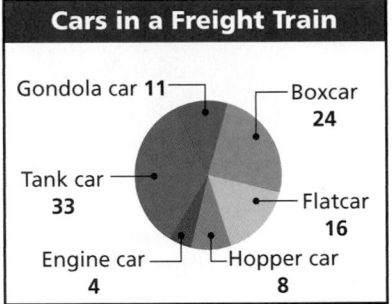

Cars in a Freight Train

27. About what percent of the total number of cars are hopper cars?

28. About what percent of the total number of cars are gondola or tank cars?

29. The table shows the weight of twin babies at various times from birth to four weeks old. Use the given data to make a graph. Explain why you chose that type of graph.

Age (days)	Boy's Weight (lb)	Girl's Weight (lb)
1	5.3	5.7
3	5.0	5.2
7	5.5	5.9
14	6.2	6.8
28	7.9	7.5

Write *bar, double-bar, line, double-line*, or *circle* to indicate the type of graph that would best display the data described.

30. attendance at a carnival each year over a ten-year period

31. attendance at two different carnivals each year over a ten-year period

32. attendance at five different carnivals during the same year

33. attendance at a carnival by age group as it relates to total attendance

34. **Critical Thinking** Give an example of real-world data that would best be displayed by each type of graph: line graph, circle graph, double-bar graph.

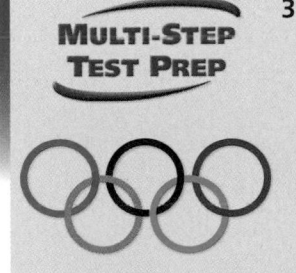

MULTI-STEP TEST PREP

35. This problem will prepare you for the Multi-Step Test Prep on page 734.

The first modern Olympic Games took place in 1896 in Athens, Greece. The circle graph shows the total number of medals won by several countries at the Olympic Games of 1896.

a. Which country won the most medals? Estimate the percent of the medals won by this country.

b. Which country won the second most medals? Estimate the percent of the medals won by this country.

Olympic Medals, 1896

36. Write About It Explain how you could use a line graph to make predictions.

37. Which type of graph would best display the contribution of each high school basketball player to the team, in terms of points scored?

   Ⓐ Bar graph   Ⓑ Line graph   Ⓒ Double-line graph   Ⓓ Circle graph

38. At what age did Marianna have 75% more magazine subscriptions than she did at age 40?

  Ⓕ 25

  Ⓖ 30

  Ⓗ 35

  Ⓙ 45

39. Short Response The table shows the number of students in each algebra class. Make a graph to display the data. Explain why you chose that type of graph.

Teacher	Students
Mr. Abrams	34
Ms. Belle	29
Mr. Marvin	25
Ms. Swanson	27

CHALLENGE AND EXTEND

Students and teachers at Lauren's school went on one of three field trips.

40. On which trip were there more boys than girls?

41. A total of 60 people went to the museum. Estimate the number of girls who went to the museum.

42. Explain why it is not possible to determine whether fewer teachers went to the museum than to the zoo or the opera.

SPIRAL REVIEW

Find the domain and range for each relation and tell whether the relation is a function. *(Lesson 4-2)*

43. $\{(-3, 3), (-1, 1), (0, 0), (1, 1), (3, 3)\}$

44.

x	1	2	3	4	5
y	2	4	6	8	10

45. Triangle ABC has vertices on a coordinate plane as follows:

  $A = (0, 5)$, $B = (3, 0)$, $C = (8, 3)$. Show that $\triangle ABC$ is a right triangle. *(Lesson 5-9)*

Classify each polynomial according to its degree and number of terms. *(Lesson 7-6)*

46. $24y$ **47.** $3x^2 + 6$ **48.** $4m - 18m^2 - 45m^3 + 120$

10-2 Frequency and Histograms

Objectives
Create stem-and-leaf plots.

Create frequency tables and histograms.

Vocabulary
stem-and-leaf plot
frequency
frequency table
histogram
cumulative frequency

Why learn this?

Stem-and-leaf plots can be used to organize data, like the number of students in elective classes. (See Example 1.)

A **stem-and-leaf plot** arranges data by dividing each data value into two parts. This allows you to see each data value.

The digits other than the last digit of each value are called a stem. $\longrightarrow$ 2 | 3 $\longleftarrow$ The last digit of a value is called a leaf.

Key: 2|3 means 23 $\longleftarrow$ The key tells you how to read each value.

EXAMPLE 1   Making a Stem-and-Leaf Plot

A The numbers of students in each of the elective classes at a school are given below. Use the data to make a stem-and-leaf plot.

24, 14, 12, 25, 32, 18, 23, 24, 9, 18, 34, 28, 24, 27

Number of Students in Elective Classes

Stem	Leaves
0	9
1	2 4 8 8
2	3 4 4 4 5 7 8
3	2 4

Key: 2|3 means 23

The tens digits are the stems.

The ones digits are the leaves. List the leaves from least to greatest within each row.

Title the graph and add a key.

B Marty's and Bill's scores for ten games of bowling are given below. Use the data to make a back-to-back stem-and-leaf plot.

Marty: 137, 149, 167, 134, 121, 127, 143, 123, 168, 162
Bill: 129, 138, 141, 124, 139, 160, 149, 145, 128, 130

Bowling Scores

Marty		Bill
7 3 1	12	4 8 9
7 4	13	0 8 9
9 3	14	1 5 9
	15	
8 7 2	16	0

Key: |14|1 means 141
3|14| means 143

The first two digits are the stems.

The ones digits are the leaves.

Put Marty's scores on the left side and Bill's scores on the right.

Title the graph and add a key.

The graph shows that three of Marty's scores were higher than Bill's highest score.

> **Writing Math**
>
> Stems are always consecutive numbers. In Example 1B, neither player has scores that start with 15, so there are no leaves in that row.

CHECK IT OUT!

1. The temperatures in degrees Celsius for two weeks are given below. Use the data to make a stem-and-leaf plot.

7, 32, 34, 31, 26, 27, 23, 19, 22, 29, 30, 36, 35, 31

10-2 Frequency and Histograms   **709**

The **frequency** of a data value is the number of times it occurs. A **frequency table** shows the frequency of each data value. If the data is divided into intervals, the table shows the frequency of each interval.

E X A M P L E **2** **Making a Frequency Table**

The final scores for each golfer in a tournament are given below. Use the data to make a frequency table with intervals.

77, 71, 70, 82, 75, 76, 72, 70, 77, 74, 71, 75, 68, 72, 75, 74

Step 1 Identify the least and greatest values.

The least value is 68. The greatest value is 82.

Step 2 Divide the data into equal intervals.

For this data set, use an interval of 3.

Step 3 List the intervals in the first column of the table. Count the number of data values in each interval and list the count in the last column. Give the table a title.

Golf Tournament Scores	
Scores	Frequency
68–70	3
71–73	4
74–76	6
77–79	2
80–82	1

 2. The numbers of days of Maria's last 15 vacations are listed below. Use the data to make a frequency table with intervals.

4, 8, 6, 7, 5, 4, 10, 6, 7, 14, 12, 8, 10, 15, 12

A **histogram** is a bar graph used to display the frequency of data divided into equal intervals. The bars must be of equal width and should touch, but not overlap.

E X A M P L E **3** **Making a Histogram**

Use the frequency table in Example 2 to make a histogram.

Step 1 Use the scale and interval from the frequency table.

Step 2 Draw a bar for the number of scores in each interval.

All bars should be the same width. The bars should touch, but not overlap.

Step 3 Title the graph and label the horizontal and vertical scales.

 3. Make a histogram for the number of days of Maria's last 15 vacations.

4, 8, 6, 7, 5, 4, 10, 6, 7, 14, 12, 8, 10, 15, 12

Cumulative frequency shows the frequency of all data values less than or equal to a given value. You could just count the number of values, but if the data set has many values, you might lose track. Recording the data in a cumulative frequency table can help you keep track of the data values as you count.

EXAMPLE 4   Making a Cumulative Frequency Table

The heights in inches of the players on a school basketball team are given below.

72, 68, 71, 70, 73, 69, 79, 76, 72, 75, 72, 74, 68, 70, 69, 75, 72, 71, 73, 76

a. Use the data to make a cumulative frequency table.

Step 1 Choose intervals for the first column of the table.

Step 2 Record the frequency of values in each interval for the second column.

Step 3 Add the frequency of each interval to the frequencies of all the intervals before it. Put that number in the third column of the table.

Step 4 Title the table.

Basketball Players' Heights		
Height (in.)	Frequency	Cumulative Frequency
68–70	6	6
71–73	8	14
74–76	5	19
77–79	1	20

b. How many players have heights under 74 in?

All heights under 74 in. are displayed in the first two rows of the table, so look at the cumulative frequency shown in the second row.

There are 14 players with heights under 74 in.

CHECK IT OUT!

4. The numbers of vowels in each sentence of a short essay are listed below.

33, 36, 39, 37, 34, 35, 43, 35, 28, 32, 36, 35, 29, 40, 33, 41, 37

a. Use the data to make a cumulative frequency table.

b. How many sentences contain 35 vowels or fewer?

THINK AND DISCUSS

1. In a stem-and-leaf plot, the number of ____?____ is always the same as the number of data values. (*stems* or *leaves*)

2. Explain how to make a histogram from a stem-and-leaf plot.

3. GET ORGANIZED Copy and complete the graphic organizer.

Bar Graphs vs Histograms

How are they alike?   How are they different?

go.hrw.com
Homework Help Online
KEYWORD: MA7 10-2
Parent Resources Online
KEYWORD: MA7 Parent

GUIDED PRACTICE

1. **Vocabulary** A(n) _____?_____ is a data display that shows individual data values. (*stem-and-leaf plot* or *histogram*)

SEE EXAMPLE **1**
p. 709

2. **Sports** The ages of professional basketball players at the time the players were recruited are given. Use the data to make a stem-and-leaf plot.

Ages When Recruited
21 23 21 18 22 19 24 22 21 22 20 21

3. **Weather** The average monthly rainfall for two cities (in inches) is given below. Use the data to make a back-to-back stem-and-leaf plot.

Average Monthly Rainfall (in.)											
Austin, TX	1.9	2.4	1.9	3.0	3.6	3.3	1.9	2.1	3.2	3.5	2.2	2.3
New York, NY	3.3	3.1	3.9	3.7	4.2	3.3	4.1	4.1	3.6	3.3	4.2	3.6

SEE EXAMPLE **2**
p. 710

4. **Sports** The finishing times of runners in a 5K race, to the nearest minute, are given. Use the data to make a frequency table with intervals.

Finishing Times in 5K Race (to the nearest minute)
19 25 23 29 32 30 21 22 24
19 28 26 31 34 30 28 25 24

SEE EXAMPLE **3**
p. 710

5. **Biology** The breathing intervals of gray whales are given. Use the frequency table to make a histogram for the data.

Breathing Intervals (min)	
Interval	**Frequency**
5–7	4
8–10	7
11–13	7
14–16	8

SEE EXAMPLE **4**
p. 711

6. The scores made by a group of eleventh-grade students on the mathematics portion of the SAT are given.

Scores on Mathematics Portion of SAT
520 560 720 690 540 630 790 540
600 580 710 500 540 660 630

a. Use the data to make a cumulative frequency table.

b. How many students scored 650 or higher on the mathematics portion of the SAT?

PRACTICE AND PROBLEM SOLVING

7. The numbers of people who visited a park each day over two weeks during different seasons are given below. Use the data to make a back-to-back stem-and-leaf plot.

Visitors to a Park													
Summer	25	25	26	27	27	57	59	22	23	29	22	23	54	53
Winter	11	12	13	9	30	27	4	19	14	19	21	33	35	9

Independent Practice

For Exercises	See Example
7–8	1
9	2
10	3
11	4

Extra Practice

Skills Practice p. S22

Application Practice p. S37

8. Weather The daily high temperatures in degrees Fahrenheit in a town during one month are given. Use the data to make a stem-and-leaf plot.

Daily High Temperatures (°F)									
68	72	79	77	70	72	75	71	64	64
68	62	70	71	78	83	83	87	91	89
87	75	73	70	69	69	62	58	71	76

9. The overall GPAs of several high school seniors are given. Use the data to make a frequency table with intervals.

Overall GPAs							
3.6	2.9	3.1	3.0	2.5	2.6	3.8	2.9
2.2	2.9	3.1	3.3	3.6	3.0	2.3	2.8	2.9

10. Chemistry The atomic masses of the nonmetal elements are given in the table. Use the frequency table to make a histogram for the data.

Atomic Masses of Nonmetal Elements					
Interval	0–49.9	50–99.9	100–149.9	150–199.9	200–249.9
Frequency	11	3	2	0	2

11. The numbers of pretzels found in several samples of snack mix are given in the table.

a. Use the data to make a cumulative frequency table.

b. How many samples of snack mix had fewer than 42 pretzels?

Numbers of Pretzels				
42	39	39	38	40
41	44	42	38	44
47	36	40	40	43	38

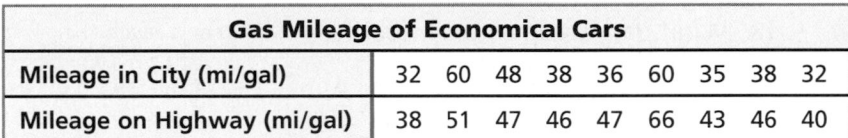

12. Automobiles The table shows gas mileage for the most economical cars in July 2004, including three hybrids.

Gas Mileage of Economical Cars									
Mileage in City (mi/gal)	32	60	48	38	36	60	35	38	32
Mileage on Highway (mi/gal)	38	51	47	46	47	66	43	46	40

Make a back-to-back stem-and-leaf plot for the data.

13. Damien's math test scores are given in the table:

a. Make a stem-and-leaf plot of Damien's test scores.

b. Make a histogram of the test scores using intervals of 5.

c. Make a histogram of the test scores using intervals of 10.

d. Make a histogram of the test scores using intervals of 20.

e. How does the size of the interval affect the appearance of the histogram?

 f. Write About It Which histogram makes Damien's grades look highest? Explain.

Damien's Math Test Scores		
75	84	68
72	59	88
72	77	81
84	60	70

14. ///**ERROR ANALYSIS**/// Two students made stem-and-leaf plots for the following data: 530, 545, 550, 555, 570. Which is incorrect? Explain the error.

A

Stem	Leaves
53	0
54	5
55	0 5
57	0

Key: 52|5 means 525

B

Stem	Leaves
53	0
54	5
55	0 5
56	
57	0

Key: 52|5 means 525

Automobiles

Solar cars usually weigh between 330 and 880 pounds. A conventional car weighs over 4000 pounds.

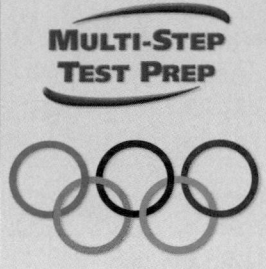
15. This problem will prepare you for the Multi-Step Test Prep on page 734.

The 2004 Olympic results for women's weightlifting in the 48 kg weight class are 210, 205, 200, 190, 187.5, 182.5, 180, 177.5, 175, 172.5, 170, 167.5, and 165, measured in kilograms. Medals are awarded to the athletes who can lift the most weight.

a. Create a frequency table beginning at 160 and using intervals of 10 kg.

b. Create a histogram of the data.

c. Tara Cunningham from the United States lifted 172.5 kg. Did she win a medal? How do you know?

16. Entertainment The top ten movies in United States theaters for the weekend of June 25–27, 2004, grossed the following amounts (in millions of dollars). Create a histogram for the data. Make the first interval 5–9.9.

Ticket Sales (million $)				
23.9	19.7	18.8	13.5	13.1
11.2	10.2	7.5	6.1	5.1

17. Critical Thinking Margo's homework assignment is to make a data display of some data she finds in a newspaper. She found a frequency table with the given intervals.

Explain why Margo must be careful when drawing the bars of the histogram.

Age
Under 18
18–30
31–54
55 and older

18. What data value occurs most often in the stem-and-leaf plot?

Ⓐ 7

Ⓒ 47

Ⓑ 4.7

Ⓓ 777

Stem	Leaves
3	2 3 4 4 7 9
4	0 1 5 7 7 7 8
5	1 2 2 3

Key: 3|2 means 3.2

19. The table shows the results of a survey about time spent on the Internet each month. Which statement is NOT supported by the data in the table?

Time Spent on the Internet per Month		
Time (h)	Frequency	Cumulative Frequency
0–4	4	4
5–9	6	10
10–14	3	13
15–19	16	29
20–24	12	41
25–29	7	48
30–34	2	50

Ⓕ The interval of 30 to 34 h/mo has the lowest frequency.

Ⓖ More than half of those who responded spend more than 20 h/mo on the Internet.

Ⓗ Only four people responded that they spend less than 5 h/mo on the Internet.

Ⓙ Sixteen people responded that they spend less than 20 h/mo on the Internet.

20. The frequencies of starting salary ranges for college graduates are noted in the table. Which histogram best reflects the data?

Starting Salaries	
Salary Range ($)	Frequency
20,000–29,000	JHT JHT JHT JHT II
30,000–39,000	JHT JHT JHT JHT JHT JHT
40,000–49,000	JHT JHT JHT I
50,000–59,000	I

Ⓐ

Ⓒ

Ⓑ

Ⓓ

CHALLENGE AND EXTEND

21. The cumulative frequencies of each interval have been given. Use this information to complete the frequency column.

Interval	Frequency	Cumulative Frequency
13–16		8
17–20		16
21–24		57
25–28		123

SPIRAL REVIEW

Solve each equation. *(Lessons 2-3 and 2-4)*

22. $19 = -2c + 5$ **23.** $4(m + 2) = -1.2$ **24.** $2(x - 3) + 7 = 3x - 9$

25. The U.S. standard railroad gauge is 56.5 inches, which is the distance between the track's rails. Charles has a model train whose scale is 113:1. What is the distance between the rails on his model train track? *(Lesson 2-7)*

Use the circle graph for Exercises 26–28. *(Lesson 10-1)*

26. Which two types of gifts make up just over half of the donated gifts?

27. Which type of gift represents $\frac{1}{5}$ of the total donated gifts?

28. If there were 160 gifts donated, how many were books?

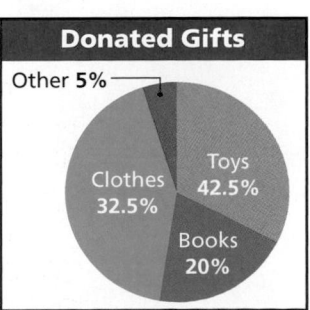

10-3 Data Distributions

(See Example 4.)

Objectives
Describe the central
tendency of a data set.

Create and interpret box-
and-whisker plots.

Vocabulary
mean
median
mode
range
outlier
first quartile
third quartile
interquartile range (IQR)
box-and-whisker plot

Who uses this?
Sports analysts examine data
distributions to make predictions.
(See Example 4.)

A *measure of central tendency* describes
the center of a set of data. Measures of
central tendency include the *mean*,
median, and *mode*.

- The **mean** is the average of the data
  values, or the sum of the values in the
  set divided by the number of values in the set.

- The **median** is the middle value when the values are in numerical order, or
  the mean of the two middle numbers if there are an even number of values.

- The **mode** is the value or values that occur most often. A data set may
  have one mode or more than one mode. If no value occurs more often than
  another, the data set has no mode.

The **range** of a set of data is the difference between the greatest and least values
in the set. The range is one measure of the spread of a data set.

E X A M P L E 1 Finding Mean, Median, Mode, and Range of a Data Set

The numbers of hours Isaac did homework on six days are 3, 8, 4, 6, 5,
and 4. Find the mean, median, mode, and range of the data set.

3, 4, 4, 5, 6, 8   *Write the data in numerical order.*

mean: $\dfrac{3 + 4 + 4 + 5 + 6 + 8}{6} = \dfrac{30}{6} = 5$ *Add all the values and divide by the number of values.*

median: 3, 4, (4, 5,) 6, 8   *There is an even number of values. Find the*
         The median is 4.5.   *mean of the two middle values.*

mode: 4   *4 occurs more than any other value.*

range: $8 - 3 = 5$ *Subtract the least value from the greatest value.*

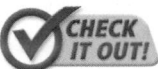
1. The weights in pounds of five cats are 12, 14, 12, 16, and 16.
Find the mean, median, mode, and range of the data set.

A value that is very different from the other values in a data set is called
an **outlier**. In the data set below, one value is much greater than the other
values.

Most of data   Mean   Much different value

EXAMPLE 2 **Determining the Effects of Outliers**

Identify the outlier in the data set {7, 10, 54, 9, 12, 8, 5}, and determine how the outlier affects the mean, median, mode, and range of the data.

5, 7, 8, 9, 10, 12, 54   *Write the data in numerical order.*

The outlier is 54.   *Look for a value much greater or less than the rest.*

With the Outlier:

mean: $\dfrac{5 + 7 + 8 + 9 + 10 + 12 + 54}{7}$

$= 15$

median: 5, 7, 8, (9,) 10, 12, 54
The median is 9.
mode: Each value occurs once.
There is no mode.
range: $54 - 5 = 49$

Without the Outlier:

mean: $\dfrac{5 + 7 + 8 + 9 + 10 + 12}{6}$

$= 8.5$

median: 5, 7, (8, 9,) 10, 12
The median is 8.5.
mode: Each value occurs once.
There is no mode.
range: $12 - 5 = 7$

The outlier increases the mean by 6.5, the median by 0.5, and the range by 42. It has no effect on the mode.

 2. Identify the outlier in the data set {21, 24, 3, 27, 30, 24}, and determine how the outlier affects the mean, median, mode, and range of the data.

As you can see in Example 2, an outlier can strongly affect the mean of a data set, while having little or no impact on the median and mode. Therefore, the mean may not be the best measure to describe a data set that contains an outlier. In such cases, the median or mode may better describe the center of the data set.

EXAMPLE 3 **Choosing a Measure of Central Tendency**

Niles scored 70, 74, 72, 71, 73, and 96 on his six geography tests. For each question, choose the mean, median, or mode, and give its value.

A Which measure gives Niles's test average?
The average of Niles's scores is the mean.
mean: $\dfrac{70 + 74 + 72 + 71 + 73 + 96}{6} = 76$

B Which measure best describes Niles's typical score? Explain.
The outlier of 96 causes the mean to be greater than all but one of the test scores, so it is not the best measure in this situation.

The data set has no mode.

The median best describes the typical score.

median: 70, 71, (72, 73,) 74, 96   *Find the mean of the two middle values.*
The median is 72.5.

 Josh scored 75, 75, 81, 84, and 85 on five tests. For each question, choose the mean, median, or mode, and give its value.

3a. Which measure describes the score Josh received most often?

3b. Which measure should Josh use to convince his parents that he is doing well in school? Explain.

Measures of central tendency describe how data cluster around one value. Another way to describe a data set is by its spread—how the data values are spread out from the center.

Quartiles divide a data set into four equal parts. Each quartile contains one-fourth of the values in the set. The **first quartile** is the median of the lower half of the data set. The second quartile is the median of the data set, and the **third quartile** is the median of the upper half of the data set.

The **interquartile range (IQR)** of a data set is the difference between the third and first quartiles. It represents the range of the middle half of the data.

Reading Math

The first quartile is sometimes called the lower quartile, and the third quartile is sometimes called the upper quartile.

A **box-and-whisker plot** can be used to show how the values in a data set are distributed. You need five values to make a box-and-whisker plot: the minimum (or least value), first quartile, median, third quartile, and maximum (or greatest value).

EXAMPLE 4 *Sports Application*

The numbers of runs scored by a softball team in 20 games are given. Use the data to make a box-and-whisker plot.

3, 4, 8, 12, 7, 5, 4, 12, 3, 9, 11, 4, 14, 8, 2, 10, 3, 10, 9, 7

Step 1 Order the data from least to greatest.

2, 3, 3, 3, 4, 4, 4, 5, 7, 7, 8, 8, 9, 9, 10, 10, 11, 12, 12, 14

Step 2 Identify the five needed values.

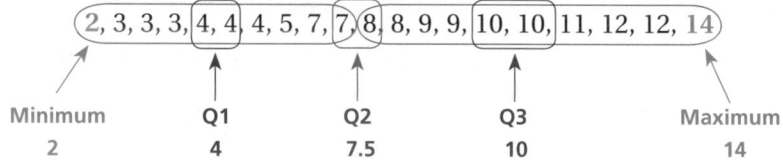

Step 3 Draw a number line and plot a point above each of the five needed values. Draw a box through the first and third quartiles and a vertical line through the median. Draw lines from the box to the minimum and maximum.

4. Use the data to make a box-and-whisker plot.

13, 14, 18, 13, 12, 17, 15, 12, 13, 19, 11, 14, 14, 18, 22, 23

EXAMPLE 5 **Reading and Interpreting Box-and-Whisker Plots**

The box-and-whisker plots show the ticket sales, in millions of dollars, of the top 25 movies in 2000 and 2007 (for the United States only).

Year 2000

Year 2007

0   50   100   150   200   250   300   350

A **Which data set has a greater median? Explain.**

The vertical line in the box for 2007 is farther to the right than the vertical line in the box for 2000.

The data set for 2007 has a greater median.

B **Which data set has a greater interquartile range? Explain.**

The length of the box for 2007 is greater than the length of the box for 2000.

The data set for 2007 has a greater interquartile range.

C **About how much more were the ticket sales for the top movie in 2007 than for the top movie in 2000?**

2007 maximum: **about $335 million**   *Read the maximum values from*
2000 maximum: **about $260 million**   *the box-and-whisker plots.*
335 − 260 − 75   *Subtract the maximum values.*

The ticket sales for the top movie in 2007 were about $75 million more than for the top movie in 2000.

 Use the box-and-whisker plots above to answer each question.

5a. Which data set has a smaller range? Explain.

5b. About how much more was the median ticket sales for the top 25 movies in 2007 than in 2000?

THINK AND DISCUSS

1. Explain when the median is a value in the data set.

2. Give an example of a data set for which the mean is twice the median. Explain how you determined your answer.

3. Suppose the minimum in a data set is the same as the first quartile. How would this affect a box-and-whisker plot of the data?

 4. GET ORGANIZED Copy and complete the graphic organizer. Tell which measure of central tendency answers each question.

Measures of Central Tendency	
Measure	**Used to Answer**
	What is the average?
	What is the halfway point of the data?
	What is the most common value?

GUIDED PRACTICE

1. **Vocabulary** What is the difference between the *range* and the *interquartile range* of a data set?

SEE EXAMPLE **1**
p. 716

Find the mean, median, mode, and range of each data set.

2. 85, 83, 85, 82

3. 12, 22, 33, 34, 44, 44

4. 10, 26, 25, 10, 20, 22, 25, 20

5. 71, 73, 75, 78, 78, 80, 85, 86

SEE EXAMPLE **1**
p. 717

Identify the outlier in each data set, and determine how the outlier affects the mean, median, mode, and range of the data.

6. 10, 96, 12, 17, 15

7. 64, 75, 72, 13, 64

SEE EXAMPLE **3**
p. 717

Adrienne scored 82, 54, 85, 91, and 83 on her last five science tests. For each question, choose the mean, median, or mode, and give its value.

8. Which measure best describes Adrienne's typical score? Explain.

9. Which measure should Adrienne use to convince her soccer coach she is doing well in science? Explain.

SEE EXAMPLE **4**
p. 718

Use the data to make a box-and-whisker plot.

10. 21, 31, 26, 24, 28, 26

11. 12, 13, 42, 62, 62, 82

SEE EXAMPLE **5**
p. 719

The box-and-whisker plots show the scores, in thousands of points, of two players on a video game. Use the box-and-whisker plots to answer each question.

12. Which player has a higher median score? Explain.

13. Which player had the lowest score? Estimate this score.

PRACTICE AND PROBLEM SOLVING

Find the mean, median, mode, and range of each data set.

Independent Practice	
For Exercises	See Example
14–17	1
18–19	2
20–21	3
22–23	4
24-26	5

14. 75, 63, 89, 91

15. 1, 2, 2, 2, 3, 3, 3, 4

16. 19, 25, 31, 19, 34, 22, 31, 34

17. 58, 58, 60, 60, 60, 61, 63

Identify the outlier in each data set, and determine how the outlier affects the mean, median, mode, and range of the data.

18. 42, 8, 54, 37, 29

19. 3, 8, 3, 3, 23, 8

Extra Practice
Skills Practice p. S22
Application Practice p. S37

Lamont bowled 153, 145, 148, and 166 in four games. For each question, choose the mean, median, or mode, and give its value.

20. Which measure gives Lamont's average score?

21. Which measure should Lamont use to convince his parents to let him join a bowling league? Explain.

Use the data to make a box-and-whisker plot.

22. 62, 63, 62, 64, 68, 62, 62

23. 85, 90, 81, 100, 92, 85

The box-and-whisker plots show the prices, in dollars, of athletic shoes at two sports apparel stores. Use the box-and-whisker plots to answer each question.

24. Which store has the greater median price? About how much greater?

25. Which store has the smaller interquartile range? What does this tell you about the data sets?

26. Estimate the difference in price between the most expensive shoe type at Jump N Run and the most expensive shoe at Sneaks R Us.

Find the mean, median, mode, and range of each data set.

27. 1, 2, 3, 4, 5, 6, 7, 8, 9, 10

28. 5, 6, 6, 5, 5

29. 2.1, 4.3, 6.5, 1.2, 3.4

30. $0, \frac{1}{4}, \frac{1}{2}, \frac{3}{4}, 1$

31. 23, 25, 26, 25, 23

32. −3, −3, −3, −2, −2, −1

33. 1, 4, 9, 16, 25, 36

34. 1, 0, 0, 1, 1, 4

35. Estimation Estimate the mean of $16\frac{7}{8}$, $12\frac{1}{4}$, $22\frac{1}{10}$, $18\frac{5}{7}$, $19\frac{1}{3}$, $13\frac{8}{11}$, and $13\frac{8}{11}$.

Tell whether each statement is sometimes, always, or never true.

36. The mean is a value in the data set.

37. The median is a value in the data set.

38. If a data set has one mode, the mode is a value in the data set.

39. The mean is affected by including an outlier.

40. The mode is affected by including an outlier.

41. Sports The table shows the attendance at six football games at Jefferson High School. Which measure of central tendency best indicates the typical attendance at a football game? Why?

42. Weather The high temperatures in degrees Fahrenheit on 11 consecutive days were 68, 71, 75, 74, 75, 71, 73, 71, 72, 74, and 79. Find the mean, median, mode, and range of the temperatures. Describe the effect on the mean, median, mode, and range if the next day's temperature was 70 °F.

Attendance at Football Games	
Eagles vs. Bulldogs	743
Eagles vs. Panthers	768
Eagles vs. Coyotes	835
Eagles vs. Bears*	1218
Eagles vs. Colts	797
Eagles vs. Mustangs	854

*Homecoming Game

43. Advertising A home-decorating store sells five types of candles, which are priced at $3, $2, $2, $2, and $15. If the store puts an ad in the paper titled "Best Local Candle Prices," which measure of central tendency should it advertise? Justify your answer.

Use the data to make a box-and-whisker plot.

44. 25, 28, 26, 16, 18, 15, 25, 28, 26, 16

45. 2, 3, 5, 7, 11, 13, 17, 19, 23, 29, 31

46. 1, 1, 1, 1, 2, 2, 2, 2, 3, 3, 4, 4, 4, 4, 4

47. 50, 52, 45, 62, 36, 55, 40, 50, 65, 33

48. This problem will prepare you for the Multi-Step Test Prep on page 734.

The results in Olympic pole-vaulting are given as heights in meters. In the 2008 Olympic Games in Beijing, the following results occurred for the men's pole-vault finals: 5.96, 5.85, 5.70, 5.70, 5.70, 5.70, 5.60, 5.60, 5.60, 5.45, 5.45.

a. Find the mean, median, mode, and range of this data set. Round to the nearest hundredth if needed.

b. The gold medal was won by Steve Hooker of Australia. What was his height in the pole-vault finals?

49. Business The salaries for the eight employees at a small company are shown in the stem-and-leaf plot. Find the mean and median of the salaries. Which measure better describes the typical salary of an employee at this company? Explain.

Salaries ($1000)

Stem	Leaves
2	0 0 3 5 5
3	0 5
4	
5	
6	
7	8

Key: 2|0 means $20,000

50. Critical Thinking Use the data set {1, 2, 3, 5, 8, 13, 21, 34} to complete the following.

a. Find the mean of the data set.

b. What happens to the mean of the data set if every number is increased by 2?

c. What happens to the mean of the data set if every number is multiplied by 2?

51. Allison has taken 5 tests worth 100 points each. Her scores are shown in the grade book below. What score does she need on her next test to have a mean of 90%?

Student	Test 1	Test 2	Test 3	Test 4	Test 5	Test 6	Average
Allison	88	85	89	92	90		

52. Astronomy The table shows the number of moons of the planets in our solar system. What is the mean number of moons per planet? Is Earth's value of one moon typical for the solar system? Explain.

Planet	Mercury	Venus	Earth	Mars	Jupiter	Saturn	Uranus	Neptune
Moons	0	0	1	2	63	60	27	13

53. Write About It Explain how an outlier with a large value will affect the mean. Explain how an outlier with a small value will affect the mean.

54. Which value is always represented on a box-and-whisker plot?

   Ⓐ Mean   Ⓑ Median   Ⓒ Mode   Ⓓ Range

55. The lengths in feet of the alligators at a zoo are 9, 7, 12, 6, and 10. The lengths in feet of the crocodiles at the zoo are 13, 10, 8, 19, 18, and 16. What is the difference between the mean length of the crocodiles and the mean length of the alligators?

   Ⓕ 0.5 foot   Ⓖ 5.2 feet   Ⓗ 8 feet   Ⓙ 11.4 feet

56. The mean score on a test is 50. Which CANNOT be true?

    Ⓐ Half the scores are 0, and half the scores are 100.

    Ⓑ The range is 50.

    Ⓒ Half the scores are 25, and half the scores are 50.

    Ⓓ Every score is 50.

57. Short Response The table shows the weights in pounds of six dogs. How does the mean weight of the dogs change if Rex's weight is not included in the data set?

Weights of Dogs (lb)			
Duffy	23	Rex	62
Rocky	15	Skipper	34
Pepper	21	Sunny	19

CHALLENGE AND EXTEND

58. List a set of data values with the following measures of central tendency:

    mean: 8   median: 7   mode: 6

59. Collect a set of data about your classmates or your school. For example, you might collect data about the number of points per game scored by your school's basketball team. Use the data you collect to make a box-and-whisker plot.

60. A *weighted average* is an average in which each data value has an importance, or weight, assigned to it. A teacher uses the following weights when determining course grades: homework 25%, tests 30%, and final exam 45%. The table shows Nathalie's scores in the class.

Homework	78, 83, 95, 82, 79, 93
Tests	88, 92, 81
Final exam	90

    a. Find the mean of Nathalie's homework scores and the mean of her test scores.

    b. Find Nathalie's weighted average for the class. To do so, multiply the homework mean, the test mean, and the final exam score by their corresponding weights. Then add the products.

    c. What if...? What would Nathalie's mean score for the class be if her teacher did not use a weighted average?

SPIRAL REVIEW

Find the slope of each line. Then tell what the slope represents. *(Lesson 5-4)*

61.

62.

Simplify each expression. *(Lesson 7-5)*

63. $32^{\frac{1}{5}}$ **64.** $81^{\frac{1}{4}}$ **65.** $125^{\frac{1}{3}}$ **66.** $64^{\frac{1}{3}}$

67. The length of a rectangle is 1 yard less than two times the width. The area is 15 square yards. What are the dimensions of the rectangle? *(Lesson 9-9)*

10-3 Technology LAB

Use Technology to Make Graphs

You can use a spreadsheet program to create bar graphs, line graphs, and circle graphs. You can also use a graphing calculator to make a box-and-whisker plot.

Use with Lesson 10-3

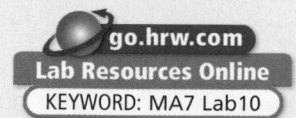

go.hrw.com
Lab Resources Online
KEYWORD: MA7 Lab10

Activity 1

Many colors are used on the flags of the 50 United States. The table shows the number of flags that use each color. Use a spreadsheet program to make a bar graph to display the data.

Color	Black	Blue	Brown	Gold	Green	Purple	Red	White
Number	27	46	20	36	24	4	34	42

1 Enter the data from the table in the first two columns of the spreadsheet.

2 Select the cells containing the titles and the data.

Then click the Chart Wizard icon, 📊. Click Column from the list on the left, and then choose the small picture of a vertical bar graph. Click Next.

3 The next screen shows the range of cells used to make the graph. Click Next.

4 Give the chart a title and enter titles for the *x*-axis and *y*-axis. Click the Legend tab, and then click the box next to Show Legend to turn off the key. (A key is needed when making a double-bar graph.) Click Next.

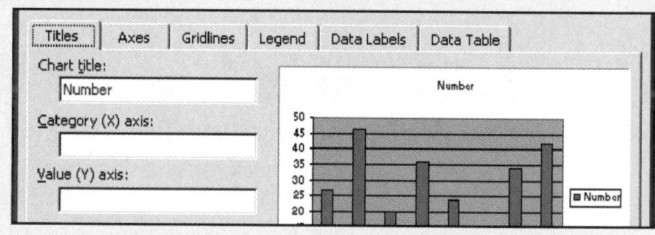

5 Click Finish to place the chart in the spreadsheet.

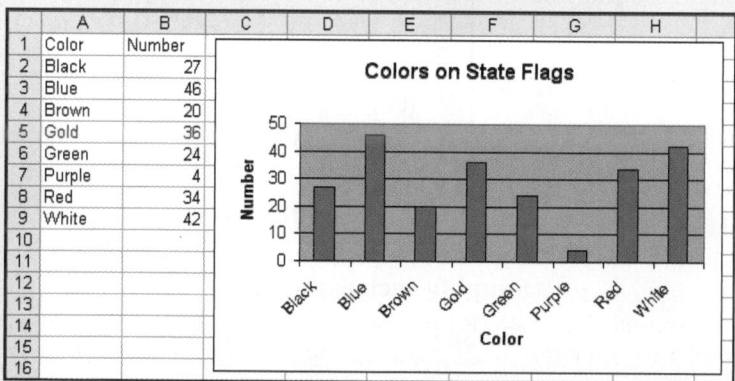

Try This

1. The table shows the average number of hours of sleep people at different ages get each night. Use a spreadsheet program to make a bar graph to display the data.

Age (yr)	3–9	10–13	14–18	19–30	31–45	46–50	51+
Sleep (h)	11	10	9	8	7.5	6	5.5

Activity 2

Adrianne is a waitress at a restaurant. The amounts Adrianne made in tips during her last 15 shifts are listed below. Use a graphing calculator to make a box-and-whisker plot to display the data. Give the minimum, first quartile, median, third quartile, and maximum values.

$58, $63, $40, $44, $57, $59, $61, $53, $54, $58, $57, $57, $58, $58, $56

1 To make a list of the data, press **STAT**, select **Edit**, and enter the values in List 1 (**L1**). Press **ENTER** after each value.

2 To use the **STAT PLOT** editor to set up the box-and-whisker plot, press **2nd** **Y=** , and then **ENTER**.

Press **ENTER** to select **Plot 1**.

3 Select **On**. Then use the arrow keys to choose the fifth type of graph, a box-and-whisker plot.

Xlist should be **L1** and **Freq:** should be 1.

4 Press **ZOOM** and select **9: ZoomStat** to see the graph in the statistics window.

5 Use **TRACE** and the arrow keys to move the cursor along the graph to the five important values: minimum (**MinX**), first quartile (**Q1**), median (**MED**), third quartile (**Q3**), and maximum (**MaxX**).

minimum: 40

first quartile: 54

median: 57

third quartile: 58

maximum: 63

Try This

2. The average length in inches of the ten longest bones in the human body are listed. Use a graphing calculator to make a box-and-whisker plot to display the data. What are the minimum, first quartile, median, third quartile, and maximum values of the data set?

19.88, 16.94, 15.94, 14.35, 11.10, 10.40, 9.45, 9.06, 7.28, 6.69

10-4 Misleading Graphs and Statistics

Objectives
Recognize misleading graphs.

Recognize misleading statistics.

Vocabulary
random sample

Graphs can be used to influence what people believe. The way a data set is displayed can influence how the data are interpreted.

EXAMPLE 1 Misleading Bar Graphs

The graph shows the size of tomatoes on plants that were treated with different fertilizers.

A Explain why the graph is misleading.

The scale on the vertical axis begins at 80. This exaggerates the differences between the sizes of the bars.

B What might someone believe because of the graph?

Someone might believe that the tomato treated with fertilizer D is much larger than the other tomatoes. It is only 3.3 grams larger than the tomato treated with fertilizer B.

 1. Who might want to use the graph above? Explain.

EXAMPLE 2 Misleading Line Graphs

The graph shows the average price of gasoline in the U.S. in September.

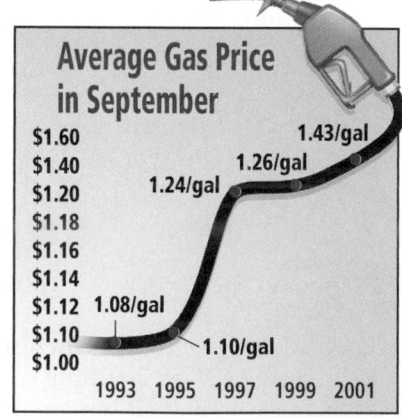

A Explain why the graph is misleading.

The intervals on the vertical axis are not equal.

B What might people be influenced to believe by the graph?

Someone might believe that the price of gasoline increased the most between 1995 and 1997. However, the change between 1995 and 1997 was only $0.14/gal while the change between 1999 and 2001 was $0.17/gal.

 2. Who might want to use the graph above? Explain.

A circle graph compares each category of a data set to the whole. When any category is not represented in the graph, it may appear that another category represents a greater percentage of the total than it should.

 3 **Misleading Circle Graphs**

The graph shows what percent of the total votes were received by three candidates for student council president.

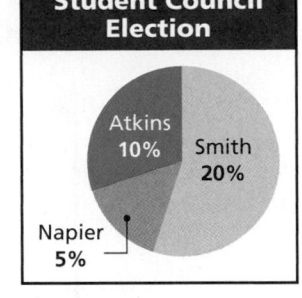

A **Explain why the graph is misleading.**

The sections of the graph do not add to 100%, so the votes for at least one of the candidates is not represented.

B **What might people be influenced to believe by the graph?**

Someone might believe that Smith won the election.

3. Who might want to use the graph above? Explain.

Statistics can be misleading because of the way the data is collected or the way the results are reported. A sufficiently large *random sample* is a good way to collect unbiased data. In a **random sample**, all members of the group being surveyed have an equal chance of being selected.

 4 **Misleading Statistics**

A researcher surveys people leaving a basketball game about what they like to watch on TV. Explain why the following statement is misleading: "80% of people like to watch sports on TV."

The sample is biased because people who attend sporting events are more likely to watch sports on TV than people who watch TV but do not attend sporting events.

4. A researcher asks 4 people if they have seasonal allergies. Three people respond yes. Explain why the following statement is misleading: "75% of people have seasonal allergies."

THINK AND DISCUSS

1. Give an example of a situation in which someone might intentionally try to make a graph misleading.

2. **GET ORGANIZED** Copy and complete the graphic organizer. Add more boxes if needed.

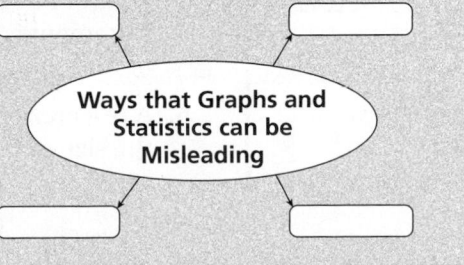

Ways that Graphs and Statistics can be Misleading

go.hrw.com
Homework Help Online
KEYWORD: MA7 10-4
Parent Resources Online
KEYWORD: MA7 Parent

GUIDED PRACTICE

1. **Vocabulary** Explain in your own words what the term *random sample* means.

SEE EXAMPLE **1**
p. 726

2. The graph shows the average salaries of employees at three companies.

   a. Explain why the graph is misleading.

   b. What might someone believe because of the graph?

   c. Who might want to use this graph? Explain.

SEE EXAMPLE **2**
p. 726

3. The graph shows hotel occupancy in San Francisco over four years.

   a. Explain why the graph is misleading.

   b. What might someone believe because of the graph?

   c. Who might want to use this graph? Explain.

SEE EXAMPLE **3**
p. 727

4. The graph shows the nutritional information for a granola bar.

   a. Explain why the graph is misleading.

   b. What might someone believe because of the graph?

   c. Who might want to use this graph? Explain.

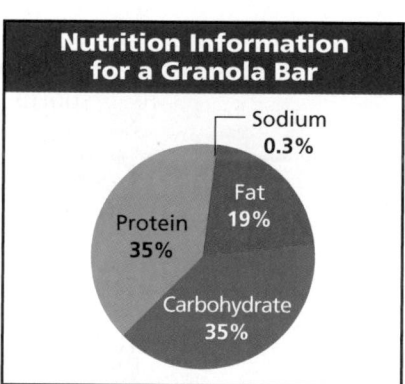

SEE EXAMPLE **4**
p. 727

5. Three students were surveyed about their favorite teacher. Two students answer Mr. Gregory, and one answers Mr. Blaine. Explain why the following statement is misleading: "Mr. Gregory is the favorite teacher of a majority of the students."

6. A researcher surveys people at a shopping mall about whether they favor enlarging the size of the mall parking lot. Explain why the following statement is misleading: "85% of the community is in favor of enlarging the parking lot."

PRACTICE AND PROBLEM SOLVING

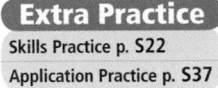

Independent Practice

For Exercises	See Example
7	1
8	2
9	3
10	4

Extra Practice

Skills Practice p. S22

Application Practice p. S37

7. The graph shows the median rent for men and women in a metropolitan area.

   a. Explain why the graph is misleading.

   b. What might someone believe because of the graph?

   c. Who might want to use this graph? Explain.

8. The graph shows the export prices of Colombian arabica coffee over nine years.

   a. Explain why the graph is misleading.

   b. What might someone believe because of the graph?

   c. Who might want to use this graph? Explain.

9. The graph shows how the state spent tax dollars during 1999 and 2000.

   a. Explain why the graph is misleading.

   b. What might someone believe because of the graph?

   c. Who might want to use this graph? Explain.

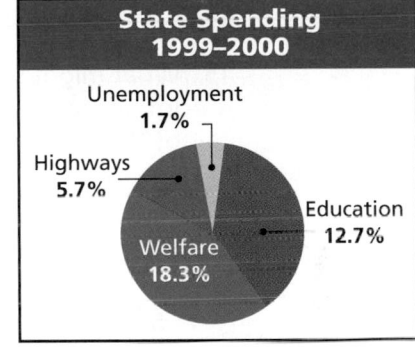

10. A college math course has one section with 240 students and 8 sections with 30 students. Explain why the following statement is misleading: "The average class size for the course is 53 students."

---

11. This problem will prepare you for the Multi-Step Test Prep on page 734.

The table shows scores from the women's gymnastics finals in the floor exercise at the 2004 Summer Olympic Games.

   a. Find the average score for the women in the finals.

   b. Would it be misleading to describe the data using the average score? Explain.

   c. Make a graph for this data that could convince someone that the difference between the first place score and the eighth place score was very small.

Rank	Name	Score
1	Catalina Ponor	9.750
2	Nicoleta Sofronie	9.562
3	Patricia Moreno	9.487
4	Fei Cheng	9.412
5	Daiane dos Santos	9.375
6	Mohini Bhardwaj	9.312
7	Kate Richardson	9.312
8	Alina Kozich	8.500

12. **///ERROR ANALYSIS///** The graph shows the population of a city over time. Which conclusion is incorrect? Explain why the conclusion is incorrect and how the graph was misleading.

A
	The population has grown rapidly over 20 years.

B
	The population has grown slowly over 20 years.

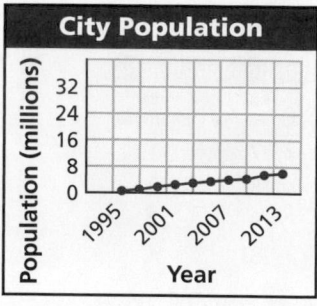

13. The table shows the average connection speeds of some broadband Internet service providers.

Provider	Connection Speed (Kbps)
Speedy Online	954
TelQuick	914
Alacrity	858

a. Construct a display that suggests that Speedy Online is much faster than the other services.

b. Construct a display that suggests that all of the services offer about the same connection speeds.

c. **Write About It** Where might you expect to see your graph from part **b**? Explain.

14. **Critical Thinking** Explain how a graph can show truthful data but still be misleading.

TEST PREP

15. What might someone be influenced to believe because of the graph?

   Ⓐ The measles vaccine was introduced when the mortality rate was at its highest.

   Ⓑ The measles vaccine was unnecessary.

   Ⓒ The measles vaccine dramatically decreased the mortality rate.

   Ⓓ The measles vaccine increased the mortality rate.

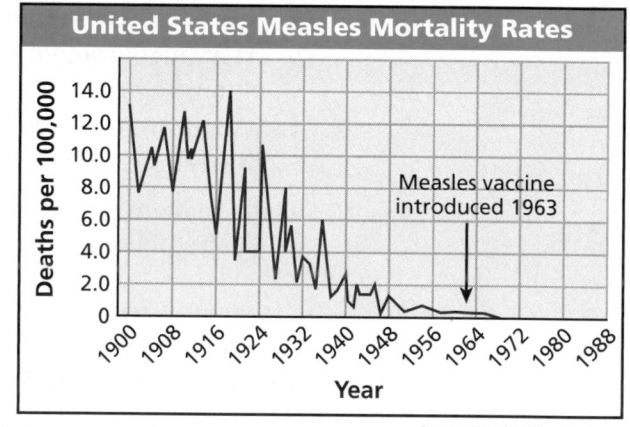

16. The table shows the number of votes cast in the 2000 U.S. presidential election and in the 2002 French presidential election. What additional information is needed to determine whether the following statement is misleading?

Country	Votes Cast
United States	105,405,100
France	29,497,272

"American voters are more likely to vote than French voters."

   Ⓕ The number of candidates in each election

   Ⓖ The legal voting age in France

   Ⓗ The number of registered voters in the United States in 2000 and France in 2002

   Ⓙ The number of polling locations in the United States in 2000 and France in 2002

CHALLENGE AND EXTEND

17. Logic A fingerprint analyst is studying a fingerprint that was found in the chemistry lab. He reports that the fingerprint belongs to Dr. Arenson. Below are two questions the analyst was asked and the answers he gave.

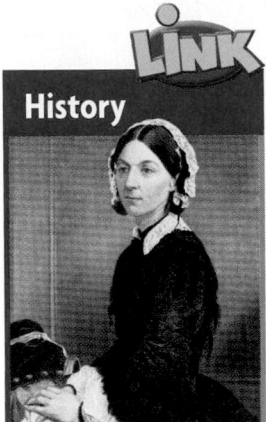

Florence Nightingale (1820–1910) served as a nurse in the Crimean War. In 1854, she brought the first female nurses to military hospitals.

> **Question 1:** What are the chances that the fingerprint belongs to someone else who has the same fingerprint as Dr. Arenson?
>
> **Answer:** One in several billion.

> **Question 2:** What are the chances that the fingerprint was wrongly identified?
>
> **Answer:** About 1 in 100.

a. What is the difference between the two questions?

b. What does the answer to question 1 lead you to believe?

c. Who do you think might have asked question 1?

d. What does the answer to question 2 lead you to believe?

e. Who do you think might have asked question 2?

18. History Graphs like the one at right were created by Florence Nightingale. Nightingale served as a nurse during the Crimean War and was concerned with the unsanitary conditions the soldiers lived in. Each "wedge" of the circle represents a month between April 1854 and March 1855.

a. What do you think Florence Nightingale wanted to show with this graph?

b. Who do you think Nightingale showed the graph to?

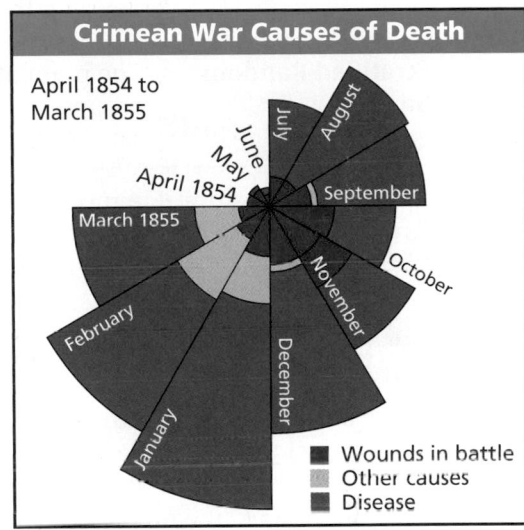

Source: The Florence Nightingale Museum

SPIRAL REVIEW

Write an inequality for each situation. *(Lesson 3-1)*

19. The maximum weight for a certain truck load is 1500 pounds.

20. Isaac's research paper must be at least 12 pages.

21. A moving company will transport up to 20 boxes for no fee.

Solve each inequality and graph the solutions. *(Lesson 3-4)*

22. $2x - 3 < 7$ **23.** $3(t - 1) \geq -15$ **24.** $6 - n < 2n + 9$

25. The table shows the weight of a golden retriever at different ages. Choose a type of graph to display the given data. Make the graph, and explain why you chose that type of graph. *(Lesson 10-1)*

Age (mo)	1	3	6	12
Weight (lb)	8	23	45	66

Sampling and Bias

If you wanted to collect data about a very large group of people, you would most likely need to survey a smaller group. The large group that contains all the people you could survey is called a *population*. The smaller group is called a *sample*.

You have learned that a random sample is a good way of collecting data that is unbiased. There are different ways of selecting a random sample.

Random Samples		
Type	**Definition**	**Example**
Simple Random Sample	Every member of the population has an equal chance of being chosen for the sample.	The names of all students in your class are placed in a hat and three names are chosen at random.
Stratified Random Sample	The population is divided into similar groups. Then a simple random sample is chosen from each group.	Your class is divided into boys and girls and two students are chosen at random from each group.
Systematic Random Sample	A member of the population is chosen for the sample at a regular interval.	Every third student who comes into the classroom is chosen.

Example 1

In each situation, identify the population and the sample. Tell whether each sample is a simple, stratified, or systematic random sample.

A For one week, the manager of a pet supplies store asks every tenth customer what brand of pet food they buy.

population: all customers at the pet supplies store during one week

sample: every tenth customer during that same week

The sample is systematic because one member of the population is chosen for the sample at a regular interval.

B Every person who enters a theater one evening places their ticket stub in a bowl. The theater owner chooses five ticket stubs to award prizes.

population: all people who put their ticket stub in the bowl

sample: five ticket stubs chosen from the bowl

The sample is simple because every member of the population has the same chance of being chosen.

C One student from each classroom at a school is chosen at random for a committee.

population: all students at a school

sample: one student from each classroom

The sample is stratified because the population is divided into similar groups and one member is chosen at random from each group.

Try This

1. Choose a topic to research. Describe the population, why you need to choose a sample, and the sample.
2. Choose whether to use a simple, stratified, or systematic random sample. Explain your choice and the process you would use to choose your sample.

A random sample is not biased because no part of the population is favored over another. In a biased sample, one or more parts of the population have an advantage for being chosen for the sample.

There are two main types of biased samples.

Biased Samples		
Type	**Definition**	**Example**
Convenience Sample	Those members of the population that are easily accessed are chosen for the sample.	A reporter questions people he personally knows.
Voluntary Response Sample	Members of the population who want to participate make up the sample.	A reporter questions people who fill out comment cards and indicate that they would like to be contacted.

Example 2

In each situation, identify the population and the sample. Tell whether each sample is a convenience or voluntary response sample. Explain why the sample is biased.

A A website asks visitors to complete a survey about Internet usage.

population: all visitors to the website

sample: those visitors who choose to complete the survey

The sample is a voluntary response sample because visitors to the website chose whether to complete the survey. The sample is biased because those visitors who choose to complete the survey may not be representative of all visitors to the website.

B A reporter asks people leaving a shopping center through one door about their shopping habits.

population: all people at the shopping center

sample: people who leave from one door at the shopping center

The sample is a convenience sample because the people leaving through the chosen door are easily accessed. The sample is biased because people leaving through another door do not have an opportunity to be chosen.

Try This

3. Choose a topic to research. Describe the population, why you need to choose a sample, and the sample.
4. Assume that you want an unbiased sample. Choose whether to use a simple, stratified, or systematic random sample. Explain your choice and the process you would use to choose your sample.
5. Describe how a biased sample could be chosen for this same situation.

MULTI-STEP TEST PREP

Data Analysis

USA! USA! USA! In 708 B.C.E., the Olympic Games included the pentathlon. This event included the discus, javelin, long jump, running, and wrestling. The winner of the pentathlon was considered a "super athlete." The modern pentathlon of the Olympic Games includes five disciplines: target shooting, fencing, swimming, horseback riding, and cross-country running.

1. The pentathlon includes five events. What type of graph should be used to show what percent of this event is made up of each discipline?

2. Do you think the winner of the modern pentathlon must win each of the five events? Explain.

3. Thirty-two men competed in the modern pentathlon in the 2004 Olympic Games. The chart shows the total points for the competitors.

Pentathlon Scores
5480 5428 5392 5356 5340
5332 5320 5295 5276 5252 5200 5196
5192 5184 5180 5172 5144 5132 5084
5084 5068 5016 4976 4936 4932 4916
4904 4848 4732 4676 4420 4388

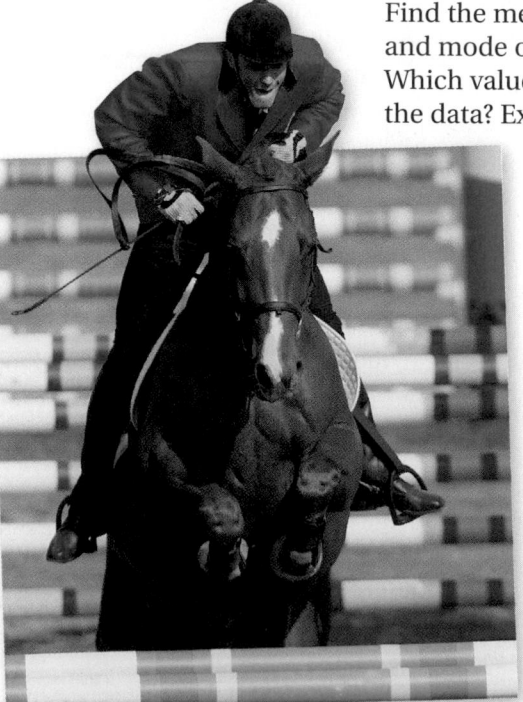

Find the mean, median, and mode of this data set. Which value best describes the data? Explain.

4. Find the minimum, first quartile, third quartile, and maximum values of the data set above. Use these values and the median to make a box-and-whisker plot of the data.

READY TO GO ON?

Quiz for Lessons 10-1 Through 10-4

✓ 10-1 Organizing and Displaying Data

Use the circle graph for 1–3.

1. Which material represents over 50% of Don's recyclables?

2. How many pounds of materials does Don recycle?

3. What percent of Don's recyclables are glass?

4. The table shows the total proceeds for a fund-raiser at various times during the day. Choose a type of graph to display the given data. Make the graph, and explain why you chose that type of graph.

Don's Recyclables (lb)

Metals 3
Plastic 1
Paper/cardboard 11
Glass 5

Time	Total Proceeds (thousand $)	Time	Total Proceeds (thousand $)
3:00 P.M.	1.5	6:00 P.M.	6.5
4:00 P.M.	2	7:00 P.M.	8
5:00 P.M.	4	8:00 P.M.	9.5

✓ 10-2 Frequency and Histograms

5. The Miller family is going to buy a new car. The approximate prices of the cars they are considering are given. Use the data to make a stem-and-leaf plot.

   $24,000, $28,000, $26,000, $32,000, $30,000, $41,000, $27,000, $22,000, $26,000, $33,000

6. The number of people at a caterer's last 12 parties are given below.

   16, 18, 17, 19, 15, 25, 18, 17, 18, 16, 17, 19

   a. Use the data to make a frequency table with intervals.

   b. Use your frequency table from part a to make a histogram.

✓ 10-3 Data Distributions

7. The daily high temperatures on 14 consecutive days in one city were 59 °F, 49 °F, 48 °F, 46 °F, 47 °F, 51 °F, 49 °F, 43 °F, 45 °F, 52 °F, 51 °F, 51 °F, 51 °F, and 38 °F.

   a. Find the mean, median, and mode of the temperatures.

   b. Which value describes the average high temperature for the 14 days?

   c. Which value best describes the high temperatures? Explain.

8. Use the temperature data above to make a box-and-whisker plot.

✓ 10-4 Misleading Graphs and Statistics

9. The graph shows the value of a company's stock over time. Explain why the graph is misleading. What might people be influenced to believe because of the graph? Who might want to use this graph?

10. The results of an online survey of 230 people showed that 92% of the population felt very comfortable using technology. Explain why this statistic is misleading.

Company B Stocks

Value of stock per share ($)
120
110
100
90
80
2000 2001 2002 2003 2004
Year

10-5 Algebra LAB

Simulations

A simulation can be used to model an experiment that would be difficult or inconvenient to actually perform. In this lab, you will conduct simulations.

Use with Lesson 10-5

Activity

The local movie theater is offering an opportunity for customers to win a free night at the movies. To win, you must collect six different letters to spell CINEMA. Each movie ticket sold during this promotion will have one of the six letters stamped on the back of the ticket. An equal number of tickets will be stamped with each of the letters.

1 Since there are six different letters that appear on the tickets an equal number of times, you can use a number cube to simulate collecting the six letters.

Each of the numbers on the number cube will represent a letter. Each roll of the number cube will represent purchasing one movie ticket, and the number rolled will represent the letter stamped on the ticket.

2 The table shows the results of rolling the number cube until each number has been rolled once.

  a. Based on the results shown in the table, how many rolls did it take to get all six numbers?

  b. Based on the results in the table, how many movie tickets would you expect to have to buy to get all six letters? If you purchased this number of tickets, would you be sure to win? Explain.

Number on Cube	Letter on Ticket	Frequency
1	C	I
2	I	IIII I
3	N	IIII
4	E	II
5	M	II
6	A	III

Try This

1. Repeat the simulation four more times and record the results.

2. Find the average number of rolls from all five simulations $\left(\dfrac{\text{total number of rolls from 5 simulations}}{5}\right)$.

3. Based on your answer to Problem 2, how many movie tickets would you expect to have to buy to get all six letters? Is this number different from the answer you gave based on the results in the table above?

4. Would any of your answers have been different if you had used a different correspondence between the numbers and letters? Explain.

10-5 Experimental Probability

Objectives
Determine the experimental probability of an event.

Use experimental probability to make predictions.

Vocabulary
experiment
trial
outcome
sample space
event
probability
experimental probability
prediction

Why learn this?
Experimental probability can be used by manufacturers for quality control. (See Example 4.)

An **experiment** is an activity involving chance. Each repetition or observation of an experiment is a **trial**, and each possible result is an **outcome**. The **sample space** of an experiment is the set of all possible outcomes.

Experiment	Rolling a number cube	Tossing a coin	Spinning a game spinner
Sample Space	{1, 2, 3, 4, 5, 6}	{heads, tails}	{red, blue, green, yellow}

EXAMPLE 1 Identifying Sample Spaces and Outcomes

Identify the sample space and the outcome shown for each experiment.

A tossing two coins
Sample space: {HH, HT, TH, TT}
Outcome shown: heads, tails (H, T)

B spinning a game spinner
Sample space: {yellow, red, blue, green}
Outcome shown: green

CHECK IT OUT!
1. Identify the sample space and the outcome shown for the experiment: rolling a number cube.

An **event** is an outcome or set of outcomes in an experiment. **Probability** is the measure of how likely an event is to occur. Probabilities are written as fractions or decimals from 0 to 1, or as percents from 0% to 100%.

EXAMPLE 2 Estimating the Likelihood of an Event

Write *impossible, unlikely, as likely as not, likely,* or *certain* to describe each event.

A There are 31 days in August.

August always has 31 days. This event is *certain*.

B Carlos correctly guesses a number between 1 and 1000.

Carlos must pick one outcome out of 1000 possible outcomes. This event is *unlikely*.

C A coin lands heads up.

Heads is one of two possible outcomes. This event is *as likely as not*.

D Cecilia rolls a 10 on a standard number cube.

A standard number cube is numbered 1 through 6. This event is *impossible*.

 CHECK IT OUT!

2. Write *impossible, unlikely, as likely as not, likely,* or *certain* to describe the event: Anthony rolls a number less than 7 on a standard number cube.

You can estimate the probability of an event by performing an experiment. The **experimental probability** of an event is the ratio of the number of times the event occurs to the number of trials. The more trials performed, the more accurate the estimate is likely to be.

 Know it! Note

Experimental Probability

$$\text{experimental probability} = \frac{\text{number of times the event occurs}}{\text{number of trials}}$$

EXAMPLE 3 Finding Experimental Probability

An experiment consists of spinning a spinner. Use the results in the table to find the experimental probability of each event.

Outcome	Frequency
Red	7
Blue	8
Green	5

Helpful Hint

Probabilities can be expressed as fractions, decimals, or percents. For Example 3, the probabilities are:

3A: $\frac{2}{5} = 0.4 = 40\%$

3B: $\frac{3}{4} = 0.75 = 75\%$

A spinner lands on blue

$$\frac{\text{number of times the event occurs}}{\text{number of trials}} = \frac{8}{7+8+5}$$
$$= \frac{8}{20}$$
$$= \frac{2}{5}$$

B spinner does not land on green

When the spinner does not land on green, it must land on red or blue.

$$\frac{\text{number of times the event occurs}}{\text{number of trials}} = \frac{7+8}{7+8+5}$$
$$= \frac{15}{20}$$
$$= \frac{3}{4}$$

Use the information in Example 3 to find the experimental probability of each event.

3a. spinner lands on red

3b. spinner does not land on red

You can use experimental probability to make *predictions*. A **prediction** is an estimate or guess about something that has not yet happened.

EXAMPLE **4** *Quality Control Application*

A manufacturer inspects 800 light bulbs and finds that 796 of them have no defects.

A What is the experimental probability that a light bulb chosen at random has no defects?

Find the experimental probability that a light bulb has no defects.

$$\frac{\text{number of times the event occurs}}{\text{number of trials}} = \frac{796}{800}$$

$$= 99.5\%$$

The experimental probability that a light bulb has no defects is 99.5%.

B The manufacturer sent a shipment of 2400 light bulbs to a retail store. Predict the number of light bulbs in the shipment that are likely to have no defects.

Find 99.5% of 2400.

$$0.995(2400) = 2388$$

The manufacturer predicts that 2388 light bulbs have no defects.

 4. A manufacturer inspects 1500 electric toothbrush motors and finds that 1497 of them have no defects.

a. What is the experimental probability that a motor chosen at random will have no defects?

b. There are 35,000 motors in a warehouse. Predict the number of motors that are likely to have no defects.

THINK AND DISCUSS

1. Explain the difference between an outcome and an event.

2. Is the experimental probability of an event always the same? Explain why or why not.

 3. GET ORGANIZED Copy and complete the graphic organizer. In each box, write an example of an event that has the given likelihood.

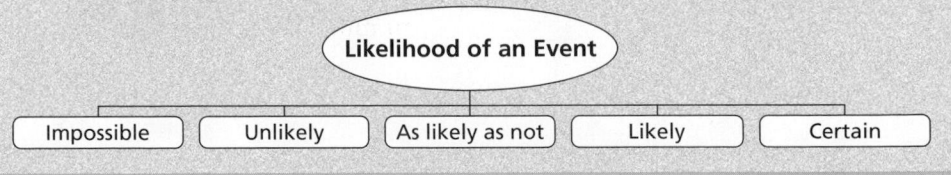

Likelihood of an Event

| Impossible | Unlikely | As likely as not | Likely | Certain |

go.hrw.com

Homework Help Online
KEYWORD: MA7 10-5

Parent Resources Online
KEYWORD: MA7 Parent

GUIDED PRACTICE

1. **Vocabulary** Give an example of an *event* that has two possible *outcomes*.

SEE EXAMPLE **1**
p. 737

Identify the sample space and the outcome shown for each experiment.

2. rolling a number cube   3. spinning a spinner   4. tossing 3 coins

SEE EXAMPLE **2**
p. 738

Write *impossible, unlikely, as likely as not, likely,* or *certain* to describe each event.

5. Peter was born in January. Thomas was born in June. Peter and Thomas have the same birthday.

6. The football team won 9 of its last 10 games. The team will win the next game.

7. A board game has a rule that if you roll the game cube and get a 6, you get an extra turn. You get an extra turn on your first roll.

SEE EXAMPLE **3**
p. 738

An experiment consists of rolling a number cube. Use the results in the table to find the experimental probability of each event.

Outcome	1	2	3	4	5	6
Frequency	5	6	2	2	3	7

8. rolling a 6

9. rolling an even number

10. not rolling a 6

SEE EXAMPLE **4**
p. 739

11. **Sports** One game of bowling consists of ten frames. Elyse usually rolls 3 strikes in each game.

a. What is the experimental probability that Elyse will roll a strike on any frame?

b. Predict the number of strikes Elyse will roll in 18 games.

PRACTICE AND PROBLEM SOLVING

Independent Practice

For Exercises	See Example
12–14	1
15–17	2
18–20	3
21	4

Extra Practice

Skills Practice p. S23

Application Practice p. S37

Identify the sample space and the outcome shown for each experiment.

12. tossing two coins   13. spinning a spinner   14. selecting a marble

Write *impossible, unlikely, as likely as not, likely,* **or** *certain* **to describe each event.**

15. Marlo purchased a new pair of shoes. She takes one shoe out of the box. The shoe is for the left foot.

16. Sam takes the bus to school. The bus came late twice in the last two weeks. The bus will be late today.

17. Tammy dropped two quarters on the floor. At least one of them lands heads up.

An experiment consists of randomly choosing a marble from a bag. Use the results in the table to find the experimental probability of each event.

Outcome	Frequency
Red	4
Blue	6
Green	6
Yellow	9

18. choosing a yellow marble

19. choosing a blue marble

20. not choosing a green marble

21. **Sports** A ski lodge inspects 80 skis and finds 4 to be defective.
    a. What is the experimental probability that a ski chosen at random will be defective?
    b. The lodge has 420 skis. Predict the number of skis that are likely to be defective.

22. The table shows the results of a survey asking students the season of their birthday. What is the experimental probability that a student has a birthday during the summer?

Season	Birthdays
Fall	39
Winter	27
Spring	33
Summer	51

23. You and your friend can either go swimming or to a movie on Thursday. The weather forecast says there is a 70% chance of rain on Thursday. Should you plan on going swimming or to a movie? Explain.

24. **Critical Thinking** Tell why it is important to repeat an experiment many times.

25. **Write About It** Explain what it means for an event to have a 50-50 chance of happening.

26. How many outcomes are in the sample space for an experiment consisting of rolling two standard number cubes?

27. **Estimation** A manufacturing company produced 986 units in one day. Of those, 9 units were found to be defective. Estimate the experimental probability that a unit produced that day was defective. Then predict approximately how many units will be defective when 5680 units are produced in one week.

MULTI-STEP TEST PREP

28. This problem will prepare you for the Multi-Step Test Prep on page 768.

In a standard deck of cards, there are 13 cards in each of four suits: hearts, diamonds, clubs, and spades. The hearts and diamonds are red and the clubs and spades are black. Ricardo randomly drew cards from a standard deck of 52 cards. The table shows the results.

Outcome	Frequency
Hearts	7
Diamonds	7
Clubs	8
Spades	6

a. Find the experimental probability of drawing a club.

b. Find the experimental probability of drawing a black suit.

29. Alex rolls two standard number cubes. What is the likelihood that the sum of the numbers is less than 4?

    Ⓐ Impossible   Ⓑ Unlikely   Ⓒ As likely as not   Ⓓ Likely

30. A community reported that $\frac{2}{3}$ of the residents had a pet and $\frac{1}{2}$ of the pet owners had a dog. If there are 84 residents in the community, how many residents are likely to have a dog?

    Ⓕ 14   Ⓖ 28   Ⓗ 42   Ⓙ 56

31. What is the probability that a number chosen at random from the list below will be a solution of the inequality $3x + 2 \le 23$?

    −8, −7, −6, −5, −4, −3, −2, −1, 0, 1, 2, 3, 4, 5, 6, 7, 8, 9

    Ⓐ $\frac{17}{18}$ Ⓑ $\frac{8}{9}$ Ⓒ $\frac{1}{9}$ Ⓓ $\frac{1}{18}$

32. Short Response A coin was tossed 50 times. It landed showing heads 6 more times than it landed showing tails. What is the experimental probability of the coin landing on heads? Show your work.

CHALLENGE AND EXTEND

A coin is tossed 3 times. Use the sample space for this experiment to describe each event below as *impossible, unlikely, as likely as not, likely,* or *certain*. Justify each answer.

33. At least 2 heads   **34.** 2 heads and 1 tail

35. 2 tails and 1 head   **36.** 3 tails

37. One coin is tossed 20 times.

    a. The experimental probability of the coin showing heads is 65%. How many times did the coin show tails?

    b. If the coin is tossed ten more times, how many more times must the coin land showing tails for the experimental probability of tails to be 50%?

SPIRAL REVIEW

38. A sales representative earns 4.5% commission on sales. Find the commission earned when the total sales are $124,000. *(Lesson 2-10)*

39. Estimate the tax on a $255 printer when the tax rate is 5.5%. *(Lesson 2-10)*

Compare the graph of each function to the graph of $f(x) = x^2$. *(Lesson 9-4)*

40. $g(x) = \frac{1}{3}x^2$ **41.** $g(x) = -x^2$ **42.** $g(x) = x^2 - 12$

The data shows the number of books read by seven students over the summer:
5, 5, 14, 2, 5, 5, 6. *(Lesson 10-3)*

43. Give the mean, median, and mode of the data.

44. Which measure of central tendency best describes the data? Explain.

45. Create a box-and-whisker plot of the data.

10-5
Technology LAB
Use Random Numbers

A calculator can be used to model an experiment that would be difficult or inconvenient to perform. To do this, you will use random numbers.

Use with Lesson 10-5

Activity

You can use a calculator to explore the experimental probability that at least 2 people in a group of 6 people were born in the same month. Assume that all months are equally likely to be a person's birth month.

1 Represent each month with an integer. Since there are 12 months, use the numbers 1–12.

To set your calculator up to generate random numbers, press **MATH**. Then use the arrow keys to highlight **PRB**. Select **5: randInt(**.

```
MATH NUM CPX PRB
1:rand
2:nPr
3:nCr
4:!
5:randInt(
6:randNorm(
7:randBin(
```

2 Now give the start number, 1, press **,**, and give the end number, 12.

Each time you press **ENTER** the calculator will return an integer from 1 to 12.

3 You are considering a group of 6 people. This means you need 6 random numbers.

```
randInt(1,12
              11
               4
               9
               3
               2
               9
```

	Person					
	1	**2**	**3**	**4**	**5**	**6**
Trial 1	11	4	9	3	2	9
Trial 2	3	8	10	12	6	2

In the first trial, the number 9 appears twice. This means that two people have a birth day in the ninth month, September.

In the second trial, no number appears more than once. This means that none of the people were born in the same month.

Try This

1. Repeat the experiment until you have 10 trials of the experiment. Count the number of trials in which a number appears more than once. Divide this number by the number of trials, 10, to find the experimental probability that at least 2 people in a group of 6 people will have the same birth month.

2. Gather the results from at least 100 trials of the experiment. (Either perform all of the trials yourself or combine data with your classmates.) Using your results, what is the experimental probability that at least 2 people in a group of 6 people will have the same birth month? Compare the results from 100 trials to the results of 10 trials.

3. How could you set up the experiment to find the experimental probability that at least 2 people in a group of 6 people will have the same birthday (same month and same date)?

Theoretical Probability

Objectives
Determine the theoretical probability of an event.

Convert between probabilities and odds.

Vocabulary
equally likely
theoretical probability
fair
complement
odds

Why learn this?
Theoretical probability can be used to determine the likelihood of different weather conditions. (See Example 2.)

When the outcomes in the sample space of an experiment have the same chance of occurring, the outcomes are said to be **equally likely**.

Equally likely outcomes	Not equally likely outcomes
There is the same chance that the spinner will land on any of the colors.	There is a greater chance that the spinner will land on blue than on any other color.

The **theoretical probability** of an event is the ratio of the number of ways the event can occur to the total number of equally likely outcomes.

> ### Theoretical Probability
>
> $$\text{theoretical probability} = \frac{\text{number of ways the event can occur}}{\text{total number of equally likely outcomes}}$$

An experiment in which all outcomes are equally likely is said to be **fair**. You can usually assume that experiments involving coins and number cubes are fair.

EXAMPLE 1 Finding Theoretical Probability

An experiment consists of rolling a number cube. Find the theoretical probability of each outcome.

A rolling a 3

$$\frac{\text{number of ways the event can occur}}{\text{total number of equally likely outcomes}} = \frac{1}{6}$$

$$= 0.1\overline{6}$$

$$= 16\frac{2}{3}\%$$

There is one 3 on a number cube.

Caution!

The use of the word *experiment* does not necessarily mean you are looking for experimental probability.

An experiment consists of rolling a number cube. Find the theoretical probability of each outcome.

B rolling a number greater than 3

$$\frac{\text{number of ways the event can occur}}{\text{total number of equally likely outcomes}} = \frac{3}{6} = \frac{1}{2}$$ *There are 3 numbers greater than 3.*

$$= 0.5 = 50\%$$

 CHECK IT OUT! An experiment consists of rolling a number cube. Find the theoretical probability of each outcome.

1a. rolling an even number   **1b.** rolling a multiple of 3

When you toss a coin, there are two possible outcomes, heads or tails. The table below shows the theoretical probabilities and experimental results of tossing a coin 10 times.

	P(heads)	*P*(tails)	*P*(heads) + *P*(tails)
Experimental Probability	$\frac{3}{10}$	$\frac{7}{10}$	$\frac{3}{10} + \frac{7}{10} = \frac{10}{10} = 1$
Theoretical Probability	$\frac{1}{2}$	$\frac{1}{2}$	$\frac{1}{2} + \frac{1}{2} = \frac{2}{2} = 1$

Reading Math

The probability of an event can be written as *P*(event). *P*(heads) means "the probability that heads will be the outcome."

The sum of the probability of heads and the probability of tails is 1, or 100%. This is because it is certain that one of the two outcomes will always occur.

$$P(\text{event happening}) + P(\text{event not happening}) = 1$$

The **complement** of an event is all the outcomes in the sample space that are not included in the event. The sum of the probabilities of an event and its complement is 1, or 100%, because the event will either happen or not happen. Two events are *complementary events* if the sum of their probabilities equals 1 and if one event occurs if and only if the other does not.

$$P(\text{event}) + P(\text{complement of event}) = 1$$

EXAMPLE 2 **Finding Probability by Using the Complement**

The weather forecaster predicts a 20% chance of snow. What is the probability that it will not snow?

$$P(\text{snow}) + P(\text{not snow}) = 100\%$$ *Either it will snow or it will not snow.*

$$20\% + P(\text{not snow}) = 100\%$$

$$\underline{-20\% \qquad\qquad\qquad -20\%}$$ *Subtract 20% from both sides.*

$$P(\text{not snow}) = 80\%$$

 CHECK IT OUT! **2.** A jar has green, blue, purple, and white marbles. The probability of choosing a green marble is 0.2, the probability of choosing blue is 0.3, and the probability of choosing purple is 0.1. What is the probability of choosing white?

Odds are another way to indicate the likelihood of an event. **Odds** express likelihood by comparing the number of ways an event can happen to the number of ways an event can fail to happen. The *odds in favor of an event* describe the likelihood that the event will occur. The *odds against an event* describe the likelihood that the event will not occur.

Odds are usually written with a colon in the form $a:b$, but can also be written as a to b or $\frac{a}{b}$.

Odds

ODDS IN FAVOR OF AN EVENT WITH EQUALLY LIKELY OUTCOMES

odds in favor $= \dfrac{\text{number of ways an event can happen}}{\text{number of ways an event can fail to happen}}$

$= a:b$

ODDS AGAINST AN EVENT WITH EQUALLY LIKELY OUTCOMES

odds against $= \dfrac{\text{number of ways an event can fail to happen}}{\text{number of ways an event can happen}}$

$= b:a$

---

a represents the number of ways an event can occur.

b represents the number of ways an event can fail to occur.

The two numbers given as the odds will add up to the total number of possible outcomes. You can use this relationship to convert between odds and probabilities.

EXAMPLE **3** **Converting Between Odds and Probabilities**

A **The probability of choosing a red card from a standard deck of playing cards is 50%. What are the odds of choosing a red card?**

The probability of choosing a red card is 50%, so the probability of not drawing a red card is 100% − 50% = 50%.

Odds in favor $= 50:50$, or $1:1$

The odds in favor of choosing a red card are $1:1$.

B **The odds against choosing a green marble from a bag are 5:3. What is the probability of choosing a green marble?**

The odds against green are 5:3, so the odds in favor of green are 3:5. This means there are 3 favorable outcomes and 5 unfavorable outcomes for a total of 8 possible outcomes.

$\dfrac{\text{number of ways event can happen}}{\text{total possible outcomes}} = \dfrac{3}{8}$

The probability of choosing a green marble is $\frac{3}{8}$.

Reading Math

You may see an outcome called "favorable." This does not mean that the outcome is good or bad. A favorable outcome is the outcome you are looking for in a probability experiment.

CHECK IT OUT!

3. The odds in favor of winning a free drink are $1:24$. What is the probability of winning a free drink?

THINK AND DISCUSS

1. Tell how to find the probability of the complement of an event.

2. GET ORGANIZED Copy and complete the graphic organizer using the spinner.

Probabilities on Spinner	
P(gray)	
P(not gray)	
Odds in favor of gray	
Odds against gray	

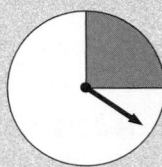

10-6 Exercises

go.hrw.com
Homework Help Online
KEYWORD: MA7 10-6
Parent Resources Online
KEYWORD: MA7 Parent

GUIDED PRACTICE

1. Vocabulary All of the outcomes in the sample space that are not included in the event are called the ___?___. (*theoretical probability*, *complement*, or *odds*)

SEE EXAMPLE 1
p. 744

Find the theoretical probability of each outcome.

2. rolling a number divisible by 3 on a number cube

3. tossing 2 coins and both landing with tails showing

4. randomly choosing the letter S from the letters in STARS

5. rolling a prime number on a number cube

SEE EXAMPLE 2
p. 745

6. A spinner is green, red, and blue. The probability that the spinner will land on green is 15% and red is 35%. What is the probability the spinner will land on blue?

7. The probability of choosing a red marble from a bag is $\frac{1}{3}$. What is the probability of not choosing a red marble?

8. You have a $\frac{1}{50}$ chance of winning. What is the probability you will not win?

9. There is a $\frac{1}{10}$ chance that you will be chosen as class representative. What is the probability that you will not be chosen?

SEE EXAMPLE 3
p. 746

10. The odds against a spinner landing on blue are 3 : 1. What is the probability of the spinner landing on blue?

11. The probability of choosing an ace from a deck of cards is $\frac{1}{13}$. What are the odds of choosing an ace?

12. The probability of not winning a game is 80%. What are the odds of winning?

13. The odds in favor of a spinner landing on blue are 1 : 3. What is the probability of landing on blue?

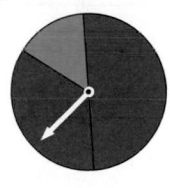

PRACTICE AND PROBLEM SOLVING

Independent Practice

For Exercises	See Example
14–16	1
17–19	2
20–22	3

Extra Practice

Skills Practice p. S23

Application Practice p. S37

Find the theoretical probability of each outcome.

14. rolling a 5 on a number cube

15. tossing 2 coins and 1 landing with heads showing, the other with tails showing

16. randomly choosing a blue marble from a bag of 5 blue marbles, 8 red marbles, and 7 yellow marbles

17. The probability of a spinner landing on yellow is $\frac{4}{9}$. What is the probability of it not landing on yellow?

18. There is a 3% probability of winning a game. Find the probability of not winning the game.

19. There is a 15% chance it will snow and a 15% chance it will rain. What is the probability that it will neither snow nor rain?

20. The odds against winning a contest are 99 : 1. What is the probability of not winning the contest?

21. The odds of choosing a white marble from a bag are 1 : 9. Find the probability of not choosing a white marble.

22. The probability of a spinner landing on green is 25%. What are the odds of the spinner not landing on green?

Use the spinner for Exercises 23–28.

23. P(red) **24.** P(green)

25. P(not blue) **26.** odds in favor of yellow

27. odds against red **28.** odds against green

 29. Write About It A number cube is rolled. Which event has a greater theoretical probability: rolling a number less than 3 or rolling a number greater than three? Explain.

30. ///**ERROR ANALYSIS**/// The odds in favor of an event are 1 : 4. Two students converted these odds into the probability of the event NOT happening. Which is incorrect? Explain the error.

Ⓐ

Odds in favor of event	1:4
Probability that event will not happen	$\frac{1}{5}$

Ⓑ

Odds in favor of event	1:4
Probability that event will not happen	$\frac{4}{5}$

31. Critical Thinking The odds in favor of a certain event are the same as the odds against that event. What is the probability of the event occurring?

MULTI-STEP TEST PREP

32. This problem will prepare you for the Multi-Step Test Prep on page 768.

Chutes and Ladders is a children's game that uses a spinner with the numbers 1 through 6.

a. What is the probability of spinning a 3?

b. What is the probability of spinning an odd number?

c. What is the probability of spinning a number that is less than or equal to 4?

33. Write About It Explain how to convert odds to probability.

 34. Geometry The radius of each circle in the diagram is given. Find the probability that a point chosen at random will lie in the red area of the diagram. (*Hint:* Find the ratio of the red area to the total area of the diagram.)

35. Two coins are tossed. What is the probability that at least one of the coins lands with heads showing?

  (A) 25%   (B) $33\frac{1}{3}$%   (C) 50%   (D) 75%

36. A standard number cube is rolled. Which has the greatest probability?

  (F) *P*(even) (G) *P*(less than 5) (H) *P*(not 2) (J) *P*(greater than 3)

37. Find the probability that a point chosen at random would fall in the yellow area.

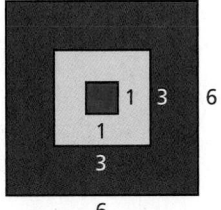

  (A) $\frac{1}{6}$ (C) $\frac{4}{9}$

  (B) $\frac{2}{9}$ (D) $\frac{2}{3}$

CHALLENGE AND EXTEND

Use the results of 3 coin-tossing experiments in the table for Exercise 38.

38. Find the experimental probability of the coin showing heads for

 a. experiment 1.

 b. experiment 2.

 c. experiment 3.

 d. Find the theoretical probability of the coin showing heads.

  e. Write About It How do the experimental probabilities of each experiment compare to the theoretical probability?

	Experiment		
	1	**2**	**3**
Number of Tosses	10	100	1000
Heads	4	48	502

SPIRAL REVIEW

39. The table shows the volume of water in an office water cooler over time. Find the rate of change for each time period. For which time period did the volume of water decrease at the slowest rate? *(Lesson 5-3)*

Time of day	7:00 A.M.	9:00 A.M.	1:00 P.M.	4:00 P.M.	5:00 P.M.
Volume (gal)	4.2	3.8	2.7	1.2	0.8

Factor each trinomial. *(Lesson 8-4)*

40. $2x^2 + x - 21$ **41.** $4x^2 - 7x + 3$ **42.** $6x^2 + 23x + 20$

An experiment consists of choosing a card out of a deck and recording the results. Use the table to find the experimental probability of each event. *(Lesson 10-5)*

Outcome	Frequency
Hearts	2
Diamonds	6
Spades	5
Clubs	7

43. choosing a heart

44. choosing a heart or a diamond

45. not choosing a club

10-7 Independent and Dependent Events

Objectives
Find the probability of independent events.

Find the probability of dependent events.

Vocabulary
independent events
dependent events

Why learn this?
You may need to understand independent and dependent events to determine the number of reading selections available.

Adam's teacher gives the class two lists of titles and asks each student to choose two of them to read. Adam can choose one title from each list or two titles from the same list.

One title from each list		Two titles from the same list	
Animal Farm (circled)	*Never Cry Wolf*	*Animal Farm* (circled)	*Animal Farm* (crossed out)
Ethan Frome	*Night*	*Ethan Frome*	*Ethan Frome*
Frankenstein	*Things Fall Apart*	*Frankenstein*	*Frankenstein* (circled)
Great Expectations	*Wish You Well*	*Great Expectations*	*Great Expectations*
Jane Eyre	*Wuthering Heights* (circled)	*Jane Eyre*	*Jane Eyre*

Choosing a title from one list does not affect the number of titles to choose from on the other list. The events are *independent*.

Choosing a title from one of the lists changes the number of titles that can be chosen from the same list. The events are *dependent*.

Events are **independent events** if the occurrence of one event does not affect the probability of the other. Events are **dependent events** if the occurrence of one event does affect the probability of the other.

EXAMPLE 1 Classifying Events as Independent or Dependent

Tell whether each set of events is independent or dependent. Explain your answer.

A A dime lands heads up and a nickel lands heads up.

The result of tossing a dime does not affect the result of tossing a nickel, so the events are independent.

B You choose a colored game piece in a board game, and then your sister picks another color.

Your sister cannot pick the same color you picked, and there are fewer game pieces for your sister to choose from after you choose, so the events are dependent.

 Tell whether each set of events is independent or dependent. Explain your answer.

1a. A number cube lands showing an odd number. It is rolled a second time and lands showing 6.

1b. One student in your class is chosen for a project. Then another student in the class is chosen.

Lydia Delgado
Northridge High
School

I use the everyday meanings of independent and dependent to remember their mathematical meanings.

The math class I take next year depends on which math classes I have already taken.

The history class I take next year is independent from (does not depend on) which math classes I have taken.

For dependent events, the occurrence of one affects the probability of the other.

For independent events, the occurrence of one does not affect the occurrence of the other.

Suppose an experiment involves tossing two fair coins. The sample space of outcomes is shown by the tree diagram. Determine the theoretical probability of both coins landing heads up.

1st Coin   **2nd Coin**

H —————< H
          T

T —————< H
          T

There are four possible outcomes in the sample space: $\{(H, H), (H, T), (T, H), (T, T)\}$

Only one outcome includes both coins landing heads up.

The theoretical probability of both coins landing heads up is $\frac{1}{4}$.

Now look back at the separate theoretical probabilities of each coin landing heads up. The theoretical probability in each case is $\frac{1}{2}$. The product of these two probabilities is $\frac{1}{4}$, the same probability shown by the tree diagram.

To determine the probability of two independent events, multiply the probabilities of the two events.

Know it!
Note

Probability of Independent Events

If A and B are independent events, then $P(A \text{ and } B) = P(A) \cdot P(B)$.

EXAMPLE 2 **Finding the Probability of Independent Events**

A An experiment consists of randomly selecting a marble from a bag, replacing it, and then selecting another marble. The bag contains 7 blue marbles and 3 yellow marbles. What is the probability of selecting a yellow marble and then a blue marble?

Because the first marble is replaced after it is selected, the sample space for each selection is the same. The events are independent.

$P(\text{yellow, blue}) = P(\text{yellow}) \cdot P(\text{blue})$

$\qquad\qquad = \frac{3}{10} \cdot \frac{7}{10}$ *The probability of selecting yellow is $\frac{3}{10}$, and the probability of selecting blue is $\frac{7}{10}$.*

$\qquad\qquad = \frac{21}{100}$

B When a person rolls 2 number cubes and they land showing the same number, we say the person rolled doubles. What is the probability of rolling doubles 3 times in a row?

The result of one roll does not affect any following rolls. The events are independent.

When you roll 2 number cubes, there are 36 possible outcomes, six of which are doubles:

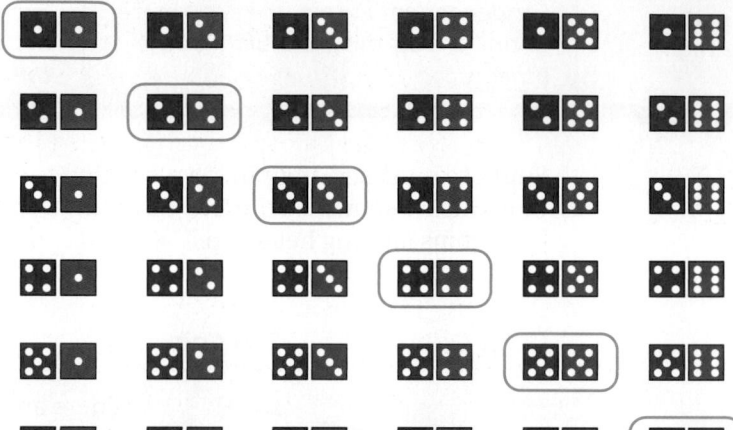

So, the probability of rolling doubles once is $P(\text{double}) = \dfrac{6}{36} = \dfrac{1}{6}$.

$$P(\text{double, double, double}) = P(\text{double}) \cdot P(\text{double}) \cdot P(\text{double})$$

$$= \frac{1}{6} \cdot \frac{1}{6} \cdot \frac{1}{6}$$

$$= \frac{1}{216}$$

 2. An experiment consists of spinning the spinner twice. What is the probability of spinning two odd numbers?

Suppose an experiment involves drawing marbles from a bag. Determine the theoretical probability of drawing a red marble and then drawing a second red marble *without replacing the first one*.

1st Draw   **2nd Draw**

The sample space for the second draw is not the same as the sample space for the first draw. There are fewer marbles in the bag for the second draw.

This means the events are dependent.

Probability of drawing a red marble on the first draw $= \dfrac{3}{9} = \dfrac{1}{3}$

Probability of drawing a red marble on the second draw $= \dfrac{2}{8} = \dfrac{1}{4}$

To determine the probability of two dependent events, multiply the probability of the first event times the probability of the second event after the first event has occurred.

Probability of Dependent Events

If A and B are dependent events, then $P(A \text{ and } B) = P(A) \cdot P(B \text{ after } A)$.

EXAMPLE **3** *Problem-Solving Application*

There are 7 pink flowers and 5 yellow flowers in a bunch. Jane selects a flower at random, and then Leah selects a flower at random from the remaining flowers. What is the probability that Jane selects a pink flower and Leah selects a yellow flower?

1 **Understand the Problem**

The **answer** will be the probability that a yellow flower is chosen after a pink flower is chosen.

List the **important information:**
- Jane chooses a pink flower from 7 pink flowers and 5 yellow flowers.
- Leah chooses a yellow flower from 6 pink flowers and 5 yellow flowers.

2 **Make a Plan**

Draw a diagram.

Flowers Jane can choose from:

●●●●●●●   7 pink
○○○○○   5 yellow
             12 total

Flowers Leah can choose from:

●●●●●●   6 pink
○○○○○   5 yellow
             11 total

After Jane selects a flower, the sample space changes. So the events are dependent.

3 **Solve**

$P(\text{pink and yellow}) = P(\text{pink}) \cdot P(\text{yellow after pink})$

$$= \frac{7}{12} \cdot \frac{5}{11}$$ *Jane selects one of 7 pink flowers from 12 total flowers. Then Leah selects one of 5 yellow flowers from the 11 flowers left.*

$$= \frac{35}{132}$$

The probability that Jane selects a pink flower and Leah selects a yellow flower is $\frac{35}{132}$.

4 **Look Back**

Drawing a diagram helps you see how the sample space changes. This means the events are dependent, so you can use the formula for probability of dependent events.

3. A bag has 10 red marbles, 12 white marbles, and 8 blue marbles. Two marbles are randomly drawn from the bag. What is the probability of drawing a blue marble and then a red marble?

THINK AND DISCUSS

1. Give an example of two events that are dependent. Explain why the events are dependent.

2. GET ORGANIZED Copy and complete the graphic organizer.

	Example	Probability
Dependent Events	$A =$ $B =$	$P(A \text{ and } B) =$
Independent Events	$A =$ $B =$	$P(A \text{ and } B) =$

10-7 Exercises

go.hrw.com
Homework Help Online
KEYWORD: MA7 10-7
Parent Resources Online
KEYWORD: MA7 Parent

GUIDED PRACTICE

1. Vocabulary Two events are ____?____ if the occurrence of one event affects the probability of the other event. (*independent* or *dependent*)

SEE EXAMPLE **1**
p. 750

Tell whether each set of events is independent or dependent. Explain your answers.

2. You draw a heart from a deck of cards and set it aside. Then you draw a club from the deck of cards.

3. You guess "true" on two true-false questions.

4. You select a kitten to adopt from an animal shelter. Then your friend selects a kitten to adopt.

5. You order from a menu, and then your friend orders.

6. A doctors' office schedules several patients. Then you make an appointment.

SEE EXAMPLE **2**
p. 751

7. A coin is tossed three times. What is the probability of the coin landing heads up three times?

8. Seven cards are numbered from 1 to 7 and placed in a box. One card is selected at random and replaced. Another card is randomly selected. What is the probability of selecting two odd numbers?

9. Stacey rolls two number cubes. What is the probability that the sum of the numbers on the two number cubes is 7?

10. A number cube is rolled twice and a coin is tossed once. What is the probability of the coin landing heads up and the number cube landing with 2 showing both times?

11. A spinner with four equal sections of red, yellow, green, and blue is spun twice. What is the probability that it lands on yellow and then on green?

SEE EXAMPLE **3**

p. 753

12. A bag contains 4 red marbles, 3 white marbles, and 6 blue marbles. What is the probability of randomly selecting a red marble, setting it aside, and then randomly selecting a white marble from the bag?

13. Seven cards are numbered from 1 to 7 and placed in a box. One card is selected at random and not replaced. Another card is randomly selected. What is the probability of selecting two odd numbers?

14. There are 15 boys and 14 girls in a room. Two of them are selected at random to take a survey. What is the probability that the two people selected will be girls?

PRACTICE AND PROBLEM SOLVING

Independent Practice

For Exercises	See Example
15–16	1
17–19	2
20–22	3

Extra Practice

Skills Practice p. S23
Application Practice p. S37

Tell whether each set of events is independent or dependent. Explain your answer.

15. The teacher randomly selects two students from the class.

16. You roll a 3 on a number cube and choose a 3 from a deck of cards.

17. A number cube is rolled three times. What is the probability of rolling three even numbers?

18. Ten cards are numbered from 1 to 10 and placed in a box. One card is selected at random and replaced. Another card is randomly selected. What is the probability of selecting two even numbers?

19. Stacey rolls a number cube and tosses a coin. What is the probability that she rolls a 5 and the coin lands heads up?

20. A bag contains 5 red marbles, 3 white marbles, and 4 blue marbles. What is the probability of randomly selecting a red marble, setting it aside, and then randomly selecting another red marble from the bag?

21. Ten cards are numbered from 1 to 10 and placed in a box. One card is selected at random and not replaced. Another card is randomly selected. What is the probability of selecting two even numbers?

22. A game has 6 colored playing pieces. They are red, yellow, green, blue, purple, and white. You and a friend each pick a game piece without looking. What is the probability that your friend picks the blue piece and then you pick the yellow piece?

23. **School** On a multiple-choice test, each question has 4 possible answers. A student does not know the answers to three questions, so the student guesses.

   a. What is the probability that the student gets all three questions wrong?

   b. What is the probability that the student gets all three questions right?

School

On some standardized tests, there is no penalty for a wrong answer. On these tests, it is better to guess than to leave the answer blank, especially if some choices can be eliminated.

Tell whether each set of events is independent or dependent. Explain your answer.

24. Pick "Joe" from a box of names, replace it, and then pick "Craig."

25. Pick "Joe" from a box of names, set it aside, and then pick "Craig."

26. Roll a prime number on a number cube and get tails when tossing a coin.

27. Roll an even number, then an odd number, and then a 1 on a number cube.

28. This problem will prepare you for the Multi-Step Test Prep on page 768.

Yahtzee is a game that involves rolling five dice. On his or her turn, a player can roll up to three times to try to score points in various categories. Rolling a "Yahtzee" means rolling five of a kind, or five of the same number.

a. Juan has rolled twice and has three 5's showing. He rolls the remaining two dice. What is the probability that both dice will land showing 5?

b. Shauna has two 3's showing. She has one more roll with the remaining three dice. What is the probability that all three dice will land showing 3?

c. Mike rolls all five number cubes and all of them land showing 6. What is the probability of getting five 6's in one roll?

29. A bag contains 3 red, 5 blue, and 2 white marbles.

a. Find the probability of randomly picking a red marble, replacing it, and then picking a blue marble.

b. Find the probability of randomly picking a red marble, setting it aside, and then picking a blue marble.

c. Find the probability of randomly picking a red marble, replacing it, and then picking another red marble.

d. Find the probability of randomly picking a red marble, setting it aside, and then picking another red marble.

30. Entertainment Joe and Maria are playing a board game. On each turn, the player rolls two number cubes. Both players have two turns remaining.

a. Joe will win if he rolls double 6's on both turns. What is the probability that Joe will roll double 6's on both turns?

b. Maria will win if she rolls 2 on the first turn and 12 on the second turn. What is the probability that Maria will roll 2 on the first turn and 12 on the second turn?

 c. Write About It Who has the better probability of winning? Explain.

31. Tamika has $2.50 in quarters in her pocket, including four state quarters. She reaches into her pocket and takes out two quarters, one at a time. What is the probability that they are both state quarters?

32. Ten cards are numbered 1 through 10 and placed in a bag. You draw a card, set it aside, and draw another card. What is the probability that you will draw two numbers that are divisible by 3?

33. Critical Thinking What is the probability of a coin landing heads up on two tosses if it lands tails up on the first toss? Explain.

 34. Write About It Explain what it means for two events to be independent.

 TEST PREP

35. A number cube is rolled twice. What is the probability of getting a 2 on both rolls?

    Ⓐ $\frac{1}{3}$ Ⓑ $\frac{1}{4}$ Ⓒ $\frac{1}{9}$ Ⓓ $\frac{1}{36}$

36. In baseball, Julio averages 3 hits in every 10 at bats. What is the probability that he will get hits in both of his next two at bats?

    Ⓕ 0.03   Ⓖ 0.09   Ⓗ 0.3   Ⓙ 0.9

37. Two people from a group of 30 will be selected at random for a prize. Twenty people in the group are women. What is the probability that both people selected will be men?

(A) $\dfrac{3}{29}$ (B) $\dfrac{38}{87}$ (C) $\dfrac{56}{87}$ (D) $\dfrac{1}{10}$

38. Ravi has 10 pairs of socks in a drawer, but none of the pairs are matched up. Each pair is a different color, and one pair is blue. Ravi has to pick his socks in the dark so he does not wake his brother. Which expression can be used to find the probability that Ravi will choose a blue sock and then the matching sock?

(F) $\dfrac{1}{20}+\dfrac{1}{20}$ (G) $\dfrac{1}{10}\cdot\dfrac{1}{20}$ (H) $\dfrac{1}{20}+\dfrac{1}{19}$ (J) $\dfrac{1}{10}\cdot\dfrac{1}{19}$

CHALLENGE AND EXTEND

39. Basketball Terrance has made 90% of the free throws he has attempted at basketball practice. What is the probability that he will make the next three free throws he attempts?

40. A number cube is rolled three times. What is the probability of rolling a 5 at least once?

Geometry Use the grid for Exercises 41–44.

On the grid at right, one small square represents 1% probability.

The shaded rows represent the probability that event A occurs.

The shaded columns represent the probability that event B occurs.

The area where the shaded rows and columns overlap represents the probability that both events occur.

Use the grid to find each probability.

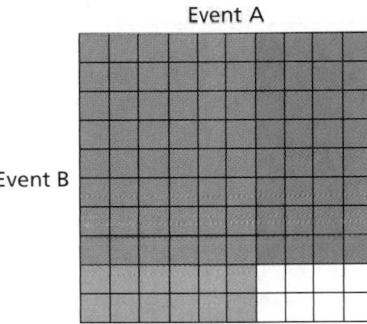

41. Event A occurs.

42. Event B occurs.

43. Event A occurs AND event B occurs.

44. Neither event A nor event B occurs.

SPIRAL REVIEW

45. A tennis player serves 2 aces (unreturned serves) for every 17 serves. If the player serves 204 times in the next match, how many serves would you expect to be aces? *(Lesson 2-7)*

Compare the graph of each function to the graph of $f(x) = x^2$. *(Lesson 9-4)*

46. $g(x) = 4x^2 - 1$ **47.** $g(x) = \dfrac{1}{5}x^2$ **48.** $g(x) = -x^2 + 3$

Find the theoretical probability of each outcome. *(Lesson 10-6)*

49. Randomly selecting a blue marble out of a bag with 6 red and 9 blue marbles

50. Rolling a number less than 10 on a number cube

51. Randomly selecting A, E, I, O, or U from all letters of the alphabet

10-7 Algebra LAB

Use with Lesson 10-7

Compound Events

When two events cannot happen at the same time, they are called *mutually exclusive* events. When two events can happen at the same time, they are called *inclusive* events. You can use sample spaces to determine the probabilities of mutually exclusive events and inclusive events.

When finding the probablity of a compound event, you should first determine whether the simple events involved are dependent or independent.

Activity 1

Suppose you are playing Monopoly and are "just visiting" the Jail. If you roll 7 on your next turn, you will land on Community Chest. If you roll 12, you will land on Chance. What is the probability that on your next roll you land on either Community Chest or Chance?

You cannot land on Community Chest and Chance at the same time, so the events are mutually exclusive. You cannot roll 7 and 12 at the same time, so those events are also mutually exclusive.

The table shows some of the totals when rolling two fair dice. Copy and complete the table. Use one color to circle all rolls with a total of 7. Use a second color to circle all rolls with a total of 12.

+	1	2	3	4	5	6
1	2	3	4	5		
2	3	4				
3	4	5				
4	5					
5	6					
6	7					

Try This

1. What is the total number of possible rolls?

2. What is the probability that the total will be 7?

3. What is the probability that the total will be 12?

4. What is the probability that the total will be 7 or 12?

5. What do you notice about the probabilities in Problems 2, 3, and 4?

Suppose you are three spaces away from Community Chest and eight spaces away from Chance.

6. What is the probability that on your next roll the total will be 3?

7. What is the probability that on your next roll the total will be 8?

8. What is the probability that on your next roll the total will be 3 or 8?

9. Complete the following statement:

The probability that one of two mutually exclusive events will occur is the ___?___ of the probabilities of the individual events.

In this lab, you discovered this rule: If A and B are mutually exclusive events, then $P(A \text{ or } B) = P(A) + P(B)$.

Activity 2

Suppose you are playing Yahtzee and on the last roll of your turn, you roll two of the five dice. You need to roll either a 1 or a 5 to make what is called a "small straight" (four consecutive numbers).

What is the probability that you will make a small straight?

You can roll a 1 and a 5 at the same time on different dice. These events are inclusive.

(If you roll a 1 and a 5, you will need to look at only four of the dice to make a small straight.)

There are three outcomes that involve rolling a 1 or rolling a 5.

Case 1	Case 2	Case 3
At least one 1	At least one 5	Both a 1 and a 5

Try This

10. Find the probability of Case 1, rolling at least one 1.

   a. What is the probability of rolling ⊡ on the first die and any number on the second die?

   b. What is the probability of rolling any number on the first die and ⊡ on the second die?

   c. What is the probability of rolling ⊡ on the first die and ⊡ on the second die?

   d. Parts **a** and **b** both include rolling ⊡ on the first die and ⊡ on the second die. You need to count this outcome only once, so subtract the probability from part **c** from the sum of parts **a** and **b**.

11. Find the probability of Case 2, rolling at least one 5. (*Hint:* Repeat the steps in Problem 10.)

12. Find the probability of Case 3, rolling a 1 and a 5.

13. The probability of rolling a small straight, is the probability of rolling ⊡ *or* ⁙.

   Subtract the probability of rolling both ⊡ *and* ⁙ from the sum of the probabilities of rolling ⊡ on one of the dice (Problem 10) and rolling ⁙ on one of the dice (Problem 11).

14. Complete the following statement:

   The probability that one of two inclusive events will occur is the ___?___ of the probabilities of the individual events ___?___ the probability of the intersection of the two events.

In this lab, you discovered this rule:

If A and B are inclusive events, then $P(A \text{ or } B) = P(A) + P(B) - P(A \text{ and } B)$.

10-8 Combinations and Permutations

Objectives
Solve problems involving permutations.

Solve problems involving combinations.

Vocabulary
compound event
combination
permutation

Who uses this?
Security companies use permutations to create many security codes using a limited number of digits or letters. (See Exercise 8.)

Sometimes there are too many possible outcomes to make a tree diagram or a list. The *Fundamental Counting Principle* is one method of finding the number of possible outcomes.

Know it!
Note

Fundamental Counting Principle

If there are *m* ways to choose a first item and *n* ways to choose a second item after the first item has been chosen, then there are *m · n* ways to choose both items.

The Fundamental Counting Principle can also be used when there are more than two items to choose.

EXAMPLE 1 **Using the Fundamental Counting Principle**

A florist is arranging centerpieces that include 1 flower, 1 plant, and 1 vase. The florist has 2 kinds of vases, 2 kinds of plants, and 3 kinds of flowers to choose from. How many different centerpieces are possible?

Method 1 Use a tree diagram. *Follow each branch of the tree diagram to find all of the possible centerpieces.*

There are 12 possible centerpieces.

Method 2 Use the Fundamental Counting Principle.

2 · 2 · 3   *There are 2 choices for the first item, 2 choices for the*
     12   *second item, and 3 choices for the third item.*

There are 12 possible centerpieces.

 CHECK IT OUT!
1. A voicemail system password is 1 letter followed by a 3-digit number less than 600. How many different voicemail passwords are possible?

A **compound event** consists of two or more simple events, such as a rolled number cube landing with 3 showing and a tossed coin landing heads up. (A simple event has only one outcome, such as rolling a 3 on a number cube.) For some compound events, the order in which the simple events occur is important.

A **combination** is a grouping of outcomes in which the order does not matter.
A **permutation** is an arrangement of outcomes in which the order does matter.

EXAMPLE 2 **Finding Combinations and Permutations**

Tell whether each situation involves combinations or permutations. Then give the number of possible outcomes.

A **A street vendor sells cashews, peanuts, and almonds. How many different ways are there to mix two kinds of nuts?**

List all of the possible groupings:

| cashews and peanuts | peanuts and almonds | almonds and cashews |
| peanuts and cashews | almonds and peanuts | cashews and almonds |

The order of the outcomes is not important, so this situation involves combinations. Eliminate the groupings that are duplicates.

| cashews and peanuts | peanuts and almonds | almonds and cashews |
| ~~peanuts and cashews~~ | ~~almonds and peanuts~~ | ~~cashews and almonds~~ |

There are 3 different ways to mix two kinds of nuts.

B **Karen is painting her bedroom. She has orange, green, blue, and purple paint. She plans to use one color as a base coat and stencil a design with another color. How many different ways can she do this?**

List all of the possible groupings:

The order of the outcomes is important, because one color is painted on top of the other. This situation involves permutations.

There are 12 different ways for Karen to paint her room.

 CHECK IT OUT! **Tell whether each situation involves combinations or permutations. Then give the number of possible outcomes.**

2a. Ingrid is stringing three different types of beads on a bracelet. How many ways can she use one bead of each type to string the next three beads?

2b. Nathan wants to order a sandwich with two of the following ingredients: mushroom, eggplant, tomato, and avocado. How many different sandwiches can Nathan choose?

The factorial of a number is the product of the number and all the natural numbers less than the number. The factorial of 5 is written 5! and is read "five factorial." $5! = 5 \cdot 4 \cdot 3 \cdot 2 \cdot 1 = 120$. Factorials can be used to find the number of combinations and permutations that can be made from a set of choices.

Suppose you want to make a five-letter password from the letters A, B, C, D, and E without repeating a letter. You have 5 choices for the first letter, but only 4 choices for the second letter. You have one fewer choice for each letter of the password.

First letter	Second letter	Third letter	Fourth letter	Fifth letter

5 choices ✕ 4 choices ✕ 3 choices ✕ 2 choices ✕ 1 choice ═ 120 permutations

Suppose you want to make a three-letter password from the 5 letters A, B, C, D, and E without repeating a letter. Again, you have one fewer choice for each letter of the password.

First letter	Second letter	Third letter

There are 5 choices (A, B, C, D, E), and you are choosing 3 of them.

5 choices ✕ 4 choices ✕ 3 choices ═ 60 permutations

The number of permutations is $\frac{5!}{2!}$, or $\frac{5 \cdot 4 \cdot 3 \cdot \cancel{2} \cdot \cancel{1}}{\cancel{2} \cdot \cancel{1}} = 5 \cdot 4 \cdot 3 = 60$.

Permutations

FORMULA	The number of permutations of n things chosen r at a time:	$_nP_r = \dfrac{n!}{(n-r)!}.$
EXAMPLE	A club will choose a president, a vice president, and a secretary from a list of 8 people. How many ways can the club choose the 3 officers?	
	The position that each person takes matters, so this situation involves permutations.	
	Think: There are 8 people, and the club will choose 3 of them.	$_8P_3 = \dfrac{8!}{(8-3)!} = \dfrac{8!}{5!} = 336$

EXAMPLE 3 **Finding Permutations**

Lee brings 7 CDs numbered 1–7 to a party. How many different ways can he choose the first 4 CDs to play?

The order in which the CDs are played matters, so use the formula for permutations.

$$_7P_4 = \frac{7!}{(7-4)!} = \frac{7!}{3!}$$

$n = 7$ and $r = 4$.

$$= \frac{7 \cdot 6 \cdot 5 \cdot 4 \cdot \cancel{3} \cdot \cancel{2} \cdot \cancel{1}}{\cancel{3} \cdot \cancel{2} \cdot \cancel{1}}$$

A number divided by itself is 1, so you can divide out common factors in the numerator and denominator.

$$= 7 \cdot 6 \cdot 5 \cdot 4 = 840$$

There are 840 different ways Lee can choose to play the 4 CDs.

 CHECK IT OUT! **3.** How many different ways can 9 people line up for a picture?

The formula for combinations also involves factorials.

Combinations

FORMULA	The number of combinations of n things chosen r at a time: $\quad {}_nC_r = \dfrac{n!}{r!(n-r)!}.$
EXAMPLE	A club will form a 3-person committee from a list of 8 people. How many ways can the club choose the 3 people? The position that each person takes does not matter, so this situation involves combinations. Think: There are 8 people, and the club will choose 3 of them. $\quad {}_8C_3 = \dfrac{8!}{3!(8-3)!} = \dfrac{8!}{3!5!} = 56$

E X A M P L E **4** **Finding Combinations**

There are 11 different cereals for sale at a grocery store. How many different ways can a shopper select 4 different cereals?

The order in which the cereals are selected does not matter, so use the formula for combinations.

Method 1 Use the formula for combinations.

$${}_{11}C_4 = \frac{11!}{4!\,(11-4)!} = \frac{11!}{4!7!} \qquad n = 11 \text{ and } r = 4.$$

$$= \frac{11 \cdot 10 \cdot 9 \cdot 8 \cdot \cancel{7} \cdot \cancel{6} \cdot \cancel{5} \cdot \cancel{4} \cdot \cancel{3} \cdot \cancel{2} \cdot \cancel{1}}{(4 \cdot 3 \cdot 2 \cdot 1)(\cancel{7} \cdot \cancel{6} \cdot \cancel{5} \cdot \cancel{4} \cdot \cancel{3} \cdot \cancel{2} \cdot \cancel{1})}$$

$$= \frac{7920}{24} = 330$$

Helpful Hint

You can also use a calculator to find permutations. Look for the **nPr** function on your calculator.

Method 2 Use the **nCr** function of a calculator.

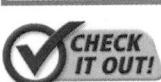

```
11 nCr 4
              330
```

There are 330 different ways the shopper can choose 4 different cereals.

CHECK IT OUT! **4.** A basketball team has 12 members who can play any position. How many different ways can the coach choose 5 starting players?

THINK AND DISCUSS

1. Explain how to find $\frac{10!}{9!}$ without a calculator.

2. GET ORGANIZED Copy and complete the graphic organizer.

	Fundamental Counting Principle	Permutation	Combination
When to Use			
Formula			

go.hrw.com
Homework Help Online
KEYWORD: MA7 10-8
Parent Resources Online
KEYWORD: MA7 Parent

GUIDED PRACTICE

1. **Vocabulary** A ____?____ is an arrangement of outcomes in which the order does not matter. (*compound event*, *permutation*, or *combination*)

SEE EXAMPLE **1**
p. 760

2. The menu for a restaurant is shown. How many different meals with one salad, one soup, one entree, and one dessert are possible?

3. You have 4 colors of wrapping paper and 2 kinds of ribbon. How many different ways are there to use one color of paper and one type of ribbon to wrap a package?

SEE EXAMPLE **2**
p. 761

Tell whether each situation involves combinations or permutations. Then give the number of possible outcomes.

4. How many different ways can 4 people be seated in a row of 4 seats?

5. How many different kinds of punch can be made from 2 of the following: cranberry juice, apple juice, orange juice, and grape juice?

SEE EXAMPLE **3**
p. 762

6. An airport identification code is made up of three letters, like the examples shown. How many different airport identification codes are possible? (Assume any letter can be repeated and can appear in any position.)

7. A manager is scheduling interviews for job applicants. She has 8 time slots and 6 applicants to interview. How many different interview schedules are possible?

8. An e-mail server password must be 6 different lowercase letters. How many different e-mail server passwords are possible?

 Albuquerque International Airport, New Mexico

 Dallas/Fort Worth International Airport, Texas

 John F. Kennedy International Airport, New York

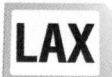 Los Angeles International Airport, California

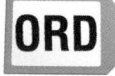 O'Hare International Airport, Illinois

SEE EXAMPLE **4**
p. 763

9. Francine is deciding which after-school clubs to join. She has time to participate in 3. How many different ways can Francine choose which 3 clubs to join?

10. Laura is making gift baskets. Each basket has 2 gifts, and she has 5 gifts to choose from. How many different gift baskets can Laura make?

11. How many different ways can a contest judge select 5 finalists from 20 contestants?

Join a Club!
Science Club   Math Club
Drama Club   Dance Club
Chess Club   Spanish Club
Student Government

PRACTICE AND PROBLEM SOLVING

Independent Practice

For Exercises	See Example
12–13	1
14–15	2
16–17	3
18–19	4

Extra Practice

Skills Practice p. S23

Application Practice p. S37

12. Maria looks in her closet and exclaims, "I have nothing to wear!" How many different outfits of one shirt, one pair of shorts, and one pair of sandals are possible using the items shown?

13. When a customer buys tickets for a concert, the ticket office assigns a confirmation code that is made up of 2 lowercase consonants, followed by a 3-digit number from 000 to 999. A letter or digit may be repeated. How many different confirmation codes are possible?

For Exercises 14 and 15, tell whether each situation involves combinations or permutations. Then give the number of possible outcomes.

14. A team of archeologists divides a dig site into 3 areas. They dig one area at a time. How many different ways can they order the 3 areas?

15. To decide which team will lead the class discussion, a teacher writes the names of 5 students on slips of paper and puts them in a hat. Then she draws 2 names. How many teams of two are possible?

16. The code for a bicycle lock is made up of 4 digits from 0 through 9. How many different codes are possible?

17. A television station has 5 different commercials to play during the news. In how many different ways can they order the commercials?

18. David's summer reading list has 9 books. How many different ways can David select 3 books to read?

19. Steve draws a hand of 7 cards from a deck of 52 different cards. How many different hands are possible?

20. **History** The North American Numbering Plan (NANP) was first used in 1947. It is a system for assigning telephone numbers and area codes.

   a. Originally, the NANP allowed only 3-digit area codes whose first digit was not 0 or 1, and whose second digit was always 0 or 1. How many different area codes were possible under this system?

   b. In 1995, because of increased demand, the NANP removed the restriction that the second digit of the area code must be 0 or 1. How many more area codes did this make possible?

21. **Critical Thinking** For $n = 6$ and $r = 2$, which is larger: $_nP_r$ or $_nC_r$? Explain why this is true.

22. **Write About It** Explain why a "combination lock" should be called a "permutation lock."

23. **Write About It** You roll a number cube 6 times. Explain how to determine the number of possible outcomes. Would a tree diagram be useful in solving this problem? Explain why or why not.

24. This problem will prepare you for the Multi-Step Test Prep on page 768.

Many states have lotteries to raise money. In one lottery, the players choose 6 different numbers from the numbers 1–49. The order of the numbers does not matter.

a. How many combinations are there?

b. The probability that your first number is on the winning ticket is $\frac{6}{49}$. The probability that your second number matches is $\frac{5}{48}$. The probabilities of the third, fourth, fifth, and sixth numbers matching are $\frac{4}{47}$, $\frac{3}{46}$, $\frac{2}{45}$, and $\frac{1}{44}$. The product of these probabilities is the probability of winning the lottery with one ticket. Find that probability. How does it relate to the number of combinations shown in part **a?**

25. Technology Nancy's password for her online banking program is made up of 6 letters. It does not matter whether the letters are uppercase or lowercase and any letter may be repeated.

a. What is the probability of someone correctly guessing Nancy's password?

b. How many hours would it take for someone to try all the possible passwords if the person could guess one password each second?

 c. Write About It Explain why you think some Internet companies require that passwords be at least 6 characters long.

 TEST PREP

26. Which situation is best modeled by the expression $_{10}C_4$?

(A) Lisa's salon offers 10 kinds of shampoo and 4 kinds of conditioner. How many different ways can she shampoo and condition a client's hair?

(B) Sara has a box of 10 colored pencils. How many different ways can she choose 4 colored pencils from the box?

(C) A personal identification number (PIN) is a 4-digit number. Digits can be repeated in a PIN. How many different PINs are possible?

(D) There are 10 chairs placed around a table. How many different ways can 4 people seat themselves around the table?

27. Which of the following is equal to 4!?

(F) $10! - 6!$ (G) $\frac{8!}{2!}$ (H) $(2!)(2!)$ (J) $\frac{24!}{23!}$

28. Which table represents the values of $_xC_4$ for the given values of x?

(A)
x	$_xC_4$
5	5
6	30
7	210
8	1680

(B)
x	$_xC_4$
5	120
6	360
7	840
8	1680

(C)
x	$_xC_4$
5	5
6	15
7	35
8	70

(D)
x	$_xC_4$
5	30
6	90
7	210
8	240

29. Short Response The periodic table of the elements is a chart listing 117 different elements. Maria must give a presentation on 3 different elements from the periodic table. How many ways can she choose which elements to present? Show your work and explain each step.

CHALLENGE AND EXTEND

Simplify each expression.

30. $\dfrac{8!}{3!}$

31. $\dfrac{7!4!}{6!}$

32. $\dfrac{_7P_5}{_7P_3}$

33. The chart shows the different toppings offered by a pizza shop.

   a. How many different pizzas with 2 toppings are possible?

   b. How many different pizzas with 6 toppings are possible?

   c. What do you notice about your answers to parts **a** and **b**? Explain why you think this is.

Pizza Ingredients

- Extra Cheese
- Green Peppers
- Mushrooms
- Pepperoni
- Sausage
- Onions
- Pineapple
- Green Olives

34. Use the permutation and combination formulas you learned in this lesson.

   a. What is the number of permutations when $n = r$?

   b. What is the number of combinations when $n = r$?

35. You roll a number cube six times in a row. What is the probability that you roll the numbers 1 through 6 in order?

SPIRAL REVIEW

Simplify each expression. *(Lesson 1-7)*

36. $4.9m + 3.8 - 2.1m - 3.9$

37. $4(2x - 1) + 9 - 3x$

38. $3a^2 - 5a - 7a^2$

Identify the independent and dependent variables. Write an equation in function notation for each situation. *(Lesson 4-3)*

39. A bathtub fills at a rate of 15 gallons per minute.

40. About 5 seeds should be planted per square inch.

41. A snow removal company charges a contract fee of $300 plus $80 per hour.

42. Five people responded that they spend the following amounts for haircuts during one year: $150, $120, $135, $0, and $145. A researcher concluded that "people spend an average of $110 per year on haircuts." Why is this statistic misleading? *(Lesson 10-4)*

Career Path

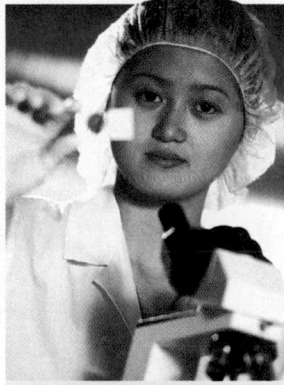

Erika Sheehan
Biostatistics major

Q: What math classes did you take in high school?
A: Algebra, Geometry, Precalculus, Calculus

Q: What math classes have you taken in college?
A: Statistics, Linear Algebra, Problem Solving

Q: What do Biostatisticians do?
A: Biostatisticians apply statistical methods to research scientific questions relating to health and medicine.

Q: What are your plans for the future?
A: After graduating, I would like to get a job at a pharmaceutical company testing the safety and effectiveness of new medicines.

MULTI-STEP TEST PREP

Probability

The Games People Play Probability is involved in most board and card games.

1. There are 108 cards in a deck for the game Uno. The table shows the number of each type of card found in an Uno deck. What is the probability of randomly selecting a red card from a complete deck of Uno cards?

Type of Card	Number in Deck
Blue cards, 0–9	19
Green cards, 0–9	19
Red cards, 0–9	19
Yellow cards, 0–9	19
Draw Two	8 (2 in each color)
Reverse	8 (2 in each color)
Skip	8 (2 in each color)
Wild	4
Wild Draw Four	4

2. Robert is playing Monopoly. He starts the game on the GO space. He wants to avoid the Income Tax space, which he will land on if he rolls a 4 with the two dice. What is the probability that he will land on the Income Tax space?

3. In the game Battleship, each player chooses locations for small ships on a 10-by-10 grid. Each player guesses grid spaces to try to locate the other player's ships. A correct guess equals a hit, and by hitting each space occupied by a ship, the ship is sunk. The battleship piece occupies four grid spaces. What is the probability that a player randomly guesses a correct grid space and hits the other player's battleship?

4. In the game Set, each card can be characterized in four ways. Cards are either red, green, or purple. The design on each card is either an oval, a squiggle, or a diamond. There are either one, two, or three of the design on the card. The designs are either solid, empty, or striped. How many different cards are possible?

Quiz for Lessons 10-5 Through 10-8

✓ 10-5 Experimental Probability

An experiment consists of pushing the random select button on a CD player for a disc with five tracks. Use the results in the table to find the experimental probability of each event.

Outcome	Frequency
Track 1	4
Track 2	6
Track 3	2
Track 4	5
Track 5	3

1. Selecting track 4

2. Selecting track 3

3. Not selecting track 2

4. Selecting an odd numbered track

5. Selecting one of the first 3 tracks

6. Ms. Bleakman checks 32 papers and finds 2 with no name. What is the experimental probability that a paper chosen at random will have no name? Ms. Bleakman has the papers of 176 students. Predict the number of papers she will find with no name.

✓ 10-6 Theoretical Probability

Find the theoretical probability of each outcome.

7. Landing on an odd number when spinning a spinner with 4 equal spaces marked 1, 4, 6, 8

8. Randomly selecting a vowel from all the letters in the word VOWELS

9. Picking a red marble out of a bag with 3 green, 5 blue, 2 red, and 6 yellow marbles

10. The probability of winning a certain prize is 5%. What are the odds of winning the prize?

11. The odds of choosing a winning ticket are 2:8. What is the probability of choosing a winning ticket?

12. The probability of snow is 70%. What are the odds of it not snowing?

✓ 10-7 Independent and Dependent Events

13. A physical education class has 12 boys and 18 girls. Each day, the teacher randomly selects a team captain. Assume that no student is absent. What is the probability that the team captain is a girl two days in a row?

14. After reading to a kindergarten class at the library, Tobey gives out stickers. He has 9 zoo animal stickers and 16 scratch-n-sniff stickers. If Tobey gives the stickers out at random, what is the probability that the first child gets a scratch-n-sniff sticker and the second child gets a zoo animal sticker?

✓ 10-8 Combinations and Permutations

15. Luisa is choosing a line-up of CDs to play from beginning to end at her party. She has 12 CDs from which to choose and time to play only 5. How many ways are there for Luisa to arrange the musical line-up?

16. Gavin is shopping for school clothes with his father. After trying on several shirts, Gavin has identified 8 shirts that he likes. His father says Gavin must narrow it down to 5 shirts. How many ways can Gavin choose 5 shirts from the 8 he likes?

Matrix A

$$\begin{bmatrix} 1 & 8 \\ 6 & -1 \\ 5 & 0 \end{bmatrix}$$ 3 rows

2 columns

Matrix B

$$\begin{bmatrix} 1 & 6 & 5 \\ 8 & -1 & 0 \end{bmatrix}$$ 2 rows

3 columns

EXTENSION Matrices

Objectives
Organize data in a matrix.

Add and subtract matrices and multiply a matrix by a scalar.

Vocabulary
matrix
entry
scalar

A **matrix** is a rectangular arrangement of numbers in rows and columns. Each number in the matrix is called an **entry**.

Matrices are described by the number of rows and columns in the matrix. Matrix A is called a 3 × 2 (3 by 2) matrix because it has 3 rows and 2 columns. Matrix B contains the same data, but it is arranged in 2 rows and 3 columns, so it is called a 2 × 3 (2 by 3) matrix.

EXAMPLE 1 **Organizing Data in a Matrix**

The table shows the number of members in each section of two marching bands. Arrange the data in a matrix. Give the dimensions of the matrix.

Table

	Percussion	Brass	Woodwinds
Northmount High	14	23	16
Western High	19	36	41

Matrix

$$\begin{array}{c} \\ \text{North} \\ \text{West} \end{array} \begin{array}{ccc} P & B & W \\ \end{array}$$
$$\begin{array}{c} \text{North} \\ \text{West} \end{array} \begin{bmatrix} 14 & 23 & 16 \\ 19 & 36 & 41 \end{bmatrix}$$

The matrix has 2 rows and 3 columns, so its dimensions are 2 × 3.

 1. Use the information above to make a 3 × 2 matrix.

If two matrices have the same dimensions, they can be added or subtracted by finding the sum or difference of the corresponding entries.

EXAMPLE 2 **Adding and Subtracting Matrices**

The matrices show the enrollment by grade level at two high schools during the same year.

A Add the two matrices to find the total enrollment of girls in the tenth grade.

Washington
Boys Girls
$$\begin{array}{c} \text{10th} \\ \text{11th} \\ \text{12th} \end{array} \begin{bmatrix} 141 & 148 \\ 132 & 115 \\ 105 & 128 \end{bmatrix}$$

Central
Boys Girls
$$\begin{array}{c} \text{10th} \\ \text{11th} \\ \text{12th} \end{array} \begin{bmatrix} 139 & 127 \\ 141 & 136 \\ 112 & 98 \end{bmatrix}$$

$$\begin{bmatrix} 141 & 148 \\ 132 & 115 \\ 105 & 128 \end{bmatrix} + \begin{bmatrix} 139 & 127 \\ 141 & 136 \\ 112 & 98 \end{bmatrix} = \begin{bmatrix} 141+139 & 148+127 \\ 132+141 & 115+136 \\ 105+112 & 128+98 \end{bmatrix}$$

Total
Boys Girls
$$= \begin{array}{c} \text{10th} \\ \text{11th} \\ \text{12th} \end{array} \begin{bmatrix} 280 & 275 \\ 273 & 251 \\ 217 & 226 \end{bmatrix}$$

The total enrollment of girls in the tenth grade was 275.

770 *Chapter 10 Data Analysis and Probability*

The matrices show the enrollment by grade level at two high schools during the same year.

	Washington	
	Boys	Girls
10th	141	148
11th	141	136
12th	112	128

	Central	
	Boys	Girls
10th	139	127
11th	132	115
12th	105	98

B Subtract the two matrices to find how many more eleventh-grade boys were enrolled at Washington High than at Central High.

$$\begin{bmatrix} 141 & 148 \\ 141 & 136 \\ 112 & 128 \end{bmatrix} - \begin{bmatrix} 139 & 127 \\ 132 & 115 \\ 105 & 98 \end{bmatrix} = \begin{bmatrix} 141-139 & 148-127 \\ 141-132 & 136-115 \\ 112-105 & 128-98 \end{bmatrix} = \begin{matrix} \\ 10\text{th} \\ 11\text{th} \\ 12\text{th} \end{matrix} \overset{\textstyle \begin{matrix} \textbf{Total} \\ \text{Boys} \ \ \text{Girls} \end{matrix}}{\begin{bmatrix} 2 & 21 \\ 9 & 21 \\ 7 & 30 \end{bmatrix}}$$

There were 9 more eleventh-grade boys enrolled at Washington High than at Central High.

Use the information above to answer the following.

2a. What was the total enrollment of boys in the twelfth grade that year?

2b. How many more tenth-grade girls were enrolled at Washington High than at Central High that year?

To multiply a matrix by a number, multiply each entry in the matrix by the number. This kind of multiplication is called *scalar* multiplication. The **scalar** is the number by which the matrix is multiplied.

EXAMPLE 3 **Scalar Multiplication of a Matrix**

The matrix shows the number of field goals (FG) and touchdowns (TD) scored by a football team in each quarter of last week's game. This week they scored twice as many field goals and touchdowns in each quarter of the game. Multiply the matrix by 2 to show the number of scores from this week's game.

	Points per Quarter			
	1st	2nd	3rd	4th
FG	1	0	2	1
TD	0	0	1	1

$$2\begin{bmatrix} 1 & 0 & 2 & 1 \\ 0 & 0 & 1 & 1 \end{bmatrix} = \begin{bmatrix} 2(1) & 2(0) & 2(2) & 2(1) \\ 2(0) & 2(0) & 2(1) & 2(1) \end{bmatrix}$$

Multiply each entry in the matrix by the scalar 2.

	Points per Quarter			
	1st	2nd	3rd	4th
FG	2	0	4	2
TD	0	0	2	2

3. The matrix shows the number of short sleeve and long sleeve T-shirts a store has in its inventory. A second store has 3 times as many shirts in inventory. How many of each shirt and size does the second store have in its inventory?

	Inventory	
	Short sleeve	Long sleeve
Small	42	52
Medium	76	43
Large	19	26

Arrange the data in each table in a matrix.

1.

Polyhedra			
	Faces	Vertices	Edges
Tetrahedron	4	4	6
Cube	6	8	12
Octahedron	8	6	12
Icosahedron	20	12	30

2.

Tourism in Burma, 1998–99	
	Number of Visitors
From Europe	52,790
From N. America	13,041
From Asia	126,441
From Africa	354

3.

Batting Statistics		
	At Bats	Hits
Johnson	69	22
Crabtree	108	31
Aguirre	47	13

4.

Video Inventory			
	Comedy	Drama	Horror
New Releases	16	19	8
Weekly Rentals	57	62	39

Give the dimensions of each matrix.

5. $\begin{bmatrix} -6 \end{bmatrix}$

6. $\begin{bmatrix} -1 & 0 \\ 0 & -1 \end{bmatrix}$

7. $\begin{bmatrix} 9 & 11 & 7 & 6 \\ 2 & -3 & 4 & 6 \end{bmatrix}$

8. $\begin{bmatrix} 0 \\ 15 \\ 22 \end{bmatrix}$

9. $\begin{bmatrix} 2 & 1 & 1 \\ 1 & 2 & 1 \\ 1 & 1 & 2 \end{bmatrix}$

10. Write About It The matrices show the revenue and expenses, in millions of dollars, generated by the three different products that a company sells during two months of the year. Explain how to find the company's total profit for each of the products for those two months. (*Hint:* Profit is revenue minus expenses.)

$$\begin{array}{c} \textbf{Revenue} \\ \begin{array}{ccc} \text{A} & \text{B} & \text{C} \end{array} \\ \begin{array}{c} \text{Month 1} \\ \text{Month 2} \end{array} \begin{bmatrix} 2.3 & 0.7 & 3.0 \\ 2.1 & 1.1 & 2.8 \end{bmatrix} \end{array} \qquad \begin{array}{c} \textbf{Expenses} \\ \begin{array}{ccc} \text{A} & \text{B} & \text{C} \end{array} \\ \begin{array}{c} \text{Month 1} \\ \text{Month 2} \end{array} \begin{bmatrix} 1.8 & 1.6 & 2.1 \\ 1.9 & 1.2 & 2.0 \end{bmatrix} \end{array}$$

Add or subtract.

11. $\begin{bmatrix} -1 & 4 \\ -3 & 6 \end{bmatrix} + \begin{bmatrix} 4 & 6 \\ 2 & -4 \end{bmatrix}$

12. $\begin{bmatrix} 5 & 7 & 3 \\ -4 & 6 & -2 \end{bmatrix} - \begin{bmatrix} 9 & 19 & 6 \\ -3 & 7 & 2 \end{bmatrix}$

13. $\begin{bmatrix} 1.4 \\ -0.6 \end{bmatrix} - \begin{bmatrix} 2.8 \\ -1.3 \end{bmatrix}$

14. $\begin{bmatrix} \frac{3}{5} & \frac{1}{3} & \frac{4}{5} \end{bmatrix} - \begin{bmatrix} \frac{1}{5} & \frac{5}{6} & \frac{3}{10} \end{bmatrix}$

15. Hiking The matrix shows the number of miles hiked on each day of a three-day hiking trip.

a. Use scalar multiplication to convert the distances to kilometers. Write your answer as a matrix. (*Hint:* A mile is about 1.6 kilometers.)

b. What is the total length of the hiking trip in kilometers?

$$\begin{array}{c} \text{Miles} \\ \begin{array}{c} \text{Day 1} \\ \text{Day 2} \\ \text{Day 3} \end{array} \begin{bmatrix} 10.2 \\ 18.6 \\ 4.3 \end{bmatrix} \end{array}$$

Multiply.

16. $6 \begin{bmatrix} 3 & 2 \\ -2 & -9 \end{bmatrix}$

17. $-4 \begin{bmatrix} 1 & 0 & -4 \\ 3 & -3 & 5 \\ 0 & 6 & -1 \end{bmatrix}$

18. $2.7 \begin{bmatrix} 1.9 & 2.7 \\ -0.8 & -3.6 \\ 1.4 & 4.2 \end{bmatrix}$

19. $-0.6 \begin{bmatrix} 8.2 & 10 & -2.8 \end{bmatrix}$

20. $\frac{2}{3} \begin{bmatrix} \frac{1}{4} & -6 \\ -4 & \frac{3}{2} \end{bmatrix}$

21. $-2\frac{1}{2} \begin{bmatrix} -5 & 3 & \frac{4}{5} \\ \frac{1}{5} & -4 & 2 \end{bmatrix}$

22. Entertainment Two teams are competing in a scavenger hunt. Each item on the list is worth 1, 5, or 10 points. The matrix shows the number of items of each point value that was found by the two teams.

	Red team	Blue team
1-point	22	7
5-point	13	18
10-point	4	6

a. How many items did the red team find?

b. How many total points were scored by the red team?

c. How many items did the blue team find?

d. How many total points were scored by the blue team?

e. What is the total number of 5-point items found by the two teams?

f. How many more 1-point items did the red team find than the blue team?

23. Technology Computer animation programs store data in matrices. The data may describe how a figure moves across the screen. Matrix *A* represents the coordinates of the vertices of a polygon. Matrices *E* and *F* represent translations of the polygon.

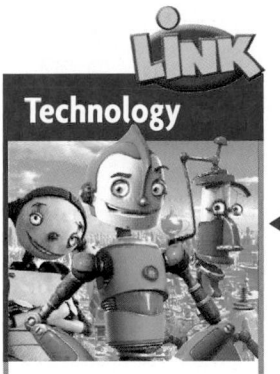

Matrix *A*		Matrix *E*		Matrix *F*	
x	*y*	*x*	*y*	*x*	*y*
0	0	0	3	−2	0
4	1	0	3	−2	0
2	5	0	3	−2	0
−2	3	0	3	−2	0

a. Graph the ordered pairs given by matrix *A* and connect them in the order they are listed. Connect the last point to the first point.

b. Add matrices *A* and *E* and graph the new ordered pairs. Connect the points as in part **a** and describe how the graph is different from part **a**.

c. Subtract matrix *F* from matrix *A* and graph the new ordered pairs. Connect the points and describe how the graph is different from part **a**.

d. Multiply matrix *A* by 2 and graph the new ordered pairs. Connect the points and describe how the graph is different from part **a**.

e. Add matrices *A* and *F*, and then multiply the result by $\frac{1}{2}$. Graph the new ordered pairs and connect the points. Describe how the graph is different from part **a**.

f. **Challenge** Use the following information to write matrix *G*:
Matrices *A* and *G* are added and the new ordered pairs are graphed. The points are connected as in part **a**. The graph looks like the graph from part **a** has been shifted down 2 units and to the right 3 units.

Study Guide: Review

Vocabulary

Complete the sentences below with vocabulary words from the list above.

1. A(n) ____?____ is one possible result of an experiment.

2. The ____?____ is the difference between the third and first quartiles.

3. Two events are ____?____ if the occurrence of one event does not affect the probability of the other.

10-1 Organizing and Displaying Data (*pp. 700–708*)

EXAMPLE

The circle graph shows the post-graduation plans for a high school's 500 graduating seniors.

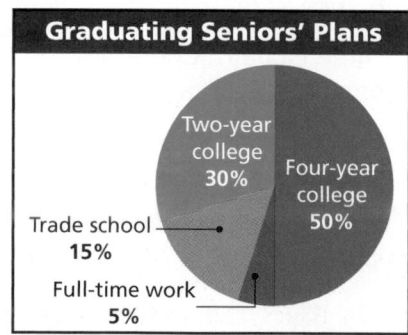

■ How many seniors plan to attend a four-year college?
50% of 500   *Find the percentage.*
$0.50 \times 500 = 250$
250 students plan to attend a four-year college.

EXERCISES

Use the double-bar graph for Exercises 4 and 5.

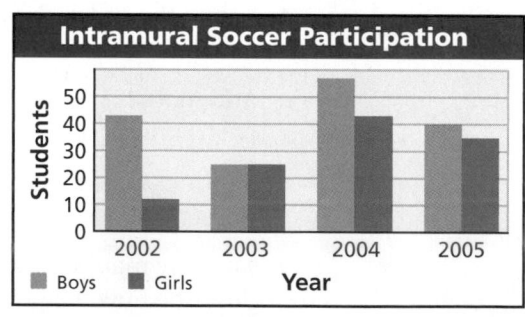

4. In which year did the same number of boys and girls participate?

5. How many more boys than girls participated during 2004?

10-2 Frequency and Histograms (pp. 709–715)

EXAMPLE

- The lives (in hours) of each light bulb in a test are given below. Use the data to make a frequency table and a histogram.

  22, 28, 25, 21, 19, 21, 25,
  21, 22, 18, 20, 29, 25, 26

  Identify the least and greatest values. Divide the data into equal intervals.

Light Bulb Life (h)	
Life	Frequency
18–20	3
21–23	5
24–26	4
27–29	2

  Draw a bar for the number of hours in each interval. The bars touch, but do not overlap.

EXERCISES

6. The weights of packages shipped by an online retailer are given below. Use the data to make a stem-and-leaf plot.

Package Weight (lb)										
14	9	22	24	7	1	19	22	28	18	12

7. The numbers of people who attended two different plays are shown in the table below. Make a back-to-back stem-and-leaf plot.

Play Attendance	
Comedy Camp	Days and Days
104 62 83 102	103 105 80 135
104 120 81	109 128 82
126 122	132 139

8. The capacities of the gas tanks on several new vehicles are shown below. Use the data to make a frequency table with intervals.

Gas Tank Capacity (gal)										
15	12	12	15	18	26	25	12	15	18	11
10	12	16	15	16	18	25	21	18	20	21

9. Use your frequency table from Exercise 9 to make a histogram.

10-3 Data Distributions (pp. 716–723)

EXAMPLE

- Consider the following ages of the winners of an art contest: 13, 15, 14, 18, 12, 10, 11, 13. Find the mean and mode of the data.

  mean:

  $$\frac{10 + 11 + 12 + 13 + 13 + 14 + 15 + 18}{8}$$

  $$= \frac{106}{8}$$

  $$= 13.25$$

  mode: 13   *13 occurs most often.*

EXERCISES

Find the mean, median, mode, and range of each data set.

10. Years of playing experience of the members of a musical ensemble:

    5, 14, 25, 7, 8, 10, 12, 33, 12

Herman has five pairs of cowboy boots. The prices were $120, $137, $120, $145, and $482.
mean: $200.80   median: $137   mode: $120

11. Which value best describes the price Herman paid? Explain.

Use the data to make a box-and-whisker plot.

12. 25, 28, 2, 24, 28, 21, 18, 29, 31, 12, 6, 19, 27, 3

10-4 Misleading Graphs and Statistics (pp. 726–731)

EXAMPLE

- Explain why the graph is misleading.

The vertical axis begins at 71. This exaggerates the difference in the heights of the bars.

EXERCISES

The graph shows the cost of admission to an amusement park over 20 years.

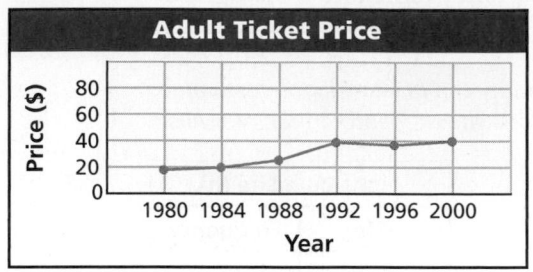

13. Explain why the graph is misleading.

14. What might someone believe because of the graph?

10-5 Experimental Probability (pp. 737–742)

EXAMPLES

The manager of a photo processing lab inspects 500 photos and finds that 4 have flaws.

- What is the experimental probability that a photo is flawed?

$$\frac{\text{number of times the event occurs}}{\text{number of trials}} = \frac{4}{500} = 0.8\%$$

- In one month, the lab processes 13,000 photos. Predict the number that are likely to be flawed.
  $0.008 \cdot 13,000 = 104$ *Find 0.8% of 13,000.*
  104 photos are likely to be flawed.

EXERCISES

A manufacturer inspects 800 batteries and finds that 796 have no defects.

15. What is the experimental probability that a battery chosen at random has no defects?

16. There are 25,000 batteries in storage. How many batteries are likely to have no defects?

17. Another storage area holds 50,000 batteries. How many batteries are likely to have a defect?

10-6 Theoretical Probability (pp. 744–749)

EXAMPLE

- A jar contains red, green, brown, and blue marbles. The probability of choosing red is 0.30, of choosing green is 0.20, and of choosing brown is 0.25. Find the probability of choosing blue.

$$P(\text{blue}) + P(\text{not blue}) = 1$$
$$P(\text{blue}) + P(\text{red, green, or brown}) = 1$$
$$P(\text{blue}) + (0.30 + 0.20 + 0.25) = 1$$
$$P(\text{blue}) + 0.75 = 1$$
$$P(\text{blue}) = 0.25$$

EXERCISES

Find the theoretical probability of each outcome.

18. Rolling a number less than 4 on a standard number cube

19. Randomly selecting a month that starts with "J" from all month names

20. Randomly selecting a vowel from the letters in EQUATION

10-7 Independent and Dependent Events (pp. 750–757)

EXAMPLES

A hardware store shelf holds 12 cans of red paint, 4 cans of yellow paint, and 6 cans of black paint.

■ Syd selects one can at random and replaces it. Then she selects another can at random. What is the probability that Syd selects a red can and then a yellow can?

$P(\text{red, yellow}) = P(\text{red}) \cdot P(\text{yellow})$

$= \dfrac{12}{22} \cdot \dfrac{4}{22}$ *Independent events*

$= \dfrac{48}{484} = \dfrac{12}{121}$

■ Gene selects one can at random and then selects another can at random from the remaining cans. What is the probability that Gene selects two cans of black paint?

$P(\text{black, black}) = P(\text{black}) \cdot P(\text{black after black})$

$= \dfrac{6}{22} \cdot \dfrac{5}{21}$ *Dependent events*

$= \dfrac{30}{462} = \dfrac{5}{77}$

EXERCISES

Tell whether each set of events is independent or dependent. Explain your answers.

21. A computer generates a random number and then generates another random number.

22. You roll two number cubes. One is a 6 and the other is a 1.

23. Two audience members are called to the stage.

A lottery machine contains different-colored balls. There are 64 green, 128 yellow, 1 golden, and 3 silver balls. Find the probability of each event.

24. A yellow ball is drawn and set aside. Then a green ball is drawn.

25. A golden ball is drawn and set aside. Then another golden ball is drawn.

26. A green ball is drawn and replaced. Then another green ball is drawn.

10-8 Combinations and Permutations (pp. 760–767)

EXAMPLES

A sporting goods store carries sweatshirts for 8 local high school football teams.

■ How many different packages of 4 different high school sweatshirts are possible?
Use a combination. The order does not matter.

$_8C_4 = \dfrac{8!}{4!(8-4)!} = \dfrac{8!}{4!(4)!}$

$= \dfrac{8 \cdot 7 \cdot 6 \cdot 5 \cdot \cancel{4} \cdot \cancel{3} \cdot \cancel{2} \cdot \cancel{1}}{(4 \cdot 3 \cdot 2 \cdot 1)(\cancel{4} \cdot \cancel{3} \cdot \cancel{2} \cdot \cancel{1})} = \dfrac{1680}{24} = 70$

Seventy different packages are possible.

■ Three different high school sweatshirts will be hung in a row. How many displays are possible?
Use a permutation. The order matters.

$_8P_3 = \dfrac{8!}{(8-3)!} = \dfrac{8!}{5!} =$

$\dfrac{8 \cdot 7 \cdot 6 \cdot \cancel{5} \cdot \cancel{4} \cdot \cancel{3} \cdot \cancel{2} \cdot \cancel{1}}{\cancel{5} \cdot \cancel{4} \cdot \cancel{3} \cdot \cancel{2} \cdot \cancel{1}} = 336$

There are 336 different possible displays.

EXERCISES

27. A catering hall offers 4 different plates, 3 different silverware patterns, and 5 different types of glassware. How many place settings of one plate, one silverware pattern, and one type of glassware are possible?

Tell whether each situation involves combinations or permutations. Then give the number of possible outcomes.

28. Shelly is making up a 7-digit phone number to use in a play. She can choose any digit from 0–9 but does not want to repeat a number. How many different phone numbers are possible?

29. A restaurant offers 12 different appetizers. How many ways can a group of friends share 3 different appetizers?

30. A group of 15 friends is at an amusement park. In how many ways can a group be chosen to ride in a four-person gondola?

CHAPTER TEST

1. The table shows the population of Oakville. Use the data to make a graph. Explain why you chose that type of graph.

2. Which ten-year period saw the greatest change in population?

3. Describe the trend in Oakville's population.

Population of Oakville	
Year	Population
1970	20,851
1980	14,229
1990	11,198
2000	9,579

The high temperatures in degrees Fahrenheit for two weeks are given:
64, 66, 63, 58, 59, 55, 51, 54, 61, 62, 68, 70, 63, 63.

4. Use the data to make a stem-and-leaf plot.

5. Use the data to make a frequency table with intervals.

6. Use your frequency table from Problem 5 to make a histogram.

The lengths of statements during a town council meeting are given.

7. Find the mean, median, mode, and range of the data.

8. Use the data to make a box-and-whisker plot.

Length of Statement (min)						
6	25	12	14	2	13	38
22	21	14	3	8	5	17

A manufacturer inspects 500 watches and finds that 498 have no defects.

9. What is the experimental probability that a watch chosen at random has no defects?

10. There are 30,000 watches in a warehouse. Predict the number of watches that are likely to have no defects.

The graph shows how the money raised by a charity is spent.

11. Explain why the graph is misleading.

12. What might someone believe because of the graph?

13. Who might want to use this graph?

14. A bag contains 12 cards, each with a different month of the year printed on it. A card is selected at random. What is the probability that the month begins with *A*?

15. The odds of spinning red on a spinner are 2 : 7. What is the probability of not spinning red?

16. A bag has 14 red marbles and 10 white marbles. Rosa randomly picks two marbles from the bag, one at a time. What is the probability that Rosa picks two white marbles?

Tell whether each situation involves combinations or permutations. Then give the number of possible outcomes.

17. Sara is ordering a deli platter for a party. The deli offers 9 kinds of meats. Sara must select 4 kinds for the platter. How many different platters can Sara choose?

18. Armando has 12 antique books. He will select 3 books and put one up for auction each day for three days. How many different ways can he do this?

COLLEGE ENTRANCE EXAM PRACTICE

FOCUS ON SAT MATHEMATICS SUBJECT TEST

There are two levels of SAT Subject Tests: Mathematics Level 1 and Mathematics Level 2. Each test has 50 multiple-choice questions. The content of each test is very different. Getting a high score on one test does not mean you will get a high score on the other test.

You can write all over the test book to sketch figures, do scratch work, or cross out incorrect answers to help you eliminate choices. Remember to mark your final answer on the answer sheet because the test book is not used for scoring.

You may want to time yourself as you take this practice test. It should take you about 6 minutes to complete.

---

1. Which of the following represents the number of ways 6 committee members can be selected from a group of 25 teachers?

    (A) $_6C_{25}$

    (B) $_{19}C_6$

    (C) $_{25}C_6$

    (D) $_6P_{25}$

    (E) $_{25}P_6$

---

2. Your friend randomly selects 2 movies from your collection to borrow. Your collection includes 9 comedies, 5 dramas, 3 mysteries, 1 musical, and 2 horror movies. What is the probability that both movies are comedies?

    (A) $\dfrac{1}{36}$

    (B) $\dfrac{18}{95}$

    (C) $\dfrac{81}{400}$

    (D) $\dfrac{2}{9}$

    (E) $\dfrac{331}{380}$

---

3. A student's test scores are 88, 87, 82, 95, and 89. If the student needs an average test score of at least 90 to obtain a grade of A, what must the minimum score be on the last test of the semester?

    (A) 88

    (B) 88.2

    (C) 91

    (D) 99

    (E) 100

---

4. What is the probability of not getting a 2 on the spinner?

    (A) 0.10

    (B) 0.25

    (C) 0.50

    (D) 0.75

    (E) 1

---

5. What is the value of $\dfrac{(n+1)!}{(n-1)!}$?

    (A) $n^2 + n$

    (B) $2n + 1$

    (C) $n!$

    (D) $n^2 - 1$

    (E) -1

TEST TACKLER

Standardized Test Strategies

Any Question Type: Spatial Reasoning

Some test questions include a three-dimensional figure. You must use spatial reasoning to correctly interpret the figure.

EXAMPLE 1

Which of the following shows the top view of the solid figure?

Ⓐ   Ⓑ   Ⓒ   Ⓓ

Notice that the isometric drawing shows three sides of the figure: the top, front, and right side. Use the isometric drawing to make a foundation plan of the figure.

Count the number of cubes at the widest part of the figure and at the longest part of the figure.

The widest part is 3 cubes across.
The longest part is 4 cubes deep.

Draw a 3-by-4 grid.

Each cube on the bottom level of the figure corresponds to a square on the grid.

Start at the front of the figure. Shade in each square of the grid that corresponds to a cube on the bottom level of the figure.

Using the foundation plan, you can see that choice B shows the top view of the solid.

Imagine that you are stacking blocks to help you to visualize the solid figure. Each square shown in the drawing represents a face of one block.

Read each test item and answer the questions that follow.

Item A
Multiple Choice Which solid is represented by these top, side, and front views?

Top   Front   Right side

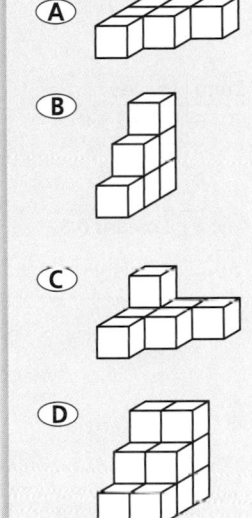

Ⓐ

Ⓑ

Ⓒ

Ⓓ

1. How many cubes can you see if you are looking down on the figure? How do you know?

2. How many cubes can you see if you are looking at the front of the figure? How do you know?

3. How many cubes high is the highest stack of the figure? Explain how you know.

4. Using your answers from Problems 1–3, what is the correct answer choice?

Item B
Short Response The drawing shows a foundation plan of a solid figure made of stacked cubes. The numbers in the squares identify the number of cubes in each stack. Draw a three-dimensional view of this solid figure.

2	4	6
2	2	3
2	1	1

5. Draw the top view of the figure.

6. If you were to look at the figure from the right or from the front, how many cubes high is the highest stack? Explain how you know.

7. A student drew this figure as his response. Do you agree that this is the correct drawing? If so, explain how you know. If not, what did the student do wrong?

Item C
Short Response Draw the top view and front view of the solid figure.

8. If you look down on the figure, how many cubes do you see?

9. Create a base plan or foundation plan for the figure.

10. Nolan drew his version of the top view of the figure. Is he correct? If not, show how you would change his drawing so that it is correct.

11. If you look at the figure from the front, how tall is the highest stack of cubes and how short is the shortest stack of cubes?

12. Draw the front view of the figure.

STANDARDIZED TEST PREP

CUMULATIVE ASSESSMENT, CHAPTERS 1–10

Multiple Choice

1. Josephine has 9 cousins. Her friend Summer has *s* more cousins. Which expression can be used to show the number of cousins Summer has?

Ⓐ $9 \div s$ Ⓒ $9 + s$

Ⓑ $9s$ Ⓓ $9 - s$

2. A negative number raised to an exponent is positive. Which of the following is NOT true?

Ⓕ The number could be even.

Ⓖ The number could be odd.

Ⓗ The exponent could be even.

Ⓙ The exponent could be odd.

3. A computer game normally sells for $40. Niko bought it when it went on sale for 25% off. The sales tax was 6%. How much did Niko pay for the game?

Ⓐ $10.60   Ⓒ $31.80

Ⓑ $12.40   Ⓓ $32.40

4. The graph shows the profit made at a family yard sale that lasted 8 hours. Between which hours did the profit increase at the slowest rate?

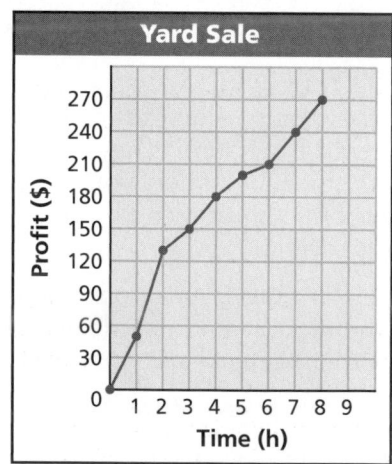

Ⓕ 0–1   Ⓗ 5–6

Ⓖ 1–2   Ⓙ 7–8

5. Which of the following is one of the five values needed to make a box-and-whisker plot?

Ⓐ Mean   Ⓒ Mode

Ⓑ Median   Ⓓ Average

6. Which value is a solution of $2(1 - x) < 12$?

Ⓕ −7   Ⓗ −5

Ⓖ −6   Ⓙ −4

7. What is the median of the data presented in this stem-and-leaf plot?

Stem	Leaves
6	0 2 2 2 5 8
7	3 4 4 6 7
8	2 5 8 9

Key: 8 | 2 means 0.82

Ⓐ 0.62

Ⓑ 0.74

Ⓒ 6.2

Ⓓ 7.4

8. Which of the following does NOT represent a function?

Ⓕ $\{(-4, 3), (-2, 1), (-2, -1), (-4, -3)\}$

Ⓖ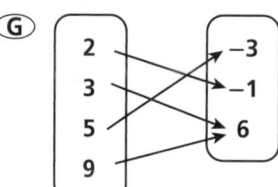

Ⓗ

x	−4	−3	−2	−1	0	1
y	4	3	2	1	0	−1

Ⓙ

If you are allowed to write in your test booklet, you may want to add additional information to a given diagram. Be sure to mark your answer on the answer sheet since your marks on the test booklet will not be graded.

9. Which of these equations describes a line parallel to $x + 2y = 6$?

 (A) $y = \frac{1}{2}x$ (C) $y = -2x + 6$

 (B) $y = -\frac{1}{2}x + 4$ (D) $y = 2x + 3$

10. What is the probability that the spinner will NOT land on white?

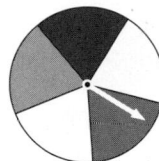

 (F) 20%

 (G) 40%

 (H) 50%

 (J) 60%

11. A CD-ROM is storing 4.2×10^8 bytes of information. What is this number in standard form?

 (A) 0.0000000042

 (B) 0.00000042

 (C) 420,000,000

 (D) 4,200,000,000

12. Which is a factor of $4x^2 + 24x + 36$?

 (F) $x + 12$

 (G) $2x + 6$

 (H) $2x + 18$

 (J) $4x + 18$

Gridded Response

13. Yvette is choosing between two stores to get her family pictures taken. Say Cheese charges a $20 sitting fee and $14 per sheet of pictures. Picture Me charges a $12 sitting fee and $18 per sheet of pictures. For how many sheets will the total cost be the same at both stores?

14. Brian plays basketball. In the past, he has made 4 out of every 5 free throws. What is the probability, as a decimal, that Brian will make the next two free throws?

15. A password for a security system must consist of a letter followed by two digits. How many possible passwords are there?

Short Response

16. An experiment consists of tossing 3 coins at the same time.

 a. Identify the sample space.

 b. What is the probability of tossing 2 tails and 1 head?

 c. Which is more likely to occur: tossing exactly 1 tail or tossing at least 2 heads? Explain.

17. If 8% of a number is 4, what is 12% of the number? Explain your reasoning.

18. Nat surveyed 30 twelfth-grade students and found that 27 of them were in favor of allowing seniors to leave campus for lunch. As a result, Nat reported that "90% of the student body supports off-campus lunch privileges for seniors." Was Nat's statistic misleading? Explain.

19. A service technician is scheduling house calls to make repairs. He has 9 time slots in his work day. He has 7 house calls to make. How many different schedules of his day are possible? Show and explain your work.

20. For her scrapbook page, Denise has 5 different background colors, 4 different framing styles, and 2 different accents. How many possible scrapbook layouts can Denise create with the available materials? Show and explain your work.

Extended Response

21. The ages of the first 15 people to enter a community center for bingo one evening are 77, 85, 76, 73, 69, 70, 84, 82, 76, 74, 89, 83, 68, 91, and 88.

 a. Find the mean, median, mode, and range of the data.

 b. Create a box-and-whisker plot of the data.

 c. The sixteenth person to enter the center is 39 years old. Calculate the mean, median, mode, and range of the data with the 16 people.

 d. Create a box-and-whisker plot with the 16 people.

 e. When the sixteenth person was added, which measure of central tendency changed the most? Which measure changed the least? Explain.

 f. How did the addition of the sixteenth person affect the box-and-whisker plot?

Real-World CONNECTIONS

Pennsylvania

Shartlesville

Pittsburgh

⭐ Roadside America Indoor Miniature Village

The Roadside America Indoor Miniature Village in Shartlesville, Pennsylvania, is sometimes referred to as the World's Greatest Indoor Miniature Village. The exhibit uses miniature buildings and realistic landscaping to show what life was like in the 1700s, 1800s, and 1900s. Laurence Gieringer built the village using a $\frac{3}{8}$-inch-to-1-foot scale.

Choose one or more strategies to solve each problem.

1. Suppose a model of a building is made of 180 one-inch cubes. The area of the base of the model is 15 in². How tall is the miniature building? Using a scale of $\frac{3}{8}$ inch to 1 foot, how tall is the actual building?

2. There are about 4000 miniature people in the village. This number is about 100 more than thirteen times the number of buildings in the village. Estimate the number of miniature buildings in the village.

For 3, use the map.

3. It might be helpful to use a coordinate grid when designing a miniature village. Suppose you decide to arrange it as shown. About how far is it from the school to the post office along a straight line?

1 unit : 1 mile

⭐ The National Aviary

The National Aviary is located on the north side of Pittsburgh. It is America's only independent indoor nonprofit bird zoo. The aviary is home to more than 600 birds of over 200 species, many of which are threatened or endangered in the wild. Visitors can see birds from almost every continent. Visitors can even feed the birds flying around in a 200,000-cubic-foot indoor rainforest where it actually rains every 15 minutes.

Choose one or more strategies to solve each problem.

For 1 and 2, use the circle graph.

1. The red-crowned crane is the second rarest crane species. The total population of red-crowned cranes in the wild is about 2000 birds. The circle graph shows the approximate percent of this population in four countries where they are found. About how many red-crowned cranes live in Japan?

2. About how many of the total population of red-crowned cranes living in the wild do not live in North Korea or South Korea?

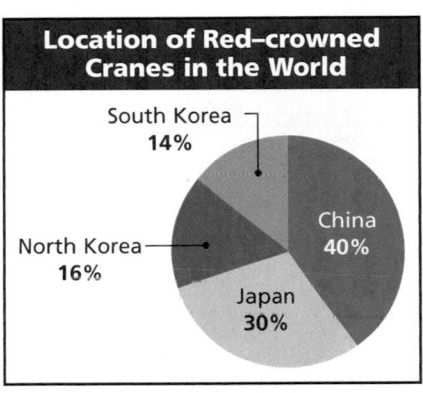

Location of Red–crowned Cranes in the World

South Korea 14%
China 40%
North Korea 16%
Japan 30%

3. One exhibit at the aviary contains bald eagles. An eagle can see a rabbit from about one mile away. The average person must be 1650 feet away to see the same rabbit. Do humans or eagles see farther? How many times as far?

4. It is estimated that only one of every 18 attempts by an eagle to hunt for food is successful. Because of this, eagles use a great deal of energy hunting and have to spend a lot of time resting quietly. According to this information, if you observe an eagle diving for a fish, what is the probability that he is not going to catch the fish on the first try?

11A Exponential Functions

11B Radical Functions and Equations

Chapter

- Graph and use exponential functions to model real-world problems.
- Simplify radical expressions.
- Use radical equations to solve real-world problems.

Population Explosion

The concepts in this chapter are used to model many real-world phenomena, such as changes in wildlife populations.

go.hrw.com

Chapter Project Online

KEYWORD: MA7 ChProj

ARE YOU READY?

✓ Vocabulary

Match each term on the left with a definition on the right.

1. like terms
2. square root
3. domain
4. perfect square
5. exponent

A. the set of second elements of a relation

B. terms that contain the same variables raised to the same powers

C. the set of first elements of a relation

D. a number that tells how many times a base is used as a factor

E. a number whose positive square root is a whole number

F. one of two equal factors of a number

✓ Evaluate Powers

Find the value of each expression.

6. 2^4
7. 5^0
8. $7 \cdot 3^2$
9. $3 \cdot 5^3$
10. 3^5
11. $-6^2 + 8^1$
12. $40 \cdot 2^3$
13. $7^2 \cdot 3^1$

✓ Graph Functions

Graph each function.

14. $y = 8$
15. $y = x + 3$
16. $y = x^2 - 4$
17. $y = x^2 + 2$

✓ Fractions, Decimals, and Percents

Write each percent as a decimal.

18. 50%
19. 25%
20. 15.2%
21. 200%
22. 1.9%
23. 0.3%
24. 0.1%
25. 1.04%

✓ Squares and Square Roots

Find each square root.

26. $\sqrt{36}$
27. $\sqrt{81}$
28. $\sqrt{25}$
29. $\sqrt{64}$

✓ Pythagorean Theorem

Find the length of the hypotenuse in each right triangle.

30.
3 cm, 4 cm

31.
5 in., 12 in.

32.
6 ft, 8 ft

✓ Multiply Monomials and Polynomials

Multiply.

33. $5(2m - 3)$
34. $3x(8x + 9)$
35. $2t(3t - 1)$
36. $4r(4r - 5)$

Study Guide: Preview

Where You've Been

Previously, you
- identified and extended arithmetic sequences.
- identified and graphed linear functions and quadratic functions.
- solved linear and quadratic equations.

In This Chapter

You will study
- another type of sequence—geometric sequences.
- two more types of functions—exponential functions and square-root functions.
- radical equations.

Where You're Going

You can use the skills in this chapter
- to analyze more complicated functions in later math courses, such as Calculus.
- to explore exponential growth and decay models that are used in science.
- to make informed decisions about finances.

Key Vocabulary/Vocabulario

common ratio	razón común
compound interest	interés compuesto
exponential decay	decrecimiento exponencial
exponential function	función exponencial
exponential growth	crecimiento exponencial
extraneous solution	solución extraña
geometric sequence	sucesión geométrica
like radicals	radicales semejantes
radical equation	ecuación radical
radical expression	expresión radical
radicand	radicando
square-root function	función de raíz cuadrada

Vocabulary Connections

To become familiar with some of the vocabulary terms in the chapter, consider the following. You may refer to the chapter, the glossary, or a dictionary if you like.

1. What does it mean when several items have something "in common"? What is a ratio? What do you think **common ratio** means?

2. In the division problem $2\overline{)50}$ with quotient 25, the *dividend* is 50. If a *radicand* is similar to a dividend, then what is the **radicand** in $\sqrt{16} = 4$?

3. A square-root sign is also known as a *radical*. Use this knowledge to define **radical expression** and **radical equation**.

4. The root word of *extraneous* is *extra*. *Extraneous* means *irrelevant* or *unrelated*. Use this information to define **extraneous solution**.

Study Strategy: Remember Formulas

In math, there are many formulas, properties, and rules that you should commit to memory.

To memorize a formula, create flash cards. Write the name of the formula on one side of a card. Write the formula on the other side of the card. You might also include a diagram or an example if helpful. Study your flash cards on a regular basis.

Sample Flash Card

Front

Back

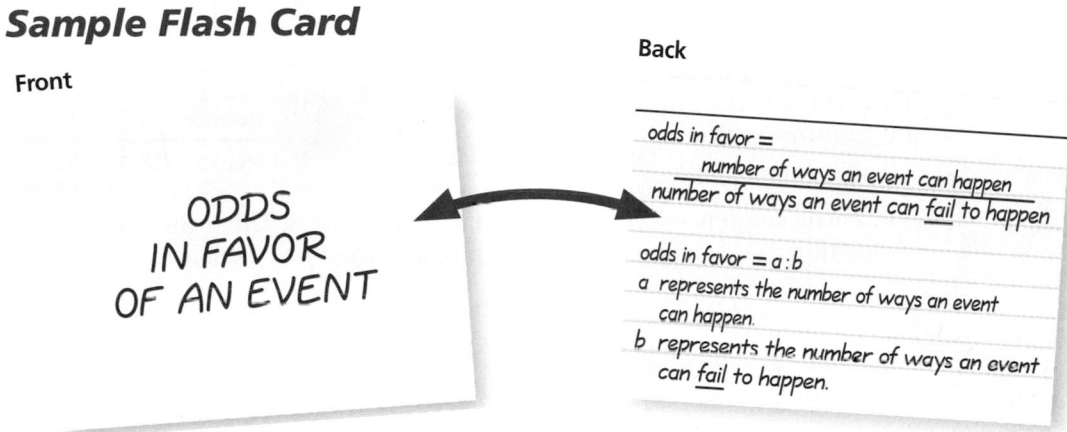

Knowing when and how to apply a mathematical formula is as important as memorizing the formula itself.

To know what formula to apply, read the problem carefully and look for key words.

From Lesson 10-6

> The **probability** of choosing an ace from a deck of cards is $\frac{1}{13}$.
> What are the **odds of choosing an ace**?

The key words have been highlighted. The probability is given, and you are asked to find the odds. You should use the formula for *odds in favor of an event*.

Try This

Read each problem. Then write the formula(s) needed to solve it. What key words helped you identify the formula?

1. A manufacturer inspects 450 computer chips and finds that 22 are defective. What is the experimental probability that a chip chosen at random is defective?

2. The area of a rectangular pool is 120 square feet. The length is 1 foot less than twice the width. What is the perimeter of the pool?

Geometric Sequences

Objectives
Recognize and extend geometric sequences.

Find the *n*th term of a geometric sequence.

Vocabulary
geometric sequence
common ratio

Who uses this?
Bungee jumpers can use geometric sequences to calculate how high they will bounce.

The table shows the heights of a bungee jumper's bounces.

The height of the bounces shown in the table form a *geometric sequence*. In a **geometric sequence**, the ratio of successive terms is the same number *r*, called the **common ratio**.

Bounce	1	2	3
Height (ft)	200	80	32

Writing Math

The variable *a* is often used to represent terms in a sequence. The variable a_4 (read "a sub 4") is the fourth term in a sequence.

Geometric sequences can be thought of as functions. The term number, or position in the sequence, is the input, and the term itself is the output.

$$\begin{array}{cccc} 1 & 2 & 3 & 4 \quad \leftarrow \text{Position} \\ \downarrow & \downarrow & \downarrow & \downarrow \\ 3 & 6 & 12 & 24 \quad \leftarrow \text{Term} \\ a_1 & a_2 & a_3 & a_4 \end{array}$$

To find a term in a geometric sequence, multiply the previous term by *r*.

Finding a Term of a Geometric Sequence

The *n*th term of a geometric sequence with **common ratio** *r* is

$$a_n = a_{n-1}r$$

EXAMPLE 1 **Extending Geometric Sequences**

Find the next three terms in each geometric sequence.

A 1, 3, 9, 27, ...

Step 1 Find the value of *r* by dividing each term by the one before it.

$\frac{3}{1} = 3 \qquad \frac{9}{3} = 3 \qquad \frac{27}{9} = 3 \quad \leftarrow$ The value of *r* is 3.

Step 2 Multiply each term by 3 to find the next three terms.

$\times 3 \qquad \times 3 \qquad \times 3 \qquad a_n = a_{n-1}r$

The next three terms are 81, 243, and 729.

B $-16, 4, -1, \frac{1}{4}, \ldots$

Step 1 Find the value of r by dividing each term by the one before it.

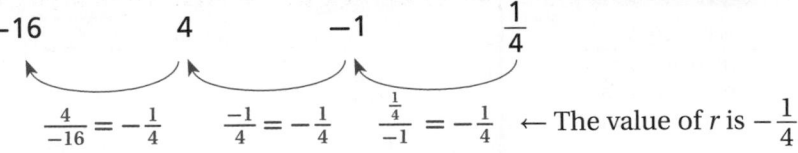

$$\frac{4}{-16} = -\frac{1}{4} \qquad \frac{-1}{4} = -\frac{1}{4} \qquad \frac{\frac{1}{4}}{-1} = -\frac{1}{4} \leftarrow \text{The value of } r \text{ is } -\frac{1}{4}.$$

Step 2 Multiply each term by $-\frac{1}{4}$ to find the next three terms.

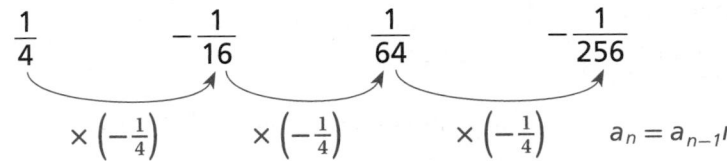

$$\times \left(-\frac{1}{4}\right) \qquad \times \left(-\frac{1}{4}\right) \qquad \times \left(-\frac{1}{4}\right) \qquad a_n = a_{n-1}r$$

The next three terms are $-\frac{1}{16}, \frac{1}{64},$ and $-\frac{1}{256}$.

Find the next three terms in each geometric sequence.

1a. $5, -10, 20, -40, \ldots$ **1b.** $512, 384, 288, \ldots$

To find the output a_n of a geometric sequence when n is a large number, you need an equation, or function rule.

The pattern in the table shows that to get the nth term, multiply the first term by the common ratio raised to the power $n - 1$.

Words	Numbers	Algebra
1st term	3	a_1
2nd term	$3 \cdot 2^1 = 6$	$a_1 \cdot r^1$
3rd term	$3 \cdot 2^2 = 12$	$a_1 \cdot r^2$
4th term	$3 \cdot 2^3 = 24$	$a_1 \cdot r^3$
nth term	$3 \cdot 2^{n-1}$	$a_1 \cdot r^{n-1}$

If the first term of a geometric sequence is a_1, the nth term is a_n, and the common ratio is r, then

$$a_n = a_1 r^{n-1}$$

nth term   1st term   Common ratio

EXAMPLE 2   **Finding the nth Term of a Geometric Sequence**

A The first term of a geometric sequence is 128, and the common ratio is 0.5. What is the 10th term of the sequence?

$a_n = a_1 r^{n-1}$ *Write the formula.*

$a_{10} = 128(0.5)^{10-1}$ *Substitute 128 for a_1, 10 for n, and 0.5 for r.*

$\quad = 128(0.5)^9$ *Simplify the exponent.*

$\quad = 0.25$ *Use a calculator.*

B For a geometric sequence, $a_1 = 8$ and $r = 3$. Find the 5th term of this sequence.

$a_n = a_1 r^{n-1}$ *Write the formula.*

$a_5 = 8(3)^{5-1}$ *Substitute 8 for a_1, 5 for n, and 3 for r.*

$\quad = 8(3)^4$ *Simplify the exponent.*

$\quad = 648$ *Use a calculator.*

C What is the 13th term of the geometric sequence $8, -16, 32, -64, \dots$?

$\dfrac{-16}{8} = -2 \qquad \dfrac{32}{-16} = -2 \qquad \dfrac{-64}{32} = -2 \qquad$ *The value of r is -2.*

$a_n = a_1 r^{n-1}$ *Write the formula.*

$a_{13} = 8(-2)^{13-1}$ *Substitute 8 for a_1, 13 for n, and -2 for r.*

$\quad\; = 8(-2)^{12}$ *Simplify the exponent.*

$\quad\; = 32{,}768$ *Use a calculator.*

 2. What is the 8th term of the sequence $1000, 500, 250, 125, \dots$?

EXAMPLE 3   *Sports Application*

A bungee jumper jumps from a bridge. The diagram shows the bungee jumper's height above the ground at the top of each bounce. The heights form a geometric sequence. What is the bungee jumper's height at the top of the 5th bounce?

First bounce 200 ft

Second bounce 80 ft

Third bounce 32 ft

$200 \qquad\qquad 80 \qquad\qquad 32$

$\dfrac{80}{200} = 0.4 \qquad \dfrac{32}{80} = 0.4$

$a_n = a_1 r^{n-1}$ *Write the formula.*

$a_5 = 200(0.4)^{5-1}$ *Substitute 200 for a_1, 5 for n, and 0.4 for r.*

$\quad = 200(0.4)^4$ *Simplify the exponent.*

$\quad = 5.12$ *Use a calculator.*

The height of the 5th bounce is 5.12 feet.

 3. The table shows a car's value for 3 years after it is purchased. The values form a geometric sequence. How much will the car be worth in the 10th year?

Year	Value ($)
1	10,000
2	8,000
3	6,400

THINK AND DISCUSS

1. How do you determine whether a sequence is geometric?

2. **GET ORGANIZED** Copy and complete the graphic organizer. In each box, write a way to represent the geometric sequence.

Ways to Represent Geometric Sequence 1, 2, 4, 8, …

Table   Formula   Words

go.hrw.com
Homework Help Online
KEYWORD: MA7 11-1
Parent Resources Online
KEYWORD: MA7 Parent

GUIDED PRACTICE

1. **Vocabulary** What is the *common ratio* of a geometric sequence?

SEE EXAMPLE 1 p. 790

Find the next three terms in each geometric sequence.

2. 2, 4, 8, 16, …   **3.** 400, 200, 100, 50, …   **4.** 4, −12, 36, −108, …

SEE EXAMPLE 2 p. 791

5. The first term of a geometric sequence is 1, and the common ratio is 10. What is the 10th term of the sequence?

6. What is the 11th term of the geometric sequence 3, 6, 12, 24, … ?

SEE EXAMPLE 3 p. 792

7. Sports In the NCAA men's basketball tournament, 64 teams compete in round 1. Fewer teams remain in each following round, as shown in the graph, until all but one team have been eliminated. The numbers of teams in each round form a geometric sequence. How many teams compete in round 5?

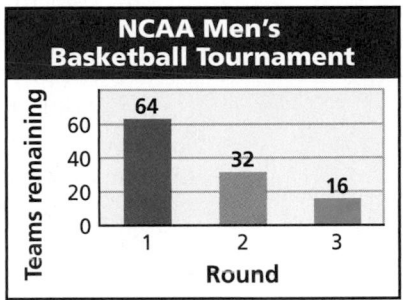

PRACTICE AND PROBLEM SOLVING

Independent Practice

For Exercises	See Example
8–13	1
14–15	2
16	3

Extra Practice
Skills Practice p. S24
Application Practice p. S38

Find the next three terms in each geometric sequence.

8. −2, 10, −50, 250, …   **9.** 32, 48, 72, 108, …   **10.** 625, 500, 400, 320, …

11. 6, 42, 294, …   **12.** 6, −12, 24, −48, …   **13.** $40, 10, \frac{5}{2}, \frac{5}{8}, \dots$

14. The first term of a geometric sequence is 18 and the common ratio is 3.5. What is the 5th term of the sequence?

15. What is the 14th term of the geometric sequence 1000, 100, 10, 1, … ?

16. Physical Science A ball is dropped from a height of 500 meters. The table shows the height of each bounce, and the heights form a geometric sequence. How high does the ball bounce on the 8th bounce? Round your answer to the nearest tenth of a meter.

Bounce	Height (m)
1	400
2	320
3	256

Find the missing term(s) in each geometric sequence.

17. 20, 40, ■, ■, …   **18.** ■, 6, 18, ■, …   **19.** 9, 3, 1, ■, …

20. 3, 12, ■, 192, ■, …   **21.** $7, 1, ■, ■, \frac{1}{343}, \dots$ **22.** $■, 100, 25, ■, \frac{25}{16}, \dots$

23. −3, ■, −12, 24, ■, …   **24.** ■, ■, 1, −3, 9, …   **25.** 1, 17, 289, ■, …

Determine whether each sequence could be geometric. If so, give the common ratio.

26. 2, 10, 50, 250, …   **27.** $15, 5, \frac{5}{3}, \frac{5}{9}, \dots$ **28.** 6, 18, 24, 38, …

29. 9, 3, −1, −5, …   **30.** 7, 21, 63, 189, …   **31.** 4, 1, −2, −4, …

32. **Multi-Step** Billy earns money by mowing lawns for the summer. He offers two payment plans, as shown at right.

a. Do the payments for plan 2 form a geometric sequence? Explain.

b. If you were one of Billy's customers, which plan would you choose? (Assume that the summer is 10 weeks long.) Explain your choice.

33. **Measurement** When you fold a piece of paper in half, the thickness of the folded piece is twice the thickness of the original piece. A piece of copy paper is about 0.1 mm thick.

a. How thick is a piece of copy paper that has been folded in half 7 times?

b. Suppose that you could fold a piece of copy paper in half 12 times. How thick would it be? Write your answer in centimeters.

List the first four terms of each geometric sequence.

34. $a_1 = 3, a_n = 3(2)^{n-1}$

35. $a_1 = -2, a_n = -2(4)^{n-1}$

36. $a_1 = 5, a_n = 5(-2)^{n-1}$

37. $a_1 = 2, a_n = 2(2)^{n-1}$

38. $a_1 = 2, a_n = 2(5)^{n-1}$

39. $a_1 = 12, a_n = 12\left(\frac{1}{4}\right)^{n-1}$

40. **Critical Thinking** What happens to the terms of a geometric sequence when r is doubled? Use an example to support your answer.

41. **Geometry** The steps below describe how to make a geometric figure by repeating the same process over and over on a smaller and smaller scale.

Step 1 (stage 0) Draw a large square.

Step 2 (stage 1) Divide the square into four equal squares.

Step 3 (stage 2) Divide each small square into four equal squares.

Step 4 Repeat Step 3 indefinitely.

a. Draw stages 0, 1, 2, and 3.

b. How many small squares are in each stage? Organize your data relating stage and number of small squares in a table.

c. Does the data in part **b** form a geometric sequence? Explain.

d. Write a rule to find the number of small squares in stage n.

 42. **Write About It** Write a series of steps for finding the nth term of a geometric sequence when you are given the first several terms.

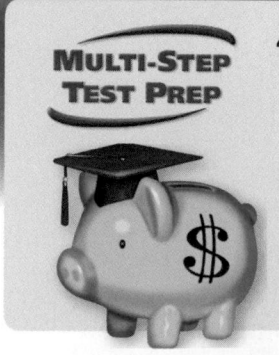

MULTI-STEP TEST PREP

43. This problem will prepare you for the Multi-Step Test Prep on page 820.

a. Three years ago, the annual tuition at a university was $3000. The following year, the tuition was $3300, and last year, the tuition was $3630. If the tuition has continued to grow in the same manner, what is the tuition this year? What do you expect it to be next year?

b. What is the common ratio?

c. What would you predict the tuition was 4 years ago? How did you find that value?

44. Which of the following is a geometric sequence?

  Ⓐ $\dfrac{1}{2}$, 1, $\dfrac{3}{2}$, 2, …   Ⓒ 3, 8, 13, 18, …

  Ⓑ −2, −6, −10, −14, …   Ⓓ 5, 10, 20, 40, …

45. Which equation represents the nth term in the geometric sequence 2, −8, 32, −128, …?

  Ⓕ $a_n = (-4)^n$ Ⓖ $a_n = (-4)^{n-1}$ Ⓗ $a_n = 2(-4)^n$ Ⓙ $a_n = 2(-4)^{n-1}$

46. The frequency of a musical note, measured in hertz (Hz), is called its pitch. The pitches of the A keys on a piano form a geometric sequence, as shown.

           A₁   A₂   A₃   A₄

       55 Hz   110 Hz   220 Hz   440 Hz

What is the frequency of A₇?

  Ⓐ 880 Hz   Ⓑ 1760 Hz   Ⓒ 3520 Hz   Ⓓ 7040 Hz

CHALLENGE AND EXTEND

Find the next three terms in each geometric sequence.

47. $x, x^2, x^3, \ldots$ **48.** $2x^2, 6x^3, 18x^4, \ldots$ **49.** $\dfrac{1}{y^3}, \dfrac{1}{y^2}, \dfrac{1}{y}, \ldots$ **50.** $\dfrac{1}{(x+1)^2}, \dfrac{1}{x+1}, 1, \ldots$

51. The 10th term of a geometric sequence is 0.78125. The common ratio is −0.5. Find the first term of the sequence.

52. The first term of a geometric sequence is 12 and the common ratio is $\dfrac{1}{2}$. Is 0 a term in this sequence? Explain.

53. A geometric sequence starts with 14 and has a common ration of 0.4. Colin finds that another number in the sequence is 0.057344. Which term in the sequence did Colin find?

54. The first three terms of a sequence are 1, 2, and 4. Susanna said the 8th term of this sequence is 128. Paul said the 8th term is 29. Explain how the students found their answers. Why could these both be considered correct answers?

SPIRAL REVIEW

Solve each inequality and graph the solutions. *(Lesson 3-2)*

55. $b - 4 > 6$ **56.** $-12 + x \le -8$ **57.** $c + \dfrac{2}{3} < \dfrac{1}{3}$

Graph the solutions of each linear inequality. *(Lesson 6-5)*

58. $y < 2x - 4$ **59.** $3x + y > 6$ **60.** $-y \le 2x + 1$

Write a function to describe each of the following graphs. *(Lesson 9-4)*

61. The graph of $f(x) = x^2 - 3$ translated 7 units up

62. The graph of $f(x) = 2x^2 + 6$ narrowed and translated 2 units down

11-2 Exponential Functions

Objectives
Evaluate exponential functions.

Identify and graph exponential functions.

Vocabulary
exponential function

Who uses this?
Scientists model populations with exponential functions.

The table and the graph show an insect population that increases over time.

Time (days)	Population
0	2
1	6
2	18
3	54

$\times 3$
$\times 3$
$\times 3$

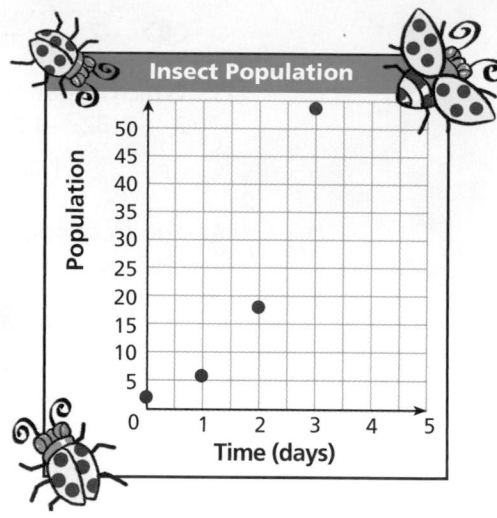

Insect Population

A function rule that describes the pattern above is $f(x) = 2(3)^x$. This type of function, in which the independent variable appears in an exponent, is an **exponential function**. Notice that 2 is the starting population and 3 is the amount by which the population is multiplied each day.

Know it!
Note

Exponential Functions

An exponential function has the form $f(x) = ab^x$, where $a \neq 0$, $b \neq 1$, and $b > 0$.

EXAMPLE 1 **Evaluating an Exponential Function**

A The function $f(x) = 2(3)^x$ models an insect population after x days. What will the population be on the 5th day?

$f(x) = 2(3)^x$ *Write the function.*
$f(5) = 2(3)^5$ *Substitute 5 for x.*
$\quad = 2(243)$ *Evaluate 3^5.*
$\quad = 486$ *Multiply.*

There will be 486 insects on the 5th day.

Helpful Hint

In Example 1B, round your answer to the nearest whole number because there can only be a whole number of prairie dogs.

B The function $f(x) = 1500(0.995)^x$, where x is the time in years, models a prairie dog population. How many prairie dogs will there be in 8 years?

$f(x) = 1500(0.995)^x$
$f(8) = 1500(0.995)^8$ *Substitute 8 for x.*
$\quad \approx 1441$ *Use a calculator. Round to the nearest whole number.*

There will be about 1441 prairie dogs in 8 years.

CHECK IT OUT!

1. The function $f(x) = 8(0.75)^x$ models the width of a photograph in inches after it has been reduced by 25% x times. What is the width of the photograph after it has been reduced 3 times?

Remember that linear functions have constant first differences and quadratic functions have constant second differences. Exponential functions do not have constant differences, but they do have *constant ratios*.

As the *x*-values increase by a constant amount, the *y*-values are multiplied by a constant amount. This amount is the constant ratio and is the value of *b* in $f(x) = ab^x$.

	x	f(x) = 2(3)ˣ	
+1	1	6	×3
+1	2	18	×3
+1	3	54	×3
	4	162	

EXAMPLE 2 **Identifying an Exponential Function**

Tell whether each set of ordered pairs satisfies an exponential function. Explain your answer.

A $\{(-1, 1.5), (0, 3), (1, 6), (2, 12)\}$

	x	y	
+1	−1	1.5	×2
+1	0	3	×2
+1	1	6	×2
	2	12	

This is an exponential function. As the *x*-values increase by a constant amount, the *y*-values are multiplied by a constant amount.

B $\{(-1, -9), (1, 9), (3, 27), (5, 45)\}$

	x	y	
+2	−1	−9	×(−1)
+2	1	9	×3
+2	3	27	×$\frac{5}{3}$
	5	45	

This is *not* an exponential function. As the *x*-values increase by a constant amount, the *y*-values are *not* multiplied by a constant amount.

 CHECK IT OUT! Tell whether each set of ordered pairs satisfies an exponential function. Explain your answer.

2a. $\{(-1, 1), (0, 0), (1, 1), (2, 4)\}$ **2b.** $\{(-2, 4), (-1, 2), (0, 1), (1, 0.5)\}$

To graph an exponential function, choose several values of *x* (positive, negative, and 0) and generate ordered pairs. Plot the points and connect them with a smooth curve.

EXAMPLE 3 **Graphing $y = ab^x$ with $a > 0$ and $b > 1$**

Graph $y = 3(4)^x$.

Choose several values of x and generate ordered pairs.

x	y = 3(4)ˣ
−1	0.75
0	3
1	12
2	48

Graph the ordered pairs and connect with a smooth curve.

 CHECK IT OUT! **3a.** Graph $y = 2^x$. **3b.** Graph $y = 0.2(5)^x$.

EXAMPLE 4 Graphing $y = ab^x$ with $a < 0$ and $b > 1$

Graph $y = -5(2)^x$.

Choose several values of x and generate ordered pairs.

x	$y = -5(2)^x$
−1	−2.5
0	−5
1	−10
2	−20

Graph the ordered pairs and connect with a smooth curve.

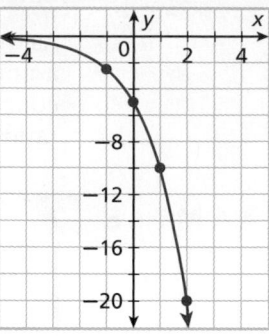

CHECK IT OUT!   **4a.** Graph $y = -6^x$.   **4b.** Graph $y = -3(3)^x$.

EXAMPLE 5 Graphing $y = ab^x$ with $0 < b < 1$

Graph each exponential function.

A $y = 3\left(\dfrac{1}{2}\right)^x$

Choose several values of x and generate ordered pairs.

x	$y = 3\left(\frac{1}{2}\right)^x$
−1	6
0	3
1	1.5
2	0.75

Graph the ordered pairs and connect with a smooth curve.

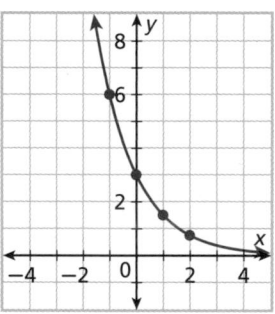

B $y = -2(0.4)^x$

Choose several values of x and generate ordered pairs.

x	$y = -2(0.4)^x$
−2	−12.5
−1	−5
0	−2
1	−0.8

Graph the ordered pairs and connect with a smooth curve.

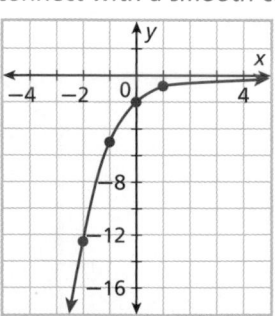

CHECK IT OUT!   **Graph each exponential function.**

   5a. $y = 4\left(\dfrac{1}{4}\right)^x$ **5b.** $y = -2(0.1)^x$

The box summarizes the general shapes of exponential function graphs.

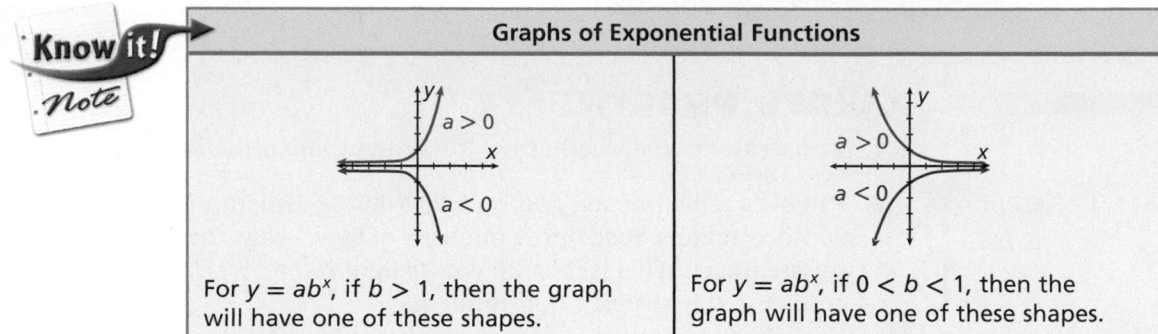

Graphs of Exponential Functions	
For $y = ab^x$, if $b > 1$, then the graph will have one of these shapes.	For $y = ab^x$, if $0 < b < 1$, then the graph will have one of these shapes.

EXAMPLE 6 *Statistics Application*

In the year 2000, the world population was about 6 billion, and it was growing by 1.21% each year. At this growth rate, the function $f(x) = 6(1.0121)^x$ gives the population, in billions, x years after 2000. Using this model, in about what year does the population reach 7 billion?

Enter the function into the Y= editor of a graphing calculator.

Caution!

The function values give the population *in billions*, so a *y*-value of 7 means 7 billion.

TABLE

Press **2nd** **GRAPH**. *Use the arrow keys to find a y-value as close to 7 as possible. The corresponding x-value is 13.*

The world population reaches 7 billion in about 2013.

CHECK IT OUT!

6. An accountant uses $f(x) = 12,330(0.869)^x$, where x is the time in years since the purchase, to model the value of a car. When will the car be worth $2000?

THINK AND DISCUSS

1. How can you find the constant ratio of a set of exponential data?

2. **GET ORGANIZED** Copy and complete the graphic organizer. In each box, give an example of an appropriate exponential function and sketch its graph.

Exponential Functions: $y = ab^x$

| $a > 0, b > 1$ | $a < 0, b > 1$ | $a > 0, 0 < b < 1$ | $a < 0, 0 < b < 1$ |

go.hrw.com
Homework Help Online
KEYWORD: MA7 11-2
Parent Resources Online
KEYWORD: MA7 Parent

GUIDED PRACTICE

1. **Vocabulary** Tell whether $y = 3x^4$ is an *exponential function*. Explain your answer.

SEE EXAMPLE **1**
p. 796

2. **Physics** The function $f(x) = 50,000(0.975)^x$, where x represents the underwater depth in meters, models the intensity of light below the water's surface in lumens per square meter. What is the intensity of light 200 meters below the surface? Round your answer to the nearest whole number.

SEE EXAMPLE **2**
p. 797

Tell whether each set of ordered pairs satisfies an exponential function. Explain your answer.

3. $\{(-1, -1), (0, 0), (1, -1), (2, -4)\}$

4. $\{(0, 1), (1, 4), (2, 16), (3, 64)\}$

Graph each exponential function.

SEE EXAMPLE **3**
p. 797

5. $y = 3^x$

6. $y = 5^x$

7. $y = 10(3)^x$

8. $y = 5(2)^x$

SEE EXAMPLE **4**
p. 798

9. $y = -2(3)^x$

10. $y = -4(2)^x$

11. $y = -3(2)^x$

12. $y = 2(3)^x$

SEE EXAMPLE **5**
p. 798

13. $y = -\left(\frac{1}{4}\right)^x$

14. $y = \left(\frac{1}{3}\right)^x$

15. $y = 2\left(\frac{1}{4}\right)^x$

16. $y = -2(0.25)^x$

SEE EXAMPLE **6**
p. 799

17. The function $f(x) = 57.8(1.02)^x$ gives the number of passenger cars, in millions, in the United States x years after 1960. Using this model, in about what year does the number of passenger cars reach 200 million?

PRACTICE AND PROBLEM SOLVING

Independent Practice

For Exercises	See Example
18–20	1
21–24	2
25–27	3
28–30	4
31–33	5
34	6

Extra Practice

Skills Practice p. S24

Application Practice p. S38

18. **Sports** If a golf ball is dropped from a height of 27 feet, the function $f(x) = 27\left(\frac{2}{3}\right)^x$ gives the height in feet of each bounce, where x is the bounce number. What will be the height of the 4th bounce?

19. Suppose the depth of a lake can be described by the function $y = 334(0.976)^x$, where x represents the number of weeks from today. Today, the depth of the lake is 334 ft. What will the depth be in 6 weeks? Round your answer to the nearest whole number.

20. **Physics** A ball rolling down a slope travels continuously faster. Suppose the function $y = 1.3(1.41)^x$ describes the speed of the ball in inches per minute. How fast will the ball be rolling in 15 minutes? Round your answer to the nearest hundredth.

Tell whether each set of ordered pairs satisfies an exponential function. Explain your answer.

21. $\left\{(-2, 9), (-1, 3), (0, 1), \left(1, \frac{1}{3}\right)\right\}$

22. $\{(-1, 0), (0, 1), (1, 4), (2, 9)\}$

23. $\{(-1, -5), (0, -3), (1, -1), (2, 1)\}$

24. $\{(-3, 6.25), (-2, 12.5), (-1, 25), (0, 50)\}$

Graph each exponential function.

25. $y = 1.5^x$

26. $y = \frac{1}{3}(3)^x$

27. $y = 100(0.7)^x$

28. $y = -2(4)^x$

29. $y = -1(5)^x$

30. $y = -\frac{1}{2}(4)^x$

31. $y = 4\left(\frac{1}{2}\right)^x$

32. $y = -2\left(\frac{1}{3}\right)^x$

33. $y = 0.5(0.25)^x$

34. **Technology** Moore's law states that the maximum number of transistors that can fit on a silicon chip doubles every two years. The function $f(x) = 42(1.41)^x$ models the number of transistors, in millions, that can fit on a chip, where x is the number of years since 2000. Using this model, in what year can a chip hold 1 billion transistors?

35. **Multi-Step** A computer randomly creates three different functions. The functions are $y = (3.1x + 7)^2$, $y = 4.8(2)^x$, and $y = \frac{1}{5}(6)^x$. The computer then generates the y value 38.4. Given the three different functions, determine which one is exponential *and* produces the generated number.

36. **Contests** As a promotion, a clothing store draws the name of one of its customers each week. The prize is a coupon for the store. If the winner is not present at the drawing, he or she cannot claim the prize, and the amount of the coupon increases for the following week's drawing. The function $f(x) = 20(1.2)^x$ gives the amount of the coupon in dollars after x weeks of the prize going unclaimed.

Clothes for everyone!
Math Apparel
Win Valuable Store Coupon
Must be present to win!

   a. What is the amount of the coupon after 2 weeks of the prize going unclaimed?

   b. After how many weeks of the prize going unclaimed will the amount of the coupon be greater than $100?

   c. What is the original amount of the coupon?

   d. Find the percent increase each week.

37. **Critical Thinking** In the definition of exponential function, the value of b cannot be 1, and the value of a cannot be 0. Why?

Graphing Calculator Graph each group of functions on the same screen. How are their graphs alike? How are they different?

38. $y = 2^x, y = 3^x, y = 4^x$

39. $y = \left(\frac{1}{2}\right)^x, y = \left(\frac{1}{3}\right)^x, y = \left(\frac{1}{4}\right)^x$

Evaluate each of the following for the given value of x.

40. $f(x) = 4^x; x = 3$

41. $f(x) = -(0.25)^x; x = 1.5$

42. $f(x) = 0.4(10)^x; x = -3$

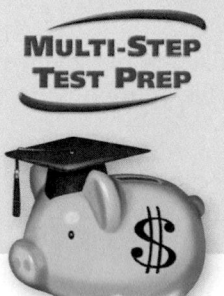

MULTI-STEP TEST PREP

43. This problem will prepare you for the Multi-Step Test Prep on page 820.

   a. The annual tuition at a community college since 2001 is modeled by the equation $C = 2000(1.08)^n$, where C is the tuition cost and n is the number of years since 2001. What was the tuition cost in 2001?

   b. What is the annual percentage of tuition increase?

   c. Find the tuition cost in 2006.

44. Write About It Your employer offers two salary plans. With plan A, your salary is $f(x) = 10{,}000(2x)$, where x is the number of years you have worked for the company. With plan B, your salary is $g(x) = 10{,}000(2)^x$. Which plan would you choose? Why?

45. Which graph shows an exponential function?

Ⓐ

Ⓒ

Ⓑ

Ⓓ

46. The function $f(x) = 15(1.4)^x$ represents the area in square inches of a photograph after it has been enlarged x times by a factor of 140%. What is the area of the photograph after it has been enlarged 4 times?

Ⓕ 5.6 square inches

Ⓖ 57.624 square inches

Ⓗ 41.16 square inches

Ⓙ 560 square inches

47. Look at the pattern. How many squares will there be in the nth stage?

Stage 0   Stage 1   Stage 2

Ⓐ $5n$ Ⓑ $2.5 \cdot 2^n$ Ⓒ 25^{n-1} Ⓓ 5^n

CHALLENGE AND EXTEND

Solve each equation.

48. $4^x = 64$

49. $\left(\dfrac{1}{3}\right)^x = \dfrac{1}{27}$

50. $2^x = \dfrac{1}{16}$

51. Graph the following functions: $y = 2(2)^x$, $y = 3(2)^x$, $y = -2(2)^x$. Then make a conjecture about the relationship between the value of a and the y-intercept of $y = ab^x$.

SPIRAL REVIEW

52. The average of Roger's three test scores must be at least 90 to earn an A in his science class. Roger has scored 88 and 89 on his first two tests. Write and solve an inequality to find what he must score on the third test to earn an A. *(Lesson 3-4)*

Find the missing term in each perfect-square trinomial. *(Lesson 8-5)*

53. $x^2 + 10x + \blacksquare$

54. $4x^2 + \blacksquare + 64$

55. $\blacksquare + 42x + 49$

56. What is the 12th term of the sequence 4, 12, 36, 108, …? *(Lesson 11-1)*

Changing Dimensions

What happens to the volume of a three-dimensional figure when you repeatedly double the dimensions?

Recall these formulas for the volumes of common three-dimensional figures.

Cube $V = s^3$

s

Rectangular Prism $V = \ell wh$

h

ℓ

w

Pyramid $V = \frac{1}{3}(\text{area of base}) \cdot h$

h

Base

Changing the dimensions of three-dimensional figures results in geometric sequences.

Example

Find the volume of a cube with a side length of 3 cm. Double the side length and find the new volume. Repeat two more times. Show the patterns for the side lengths and volumes as geometric sequences. Identify the common ratios.

Cube	Side Length (cm)	Volume (cm³)
1	3	27
2	6	216
3	12	1,728
4	24	13,824

(Side Length: ×2 between rows; Volume: ×8 between rows)

The side lengths and the volumes form geometric sequences. The sequence of the side lengths has a common ratio of 2. The sequence of the volumes has a common ratio of 2^3, or 8.

The patterns in the example above are a specific instance of a general rule.

> When the dimensions of a solid figure are multiplied by x, the volume of the figure is multiplied by x^3.

Try This

1. The large rectangular prism at right is 8 in. wide, 16 in. long, and 32 in. tall. The dimensions are multiplied by $\frac{1}{2}$ to create each next smaller prism. Show the patterns for the dimensions and the volumes as geometric sequences. Identify the common ratios.

2. A pyramid has a height of 8 cm and a square base of 3 cm on each edge. Triple the dimensions two times. Show the patterns for the dimensions and the volumes as geometric sequences. Identify the common ratios.

11-3 Algebra LAB

Model Growth and Decay

You can fold and cut paper to model quantities that increase or decrease exponentially.

Use with Lesson 11-3

Activity 1

❶ Copy the table at right.

❷ Fold a piece of notebook paper in half. Then open it back up. Count the number of regions created by the fold. Record your answer in the table.

❸ Now fold the paper in half twice. Record the number of regions created by the folds in the table.

❹ Repeat this process for 3, 4, and 5 folds.

Folds	Regions
0	1
1	
2	
3	
4	
5	

Try This

1. When the number of folds increases by 1, the number of regions ___?___ .

2. For each row of the table, write the number of regions as a power of 2.

3. Write an exponential expression for the number of regions formed by n folds.

4. If you could fold the paper 8 times, how many regions would be formed?

5. How many times would you have to fold the paper to make 512 regions?

Activity 2

❶ Copy the table at right.

❷ Begin with a square piece of paper. The area of the paper is 1 square unit. Cut the paper in half. Each piece has an area of $\frac{1}{2}$ square unit. Record the result in the table.

❸ Cut one of those pieces in half again, and record the area of one of the new, smaller pieces in the table.

❹ Repeat this process for 3, 4, and 5 cuts.

Cuts	Area
0	1
1	
2	
3	
4	
5	

Try This

6. When the number of cuts increases by 1, the area ___?___ .

7. For each row of the table, write the area as a power of 2.

8. Write an exponential expression for the area after n cuts.

9. What would be the area after 7 cuts?

10. How many cuts would you have to make to get an area of $\frac{1}{256}$ square unit?

Exponential Growth and Decay

Objective
Solve problems involving exponential growth and decay.

Vocabulary
exponential growth
compound interest
exponential decay
half-life

Why learn this?
Exponential growth and decay describe many real-world situations, such as the value of artwork. (See Example 1.)

Exponential growth occurs when a quantity increases by the same rate r in each time period t. When this happens, the value of the quantity at any given time can be calculated as a function of the rate and the original amount.

Exponential Growth

An exponential growth function has the form $y = a(1 + r)^t$, where $a > 0$.

  y represents the final amount.

  a represents the original amount.

  r represents the rate of growth expressed as a decimal.

  t represents time.

EXAMPLE 1 **Exponential Growth**

The original value of a painting is $1400, and the value increases by 9% each year. Write an exponential growth function to model this situation. Then find the value of the painting in 25 years.

Helpful Hint

In Example 1, round to the nearest hundredth because the problem deals with money. This means you are rounding to the nearest cent.

Step 1 Write the exponential growth function for this situation.

$$y = a(1 + r)^t \qquad \textit{Write the formula.}$$
$$= 1400(1 + 0.09)^t \qquad \textit{Substitute 1400 for a and 0.09 for r.}$$
$$= 1400(1.09)^t \qquad \textit{Simplify.}$$

Step 2 Find the value in 25 years.

$$y = 1400(1.09)^t$$
$$= 1400(1.09)^{25} \qquad \textit{Substitute 25 for t.}$$
$$\approx 12{,}072.31 \qquad \textit{Use a calculator and round to the nearest hundredth.}$$

The value of the painting in 25 years is $12,072.31.

 1. A sculpture is increasing in value at a rate of 8% per year, and its value in 2000 was $1200. Write an exponential growth function to model this situation. Then find the sculpture's value in 2006.

A common application of exponential growth is *compound interest*. Recall that simple interest is earned or paid only on the principal. **Compound interest** is interest earned or paid on *both* the principal and previously earned interest.

Compound Interest

$$A = P\left(1 + \frac{r}{n}\right)^{nt}$$

A represents the balance after *t* years.

P represents the principal, or original amount.

r represents the annual interest rate expressed as a decimal.

n represents the number of times interest is compounded per year.

t represents time in years.

EXAMPLE 2 *Finance Application*

Write a compound interest function to model each situation. Then find the balance after the given number of years.

A **$1000 invested at a rate of 3% compounded quarterly; 5 years**

Step 1 Write the compound interest function for this situation.

$A = P\left(1 + \frac{r}{n}\right)^{nt}$ *Write the formula.*

$= 1000\left(1 + \frac{0.03}{4}\right)^{4t}$ *Substitute 1000 for P, 0.03 for r, and 4 for n.*

$= 1000(1.0075)^{4t}$ *Simplify.*

Reading Math

For compound interest,
- *annually* means "once per year" ($n = 1$).
- *quarterly* means "4 times per year" ($n = 4$).
- *monthly* means "12 times per year" ($n = 12$).

Step 2 Find the balance after 5 years.

$A = 1000(1.0075)^{4(5)}$ *Substitute 5 for t.*

$= 1000(1.0075)^{20}$

≈ 1161.18 *Use a calculator and round to the nearest hundredth.*

The balance after 5 years is $1161.18.

B **$18,000 invested at a rate of 4.5% compounded annually; 6 years**

Step 1 Write the compound interest function for this situation.

$A = P\left(1 + \frac{r}{n}\right)^{nt}$ *Write the formula.*

$= 18{,}000\left(1 + \frac{0.045}{1}\right)^{t}$ *Substitute 18,000 for P, 0.045 for r, and 1 for n.*

$= 18{,}000(1.045)^{t}$ *Simplify.*

Step 2 Find the balance after 6 years.

$A = 18{,}000(1.045)^{6}$ *Substitute 6 for t.*

$\approx 23{,}440.68$ *Use a calculator and round to the nearest hundredth.*

The balance after 6 years is $23,440.68.

Write a compound interest function to model each situation. Then find the balance after the given number of years.

2a. $1200 invested at a rate of 3.5% compounded quarterly; 4 years

2b. $4000 invested at a rate of 3% compounded monthly; 8 years

Exponential decay occurs when a quantity decreases by the same rate r in each time period t. Just like exponential growth, the value of the quantity at any given time can be calculated by using the rate and the original amount.

Exponential Decay

An exponential decay function has the form $y = a(1 - r)^t$, where $a > 0$.

   y represents the final amount.

   a represents the original amount.

   r represents the rate of decay as a decimal.

   t represents time.

Notice an important difference between exponential growth functions and exponential decay functions. For exponential growth, the value inside the parentheses will be greater than 1 because r is added to 1. For exponential decay, the value inside the parentheses will be less than 1 because r is subtracted from 1.

EXAMPLE **3** **Exponential Decay**

The population of a town is decreasing at a rate of 1% per year. In 2000 there were 1300 people. Write an exponential decay function to model this situation. Then find the population in 2008.

Step 1 Write the exponential decay function for this situation.

$$y = a(1 - r)^t \qquad \textit{Write the formula.}$$

$$= 1300(1 - 0.01)^t \qquad \textit{Substitute 1300 for a and 0.01 for r.}$$

$$= 1300(0.99)^t \qquad \textit{Simplify.}$$

Step 2 Find the population in 2008.

$$y = 1300(0.99)^8 \qquad \textit{Substitute 8 for t.}$$

$$\approx 1200 \qquad \textit{Use a calculator and round to the nearest whole number.}$$

The population in 2008 is approximately 1200 people.

> **Helpful Hint**
>
> In Example 3, round your answer to the nearest whole number because there can only be a whole number of people.

3. The fish population in a local stream is decreasing at a rate of 3% per year. The original population was 48,000. Write an exponential decay function to model this situation. Then find the population after 7 years.

A common application of exponential decay is *half-life*. The **half-life** of a substance is the time it takes for one-half of the substance to decay into another substance.

Half-life

$A = P(0.5)^t$

   A represents the final amount.

   P represents the original amount.

   t represents the number of half-lives in a given time period.

EXAMPLE 4 *Science Application*

Fluorine-20 has a half-life of 11 seconds.

A **Find the amount of fluorine-20 left from a 40-gram sample after 44 seconds.**

Step 1 Find t, the number of half-lives in the given time period.

$$\frac{44 \text{ s}}{11 \text{ s}} = 4$$ *Divide the time period by the half-life.*
The value of t is 4.

Step 2 $A = P(0.5)^t$ *Write the formula.*

$= 40(0.5)^4$ *Substitute 40 for P and 4 for t.*

$= 2.5$ *Use a calculator.*

There are 2.5 grams of fluorine-20 remaining after 44 seconds.

B **Find the amount of fluorine-20 left from a 40-gram sample after 2.2 minutes. Round your answer to the nearest hundredth.**

Step 1 Find t, the number of half-lives in the given time period.

$2.2(60) = 132$ *Find the number of seconds in 2.2 minutes.*

$\frac{132 \text{ s}}{11 \text{ s}} = 12$ *Divide the time period by the half-life.*
The value of t is $\frac{132}{11} = 12$.

Step 2 $A = P(0.5)^t$ *Write the formula.*

$= 40(0.5)^{12}$ *Substitute 40 for P and 12 for t.*

≈ 0.01 *Use a calculator. Round to the nearest hundredth.*

There is about 0.01 gram of fluorine-20 remaining after 2.2 minutes.

CHECK IT OUT!

4a. Cesium-137 has a half-life of 30 years. Find the amount of cesium-137 left from a 100-milligram sample after 180 years.

4b. Bismuth-210 has a half-life of 5 days. Find the amount of bismuth-210 left from a 100-gram sample after 5 weeks. (*Hint:* Change 5 weeks to days.)

THINK AND DISCUSS

1. Describe three real-world situations that can be described by exponential growth or exponential decay functions.

2. The population of a town after t years can be modeled by $P = 1000(1.02)^t$. Is the population increasing or decreasing? By what percentage rate?

3. An exponential function is a function of the form $y = ab^x$. Explain why both exponential growth functions and exponential decay functions are exponential functions.

4. GET ORGANIZED Copy and complete the graphic organizer.

go.hrw.com
Homework Help Online
KEYWORD: MA7 11-3
Parent Resources Online
KEYWORD: MA7 Parent

GUIDED PRACTICE

1. **Vocabulary** The function $y = 0.68(2)^x$ is an example of _____?_____.
   (*exponential growth* or *exponential decay*)

SEE EXAMPLE 1
p. 805

Write an exponential growth function to model each situation. Then find the value of the function after the given amount of time.

2. The cost of tuition at a college is $12,000 and is increasing at a rate of 6% per year; 4 years.

3. The number of student-athletes at a local high school is 300 and is increasing at a rate of 8% per year; 5 years.

SEE EXAMPLE 2
p. 806

Write a compound interest function to model each situation. Then find the balance after the given number of years.

4. $1500 invested at a rate of 3.5% compounded annually; 4 years

5. $4200 invested at a rate of 2.8% compounded quarterly; 6 years

SEE EXAMPLE 3
p. 807

Write an exponential decay function to model each situation. Then find the value of the function after the given amount of time.

6. The value of a car is $18,000 and is depreciating at a rate of 12% per year; 10 years.

7. The amount (to the nearest hundredth) of a 10-mg dose of a certain antibiotic decreases in your bloodstream at a rate of 16% per hour; 4 hours.

SEE EXAMPLE 4
p. 808

8. Bismuth-214 has a half-life of approximately 20 minutes. Find the amount of bismuth-214 left from a 30-gram sample after 1 hour.

9. Mendelevium-258 has a half-life of approximately 52 days. Find the amount of mendelevium-258 left from a 44-gram sample after 156 days.

PRACTICE AND PROBLEM SOLVING

Independent Practice

For Exercises	See Example
10–13	1
14–17	2
18–19	3
20	4

Extra Practice

Skills Practice p. S24
Application Practice p. S38

Write an exponential growth function to model each situation. Then find the value of the function after the given amount of time.

10. Annual sales for a company are $149,000 and are increasing at a rate of 6% per year; 7 years.

11. The population of a small town is 1600 and is increasing at a rate of 3% per year; 10 years.

12. A new savings account starts at $700 and increases at 1.2% yearly; 8 years.

13. Membership of a local club grows at a rate of 7.8% yearly and currently has 30 members; 6 years.

Write a compound interest function to model each situation. Then find the balance after the given number of years.

14. $28,000 invested at a rate of 4% compounded annually; 5 years

15. $7000 invested at a rate of 3% compounded quarterly; 10 years

16. $3500 invested at a rate of 1.8% compounded monthly; 4 years

17. $12,000 invested at a rate of 2.6% compounded annually; 15 years

Write an exponential decay function to model each situation. Then find the value of the function after the given amount of time.

18. The population of a town is 18,000 and is decreasing at a rate of 2% per year; 6 years.

19. The value of a book is $58 and decreases at a rate of 10% per year; 8 years.

20. The half-life of bromine-82 is approximately 36 hours. Find the amount of bromine-82 left from an 80-gram sample after 6 days.

Identify each of the following functions as exponential growth or decay. Then give the rate of growth or decay as a percent.

21. $y = 3(1.61)^t$ 22. $y = 39(0.098)^t$ 23. $y = a\left(\frac{2}{3}\right)^t$ 24. $y = a\left(\frac{3}{2}\right)^t$

25. $y = a(1.1)^t$ 26. $y = a(0.8)^t$ 27. $y = a\left(\frac{5}{4}\right)^t$ 28. $y = a\left(\frac{1}{2}\right)^t$

Write an exponential growth or decay function to model each situation. Then find the value of the function after the given amount of time.

29. The population of a country is 58,000,000 and grows by 0.1% per year; 3 years.

30. An antique car is worth $32,000, and its value grows by 7% per year; 5 years.

31. An investment of $8200 loses value at a rate of 2% per year; 7 years.

32. A new car is worth $25,000, and its value decreases by 15% each year; 6 years.

33. The student enrollment in a local high school is 970 students and increases by 1.2% per year; 5 years.

Atlantic Ocean

North Sea

England

Testwood •

34. **Archaeology** Carbon-14 dating is a way to determine the age of very old organic objects. Carbon-14 has a half-life of about 5700 years. An organic object with $\frac{1}{2}$ as much carbon-14 as its living counterpart died 5700 years ago. In 1999, archaeologists discovered the oldest bridge in England near Testwood, Hampshire. Carbon dating of the wood revealed that the bridge was 3500 years old. Suppose that when the bridge was built, the wood contained 15 grams of carbon-14. How much carbon-14 would it have contained when it was found by the archaeologists? Round to the nearest hundredth.

A computer-generated image of what the bridge at Testwood might have looked like

35. **///ERROR ANALYSIS///** Two students were asked to find the value of a $1000-item after 3 years. The item was depreciating (losing value) at a rate of 40% per year. Which is incorrect? Explain the error.

A

$1000(0.6)^3$

$216

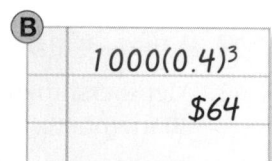

B

$1000(0.4)^3$

$64

36. **Critical Thinking** The value of a certain car can be modeled by the function $y = 20,000(0.84)^t$, where t is time in years. Will the value ever be zero? Explain.

37. The value of a rare baseball card increases every year at a rate of 4%. Today, the card is worth $300. The owner expects to sell the card as soon as the value is over $600. How many years will the owner wait before selling the card? Round your answer to the nearest whole number.

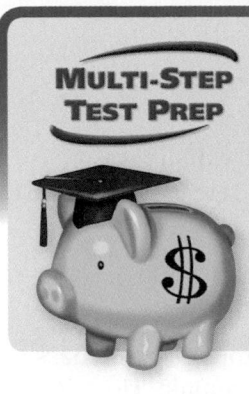

MULTI-STEP TEST PREP

38. This problem will prepare you for the Multi-Step Test Prep on page 820.

    a. The annual tuition at a prestigious university was $20,000 in 2002. It generally increases at a rate of 9% each year. Write a function to describe the cost as a function of the number of years since 2002. Use 2002 as year zero when writing the function rule.

    b. What do you predict the cost of tuition will be in 2008?

    c. Use a table of values to find the first year that the cost of the tuition is more than twice the cost in 2002.

39. Multi-Step At bank A, $600 is invested with an interest rate of 5% compounded annually. At bank B, $500 is invested with an interest rate of 6% compounded quarterly. Which account will have a larger balance after 10 years? 20 years?

40. Estimation The graph shows the decay of 100 grams of sodium-24. Use the graph to estimate the number of hours it will take the sample to decay to 10 grams. Then estimate the half-life of sodium-24.

41. Graphing Calculator Use a graphing calculator to graph $y = 10(1 + r)^x$ for $r = 10\%$ and $r = 20\%$. Compare the two graphs. How does the value of r affect the graphs?

Sodium-24

Amount remaining (g) vs. Time (h)

42. Write About It Write a real-world situation that could be modeled by $y = 400(1.08)^t$.

43. Write About It Write a real-world situation that could be modeled by $y = 800(0.96)^t$.

44. Critical Thinking The amount of water in a container doubles every minute. After 6 minutes, the container is full. Your friend says it was half full after 3 minutes. Do you agree? Why or why not?

TEST PREP

45. A population of 500 is decreasing by 1% per year. Which function models this situation?

    Ⓐ $y = 500(0.01)^t$ Ⓑ $y = 500(0.1)^t$ Ⓒ $y = 500(0.9)^t$ Ⓓ $y = 500(0.99)^t$

46. Which function is NOT an exponential decay model?

    Ⓕ $y = 5\left(\frac{1}{3}\right)^x$ Ⓖ $y = -5\left(\frac{1}{3}\right)^x$ Ⓗ $y = 5(3)^{-x}$ Ⓙ $y = 5(3^{-1})^x$

47. Stephanie wants to save $1000 for a down payment on a car that she wants to buy in 3 years. She opens a savings account that pays 5% interest compounded annually. About how much should Stephanie deposit now to have enough money for the down payment in 3 years?

    Ⓐ $295   Ⓑ $333   Ⓒ $500   Ⓓ $865

48. Short Response In 2000, the population of a town was 1000 and was growing at a rate of 5% per year.

    a. Write an exponential growth function to model this situation.

    b. In what year is the population 1300? Show how you found your answer.

49. You invest $700 at a rate of 6% compounded quarterly. Use a graph to estimate the number of years it will take for your investment to increase to $2300.

50. Omar invested $500 at a rate of 4% compounded annually. How long will it take for Omar's money to double? How long would it take if the interest were 8% compounded annually?

51. An 80-gram sample of a radioactive substance decayed to 10 grams after 300 minutes. Find the half-life of the substance.

52. Praseodymium-143 has a half-life of 2 weeks. The original measurement for the mass of a sample was lost. After 6 weeks, 15 grams of praseodymium-143 remain. How many grams was the original sample?

53. Phillip invested some money in a business 8 years ago. Since then, his investment has grown at an average rate of 1.3% compounded quarterly. Phillip's investment is now worth $250,000. How much was his original investment? Round your answer to the nearest dollar.

54. **Personal Finance** Anna has a balance of $200 that she owes on her credit card. She plans to make a $30 payment each month. There is also a 1.5% finance charge (interest) on the remaining balance each month. Copy and complete the table to answer the questions below. You may add more rows to the table as necessary.

Month	Balance ($)	Monthly Payment ($)	Remaining Balance ($)	1.5% Finance Charge ($)	New Balance ($)
1	200	30	170	2.55	172.55
2	172.55	30			
3		30			
4		30			

a. How many months will it take Anna to pay the entire balance?

b. By the time Anna pays the entire balance, how much total interest will she have paid?

SPIRAL REVIEW

Write and solve a proportion for each situation. *(Lesson 2-8)*

55. A daffodil that is 1.2 feet tall casts a shadow that is 1.5 feet long. At the same time, a nearby lamppost casts a shadow that is 20 feet long. What is the height of the the lamppost?

56. A green rectangular throw pillow measures 20 inches long by 10 inches wide. A proportionally similar yellow throw pillow is 12 inches long. What is the width of the yellow pillow?

Graph each function. *(Lesson 4-4)*

57. $f(x) = 2x + 1$

58. $f(x) = |x - 4|$

59. $f(x) = x^2 - 1$

60. The function $f(x) = 0.10(2)^x$ describes the total cost in dollars of a library book fine, where x is the number of days that the book is overdue. What is the amount of the fine if a book is 4 days overdue? How many days overdue is a book if the fine is $12.80? *(Lesson 11-2)*

11-4 Linear, Quadratic, and Exponential Models

Objectives
Compare linear, quadratic, and exponential models.

Given a set of data, decide which type of function models the data and write an equation to describe the function.

Why learn this?
Different situations in sports can be described by linear, quadratic, or exponential models.

Look at the tables and graphs below. The data show three ways you have learned that variable quantities can be related. The relationships shown are linear, quadratic, and exponential.

Linear

Training Heart Rate	
Age (yr)	Beats/min
20	170
30	161.5
40	153
50	144.5

Quadratic

Volleyball Height	
Time (s)	Height (ft)
0.4	10.44
0.8	12.76
1	12
1.2	9.96

Exponential

Volleyball Tournament	
Round	Teams Left
1	16
2	8
3	4
4	2

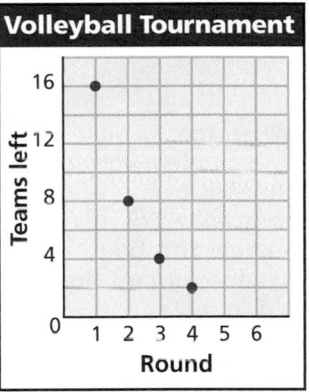

In the real world, people often gather data and then must decide what kind of relationship (if any) they think best describes their data.

EXAMPLE 1 Graphing Data to Choose a Model

Graph each data set. Which kind of model best describes the data?

A

Time (h)	0	1	2	3
Bacteria	10	20	40	80

Plot the data points and connect them.
The data appear to be exponential.

Bacteria Population

Graph each data set. Which kind of model best describes the data?

Celsius to Fahrenheit

B | °C | 0 | 5 | 10 | 15 | 20 |
| --- | --- | --- | --- | --- | --- |
| °F | 32 | 41 | 50 | 59 | 68 |

Plot the data points and connect them.
The data appear to be linear.

 Graph each data set. Which kind of model best describes the data?

1a. $\{(-3, 0.30), (-2, 0.44), (0, 1), (1, 1.5), (2, 2.25), (3, 3.38)\}$

1b. $\{(-3, -14), (-2, -9), (-1, -6), (0, -5), (1, -6), (2, -9), (3, -14)\}$

Another way to decide which kind of relationship (if any) best describes a data set is to use patterns.

EXAMPLE 2   Using Patterns to Choose a Model

Look for a pattern in each data set to determine which kind of model best describes the data.

A

Height of Bridge Suspension Cables

Cable's Distance from Tower (ft)	Cable's Height (ft)
0	400
100	256
200	144
300	64

+ 100 (between each distance row)
− 144, − 112, − 80 (first differences)
+ 32, + 32 (second differences)

For every constant change in distance of +100 feet, there is a constant second difference of +32.
The data appear to be quadratic.

Remember!

When the independent variable changes by a constant amount,
• linear functions have constant first differences.
• quadratic functions have constant second differences.
• exponential functions have a constant ratio.

B

Value of a Car

Car's Age (yr)	Value ($)
0	20,000
1	17,000
2	14,450
3	12,282.50

+ 1 (between each age row)
× 0.85, × 0.85, × 0.85

For every constant change in age of +1 year, there is a constant ratio of 0.85.
The data appear to be exponential.

 2. Look for a pattern in the data set $\{(-2, 10), (-1, 1), (0, -2), (1, 1), (2, 10)\}$ to determine which kind of model best describes the data.

After deciding which model best fits the data, you can write a function. Recall the general forms of linear, quadratic, and exponential functions.

General Forms of Functions

LINEAR	QUADRATIC	EXPONENTIAL
$y = mx + b$	$y = ax^2 + bx + c$	$y = ab^x$

EXAMPLE 3

Problem-Solving Application

Use the data in the table to describe how the ladybug population is changing. Then write a function that models the data. Use your function to predict the ladybug population after one year.

Ladybug Population	
Time (mo)	Ladybugs
0	10
1	30
2	90
3	270

1 Understand the Problem

The **answer** will have three parts—a description, a function, and a prediction.

2 Make a Plan

Determine whether the data is linear, quadratic, or exponential. Use the general form to write a function. Then use the function to find the population after one year.

3 Solve

Step 1 Describe the situation in words.

Ladybug Population	
Time (mo)	Ladybugs
0	10
1	30
2	90
3	270

+1 ⟨ ... ⟩ × 3

Each month, the ladybug population is multiplied by 3. In other words, the population triples each month.

Step 2 Write the function.

There is a constant ratio of 3. The data appear to be exponential.

$y = ab^x$	*Write the general form of an exponential function.*
$y = a(3)^x$	*Substitute the constant ratio, 3, for b.*
$10 = a(3)^0$	*Choose an ordered pair from the table, such as (0, 10). Substitute for x and y.*
$10 = a(1)$	*Simplify. $3^0 = 1$*
$10 = a$	*The value of a is 10.*
$y = 10(3)^x$	*Substitute 10 for a in $y = a(3)^x$.*

Step 3 Predict the ladybug population after one year.

$y = 10(3)^x$ *Write the function.*

$\quad = 10(3)^{12}$ *Substitute 12 for x (1 year = 12 mo).*

$\quad = 5,314,410$ *Use a calculator.*

There will be 5,314,410 ladybugs after one year.

4 **Look Back**

You chose the ordered pair $(0, 10)$ to write the function. Check that every other ordered pair in the table satisfies your function.

$y = 10(3)^x$	
30	$10(3)^1$
30	$10(3)$
30	30 ✓

$y = 10(3)^x$	
90	$10(3)^2$
90	$10(9)$
90	90 ✓

$y = 10(3)^x$	
270	$10(3)^3$
270	$10(27)$
270	270 ✓

3. Use the data in the table to describe how the oven temperature is changing. Then write a function that models the data. Use your function to predict the temperature after 1 hour.

Oven Temperature				
Time (min)	0	10	20	30
Temperature (°F)	375	325	275	225

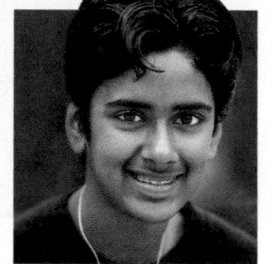

Student to Student

Checking Units

I used to get a lot of answers wrong because of the units. If a question asked for the value of something after 1 year, I would always just substitute 1 into the function.

I finally figured out that you have to check what x is. If x represents months and you're trying to find the value after 1 year, then you have to substitute 12, not 1, because there are 12 months in a year.

Michael Gambhir
Warren High School

THINK AND DISCUSS

1. Do you think that every data set will be able to be modeled by a linear, quadratic, or exponential function? Why or why not?

2. In Example 3, is it certain that there will be 5,314,410 ladybugs after one year? Explain.

3. GET ORGANIZED Copy and complete the graphic organizer. In each box, list some characteristics and sketch a graph of each type of model.

GUIDED PRACTICE

SEE EXAMPLE 1
p. 813

Graph each data set. Which kind of model best describes the data?

1. $\{(-1, 4), (-2, 0.8), (0, 20), (1, 100), (-3, 0.16)\}$

2. $\{(0, 3), (1, 9), (2, 11), (3, 9), (4, 3)\}$

3. $\{(2, -7), (-2, -9), (0, -8), (4, -6), (6, -5)\}$

SEE EXAMPLE 2
p. 814

Look for a pattern in each data set to determine which kind of model best describes the data.

4. $\{(-2, 1), (-1, 2.5), (0, 3), (1, 2.5), (2, 1)\}$

5. $\{(-2, 0.75), (-1, 1.5), (0, 3), (1, 6), (2, 12)\}$

6. $\{(-2, 2), (-1, 4), (0, 6), (1, 8), (2, 10)\}$

SEE EXAMPLE 3
p. 815

7. **Consumer Economics** Use the data in the table to describe the cost of grapes. Then write a function that models the data. Use your function to predict the cost of 6 pounds of grapes.

Total Cost of Grapes				
Amount (lb)	1	2	3	4
Cost ($)	1.79	3.58	5.37	7.16

PRACTICE AND PROBLEM SOLVING

Independent Practice
For Exercises	See Example
8–10	1
11–13	2
14	3

Extra Practice
Skills Practice p. S24
Application Practice p. S38

Graph each data set. Which kind of model best describes the data?

8. $\{(-3, -5), (-2, -8), (-1, -9), (0, -8), (1, -5), (2, 0), (3, 7)\}$

9. $\{(-3, -1), (-2, 0), (-1, 1), (0, 2), (1, 3), (2, 4), (3, 5)\}$

10. $\{(0, 0.1), (2, 0.9), (3, 2.7), (4, 8.1)\}$

Look for a pattern in each data set to determine which kind of model best describes the data.

11. $\{(-2, 5), (-1, 4), (0, 3), (1, 2), (2, 1)\}$

12. $\{(-2, 12), (-1, 15), (0, 16), (1, 15), (2, 12)\}$

13. $\{(-2, 8), (-1, 4), (0, 2), (1, 1), (2, 0.5)\}$

14. **Business** Use the data in the table to describe how the company's sales are changing. Then write a function that models the data. Use your function to predict the amount of sales after 10 years.

Company Sales				
Year	0	1	2	3
Sales ($)	25,000	30,000	36,000	43,200

15. **Multi-Step** Jay's hair grows about 6 inches each year. Write a function that describes the length ℓ in inches that Jay's hair will grow for each year k. Which kind of model best describes the function?

Tell which kind of model best describes each situation.

16. The height of a plant at weekly intervals over the last 6 weeks was 1 inches, 1.5 inches, 2 inches, 2.5 inches, 3 inches., and 3.5 inches.

17. The number of games a baseball player played in the last four years was 162, 162, 162, and 162.

18. The height of a ball in a certain time interval was recorded as 30.64 feet, 30.96 feet, 31 feet, 30.96 feet, and 30.64 feet.

Write a function to model each set of data.

19.

x	−1	0	1	2	4
y	0.05	0.2	0.8	3.2	51.2

20.

x	−2	0	2	4	8
y	5	4	3	2	0

Tell which kind of model best describes each graph.

21.

22.

23. Write About It Write a set of data that you could model with an exponential function. Explain why the exponential model would work.

24. ///**ERROR ANALYSIS**/// A student concluded that the data set would best be modeled by a quadratic function. Explain the student's error.

25. Critical Thinking Sometimes the graphs of quadratic data and exponential data can look very similar. Describe how you can tell them apart.

MULTI-STEP TEST PREP

26. This problem will prepare you for the Multi-Step Test Prep on page 820.

a. Examine the two models that represent annual tuition for two colleges. Describe each model as linear, quadratic, or exponential.

b. Write a function rule for each model.

c. Both models have the same values for 2004. What does this mean?

d. Why do both models have the same value for year 1?

Years After 2004	Tuition at College 1 ($)	Tuition at College 2 ($)
0	2000.00	2000.00
1	2200.00	2200.00
2	2400.00	2420.00
3	2600.00	2662.00
4	2800.00	2928.20

27. Which function best models the data: $\{(-4, -2), (-2, -1), (0, 0), (2, 1), (4, 2)\}$?

    Ⓐ $y = \left(\dfrac{1}{2}\right)^x$ Ⓑ $y = \dfrac{1}{2}x^2$ Ⓒ $y = \dfrac{1}{2}x$ Ⓓ $y = \left(\dfrac{1}{2}x\right)^2$

28. A city's population is increasing at a rate of 2% per year. Which type of model describes this situation?

    Ⓕ Exponential   Ⓖ Quadratic   Ⓗ Linear   Ⓙ None of these

29. Which data set is best modeled by a linear function?

    Ⓐ $\{(-2, 0), (-1, 2), (0, -4), (1, -1), (2, 2)\}$

    Ⓑ $\{(-2, 2), (-1, 4), (0, 6), (1, 16), (2, 32)\}$

    Ⓒ $\{(-2, 2), (-1, 4), (0, 6), (1, 8), (2, 10)\}$

    Ⓓ $\{(-2, 0), (-1, 5), (0, 7), (1, 5), (2, 0)\}$

CHALLENGE AND EXTEND

30. Finance An accountant estimates that a certain new automobile worth $18,000 will lose value at a rate of 16% per year.

    a. Make a table that shows the worth of the car for years 0, 1, 2, 3, and 4. What is the real-world meaning of year 0?

    b. Which type of model best represents the data in your table? Explain.

    c. Write a function for your data.

    d. What is the value of the car after $5\frac{1}{2}$ years?

    e. What is the value of the car after 8 years?

31. Pet Care The table shows general guidelines for the weight of a Great Dane at various ages.

    a. None of the three models in this lesson—linear, quadratic, or exponential—fits this data exactly. Which of these is the *best* model for the data? Explain your choice.

    b. What would you predict for the weight of a Great Dane who is 1 year old?

    c. Do you think you could use your model to find the weight of a Great Dane at any age? Why or why not?

Great Dane	
Age (mo)	Weight (kg)
2	12
4	23
6	33
8	40
10	45

SPIRAL REVIEW

Write an algebraic expression for each situation. *(Lesson 1-1)*

32. the total number of kilometers run by Helen in n 5-kilometer races

33. the average gas mileage of a car that travels 145 miles on g gallons of gasoline

34. Lorraine's height if she is b inches shorter than Gene, who is 74 inches tall

Solve by using square roots. *(Lesson 9-7)*

35. $4x^2 = 100$ **36.** $10 - x^2 = 10$ **37.** $16x^2 + 5 = 86$

Graph each exponential function. *(Lesson 11-2)*

38. $y = 6^x$ **39.** $y = -2(5)^x$ **40.** $y = \left(\dfrac{1}{3}\right)^x$

MULTI-STEP TEST PREP

Exponential Functions

Dollars for Scholars In 1980, the average annual tuition at two-year colleges was $350. Since then, the cost of tuition has increased by an average of 9% each year.

1. Write a function rule that models the annual growth in tuition at two-year colleges since 1980. Let 1980 be year zero in your function. Identify the variables, and tell which is independent and which is dependent.

2. Use your function to determine the average annual tuition in 2006. Use a table and a graph to support your answer.

3. Use your function to predict the average annual tuition at two-year colleges for the year you plan to graduate from high school.

4. In what year is the average annual tuition twice as much as in 1980? Use a table and a graph to support your answer.

5. In what year does the average annual tuition reach $1000? Use a table and a graph to support your answer.

Quiz for Lessons 11-1 Through 11-4

11-1 Geometric Sequences

Find the next three terms in each geometric sequence.

1. 3, 6, 12, 24, …

2. −1, 2, −4, 8, …

3. −2400, −1200, −600, −300, …

4. The first term of a geometric sequence is 2 and the common ratio is 3. What is the 8th term of the sequence?

5. The table shows the distance swung by a pendulum during its first three swings. The values form a geometric sequence. What will be the length of the 7th swing?

Swing	Length (cm)
1	1000
2	800
3	640

11-2 Exponential Functions

6. The function $f(x) = 3(1.1)^x$ gives the length (in inches) of an image after being enlarged by 10% x times. What is the length of the image after it has been enlarged 4 times? Round your answer to the nearest hundredth.

Graph each exponential function.

7. $y = 3^x$

8. $y = 2(2)^x$

9. $y = -2(4)^x$

10. $y = -(0.5)^x$

11. The function $f(x) = 40(0.8)^x$ gives the amount of a medication in milligrams present in a patient's system x hours after taking a 40-mg dose. In how many hours will there be less than 2 mg of the drug in a patient's system?

11-3 Exponential Growth and Decay

Write a function to model each situation. Then find the value of the function after the given amount of time.

12. Fiona's salary is $30,000, and she expects to receive a 3% raise each year; 10 years.

13. $2000 is invested at a rate of 4.5% compounded monthly; 3 years.

14. A $1200 computer is losing value at a rate of 20% per year; 4 years.

15. Strontium-90 has a half-life of 29 years. About how much strontium-90 will be left from a 100-mg sample after 290 years? Round your answer to the nearest thousandth.

11-4 Linear, Quadratic, and Exponential Models

Graph each data set. Which kind of model best describes the data?

16. $\{(-2, 5), (3, 10), (0, 1), (1, 2), (0.5, 1.25)\}$

17. $\{(0, 3), (2, 12), (-1, 1.5), (-3, 0.375), (4, 48)\}$

Look for a pattern in each data set to determine which kind of model best describes the data.

18. $\{(-2, -6), (-1, -5), (0, -4), (1, -3), (2, -2)\}$

19. $\{(-2, -24), (-1, -12), (0, -6), (1, -3)\}$

20. Use the data in the table to describe how the value of the stamp is changing. Then write a function that models the data. Use your function to predict the value of the stamp in 11 years.

Value of Collectible Stamp				
Year	0	1	2	3
Value ($)	5.00	6.00	7.20	8.64

Square-Root Functions

Objectives
Identify square-root functions and their domains and ranges.

Graph square-root functions.

Vocabulary
square-root function

Who uses this?
Astronauts can use square-root functions to calculate their speed in free fall.

Astronauts at NASA practice living in the weightlessness of space by training in the KC-135, also known as the "Vomit Comet." This aircraft flies to a certain altitude and then free falls for a period of time, simulating a zero-gravity environment.

The function $y = 8\sqrt{x}$ gives the speed in feet per second of an object in free fall after falling x feet. This function is different from others you have seen so far. It contains a variable under the square-root sign, $\sqrt{}$.

Know it! Note

Square-Root Function

WORDS	EXAMPLES	NONEXAMPLES
A **square-root function** is a function whose rule contains a variable under a square-root sign.	$y = \sqrt{x}$ $y = \sqrt{2x+1}$ $y = 3\sqrt{\dfrac{x}{2}} - 6$	$y = x^2$ $y = \dfrac{2}{x+1}$ $y = \sqrt{3}x$

EXAMPLE 1 Evaluating Square-Root Functions

A Find the speed of an object in free fall after it has fallen 4 feet.

$y = 8\sqrt{x}$ *Write the speed function.*
$ = 8\sqrt{4}$ *Substitute 4 for x.*
$ = 8(2)$ *Simplify.*
$ = 16$

After an object has fallen 4 feet, its speed is 16 ft/s.

Helpful Hint

Check that your answer is reasonable. In Example 1B, $8\sqrt{49} = 8(7) = 56$, so $8\sqrt{50} \approx 56.6$ is reasonable.

B Find the speed of an object in free fall after it has fallen 50 feet. Round your answer to the nearest tenth.

$y = 8\sqrt{x}$ *Write the speed function.*
$ = 8\sqrt{50}$ *Substitute 50 for x.*
$ \approx 56.6$ *Use a calculator.*

After an object has fallen 50 feet, its speed is about 56.6 ft/s.

 CHECK IT OUT!

1a. Find the speed of an object in free fall after it has fallen 25 feet.

1b. Find the speed of an object in free fall after it has fallen 15 feet. Round your answer to the nearest hundredth.

Recall that the square root of a negative number is not a real number. The domain (*x*-values) of a square-root function is restricted to numbers that make the value under the radical sign greater than or equal to 0.

EXAMPLE 2 **Finding the Domain of Square-Root Functions**

Find the domain of each square-root function.

A $y = \sqrt{x + 4} - 3$

$x + 4 \geq 0$ *The expression under the radical sign must be greater than or equal to 0.*

$$\frac{-4 \quad -4}{x \quad \geq -4}$$ *Solve the inequality. Subtract 4 from both sides.*

The domain is the set of all real numbers greater than or equal to −4.

B $y = \sqrt{3(x - 2)}$

$3(x - 2) \geq 0$ *The expression under the radical sign must be greater than or equal to 0.*

$3x - 6 \geq 0$ *Solve the inequality. Distribute 3 on the left side.*

$$\frac{+6 \quad +6}{3x \quad \geq \quad 6}$$ *Add 6 to both sides.*

$x \geq 2$ *Divide both sides by 3.*

The domain is the set of all real numbers greater than or equal to 2.

CHECK IT OUT! **Find the domain of each square-root function.**

2a. $y = \sqrt{2x - 1}$ **2b.** $y = \sqrt{3x - 5}$

The parent function for square-root functions, $f(x) = \sqrt{x}$, is graphed at right. Notice there are no *x*-values to the left of 0 because the domain is $x \geq 0$.

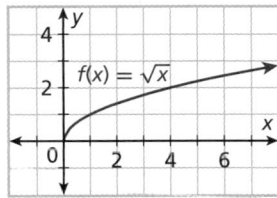

Know it! Note

Translations of the Graph of $f(x) = \sqrt{x}$	
The graph of $f(x) = \sqrt{x} + c$ is a vertical translation of the graph of $f(x) = \sqrt{x}$.	The graph of $f(x) = \sqrt{x - a}$ is a horizontal translation of the graph of $f(x) = \sqrt{x}$.
	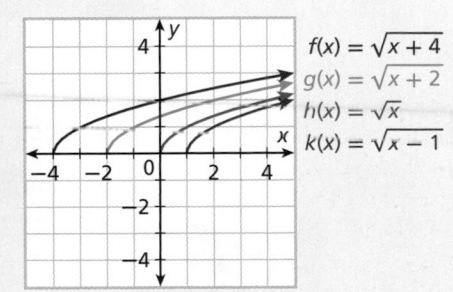
The graph is translated *c* units up for $c > 0$ and *c* units down for $c < 0$.	The graph is translated *a* units right for $a > 0$ and *a* units left for $a < 0$.

If a square-root function is given in one of these forms, you can graph the parent function $f(x) = \sqrt{x}$ and translate it vertically or horizontally.

EXAMPLE 3 **Graphing Square-Root Functions**

A Graph $f(x) = \sqrt{x - 4}$.

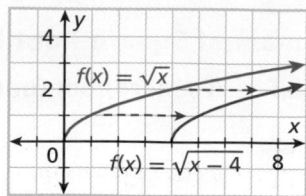

Since this function is in the form $f(x) = \sqrt{x - a}$, you can graph it as a horizontal translation of the graph of $f(x) = \sqrt{x}$.

Graph $f(x) = \sqrt{x}$ and then shift the graph 4 units to the right.

B Graph $f(x) = \sqrt{2x} + 3$.

This is not a horizontal or vertical translation of the graph of $f(x) = \sqrt{x}$.

Step 1 Find the domain of the function.

$2x \geq 0$ *The expression under the radical sign must be greater than or equal to 0.*

$x \geq 0$ *Solve the inequality by dividing both sides by 2.*

The domain is the set of all real numbers greater than or equal to 0.

Step 2 Choose x-values greater than or equal to 0 and generate ordered pairs.

x	$f(x) = \sqrt{2x} + 3$
0	3
2	5
8	7
18	9
32	11

Step 3 Plot the points. Then connect them with a smooth curve.

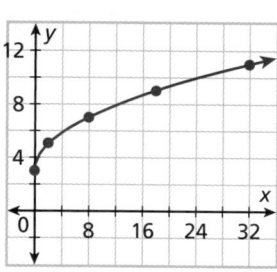

> **Helpful Hint**
>
> In Example 3B, when generating ordered pairs, choose x-values that make the expression under the radical sign a perfect square.

 CHECK IT OUT! Graph each square-root function.

3a. $f(x) = \sqrt{x} + 2$ **3b.** $f(x) = 2\sqrt{x} + 3$

THINK AND DISCUSS

1. How do you find the domain of a square-root function?

2. Compare the graph of $f(x) = \sqrt{x + 8}$ with the graph of $f(x) = \sqrt{x}$.

3. Compare the graph of $f(x) = \sqrt{x + 8}$ with the graph of $f(x) = \sqrt{x} + 8$.

4. GET ORGANIZED Copy and complete the graphic organizer. In each box, graph the function and give its domain.

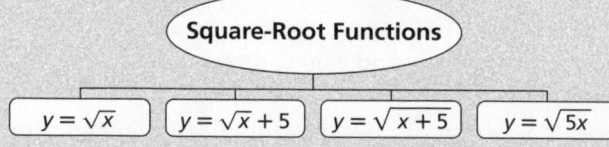

Square-Root Functions

$y = \sqrt{x}$ $y = \sqrt{x} + 5$ $y = \sqrt{x + 5}$ $y = \sqrt{5x}$

11-5
Exercises

go.hrw.com
Homework Help Online
KEYWORD: MA7 11-5
Parent Resources Online
KEYWORD: MA7 Parent

GUIDED PRACTICE

1. **Vocabulary** Explain why $y = x + \sqrt{3}$ is not a *square-root function*.

SEE EXAMPLE 1
p. 822

2. **Geometry** In a right triangle, $c = \sqrt{a^2 + b^2}$, where c is the length of the hypotenuse (the longest side) and a and b are the lengths of the other two sides, called the legs. What is the length of the hypotenuse of a right triangle if its legs measure 14 cm and 8 cm? Round your answer to the nearest hundredth.

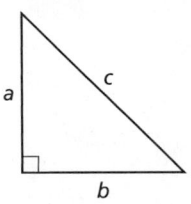

SEE EXAMPLE 2
p. 823

Find the domain of each square-root function.

3. $y = \sqrt{x + 6}$

4. $y = 4 - \sqrt{3 - x}$

5. $y = \sqrt{2x} - 5$

6. $y = \sqrt{x + 2}$

7. $y = \sqrt{3x + 9}$

8. $y = x + \sqrt{x - 5}$

SEE EXAMPLE 3
p. 824

Graph each square-root function.

9. $f(x) = \sqrt{x - 1}$

10. $f(x) = -\sqrt{2x}$

11. $f(x) = \sqrt{x} + 1$

12. $f(x) = \sqrt{x} - 12$

13. $f(x) = \sqrt{4 - x}$

14. $f(x) = \sqrt{x + 4}$

PRACTICE AND PROBLEM SOLVING

Independent Practice

For Exercises	See Example
15	1
16–27	2
28–33	3

15. **Law Enforcement** At the scene of a car accident, police measure the length of the skid marks to estimate the speed that the car was traveling. On dry concrete, $f(x) = \sqrt{24x}$ gives the speed in mi/h when the length of the skid mark is x feet. Find the speed that a car was traveling if it left a skid mark that was 104 ft long. Round your answer to the nearest hundredth.

Extra Practice
Skills Practice p. S25
Application Practice p. S38

Find the domain of each square-root function.

16. $y = \sqrt{8 - 2x}$

17. $y = 4 - \sqrt{\dfrac{x}{2}}$

18. $y = \sqrt{3x + 2}$

19. $y = \sqrt{-2x + 3}$

20. $y = 2\sqrt{x + 1} - 2$

21. $y = \sqrt{3(x + 2)} - 1$

22. $y = \sqrt{2(x + 4)} - 3$

23. $y = 7\sqrt{\dfrac{x}{5} - 8}$

24. $y = \sqrt{2(3x - 6)}$

25. $y = \sqrt{\dfrac{1}{3}(x - 9)}$

26. $y = \sqrt{2(x + 7)} - 6$

27. $y = 4 + \sqrt{3x + 2}$

Graph each square-root function.

28. $f(x) = \sqrt{x - 5}$

29. $f(x) = \sqrt{2x} - 4$

30. $f(x) = -1 - \sqrt{x}$

31. $f(x) = \sqrt{x} - 4$

32. $f(x) = 3\sqrt{x - 6}$

33. $f(x) = \dfrac{1}{2}\sqrt{x + 4}$

34. **Geometry** If you know a circle's area, you can use the formula $r = \sqrt{\dfrac{A}{\pi}}$ to find the radius. What is the radius of a circle whose area is 60 cm²? Use 3.14 for π. Round your answer to the nearest hundredth of a centimeter.

35. **Graphing Calculator** Use a graphing calculator for the following.
   a. Graph $y = \sqrt{x}$, $y = \frac{1}{2}\sqrt{x}$, $y = 2\sqrt{x}$, $y = 3\sqrt{x}$, and $y = 4\sqrt{x}$ on the same screen.
   b. What is the domain of each function?
   c. What is the range of each function?
   d. Describe the characteristics of $y = a\sqrt{x}$ for $a > 0$.

36. **Graphing Calculator** Use a graphing calculator for the following.
    a. Graph $y = -\sqrt{x}$, $y = -\frac{1}{2}\sqrt{x}$, $y = -2\sqrt{x}$, $y = -3\sqrt{x}$, and $y = -4\sqrt{x}$ on the same screen.
    b. What is the domain of each function?
    c. What is the range of each function?
    d. Describe the characteristics of $y = a\sqrt{x}$ for $a < 0$.

37. The distance d between two points (x, y) and (w, z) in the coordinate plane can be found by using the formula $d = \sqrt{(w - x)^2 + (z - y)^2}$. What is the distance between the points $(2, 1)$ and $(5, 3)$? Round your answer to the nearest hundredth.

38. **Geology** Tsunamis are large waves that move across deep oceans at high speeds. When tsunamis hit shallow water, their energy moves them upward into a destructive force. The speed of a tsunami in meters per second can be found using the function $f(x) = \sqrt{9.8x}$, where x is the depth of the water in meters. Graph this function. Then find the speed of a tsunami when the water depth is 500 meters.

39. **Astronomy** A planet's *escape velocity* is the initial velocity that an object must have to escape the planet's gravity. Escape velocity v in meters per second can be found by using the formula $v = \sqrt{2gr}$, where g is the planet's surface gravity and r is the planet's radius. Find the escape velocity for each planet in the table. Round your answers to the nearest whole number.

Planet	g (m/s²)	r (m)
Mercury	3.7	2.4×10^6
Venus	8.8	6.1×10^6
Earth	9.8	6.4×10^6
Mars	3.7	3.4×10^6

40. **Geometry** The volume V of a cylinder can be found by using the formula $V = \pi r^2 h$, where r represents the radius of the cylinder and h represents its height. Find the radius of a cylinder whose volume is 1212 in³ and whose height is 10 inches. Use 3.14 for π.

41. **Write About It** Explain how to find the domain of a square-root function. Why is the domain not all real numbers?

42. **Multi-Step** For the function $y = \sqrt{3(x - 5)}$, find the value of y that corresponds to the least possible value for x.

43. **Critical Thinking** Can the range of a square-root function be all real numbers? Explain.

MULTI-STEP TEST PREP

44. This problem will prepare you for the Multi-Step Test Prep on page 854.
    a. The Ocean Motion ride at Ohio's Cedar Point amusement park is a giant ship that swings like a pendulum. If a pendulum is under the influence of gravity only, then the time in seconds that it takes for one complete swing back and forth (called the pendulum's period) is $T = 2\pi\sqrt{\frac{\ell}{32}}$, where ℓ is the length of the pendulum in feet. What is the domain of this function?
    b. What is the period of a pendulum whose length is 80 feet? Use 3.14 for π and round your answer to the nearest hundredth.
    c. The length of the Ocean Motion pendulum is about 80 feet. Do you think your answer to part b is its period? Explain why or why not.

45. Which function is graphed at right?

   Ⓐ $f(x) = \sqrt{x} + 3$ Ⓒ $f(x) = \sqrt{x} - 3$

   Ⓑ $f(x) = \sqrt{x} + 3$ Ⓓ $f(x) = \sqrt{x} - 3$

46. Which function has domain $x \geq 2$?

   Ⓕ $y = \sqrt{2x}$ Ⓗ $y = \sqrt{\dfrac{x}{2}}$

   Ⓖ $y = \sqrt{x + 2}$ Ⓙ $y = \sqrt{x - 2}$

47. The function $y = \sqrt{\frac{1}{5}x}$ gives the approximate time y in seconds that it takes an object to fall to the ground from a height of x meters. About how long will it take an object 25 meters above the ground to fall to the ground?

   Ⓐ 11.2 seconds   Ⓒ 2.2 seconds

   Ⓑ 5 seconds   Ⓓ 0.4 seconds

48. Gridded Response If $g(x) = \sqrt{4x} - 1$, what is $g(9)$?

CHALLENGE AND EXTEND

Find the domain of each function.

49. $y = \sqrt{x^2 - 25}$ **50.** $y = \sqrt{x^2 + 5x + 6}$ **51.** $y = \sqrt{2x^2 + 5x - 12}$

Find the domain and range of each function.

52. $y = 2 - \sqrt{x + 3}$ **53.** $y = 4 - \sqrt{3 - x}$ **54.** $y = 6 - \sqrt{\dfrac{x}{2}}$

55. Give an example of a square-root function whose graph is above the x-axis.

56. Give an example of a square-root function whose graph is in Quadrant IV.

57. Multi-Step Justin is given the function $y = 3 - \sqrt{2(x - 5)}$ and $x = 2, 4, 5,$ and 7. He notices that two of these values are not in the function's domain.

   a. Which two values are not in the domain? How do you know?

   b. What are the values of y for the two given x-values that are in the domain?

SPIRAL REVIEW

Write each equation in slope-intercept form, and then graph. *(Lesson 5-7)*

58. $2y = 4x - 8$ **59.** $3x + 6y = 12$ **60.** $2x = -y - 9$

Find each product. *(Lesson 7-9)*

61. $(3x - 1)^2$ **62.** $(2x - 5)(2x + 5)$ **63.** $(a - b^2c)^2$

64. $(x^2 + 2y)^2$ **65.** $(3r - 2s)(3r + 2s)$ **66.** $(a^3b^2 - c^4)(a^3b^2 + c^4)$

67. Blake invested $42,000 at a rate of 5% compounded quarterly. Write a function to model this situation. Then find the value of Blake's investment after 3 years. *(Lesson 11-3)*

68. Lead-209 has a half-life of about 3.25 hours. Find the amount of lead-209 left from a 230-mg sample after 1 day. Round your answer to the nearest hundredth. *(Lesson 11-3)*

11-5
Technology LAB
Graph Radical Functions

You can use a graphing calculator to graph radical functions or to quickly check that a graph drawn by hand is reasonable.

Use with Lesson 11-5

Activity

Graph $f(x) = \sqrt{x - 1}$ without using a graphing calculator. Then graph the same function on a graphing calculator and compare.

1 The graph will be a shift of the graph of the parent function $f(x) = \sqrt{x}$ one unit right. Graph $f(x) = \sqrt{x}$ and then shift the graph one unit right.

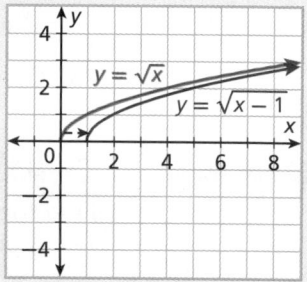

2 Enter the function into the **Y=** editor.

Press **WINDOW** and enter -1 for **Xmin**, 9 for **Xmax**, -5 for **Ymin**, and 5 for **Ymax**.

Press **GRAPH** and compare the graph on the screen to the graph done by hand.

The graph on the screen indicates that the graph done by hand is reasonable.

Try This

1. Graph $f(x) = \sqrt{x + 3}$ without using a graphing calculator. Then graph the same function on a graphing calculator and compare.

2. Graph $f(x) = \sqrt{x} - 2$ without using a graphing calculator. Then graph the same function on a graphing calculator and compare.

3. **Make a Conjecture** How do you think the graph of $f(x) = \sqrt{x + 1} + 4$ compares to the graph of $f(x) = \sqrt{x}$? Use a graphing calculator to check your conjecture.

4. **Make a Conjecture** How do you think the graph of $f(x) = 2\sqrt{x}$ compares to the graph of $f(x) = \sqrt{x}$? Use a graphing calculator to check your conjecture.

11-6 Radical Expressions

Objective
Simplify radical expressions.

Vocabulary
radical expression
radicand

Why learn this?
You can use a radical expression to find the length of a throw in baseball. (See Example 5.)

An expression that contains a radical sign $(\sqrt{\ })$ is a **radical expression**. There are many different types of radical expressions, but in this chapter, you will only study radical expressions that contain square roots.

Examples of radical expressions:

$$\sqrt{14} \quad \sqrt{\ell^2 + w^2} \quad \sqrt{2gd} \quad \frac{\sqrt{d}}{4} \quad 5\sqrt{2} \quad \sqrt{18}$$

The expression under a radical sign is the **radicand**. A radicand may contain numbers, variables, or both. It may contain one term or more than one term.

Know it! Note

Simplest Form of a Square-Root Expression

An expression containing square roots is in simplest form when
- the radicand has no perfect square factors other than 1.
- the radicand has no fractions.
- there are no square roots in any denominator.

Remember that positive numbers have two square roots, one positive and one negative. However, $\sqrt{\ }$ indicates a nonnegative square root. When you simplify, be sure that your answer is not negative. To simplify $\sqrt{x^2}$, you should write $\sqrt{x^2} = |x|$, because you do not know whether x is positive or negative.

Below are some simplified square-root expressions:

$$\sqrt{x^2} = |x| \qquad \sqrt{x^3} = x\sqrt{x} \qquad \sqrt{x^4} = x^2 \qquad \sqrt{x^5} = x^2\sqrt{x} \qquad \sqrt{x^6} = |x^3|$$

EXAMPLE 1 Simplifying Square-Root Expressions

Simplify each expression.

A $\sqrt{\dfrac{2}{72}}$

$\sqrt{\dfrac{2}{72}} = \sqrt{\dfrac{1}{36}}$

$= \dfrac{1}{6}$

B $\sqrt{3^2 + 4^2}$

$\sqrt{3^2 + 4^2} = \sqrt{9 + 16}$

$= \sqrt{25}$

$= 5$

C $\sqrt{x^2 + 8x + 16}$

$\sqrt{x^2 + 8x + 16} = \sqrt{(x + 4)^2}$

$= |x + 4|$

Simplify each expression.

1a. $\sqrt{\dfrac{256}{4}}$ **1b.** $\sqrt{40 + 9}$ **1c.** $\sqrt{5^2 + 12^2}$ **1d.** $\sqrt{(3 - x)^2}$

Product Property of Square Roots

WORDS	NUMBERS	ALGEBRA
For any nonnegative real numbers a and b, the square root of ab is equal to the square root of a times the square root of b.	$\sqrt{4(25)} = \sqrt{100} = 10$ $\sqrt{4(25)} = \sqrt{4}\sqrt{25} = 2(5) = 10$	$\sqrt{ab} = \sqrt{a}\sqrt{b}$, where $a \geq 0$ and $b \geq 0$

Using the Product Property of Square Roots

Simplify. All variables represent nonnegative numbers.

A $\sqrt{18}$

$$\sqrt{18} = \sqrt{9(2)}$$ *Factor the radicand using perfect squares.*
$$= \sqrt{9}\sqrt{2}$$ *Product Property of Square Roots*
$$= 3\sqrt{2}$$ *Simplify.*

B $\sqrt{x^4 y^3}$

$$\sqrt{x^4 y^3} = \sqrt{x^4}\sqrt{y^3}$$ *Product Property of Square Roots*
$$= \sqrt{x^4}\sqrt{y^2}\sqrt{y}$$ *Product Property of Square Roots*
$$= x^2 y\sqrt{y}$$ *Since y is nonnegative, $\sqrt{y^2} = y$.*

CHECK IT OUT! Simplify. All variables represent nonnegative numbers.

2a. $\sqrt{128}$ **2b.** $\sqrt{x^3 y^2}$ **2c.** $\sqrt{48a^2 b}$

Quotient Property of Square Roots

WORDS	NUMBERS	ALGEBRA
For any real numbers a and b ($a \geq 0$ and $b > 0$), the square root of $\frac{a}{b}$ is equal to the square root of a divided by the square root of b.	$\sqrt{\dfrac{36}{4}} = \sqrt{9} = 3$ $\sqrt{\dfrac{36}{4}} = \dfrac{\sqrt{36}}{\sqrt{4}} = \dfrac{6}{2} = 3$	$\sqrt{\dfrac{a}{b}} = \dfrac{\sqrt{a}}{\sqrt{b}}$, where $a \geq 0$ and $b > 0$

EXAMPLE 3 **Using the Quotient Property of Square Roots**

Simplify. All variables represent nonnegative numbers.

A $\sqrt{\dfrac{5}{9}}$

$$\sqrt{\frac{5}{9}} = \frac{\sqrt{5}}{\sqrt{9}}$$ *Quotient Property of Square Roots*
$$= \frac{\sqrt{5}}{3}$$ *Simplify.*

B $\sqrt{\dfrac{a^5}{81a}}$

$$\sqrt{\frac{a^5}{81a}} = \sqrt{\frac{a^4}{81}}$$ *Simplify.*
$$= \frac{\sqrt{a^4}}{\sqrt{81}}$$ *Quotient Property of Square Roots*
$$= \frac{a^2}{9}$$ *Simplify.*

Simplify. All variables represent nonnegative numbers.

3a. $\sqrt{\dfrac{12}{27}}$ **3b.** $\sqrt{\dfrac{36}{x^4}}$ **3c.** $\sqrt{\dfrac{y^6}{4}}$

EXAMPLE 4 Using the Product and Quotient Properties Together

Simplify. All variables represent nonnegative numbers.

A $\sqrt{\dfrac{80}{25}}$

$\dfrac{\sqrt{80}}{\sqrt{25}}$ *Quotient Property of Square Roots*

$\dfrac{\sqrt{16(5)}}{\sqrt{25}}$ *Write 80 as 16(5).*

$\dfrac{\sqrt{16}\,\sqrt{5}}{\sqrt{25}}$ *Product Property of Square Roots*

$\dfrac{4\sqrt{5}}{5}$ *Simplify.*

B $\sqrt{\dfrac{4x^5}{9}}$

$\dfrac{\sqrt{4x^5}}{\sqrt{9}}$ *Quotient Property of Square Roots*

$\dfrac{\sqrt{4}\,\sqrt{x^5}}{\sqrt{9}}$ *Product Property of Square Roots*

$\dfrac{\sqrt{4}\,\sqrt{x^4}\,\sqrt{x}}{\sqrt{9}}$

$\dfrac{2x^2\sqrt{x}}{3}$ *Simplify.*

> **Caution!** //////
>
> In the expression $\dfrac{4\sqrt{5}}{5}$, $\sqrt{5}$ and 5 are not common factors. $\dfrac{4\sqrt{5}}{5}$ is completely simplified.

 Simplify. All variables represent nonnegative numbers.

4a. $\sqrt{\dfrac{20}{49}}$ **4b.** $\sqrt{\dfrac{z^5}{25y^2}}$ **4c.** $\sqrt{\dfrac{p^6}{q^{10}}}$

EXAMPLE 5 *Sports Application*

A baseball diamond is a square with sides of 90 feet. How far is a throw from third base to first base? Give the answer as a radical expression in simplest form. Then estimate the length to the nearest tenth of a foot.

3rd base   1st base

?   90 ft   90 ft

The distance from third base to first base is the hypotenuse of a right triangle. Use the Pythagorean Theorem: $c^2 = a^2 + b^2$.

$c = \sqrt{a^2 + b^2}$ *Solve for c.*

$= \sqrt{(90)^2 + (90)^2}$ *Substitute 90 for a and b.*

$= \sqrt{8100 + 8100}$ *Simplify.*

$= \sqrt{16,200}$

$= \sqrt{100(81)(2)}$ *Factor 16,200 using perfect squares.*

$= \sqrt{100}\,\sqrt{81}\,\sqrt{2}$ *Use the Product Property of Square Roots.*

$= 10(9)\sqrt{2}$

$= 90\sqrt{2}$ *Simplify.*

≈ 127.3 *Use a calculator and round to the nearest tenth.*

The distance is $90\sqrt{2}$, or about 127.3, feet.

 5. A softball diamond is a square with sides of 60 feet. How long is a throw from third base to first base in softball? Give the answer as a radical expression in simplest form. Then estimate the length to the nearest tenth of a foot.

THINK AND DISCUSS

1. Show two ways to evaluate $\sqrt{16(9)}$.

2. Show two ways to evaluate $\sqrt{\dfrac{100}{4}}$.

3. GET ORGANIZED Copy and complete the graphic organizer. In each box, write the property and give an example.

	Product Property of Square Roots	Quotient Property of Square Roots
Words		
Example		

11-6 Exercises

go.hrw.com
Homework Help Online
KEYWORD: MA7 11-6
Parent Resources Online
KEYWORD: MA7 Parent

GUIDED PRACTICE

1. Vocabulary In the expression $\sqrt{3x - 6} + 7$, what is the *radicand*?

SEE EXAMPLE **1**
p. 829

Simplify each expression.

2. $\sqrt{81}$

3. $\sqrt{\dfrac{98}{2}}$

4. $\sqrt{(a + 7)^2}$

Simplify. All variables represent nonnegative numbers.

SEE EXAMPLE **2**
p. 830

5. $\sqrt{180}$

6. $\sqrt{40}$

7. $\sqrt{648}$

8. $\sqrt{m^5 n^3}$

9. $\sqrt{32x^4 y^3}$

10. $\sqrt{200a^2 b}$

SEE EXAMPLE **3**
p. 830

11. $\sqrt{\dfrac{17}{25}}$

12. $\sqrt{\dfrac{7}{16}}$

13. $\sqrt{\dfrac{6}{49}}$

14. $\sqrt{\dfrac{b}{c^2}}$

15. $\sqrt{\dfrac{4x^2}{36x}}$

16. $\sqrt{\dfrac{7a^4}{9a^3}}$

SEE EXAMPLE **4**
p. 831

17. $\sqrt{\dfrac{108}{49}}$

18. $\sqrt{\dfrac{204}{25}}$

19. $\sqrt{\dfrac{512}{81}}$

20. $\sqrt{\dfrac{1}{36x^2}}$

21. $\sqrt{\dfrac{50x^2}{169}}$

22. $\sqrt{\dfrac{72x^7}{4x^4}}$

SEE EXAMPLE **5**
p. 831

23. Recreation Your boat is traveling due north from a dock. Your friend's boat left at the same time from the same dock and is headed due east. After an hour, your friend calls and tells you that he has just stopped because of engine trouble. How far must you travel to meet your friend? Give your answer as a radical expression in simplest form. Then estimate the distance to the nearest mile.

PRACTICE AND PROBLEM SOLVING

Independent Practice

For Exercises	See Example
24–31	1
32–35	2
36–39	3
40–43	4
44	5

Extra Practice

Skills Practice p. S25

Application Practice p. S38

Simplify.

24. $\sqrt{100}$

25. $\sqrt{\dfrac{800}{2}}$

26. $\sqrt{3^2 + 4^2}$

27. $\sqrt{3 \cdot 27}$

28. $\sqrt{a^4}$

29. $\sqrt{(x+1)^2}$

30. $\sqrt{(5-x)^2}$

31. $\sqrt{(x-3)^2}$

Simplify. All variables represent nonnegative numbers.

32. $\sqrt{125}$

33. $\sqrt{4000}$

34. $\sqrt{216a^2b^2}$

35. $\sqrt{320r^2s^2}$

36. $\sqrt{\dfrac{15}{64}}$

37. $\sqrt{\dfrac{45}{4}}$

38. $\sqrt{\dfrac{64a^4}{4a^6}}$

39. $\sqrt{\dfrac{14z^3}{9z^3}}$

40. $\sqrt{\dfrac{128}{81}}$

41. $\sqrt{\dfrac{x^3}{y^6}}$

42. $\sqrt{\dfrac{150}{196x^2}}$

43. $\sqrt{\dfrac{192s^3}{49s}}$

44. Amusement Parks A thrill ride at an amusement park carries riders 160 feet straight up and then releases them for a free fall. The time t in seconds that it takes an object in free fall to reach the ground is $t = \sqrt{\dfrac{d}{16}}$, where d is the distance in feet that it falls. How long does it take the riders to reach the ground? Give your answer as a radical expression in simplest form. Then estimate the answer to the nearest tenth of a second.

Simplify. All variables represent nonnegative numbers.

45. $-4\sqrt{75}$

46. $-\sqrt{80}$

47. $5x\sqrt{63}$

48. $3\sqrt{48x}$

49. $2\sqrt{\dfrac{x^2}{4}}$

50. $\dfrac{1}{2}\sqrt{\dfrac{1}{25}}$

51. $3x\sqrt{\dfrac{x^5}{81}}$

52. $\dfrac{12}{x}\sqrt{\dfrac{x^2y}{36}}$

Use the Product Property or the Quotient Property of Square Roots to write each expression as a single square root. Then simplify if possible.

53. $\sqrt{12}\,\sqrt{3}$

54. $\sqrt{18}\,\sqrt{8}$

55. $\sqrt{10}\,\sqrt{5}$

56. $\sqrt{8}\,\sqrt{14}$

57. $\dfrac{\sqrt{33}}{\sqrt{11}}$

58. $\dfrac{\sqrt{24}}{\sqrt{2}}$

59. $\dfrac{\sqrt{60}}{\sqrt{3}}$

60. $\dfrac{\sqrt{72}}{\sqrt{9}}$

61. Multi-Step How many whole feet of fencing would be needed to enclose the triangular garden that is sketched at right? Explain your answer.

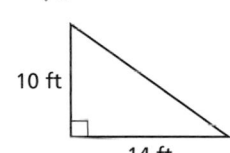

10 ft

14 ft

62. Write About It Write a series of steps that you could use to simplify $\sqrt{\dfrac{28}{49}}$.

MULTI-STEP TEST PREP

63. This problem will prepare you for the Multi-Step Test Prep on page 854.

a. The vertical component of a roller coaster's speed in feet per second at the bottom of a hill is $v = \sqrt{64h}$, where h is the hill's height in feet. Simplify this expression. Then estimate the velocity at the bottom of a 137-foot hill.

b. The distance along the track of a hill is $d = \sqrt{x^2 + h^2}$, where x is the horizontal distance along the ground and h is the hill's height. Where does this equation come from?

c. For the hill in part **a**, the horizontal distance along the ground is 103 feet. What is the distance along the track? Round your answer to the nearest tenth.

64. Critical Thinking The Product Property of Square Roots states that $\sqrt{ab} = \sqrt{a}\sqrt{b}$, where $a \geq 0$ and $b \geq 0$. Why must a and b be greater than or equal to zero?

65. Architecture The formula $d = \frac{\sqrt{6h}}{3}$ estimates the distance d in miles that a person can see to the horizon from h feet above the ground. Find the distance you could see to the horizon from the top of each building in the graph. Give your answers as radical expressions in simplest form and as estimates to the nearest tenth of a mile.

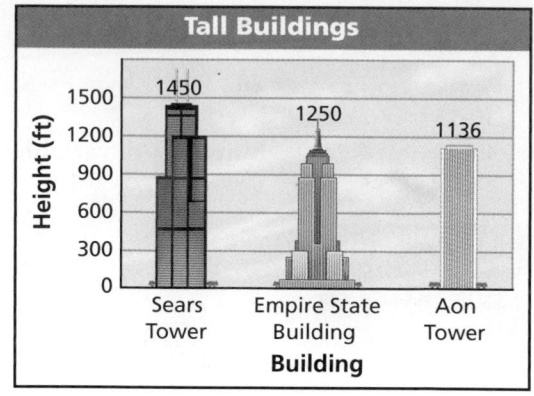

Tall Buildings

Height (ft) — Sears Tower: 1450; Empire State Building: 1250; Aon Tower: 1136

Building

66. Math History Heron's formula for the area A of a triangle is $A = \sqrt{s(s-a)(s-b)(s-c)}$, where a, b, and c are the side lengths and $s = \frac{1}{2}(a+b+c)$. Find the area of a triangle with side lengths of 7 m, 9 m, and 12 m. Give your answer as a radical expression in simplest form and as an estimate to the nearest tenth.

TEST PREP

67. Which expression is in simplest form?

Ⓐ $\sqrt{49}$ Ⓑ $\sqrt{48}$ Ⓒ $\sqrt{35}$ Ⓓ $\sqrt{36}$

68. Which expression is equal to $\sqrt{60}$?

Ⓕ $2\sqrt{15}$ Ⓖ $6\sqrt{10}$ Ⓗ $15\sqrt{2}$ Ⓙ $10\sqrt{60}$

69. How long is the diagonal of a square whose area is 100 square feet?

Ⓐ $2\sqrt{10}$ feet   Ⓑ 10 feet   Ⓒ $10\sqrt{2}$ feet   Ⓓ 20 feet

CHALLENGE AND EXTEND

Simplify. All variables represent nonnegative numbers.

70. $\sqrt{4x + 16}$ **71.** $\sqrt{x^3 + x^2}$ **72.** $\sqrt{9x^3 - 18x^2}$

73. Let x represent any real number (including negative numbers). Simplify each of the following expressions, using absolute-value symbols when necessary.

a. $\sqrt{x^2}$ **b.** $\sqrt{x^4}$ **c.** $\sqrt{x^6}$ **d.** $\sqrt{x^8}$ **e.** $\sqrt{x^{10}}$

f. For any nonnegative integer n, $\sqrt{x^{2n}} = $ ▨ if n is even, and $\sqrt{x^{2n}} = $ ▨ if n is odd.

SPIRAL REVIEW

Tell whether each relationship is a direct variation. Explain. *(Lesson 5-6)*

74.

x	2	3	4
y	12	18	24

75.

x	2	3	4
y	−6	−5	−4

76. Write an equation in slope-intercept form for the line through $(3, 1)$ and $(2, -5)$. *(Lesson 5-7)*

Graph each data set. Which kind of model best describes the data? *(Lesson 11-4)*

77. $\{(-3, 16), (-2, 8), (0, 2), (1, 1), (3, 0.25)\}$

78. $\{(-5, 15), (-2, -6), (0, -10), (3, -1), (4, 6)\}$

11-7 Adding and Subtracting Radical Expressions

Objective
Add and subtract radical expressions.

Vocabulary
like radicals

Why learn this?
You can add or subtract radical expressions to find perimeter. (See Example 3.)

Square-root expressions with the same radicand are examples of **like radicals** .

Like Radicals	$2\sqrt{5}$ and $4\sqrt{5}$	$6\sqrt{x}$ and $-2\sqrt{x}$	$3\sqrt{4t}$ and $\sqrt{4t}$
Unlike Radicals	2 and $\sqrt{15}$	$6\sqrt{x}$ and $\sqrt{6x}$	$3\sqrt{2}$ and $2\sqrt{3}$

Like radicals can be combined by adding or subtracting. You can use the Distributive Property to show how this is done:

$$2\sqrt{5} + 4\sqrt{5} = (2 + 4)\sqrt{5} = 6\sqrt{5}$$

$$6\sqrt{x} - 2\sqrt{x} = (6 - 2)\sqrt{x} = 4\sqrt{x}$$

Notice that you can combine like radicals by adding or subtracting the numbers multiplied by the radical and keeping the radical the same.

EXAMPLE 1 Adding and Subtracting Square-Root Expressions

Add or subtract.

Helpful Hint

Combining like radicals is similar to combining like terms.
$2\sqrt{5} + 4\sqrt{5} = 6\sqrt{5}$
$2x + 4x = 6x$

A $3\sqrt{7} + 8\sqrt{7}$
$3\sqrt{7} + 8\sqrt{7}$ *The terms are like radicals.*
$11\sqrt{7}$

B $9\sqrt{y} - \sqrt{y}$
$9\sqrt{y} - 1\sqrt{y}$ $\sqrt{y} = 1\sqrt{y}$; *the terms are like radicals.*
$8\sqrt{y}$

C $12\sqrt{2} - 4\sqrt{11}$
$12\sqrt{2} - 4\sqrt{11}$ *The terms are unlike radicals. Do not combine.*

D $-8\sqrt{3d} + 6\sqrt{2d} + 10\sqrt{3d}$
$-8\sqrt{3d} + 6\sqrt{2d} + 10\sqrt{3d}$ *Identify like radicals.*
$2\sqrt{3d} + 6\sqrt{2d}$ *Combine like radicals.*

 CHECK IT OUT! Add or subtract.
1a. $5\sqrt{7} - 6\sqrt{7}$ **1b.** $8\sqrt{3} - 5\sqrt{3}$
1c. $4\sqrt{n} + 4\sqrt{n}$ **1d.** $\sqrt{2s} - \sqrt{5s} + 9\sqrt{5s}$

Sometimes radicals do not appear to be like until they are simplified. Simplify all radicals in an expression before trying to identify like radicals.

EXAMPLE 2

Simplifying Before Adding or Subtracting

Simplify each expression.

A $\sqrt{12} + \sqrt{27}$

$\sqrt{4(3)} + \sqrt{9(3)}$ *Factor the radicands using perfect squares.*

$\sqrt{4}\sqrt{3} + \sqrt{9}\sqrt{3}$ *Product Property of Square Roots*

$2\sqrt{3} + 3\sqrt{3}$ *Simplify.*

$5\sqrt{3}$ *Combine like radicals.*

B $3\sqrt{8} + \sqrt{45}$

$3\sqrt{4(2)} + \sqrt{9(5)}$ *Factor the radicands using perfect squares.*

$3\sqrt{4}\sqrt{2} + \sqrt{9}\sqrt{5}$ *Product Property of Square Roots*

$3(2)\sqrt{2} + 3\sqrt{5}$ *Simplify.*

$6\sqrt{2} + 3\sqrt{5}$ *The terms are unlike radicals. Do not combine.*

C $5\sqrt{28x} - 8\sqrt{7x}$

$5\sqrt{4(7x)} - 8\sqrt{7x}$ *Factor 28x using a perfect square.*

$5\sqrt{4}\sqrt{7x} - 8\sqrt{7x}$ *Product Property of Square Roots*

$5(2)\sqrt{7x} - 8\sqrt{7x}$ *Simplify.*

$10\sqrt{7x} - 8\sqrt{7x}$

$2\sqrt{7x}$ *Combine like radicals.*

D $\sqrt{125b} + 3\sqrt{20b} - \sqrt{45b}$

$\sqrt{25(5b)} + 3\sqrt{4(5b)} - \sqrt{9(5b)}$ *Factor the radicands using perfect squares.*

$\sqrt{25}\sqrt{5b} + 3\sqrt{4}\sqrt{5b} - \sqrt{9}\sqrt{5b}$ *Product Property of Square Roots*

$5\sqrt{5b} + 3(2)\sqrt{5b} - 3\sqrt{5b}$ *Simplify.*

$5\sqrt{5b} + 6\sqrt{5b} - 3\sqrt{5b}$

$8\sqrt{5b}$ *Combine like radicals.*

> **Remember!**
>
> When you write a radicand as a product, make at least one factor a perfect square.

 CHECK IT OUT! Simplify each expression.

2a. $\sqrt{54} + \sqrt{24}$ **2b.** $4\sqrt{27} - \sqrt{18}$ **2c.** $\sqrt{12y} + \sqrt{27y}$

EXAMPLE 3

Geometry Application

Find the perimeter of the triangle. Give your answer as a radical expression in simplest form.

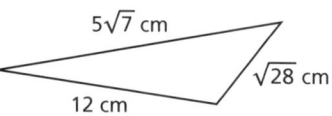

$12 + 5\sqrt{7} + \sqrt{28}$ *Write an expression for perimeter.*

$12 + 5\sqrt{7} + \sqrt{4(7)}$ *Factor 28 using a perfect square.*

$12 + 5\sqrt{7} + \sqrt{4}\sqrt{7}$ *Product Property of Square Roots*

$12 + 5\sqrt{7} + 2\sqrt{7}$ *Simplify.*

$12 + 7\sqrt{7}$ *Combine like radicals.*

The perimeter is $\left(12 + 7\sqrt{7}\right)$ cm.

 CHECK IT OUT! **3.** Find the perimeter of a rectangle whose length is $2\sqrt{b}$ inches and whose width is $3\sqrt{b}$ inches. Give your answer as a radical expression in simplest form.

1. Rearrange the following into two groups of like radicals: $2\sqrt{6}$, $6\sqrt{5}$, $\sqrt{600}$, $\sqrt{150}$, $-\sqrt{20}$, $\sqrt{5}$.

2. Tell why you should simplify radicals when adding and subtracting expressions with radicals.

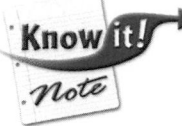

3. GET ORGANIZED Copy and complete the graphic organizer.

11-7 Exercises

go.hrw.com
Homework Help Online
KEYWORD: MA7 11-7
Parent Resources Online
KEYWORD: MA7 Parent

GUIDED PRACTICE

1. Vocabulary Give an example of *like radicals*.

SEE EXAMPLE **1**
p. 835

Add or subtract.

2. $14\sqrt{3} - 6\sqrt{3}$

3. $9\sqrt{5} + \sqrt{5}$

4. $6\sqrt{2} + 5\sqrt{2} - 15\sqrt{2}$

5. $3\sqrt{7} + 5\sqrt{2}$

6. $5\sqrt{a} - 9\sqrt{a}$

7. $9\sqrt{6a} + 6\sqrt{5a} - 4\sqrt{6a}$

SEE EXAMPLE **2**
p. 836

Simplify each expression.

8. $\sqrt{32} - \sqrt{8}$

9. $4\sqrt{12} + \sqrt{75}$

10. $2\sqrt{3} + 5\sqrt{12} - \sqrt{27}$

11. $\sqrt{20x} - \sqrt{45x}$

12. $\sqrt{28c} + 9\sqrt{24c}$

13. $\sqrt{50t} - 2\sqrt{12t} + 3\sqrt{2t}$

SEE EXAMPLE **3**
p. 836

14. Geometry Find the perimeter of the trapezoid shown. Give your answer as a radical expression in simplest form.

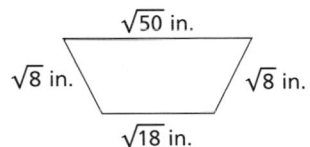

$\sqrt{50}$ in.

$\sqrt{8}$ in. $\sqrt{8}$ in.

$\sqrt{18}$ in.

PRACTICE AND PROBLEM SOLVING

Independent Practice

For Exercises	See Example
15–20	1
21–29	2
30	3

Extra Practice
Skills Practice p. S25
Application Practice p. S38

Add or subtract.

15. $4\sqrt{3} + 2\sqrt{3}$

16. $\frac{1}{2}\sqrt{72} - 12$

17. $2\sqrt{11} + \sqrt{11} - 6\sqrt{11}$

18. $6\sqrt{7} + 7\sqrt{6}$

19. $-3\sqrt{n} - \sqrt{n}$

20. $2\sqrt{2y} + 3\sqrt{2y} - 2\sqrt{3y}$

Simplify each expression.

21. $\sqrt{175} + \sqrt{28}$

22. $2\sqrt{80} - \sqrt{20}$

23. $5\sqrt{8} - \sqrt{32} + 2\sqrt{18}$

24. $\sqrt{150r} + \sqrt{54r}$

25. $\sqrt{63x} - 4\sqrt{27x}$

26. $\sqrt{48p} + 3\sqrt{18p} - 2\sqrt{27p}$

27. $\sqrt{180j} - \sqrt{45j}$

28. $3\sqrt{90c} - \sqrt{40c}$

29. $2\sqrt{75m} - \sqrt{12m} - \sqrt{108m}$

30. **Fitness** What is the total length of the jogging path? Give your answer as a radical expression in simplest form.

Simplify each expression.

31. $5\sqrt{7} + 7\sqrt{7}$ 32. $18\sqrt{ab} - 10\sqrt{ab}$

33. $-3\sqrt{3} + 3\sqrt{3}$ 34. $\sqrt{98} + \sqrt{128}$

35. $\sqrt{300} - \sqrt{27}$ 36. $\sqrt{45x} + \sqrt{500x}$

37. $\dfrac{5}{2}\sqrt{8} + \dfrac{\sqrt{32}}{2}$ 38. $\dfrac{1}{6}\sqrt{18} - \dfrac{\sqrt{2}}{2}$

 39. **Geometry** Use the diagram to answer the following:

a. What is the area of section A? section B? section C?

b. What is the combined area of the three sections?

c. Explain how this model relates to adding like radicals.

Simplify each expression.

40. $\sqrt{450ab} - \sqrt{50ab}$ 41. $\sqrt{12} + \sqrt{125} + \sqrt{25}$

42. $\sqrt{338} - \sqrt{18}$ 43. $\sqrt{700x} - \sqrt{28x} - \sqrt{70x}$

44. $-3\sqrt{90} - 3\sqrt{160}$ 45. $7\sqrt{80k} + 2\sqrt{20k} + \sqrt{45k}$

46. $\sqrt{24abc} + \sqrt{600abc}$ 47. $\sqrt{12} + \sqrt{20} + \sqrt{27} + \sqrt{45}$

48. **///ERROR ANALYSIS///** Which expressions are simplified incorrectly? Explain the error in each incorrect simplification.

Ⓐ	Ⓑ	Ⓒ
$4\sqrt{5} + 5\sqrt{5}$	$8\sqrt{3} - 7\sqrt{3}$	$7\sqrt{11} - 3\sqrt{6}$
$9\sqrt{10}$	$\sqrt{3}$	$4\sqrt{5}$

49. **Write About It** Tell how to identify like radicals. Give examples and nonexamples of like radicals in your answer.

Complete each box to make a true statement.

50. $5\sqrt{ab} + 2\sqrt{\boxed{}} - 3\sqrt{a} = 7\sqrt{ab} - 3\sqrt{a}$ 51. $4\sqrt{x} - \sqrt{\boxed{}\,}x = \sqrt{x}$

52. $5\sqrt{2} - \sqrt{\boxed{}} + \sqrt{2} = 4\sqrt{2}$ 53. $\sqrt{\boxed{}} + 8\sqrt{2} = 11\sqrt{2}$

54. $3\sqrt{3} + 2\sqrt{3} + \sqrt{\boxed{}} = 9\sqrt{3}$ 55. $2x - \sqrt{\boxed{}} = -4x$

MULTI-STEP TEST PREP

56. This problem will prepare you for the Multi-Step Test Prep on page 854.

a. The first Ferris wheel was designed by George W. Ferris and introduced at the 1893 Chicago World's Fair. Its diameter was 250 feet. What was its radius?

b. For a rider halfway up on the ride, the distance from the boarding point can be found by using the equation $d = \sqrt{2r^2}$, where r is the radius of the wheel. Explain where this equation comes from. (*Hint:* Draw a picture.)

57. **Multi-Step** A square has an area of 48 in². Another square has an area of 12 in².
Write a simplified radical expression for the perimeter of each square. Then
write a simplified radical expression for the combined perimeters of the
two squares.

58. **Critical Thinking** How are like radicals similar to like terms?

59. Which of the following expressions CANNOT be simplified?
   Ⓐ $3\sqrt{5} + 4\sqrt{5}$ Ⓒ $2\sqrt{8} + 3\sqrt{2}$
   Ⓑ $5\sqrt{6} + 6\sqrt{5}$ Ⓓ $3\sqrt{12} + \sqrt{27}$

60. What is $-5\sqrt{7x} + 6\sqrt{7x}$?
   Ⓕ $\sqrt{7x}$ Ⓖ $\sqrt{14x^2}$ Ⓗ $\sqrt{14x}$ Ⓙ $7x$

61. What is $\sqrt{18} - \sqrt{2}$?
   Ⓐ $2\sqrt{2}$ Ⓑ 4 Ⓒ $4\sqrt{2}$ Ⓓ $8\sqrt{2}$

CHALLENGE AND EXTEND

Simplify. All radicands represent nonnegative numbers.

62. $5\sqrt{x-5} + 2\sqrt{x-5}$

63. $x\sqrt{x} + 2\sqrt{x}$

64. $4\sqrt{x-3} + \sqrt{25x-75}$

65. $2\sqrt{x+7} - \sqrt{4x+28}$

66. $\sqrt{4x^3 + 24x^2} + \sqrt{x^3 + 6x^2}$

67. $\sqrt{x^3 - x^2} + \sqrt{4x-4}$

68. $\sqrt{x^3 + 2x^2} - \sqrt{x+2}$

69. $\sqrt{9x+9} - \sqrt{x^3 + 2x^2}$

70. **Geometry** Find the area of the trapezoid.
Use the formula $A = \frac{1}{2}h(b_1 + b_2)$.

SPIRAL REVIEW

71. Use slope to show that *ABCD* is
a parallelogram. *(Lesson 5-9)*

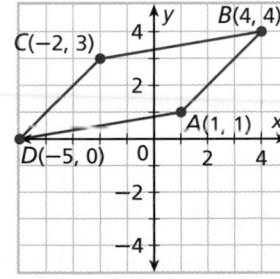

72. Use slope to show that *XYZ* is a
right triangle. *(Lesson 5-9)*

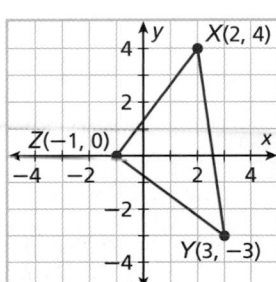

73. A number cube is rolled and a coin is tossed. What is the probability of rolling a
6 and tossing heads? *(Lesson 10-7)*

Find the domain of each square-root function. *(Lesson 11-5)*

74. $y = \sqrt{4x-2}$ 75. $y = -2\sqrt{x+3}$ 76. $y = 1 + \sqrt{x+6}$

Multiplying and Dividing Radical Expressions

Objectives
Multiply and divide radical expressions.

Rationalize denominators.

Who uses this?
Electricians can divide radical expressions to find how much current runs through an appliance. (See Exercise 64.)

You can use the Product and Quotient Properties of square roots you have already learned to multiply and divide expressions containing square roots.

DON'T GO IN THERE!

Off the Mark. Cartoon copyrighted by Mark Parisi, printed with permission.

EXAMPLE 1 **Multiplying Square Roots**

Multiply. Write each product in simplest form.

A $\sqrt{3}\sqrt{6}$

$\sqrt{3(6)}$ *Product Property of Square Roots*

$\sqrt{18}$ *Multiply the factors in the radicand.*

$\sqrt{9(2)}$ *Factor 18 using a perfect-square factor.*

$\sqrt{9}\sqrt{2}$ *Product Property of Square Roots*

$3\sqrt{2}$ *Simplify.*

B $\left(5\sqrt{3}\right)^2$

$5\sqrt{3} \cdot 5\sqrt{3}$ *Expand the expression.*

$5(5)\sqrt{3}\sqrt{3}$ *Commutative Property of Multiplication*

$25\sqrt{3(3)}$ *Product Property of Square Roots*

$25\sqrt{9}$ *Simplify the radicand.*

$25(3)$ *Simplify the square root.*

75 *Multiply.*

C $2\sqrt{8x}\sqrt{4x}$

$2\sqrt{8x(4x)}$ *Product Property of Square Roots*

$2\sqrt{32x^2}$ *Multiply the factors in the radicand.*

$2\sqrt{16(2)x^2}$ *Factor 32 using a perfect-square factor.*

$2\sqrt{16}\sqrt{2}\sqrt{x^2}$ *Product Property of Square Roots*

$2(4)\sqrt{2}(x)$

$8x\sqrt{2}$

> **Helpful Hint**
>
> In Example 1C, $\sqrt{8x}$ and $\sqrt{4x}$ represent real numbers only if $x \geq 0$, so, in this case, $\sqrt{x^2} = x$.

Multiply. Write each product in simplest form.

1a. $\sqrt{5}\sqrt{10}$ **1b.** $\left(3\sqrt{7}\right)^2$ **1c.** $\sqrt{2m}\sqrt{14m}$

EXAMPLE 2 **Using the Distributive Property**

Multiply. Write each product in simplest form.

A $\sqrt{2}\left(5 + \sqrt{12}\right)$

$\sqrt{2}\left(5 + \sqrt{12}\right)$

$\sqrt{2}(5) + \sqrt{2}\sqrt{12}$ *Distribute* $\sqrt{2}$.

$5\sqrt{2} + \sqrt{2(12)}$ *Product Property of Square Roots*

$5\sqrt{2} + \sqrt{24}$ *Multiply the factors in the second radicand.*

$5\sqrt{2} + \sqrt{4(6)}$ *Factor 24 using a perfect-square factor.*

$5\sqrt{2} + \sqrt{4}\sqrt{6}$ *Product Property of Square Roots*

$5\sqrt{2} + 2\sqrt{6}$ *Simplify.*

B $\sqrt{3}\left(\sqrt{3} - \sqrt{5}\right)$

$\sqrt{3}\left(\sqrt{3} - \sqrt{5}\right)$

$\sqrt{3}\sqrt{3} - \sqrt{3}\sqrt{5}$ *Distribute* $\sqrt{3}$.

$\sqrt{3(3)} - \sqrt{3(5)}$ *Product Property of Square Roots*

$\sqrt{9} - \sqrt{15}$ *Simplify the radicands.*

$3 - \sqrt{15}$ *Simplify.*

 Multiply. Write each product in simplest form.

2a. $\sqrt{6}\left(\sqrt{8} - 3\right)$ **2b.** $\sqrt{5}\left(\sqrt{10} + 4\sqrt{3}\right)$

2c. $\sqrt{7k}\left(\sqrt{7} - 5\right)$ **2d.** $5\sqrt{5}\left(-4 + 6\sqrt{5}\right)$

Remember!

First terms
Outer terms
Inner terms
Last terms

See Lesson 7-8.

In Chapter 7, you learned to multiply binomials by using the FOIL method. The same method can be used to multiply square-root expressions that contain two terms.

$$\left(4 + \sqrt{3}\right)\left(5 + \sqrt{3}\right) = 4(5) + 4\sqrt{3} + 5\sqrt{3} + \sqrt{3}\sqrt{3}$$

$$= 20 \qquad + 9\sqrt{3} \qquad + 3 \quad = \quad 23 + 9\sqrt{3}$$

EXAMPLE 3 **Multiplying Sums and Differences of Radicals**

Multiply. Write each product in simplest form.

A $\left(4 + \sqrt{5}\right)\left(3 - \sqrt{5}\right)$

$12 - 4\sqrt{5} + 3\sqrt{5} - 5$ *Use the FOIL method.*

$7 - \sqrt{5}$ *Simplify by combining like terms.*

B $\left(\sqrt{7} - 5\right)^2$

$\left(\sqrt{7} - 5\right)\left(\sqrt{7} - 5\right)$ *Expand the expression.*

$7 - 5\sqrt{7} - 5\sqrt{7} + 25$ *Use the FOIL method.*

$32 - 10\sqrt{7}$ *Simplify by combining like terms.*

 Multiply. Write each product in simplest form.

3a. $\left(3 + \sqrt{3}\right)\left(8 - \sqrt{3}\right)$ **3b.** $\left(9 + \sqrt{2}\right)^2$

3c. $\left(3 - \sqrt{2}\right)^2$ **3d.** $\left(4 - \sqrt{3}\right)\left(\sqrt{3} + 5\right)$

A quotient with a square root in the denominator is **not** simplified. To simplify these expressions, multiply by a form of 1 to get a perfect-square radicand in the denominator. This is called *rationalizing the denominator*.

E X A M P L E 4 **Rationalizing the Denominator**

Simplify each quotient.

A $\dfrac{\sqrt{7}}{\sqrt{2}}$

$\dfrac{\sqrt{7}}{\sqrt{2}}\left(\dfrac{\sqrt{2}}{\sqrt{2}}\right)$ *Multiply by a form of 1 to get a perfect-square radicand in the denominator.*

$\dfrac{\sqrt{14}}{\sqrt{4}}$ *Product Property of Square Roots*

$\dfrac{\sqrt{14}}{2}$ *Simplify the denominator.*

Helpful Hint

Use the square root in the denominator to find the appropriate form of 1 for multiplication.

B $\dfrac{\sqrt{7}}{\sqrt{8n}}$

$\dfrac{\sqrt{7}}{\sqrt{4(2n)}}$ *Write 8n using a perfect-square factor.*

$\dfrac{\sqrt{7}}{2\sqrt{2n}}$ *Simplify the denominator.*

$\dfrac{\sqrt{7}}{2\sqrt{2n}}\left(\dfrac{\sqrt{2n}}{\sqrt{2n}}\right)$ *Multiply by a form of 1 to get a perfect-square radicand in the denominator.*

$\dfrac{\sqrt{14n}}{2\sqrt{4n^2}}$ *Product Property of Square Roots*

$\dfrac{\sqrt{14n}}{2(2n)}$ *Simplify the square root in the denominator.*

$\dfrac{\sqrt{14n}}{4n}$ *Simplify the denominator.*

 CHECK IT OUT! Simplify each quotient.

4a. $\dfrac{\sqrt{13}}{\sqrt{5}}$ **4b.** $\dfrac{\sqrt{7a}}{\sqrt{12}}$ **4c.** $\dfrac{2\sqrt{80}}{\sqrt{7}}$

THINK AND DISCUSS

1. Explain why multiplying $\dfrac{\sqrt{6}}{\sqrt{5}}$ by $\dfrac{\sqrt{5}}{\sqrt{5}}$ does not change the value of $\dfrac{\sqrt{6}}{\sqrt{5}}$.

 2. GET ORGANIZED Copy and complete the graphic organizer. In each box, give an example and show how to simplify it.

Multiplying Radical Expressions

| Multiplying two square roots | Using the Distributive Property | Using FOIL |

go.hrw.com
Homework Help Online
KEYWORD: MA7 11-8
Parent Resources Online
KEYWORD: MA7 Parent

GUIDED PRACTICE

Multiply. Write each product in simplest form.

SEE EXAMPLE **1**
p. 840

1. $\sqrt{2}\sqrt{3}$ 2. $\sqrt{3}\sqrt{8}$ 3. $\left(5\sqrt{5}\right)^2$

4. $\left(4\sqrt{2}\right)^2$ 5. $3\sqrt{3a}\sqrt{10}$ 6. $2\sqrt{15p}\sqrt{3p}$

SEE EXAMPLE **2**
p. 841

7. $\sqrt{6}\left(2+\sqrt{7}\right)$ 8. $\sqrt{3}\left(5-\sqrt{3}\right)$ 9. $\sqrt{7}\left(\sqrt{5}-\sqrt{3}\right)$

10. $\sqrt{2}\left(\sqrt{10}+8\sqrt{2}\right)$ 11. $\sqrt{5y}\left(\sqrt{15}+4\right)$ 12. $\sqrt{2t}\left(\sqrt{6t}-\sqrt{2t}\right)$

SEE EXAMPLE **3**
p. 841

13. $\left(2+\sqrt{2}\right)\left(5+\sqrt{2}\right)$ 14. $\left(4+\sqrt{6}\right)\left(3-\sqrt{6}\right)$ 15. $\left(\sqrt{3}-4\right)\left(\sqrt{3}+2\right)$

16. $\left(5+\sqrt{3}\right)^2$ 17. $\left(\sqrt{6}-5\sqrt{3}\right)^2$ 18. $\left(6+3\sqrt{2}\right)^2$

SEE EXAMPLE **4**
p. 842

Simplify each quotient.

19. $\dfrac{\sqrt{13}}{\sqrt{2}}$ 20. $\dfrac{\sqrt{20}}{\sqrt{8}}$ 21. $\dfrac{\sqrt{11}}{6\sqrt{3}}$ 22. $\dfrac{\sqrt{28}}{\sqrt{3s}}$

23. $\dfrac{2}{\sqrt{7}}$ 24. $\dfrac{3}{\sqrt{6}}$ 25. $\dfrac{1}{\sqrt{5x}}$ 26. $\dfrac{\sqrt{3}}{\sqrt{x}}$

PRACTICE AND PROBLEM SOLVING

Independent Practice	
For Exercises	See Example
27–32	1
33–38	2
39–44	3
45–52	4

Extra Practice
Skills Practice p. S25
Application Practice p. S38

Multiply. Write each product in simplest form.

27. $\sqrt{3}\sqrt{5}\sqrt{6}$ 28. $3\sqrt{6}\left(5\sqrt{6}\right)$ 29. $\left(2\sqrt{2}\right)^2$

30. $\left(3\sqrt{6}\right)^2$ 31. $\sqrt{21d}\left(2\sqrt{3d}\right)$ 32. $4\sqrt{5n}\left(2\sqrt{5n}\right)\left(3\sqrt{3n}\right)$

33. $\sqrt{5}\left(4-\sqrt{10}\right)$ 34. $\sqrt{2}\left(\sqrt{6}+2\right)$ 35. $\sqrt{2}\left(\sqrt{6}-\sqrt{10}\right)$

36. $3\sqrt{3}\left(\sqrt{8}-2\sqrt{6}\right)$ 37. $\sqrt{3f}\left(\sqrt{3}+12\right)$ 38. $\sqrt{8m}\left(\sqrt{10}+\sqrt{2m}\right)$

39. $\left(15+\sqrt{15}\right)\left(4+\sqrt{15}\right)$ 40. $\left(\sqrt{6}+4\right)\left(\sqrt{2}-7\right)$ 41. $\left(3-\sqrt{2}\right)\left(4+\sqrt{2}\right)$

42. $\left(\sqrt{5}-5\right)^2$ 43. $\left(\sqrt{3}+8\right)^2$ 44. $\left(2\sqrt{3}+4\sqrt{5}\right)^2$

Simplify each quotient.

45. $\dfrac{\sqrt{75}}{\sqrt{2}}$ 46. $\dfrac{\sqrt{5}}{4\sqrt{8}}$ 47. $\dfrac{\sqrt{27}}{3\sqrt{x}}$ 48. $\dfrac{\sqrt{48k}}{\sqrt{5}}$

49. $\dfrac{\sqrt{49x}}{\sqrt{2}}$ 50. $\dfrac{3\sqrt{27}}{\sqrt{b}}$ 51. $\dfrac{\sqrt{12y}}{\sqrt{3}}$ 52. $\dfrac{\sqrt{12t}}{\sqrt{6}}$

Geometry Find the area of each figure. Give your answer as a radical expression in simplest form.

53.
$6\sqrt{5}$ in.
$6\sqrt{5}$ in.

54.

$\sqrt{6}$ m
$2\sqrt{3}$ m

55.

$\left(6\sqrt{2}-2\right)$ cm
$\sqrt{5}$ cm

Simplify.

56. $\sqrt{3}\left(\dfrac{\sqrt{2}}{\sqrt{7}}\right)$

57. $\dfrac{15\sqrt{10}}{5\sqrt{3}}$

58. $\dfrac{6+\sqrt{18}}{3}$

59. $\left(\sqrt{3}-4\right)\left(\sqrt{3}+2\right)$

60. $\sqrt{2}\left(6+\sqrt{12}\right)$

61. $\dfrac{\sqrt{1}+\sqrt{25}}{\sqrt{2}}$

62. $\dfrac{\sqrt{15}+\sqrt{10}}{\sqrt{5}}$

63. $\sqrt{12}\left(\sqrt{3}+8\right)^{2}$

64. $\sqrt{3}\left(4-2\sqrt{5}\right)$

65. $\left(\sqrt{x}-\sqrt{y}\right)^{2}$

66. $\left(\sqrt{x}-5\right)\left(3\sqrt{x}+7\right)$

67. $\left(\sqrt{3}+\sqrt{x}\right)^{2}$

68. Electricity Electrical current in amps can be represented by $\dfrac{\sqrt{W}}{\sqrt{R}}$, where W is power in watts and R is resistance in ohms. How much electrical current is running through a microwave oven that has 850 watts of power and 5 ohms of resistance? Give the answer as a radical expression in simplest form. Then estimate the amount of current to the nearest tenth.

69. Physics The *period* of a pendulum is the amount of time it takes the pendulum to make one complete swing and return to its starting point. The period of a pendulum in seconds can be represented by $2\pi\sqrt{\dfrac{\ell}{32}}$, where ℓ is the length of the pendulum in feet. What is the period of a pendulum whose length is 3 feet? Give the answer as a radical expression in simplest form. Then estimate the period to the nearest tenth.

Geometry Find the area of each triangle. Give the exact answer in simplest form. (*Hint:* The formula for the area of a triangle is $A=\frac{1}{2}bh$.)

70.

$\sqrt{3}$ yd

$2\sqrt{6}$ yd

71.

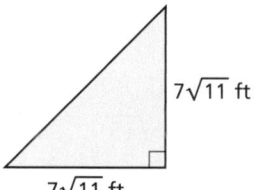

$7\sqrt{11}$ ft

$7\sqrt{11}$ ft

72.

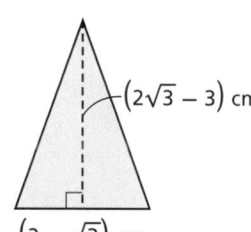

$\left(2\sqrt{3}-3\right)$ cm

$\left(2-\sqrt{3}\right)$ cm

73. Write About It Describe an expression for which you would have to rationalize the denominator. How would you do it? Include an explanation of how you would choose what to multiply the original expression by.

MULTI-STEP TEST PREP

74. This problem will prepare you for the Multi-Step Test Prep on page 854.

a. Many amusement parks have free-fall rides in which cars travel straight up a tower and then are allowed to fall back to the ground. The time in seconds for any object in free fall is $t=\sqrt{\dfrac{d}{16}}$, where d is the distance that the object falls in feet. On a particular free-fall ride, the cars are in free fall for 100 feet. How long does free fall last on this ride?

b. The cars in the ride from part **a** travel up the tower at a speed of 18 feet per second. How long does this trip take? Round your answer to the nearest tenth. How does this time compare with the time spent in free fall?

75. What is the product of $3\sqrt{5}$ and $\sqrt{15}$?

   Ⓐ $5\sqrt{3}$ Ⓑ $15\sqrt{3}$ Ⓒ $15\sqrt{15}$ Ⓓ $45\sqrt{5}$

76. Which of the following is the result of rationalizing the denominator in the expression $\frac{4}{3\sqrt{2}}$?

   Ⓕ $\frac{\sqrt{2}}{3}$ Ⓖ $2\sqrt{2}$ Ⓗ $\frac{2\sqrt{2}}{3}$ Ⓙ $\frac{3\sqrt{2}}{2}$

77. Which of the following is equivalent to $\left(5\sqrt{10}\right)^2$?

   Ⓐ 50 Ⓑ 100 Ⓒ 125 Ⓓ 250

CHALLENGE AND EXTEND

The expressions $\sqrt{a} + \sqrt{b}$ and $\sqrt{a} - \sqrt{b}$ are called *conjugates*. When a and b are nonnegative, you can use the FOIL method to multiply conjugates as follows:

$$\left(\sqrt{a} - \sqrt{b}\right)\left(\sqrt{a} + \sqrt{b}\right) = a + \sqrt{ab} - \sqrt{ab} - b = a - b$$

$$\left(\sqrt{3} - \sqrt{5}\right)\left(\sqrt{3} + \sqrt{5}\right) = 3 + \sqrt{15} - \sqrt{15} - 5 = 3 - 5 = -2$$

Notice that the product does not contain any square roots. This means that you can use conjugates to rationalize denominators that contain sums or differences of square roots:

$$\frac{\sqrt{2}}{\sqrt{7} + \sqrt{2}}\left(\frac{\sqrt{7} - \sqrt{2}}{\sqrt{7} - \sqrt{2}}\right) = \frac{\sqrt{2}\left(\sqrt{7} - \sqrt{2}\right)}{\left(\sqrt{7} + \sqrt{2}\right)\left(\sqrt{7} - \sqrt{2}\right)} = \frac{\sqrt{14} - \sqrt{4}}{7 - 2} = \frac{\sqrt{14} - 2}{5}$$

Simplify.

78. $\dfrac{4}{\sqrt{3} - \sqrt{2}}$ **79.** $\dfrac{8}{\sqrt{3} + \sqrt{5}}$ **80.** $\dfrac{\sqrt{5}}{\sqrt{10} + \sqrt{3}}$ **81.** $\dfrac{\sqrt{2} + \sqrt{3}}{\sqrt{2} - \sqrt{3}}$

82. $\dfrac{\sqrt{3}}{\sqrt{2} + \sqrt{3}}$ **83.** $\dfrac{\sqrt{2}}{\sqrt{8} + \sqrt{6}}$ **84.** $\dfrac{6}{\sqrt{2} + \sqrt{3}}$ **85.** $\dfrac{2}{\sqrt{6} - \sqrt{5}}$

86. Geometry One rectangle is $4\sqrt{6}$ feet long and $\sqrt{2}$ feet wide. Another rectangle is $8\sqrt{2}$ feet long and $2\sqrt{6}$ feet wide. How much more area does the larger rectangle cover than the smaller rectangle? (*Hint:* The formula for the area of a rectangle is $A = \ell w$.)

SPIRAL REVIEW

Describe the transformation(s) from the graph of $f(x)$ to the graph of $g(x)$. *(Lesson 5-10)*

87. $f(x) = -2x + 3; g(x) = -2x - 1$ **88.** $f(x) = 4x; g(x) = 5x$

Factor each polynomial completely. Check your answer. *(Lesson 8-6)*

89. $x^2 + 7x - 30$ **90.** $6x^2 + 11x + 3$ **91.** $x^2 - 16$

92. $3x^2 + 30x + 75$ **93.** $2x^4 - 18$ **94.** $8x^3 - 20x^2 - 12x$

Simplify. All variables represent nonnegative numbers. *(Lesson 11-6)*

95. $\sqrt{360}$ **96.** $\sqrt{\dfrac{72}{16}}$ **97.** $\sqrt{\dfrac{49x^2}{64y^4}}$ **98.** $\sqrt{\dfrac{50a^7}{9a^3}}$

Solving Radical Equations

Objective
Solve radical equations.

Vocabulary
radical equation
extraneous solution

Who uses this?
Meteorologists can use radical equations to estimate the size of a storm. (See Exercise 76.)

A **radical equation** is an equation that contains a variable within a radical. In this course, you will only study radical equations that contain square roots.

Recall that you use inverse operations to solve equations. For nonnegative numbers, squaring and taking the square root are inverse operations. When an equation contains a variable within a square root, square both sides of the equation to solve.

Power Property of Equality

WORDS	NUMBERS	ALGEBRA
You can square both sides of an equation, and the resulting equation is still true.	$3 = 1 + 2$ $(3)^2 = (1 + 2)^2$ $9 = 9$	If a and b are real numbers and $a = b$, then $a^2 = b^2$.

EXAMPLE **1** **Solving Simple Radical Equations**

Solve each equation. Check your answer.

A $\sqrt{x} = 8$

$(\sqrt{x})^2 = (8)^2$ *Square both sides.*

$x = 64$

Check $\sqrt{x} = 8$

$\begin{array}{c|c} \sqrt{64} & 8 \\ 8 & 8 \checkmark \end{array}$ *Substitute 64 for x in the original equation.*
     Simplify.

B $6 = \sqrt{4x}$

$(6)^2 = (\sqrt{4x})^2$ *Square both sides.*

$36 = 4x$

$9 = x$ *Divide both sides by 4.*

Check $6 = \sqrt{4x}$

$\begin{array}{c|c} 6 & \sqrt{4(9)} \\ 6 & \sqrt{36} \\ 6 & 6 \checkmark \end{array}$ *Substitute 9 for x in the original equation.*
     Simplify.

 Solve each equation. Check your answer.

1a. $\sqrt{x} = 6$ **1b.** $9 = \sqrt{27x}$ **1c.** $\sqrt{3x} = 1$

Some square-root equations do not have the square root isolated. To solve these equations, you may have to isolate the square root before squaring both sides. You can do this by using one or more inverse operations.

EXAMPLE 2 **Solving Radical Equations by Adding or Subtracting**

Solve each equation. Check your answer.

A $\sqrt{x} + 3 = 10$

$\sqrt{x} = 7$	Subtract 3 from both sides.
$\left(\sqrt{x}\right)^2 = (7)^2$	Square both sides.
$x = 49$	

Check $\sqrt{x} + 3 = 10$

$\sqrt{49} + 3$	10
$7 + 3$	10
10	$10 \checkmark$

B $\sqrt{x-5} = 4$

$\left(\sqrt{x-5}\right)^2 = (4)^2$	Square both sides.
$x - 5 = 16$	
$x = 21$	Add 5 to both sides.

Check $\sqrt{x-5} = 4$

$\sqrt{21-5}$	4
$\sqrt{16}$	4
4	$4 \checkmark$

C $\sqrt{2x-1} + 4 = 7$

$\sqrt{2x-1} = 3$	Subtract 4 from both sides.
$\left(\sqrt{2x-1}\right)^2 = (3)^2$	Square both sides.
$2x - 1 = 9$	
$2x = 10$	Add 1 to both sides.
$x = 5$	Divide both sides by 2.

Check $\sqrt{2x-1} + 4 = 7$

$\sqrt{2(5)-1} + 4$	7
$\sqrt{10-1} + 4$	7
$\sqrt{9} + 4$	7
$3 + 4$	7
7	$7 \checkmark$

 Solve each equation. Check your answer.

2a. $\sqrt{x} - 2 = 1$ **2b.** $\sqrt{x+7} = 5$ **2c.** $\sqrt{3x+7} - 1 = 3$

EXAMPLE 3 **Solving Radical Equations by Multiplying or Dividing**

Solve each equation. Check your answer.

A $3\sqrt{x} = 21$

Method 1

$3\sqrt{x} = 21$	
$\sqrt{x} = 7$	Divide both sides by 3.
$\left(\sqrt{x}\right)^2 = (7)^2$	Square both sides.
$x = 49$	

Method 2

$3\sqrt{x} = 21$	
$\left(3\sqrt{x}\right)^2 = 21^2$	Square both sides.
$9x = 441$	
$x = 49$	Divide both sides by 9.

Check $3\sqrt{x} = 21$

$3\sqrt{49}$	21	Substitute 49 for x in the original equation.
$3(7)$	21	Simplify.
21	$21 \checkmark$	

Solve each equation. Check your answer.

B $\dfrac{\sqrt{x}}{3} = 5$

Method 1		**Method 2**	
$\sqrt{x} = 15$	*Multiply both sides by 3.*	$\left(\dfrac{\sqrt{x}}{3}\right)^2 = (5)^2$	*Square both sides.*
$\left(\sqrt{x}\right)^2 = (15)^2$	*Square both sides.*	$\dfrac{x}{9} = 25$	
$x = 225$		$x = 225$	*Multiply both sides by 9.*

Check $\dfrac{\sqrt{x}}{3} = 5$

$$\begin{array}{c|c}
\dfrac{\sqrt{225}}{3} & 5 \\
\hline
\dfrac{15}{3} & 5 \\
5 & 5 \checkmark
\end{array}$$

Substitute 225 for x in the original equation.

Simplify.

 Solve each equation. Check your answer.

3a. $2\sqrt{x} = 22$ **3b.** $2 = \dfrac{\sqrt{x}}{4}$ **3c.** $\dfrac{2\sqrt{x}}{5} = 4$

EXAMPLE 4   **Solving Radical Equations with Square Roots on Both Sides**

Solve each equation. Check your answer.

A $\sqrt{x+1} = \sqrt{3}$

$\left(\sqrt{x+1}\right)^2 = \left(\sqrt{3}\right)^2$ *Square both sides.*   **Check** $\sqrt{x+1} = \sqrt{3}$

$x + 1 = 3$ $\begin{array}{c|c} \sqrt{2+1} & \sqrt{3} \\ \sqrt{3} & \sqrt{3} \checkmark \end{array}$

$x = 2$ *Subtract 1 from both sides.*

B $\sqrt{x+8} - \sqrt{3x} = 0$

$\sqrt{x+8} = \sqrt{3x}$ *Add $\sqrt{3x}$ to both sides.*   **Check** $\sqrt{x+8} - \sqrt{3x} = 0$

$\left(\sqrt{x+8}\right)^2 = \left(\sqrt{3x}\right)^2$ *Square both sides.* $\begin{array}{c|c} \sqrt{4+8} - \sqrt{3(4)} & 0 \\ \sqrt{12} - \sqrt{12} & 0 \\ 0 & 0 \checkmark \end{array}$

$x + 8 = 3x$

$8 = 2x$ *Subtract x from both sides.*

$4 = x$ *Divide both sides by 2.*

 Solve each equation. Check your answer.

4a. $\sqrt{3x+2} = \sqrt{x+6}$ **4b.** $\sqrt{2x-5} - \sqrt{6} = 0$

Squaring both sides of an equation may result in an **extraneous solution** — a number that is not a solution of the original equation.

Suppose your original equation is $x = 3$.	$x = 3$
Square both sides. Now you have a new equation.	$x^2 = 9$
Solve this new equation for x by taking the square root of both sides.	$\sqrt{x^2} = \sqrt{9}$ $x = 3$ or $x = -3$

Now there are two solutions of the new equation. One $(x = 3)$ is a solution of the original equation. The other $(x = -3)$ is extraneous—it is not a solution of the original equation. Because of extraneous solutions, it is important to check your answers.

EXAMPLE 5 **Extraneous Solutions**

Solve $\sqrt{6-x} = x$. Check your answer.

$$\left(\sqrt{6-x}\right)^2 = (x)^2$$ *Square both sides.*

$$6 - x = x^2$$

$$x^2 + x - 6 = 0$$ *Write in standard form.*

$$(x-2)(x+3) = 0$$ *Factor.*

$$x - 2 = 0 \text{ or } x + 3 = 0$$ *Zero-Product Property*

$$x = 2 \text{ or } \qquad x = -3$$ *Solve for x.*

Helpful Hint

The equation in Example 5 has one solution. When all of the solutions of an equation are extraneous, the original equation has no solutions.

Check

$$\dfrac{\sqrt{6-x} = x}{}$$

$\sqrt{6-2}$	2	*Substitute 2 for x in the equation.*
$\sqrt{4}$	2	
2	2 ✓	

$$\dfrac{\sqrt{6-x} = x}{}$$

$\sqrt{6-(-3)}$	-3	*Substitute −3 for x in the equation.*
$\sqrt{9}$	-3	
3	-3 ✗	

−3 does not check; it is extraneous. The only solution is 2.

 Solve each equation. Check your answer.

5a. $11 + \sqrt{5x} = 6$ **5b.** $x = \sqrt{-3x-2}$ **5c.** $x - 2 = \sqrt{x}$

EXAMPLE 6 *Geometry Application*

Geometry

A rectangle has an area of 52 square feet. Its length is 13 feet, and its width is $\sqrt{x}$ feet. What is the value of x? What is the width of the rectangle?

| $A = 52$ ft^2 | $\sqrt{x}$ ft |

13 ft

$$A = \ell w$$ *Use the formula for area of a rectangle.*

$$52 = 13\sqrt{x}$$ *Substitute 52 for A, 13 for ℓ, and $\sqrt{x}$ for w.*

$$\dfrac{52}{13} = \dfrac{13\sqrt{x}}{13}$$ *Divide both sides by 13.*

$$4 = \sqrt{x}$$

$$4^2 = \left(\sqrt{x}\right)^2$$ *Square both sides.*

$$16 = x$$

Check $A = \ell w$

$$52 = 13\sqrt{x}$$

52	$13\sqrt{16}$	*Substitute 16 for x in the equation.*
52	$13(4)$	
52	52 ✓	

The value of x is 16. The width of the rectangle is $\sqrt{16} = 4$ feet.

 6. A rectangle has an area of 15 cm^2. Its width is 5 cm, and its length is $\left(\sqrt{x+1}\right)$ cm. What is the value of x? What is the length of the rectangle?

THINK AND DISCUSS

1. Compare the two methods used in Example 3A. Which method do you prefer? Why?

2. What is the first step to solve $\sqrt{x-2} + 3 = 8$? Why?

3. **GET ORGANIZED** Copy and complete the graphic organizer. Write and solve a radical equation, using the boxes to show each step.

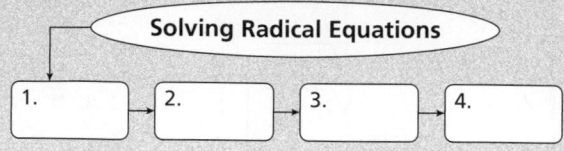

Solving Radical Equations

| 1. | → | 2. | → | 3. | → | 4. |

11-9 Exercises

go.hrw.com
Homework Help Online
KEYWORD: MA7 11-9
Parent Resources Online
KEYWORD: MA7 Parent

GUIDED PRACTICE

1. Vocabulary Is $x = \sqrt{3}$ a *radical equation*? Why or why not?

SEE EXAMPLE **1**
p. 846

Solve each equation. Check your answer.

2. $\sqrt{x} = 7$

3. $4 = \sqrt{-2y}$

4. $\sqrt{20a} = 10$

5. $12 = \sqrt{-x}$

SEE EXAMPLE **2**
p. 847

6. $\sqrt{x} + 6 = 11$

7. $\sqrt{2x-5} = 7$

8. $\sqrt{2-a} = 3$

9. $\sqrt{2x} - 3 = 7$

10. $\sqrt{x-2} = 3$

11. $\sqrt{x+3} = 1$

12. $\sqrt{x-1} = 2$

13. $\sqrt{4y+13} - 1 = 6$

SEE EXAMPLE **3**
p. 847

14. $-2\sqrt{x} = -10$

15. $\dfrac{\sqrt{a}}{2} = 4$

16. $5\sqrt{-x} = 20$

17. $\dfrac{3\sqrt{x}}{4} = 3$

18. $\dfrac{5\sqrt{x}}{6} = 10$

19. $2\sqrt{x} = 8$

20. $\dfrac{\sqrt{x}}{3} = 3$

21. $\dfrac{3\sqrt{x}}{2} = 1$

22. $13\sqrt{2x} = 26$

23. $\dfrac{\sqrt{x}}{5} = 2$

24. $\dfrac{\sqrt{x-7}}{3} = 1$

25. $4\sqrt{2x-1} = 12$

SEE EXAMPLE **4**
p. 848

Solve each equation. Check your answer.

26. $\sqrt{5-x} = \sqrt{6x-2}$

27. $\sqrt{x+7} = \sqrt{3x-19}$

28. $0 = \sqrt{2x} - \sqrt{x+3}$

29. $\sqrt{x-5} = \sqrt{7-x}$

30. $\sqrt{-x} = \sqrt{2x+1}$

31. $\sqrt{3x+1} - \sqrt{2x+3} = 0$

SEE EXAMPLE **5**
p. 849

Solve each equation. Check your answer.

32. $\sqrt{x-5} + 5 = 0$

33. $\sqrt{3x} + 5 = 3$

34. $\sqrt{2-7x} = 2x$

35. $x = \sqrt{12+x}$

36. $6 + \sqrt{x-1} = 4$

37. $\sqrt{6-3x} + 2 = x$

38. $\sqrt{x-2} = 2 - x$

39. $10 + \sqrt{x} = 5$

SEE EXAMPLE **6**
p. 849

40. Geometry A trapezoid has an area of 14 cm². The length of one base is 4 cm and the length of the other base is 10 cm. The height is $\left(\sqrt{2x+3}\right)$ cm. What is the value of x? What is the height of the trapezoid? (*Hint:* The formula for the area of a trapezoid is $A = \frac{1}{2}\left(b_1 + b_2\right)h$.)

PRACTICE AND PROBLEM SOLVING

Independent Practice

For Exercises	See Example
41–44	1
45–48	2
49–52	3
53–58	4
59–66	5
67	6

Extra Practice

Skills Practice p. S25

Application Practice p. S38

Solve each equation. Check your answer.

41. $\sqrt{3x} = 12$

42. $2 = \sqrt{-2x}$

43. $\sqrt{-a} = 5$

44. $11 = \sqrt{c}$

45. $\sqrt{x-7} = 8$

46. $\sqrt{x} - 4 = 0$

47. $\sqrt{1-3x} = 5$

48. $\sqrt{5x+1} + 2 = 6$

49. $5\sqrt{x} = 30$

50. $\dfrac{\sqrt{2x}}{2} = 4$

51. $5\sqrt{-x} = 20$

52. $3\sqrt{3p} = 9$

Solve each equation. Check your answer.

53. $\sqrt{3x-13} = \sqrt{x+3}$

54. $\sqrt{x} - \sqrt{6-x} = 0$

55. $\sqrt{x+5} = \sqrt{2x-4}$

56. $\sqrt{4x-2} = \sqrt{3x+4}$

57. $\sqrt{5x-6} = \sqrt{16-6x}$

58. $\sqrt{12x-3} = \sqrt{4x+93}$

Solve each equation. Check your answer.

59. $\sqrt{x+6} = 1$

60. $-2\sqrt{x} = 6$

61. $x = \sqrt{2x+15}$

62. $\sqrt{6x} + 9 = 2$

63. $\sqrt{4-3x} = x$

64. $\sqrt{5x+4} = x - 4$

65. $\sqrt{2x+2} = 2x$

66. $\sqrt{x+3} + 10 = 7$

67. Geometry A triangle has an area of 60 in². Its base is 10 inches and its height is $\sqrt{x}$ inches. What is the value of x? What is the height of the triangle? (*Hint:* The formula for the area of a triangle is $A = \frac{1}{2}bh$.)

Translate each sentence into an equation. Then solve the equation and check your answer.

68. The square root of three times a number is nine.

69. The difference of the square root of a number and three is four.

70. The square root of the difference of a number and three is four.

71. A number is equal to the square root of the sum of that number and six.

Geometry Find the dimensions of each rectangle given its perimeter.

72.

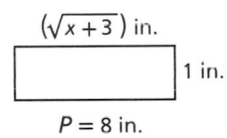

$P = 18$ m

73.

$(\sqrt{x+3})$ in.

1 in.

$P = 8$ in.

74.

$P = 30$ cm

75. Physics The formula $v = \dfrac{\sqrt{2Em}}{m}$ describes the relationship between an object's mass m in kilograms, its velocity v in meters per second, and its kinetic energy E in joules.

  a. A baseball with a mass of 0.14 kg is thrown with a velocity of 28 m/s. How much kinetic energy does the baseball have?

  b. What is the kinetic energy of an object at rest $(v = 0)$?

76. Meteorology The formula $t = \sqrt{\dfrac{d^2}{216}}$ gives the time t in hours that a storm with diameter d miles will last. What is the diameter of a storm that lasts 1 hour? Round your answer to the nearest hundredth.

77. Transportation A sharp curve may require a driver to slow down to avoid going off the road. The equation $v = \sqrt{2.5r}$ describes the relationship between the radius r in feet of an unbanked curve and the maximum velocity v in miles per hour that a car can safely go around the curve. An engineer is designing a highway with a maximum speed limit of 65 mi/h. What is the radius of an unbanked curve for which this is the maximum safe speed?

78. **Write About It** Explain why it is important to check solutions when solving radical equations.

79. **Multi-Step** Solve for x and y in the equations $\sqrt{x} + \sqrt{y} = \sqrt{81}$ and $6\sqrt{y} = 24$. (*Hint: Solve for y first, and then use substitution to solve for x.*)

Tell whether the following statements are *always*, *sometimes*, or *never* true. If the answer is *sometimes*, give one example that is true and one that is false.

80. If $a = b$, then $a^2 = b^2$.

81. If $a^2 = b^2$, then $a = b$.

82. When solving radical equations, the value of the variable is nonnegative.

83. **///ERROR ANALYSIS///** Two students solved $\sqrt{5 - x} = \sqrt{x + 9}$. Which is incorrect? Explain the error.

Ⓐ
$$\sqrt{5 - x} = \sqrt{x + 9}$$
$$\left(\sqrt{5 - x}\right)^2 = \left(\sqrt{x + 9}\right)^2$$
$$5 - x = x + 9$$
$$-2x = 4$$
$$x = -2$$

Check $\sqrt{5 - (-2)}$? $\sqrt{(-2) + 9}$
$$\sqrt{7} = \sqrt{7} \checkmark$$

Ⓑ
$$\sqrt{5 - x} = \sqrt{x + 9}$$
$$\left(\sqrt{5 - x}\right)^2 = \left(\sqrt{x + 9}\right)^2$$
$$5 - x = x + 9$$
$$4 = 2x$$
$$2 = x$$

Check $\sqrt{5 - 2}$? $\sqrt{2 + 9}$
$$\sqrt{3} \neq \sqrt{11} \ X$$

no solution

84. **Estimation** The relationship between a circle's radius and its area can be modeled by $r = \sqrt{\dfrac{A}{\pi}}$, where r is the radius and A is the area. Solutions to this equation are graphed at right. Use the graph to estimate the radius of a circle with an area of 29 m².

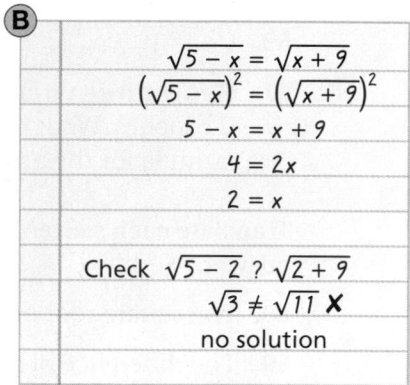

Area and Radius of a Circle

85. **Critical Thinking** Suppose that the equation $\sqrt{-x} = k$ has a solution. What does that tell you about the value of x? the value of k? Explain.

86. This problem will prepare you for the Multi-Step Test Prep on page 854.

a. The Demon Drop is a free-fall ride at Ohio's Cedar Point amusement park. The maximum speed on the Demon Drop is 42 miles per hour. Convert this speed to feet per second. (*Hint: There are 5280 feet in a mile.*)

b. The Demon Drop is 131 feet tall. Most of the drop is a vertical free fall, but near the bottom, the track curves so that the cars slow down gradually. The velocity of any object in free fall is $v = 8\sqrt{d}$, where v is the velocity in feet per second and d is the distance the object has fallen in feet. Use this equation and your answer to part **a** to estimate the free-fall distance.

87. Which of the following is the solution of $\sqrt{8 - 2x} - 2 = 2$?

    (A) −4   (B) −2   (C) 2   (D) 4

88. For which of the following values of k does the equation $\sqrt{x + 1} + k = 0$ have no real solution?

    (F) −2   (G) −1   (H) 0   (J) 1

89. Which of the following is the solution of $x = \sqrt{12 - x}$?

    (A) −4   (B) −3   (C) 3   (D) 4

90. Which of the following is the solution of $\sqrt{x + 13} = 5\sqrt{x - 11}$?

    (F) 9   (G) 12   (H) 16   (J) 17

91. Which of the following is an extraneous solution of $\sqrt{3x - 2} = x - 2$?

    (A) 1   (B) 2   (C) 3   (D) 6

CHALLENGE AND EXTEND

Solve each equation. Check your answer.

92. $\sqrt{x + 3} = x + 1$ **93.** $\sqrt{x - 1} = x - 1$ **94.** $x - 1 = \sqrt{2x + 6}$

95. $\sqrt{x^2 + 5x + 11} = x + 3$ **96.** $\sqrt{x^2 + 9x + 14} = x + 4$ **97.** $x + 2 = \sqrt{x^2 + 5x + 4}$

98. Graphing Calculator Solve $\sqrt{2x - 2} = -\sqrt{x}$ and check your answer. Then use your graphing calculator for the following:

    a. Graph $y = \sqrt{2x - 2}$ and $y = -\sqrt{x}$ on the same screen. Make a sketch of the graphs.

    b. Use the graphs in part **a** to explain your solution to $\sqrt{2x - 2} = -\sqrt{x}$.

99. Graphing Calculator Solve $x = \sqrt{x + 6}$ and check your answer. Then use your graphing calculator for the following:

    a. Graph $y = x$ and $y = \sqrt{x + 6}$ on the same screen. Make a sketch of the graphs.

    b. Use the graphs in part **a** to explain your solution to $x = \sqrt{x + 6}$.

100. Find the domain for the function $y = \dfrac{4}{\sqrt{x - 2}}$. Is the domain for this function different from the domain for the function $y = \sqrt{x - 2}$? Why or why not?

SPIRAL REVIEW

101. On a map, the distance between two towns is 3.2 inches. If the map uses the scale 2.5 in : 40 mi, what is the actual distance between the towns? *(Lesson 2-7)*

102. In model railroading, O-scale trains use the scale 1 : 48. An O-scale boxcar measures 12.5 inches. How many feet long is the boxcar that it models? *(Lesson 2-7)*

103. The personal identification number (PIN) for a debit card is made up of four numbers. How many PINs are possible? *(Lesson 10-8)*

104. A dessert menu offers 6 different selections. The restaurant offers a dessert sampler that includes small portions of any 4 different choices from the dessert menu. How many different dessert samplers are possible? *(Lesson 10-8)*

Graph each square-root function. *(Lesson 11-5)*

105. $f(x) = \sqrt{x + 3}$ **106.** $f(x) = \sqrt{3x - 6}$ **107.** $f(x) = 2\sqrt{x} + 1$

MULTI-STEP TEST PREP

Radical Functions and Equations

Eye in the Sky The London Eye is a giant observation wheel in London, England. It carries people in enclosed capsules around its circumference. Opened on December 31, 1999, to welcome the new millennium, its diameter is 135 meters. On the London Eye, riders can see a distance of 40 kilometers.

1. What is the circumference of the London Eye? Use 3.14 for π.

2. The London Eye's velocity in meters per second can be found using the equation $v = \sqrt{0.001r}$, where r is the radius of the wheel in meters. Find the velocity in meters per second. Round to the nearest hundredth.

3. Another way to find the velocity is to divide the distance around the wheel by the time for the ride. A ride on the London Eye lasts 30 minutes. Use this method to find the velocity of the wheel in meters per second to the nearest hundredth.

4. Are your answers to problems 2 and 3 the same? If not, explain any differences.

5. When a rider is at the highest point on the London Eye, how far is he from the bottom of the ride? Explain.

6. When a rider is at half the maximum height, her distance from the bottom of the ride can be found using the equation $d = \sqrt{2r^2}$. Explain where this equation comes from. Then find this distance. Round to the nearest hundredth.

READY TO GO ON?

Quiz for Lessons 11-5 Through 11-9

✓ **11-5** **Square-Root Functions**

1. The distance in kilometers that a person can see to the horizon can be approximated by the formula $D = 113\sqrt{h}$, where h is the person's height in kilometers above sea level. What is the distance to the horizon observed by a mountain climber who is 0.3 km above sea level?

Find the domain of each square-root function.

2. $y = \sqrt{3x} - 7$

3. $y = \sqrt{x - 5}$

4. $y = \sqrt{2x - 6}$

Graph each square-root function.

5. $f(x) = \sqrt{x - 6}$

6. $f(x) = \sqrt{x} + 5$

7. $f(x) = \sqrt{8 - 4x}$

✓ **11-6** **Radical Expressions**

Simplify. All variables represent nonnegative numbers.

8. $\sqrt{75}$

9. $\sqrt{\dfrac{300}{3}}$

10. $\sqrt{a^2 b^3}$

11. $\sqrt{98xy^2}$

12. $\sqrt{\dfrac{32}{25}}$

13. $\sqrt{\dfrac{128}{121}}$

14. $\sqrt{\dfrac{4b^2}{81}}$

15. $\sqrt{\dfrac{75a^9}{49a^3}}$

16. How long is the diagonal of a rectangular television screen that is 19.2 inches long and 14.4 inches high?

✓ **11-7** **Adding and Subtracting Radical Expressions**

Simplify each expression.

17. $12\sqrt{7} - 5\sqrt{7}$

18. $3\sqrt{x} + 3\sqrt{x}$

19. $\sqrt{12} + \sqrt{75}$

20. $5\sqrt{50} + \sqrt{98}$

21. $4\sqrt{3} - 3\sqrt{4}$

22. $\sqrt{98x} + \sqrt{18x} - \sqrt{200x}$

✓ **11-8** **Multiplying and Dividing Radical Expressions**

Multiply. Write each product in simplest form.

23. $\sqrt{6} \sqrt{11}$

24. $\sqrt{3} \sqrt{8}$

25. $4\sqrt{12x} \sqrt{3x}$

26. $(3 - \sqrt{3})(5 + \sqrt{3})$

Simplify each quotient.

27. $\dfrac{\sqrt{19}}{\sqrt{3}}$

28. $\dfrac{\sqrt{14}}{\sqrt{8}}$

29. $\dfrac{\sqrt{6b}}{\sqrt{8}}$

30. $\dfrac{\sqrt{27}}{\sqrt{3t}}$

✓ **11-9** **Solving Radical Equations**

Solve each equation. Check your answer.

31. $\sqrt{x} - 4 = 21$

32. $-3\sqrt{x} = -12$

33. $\dfrac{5\sqrt{x}}{2} = 40$

34. $\sqrt{4x - 2} - \sqrt{43 - x} = 0$

35. $\sqrt{20 + x} = x$

36. $\sqrt{4x} + 12 = 10$

Study Guide: Review

Vocabulary

Complete the sentences below with vocabulary words from the list above.

1. $f(x) = \sqrt{2x}$ is an example of a(n) ____?____.

2. A(n) ____?____ function has the form $y = a(1 - r)^t$, where $a > 0$.

3. In the formula $a_n = a_1 r^{n-1}$, the variable r represents the ____?____.

4. $f(x) = 2^x$ is an example of a(n) ____?____.

11-1 Geometric Sequences (pp. 790–795)

EXAMPLE

■ What is the 10th term of the geometric sequence $-6400, 3200, -1600, 800, \ldots$?

Find the common ratio by dividing consecutive terms.

$\dfrac{3200}{-6400} = -0.5 \quad \dfrac{-1600}{3200} = -0.5$

$a_n = a_1 r^{n-1}$ *Write the formula.*

$a_{10} = -6400(-0.5)^{10-1}$ *Substitute.*

$\phantom{a_{10}} = -6400(-0.5)^9$ *Simplify.*

$\phantom{a_{10}} = 12.5$

EXERCISES

Find the next three terms in each geometric sequence.

5. $1, 3, 9, 27, \ldots$ **6.** $3, -6, 12, -24, \ldots$

7. $80, 40, 20, 10, \ldots$ **8.** $-1, -4, -16, -64, \ldots$

9. The first term of a geometric sequence is 4 and the common ratio is 5. What is the 10th term?

10. What is the 15th term of the geometric sequence $4, 12, 36, 108, \ldots$?

11-2 Exponential Functions (pp. 796–802)

EXAMPLE

■ Tell whether the ordered pairs $\{(1, 4), (2, 16), (3, 36), (4, 64)\}$ satisfy an exponential function. Explain.

x	y
1	4
2	16
3	36
4	64

As the x-values increase by a constant amount, the y-values are not multiplied by a constant amount. This function is not exponential.

EXERCISES

Tell whether each set of ordered pairs satisfies an exponential function. Explain.

11. $\{(0, 1), (2, 9), (4, 81), (6, 729)\}$

12. $\{(-2, -8), (-1, -4), (0, 0), (1, 4)\}$

Graph each exponential function.

13. $y = 4^x$ **14.** $y = \left(\dfrac{1}{4}\right)^x$

11-3 Exponential Growth and Decay (pp. 805–812)

EXAMPLE

■ The value of a piece of antique furniture has been increasing at a rate of 2% per year. In 1990, its value was $800. Write an exponential growth function to model the situation. Then find the value of the furniture in the year 2010.

Step 1 $y = a(1 + r)^t$ *Write the formula.*

$y = 800(1 + 0.02)^t$ *Substitute.*

$y = 800(1.02)^t$ *Simplify.*

Step 2 $y = 800(1.02)^{20}$ *Substitute 20 for t.*

≈ 1188.76 *Simplify and round.*

The furniture's value will be $1188.76.

EXERCISES

15. The number of students in the book club is increasing at a rate of 15% per year. In 2001, there were 9 students in the book club. Write an exponential growth function to model the situation. Then find the number of students in the book club in the year 2008.

16. The population of a small town is decreasing at a rate of 4% per year. In 1970, the population was 24,500. Write an exponential decay function to model the situation. Then find the population in the year 2020.

11-4 Linear, Quadratic, and Exponential Models (pp. 813–819)

EXAMPLE

■ Use the data in the table to describe how Jasmin's debt is changing. Then write a function that models the data. Use your function to predict Jasmin's debt after 8 years.

Jasmin's Debt

Years	Debt ($)
1	130
2	260
3	520
4	1040

+1 ... ×2
+1 ... ×2
+1 ... ×2

Jasmin's debt doubles every year.

For a constant change in time $(+1)$, there is a constant ratio of 2, so the data is exponential.

$y = ab^x$ *Write the general form.*

$y = a(2)^x$ *Substitute 2 for b.*

$130 = a(2)^1$ *Substitute (1, 130) for x and y.*

$a = 65$ *Solve for a.*

$y = 65(2)^x$ *Replace a and b in $y = ab^x$.*

$y = 65(2)^8$ *Substitute 8 for x.*

$y = 16,640$ *Simplify with a calculator.*

Jasmin's debt in 8 years will be $16,640.

EXERCISES

Graph each data set. Which kind of model best describes the data?

17. $\{(-2, -12), (-1, -3), (0, 0), (1, -3), (2, -12)\}$

18. $\{(-2, -2), (-1, 2), (0, 6), (1, 10), (2, 14)\}$

19. $\left\{\left(-2, -\frac{1}{4}\right), \left(-1, -\frac{1}{2}\right), (0, -1), (1, -2), (2, -4)\right\}$

Look for a pattern in each data set to determine which kind of model best describes the data.

20. $\{(0, 2), (1, 6), (2, 18), (3, 54), (4, 162)\}$

21. $\{(0, 0), (2, -20), (4, -80), (6, -180), (8, -320)\}$

22. $\{(-8, 5), (-4, 3), (0, 1), (4, -1), (8, -3)\}$

23. Write a function that models the data. Then use your function to predict how long the humidifier will produce steam with 10 quarts of water.

Input and Output of a Humidifier

Water Volume (qt)	Steam Time (h)
3	4.5
4	6
5	7.5
6	9

11-5 Square-Root Functions (pp. 822–827)

EXAMPLE

- Graph $f(x) = 3\sqrt{x-2}$.

Step 1 Find the domain of the function.

$x - 2 \geq 0$ *The radicand must be greater*

   $x \geq 2$ *than or equal to 0.*

Step 2 Generate ordered pairs.

x	$f(x) = 3\sqrt{x-2}$
2	0
3	3
6	6
11	9
18	12

Choose x-values greater than or equal to 2 that form a perfect square under the radical sign.

Step 3 Plot and connect the points.

EXERCISES

24. If you know the surface area S of a cube, you can use the formula $\ell = \sqrt{\frac{S}{6}}$ to find the length ℓ of a side. What is the side length of a cube whose surface area is 135 cm²? Round your answer to the nearest hundredth of a centimeter.

Find the domain of each square-root function.

25. $y = \sqrt{x} + 5$ **26.** $y = \sqrt{x+4}$

27. $y = 8 - \sqrt{3x}$ **28.** $y = 2\sqrt{x+2}$

29. $y = 1 + \sqrt{3x-4}$ **30.** $y = \sqrt{2x+6}$

31. $y = \sqrt{2x-7}$ **32.** $y = \sqrt{5x+18}$

33. $y = \sqrt{4x-3}$ **34.** $y = 3\sqrt{x-1}$

Graph each square-root function.

35. $f(x) = \sqrt{x} + 8$ **36.** $f(x) = \sqrt{x-3}$

37. $f(x) = -\sqrt{2x}$ **38.** $f(x) = \sqrt{x} - 1$

39. $f(x) = 2\sqrt{x+3}$ **40.** $f(x) = \sqrt{5-x}$

41. $f(x) = \sqrt{7-4x}$ **42.** $f(x) = 3\sqrt{x-1}$

43. $f(x) = 1 + \sqrt{x+1}$ **44.** $f(x) = \frac{1}{2}\sqrt{x-2}$

11-6 Radical Expressions (pp. 829–834)

EXAMPLES

Simplify. All variables represent nonnegative numbers.

- $\sqrt{50x^4}$

  $\sqrt{(25)(2)x^4}$ *Factor the radicand.*

  $\sqrt{25}\sqrt{2}\sqrt{x^4}$ *Use the Product Property.*

  $5x^2\sqrt{2}$ *Simplify.*

- $\sqrt{\dfrac{16m^6}{64m^3}}$

  $\sqrt{\dfrac{m^3}{4}}$ *Simplify the radicand.*

  $\dfrac{\sqrt{m^3}}{\sqrt{4}}$ *Use the Quotient Property of Square Roots.*

  $\dfrac{\sqrt{m^2}\sqrt{m}}{\sqrt{4}}$ *Use the Product Property of Square Roots.*

  $\dfrac{m\sqrt{m}}{2}$ *Simplify.*

EXERCISES

Simplify. All variables represent nonnegative numbers.

45. $\sqrt{121}$ **46.** $\sqrt{n^4}$

47. $\sqrt{(x+3)^2}$ **48.** $\sqrt{\dfrac{75}{3}}$

49. $\sqrt{36d^2}$ **50.** $\sqrt{y^6x}$

51. $\sqrt{12}$ **52.** $\sqrt{32ab^5}$

53. $\sqrt{\dfrac{5}{4}}$ **54.** $\sqrt{\dfrac{t^3}{100t}}$

55. $\sqrt{\dfrac{8}{18}}$ **56.** $\sqrt{\dfrac{32p^4}{49}}$

57. $\sqrt{\dfrac{s^2t^9}{s^4}}$ **58.** $\sqrt{\dfrac{72b^6}{225}}$

11-7 Adding and Subtracting Radical Expressions (pp. 835–839)

EXAMPLE

■ Simplify $\sqrt{50x} - \sqrt{2x} + \sqrt{12x}$.

$$\sqrt{50x} - 1\sqrt{2x} + \sqrt{12x}$$

$$\sqrt{(25)(2)x} - 1\sqrt{2x} + \sqrt{(4)(3)x}$$

$$\sqrt{25}\sqrt{2x} - 1\sqrt{2x} + \sqrt{4}\sqrt{3x}$$

$$5\sqrt{2x} - 1\sqrt{2x} + 2\sqrt{3x}$$

$$4\sqrt{2x} + 2\sqrt{3x}$$

EXERCISES

Simplify each expression.

59. $6\sqrt{7} + 3\sqrt{7}$

60. $4\sqrt{3} - \sqrt{3}$

61. $3\sqrt{2} + 2\sqrt{3}$

62. $9\sqrt{5t} - 8\sqrt{5t}$

63. $\sqrt{50} - \sqrt{18}$

64. $\sqrt{12} + \sqrt{20}$

65. $\sqrt{20x} - \sqrt{80x}$

66. $4\sqrt{54} - \sqrt{24}$

11-8 Multiplying and Dividing Radical Expressions (pp. 840–845)

EXAMPLES

■ Multiply $\left(\sqrt{3} + 6\right)^2$. Write the product in simplest form.

$$\left(\sqrt{3} + 6\right)^2$$

$$\left(\sqrt{3} + 6\right)\left(\sqrt{3} + 6\right) \qquad \textit{Expand the expression.}$$

$$3 + 6\sqrt{3} + 6\sqrt{3} + 36 \qquad \textit{Use the FOIL method.}$$

$$39 + 12\sqrt{3} \qquad \textit{Simplify.}$$

■ Simplify the quotient $\dfrac{\sqrt{5}}{\sqrt{3}}$.

$$\dfrac{\sqrt{5}}{\sqrt{3}}\left(\dfrac{\sqrt{3}}{\sqrt{3}}\right) = \dfrac{\sqrt{15}}{3} \qquad \begin{array}{l}\textit{Rationalize the}\\ \textit{denominator.}\end{array}$$

EXERCISES

Multiply. Write each product in simplest form.

67. $\sqrt{2}\,\sqrt{7}$

68. $\sqrt{3}\,\sqrt{6}$

69. $3\sqrt{2x}\,\sqrt{14}$

70. $\left(5\sqrt{6}\right)^2$

71. $\sqrt{2}\left(4 - \sqrt{8}\right)$

72. $\left(8 + \sqrt{7}\right)^2$

Simplify each quotient.

73. $\dfrac{4}{\sqrt{5}}$

74. $\dfrac{a\sqrt{9}}{\sqrt{2}}$

75. $\dfrac{\sqrt{8}}{2\sqrt{6}}$

76. $\dfrac{\sqrt{5}}{\sqrt{2n}}$

77. $\dfrac{\sqrt{10}}{\sqrt{12}}$

78. $\dfrac{-3}{\sqrt{3}}$

11-9 Solving Radical Equations (pp. 846–853)

EXAMPLE

■ Solve $\sqrt{4x + 1} - 8 = -3$. Check your answer.

$$\sqrt{4x + 1} - 8 = -3$$

$$\sqrt{4x + 1} = 5 \qquad \textit{Add 8 to both sides.}$$

$$\left(\sqrt{4x + 1}\right)^2 = \left(5\right)^2 \qquad \textit{Square both sides.}$$

$$4x + 1 = 25$$

$$4x = 24 \qquad \textit{Subtract 1 from both sides.}$$

$$x = 6 \qquad \textit{Divide both sides by 4.}$$

$$\begin{array}{r|l}\textbf{Check} \quad \sqrt{4x + 1} - 8 = -3 & \\ \hline \sqrt{4(6) + 1} - 8 & -3 \\ \sqrt{25} - 8 & -3 \\ 5 - 8 & -3 \\ -3 & -3 \checkmark \end{array}$$

EXERCISES

Solve each equation. Check your answer.

79. $\sqrt{x} = 8$

80. $\sqrt{2x} = 4$

81. $\sqrt{x + 6} = 3$

82. $-3\sqrt{x} = -15$

83. $3\sqrt{-x} = 27$

84. $\dfrac{4\sqrt{x}}{5} = 8$

85. $\sqrt{x + 1} = \sqrt{3x - 5}$

86. $\sqrt{x - 2} + 4 = 3$

87. $12 = 4\sqrt{2x + 1}$

88. $\sqrt{x - 5} = \sqrt{7 - x}$

89. $\sqrt{x + 2} = 3$

90. $\sqrt{2x - 3} = 4$

91. $4\sqrt{x - 3} = 12$

92. $\sqrt{x + 6} = x$

93. $\sqrt{3x + 4} = x$

94. $\sqrt{2x + 6} = x - 1$

Find the next three terms in each geometric sequence.

1. 2, 6, 18, 54, …

2. 4800, 2400, 1200, 600, …

3. −4, 20, −100, 500, …

4. Communication If school is cancelled, the school secretary calls 2 families. Each of those families calls 2 other families. In the third round of calls, each of the 4 families calls 2 more families. If this pattern continues, how many families are called in the seventh round of calls?

Graph each exponential function.

5. $y = -2(4)^x$

6. $y = 3(2)^x$

7. $y = 4\left(\dfrac{1}{2}\right)^x$

8. $-\left(\dfrac{1}{3}\right)^x$

9. A teacher is repeatedly enlarging a diagram on a photocopier. The function $f(x) = 3(1.25)^x$ represents the length of the diagram, in centimeters, after x enlargements. What is the length after 5 enlargements? Round to the nearest centimeter.

10. Chelsea invested $5600 at a rate of 3.6% compounded quarterly. Write a compound interest function to model the situation. Then find the balance after 6 years.

11. The number of trees in a forest is decreasing at a rate of 5% per year. The forest had 24,000 trees 15 years ago. Write an exponential decay function to model the situation. Then find the number of trees now.

Look for a pattern in each data set to determine which kind of model best describes the data.

12. $\{(-10, -17), (-5, -7), (0, 3), (5, 13), (10, 23)\}$

13. $\{(1, 3), (2, 9), (3, 27), (4, 81), (5, 243)\}$

14. Use the data in the table to describe how the bacteria population is changing. Then write a function that models the data. Use your function to predict the bacteria population after 10 hours.

Bacteria Population				
Time (h)	0	1	2	3
Bacteria	6	18	54	162

Find the domain of each square-root function.

15. $y = 6 + \sqrt{x}$

16. $y = -2\sqrt{x + 9}$

17. $y = x + \sqrt{3x - 3}$

Graph each square-root function.

18. $f(x) = \sqrt{x} + 2$

19. $f(x) = \sqrt{x - 1}$

20. $f(x) = -3\sqrt{2x}$

Simplify. All variables represent nonnegative numbers.

21. $\sqrt{27}$

22. $\sqrt{75m^4}$

23. $\sqrt{\dfrac{x^6}{y^2}}$

24. $\sqrt{\dfrac{p^9}{144p}}$

25. $4\sqrt{10} - 2\sqrt{10}$

26. $5\sqrt{3y} + \sqrt{3y}$

27. $\sqrt{8} - \sqrt{50}$

28. $2\sqrt{75} - \sqrt{32} + \sqrt{48}$

29. $\sqrt{2}\sqrt{3m}$

30. $\dfrac{\sqrt{128d}}{\sqrt{5}}$

31. $\sqrt{3}\left(\sqrt{21} - 2\right)$

32. $\left(\sqrt{3} - 2\right)\left(\sqrt{3} + 4\right)$

Solve each equation. Check your answer.

33. $\sqrt{2x} = 6$

34. $\sqrt{3x + 4} - 2 = 5$

35. $\dfrac{2\sqrt{x}}{3} = 8$

36. $\sqrt{5x + 1} = \sqrt{2x - 2}$

COLLEGE ENTRANCE EXAM PRACTICE

FOCUS ON SAT MATHEMATICS SUBJECT TESTS

Colleges use standardized test scores to confirm what your academic record indicates. Because courses and instruction differ from school to school, standardized tests are one way in which colleges try to compare students fairly when making admissions decisions.

You will need to use a calculator on the SAT Mathematics Subject Tests. If you do not already have a graphing calculator, consider getting one because it may give you an advantage when solving some problems. Spend time getting used to your calculator before the test.

You may want to time yourself as you take this practice test. It should take you about 6 minutes to complete.

---

1. What is the domain of $y = \sqrt{x - 4}$?

    (A) $x \geq -2$

    (B) $x \geq 2$

    (C) $x \geq -4$

    (D) $x \geq 4$

    (E) $x > 4$

---

2. $\dfrac{\sqrt{8}\sqrt{3}}{\sqrt{5}} =$

    (A) $2\sqrt{3}$

    (B) $\dfrac{2\sqrt{3}}{5}$

    (C) $\sqrt{12}$

    (D) $\dfrac{4\sqrt{30}}{5}$

    (E) $\dfrac{2\sqrt{30}}{5}$

---

3. If $\dfrac{\sqrt{6 - 3x}}{5} = 3$, what is the value of x?

    (A) -3

    (B) -13

    (C) -73

    (D) -77

    (E) -89

---

4. The third term of a geometric sequence is 32 and the fifth term is 512. What is the eighth term of the sequence?

    (A) 544

    (B) 1232

    (C) 8192

    (D) 32,768

    (E) 2,097,152

---

5. A band releases a new CD and tracks its sales. The table shows the number of copies sold each week (in thousands). Which type of function best models this data?

CD Sales	
Week	Copies Sold (thousands)
1	129.5
2	155
3	179.5
4	203
5	225.5
6	247

    (A) Linear function

    (B) Quadratic function

    (C) Exponential function

    (D) Square-root function

    (E) Absolute-value function

TEST TACKLER

Standardized Test Strategies

Multiple Choice: *None of the Above* or *All of the Above*

In some multiple-choice test items, one of the options is *None of the above* or *All of the above*. To answer these types of items, first determine whether each of the other options is true or false. If you find that more than one option is true, then the correct choice is likely to be *All of the above*. If none of the options are true, the correct choice is *None of the above*.

If you do not know how to solve the problem and have to guess, *All of the above* is most often correct, and *None of the above* is usually incorrect.

EXAMPLE

There are 8 players on the chess team. Which of the following expressions gives the number of ways in which the coach can choose 2 players to start the game?

   (A) $_8C_2$ **(C)** 28

   (B) $\dfrac{8!}{2!(6!)}$ **(D)** All of the above

Notice that choice D is All of the above. *This means that you must look at each option. As you consider each option, mark it true or false in your test booklet.*

A Because order does not matter, this is a combination problem. The number of combinations of 8 players, taken 2 at a time, is given by $_nC_r$, where $n = 8$ and $r = 2$, so $_8C_2$ is a correct model of the combination. Choice A is true.

B The number of combinations of 8 players, taken 2 at a time, is given by $_nC_r = \dfrac{n!}{r!(n-r)!}$, where $n = 8$ and $r = 2$.

$$_nC_r = \frac{n!}{r!(n-r)!} = \frac{8!}{2!(8-2)!} = \frac{8!}{2!(6)!}$$

Choice B is a correct model of the combination. Choice B is also true. The answer is likely to be choice D, *All of the above*, but you should also check whether choice C is true.

C The number of combinations of 8 players, taken 2 at a time, is given by $_nC_r = \dfrac{n!}{r!(n-r)!}$, where $n = 8$ and $r = 2$.

$$_nC_r = \frac{n!}{r!(n-r)!} = \frac{8!}{2!(8-2)!} = \frac{8!}{2!(6)!} = 28$$

Choice C is a correct model of the combination. Choice C is true as well.

Because A, B, and C are all true, the correct response is D, *All of the above*.

Be careful of problems that contain more than one negative word, such as *no*, *not*, or *never*. Read the problem and each option twice before selecting an answer.

Read each test item and answer the questions that follow.

Item A
The mean score on a test is 68. Which CANNOT be true?

Ⓐ Every score is 68.

Ⓑ Half of the scores are 68, and half of the scores are 0.

Ⓒ Half of the scores are 94, and half of the scores are 42.

Ⓓ None of the above

1. What is the definition of *mean*?

2. If you find that an option is true, is that the correct response? Explain.

3. Willie determined that A and C could both be true, so he chose D as his response. Do you agree? Why or why not?

Item B
What is the probability of rolling a 2 on a number cube?

Ⓕ 16.$\overline{6}$%

Ⓖ $1 - P(\text{rolling } 1, 3, 4, 5, \text{ or } 6)$

Ⓗ $\dfrac{1}{6}$

Ⓙ All of the above

4. What is the complement of rolling a 2? Is choice G correct? Explain.

5. If you roll a number cube, how many possible outcomes are there? How does this information help you solve this problem?

6. Is the value given in choice H equivalent to any other choice? If so, which one(s)?

7. How many choices are true? What is the correct response to the test item?

Item C
Suppose that a dart lands at a random point on the circular dartboard. Find the probability that the dart does NOT land inside the center circle.

Ⓐ $\dfrac{1}{9}$ Ⓒ $\dfrac{8}{9}$

Ⓑ 8π Ⓓ None of the above

8. Kyle finds that choices A and B are both false. To save time, he selects choice D as his answer because he figures it is likely that choice C will also be false. Do you think Kyle made a wise decision? Why or why not?

9. What is the formula for the area of a circle? What is the total area of this dartboard? How can you determine the area of the dartboard outside the center circle?

10. Determine whether choices A, B, and C are true, and then give the correct response to this test item.

Item D
Each gym member receives a 3-digit locker combination. Digits are from 0–9 and may repeat. What is the probability that you will receive a code consisting of three identical numbers?

Ⓕ $\dfrac{1}{100}$ Ⓗ $_{10}P_3 = \dfrac{10!}{7!}$

Ⓖ $\dfrac{10}{_{10}C_3}$ Ⓙ All of the above

11. How can you determine whether choice J is the correct response to the test item?

12. Are the values given in choices F, G, and H equivalent? What does this tell you about choice J?

STANDARDIZED TEST PREP

CUMULATIVE ASSESSMENT, CHAPTERS 1–11

Multiple Choice

1. A sequence is defined by the rule $a_n = -3(2)^{n-1}$. What is the 5th term of the sequence?

- (A) 5
- (B) -30
- (C) -48
- (D) -216

2. Which could be the graph of $y = -2^x$?

(F)

(G)

(H)

(J)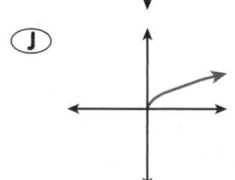

3. What is the slope of the line described by $4x - 3y = 12$?

- (A) 4
- (B) 3
- (C) $\frac{4}{3}$
- (D) $-\frac{3}{4}$

4. The odds in favor of a spinner landing on blue are 2:7. What is the probability of the spinner NOT landing on blue?

- (F) $\frac{7}{9}$
- (H) $\frac{2}{7}$
- (G) $\frac{5}{7}$
- (J) $\frac{2}{9}$

5. Which rule can be used to find any term in the sequence 8, 4, 2, 1, …?

- (A) $a_n = 8\left(\frac{1}{2}\right)^n$
- (C) $a_n = \left(\frac{1}{2}\right)^{n-1}$
- (B) $a_n = 2(1)^n$
- (D) $a_n = 8\left(\frac{1}{2}\right)^{n-1}$

6. Jerome walked on a treadmill for 45 minutes at a speed of 4.2 miles per hour. Approximately how far did Jerome walk?

- (F) 1.89 miles
- (G) 2.1 miles
- (H) 3.15 miles
- (J) 5.6 miles

7. What is the solution to the system of equations below?

$$\begin{cases} 2x - y = 2 \\ y = 3x - 5 \end{cases}$$

- (A) $(4, 6)$
- (C) $(2, 1)$
- (B) $(3, 4)$
- (D) $(0, 2)$

8. What is the complete factorization of $2x^3 + 18x$?

- (F) $2x(x^2 + 9)$
- (G) $2x(x + 3)^2$
- (H) $2x(x + 3)(x - 3)$
- (J) $2(x^3 + 18)$

9. Which ordered pair lies on the graph of $y = 3(2)^{x+1}$?

- (A) $(-1, 0)$
- (C) $(1, 12)$
- (B) $(0, 9)$
- (D) $(3, 24)$

When a test item gives an equation to be solved, it may be quicker to work backward from the answer choices by substituting them into the equation. If time remains, check your answer by solving the equation.

10. Which shows the product of 5.1×10^4 and 3×10^9 written in scientific notation?

  (F) 1.53×10^{12}

  (G) 1.53×10^{14}

  (H) 15.3×10^{12}

  (J) 15.3×10^{13}

11. Which is an arithmetic sequence?

  I 3, 6, 9, 12, 15, …

  II 1, 10, 100, 1000, …

  III 4000, −2000, 1000, −500, …

  (A) I only

  (B) II and III

  (C) I and III

  (D) III only

Gridded Response

12. The function $f(x) = 30{,}000(0.8)^x$ gives the value of a vehicle, where x is the number of years after purchase. According to the function, what will be the value of the car in dollars 8 years after purchase? Round your answer to the nearest whole dollar.

13. The graph of $f(x)$ is shown below. How many zeros does $f(x)$ have?

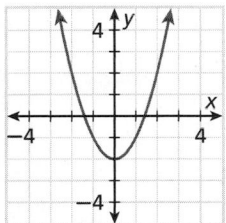

14. Rosalind purchased a sewing machine at a 20%-off sale. The original selling price of the machine was $340. What was the sale price in dollars?

15. Two planes leave an airport, one heading due north and the other heading due west. After several minutes, the first plane is 12 miles north of the airport, and the second plane is 15 miles west of the airport. Estimate the distance between the two planes to the nearest hundredth of a mile.

Short Response

16. The table shows the number of people newly infected by a certain virus with one person as the original source.

Week	1	2	3	4	5	6	7
Newly Infected People	1	3	9	27	81	243	729

  a. Is the data set best described by a linear function, a quadratic function, or an exponential function? Write a function to model the data.

  b. Use the function to predict the number of people that will become infected in the 10th week. Show your work.

17. Ella and Mia went on a camping trip. The total cost for their trip was $124, which the girls divided evenly. Ella paid for 4 nights at the campsite and $30 for supplies. Mia paid for 2 nights at the campsite and $46 for supplies.

  a. Write an equation that could be used to find the cost of one night's stay at the campsite. Explain what each variable in your equation represents.

  b. Solve your equation from part **a** to find the cost of one night's stay at the campsite. Show your work.

Extended Response

18. Regina is beginning a training program to prepare for a race. In week 1, she will run 3 miles during each workout. Each week thereafter, she plans to increase the distance of her runs by 20%.

  a. Write an equation to show the number of miles Regina plans to run during her workouts each week. Use the variable n to represent the week number.

  b. Make a table of values to show the distances of the runs in Regina's workouts for the first 6 weeks. Round each distance to the nearest hundredth of a mile. Then graph the points.

  c. Explain how to use your equation from part **a** to determine how many miles Regina will run during each workout in week 8. Then find this number.

  d. Explain how to the use your graph from part **b** to determine how many miles Regina will run during each workout in week 8. How does the graph verify the answer you found in part **c**?

Rational Functions and Equations

Chapter

- Graph and use rational functions to solve real-world problems.
- Simplify rational expressions.
- Use rational equations to solve real-world problems.

By DESIGN

Ratios and rational expressions can be used to explore perspective in art and dimensions in package design. Try your hand at both.

go.hrw.com
Chapter Project Online
KEYWORD: MA7 ChProj

ARE YOU READY?

✓ Vocabulary

Match each term on the left with a definition on the right.

1. perfect-square trinomial

2. greatest common factor

3. monomial

4. polynomial

5. reciprocals

A. the greatest factor that is shared by two or more terms

B. a number, a variable, or a product of numbers and variables with whole-number exponents

C. two numbers whose product is 1

D. a polynomial with three terms

E. the sum or difference of monomials

F. a trinomial that is the result of squaring a binomial

✓ Simplify Fractions

Simplify.

6. $\dfrac{12}{4}$

7. $\dfrac{100}{36}$

8. $\dfrac{240}{18}$

9. $\dfrac{121}{66}$

✓ Add and Subtract Fractions

Add or subtract.

10. $\dfrac{1}{3} + \dfrac{1}{2}$

11. $\dfrac{7}{8} - \dfrac{1}{6}$

12. $\dfrac{3}{4} + \dfrac{2}{3} + \dfrac{1}{2}$

13. $\dfrac{5}{9} + \dfrac{1}{12} - \dfrac{1}{3}$

✓ Factor GCF from Polynomials

Factor each polynomial.

14. $x^2 + 2x$

15. $x^2 + x$

16. $2x^2 + x$

17. $x^2 - x$

18. $3x^2 + 2x$

19. $4x^2 - 4$

20. $3x^2 - 6x$

21. $x^3 - x^2$

✓ Properties of Exponents

Simplify each expression.

22. $4x \cdot 3x^2$

23. $-5 \cdot 2jk$

24. $-2a^3 \cdot 3a^4$

25. $3ab \cdot 4a^2b$

26. $2x \cdot 3y \cdot xy$

27. $a^2b \cdot 3ab^3$

28. $3rs \cdot 3rs^3$

29. $5m^2n^2 \cdot 4mn^2$

✓ Simplify Polynomial Expressions

Simplify each expression.

30. $4x - 2y - 8y$

31. $2r - 4s + 3s - 8r$

32. $ab^2 - ab + 4ab^2 + 2a^2b + a^2b^2$

33. $3g(g - 4) + g^2 + g$

Where You've Been

Previously you

- identified, wrote, and graphed equations of direct variation.
- identified and graphed quadratic, exponential, and square-root functions.
- used factoring to solve quadratic equations.
- simplified radical expressions and solved radical equations.

In This Chapter

You will study

- how to identify, write, and graph equations of inverse variation.
- how to graph rational functions and simplify rational expressions.
- how to solve rational equations.

Where You're Going

You can use the skills in this chapter

- to build upon your knowledge of graphing and transforming various types of functions.
- to solve problems involving inverse variation in classes such as Physics and Chemistry.
- to calculate costs when working with a fixed budget.

Key Vocabulary/Vocabulario

asymptote	asíntota
discontinuous function	función discontinua
excluded values	valores excluidos
inverse variation	variación inversa
rational equation	ecuación racional
rational expression	expresión racional
rational function	función racional

Vocabulary Connections

To become familiar with some of the vocabulary terms in the chapter, consider the following. You may refer to the chapter, the glossary, or a dictionary if you like.

1. What are some other words that mean the same as *continuous*? The prefix *dis-* generally means "not." Describe what the graph of a **discontinuous function** might look like.

2. What does it mean for someone or something to be *included* in a group? What about *excluded*? What might it mean for some values to be **excluded values** for a particular function?

3. A *direct variation* is a relationship between two variables, x and y, that can be written in the form $y = kx$ where k is a nonzero constant. The inverse of a number x is $\frac{1}{x}$. Use this information to write the form of an **inverse variation**.

4. You learned in Chapter 1 that an *algebraic expression* is an expression that contains one or more variables, numbers, or operations. You also learned that a *rational number* is a number that can be written in the form of a fraction. Combine these terms to define **rational expression**. Give an example.

Study Strategy: Prepare for Your Final Exam

Math is a cumulative subject, so your final exam will probably cover all of the material you have learned since the beginning of the course. Preparation is essential for you to be successful on your final exam. It may help you to make a study timeline like the one below.

2 weeks before the final:

- Look at previous exams and homework to determine areas I need to focus on; rework problems that were incorrect or incomplete.
- Make a list of all formulas, definitions, and properties I need to know for the final.
- Create a practice exam using problems from the book that are similar to problems from each exam.

1 week before the final:

- Take the practice exam and check it. For each problem I miss, find 2 or 3 similar ones and work those.
- Work with a friend in the class to quiz each other on formulas, definitions, and properties from my list.

1 day before the final:

- Make sure I have pencils, calculator (check batteries!), and ruler.

FINAL

Try This

1. Create a timeline that you will use to study for your final exam.

12-1
Algebra LAB

Model Inverse Variation

The relationship between the width and the length of a rectangle with a constant area is an inverse variation. In this activity, you will study this relationship by modeling rectangles with square tiles or grid paper.

Use with Lesson 12-1

Activity

Use 12 square tiles to form a rectangle with an area of 12 square units, or draw the rectangle on grid paper. Use a width of 1 unit and a length of 12 units.

Your rectangle should look like the one shown.

Using the same 12 square tiles, continue forming rectangles by changing the width and length until you have formed all the different rectangles you can that have an area of 12 square units. Copy and complete the table as you form each rectangle.

Width (x)	Length (y)	Area (xy)
1	12	12
		12
		12
		12
		12
		12

Plot the ordered pairs from the table on a graph. Draw a smooth curve through the points.

Try This

1. Look at the table and graph above. What happens to the length as the width increases? Why?

2. This type of relationship is called an *inverse variation*. Why do you think it is called that?

3. For each point, what does xy equal? Complete the equation $xy =$ ▊. Solve this equation for y.

4. Form all the different rectangles that have an area of 24 square units. Record their widths and lengths in a table. Graph your results. Write an equation relating the width x and length y.

5. **Make a Conjecture** Using the equations you wrote in 3 and 4, what do you think the equation of any inverse variation might look like when solved for y?

12-1 Inverse Variation

Objective
Identify, write, and graph inverse variations.

Vocabulary
inverse variation

Remember!

A direct variation is an equation that can be written in the form $y = kx$, where k is a nonzero constant.

Why learn this?

Inverse variation can be used to find the frequency at which a guitar string vibrates. (See Example 3.)

A relationship that can be written in the form $y = \frac{k}{x}$, where k is a nonzero constant and $x \neq 0$, is an **inverse variation**. The constant k is the constant of variation.

Multiplying both sides of $y = \frac{k}{x}$ by x gives $xy = k$. So, for any inverse variation, the product of x and y is a nonzero constant.

Know it!
Note

Inverse Variations

WORDS	NUMBERS	ALGEBRA
y varies inversely as x.	$y = \frac{3}{x}$	$y = \frac{k}{x}$
y is inversely proportional to x.	$xy = 3$	$xy = k \; (k \neq 0)$

There are two methods to determine whether a relationship between data is an inverse variation. You can write a function rule in $y = \frac{k}{x}$ form, or you can check whether xy is constant for each ordered pair.

EXAMPLE 1 **Identifying an Inverse Variation**

Tell whether each relationship is an inverse variation. Explain.

A

x	y
1	20
2	10
4	5

B

x	y
2	6
3	9
6	18

Method 1 Write a function rule.

$y = \dfrac{20}{x}$ *Can write in $y = \frac{k}{x}$ form.*

The relationship is an inverse variation.

Method 2 Find xy for each ordered pair.

$1(20) = 20$, $2(10) = 20$, $4(5) = 20$

The product xy is constant, so the relationship is an inverse variation.

Method 1 Write a function rule.

$y = 3x$ *Cannot write in $y = \frac{k}{x}$ form.*

The relationship is not an inverse variation.

Method 2 Find xy for each ordered pair.

$2(6) = 12$, $3(9) = 27$, $6(18) = 108$

The product xy is not constant, so the relationship is not an inverse variation.

Tell whether each relationship is an inverse variation. Explain.

 $5xy = -21$

$\dfrac{5xy}{5} = \dfrac{-21}{5}$ *Find xy. Since xy is multiplied by 5, divide both sides by 5 to undo the multiplication.*

$xy = \dfrac{-21}{5}$ *Simplify.*

xy equals the constant $\dfrac{-21}{5}$, so the relationship is an inverse variation.

CHECK IT OUT!

Tell whether each relationship is an inverse variation. Explain.

1a.

x	y
−12	24
1	−2
8	−16

1b.

x	y
3	3
9	1
18	0.5

1c. $2x + y = 10$

Helpful Hint

Since k is a nonzero constant, $xy \ne 0$. Therefore, neither x nor y can equal 0, and no solution points will be on the x- or y-axes.

An inverse variation can also be identified by its graph. Some inverse variation graphs are shown. Notice that each graph has two parts that are not connected.

Also notice that none of the graphs contain $(0, 0)$. This is because $(0, 0)$ can never be a solution of an inverse variation equation.

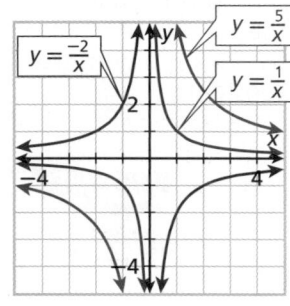

EXAMPLE 2

Graphing an Inverse Variation

Write and graph the inverse variation in which $y = 2$ when $x = 4$.

Step 1 Find k.

$k = xy$ *Write the rule for constant of variation.*

$= 4(2)$ *Substitute 4 for x and 2 for y.*

$= 8$

Step 2 Use the value of k to write an inverse variation equation.

$y = \dfrac{k}{x}$ *Write the rule for inverse variation.*

$y = \dfrac{8}{x}$ *Substitute 8 for k.*

Step 3 Use the equation to make a table of values.

x	−4	−2	−1	0	1	2	4
y	−2	−4	−8	undef.	8	4	2

Step 4 Plot the points and connect them with smooth curves.

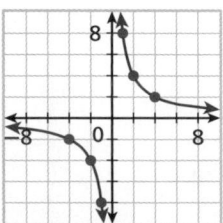

CHECK IT OUT!

2. Write and graph the inverse variation in which $y = \frac{1}{2}$ when $x = 10$.

EXAMPLE 3 *Music Application*

The inverse variation $xy = 2400$ relates the vibration frequency y in hertz (Hz) to the length x in centimeters of a guitar string. Determine a reasonable domain and range and then graph this inverse variation. Use the graph to estimate the frequency of vibration when the string length is 100 centimeters.

Step 1 Solve the function for y so you can graph it.

$$xy = 2400$$

$$y = \frac{2400}{x}$$ *Divide both sides by x.*

Step 2 Decide on a reasonable domain and range.

$x > 0$ *Length is never negative and $x \neq 0$.*

$y > 0$ *Because x and xy are both positive, y is also positive.*

Remember!

Recall that sometimes domain and range are restricted in real-world situations.

Step 3 Use values of the domain to generate reasonable ordered pairs.

x	20	40	60	120
y	120	60	40	20

Guitar String Vibration

Step 4 Plot the points. Connect them with a smooth curve.

Step 5 Find the y-value where $x = 100$. When the string length is 100 cm, the frequency of vibration is about 24 Hz.

 3. The inverse variation $xy = 100$ represents the relationship between the pressure x in atmospheres (atm) and the volume y in mm³ of a certain gas. Determine a reasonable domain and range and then graph this inverse variation. Use the graph to estimate the volume of the gas when the pressure is 40 atmospheric units.

The fact that $xy = k$ is the same for every ordered pair in any inverse variation can help you find missing values in the relationship.

Know it!
Note

Product Rule for Inverse Variation

If (x_1, y_1) and (x_2, y_2) are solutions of an inverse variation, then $x_1y_1 = x_2y_2$.

EXAMPLE 4 **Using the Product Rule**

Let $x_1 = 3$, $y_1 = 2$, and $y_2 = 6$. Let y vary inversely as x. Find x_2.

$$x_1y_1 = x_2y_2$$ *Write the Product Rule for Inverse Variation.*

$$(3)(2) = x_2(6)$$ *Substitute 3 for x_1, 2 for y_1, and 6 for y_2.*

$$6 = 6x_2$$ *Simplify.*

$$\frac{6}{6} = \frac{6x_2}{6}$$ *Solve for x_2 by dividing both sides by 6.*

$$1 = x_2$$ *Simplify.*

CHECK IT OUT! **4.** Let $x_1 = 2$, $y_1 = -6$, and $x_2 = -4$. Let y vary inversely as x. Find y_2.

EXAMPLE 5 Physics Application

Boyle's law states that the pressure of a quantity of gas x varies inversely as the volume of the gas y. The volume of air inside a bicycle pump is 5.2 in³, and the pressure is 15.5 psi. Assuming no air escapes, what is the pressure of the air inside the pump after the handle is pushed in, and the air is compressed to a volume of 2.6 in³?

Reading Math

In Example 5, x_1 and y_1 represent volume and pressure **before** the handle is pushed in, and x_2 and y_2 represent volume and pressure **after** the handle is pushed in.

Volume = 5.2 in3
Pressure = 15.5 psi

Volume = 2.6 in3
Pressure = ?

$$x_1 y_1 = x_2 y_2 \qquad \textit{Use the Product Rule for Inverse Variation.}$$

$$(5.2)(15.5) = (2.6)y_2 \qquad \textit{Substitute 5.2 for } x_1, \textit{ 15.5 for } y_1, \textit{ and 2.6 for } x_2.$$

$$80.6 = 2.6y_2 \qquad \textit{Simplify.}$$

$$\frac{80.6}{2.6} = \frac{2.6y_2}{2.6} \qquad \textit{Solve for } y_2 \textit{ by dividing both sides by 2.6.}$$

$$31 = y_2 \qquad \textit{Simplify.}$$

The pressure after the handle is pushed in is 31 psi.

CHECK IT OUT! **5.** On a balanced lever, weight varies inversely as the distance from the fulcrum to the weight. The diagram shows a balanced lever. How much does the child weigh?

60 lb

3.2 ft

4.3 ft

Fulcrum

THINK AND DISCUSS

1. Name two ways you can identify an inverse variation.

2. GET ORGANIZED Copy and complete the graphic organizer. In each box, write an example of the parts of the given inverse variation.

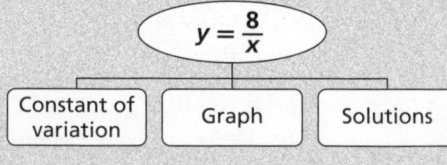

$$y = \frac{8}{x}$$

| Constant of variation | Graph | Solutions |

go.hrw.com
Homework Help Online
KEYWORD: MA7 12-1
Parent Resources Online
KEYWORD: MA7 Parent

GUIDED PRACTICE

1. **Vocabulary** Describe the graph of an *inverse variation*.

SEE EXAMPLE 1
p. 871

Tell whether each relationship is an inverse variation. Explain.

2.

x	y
1	8
4	2
2	4

3.

x	y
$\frac{1}{6}$	1
$\frac{1}{3}$	2
2	12

4. $x + y = 8$

5. $4xy = 3$

SEE EXAMPLE 2
p. 872

6. Write and graph the inverse variation in which $y = 2$ when $x = 2$.

7. Write and graph the inverse variation in which $y = 6$ when $x = -1$.

SEE EXAMPLE 3
p. 873

8. **Travel** The inverse variation $xy = 30$ relates the constant speed x in mi/h to the time y in hours that it takes to travel 30 miles. Determine a reasonable domain and range and then graph this inverse variation. Use the graph to estimate how many hours it would take traveling 4 mi/h.

SEE EXAMPLE 4
p. 873

9. Let $x_1 = 3$, $y_1 = 12$, and $x_2 = 9$. Let y vary inversely as x. Find y_2.

10. Let $x_1 = 1$, $y_1 = 4$, and $y_2 = 16$. Let y vary inversely as x. Find x_2.

SEE EXAMPLE 5
p. 874

11. **Mechanics** The rotational speed of a gear varies inversely as the number of teeth on the gear. A gear with 12 teeth has a rotational speed of 60 rpm. How many teeth are on a gear that has a rotational speed of 45 rpm?

PRACTICE AND PROBLEM SOLVING

Independent Practice

For Exercises	See Example
12–15	1
16–17	2
18	3
19–20	4
21	5

Extra Practice

Skills Practice p. S26

Application Practice p. S39

Tell whether each relationship is an inverse variation. Explain.

12.

x	y
3	-3
-5	5
7	-7

13.

x	y
2	5
0.5	20
8	1.25

14. $x = \frac{13}{y}$

15. $y = 5x$

16. Write and graph the inverse variation in which $y = -2$ when $x = 5$.

17. Write and graph the inverse variation in which $y = -6$ when $x = -\frac{1}{3}$.

18. **Engineering** The inverse variation $xy = 12$ relates the current x in amps to the resistance y in ohms of a circuit attached to a 12-volt battery. Determine a reasonable domain and range and then graph this inverse variation. Use the graph to estimate the resistance of a circuit when the current is 5 amps.

19. Let $x_1 = -3$, $y_1 = -4$, and $y_2 = 6$. Let y vary inversely as x. Find x_2.

20. Let $x_1 = 7$, $y_1 = 9$, and $x_2 = 6$. Let y vary inversely as x. Find y_2.

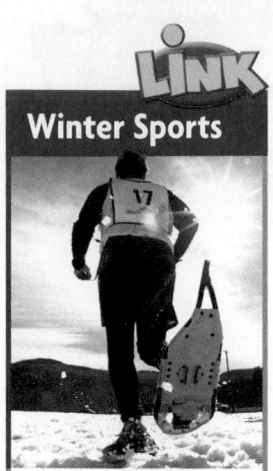
21. **Home Economics** The length of fabric that June can afford varies inversely as the price per yard of the fabric. June can afford exactly 5 yards of fabric that costs $10.50 per yard. How many yards of fabric that costs $4.25 per yard can June buy? (Assume that she can only buy whole yards.)

22. **Winter Sports** When a person is snowshoeing, the pressure on the top of the snow in psi varies inversely as the area of the bottom of the snowshoe in square inches. The constant of variation is the weight of the person wearing the snowshoes in pounds.

   a. Helen weighs 120 pounds. About how much pressure does she put on top of the snow if she wears snowshoes that cover 360 in²?

   b. Max weighs 207 pounds. If he exerts 0.4 psi of pressure on top of the snow, what is the area of the bottom of his snowshoes in square inches?

Determine if each equation represents a direct variation, an inverse variation, or neither. Find the constant of variation when one exists.

23. $y = 8x$

24. $y = \dfrac{14}{x}$

25. $y = \dfrac{1}{3}x - 2$

26. $y = \dfrac{1}{5}x$

27. $y = 4\dfrac{3}{x}$

28. $y = \dfrac{x}{2} + 7$

29. $y = \dfrac{15}{x}$

30. $y = 5x$

31. **Multi-Step** A track team is competing in a 10 km race. The distance will be evenly divided among the team members. Write an equation that represents the distance d each runner will run if there are n runners. Does this represent a direct variation, inverse variation, or neither?

Determine whether each data set represents a direct variation, an inverse variation, or neither.

32.

x	2	4	8
y	5	10	20

33.

x	6	12	15
y	6	8	9

34.

x	1	2	3
y	12	6	4

35. **Multi-Step** Your club awards one student a $2000 scholarship each year, and each member contributes an equal amount. Your contribution y depends on the number of members x. Write and graph an inverse variation equation that represents this situation. What are a reasonable domain and range?

36. **Estimation** Estimate the value of y if y is inversely proportional to x, $x = 4$, and the constant of variation is 6π.

37. **Critical Thinking** Why will the point $(0, 0)$ never be a solution to an inverse variation?

38. **Write About It** Explain how to write an inverse variation equation of the form $y = \dfrac{k}{x}$ when values of x and y are known.

39. **Write About It** List all the mathematical terms you know that contain the word *inverse*. How are these terms all similar? How is *inverse variation* similar to these terms?

MULTI-STEP TEST PREP

40. This problem will prepare you for the Multi-Step Test Prep on page 896. The total number of workdays it takes to build the frame of a house varies inversely as the number of people working in a crew. Let x be the number of people in the crew and let y be the number of workdays.

   a. Find the constant of variation when $y = 75$ and $x = 2$.

   b. Write the rule for the inverse of variation equation.

   c. Graph the equation of this inverse variation.

41. Which equation best represents the graph?

   (A) $y = -\frac{1}{4}x$ (C) $y = -\frac{4}{x}$

   (B) $y = \frac{1}{4}x$ (D) $y = \frac{4}{x}$

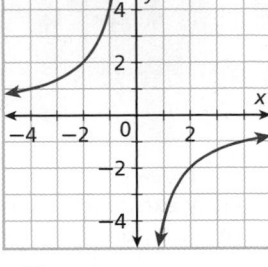

42. Determine the constant of variation if y varies inversely as x and $y = 2$ when $x = 7$.

   (F) $\frac{2}{7}$ (G) $\frac{7}{2}$ (H) 3.5   (J) 14

43. Which of the following relationships does NOT represent an inverse variation?

(A)

x	2	4	5
y	10	5	4

(C)

x	2	4	5
y	8	16	20

   (B) $y = \frac{17.5}{x}$ (D) $\frac{11}{2} = xy$

44. Gridded Response At a carnival, the number of tickets Brad can buy is inversely proportional to the price of the tickets. He can afford 12 tickets that cost $2.50 each. How many tickets can Brad buy if each costs $3.00?

CHALLENGE AND EXTEND

45. The definition of inverse variation says that k is a nonzero constant. What function would $y = \frac{k}{x}$ represent if $k = 0$?

46. Mechanics A part of a car's braking system uses a lever to multiply the force applied to the brake pedal. The force at the end of a lever varies inversely with the distance from the fulcrum. Point P is the end of the lever. A force of 2 lb is applied to the brake pedal. What is the force created at the point P?

47. Communication The strength of a radio signal varies inversely with the square of the distance from the transmitter. A signal has a strength of 2000 watts when it is 4 kilometers from the transmitter. What is the strength of the signal 6 kilometers from the transmitter?

SPIRAL REVIEW

Find the domain and range for each relation. Tell whether the relation is a function. *(Lesson 4-2)*

48. $\{(-2, -4), (-2, -2), (-2, 0), (-2, 2)\}$ **49.** $\{(-4, 5), (-2, 3), (0, 1), (2, 3), (4, 5)\}$

Solve by completing the square. *(Lesson 9-8)*

50. $x^2 + 12x = 45$ **51.** $d^2 - 6d - 7 = 0$ **52.** $2y^2 + 6y = -\frac{5}{2}$

53. A rectangle has a length of 6 cm and a width of 2 cm. Find the length of the diagonal and write it as a simplified radical expression. *(Lesson 11-6)*

12-2 Rational Functions

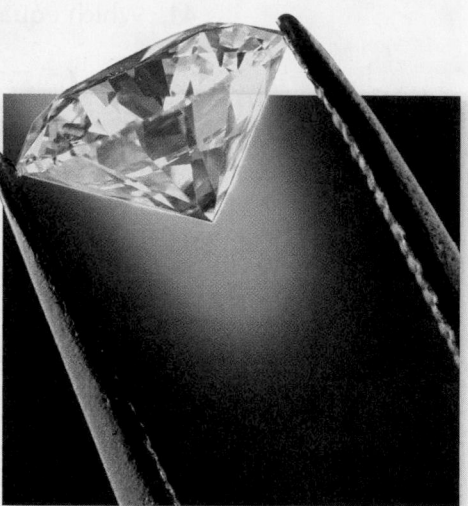

Objectives
Identify excluded values of rational functions.

Graph rational functions.

Vocabulary
rational function
excluded value
discontinuous function
asymptote

Who uses this?
Gemologists can use rational functions to maximize reflected light. (See Example 4.)

A **rational function** is a function whose rule is a quotient of polynomials. The inverse variations you studied in the previous lesson are a special type of rational function.

Rational functions: $y = \dfrac{2}{x}$, $y = \dfrac{3}{4 - 2x}$, $y = \dfrac{1}{x^2}$

For any function involving x and y, an **excluded value** is any x-value that makes the function value y undefined. For a rational function, an excluded value is any value that makes the denominator equal 0.

EXAMPLE 1 **Identifying Excluded Values**

Identify the excluded value for each rational function.

A $y = \dfrac{8}{x}$

$x = 0$ *Set the denominator equal to 0.*

The excluded value is 0.

B $y = \dfrac{3}{x + 3}$

$x + 3 = 0$ *Set the denominator equal to 0.*

$x = -3$ *Solve for x.*

The excluded value is -3.

 CHECK IT OUT! Identify the excluded value for each rational function.

1a. $y = \dfrac{10}{x}$ **1b.** $y = \dfrac{4}{x - 1}$ **1c.** $y = -\dfrac{5}{x + 4}$

Most rational functions are **discontinuous functions**, meaning their graphs contain one or more jumps, breaks, or holes. This occurs at an excluded value.

One place that a graph of a rational function is discontinuous is at an *asymptote*. An **asymptote** is a line that a graph gets closer to as the absolute value of a variable increases. In the graph shown, both the x- and y-axes are asymptotes. The graphs of rational functions will get closer and closer to but never touch the asymptotes.

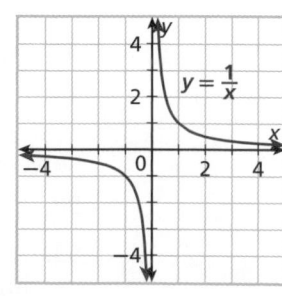

For rational functions, vertical asymptotes will occur at excluded values.

Look at the graph of $y = \frac{1}{x}$. The denominator is 0 when $x = 0$ so 0 is an excluded value. This means there is a vertical asymptote at $x = 0$. Notice the horizontal asymptote at $y = 0$.

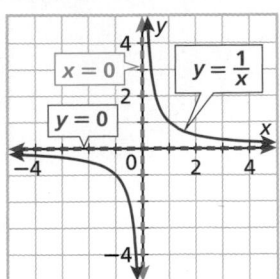

Look at the graph of $y = \frac{1}{x - 3} + 2$. Notice that the graph of the parent function $y = \frac{1}{x}$ has been translated **3 units right** and there is a vertical asymptote at $x = 3$. The graph has also been translated **2 units up** and there is a horizontal asymptote at $y = 2$.

These translations lead to the following formulas for identifying asymptotes in rational functions.

Know it! Note

Identifying Asymptotes

WORDS	EXAMPLES	
A rational function in the form $$y = \frac{a}{x - b} + c$$ has a vertical asymptote at the excluded value, or $x = b$, and a horizontal asymptote at $y = c$.	$y = \frac{2}{x}$ $= \frac{2}{x - 0} + 0$ Vertical asymptote: $x = 0$ Horizontal asymptote: $y = 0$	$y = \frac{1}{x + 2} + 4$ $= \frac{1}{x - (-2)} + 4$ Vertical asymptote: $x = -2$ Horizontal asymptote: $y = 4$

EXAMPLE 2 **Identifying Asymptotes**

Identify the asymptotes.

A $y = \frac{1}{x - 6}$

Step 1 Write in $y = \frac{1}{x - b} + c$ form.

$$y = \frac{1}{x - 6} + 0$$

Step 2 Identify the asymptotes.
vertical: $x = 6$
horizontal: $y = 0$

B $y = \frac{2}{3x - 10} - 7$

Step 1 Identify the vertical asymptote.

$$3x - 10 = 0 \qquad \textit{Find the excluded value. Set the denominator equal to 0.}$$

$$\underline{ +10 \quad +10} \qquad \textit{Add 10 to both sides.}$$

$$3x = 10$$

$$x = \frac{10}{3} \qquad \textit{Solve for x. } \frac{10}{3} \textit{ is an excluded value.}$$

Step 2 Identify the horizontal asymptote.

$c = -7$ *−7 can be written as + (−7)*

$y = -7$ *y = c*

vertical asymptote: $x = \frac{10}{3}$; horizontal asymptote: $y = -7$

 Identify the asymptotes.

2a. $y = \dfrac{2}{x - 5}$ **2b.** $y = \dfrac{1}{4x + 16} + 5$ **2c.** $y = \dfrac{3}{x + 77} - 15$

To graph a rational function in the form $y = \dfrac{a}{x - b} + c$ when $a = 1$, you can graph the asymptotes and then translate the parent function $y = \frac{1}{x}$. However, if $a \neq 1$, the graph is not a translation of the parent function. In this case, you can use the asymptotes and a table of values.

EXAMPLE **3**   **Graphing Rational Functions Using Asymptotes**

Graph each function.

A $y = \dfrac{2}{x + 1}$

Since the numerator is not 1, use the asymptotes and a table of values.

Step 1 Identify the vertical and horizontal asymptotes.

vertical: $x = -1$ *Use x = b. x + 1 = x − (−1), so b = −1.*

horizontal : $y = 0$ *Use y = c. c = 0*

Step 2 Graph the asymptotes using dashed lines.

Step 3 Make a table of values. Choose x-values on both sides of the vertical asymptote.

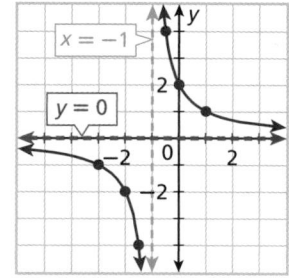

x	-3	-2	$-\frac{3}{2}$	$-\frac{1}{2}$	0	1
y	-1	-2	-4	4	2	1

Step 4 Plot the points and connect them with smooth curves. The curves will get very close to the asymptotes, but will not touch them.

B $y = \dfrac{1}{x - 2} - 4$

Since the numerator is 1, use the asymptotes and translate $y = \frac{1}{x}$.

Step 1 Identify the vertical and horizontal asymptotes.

vertical: $x = 2$ *Use x = b. b = 2*

horizontal: $y = -4$ *Use y = c. c = −4*

Step 2 Graph the asymptotes using dashed lines.

Step 3 Draw smooth curves to show the translation.

 Graph each function.

3a. $y = \dfrac{1}{x + 7} + 3$ **3b.** $y = \dfrac{2}{x - 3} + 2$

EXAMPLE 4 *Gemology Application*

Some diamonds are cut using ratios calculated by a mathematician, Marcel Tolkowsky, in 1919. The amount of light reflected up through the top of a diamond (brilliancy) can be maximized using the ratio between the width of the diamond and the depth of the diamond. A gemologist has a diamond with a width of 90 millimeters. If x represents the depth of the diamond, then $y = \frac{90}{x}$ represents the brilliancy ratio y.

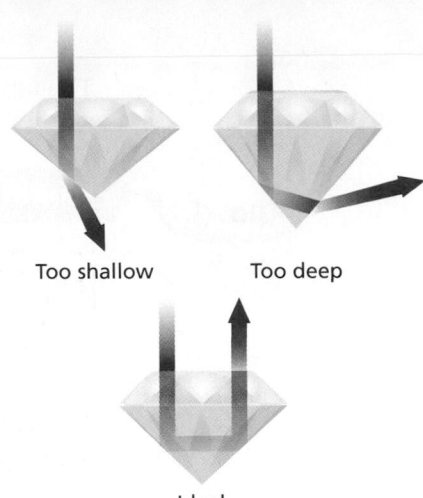

Too shallow   Too deep

Ideal

a. **Describe the reasonable domain and range values.**

Both the depth of the diamond and the brilliancy ratio will be nonnegative, so nonnegative values are reasonable for the domain and range.

b. **Graph the function.**

Step 1 Identify the vertical and horizontal asymptotes.

vertical: $x = 0$ *Use x = b. b = 0*
horizontal: $y = 0$ *Use y = c. c = 0*

Step 2 Graph the asymptotes.
The asymptotes will be the x- and y-axes.

Step 3 Since the domain is restricted to nonnegative values, only choose x-values on the right side of the vertical asymptote.

Depth of Diamond (mm)	2	10	20	45
Brilliancy Ratio	45	9	4.5	2

Step 4 Plot the points and connect them with smooth curves.

Brilliancy of a Diamond Cut

 CHECK IT OUT!

4. A librarian has a budget of $500 to buy copies of a software program. She will receive 10 free copies when she sets up an account with the supplier. The number of copies y of the program that she can buy is given by $y = \frac{500}{x} + 10$, where x is the price per copy.

a. Describe the reasonable domain and range values.

b. Graph the function.

The table shows some of the properties of the four families of functions you have studied and their graphs.

LINEAR FUNCTION	QUADRATIC FUNCTION
$y = mx + b$	$y = ax^2 + bx + c$
• Parent function: $y = x$	• Parent function: $y = x^2$
• m is the slope. It rotates the graph about $(0, b)$.	• a determines the width of the parabola and the direction it opens.
• b is the y-intercept. It translates the graph of $y = x$ vertically.	• c translates the graph of $y = ax^2$ vertically.
	• The axis of symmetry is the vertical line $x = -\frac{b}{2a}$.

SQUARE-ROOT FUNCTION	RATIONAL FUNCTION
$y = \sqrt{x - a} + b$	$y = \dfrac{a}{x - b} + c$
• Parent function: $y = \sqrt{x}$	• Parent function: $y = \frac{1}{x}$
• a translates the graph of $y = \sqrt{x}$ horizontally.	• b translates the graph $y = \frac{1}{x}$ horizontally.
• b translates the graph of $y = \sqrt{x}$ vertically.	• c translates the graph of $y = \frac{1}{x}$ vertically.

THINK AND DISCUSS

1. Does $y = \frac{1}{x - 5}$ have any excluded values? Explain.

2. Tell how to find the vertical and horizontal asymptotes of $y = \frac{1}{x + 9} - 5$.

3. GET ORGANIZED Copy and complete the graphic organizer. In each box, find the asymptotes for the given rational function.

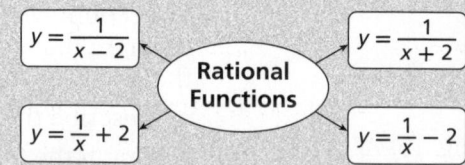

12-2

Exercises

go.hrw.com
Homework Help Online
KEYWORD: MA7 12-2
Parent Resources Online
KEYWORD: MA7 Parent

GUIDED PRACTICE

1. **Vocabulary** An x-value that makes a function undefined is a(n)_____?_____.
   (*asymptote* or *excluded value*)

SEE EXAMPLE **1**
p. 878

Identify the excluded value for each rational function.

2. $y = \frac{4}{x}$

3. $y = \frac{2}{x + 3}$

4. $y = -\frac{2}{x}$

5. $y = \frac{16}{x - 4}$

SEE EXAMPLE **2**
p. 879

Identify the asymptotes.

6. $y = \frac{1}{x - 3}$

7. $y = \frac{4}{3x + 15}$

8. $y = \frac{2}{3x - 5} + 2$

9. $y = \frac{1}{x + 9} - 10$

SEE EXAMPLE **3**
p. 880

Graph each function.

10. $y = \frac{2}{x + 6}$

11. $y = \frac{1}{x - 2} - 6$

12. $y = \frac{1}{x} + 2$

13. $y = \frac{1}{x - 3} - 2$

SEE EXAMPLE **4**
p. 881

14. **Catering** A caterer has $100 in her budget for fruit. Slicing and delivery of each pound of fruit costs $5. If x represents the cost per pound of the fruit itself, then $y = \frac{100}{x + 5}$ represents the number of pounds y she can buy.
    a. Describe the reasonable domain and range values.
    b. Graph the function.

PRACTICE AND PROBLEM SOLVING

Independent Practice

For Exercises	See Example
15–18	1
19–22	2
23–26	3
27	4

Extra Practice
Skills Practice p. S26
Application Practice p. S39

Identify the excluded value for each rational function.

15. $y = \frac{7}{x}$

16. $y = \frac{1}{x - 4}$

17. $y = -\frac{15}{x}$

18. $y = \frac{12}{x - 5}$

Identify the asymptotes.

19. $y = \frac{9}{x - 4}$

20. $y = \frac{2}{x + 4}$

21. $y = \frac{7}{4x - 12} + 4$

22. $y = \frac{7}{3x + 5} - 9$

Graph each function.

23. $y = \frac{5}{x - 5}$

24. $y = \frac{1}{x + 5} - 6$

25. $y = \frac{1}{x + 4}$

26. $y = \frac{1}{x - 4} + 2$

27. **Business** A wholesaler is buying auto parts. He has $200 to spend. He receives 5 parts free with the order. The number of parts y he can buy, if the average price of the parts is x dollars, is $y = \frac{200}{x} + 5$.
    a. Describe the reasonable domain and range values.
    b. Graph the function.

Find the excluded value for each rational function.

28. $y = \frac{4}{x}$

29. $y = \frac{1}{x - 7}$

30. $y = \frac{2}{x + 4}$

31. $y = \frac{3}{2x + 1}$

Graph each rational function. Show the asymptotes.

32. $y = \frac{1}{x - 2}$

33. $y = \frac{2}{x} + 3$

34. $y = \frac{3}{x + 1} + 2$

35. $y = \frac{1}{x - 4} - 1$

36. **Multi-Step** The function $y = \frac{60}{x^2}$ relates the luminescence in lumens y of a 60-watt lightbulb viewed from a distance of x ft. Graph the function. Use the graph to find the luminescence of a 60-watt lightbulb viewed from a distance of 6 ft.

Identify the asymptotes of each rational function.

37. $y = \dfrac{7}{x+1}$ 　　　　 **38.** $y = \dfrac{1}{x} - 5$ 　　　　 **39.** $y = \dfrac{12}{x-2} + 5$ 　　 **40.** $y = \dfrac{18}{x+3} - 9$

Match each graph with one of the following functions.

A. $y = \dfrac{1}{x+1} + 2$ 　　　　 **B.** $y = \dfrac{1}{x+2} - 1$ 　　　　 **C.** $y = \dfrac{1}{x-2} + 1$

41.

42.

43.

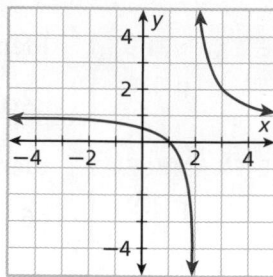

44. ///ERROR ANALYSIS/// In finding the horizontal asymptote of $y = \frac{1}{x+2} - 3$, student A said the asymptote is at $y = -3$, and student B said it is at $y = -2$. Who is incorrect? Explain the error.

45. Finance The time in months y that it will take to pay off a bill of $1200, when x dollars are paid each month and the finance charge is $15 per month, is $y = \frac{1200}{x-15}$. Describe the reasonable domain and range values and graph the function.

46. The table shows how long it takes different size landscaping teams to complete a project.

　a. Graph the data.

　b. Write a rational function to represent the data.

　c. How many hours would it take 12 landscapers to complete the project?

Landscapers	Time (h)
2	30
4	15
5	12
10	6

Graph each function. Compare its graph to the graph of $y = \frac{1}{x}$.

47. $y = \dfrac{1}{x-6}$ 　　 **48.** $y = \dfrac{1}{x+7}$ 　　 **49.** $y = \dfrac{1}{x} + 4$ 　　 **50.** $y = \dfrac{1}{x-2} - 9$

Find the domain that makes the range positive.

51. $y = \dfrac{10}{x-2}$ 　　 **52.** $y = \dfrac{10}{x+2}$ 　　 **53.** $y = \dfrac{5}{5x+1}$ 　　 **54.** $y = \dfrac{4}{3x-7}$

55. Critical Thinking In which quadrants would you find the graph of $y = \frac{a}{x}$ when a is positive? when a is negative?

MULTI-STEP TEST PREP

56. This problem will prepare you for the Multi-Step Test Prep on page 896.

It takes a total of 250 workdays to build a house for charity. For example, if 2 workers build the house, it takes them 125 actual construction days. If 10 workers are present, it takes 25 construction days to build the house.

　a. Write a function that represents the number of construction days to build as a function of the number of workers.

　b. What is the domain of this function?

　c. Sketch a graph of the function.

57. Write About It Graph each pair of functions on a graphing calculator. Then make a conjecture about the relationship between the graphs of the rational functions $y = \frac{k}{x}$ and $y = \frac{-k}{x}$.

a. $y = \frac{1}{x}$; $y = \frac{-1}{x}$ **b.** $y = \frac{3}{x}$; $y = \frac{-3}{x}$ **c.** $y = \frac{5}{x}$; $y = \frac{-5}{x}$

58. Which function is graphed?

Ⓐ $y = \dfrac{2}{x+3} - 4$ Ⓒ $y = \dfrac{2}{x-3} + 4$

Ⓑ $y = \dfrac{2}{x+4} - 3$ Ⓓ $y = \dfrac{2}{x-4} + 3$

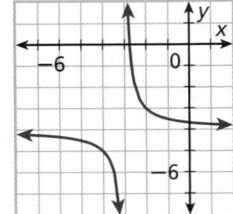

59. Which rational function has a graph with the horizontal asymptote $y = -1$?

Ⓕ $y = \dfrac{-1}{x}$ Ⓗ $y = \dfrac{1}{x+1}$

Ⓖ $y = \dfrac{1}{x-1}$ Ⓙ $y = \dfrac{1}{x} - 1$

60. Short Response Write a rational function whose graph is the same shape as the graph of $f(x) = \frac{1}{x}$, but is translated 2 units left and 3 units down. Graph the function.

CHALLENGE AND EXTEND

61. Graph the equation $y = \dfrac{1}{x^2+1}$.
   a. Does this equation represent a rational function? Explain.
   b. What is the domain of the function?
   c. What is the range of the function?
   d. Is the graph discontinuous?

62. Graphing Calculator Are the graphs of $f(x) = \dfrac{(x-3)(x-1)}{x-3}$ and $g(x) = x - 1$ identical? Explain. (*Hint:* Are there any excluded values?)

63. Critical Thinking Write the equation of the rational function that has a horizontal asymptote at $y = 3$ and a vertical asymptote at $x = -2$ and contains the point $(1, 4)$.

SPIRAL REVIEW

Solve each equation by graphing the related function. *(Lesson 9-5)*

64. $4 - x^2 = 0$ **65.** $3x^2 = x^2 + 2x + 12$ **66.** $-x^2 = -6x + 9$

67. In the first five stages of a fractal design, a line segment has the following lengths, in centimeters: 240, 120, 60, 30, 15. Use this pattern and your knowledge of geometric sequences to determine the length of the segment in the tenth stage. *(Lesson 11-1)*

Determine whether each function represents an inverse variation. Explain. *(Lesson 12-1)*

68. $x + y = 12$ **69.**

x	30	60	90	120
y	10	20	30	40

      70. $xy = -4$

Simplifying Rational Expressions

Objectives
Simplify rational expressions.

Identify excluded values of rational expressions.

Vocabulary
rational expression

Why learn this?
The shapes and sizes of plants and animals are partly determined by the ratio of surface area to volume.

If an animal's body is small and its surface area is large, the rate of heat loss will be high. Hummingbirds must maintain a high metabolism to compensate for the loss of body heat due to having a high surface-area-to-volume ratio. Formulas for surface-area-to-volume ratios are *rational expressions*.

A **rational expression** is an algebraic expression whose numerator and denominator are polynomials. The value of the polynomial expression in the denominator cannot be zero since division by zero is undefined. This means that rational expressions may have excluded values.

EXAMPLE 1 **Identifying Excluded Values**

Find any excluded values of each rational expression.

A $\dfrac{5}{8r}$

$8r = 0$ *Set the denominator equal to 0.*

$r = \dfrac{0}{8} = 0$ *Solve for r by dividing both sides by 8.*

The excluded value is 0.

B $\dfrac{9d + 1}{d^2 - 2d}$

$d^2 - 2d = 0$ *Set the denominator equal to 0.*

$d(d - 2) = 0$ *Factor.*

$d = 0$ or $d - 2 = 0$ *Use the Zero Product Property.*

       $d = 2$ *Solve for d.*

The excluded values are 0 and 2.

To review the Zero Product Property, see Lesson 9-6.

To review factoring trinomials, see Chapter 8.

C $\dfrac{x + 4}{x^2 + 5x + 6}$

$x^2 + 5x + 6 = 0$ *Set the denominator equal to 0.*

$(x + 3)(x + 2) = 0$ *Factor.*

$x + 3 = 0$ or $x + 2 = 0$ *Use the Zero Product Property.*

$x = -3$ or $x = -2$ *Solve each equation for x.*

The excluded values are -3 and -2.

 Find any excluded values of each rational expression.

1a. $\dfrac{12}{t + 5}$ **1b.** $\dfrac{3b}{b^2 + 5b}$ **1c.** $\dfrac{3k^2}{k^2 + 7k + 12}$

A rational expression is in its simplest form when the numerator and denominator have no common factors except 1. Remember that to simplify fractions you can divide out common factors that appear in both the numerator and the denominator. You can do the same to simplify rational expressions.

EXAMPLE 2   **Simplifying Rational Expressions**

Simplify each rational expression, if possible. Identify any excluded values.

A $\dfrac{3t^3}{12t}$

$\dfrac{3t^3}{3 \cdot 4t}$ *Factor 12.*

$\dfrac{{}^{1}\cancel{3}t^{\cancel{3}^{t^2}}}{{}_{1}\cancel{3} \cdot 4\cancel{t}^1}$ *Divide out common factors. Note that if t = 0, the expression is undefined.*

$\dfrac{t^2}{4};\ t \neq 0$ *Simplify. The excluded value is 0.*

Caution! ///////

Be sure to use the original denominator when finding excluded values. The excluded values may not be "seen" in the simplified denominator.

B $\dfrac{3x^2 - 9x}{x - 3}$

$\dfrac{3x(x - 3)}{x - 3}$ *Factor the numerator.*

$\dfrac{3x\cancel{(x - 3)}^1}{\cancel{x - 3}^1}$ *Divide out common factors. Note that if x = 3, the expression is undefined.*

    Simplify. The excluded value is 3.

$3x;\ x \neq 3$

C $\dfrac{c}{c + 5}$ *The numerator and denominator have no common factors. The excluded value is −5.*

$\dfrac{c}{c + 5};\ c \neq -5$

CHECK IT OUT!   Simplify each rational expression, if possible. Identify any excluded values.

2a. $\dfrac{5m^2}{15m}$ **2b.** $\dfrac{6p^3 + 12p}{p^2 + 2}$ **2c.** $\dfrac{3n}{n - 2}$

From now on in this chapter, you may assume that the values of the variables that make the denominator equal to 0 are excluded values. You do not need to include excluded values in your answers unless they are asked for.

EXAMPLE 3   **Simplifying Rational Expressions with Trinomials**

Simplify each rational expression, if possible.

A $\dfrac{k + 1}{k^2 - 4k - 5}$ **B** $\dfrac{y^2 - 16}{y^2 - 8y + 16}$

$\dfrac{k + 1}{(k + 1)(k - 5)}$ *Factor the numerator and the denominator when possible.* $\dfrac{(y + 4)(y - 4)}{(y - 4)(y - 4)}$

$\dfrac{\cancel{k + 1}^1}{\cancel{(k + 1)}^1(k - 5)}$ *Divide out common factors.* $\dfrac{(y + 4)\cancel{(y - 4)}^1}{(y - 4)\cancel{(y - 4)}^1}$

$\dfrac{1}{k - 5}$ *Simplify.* $\dfrac{y + 4}{y - 4}$

CHECK IT OUT! Simplify each rational expression, if possible.

3a. $\dfrac{r+2}{r^2+7r+10}$

3b. $\dfrac{b^2-25}{b^2+10b+25}$

Recall from Chapter 8 that opposite binomials can help you factor polynomials. Recognizing opposite binomials can also help you simplify rational expressions.

Consider $\frac{x-3}{3-x}$. The numerator and denominator are opposite binomials. Therefore,

$$\frac{x-3}{3-x} = \frac{x-3}{-x+3} = \frac{x-3^1}{-1(x-3)^1} = \frac{1}{-1} = -1.$$

EXAMPLE 4 **Simplifying Rational Expressions Using Opposite Binomials**

Simplify each rational expression, if possible.

A $\dfrac{2x-10}{25-x^2}$

$\dfrac{2(x-5)}{(5-x)(5+x)}$ *Factor.*

$\dfrac{2(x-5)}{(5-x)(5+x)}$ *Identify opposite binomials.*

$\dfrac{2(x-5)}{-1(x-5)(5+x)}$ *Rewrite one opposite binomial.*

$\dfrac{2(x-5)^1}{-1(x-5)^1(5+x)}$ *Divide out common factors.*

$-\dfrac{2}{5+x}$ *Simplify.*

B $\dfrac{2-2m}{2m^2+2m-4}$

$\dfrac{2(1-m)}{2(m+2)(m-1)}$

$\dfrac{2(1-m)}{2(m+2)(m-1)}$

$\dfrac{2(1-m)}{2(m+2)(-1)(1-m)}$

$\dfrac{2^1(1-m)^1}{2^1(m+2)(-1)(1-m)^1}$

$-\dfrac{1}{m+2}$

CHECK IT OUT! Simplify each rational expression, if possible.

4a. $\dfrac{3x-12}{16-x^2}$

4b. $\dfrac{6-2x}{2x^2-4x-6}$

4c. $\dfrac{3x-33}{x^2-121}$

Student to Student   *Simplifying Rational Expressions*

Tanika Brown,
Washington High
School

When I can't tell if I'm allowed to divide out part of an expression, I substitute a number into the original expression and simplify it. Then I simplify the original expression by dividing out the term in question. I check by seeing if the results are the same.

For example, I'll use $x = 2$ to see if I can divide out $4x$ in $\frac{4x}{4x-7}$.

Substitute $x = 2$.

$\dfrac{4x}{4x-7}$

$\dfrac{4(2)}{4(2)-7}$

$\dfrac{8}{8-7} = \dfrac{8}{1} = 8$

Divide out $4x$.

$\dfrac{4^1x^1}{4^1x^1-7}$

$\dfrac{1}{1-7}$

$\dfrac{1}{-6}$

$4x$ cannot be divided out because $8 \neq \frac{1}{-6}$.

EXAMPLE 5 *Biology Application*

Desert plants must conserve water. Water evaporates from the surface of a plant. The volume determines how much water is in a plant. So the greater the surface-area-to-volume ratio, the less likely a plant is to survive in the desert. A barrel cactus is a desert plant that is close to spherical in shape.

a. What is the surface-area-to-volume ratio of a spherical barrel cactus? (*Hint:* For a sphere, $S = 4\pi r^2$ and $V = \frac{4}{3}\pi r^3$.)

$\dfrac{4\pi r^2}{\frac{4}{3}\pi r^3}$ *Write the ratio of surface area to volume.*

$\dfrac{4\pi^1 r^2}{\frac{4}{3}\pi^1 r^3}$ *Divide out common factors.*

$\dfrac{4r^{2^1}}{\frac{4}{3}r^{3^r}}$ *Use properties of exponents.*

$\dfrac{4}{r} \cdot \dfrac{3}{4}$ *Multiply by the reciprocal of $\frac{4}{3}$.*

$\dfrac{4^1}{r} \cdot \dfrac{3}{4^1}$ *Divide out common factors.*

$\dfrac{3}{r}$ *Simplify.*

b. Which barrel cactus has a greater chance of survival in the desert, one with a radius of 4 inches or one with a radius of 7 inches? Explain.

$\dfrac{3}{r} = \dfrac{3}{4}$ $\dfrac{3}{r} = \dfrac{3}{7}$ *Write the ratio of surface area to volume twice. Substitute 4 and 7 for r.*

$\dfrac{3}{4} > \dfrac{3}{7}$ *Compare the ratios.*

The barrel cactus with a radius of 7 inches has a greater chance of survival. Its surface-area-to-volume ratio is less than for a cactus with a radius of 4 inches.

> **Remember!**
>
> For two fractions with the same numerator, the value of the fraction with a greater denominator is less than the value of the other fraction.
>
> $9 > 3$
>
> $\dfrac{2}{9} < \dfrac{2}{3}$

CHECK IT OUT!

5. Which barrel cactus has less of a chance to survive in the desert, one with a radius of 6 inches or one with a radius of 3 inches? Explain.

THINK AND DISCUSS

1. Write a rational expression that has an excluded value that cannot be identified when the expression is in its simplified form.

2. **GET ORGANIZED** Copy and complete the graphic organizer. In each box, write and simplify one of the given rational expressions using the most appropriate method. $\dfrac{x-3}{x^2-6x+9}, \dfrac{5x^4}{x^2}, \dfrac{4-x}{x-4}, \dfrac{4x^2-4x}{8x}$

```
┌─────────────────────────────┐   ┌─────────────────────────────┐
│ Using properties of exponents│   │  Using opposite binomials   │
└─────────────────────────────┘   └─────────────────────────────┘
              ↖                       ↗
          ╭───────────────────────────╮
          │    Ways of Simplifying    │
          │   Rational Expressions    │
          ╰───────────────────────────╯
              ↙                       ↘
┌─────────────────────────────┐   ┌─────────────────────────────┐
│  Factoring the numerator    │   │  Factoring the denominator  │
└─────────────────────────────┘   └─────────────────────────────┘
```

12-3

Exercises

go.hrw.com
Homework Help Online
KEYWORD: MA7 12-3
Parent Resources Online
KEYWORD: MA7 Parent

GUIDED PRACTICE

1. **Vocabulary** What is true about both the numerator and denominator of rational expressions?

SEE EXAMPLE **1**
p. 886

Find any excluded values of each rational expression.

2. $\dfrac{5}{m}$

3. $\dfrac{x+2}{x^2-8x}$

4. $\dfrac{p^2}{p^2-2p-15}$

SEE EXAMPLE **2**
p. 887

Simplify each rational expression, if possible. Identify any excluded values.

5. $\dfrac{4a^2}{8a}$

6. $\dfrac{2d^2+12d}{d+6}$

7. $\dfrac{2}{y+3}$

8. $\dfrac{10}{5-y}$

9. $\dfrac{2h}{2h+4}$

10. $\dfrac{3(x+4)}{6x}$

Simplify each rational expression, if possible.

SEE EXAMPLE **3**
p. 887

11. $\dfrac{b+4}{b^2+5b+4}$

12. $\dfrac{s^2-4}{s^2+4s+4}$

13. $\dfrac{c^2+5c+6}{(c+3)(c-4)}$

14. $\dfrac{(x-2)(x+1)}{x^2+4x+3}$

15. $\dfrac{j^2-25}{j^2+2j-15}$

16. $\dfrac{p+1}{p^2-4p-5}$

SEE EXAMPLE **4**
p. 888

17. $\dfrac{2n-16}{64-n^2}$

18. $\dfrac{8-4x}{2x^2-12x+16}$

19. $\dfrac{10-5r}{r^2-4r-12}$

20. $\dfrac{2x-14}{49-x^2}$

21. $\dfrac{5q-50}{100-q^2}$

22. $\dfrac{36-12a}{a^2+2a-15}$

SEE EXAMPLE **5**
p. 889

23. **Construction** The side of a triangular roof will have the same height h and base b_2 as the side of a trapezoidal roof.

a. What is the ratio of the area of the triangular roof to the area of the trapezoidal roof?

$\left(\textit{Hint:} \text{ For a triangle, } A = \frac{1}{2}b_2 h. \right.$

$\left. \text{For a trapezoid, } A = \frac{b_1+b_2}{2}h. \right)$

b. Compare the ratio from part **a** to what the ratio will be if b_1 is doubled for the trapezoidal roof and b_2 is doubled for both roofs.

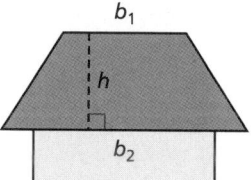

PRACTICE AND PROBLEM SOLVING

Find any excluded values of each rational expression.

24. $\dfrac{c}{c^2+c}$

25. $\dfrac{2}{-3x}$

26. $\dfrac{4}{x^2-3x-10}$

27. $\dfrac{n^2-1}{2n^2-7n-4}$

Simplify each rational expression, if possible. Identify any excluded values.

28. $\dfrac{4d^3+4d^2}{d+1}$

29. $\dfrac{3m^2}{m-4}$

30. $\dfrac{10y^4}{2y}$

31. $\dfrac{2t^2}{16t}$

Independent Practice

For Exercises	See Example
24–27	1
28–31	2
32–37	3
38–40	4
41	5

Extra Practice

Skills Practice p. S26

Application Practice p. S39

Simplify each rational expression, if possible.

32. $\dfrac{q-6}{q^2-9q+18}$

33. $\dfrac{z^2-2z+1}{z^2-1}$

34. $\dfrac{t-3}{t^2-5t+6}$

35. $\dfrac{p^2-6p-7}{p^2-4p-5}$

36. $\dfrac{x^2-1}{x^2+4x+3}$

37. $\dfrac{2x-4}{x^2-6x+8}$

38. $\dfrac{20-4x}{x^2-25}$

39. $\dfrac{3-3b}{3b^2+18b-21}$

40. $\dfrac{3v-36}{144-v^2}$

41. Geometry When choosing package sizes, a company wants a package that uses the least amount of material to hold the greatest volume of product.

a. What is the surface-area-to-volume ratio for a rectangular prism? (*Hint:* For a rectangular prism, $S = 2\ell w + 2\ell h + 2wh$ and $V = \ell wh$.)

b. Which box should the company choose? Explain.

Box A   Box B

8 in.   10 in.

4 in.   5 in.   2 in.   8 in.

42. Biology The table gives information on two populations of animals that were released into the wild. Suppose 16 more predators and 20 more prey are released into the area. Write and simplify a rational expression to show the ratio of predator to prey.

	Predator	Prey
Original Population	x	x
Population 5 Years Later	$4x$	$5x$

Biology

As a result of a nation-wide policy of protection and reintroduction, the population of bald eagles in the lower 48 states grew from 417 nesting pairs in 1963 to more than 6400 nesting pairs in 2000.

Source: U.S. Fish and Wildlife Service

Simplify each rational expression, if possible.

43. $\dfrac{p^2+12p+36}{12p+72}$

44. $\dfrac{3n^3+33n^2+15n}{3n^3+15n}$

45. $\dfrac{a}{2a+a}$

46. $\dfrac{j-5}{j^2-25}$

47. $\dfrac{6w^2+11w-7}{6w-3}$

48. $\dfrac{n^2-n-56}{n^2-16n+64}$

49. $\dfrac{(x+1)^2}{x^2+2x+1}$

50. $\dfrac{5}{(x+5)^2}$

51. $\dfrac{25-x^2}{x^2-3x-10}$

MULTI-STEP TEST PREP

52. This problem will prepare you for the Multi-Step Test Prep on page 896.

It takes 250 workdays to build a house. The number of construction days is determined by the size of the crew. The crew includes one manager who supervises workers and checks for problems, but does not do any building.

a. The table shows the number of construction days as a function of the number of workers. Copy and complete the table.

b. Use the table to write a function that represents the number of construction days.

c. Identify the excluded values of the function.

Crew Size (x)	Workdays / Workers	Construction Days (y)
2	$\dfrac{250}{2-1}$	250
3	$\dfrac{250}{3-1}$	■
6	■	■
11	■	25

53. **Geometry** Let s represent the length of an edge of a cube.

   a. Write the ratio of a cube's surface area to volume in simplified form. (*Hint:* For a cube, $S = 6s^2$.)

   b. What is the ratio of the cube's surface area to volume when $s = 2$?

   c. What is the ratio of the cube's surface area to volume when $s = 6$?

54. **Write About It** Explain how to find excluded values for a rational expression.

55. **Critical Thinking** Give an example of a rational expression that has x in both the numerator and denominator, but cannot be simplified.

TEST PREP

56. Which expression is undefined for $x = 4$ and $x = -1$?

   (A) $\dfrac{x-1}{x+4}$

   (B) $\dfrac{x-4}{x+4}$

   (C) $\dfrac{x}{x^2+3x-4}$

   (D) $\dfrac{x}{x^2-3x-4}$

57. Which expression is the ratio of the area of a triangle to the area of a rectangle that has the same base and height?

   (F) $\dfrac{1}{2}$

   (G) $\dfrac{bh}{2}$

   (H) $\dfrac{(bh)^2}{2}$

   (J) 2

58. **Gridded Response** What is the excluded value for $\dfrac{x-4}{x^2-8x+16}$?

CHALLENGE AND EXTEND

Tell whether each statement is sometimes, always, or never true. Explain.

59. A rational expression has an excluded value.

60. A rational expression has a variable in a square root in the numerator.

61. The graph of a rational function has at least one asymptote.

Simplify each rational expression.

62. $\dfrac{9v - 6v^2}{4v^2 - 4v - 3}$

63. $\dfrac{2a^2 - 7a + 3}{2a^2 + 9a - 5}$

64. $\dfrac{0.25y - 0.10}{0.25y^2 - 0.04}$

Identify any excluded values of each rational expression.

65. $\dfrac{\frac{1}{4}x^2 - 7x + 49}{\frac{1}{4}x^2 - 49}$

66. $\dfrac{-80x + 40x^2 + 40}{-30 - 30x^2 + 60x}$

67. $\dfrac{6x + 12}{12x + 6x^2}$

SPIRAL REVIEW

68. A rectangle has an area of 24 square feet. Every dimension is multiplied by a scale factor, and the new rectangle has an area of 864 square feet. What is the scale factor? *(Lesson 2-8)*

Use intercepts to graph the line described by each equation. *(Lesson 5-2)*

69. $5x - 3y = -15$

70. $y = 8x - 8$

71. $\dfrac{1}{2}x + y = 2$

For each of the following, let y vary inversely as x. *(Lesson 12-1)*

72. $x_1 = 2$, $y_1 = 4$, and $x_2 = 1$. Find y_2.

73. $x_1 = 2$, $y_1 = -1$, and $y_2 = \dfrac{1}{3}$. Find x_2.

12-3 Technology LAB

Graph Rational Functions

You can use a graphing calculator to graph rational functions and to compare graphs of rational functions before and after they are simplified.

Use with Lesson 12-3

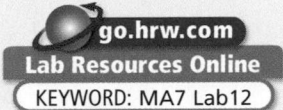

go.hrw.com
Lab Resources Online
KEYWORD: MA7 Lab12

Activity

Simplify $y = \dfrac{x-1}{x^2 - 5x + 4}$ and give any excluded values. Then graph both the original function and the simplified function and compare the graphs.

1 Simplify the function and find the excluded values.

$$\frac{x-1}{x^2 - 5x + 4} = \frac{x-1}{(x-1)(x-4)} = \frac{1}{x-4}; \text{ excluded values: } 4, 1$$

2 Enter $y = \dfrac{x-1}{x^2 - 5x + 4}$ and $y = \dfrac{1}{x-4}$ into your calculator as shown and press **GRAPH**.

3 To compare the graphs, press **TRACE**. At the top of the screen, you can see which graph the cursor is on. To change between graphs, press ▲ and ▼.

4 The graphs appear to be the same, but check the excluded values, 4 and 1. While on **Y1,** press 4 **ENTER**. Notice that there is no *y*-value at $x = 4$. The function is undefined.

5 Press ▼ to switch to **Y2** and press 4 **ENTER**. This function is also undefined at $x = 4$. The graphs are the same at this excluded value.

6 Return to **Y1** and press 1 **ENTER**. This function is undefined at $x = 1$. However, this is not a vertical asymptote. Instead, this graph has a "hole" at $x = 1$.

7 Switch to **Y2** and press 1 **ENTER**. This function is defined at $x = 1$. So the two graphs are the same except at $x = 1$.

Try This

1. Why is $x = 1$ an excluded value for one function but not for the other?

2. Are the functions $y = \dfrac{x-1}{x^2 - 5x + 4}$ and $y = \dfrac{1}{x-4}$ truly equivalent for all values of *x*? Explain.

3. Make a Conjecture Complete each statement.
  a. If a value of *x* is excluded from a function and its simplified form, it appears on the graph as a(n) ___?___ .
  b. If a value of *x* is excluded from a function but not its simplified form, it appears on the graph as a ___?___ .

Representing Solid Figures

A *net* is a flat pattern that can be folded to make a solid figure. The net shows all of the faces and surfaces of the solid.

To identify the solid shown by a net, remember these properties of solids.

| Prisms | Pyramids | Cylinder | Cone |

- A *prism* has two parallel, congruent bases that are polygons. The other faces are rectangles or parallelograms.

- A base of a *pyramid* is a polygon. The other faces are triangles.

- A *cylinder* has two congruent circles as its bases.

- A *cone* has one circle as its base.

Example 1

Identify the solid shown by this net.

The faces are all polygons, so this is either a prism or a pyramid. Look for a pair of congruent polygons. There are two congruent right triangles. The solid is a *prism*.

A prism is named by the shape of its bases, so this is a *triangular prism*.

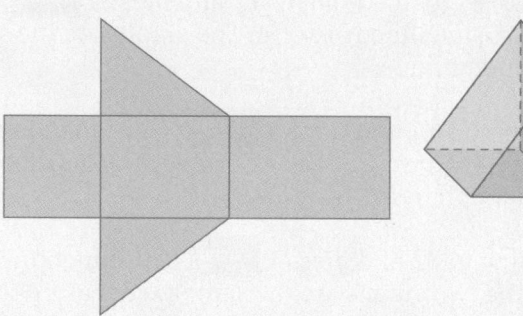

Try This

Identify the solid shown by each net.

1.

2.

3.

Identify the solid shown by each net.

4.

5.

6.

A foundation plan is a drawing that represents a solid made from cubes. The squares in the foundation plan are a top view of the solid. The number in each square shows the height of the solid at that point. The foundation plan shown is like a set of instructions for building the solid next to it.

Example 2

Draw a foundation plan for this solid figure.

Use squares to show a top view of the solid.

Put a number in each square to show the height at that point.

```
1 3 1 2
1
```

Try This

Draw a foundation plan for each solid figure.

7.

8.

9.

10.

11.

12.

MULTI-STEP TEST PREP

Rational Functions and Expressions

Construction Daze
Robert is part of a volunteer crew constructing houses for low-income families. The table shows how many construction days it takes to complete a house for work crews of various sizes.

Crew Size	Construction Days	Workdays
2	100	200
4	50	200
8	25	200
10	20	200
20	10	200

1. Working at the same rate, how many construction days should it take a crew of 40 people to build the house?

2. Express the number of construction days as a function of the crew size. Define the variables. What type of relationship is formed in the situation?

3. Explain how the crew size affects the number of construction days.

4. About how many construction days would it take a crew of 32 to complete a house?

5. If a crew can complete a house in 12.5 days, how many people are in the crew?

6. What are a reasonable domain and range of the function?

7. Suppose there are two managers that do not contribute to the work of building the house, yet are counted as part of the crew. Express the number of construction days as a function of the crew size. What are the asymptotes of this function? Graph the function.

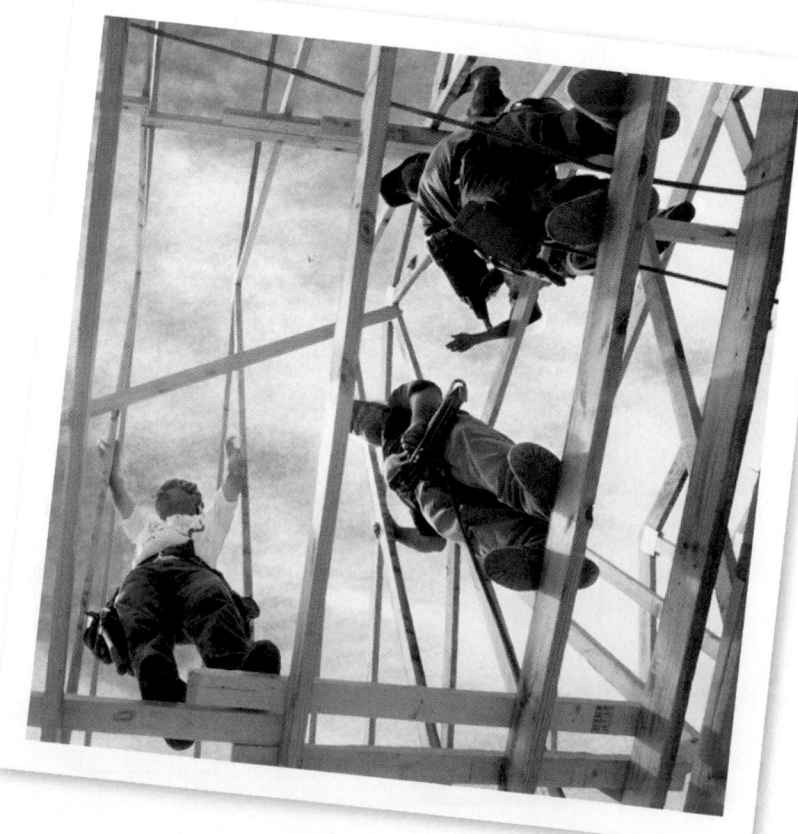

READY TO GO ON?

Quiz for Lessons 12-1 Through 12-3

✓ 12-1 Inverse Variation

Tell whether each relationship represents an inverse variation. Explain.

1.

x	−5	−4	−3
y	10	−8	6

2.

x	18	9	6
y	2	4	6

3. $y = \dfrac{3}{x}$ **4.** $y + x = \dfrac{3}{4}$ **5.** $xy = -2$ **6.** $y = \dfrac{x}{5}$

7. Write and graph the inverse variation in which $y = 3$ when $x = 2$.

8. Write and graph the inverse variation in which $y = 4$ when $x = -1$.

9. The number of calculators Mrs. Hopkins can buy for the classroom varies inversely as the cost of each calculator. She can buy 24 calculators that cost $60 each. How many calculators can she buy if they cost $80 each?

✓ 12-2 Rational Functions

Identify the excluded value and the vertical and horizontal asymptotes for each rational function. Then graph each function.

10. $y = \dfrac{12}{x}$ **11.** $y = \dfrac{6}{x + 2}$ **12.** $y = \dfrac{4}{x - 1}$ **13.** $y = \dfrac{2}{x + 1} - 3$

14. Jeff builds model train layouts. He has $75 to spend on packages of miniature landscape items. He receives 6 free packages with each order. The number of packages y that Jeff can buy is given by $y = \dfrac{75}{x} + 6$, where x represents the cost of each package in dollars. Describe the reasonable domain and range values and graph the function.

✓ 12-3 Simplifying Rational Expressions

Find any excluded values of each rational expression.

15. $\dfrac{15}{n}$ **16.** $\dfrac{p}{p - 8}$ **17.** $\dfrac{x + 2}{x^2 + 6x + 8}$ **18.** $\dfrac{t - 1}{t^2 + t}$

Simplify each rational expression, if possible. Identify any excluded values.

19. $\dfrac{3x^2}{6x^3}$ **20.** $\dfrac{2n}{n^2 - 3n}$ **21.** $\dfrac{s + 1}{s^2 - 4s - 5}$ **22.** $\dfrac{12 - 3x}{x^2 - 8x + 16}$

23. Suppose a cone and a cylinder have the same radius and that the slant height ℓ of the cone is the same as the height h of the cylinder. Find the ratio of the cone's surface area to the cylinder's surface area.

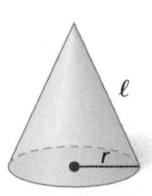

$S = \pi r \ell + \pi r^2$

$S = 2\pi rh + 2\pi r^2$

<table>
<tr><td>

12-4

</td><td>

Multiplying and Dividing Rational Expressions

</td></tr>
</table>

Objective
Multiply and divide rational expressions.

Why learn this?

You can multiply rational expressions to determine the probabilities of winning prizes at carnivals. (See Example 5.)

The rules for multiplying rational expressions are the same as the rules for multiplying fractions. You multiply the numerators, and you multiply the denominators.

Know it!
Note

> **Multiplying Rational Expressions**
>
> If a, b, c, and d are nonzero polynomials, then $\dfrac{a}{b} \cdot \dfrac{c}{d} = \dfrac{ac}{bd}$.

EXAMPLE 1 **Multiplying Rational Expressions**

Multiply. Simplify your answer.

A $\dfrac{a+3}{2} \cdot \dfrac{6}{3a+9}$

$\dfrac{6(a+3)}{2(3a+9)}$ *Multiply the numerators and denominators.*

$\dfrac{6(a+3)}{2 \cdot 3(a+3)}$ *Factor.*

$\dfrac{\cancel{6}^{1}\cancel{(a+3)}^{1}}{\cancel{6}^{1}\cancel{(a+3)}^{1}}$ *Divide out the common factors.*

1 *Simplify.*

Remember!

See the Quotient of Powers Property in Lesson 7-4.
$$\dfrac{a^m}{a^n} = a^{m-n}$$

B $\dfrac{12b^3c^2}{5ac} \cdot \dfrac{15a^2b}{3b^2c}$

$\dfrac{(12)(15)a^2(b^3 \cdot b)c^2}{(5)(3)ab^2(c \cdot c)}$ *Multiply the numerators and the denominators. Arrange the expression so like variables are together.*

$\dfrac{180a^2b^4c^2}{15ab^2c^2}$ *Simplify.*

$12a^1b^2c^0$ *Divide out common factors. Use properties of exponents.*

$12ab^2$ *Simplify. Remember that $c^0 = 1$.*

C $\dfrac{5x^2}{2y^3} \cdot \dfrac{3x}{2y^2}$

$\dfrac{15x^3}{4y^5}$ *Multiply. There are no common factors, so the product cannot be simplified.*

1a. $\dfrac{(c-4)}{5} \cdot \dfrac{45}{(-4c+16)}$

1b. $\dfrac{5y^5z}{3xy^2z} \cdot \dfrac{2x^4y^2}{4xy}$

EXAMPLE 2   Multiplying a Rational Expression by a Polynomial

Multiply $\left(x^2+8x+15\right)\dfrac{4}{2x+6}$. Simplify your answer.

$\dfrac{x^2+8x+15}{1} \cdot \dfrac{4}{2x+6}$ *Write the polynomial over 1.*

$\dfrac{(x+3)(x+5)}{1} \cdot \dfrac{4}{2(x+3)}$ *Factor the numerator and denominator.*

$\dfrac{\cancel{(x+3)}^1(x+5)\cancel{4}^2}{\cancel{2}^1\cancel{(x+3)}^1}$ *Divide out common factors.*

$2x+10$ *Multiply remaining factors.*

> **Remember!**
>
> Just as you can write an integer as a fraction, you can write any expression as a rational expression by writing it with a denominator of 1.

2. Multiply $\dfrac{m-5}{m^2-4m-12} \cdot (3m+6)$. Simplify your answer.

There are two methods for simplifying rational expressions. You can **simplify first** by dividing out common factors and **then multiply** the remaining factors. You can also **multiply first** and **then simplify**. Using either method will result in the same answer.

EXAMPLE 3   Multiplying Rational Expressions Containing Polynomials

Multiply $\dfrac{4d^3+4d}{16f} \cdot \dfrac{2f}{7d^2f+7f}$. Simplify your answer.

Method 1   Simplify first.

$\dfrac{4d^3+4d}{16f} \cdot \dfrac{2f}{7d^2f+7f}$

$\dfrac{4d(d^2+1)}{16f} \cdot \dfrac{2f}{7f(d^2+1)}$ *Factor.*

$\dfrac{\cancel{4}^1d(\cancel{d^2+1})^1}{\cancel{16}^2f^1} \cdot \dfrac{\cancel{2}^1f^1}{7f(\cancel{d^2+1})^1}$ *Divide out common factors.*

Then multiply.

$\dfrac{d}{14f}$ *Simplify.*

Method 2   Multiply first.

$\dfrac{4d^3+4d}{16f} \cdot \dfrac{2f}{7d^2f+7f}$

$\dfrac{(4d^3+4d)2f}{16f(7d^2f+7f)}$ *Multiply.*

$\dfrac{8d^3f+8df}{112d^2f^2+112f^2}$ *Distribute.*

Then simplify.

$\dfrac{8df(d^2+1)}{112f^2(d^2+1)}$ *Factor.*

$\dfrac{\cancel{8}^1d\cancel{f}^1(\cancel{d^2+1})^1}{\cancel{112}^{14}\,f^{\cancel{2}f}(\cancel{d^2+1})^1}$ *Divide out common factors.*

$\dfrac{d}{14f}$ *Simplify.*

Multiply. Simplify your answer.

3a. $\dfrac{n-5}{n^2+4n} \cdot \dfrac{n^2+8n+16}{n^2-3n-10}$ **3b.** $\dfrac{p+4}{p^2+2p} \cdot \dfrac{p^2-3p-10}{p^2+16}$

The rules for dividing rational expressions are the same as the rules for dividing fractions. To divide by a rational expression, multiply by its reciprocal.

Dividing Rational Expressions

If a, b, c, and d are nonzero polynomials, then $\dfrac{a}{b} \div \dfrac{c}{d} = \dfrac{a}{b} \cdot \dfrac{d}{c} = \dfrac{ad}{bc}$.

EXAMPLE 4 **Dividing by Rational Expressions and Polynomials**

Divide. Simplify your answer.

A $\dfrac{1}{x} \div \dfrac{x-2}{2x}$

$\dfrac{1}{x} \cdot \dfrac{2x}{x-2}$ *Write as multiplication by the reciprocal.*

$\dfrac{1(2x)}{x(x-2)}$ *Multiply the numerators and the denominators.*

$\dfrac{2\cancel{x}^1}{\cancel{x}^1(x-2)}$ *Divide out common factors.*

$\dfrac{2}{x-2}$ *Simplify.*

B $\dfrac{x^2-2x}{x} \div \dfrac{2-x}{x^2+2x+1}$

$\dfrac{x^2-2x}{x} \cdot \dfrac{x^2+2x+1}{2-x}$ *Write as multiplication by the reciprocal.*

$\dfrac{x(x-2)}{x} \cdot \dfrac{(x+1)(x+1)}{2-x}$ *Factor.*

$\dfrac{x(x-2)}{x} \cdot \dfrac{(x+1)(x+1)}{-1(x-2)}$ *Rewrite one opposite binomial.*

$\dfrac{\cancel{x}^1\cancel{(x-2)}^1}{\cancel{x}^1} \cdot \dfrac{(x+1)(x+1)}{-1\cancel{(x-2)}^1}$ *Divide out common factors.*

$-(x+1)^2$ *Multiply.*

C $\dfrac{3a^2b}{b} \div (3a^2+6a)$

$\dfrac{3a^2b}{b} \div \dfrac{3a^2+6a}{1}$ *Write the binomial over 1.*

$\dfrac{3a^2b}{b} \cdot \dfrac{1}{3a^2+6a}$ *Write as multiplication by the reciprocal.*

$\dfrac{3a^2b}{b(3a^2+6a)}$ *Multiply the numerators and the denominators.*

$\dfrac{\cancel{3}^1\cancel{a^2}^a\cancel{b}^1}{\cancel{b}^1[\cancel{3}^1\cancel{a}^1(a+2)]}$ *Factor. Divide out common factors.*

$\dfrac{a}{a+2}$ *Simplify.*

 Divide. Simplify your answer.

4a. $\dfrac{3}{x^2} \div \dfrac{x^3}{x-5}$

4b. $\dfrac{18vw^2}{6v} \div \dfrac{3v^2x^4}{2w^4x}$

4c. $\dfrac{x^2-x}{x+2} \div (x^2+2x-3)$

EXAMPLE 5 *Probability Application*

Marty is playing a carnival game. He needs to pick two items out of a bag without looking. The bag has red and blue items. There are three more red items than blue items.

a. Write and simplify an expression that represents the probability that Marty will pick two blue items without replacing the first item.

Let x = the number of blue items.

Blue	+	Red	=	Total
x	+	$x + 3$	=	$2x + 3$

Write expressions for the number of each color item and for the total number of items.

The probability of picking a blue item and then another blue item is the product of the probabilities of the individual events.

1st pick: blue items   2nd pick: blue items

$$P(\text{blue, blue}) = \frac{x}{2x+3} \cdot \frac{x-1}{2x+2}$$

1st pick: total items   2nd pick: total items

$$= \frac{x}{2x+3} \cdot \frac{x-1}{2(x+1)}$$

$$= \frac{x(x-1)}{2(2x+3)(x+1)}$$

Remember!

For a review of probability topics, see Chapter 10.

b. What is the probability that Marty picks two blue items if there are 10 blue items in the bag before his first pick?

Use the probability of picking two blue items. Since x represents the number of blue items, substitute 10 for x.

$$P(\text{blue, blue}) = \frac{10(10-1)}{2(2 \cdot 10 + 3)(10 + 1)} \qquad \textit{Substitute.}$$

$$= \frac{10(9)}{2(23)(11)} = \frac{90}{506} \approx 0.18 \qquad \begin{array}{l}\textit{Use the order of operations}\\ \textit{to simplify.}\end{array}$$

The probability of picking two blue items if there are 10 blue items in the bag before the first pick is approximately 0.18.

5. What if...? There are 50 blue items in the bag before Marty's first pick. What is the probability that Marty picks two blue items?

THINK AND DISCUSS

1. Explain how to divide by a polynomial.

2. GET ORGANIZED Copy and complete the graphic organizer. In each box, describe how to perform the operation with rational expressions.

```
        Rational Expressions
        ┌───────────┴───────────┐
   Multiplying            Dividing
```

Exercises

go.hrw.com
Homework Help Online
KEYWORD: MA7 12-4
Parent Resources Online
KEYWORD: MA7 Parent

GUIDED PRACTICE

Multiply. Simplify your answer.

SEE EXAMPLE **1**
p. 898

1. $\dfrac{4hj^2}{10j^3} \cdot \dfrac{3h^3k}{h^3k^3}$

2. $\dfrac{4y}{x^5} \cdot \dfrac{2yz^2}{9x^2}$

3. $\dfrac{x-2}{x+3} \cdot \dfrac{4x+12}{6}$

4. $\dfrac{ab}{c} \cdot \dfrac{2a^2}{3c}$

5. $\dfrac{7c^4d}{10c} \cdot \dfrac{5a}{21c^3d}$

6. $\dfrac{12p^2q}{5p} \cdot \dfrac{15p^4q^3}{12q}$

SEE EXAMPLE **2**
p. 899

7. $\dfrac{12}{4y+8}\left(y^2-4\right)$

8. $\dfrac{x+2}{6x^2}\left(5x+10\right)$

9. $\dfrac{3m}{6m+18}\left(m^2-7m-30\right)$

10. $\dfrac{4p}{8p+16}\left(p^2-5p-14\right)$

11. $\dfrac{a^2}{a}\left(a^2+10a+25\right)$

12. $\dfrac{-c}{4c+4}\left(c^2-c-2\right)$

SEE EXAMPLE **3**
p. 899

13. $\dfrac{a^2+6ab}{b} \cdot \dfrac{5+3a}{3a^2b+5ab}$

14. $\dfrac{x^2+5x+4}{x-4} \cdot \dfrac{x^2-2x-8}{x^2+6x+8}$

15. $\dfrac{j-1}{j^2-4j+3} \cdot \dfrac{j^2-5j+6}{2j-4}$

16. $\dfrac{p^3+4pq}{p} \cdot \dfrac{6q^3-8}{2q}$

17. $\dfrac{r^2+15r+14}{r^2-16} \cdot \dfrac{2r+8}{r+1}$

18. $\dfrac{y-8}{y^2-1} \cdot \dfrac{y+2}{y^2-49}$

SEE EXAMPLE **4**
p. 900

Divide. Simplify your answer.

19. $\dfrac{3a^4b}{2a^2c^3} \div \dfrac{12a^2c}{8c^4}$

20. $\dfrac{2m^3+2m}{m^2-2m} \div \dfrac{4m^2+4}{m-1}$

21. $\dfrac{x^2+4x-5}{3x-3} \div \left(x^2-25\right)$

SEE EXAMPLE **5**
p. 901

22. Probability While playing a game, Rachel pulls two tiles out of a bag without looking and without replacing the first tile. The bag has two colors of tiles—black and white. There are 10 more white tiles than black tiles.

  a. Write and simplify an expression that represents the probability that Rachel will pick a black tile, then a white tile.

  b. What is the probability that Rachel pulls a black tile and then a white tile if there are 5 black tiles in the bag before her first pick?

PRACTICE AND PROBLEM SOLVING

Independent Practice	
For Exercises	See Example
23–25	1
26–28	2
29–31	3
32–34	4
35	5

Extra Practice
Skills Practice p. S27
Application Practice p. S39

Multiply. Simplify your answer.

23. $\dfrac{p^6q^2}{7r^3} \cdot \dfrac{-3p^2}{r}$

24. $\dfrac{3r^2t}{6st^3} \cdot \dfrac{2r^2s^3t^2}{8r^4s^2}$

25. $\dfrac{10}{y+5} \cdot \dfrac{y+2}{3}$

26. $\dfrac{3}{2a+6}\left(a^2+4a+3\right)$

27. $\dfrac{4m^2-8m}{m^2+6m-16}\left(m^2+7m-8\right)$

28. $\dfrac{x}{2x^2-12x+18}\left(2x^2-4x-6\right)$

29. $\dfrac{6n^2+18n}{n^2+9n+8} \cdot \dfrac{n^2-1}{2n+6}$

30. $\dfrac{3a^2b}{5a^3+10a^2b} \cdot \dfrac{2a+4b}{6a^3b+6a^2b^2}$

31. $\dfrac{t^2-100}{5t+50} \cdot \dfrac{5}{t-10}$

Divide. Simplify your answer.

32. $\dfrac{6j^2k^5}{5j} \div \dfrac{4j^3k^3}{3j}$

33. $\dfrac{a-4}{a^2} \div \left(8a-2a^2\right)$

34. $\dfrac{x^2-9}{x^2+6x+9} \div \dfrac{4x^2-12x}{16x}$

35. **Entertainment** A carnival game board is covered completely in small balloons. You throw darts at the board and try to pop the balloons.

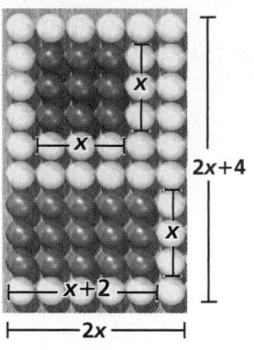

   a. Write and simplify an expression describing the probability that the next two balloons popped are red and then blue. (*Hint:* Write the probabilities as ratios of the areas of rectangles.)

   b. What is the probability that the next two balloons popped are red and then blue if $x = 3$?

36. **/// ERROR ANALYSIS ///** Which is incorrect? Explain the error.

   (A)
$$\frac{4a^2 - b^2}{a^2} \cdot \frac{a}{2a - b}$$

$$\frac{{}^{2}\cancel{4}a^2 - b^2}{\cancel{a^2}} \cdot \frac{\cancel{a}}{2\cancel{a} - b} = -\frac{2 - b^2}{b}$$

   (B)
$$\frac{4a^2 - b^2}{a^2} \cdot \frac{a}{2a - b}$$

$$\frac{(2a - b)(2a + b)}{{}_{a}\cancel{a^2}} \cdot \frac{\cancel{a}}{2a - b} = \frac{2a + b}{a}$$

37. **Critical Thinking** Which of the following expressions is NOT equivalent to the other three? Explain why.

   a. $\dfrac{4x^2}{x^2 - 3x} \cdot \dfrac{2x - 6}{8y^2}$

   b. $\dfrac{6xy^2}{x^2} \div \dfrac{3y^4}{2x^2}$

   c. $\dfrac{10x^4y}{5xy^2} \div 2x^2y$

   d. $\dfrac{4x}{xy^2 + 2y^2} \cdot \dfrac{x^2 - 4}{4x - 8}$

Multiply or divide. Simplify your answer.

38. $\dfrac{5p^3}{p^2q} \cdot \dfrac{2q^3}{p^2}$

39. $\dfrac{6m^2 - 18m}{12m^3 + 12m^2} \div \dfrac{m^2 - 9}{m^2 + 4m + 3}$

40. $\dfrac{2x^2}{4x - 8} \cdot \dfrac{x^2 - 5x + 6}{x^5}$

41. $\dfrac{x^2 - 9}{4x} \div \left(4x^2 - 36\right)$

42. $\dfrac{33m - 3m^2}{-2m - 4} \div \dfrac{6m - 66}{m^2 - 4m}$

43. $\dfrac{12w^4x^7}{3w^3} \cdot \dfrac{w^{-1}x^{-7}}{4}$

44. **Write About It** Explain how to divide $\frac{1}{m} \div \frac{3}{4m}$.

45. This problem will prepare you for the Multi-Step Test Prep on page 926.

MULTI-STEP TEST PREP

The size of an image projected on a screen depends on how far the object is from the lens, the magnification of the lens, and the distance between the image and the lens. Magnification of a lens is $M = \frac{I}{O} = \frac{y}{x}$ where I is the height of the image, O is the height of the object, x is the distance of the object from the lens, and y is the distance of the image from the lens.

   a. If an object 16 cm high is placed 15 cm from the lens, it forms an image 60 cm from the lens. What is the height of the image?

   b. Marie moves the same object to a distance of 20 cm from the lens. If the image is the same size as part **a,** what is the distance between the image and the lens?

   c. What is the magnification of the lens?

46. Which expression is equivalent to $\dfrac{t+4}{9} \cdot \dfrac{t+4}{3}$?

    Ⓐ $\dfrac{(t+4)^2}{27}$ Ⓑ $\dfrac{t^2+16}{27}$ Ⓒ $\dfrac{1}{3}$ Ⓓ $\dfrac{1}{27}$

47. Identify the product $-\dfrac{20b^2}{a^2} \cdot \dfrac{3ab}{15b}$.

    Ⓕ $-\dfrac{a}{4b^2}$ Ⓖ $-4b^2$ Ⓗ $-\dfrac{4b^2}{a}$ Ⓙ $-\dfrac{b^2}{4a}$

48. Which of the following is equivalent to $\dfrac{2x}{x+5}$?

    Ⓐ $\dfrac{x-2}{8x} \cdot \dfrac{4}{x^2+3x-10}$ Ⓒ $\dfrac{x-2}{4} \div \dfrac{x^2+3x-10}{8x}$

    Ⓑ $\dfrac{x^2-3x-10}{8x} \cdot \dfrac{4}{x-2}$ Ⓓ $\dfrac{x^2-3x-10}{4} \div \dfrac{x-2}{8x}$

49. Short Response Simplify $\dfrac{x^2-10x+24}{3x^2-12x} \div (x^2-3x-18)$. Show your work.

CHALLENGE AND EXTEND

Simplify.

50. $\dfrac{x-3}{3x-6} \cdot \dfrac{3x+12}{x+1} \cdot \dfrac{2x-4}{x^2+x-12}$ **51.** $\dfrac{x^2-1}{x+2} \div \dfrac{3x+3}{x+2} \div (x-1)$

A *complex fraction* is a fraction that contains one or more fractions in the numerator or the denominator. Simplify each complex fraction.

$\left(\textit{Hint: Use the rule } \dfrac{\frac{a}{b}}{\frac{c}{d}} = \dfrac{a}{b} \div \dfrac{c}{d}. \right)$

52. $\dfrac{\dfrac{c+5}{c^2-4}}{\dfrac{c^2+6c+5}{c+2}}$ **53.** $\dfrac{\dfrac{x^2y}{xz^3}}{\dfrac{x^2y}{x^2z}}$ **54.** $\dfrac{\dfrac{x^2}{2} \cdot \dfrac{x}{3}}{\dfrac{x}{6}}$ **55.** $\dfrac{\dfrac{a+1}{a^2+6a+5}}{\dfrac{2a+2}{a+5}}$

SPIRAL REVIEW

56. Jillian's mother told her to preheat the oven to at least 325 °F. When Jillian went into the kitchen, the oven was already set to 200 °F. Write and solve an inequality to determine how many more degrees Jillian should increase the temperature. *(Lesson 3-2)*

57. Pierce has $30 to spend on a night out. He already spent $12 on dinner and $9 on a movie ticket. He will spend some money m on snacks. Write and solve an inequality that will show all the values of m that Pierce can spend on snacks. *(Lesson 3-2)*

Simplify each radical. Then add or subtract, if possible. *(Lesson 11-7)*

58. $\sqrt{18} - \sqrt{8}$ **59.** $\sqrt{3t} + 5\sqrt{3t} + \sqrt{12t}$ **60.** $\sqrt{20} - \sqrt{80} + \sqrt{3}$

Identify the excluded value and asymptotes for each rational function. *(Lesson 12-2)*

61. $y = \dfrac{4}{x-3}$ **62.** $y = \dfrac{1}{2x+4}$ **63.** $y = -\dfrac{1}{x} + 3$

64. $y = -\dfrac{2}{x+5}$ **65.** $y = \dfrac{12}{4x}$ **66.** $y = -\dfrac{1}{3x-2}$

Adding and Subtracting Rational Expressions

Objectives
Add and subtract rational expressions with like denominators.

Add and subtract rational expressions with unlike denominators.

Who uses this?
Kayakers can use rational expressions to figure out travel time for different river trips. (See Example 5.)

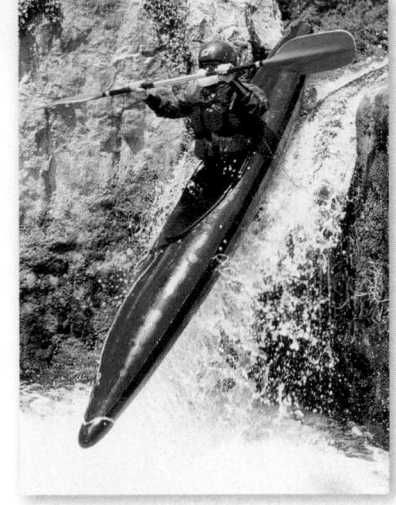

The rules for adding rational expressions are the same as the rules for adding fractions. If the denominators are the same, you add the numerators and keep the common denominator.

$$\frac{3}{8} + \frac{2}{8} = \frac{3+2}{8} = \frac{5}{8}$$

Know it!
Note

> **Adding Rational Expressions with Like Denominators**
>
> If a, b, and c represent polynomials and $c \neq 0$, then $\frac{a}{c} + \frac{b}{c} = \frac{a+b}{c}$.

EXAMPLE 1 **Adding Rational Expressions with Like Denominators**

Add. Simplify your answer.

A $\dfrac{3b}{b^2} + \dfrac{5b}{b^2}$

$$\frac{3b + 5b}{b^2} = \frac{8b^1}{b^{2^b}}$$ *Combine like terms in the numerator. Divide out common factors.*

$$= \frac{8}{b}$$ *Simplify.*

B $\dfrac{x^2 - 8x}{x - 4} + \dfrac{2x + 8}{x - 4}$

$$\frac{x^2 - 8x + 2x + 8}{x - 4} = \frac{x^2 - 6x + 8}{x - 4}$$ *Combine like terms in the numerator.*

$$= \frac{(x - 2)(x - 4)^1}{x - 4^1}$$ *Factor. Divide out common factors.*

$$= x - 2$$ *Simplify.*

C $\dfrac{2m + 4}{m^2 - 9} + \dfrac{2}{m^2 - 9}$

$$\frac{2m + 4 + 2}{m^2 - 9} = \frac{2m + 6}{m^2 - 9}$$ *Combine like terms in the numerator.*

$$= \frac{2(m + 3)^1}{(m - 3)(m + 3)^1}$$ *Factor. Divide out common factors.*

$$= \frac{2}{m - 3}$$ *Simplify.*

CHECK IT OUT! Add. Simplify your answer.

1a. $\dfrac{n}{2n} + \dfrac{3n}{2n}$

1b. $\dfrac{3y^2}{y + 1} + \dfrac{3y}{y + 1}$

To subtract rational expressions with like denominators, remember to add the opposite of *each* term in the second numerator.

EXAMPLE 2 **Subtracting Rational Expressions with Like Denominators**

Subtract. Simplify your answer.

$$\frac{3m-6}{m^2+m-6} - \frac{-m+2}{m^2+m-6}$$

Caution!

Make sure you add the opposite of all the terms in the numerator of the second expression when subtracting rational expressions.

$$\frac{3m-6-(-m+2)}{m^2+m-6} = \frac{3m-6+m-2}{m^2+m-6}$$ *Subtract numerators.*

$$= \frac{4m-8}{m^2+m-6}$$ *Combine like terms.*

$$= \frac{4(m-2)^1}{(m+3)(m-2)^1}$$ *Factor. Divide out common factors.*

$$= \frac{4}{m+3}$$ *Simplify.*

CHECK IT OUT! Subtract. Simplify your answer.

2a. $\dfrac{5a+2}{a^2-4} - \dfrac{2a-4}{a^2-4}$ **2b.** $\dfrac{2b+14}{b^2+3b-4} - \dfrac{-2b+2}{b^2+3b-4}$

As with fractions, rational expressions must have a common denominator before they can be added or subtracted. If they do not have a common denominator, you can use the least common multiple, or LCM, of the denominators to find one.

To find the LCM, write the prime factorization of both expressions. Use each factor the greatest number of times it appears in either expression.

$$6x^2 = 2 \cdot \boxed{3} \cdot \boxed{x \cdot x}$$ $$5x + 15 = \boxed{5}(x+3)$$

$$8x = \boxed{2 \cdot 2 \cdot 2} \cdot \quad \cdot x$$ $$x^2 - 9 = \boxed{(x+3)}\boxed{(x-3)}$$

$$\text{LCM} = 2 \cdot 2 \cdot 2 \cdot 3 \cdot x \cdot x = 24x^2$$ $$\text{LCM} = 5(x+3)(x-3)$$

EXAMPLE 3 **Identifying the Least Common Multiple**

Find the LCM of the given expressions.

A $24a^3, 4a$

$$24a^3 = 2 \cdot 2 \cdot 2 \cdot 3 \cdot a \cdot a \cdot a$$

$$4a = 2 \cdot 2 \cdot \qquad a$$

$$\text{LCM} = 2 \cdot 2 \cdot 2 \cdot 3 \cdot a \cdot a \cdot a = 24a^3$$

Write the prime factorization of each expression. Use every factor of both expressions the greatest number of times it appears in either expression.

B $2d^2 + 10d + 12, d^2 + 7d + 12$

$$2d^2 + 10d + 12 = 2(d^2 + 5d + 6)$$ *Factor each expression.*

$$= 2(d+3)(d+2)$$ *Use every factor of both expressions the greatest number of times it*

$$d^2 + 7d + 12 = (d+3) \qquad (d+4)$$ *appears in either expression.*

$$\text{LCM} = 2(d+3)(d+2)(d+4)$$

CHECK IT OUT! Find the LCM of the given expressions.

3a. $5f^2h, 15fh^2$ **3b.** $x^2 - 4x - 12, (x-6)(x+5)$

The LCM of the denominators of fractions or rational expressions is also called the least common denominator, or LCD. You use the same method to add or subtract rational expressions.

Adding or Subtracting Rational Expressions
Step 1 Identify the LCD.
Step 2 Multiply each expression by an appropriate form of 1 so that each term has the LCD as its denominator.
Step 3 Write each expression using the LCD.
Step 4 Add or subtract the numerators, combining like terms as needed.
Step 5 Factor.
Step 6 Simplify as needed.

E X A M P L E 4 **Adding and Subtracting with Unlike Denominators**

Add or subtract. Simplify your answer.

A $\dfrac{3x}{6x^2} + \dfrac{2x}{4x}$

$$6x^2 = 2 \quad \cdot 3 \cdot x \cdot x$$

Step 1 $\quad 4x = 2 \cdot 2 \quad \cdot x$ *Identify the LCD.*

$$\text{LCD} = 2 \cdot 2 \cdot 3 \cdot x \cdot x = 12x^2$$

Step 2 $\dfrac{3x}{6x^2}\left(\dfrac{2}{2}\right) + \dfrac{2x}{4x}\left(\dfrac{3x}{3x}\right)$ *Multiply each expression by an appropriate form of 1.*

Step 3 $\quad \dfrac{6x}{12x^2} + \dfrac{6x^2}{12x^2}$ *Write each expression using the LCD.*

Step 4 $\quad \dfrac{6x + 6x^2}{12x^2}$ *Add the numerators.*

Step 5 $\quad \dfrac{\cancel{6}^{1}\cancel{x}^{1}(1 + x)}{\cancel{6}^{1} \cdot 2\cancel{x}^{2x}}$ *Factor and divide out common factors.*

Step 6 $\quad \dfrac{1 + x}{2x}$ *Simplify.*

Remember!

Expressions like
$m - 3$ and $3 - m$ are
opposite binominals.
$3 - m = -1(m - 3)$
and
$m - 3 = -1(3 - m)$

B $\dfrac{1}{m - 3} - \dfrac{5}{3 - m}$

Step 1 The denominators are **opposite binomials**.
The LCD can be either $m - 3$ or $3 - m$.   *Identify the LCD.*

Step 2 $\dfrac{1}{m - 3} - \dfrac{5}{3 - m}\left(\dfrac{-1}{-1}\right)$ *Multiply the second expression by $\frac{-1}{-1}$ to get an LCD of $m - 3$.*

Step 3 $\quad \dfrac{1}{m - 3} - \dfrac{-5}{m - 3}$ *Write each expression using the LCD.*

Step 4 $\quad \dfrac{1 - (-5)}{m - 3}$ *Subtract the numerators.*

Steps 5, 6 $\quad \dfrac{6}{m - 3}$ *No factoring is needed, so just simplify.*

CHECK IT OUT! Add or subtract. Simplify your answer.

4a. $\dfrac{4}{3d} - \dfrac{2d}{2d^3}$ **4b.** $\dfrac{a^2 + 4a}{a^2 + 2a - 8} + \dfrac{8}{a - 2}$

EXAMPLE **5** *Recreation Application*

Katy wants to find out how long it will take to kayak 1 mile up a river and return to her starting point. Katy's average paddling rate is 4 times the speed of the river's current.

   a. **Write and simplify an expression for the time it will take Katy to kayak the round-trip in terms of the rate of the river's current.**

      Step 1 Write expressions for the distances and rates in the problem. The **distance** in both directions is **1 mile.**

        Let x represent the rate of the current, and let $4x$ represent Katy's paddling rate.

        Katy's **rate against the current** is $4x - x$, or $3x$.

        Katy's **rate with the current** is $4x + x$, or $5x$.

      Step 2 Use a table to write expressions for time.

Helpful Hint

To write expressions for time in terms of distance and rate, solve $d = rt$ for t.

$$t = \frac{d}{r}$$

Direction	Distance (mi)	Rate (mi/h)	Time (h) = $\frac{\text{distance}}{\text{rate}}$
Upstream (against current)	1	$3x$	$\frac{1}{3x}$
Downstream (with current)	1	$5x$	$\frac{1}{5x}$

      Step 3 Write and simplify an expression for the total time.

        total time = time upstream + time downstream

        $\text{total time} = \dfrac{1}{3x} + \dfrac{1}{5x}$ *Substitute known values.*

        $= \dfrac{1}{3x}\left(\dfrac{5}{5}\right) + \dfrac{1}{5x}\left(\dfrac{3}{3}\right)$ *Multiply each fraction by an appropriate form of 1.*

        $= \dfrac{5}{15x} + \dfrac{3}{15x}$ *Write each expression using the LCD, 15x.*

        $= \dfrac{8}{15x}$ *Add the numerators.*

   b. **If the rate of the river is 2 miles per hour, how long will it take Katy to kayak round trip?**

      $\dfrac{8}{15(2)} = \dfrac{4}{15}$ *Substitute 2 for x. Simplify.*

      It will take Katy $\frac{4}{15}$ of an hour, or 16 minutes, to kayak the round-trip.

 5. What if?... Katy's average paddling rate increases to 5 times the speed of the current. Now how long will it take Katy to kayak the round trip?

THINK AND DISCUSS

1. Explain how to find the least common denominator of rational expressions.

2. GET ORGANIZED Copy and complete the graphic organizer. In each box, compare and contrast operations with fractions and rational expressions.

go.hrw.com
Homework Help Online
KEYWORD: MA7 12-5
Parent Resources Online
KEYWORD: MA7 Parent

GUIDED PRACTICE

SEE EXAMPLE 1
p. 905

Add. Simplify your answer.

1. $\dfrac{y}{3y^2} + \dfrac{5y}{3y^2}$

2. $\dfrac{4m + 30}{m + 5} + \dfrac{m^2 + 8m + 5}{m + 5}$

3. $\dfrac{x}{x^2 - 16} + \dfrac{4}{x^2 - 16}$

SEE EXAMPLE 2
p. 906

Subtract. Simplify your answer.

4. $\dfrac{7}{2x^3} - \dfrac{3}{2x^3}$

5. $\dfrac{7a - 2}{a^2 + 3a + 2} - \dfrac{5a - 6}{a^2 + 3a + 2}$

6. $\dfrac{3x^2 + 1}{2x + 2} - \dfrac{2x^2 - 2x}{2x + 2}$

SEE EXAMPLE 3
p. 906

Find the LCM of the given expressions.

7. $3xy^2, 6x^3yz$

8. $x^2 + 9x + 20, (x + 5)(x - 4)$

9. $y^2 - 16, (y + 9)(y - 4)$

SEE EXAMPLE 4
p. 907

Add or subtract. Simplify your answer.

10. $\dfrac{3}{c} - \dfrac{4}{3c}$

11. $\dfrac{x^2 + x}{x^2 + 3x + 2} + \dfrac{3}{x + 2}$

12. $\dfrac{2x}{x - 5} + \dfrac{x}{5 - x}$

SEE EXAMPLE 5
p. 908

13. Travel The Escobar family went on a car trip. They drove 100 miles on country roads and 240 miles on the highway. They drove 50% faster on the highway than on the country roads. Let r represent their rate on country roads in miles per hour.

a. Write and simplify an expression that represents the number of hours it took the Escobar family to complete their trip in terms of r. (*Hint:* 50% faster means 150% of the original rate.)

b. Find their total travel time if they drove the posted speed limit.

PRACTICE AND PROBLEM SOLVING

Independent Practice

For Exercises	See Example
14–16	1
17–19	2
20–25	3
26–31	4
32	5

Extra Practice
Skills Practice p. S27
Application Practice p. S39

Add. Simplify your answer.

14. $\dfrac{4y}{y^3} + \dfrac{4y}{y^3}$

15. $\dfrac{a^2 - 3}{a + 3} + \dfrac{2a}{a + 3}$

16. $\dfrac{4x - 13}{x^2 - 5x + 6} + \dfrac{1}{x^2 - 5x + 6}$

Subtract. Simplify your answer.

17. $\dfrac{m^2}{m - 6} - \dfrac{6m}{m - 6}$

18. $\dfrac{c + 3}{4c^2 - 25} - \dfrac{-c + 8}{4c^2 - 25}$

19. $\dfrac{-2a^2 - 9a}{a - 2} - \dfrac{-5a^2 - 4a + 2}{a - 2}$

Find the LCM of the given expressions.

20. $4jk^4m, 25jm$

21. $12a^2 + 4a, 27a + 9$

22. $p^2 - 3p, pqr^2$

23. $5xy^2z, 10y^3$

24. $5x^2, 7x - 14$

25. $y^2 + 7y + 10, y^2 + 9y + 20$

Add or subtract. Simplify your answer.

26. $\dfrac{2x}{5x} + \dfrac{10x}{3x^2}$

27. $\dfrac{y^2 - y}{y^2 - 4y + 3} - \dfrac{2y - 2}{3y - 9}$

28. $\dfrac{-3t}{t - 4} - \dfrac{2t + 4}{4 - t}$

29. $\dfrac{z}{3z^2} + \dfrac{4}{7z}$

30. $\dfrac{5x}{2x - 6} + \dfrac{x + 2}{3 - x}$

31. $\dfrac{3m}{4m - 8} - \dfrac{m^2}{m^2 - 4m + 4}$

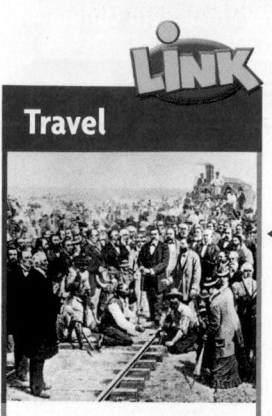
32. **Fitness** Ira walks one mile from his house to the recreation center. After playing basketball, he walks home at only 85% of his normal walking speed. Let w be Ira's normal rate of walking.

 a. Write an expression to represent Ira's round-trip walking time.

 b. If Ira's normal rate of walking is 3 miles per hour, how long did it take for him to complete his walking?

33. **Travel** A train travels 500 miles across the Midwest—50 miles through cities and 450 miles through open country. As it passes through cities, it slows to one-fifth the speed it travels through open country. Let r represent the rate in open country in miles per hour.

 a. Write and simplify an expression in terms of r that represents the number of hours it takes the train to travel 500 miles.

 b. Find the total travel time if the train's rate through open country is 50 miles per hour.

 c. **Critical Thinking** If you knew the time it took the train to make the trip, how could you find its average rate?

Add or subtract. Simplify your answer.

34. $\dfrac{10}{5+y} + \dfrac{2y}{5+y}$

35. $\dfrac{7}{49-c^2} - \dfrac{c}{49-c^2}$

36. $\dfrac{6a}{a-12} + \dfrac{4}{12-a}$

37. $\dfrac{b}{2b^3} + \dfrac{3}{3b^2}$

38. $\dfrac{r^2+2r}{r+3} - \dfrac{2r+9}{r+3}$

39. $\dfrac{x^2-2x}{3x-15} - \dfrac{8x-25}{3x-15}$

40. $\dfrac{2y}{8y^2} + \dfrac{9}{4y^3}$

41. $\dfrac{2}{x+2} + \dfrac{6}{x+4}$

42. $\dfrac{2y}{3y-9} - \dfrac{y+1}{y^2-9}$

43. **///ERROR ANALYSIS///** Two students were asked to find the excluded values of the expression $\dfrac{p}{p^2-p-12} - \dfrac{4}{p^2-p-12}$. Student A identified the excluded value as $p = -3$. Student B identified the excluded values as $p = -3$ and $p = 4$. Who is incorrect? What is the error?

44. **Multi-Step** At the spring fair there is a square Velcro target as shown. A player tosses a ball, which will stick to the target in some random spot. If the ball sticks to a spot in either the small square or the circle, the player wins a prize. What is the probability that a player will win a prize, assuming the ball sticks somewhere on the target? Round your answer to the nearest hundredth.

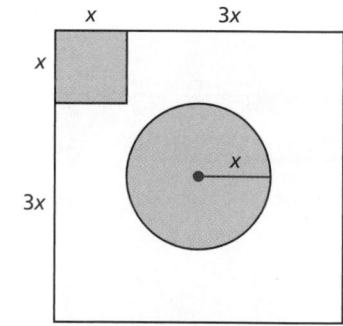

45. **Critical Thinking** Write two expressions whose sum is $\dfrac{x}{x+1}$.

46. This problem will prepare you for the Multi-Step Test Prep on page 926.

 Jonathan is studying light in his science class. He finds that a magnifying glass can be used to project upside-down images onto a piece of paper. The equation $\frac{1}{f} = \frac{1}{x} + \frac{1}{y}$ relates the focal length of the lens f, the distance of the object from the lens x, and the distance of the image from the lens y. The focal length of Jonathan's lens is 12 cm.

 a. Jonathan wants to write y, the distance of the image from the lens, as a function of x, the distance of the object from the lens. To begin, he rewrote the equation above as $\frac{1}{y} = \frac{1}{12} - \frac{1}{x}$. Explain how he did this.

 b. Explain how Jonathan simplified the equation in part **a** to $\frac{1}{y} = \frac{x-12}{12x}$.

47. Critical Thinking Identify three common denominators that could be used to add $\frac{3}{2x^2}$ to $\frac{3}{4x}$.

 48. Write About It Explain how to find the least common denominator of two rational expressions when the denominators are opposite binomials.

49. What is the LCD of $\dfrac{6}{3p+3}$ and $\dfrac{4}{p+1}$?

   Ⓐ $p+1$ Ⓑ 12   Ⓒ $3p+1$ Ⓓ $3p+3$

50. Simplify $\dfrac{4}{2x} - \dfrac{1}{x}$.

   Ⓕ $\dfrac{1}{x}$ Ⓖ $\dfrac{3}{x}$ Ⓗ $\dfrac{5}{x}$ Ⓙ $\dfrac{3}{2x}$

51. Which of the following is equivalent to $\dfrac{2x}{x-2}$?

   Ⓐ $\dfrac{x}{x+2} + \dfrac{x}{x-2}$ Ⓒ $\dfrac{x^2+4x}{x^2-4} + \dfrac{x}{x+2}$

   Ⓑ $\dfrac{2x}{x^2-4} + \dfrac{4}{x-2}$ Ⓓ $\dfrac{x}{x+2} + \dfrac{x^2+6x}{x^2-4}$

52. Extended Response Andrea biked 3 miles to the post office and 5 miles to the library. The rate at which she biked to the library was three times faster than her rate to the post office r.

   a. Write an expression that represents Andrea's total biking time in hours. Explain what each part of your expression means in the situation.

   b. Simplify the expression.

   c. How long did it take Andrea to bike the 8 miles if her biking rate to the post office was 3 miles per hour?

CHALLENGE AND EXTEND

Add or subtract and simplify. Find the excluded values.

53. $\dfrac{3}{x+y} - \dfrac{2x+y}{x^2-y^2}$ **54.** $\dfrac{3}{2m} + \dfrac{4}{m^2} + \dfrac{2}{5m}$ **55.** $\dfrac{a}{xy} + \dfrac{b}{xz} + \dfrac{c}{yz}$

56. Simplify the complex fraction $\dfrac{\frac{1}{x} - \frac{1}{y}}{\frac{x}{xy} - \frac{1}{x}}$. (*Hint:* Simplify the numerator and denominator of the complex fraction first.)

SPIRAL REVIEW

Sketch a graph for each situation. *(Lesson 4-1)*

57. Snow falls lightly at first, then falls heavily at a steady rate.

58. Snow melts quickly during the afternoon, then stops melting at night.

59. Snow falls heavily, is shoveled away, and then a light snow falls.

Solve each quadratic equation by factoring. *(Lesson 9-6)*

60. $d^2 - 4d - 12 = 0$ **61.** $2g^2 - 9g = -4$ **62.** $9x^2 + 6x + 1 = 0$

Simplify each rational expression, if possible. Identify any excluded values. *(Lesson 12-3)*

63. $\dfrac{2t^2-8}{t^2-4}$ **64.** $\dfrac{n^2+5n}{n^2+3n-10}$ **65.** $\dfrac{4-x}{x^2-16}$

12-6
Algebra LAB

Model Polynomial Division

Some polynomial divisions can be modeled by algebra tiles. If a polynomial can be modeled by a rectangle, then its factors are represented by the length and width of the rectangle. If one factor is a divisor, then the other factor is a quotient.

Use with Lesson 12-6

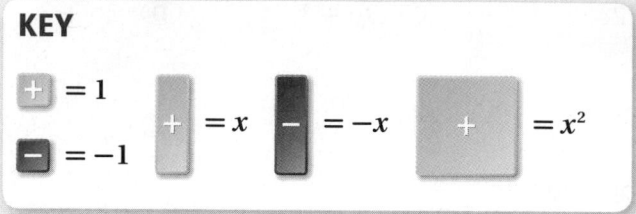
Activity 1

Use algebra tiles to find the quotient $(x^2 + 5x + 6) \div (x + 2)$.

[tiles: one x²-tile and five x-tiles and six unit tiles]	*Model $x^2 + 5x + 6$.*

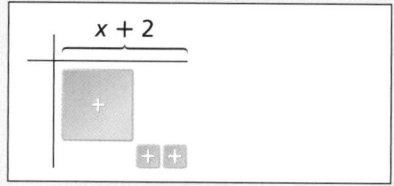

Try to form a rectangle with a length of x + 2.

Place the x^2-tile in the upper-left corner. Then place two unit tiles in a row at the lower-right corner.

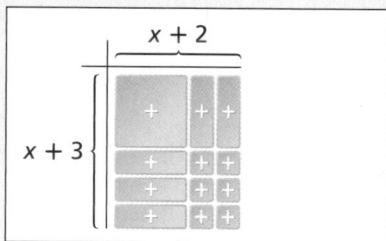

Try to use all the remaining tiles to complete a rectangle.

If you can complete a rectangle, then the width of the rectangle is the quotient.

The rectangle has length $x + 2$ and width $x + 3$. So, $(x^2 + 5x + 6) \div (x + 2) = x + 3$.

You can check your answer by multiplying.	$(x + 3)(x + 2)$	
	$x^2 + 2x + 3x + 6$	*Use the FOIL method.*
	$x^2 + 5x + 6$ ✓	

Try This

Use algebra tiles to find each quotient.

1. $(x^2 + 5x + 4) \div (x + 1)$ **2.** $(x^2 + 7x + 10) \div (x + 5)$ **3.** $(x^2 + 4x - 5) \div (x - 1)$

4. $(2x^2 + 5x + 2) \div (x + 2)$ **5.** $(x^2 - 6x + 8) \div (x - 2)$ **6.** $(2x^2 - x - 3) \div (x + 1)$

7. Describe what happens when you try to model $(x^2 - 4x + 3) \div (x + 1)$.

12-6 Dividing Polynomials

Objective
Divide a polynomial by a monomial or binomial.

Why learn this?
Division of polynomials can be used to compare the energy produced by solar panels. (See Exercise 51.)

The electrical power (in watts) produced by a solar panel is directly proportional to the surface area of the solar panel. Division of polynomials can be used to compare energy production by solar panels of different sizes.

To divide a polynomial by a monomial, you can first write the division as a rational expression. Then divide each term in the polynomial by the monomial.

EXAMPLE 1   **Dividing a Polynomial by a Monomial**

Divide $(6x^3 + 8x^2 - 4x) \div 2x$.

$$\dfrac{6x^3 + 8x^2 - 4x}{2x}$$ *Write as a rational expression.*

$$\dfrac{6x^3}{2x} + \dfrac{8x^2}{2x} - \dfrac{4x}{2x}$$ *Divide each term in the polynomial by the monomial 2x.*

$$\dfrac{\cancel{6}^3 \, x^{\cancel{3}\,x^2}}{\cancel{2}^1 \, \cancel{x}^1} + \dfrac{\cancel{8}^4 \, x^{\cancel{2}\,x}}{\cancel{2}^1 \, \cancel{x}^1} - \dfrac{\cancel{4}^2 \, x^1}{\cancel{2}^1 \, x^1}$$ *Divide out common factors.*

$$3x^2 + 4x - 2$$ *Simplify.*

CHECK IT OUT!   **Divide.**

1a. $(8p^3 - 4p^2 + 12p) \div (-4p^2)$

1b. $(6x^3 + 2x - 15) \div 6x$

Division of a polynomial by a binomial is similar to division of whole numbers.

Dividing Polynomials

	WORDS	NUMBERS	POLYNOMIALS
Step 1	Factor the numerator and/or denominator if possible.	$\dfrac{168}{3} = \dfrac{56 \cdot 3}{3}$	$\dfrac{r^2 + 3r + 2}{r + 2} = \dfrac{(r + 2)(r + 1)}{(r + 2)}$
Step 2	Divide out any common factors.	$\dfrac{56 \cdot \cancel{3}}{\cancel{3}}$	$\dfrac{\cancel{(r + 2)}\,(r + 1)}{\cancel{(r + 2)}}$
Step 3	Simplify.	56	$r + 1$

EXAMPLE 2 **Dividing a Polynomial by a Binomial**

Divide.

A $\dfrac{c^2 + 4c - 5}{c - 1}$

$\dfrac{(c + 5)(c - 1)}{c - 1}$ *Factor the numerator.*

$\dfrac{(c + 5)(\cancel{c - 1})^1}{(\cancel{c - 1})^1}$ *Divide out common factors.*

$c + 5$ *Simplify.*

B $\dfrac{3x^2 - 10x - 8}{4 - x}$

$\dfrac{(3x + 2)(x - 4)}{4 - x}$ *Factor the numerator.*

$\dfrac{(3x + 2)(x - 4)}{-1(x - 4)}$ *Factor one opposite binomial.*

$\dfrac{(3x + 2)(\cancel{x - 4})^1}{-1(\cancel{x - 4})^1}$ *Divide out common factors.*

$-3x - 2$ *Simplify.*

 Divide.

2a. $\dfrac{10 + 7k + k^2}{k + 2}$ **2b.** $\dfrac{b^2 - 49}{b + 7}$ **2c.** $\dfrac{s^2 + 12s + 36}{s + 6}$

Recall how you used long division to divide whole numbers as shown at right. You can also use long division to divide polynomials. An example is shown below.

$$\begin{array}{r} 15 \\ 23{\overline{\smash{\big)}\,345}} \\ \underline{-23} \\ 115 \\ \underline{-115} \\ 0 \end{array}$$

$$\left(x^2 + 3x + 2\right) \div \left(x + 2\right)$$

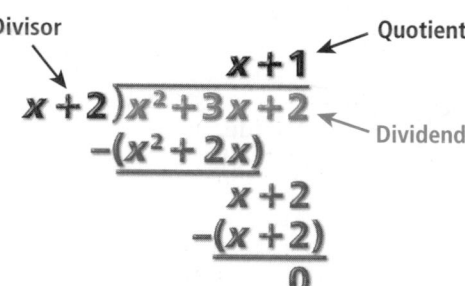

Using Long Division to Divide a Polynomial by a Binomial
Step 1 Write the binomial and polynomial in long division form.
Step 2 Divide the first term of the dividend by the first term of the divisor. This is the first term of the quotient.
Step 3 Multiply this first term of the quotient by the binomial divisor and place the product under the dividend, aligning like terms.
Step 4 Subtract the product from the dividend.
Step 5 Bring down the next term in the dividend.
Step 6 Repeat Steps 2–5 as necessary until you get 0 or until the degree of the remainder is less than the degree of the binomial.

EXAMPLE **3** **Polynomial Long Division**

Divide using long division.

A $\left(x^2 + 2 + 3x\right) \div (x + 2)$

Step 1 $x + 2\overline{)x^2 + 3x + 2}$

Write in long division form with expressions in standard form.

Step 2 $x + 2\overline{)x^2 + 3x + 2}^{x}$

Divide the first term of the dividend by the first term of the divisor to get the first term of the quotient.

Step 3 $\begin{array}{r} x \\ x + 2\overline{)x^2 + 3x + 2} \\ x^2 + 2x \end{array}$

Multiply the first term of the quotient by the binomial divisor. Place the product under the dividend, aligning like terms.

Step 4 $\begin{array}{r} x \\ x + 2\overline{)x^2 + 3x + 2} \\ -\left(x^2 + 2x\right) \\ \hline 0 + x \end{array}$

Subtract the product from the dividend.

Step 5 $\begin{array}{r} x \\ x + 2\overline{)x^2 + 3x + 2} \\ -\left(x^2 + 2x\right)\downarrow \\ \hline x + 2 \end{array}$

Bring down the next term in the dividend.

Step 6 $\begin{array}{r} x + 1 \\ x + 2\overline{)x^2 + 3x + 2} \\ -\left(x^2 + 2x\right) \\ \hline x + 2 \\ -\,(x + 2) \\ \hline 0 \end{array}$

Repeat Steps 2–5 as necessary.
The remainder is 0.

Check Multiply the answer and the divisor.

$(x + 2)(x + 1)$
$x^2 + x + 2x + 2$
$x^2 + 3x + 2 \checkmark$

B $\dfrac{x^2 + 4x + 3}{x + 1}$

$x + 1\overline{)x^2 + 4x + 3}$

Write in long division form.

$\begin{array}{r} x + 3 \\ x + 1\overline{)x^2 + 4x + 3} \\ -\left(x^2 + x\right)\downarrow \\ \hline 3x + 3 \\ -(3x + 3) \\ \hline 0 \end{array}$

$x^2 \div x = x$
Multiply $x \cdot (x + 1)$. Subtract.
Bring down the 3. $3x \div x = 3$
Multiply $3(x + 1)$. Subtract.
The remainder is 0.

Check Multiply the answer and the divisor.

$(x + 1)(x + 3)$
$x^2 + 3x + 1x + 3$
$x^2 + 4x + 3 \checkmark$

 CHECK IT OUT! Divide using long division.

3a. $\left(2y^2 - 5y - 3\right) \div (y - 3)$ **3b.** $\left(a^2 - 8a + 12\right) \div (a - 6)$

Helpful Hint

You can check your simplified answer by multiplying it by the divisor. When the remainder is 0, the product should be the numerator.

Sometimes the divisor is not a factor of the dividend, so the remainder is not 0. Then the remainder can be written as a rational expression.

EXAMPLE **4** **Long Division with a Remainder**

Divide $(2x^2 + 3x - 6) \div (x - 2)$.

$x - 2\overline{)2x^2 + 3x - 6}$ *Write in long division form.*

$$\begin{array}{r} 2x + 7 \\ x - 2\overline{)2x^2 + 3x - 6} \\ -(2x^2 - 4x) \\ \hline 7x - 6 \\ -(7x - 14) \\ \hline 8 \end{array}$$

$2x^2 \div x = 2x$

Multiply $2x(x - 2)$. Subtract.

Bring down the -6. $7x \div x = 7$

Multiply $7(x - 2)$. Subtract.

The remainder is 8.

$\dfrac{8}{x - 2}$ *Write the remainder as a rational expression using the divisor as the denominator.*

$2x + 7 + \dfrac{8}{x - 2}$ *Write the quotient with the remainder.*

 Divide.

4a. $(3m^2 + 4m - 2) \div (m + 3)$ **4b.** $(y^2 + 3y + 2) \div (y - 3)$

Sometimes you need to write a placeholder for a term using a zero coefficient. This is best seen if you write the polynomials in standard form.

EXAMPLE **5** **Dividing Polynomials That Have a Zero Coefficient**

Divide $(3x - 4x^3 - 15) \div (2x + 3)$.

$(-4x^3 + 3x - 15) \div (2x + 3)$ *Write the polynomials in standard form.*

$2x + 3\overline{)-4x^3 + 0x^2 + 3x - 15}$ *Write in long division form. Use $0x^2$ as a placeholder for the x^2 term.*

Remember!

Recall from Chapter 7 that a polynomial in one variable is written in standard form when the degrees of the terms go from greatest to least.

$$\begin{array}{r} -2x^2 + 3x - 3 \\ 2x + 3\overline{)-4x^3 + 0x^2 + 3x - 15} \\ -(-4x^3 - 6x^2) \\ \hline 6x^2 + 3x \\ -(6x^2 + 9x) \\ \hline -6x - 15 \\ -(-6x - 9) \\ \hline -6 \end{array}$$

$-4x^3 \div 2x = -2x^2$

Multiply $-2x^2(2x + 3)$. Subtract.

Bring down $3x$. $6x^2 \div 2x = 3x$

Multiply $3x(2x + 3)$. Subtract.

Bring down -15. $-6x \div 2x = -3$

Multiply $-3(2x + 3)$. Subtract.

The remainder is -6.

$(3x - 4x^3 - 15) \div (2x + 3) = -2x^2 + 3x - 3 + \dfrac{-6}{2x + 3}$.

 Divide.

5a. $(1 - 4x^2 + x^3) \div (x - 2)$

5b. $(4p - 1 + 2p^3) \div (p + 1)$

THINK AND DISCUSS

1. When dividing a polynomial by a binomial, what does it mean when the remainder is 0?

2. Suppose that the final answer to a polynomial division problem is $x - 5 + \frac{3}{x+2}$. Find an excluded value. Justify your answer.

3. **GET ORGANIZED** Copy and complete the graphic organizer. In each box, show an example.

```
        Long Division
        /          \
  Polynomials   Whole numbers
```

12-6 Exercises

go.hrw.com
Homework Help Online
KEYWORD: MA7 12-6
Parent Resources Online
KEYWORD: MA7 Parent

GUIDED PRACTICE

Divide.

SEE EXAMPLE 1
p. 913

1. $\left(4x^2 - x\right) \div 2x$

2. $\left(16a^4 - 4a^3\right) \div 4a$

3. $\left(21b^2 - 14b + 24\right) \div 3b$

4. $\left(18r^2 - 12r + 6\right) \div (-6r)$

5. $\left(6x^3 + 12x^2 + 9x\right) \div 3x^2$

6. $\left(5m^4 + 15m^2 - 10\right) \div 5m^3$

SEE EXAMPLE 2
p. 914

7. $\dfrac{2x^2 - x - 3}{x + 1}$

8. $\dfrac{a^2 - a - 12}{a - 4}$

9. $\dfrac{6y^2 + 11y - 10}{3y - 2}$

10. $\dfrac{t^2 - 6t + 8}{t - 4}$

11. $\dfrac{x^2 + 16x + 15}{x + 15}$

12. $\dfrac{p^2 - p - 20}{p + 4}$

Divide using long division.

SEE EXAMPLE 3
p. 915

13. $\left(c^2 + 7c + 12\right) \div (c + 4)$

14. $\left(3s^2 - 12s - 15\right) \div (s - 5)$

15. $\dfrac{x^2 + 5x - 14}{x + 7}$

16. $\dfrac{x^2 + 4x - 12}{x - 2}$

SEE EXAMPLE 4
p. 916

17. $\left(a^2 + 4a + 3\right) \div (a + 2)$

18. $\left(2r^2 + 11r + 5\right) \div (r - 3)$

19. $\left(n^2 + 8n + 15\right) \div (n + 4)$

20. $\left(2t^2 - t + 4\right) \div (t - 1)$

21. $\left(8n^2 - 6n - 7\right) \div (2n + 1)$

22. $\left(b^2 - b + 1\right) \div (b + 2)$

SEE EXAMPLE 5
p. 916

23. $\left(3x - 2x^3 - 10\right) \div (3 + x)$

24. $\left(3p^3 - 2p^2 - 4\right) \div (p - 2)$

25. $\left(m^2 + 2\right) \div (m - 1)$

26. $\left(3x^2 + 4x^3 - 5\right) \div (5 + x)$

27. $\left(4k^3 - 2k - 8\right) \div (k + 1)$

28. $\left(j^3 + 6j + 2\right) \div (j + 4)$

PRACTICE AND PROBLEM SOLVING

Divide.

29. $\left(9t^3 + 12t^2 - 6t\right) \div 3t^2$

30. $\left(5n^3 - 10n + 15\right) \div (-5n)$

31. $\left(-16p^4 + 4p^3 + 8\right) \div 4p^3$

32. $\dfrac{4r^2 - 9r + 2}{r - 2}$

33. $\dfrac{8t^2 + 2t - 3}{2t - 1}$

34. $\dfrac{3g^2 + 7g - 6}{g + 3}$

<table>
<tr><td colspan="2">Independent Practice</td></tr>
<tr><td>For
Exercises</td><td>See
Example</td></tr>
<tr><td>29–31</td><td>1</td></tr>
<tr><td>32–34</td><td>2</td></tr>
<tr><td>35–38</td><td>3</td></tr>
<tr><td>39–41</td><td>4</td></tr>
<tr><td>42–44</td><td>5</td></tr>
</table>

Extra Practice

Skills Practice p. S27

Application Practice p. S39

Divide using long division.

35. $\left(x^2 - 5x + 6\right) \div (x - 2)$

36. $\left(2m^2 + 8m + 8\right) \div (m + 2)$

37. $\left(6a^2 + 7a - 3\right) \div (2a + 3)$

38. $\left(3x^2 - 10x - 8\right) \div (x - 4)$

39. $\left(3x^2 - 2x + 6\right) \div (x - 2)$

40. $\left(2m^2 + 5m + 8\right) \div (m + 1)$

41. $\left(6x^2 - x - 3\right) \div (2x - 1)$

42. $\left(2m^3 - 4m - 30\right) \div (2m - 10)$

43. $\left(6t^3 + 21t + 9\right) \div (3t + 9)$

44. $\left(p^4 - 7p^2 + p + 1\right) \div (p - 3)$

45. Multi-Step Find the value of n, so that $x - 4$ is a factor of $x^2 + x + n$.

Geometry The area of each of three rectangles is $2x^2 - 3x - 2$ cm². Below are the different widths of the rectangles. Find each corresponding length.

46. $x - 2$

47. $x + 1$

48. $2x + 1$

49. Graphing Calculator Use the table of values for $f(x) = \dfrac{x^2 + 3x + 4}{x - 5}$ to answer the following.

   a. Describe what is happening to the values of y as x increases from 2 to 4.

   b. Describe what is happening to the values of y as x increases from 6 to 8.

   c. Explain why there is no value in the y column when x is 5.

Solar Energy

50. Estimation Estimate the value of $\dfrac{x^2 + 10x + 25}{x^2 - 25} \div \dfrac{x^4 - 4x^3 - 45x^2}{x^2 - 14x + 45}$ for $x = 2.88$.

51. Solar Energy The greater the area of a solar panel, the greater the number of watts of energy produced. The area of two solar panels A and B, in square meters, can be represented by $A = m^2 + 3m + 2$ and $B = 2m + 2$. Divide the polynomials to find an expression that represents the ratio of the area of A to the area of B.

NASA is researching unmanned solar-powered aircraft. In the future, these aircraft may be able to stay in the air indefinitely.

52. ///ERROR ANALYSIS/// Two students attempted to divide $\dfrac{4x^2 - 6x + 12}{-2x}$. Which is incorrect? Explain the error.

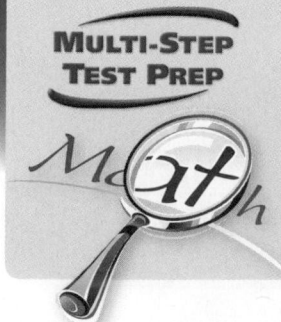

53. This problem will prepare you for the Multi-Step Test Prep on page 926.

Jonathan continues to study lenses and uses the equation $\frac{1}{y} = \frac{x - 12}{12x}$.

   a. Jonathan wants to write y, the distance of the image from the lens, as a function of x, the distance of the object from the lens. What is the equation solved for y?

   b. Use a graphing calculator to create a table of values for the function $y(x)$. For which value of x is the function undefined?

54. **Write About It** When dividing a polynomial by a binomial, what does it mean when there is a remainder?

55. **Critical Thinking** Divide $2x + 3\overline{)2x^2 + 7x + 6}$. Find a value for each expression by substituting 10 for x in the original problem. Repeat the division. Compare the results of each division.

56. **Write About It** Is $3x + 2$ a factor of $3x^2 + 14x + 8$? Explain.

 TEST PREP

57. Which expression has an excluded value of $-\frac{1}{2}$?

   (A) $\dfrac{4x^2 - 2x - 2}{4x - 2}$ (B) $\dfrac{4x^2 - 2x - 2}{2x - 4}$ (C) $\dfrac{4x^2 - 2x - 2}{4x + 2}$ (D) $\dfrac{4x^2 - 2x - 2}{2x + 4}$

58. Find $(x^2 - 1) \div (x + 2)$.

   (F) $x - 2 + \dfrac{-5}{x + 2}$ (G) $x - 2 + \dfrac{3}{x + 2}$ (H) $x + 2 + \dfrac{-5}{x - 2}$ (J) $x + 2 + \dfrac{3}{x - 2}$

59. Which expression is a factor of $x^2 - 4x - 5$?

   (A) $x - 1$ (B) $x + 1$ (C) $x - 4$ (D) $x + 5$

60. Which of the following expressions is equivalent to $(x^3 + 2x^2 + 3x + 1) \div (x - 1)$?

   (F) $x^2 + 3x + 6 + \dfrac{7}{x - 1}$ (H) $x^2 + 3x + 6 + \dfrac{-5}{x - 1}$

   (G) $x^2 + x + 2 + \dfrac{-1}{x - 1}$ (J) $x^2 + x + 2 + \dfrac{3}{x - 1}$

CHALLENGE AND EXTEND

Divide. Simplify your answer.

61. $(6x^3y - x^2 + 4xy^2) \div (2x^2y)$ 62. $(x^3 - 1) \div (x - 1)$

63. $(x^3 + 2x^2 - x - 2) \div (x^2 - 1)$ 64. $(x^3 + 8) \div (x + 2)$

65. **Geometry** The base of a triangle is $2x + 4$ m and the area is $2x^2 + 5x + 2$ m². How much longer is the base than the height?

66. **Geometry** The formula for finding the volume of a cylinder is $V = BH$, where B is the area of the base of the cylinder and H is the height.

   a. Find the height of the cylinder given that $V = \pi(x^3 + 4x^2 + 5x + 2)$ and $B = \pi(x^2 + 2x + 1)$.

   b. Find an expression for the radius of the base.

SPIRAL REVIEW

67. Find the probability that a point within the boundaries of the larger rectangle is in the shaded region. Express your answer as a simplified radical expression. *(Lesson 11-8)*

Multiply. Write each product in simplest form. *(Lesson 11-8)*

68. $3\sqrt{3} \cdot \sqrt{6}$ 69. $\sqrt{5}(6 - \sqrt{10})$ 70. $(\sqrt{3} + 2)(\sqrt{3} + 5)$

Multiply. Simplify your answer. *(Lesson 12-4)*

71. $(x^2 + 4x + 3) \cdot \dfrac{8}{2(x + 3)}$ 72. $\dfrac{9xy^2}{2x^3} \cdot \dfrac{8y}{3x^4}$ 73. $\dfrac{2k^2 + 4k^3}{k + 1} \cdot \dfrac{k^2 + 3k + 2}{2k^2}$

12-7 Solving Rational Equations

Objectives
Solve rational equations.

Identify extraneous solutions.

Vocabulary
rational equation

Why learn this?
Rational equations can be used to find how much time it takes two or more people working together to complete a job. (See Example 3.)

A **rational equation** is an equation that contains one or more rational expressions. If a rational equation is a proportion, it can be solved using the Cross Product Property.

EXAMPLE 1 Solving Rational Equations by Using Cross Products

Solve $\dfrac{3}{t-3} = \dfrac{2}{t}$. Check your answer.

$\dfrac{3}{t-3} = \dfrac{2}{t}$ *Use cross products.*

$3t = (t-3)(2)$

$3t = 2t - 6$ *Distribute 2 on the right side.*

$t = -6$ *Subtract 2t from both sides.*

Check

$\dfrac{3}{t-3} = \dfrac{2}{t}$

$\begin{array}{c|c} \dfrac{3}{-6-3} & \dfrac{2}{-6} \\ \dfrac{3}{-9} & \dfrac{2}{-6} \\ -\dfrac{1}{3} & -\dfrac{1}{3} \end{array}$ ✓

 Solve. Check your answer.

1a. $\dfrac{1}{n} = \dfrac{3}{n+4}$ **1b.** $\dfrac{4}{h+1} = \dfrac{2}{h}$ **1c.** $\dfrac{21}{x-7} = \dfrac{3}{x}$

Some rational equations contain sums or differences of rational expressions. To solve these, you must find the LCD of all the rational expressions in the equation.

EXAMPLE 2 Solving Rational Equations by Using the LCD

Solve $\dfrac{1}{c} + \dfrac{3}{2c} = \dfrac{2}{c+1}$.

Step 1 Find the LCD.

$2c(c+1)$ *Include every factor of the denominators.*

Step 2 Multiply both sides by the LCD.

$$2c(c+1)\left(\dfrac{1}{c} + \dfrac{3}{2c}\right) = 2c(c+1)\left(\dfrac{2}{c+1}\right)$$

$$2c(c+1)\left(\dfrac{1}{c}\right) + 2c(c+1)\left(\dfrac{3}{2c}\right) = 2c(c+1)\left(\dfrac{2}{c+1}\right)$$ *Distribute on the left side.*

Step 3 Simplify and solve.

$$2\cancel{c}^{1}(c+1)\left(\frac{1}{\cancel{c}^{1}}\right) + 2c^{1}(c+1)\left(\frac{3}{2\cancel{c}^{1}}\right) = 2c\cancel{(c+1)}^{1}\left(\frac{2}{\cancel{c+1}^{1}}\right)$$
Divide out common factors.

$$2(c+1) + (c+1)3 = (2c)2 \qquad \textit{Simplify.}$$
$$2c + 2 + 3c + 3 = 4c \qquad \textit{Distribute and multiply.}$$
$$5c + 5 = 4c \qquad \textit{Combine like terms.}$$
$$c + 5 = 0 \qquad \textit{Subtract 4c from both sides.}$$
$$c = -5 \qquad \textit{Subtract 5 from both sides.}$$

Check Verify that your solution is not extraneous.

$$\frac{1}{c} + \frac{3}{2c} = \frac{2}{c+1}$$

$\dfrac{1}{-5} + \dfrac{3}{2(-5)}$	$\dfrac{2}{-5+1}$
$\dfrac{2}{-10} + \dfrac{3}{-10}$	$\dfrac{2}{-4}$
$-\dfrac{5}{10}$	$-\dfrac{1}{2}$
$-\dfrac{1}{2}$	$-\dfrac{1}{2}$ ✓

 Solve each equation. Check your answer.

2a. $\dfrac{2}{a+1} + \dfrac{1}{a+1} = \dfrac{4}{a}$ **2b.** $\dfrac{6}{j+2} - \dfrac{10}{j} = \dfrac{4}{2j}$

2c. $\dfrac{8}{t+3} = \dfrac{1}{t} + 1$

EXAMPLE 3 **_Problem-Solving Application_**

Greg can clean a house in 5 hours. It takes Armin 7 hours to clean the same house. How long will it take them to clean the house if they work together?

 Understand the Problem

The **answer** will be the number of hours h Greg and Armin need to clean the house.

Armin
7 hours

Greg
5 hours

List the important information:
- Greg cleans the house in 5 hours, so he cleans $\frac{1}{5}$ of the house per hour.
- Armin cleans the house in 7 hours, so he cleans $\frac{1}{7}$ of the house per hour.

2 **Make a Plan**

The part of the house Greg cleans plus the part of the house Armin cleans equals the complete job. Greg's rate times the number of hours worked plus Armin's rate times the number of hours worked will give the complete time to clean the house. Let h represent the number of hours worked.

(Greg's rate) h	$+$	(Armin's rate) h	$=$	complete job
$\frac{1}{5} h$	$+$	$\frac{1}{7} h$	$=$	1

Solve

$$35\left(\frac{1}{5}h + \frac{1}{7}h\right) = 35(1)$$ *Multiply both sides by the LCD, 35.*

$$7h + 5h = 35$$ *Distribute 35 on the left side.*

$$12h = 35$$ *Combine like terms.*

$$h = \frac{35}{12} = 2\frac{11}{12}$$ *Divide by 12 on both sides.*

Greg and Armin working together can clean the house in $2\frac{11}{12}$ hours, or 2 hours 55 minutes.

4 Look Back

Greg cleans $\frac{1}{5}$ of the house per hour and Armin cleans $\frac{1}{7}$ of the house per hour. So, in $2\frac{11}{12}$ hours, Greg cleans $\frac{35}{12} \cdot \frac{1}{5} = \frac{7}{12}$ of the house and Armin cleans $\frac{35}{12} \cdot \frac{1}{7} = \frac{5}{12}$ of the house. Together, they clean $\frac{7}{12} + \frac{5}{12} = 1$ house.

CHECK IT OUT!

3. Cindy mows a lawn in 50 minutes. It takes Sara 40 minutes to mow the same lawn. How long will it take them to mow the lawn if they work together?

When you multiply each side of an equation by the LCD, you may get an extraneous solution. Recall from Chapter 11 that an extraneous solution is a solution to a resulting equation that is not a solution to the original equation.

EXAMPLE 4 **Extraneous Solutions**

Solve $\frac{x-9}{x^2-9} = \frac{-3}{x-3}$. **Identify any extraneous solutions.**

Step 1 Solve.

$$(x-9)(x-3) = -3(x^2-9)$$ *Use cross products.*

$$x^2 - 12x + 27 = -3x^2 + 27$$ *Multiply the left side. Distribute −3 on the right side.*

$$4x^2 - 12x + 27 = 27$$ *Add $3x^2$ to both sides.*

$$4x^2 - 12x = 0$$ *Subtract 27 from both sides.*

$$4x(x-3) = 0$$ *Factor the quadratic expression.*

$$4x = 0 \text{ or } x - 3 = 0$$ *Use the Zero Product Property.*

$$x = 0 \text{ or } x = 3$$ *Solve for x.*

Helpful Hint

Extraneous solutions may be introduced by squaring both sides of an equation or by multiplying both sides of an equation by a variable expression.

Step 2 Find extraneous solutions.

$$\frac{x-9}{x^2-9} = \frac{-3}{x-3}$$

$\frac{0-9}{0^2-9}$	$\frac{-3}{0-3}$
$\frac{-9}{-9}$	$\frac{-3}{-3}$
1	1 ✓

$$\frac{x-9}{x^2-9} = \frac{-3}{x-3}$$

$\frac{3-9}{3^2-9}$	$\frac{-3}{3-3}$
$\frac{-6}{0}$	$\frac{-3}{0}$

Because both $\frac{-6}{0}$ and $\frac{-3}{0}$ are undefined, 3 is not a solution.

The only solution is 0, so 3 is an extraneous solution.

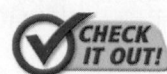 Solve. Identify any extraneous solutions.

4a. $\frac{3}{x-7} = \frac{x-2}{x-7}$ **4b.** $\frac{x+1}{x-2} = \frac{4}{x-3}$ **4c.** $\frac{9}{x^2+2x} = \frac{6}{x^2}$

THINK AND DISCUSS

1. Why is it important to check your answers to rational equations?

2. For what values of x are the rational expressions in the equation $\frac{x}{x-3} = \frac{2}{x+3}$ undefined?

3. Explain why some rational equations, such as $\frac{x}{x-4} = \frac{4}{x-4}$, have no solutions.

4. GET ORGANIZED Copy and complete the graphic organizer. In each box, write the solution and check.

Solving Rational Equations

Solve by using cross products.	Solve by using the LCD.
$\frac{3}{x} = \frac{2}{x+1}$	$\frac{7}{x-1} - \frac{4}{x-1} = \frac{6}{x}$

12-7 Exercises

go.hrw.com
Homework Help Online
KEYWORD: MA7 12-7
Parent Resources Online
KEYWORD: MA7 Parent

GUIDED PRACTICE

1. Vocabulary A(n) ____?____ contains one or more rational expressions. (*extraneous solution* or *rational equation*)

Solve. Check your answer.

SEE EXAMPLE **1**
p. 920

2. $\frac{3}{x+4} = \frac{2}{x}$

3. $\frac{5}{s-6} = \frac{4}{s}$

4. $\frac{20}{p+100} = \frac{-10}{2p}$

5. $\frac{4}{j} = \frac{1}{j+2}$

6. $\frac{3}{x-4} = \frac{9}{x-2}$

7. $\frac{6}{2x-1} = 3$

SEE EXAMPLE **2**
p. 920

8. $\frac{6}{x} - \frac{5}{x} = \frac{1}{3}$

9. $\frac{a}{9} + \frac{1}{3} = \frac{2}{5}$

10. $\frac{3}{x+1} = \frac{2}{x} + \frac{3}{x}$

11. $\frac{8}{d} = \frac{1}{d+2} - \frac{3}{d}$

12. $\frac{3}{s-6} = \frac{4}{s} + \frac{1}{2s}$

13. $\frac{7}{r} + \frac{2}{r-1} = \frac{-1}{2r}$

14. $\frac{3}{a-4} = \frac{a}{a-2}$

15. $\frac{r}{2} - \frac{2}{r} = \frac{5}{6}$

16. $\frac{6}{n} = \frac{7}{n^2} - 1$

17. $\frac{4}{x+1} = x - 2$

18. $\frac{5}{a^2} = \frac{4}{a} + 1$

19. $\frac{1}{p} = \frac{-3}{p^2} + 2$

SEE EXAMPLE **3**
p. 921

20. Painting Summer can paint a room in 3 hours. Louise can paint the room in 5 hours. How many hours will it take to paint the room if they work together?

21. Technology Lawrence's old robotic vacuum can clean his apartment in $1\frac{1}{2}$ hours. His new robotic vacuum can clean his apartment in 45 minutes. How long will it take both vacuums, working together, to clean his apartment?

SEE EXAMPLE **4**
p. 922

Solve. Identify any extraneous solutions.

22. $\frac{3}{c-4} = \frac{c-1}{c-4}$

23. $\frac{w+3}{w^2-1} - \frac{2w}{w-1} = 1$

24. $\frac{3x-7}{x-5} + \frac{x}{2} = \frac{8}{x-5}$

PRACTICE AND PROBLEM SOLVING

Independent Practice

For Exercises	See Example
25–28	1
29–36	2
37	3
38–41	4

Extra Practice

Skills Practice p. S27

Application Practice p. S39

Solve. Check your answer.

25. $\dfrac{8}{x-2} = \dfrac{2}{x+1}$

26. $\dfrac{12}{3n-1} = \dfrac{3}{n}$

27. $\dfrac{x}{x+4} = \dfrac{x}{x-1}$

28. $\dfrac{9}{x+5} = \dfrac{4}{x}$

29. $\dfrac{6}{s} - \dfrac{2}{s} = 5$

30. $\dfrac{1}{2x} + \dfrac{1}{4x} = \dfrac{7}{8x}$

31. $\dfrac{7}{c} - \dfrac{2}{c} = \dfrac{4}{c-1}$

32. $\dfrac{9}{m} - \dfrac{3}{2m} = \dfrac{15}{m}$

33. $\dfrac{3}{x^2} = \dfrac{2}{x}$

34. $\dfrac{r}{3} - 3 = -\dfrac{6}{r}$

35. $\dfrac{6}{x^2} = \dfrac{1}{2} + \dfrac{1}{2x}$

36. $\dfrac{8}{3x^2} = \dfrac{2}{x} - \dfrac{1}{3}$

37. Mel can carpet a floor in 10 hours. Sandy can carpet the same floor in 15 hours. How many hours will it take them to carpet the floor if they work together?

Solve. Identify any extraneous solutions.

38. $\dfrac{5x}{x-3} = 8 + \dfrac{15}{x-3}$

39. $\dfrac{3t}{t-3} = \dfrac{t+4}{t-3}$

40. $\dfrac{2}{x} = \dfrac{x+1}{x^2-1}$

41. $\dfrac{1}{x} = \dfrac{x-4}{x^2-16}$

42. Multi-Step Clancy has been keeping his free throw statistics. Use his data to write the ratio of the number of free throws Clancy has made to the number of attempts.

Clancy's Free Throws	
Attempts	**Made**
45	39

   a. What percentage has he made?

   b. Write and solve an equation to find how many free throws *f* Clancy would have to make in a row to improve his free-throw percentage to 90%. (*Hint:* Clancy needs to make *f* more free throws in *f* more attempts.)

43. Travel A passenger train travels 20 mi/h faster than a freight train. It took the passenger train 2 hours less time than the freight train to travel 240 miles. The freight train took *t* hours. Copy and complete the chart. Then find the rate of the freight train.

	Distance	Rate	Time
Passenger train	240	$\dfrac{240}{t-2}$	
Freight train	240		t

OK, LET'S SEE... WILL IS ON A TRAIN TRAVELING NORTH AT 50 MPH. PETER IS ON A TRAIN TRAVELING WEST AT...

Suspecting that just such a word problem might be on the algebra midterm, Gary came prepared.

44. Pipe A fills a storage tank with a certain chemical in 12 hours. Pipe B fills the tank in 18 hours. How long would it take both pipes to fill the tank?

MULTI-STEP TEST PREP

45. This problem will prepare you for the Multi-Step Test Prep on page 926.

Blanca sets up a lens with a focal length *f* of 15 cm and places a candle 24 cm from the lens. She knows that $\dfrac{1}{f} = \dfrac{1}{x} + \dfrac{1}{y}$ where *x* is the distance of the object from the lens and *y* is the distance of the image from the lens.

   a. Write the equation using the given values.

   b. For the values of *f* and *x* given above, how far will the image appear from the lens?

   c. How will distance between the image and the lens be affected if Blanca uses a lens with a focal length of 18 cm?

46. Critical Thinking Can you cross multiply to solve all rational equations? If so, explain. If not, how do you identify which ones can be solved using cross products?

47. Write About It Solve $\frac{1}{x} + \frac{3}{x} = \frac{3}{x-1}$. Explain each step and why you chose the method you used.

48. Which value is an extraneous solution to $\dfrac{x}{x+4} - \dfrac{4}{x-4} = \dfrac{x^2+16}{x^2-16}$?

   Ⓐ −16   Ⓑ −4   Ⓒ 4   Ⓓ 16

49. Which is a solution to $\dfrac{x+2}{x-3} - \dfrac{1}{x} = \dfrac{3}{x^2-3x}$?

   Ⓕ −1   Ⓖ 0   Ⓗ 1   Ⓙ 3

50. What are the solutions of $\dfrac{5}{x^2} = \dfrac{1}{3} + \dfrac{2}{3x}$?

   Ⓐ −3 and 5   Ⓑ −3 and 2   Ⓒ 2 and 3   Ⓓ 3 and −5

CHALLENGE AND EXTEND

51. Below is a solution to a rational equation. Use an algebraic property to justify each step.

Solve $\dfrac{3}{x} = \dfrac{6}{x+4}$.

Statements	Reasons
a. $3(x+4) = 6x$	
b. $3x + 12 = 6x$	
c. $12 = 3x$	
d. $4 = x$	

52. For what value of a will the equation $\dfrac{x+4}{x-a} = \dfrac{7}{x-a}$ have no solution?

53. Luke, Eddie, and Ryan can do a job in 1 hour and 20 minutes if they work together. Working alone, it takes Ryan 1 hour more to do the job than it takes Luke, and Luke does the job twice as fast as Eddie. How much time would it take each to do the job working alone?

SPIRAL REVIEW

Identify which lines are parallel and which lines are perpendicular. *(Lesson 5-9)*

54. $y = \dfrac{1}{3}x$; $y = 3x + 1$; $y = 3x - 1$ **55.** $y = -2x$; $y = 2x - 2$; $y = \dfrac{1}{2}x + 4$

56. $y = -x - 3$; $y = x - 2$; $y = x + 3$ **57.** $y = -\dfrac{2}{3}x + 2$; $y = \dfrac{3}{2}x + 3$; $y = -\dfrac{3}{2}x - 1$

Solve each equation. Check your answer. *(Lesson 11-9)*

58. $2\sqrt{x} = 24$ **59.** $\sqrt{x+15} = \sqrt{4x}$ **60.** $\sqrt{2-x} = x$

Graph each rational function. *(Lesson 12-2)*

61. $y = \dfrac{4}{x}$ **62.** $y = \dfrac{2}{x+1}$ **63.** $y = -\dfrac{1}{x} + 3$

MULTI-STEP TEST PREP

Operations with Rational Expressions and Equations

An Upside-Down World Jamal is studying lenses and their images for a science project. He finds in a science book that a magnifying glass can be used to project upside-down images on a screen. The equation $\frac{1}{f} = \frac{1}{x} + \frac{1}{y}$ relates the focal length of the lens f, the distance of the object from the lens x, and the distance of the image from the lens y. The focal length of Jamal's lens is 10 cm.

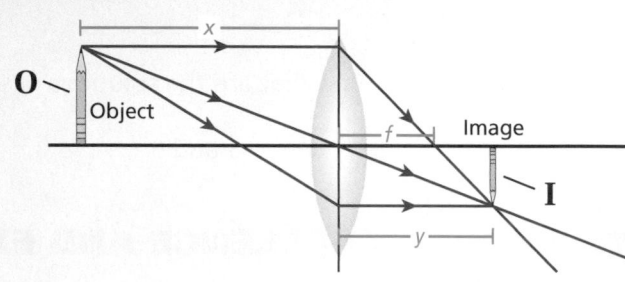

1. Solve the given equation for y using the given value of f.

2. Jamal experiments with a candle, the lens, and a screen. Given that the focal length remains constant, use a table for the x-values 0, 2, 4, 6, 8, 10, 12, 14, and 16 cm. For which x-values are the y-values positive?

3. Graph the function $y(x)$. Label the axes.

Magnification for images is the ratio of the height of the image to the height of the object. This is also equal to the ratio of the distance between the image and the lens and the distance between the object and the lens: $M = \frac{I}{O} = \frac{y}{x}$. I is the height of the image, O is the height of the object, y is the distance of the image from the lens, and x is the distance of the object from the lens.

4. If the height of a candle is 15 cm and the projected image of that candle is 37.5 cm, what is the magnification of the lens?

5. As Jamal moves the candle further from the lens (increases x), and the distance between the lens and the screen decreases (y decreases), does the magnification M stay the same, increase, or decrease?

READY TO GO ON?

Quiz for Lessons 12-4 Through 12-7

✓ 12-4 Multiplying and Dividing Rational Expressions

Multiply. Simplify your answer.

1. $\dfrac{n+3}{n-5} \cdot (n^2 - 5n)$

2. $\dfrac{8}{2x+6} \cdot (x^2 + 6x + 9)$

3. $\dfrac{5a^2 b^3}{ab^5} \cdot \dfrac{2a^4 bc^5}{20c}$

4. $\dfrac{6xy^2}{2x^2 y^6} \cdot \dfrac{6x^4 y^4}{9x^3}$

5. $\dfrac{3h^3 - 6h}{10g^2} \cdot \dfrac{4g}{gh^2 - 2g}$

6. $\dfrac{m^2 + m - 2}{m^2 - 2m - 8} \cdot \dfrac{m^2 - 8m + 16}{3m - 3}$

Divide. Simplify your answer.

7. $\dfrac{2}{n^3} \div \dfrac{n-6}{n^5}$

8. $\dfrac{2x^2 + 8x + 6}{x} \div \dfrac{2x^2 + 2x}{x^3 - x^2}$

9. $\dfrac{8b^3 c}{b^2 c} \div (4b^2 + 4b)$

✓ 12-5 Adding and Subtracting Rational Expressions

Add or subtract. Simplify your answer.

10. $\dfrac{15}{2p} - \dfrac{13}{2p}$

11. $\dfrac{3m^2}{4m^5} + \dfrac{5m^2}{4m^5}$

12. $\dfrac{x^2 + 8x}{x - 2} - \dfrac{3x + 14}{x - 2}$

13. $\dfrac{2t}{4t^2} + \dfrac{2}{t}$

14. $\dfrac{m^2 - m - 2}{m^2 + 6m + 5} - \dfrac{2}{m + 5}$

15. $\dfrac{4x}{x - 2} + \dfrac{3x}{2 - x}$

16. Julianne competes in a biathlon that consists of a 25-mile running leg and a 45-mile biking leg. Julianne averages 3 times the rate of speed on her bike that she does on her feet. Let r represent Julianne's running rate of speed. Write and simplify an expression, in terms of r, that represents the time it takes for Julianne to complete both legs of the race. Then determine how long it will take Julianne to complete the race if she runs an average of 10 mi/h.

✓ 12-6 Dividing Polynomials

Divide.

17. $(6d^2 + 4d) \div 2d$

18. $(15x^4 + 3x^3 - x) \div (-3x^2)$

19. $(2x^2 - 7x - 4) \div (2x + 1)$

Divide using long division.

20. $(a^2 + 3a - 10) \div (a - 2)$

21. $(4y^2 - 9) \div (2y - 3)$

22. $(2x^2 + 5x - 8) \div (x + 2)$

✓ 12-7 Solving Rational Equations

Solve. Identify any extraneous solutions.

23. $\dfrac{3}{x} = \dfrac{4}{x - 1}$

24. $\dfrac{1}{x} = \dfrac{2}{x^2}$

25. $\dfrac{2}{t} + \dfrac{4}{3t} = \dfrac{4}{t + 2}$

26. $\dfrac{4}{n^2} = \dfrac{7}{n} + 2$

27. $\dfrac{d + 2}{d + 8} = \dfrac{-6}{d + 8}$

28. $\dfrac{x - 6}{x^2 - 6} = \dfrac{-4}{x - 4}$

29. It takes Dustin 2 hours to shovel the snow from his driveway and sidewalk. It takes his sister 3 hours to shovel the same area. How long will it take them to shovel the walk if they work together?

Trigonometric Ratios

Objectives
Find the three basic trigonometric ratios in a right triangle.

Use trigonometric ratios to find missing lengths.

Vocabulary
trigonometric ratios
sine
cosine
tangent

A **trigonometric ratio** is a ratio of the lengths of two sides in a right triangle. Three basic trigonometric ratios are *sine, cosine,* and *tangent,* abbreviated *sin, cos,* and *tan,* respectively.

Trigonometric Ratios

$$\sin A = \frac{\text{leg opposite } \angle A}{\text{hypotenuse}} = \frac{a}{c}$$

$$\cos A = \frac{\text{leg adjacent to } \angle A}{\text{hypotenuse}} = \frac{b}{c}$$

$$\tan A = \frac{\text{leg opposite } \angle A}{\text{side adjacent to } \angle A} = \frac{a}{b}$$

EXAMPLE 1 Finding the Value of a Trigonometric Ratio

Find each trigonometric ratio to the nearest thousandth.

A $\sin A$
$$\sin A = \frac{\text{opposite}}{\text{hypotenuse}} = \frac{3}{5} = 0.600$$

B $\cos A$
$$\cos A = \frac{\text{adjacent}}{\text{hypotenuse}} = \frac{4}{5} = 0.800$$

C $\tan A$
$$\tan A = \frac{\text{opposite}}{\text{adjacent}} = \frac{3}{4} = 0.750$$

 1. Use the figure above to find $\sin B$, $\cos B$ and $\tan B$.

EXAMPLE 2 *Aviation Application*

A plane takes off with a 9° angle of ascent. What is the plane's altitude when it has covered a horizontal distance of 184,800 feet? Round your answer to the nearest foot.

Helpful Hint

To find trigonometric ratios on a graphing calculator, press
SIN, **COS**, or **TAN**
and then the value of the degree. Be sure your calculator is in Degree mode.

Draw a diagram to model the problem.

$$\tan A = \frac{\text{opposite}}{\text{adjacent}}$$

$$\tan 9° = \frac{h}{184,800}$$

$184,800(\tan 9°) = h$ *Multiply both sides by 184,800.*

$29,269.4 \approx h$ *Simplify the left side with a calculator.*

The plane's altitude is about 29,269 feet.

2. Construction A 14-foot ladder is leaning against a building. The ladder makes a 70° angle with the ground. How far is the base of the ladder from the building? Round your answer to the nearest tenth of a foot.

EXTENSION
Exercises

Use the diagram for Exercises 1 and 2.

1. Find sin A, cos A, and tan A to the nearest thousandth.

2. Find sin B, cos B, and tan B to the nearest thousandth.

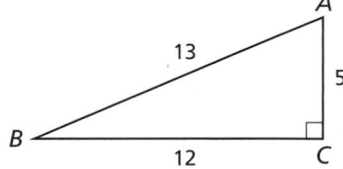

Find the value of x. Round answers to the nearest tenth.

3.

4.

5.

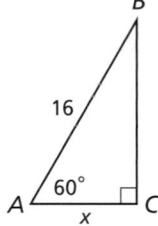

6. Diving If a submarine travels 3 miles while rising to the surface at a 9° angle, how deep was the submarine when it started? Round your answer to the nearest tenth of a mile.

7. Construction A wheelchair ramp is to have an angle of 4.5° with the ground. The deck at the top of the ramp is 20 inches above ground level.

a. Draw a diagram to illustrate the situation.

b. How long should the ramp be? Round your answer to the nearest tenth of an inch.

c. How far from the deck should the ramp begin? Round your answer to the nearest tenth of an inch.

8. Navigation The top of a lighthouse is 40 meters above sea level. The angle of elevation from a fishing boat to the top of the lighthouse is 20°. How far is the fishing boat from the base of the lighthouse? Round your answer to the nearest tenth of a meter.

 9. Write About It What would have to be true about the legs of a right triangle for an angle to have a tangent of 1? What would be the measure of that angle?

Study Guide: Review

Vocabulary

Complete the sentences below with vocabulary words from the list above.

1. A(n) ___?___ is an algebraic expression whose numerator and denominator are polynomials.

2. A function whose rule is a quotient of polynomials in which the denominator has a degree of at least 1 is a(n) ___?___ .

3. A(n) ___?___ is an equation that contains one or more rational expressions.

4. A(n) ___?___ is a relationship that can be written in the form $y = \frac{k}{x}$, where k is a nonzero constant.

5. A function is a ___?___ if its graph contains one or more jumps, breaks, or holes.

12-1 Inverse Variation (pp. 871–877)

EXAMPLE

■ Write and graph the inverse variation in which $y = 2$ when $x = 3$.

$y = \frac{k}{x}$ *Use the form $y = \frac{k}{x}$.*

$2 = \frac{k}{3}$ *Substitute known values.*

$6 = k$ *Multiply by 3 to find the value of k.*

$y = \frac{6}{x}$ *Substitute 6 for k in $y = \frac{k}{x}$.*

x	−6	−3	−2	−1	0	1	2	3	6
y	−1	−2	−3	−6	und.	6	3	2	1

Make a table of values and plot the points.

EXERCISES

Tell whether each relationship represents an inverse variation. Explain.

6.

x	y
4	−3
−12	1
6	−2

7.

x	y
2	4
6	8
10	12

8. Write and graph the inverse variation in which $y = 4$ when $x = -1$.

9. Write and graph the inverse variation in which $y = \frac{1}{2}$ when $x = 2$.

10. Let $x_1 = 5$, $y_1 = -6$, and $x_2 = 2$. Let y vary inversely as x. Find y_2.

11. The number of fleet vehicles a town can afford to buy varies inversely as the price of each car. If the town can afford 3 cars priced at $22,000 each, what must the price of a car be in order for the town to purchase 5 of them?

12-2 Rational Functions (pp. 878–885)

EXAMPLE

■ Graph the function $y = \dfrac{1}{x+1} + 3$.

Since the numerator is 1, use the asymptotes and translate $y = \dfrac{1}{x}$.

Find the asymptotes.

$x = -1 \qquad b = -1$
$y = 3 \qquad c = 3$

Graph the asymptotes. Draw smooth curves to show the translation.

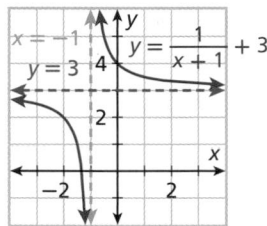

EXERCISES

Identify the excluded values and the vertical and horizontal asymptotes for each rational function.

12. $y = \dfrac{1}{x+4}$

13. $y = \dfrac{1}{x+1} + 3$

14. $y = \dfrac{-5}{2x+6} - 4$

15. $y = \dfrac{2}{4x-7} + 5$

Graph each function.

16. $y = \dfrac{3}{x}$

17. $y = \dfrac{4}{x+5}$

18. $y = \dfrac{1}{x+4} - 2$

19. $y = \dfrac{1}{x-6} + 2$

20. A rectangle has an area of 24 cm². If x represents the width, then $y = \dfrac{24}{x}$ represents the length y. Describe the reasonable domain and range values and graph the function.

12-3 Simplifying Rational Expressions (pp. 886–892)

EXAMPLE

Simplify the rational expression, if possible. Identify any excluded values.

■ $\dfrac{x-1}{x^2 + 2x - 3}$

$\dfrac{x-1}{(x+3)(x-1)}$ *Factor the denominator.*

$\dfrac{x-1^{1}}{(x+3)(x-1)^{1}}$ *Divide out common factors.*

$\dfrac{1}{x+3}$ *Simplify.*

Identify the excluded values.

$x^2 + 2x - 3 = 0$ *To find excluded values, set the denominator equal to 0.*

$(x+3)(x-1) = 0$ *Factor.*

$x + 3 = 0 \text{ or } x - 1 = 0$ *Use the Zero Product Property.*

$x = -3 \text{ or } x = 1$ *Solve each equation for x.*

The excluded values are −3 and 1.

EXERCISES

Find any excluded values of each rational expression.

21. $\dfrac{3}{5p}$

22. $\dfrac{-2}{r-7}$

23. $\dfrac{t}{t^2 - t}$

24. $\dfrac{-4}{x^2 - 4x - 5}$

25. $\dfrac{x-1}{x^2 - 25}$

26. $\dfrac{x+4}{x^2 - 11x + 28}$

Simplify each rational expression, if possible. Identify any excluded values.

27. $\dfrac{7r^2}{21r^3}$

28. $\dfrac{3k^2}{6k^3 - 9k^2}$

29. $\dfrac{x+6}{x^2 + 4x - 12}$

30. $\dfrac{2x-6}{9 - x^2}$

31. $\dfrac{3x+15}{x^2 + 4x - 5}$

32. $\dfrac{x^2 + 9x + 18}{x^2 + x - 30}$

33. What is the ratio of the area of the square to the area of the circle?

12-4 Multiplying and Dividing Rational Expressions (pp. 898–904)

EXAMPLES

■ Multiply. Simplify your answer.

$$\frac{5x^3 - 10x}{4x} \cdot \frac{6x^2}{7x^4 - 14x^2}$$

$$\frac{5x(x^2 - 2)}{4x} \cdot \frac{6x^2}{7x^2(x^2 - 2)} \qquad \textit{Factor.}$$

$$\frac{5\cancel{x}^1 (\cancel{x^2 - 2})^1}{\cancel{4}^2\cancel{x}^1} \cdot \frac{\cancel{6}^3\cancel{x}^{2^1}}{7\cancel{x}^{2^1} (\cancel{x^2 - 2})^1} \qquad \begin{array}{l}\textit{Divide out}\\ \textit{common factors.}\end{array}$$

$$\frac{15}{14} \qquad \textit{Simplify.}$$

■ Divide. Simplify your answer.

$$\frac{32x^2y^2}{7z} \div \frac{2xy^2}{28xz^3}$$

$$\frac{32x^2y^2}{7z} \cdot \frac{28xz^3}{2xy^2} \qquad \begin{array}{l}\textit{Multiply by the}\\ \textit{reciprocal.}\end{array}$$

$$\cdot \frac{\cancel{32}^{16} x^2 y^{2^1}}{\cancel{7}^1 \cancel{z}^1} \cdot \frac{\cancel{28}^4 \cancel{x}^1 z^{3^{z^2}}}{\cancel{2}^1 \cancel{x}^1 \cancel{y}^{2^1}} \qquad \begin{array}{l}\textit{Divide out common}\\ \textit{factors.}\end{array}$$

$$64x^2z^2 \qquad \textit{Simplify.}$$

EXERCISES

Multiply. Simplify your answer.

34. $\frac{2b}{3b - 6} \cdot (b^2 - b - 2)$ **35.** $\frac{4x}{3x + 9} \cdot (x^2 - 9)$

36. $\frac{5ab^2}{2ab} \cdot \frac{3a^2b^2}{a^2b}$ **37.** $\frac{3c}{2d} \cdot \frac{-4c^2d}{8d^2}$

38. $\frac{b + 2}{2b^2 + 12b} \cdot \frac{b^2 + 2b - 24}{b^2 - 16}$

39. $\frac{n^2 - n - 12}{n^2 + 2n - 24} \cdot \frac{n^2 + 3n + 2}{n^2 - 4n - 21}$

Divide. Simplify your answer.

40. $\frac{3b + b^2}{b + 3b^2} \div \frac{b^2 - 9}{3b + 1}$ **41.** $\frac{7}{y} \div \frac{21}{y^3}$

42. $16n^3 \div \frac{4m^2n}{3mn}$ **43.** $\frac{x^2 + 2x - 3}{4x} \div \frac{x^2 - 4}{x}$

44. A bag contains red and blue marbles. It has 8 more red marbles than blue marbles. Veronica reaches into the bag and selects one marble at random. She sets the marble aside and then selects another. What is the probability that she selects two red marbles?

12-5 Adding and Subtracting Rational Expressions (pp. 905–911)

EXAMPLES

Add or subtract. Simplify your answer.

■ $\frac{7x}{3xy} - \frac{x^2 - 3x}{3xy}$

$$\frac{7x - (x^2 - 3x)}{3xy} \qquad \textit{Subtract numerators.}$$

$$\frac{7x - x^2 + 3x}{3xy} \qquad \textit{Distribute.}$$

$$\frac{10x - x^2}{3xy} \qquad \textit{Simplify.}$$

■ $\frac{3w}{w - 5} + \frac{4}{w^2 - 2w - 15}$

$$\frac{3w}{w - 5} + \frac{4}{(w - 5)(w + 3)} \qquad \begin{array}{l}\textit{Factor to find the}\\ \textit{LCD.}\end{array}$$

$$\frac{3w(w + 3)}{(w - 5)(w + 3)} + \frac{4}{(w - 5)(w + 3)} \qquad \begin{array}{l}\textit{Write each}\\ \textit{expression}\\ \textit{using the}\\ \textit{LCD.}\end{array}$$

$$\frac{3w^2 + 9w}{(w - 5)(w + 3)} + \frac{4}{(w - 5)(w + 3)}$$

$$\frac{3w^2 + 9w + 4}{(w - 5)(w + 3)} \qquad \textit{Add and simplify.}$$

EXERCISES

Find the LCM of the given expressions.

45. $5a^2b, 10ab^2$ **46.** $2x^2 - 6x, 5x - 15$

Add or subtract. Simplify your answer.

47. $\frac{b^2}{2b} + \frac{8}{2b}$ **48.** $\frac{3x^2 - 4}{x^2 - 2} + \frac{2x}{x^2 - 2}$

49. $\frac{8p}{p^2 - 4p + 2} - \frac{2}{p^2 - 4p + 2}$

50. $\frac{3b + 4}{7 - b} - \frac{5 - 2b}{7 - b}$ **51.** $\frac{n - 5}{n^2 - 1} - \frac{n + 5}{n^2 - 1}$

52. $\frac{3}{5m} + \frac{m + 2}{10m^2}$ **53.** $\frac{h^2 + 2h}{h - 5} - \frac{3h - 1}{5 - h}$

54. A scout troop hikes 10 miles to the top of a mountain. Because the return trip is downhill, the troop is able to hike 3 times faster on their way down. Let r represent the troop's rate to the mountaintop. Write and simplify an expression for the round-trip hiking time in terms of r.

12-6 Dividing Polynomials (pp. 913–919)

EXAMPLES

Divide.

- $(6x^4 - 9x^3 + 3x^2) \div 3x$

$$\frac{6x^4 - 9x^3 + 3x^2}{3x}$$ *Write as a rational expression.*

$$\frac{6x^4}{3x} - \frac{9x^3}{3x} + \frac{3x^2}{3x}$$ *Divide each term separately.*

$$\frac{\cancel{6}^2 x^{\cancel{4}x^3}}{\cancel{3}^1 x^{\cancel{1}}} - \frac{\cancel{9}^3 x^{\cancel{3}x^2}}{\cancel{3}^1 x^{\cancel{1}}} + \frac{\cancel{3}^1 x^{\cancel{2}x}}{\cancel{3}^1 x^{\cancel{1}}}$$ *Divide out common factors.*

$$2x^3 - 3x^2 + x$$ *Simplify.*

- $(4x^3 - 2x^2 + 5x - 1) \div (x - 2)$

$$
\begin{array}{r}
4x^2 + 6x + 17 \\
x - 2 \overline{)\, 4x^3 - 2x^2 + 5x - 1} \\
\underline{-(4x^3 - 8x^2)} \\
6x^2 + 5x \\
\underline{-(6x^2 - 12x)} \\
17x - 1 \\
\underline{-(17x - 34)} \\
33
\end{array}
$$

$$4x^2 + 6x + 17 + \frac{33}{x - 2}$$

EXERCISES

Divide.

55. $(4n^3 - 6n^2 - 10n) \div 2n$

56. $(-5x^3 + 10x - 25) \div (-5x^2)$

57. $\dfrac{x^2 - 8x - 20}{x - 10}$

58. $\dfrac{6n^2 - 13n - 5}{2n - 5}$

59. $\dfrac{h^2 - 144}{h - 12}$

60. $\dfrac{9x^2 + 12x + 4}{3x + 2}$

61. $\dfrac{m^2 - 2m - 24}{m + 4}$

62. $\dfrac{3m^2 + m - 4}{m - 1}$

Divide using long division.

63. $(x^2 + 5x + 6) \div (x + 3)$

64. $(x^2 + x - 30) \div (x - 5)$

65. $(p^2 + 2p - 8) \div (p + 4)$

66. $(2x^2 + 3x - 5) \div (x + 2)$

67. $(2n^2 - 3n + 1) \div (n - 5)$

68. $(3b^3 - 4b + 2) \div (b - 2)$

69. $(2x^2 - 4x^3 + 3x) \div (x + 2)$

12-7 Solving Rational Equations (pp. 920–925)

EXAMPLE

Solve. Identify any extraneous solutions.

- $\dfrac{3}{x + 3} - 4 = \dfrac{2}{x}$

$$x(x+3)\left(\frac{3}{x+3} - 4\right) = x(x+3)\frac{2}{x}$$

$$x(x+3)\left(\frac{3}{x+3}\right) - x(x+3)4 = x(x+3)\frac{2}{x}$$

$$x\cancel{(x+3)}^1\left(\frac{3}{\cancel{x+3}^1}\right) - x(x+3)4 = \cancel{x}^1(x+3)\frac{2}{\cancel{x}^1}$$

$$3x - 4x(x+3) = 2(x+3)$$
$$3x - 4x^2 - 12x = 2x + 6$$
$$0 = 4x^2 + 11x + 6$$
$$0 = (4x+3)(x+2)$$

$$4x + 3 = 0 \text{ or } x + 2 = 0$$
$$x = -\frac{3}{4} \text{ or } x = -2$$ *$x \neq -3$ or 0, so there are no extraneous solutions.*

EXERCISES

Solve. Identify any extraneous solutions.

70. $-4 = \dfrac{3}{r}$

71. $\dfrac{6}{7} = \dfrac{x}{2}$

72. $\dfrac{6}{b} = \dfrac{-5}{3 + b}$

73. $\dfrac{7}{3y^2} = \dfrac{-2}{y}$

74. $\dfrac{2}{x - 1} = \dfrac{3x}{1 - x}$

75. $\dfrac{2x}{x^2} + \dfrac{1}{x^2} = 3$

76. $\dfrac{2}{3} + \dfrac{4}{x} = \dfrac{6}{3x}$

77. $-\dfrac{1}{3x} + \dfrac{x}{4} = -\dfrac{1}{12x}$

78. $\dfrac{2}{3b} + 4 = \dfrac{1}{3b}$

79. $\dfrac{4}{x - 4} = \dfrac{8}{x^2 - 16}$

80. $\dfrac{5x - 10}{x + 1} = \dfrac{x}{2}$

81. $\dfrac{2x}{x + 3} + \dfrac{x}{4} = \dfrac{3}{x + 3}$

82. $\dfrac{9m}{m - 5} = 7 - \dfrac{3}{m - 5}$

83. $\dfrac{x - 4}{x^2 - 4} = \dfrac{-2}{x - 2}$

Study Guide: Review   **933**

1. Write and graph the inverse variation in which $y = -4$ when $x = 2$.

2. The number of posters the Spanish Club can buy varies inversely as the cost of each poster. The club can buy 15 posters that cost $2.60 each. How many posters can the club buy if they cost $3.25 each?

Identify the excluded values and the vertical and horizontal asymptotes for each rational function.

3. $y = \dfrac{3}{x + 1}$

4. $y = \dfrac{1}{2x - 1} + 5$

5. $y = \dfrac{1}{x + 3} - 3$

Simplify each rational expression, if possible. Identify any excluded values.

6. $\dfrac{2b}{4b^2}$

7. $\dfrac{x^2 - 16}{x^2 + 3x - 4}$

8. $\dfrac{b^2 - 2b - 15}{5 - b}$

9. $\dfrac{x^2 + 4x - 5}{x^2 - 25}$

Multiply. Simplify your answer.

10. $\dfrac{-4}{x^2 - 9} \cdot (x - 3)$

11. $\dfrac{2a^2b^2}{5b^3} \cdot \dfrac{15a^2b}{8a^4}$

12. $\dfrac{x^2 - x - 12}{x^2 - 16} \cdot \dfrac{x^2 + x - 12}{x^2 + 3x + 2}$

Divide. Simplify your answer.

13. $\dfrac{4x^2y^4}{3xy^2} \div \dfrac{12xy}{15x^3y^2}$

14. $\dfrac{3b^2 - 6b}{2b^3 + 3b^2} \div \dfrac{2b - 4}{8b + 12}$

15. $\dfrac{x^2 + 2x - 15}{x^2 - 9} \div \dfrac{x^2 - 25}{x^2 + 3x + 2}$

Add or subtract. Simplify your answer.

16. $\dfrac{b^2 + 3}{5b} + \dfrac{4}{5b}$

17. $\dfrac{5x - 2}{x^2 + 2} - \dfrac{2x}{x^2 + 2}$

18. $\dfrac{2}{3x^2} - \dfrac{5 - 2x}{3x^2}$

19. $\dfrac{3m}{2m^2} + \dfrac{1}{2m}$

20. $\dfrac{3x}{2x + 4} - \dfrac{1}{x + 2}$

21. $\dfrac{y^2 + 4}{y - 3} + \dfrac{y^2}{3 - y}$

Divide.

22. $(8t^2 - 2t) \div 2t$

23. $\dfrac{3x^2 + 2x - 8}{x + 2}$

24. $\dfrac{k^2 - 2k - 35}{k + 5}$

Divide using long division.

25. $(2w^2 + 5w - 12) \div (w + 4)$

26. $(x^2 - 4x + 9) \div (x + 2)$

27. The area of a rectangle can be modeled by $A(x) = x^3 - 1$. The length is $x - 1$.

    a. Find a polynomial to represent the width of the rectangle.

    b. Find the width when x is 6 cm.

Solve. Identify any extraneous solutions.

28. $\dfrac{2}{x - 1} = \dfrac{9}{2x - 3}$

29. $\dfrac{3}{n - 1} = \dfrac{n}{n + 4}$

30. $\dfrac{2}{n + 2} = \dfrac{n - 4}{n^2 - 4}$

31. Julio can wash and wax the family car in 2 hours. It takes Leo 4 hours to wash and wax the same car. How long will it take them to wash and wax the car if they work together?

COLLEGE ENTRANCE EXAM PRACTICE

FOCUS ON SAT MATHEMATICS SUBJECT TESTS

The topics covered on each SAT Mathematics Subject Test vary only slightly each time the test is given. Find out the general distribution of test items across topics, and then identify the areas you need to concentrate on while studying.

HOT TIP!

To prepare for the SAT Math Subject Tests, start reviewing material several months before your test date. Take sample tests to find the areas you need to focus on. You are not expected to have studied all topics on the test.

You may want to time yourself as you take this practice test. It should take you about 6 minutes to complete.

---

1. Which set of ordered pairs satisfies an inverse variation?

   (A) $(6, 3)$ and $(8, 4)$

   (B) $(2, -3)$ and $(4, 5)$

   (C) $(4, -2)$ and $(-5, 10)$

   (D) $(2, 6)$ and $(-3, -4)$

   (E) $\left(4, \frac{1}{4}\right)$ and $\left(-4, \frac{1}{4}\right)$

---

2. If $\dfrac{3}{x+3} = \dfrac{7x}{x^2-9}$, what is x?

   (A) -12

   (B) -3

   (C) $-\dfrac{9}{4}$

   (D) $\dfrac{9}{4}$

   (E) 3

---

3. What is h if $\left(x^3 + 2x^2 - 4x + h\right) \div (x + 1)$ has a remainder of 15?

   (A) -10

   (B) -5

   (C) 5

   (D) 10

   (E) 20

---

4. The graph of which function is shown?

   (A) $f(x) = \dfrac{2}{x+4} + 1$

   (B) $f(x) = \dfrac{4}{x+2} - 1$

   (C) $f(x) = \dfrac{4}{x-2} + 1$

   (D) $f(x) = \dfrac{4}{x-2} - 1$

   (E) $f(x) = \dfrac{2}{x-4} + 1$

---

5. Which function has the same graph as $f(x) = \dfrac{x^2 - 4x - 5}{x^2 - 3x - 10}$ except at $x = 5$?

   (A) $g(x) = \dfrac{x-1}{x-2}$

   (B) $g(x) = \dfrac{x+1}{x+2}$

   (C) $g(x) = \dfrac{x+1}{(x-5)(x+2)}$

   (D) $g(x) = \dfrac{(x+5)(x-1)}{x+2}$

   (E) $g(x) = \dfrac{(x-5)(x+1)}{x-2}$

TEST TACKLER

Standardized Test Strategies

Multiple Choice: Choose Combinations of Answers

Some multiple-choice test items require selecting a combination of correct answers. The correct response is the most complete option available. To solve this type of test item, determine if each statement is true or false. Then choose the option that includes each correct statement.

EXAMPLE

Which of the following has an excluded value of -5?

I. $\dfrac{5}{x-5}$

III. $\dfrac{x^2-10}{5x+25} \cdot \dfrac{5}{x+10}$

II. $\dfrac{8x^2+36x-20}{2(x+5)}$

IV. $\dfrac{2(x+2)}{2x^2+12x+10}$

(A) I only

(C) II, III, and IV

(B) II and III

(D) III and IV

Look at each statement separately and determine whether it is true. You can keep track of which statements are true in a table.

Statement I
The denominator, $x-5$, equals 0 when $x=5$.

Statement I does not answer the question, so it is false.

Statement II
The denominator, $2(x+5)$, equals 0 when $x=-5$.

Statement II does answer the question, so it is true.

Statement	True/False
I	False
II	True
III	True
IV	True

Statement III
The denominator, $(5x+25)(x+10)$, equals 0 when $x=-5$ or $x=-10$.

Statement III does answer the question, so it is true.

Statement IV
The denominator, $2x^2+12x+10$, can be factored as $2(x+5)(x+1)$. This expression equals 0 when $x=-5$ or $x=-1$.

Statement IV does answer the question, so it is true.

Statements II, III, and IV are all true. Option C is the correct response because it includes all the true statements.

Options B and D contain some of the true statements, but option C is the **most complete** answer.

Evaluate all of the statements before deciding on an answer choice. Make a table to keep track of whether each statement is true or false.

Read each test item and answer the questions that follow.

Item A

Which dimensions represent a rectangle that has an area equivalent to the expression $2x^2 + 18x + 16$?

I. $\ell = x + 8$

  $w = 2(x + 1)$

II. $\ell = 2x + 2$

  $w = \dfrac{x^2 + 3x - 40}{x - 5}$

III. $\ell = x + 2$

  $w = \dfrac{(2x + 2)(x + 4)}{1} \cdot \dfrac{3x - 1}{3x^2 - 11x - 4}$

(A) I only

(B) III only

(C) I and II

(D) I, II, and III

---

1. How do you determine the area of a rectangle?

2. Daisy realized that the area of rectangle I was equivalent to the given area and selected option A as her response. Do you agree? Explain your reasoning.

3. Write a simplified expression for the width of rectangle II.

4. Explain each step for determining the area of rectangle III.

5. If rectangle II has an area equivalent to the given expression, then which options can you eliminate?

Item B

Which expression is undefined for $x = 3$ or $x = -2$?

I. $2x + 12 \cdot \dfrac{4}{2(x - 3)(x + 6)}$

III. $\dfrac{x - 2}{(x + 2)(x - 1)}$

II. $\dfrac{9x - 1}{x^2 + 3}$

IV. $\dfrac{14}{x^2 - x - 6}$

(F) I, III, and IV

(H) III and IV

(G) I and II

(J) I and IV

---

6. When is an expression undefined?

7. Henry determined that statement I is undefined when $x = 3$. He decides it is an incorrect answer because the expression is defined when $x = -2$. Should he select option H by process of elimination? Explain your reasoning.

8. Make a table to determine the correct response.

Item C

Which rational function has a graph with a horizontal asymptote of $y = 4$?

I. $y = \dfrac{-4}{x}$

III. $y = \dfrac{1}{x - 4}$

II. $y = \dfrac{1}{x} + 4$

IV. $y = -\dfrac{1}{x} + 4$

(A) I and III

(C) I and II

(B) II only

(D) II and IV

---

9. Where does the horizontal asymptote of the function in statement I occur?

10. Using your answer from Problem 9, which option(s) can you eliminate? Explain your reasoning.

11. Look at the options remaining. Which statement would be best to check next? Explain your reasoning.

STANDARDIZED TEST PREP

CUMULATIVE ASSESSMENT, CHAPTERS 1–12

Multiple Choice

1. Simplify the expression $4(2d - 1) - 6d$.

  (A) $2d$ **(C)** $-4d + 3$

  (B) $2d - 4$ **(D)** $2d - 1$

2. Which equation is the result of solving $3x + 2y = 8$ for y?

  (F) $y = \frac{3}{2}x - 4$ **(H)** $y = -3x + 8$

  (G) $y = 3x + 4$ **(J)** $y = -\frac{3}{2}x + 4$

3. Which function is shown in the graph?

  (A) $y = 3x$

  (B) $y = \frac{x}{3}$

  (C) $y = \sqrt{x} + 3$

  (D) $y = \frac{1}{x} + 3$

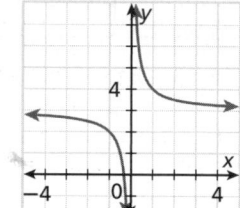

4. The drama club needs to raise at least $1400 for a field trip. The club was given $150 by the school administration. Club members are selling key chains for $5 each. Which inequality represents the number of key chains k that the drama club needs to sell to go on its field trip?

  (F) $150 + 5k \geq 1400$

  (G) $5k - 150 \geq 1400$

  (H) $5k + 150 \leq 1400$

  (J) $150 \leq 5k + 1400$

5. Which expression is NOT equivalent to $\frac{3}{x - 1}$?

  (A) $\frac{3x + 6}{x^2 + x - 2}$ **(C)** $\frac{3x + 3}{x^2 - 1}$

  (B) $\frac{3x - 3}{x^2 - 2x + 1}$ **(D)** $\frac{3x - 3}{x - 1}$

6. Which situation best describes a negative correlation?

  (F) The intensity level of an exercise and the number of Calories burned per minute

  (G) The amount of time that an electronic game is on and the amount of power remaining in the game's batteries

  (H) The height of a tree and the amount of ink in a ballpoint pen

  (J) The daytime temperature and the number of people at an ice cream stand

7. Which expression is equivalent to $\frac{3m^2n}{5m} \cdot \frac{20mn}{n^6}$?

  (A) $\frac{12m^2}{n^4}$ **(C)** $12m^2n^3$

  (B) $\frac{12m^3}{n^3}$ **(D)** $\frac{12m}{n}$

8. Simplify $\frac{3}{x} + \frac{3}{5x}$.

  (F) $\frac{1}{x}$ **(H)** $\frac{18}{5x}$

  (G) $\frac{9}{5x}$ **(J)** $\frac{1}{2x}$

9. Which of the following has a slope of -3?

  (A)   **(C)**

  (B)   **(D)**

10. What is $(-12x^6 + x) \div (-4x^2)$?

  (F) $3x^3 - \frac{1}{4x}$ **(H)** $3x^5$

  (G) $3x^4 - \frac{1}{4x}$ **(J)** $3x^4 + x$

11. Abe flips two coins. What is the probability of both coins landing heads up?

　Ⓐ $\frac{1}{2}$　　　　　Ⓒ $\frac{1}{8}$

　Ⓑ $\frac{1}{4}$　　　　　Ⓓ $\frac{1}{16}$

12. Which is a solution to $\frac{n}{n+2} = \frac{-8}{n}$?

　Ⓕ -4　　　　　Ⓗ 2

　Ⓖ -2　　　　　Ⓙ 4

13. Which of the following is equivalent to $\left(\frac{2x^5y^2}{8x}\right)^{-2}$?

　Ⓐ $\frac{16}{x^8y^4}$　　　　Ⓒ $\frac{4}{x^4y^2}$

　Ⓑ $\frac{x^8}{16y^4}$　　　　Ⓓ $\frac{x^5}{16}$

14. What situation can be modeled by the function $y = \frac{140}{x}$?

　Ⓕ The cost of attending a ski trip is $140 for each person who attends.

　Ⓖ The area of a rectangle with a width of 140 meters varies directly as its length.

　Ⓗ The cost per person of a boat rental is $140 divided by the number of people.

　Ⓙ Attendance at this year's concert was 140 people more than at last year's concert.

Know the rules for writing gridded-response answers. For example, can you write the fraction $\frac{2}{3}$ as 0.6666 or as 0.67? Different tests may have different rules, so pay close attention to the directions.

Gridded Response

15. What is the excluded value for the rational expression $\frac{x^2-4}{3x-6}$?

16. What is the next term in the geometric sequence 2000, 1600, 1280, 1024,…?

17. What is the constant of variation if y varies inversely as x and $y = 3$ when $x = 6$?

18. What is the value of $4^0 - (2^{-3})$?

19. Identify the excluded value for $y = \frac{x-4}{x-2}$.

Short Response

20. Mr. Lui wrote $\dfrac{15 - 5x}{x^2 - 9x + 18}$ on the board.

　a. Explain what kind of expression it is.

　b. Simplify the expression. Show your work.

　c. Identify any excluded values.

21. Describe the similarities and differences between the graph of $f(x) = x^2 + 4$ and the graph of

　$g(x) = \frac{1}{2}x^2 + 3$.

22. What are 2 values of b that will make $2x^2 - bx - 20$ factorable? Explain your answer.

23. Brandee makes an hourly wage. In the last pay period, she earned $800 for regular hours and $240 for overtime hours. Her overtime rate of pay is 50% more per hour than her regular rate of pay r. Write and simplify an expression, in terms of r, that represents the number of hours h Brandee worked in the pay period. Show your work.

Extended Response

24. Principal Farley has $200 to pay for some teachers to attend a technology conference. The company hosting the conference is allowing 2 teachers to attend for free. The number of teachers y that can be sent to the conference is given by the function $y = \frac{200}{x} + 2$, where x is the cost per teacher.

　a. Describe the reasonable domain and range values for this function.

　b. Identify the vertical and horizontal asymptotes.

　c. Graph the function.

　d. Give two whole-number solutions to the equation and describe what they mean in the context of this situation.

Real-World CONNECTIONS

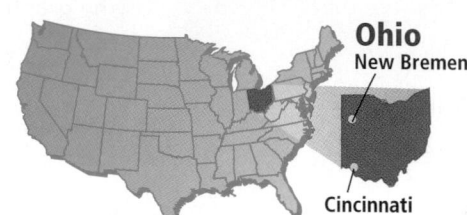

Ohio
New Bremen

Cincinnati

⭐ Cincinnati Reds

Organized in 1866, the Cincinnati Reds, known then as the Cincinnati Red Stockings, were the first major league baseball team. They now play in a stadium built in 2003 called the Great American Ballpark.

Choose one or more strategies to solve each problem.

1. The table shows the total payroll for the Reds from 2000 to 2005. What percent did the total payroll increase from 2000 to 2005?

2. Assume the payroll percent increase for the next x years is the same as from 2004 to 2005. Write an exponential growth function to model this situation.

3. Using the function found in Problem 2, what is the expected total payroll for the Reds in the year 2010?

4. Suppose that at a Cincinnati Reds game, tickets in the blue zone average $28 and tickets in the green zone average $20. Suppose twice as many tickets were sold to fans in the green zone as in the blue zone and the total ticket sales for these two zones was $204,000. Fans bought 14,197 tickets in other zones and sections. How many people had tickets to the game?

Payroll for The Cincinnati Reds	
Year	Total Payroll ($)
2000	44,217,500
2001	48,784,000
2002	45,050,390
2003	59,355,667
2004	46,615,250
2005	61,892,583

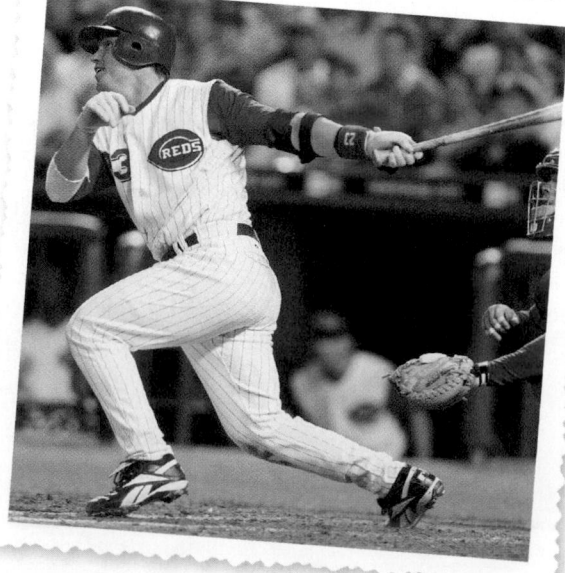

⭐ Bicycle Museum of America

The Bicycle Museum of America in New Bremen, Ohio, is home to one of the largest private collections of bicycles and bicycle memorabilia in the world. The collection represents every era, including antique bicycles from the 1800s, balloon-tire classics of the 1940s and 1950s, and banana-seat bikes with high-rise handlebars from the 1960s.

Choose one or more strategies to solve each problem.

1. Alfred Letourner was one of the top racers of his era. On May 17, 1941, at an event sponsored by Schwinn, Letourner rode a bike similar to the one in the photo with a gear ratio of $9\frac{1}{2}$ to 1. The bike only weighed 20 pounds. At this event, Letourner shattered speed records when he rode a mile in 33.05 seconds. At this pace, about how many miles per hour was Letourner riding?

The diagram shows the relationship between the number of teeth on the pedal gear and the number of teeth on the wheel gear of a bicycle. This relationship affects the speed and effort of pedaling. For example, if the pedal gear has 39 teeth and the wheel gear has 17 teeth, then the gear ratio is $\frac{39}{17} = 2.294$. This number represents the number of turns of the wheel for every full turn of the pedal.

Pedal gears   Wheel gears

39 teeth
53 teeth

14 teeth
16 teeth
19 teeth
21 teeth
23 teeth

2. Which gear combination shown in the diagram would yield the highest number of rotations of the tires to the turn of the pedal? About how many turns of the wheel for every full turn of the pedal can be expected with this combination?

3. If a mountain bike has tires with a diameter of 26 inches, how far, in feet, will a rider travel for each full turn of the pedal if the pedal gear has 39 teeth and the wheel gear has 14 teeth?

Additional Topics

Introduction to Power Functions

Objective
Analyze the characteristics of power functions.

Vocabulary
power function

A **power function** is a function that can be written in the form $f(x) = ax^n$, where a and n are real numbers and $a \neq 0$. This lesson will only address power functions for which n is a positive integer.

Power Functions				
$n = 1$ $y = ax$	$n = 2$ $y = ax^2$	$n = 3$ $y = ax^3$	$n = 4$ $y = ax^4$	$n = 5$ $y = ax^5$

EXAMPLE 1 **Graphing Power Functions**

Graph the power function $y = x^5$, and then describe the graph.

Step 1 Make a table of values.

x	$x^5 = y$
-2	$(-2)^5 = -32$
-1	$(-1)^5 = -1$
0	$0^5 = 0$
1	$1^5 = 1$
2	$2^5 = 32$

The ordered pairs $(-2, -32)$, $(-1, -1)$, $(0, 0)$, $(1, 1)$ and $(2, 32)$ lie on the graph.

Step 2 Sketch the graph by plotting the ordered pairs from the table.

From left to right, the graph increases. It crosses the x-axis once, at the origin.

 1. Graph the power function $y = x^4$, and then describe the graph.

Substituting any real value of x into a power function results in a real number. Therefore, the domain of any power function is all real numbers. The range of a power function depends on the *degree* of the function. The degree of the power function $f(x) = ax^n$ is n.

The table summarizes the possibilities for the range and the maximum and minimum values of a power function.

Range, Maximum Value, and Minimum Value		
Odd Degree	**Even Degree, $a > 0$**	**Even Degree, $a < 0$**
The range is all real numbers. There is no maximum or minimum value.	The graph opens upward. The minimum value is 0. The range is $y \geq 0$.	The graph opens downward. The maximum value is 0. The range is $y \leq 0$.

EXAMPLE 2 Finding Maximum or Minimum Values

Give the domain and range of each power function. Then give the minimum or maximum value, if any.

A $f(x) = -0.5x^7$

The degree, 7, is odd.

The domain is all real numbers. The range is all real numbers. There is no minimum or maximum value.

B $f(x) = -2x^4$

The degree, 4, is even, and $a < 0$.
The domain is all real numbers.
The range is $y \leq 0$.
The maximum value is 0.

Check The graph supports the answer.

C $f(x) = \frac{1}{20}x^6$

The degree, 6, is even, and $a > 0$.
The domain is all real numbers.
The range is $y \geq 0$.
The minimum value is 0.

Check The graph supports the answer.

 CHECK IT OUT! Give the domain and range of each power function. Then give the minimum or maximum value, if any.

2a. $f(x) = -x^8$ **2b.** $f(x) = -2.5x^5$ **2c.** $f(x) = \frac{1}{4}x^{10}$

Graph each power function, and then describe the graph.

1. $y = x^3$

2. $y = x^6$

3. $y = x^7$

Give the domain and range of each power function. Then give the minimum or maximum value, if any.

4. $f(x) = -2x^{11}$

5. $f(x) = -\frac{1}{8}x^{16}$

6. $f(x) = 0.05x^8$

7. Geometry A cube has sides of length x.

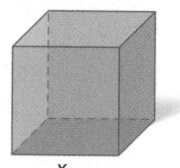

  a. Write a power function f that gives the area of each face of the cube.

  b. Write a power function g that gives the surface area of the cube.

  x

8. Geometry The volume V of a sphere of radius x is given by the power function $V(x) = \frac{4}{3}\pi x^3$. Use a graphing calculator to determine the radius of a sphere that has a volume of 100 cm³. Round your answer to the nearest tenth of a centimeter and explain your method.

Determine whether each statement is always, sometimes, or never true. Explain.

9. A power function has two x-intercepts.

10. A power function has a minimum value of 1.

11. The graph of a power function that passes through the point (a, b) also passes through the point $(-a, -b)$.

12. A power function that has a minimum value has an even degree.

The *end behavior* of a function is a description of the function's values as x increases or decreases. For example, you can describe the end behavior of $f(x) = x^3$ as follows: As x increases, $f(x)$ increases. As x decreases, $f(x)$ decreases.

Describe the end behavior of each power function.

13. $f(x) = -4x^4$

14. $f(x) = \frac{1}{3}x^7$

15. $f(x) = -2x^9$

16. Physics A certain metal sphere sinks in a lake according to the function $d(t) = 2.1t^2$ where t is the time in seconds and $d(t)$ is the depth of the sphere in meters. Sketch a graph of the function. Then give a reasonable domain and range for the function when the sphere is dropped in a lake with a maximum depth of 100 meters.

17. Determine whether the power function $f(x) = -3x^3$ is increasing or decreasing on the interval $-5 \le x \le -1$.

18. Critical Thinking Is a direct variation a power function? Explain why or why not.

19. Graph $f(x) = x^3$, $g(x) = x^3 + 1$, and $h(x) = x^3 - 2$. Make a conjecture, in terms of a transformation, about the effect of b on the graph of $f(x) = ax^3 + b$.

Piecewise and Step Functions

Objective
Recognize, identify, and graph piecewise and step functions.

Vocabulary
piecewise function
step function
greatest-integer function

A **piecewise function** is a function that is a combination of one or more functions. The rule for a piecewise function may be different for different parts of the function's domain.

For example, the absolute value function $y = |x|$ is a piecewise function and can be defined by the following rule:

$$y = \begin{cases} -x \text{ if } x < 0 \\ x \ \ \text{ if } x \geq 0 \end{cases}$$

To evaluate a piecewise function for a given input value, find the interval of the domain that contains the input value and apply the rule for that interval.

EXAMPLE 1   Evaluating a Piecewise Function

For $f(x) = \begin{cases} x^2 + 1 & \text{if } x < 2 \\ -3x + 4 & \text{if } x \geq 2 \end{cases}$, evaluate $f(x)$ for $x = -3$ and $x = 6$.

$f(-3) = (-3)^2 + 1 = 10$ *Because −3 < 2, use the rule for x < 2.*

$f(6) = -3(6) + 4 = -14$ *Because 6 ≥ 2, use the rule for x ≥ 2.*

 1. For $g(x) = \begin{cases} 3x - 3 & \text{if } x < -1 \\ -x^2 & \text{if } x \geq -1 \end{cases}$, evaluate $g(x)$ for $x = -4$ and $x = -1$.

EXAMPLE 2   Graphing a Piecewise Function

Graph $f(x) = \begin{cases} -3 & \text{if } x < 0 \\ x^2 + 1 & \text{if } x \geq 0 \end{cases}$.

This function is composed of two pieces.

For $x < 0$, the function is the constant function $f(x) = -3$. Draw a horizontal ray to the left of $(0, -3)$. Draw an open circle at $(0, -3)$ to show that this point is not part of the graph.

For $x \geq 0$, the function is the quadratic function $f(x) = x^2 + 1$. Draw half of a parabola to the right of $(0, 1)$. Draw a solid circle at $(0, 1)$ to show that this point is part of the graph.

 **2.** Graph $g(x) = \begin{cases} 2x & \text{if } x < 1 \\ x - 1 & \text{if } x \geq 1 \end{cases}$.

The graph and table at right give the price of admission to a theme park. The function is defined differently over different domain intervals (age groups), so the function is a piecewise function.

Theme Park Admission Prices	
Regular admission	$25
Youth (under 15)	$10
Seniors (55 and older)	$20

The function that describes the theme park admission prices is a *step function*. A **step function** is a piecewise function that is constant over each interval in its domain.

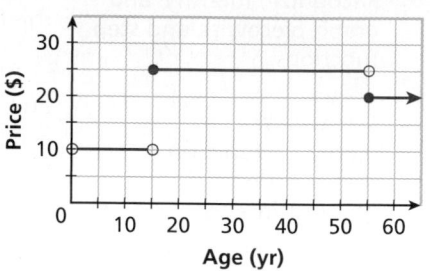

Theme Park Admission Prices

EXAMPLE 3 **Step Functions**

Parking Fees

The graph shows parking fees at a garage. Create a table and a verbal description to represent the graph.

Step 1 Create a table.

Use the endpoints of the segments of the graph to identify the intervals of the domain.

Parking Fees	
Hours x	**Fee** y **($)**
$0 < x \le 2$	3
$2 < x \le 4$	4
$4 < x \le 6$	5
$x > 6$	6

On the graph, an open circle means that a value is not included in the interval. A solid circle means that a value is included in the interval.

Step 2 Write a verbal description.

For any amount of time up to 2 hours, the parking fee is $3. For more than 2 hours and no more than 4 hours, the fee is $4. For more than 4 hours and no more than 6 hours, the fee is $5. For more than 6 hours, the fee is $6.

---

3. The graph shows the shipping costs for books that are ordered online. Create a table and a verbal description to represent the graph.

Shipping Costs

The **greatest-integer function** is a piecewise function, written $f(x) = \lfloor x \rfloor$, in which the number x is rounded down to the greatest integer that is less than or equal to x. For example, $f(3.14) = \lfloor 3.14 \rfloor = 3$. The graph of the greatest-integer function shows that it is a step function.

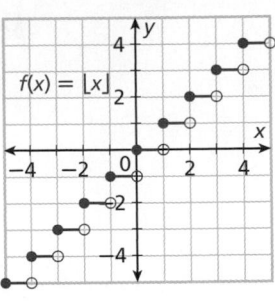

EXAMPLE 4   Using the Greatest-Integer Function

Write a function that gives the number of magazines that you can buy with x dollars if a magazine costs \$3.75. Then use the function to find the number of magazines you can buy with \$20.

The number of magazines you can buy with x dollars is $\frac{x}{3.75}$, rounded down to the greatest integer that is less than or equal to this quotient.

The function is $f(x) = \left\lfloor \dfrac{x}{3.75} \right\rfloor$.

To find how many magazines you can buy with \$20, evaluate $f(x)$ for $x = 20$.

$$f(20) = \left\lfloor \frac{20}{3.75} \right\rfloor = \lfloor 5.\overline{3} \rfloor = 5$$

You can buy 5 magazines with \$20.

CHECK IT OUT!

4. Write a function that gives the number of movie tickets that you can buy with x dollars if a movie ticket costs \$10.95. Then use the function to find the number of movie tickets you can buy with \$50.

A-2   Exercises

Evaluate each function for $x = -2$ and $x = 3$.

1. $f(x) = \begin{cases} 2x + 1 & \text{if } x < 0 \\ -x + 2 & \text{if } x \geq 0 \end{cases}$

2. $g(x) = \begin{cases} -x^2 & \text{if } x \leq -1 \\ 5x & \text{if } x > -1 \end{cases}$

3. $h(x) = \begin{cases} x^2 + 1 & \text{if } x < -3 \\ 2x - 5 & \text{if } x \geq -3 \end{cases}$

4. $f(x) = \begin{cases} -5 & \text{if } x < 3 \\ 3x^2 + 1 & \text{if } x \geq 3 \end{cases}$

Evaluate each function for $x = -1$ and $x = 2$.

5. $f(x) = \begin{cases} 4x - 1 & \text{if } x < -1 \\ -x + 5 & \text{if } -1 \leq x < 2 \\ 3x & \text{if } x \geq 2 \end{cases}$

6. $f(x) = \begin{cases} x^2 & \text{if } x \leq -2 \\ 4x + 6 & \text{if } -2 \leq x \leq 1 \\ \frac{1}{2}x & \text{if } x \geq 1 \end{cases}$

Graph each function.

7. $f(x) = \begin{cases} x - 1 & \text{if } x < 0 \\ 4 & \text{if } x \geq 0 \end{cases}$

8. $f(x) = \begin{cases} -1 & \text{if } x \leq -1 \\ 2x & \text{if } -1 < x \leq 2 \\ x - 4 & \text{if } x > 2 \end{cases}$

Create a table and a verbal description to represent each graph.

9.
Admission Prices

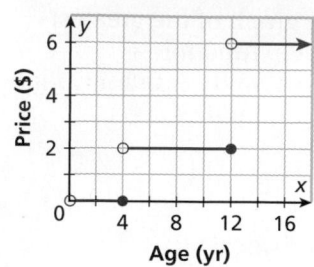

10.
Weeks of Paid Vacation

11. Write a function that gives the number of energy bars that you can buy with x dollars if an energy bar costs $1.35. Then use the function to find the number of energy bars you can buy with $10.

12. The function $g(x) = \left\lfloor \frac{x}{3.95} \right\rfloor$ gives the number of gel pens you can buy with x dollars. What is the price of one gel pen? How many gel pens can you buy with $15?

Write a piecewise function for each graph.

13.

14.

15.

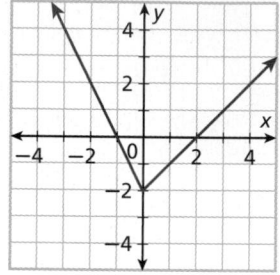

16. Entertainment The cost of admission to a state fair is $4 for children less than 12 years old and $8 for everyone 12 or older.

    a. Write a function that gives the cost of admission for a person who is x years old.

    b. Graph the function.

17. Pet Care The table shows the recommended amount of dog food based on a dog's weight.

    a. Write a function that gives the amount of dog food in cups for a dog that weighs x pounds.

    b. Graph the function.

Recommended Amount of Dog Food	
Weight of dog (lb)	Amount of food (c)
Less than 10	$\frac{1}{2}$
At least 10 and no more than 20	1
More than 20	$1\frac{1}{2}$

18. Travel Carolyn leaves her house and drives for 3 hours at a constant rate of 60 mi/h. Then she stops for 1 hour to have lunch. After lunch, she continues to drive away from her house at a constant rate of 60 mi/h for another 2 hours. Graph a piecewise function that gives Carolyn's distance in miles from her house after x hours.

19. Critical Thinking What are the domain and range of the piecewise function

$$f(x) = \begin{cases} x & \text{if } x < 0 \\ x^2 & \text{if } x \geq 0 \end{cases} ?$$

A-3
Technology LAB
Graphing to Solve Nonlinear Equations

You can use a graphing calculator to solve nonlinear equations, including quadratic and exponential equations.

Activity

Use a graph to solve $x^2 - x - 5 = -3$.

Enter the left side of the equation as **Y1** and the right side as **Y2**.

Press **GRAPH**. The x-values of the points where the graphs intersect (where **Y1 = Y2**) are the solutions of the equation. Notice that there is more than one solution.

To find the coordinates of an intersection point:

CALC
Press **2nd** **TRACE** and select **5:intersect.**

Press **ENTER** to select **Y1**.

Press **ENTER** again to select **Y2**.

Use ◀ and ▶ to move the cursor close to the intersection point.

Press **ENTER**.

One point of intersection is $(-1, -3)$, so one solution is $x = -1$.

Repeat these steps to find the coordinates of the second intersection point. This point is $(2, -3)$, so the second solution is $x = 2$.

The solutions of $x^2 - x - 5 = -3$ are -1 and 2.

Check

$x^2 - x - 5 = -3$	
$(-1)^2 - (-1) - 5$	-3
$1 + 1 - 5$	-3
-3	-3 ✔

$x^2 - x - 5 = -3$	
$(2)^2 - 2 - 5$	-3
$4 - 2 - 5$	-3
-3	-3 ✔

Try This

Use a graph to solve each equation.

1. $x^2 + 6x + 9 = 1$ **2.** $1.5(2)^x = 6$ **3.** $-x^2 + 3x - 4 = -4$

4. $2\left(\dfrac{1}{2}\right)^x = 4$ **5.** $2x^2 + 2x - 12 = -8$ **6.** $\dfrac{2}{3}\left(\dfrac{1}{3}\right)^x = 6$

7. Critical Thinking Explain how you could use a graphing calculator to show that the equation $x^2 - 2x + 4 = 1$ has no real solutions.

8. Critical Thinking Could you use the method described in the activity to solve an equation like $x^2 + 4x = x + 4$? Explain.

Patterns and Recursion

Objective
Identify and extend patterns using recursion.

Vocabulary
recursive pattern

In a **recursive pattern** or *recursive sequence*, each term is defined using one or more previous terms. For example, the sequence 1, 4, 7, 10, 13, ... can be defined recursively as follows: The first term is 1 and each term after the first is equal to the preceding term plus 3.

You can use recursive techniques to identify patterns. The table summarizes the characteristics of four types of patterns.

Using Recursive Techniques to Identify Patterns	
Type of Pattern	**Characteristics**
Linear	First differences are constant.
Quadratic	Second differences are constant.
Cubic	Third differences are constant.
Exponential	Ratios between successive terms are constant.

EXAMPLE 1

Identifying and Extending a Pattern

Identify the type of pattern. Then find the next three numbers in the pattern.

Helpful Hint

You may need to use trial and error when identifying a pattern. If first, second, and third differences are not constant, check for constant ratios.

A 4, 6, 10, 16, 24, ...

Find first, second, and, if necessary, third differences.

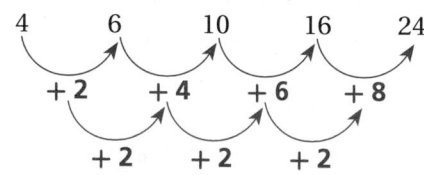

Second differences are constant, so the pattern is quadratic.

Extend the pattern by continuing the sequence of first and second differences.

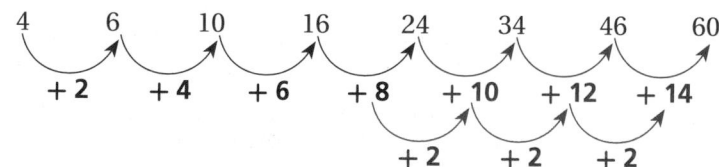

The next three numbers in the pattern are 34, 46, and 60.

B $\frac{1}{8}, \frac{1}{2}, 2, 8, 32$

Find the ratio between successive terms.

$\frac{1}{8} \quad \frac{1}{2} \quad 2 \quad 8 \quad 32$

$\times 4 \quad \times 4 \quad \times 4 \quad \times 4$

Ratios between terms are constant, so the pattern is exponential.

Extend the pattern by continuing the sequence of ratios.

The next three numbers in the pattern are 128, 512, and 2048.

CHECK IT OUT! Identify the type of pattern. Then find the next three numbers in the pattern.

1a. 56, 47, 38, 29, 20, ...   **1b.** 1, 8, 27, 64, 125, ...

You can use a similar process to determine whether a function is linear, quadratic, cubic, or exponential. Note that before comparing y-values, you must first make sure there is a constant change in the corresponding x-values.

Using Recursive Techniques to Identify Functions	
Type of Function	**Characteristics** **(Given a Constant Change in x-values)**
Linear	First differences of y-values are constant.
Quadratic	Second differences of y-values are constant.
Cubic	Third differences of y-values are constant.
Exponential	Ratios between successive y-values are constant.

EXAMPLE 2   Identifying a Function

The ordered pairs {(–4, –4), (0, 0), (4, 4), (8, 32), (12, 108)} satisfy a function. Determine whether the function is linear, quadratic, cubic, or exponential. Then find three additional ordered pairs that satisfy the function.

Make a table. Check for a constant change in the x-values. Then find first, second, and third differences of y-values.

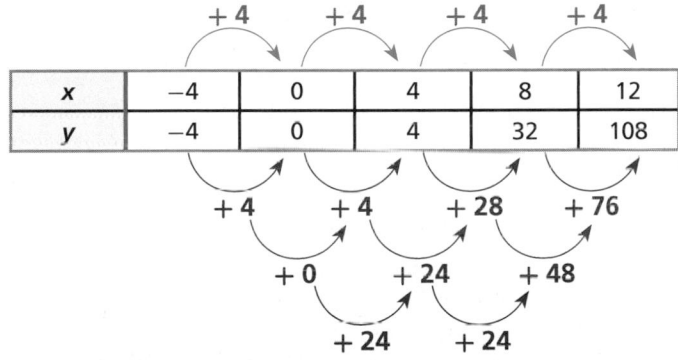

There is a constant change in the x-values. Third differences are constant. The function is a cubic function.

To find additional ordered pairs, extend the pattern by working backward from the constant third differences.

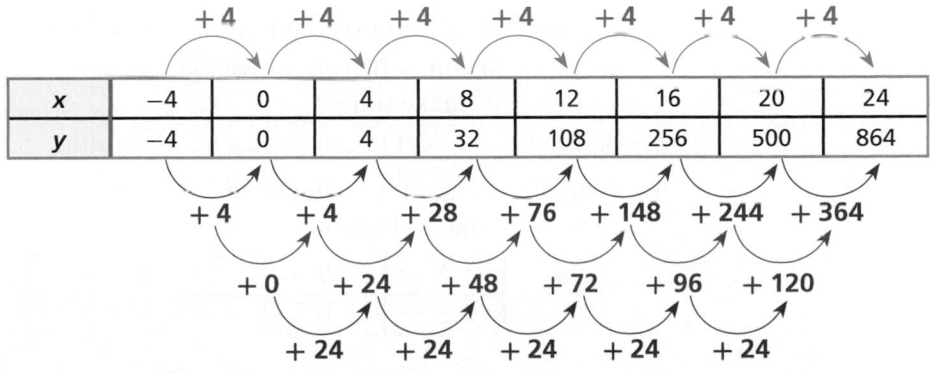

Helpful Hint

In Example 2, the constant third differences are 24. To extend the pattern, first find each second difference by adding 24 to the previous second difference. Then find each first difference by adding the second difference below to the previous first difference.

Three additional ordered pairs that satisfy this function are (16, 256), (20, 500), and (24, 864).

CHECK IT OUT! Several ordered pairs that satisfy a function are given. Determine whether the function is linear, quadratic, cubic, or exponential. Then find three additional ordered pairs that satisfy the function.

2a. {(0, 1), (1, 3), (2, 9), (3, 19), (4, 33)}

2b. $\left\{\left(1, \frac{1}{2}\right), \left(3, \frac{1}{6}\right), \left(5, \frac{1}{18}\right), \left(7, \frac{1}{54}\right), \left(9, \frac{1}{162}\right)\right\}$

A-4 Exercises

Identify the type of pattern. Then find the next three numbers in the pattern.

1. 25, 28, 31, 34, 37, ...

2. 20, 45, 80, 125, 180, ...

3. 128, 64, 32, 16, 8, ...

4. 4, 32, 108, 256, 500, ...

5. $\frac{1}{2}, \frac{3}{4}, 1, 1\frac{1}{4}, 1\frac{1}{2}, \ldots$

6. 0.3, 0.03, 0.003, 0.0003, 0.00003, ...

7. 127, 66, 29, 10, 3, ...

8. 2, 8, 18, 32, 50, ...

Several ordered pairs that satisfy a function are given. Determine whether the function is linear, quadratic, cubic, or exponential. Then find three additional ordered pairs that satisfy the function.

9. {(3, 1), (5, –3), (7, –7), (9, –11), (11, –15)}

10. {(–1, –2), (2, 7), (5, 124), (8, 511), (11, 1330)}

11. $\left\{\left(2, \frac{1}{4}\right), \left(3, \frac{1}{8}\right), \left(4, \frac{1}{16}\right), \left(5, \frac{1}{32}\right), \left(6, \frac{1}{64}\right)\right\}$

12. {(–3, –7), (0, 2), (3, –7), (6, –34), (9, –79)}

13. {(0, 600), (10, 480), (20, 384), (30, 307.2), (40, 245.76)}

14. {(–8, 2), (–5, 7), (–2, 12), (1, 17), (4, 22)}

15. Entertainment The table shows the cost of using an online DVD rental service for different numbers of months.

Online DVD Rentals	
Months	Cost ($)
3	50
6	92
9	134
12	176
15	218

a. Determine whether the function that models the data is linear, quadratic, cubic, or exponential. Explain.

b. Graph the data in the table.

c. What do you notice about your graph? Why does this make sense?

d. Predict the cost of the service for 18 months.

16. A student claimed that the function shown in the table is a quadratic function. Do you agree or disagree? Explain.

x	3	7	10	14	17
y	2	6	12	20	30

+4   +6   +8   +10

+2   +2   +2

17. **Business** The table shows the annual sales for a small company.

Annual Sales	
Year	Sales ($)
2006	513,000
2007	516,000
2008	521,000
2009	528,000
2010	537,000

a. Determine whether the function that models the data is linear, quadratic, cubic, or exponential. Explain.

b. Suppose sales continue to grow according to the pattern in the table. Predict the annual sales for 2011, 2012, and 2013.

c. If the pattern continues, in what year will annual sales be $17,000 greater than the previous year's sales?

18. **Critical Thinking** Use the table for the following problems.

x	0	1	2	3	4
y	3	6			

a. Copy and complete the table so that the function is a linear function.

b. Copy and complete the table so that the function is a quadratic function.

c. Copy and complete the table so that the function is an exponential function.

d. For which of these three types of functions is there more than one correct way to complete the table? Explain.

Use the description to write the first five terms in each numerical pattern.

19. The first term is 8. Each following term is 11 less than the term before it.

20. The first term is 1000. Each following term is 40% of the term before it.

21. The first two terms are 1 and 2. Each following term is the sum of the two terms before it.

Make a table for a function that has the given characteristics. Include at least five ordered pairs.

22. The function is linear. The first differences are -3.

23. The function is quadratic. The second differences are 6.

24. The function is cubic. The third differences are 1.

A *recursive formula* for a sequence shows how to find the value of a term from one or more terms that come before it. For example, the recursive formula $a_n = a_{n-1} + 3$ tells you that each term is equal to the preceding term plus 3. Given that $a_1 = 5$, you can use the formula to generate the sequence 5, 8, 11, 14, ...

Write the first four terms of each sequence.

25. $a_n = a_{n-1} + 2; a_1 = 12$

26. $a_n = a_{n-1} - 7; a_1 = -16$

27. $a_n = 2a_{n-1}; a_1 = 4$

28. $a_n = 0.6a_{n-1}; a_1 = 100$

29. $a_n = 5a_{n-1} - 2; a_1 = 0$

30. $a_n = (a_{n-1})^2; a_1 = -2$

31. A *recursive function* defines a function for whole numbers by referring to the value of the function at previous whole numbers. Consider the recursive function $f(n) = f(n-1) + 5$ with $f(0) = 1$.

a. According to the formula, $f(1) = f(0) + 5$. What is the value of $f(1)$?

b. Use the formula to find $f(2), f(3), f(4)$, and $f(5)$.

c. Graph $f(n)$ by plotting points at $x = 0$, $x = 1$, $x = 2$, $x = 3$, $x = 4$, and $x = 5$.

d. What do you notice about your graph? What does this tell you about $f(n)$?

Linear and Nonlinear Rates of Change

Objectives
Identify linear and nonlinear rates of change.

Compare rates of change.

Recall that a *rate of change* is a ratio that compares the amount of change in a dependent variable to the amount of change in an independent variable.

$$\text{rate of change} = \frac{\text{change in dependent variable}}{\text{change in independent variable}}$$

The table shows the price of one ounce of gold in 2005 and 2008. The year is the independent variable and the price is the dependent variable. The rate of change is $\frac{870-513}{2008-2005} = \frac{357}{3} = 119$, or $119 per year.

Price of Gold	
Year	Price ($/oz)
2005	513
2008	870

E X A M P L E   1   Identifying Constant and Variable Rates of Change

Determine whether each function has a constant or variable rate of change.

A {(0, 0), (1, 4), (3, 8), (6, 8), (8, 6)}

Find the ratio of the amount of change in the dependent variable y to the corresponding amount of change in the independent variable x.

x	y
0	0
1	4
3	8
6	8
8	6

+1) +4
+2) +4
+3) +0
+2) −2

The rates of change are
$\frac{4}{1} = 4, \frac{4}{2} = 2, \frac{0}{3} = 0,$ and $\frac{-2}{2} = -1.$
The function has a variable rate of change.

B {(0, 1), (1, 2), (4, 5), (6, 7), (7, 8)}

Find the ratio of the amount of change in the dependent variable y to the corresponding amount of change in the independent variable x.

x	y
0	1
1	2
4	5
6	7
7	8

+1) +1
+3) +3
+2) +2
+1) +1

The rates of change are
$\frac{1}{1} = 1, \frac{3}{3} = 1, \frac{2}{2} = 1,$ and $\frac{1}{1} = 1.$
The function has a constant rate of change.

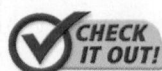

Determine whether each function has a constant or variable rate of change.

1a. {(−3, 10), (0, 7), (1, 6), (4, 3), (7, 0)}

1b. {(−2, −3), (2, 5), (3, 7), (5, 9), (8, 12)}

The functions in Examples 1A and 1B are graphed below.

Example 1A (variable rate of change)

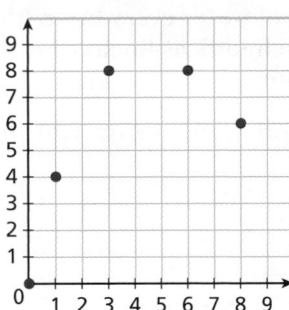

Example 1B (constant rate of change)

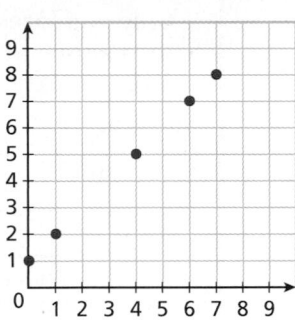

Recall from Chapter 5 that a function is a *linear function* if and only if the function has a constant rate of change. The graph of such a function is a straight line and the rate of change is the slope of the line, as in Example 1B.

A function with a variable rate of change, as in Example 1A, is a *nonlinear function*. Examples of nonlinear functions include quadratic functions and exponential functions.

EXAMPLE 2 **Identifying Linear and Nonlinear Functions**

Use rates of change to determine whether each function is linear or nonlinear.

A

x	y
−2	0
0	1
1	1.5
4	3
10	6

+2 (−2 → 0) +1
+1 (0 → 1) +0.5
+3 (1 → 4) +1.5
+6 (4 → 10) +3

Find the rates of change.

$$\frac{1}{2} \quad \frac{0.5}{1}=\frac{1}{2} \quad \frac{1.5}{3}=\frac{1}{2} \quad \frac{3}{6}=\frac{1}{2}$$

There is a constant rate of change, $\frac{1}{2}$, so this function is linear.

B

x	y
−6	18
−2	2
2	2
0	0
4	8

+4 (−6 → −2) − 16
+4 (−2 → 2) +0
−2 (2 → 0) − 2
+4 (0 → 4) +8

Find the rates of change.

$$\frac{-16}{4}=-4 \quad \frac{0}{4}=0 \quad \frac{-2}{-2}=1 \quad \frac{8}{4}=\frac{1}{2}$$

The rates of change are not constant, so this function is nonlinear.

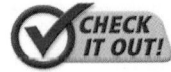 Use rates of change to determine whether each function is linear or nonlinear.

2a.

x	y
−2	$\frac{1}{4}$
−1	$\frac{1}{2}$
0	1
3	8
4	16

2b.

x	y
−5	3
−1	3
1	3
3	3
7	3

When you are given a verbal description of a function, you can determine whether the function is linear or nonlinear by making a table of values and examining the rates of change. You can compare two functions by comparing their rates of change.

EXAMPLE 3 *Physical Science Application*

Two water tanks contain 512 gallons of water each. Tank A begins to drain, losing half of its volume of water every hour. Tank B begins to drain at the same time and loses 40 gallons of water every hour. Identify the function that gives the volume of water in each tank as linear or nonlinear. Which tank loses water more quickly between hour 4 and hour 5?

Use the verbal descriptions to make a table for the volume of water in each tank.

Time (h)	0	1	2	3	4	5
Water in Tank A (gal)	512	256	128	64	32	16

Time (h)	0	1	2	3	4	5
Water in Tank B (gal)	512	472	432	392	352	312

For tank A, the rates of change are –256, –128, –64, –32, and –16, so the rate of change is variable and the function is nonlinear.

For tank B, the rates of change are all –40, so the rate of change is constant and the function is linear.

Between hours 4 and 5, the volume of water in tank A decreases at a rate of 16 gallons per hour. The volume of water in tank B decreases at a rate of 40 gallons per hour. Tank B loses water more quickly.

 CHECK IT OUT!

3. Reka and Charlotte each invest $500. Each month, Charlotte's investment grows by $25, while Reka's investment grows by 5% of the previous month's amount. Identify the function that gives the value of each investment as linear or nonlinear. Who is earning money more quickly between month 3 and month 4?

A-5 Exercises

Use rates of change to determine whether each function is linear or nonlinear.

1.

x	4	5	7	10	12
y	–2	–1	1	4	6

2.

x	–2	3	4	6	8
y	–4	6	8	14	20

3.

x	0	3	9	12	18
y	14	12	8	6	2

4.

x	–8	–6	–4	–2	0
y	–3	1	3	5	9

5. Hobbies Caitlin and Greg collect stamps. Each starts with a collection of 50 stamps. Caitlin adds 15 stamps to her collection each week. Greg adds 1 stamp to his collection the first week, 3 stamps the second week, 5 stamps the third week, and so on. Identify the function that gives the number of stamps in each collection as linear or nonlinear. Which collection is growing more quickly between week 5 and week 6?

Determine whether each function has a constant or variable rate of change.

6.

7.

8.
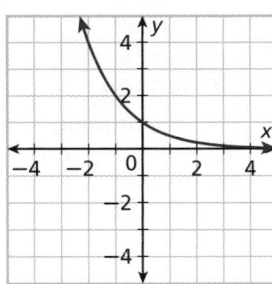

9. $y = 2x^2$

10. $y + 1 = 3x$

11. $y = -7$

12. $y = \frac{1}{5}x$

13. $y = 5^x$

14. $y = x^2 + 1$

15. $y = 3\sqrt{x}$

16. $y = \frac{x - 3}{2x}$

17. $x + y = 6.25$

Determine whether each statement is sometimes, always, or never true.

18. A function whose graph is a straight line has a variable rate of change.

19. A quadratic function has a constant rate of change.

20. The rate of change of a linear function is negative.

21. The rate of change between two points on the graph of a nonlinear function is 0.

22. Critical Thinking The figure shows the graph of the exponential function $y = \left(\frac{1}{2}\right)^x$.

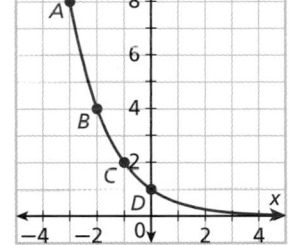

  a. Find the rates of change between points A and B, between points B and C, and between points A and D.

  b. What do you notice about the rates of change you found in part **a**? Do you think this would be true for the rate of change between any two points on the graph?

  c. How do your findings about the rates of change relate to the shape of the graph?

23. A model rocket is launched from the ground. The graph shows the height of the rocket at various times.

Model Rocket

  a. Find the rates of change between points A and B and between points B and C.

  b. Which rate of change is greater? What does this tell you about the motion of the rocket?

  c. Find the rates of change between points C and D and between points D and E.

  d. What does the sign of the rates of change you found in part **c** tell you about the motion of the rocket? Explain.

Reasoning and Counterexamples

Objectives

Use inductive reasoning to make conjectures.

Use deductive reasoning to prove conjectures, and find counterexamples to disprove conjectures.

Inductive reasoning is the process of concluding that a general rule or statement is true because specific cases are true. A statement based on inductive reasoning is called a **conjecture**.

Row 1
Row 2
Row 3

When several numbers or geometric figures form a pattern and you assume the pattern will continue, you are using inductive reasoning. For example, you might use inductive reasoning to make the conjecture that the fourth row of the pattern at right will contain seven stars.

EXAMPLE 1 **Using Inductive Reasoning**

Vocabulary

inductive reasoning
conjecture
counterexample
deductive reasoning

Use inductive reasoning to make a conjecture about the value of the 100th term in the sequence 5, 9, 13, 17, 21, ...

Make a table. Examine the values and look for a pattern.

Term	1st	2nd	3rd	4th	5th
Value	5	9	13	17	21
Pattern	4(1) + 1	4(2) + 1	4(3) + 1	4(4) + 1	4(5) + 1

Each value in the sequence is 4 times its position in the sequence, plus 1. The rule $4n + 1$ can be used to find the nth term. A reasonable conjecture for the value of the 100th term is $4(100) + 1 = 401$.

 1. Use inductive reasoning to make a conjecture about the value of the 45th term in the sequence 1, 4, 9, 16, 25, ...

A **counterexample** is a case that proves that a conjecture or statement is false. One counterexample is enough to disprove a statement.

Counterexamples	
Statement	**Counterexample**
No month has fewer than 30 days.	February has fewer than 30 days, so the statement is false.
All prime numbers are odd.	The number 2 is a prime number, but it is not odd. This example shows that the statement is false.
Every integer that is divisible by 2 is also divisible by 4.	The integer 18 is divisible by 2, but it is not divisible by 4. This example shows that the statement is false.

Recall that the Commutative and Associative Properties are true for addition and multiplication. The following example shows how you can use a counterexample to demonstrate that those properties are not true for other operations.

EXAMPLE 2 Finding a Counterexample

Find a counterexample to disprove the statement "The Associative Property is true for subtraction."

Find three real numbers a, b, and c such that $a - (b - c) \neq (a - b) - c$.
Try $a = 10$, $b = 7$, and $c = 2$.

$a - (b - c)$	$(a - b) - c$
$10 - (7 - 2)$	$(10 - 7) - 2$
$10 - 5 = 5$	$3 - 2 = 1$

Since $10 - (7 - 2) \neq (10 - 7) - 2$, this is a counterexample that shows that the statement is false.

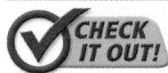 **2.** Find a counterexample to disprove the statement "The Commutative Property is true for division."

Inductive reasoning can be used to make conjectures, but it cannot be used to prove a statement. To prove a statement, you must use *deductive reasoning*. **Deductive reasoning** is the process of drawing conclusions from given facts, definitions, and properties.

You may not realize it, but you use deductive reasoning every time you solve an equation. In fact, solving an equation can be thought of as a proof.

EXAMPLE 3 Using Deductive Reasoning

Use deductive reasoning to prove each statement.

Writing Math

Notice that each step of a proof is justified with a definition, a property, an operation, or a piece of given information.

A If $3x + 4 = 19$, then $x = 5$.

Statements	Reasons
1. $3x + 4 = 19$	Given
2. $3x + 4 - 4 = 19 - 4$	Subtraction Property of Equality
3. $3x = 15$	Subtraction
4. $\frac{3x}{3} = \frac{15}{3}$	Division Property of Equality
5. $x = 5$	Division

B If $5(x - 3) = -20$, then $x = -1$.

Statements	Reasons
1. $5(x - 3) = -20$	Given
2. $5x - 5(3) = -20$	Distributive Property
3. $5x - 15 = -20$	Multiplication
4. $5x - 15 + 15 = -20 + 15$	Addition Property of Equality
5. $5x = -5$	Addition
6. $\frac{5x}{5} = \frac{-5}{5}$	Division Property of Equality
7. $x = -1$	Division

 Use deductive reasoning to prove each statement.
3a. If $\frac{x}{2} - 1 = 7$, then $x = 16$.
3b. If $4(x + 2) = 8$, then $x = 0$.

Exercises

Use inductive reasoning to make a conjecture about the value of the 40th term in each sequence.

1. 7, 8, 9, 10, 11, ...

2. 4, 7, 10, 13, 16, ...

3. 5, 10, 15, 20, 25, 30, ...

4. 0, 3, 6, 9, 12, ...

5. 3, 5, 3, 5, 3, ...

6. 1, 2, 3, 1, 2, 3, 1, ...

Use inductive reasoning to make a conjecture about the next item in each pattern.

7. d, e, f, d, e, f, ...

8. $\frac{1}{2}, \frac{3}{4}, \frac{7}{8}, \frac{15}{16}, ...$

9. 0.1, 0.02, 0.003, ...

10. 66, 57, 48, 39, ...

11. −1, 5, −3, 5, −5, 5, ...

12. △, □, ⬠, ...

Find a counterexample to disprove each statement.

13. The Associative Property is true for division.

14. The Commutative Property is true for subtraction.

Use deductive reasoning to fill in each missing term.

15. The Red-Q company makes only red clothes. This shirt is made by Red-Q. Therefore, this shirt is ___?___.

16. Lance goes to the library every ___?___. Today is Wednesday. Therefore, Lance went to the library today.

Tell whether each statement is true or false. If the statement is false, give a counterexample to disprove the statement.

17. If n is an even number, then $3n$ is also an even number.

18. The sum of two odd numbers is also an odd number.

19. If a number is divisible by 6, then it is divisible by 12.

20. The product of two odd numbers is an odd number.

21. Every number that is a multiple of 4 is a multiple of 2.

22. If m is a multiple of 3 and n is a multiple of 4, then $m + n$ is a multiple of 7.

23. Fill in the missing statement or reason to complete the proof of the following statement: If $-2(x + 6) = -18$, then $x = 3$.

Statements	Reasons
1. $-2(x + 6) = -18$	Given
2. $(-2)x + (-2)6 = -18$	Distributive Property
3. a. _____?_____	Multiplication
4. $-2x - 12 + 12 = -18 + 12$	**b.** _____?_____
5. $-2x = -6$	Addition
6. $\frac{-2x}{-2} = \frac{-6}{-2}$	**c.** _____?_____
7. $x = 3$	Division

Use deductive reasoning to prove each statement.

24. If $x - 16 = 41$, then $x = 57$.

25. If $3x - 17 = 13$, then $x = 10$.

26. If $7(x - 2) = 21$, then $x = 5$.

27. If $3(x + 1) = -9$, then $x = -4$.

28. **Geometry** A student drew the set of figures shown below. Then the student made the following conjecture: Given three points in a plane, it is possible to draw exactly three distinct lines through the points. Do you agree or disagree? Explain.

29. **Geometry** An *exterior angle* of a triangle is the angle formed by extending one side of the triangle. An exterior angle of a triangle has two *remote interior angles*. In the figure, ∠4 is an exterior angle. Its remote interior angles are ∠1 and ∠2 .

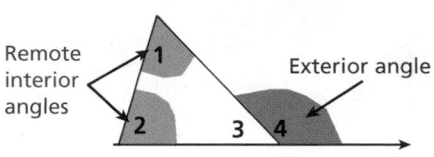

a. Draw a triangle and an exterior angle. Use a protractor to measure the exterior angle and its remote interior angles. What do you notice about the sum of the measures of the remote interior angles?

b. Repeat the process in part **a** several more times. Make a conjecture.

c. What type of reasoning did you use to make your conjecture? Explain.

Determine whether inductive or deductive reasoning was used in each situation. Explain.

30. Christine visited San Diego four times. Each time it was raining. Christine concludes, "San Diego is a very rainy city."

31. Stephanic knows that her cousin's new pet is a lizard. She also knows that every lizard is a reptile and that every reptile has scales. Stephanie concludes that her cousin's new pet has scales.

32. According to Aaron's textbook, the sum of the angle measures in any triangle is 180°. Aaron finds that two angles of a triangle measure 50° and 60°. Aaron concludes that the third angle must measure 70°.

33. Looking at the sequence 3, 9, 27, 81, ..., David concludes that the next number must be 243 because each term is 3 times the previous term.

A *conditional statement* is a statement that can be written in the form "If *p*, then *q*." The *contrapositive* of a conditional statement is the statement "If not *q*, then not *p*." The contrapositive of a true conditional statement is also true. Use the contrapositive to make a true conjecture based on each conditional statement.

34. If today is Tuesday, then tomorrow is Wednesday.

35. If Sam lives in Detroit, then Sam lives in Michigan.

36. If *n* is an even number, then *n* + 1 is an odd number.

37. If $8x + 3 = 19$, then $x = 2$.

38. **Logic** The mockingbird, the cardinal, the goldfinch, and the grouse are the state birds of Illinois, New Jersey, Pennsylvania, and Tennessee, but not necessarily in that order. Use deductive reasoning and the following clues to match each bird with its state.

- The cardinal is not the state bird of Tennessee.

- The state bird of Pennsylvania begins with the same letter as the state bird of New Jersey.

- The state whose capital is Trenton has the goldfinch as its state bird.

Student Handbook

Student Handbook

Extra Practice

Lesson 1-1

Give two ways to write each algebraic expression in words.

1. $x + 8$ **2.** $6(y)$ **3.** $g - 4$ **4.** $\dfrac{12}{h}$

Evaluate each expression for $a = 4$, $b = 2$, and $c = 5$.

5. $b + c$ **6.** $\dfrac{a}{b}$ **7.** $c - a$ **8.** ab

Write an algebraic expression for each verbal expression. Then evaluate the algebraic expression for the given values of y.

	Verbal	Algebraic	$y = 9$	$y = 6$
9.	y reduced by 4	■	■	■
10.	the quotient of y and 3	■	■	■
11.	5 more than y	■	■	■
12.	the sum of y and 2	■	■	■

Lesson 1-2

Add or subtract using a number line.

13. $-7 - 9$ **14.** $-2.2 + 4.3$ **15.** $-5\dfrac{1}{2} - 2\dfrac{1}{2}$ **16.** $3.4 - 6.5$

Subtract.

17. $12 - 47$ **18.** $1.3 - 9.2$ **19.** $1\dfrac{1}{3} - 4\dfrac{2}{3}$

Compare. Write $<$, $>$, or $=$.

20. $-5 - (-8)$ ■ $-4 - 9$ **21.** $\left|-6 - (-2)\right|$ ■ $7 - 4$ **22.** $-2 - 5$ ■ $7 - 14$

Evaluate the expression $g - (-7)$ for each value of g.

23. $g = 121$ **24.** $g = 1.25$ **25.** $g = -\dfrac{2}{5}$ **26.** $g = -8\dfrac{1}{3}$

Lesson 1-3

Find the value of each expression.

27. $-24 \div (-8)$ **28.** $5(-9)$ **29.** $-5.2 \div (-1.3)$

30. $\dfrac{2}{7} \div \left(-\dfrac{6}{7}\right)$ **31.** $0 \div \left(-\dfrac{4}{5}\right)$ **32.** $\dfrac{9}{10} \div 0$

Evaluate each expression for $x = -8$, $y = 6$, and $z = -4$.

33. xy **34.** yz **35.** $\dfrac{y}{z}$ **36.** $\dfrac{z}{x}$

Let a represent a positive number, b represent a negative number, and z represent zero. Tell whether each expression is positive, negative, zero, or undefined.

37. ab **38.** $-bz$ **39.** $-\dfrac{a}{b}$ **40.** $\dfrac{ab}{z}$

Lesson 1-4

Write each expression as repeated multiplication. Then simplify the expression.

41. 3^3 **42.** -2^4 **43.** $(-5)^3$ **44.** $(-1)^5$

Write each expression using a base and an exponent.

45. $5 \cdot 5 \cdot 5 \cdot 5 \cdot 5$ **46.** $4 \cdot 4 \cdot 4$ **47.** $2 \cdot 2 \cdot 2 \cdot 2$

Write the exponent that makes each equation true.

48. $2^{\blacksquare} = 16$ **49.** $4^{\blacksquare} = 256$ **50.** $(-3)^{\blacksquare} = 81$ **51.** $-5^{\blacksquare} = -125$

Lesson 1-5

Find each root.

52. $-\sqrt{64}$ **53.** $\sqrt{144}$ **54.** $\sqrt[3]{\dfrac{8}{125}}$

Compare. Write $<$, $>$, or $=$.

55. $\sqrt{118}$ ▨ 11 **56.** 6 ▨ $\sqrt{35}$ **57.** 14 ▨ $\sqrt{196}$ **58.** $\sqrt{50}$ ▨ 7

Write all classifications that apply to each real number.

59. -44 **60.** $\sqrt{49}$ **61.** 15.982 **62.** $\dfrac{1}{9}$

Lesson 1-6

Evaluate each expression for the given value of the variable.

63. $22 - 3g + 5$ for $g = 4$ **64.** $12 - 30 \div h$ for $h = 6$ **65.** $\sqrt{(11j + j)} + 6$ for $j = 3$

Simplify each expression.

66. $4 + 12 \div |3 - 9|$ **67.** $-36 - \sqrt{4 + 15 \div 3}$ **68.** $\dfrac{5 - \sqrt{12(3)}}{-4 + \sqrt{2(8)}}$

Translate each word phrase into an algebraic expression.

69. the quotient of 8 and the difference of a and 5

70. the sum of -9 and the square root of the product of 7 and c

Lesson 1-7

Simplify each expression.

71. $-5 + 38 + 5 + 62$ **72.** $2\dfrac{1}{3} - 42 + 7\dfrac{2}{3}$ **73.** $\dfrac{1}{5} \cdot 4 \cdot 25$

Write each product using the Distributive Property. Then simplify.

74. $12(108)$ **75.** $7(89)$ **76.** $11(33)$

Simplify each expression by combining like terms.

77. $7a - 3a$ **78.** $-2b - 12b$ **79.** $4c + 5c^2 - c$

Simplify each expression. Justify each step with an operation or property.

80. $6(p - 2) + 3p$ **81.** $8q - 3 + 5q(2 + q)$ **82.** $-4 + 3r - 7(2s - r)$

Lesson 1-8

Graph each point.

83. $A(2, 3)$ **84.** $B(-4, 1)$ **85.** $C(0, -2)$ **86.** $D(-4, -1)$

Name the quadrant in which each point lies.

87. J **88.** K **89.** L

90. M **91.** N **92.** P

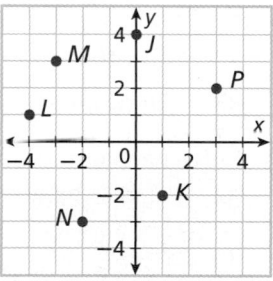

Generate ordered pairs for each function for $x = -2, -1, 0, 1$, and 2. Graph the ordered pairs and describe the pattern.

93. $y = x - 3$ **94.** $y = -2x$ **95.** $y = -x^2$ **96.** $y = |3x|$

Write an equation for each rule. Use the given values for x to generate ordered pairs. Graph the ordered pairs and describe the pattern.

97. y is equal to the sum of one-third of x and -2; $x = -6, -3, 0, 3$, and 6.

98. y is equal to 4 less than x squared; $x = -2, -1, 0, 1$, and 2.

Lesson 2-1

Solve each equation. Check your answer.

1. $x - 9 = 5$ **2.** $4 = y - 12$ **3.** $a + \dfrac{3}{5} = 7$

4. $7.3 = b + 3.4$ **5.** $-6 + j = 5$ **6.** $-1.7 = -6.1 + k$

Write an equation to represent each relationship. Then solve the equation.

7. A number decreased by 7 is equal to 10. **8.** The sum of 6 and a number is −3.

Lesson 2-2

Solve each equation. Check your answer.

9. $\dfrac{n}{5} = 15$ **10.** $-6 = \dfrac{k}{4}$ **11.** $\dfrac{r}{2.6} = 5$

12. $3b = 27$ **13.** $56 = -7d$ **14.** $-3.6 = -2f$

15. $\dfrac{1}{4}z = 3$ **16.** $12 = \dfrac{4}{5}g$ **17.** $\dfrac{1}{3}a = -5$

Write an equation to represent each relationship. Then solve the equation.

18. A number multiplied by 4 is −20. **19.** The quotient of a number and 5 is 7.

Lesson 2-3

Solve each equation. Check your answer.

20. $2k + 7 = 15$ **21.** $11 - 5m = -4$ **22.** $23 = 9 - 2d$

23. $\dfrac{2}{5}b + 6 = 10$ **24.** $\dfrac{f}{3} - 4 = 2$ **25.** $6n + 4 = 22$

Write an equation to represent each relationship. Solve each equation.

26. The difference of 11 and 4 times a number equals 3.

27. Thirteen less than 5 times a number is equal to 7.

Lesson 2-4

Solve each equation. Check your answer.

28. $5b - 3 = 4b + 1$ **29.** $3g + 7 = 11g - 17$

30. $-8 + 4y = y - 6 + 3y - 2$ **31.** $7 + 3d - 5 = -1 + 2d - 12 + d$

Write an equation to represent each relationship. Then solve the equation.

32. Three more than one-half a number is the same as 17 minus three times the number.

33. Two times the difference of a number and 4 is the same as 5 less than the number.

Lesson 2-5

Solve each equation for the indicated variable.

34. $q - 3r = 2$ for r **35.** $\dfrac{5 - c}{6} = d - 7$ for c

36. $2x + 3\dfrac{y}{4} = 5$ for y **37.** $2fgh - 3g = 10$ for h

Lesson 2-6

Solve each equation. Check your answer.

38. $|a| = 13$ **39.** $|x| - 16 = 3$ **40.** $|g + 5| = 11$

41. $|7s| - 6 = 8$ **42.** $\left|\dfrac{f}{2} + 1\right| = 15$ **43.** $|p - 5| - 12 = -9$

44. $500 = 25|z| + 200$ **45.** $|7j + 14| - 5 = 16$ **46.** $\dfrac{|p - 2| - 15}{5} = -1$

Extra Practice

Lesson 2-7

47. A long-distance runner ran 9000 meters in 30 minutes. Find the unit rate in meters per minute.

48. A hummingbird flapped its wings 770 times in 14 seconds. Find the unit rate in flaps per second.

49. A car traveled 210 miles in 3 hours. Find the unit rate in miles per hour.

50. A printer printed 60 pages in 5 minutes. Find the unit rate in pages per minute.

Solve each proportion.

51. $\dfrac{h}{4} = \dfrac{5}{6}$

52. $\dfrac{5}{m} = \dfrac{2}{5}$

53. $\dfrac{r}{3} = \dfrac{10}{7}$

54. $\dfrac{2}{3} = \dfrac{2x}{8}$

55. $\dfrac{5}{x-3} = \dfrac{3}{10}$

56. $\dfrac{b-2}{4} = \dfrac{7}{12}$

Lesson 2-8

Find the value of x in each diagram.

57. $ABCD \sim EFGH$

58. $\triangle JKL \sim \triangle MNO$

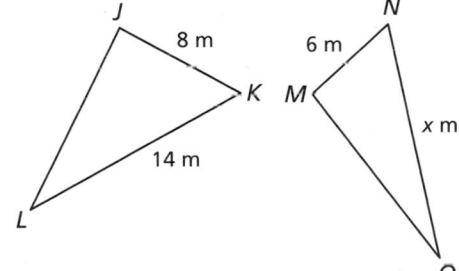

Lesson 2-9

59. Find 25% of 60.

60. Find 40% of 95.

61. What percent of 75 is 15?

62. What percent of 60 is 33?

63. 91 is what percent of 65?

64. 35% of what number is 24.5?

Write each decimal or fraction as a percent.

65. $\dfrac{4}{5}$

66. 0.55

67. $\dfrac{9}{6}$

68. 0.0375

Write each percent as a decimal and as a fraction.

69. 32%

70. 24%

71. 37.5%

72. 118.75%

Write each list in order from least to greatest.

73. $\dfrac{2}{17}$, 0.28, 1.9%, $\dfrac{6}{25}$, 0.19

74. $\dfrac{5}{3}$, 9.2, 117%, $\dfrac{9}{11}$, 8.8%

Lesson 2-10

75. Estimate the tax on a $2438.00 clarinet when the sales tax is 7.9%.

76. Estimate the tip on a $21.32 check using a tip rate of 20%.

Lesson 2-11

Find each percent change. Tell whether it is a percent increase or decrease.

77. 10 to 25

78. 40 to 2

79. 800 to 160

80. 4 to 14

81. 8 to 30

82. 60 to 36

83. Find the result when 45 is increased by 40%.

84. Find the result when 120 is decreased by 70%.

Extra Practice

Lesson 3-1

Describe the solutions of each inequality in words.

1. $3 + v < -2$ **2.** $15 \le k + 4$ **3.** $-3 + n > 6$ **4.** $1 - 4x \ge -2$

Graph each inequality.

5. $f \ge 2$ **6.** $m < -1$ **7.** $\sqrt{4^2 + 3^2} > c$ **8.** $(-1 - 1)^2 \le p$

Write the inequality shown by each graph.

9.

10.

11.

12.

13.

14.

Write each inequality with the variable on the left. Graph the solutions.

15. $14 > b$ **16.** $9 \le g$ **17.** $-2 < x$ **18.** $-4 \ge k$

Lesson 3-2

Solve each inequality and graph the solutions.

19. $8 \ge d - 4$ **20.** $-5 < 10 + w$ **21.** $a + 4 \le 7$ **22.** $9 + j > 2$

Write an inequality to represent each statement. Solve the inequality and graph the solutions.

23. Five more than a number v is less than or equal to 9.

24. A number t decreased by 2 is at least 7.

25. Three less than a number r is less than -1.

26. A number k increased by 1 is at most -2.

Use the inequality $4 + z \le 11$ to fill in the missing numbers.

27. $z \le \blacksquare$ **28.** $z - \blacksquare \le 4$ **29.** $z - 3 \le \blacksquare$

Lesson 3-3

Solve each inequality and graph the solutions.

30. $24 > 4b$ **31.** $27g \le 81$ **32.** $\dfrac{x}{5} < 3$ **33.** $10y \ge 2$

34. $4p < -2$ **35.** $\dfrac{3s}{8} > 3$ **36.** $0 \ge \dfrac{3}{7}d$ **37.** $\dfrac{a}{8} \ge \dfrac{3}{4}$

38. $-3k \le -12$ **39.** $\dfrac{-2e}{5} \ge 4$ **40.** $8 < -12y$ **41.** $-3.5 > 14c$

42. $9 > \dfrac{h}{-2}$ **43.** $49 > -7m$ **44.** $60 \le -12c$ **45.** $-\dfrac{1}{3}q < -6$

Write an inequality for each statement. Solve the inequality and graph the solutions.

46. The product of $\dfrac{1}{2}$ and a number is not more than 6.

47. The quotient of r and -5 is greater than 3.

48. The product of -11 and a number is greater than -33.

49. The quotient of w and -4 is less than or equal to -6.

Lesson 3-4

Solve each inequality and graph the solutions.

50. $3t - 2 < 5$

51. $-6 < 5b - 4$

52. $4 < \dfrac{2f + 3}{2}$

53. $10 \le 3(4 - r)$

54. $\dfrac{2}{3} + \dfrac{3}{4}h < \dfrac{4}{3}$

55. $\dfrac{1}{5}(10k - 2) > 1$

56. $-n - 3 < -2^3$

57. $37 - 4d \le \sqrt{3^2 + 4^2}$

58. $-\dfrac{3}{4}(8q - 2^2) < -3$

Use the inequality $-6 - 2w \ge 10$ to fill in the missing numbers.

59. $w \le \blacksquare$

60. $w - 3 \le \blacksquare$

61. $\blacksquare + w \le 1$

Write an inequality for each statement. Solve the inequality and graph the solutions.

62. Twelve is less than or equal to the product of 6 and the difference of 5 and a number.

63. The difference of one-third a number and 8 is more than -4.

64. One-fourth of the sum of $2x$ and 4 is more than 5.

Lesson 3-5

Solve each inequality and graph the solutions.

65. $4v - 2 \le 3v$

66. $2(7 - s) > 4(s + 2)$

67. $\dfrac{1}{3}u - \dfrac{5}{2} \ge \dfrac{1}{6}u$

Solve each inequality.

68. $3 + 3c < 6 + 3c$

69. $4(k + 2) \ge 4k + 5$

70. $2(5 - b) \le 3 - 2b$

Write an inequality to represent each relationship. Solve your inequality.

71. The difference of three times a number and 5 is more than the number times 4.

72. One less than a number is greater than the product of 3 and the difference of 5 and the number.

Lesson 3-6

Solve each compound inequality and graph the solutions.

73. $6 < 3 + x < 8$

74. $-1 \le b + 4 \le 3$

75. $k + 5 \le -3$ OR $k + 5 \ge 1$

76. $r - 3 > 2$ OR $r + 1 < 4$

Write the compound inequality shown by each graph.

77.

78.

Write and graph a compound inequality for the numbers described.

79. all real numbers less than 2 and greater than or equal to -1

80. all real numbers between -3 and 1

Lesson 3-7

Solve each inequality and graph the solutions.

81. $|n + 5| \le 26$

82. $|x| + 6 < 13$

83. $4|k| \le 12$

84. $|c - 8| > 18$

85. $6|p| \ge 48$

86. $|3 + t| - 1 \ge 5$

Solve each inequality.

87. $|a| - 2 \le -5$

88. $2|w| + 5 < 3$

89. $|s| + 12 > 8$

Write and solve an absolute-value inequality for each expression. Graph the solutions on a number line.

90. All numbers whose absolute value is greater than 14.

91. All numbers whose absolute value multiplied by 3 is less than 27.

Extra Practice

Lesson 4-1

Choose the graph that best represents each situation.

1. A person blows up a balloon with a steady airstream.

2. A person blows up a balloon and then lets it deflate.

3. A person blows up a balloon slowly at first and then uses more and more air.

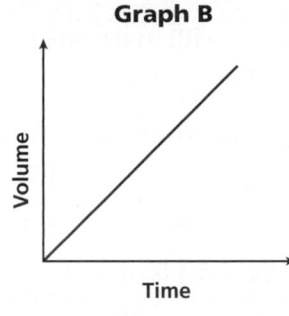

Lesson 4-2

Express each relation as a table, as a graph, and as a mapping diagram.

4. $\{(0, 2), (-1, 3), (-2, 5)\}$

5. $\{(2, 8), (4, 6), (6, 4), (8, 2)\}$

Give the domain and range of each relation. Tell whether the relation is a function. Explain.

6. $\{(3, 4), (-1, 2), (2, -3), (5, 0)\}$

7. $\{(5, 4), (0, 2), (5, -3), (0, 1)\}$

8.

x	2	0	1	2	−1
y	1	0	−1	−2	−3

9.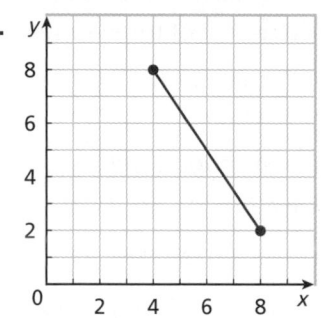

Lesson 4-3

Determine a relationship between the x- and y-variables. Write an equation.

10. $\{(1, 3), (2, 6), (3, 9), (4, 12)\}$

11.

x	1	2	3	4
y	1	4	9	16

Identify the independent and dependent variables. Write an equation in function notation for each situation.

12. A science tutor charges students $15 per hour.

13. A circus charges a $10 entry fee and $1.50 for each pony ride.

14. For $f(a) = 6 - 4a$, find $f(a)$ when $a = 2$ and when $a = -3$.

15. For $g(d) = \frac{2}{5}d + 3$, find $g(d)$ when $d = 10$ and when $d = -5$.

16. For $h(w) = 2 - w^2$, find $h(w)$ when $w = -1$ and when $w = -2$.

17. Complete the table for $f(t) = 7 + 3t$.

t	0	1	2	3
f(t)				

18. Complete the table for $h(s) = 2s + s^3 - 6$.

s	−1	0	1	2
h(s)				

Lesson 4-4

Graph each function for the given domain.

19. $2x - y = 2$; D: $\{-2, -1, 0, 1\}$

20. $f(x) = x^2 - 1$; D: $\{-3, -1, 0, 2\}$

Graph each function.

21. $f(x) = 4 - 2x$

22. $y + 3 = 2x$

23. $y = -5 + x^2$

24. Use a graph of the function $y = \frac{5}{2} - 2x$ to find the value of y when $x = \frac{1}{2}$. Check your answer.

25. Find the value of x so that $(x, 4)$ satisfies $y = -x + 8$.

26. Find the value of y so that $(-3, y)$ satisfies $y = 15 - 2x^2$.

For each function, determine whether the given points are on the graph.

27. $y = \frac{x}{3} + 4$; $(-3, 3)$ and $(3, 5)$

28. $y = x^2 - 1$; $(-2, 3)$ and $(2, 5)$

Lesson 4-5

Describe the correlation illustrated by each scatter plot.

29.

30.

31.

Identify the correlation you would expect to see between each pair of data sets. Explain.

32. the number of chess pieces captured and the number of pieces still on the board

33. a person's height and the color of the person's eyes

Choose the scatter plot that best represents the described relationship. Explain.

34. the number of students in a class and the grades on a test

35. the number of students in a class and the number of empty desks

Graph A   Graph B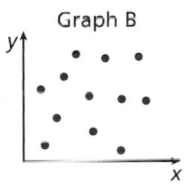

Lesson 4-6

Determine whether each sequence appears to be an arithmetic sequence. If so, find the common difference and the next three terms.

36. $-10, -7, -4, -1, \ldots$

37. $8, 5, 1, -4, \ldots$

38. $1, -2, 3, -4, \ldots$

39. $-19, -9, 1, 11, \ldots$

Find the indicated term of each arithmetic sequence.

40. 15th term: $-5, -1, 3, 7, \ldots$

41. 20th term: $a_1 = 2$; $d = -5$

42. 12th term: $8, 16, 24, 32, \ldots$

43. 21st term: $5.2, 5.17, 5.14, 5.11, \ldots$

Find the common difference for each arithmetic sequence.

44. $0, 7, 14, 21, \ldots$

45. $132, 121, 110, 99, \ldots$

46. $\frac{1}{4}, 1, \frac{7}{4}, \frac{10}{4}, \ldots$

47. $1.4, 2.2, 3, 3.8, \ldots$

48. $-7, -2, 3, 8, \ldots$

49. $7.28, 7.21, 7.14, 7.07, \ldots$

Find the next four terms in each arithmetic sequence.

50. $-3, -6, -9, -12, \ldots$

51. $2, 9, 16, 23, \ldots$

52. $-\frac{1}{3}, \frac{1}{3}, 1, \frac{5}{3}, \ldots$

53. $-4.3, -3.2, -2.1, -1, \ldots$

Extra Practice

Lesson 5-1

Identify whether each graph represents a function. Explain. If the graph does represent a function, is the function linear?

1.

2.

3.
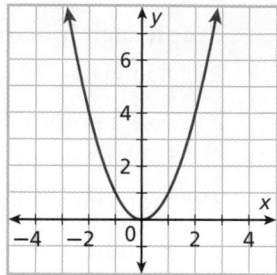

Tell whether the given ordered pairs satisfy a linear function. Explain.

4.

x	−4	−2	0	2	4
y	7	6	5	4	3

5.

x	2	5	8	11	14
y	12	8	7	3	3

Tell whether each equation is linear. If so, write the equation in standard form and give the values of *A*, *B*, and *C*.

6. $y = 8 - 3x$

7. $\frac{x}{3} = 4 - 2y$

8. $-3 + xy = 2$

9. $4x = -3 - 3y$

Lesson 5-2

Find the *x*- and *y*-intercepts.

10. $-4x = 2y - 1$

11. $x - y = 3$

12. $2x - 3y = 12$

13. $2.5x + 2.5y = 5$

Use intercepts to graph the line described by each equation.

14. $15 = -3x - 5y$

15. $4y = 2x + 8$

16. $y = 6 - 3x$

17. $-2y = x + 2$

Lesson 5-3

Find the slope of each line.

18.

19.
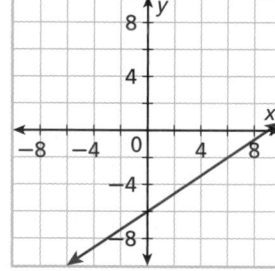

Lesson 5-4

Find the slope of the line that contains each pair of points.

20. $(-1, 2)$ and $(-4, 8)$

21. $(2, 6)$ and $(0, 1)$

22. $(-2, 3)$ and $(4, 0)$

Find the slope of the line described by each equation.

23. $2y = 42 - 6x$

24. $3x + 4y = 12$

25. $3x = 15 + 5y$

Lesson 5-5

Find the coordinates of the midpoint of each segment.

26. $\overline{AB}$ with endpoints $A(-3, 4)$ and $B(1, 5)$

27. $\overline{CD}$ with endpoints $C(9, -8)$ and $D(9, -2)$

Find the distance, to the nearest hundredth, between each pair of points.

28. $A(0, 6)$ and $B(4, 8)$

29. $J(-1, 7)$ and $K(-4, 5)$

30. $S(-3, -9)$ and $T(2, 3)$

Extra Practice

Lesson 5-6

Tell whether each equation represents a direct variation. If so, identify the constant of variation.

31. $x - 2y = 0$ **32.** $x - y = 3$ **33.** $3y = 2x$

34. The value of y varies directly with x, and $y = 2$ when $x = -3$. Find y when $x = 6$.

35. The value of y varies directly with x, and $y = -3$ when $x = 9$. Find y when $x = 12$.

Lesson 5-7

Write the equation that describes each line in slope-intercept form.

36. slope $= 2$, y-intercept $= -2$ **37.** slope $= 0.25$, y-intercept $= 4$

38. slope $= -2$, $(5, 4)$ is on the line.   **39.** slope $= \frac{1}{3}$, $(-8, 0)$ is on the line.

40.

41.
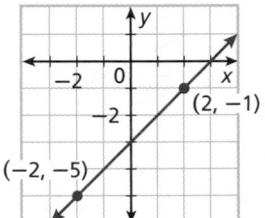

Write each equation in slope-intercept form. Then graph the line described by the equation.

42. $2y = x - 3$ **43.** $-3x - 2y = 1$ **44.** $2y - \frac{1}{2}x = 2$

Lesson 5-8

Write an equation in point-slope form for the line with the given slope that contains the given point.

45. slope $= 2$; $(0, 3)$ **46.** slope $= -1$; $(1, -1)$ **47.** slope $= \frac{1}{2}$; $(2, 4)$

Write the equation that describes each line in slope-intercept form.

48. slope $= 3$, $(-2, -5)$ is on the line.   **49.** $(-1, 1)$ and $(1, -2)$ are on the line.

50. $(3, 1)$ and $(2, -3)$ are on the line.   **51.** x-intercept $= 4$, y-intercept $= -5$

Lesson 5-9

Write an equation in slope-intercept form for the line that is parallel to the given line and that passes through the given point.

52. $y = -2x + 3$; $(1, 4)$ **53.** $y = x - 5$; $(2, -4)$ **54.** $y = 3x$; $(-1, 5)$

Write an equation in slope-intercept form for the line that is perpendicular to the given line and that passes through the given point.

55. $y = x + 1$; $(3, -2)$ **56.** $y = -4x - 1$; $(-1, 0)$ **57.** $y = 4x + 5$; $(2, -1)$

Lesson 5-10

Graph $f(x)$ and $g(x)$. Then describe the transformation(s) from the graph of $f(x)$ to the graph of $g(x)$.

58. $f(x) = x$, $g(x) = x + 2$ **59.** $f(x) = x$, $g(x) = x - \frac{1}{2}$

60. $f(x) = 6x + 1$, $g(x) = 2x + 1$ **61.** $f(x) = 3x - 1$, $g(x) = 9x - 1$

62. $f(x) = x$, $g(x) = 2x - 1$ **63.** $f(x) = x + 1$, $g(x) = -\frac{1}{2}x$

Extra Practice

Lesson 6-1

Tell whether the ordered pair is a solution of the given system.

1. $(1, 3)$; $\begin{cases} 2x - 3y = -7 \\ -5x + 3y = 4 \end{cases}$ **2.** $(-2, 2)$; $\begin{cases} 4x + 3y = -2 \\ -2x - 2y = 2 \end{cases}$ **3.** $(4, -3)$; $\begin{cases} -2x - 3y = 1 \\ x + 2y = -2 \end{cases}$

Use the given graph to find the solution of each system.

4. $\begin{cases} y = \dfrac{1}{2}x - 1 \\ y = -\dfrac{1}{2}x + 3 \end{cases}$ **5.** $\begin{cases} y = x + 1 \\ y = -x + 1 \end{cases}$

  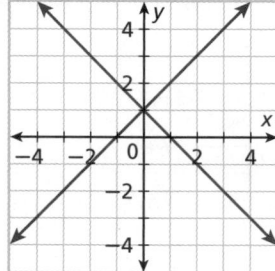

Solve each system by graphing. Check your answer.

6. $\begin{cases} y = x + 1 \\ y = -2x - 2 \end{cases}$ **7.** $\begin{cases} 3x + y = -8 \\ 3y = \dfrac{1}{2}x - 5 \end{cases}$ **8.** $\begin{cases} x = 2 - 2y \\ -1 = -2x - 3y \end{cases}$

Lesson 6-2

Solve each system by substitution.

9. $\begin{cases} y = 12 - 3x \\ y = 2x - 3 \end{cases}$ **10.** $\begin{cases} 2x + y = -6 \\ -5x + y = 1 \end{cases}$ **11.** $\begin{cases} y = 11 - 3x \\ -2x + y = 1 \end{cases}$

12. $\begin{cases} 2x + 3y = 2 \\ -\dfrac{1}{2}x + 2y = -6 \end{cases}$ **13.** $\begin{cases} 3x - 2y = -3 \\ y = 7 - 4x \end{cases}$ **14.** $\begin{cases} 4y - 2x = -2 \\ x + 3y = -4 \end{cases}$

Two angles whose measures have a sum of 90° are called complementary angles. For Exercises 15–17, x and y represent the measures of complementary angles. Use this information and the equation given in each exercise to find the measure of each angle.

15. $y = 9x - 10$ **16.** $y - 4x = 15$ **17.** $y = 2x + 15$

Lesson 6-3

Solve each system by elimination.

18. $\begin{cases} x - 3y = -1 \\ -x + 2y = -2 \end{cases}$ **19.** $\begin{cases} -3x - y = 1 \\ 5x + y = -5 \end{cases}$ **20.** $\begin{cases} -x - 3y = -1 \\ 3x + 3y = 9 \end{cases}$

21. $\begin{cases} 3x - 2y = 2 \\ 3x + y = 8 \end{cases}$ **22.** $\begin{cases} 5x - 2y = -15 \\ 2x - 2y = -12 \end{cases}$ **23.** $\begin{cases} -4x - 2y = -4 \\ -4x + 3y = -24 \end{cases}$

24. $\begin{cases} -3x - 3y = 3 \\ 2x + y = -4 \end{cases}$ **25.** $\begin{cases} 4x - 3y = -1 \\ 2x - 2y = -4 \end{cases}$ **26.** $\begin{cases} 3x + 6y = 0 \\ 7x + 4y = 20 \end{cases}$

Solve each system of linear equations.

27. $\begin{cases} y = 2x + 4 \\ -2x + y = 6 \end{cases}$

28. $\begin{cases} -y = 3 - 5x \\ y - 5x = 6 \end{cases}$

29. $\begin{cases} y + 2 = 3x \\ 3x - y = -1 \end{cases}$

30. $\begin{cases} 2y = 6 - 6x \\ 3y + 9x = 9 \end{cases}$

31. $\begin{cases} y - 1 = -3x \\ 12x + 4y = 4 \end{cases}$

32. $\begin{cases} 4x - 2y = 4 \\ 3y = 6\,(x - 1) \end{cases}$

Classify each system. Give the number of solutions.

33. $\begin{cases} 2y = 2\,(4x - 3) \\ y - 1 = 4x \end{cases}$

34. $\begin{cases} 3y + 6x = 9 \\ 2(y - 3) = -4x \end{cases}$

35. $\begin{cases} 3x - 13 = 2y \\ -3y = 2x \end{cases}$

Tell whether the ordered pair is a solution of the given inequality.

36. $(3, 6);\ y > 2x + 4$

37. $(-2, -8);\ y \le 3x - 2$

38. $(-3, 3);\ y \ge -2x + 5$

Graph the solutions of each linear inequality.

39. $y > 2x$

40. $y \le -3x + 2$

41. $y \ge 2x - 1$

42. $-y < -x + 4$

43. $y \ge -2x + 4$

44. $y > -x - 3$

45. $y < \frac{1}{2}x + 1\frac{1}{2}$

46. $y \le 4x - (-1)$

Write an inequality to represent each graph.

47.

48.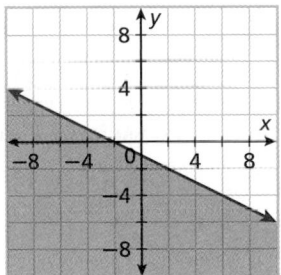

Tell whether the ordered pair is a solution of the given system.

49. $(2, 5);\ \begin{cases} y > 3x - 3 \\ y \ge x + 1 \end{cases}$

50. $(3, 9);\ \begin{cases} y > -3x - 2 \\ y < 2x + 3 \end{cases}$

51. $(2, 3);\ \begin{cases} y > 2x \\ y \le x - 3 \end{cases}$

Graph each system of linear inequalities. Give two ordered pairs that are solutions and two that are not solutions.

52. $\begin{cases} x + 4y < 2 \\ 2y > 3x + 8 \end{cases}$

53. $\begin{cases} y \le 6 - 2x \\ x - 2y < -2 \end{cases}$

54. $\begin{cases} 2x - 2 > -3y \\ -x + 3y \ge -10 \end{cases}$

Graph each system of linear inequalities. Describe the solutions.

55. $\begin{cases} y > 2x + 1 \\ y < 2x - 2 \end{cases}$

56. $\begin{cases} y < 3x - 1 \\ y > 3x - 4 \end{cases}$

57. $\begin{cases} y \ge -x + 2 \\ y \ge -x + 5 \end{cases}$

58. $\begin{cases} y \ge 2x - 3 \\ y \ge 2x + 3 \end{cases}$

59. $\begin{cases} y > -4x - 2 \\ y \le -4x - 5 \end{cases}$

60. $\begin{cases} y \ge -2x + 1 \\ y < -2x + 6 \end{cases}$

Lesson 7-1

Simplify.

1. 3^{-4} 2. 5^{-3} 3. -4^0 4. -2^{-5} 5. 6^{-3}

6. $(-2)^{-4}$ 7. 1^{-7} 8. $(-4)^{-3}$ 9. $(-5)^0$ 10. $(-1)^{-5}$

Evaluate each expression for the given value(s) of the variable(s).

11. x^{-4} for $x = 2$ 12. $(c + 3)^{-3}$ for $c = -6$

13. $3j^{-7}k^{-1}$ for $j = -2$ and $k = 3$ 14. $(2n - 2)^{-4}$ for $n = 3$

Simplify.

15. $b^4 g^{-5}$ 16. $\dfrac{k^{-3}}{r^5}$ 17. $5s^{-3}c^0$ 18. $\dfrac{z^{-4}}{5t^{-2}}$

19. $\dfrac{f^2}{3a^{-4}}$ 20. $\dfrac{-3t^4}{q^{-5}}$ 21. $\dfrac{a^0 k^{-4}}{p^2}$ 22. $3f^{-1}y^{-5}$

Lesson 7-2

Find the value of each power of 10.

23. 10^{-7} 24. 10^9 25. 10^6 26. 10^{-8}

Write each number as a power of 10.

27. $10{,}000{,}000$ 28. 0.00001 29. $10{,}000{,}000{,}000{,}000$

Find the value of each expression.

30. 72.19×10^{-2} 31. 0.096×10^{-7} 32. 7384.5×10^6

Write each number in scientific notation.

33. $3{,}605{,}000$ 34. 0.0063 35. $100{,}500{,}000$

Lesson 7-3

Simplify.

36. $3^4 \cdot 3^2$ 37. $r^7 \cdot r^0$ 38. $(k^4)^4$

39. $(b^4)^3$ 40. $(c^3 d^2)^3 \cdot (cd^2)^{-2}$ 41. $(-3q^3)^{-2}$

Find the missing exponent in each expression.

42. $a^{\blacksquare} a^6 = a^9$ 43. $(a^3 b^{\blacksquare})^3 = \dfrac{a^9}{b^6}$ 44. $(a^4 b^{-2})^{\blacksquare} \cdot a^3 = \dfrac{b^4}{a^5}$

Lesson 7-4

Simplify.

45. $\dfrac{3^{11}}{3^8}$ 46. $\dfrac{4^4 \cdot 5^3}{3^2 \cdot 4^3 \cdot 5^3}$ 47. $\dfrac{6h^4}{12h^3}$ 48. $\dfrac{r^6 s^5}{r^5 s^6}$

Simplify each quotient and write the answer in scientific notation.

49. $(4 \times 10^7) \div (1.6 \times 10^5)$ 50. $(10 \times 10^4) \div (2 \times 10^7)$ 51. $(2.5 \times 10^8) \div (5 \times 10^3)$

Simplify.

52. $\left(\dfrac{2}{3}\right)^4$ 53. $\left(\dfrac{x^2 y^2}{y^3}\right)^2$ 54. $\left(\dfrac{4}{5}\right)^{-3}$ 55. $\left(\dfrac{2xy^2}{3(xy)^2}\right)^{-3}$

Chapter 7 ▪ Skills Practice

Lesson 7-5

Simplify each expression.

56. $27^{\frac{1}{3}}$ **57.** $256^{\frac{1}{4}}$ **58.** $169^{\frac{1}{2}}$ **59.** $0^{\frac{1}{5}}$

60. $4^{\frac{3}{2}}$ **61.** $49^{\frac{3}{2}}$ **62.** $36^{\frac{3}{2}}$ **63.** $16^{\frac{5}{4}}$

Simplify. All variables represent nonnegative numbers.

64. $\sqrt{x^2 y^6}$ **65.** $\sqrt[3]{a^9 b^{15}}$ **66.** $\dfrac{(m^8)^{\frac{1}{2}}}{\sqrt{m^4}}$ **67.** $\left(\sqrt[5]{g^{60}}\right)^{\frac{1}{3}} \sqrt[7]{t^{14}}$

Lesson 7-6

Find the degree of each monomial.

68. 4^7 **69.** $x^3 y$ **70.** $\dfrac{r^6 st^2}{2}$ **71.** 9^0

Find the degree of each polynomial.

72. $a^2 b + b - 2^2$ **73.** $5x^4 y^2 - y^5 z^2$ **74.** $3g^4 h + h^2 + 4j^6$ **75.** $4nm^7 - m^6 p^3 + p$

Write each polynomial in standard form. Then give the leading coefficient.

76. $4r - 5r^3 + 2r^2$ **77.** $-3b^2 + 7b^6 + 4 - b$ **78.** $\dfrac{1}{2}t^3 + t - \dfrac{1}{3}t^5 + 4$

Classify each polynomial according to its degree and number of terms.

79. $3x^2 + 4x - 5$ **80.** $-4x^2 + x^6 - 4 + x^3$ **81.** $x^3 - 7^2$

Lesson 7-7

Add or subtract.

82. $4y^3 - 2y + 3y^3$ **83.** $9k^2 + 5 - 10k^2 - 6$

84. $7 - 3n^2 + 4 + 2n^2$ **85.** $\left(9x^6 - 5x^2 + 3\right) + \left(6x^2 - 5\right)$

86. $\left(2y^5 - 5y^2\right) + \left(3y^5 - y^3 + 2y^2\right)$ **87.** $\left(r^3 + 2r + 1\right) - \left(2r^3 - 4\right)$

88. $\left(10s^2 + 5\right) - \left(5s^2 + 3s - 2\right)$ **89.** $\left(2s^7 - 6s^3 + 2\right) - \left(3s^7 + 2\right)$

Lesson 7-7

Multiply.

90. $\left(3a^7\right)\left(2a^4\right)$ **91.** $\left(-3xy^3\right)\left(2x^2 z\right)\left(yz^4\right)$ **92.** $\left(4k\ell^3 m\right)\left(-2k^2 m^2\right)$

93. $3jk^2\left(2j^2 + k\right)$ **94.** $4q^3 r^2\left(2qr^2 + 3q\right)$ **95.** $3xy^2\left(2x^2 y - 3y\right)$

96. $(x - 3)(x + 1)$ **97.** $(x - 2)(x - 3)$ **98.** $\left(x^2 + 2xy\right)\left(3x^2 y - 2\right)$

99. $\left(x^2 - 3x\right)\left(2xy - 3y\right)$ **100.** $(x - 2)\left(x^2 + 3x - 4\right)$ **101.** $(2x - 1)\left(-2x^2 - 3x + 4\right)$

102. $(x + 3)\left(2x^4 - 3x^2 - 5\right)$ **103.** $(3a + b)\left(2a^2 + ab - 2b^2\right)$ **104.** $\left(a^2 - b\right)\left(3a^2 - 2ab + 3b^2\right)$

Lesson 7-8

Multiply.

105. $(x + 3)^2$ **106.** $(3 + 2x)^2$ **107.** $(4x + 2y)^2$

108. $(3x - 2)^2$ **109.** $(5 - 2x)^2$ **110.** $(3x - 5y)^2$

111. $(3 + x)(3 - x)$ **112.** $(x - 5)(x + 5)$ **113.** $(2x + 1)(2x - 1)$

114. $\left(x^2 + 4\right)\left(x^2 - 4\right)$ **115.** $\left(2 + 3x^3\right)\left(2 - 3x^3\right)$ **116.** $\left(4x^3 - 3y\right)\left(4x^3 + 3y\right)$

Extra Practice

min

Lesson 8-1

Write the prime factorization of each number.

1. 24   **2.** 78   **3.** 88   **4.** 63

5. 128   **6.** 102   **7.** 71   **8.** 125

Find the GCF of each pair of numbers.

9. 18 and 66   **10.** 24 and 104   **11.** 30 and 75

12. 24 and 120   **13.** 36 and 99   **14.** 42 and 72

Find the GCF of each pair of monomials.

15. $4a^3$ and $9a^4$ **16.** $6q^2$ and $15q^5$ **17.** $6x^2$ and $14y^3$

18. $4z^2$ and $10z^5$ **19.** $5g^3$ and $9g$ **20.** $12x^2$ and $21y^2$

Lesson 8-2

Factor each polynomial. Check your answer.

21. $6b^2 - 15b^3$ **22.** $11t^4 - 9t^3$ **23.** $10v^3 - 25v$

24. $12r + 16r^3$ **25.** $17a^4 - 35a^2$ **26.** $9f + 18f^5 + 12f^2$

Factor each expression.

27. $3(a + 3) + 4a(a + 3)$ **28.** $5(k - 4) - 2k(k - 4)$ **29.** $5(c - 3) + 4c^2(c - 3)$

30. $3(t - 4) + t(t - 4)$ **31.** $5(2r - 1) - s(2r - 1)$ **32.** $7(3d + 4) - 2e(3d + 4)$

Factor each polynomial by grouping. Check your answer.

33. $x^3 + 3x^2 - 2x - 6$ **34.** $2m^3 - 3m^2 + 8m - 12$ **35.** $3k^3 - k^2 + 15k - 5$

36. $15r^3 + 25r^2 - 6r - 10$ **37.** $12n^3 - 6n^2 - 10n + 5$ **38.** $4z^3 - 3z^2 + 4z - 3$

39. $2k^2 - 3k + 12 - 8k$ **40.** $3p^2 - 2p + 8 - 12p$ **41.** $10d^2 - 6d + 9 - 15d$

42. $6a^3 - 4a^2 + 10 - 15a$ **43.** $12s^3 - 2s^2 + 3 - 18s$ **44.** $4c^3 - 3c^2 + 15 - 20c$

Lesson 8-3

Factor each trinomial. Check your answer.

45. $x^2 + 15x + 36$ **46.** $x^2 + 13x + 40$ **47.** $x^2 + 10x + 16$

48. $x^2 - 9x + 18$ **49.** $x^2 - 11x + 28$ **50.** $x^2 - 13x + 42$

51. $x^2 + 4x - 21$ **52.** $x^2 - 5x - 36$ **53.** $x^2 - 7x - 30$

54. Factor $c^2 - 2c - 48$. Show that the original polynomial and the factored form describe the same sequence of values for $c = 0, 1, 2, 3,$ and 4.

Copy and complete the table.

$x^2 + bx + c$	Sign of c	Binomial factors	Sign of Numbers in Binomials
$x^2 + 9x + 20$	Positive	$(x + 4)(x + 5)$	Both positive
55. $x^2 - x - 20$	?	?	?
56. $x^2 - 2x - 8$	?	?	?
57. $x^2 - 6x + 8$	?	?	?

Extra Practice

Lesson 8-4

Factor each trinomial. Check your answer.

58. $2x^2 + 13x + 15$

59. $3x^2 + 14x + 16$

60. $8x^2 - 16x + 6$

61. $6x^2 + 11x + 4$

62. $3x^2 - 11x + 6$

63. $10x^2 - 31x + 15$

64. $6x^2 - 5x - 4$

65. $8x^2 - 14x - 15$

66. $4x^2 - 11x + 6$

67. $12x^2 - 13x + 3$

68. $6x^2 - 7x - 10$

69. $6x^2 + 7x - 3$

70. $2x^2 + 5x - 12$

71. $6x^2 - 5x - 6$

72. $8x^2 + 10x - 3$

73. $10x^2 - 11x - 6$

74. $4x^2 - x - 5$

75. $6x^2 - 7x - 20$

76. $-2x^2 + 11x - 5$

77. $-6x^2 - x + 12$

78. $-8x^2 - 10x - 3$

79. $-4x^2 + 16x - 15$

80. $-10x^2 + 21x + 10$

81. $-3x^2 + 13x - 14$

Lesson 8-5

Determine whether each trinomial is a perfect square. If so, factor. If not, explain why.

82. $x^2 - 8x + 16$

83. $4x^2 - 4x + 1$

84. $x^2 - 8x + 9$

85. $9x^2 - 14x + 4$

86. $4x^2 + 12x + 9$

87. $x^2 + 8x - 16$

88. $9x^2 - 42x + 49$

89. $4x^2 + 18x + 25$

90. $16x^2 - 24x + 9$

Determine whether each trinomial is the difference of two squares. If so, factor. If not, explain why.

91. $4 - 16x^4$

92. $-t^2 - 35$

93. $c^2 - 25$

94. $g^5 - 9$

95. $v^4 - 64$

96. $x^2 - 120$

97. $x^2 - 36$

98. $9m^2 - 15$

99. $25c^2 - 16$

Find the missing term in each perfect-square trinomial.

100. $4x^2 - 20x + \blacksquare$

101. $9x^2 + \blacksquare + 1$

102. $\blacksquare - 56x + 49$

103. $9b^2 - \blacksquare + 25$

104. $\blacksquare + 28a + 49$

105. $4a^2 + 4a + \blacksquare$

Lesson 8-6

Tell whether each expression is completely factored. If not, factor.

106. $5(16x^2 + 4)$

107. $3r(4x \quad 9)$

108. $(9d - 6)(2d - 7)$

109. $(5 - h)(6 - 5h)$

110. $12y^2 - 2y - 24$

111. $3f(2f^2 + 5fg + 2g^2)$

Factor each polynomial completely. Check your answer.

112. $12b^3 - 48b$

113. $24w^4 - 20w^3 - 16w^2$

114. $18k^3 - 32k$

115. $4a^3 + 12a^2 - a^2b - 3ab$

116. $3x^3y - 6x^2y^2 + 3xy^3$

117. $36p^2q - 64q^3$

118. $32a^4 - 8a^2$

119. $m^3 + 5m^2n + 6mn^2$

120. $4x^2 - 3x^2 - 16x + 48x$

121. $18d^2 + 3d - 6$

122. $2r^2 - 9r - 18$

123. $8y^2 + 4y - 4$

124. $81 - 36u^2$

125. $8x^4 + 12x^2 - 20$

126. $10j^3 + 15j^2 - 70j$

127. $27z^3 - 18z^2 + 3z$

128. $4b^2 + 2b - 72$

129. $3f^2 - 3g^2$

Lesson 9-1

Tell whether each function is quadratic. Explain.

1. $y + 4x^2 = 2x - 3$ **2.** $4x - y = 3$ **3.** $3x^2 - 4 = y + x$

4.

x	−6	−4	−2	0	2
y	−5	−6	−4	2	11

5.

x	0	1	2	3	4
y	−5	−5	−3	1	7

Tell whether the graph of each quadratic function opens upward or downward. Then use a table of values to graph each function.

6. $y = -3x^2$ **7.** $y = \frac{2}{3}x^2$ **8.** $y = x^2 + 2$ **9.** $y = -4x^2 + 2x$

Identify the vertex of each parabola. Then find the domain and range.

10.   **11.**   **12.**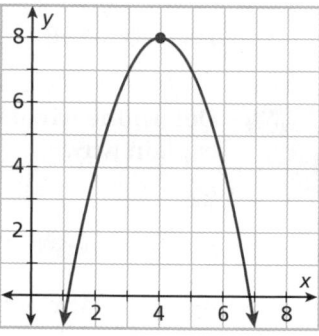

Lesson 9-2

Find the zeros of each quadratic function and the axis of symmetry of each parabola from the graph.

13.   **14.**   **15.**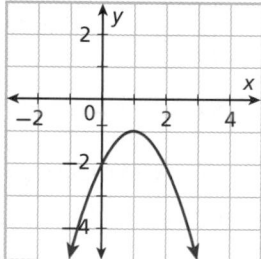

Find the vertex.

16. $y = 3x^2 - 6x + 2$ **17.** $y = -2x^2 + 8x - 3$ **18.** $y = x^2 + 2x - 4$

Lesson 9-3

Graph each quadratic function.

19. $y = x^2 - 4x + 1$ **20.** $y = -x^2 - x + 4$ **21.** $y = 3x^2 - 3x + 1$

22. $y - 2 = 2x^2$ **23.** $y + 3x^2 = 3x - 1$ **24.** $y - 4 = x^2 + 2x$

Lesson 9-4

Order the functions from narrowest to widest.

25. $f(x) = 2x^2, g(x) = -4x^2, h(x) = -x^2$ **26.** $f(x) = 3x^2, g(x) = \frac{1}{2}x^2, h(x) = -2x^2$

27. $f(x) = 4x^2, g(x) = x^2, h(x) = -\frac{1}{4}x^2$ **28.** $f(x) = 2x^2, g(x) = 5x^2, h(x) = -3x^2$

Compare the graph of each function with the graph of $f(x) = x^2$.

29. $g(x) = 2x^2 - 2$ **30.** $g(x) = -\frac{1}{2}x^2$ **31.** $g(x) = -3x^2 + 1$

Lesson 9-5

Solve each quadratic equation by graphing the related function.

32. $x^2 - x - 2 = 0$
33. $x^2 - 2x + 8 = 0$
34. $2x^2 + 4x - 6 = 0$

35. $2x^2 + 9x = -4$
36. $2x^2 + 3 = 0$
37. $2x^2 - 2x - 12 = 0$

38. $3x^2 = -3x + 6$
39. $x^2 = 4$
40. $2x^2 + 6x - 20 = 0$

41. $-3x^2 - 2 = 0$
42. $x^2 = -2x + 8$
43. $x^2 - 2x = 15$

Lesson 9-6

Use the Zero Product Property to solve each equation. Check your answer.

44. $(x + 3)(x - 2) = 0$
45. $(x - 4)(x + 2) = 0$
46. $(x)(x - 4) = 0$

47. $(2x + 6)(x - 2) = 0$
48. $(3x - 1)(x + 3) = 0$
49. $(x)(2x - 4) = 0$

Solve each quadratic equation by factoring. Check your answer.

50. $x^2 + 5x + 6 = 0$
51. $x^2 - 3x - 4 = 0$
52. $x^2 + x - 12 = 0$

53. $x^2 + x - 6 = 0$
54. $x^2 - 6x + 5 = 0$
55. $x^2 + 4x - 12 = 0$

56. $x^2 = 6x - 9$
57. $2x^2 + 4x = 6$
58. $x^2 + 2x = -1$

59. $3x^2 = 3x + 6$
60. $x^2 = x + 12$
61. $4x^2 + 8x + 4 = 0$

Lesson 9-7

Solve using square roots. Check your answer.

62. $x^2 = 169$
63. $x^2 = 121$
64. $x^2 = 289$

65. $x^2 = -64$
66. $x^2 = 81$
67. $x^2 = -441$

68. $4x^2 - 196 = 0$
69. $0 = 3x^2 - 48$
70. $24x^2 + 96 = 0$

71. $10x^2 - 75 = 15$
72. $0 = 4x^2 + 144$
73. $5x^2 - 105 = 20$

Solve. Round to the nearest hundredth.

74. $4x^2 = 160$
75. $0 = 3x^2 - 66$
76. $250 - 5x^2 = 0$

77. $0 = 9x^2 - 72$
78. $48 - 2x^2 = 42$
79. $6x^2 = 78$

Lesson 9-8

Complete the square to form a perfect-square trinomial.

80. $x^2 - 8x + $
81. $x^2 + x + $ ▧
82. $x^2 + 10x + $ ▧

83. $x^2 - 5x + $ ▧
84. $x^2 + 6x + $ ▧
85. $x^2 - 7x + $ ▧

Solve by completing the square.

86. $x^2 + 6x = 91$
87. $x^2 + 10x = -16$
88. $x^2 - 4x = 12$

89. $x^2 - 8x = -12$
90. $x^2 - 12x = -35$
91. $-x^2 - 6x = 5$

92. $-x^2 - 4x + 77 = 0$
93. $-x^2 = 10x + 9$
94. $-x^2 + 63 = -2x$

Lesson 9-9

Solve using the quadratic formula.

95. $x^2 + 3x - 4 = 0$
96. $x^2 - 2x - 8 = 0$
97. $x^2 + 2x - 3 = 0$

98. $x^2 - x - 10 = 0$
99. $2x^2 - x - 4 = 0$
100. $2x^2 + 3x - 3 = 0$

Find the number of real solutions of each equation using the discriminant.

101. $x^2 + 4x + 1 = 0$
102. $2x^2 - 3x + 2 = 0$
103. $x^2 - 5x + 2 = 0$

104. $2x^2 - 4x + 2 = 0$
105. $x^2 + 2x - 5 = 0$
106. $2x^2 - 2x - 3 = 0$

Extra Practice

Lesson 10-1

Use the line graph for Exercises 1–4.

1. In what year was the population the greatest?

2. Estimate the population in 2005.

3. During which one-year period did the population increase by the greatest amount?

4. Estimate the amount by which the population decreased from 2005 to 2006.

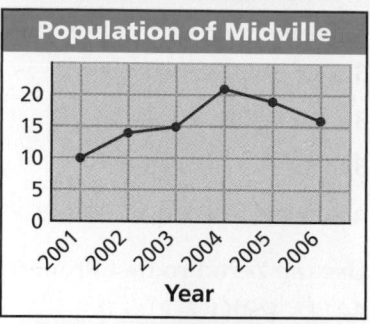

Population of Midville

Use the circle graph for Exercises 5–7.

5. Which candidate received the fewest votes?

6. Which two candidates received approximately the same number of votes?

7. A total of 400 students voted in the election. How many votes did Velez receive?

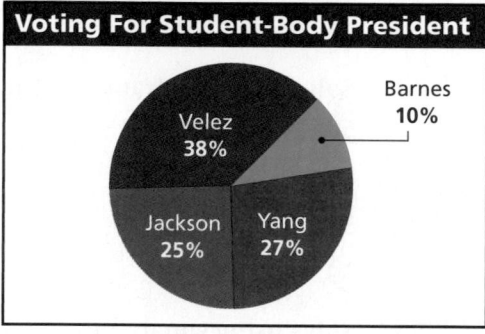

Voting For Student-Body President

Lesson 10-2

The daily high temperatures in degrees Celsius during a two-week period in Madison, Wisconsin, are given at right.

8. Use the data to make a stem-and-leaf plot.

9. Use the data to make a frequency table with intervals.

10. Use the frequency table from Exercise 9 to make a histogram for the data.

11. Use the data to make a cumulative frequency table.

High Temperatures (°C)						
22	25	28	33	29	24	19
19	18	25	32	30	32	25

Lesson 10-3

Find the mean, median, mode, and range of each data set.

12. 42, 45, 48, 45

13. 66, 68, 68, 62, 61, 68, 65, 60

Identify the outlier in each data set, and determine how the outlier affects the mean, median, mode, and range of the data.

14. 4, 8, 15, 8, 71, 7, 6   15. 36, 7, 50, 40, 38, 48, 40

Use the data to make a box-and-whisker plot.

16. 7, 8, 10, 2, 5, 1, 10, 8, 5, 5   17. 54, 64, 50, 48, 53, 55, 57

Lesson 10-4

18. The graph shows the ages of people who listen to a radio program.

   a. Explain why the graph is misleading.

   b. What might someone believe because of the graph?

   c. Who might want to use this graph? Explain.

19. A researcher surveys people at the Elmwood library about the number of hours they spend reading each day. Explain why the following statement is misleading: "People in Elmwood read for an average of 1.5 hours per day."

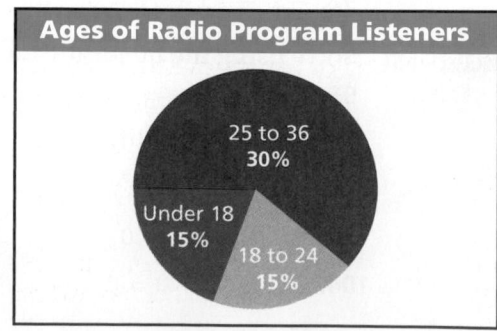

Ages of Radio Program Listeners

Lesson 10-5

20. Identify the sample space and the outcome shown for the spinner at right.

Write *impossible, unlikely, as likely as not, likely,* **or** *certain* **to describe each event.**

21. Two people sitting next to each other on a bus have the same birthday.

22. Dylan rolls a number greater than 1 on a standard number cube.

An experiment consists of randomly choosing a fruit snack from a box. Use the results in the table to find the experimental probability of each event.

Outcome	Frequency
Cherry	8
Peach	6
Blueberry	6

23. choosing a blueberry fruit snack

24. choosing a cherry fruit snack

25. not choosing a cherry fruit snack

Lesson 10-6

Find the theoretical probability of each outcome.

26. rolling an even number on a number cube

27. tossing two coins and both landing tails up

28. randomly choosing a prime number from a bag that contains ten slips of paper numbered 1 through 10

29. The probability of choosing a green marble from a bag is $\frac{3}{7}$. What is the probability of not choosing a green marble?

30. The odds against winning a game are $8:3$. What is the probability of winning the game?

Lesson 10-7

Tell whether each set of events is independent or dependent. Explain your answer.

31. You pick a bottle from a basket containing chilled drinks, and then your friend chooses a bottle.

32. You roll a 6 on a number cube and you toss a coin that lands heads up.

33. A number cube is rolled three times. What is the probability of rolling three numbers greater than 4?

34. An experiment consists of randomly selecting a marble from a bag, replacing it, and then selecting another marble. The bag contains 3 blue marbles, 2 orange marbles, and 5 yellow marbles. What is the probability of selecting a blue marble and then a yellow marble?

35. Madeleine has 3 nickels and 5 quarters in her pocket. She randomly chooses one coin and does not replace it. Then she randomly chooses another coin. What is the probability that she chooses two quarters?

Lesson 10-8

For Exercises 36 and 37, tell whether each situation involves combinations or permutations. Then give the number of possible outcomes.

36. How many different ways can three photographs be arranged in a row on a wall?

37. How many different smoothies can be made by blending two of the following fruits: oranges, bananas, strawberries, and peaches?

38. There are 6 entrants in a livestock competition at a county fair. How many different ways can the first-place, second-place, and third-place ribbons be awarded?

39. An amusement park has 7 roller coasters. How many different ways can Jacinto choose 4 different roller coasters to ride?

Extra Practice

Extra Practice

Lesson 11-1

Find the next three terms in each geometric sequence.

1. 1, 5, 25, 125 …

2. 736, 368, 184, 92, …

3. −2, 6, −18, 54, …

4. 8, 2, $\frac{1}{2}$, $\frac{1}{8}$, …

5. 7, −14, 28, −56, …

6. $\frac{1}{9}$, $\frac{1}{3}$, 1, 3, …

7. The first term of a geometric sequence is 2, and the common ratio is 3. What is the 8th term of the sequence?

8. What is the 8th term of the geometric sequence 600, 300, 150, 75, …?

Lesson 11-2

Tell whether each set of ordered pairs satisfies an exponential function. Explain your answer.

9. $\left\{\left(-1, \frac{1}{2}\right), (0, 2), (1, 8), (2, 32)\right\}$

10. $\left\{\left(-1, -\frac{1}{2}\right), (0, 0), \left(1, \frac{1}{2}\right), (2, 4)\right\}$

11. $\left\{(-1, 4), (0, 1), \left(1, \frac{1}{4}\right), \left(2, \frac{1}{16}\right)\right\}$

12. $\left\{(0, 0), (1, 3), (2, 12), (3, 27)\right\}$

Graph each exponential function.

13. $y = 3(2)^x$

14. $y = \frac{1}{2}(4)^x$

15. $y = -3^x$

16. $y = -\frac{1}{2}(2)^x$

17. $y = 5\left(\frac{1}{2}\right)^x$

18. $y = -2(0.25)^x$

Lesson 11-3

Write an exponential growth function to model each situation. Then find the value of the function after the given amount of time.

19. The rent for an apartment is $6600 per year and increasing at a rate of 4% per year; 5 years.

20. A museum has 1200 members and the number of members is increasing at a rate of 2% per year; 8 years.

Write a compound interest function to model each situation. Then find the balance after the given number of years.

21. $4000 invested at a rate of 4% compounded quarterly; 3 years

22. $5200 invested at a rate of 2.5% compounded annually; 6 years

Write an exponential decay function to model each situation. Then find the value of the function after the given amount of time.

23. The cost of a stereo system is $800 and is decreasing at a rate of 6% per year; 5 years.

24. The population of a town is 14,000 and is decreasing at a rate of 2% per year; 10 years.

Lesson 11-4

Graph each data set. Which kind of model best describes the data?

25. $\left\{(0, 3), (1, 0), (2, -1), (3, 0), (4, 3)\right\}$

26. $\left\{(-4, -4), (-3, -3.5), (-2, -3), (-1, -2.5), (0, -2), (1, -1.5)\right\}$

27. $\left\{(0, 4), (1, 2), (2, 1), (3, 0.5), (4, 0.25)\right\}$

Look for a pattern in each data set to determine which kind of model best describes the data.

28. $\left\{(-1, -5), (0, -5), (1, -3), (2, 1), (3, 7)\right\}$

29. $\left\{(0, 0.25), (1, 0.5), (2, 1), (3, 2), (4, 4)\right\}$

30. $\left\{(-2, 11), (-1, 8), (0, 5), (1, 2), (2, -1)\right\}$

Lesson 11-5

Find the domain of each square-root function.

31. $y = \sqrt{x+1}$ **32.** $y = \sqrt{x-2} + 4$ **33.** $y = \sqrt{4+x}$

34. $y = \sqrt{3x-6}$ **35.** $y = 1 + \sqrt{\dfrac{x}{3}}$ **36.** $y = \sqrt{4x-1}$

Graph each square-root function.

37. $y = \sqrt{x+2}$ **38.** $y = \sqrt{x} - 3$ **39.** $y = \sqrt{3x} + 1$

40. $y = -\sqrt{x}$ **41.** $y = 2\sqrt{x+1}$ **42.** $y = 3\sqrt{x} - 2$

Lesson 11-6

Simplify each expression.

43. $\sqrt{\dfrac{128}{2}}$ **44.** $\sqrt{7^2 + 24^2}$ **45.** $\sqrt{(4-x)^2}$

46. $\sqrt{\dfrac{3}{48}}$ **47.** $\sqrt{y^2 + 4y + 4}$ **48.** $\sqrt{5^2 - 4^2}$

Simplify. All variables represent nonnegative numbers.

49. $\sqrt{72}$ **50.** $\sqrt{75x^4y^3}$ **51.** $\sqrt{\dfrac{11}{81}}$

52. $\sqrt{\dfrac{64}{x^6}}$ **53.** $\sqrt{\dfrac{16a^4}{25b^2}}$ **54.** $\sqrt{\dfrac{18x^4}{49x^3}}$

Lesson 11-7

Add or subtract.

55. $5\sqrt{7} + 3\sqrt{7}$ **56.** $6\sqrt{2} + \sqrt{2}$ **57.** $5\sqrt{3} - 2\sqrt{3}$

58. $\sqrt{5} + 7\sqrt{5} - 9\sqrt{5}$ **59.** $2\sqrt{y} + 4\sqrt{y} - 3\sqrt{y}$ **60.** $5\sqrt{3} + 4\sqrt{2} - 3\sqrt{3}$

Simplify each expression.

61. $\sqrt{75} + \sqrt{27}$ **62.** $\sqrt{45} - \sqrt{20}$ **63.** $2\sqrt{12} + \sqrt{18}$

64. $3\sqrt{27x} + \sqrt{48x}$ **65.** $5\sqrt{20y} - 2\sqrt{80y}$ **66.** $\sqrt{28a} + 2\sqrt{63a} - \sqrt{175a}$

67. $\sqrt{50y} - 2\sqrt{18y} + 3\sqrt{8y}$ **68.** $\sqrt{12x} - \sqrt{27x} - \sqrt{5x}$ **69.** $5\sqrt{180s} - 6\sqrt{80s}$

Lesson 11-8

Multiply. Write each product in simplest form.

70. $\sqrt{5}\sqrt{10}$ **71.** $\sqrt{6}\sqrt{12}$ **72.** $\left(3\sqrt{3}\right)^2$

73. $\left(2\sqrt{7}\right)^2$ **74.** $\sqrt{6x}\sqrt{15x}$ **75.** $\sqrt{3}\left(2 + \sqrt{27}\right)$

76. $2\sqrt{5}\left(\sqrt{20} + 3\right)$ **77.** $\sqrt{2x}\left(3 + \sqrt{8x}\right)$ **78.** $\left(4 + \sqrt{3}\right)\left(1 - \sqrt{3}\right)$

79. $\left(3 + \sqrt{5}\right)\left(8 - \sqrt{5}\right)$ **80.** $\left(4 + \sqrt{2}\right)^2$ **81.** $\left(5 - \sqrt{3}\right)^2$

Simplify each quotient.

82. $\dfrac{\sqrt{5}}{\sqrt{3}}$ **83.** $\dfrac{2\sqrt{7}}{\sqrt{5}}$ **84.** $\dfrac{\sqrt{3}}{\sqrt{20}}$

85. $\dfrac{5\sqrt{7}}{\sqrt{50}}$ **86.** $\dfrac{\sqrt{12a}}{\sqrt{32}}$ **87.** $\dfrac{\sqrt{200x}}{\sqrt{28}}$

Lesson 11-9

Solve each equation. Check your answer.

88. $\sqrt{x} = 11$ **89.** $\sqrt{3x} = 9$ **90.** $\sqrt{-2x} = 10$

91. $5 = \sqrt{-4x}$ **92.** $\sqrt{x} + 5 = 12$ **93.** $\sqrt{x} - 4 = 1$

94. $\sqrt{3x+1} = 4$ **95.** $\sqrt{2x+5} = 3$ **96.** $\sqrt{x-4} + 1 = 7$

97. $\sqrt{6-3x} - 2 = 4$ **98.** $\sqrt{6-x} - 5 = -3$ **99.** $4\sqrt{x} = 20$

Extra Practice

Lesson 12-1

Tell whether each relationship is an inverse variation. Explain.

1.

x	y
4	8
8	16
16	32
32	64

2.

x	y
2	6
3	4
6	2
12	1

3.

x	y
−1	24
2	−12
4	−6
8	−3

4. $3xy = 10$

5. $y - x = 6$

6. $6xy = -1$

7. Write and graph the inverse variation in which $y = 4$ when $x = 3$.

8. Write and graph the inverse variation in which $y = \frac{1}{2}$ when $x = 6$.

9. Let $x_1 = 6$, $y_1 = 8$, and $x_2 = 12$. Let y vary inversely as x. Find y_2.

10. Let $x_1 = -4$, $y_1 = -2$, and $y_2 = 16$. Let y vary inversely as x. Find x_2.

Lesson 12-2

Identify the excluded values for each rational function.

11. $y = \frac{16}{x}$

12. $y = \frac{1}{x - 1}$

13. $y = -\frac{3}{x + 5}$

14. $y = \frac{20}{x + 20}$

Identify the asymptotes.

15. $y = \frac{2}{x - 4}$

16. $y = \frac{8}{x + 5}$

17. $y = \frac{7}{3x - 2} - 6$

18. $y = \frac{3}{2x - 2} + 4$

Graph each function.

19. $y = \frac{1}{x + 3}$

20. $y = \frac{1}{x - 2}$

21. $y = \frac{1}{x} + 4$

22. $y = \frac{3}{x - 2}$

23. $y = \frac{1}{x - 3} + 2$

24. $y = \frac{1}{x - 5} - 6$

25. $y = \frac{1}{x + 2} + 5$

26. $y = \frac{1}{x + 5} + 1$

Lesson 12-3

Find the excluded value(s) of each rational expression.

27. $\frac{3}{7x}$

28. $\frac{-2}{x^2 - x}$

29. $\frac{6}{x^2 + x - 12}$

30. $\frac{p + 1}{p^2 + 4p - 5}$

Simplify each rational expression, if possible. Identify excluded values.

31. $\frac{4m^2}{12m}$

32. $\frac{7x^5}{28x}$

33. $\frac{4x^2 - 8x}{x - 2}$

34. $\frac{2y}{y - 1}$

35. $\frac{5x^3 + 20x^2}{x + 4}$

36. $\frac{a + 1}{a - 2}$

37. $\frac{3y^3 + 3y}{y^2 + 1}$

38. $\frac{x^3 + 4x}{x^2 + 4}$

Simplify each rational expression, if possible.

39. $\frac{b + 2}{b^2 + 5b + 6}$

40. $\frac{x - 3}{x^2 - 6x + 9}$

41. $\frac{y^2 - 4y - 5}{y^2 - 2y - 3}$

42. $\frac{(m + 2)^2}{m^2 - 6m - 16}$

43. $\frac{x^2 - 9}{x^2 + x - 12}$

44. $\frac{2 - m}{3m^2 - 6m}$

45. $\frac{x - 4}{12x^2 - 3x^3}$

46. $\frac{6 - 3x}{x^2 - 6x + 8}$

Extra Practice

Lesson 12-4

Multiply. Simplify your answer.

47. $\dfrac{4a^3}{b^3} \cdot \dfrac{ab}{6a^2}$

48. $\dfrac{6x^3y}{4y^4} \cdot \dfrac{8x^2yz^2}{3xz^5}$

49. $\dfrac{x-3}{2} \cdot \dfrac{8}{4x-12}$

50. $\dfrac{x-2}{x-5} \cdot \dfrac{2x-10}{3}$

51. $\dfrac{a^2b^3}{6a^3c} \cdot \dfrac{9b^2}{12b^5c^2}$

52. $\dfrac{3x}{2x+4} \cdot \dfrac{3x+6}{9}$

53. $\dfrac{1}{2x+4}\left(x^2 - 2x - 8\right)$

54. $\dfrac{3x}{4x-20}\left(x^2 + x - 30\right)$

55. $\dfrac{2y}{3y+15}\left(y^2 + 10y + 25\right)$

56. $\dfrac{4r^3 + 8r}{r^3} \cdot \dfrac{r}{3r^2 + 6}$

57. $\dfrac{x^2 + x}{x^2 - x - 6} \cdot \dfrac{x-3}{6x^2 + 6x}$

58. $\dfrac{a^2 - 3a - 10}{a^2 - a - 6} \cdot \dfrac{a^2 - 2a - 3}{a-5}$

59. $\dfrac{4b^2 + 4}{b-1} \cdot \dfrac{b^2 - 1}{8b^2 + 8}$

60. $\dfrac{pq + 2q}{pq + 1} \cdot \dfrac{3pq + 3}{pq^2 + 2q^2}$

61. $\dfrac{r^2 + 3r + 2}{4r + 4} \cdot \dfrac{2r + 6}{r^2 - 2r - 8}$

Divide. Simplify your answer.

62. $\dfrac{3x^2y^3}{x^3z^2} \div \dfrac{6y^4}{x^2z^5}$

63. $\dfrac{x^2 + 4x + 3}{3x^3 + 9x^2} \div \left(x^2 - 1\right)$

64. $\dfrac{p-1}{p^2 + 4p - 5} \div \dfrac{p^2 - 2p}{p^2 + 3p - 10}$

Lesson 12-5

Add. Simplify your answer.

65. $\dfrac{3x}{4x^3} + \dfrac{5x}{4x^3}$

66. $\dfrac{x^2 + 1}{x-1} + \dfrac{1 - 3x}{x-1}$

67. $\dfrac{2x^2}{x^2 - 2x - 3} + \dfrac{2x}{x^2 - 2x - 3}$

Subtract. Simplify your answer.

68. $\dfrac{5}{6y^4} - \dfrac{2}{6y^4}$

69. $\dfrac{5a^2 + 1}{a^2 - a - 6} - \dfrac{15a + 1}{a^2 - a - 6}$

70. $\dfrac{m^2 + 2m}{m^2 - 9} - \dfrac{m + 12}{m^2 - 9}$

Find the LCM of the given expressions.

71. $8x^5y^8, \, 6x^4y^9$

72. $x^2 - 4, \, x^2 + 7x + 10$

73. $d^2 - 2d - 3, \, d^2 + d - 12$

Add or subtract. Simplify your answer.

74. $\dfrac{5}{y^2} - \dfrac{3}{4y^2}$

75. $\dfrac{5}{x^2 - x - 6} + \dfrac{1}{x + 2}$

76. $\dfrac{3x}{x - 2} - \dfrac{x}{2 - x}$

Lesson 12-6

Divide.

77. $\left(12y^5 - 16y^2 + 4y\right) \div 4y^2$

78. $\left(6m^4 - 18m + 3\right) \div 6m^2$

79. $\left(16x^4 + 20x^3 - 4x\right) \div -4x^3$

80. $\dfrac{b^2 - 4b - 5}{b + 1}$

81. $\dfrac{2x^2 + 9x + 4}{x + 4}$

82. $\dfrac{6a^2 - 13a - 5}{3a + 1}$

Divide using long division.

83. $\left(a^2 - 5a - 6\right) \div (a + 1)$

84. $\left(2x^2 + 10x + 8\right) \div (x + 4)$

85. $\left(3y^2 - 11y + 10\right) \div (y - 2)$

86. $\left(3x^2 - 2x - 7\right) \div (x - 2)$

87. $\left(2x^2 + 2x - 9\right) \div (x + 3)$

88. $\left(5x^3 + 2x^2 - 4\right) \div (x - 2)$

Lesson 12-7

Solve. Check your answer.

89. $\dfrac{5}{x + 1} = \dfrac{4}{x - 1}$

90. $\dfrac{4}{t} = \dfrac{10}{t + 9}$

91. $\dfrac{8}{m} = \dfrac{6}{m + 1}$

92. $\dfrac{4}{a - 2} = \dfrac{8}{a + 1}$

93. $\dfrac{3}{2y + 4} = \dfrac{1}{y}$

94. $\dfrac{5}{4w - 2} = \dfrac{6}{5w - 2}$

95. $\dfrac{1}{2} + \dfrac{3}{2m} = -\dfrac{1}{m^2}$

96. $\dfrac{x}{2} + \dfrac{3}{2} = \dfrac{2}{x}$

97. $1 - \dfrac{3}{a} = \dfrac{10}{a^2}$

Solve. Identify any extraneous solutions.

98. $\dfrac{3}{x + 4} = \dfrac{x - 5}{x + 4}$

99. $\dfrac{2}{x} = \dfrac{x + 2}{x^2 - 4}$

100. $\dfrac{4x}{x - 4} - 7 = \dfrac{16}{x - 4}$

Extra Practice

Biology Use the following information for Exercises 1 and 2.

In general, skin cells in the human body contain 46 chromosomes. *(Lesson 1-1)*

1. Write an expression for the number of chromosomes in *c* skin cells.

2. Find the number of chromosomes in 8, 15, and 50 skin cells.

3. On a winter day in Fairbanks, Alaska, the temperature dropped from 12 °F to −16 °F. How many degrees did the temperature drop? *(Lesson 1-2)*

4. **Geography** The elevation of the Dead Sea in Jordan is −411 meters. The greatest elevation on Earth is Mt. Everest, at 8850 meters. What is the difference in elevation between these two locations? *(Lesson 1-2)*

5. Jeremy is raising money for his school by selling magazine subscriptions. Each subscription costs $16.75. During the first week, he sells 12 subscriptions. How much money does he raise? *(Lesson 1-3)*

6. As a service charge, Nadine's checking account is adjusted by −$3 each month. What is the total amount of the adjustment over the course of one year? *(Lesson 1-3)*

7. To go from one figure to the next in the sequence of figures, each square is split into four smaller squares. How many squares will be in Figure 5? *(Lesson 1-4)*

Figure 0   Figure 1   Figure 2

8. When you fold a sheet of paper in half and then open it, the crease creates 2 regions. Folding the paper in half 2 times creates 4 regions. How many regions do you create when you fold a sheet of paper in half 5 times? *(Lesson 1-4)*

9. Dan began his stamp collection with just 5 stamps in the first year. Every year thereafter, his collection grew 5 times as large as the year before. How many stamps were in Dan's collection after 4 years? *(Lesson 1-4)*

10. An art museum exhibits a square painting that has an area of 75 square feet. Find its side length to the nearest tenth. *(Lesson 1-5)*

11. **Travel** The base of the Washington Monument in Washington, D.C., is a square with an area of 336 yards. Find the length of one side of the monument's base to the nearest tenth. *(Lesson 1-5)*

12. The toll to cross a bridge is $2 for cars, $5 for trucks, and $10 for buses. The total amount of money collected can be found using the expression $2C + 5T + 10B$. Use the table to find the total amount of money collected between 10 A.M. and 11 A.M. *(Lesson 1-6)*

Bridge Tolls, 10 A.M. to 11 A.M.	
Type of Vehicle	Number
Car *C*	104
Truck *T*	20
Bus *B*	3

13. The expression $\frac{5}{9}(F - 32)$ converts a temperature *F* in degrees Fahrenheit to a temperature in degrees Celsius. Convert 77 °F to degrees Celsius. *(Lesson 1-6)*

Use the following information for Exercises 14 and 15.

An airplane has 12 rows of seats in first class and 35 rows of seats in coach. Each row has the same number of seats. *(Lesson 1-7)*

14. The total number of seats in the plane is $12x + 35x$, where *x* is the number of seats in a row. Simplify the expression.

15. Find the total number of seats given that the plane has 6 seats per row.

Use the following information for Exercises 16 and 17.

A sales representative earns $680 per week plus a $40 commission for each sale. *(Lesson 1-8)*

16. Write a rule for the sales representative's weekly earnings.

17. Write ordered pairs for the representative's weekly earnings for 5, 8, and 10 sales.

1. **Economics** In 2004, the average price of an ounce of gold was $47 more than the average price in 2003. The 2004 price was $410. Write and solve an equation to find the average price of an ounce of gold in 2003. *(Lesson 2-1)*

2. During a renovation, 36 seats were removed from a theater. The theater now seats 580 people. Write and solve an equation to find the number of seats in the theater before the renovation. *(Lesson 2-1)*

3. A case of juice drinks contains 12 bottles and costs $18. Write and solve an equation to find the cost of each drink. *(Lesson 2-2)*

4. **Astronomy** Objects weigh about 3 times as much on Earth as they do on Mars. A rock weighs 42 lb on Mars. Write and solve an equation to find the rock's weight on Earth. *(Lesson 2-2)*

5. The county fair's admission fee is $8 and each ride costs $2.50. Sonia spent a total of $25.50. How many rides did she go on? *(Lesson 2-3)*

6. At the beginning of a block party, the temperature was 84°. During the party, the temperature dropped 3° every hour. At the end of the party, the temperature was 66°. How long was the party? *(Lesson 2-3)*

7. **Consumer Economics** A health insurance policy costs $700 per year, plus $15 for each visit to the doctor's office. A different plan costs $560 per year, but each office visit is $50. Find the number of office visits for which the two plans have the same total cost. *(Lesson 2-4)*

8. **Geometry** The formula $A = \frac{1}{2} bh$ gives the area A of a triangle with base b and height h. *(Lesson 2-5)*

   a. Solve $A = \frac{1}{2} bh$ for h.

   b. Find the height of a triangle with an area of 30 square feet and a base of 6 feet.

9. Charles is hanging a poster on his wall. He wants the top of the poster to be 84 inches from the floor but would be happy for it to be 3 inches higher or lower. Write and solve an absolute-value equation to find the maximum and minimum acceptable heights. *(Lesson 2-6)*

10. The ratio of students to adults on a school trip is 9:2. There are 6 adults on the trip. How many students are there? *(Lesson 2-7)*

11. A cheetah can reach speeds of up to 103 feet per second. Use dimensional analysis to convert the cheetah's speed to miles per hour. Round to the nearest tenth. *(Lesson 2-7)*

12. Write and solve a proportion to find the height of the flagpole. *(Lesson 2-8)*

13. Paul has 8 jazz CDs. The jazz CDs are 5% of his collection. How many CDs does Paul have? *(Lesson 2-9)*

14. Miguel earns an annual salary of $38,000 plus a 3.5% commission on sales. His sales for one year were $90,000. Find his total salary for the year. *(Lesson 2-10)*

15. How long would it take $3600 to earn simple interest of $450 at an annual interest rate of 5%? *(Lesson 2-10)*

16. A store sells swimsuits at a 30% discount. What is the final price of a swimsuit that originally sold for $28? *(Lesson 2-11)*

17. Mei sells jam at a farmer's market for $4.20 per jar. Each jar costs Mei $3 to make. What is the markup as a percent? *(Lesson 2-11)*

Extra Practice

Chapter 3 ■ Applications Practice

1. At a food-processing factory, each box of cereal must weigh at least 15 ounces. Define a variable and write an inequality for the acceptable weights of the cereal boxes. Graph the solutions. *(Lesson 3-1)*

2. In order to qualify for a discounted entry fee at a museum, a visitor must be less than 13 years old. Define a variable and write an inequality for the ages that qualify for the discounted entry fee. Graph the solutions. *(Lesson 3-1)*

3. A restaurant can seat no more than 102 customers at one time. There are already 96 customers in the restaurant. Write and solve an inequality to find out how many additional customers could be seated in the restaurant. *(Lesson 3-2)*

4. **Meteorology** A hurricane is a tropical storm with a wind speed of at least 74 mi/h. A meteorologist is tracking a storm whose current wind speed is 63 mi/h. Write and solve an inequality to find out how much greater the wind speed must be in order for this storm to be considered a hurricane. *(Lesson 3-2)*

Hobbies Use the following information for Exercises 5–7.

When setting up an aquarium, it is recommended that you have no more than one inch of fish per gallon of water. For example, in a 30-gallon tank, the total length of the fish should be at most 30 inches. *(Lesson 3-3)*

Freshwater Fish	
Name	Length (in.)
Red tail catfish	3.5
Blue gourami	1.5

5. Write an inequality to show the possible numbers of blue gourami you can put in a 10-gallon aquarium.

6. Find the possible numbers of blue gourami you can put in a 10-gallon aquarium.

7. Find the possible numbers of red tail catfish you can put in a 20-gallon aquarium.

8. The admission fee at an amusement park is $12, and each ride costs $3.50. The park also offers an all-day pass with unlimited rides for $33. For what numbers of rides is it cheaper to buy the all-day pass? *(Lesson 3-4)*

9. The table shows the cost of Internet access at two different cafes. For how many hours of access is the cost at Cyber Station less than the cost at Web World? *(Lesson 3-5)*

Internet Access	
Cafe	Cost
Cyber Station	$12 one-time membership fee $1.50 per hour
Web World	No membership fee $2.25 per hour

10. Larissa is considering two summer jobs. A job at the mall pays $400 per week plus $15 for every hour of overtime. A job at the movie theater pays $360 per week plus $20 for every hour of overtime. How many hours of overtime would Larissa have to work in order for the job at the movie theater to pay a higher salary than the job at the mall? *(Lesson 3-5)*

11. **Health** For maximum safety, it is recommended that food be stored at a temperature between 34 °F and 40 °F inclusive. Write a compound inequality to show the temperatures that are within the recommended range. Graph the solutions. *(Lesson 3-6)*

12. **Physics** Color is determined by the wavelength of light. Wavelengths are measured in nanometers (nm). Our eyes see the color green when light has a wavelength between 492 nm and 577 nm inclusive. Write a compound inequality to show the wavelengths that produce green light. Graph the solutions. *(Lesson 3-6)*

13. Allison ran a mile in 8 minutes. She wants to run a second mile within 0.75 minute of her time for the first mile. Write and solve an absolute-value inequality to find the range of acceptable times for the second mile. *(Lesson 3-7)*

1. Donnell drove on the highway at a constant speed and then slowed down as she approached her exit. Sketch a graph to show the speed of Donnell's car over time. Tell whether the graph is continuous or discrete. *(Lesson 4-1)*

2. Lori is buying mineral water for a party. The bottles are available in six-packs. Sketch a graph showing the number of bottles Lori will have if she buys 1, 2, 3, 4, or 5 six-packs. Tell whether the graph is continuous or discrete. *(Lesson 4-1)*

3. **Health** To exercise effectively, it is important to know your maximum heart rate. You can calculate your maximum heart rate in beats per minute by subtracting your age from 220. *(Lesson 4-2)*

   a. Express the age x and the maximum heart rate y as a relation in table form by showing the maximum heart rate for people who are 20, 30, 35, and 40 years old.

   b. Is this relation a function? Explain.

4. **Sports** The table shows the number of games won by four baseball teams and the number of home runs each team hit. Is this relation a function? Explain. *(Lesson 4-2)*

Season Statistics	
Wins	Home Runs
95	185
93	133
80	140
93	167

5. Michael uses 5.5 cups of flour for each loaf of bread that he bakes. He plans to bake a maximum of 4 loaves. Write a function to describe the number of cups of flour used. Find a reasonable domain and range for the function. *(Lesson 4-3)*

6. A gym offers the following special rate. New members pay a $425 initiation fee and then pay $90 per year for 1, 2, or 3 years. Write a function to describe the situation. Find a reasonable domain and range for the function. *(Lesson 4-3)*

7. The function $y = 3.5x$ describes the number of miles y that the average turtle can walk in x hours. Graph the function. Use the graph to estimate how many miles a turtle can walk in 4.5 hours. *(Lesson 4-4)*

8. **Earth Science** The Kangerdlugssuaq glacier in Greenland is flowing into the sea at the rate of 1.6 meters per hour. The function $y = 1.6x$ describes the number of meters y that flow into the sea in x hours. Graph the function. Use the graph to estimate the number of meters that flow into the sea in 8 hours. *(Lesson 4-4)*

9. The scatter plot shows a relationship between the number of lemonades sold in a day and the day's high temperature. Based on this relationship, predict the number of lemonades that will be sold on a day when the high temperature is 96 °F. *(Lesson 4-5)*

Lemonade Sales

10. In month 1 the Elmwood Public Library had 85 Spanish books in its collection. Each month, the librarian plans to order 8 new Spanish books. How many Spanish books will the library have in month 15? *(Lesson 4-6)*

11. Nikki purchases a card that she can use to ride the bus in her town. Each time she rides the bus $1.50 is deducted from the value of the card. After her first ride, there is $43.50 left on the card. How much money will be left on the card after Nikki has taken 12 bus rides? *(Lesson 4-6)*

Chapter 5 ▪ Applications Practice

1. Jennifer is having prints made of her photographs. Each print costs $1.50. The function $f(x) = 1.50x$ gives the total cost of the x prints. Graph this function and give its domain and range. *(Lesson 5-1)*

2. The Chang family lives 400 miles from Denver. They drive to Denver at a constant speed of 50 mi/h. The function $f(x) = 400 - 50x$ gives their distance in miles from Denver after x hours. *(Lesson 5-2)*

   a. Graph this function and find the intercepts.

   b. What does each intercept represent?

3. **History** The table shows the number of nations in the United Nations in different years. Find the rate of change for each time interval. During which time interval did the U.N. grow at the greatest rate? *(Lesson 5-3)*

Year	1945	1950	1960	1975
Number of Nations	51	60	99	144

4. The graph shows the temperature of an oven at different times. Find the slope of the line. Then tell what the slope represents. *(Lesson 5-4)*

5. A straight highway connects the towns of Dale and Winslow. On a map, the coordinates of Dale are (5, 16), and the coordinates of Winslow are (9, 24). A rest area is located on the highway at the midpoint between the towns. What are the map coordinates of the rest area? *(Lesson 5-5)*

6. On a map, a campground is at (3, 5), and a fishing area is at (8, 4). Each unit on the map represents 0.1 mile. To the nearest tenth of a mile, what is the distance between the campground and the fishing area? *(Lesson 5-5)*

7. **Sports** Competitive race-walkers move at a speed of about 9 miles per hour. Write a direct variation equation for the distance y that a race-walker will cover in x hours. Then graph. *(Lesson 5-6)*

8. A bicycle rental costs $10 plus $1.50 per hour. The cost as a function of the number of hours is shown in the graph. *(Lesson 5-7)*

   a. Write an equation that represents the cost as a function of the number of hours.

   b. Identify the slope and y-intercept and describe their meaning.

   c. Find the cost of renting a bike for 6 hours.

9. A hot-air balloon is moving at a constant rate. Its altitude is a linear function of time, as shown in the table. Write an equation in slope-intercept form that represents this function. Then find the balloon's altitude after 25 minutes. *(Lesson 5-8)*

Balloon's Altitude	
Time (min)	Altitude (m)
0	250
7	215
12	190

10. **Geometry** Show that the points $A(2, 3)$, $B(3, 1)$, $C(-1, -1)$, and $D(-2, 1)$ are the vertices of a rectangle. *(Lesson 5-9)*

11. A phone plan for international calls costs $12.50 per month plus $0.04 per minute. The monthly cost for x minutes of calls is given by the function $f(x) = 0.04x + 12.50$. How will the graph change if the phone company raises the monthly fee to $14.50? if the cost per minute is raised to $0.05? *(Lesson 5-10)*

Chapter 6 ■ Applications Practice

1. Net Sounds, an online music store, charges $12 per CD plus $3 for shipping and handling. Web Discs charges $10 per CD plus $9 for shipping and handling. For how many CDs will the cost be the same? What will that cost be? *(Lesson 6-1)*

2. At Rocco's Restaurant, a large pizza costs $12 plus $1.25 for each additional topping. At Pizza Palace, a large pizza costs $15 plus $0.75 for each additional topping. For how many toppings will the cost be the same? What will that cost be? *(Lesson 6-1)*

Use the following information for Exercises 3 and 4.

The coach of a baseball team is deciding between two companies that manufacture team jerseys. One company charges a $60 setup fee and $25 per jersey. The other company charges a $200 setup fee and $15 per jersey. *(Lesson 6-2)*

3. For how many jerseys will the cost at the two companies be the same? What will that cost be?

4. The coach is planning to purchase 20 jerseys. Which company is the better option? Why?

5. **Geometry** The length of a rectangle is 5 inches greater than the width. The sum of the length and width is 41 inches. Find the length and width of the rectangle. *(Lesson 6-2)*

6. At a movie theater, tickets cost $9.50 for adults and $6.50 for children. A group of 7 moviegoers pays a total of $54.50. How many adults and how many children are in the group? *(Lesson 6-3)*

7. **Business** A grocer is buying large quantities of fruit to resell at his store. He purchases apples at $0.50 per pound and pears at $0.75 per pound. The grocer spends a total of $17.25 for 27 pounds of fruit. How many pounds of each fruit does he buy? *(Lesson 6-3)*

8. Bricks are available in two sizes. Large bricks weigh 9 pounds, and small bricks weigh 4.5 pounds. A bricklayer has 14 bricks that weigh a total of 90 pounds. How many of each type of brick are there? *(Lesson 6-3)*

9. **Sports** The table shows the time it took two runners to complete the Boston Marathon in several different years. If the patterns continue, will Shanna ever complete the marathon in the same number of minutes as Maria? Explain. *(Lesson 6-4)*

Marathon Times (min)				
	2003	2004	2005	2006
Shanna	190	182	174	166
Maria	175	167	159	151

10. Jordan leaves his house and rides his bike at 10 mi/h. After he goes 4 miles, his brother Tim leaves the house and rides in the same direction at 12 mi/h. If their rates stay the same, will Tim ever catch up to Jordan? Explain. *(Lesson 6-4)*

11. Charmaine is buying almonds and cashews for a reception. She wants to spend no more than $18. Almonds cost $4 per pound, and cashews cost $5 per pound. Write a linear inequality to describe the situation. Graph the solutions. Then give two combinations of nuts that Charmaine could buy. *(Lesson 6-5)*

12. Luis is buying T-shirts to give out at a school fund-raiser. He must spend less than $100 for the shirts. Child shirts cost $5 each, and adult shirts cost $8 each. Write a linear inequality to describe the situation. Graph the solutions. Then give two combinations of shirts that Luis could buy. *(Lesson 6-5)*

13. Nicholas is buying treats for his dog. Beef cubes cost $3 per pound, and liver cubes cost $2 per pound. He wants to buy at least 2 pounds of each type of treat, and he wants to spend no more than $14. Graph all possible combinations of the treats that Nicholas could buy. List two possible combinations. *(Lesson 6-6)*

14. **Geometry** The perimeter of a rectangle is at most 20 inches. The length and the width are each at least 3 inches. Graph all possible combinations of lengths and widths that result in such a rectangle. List two possible combinations. *(Lesson 6-6)*

1. The eye of a bee is about 10^{-3} m in diameter. Simplify this expression. *(Lesson 7-1)*

2. A typical stroboscopic camera has a shutter speed of 10^{-6} seconds. Simplify this expression. *(Lesson 7-1)*

3. **Space Exploration** During a mission that took place in August, 2005, the Space Shuttle *Discovery* traveled a total distance of 9.3×10^6 km. The Space Shuttle's velocity was 28,000 km/h. *(Lesson 7-2)*

   a. Write the total distance that the Space Shuttle traveled in standard form.

   b. Write the Space Shuttle's velocity in scientific notation.

4. There are approximately 10,000,000 grains in a pound of salt. Write this number in scientific notation. *(Lesson 7-2)*

5. A high-speed centrifuge spins at a speed of 2×10^4 rotations per minute. How many rotations does it make in one hour? Write your answer in scientific notation. *(Lesson 7-3)*

6. **Astronomy** Earth travels approximately 5.8×10^8 miles as it makes one orbit of the Sun. How far does Earth travel in 50 years? (*Note:* One year is one orbit of the Sun.) Write your answer in scientific notation. *(Lesson 7-3)*

7. **Geography** In 2005, the population of Indonesia was 2.4×10^8. This was 8 times the population of Afghanistan. What was the population of Afghanistan in 2005? Write your answer in standard form. *(Lesson 7-4)*

8. The Golden Gate Bridge weighs about 1.8×10^9 lb. The Eiffel Tower weighs about 2.25×10^7 lb. How many times heavier is the Golden Gate Bridge than the Eiffel Tower? Write your answer in standard form. *(Lesson 7-4)*

9. Carl has 4 identical cubes lined up in a row and wants to find the total length of the cubes. He knows that the volume of one cube is 343 in^3. Use the formula $s = V^{\frac{1}{3}}$ to find the length of one cube. What is the length of the row of cubes? *(Lesson 7-5)*

10. A rock is thrown off a 220-foot cliff with an initial velocity of 50 feet per second. The height of the rock above the ground is given by the polynomial $-16t^2 - 50t + 220$, where t is the time in seconds after the rock has been thrown. What is the height of the rock above the ground after 2 seconds? *(Lesson 7-6)*

11. The sum of the first n natural numbers is given by the polynomial $\frac{1}{2}n^2 + \frac{1}{2}n$. Use this polynomial to find the sum of the first 9 natural numbers. *(Lesson 7-6)*

12. **Biology** The population of insects in a meadow depends on the temperature. A biologist models the population of insect A with the polynomial $0.02x^2 + 0.5x + 8$ and the population of insect B with the polynomial $0.04x^2 - 0.2x + 12$, where x represents the temperature in degrees Fahrenheit. *(Lesson 7-7)*

    a. Write a polynomial that represents the total population of both insects.

    b. Write a polynomial that represents the difference of the populations of insect B and insect A.

13. **Geometry** The length of the rectangle shown is 1 inch longer than 3 times the width.

    a. Write a polynomial that represents the area of the rectangle.

    b. Find the area of the rectangle when the width is 4 inches. *(Lesson 7-8)*

14. A cabinet maker starts with a square piece of wood and then cuts a square hole from its center as shown. Write a polynomial that represents the area of the remaining piece of wood. *(Lesson 7-9)*

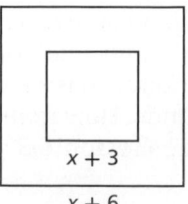

1. Ms. Andrews's class has 12 boys and 18 girls. For a class picture, the students will stand in rows on a set of steps. Each row must have the same number of students, and each row will contain only boys or girls. How many rows will there be if Ms. Andrews puts the maximum number of students in each row? *(Lesson 8-1)*

2. A museum director is planning an exhibit of Native American baskets. There are 40 baskets from North America and 32 baskets from South America. The baskets will be displayed on shelves so that each shelf has the same number of baskets. Baskets from North and South America will not be placed together on the same shelf. How many shelves will be needed if each shelf holds the maximum number of baskets? *(Lesson 8-1)*

3. The area of a rectangular painting is $\left(3x^2 + 5x\right)$ ft². Factor this polynomial to find possible expressions for the dimensions of the painting. *(Lesson 8-2)*

4. **Geometry** The surface area of a cylinder with radius r and height h is given by the expression $2\pi r^2 + 2\pi rh$. Factor this expression. *(Lesson 8-2)*

5. The area of a rectangular classroom in square feet is given by $x^2 + 9x + 18$. The width of the classroom is $(x + 3)$ ft. What is the length of the classroom? *(Lesson 8-3)*

Gardening Use the following information for Exercises 6 and 7.

A rectangular flower bed has a width of $(x + 4)$ ft. The bed will be enlarged by increasing the length, as shown. *(Lesson 8-3)*

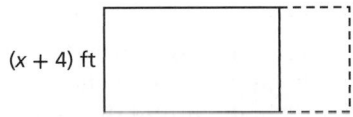

$(x + 4)$ ft

6. The original flower bed has an area of $\left(x^2 + 9x + 20\right)$ ft². What is its length?

7. The enlarged flower bed will have an area of $\left(x^2 + 12x + 32\right)$ ft². What will be the new length of the flower bed?

8. A rectangular poster has an area of $\left(6x^2 + 19x + 15\right)$ in². The width of the poster is $(2x + 3)$ in. What is the length of the poster? *(Lesson 8-4)*

9. **Physics** The height of an object thrown upward with a velocity of 38 feet per second from an initial height of 5 feet can be modeled by the polynomial $-16t^2 + 38t + 5$, where t is the time in seconds. Factor this expression. Then use the factored expression to find the object's height after $\frac{1}{2}$ second. *(Lesson 8-4)*

10. A rectangular pool has an area of $\left(9x^2 + 30x + 25\right)$ ft². The dimensions of the pool are of the form $ax + b$, where a and b are whole numbers. Find an expression for the perimeter of the pool. Then find the perimeter when $x = 5$. *(Lesson 8-5)*

11. **Geometry** The area of a square is $9x^2 - 24x + 16$. Find the length of each side of the square. Is it possible for x to equal 1 in this situation? Why or why not? *(Lesson 8-5)*

Architecture Use the following information for Exercises 12–14.

An architect is designing a rectangular hotel room. A balcony that is 5 feet wide runs along the length of the room, as shown in the figure. *(Lesson 8-6)*

2x ft   5 ft

12. The area of the room, including the balcony, is $\left(4x^2 + 12x + 5\right)$ ft². Tell whether the polynomial is fully factored. Explain.

13. Find the length and width of the room (including the balcony).

14. How long is the balcony when $x = 9$?

1. The table shows the height of a ball at various times after being thrown into the air. Tell whether the function is quadratic. Explain. *(Lesson 9-1)*

Time (s)	0	0.5	1	1.5	2
Height (ft)	4	20	28	28	20

2. The height of the curved roof of a camping tent can be modeled by $f(x) = -0.5x^2 + 3x$, where x is the width in feet. Find the height of the tent at its tallest point. *(Lesson 9-2)*

3. Engineering A small bridge passes over a stream. The height in feet of the bridge's curved arch support can be modeled by $f(x) = -0.25x^2 + 2x + 1.5$, where the x-axis represents the level of the water. Find the greatest height of the arch support. *(Lesson 9-2)*

4. Sports The height in meters of a football that is kicked from the ground is approximated by $f(x) = -5x^2 + 20x$, where x is the time in seconds after the ball is kicked. Find the ball's maximum height and the time it takes the ball to reach this height. Then find how long the ball is in the air. *(Lesson 9-3)*

5. Physics Two golf balls are dropped, one from a height of 400 feet and the other from a height of 576 feet. *(Lesson 9-4)*

  a. Compare the graphs that show the time it takes each golf ball to reach the ground.

  b. Use the graphs to tell when each golf ball reaches the ground.

6. A model rocket is launched into the air with an initial velocity of 144 feet per second. The quadratic function $y = -16x^2 + 144x$ models the height of the rocket after x seconds. How long is the rocket in the air? *(Lesson 9-5)*

7. A gymnast jumps on a trampoline. The quadratic function $y = -16x^2 + 24x$ models her height in feet above the trampoline after x seconds. How long is the gymnast in the air? *(Lesson 9-5)*

8. A child standing on a rock tosses a ball into the air. The height of the ball above the ground is modeled by $h = -16t^2 + 28t + 8$, where h is the height in feet and t is the time in seconds. Find the time it takes the ball to reach the ground. *(Lesson 9-6)*

9. A fireworks rocket is launched from the edge of a rooftop. The height of the rocket above the ground is modeled by $h = -16t^2 + 40t + 24$, where h is the height in feet and t is the time in seconds. Find the time it takes the rocket to hit the ground. *(Lesson 9-6)*

10. Geometry The base of the triangle in the figure is five times the height. The area of the triangle is 400 in². Find the height of the triangle to the nearest tenth. *(Lesson 9-7)*

11. The length of a rectangular swimming pool is 8 feet greater than the width. The pool has an area of 240 ft². Find the length and width of the pool. *(Lesson 9-8)*

12. Geometry One base of a trapezoid is 4 ft longer than the other base. The height of the trapezoid is equal to the shorter base. The trapezoid's area is 80 ft². Find the height. $\left(\text{Hint: } A = \frac{1}{2}h(b_1 + b_2)\right)$ *(Lesson 9-8)*

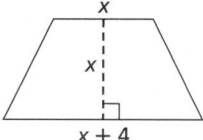

13. A referee tosses a coin into the air at the start of a football game to decide which team will get the ball. The height of the coin above the ground is modeled by $h = -16t^2 + 12t + 4$, where h is the height in feet and t is the time in seconds after the coin is tossed. Will the coin reach a height of 8 feet? Use the discriminant to explain your answer. *(Lesson 9-9)*

Geography Use the following information for Exercises 1–3.

The bar graph shows the areas of the Great Lakes. *(Lesson 10-1)*

1. Estimate the difference in the areas between the lake with the greatest area and the lake with the least area.

2. Estimate the total area of the five lakes.

3. Approximately what percent of the total area is Lake Superior?

4. The scores of 18 students on a Spanish exam are given below. Use the data to make a stem-and-leaf plot. *(Lesson 10-2)*

Exam Scores								
65	94	92	75	71	83	77	73	91
82	63	79	80	77	99	76	80	88

5. The numbers of customers who visited a hair salon each day are given below. Use the data to make a frequency table with intervals. *(Lesson 10-2)*

Number of Customers Per Day						
32	35	29	44	41	25	35
40	41	32	33	28	33	34

Sports Use the following information for Exercises 6 and 7.

The numbers of points scored by a college football team in 11 games are given below. *(Lesson 10-3)*

10 17 17 14 21 7 10 14 17 17 21

6. Find the mean, median, mode, and range of the data set.

7. Use the data to make a box-and-whisker plot.

8. The weekly salaries of five employees at a restaurant are $450, $500, $460, $980, and $520. Explain why the following statement is misleading: "The average salary is $582." *(Lesson 10-4)*

9. The graph shows the sales figures for three sales representatives. Explain why the graph is misleading. What might someone believe because of the graph? *(Lesson 10-4)*

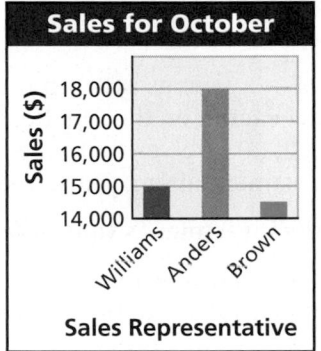

10. A manager inspects 120 stereos that were built at a factory. She finds that 6 are defective. What is the experimental probability that a stereo chosen at random will be defective? *(Lesson 10-5)*

Travel Use the following information for Exercises 11–13.

A row of an airplane has 2 window seats, 3 middle seats, and 4 aisle seats. You are randomly assigned a seat in the row. *(Lesson 10-6)*

11. Find the probability that you are assigned a window seat.

12. Find the odds in favor of being assigned a window seat.

13. Find the probability that you are not assigned a middle seat.

14. A class consists of 19 boys and 16 girls. The teacher selects one student at random to be the class president and then selects a different student to be vice president. What is the probability that both students are girls? *(Lesson 10-7)*

Extra Practice

1. Scientists who are developing a vaccine track the number of new infections of a disease each year. The values in the table form a geometric sequence. To the nearest whole number, how many new infections will there be in the 6th year? *(Lesson 11-1)*

Year	Number of New Infections
1	12,000
2	9000
3	6750

2. Finance For a savings account that earns 5% interest each year, the function $f(x) = 2000(1.05)^x$ gives the value of a $2000 investment after x years. *(Lesson 11-2)*

    a. Find the investment's value after 5 years.

    b. Approximately how many years will it take for the investment to be worth $3100?

3. Chemistry Cesium-137 has a half-life of 30 years. Find the amount left from a 200-gram sample after 150 years. *(Lesson 11-3)*

4. The cost of tuition at a dance school is $300 a year and is increasing at a rate of 3% a year. Write an exponential growth function to model the situation and find the cost of tuition after 4 years. *(Lesson 11-3)*

5. Use the data in the table to describe how the price of the company's stock is changing. Then write a function that models the data. Use your function to predict the price of the company's stock after 7 years. *(Lesson 11-4)*

Stock Prices				
Year	0	1	2	3
Price ($)	10.00	11.00	12.20	13.31

6. Use the data in the table to describe the rate at which Susan reads. Then write a function that models the data. Use your function to predict the number of pages Susan will read in 6 hours. *(Lesson 11-4)*

Total Number of Pages Read				
Time (h)	1	2	3	4
Pages	48	96	144	192

7. The function $f(x) = \sqrt{1.44x}$ gives the approximate distance in miles to the horizon as observed by a person whose eye level is x feet above the ground. Jamal stands on a tower so that his eyes are 180 ft above the ground. What is the distance to the horizon? Round your answer to the nearest tenth. *(Lesson 11-5)*

8. Geometry Given the surface area, S, of a sphere, the formula $r = \sqrt{\frac{S}{4\pi}}$ can be used to find the sphere's radius. What is the radius of a sphere with a surface area of 100 m²? Use 3.14 for π. Round your answer to the nearest hundredth of a meter. *(Lesson 11-5)*

9. Cooking A chef has a square baking pan with sides 8 inches long. She wants to know if an 11-inch fish can fit in the pan. Find the length of the diagonal of the pan. Give the answer as a radical expression in simplest form. Then estimate the length to the nearest tenth of an inch. Tell whether the fish will fit in the pan. *(Lesson 11-6)*

10. Alicia wants to put a fence around the irregular garden plot shown. Find the perimeter of the plot. Give your answer as a radical expression in simplest form. *(Lesson 11-7)*

11. Physics The velocity of an object in meters per second is given by $\frac{\sqrt{2}\sqrt{E}}{\sqrt{m}}$, where E is kinetic energy in Joules and m is mass in kilograms. What is the velocity of an object that has 40 Joules of kinetic energy and a mass of 10 kilograms? Give the answer as a radical expression in simplest form. Then estimate the velocity to the nearest tenth. *(Lesson 11-8)*

12. A rectangular window has an area of 40 ft². The window is 8 feet long and its height is $\sqrt{x+2}$ ft. What is the value of x? What is the height of the window? *(Lesson 11-9)*

1. The inverse variation $xy = 200$ relates the number of words per minute x at which a person types to the number of minutes y that it takes to type a 200-word paragraph. Determine a reasonable domain and range and then graph this inverse variation. Use the graph to estimate how many minutes it would take to type the paragraph at a rate of 60 words per minute. *(Lesson 12-1)*

2. **Business** The owner of a deli finds that the number of sandwiches sold in one day varies inversely as the price of the sandwiches. When the price is $4.50, the deli sells 60 sandwiches. How many sandwiches can the owner expect to sell when the price is $3.60? *(Lesson 12-1)*

3. A gardener has $30 in his budget to buy packets of seeds. He receives 3 free packets of seeds with his order. The number of packets y he can buy is $y = \frac{30}{x} + 3$, where x is the price per packet. Describe the reasonable domain and range values. Then graph the function. *(Lesson 12-2)*

4. Ashley wants to save $1000 for a trip to Europe. She puts aside x dollars per month, and her grandmother contributes $10 per month. The number of months y it will take to save $1000 is $y = \frac{1000}{x + 10}$. Describe the reasonable domain and range values. Then graph the function. *(Lesson 12-2)*

5. **Geometry** Find the ratio of the area of a circle to the circumference of the circle. (*Hint:* For a circle, $A = \pi r^2$ and $C = 2\pi r$). For what radius is this ratio equal to 1? *(Lesson 12-3)*

6. **Geometry** For a cylinder with radius r and height h, the volume is $V = \pi r^2 h$, and the surface area is $S = 2\pi r^2 + 2\pi rh$. What is the ratio of the volume to the surface area for a cylinder? What is this ratio when $r = h = 1$? *(Lesson 12-3)*

7. A committee consists of five more women than men. The chairperson randomly chooses one person to serve as secretary and a different person to serve as treasurer. Write and simplify an expression that represents the probability that both people who are chosen are men. What is the probability of choosing two men if there are 6 men on the committee? *(Lesson 12-4)*

8. **Transportation** A delivery truck makes a delivery to a town 150 miles away traveling r miles per hour. On the return trip, the delivery truck travels 20% faster. Write and simplify an expression for the truck's round-trip delivery time in terms of r. Then find the round-trip delivery time if the truck travels 55 mi/h on its way to the delivery. *(Lesson 12-5)*

9. **Recreation** Jordan is hiking 2 miles to a vista point at the top of a hill and then back to his campsite at the base of the hill. His downhill rate is 3 times his uphill rate, r. Write and simplify an expression in terms of r for the time that the round-trip hike will take. Then find how long the hike will take if Jordan's uphill rate is 2 mi/h. *(Lesson 12-5)*

10. **Geometry** The volume of a rectangular prism is the area of the base times the height. A rectangular prism has a volume given by $\left(2x^2 + 7x + 5\right)$ cm^3 and a height given by $(x + 1)$ cm. What is the area of the base of the rectangular prism? *(Lesson 12-6)*

11. Tanya can deliver newspapers to all of the houses on her route in 1 hour. Her brother, Nick, can deliver newspapers along the same route in 2 hours. How long will it take to deliver the newspapers if they work together? *(Lesson 12-7)*

12. **Agriculture** Grains are harvested using a combine. A farm has two combines—one that can harvest the wheat field in 9 hours and another that can harvest the wheat field in 11 hours. How long will it take to harvest the wheat field using both combines? *(Lesson 12-7)*

Problem Solving Handbook

Draw a Diagram

You can **draw a diagram** to help you visualize what the words of a problem are describing.

Problem Solving Strategies

Draw a Diagram   Make a Table
Make a Model   Solve a Simpler Problem
Guess and Test   Use Logical Reasoning
Work Backward   Use a Venn Diagram
Find a Pattern   Make an Organized List

EXAMPLE

A gardener wants to plant a 2.5-foot-wide border of flowers around a rectangular herb garden. The herb garden is 12 feet long and 7.5 feet wide. What is the area of the border?

1 **Understand the Problem**

You need to find the area of the garden's border. You are given the garden's dimensions and the width of the border.

2 **Make a Plan**

Draw and label a diagram of the herb garden with the surrounding border. Find the dimensions of the outer rectangle. Then find the area of the inner rectangle and subtract to find the area of the border.

3 **Solve**

length of outer rectangle: **2.5 ft + 12 ft + 2.5 ft = 17 ft**
width of outer rectangle: **2.5 ft + 7.5 ft + 2.5 ft = 12.5 ft**

Find the area of each rectangle:

area of outer rectangle: **17 ft × 12.5 ft = 212.5 ft²**
area of inner rectangle: 12 ft × 7.5 ft = 90 ft²

Subtract:

area of border: 212.5 ft² − 90 ft² = 122.5 ft²

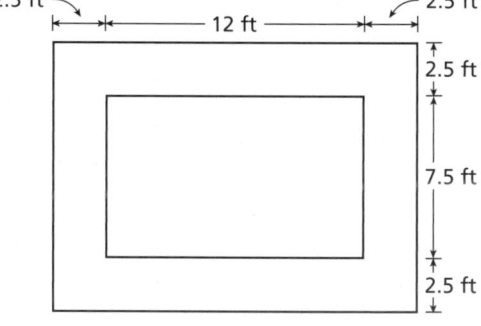

4 **Look Back**

To check your answer, solve the problem in a different way.

Divide the border into four parts and find the area of each part. Then add the areas.

$17 \text{ ft} \times 2.5 \text{ ft} = 42.5 \text{ ft}^2$ $7.5 \text{ ft} \times 2.5 \text{ ft} = 18.75 \text{ ft}^2$

$17 \text{ ft} \times 2.5 \text{ ft} = 42.5 \text{ ft}^2$ $7.5 \text{ ft} \times 2.5 \text{ ft} = 18.75 \text{ ft}^2$

$42.5 \text{ ft}^2 + 42.5 \text{ ft}^2 + 18.75 \text{ ft}^2 + 18.75 \text{ ft}^2 + = 122.5 \text{ ft}^2$

PRACTICE

1. A circular fish pond is surrounded by a circular border of stones that is 18 inches wide. The fish pond is 4 feet in diameter. What is the area of the border? (Use 3.14 for π.)

2. Thirty-two teams are in the first round of a softball tournament. A team is eliminated as soon as it loses a game. How many games need to be played to determine the winner? (*Hint:* Use a tree diagram.)

Make a Model

You can **make a model,** or representation of the objects in a problem, to help you solve it.

 Problem Solving Strategies

Draw a Diagram	Make a Table
Make a Model	Solve a Simpler Problem
Guess and Test	Use Logical Reasoning
Work Backward	Use a Venn Diagram
Find a Pattern	Make an Organized List

EXAMPLE

Mr. Duncan is using blue and white square tiles to create a pattern on his kitchen wall. The entire design will have 8 rows with 15 tiles in each row. The bottom row alternates colors starting with blue, and the row above that alternates colors starting with white. He will continue this alternating pattern so that the same two colors are never next to each other. How many of each color tile does Mr. Duncan need to complete the entire design?

1. Understand the Problem

You need to find how many of each color tile are needed. You know the number of rows and the number of tiles in each row. The colors alternate so that the same two colors are never next to each other.

2. Make a Plan

Use blocks (preferably blue and white, but any two colors would work) to make a model of the first two rows. Count how many of each color you use. Then multiply to find how many of each color would be used in the entire design.

3. Solve

Create the bottom row. Start with a blue block and alternate colors across the row until you have used 15 blocks.

Create the row above the bottom row. Start with a white block.

You could build all 8 rows and just count the number of each color, but each group of two rows will be the same, so this way is quicker.

There will be a total of 8 rows: 4 that start with blue and 4 that start with white. Count how many of each color are used above and multiply each number by 4.

$$\text{blue: } 15 \times 4 = 60$$

$$\text{white: } 15 \times 4 = 60$$

Mr. Duncan needs 60 blue tiles and 60 white tiles.

4. Look Back

The grid is 15 units by 8 units, so there are $15 \times 8 = 120$ squares in the grid. Add the number of blue and white tiles to see if the sum is 120: $60 + 60 = 120$.

PRACTICE

1. Mr. Duncan decides to tile another area of his kitchen wall. This design will have 12 rows with 10 tiles in each row. The bottom row will repeat this pattern: blue, white, blue, blue, white. The row above the bottom row will repeat this pattern: white, green, white, white, green. He will use these two patterns for each of the remaining rows so that the first colors of each row always alternate. How many of each color tile will Mr. Duncan need?

Problem Solving Handbook

Guess and Test

The **guess and test** strategy can be used when you cannot think of another way to solve the problem. Begin by making a reasonable guess, and then test it to see whether your guess is correct. If not, adjust the guess accordingly and test again. Keep guessing and testing until you correctly solve the problem.

Problem Solving Strategies

Draw a Diagram   Make a Table
Make a Model   Solve a Simpler Problem
Guess and Test   Use Logical Reasoning
Work Backward   Use a Venn Diagram
Find a Pattern   Make an Organized List

EXAMPLE

The manager of a college computer lab purchased 24 printers at a total cost of $3120. Some of the printers were laser, and some were ink jet. The laser printers cost $250 each, and the ink jet printers cost $70 each. How many of each type of printer did the manager purchase?

1. Understand the Problem

You know the cost of each type of printer and the total number of printers. You need to find the number of each type of printer purchased.

2. Make a Plan

Make reasonable first guesses for each type of printer. The sum must be 24. Then multiply each guess by the cost of each printer. Find the total and compare it to $3120. Adjust the guess as needed and continue until you find the solution.

3. Solve

Use a table to organize your guesses.

	Laser Printers	Ink Jet Printers	Total Priners	Total Cost	
1st guess	12	12	24	12($250) + 12($70) $3000 + $840 = $3840	*Too high—try fewer laser printers.*
2nd guess	6	18	24	6($250) + 18($70) $1500 + $1260 = $2760	*Too low—try more laser printers.*
3rd guess	8	16	24	8($250) + 16($70) $2000 + $1120 = $3120	*Correct!*

The manager purchased 8 laser printers and 16 ink jet printers.

4. Look Back

The total spent is $3120, and the total number of printers is 24. The solution is correct.

PRACTICE

1. All 350 seats were sold for a concert in the park. Adult tickets cost $15, and child tickets cost $5. Ticket sales totaled $4350. How many of each type of ticket were sold?

2. Jane is 3 times as old as Theo. Luke is 5 years older than Theo. Zoe is 8 years younger than twice Theo's age, and Cassie is 6 years younger than Theo. The sum of their ages is 71. How old is each person?

Problem Solving Handbook

Work Backward

You can **work backward** to solve a problem when you know the ending value and are asked to find the initial value.

Problem Solving Strategies

Draw a Diagram | Make a Table
Make a Model | Solve a Simpler Problem
Guess and Test | Use Logical Reasoning
Work Backward | Use a Venn Diagram
Find a Pattern | Make an Organized List

EXAMPLE

Lee Ann is taking a vacation in Paris, France. Her flight arrived in Paris at 9:35 A.M. on Tuesday. The plane left New York City and flew for 7 hours and 55 minutes to Nice, France, where there was a layover of 1 hour 12 minutes. From Nice the plane flew 1 hour and 25 minutes to Paris. Paris time is 6 hours ahead of New York City time. What time did the plane leave New York City?

1 Understand the Problem

You are asked to find the time that the plane left New York City. You know when the flight arrived in Paris, the length of the stops that were made along the way, and the time difference between New York City and Paris.

2 Make a Plan

Work backward from the time the plane arrived in Paris, using inverse operations. Then apply the time difference between the two cities.

3 Solve

Subtract the length of time it took to fly from Nice to Paris from the time Lee Ann arrived in Paris.
    9:35 A.M. − 1 hour 25 minutes = 8:10 A.M.
Subtract the length of the layover in Nice.
    8:10 A.M. − 1 hour 12 minutes = 6:58 A.M.
Subtract the length of the flight from New York to Nice.
    6:58 A.M. − 7 hours 55 minutes = 11:03 P.M. Monday
Since Paris time is ahead of New York time, subtract the time difference.
    11:03 P.M., Monday − 6 hours = 5:03 P.M. Monday
Lee Ann's flight left New York City on Monday at 5:03 P.M.

4 Look Back

Work forward to check your answer.
    5:03 P.M. Monday + 6 h + 7 h 55 min + 1 h 12 min + 1 h 25 min
    = 5:03 P.M. Monday + 16 h 32 min
    = 9:35 A.M. Tuesday
This matches the information given in the problem.

PRACTICE

1. A bus arrives in Dallas, Texas, at 10:59 A.M. on Friday. The bus left Atlanta, Georgia, and took 12 hours and 15 minutes to arrive in Shreveport, Louisiana, where there was a 45-minute layover. From Shreveport it took 4 hours and 29 minutes to get to Dallas. Dallas time is 1 hour behind Atlanta time. What time did the bus leave Atlanta?

2. Carolina bought a DVD player that was on sale for 90% of the original price. The total amount she paid was $135.72, which included a sales tax of $5.22. What was the original price of the DVD player?

Find a Pattern

If a problem involves a sequence of numbers or figures, it is often necessary to **find a pattern** to solve the problem.

 Problem Solving Strategies

Draw a Diagram	Make a Table
Make a Model	Solve a Simpler Problem
Guess and Test	Use Logical Reasoning
Work Backward	Use a Venn Diagram
Find a Pattern	Make an Organized List

EXAMPLE

Darian created the following sequence of stars:

How many stars will be in the 6th figure?

1 Understand the Problem

You need to find the number of stars in the 6th figure. You can find the number in the first four figures by counting.

2 Make a Plan

Count the number of stars in each of the first four figures. Use the information to find a pattern and determine a general rule.

3 Solve

Look for a pattern between the position of each figure in the sequence and the number of stars in that figure.

Position	1	2	3	4
Stars	2	6	12	20

The number of stars is the square of the position number plus the position number. This rule written algebraically is $n^2 + n$.

Evaluate the expression for $n = 6$: $n^2 + n$

$$6^2 + 6 = 36 + 6 = 42$$

There will be 42 stars in the 6th figure.

4 Look Back

Look for another pattern. The number of stars in each position increases by 4, then by 6, then by 8. That is, the amount of increase always increases by 2. So the number of stars in the 5th position will be $20 + 10$, or 30, and the number of stars in the 6th position will be $30 + 12$, or 42.

PRACTICE

1. The first three figures of a pattern are shown. How many circles will be in the 10th figure?

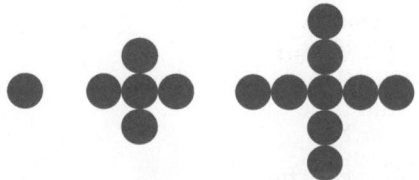

2. Lily drew the first four figures of a pattern. How many squares will be in the 7th figure?

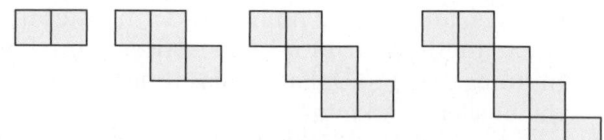

Problem Solving Handbook

Make a Table

You can **make a table** to solve problems because the rows and columns can help you arrange information. Sometimes this also allows you to discover relationships that might otherwise be hard to notice.

Problem Solving Strategies

Draw a Diagram	**Make a Table**
Make a Model	Solve a Simpler Problem
Guess and Test	Use Logical Reasoning
Work Backward	Use a Venn Diagram
Find a Pattern	Make an Organized List

EXAMPLE

A scientist begins a culture with 500 bacteria. The number of bacteria triples every 30 minutes. How many bacteria are in the culture after $2\frac{1}{2}$ hours?

1 Understand the Problem

You are asked to find the number of bacteria in the culture after $2\frac{1}{2}$ hours. You know the initial number of bacteria, and you know that the population triples every half hour.

2 Make a Plan

Make a table with rows for time and number of bacteria. Start with the initial number in the culture. Increase the time in 30-minute increments and triple the number of bacteria with each increase. Keep extending the table until the time is $2\frac{1}{2}$ hours (150 minutes).

3 Solve

Time (min)	0	30	60	90	120	150
Bacteria	500	1500	4500	13,500	40,500	**121,500**

There are 121,500 bacteria in the culture after $2\frac{1}{2}$ hours.

4 Look Back

Check your answer by solving a simpler problem. The number of bacteria in the culture triples five times (150 min ÷ 30 min = 5). Start with 5 instead of 500 and triple the number five times.

$5 \times 3 = 15$

$15 \times 3 = 45$

$45 \times 3 = 135$

$135 \times 3 = 405$

$405 \times 3 = 1215$

Multiply by 100 to find the total if you had started with 500; $1215 \times 100 = 121,500$

PRACTICE

1. A dietician's report states that a 125-pound woman needs to eat about 1750 Calories a day to maintain her weight. It also states that a 132-pound woman needs 1848 Calories and a 139-pound woman needs 1946 Calories a day. Based on these values, how many Calories does a 160-pound woman need to eat each day to maintain her weight?

2. Simon opened a savings account with an initial deposit of $200. At the end of each year, the account earns 4% interest. If he does not deposit or withdraw any additional money, what would his balance be at the end of 6 years?

Solve a Simpler Problem

Sometimes a problem contains numbers that make it seem difficult to solve. You can **solve a simpler problem** by rewriting the numbers so they are easier to compute.

Problem Solving Strategies

Draw a Diagram   Make a Table
Make a Model   **Solve a Simpler Problem**
Guess and Test   Use Logical Reasoning
Work Backward   Use a Venn Diagram
Find a Pattern   Make an Organized List

EXAMPLE

During a skating competition, Jules skated around the track 35 times. One lap is 0.9 mile. If Jules finished in 1 hour 30 minutes, what was his average speed?

1 **Understand the Problem**

You are asked to find Jules's average speed for 35 laps. You know the distance of each lap and the amount of time it took him to finish the competition.

2 **Make a Plan**

Solve a simpler problem by using easier numbers to do the computations.

3 **Solve**

Find the total distance skated.

$$35(0.9)$$ *There were 35 laps that measured 0.9 mile.*
$$35(1 - 0.1)$$ *Write 0.9 as 1 − 0.1*
$$35(1) - 3.5(0.1)$$ *Use the Distributive Property.*
$$35 - 3.5$$
$$31.5$$

Use the distance formula to find the average speed.

$$d = rt$$
$$31.5 = r \times 1.5$$ *1 hour 30 minutes = 1.5 hours*
$$\frac{31.5}{1.5} = r$$ *Solve for r.*
$$\frac{315}{15} = r$$ *Multiply the numerator and denominator by 10 to eliminate the decimals.*
$$\frac{1}{15}(315) = r$$
$$\frac{1}{15}(300 + 15) = r$$ *Write 315 as 300 + 15.*
$$\frac{1}{15}(300) + \frac{1}{15}(15) = r$$ *Use the Distributive Property.*
$$20 + 1 = r$$
$$21 = r$$

Jules skated at an average speed of 21 miles per hour.

4 **Look Back**

Each lap is a little less than 1 mile, so 35 laps is a little less than 35 miles. Round this distance to 30 miles and use $d = rt$ to find the rate when the time is 1.5 hours: $30 \text{ mi} = (1.5 \text{ h})r \longrightarrow r = 20 \text{ mi/h}$. This is close to 21 mi/h.

PRACTICE

1. Diana swam 24 laps in the pool today. One lap is 200 feet. She swam at an average rate of 4 feet per second. How many minutes did Diana swim?

Use Logical Reasoning

Use **logical reasoning** to solve problems when you are given several facts and can use common sense to find a missing fact.

Problem Solving Strategies

Draw a Diagram	Make a Table
Make a Model	Solve a Simpler Problem
Guess and Test	**Use Logical Reasoning**
Work Backward	Use a Venn Diagram
Find a Pattern	Make an Organized List

EXAMPLE 1

Five players on a baseball team wear the numbers 2, 12, 15, 34, and 42. Their positions are pitcher, catcher, first base, left field, and center field. The pitcher's number is less than the left fielder's number. The center fielder's number is greater than 25, and the left fielder wears an even number. The catcher wears number 34. What is the pitcher's number?

1. Understand the Problem

You want to find the jersey number of the pitcher. You know there are five positions and five jersey numbers. Some information about who wears which number is given.

2. Make a Plan

Organize the information in a table. Start with the fact that the catcher wears number 34 and use logical reasoning to determine the numbers of the other positions.

3. Solve

The catcher wears number 34. No other player wears 34, and the catcher wears no other number. Enter *Y's* and *N's* in the chart as shown.

The center fielder's number is greater than 25, so he must wear number 42. The left fielder cannot wear number 15 (because it is odd), and he cannot have the least number (the pitcher's number is less than his). The left fielder must wear 12.

The pitcher's number is less than 12 (the left fielder's), so he must wear number 2.

	2	12	15	34	42
Pitcher	Y	N	N	N	N
Catcher	N	N	N	Y	N
First Base	N	N	Y	N	N
Left Fielder	N	Y	N	N	N
Center Fielder	N	N	N	N	Y

Y = yes; N = no

Once you enter Y in a cell, enter N in the remaining cells for the row and the column that include it.

The pitcher wears number 2.

4. Look Back

Complete the chart if needed. Read the problem while looking at the chart to make sure there are no contradictions.

PRACTICE

1. Rose, Jill, Gaby, and Chloe bowled the scores 110, 125, 144, and 150. Jill did not bowl the 110. The person who bowled the 150 is Rose's sister and Jill's aunt. Chloe bowled the 125. What score did Jill bowl?

Use a Venn Diagram

You can **use a Venn diagram** to display
relationships among sets of numbers. Circles are used
to represent the individual sets.

Problem Solving Strategies

Draw a Diagram   Make a Table
Make a Model   Solve a Simpler Problem
Guess and Test   Use Logical Reasoning
Work Backward   **Use a Venn Diagram**
Find a Pattern   Make an Organized List

EXAMPLE

At a local supermarket, 194 people were given samples of two brands of orange
juice. Their opinions were as follows: 120 people liked brand A, 101 people liked
brand B, and 15 people did not like either brand. How many people liked only
brand A?

1 **Understand the Problem**

The total number of people was 194, and 15 of them did not like either brand. The
statement "120 people liked brand A" means some of the 120 people liked *only* brand A
and some liked brand A *and* brand B. The statement "101 people liked brand B" means
some of the 101 people liked *only* brand B and some liked brand A *and* brand B.

2 **Make a Plan**

Use a Venn diagram to show the relationship among the groups of people.

3 **Solve**

Draw and label two intersecting circles to show the sets of
people who liked brand A and brand B. Write 15 in the area
labeled "Neither."

Out of 194 people, 15 liked neither brand. Subtract 15 from
194 to find how many people liked at least one brand:
$194 - 15 = 179$.

Add the number of people who liked brand A to the number
of people who liked brand B: $120 + 101 = 221$. You know there
are only 179 people who liked at least one brand, so subtract
179 from 221: $221 - 179 = 42$. This means 42 people were
counted twice, and that 42 people liked both brands. Write 42
in the area labeled both.

Out of 120 people who liked brand A, 42 also liked brand B.
Subtract 42 from 120 to find the number of people who liked
only brand A: $120 - 42 = 78$.

So 78 people liked only brand A.

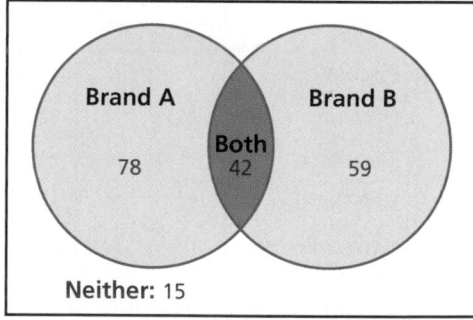

4 **Look Back**

Find the number of people who liked brand B only: $101 - 42 = 59$. Add all the
numbers in the Venn diagram. The sum of the number who liked only brand A,
the number who liked only brand B, the number who liked both brands, and the
number who liked neither brand should be the total number of people surveyed:
$78 + 59 + 42 + 15 = 194$.

PRACTICE

In a group of 138 people, 55 own a cat, 27 own a cat and a dog, and 42 own
neither pet.

1. How many people own only a cat?   **2.** How many people own a dog?

Make an Organized List

If a problem asks you to find all the possible ways in which something can happen, you can **make an organized list** to keep track of the outcomes.

 Problem Solving Strategies

Draw a Diagram	Make a Table
Make a Model	Solve a Simpler Problem
Guess and Test	Use Logical Reasoning
Work Backward	Use a Venn Diagram
Find a Pattern	**Make an Organized List**

EXAMPLE

A fair coin is tossed 4 times. What is the probability that it lands heads up at least 3 times?

1 Understand the Problem

You need to find the probability that a coin tossed 4 times lands heads up 3 or 4 times.

2 Make a Plan

The formula for probability is:

$$\text{probability} = \frac{\text{number of favorable outcomes}}{\text{total number of outcomes}}$$

The total number of outcomes is the number of items in the list. The number of favorable outcomes is the number of times the coin lands heads up 3 or 4 times.

Make an organized list of the coin tosses to find the total number of outcomes.

3 Solve

Start with heads for all 4 tosses, then heads for the first 3 tosses, then heads for the first 2 tosses, and then heads for the first toss. Repeat the pattern for tails.

HHHH	HTHH	TTTT	THTT
HHHT	HTHT	TTTH	THTH
HHTH	HTTH	TTHT	THHT
HHTT	HTTT	TTHH	THHH

There are 16 total outcomes.

There are 5 favorable outcomes.

The probability that the coin lands heads up 3 or 4 times is $\frac{5}{16}$.

4 Look Back

Double-check that each combination is listed and that no combination is written more than once. You can also use the Fundamental Counting Principle to check the total number of outcomes. For each of the 4 coin tosses, there are 2 possible outcomes, so the total number of outcomes is $2 \times 2 \times 2 \times 2 = 16$.

PRACTICE

1. A beagle, a fox terrier, an Afghan hound, and a golden retriever are competing in the finals of a dog show. How many ways can the dogs finish in first, second, and third place?

2. Two number cubes are rolled. What is the probability that the sum of the numbers rolled is an odd number?

Selected Answers

Chapter 1

1-1

Check It Out! **1a.** 4 decreased by n; n less than 4 **1b.** the quotient of t and 5; t divided by 5 **1c.** the sum of 9 and q; q added to 9 **1d.** the product of 3 and h; 3 times h **2a.** $65t$ **2b.** $m + 5$ **2c.** $32d$ **3a.** 6 **3b.** 7 **3c.** 3 **4. a.** $63s$, **b.** 756 bottles; 1575 bottles; 3150 bottles

Exercises **1.** variable **3.** the quotient of f and 3; f divided by 3 **5.** 9 decreased by y; y less than 9 **7.** the sum of t and 12; t increased by 12 **9.** x decreased by 3; the difference of x and 3 **11.** $w + 4$ **13.** 12 **15.** 6 **17.** the product of 5 and p; 5 groups of p **19.** the sum of 3 and x; 3 increased by x **21.** negative 3 times s; the product of negative 3 and s **23.** 14 decreased by t; the difference of 14 and t **25.** $t + 20$ **27.** 1 **29.** 2 **31a.** $h - 40$, **b.** 0; 4; 8; 12 **33.** $2x$ **35.** $y + 10$ **37.** $9w$; 9 in^2; 72 in^2; 81 in^2; 99 in^2 **39.** 13; 14; 15; 16 **41.** 6; 10; 13; 15 **43a.** $47.84 + m$; **b.** $58.53 - s$ **45.** $x + 7$; 19; 21 **47.** $x + 3$; 15; 17 **49.** F **51.** 36 **53.** 1 **55.** 45° **57.** 90° **59.** $\frac{1}{2}$ **61.** 1 **63.** Multiply the previous term by 3; 729, 2187, 6561.

1-2

Check It Out! **1a.** 4 **1b.** -10 **1c.** 1.5 **2a.** -12 **2b.** -35.8 **2c.** -16 **3a.** -8 **3b.** 4 **3c.** -2 **4.** 13,018 ft

Exercises **1.** opposite **3.** -8.5 **5.** $9\frac{1}{4}$ **7.** 1 **9.** $\frac{9}{16}$ **11.** -4.1 **13.** $1\frac{1}{10}$ **15.** 4 **17.** $-11\frac{3}{4}$ **19.** -30 **21.** 14 **23.** -10 **25.** 13.4 **27.** 23 °F **29.** 0.75 **31.** $-12\frac{2}{5}$ **33.** -12 **35.** 37 **37.** 0 **39.** $\frac{1}{10}$ **41.** > **43.** > **45.** < **47.** 11,331 ft **49.** never **51.** A **55.** F **57.** -9 **59.** 2 **61.** Subtract 4; $-2, -6, -10$ **63.** 12,660.5 ft **65.** $0.\overline{2}$ **67.** $0.\overline{36}$ **69.** 720°

1-3

Check It Out! **1a.** -7 **1b.** 44 **1c.** -42 **2a.** $\frac{1}{12}$ **2b.** $-\frac{1}{4}$ **2c.** $-\frac{1}{2}$ **3a.** 0 **3b.** undefined **3c.** 0 **4.** 7.875 mi

Exercises **3.** -121 **5.** 7 **7.** 2 **9.** undefined **11.** 0 **13.** about $210,000,000 **15.** -32 **17.** $\frac{9}{10}$ **19.** -3 **21.** 0 **23.** 0 **25.** -15 °F **27.** -4 **29.** -62 **31.** 18.75 **33.** 1 **35.** -12 **37.** $\frac{3}{2}$ **39.** negative **41.** negative **43.** positive **45.** undefined **47.** 1 **49.** $\frac{1}{2}$ **51.** $-\frac{1}{5}$ **53.** $\frac{9}{8}$ **55.** 15 h per semester **57.** < **59.** > **61.** = **63a.** positive **b.** negative **c.** The product of two negative numbers is positive. The product of that positive number and a negative number is negative. **d.** no **65.** $75\left(\frac{1}{15}\right)$ **67.** $-121\left(\frac{1}{11}\right)$ **69.** never **73.** C **75.** 16 quarter notes **77.** $\frac{25}{49}$ **79.** 5 **81.** 1 **83.** $-\frac{27}{64}$ **85.** Multiply by -2; $-16, 32, -64$. **87.** The numbers are alternating positive and negative multiples of 5; 30, $-35, 40$. **89.** $85 **91.** 1510 in^2 **93.** < **95.** =

1-4

Check It Out! **1a.** 2^2 **1b.** x^3 **2a.** -125 **2b.** -36 **2c.** $\frac{27}{64}$ **3a.** 8^2 **3b.** $(-3)^3$ **4.** $2^8 = 256$

Exercises **1.** the number of times to use the base as a factor **3.** 2^3 **5.** 49 **7.** -32 **9.** 9^2 **11.** $(-4)^3$ **13.** 3^4 **15.** $3^5 = 243$ **17.** 3^3 **19.** 27 **21.** -16 **23.** 7^2 **25.** $(-2)^3$ **27.** 4^3 **29.** $2^4 = 16$ **31.** < **33.** = **35.** = **37.** > **39.** 8 **41.** -64 **43.** -1 **45.** $\frac{1}{27}$ **47a.** 36 in^2 **b.** 9 in^2 **c.** 27 in^2 **49.** 6^2 **51.** $(-1)^4$ **53.** $\left(\frac{1}{9}\right)^3$ **55.** between 8000 cm^3 and 15,625 cm^3 **57.** 2 **59.** 4 **61.** 2 **63.** 4 **65a.** 100, 1000, 10,000, **b.** The exponent is the same as the number of zeros in the answer. **67.** C **69.** B **71.** 64 **73.** 65,536 **75a.** $4 \cdot 4$; $4 \cdot 4 \cdot 4$ **b.** $4 \cdot 4 \cdot 4 \cdot 4 \cdot 4 = 4^5$ **c.** $2 + 3 = 5$; the sum of the exponents in 4^2 and 4^3 is the exponent in the product 4^5. **77.** 5 **79.** 5 minus x; x less than 5

1-5

Check It Out! **1a.** 2 **1b.** -5 **1c.** 3 **2a.** $\frac{2}{3}$ **2b.** $\frac{1}{2}$ **2c.** $-\frac{2}{7}$ **3.** 3.0 ft **4a.** rational number, repeating decimal **4b.** rational number, terminating decimal, integer **4c.** irrational number **4d.** natural number, whole number, integer, rational number, terminating decimal

Exercises **3.** -15 **5.** 5 **7.** -3 **9.** -4 **11.** $\frac{2}{3}$ **13.** $\frac{3}{8}$ **15.** $\frac{1}{4}$ **17.** $-\frac{1}{5}$ **19.** rational number, terminating decimal, integer **21.** irrational number **23.** 11 **25.** -10 **31.** 4.1 cm **33.** rational number, terminating decimal, integer, whole number, natural number **35.** irrational number **37.** > **39.** < **41.** 45; rational number, terminating decimal, integer, whole number, natural number **43.** 34.625; rational number, terminating decimal **45.** always **47.** always **51.** 18 **53.** A **55.** D **57.** 0.9 **59.** -0.1 **61.** 4 **63.** 65 **65a.** no **67.** $\frac{1}{2}$ **69.** $-\frac{3}{16}$ **71.** -3.5 **73.** $-\frac{8}{125}$ **75.** 64

1-6

Check It Out! **1a.** 48 **1b.** 2.6 **1c.** 2 **2a.** 15 **2b.** 3 **3a.** 1 **3b.** -3 **3c.** 21 **4.** $6.2(9.4 + 8)$ **5.** 400

Exercises **3.** 15 **5.** -9 **7.** 14 **9.** 1 **11.** 14 **13.** 92 **15.** 1.5 **17.** -3 **19.** -22 **21.** $12(-2 + 6)$ **23.** 188.4 ft^2 **25.** 19 **27.** -15 **29.** 3 **31.** -5 **33.** 24 **35.** 17 **37.** -9 **39.** 17 **41.** -7 **43.** 0 **45.** $\frac{1}{4}$ **47.** 1 **49.** 6 **51.** $3 - \frac{2}{5}$ **53.** $8 - |3 \cdot 5|$ **55a.** 55 **b.** 498 **c.** 250 **d.** 10 **e.** 30 **f.** 70 **57.** $2[9 + (-x)]$ **59.** $\frac{\sqrt{7}}{3 \cdot 10}$ **63.** $3 \cdot 5 - 6 \cdot 2 = 3$ **69.** H **71.** -3 **73.** 6 **77.** 20 **79.** acute **81.** 100 **83.** -11 **85.** 8 **87.** $\frac{6}{7}$

1-7

Check It Out! **1a.** 21 **1b.** 560 **1c.** 28 **2a.** $9(50) + 9(2) = 468$ **2b.** $12(100) - 12(2) = 1176$

81. c divided by d; the quotient of c and d **83.** $\frac{5}{2}$ **85.** 280

2c. $7(30) + 7(4) = 238$ **3a.** $100p$
3b. $-28.5t$ **3c.** $3m^2 + m^3$
4a. $6x - 15$ **4b.** $3a - 16x$

Exercises 1. Associative Property of
Addition **3.** 24 **5.** 56 **7.** 118,000 **9.** 304
11. 456 **13.** 763 **15.** $20x$ **17.** $-9r$
19. $7.9x$ **21.** $9a - 31$ **23.** $7x - 3x^2$
25. $2a + 2$ **39.** $-3x - 14$
43. $13y - 10$ **45a.** Amy: 98:21;
Julie: 81:12; Mardi: 83:39; Sabine:
63:47 **b.** Sabine, Julie, Mardi, Amy
47. Commutative Property of
Addition **49.** Distributive
Property **51.** Distributive Property
53. $6p + 9$ **57a.** equal **b.** 96π cm^2
c. $2(16\pi) + 96\pi = 128\pi$ cm^2
59. J **61.** $12x + 116$ **63.** $-3b - 7$
65a. Commutative Property of
Addition **b.** Associative Property
of Addition **c.** Distributive
Property **d.** Rule for subtraction
67. 36 ft^2 **69.** 64 **71.** $-\frac{1}{8}$ **73.** 3
75. -2

1-8

Check It Out!
1a.
1b.
1c.

2a. none **2b.** I **2c.** III **2d.** II
3. $y = 10 + 20x$; $(1, 30)$, $(2, 50)$,
$(3, 70)$, $(4, 90)$ **4a.** $(-4, -6)$,
$(-2, -5)$, $(0, -4)$, $(2, -3)$, $(4, -2)$;
line **4b.** $(-3, 30)$, $(-1, 6)$, $(0, 3)$,
$(1, 6)$, $(3, 30)$; U shape **4c.** $(0, 2)$,
$(1, 1)$, $(2, 0)$, $(3, 1)$, $(4, 2)$; V shape

Exercises 7. none **9.** none **11.** I
13. $(-2, 0)$, $(-1, 1)$, $(0, 2)$, $(1, 3)$,
$(2, 4)$; line **15.** $(-2, -4)$, $(-1, -2)$,
$(0, 0)$, $(1, -2)$, $(2, -4)$; V shape
21. none **23.** none **25.** II
27. $y = 500 + 0.10x$; $(500, 550)$,
$(3000, 800)$, $(5000, 1000)$,
$(7500, 1250)$ **29.** $(-2, -4)$, $(-1, -1)$,
$(0, 0)$, $(1, -1)$, $(2, -4)$; U shape
31. $(-2, 7)$, $(-1, 4)$, $(0, 3)$, $(1, 4)$,
$(2, 7)$; U shape **33.** triangle
35. rectangle **37a.** $c = 2.90f$ **b.** f is
input; c is output.

c.

f	c
1	2.90
2	5.80
3	8.70
4	11.60
5	14.50
6	17.40
7	20.30
8	23.20

d. 7 yards **39.** $y = \frac{1}{2}x + (-3)$;
$(-4, -5)$, $(-2, -4)$, $(0, -3)$, $(2, -2)$,
$(4, -1)$; line **41a.** $y = 50 + 1.5x$
b. $(100, 200)$; $(150, 275)$; $(200, 350)$;
$(250, 425)$; $(300, 500)$ **43.** line
45. line **51.** G **53.** H **57.** $(-4, 4)$
59. The points make a horizontal
line at $y = 6$. **61.** $(-4, 5)$; 42 square
units **63.** cylinder **65.** pentagon
67. irrational **69.** rational,
terminating decimal, integer
71. $x^2 + 3x$

Study Guide: Review

1. constant **2.** whole numbers
3. coefficient **4.** origin **5.** $1.99g$
6. $t + 3$ **7.** 5 **8.** 5 **9.** 6 **10.** $150 \div m$;
30; 25; 15 **11.** -14 **12.** -4.6
13. $4\frac{1}{2}$ **14.** -1 **15.** -24 **16.** 14.3
17. 2231 ft **18.** 90 **19.** 0 **20.** -15.2
21. -8 **22.** 0 **23.** undefined **24.** 9
25. $-\frac{2}{3}$ **26.** $\frac{15}{7}$ **27.** 3,650,000 steps
28. 64 **29.** -27 **30.** 81 **31.** -25
32. $\frac{8}{27}$ **33.** $\frac{16}{25}$ **34.** 2^4 **35.** $(-10)^3$
36. $(-8)^2$ **37.** 12^1 **38.** 729 in^3 **39.** 6
40. 4 **41.** -7 **42.** -12 **43.** $\frac{5}{6}$ **44.** $\frac{1}{3}$
45. rational number, terminating
decimal, integer, whole number,
natural number **46.** rational
number, terminating decimal,
integer, whole number **47.** rational
number, terminating decimal,
integer **48.** rational number,
terminating decimal **49.** irrational
number **50.** rational number,
repeating decimal **51.** 3.6 ft **52.** 23
53. 8 **54.** 6 **55.** $\frac{1}{2}$ **56.** -18 **57.** 0
58. 62 **59.** 10 **60.** 8 **61.** 10
62. $8 + 7(-2)$ **63.** $\frac{12}{8+3}$ **64.** $4\sqrt{20 - x}$
65. 168 ft **66.** 40 **67.** 270
68. $13(100) + 13(3) = 1339$
69. $18(100) - 18(1) = 1782$ **70.** $4x$
71. $7y^2$ **72.** $4x + 24$ **73.** $2x^2 + 2$
74. $-4y + 3y^2$ **75.** $8y - a$
76. $9

77–80.

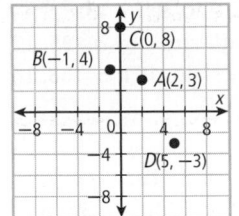

81. I **82.** IV **83.** I **84.** II **85.** III
86. IV **87.** $y = p + \frac{1}{20}p$; ($2, $2.10);
($15, $15.75); ($30, $31.50); ($40,
$42.00) **88.** $(-4, 4)$, $\left(-1, \frac{1}{4}\right)$, $(0, 0)$,
$\left(1, \frac{1}{4}\right)$, $(4, 4)$; U shape

Chapter 2

2-1

Check It Out! 1a. 8.8 **1b.** 0 **1c.** 25
2a. $\frac{1}{2}$ **2b.** -10 **2c.** 8 **3a.** 9.3 **3b.** 2
3c. 44 **4.** 35 years old

Exercises 3. 21 **5.** 16.3 **7.** $\frac{1}{2}$ **9.** 0
11. 2.3 **13.** 1.2 **15.** 32 **17.** 3.7 **19.** $\frac{17}{6}$
21. 9 **23.** 17 **25.** $\frac{4}{7}$ **27.** 10.5 **29.** 9
31. 0 **33.** -17 **35.** 3100 **37.** -0.5
39. 0.05 **41.** 15 **43.** 1545 **45.** 30
47. $\frac{1}{3}$ **49.** $a + 500 = 4732$; $4232
51. $x - 10 = 12$; $x = 22$ **53.** $x + 8 = 16$; $x = 8$ **55.** $5 + x = 6$; $x = 1$
57. $x - 4 = 9$; $x = 13$ **59.** $m + 560 = 1680$; $1120 **61.** $63 + x = 90$;
$x = 27$ **63.** $x + 15 = 90$; $x = 75$
65. $h - 47 = 28$; 75 **69.** J **71.** $-\frac{12}{5}$
73. $-\frac{13}{12}$ **75.** 10 **77.** 90 **79.** 9 **81.** 72
83. 6 ft **85.** -80 **87.** -3

2-2

Check It Out! 1a. 50 **1b.** -39
1c. 56 **2a.** 4 **2b.** -20 **2c.** 5 **3a.** $-\frac{5}{4}$
3b. 1 **3c.** 612 **4.** 15,000 ft

Exercises 1. 32 **3.** 14 **5.** 19 **7.** 7
9. 5 **11.** 2.5 **13.** 14 **15.** -9 **17.** $\frac{1}{8}$
19. $16c = 192$; $12 **21.** 24 **23.** -36
25. -150 **27.** 55 **29.** -3 **31.** 1
33. 13 **35.** 0.3 **37.** 2 **39.** -16 **41.** -3.5
43. -2 **45.** $\frac{7}{10}s = 392$; $560
49. $4s = 84$; 21 in. **51.** $4s = 16.4$;
4.1 cm **53.** $-3x = 12$; $x = -4$
55. $\frac{x}{3} = -8$; $x = -24$ **57.** $6.25h = 50$;
8 h **59.** $0.05m = 13.80$; 276 min
61. -2 **63.** 0; $8y = 0$; 0 **65a.** number
of data values **c.** 185,300 acres
67. 7 **69.** 605 **71.** $\frac{3}{16}$ **73.** 5.7
75. $\frac{2}{3}g = 2$; 3 g **77.** D **79.** B

81a. $6c = 4.80$ **b.** $c = \$0.80$ **83.** 2
85. 9 **87.** 2 **89.** −20 **91.** −132
93. Multiply both sides by a. **95.** 12
97. 25 **99.** 6 years old **101.** 6 **103.** 16

2-3

Check It Out! **1a.** 1 **1b.** 6 **1c.** 0
2a. $\frac{55}{4}$ **2b.** $\frac{1}{2}$ **2c.** 15 **3a.** $-\frac{5}{6}$ **3b.** 5
3c. 8 **4.** $60 **5.** −42

Exercises **1.** 2 **3.** −18 **5.** 2 **7.** 66
9. $\frac{5}{4}$ **11.** −12 **13.** 16 **15.** −3.2 **17.** 4
19. 15 passes **21.** 4 **23.** −4 **25.** 4
27. 5 **29.** −9 **31.** $\frac{1}{4}$ **33.** 1 **35.** 3
37. $\frac{28}{5}$ **39.** 3 **41.** 8 **43.** 7 **45.** $-\frac{1}{2}$
47. $x = 40$ **49.** $x = 35$
51. $8 - 3n = 2$; $n = 2$
53a. $1963 - 5s = 1863$; $s = 20$ **53b.** 3
55. 8 **57.** 4.5 **59.** −10 **61.** 10
63. $5k - 70 = 60$; 26 in. **65.** Stan: 36;
Mark: 37; Wayne: 38 **67a.** 45,000;
112,500; 225,000; 337,500; $225n$
67b. $c = 225n$ **71.** H **73.** 27 **75.** $6\frac{1}{5}$
77. 14.5 **79.** −6 **81.** irrational
83. repeating decimal, rational
85. $8(60) + 8(1) = 488$
87. $11(20) + 11(8) = 308$
89. 13 **91.** −18

2-4

Check It Out! **1a.** −2 **1b.** 2
2a. 4 **2b.** −2 **3a.** no solution
3b. all real numbers **4.** 10 years old

Exercises **3.** 1 **5.** 40 **7.** $-\frac{2}{3}$
9. 3 **11.** no solution **13.** all real
numbers **15.** 6 **17.** 6 **19.** 2.85
21. 10 **23.** 6 **25.** 14 **27.** $\frac{3}{4}$
29. −4 **31.** no solution **33a.** 15 weeks
33b. 180 lb **35.** $x - 30 = 14 - 3x$;
$x = 11$ **37.** −4 **39.** 7 **41.** −3 **43.** 2
45. 1 **47.** $-\frac{7}{5}$ **49.** 4 **51.** no solution
53. 9 **59.** F **61.** H **63.** 2 **65.** no
solution **67.** −20 **69.** 6, 7, 8 **71.** $1.68
73. $3y$ cm **75.** −63 **77.** 4 **79.** 2
81. −125 **83.** 15 **85.** 3

2-5

Check It Out! **1.** about 1.46 h
2. $i = f + gt$ **3a.** $t = \frac{5-b}{2}$ **3b.** $V = \frac{m}{D}$
Exercises **3.** $w = \frac{V}{\ell h}$ **5.** $m = 4n + 8$
7. $a = \frac{10}{b+c}$ **9.** $I = A - P$
11. $x = \frac{k+5}{y}$ **13.** $\frac{x-2}{z} = y$
15. $x = 5(a + g)$ **17.** $x = \frac{y-b}{m}$
19. $T = \frac{PV}{nR}$ **21.** $T = M + R$
23. $b = \frac{c-2a}{2}$ **25.** $r = 7 - ax$

27. $x = \frac{5-4y}{3}$ **31.** $a = \frac{t-g}{-0.0035}$
35. C **37.** D **39.** $a = \frac{5}{2}\left(c + \frac{3}{4}b\right)$
41. $d = 500\left(t - \frac{1}{2}\right)$ **43.** $s = \frac{v^2 - u^2}{2a}$
45. 120 s **47.** 12 **49.** −6 **51.** 20 **53.** 12

2-6

Check It Out! **1a.** −7, 7 **1b.** −5.5,
10.5 **2a.** no solutions **2b.** 4
3. $|x - 134| = 0.18$; minimum
height: 133.82 m; maximum
height: 134.18 m

Exercises **1.** −6, 6 **3.** −2, 2
5. $-\frac{3}{2}, \frac{1}{2}$ **7.** no solutions **9.** no
solutions **11.** 2.8 **13.** $|x - 207| = 2$;
mile markers 205 and 209 **15.** −9,
13 ft **17.** −2, 2 **19.** 18.8, 65.28
21. $-\frac{14}{3}$, 4 **23.** 0 **25.** 0 **27.** $\frac{2}{3}$
29. $|x - 5| = 0.001$; 4.999 mm;
5.001 mm **31.** $|x - 7| = 2$; 5, 9
33. $|x - 1500| = 75$; 1575 bricks;
1425 bricks **35.** $|x| = 3$
37. $|x - 2| = 3$ **39.** sometimes
41. always **43a.** $|t - 24| = 5$
43b. 19; 29 **43c.** yes **43d.** The
measurements are correct to within
5 mi/h. **47.** C **49.** B **51.** Division
Property of Equality; Subtraction
Property of Equality; Division
Property of Equality **53.** $1\frac{3}{4}$ ft
55. $-8\frac{1}{2}$ **57.** −1.4 **59.** $T = S - R$
61. $w = xz - 3$ **63.** $N = 6M - S$

2-7

Check It Out! **1.** 12 **2.** $7.50/h
3. 20.5 ft/s **4a.** −20 **4b.** 5.75
5. 6 in.

Exercises **1.** The ratios are
equivalent. **3.** 682 trillion **5.** 18,749
lb/cow **7.** 0.075 page/min
9. 18 mi/gal **11.** $\frac{3}{5}$ **13.** 39 **15.** 6.5
17. 23 **19.** $\frac{3}{5} = \frac{h}{4.9}$; 2.94 m **21.** 72
23. $403.90/oz **25.** 2498.4 km/h
27. 10 **29.** −1 **31.** 13 **33.** 1.2 **35.** $\frac{1}{9}$
37. 45 **39.** $84 **43.** 1.625 **45.** 3
47. $-\frac{2}{7}$ **49.** $\frac{11}{3}$ **51.** 3 **53.** 24
55. −120 **59.** A **61.** D **63.** 40°; 50°
65. 0.0006722 people/m² **67.** −27
69. $-\frac{1}{32}$ **71.** 10^2 **73.** −5 **75.** 8
77. $V = \frac{nRT}{P}$

2-8

Check It Out! **1.** 2.8 in.
2a. $\frac{150}{x} = \frac{45}{195}$; 650 cm **2b.** $\frac{5.5}{x} = \frac{3.5}{28}$;
44 ft **3.** The ratio of the perimeters

is equal to the ratio of the
corresponding sides.

Exercises **3.** 10 ft **7.** 7 in. **11.** 480 ft²
13. 4 **15.** 2.8 ft **17.** 4 cm
21. $\frac{1.5}{x} = \frac{4.5}{36}$; 12 m **23.** k^2 **25.** G
27. $w = 4$; $x = 7.5$; $y = 8$
29. 16.6 cm **31.** −12 **33.** −46
35. (−2, 4); (−1, 1); (0, 0); (1, 1);
(2, 4) **37.** (−2, −7); (−1, −4); (0, −1);
(1, 2); (2, 5) **39.** 32 **41.** 3.5

2-9

Check It Out! **1a.** 12 **1b.** 16.8
1c. 1.44 **2a.** 20% **2b.** 300% **3a.** 75
3b. 320 **4.** 10 karats

Exercises **3.** 21 **5.** 5.6 **7.** 80%
9. 12.5% **11.** 175 **13.** 36 **15.** 48
17. 2.5 **19.** 25% **21.** 50% **23.** 40
25. 511.1 **27.** 100 mg **29.** 2% **31.** 8%
33. 64% **35.** 85% **37.** 85% **39.** 0.52;
$\frac{13}{25}$ **41.** 90.0; $\frac{90}{100}$ **43.** 1.12; $\frac{28}{25}$
45. 0.06; $\frac{3}{50}$ **47.** 0.006; $\frac{3}{500}$ **49.** 0.5 is
greater than $\frac{1}{2}$% because $\frac{1}{2}$% = 0.005.
51. 0.001, 1%, $\frac{1}{10}$, 11%, 1.1 **53.** 0.49,
$\frac{5}{9}, \frac{4}{5}$, 82%, 0.94 **55a.** 40%
b. action **c.** 3% **d.** 36.9%
57. box 1: 200; 100; 50
box 2: 12; 24; 148; 96
box 3: 25; 50; 100; 200
59a. $\frac{x}{90} = \frac{40}{100}$; $36 **b.** $54 **61.** F
63. G **65.** 17.2% **67.** 88.5 **71.** 120
73. 160 **75.** 6 in. **77.** 3

2-10

Check It Out! **1.** $462.80 **2a.** $270
2b. $7650 **3a.** about $3.30
3b. about $5.60

Exercises **3.** $41,775 **5.** $4\frac{1}{2}$ yr
7. about $6.45 **9.** $462.50
11. $266.75 **13.** 5 yr **15.** about $30
17. $50,400 **19.** 2 yr **21.** $2.89 **25.** A
27. D **29.** 900 **31.** $47.17 **33.** $93
35. > **37.** > **39.** 12, 2 **41.** 2, $\frac{14}{3}$
43. 50% **45.** 80

2-11

Check It Out! **1a.** 45% decrease
1b. 20% increase **1c.** 43.75% increase
2a. 90 **2b.** 6 **3a.** $88 **3b.** 20%
4a. $15.30 **4b.** 130%

Exercises **3.** 20% decrease
5. 12.5% increase **7.** 20% decrease
9. 61.8 **11.** 8 **13.** 70% **15.** 90%
17. 25% decrease **19.** 400% increase

21. 30% increase **23.** 15% decrease
25. 20% increase **27.** $8\frac{1}{3}$% decrease
29. 252 **31.** 7.6 **33.** 15% **35.** 650%
37. 50% **41.** 18 **43.** 200% increase
45. 20 **47.** 60 **49.** 25% decrease
51a. 60% **b.** $\frac{60}{100} = \frac{18}{x}$; $x = \$30$
53. H **55.** G **57.** 200 **59.** 625
61. 64 fl oz **63.** \$9.43 **65.** 80°; 170°
67. 60°; 150° **69.** -20 **71.** 57 **73.** 36
75. -100 **77.** about \$4.20

Study Guide: Review

1. literal equation **2.** ratio **3.** 36
4. -2 **5.** -21 **6.** 18 **7.** $\frac{9}{8}$ **8.** $\frac{7}{3}$
9. $27 + s = 108$; 81 **10.** 7 **11.** $-\frac{10}{3}$
12. -90 **13.** 13 **14.** 0 **15.** -2
16. 17.5 **17.** -5 **18.** 40 **19.** -3
20. $-\frac{1}{2}$ **21.** 15 **22.** 18 **23.** 1
24. 41; 123°; 57° **25.** -2 **26.** -2 **27.** 1
28. $-\frac{2}{3}$ **29.** no solution **30.** all real
numbers **31.** 9 **32.** $n = \frac{360}{c}$
33. $a = \frac{2S}{n} - \ell$ **34.** 3.7 gal
35. $x = 15, -27$ **36.** $y = 7, 3$
37. $y = 9, -9$ **38.** $x = 17.4, -6.6$
39. $g = -4, -8$ **40.** $x = \frac{5}{7}, -\frac{5}{7}$
41. $|x - 55| = 5$; minimum speed:
50 mi/h; maximum speed: 60 mi/h
42. $3\frac{1}{3}$ c **43.** 1080 m/h **44.** 0.85 mi/
min **45.** 1.6 **46.** 54 **47.** 5 **48.** -3
49. 2.5 cm **50.** 16 ft **51.** The ratio of
the areas is the square of the ratio of
the radii. **52.** 5.29 **53.** 3105
54. 66.7% **55.** 400% **56.** 133.3
57. 240 **58.** 80% **59.** \$48,500
60. \$9000 **61.** about \$5.60
62. about \$2.20 **63.** 37% increase
64. 33% decrease **65.** 91
66. 127.5 **67.** \$3.75; \$6.25 **68.** 37.5%

Chapter 3

3-1

Check It Out! 1. all real numbers
greater than 4
2a.
2b.
2c.
3. $x < 2.5$ **4.** $d =$ amount employee
can earn per hour; $d \geq 8.25$
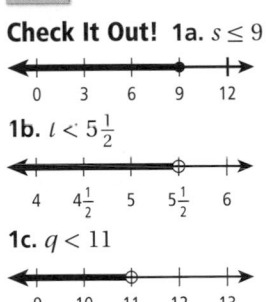

Exercises 1. A solution of an
inequality makes the inequality
true when substituted for the
variable. **3.** all real numbers greater
than -3 **5.** all real numbers greater
than or equal to 3 **11.** $b > -8\frac{1}{2}$
13. $d < -7$ **15.** $f \leq 14$ **17.** $r < 140$
where r is positive **19.** all real
numbers less than 2 **21.** all real
numbers less than or equal to 12
27. $v < -11$ **29.** $x > -3.3$ **31.** $z \geq$
9 **33.** $y =$ years of experience;
$y \geq 5$ **35.** h is less than -5. **37.** r is
greater than or equal to -2.
39. $p \leq 17$ **41.** $f > 0$ **43.** $p =$ profits;
$p < 10,000$ **45.** $e =$ elevation;
$e \leq 5000$ **51.** D **53.** C **59.** D **61.** C
65. $<$ **71.** 10 **73.** 7 **75.** $3x + 3$
77. $g = 2b$; 16
79. $b = 9$ **81.** no solutions

3-2

Check It Out! 1a. $s \leq 9$

1b. $l < 5\frac{1}{2}$

1c. $q < 11$

2. $11 + m \leq 15$; $m \leq 4$ where m is
nonnegative; Sarah can consume
4 mg or less without exceeding the
RDA. **3.** $250 + p > 282$; $p > 32$; Josh
needs to bench press more than
32 additional pounds to break the
school record.

Exercises 1. $p > 6$ **3.** $x \leq -15$
5. $102 + t \leq 104$; $t \leq 2$ where t is
nonnegative **7.** $a \geq 5$ **9.** $x < 15$
11. $1400 + 243 + w \leq 2000$;
$w \leq 357$ where w is nonnegative
13. $x - 10 > 32$; $x > 42$
15. $r - 13 \leq 15$; $r \leq 28$ **17.** $q > 51$
19. $p \leq 0.8$ **21.** $c > -202$ **23.** $x \geq 0$
25. $21 + d \leq 30$; $d \leq 9$ where d is
nonnegative **27.** $x < 3$; B
29. $x \leq 3$; D **31.** $p \leq 40,421$ where p
is nonnegative **35. a.** $411 + 411 =$
882 miles **b.** $822 + m \leq 1000$
c. $m \leq 178$, but m cannot be negative.
37. F **39.** J **41.** $r \leq 5\frac{1}{10}$
43. sometimes **45.** always
47. $y = 3 - \frac{2}{3}x$ **49.** $a = \frac{c-2}{b}$

51. $k = 2s - 11$
53. $x = 10$ **55.** $x \geq -1$

3-3

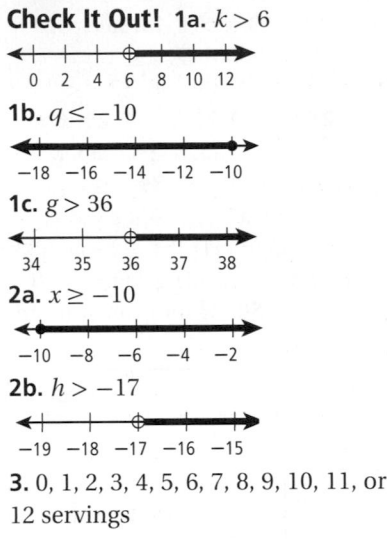

Check It Out! 1a. $k > 6$

1b. $q \leq -10$

1c. $g > 36$

2a. $x \geq -10$

2b. $h > -17$

3. 0, 1, 2, 3, 4, 5, 6, 7, 8, 9, 10, 11, or
12 servings

Exercises 1. $b > 9$ **3.** $d > 18$
5. $m \leq 1.1$ **7.** $s > -2$ **9.** $x > 5$
11. $n > -0.4$ **13.** $d > -3$ **15.** $t > -72$
17. 0, 1, 2, 3, 4, 5, or 6 nights **19.** $j \leq$
12 **21.** $d < 7$ **23.** $h \leq \frac{8}{7}$ **25.** $c \leq$
-12 **27.** $b \geq \frac{1}{10}$ **29.** $b \leq -16$
31. $r < -\frac{3}{2}$ **33.** $y < 2$ **35.** $t > 4$
37. $z < -11$ **39.** $k \leq -7$ **41.** $p \geq$
-12 **43.** $x > -3$ **45.** $x < 20$
47. $p \leq -6$ **49.** $b < 2$ **51.** $7x \geq 21$;
$x \geq 3$ **53.** $-\frac{4}{5}b \leq -16$; $b \geq 20$ **57.** C
59. A **67.** B **71.** $g \leq -\frac{14}{5}$ **73.** $m > \frac{4}{15}$
75. $x = 5$ **79.** 2^3 **81.** \$1.89/gal
83. 35 words/min **85.** $t < 1$

3-4

Check It Out! 1a. $x \leq -6$

1b. $x < -11$

1c. $n \leq -10$

2a. $m > 10$

2b. $x > -4$

2c. $x > 2\frac{1}{3}$

3. $\frac{95+x}{2} \geq 90$; $95 + x \geq 180$; $x \geq 85$; Jim's score must be at least 85.

Exercises 1. $m > 6$ **3.** $x \leq -2$
5. $x > -16$ **7.** $x \geq -9$ **9.** $x > -\frac{1}{2}$
11. $x \leq 19$ **13.** $x > 1$ **15.** sales of more than $9000 **17.** $x \leq 1$
19. $w < -2$ **21.** $x < -6$ **23.** $f < -4.5$ **25.** $w > 0$ **27.** $v > \frac{2}{3}$ **29.** $x > -5$ **31.** $x < -2$ **33.** $a \geq 11$ **35.** $x > 3$
37. starting at 29 min **39.** $x \leq 2$
41. $x < 4$ **43.** $x < -6$ **45.** $r < 8$
47. $x < 7$ **49.** $p \geq 18$ **51.** $\frac{1}{2}x + 9 < 33$; $x < 48$ **53.** $4(x + 12) \leq 16$; $x \leq -8$
55. B **57.** A **59.** 24 months or more
61a.

Number	Process	Cost
1	350 + 3	353
2	350 + 3(2)	356
3	350 + 3(3)	359
10	350 + 3(10)	380
n	350 + 3n	350 + 3n

b. $c = 350 + 3n$ **c.** $350 + 3n \leq 500$; $n \leq 50$; 50 CDs or fewer **65.** G **67.** 59
69. $x > 5$ **71.** $x > 0$ **73.** $x \geq 0$
75. $-3x > 0$ **77.** 7 **79.** $\frac{2}{3}$ **81.** -9
83. $25 + 2m = 10 + 2.5m$; $m = 30$
85. $a \geq 6$

3-5

Check It Out! 1a. $x \leq -2$
[number line]
1b. $t < -1$
[number line]
2. more than 160 flyers
3a. $r \leq 2$
[number line]
3b. $x < 3$
[number line]
4a. no solutions **4b.** all real numbers

Exercises 1. $x < 3$ **3.** $x < 2$
5. $c < -2$ **7.** at least 34 pizzas
9. $p < -17$ **11.** $x > 3$ **13.** $t < 6.8$
15. no solutions **17.** all real numbers **19.** no solutions
21. $y > -2$ **23.** $b \geq -7$ **25.** $m > 5$
27. $x \geq 2$ **29.** $w \geq 6$ **31.** $r \geq -4$
33. no solutions **35.** all real numbers
37. all real numbers **39.** $t < -7$
41. $x > 3$ **43.** $x < 2$ **45.** $x > -2$

47. $x \leq -6$ **49.** 27 s
51a. $400 + 4.50n$ **b.** $12n$ **c.** $400 + 4.50n < 12n$; $n > 53\frac{1}{3}$; 54 CDs or more **53.** $5x - 10 < 6x - 8$; $x > -2$
55. $\frac{3}{4}x \geq x - 5$; $x \leq 20$
59. x can never be greater than itself plus 1. **61.** D **63.** A
67. $x < -3$ **69.** $w \geq -1\frac{6}{7}$
73. 26 in. **75.** $y = $ years; $y \geq 14$

3-6

Check It Out! 1. $1.0 < c < 3.0$
[number line]
2a. $1 < x < 5$
[number line]
2b. $-3 \leq n < 2$
[number line]
3a. $r < 10$ OR $r > 14$
[number line]
3b. $x \geq 3$ OR $x < -1$
[number line]
4a. $-9 < y < -2$
4b. $x \leq -13$ OR $x \geq 2$

Exercises 1. intersection
3. $-5 < x < 5$ **5.** $0 < x < 3$
7. $x < -8$ OR $x > 4$ **9.** $n < 1$ OR $n > 4$
11. $-5 \leq a \leq -3$ **13.** $c < 1$ OR $c \geq 9$
15. $16 \leq k \leq 50$ **17.** $3 \leq n \leq 6$
19. $2 < x < 6$ **21.** $x < 0$ OR $x > 3$
23. $x < -3$ OR $x > 2$
25. $q < 0$ OR $q \geq 2$ **27.** $-2 < s < 1$
29a. $225 + 80n$ gives the cost of the studio and technicians; the band will spend between $200 and $550.
b. $-0.3125 \leq n \leq 4.0625$; n cannot be a negative number **c.** $155
31. $1 \leq x \leq 2$ **33.** $-10 \leq x \leq 10$
35. $t < 0$ OR $t > 100$ **37.** $-2 < x < 5$
39. $a < 0$ OR $a > 1$ **41.** $n < 2$ OR $n > 5$
43. $7 \leq m \leq 60$ **47.** D **49.** B
51. $0.5 < c < 3$ **53.** $s \leq 6$ OR $s \geq 9$
55. $-1 \leq x \leq 3$ **57.** $4x - 5$ **59.** $3a + 3$
61. $(-2, 3)$, $(-1, 0)$, $(0, -1)$, $(1, 0)$, $(2, 3)$; U-shaped **63.** $m < 2$
65. $x \leq -2$

3-7

Check It Out! 1a. $-3 \leq x \leq 3$
[number line]

1b. $-15 \leq x \leq 9$
[number line]
2a. $x \leq -2$ OR $x \geq 2$
[number line]
2b. $x \leq -6$ OR $x \geq 1$
[number line]
3. $|p - 125| \leq 75$; $50 \leq p \leq 200$
[number line]
4a. all real numbers **4b.** no solutions

Exercises 1. $-3 \leq x \leq 3$
3. $-2 < x < 2$ **5.** $4 < x < 6$
7. $x < -22$ OR $x > 22$ **9.** $x \leq -4$ OR $x \geq 4$ **11.** $x \leq 1$ OR $x \geq 5$
13. $|x - 55| \leq 25$; $30 \leq x \leq 80$
15. no solutions **17.** all real numbers **19.** no solutions
21. $2 < x < 4$ **23.** $-3 < x < 3$
25. $-6 < x < 0$ **27.** $x \leq -10$ OR $x \geq 10$ **29.** $x \leq -10$ OR $x \geq 6$
31. $x < -1$ OR $x > 2$ **33.** no solutions **35.** all real numbers
37. no solutions **39.** always
41. sometimes **43.** $|x - 2| \leq 3$; $-1 \leq x \leq 5$ **45.** $|a| \leq 2$ **47.** $|c| \geq 6\frac{1}{2}$
49a. 10,010 Hz **49b.** $|x - 10,010| \leq 9990$ **51.** $|n - 23| > 12$ **53.** $k \leq 1$; the inequality is equivalent to $|x| < k - 1$, and this has no solutions when the expression on the right side is less than or equal to 0 (i.e., when $k - 1 \leq 0$ or $k \leq 1$). **55.** B **57.** B
61. $1\frac{1}{2}$ **63.** $2\frac{1}{2}$ **65.** all real numbers less than 2 **67.** all real numbers greater than or equal to -6 **69.** $0 < x < 4$
71. $x < 1$ OR $x > 4$

Study Guide: Review

1. inequality 2. union 3. compound inequality 4. intersection
5. solution of an inequality
6. [number line]
7. [number line]
8. [number line]
9. [number line]
10. [number line]

11.

12. $a < 2$ **13.** $k \geq -3.5$
14. $q < -10$ **15.** $t = $ temperature;
$t \geq 72$ **16.** $s = $ students; $s \leq 12$
where s is a natural number
17. $m = $ minutes; $m < 30$ where m
is nonnegative **18.** $t < 7$ **19.** $k \leq 2$
20. $m > -5$ **21.** $x \geq 4.5$ **22.** $w < 9.5$
23. $a < 5$ **24.** $h < 1$ **25.** $v < -2$
26. 5.5 mi or more **27.** $18 or
less **28.** $a \leq 5$ **29.** $t > -3$ **30.** $p > 8$
31. $x \leq -25$ **32.** $n > 6$ **33.** $g < -12$
34. $k > -7$ **35.** $r < -9$ **36.** $h < -3$
37. $g < 2.5$ **38.** 0, 1, 2, 3, 4, 5,
6, 7 **39.** at least 334 lanyards
40. $x < 5$ **41.** $t \geq 6$ **42.** $m > -11$
43. $x < -1$ **44.** $h > -3$
45. $x > 1\frac{1}{2}$ **46.** $b \leq 10$ **47.** $y >$
$3\frac{1}{2}$ **48.** $n > -15$ **49.** 0, 1, 2, 3, 4, 5,
6, 7, 8, 9, 10, 11, 12, or 13 **50.** $m <$
-1 **51.** $y \geq -2$ **52.** $c < -3$
53. $q \leq -4$ **54.** $x > 2$ **55.** $t < 3$
56. no solutions **57.** all real numbers
58. $p > -\frac{1}{2}$ **59.** all real numbers
60. $k > 2$ **61.** no solutions
62. $8.75 > m$ **63.** $-10 < t < 4$
64. $-6 < k \leq 7$ **65.** $r > 7$ OR $r < -2$
66. no solutions **67.** $-2 < p \leq 5$
68. all real numbers **69.** $68 \leq t \leq 84$
70. $102 \leq n \leq 183.6$ **71.** $-22 \leq x \leq$
22 **72.** $x < -12$ OR $x > 4$ **73.** $-4 \leq$
$x \leq 4$ **74.** $-18 < x < 0$ **75.** $x \leq$
-3 OR $x > 3$ **76.** $-3 < x < 3$ **77.** x
< -13.9 OR $x > 13.9$ **78.** $-12.5 <$
$x < 2.1$ **79.** $x \leq 5$ OR $x \geq 9$ **80.** $x \leq$
-4 OR $x \geq 4$ **81.** no solutions
82. $-16.8 \leq x \leq 5.8$ **83.** $|d -$
$72| \leq 4; 68 \leq d \leq 76$

Chapter 4

4-1

Check It Out! 1. C
2a. discrete;

Keyboarding

Exercises

3.

x	y
1	1
1	2

5.

x	y
-7	7
-3	3
-1	1
5	-5

7. D: $\{-5, 0, 2, 5\}$; R: $\{-20, -8, 0,$
7$\}$ **9.** D: $\{2, 3, 5, 6, 8\}$; R: $\{4, 9, 25,$

2b. continuous;

Water Tank

3. Possible answer: When the
number of students reaches a
certain point, the number of pizzas
bought increases.

Exercises 1. continuous **3.** B
5. C **11.** A **13.** continuous **19.** The
point of intersection represents the
time of day when you will be the
same distance from the base of the
mountain on both the hike up and
the hike down. **23.** C **27.** C **29.** -8
31. $\frac{1}{9}$ **33.** $(-2, 5), (-1, 3), (0, 1),$
$(1, -1), (2, -3)$; line **35.** $(-2, 6),$
$(-1, 3), (0, 2), (1, 3), (2, 6);$
U-shape **37.** $n - 5 = -2; 3$

4-2

Check It Out! 1.

x	y
1	3
2	4
3	5

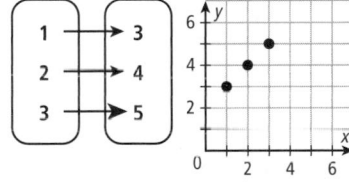

2a. D: $\{6, 5, 2, 1\}$; R: $\{-4, -1, 0\}$
2b. D: $\{1, 4, 8\}$; R: $\{1, 4\}$
3a. D: $\{-6, -4, 1, 8\}$; R: $\{1, 2, 9\}$;
yes; each domain value is paired
with exactly one range value. **3b.**
D: $\{2, 3, 4\}$; R: $\{-5, -4, -3\}$; no; the
domain value 2 is paired with both
-5 and -4.

Exercises

36, 81$\}$ **11.** D: $\{1\}$; R: $\{-2, 0, 3, 8\}$;
no **13.** D: $\{-2, -1, 0, 1, 2\}$; R: $\{1\}$;
yes

15.

x	y
-2	-4
-1	-1
0	0
1	-1
2	-4

17. D: $\{3\}$; R: $1 \leq y \leq 5$
19. D: $-2 \leq x \leq 2$; R: $0 \leq y \leq 2$;
yes **21.** yes **23.** yes **25.** yes
27. no **29a.** D: $0 \leq t \leq 5$; R: $0 \leq v \leq$
750 **b.** yes **c.** $(2, 300); (3.5, 525)$
33. G **35a.** $\{(-3, 5), (-1, 7), (0, 9),$
$(1, 11), (3, 13)\}$ **b.** D: $\{-3, -1, 0, 1,$
3$\}$; R: $\{5, 7, 9, 11, 13\}$ **c.** yes
37. all real numbers **39.** 27 cm
41. $x \geq 19$

4-3

Check It Out! 1. $y = 3x$
2a. independent: time; dependent:
cost **2b.** independent: pounds;
dependent: cost **3a.** independent:
pounds; dependent: cost; $f(x) =$
$1.69x$ **3b.** independent: people;
dependent: cost; $f(x) = 6 + 29.99x$
4a. 1; -7 **4b.** -5; 101 **5.** $f(x) =$
$500x$; D: $\{0, 1, 2, 3\}$; R: $\{0, 500, 1000,$
1500$\}$

Exercises 1. dependent
3. $y = x - 2$ **5.** independent: size of
bottle; dependent: cost of water
7. independent: hours; dependent:
cost; $f(h) = 75h$ **9.** 2; 9 **11.** $-1; -15$
13. $y = -2x$ **15.** independent: size
of lawn; dependent: cost
17. independent: days late;
dependent: total cost; $f(x) = 3.99$
$+ 0.99x$ **19.** independent: gallons
of gas; dependent: miles; $f(x) =$
$28x$ **21.** 7; 10 **23.** $f(n) - 2n + 5$;
D: $\{1, 2, 3, 4\}$; R: $\{$7, $9, $11, $13\}$
25.

z	1	2	3	4
g(z)	-3	-1	1	3

27. $f(-6.89) \approx -16$; $f(1.01) \approx 8$; $f(4.67) \approx 20$ **33.** D **35.** 3.5
37. 44.1 m **39.** $y = -3$ **41.** $x = 2$
43. D: $x \geq 0$; R: all real numbers; no

4-4

Check It Out! 1a.

1b.

2a.

2b.

3. $x = 3$ **4.** Possible answer: about 32.5 mi

Exercises

1.

3.

5.

7.

9.

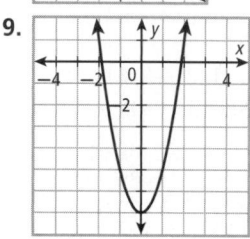

11. $y = -1$

13.

15.

17.

19.

21.

23.

25. $y = 5$

29.

31.

33.

35.

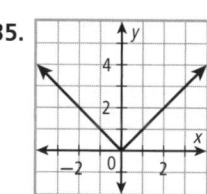

37. $x = 1$ **39.** $y = -8$ **41.** yes; yes **43.** no; yes **45.** no; yes; yes
47. yes; no; yes **55a.** $v = 10,000 - 1500h$ **b.** 8500 gal

c.

Time (h)	Volume (gal)
0	10,000
1	8,500
2	7,000
3	5,500
4	4,000

59. J **61.** J **63.** $y = 4x + 64$
65. 2^3 **67.** $p < -4$ **69.** $b \geq 20$
71. -3; 7

4-5

Check It Out!

1. Football Team Score

2. positive **3a.** No correlation; the temperature in Houston has nothing to do with the number of cars sold in Boston. **3b.** Positive; as the number of family members increases, more food is needed, so the grocery bill increases too. **3c.** Negative; as the number of times you sharpen your pencil increases, the length of the pencil decreases. **4.** Graph A; it cannot be graph B because graph B shows negative minutes; it cannot be graph C because graph C shows the temperature of the pie increasing, a positive correlation. **5.** about 75 rolls

Exercises 3. no **5.** positive **7.** negative **9.** positive **11.** A **15.** positive **17.** positive **19.** A **23.** positive **25.** B

27a. Juan's Trip

b. positive **29.** C **35.** $5(n + 2) - 2n - 8$; $n = -6$ **37.** no solution

39.

41.

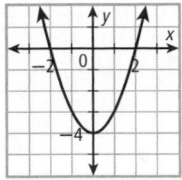

4-6

Check It Out! 1a. yes; $\frac{1}{2}$; $\frac{5}{4}, \frac{7}{4}, \frac{9}{4}$ **1b.** no **2a.** -343 **2b.** 19.6 **3.** 750 lb

Exercises 1. common difference **3.** yes; -0.7; $-0.7, -1.4, -2.1$ **5.** no **7.** -53 **9.** no **11.** yes; -9; $-58, -67, -76$ **13.** 5.9 **15.** 9500 mi **17.** $\frac{1}{4}$ **19.** -2.2 **21.** 0.07 **23.** $-\frac{3}{8}, -\frac{1}{2}, -\frac{5}{8}, -\frac{3}{4}$ **25.** -0.2, $-0.7, -1.2, -1.7$ **27.** $-0.3, -0.1$, $0.1, 0.3$ **29.** 22 **31.** 122 **33b.** $9, $11, $13, $15; $a_n = 2n + 7$ **c.** $37 **d.** no **35.** -104.5 **37.** $\frac{20}{3}$ **39a.** $a_n = 6 + 3(n - 1)$ **b.** 48 **c.** $7800 **d.** $a_n = 7 + 3(n - 1)$; $8200

41a.

Time Interval	Mile Marker
1	520
2	509
3	498
4	487
5	476
6	465

b. $a_n = 520 + (n - 1)(-11)$ **c.** number of miles per interval **d.** 421 **43.** F **45.** 173 and 182; 20th and 21st terms **47a.** session 16; yes **b.** Thursday **49.** 20 **51.** $t < -2$ OR $t > 2$ **53.** negative

Study Guide: Review

1. domain **2.** negative correlation **3.** term **4.** continuous

5. continuous

6. continuous

7. Possible answer: A family buys a fish tank and some fish. After two weeks, they buy some more fish. After two more weeks, they buy more fish. **8.** Possible answer: A monkey swings from a high branch to a lower branch. He climbs along the branch. Then he jumps to a higher branch and takes a nap.

9.

x	-1	0	2
y	0	1	1

10.

x	-2	-1	2	3
y	-1	1	3	4

11. D: $\{-4, -2, 0, 2\}$; R: $\{-1, 1, 3, 5\}$ **12.** D: $\{-2, -1, 0, 1, 2\}$; R: $\{-1, 0\}$ **13.** D: $\{0, 1, 4\}$; R: $\{-2, -1, 0, 1, 2\}$ **14.** D: $-4 \le x \le 3$; R: $-3 \le y \le 5$ **15.** D: $\{-5, 3, -1, 1\}$; R: $\{-3, -2, -1, 0\}$; yes **16.** D. $\{-4, -2, 0, 2\}$; R: $\{-2, 1\}$; yes **17.** D: $\{1, 2, 3, 4\}$; R: $\{-1, 0, 1, 2, 3\}$; no **18.** $\{(1, 5.00),$ $(2, 6.50), (3, 8.00), (4, 9.50),$ $(5, 11.00)\}$; yes **19.** yes **20.** y is 7 less than x; $y = x - 7$. **21.** y is 9 times x; $y = 9x$. **22.** independent: number of cakes; dependent: cost; $f(c) = 6c$ **23.** independent: number of CDs Raul will buy; dependent: number of CDs Tim will buy; $g(n) = 2n$ **24.** 14 **25.** -11 **26.** 6; -1

27.

28.

29.

30.

31.

32.

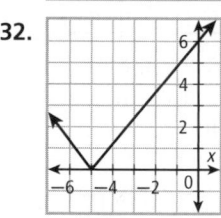

33. Possible answer: $44
34. negative **35.** Possible answer: 33 **36.** yes; −6; −4, −10, −16
37. no **38.** no **39.** yes; 2.5; 2, 4.5, 7
40. 105 **41.** −62 **42.** 20 **43.** $408
44. −15.5 °C

Chapter 5

Check It Out! 1a. Yes; each domain value is paired with exactly one range value; yes **1b.** Yes; each domain value is paired with exactly one range value; yes **1c.** No; each domain value is not paired with exactly one range value.
2. Yes; a constant change of +2 in x corresponds to a constant change of −1 in y.

3a. yes

3b. yes

3c. no

4.

D: {0, 1, 2, 3, …}
R: {$10, $13, $16, $19, …}

Exercises 1. No; it is not in the form $Ax + By = C$. **3.** yes; yes
5. yes **7.** yes **9.** yes **11.** no **15.** yes; no **17.** yes; no **19.** yes **23.** no
27. yes; yes **29.** yes; yes
31. yes; $-4x + y = 2$; $A = -4$; $B = 1$; $C = 2$ **33.** no **35.** yes; $x = 7$; $A = 1$; $B = 0$; $C = 7$ **37.** yes; $3x - y = 1$; $A = 3$; $B = -1$; $C = 1$ **39.** yes; $5x - 2y = -3$; $A = 5$, $B = -2$, $C = -3$ **41.** no **55.** no **57.** C
63. not linear **65.** −1 **67.** $\frac{1}{9}$
69. 2 **71.** 9

Check It Out! 1a. x-intercept: −2; y-intercept: 3 **1b.** x-intercept: −10; y-intercept: 6 **1c.** x-intercept: 4; y-intercept: 8

2a.

x-intercept: 30; y-intercept: 20
2b. x-intercept: number of pens that can be purchased if no

notebooks are purchased; y-intercept: number of notebooks that can be purchased if no pens are purchased

3a.

3b.

Exercises 1. y-intercept
3. x-intercept: 2; y-intercept: −4
5. x-intercept: 2; y-intercept: −1
7. x-intercept: 2; y-intercept: 8
13. x-intercept: −1; y-intercept: 3
15. x-intercept: −4; y-intercept: 2
17. x-intercept: −4; y-intercept: 2
19. x-intercept: 2; y-intercept: 8
21. x-intercept: $\frac{1}{8}$; y-intercept: −1
35. A **37.** B **41.** F **47.** x-intercept: 950; y-intercept: −55 **49.** $c > 4$
51. $m \geq -6$ **53.** yes

Check It Out! 1. day 1 to day 6: −53; day 6 to day 16: −7.5; day 16 to day 22: 0; day 22 to day 30: −4.375; from day 1 to day 6

2.

Bank Balance

−$53 day
−$7.50 day
$0 day
−$4.38 day

3. $-\frac{2}{5}$ **4a.** undefined **4b.** 0
5a. undefined **5b.** positive

Exercises 1. constant **5.** $-\frac{3}{4}$
7. undefined **9.** undefined
11. positive **15.** 1 **17.** 0
19. positive **23.** $\frac{17}{18}$ **29.** C **31.** G
35. −2 **37.** D: {3}; R: {4, 2, 0, −2}; no **39.** x-intercept: 3; y-intercept: 6
41. x-intercept: $\frac{1}{4}$; y-intercept: $\frac{1}{2}$

5-4

Check It Out! **1a.** $m = 0$ **1b.** $m = 3$
1c. $m = 2$ **2a.** $m = \frac{1}{2}$ **2b.** $m = -3$
2c. $m = 2$ **2d.** $m = -\frac{3}{2}$ **3.** $m = \frac{1}{2}$;
the height of the plant is increasing
at a rate of 1 cm every 2 days.
4. $m = -\frac{2}{3}$

Exercises **1.** 1 **3.** $-\frac{1}{2}$ **5.** 10 **7.** $\frac{1}{540}$
9. $-\frac{5}{9}$ **11.** -4 **13.** undefined
15. $-\frac{3}{4}$ **17.** $-\frac{9}{5000}$ **19.** $-\frac{13}{5}$
23a. Car 1; 20 mi/h **b.** The speed
and the slope are both equal to the
distance divided by time. **c.** 20 mi/h
25a. $y = 220 - x$ **27.** G **29.** $-\frac{b}{a}$
31. $\frac{3}{2} - y$ **33.** $x = \frac{1}{2}$ **35.** $x = -3$
37. $x = 0$ **39.** $-11 < x < -5$
41. $x \le -7$ OR $x \ge 7$ **43.** $x \le -8$ OR
$x \ge 6$ **45.** yes

5-5

Check It Out! **1.** $\left(\frac{3}{2}, 0\right)$ **2.** $(4, 3)$
3. 6.71 **4.** 17.7 mi

Exercises **3.** $\left(1\frac{1}{2}, -4\right)$ **5.** $(3, 3)$
7. 5.39 **9.** 10.82 **11.** $(-2, -3)$
13. $(17, -23)$ **15.** $(2, -8)$ **17.** 8.94
19. 9.22 **21.** 6.1 mi **25.** 13.42
27. 14.32 **29a.** 7.2 **b.** $(0, -2)$ **c.** 23
31. $\overline{CD}, \overline{EF}, \overline{AB}$ **35.** B **37.** D
39. 12.5 square units **41.** ± 8
43. 26 **45.** $x > -2$ **47.** $z > -4$
49. $\frac{1}{4}$

5-6

Check It Out! **1a.** no **1b.** yes; $-\frac{3}{4}$
1c. yes; -3 **2a.** No; possible
answer: the value of $\frac{y}{x}$ is not the
same for each ordered pair. **2b.** Yes;
possible answer: the value of $\frac{y}{x}$ is
the same for each ordered pair.
2c. No; possible answer: the value
of $\frac{y}{x}$ is not the same for each
ordered pair. **3.** 90

4. $y = 4x$

Perimeter of a Square

Exercises **1.** direct variation
3. yes; -4 **5.** no **7.** 18 **9.** $y = 7x$
11. yes; $\frac{1}{4}$ **13.** yes **15.** -16
17. $y = 2.50x$ **19.** no **21.** $y = -3x$

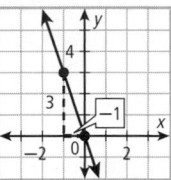

The value of k is -3, and the
graph shows that the slope of the
line is -3.
25. $y = 2x$

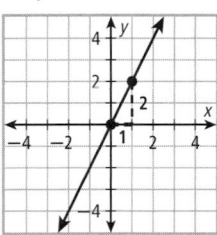

The value of k is 2, and the graph
shows that the slope of the line is 2.
29. $k = -\frac{2}{9}x$

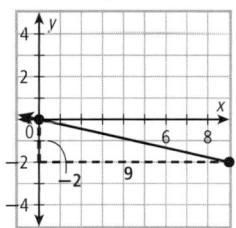

The value of k is $-\frac{2}{9}$, and the
graph shows that the slope of the
line is $-\frac{2}{9}$.
33. $y = -6x$

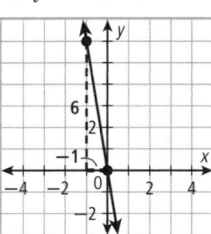

The value of k is -6, and the graph
shows that the slope of the line is
-6. **41.** C **43.** B **47.** $p = 7 - 4q$
49. $x = \frac{4 - 2y}{y}$ **51.** $y = -2x$ **53.** -4
55. $\frac{1}{2}$

5-7

Check It Out!

1a.

1b.

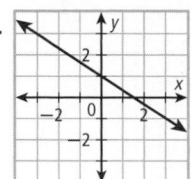

2a. $y = -12x - \frac{1}{2}$ **2b.** $y = x$
2c. $y = 8x - 25$
3a. $y = \frac{2}{3}x$

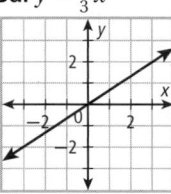

3b. $y = -3x + 5$

3c. $y = -4$

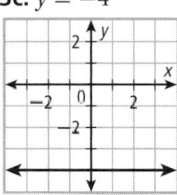

4a. $y = 18x + 200$ **4b.** slope: 18;
cost per person; y-intercept: 200;
fee **4c.** $3800

Exercises

1.

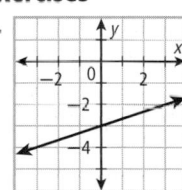

5. $y = x - 2$ **7.** $y = -3$
9. $y = -2x - 1$ **11.** $y = 3x - 1$
13a. $y = 18x + 10$ **b.** slope: 18;
Helen's speed; y-intercept: 10;
distance she has already biked
c. 46 mi

15.

17.

19. $y = 5x - 9$ **21.** $y = -\frac{1}{2}x + 7$
23. $y = \frac{1}{2}x + 4$ **25.** $y = -2x + 8$
29. possible **31.** impossible
33. C **37.** B **39.** B **41.** $y = \frac{1}{3}x - 3$
43. -6 **45.** $h =$ hours; $h \le 2$ where
h is nonnegative **47.** $n \le 8$
49. $t < -3$

5-8

Check It Out!
1a. $y - 1 = 2\left(x - \frac{1}{2}\right)$
1b. $y + 4 = 0(x - 3)$

2a.

2b.

3a. $y = \frac{1}{3}x + 2$ **3b.** $y = 6x - 8$
4. x-intercept: -3; y-intercept: 9
5. $y = 2.25x + 6$; \$53.25

Exercises 1. $y + 6 = \frac{1}{5}(x - 2)$
3. $y + 7 = 0(x - 3)$ **7.** $y = -\frac{1}{3}x + 7$
9. $y = -x$ **11.** $y = -\frac{1}{2}x + 4$
13. x-intercept: 3; y-intercept: -3
15. x-intercept: -1; y-intercept: 3
17. $y - 5 = \frac{2}{9}(x + 1)$ **19.** $y - 8 =$
$8(x - 1)$ **23.** $y = -\frac{2}{7}x + 1$ **25.** $y =$
$-6x + 57$ **27.** $y = -\frac{11}{2}x + 18$
29. $y = 2x - 6$ **31.** x-intercept: 1;
y-intercept: -2 **33.** x-intercept: -6;
y-intercept: 9 **35.** $y = -\frac{1}{500}x + 212$;
200 °F **41.** never **43a.** $y - 11 = 2.5$
$(x - 2)$ **b.** 6 in. **c.** $16\frac{5}{8}$ in.
47. $y = -8$; $x = 4$ **49.** A **53a.** $(0, 12)$
and $(6, 8)$ **b.** $y = -\frac{2}{3}x + 12$
c. 18 min **55.** H **57.** $y = -3x + \frac{11}{4}$
59. $-6 \le x \le -1$ **63.** $y = -2x + 8$

5-9

Check It Out! 1a. $y = 2x + 2$ and
$y = 2x + 1$ **1b.** $y = 3x$ and $y - 1 =$
$3(x + 2)$ **2.** slope of $\overline{AB} = 0$; slope
of $\overline{BC} = \frac{5}{3}$; slope of $\overline{CD} = 0$; slope

of $\overline{AD} = \frac{5}{3}$; $\overline{AB}$ is parallel to $\overline{CD}$
because they have the same slope.
$\overline{AD}$ is parallel to $\overline{BC}$ because
they have the same slope. Since
opposite sides are parallel, $ABCD$ is
a parallelogram. **3.** $y = -4$ and $x = 3$;
$y - 6 = 5(x + 4)$ and $y = -\frac{1}{5}x + 2$
4. slope of $\overline{PQ} = 2$; slope of $\overline{QR} = -1$;
slope of $\overline{PR} = -\frac{1}{2}$; $\overline{PQ}$ is
perpendicular to $\overline{PR}$ because the
product of their slopes is -1. Since
PQR contains a right angle, PQR is
a right triangle. **5a.** $y = \frac{4}{5}x + 3$
5b. $y = -\frac{1}{5}x + 2$

Exercises 1. parallel **3.** $y = \frac{3}{4}x - 1$
and $y - 3 = \frac{3}{4}(x - 5)$ **5.** $y = \frac{2}{3}x - 4$
and $y = -\frac{3}{2}x + 2$; $y = -1$ and $x = 3$
9. $x = 7$ and $x = -9$; $y = -\frac{5}{6}x + 8$
and $y = -\frac{5}{6}x - 4$ **11.** $y = -3x + 2$
and $3x + y = 27$; $y = \frac{1}{2}x - 1$ and
$-x + 2y = 17$ **13.** $y = 6x$ and $y = -\frac{1}{6}x$;
$y = \frac{1}{6}x$ and $y = -6x$ **15.** $x - 6y = 15$
and $y = -6x - 8$; $y = 3x - 2$ and
$3y = -x - 11$ **17.** $y = -\frac{6}{7}x$ **19.** neither
21. parallel **23.** $y = \frac{1}{2}x - 5$
25. $y = 2x + 5$ **27.** $y = 3x + 13$
29. $y = -x + 5$ **31.** $y = 4x - 23$
33. $y = -\frac{3}{4}x$ **35.** $y = -x + 1$
37. $y = \frac{2}{5}x - \frac{31}{5}$ **39.** $y = -\frac{1}{5}x - \frac{11}{5}$
41. $y = -\frac{1}{2}x - \frac{1}{2}$ **43.** $y = \frac{1}{2}x + 6$
45. $y = x - 3$ **47.** $y = -4$ **51a.** $y =$
$50x$ **b.** $y = 50x + 30$ **53.** H **57.** $-\frac{1}{5}$
59. $94 + t > 112$; $t > 18$ **63.** $y = \frac{2}{3}x - 5$
65. $y = -\frac{1}{2}x - \frac{1}{2}$ **67.** $y = 3$

5-10

Check It Out!
1.

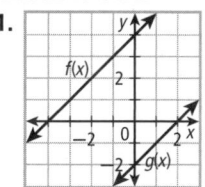

translation 6 units down

2.

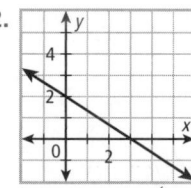

rotation about $(0, -1)$ (less steep)

3.

$g(x) = -\frac{2}{3}x + 2$

4.

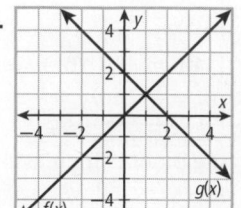

reflection across y-axis and
translation 2 units up **5.** The graph
will be rotated about $(0, 175)$ and
become less steep; the graph will
be translated 5 units up.

Exercises 1. translation
3.

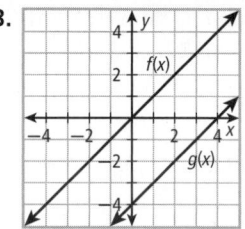

translation 4 units down

7.

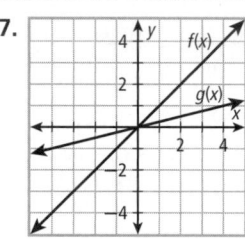

rotation about $(0, 0)$ (less steep)

9.

rotation about $(0, -2)$ (steeper)

13.

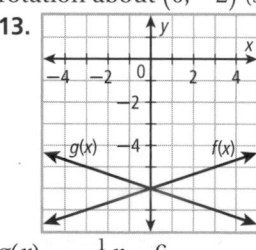

$g(x) = -\frac{1}{3}x - 6$

17.

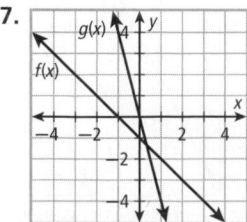

rotation about $(0, 0)$ (steeper) and
translation 1 unit up

23.

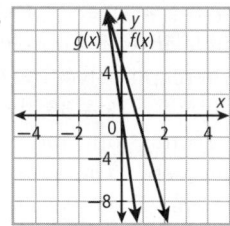

rotation about $(0, 2)$ (less steep)

27.

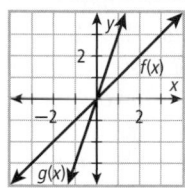

rotation about $(0, 0)$ (steeper) and translation 5 units down

31. rotation about $(0, 0)$ (steeper)

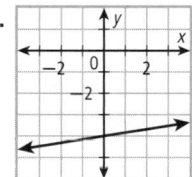

They have different slopes and the same y-intercept.

37.

$g(x) = \frac{1}{6}x - 4$ **39.** translation 9 units down **41.** rotation about $(0, 0)$ (steeper) **43.** rotation about $(0, 0)$ (steeper) **45a.** $300 **b.** 20% **c.** Commission changes to 25%. Base pay changes to $400. **49.** D **53.** $15x$ **55.** positive **57.** negative **59.** $y = -\frac{3}{5}x$ and $y + 1 = -\frac{3}{5}(x - 2)$ **61.** $x = 4$ and $y = -3$; $2y + x = 6$ and $y = 2x + 3$

Study Guide: Review

1. translation; rotation; reflection **2.** y-intercept **3.** slope; y-intercept **4.** No; a constant change of $+2$ in x corresponds to different changes in y. **5.** Yes; a constant change of $+1$ in x corresponds to a constant change of $+2$ in y. **6.** Yes; a constant change of $+1$ in x corresponds to a constant change of -2 in y. **7.** No; a constant change of -1 in y corresponds to

different changes in x. **8.** $5x + y = 1$; $A = 5$; $B = 1$; $C = 1$ **9.** $x + 6y = -2$; $A = 1$; $B = 6$; $C = -2$ **10.** $7x - 4y = 0$; $A = 7$; $B = -4$; $C = 0$ **11.** $y = 9$; $A = 0$; $B = 1$; $C = 9$

12.

Cupcake Sales

D: whole numbers;
R: nonnegative multiples of 0.5
13. x-intercept: 2; y-intercept: -4
14. x-intercept: 5; y-intercept: 6
15. x-intercept: 3; y-intercept: -9
16. x-intercept: $-\frac{1}{2}$; y-intercept: 1
17. x-intercept: -18; y-intercept: 3
18. x-intercept: $\frac{1}{3}$; y-intercept: $-\frac{1}{4}$

19.

Rate

20. 5 **21.** $-\frac{4}{3}$ **22.** -3 **23.** $-\frac{1}{2}$
24. 3 **25.** 7 **26.** 4 **27.** -5 **28.** -1
29. 1 **30.** 2 **31.** undefined **32.** 0
33. $(15, 15)$ **34.** $\left(-\frac{1}{2}, -9\right)$ **35.** 7.81 units **36.** 15.65 units **37.** 2.2 mi
38. yes; -6 **39.** yes; 1 **40.** no
41. yes; $-\frac{1}{2}$ **42.** -12
43. $y = 8x$

Maleka's Baby-sitting Earnings

44.

45.

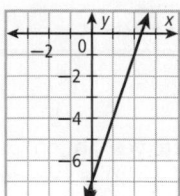

46. $y = \frac{1}{3}x + 5$ **47.** $y = 4x - 9$
48.

49.

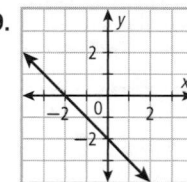

50. $y = 2x + 1$ **51.** $y = -5x - 26$
52. $y = 2x + 2$ **53.** $y = 2x + 8$
54. $y = -\frac{1}{3}x$ and $y = -\frac{1}{3}x - 6$
55. $y - 2 = -4(x - 1)$ and $y = -4x - 2$ **56.** $y - 1 = -5(x - 6)$ and $y = \frac{1}{5}x + 2$ **57.** $y - 2 = 3(x + 1)$ and $y = -\frac{1}{3}x$ **58.** $y = 2x - 3$

59.

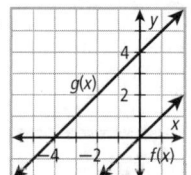

translation 4 units up

60.

reflection across y-axis

61.

reflection across y-axis
62. translation 2 units up; rotation about $(0, 3)$ (steeper)

Chapter 6

6-1

Check It Out! 1a. yes **1b.** no
2a. $(-2, 3)$ **2b.** $(3, -2)$ **3.** 5 movies; $25

Exercises 1. an ordered pair that satisfies both equations **3.** yes
5. $(2, 1)$ **7.** $(-4, 7)$ **9.** no **11.** yes
13. $(3, 3)$ **15.** $(3, -1)$

17a. $\begin{cases} y = 2x \\ y = 16 + 0.50x \end{cases}$

b.

Carnation Sales

It represents how many carnations need to be sold to break even.
c. No, because the solution is not a whole number of carnations; 11 carnations. **19.** $(-2.4, -9.3)$
21. $(0.3, -0.3)$ **23.** 45 white; 120 pink **25.** 8 yr **29.** C **31.** month 11; 400 **33.** 42 **35.** 2.2 **37.** numbers less than 5 **39.** numbers greater than 6 **41.** $c \le -9$

6-2

Check It Out! 1a. $(-2, 1)$
1b. $(0, 2)$ **1c.** $(3, -10)$ **2.** $(-1, 6)$
3. 10 months; $860; the first option; the first option is cheaper for the first 9 months; the second option is cheaper after 10 months.

Exercises 1. $(9, 35)$ **3.** $(3, 8)$
5. $(-3, -9)$ **7a.** 3 months; $136
b. Green Lawn **9.** $(-4, 2)$
11. $(-1, 2)$ **13.** $(1, 5)$
15. $(3, -2)$ **17.** 6 months; $360; the second option **19.** $(2, -2)$
21. $(8, 6)$ **23.** $(-9, -14.8)$
25. 12 nickels; 8 dimes

27. $\begin{cases} x + y = 1000 \\ 0.05x + 0.06y = 58 \end{cases}$; $200 at 5%; $800 at 6%

29. $x = 60°; y = 30°$
35. Possible estimate: $(1.75, -2.5)$; $(1.8, -2.4)$ **37.** F **39.** $r = 5; s = -2; t = 4$ **41.** $a = 9; b = 5; c = 0$
45. x-intercept: 2; y-intercept: -6

47. x-intercept: 8; y-intercept: 10
49. yes

6-3

Check It Out! 1. $(-2, 4)$ **2.** $(4, 1)$
3a. $(2, 0)$ **3b.** $(3, 4)$ **4.** 9 lilies; 4 tulips

Exercises 1. $(-4, 1)$ **3.** $(-2, -4)$
5. $(-6, 30)$ **7.** $(3, 2)$ **9.** $(4, -3)$
11. $(-1, -2)$ **13.** $(1, 5)$ **15.** $\left(6, -\frac{1}{2}\right)$
17. $(-1, 2)$ **19.** $(-1, 2)$

21. $\begin{cases} \ell - w = 2 \\ 2\ell + 2w = 40 \end{cases}$; length: 11 units; width: 9 units

25. $(3, 3)$ **27.** $\left(\frac{46}{7}, \frac{8}{7}\right)$ **29.** $\left(\frac{15}{7}, \frac{9}{7}\right)$

31a. $\begin{cases} 3A + 2B = 16 \\ 2A + 3B = 14 \end{cases}$ **b.** $A = 4; B = 2$
c. Buying the first package will save $8; buying the second package will save $7. **33.** A **35a.** $s =$ number of student tickets; $n =$ number of nonstudent tickets;

$\begin{cases} s + n = 358 \\ 1.50s + 3.25n = 752.25 \end{cases}$

b. $s = 235; n = 123$; 235 student tickets, 123 nonstudent tickets
37. $x = 4; y = -1; z = 10$

39. $\begin{cases} x + y = 5 \\ 3(10x + y) = 42 \end{cases}$; $x = 1; y = 4$; the number is 14.

41. $y = 3x$ **43.** yes; $\frac{1}{2}$ **45.** no **47.** $(4, 9)$

6-4

Check It Out! 1. Possible answer: Substitute $-2x + 5$ for y in the second equation: $2x + (-2x + 5) = 1; 5 = 1$ ✗ **2.** Possible answer: Substitute $x - 3$ for y in the second equation: $x - (x - 3) - 3 = 0; 3 - 3 = 0; 0 = 0$ ✔
3a. consistent, dependent; infinitely many solutions
3b. consistent, independent; one solution **3c.** inconsistent; no solution **4.** Yes; the graphs of the two equations have different slopes so they intersect.

Exercises 1. consistent **3.** Possible answer: Substitute $-3x + 2$ for y in the first equation: $3x + (-3x + 2) = 6; 2 = 6$ ✗ **5.** Possible answer: Substitute $-x + 3$ for y in the second equation: $x + (-x + 3) - 3 = 0; 0 = 0$ ✔ **7.** Possible answer:

Add the two equations:
$$\begin{array}{r} -7x + y = -2 \\ +7x - y = 2 \\ \hline 0 + 0 = 0 \\ 0 = 0 \ ✔ \end{array}$$

9. inconsistent; no solutions
11. yes **13.** Possible answer: Substitute $-x - 1$ for y in the first equation: $x + (-x - 1) = 3; -1 = 3$ ✗ **15.** Possible answer: Compare slopes and intercepts. $-6 + y = 2x \to y = 2x - 6; y = 2x - 36$; the lines have the same slope and different y-intercepts. Therefore the lines are parallel. **17.** Possible answer: Substitute $x - 2$ for y in the second equation: $x - (x - 2) - 2 = 0; 2 - 2 = 0; 0 = 0$ ✔
19. Possible answer: Compare slopes and intercepts. $-9x - 3y = -18 \to y = -3x + 6; 3x + y = 6 \to y = -3x + 6$; the lines have the same slope and the same y-intercepts. Therefore the graphs are one line. **21.** consistent, independent; one solution **23.** Yes; the graphs of the two equations have different slopes, so they intersect. **27.** They will always have the same number; both started with 2 and add 4 every year. **29.** The graph will be 2 parallel lines. **31.** A **33.** D **35.** $p = q; p \ne q$ **37.** 11 km **39.** no
41. $d = -1\frac{1}{2}; -6, -7\frac{1}{2}, -9$
43. $(-2, -4)$

6-5

Check It Out! 1a. no **1b.** yes
2a.

2b.

2c.

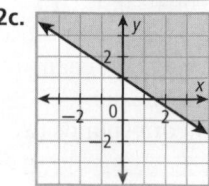

Selected Answers

3a. $2.5b + 2g \leq 6$

3b.

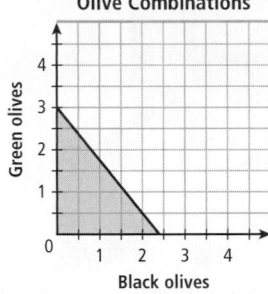

Olive Combinations

3c. Possible answer: (1 lb black, 1 lb green), (0.5 lb black, 2 lb green)

4a. $y < -x$ **4b.** $y \geq -2x - 3$

Exercises **3.** yes

5.

7.

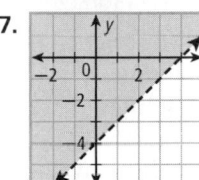

9a. $r + p \leq 16$

b.

Punch Combinations

c. Possible answer: (2 c orange, 2 c pineapple), (4 c orange, 10 c pineapple) **11.** $y \geq x + 5$ **13.** yes

15.

19a. $3x + 2y \leq 30$

b.

Food Combinations

c. Possible answer: (3 lb hamburger, 2 lb hot dogs), (5 lb hamburger, 6 lb

hot dogs) **21.** $y \leq -\frac{1}{5}x + 3$

23.

25.

29.

31.

33.

35.

37. $7a + 4s \geq 280$ **41.** A **43.** B **45.** C

47.

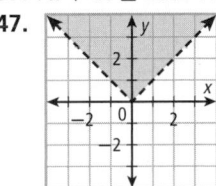

49. $y \geq \frac{1}{2}x + 3$ **51.** yes **53.** yes
55. $y = \frac{3}{4}x + \frac{7}{4}$ **57.** $y = 3x + 1$
59. $y = -\frac{1}{2}x + \frac{1}{2}$ **61.** $(-2, 15)$
63. $(2, 5)$ **65.** $(12, 3)$

6-6

Check It Out! **1a.** yes **1b.** no

2a.

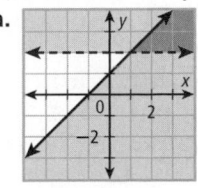

Possible answer: solutions: $(3, 3)$, $(4, 4)$; not solutions: $(-3, 1)$, $(-1, -4)$

2b.

Possible answer: solutions: $(0, 0)$, $(3, -2)$; not solutions: $(4, 4)$, $(1, -6)$

3a.

no solutions

3b.

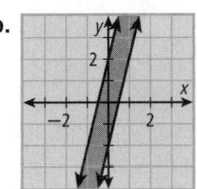

all points between and on the parallel lines

3c.

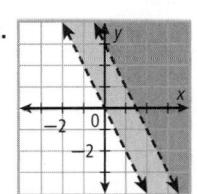

same as solutions of $y > -2x + 3$

4.

Cheese Combinations

Possible answer: (3 lb pepper jack, 2 lb cheddar), (2.5 lb pepper jack, 4 lb cheddar)

Exercises **1.** all **3.** yes

5.

Possible answer: solutions: $(3, 3)$, $(4, 3)$; not solutions: $(0, 0)$, $(2, 1)$

7.

Possible answer: solutions: (0, 4), (1, 4); not solutions: (2, −1), (3, 1)

9.

no solutions

11.

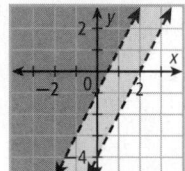

all points between the parallel lines and on the solid line

13.

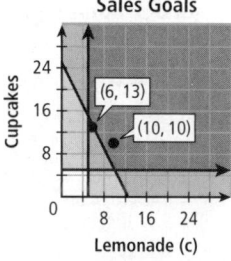

same solutions as $y > 2x − 1$

15. Sales Goals

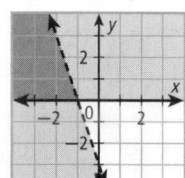

Possible answer: (6 lemonade, 13 cupcakes), (10 lemonade, 10 cupcakes) **17.** yes

19.

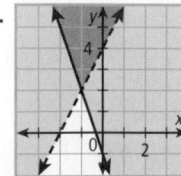

Possible answer: solutions: (−2, 0), (−3, 1); not solutions: (0, 0), (1, 4)

21.

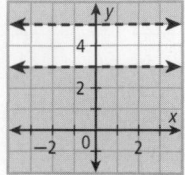

Possible answer: solutions: (−1, 3), (0, 5); not solutions: (0, 0), (1, 4)

23.

no solutions

25.

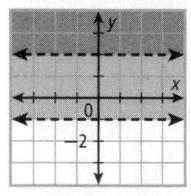

All points are solutions.

27.

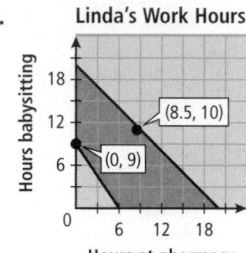

same solutions as $y > 2$

29. Linda's Work Hours

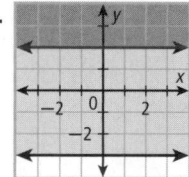

Possible answer:
(0 h at pharmacy, 9 h babysitting),
(8.5 h at pharmacy, 10 h babysitting)

31.

33.

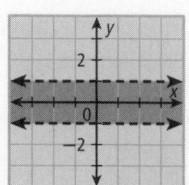

35. $\begin{cases} y > x + 1 \\ y < x + 3 \end{cases}$

37. $\begin{cases} y < 2 \\ x \geq -2 \end{cases}$

39. Student B **45.** G
47. about 12 square units

49.

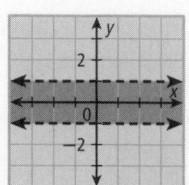

51. 25 cm² **53.** 12.5 cm² **55.** no
57. yes

Study Guide: Review

1. independent system **2.** system of linear equations **3.** solution of a system of linear inequalities
4. inconsistent system
5. independent system **6.** no

7. yes **8.** yes **9.** no **10.** (−1, −1)
11. (3, 4) **12.** 8 h; $10 **13.** (−9, −6)
14. $\left(\frac{1}{2}, -2\right)$ **15.** (−1, 6) **16.** (4, −5)
17. (−5, 2) **18.** (6, 6) **19.** 10 h;
$1350; Motor Works **20.** (−1, 3)
21. (5, −3) **22.** (11, 1) **23.** (0, 3)
24. (−2, 8) **25.** (3, −5) **26.** (4, −6)
27. (2, 2) **28.** no solution
29. infinitely many solutions
30. (−2, −4) **31.** infinitely many
solutions **32.** infinitely many
solutions **33.** (−1, −3) **34.** no
35. consistent, independent; one
solution **36.** inconsistent; no
solution **37.** consistent, dependent;
infinitely many solutions
38. inconsistent; no solution
39. consistent, independent;
one solution **40.** consistent,
dependent; infinitely many
solutions **41.** inconsistent; no
solution **42.** no **43.** yes **44.** yes
45. no

46.

47.

48.

49.

50.

51.

52. x = slices of pizza; y = bottles of soda; $2x + y \geq 450$

Fundraising Needs

Possible answer: $(200, 50)$, $(150, 150)$ **53.** no **54.** yes

55.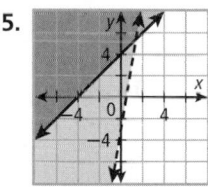

Possible answer: solutions: $(-6, 6)$, $(-10, 0)$; not solutions: $(0, 0)$, $(4, -4)$

56.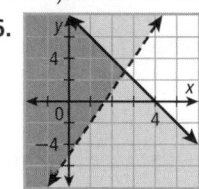

Possible answer: solutions: $(0, 0)$, $(-5, 0)$; not solutions: $(8, 0)$, $(3, -3)$

57.

Possible answer: solutions: $(-6, 2)$, $(-8, 1)$; not solutions: $(0, 0)$, $(4, 1)$

58.

Possible answer: solutions: $(8, -8)$, $(9, 0)$; not solutions: $(0, 0)$, $(0, -4)$

59.

60.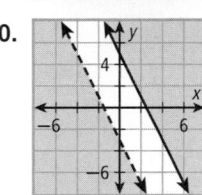

Chapter 7

7-1

Check It Out! **1.** $\frac{1}{125}$ m **2a.** $\frac{1}{10,000}$
2b. $\frac{1}{16}$ **2c.** $-\frac{1}{32}$ **2d.** $-\frac{1}{32}$ **3a.** $\frac{1}{64}$
3b. 2 **4a.** $\frac{2}{m^3}$ **4b.** $\frac{1}{7r^3}$ **4c.** $g^4 h^6$

Exercises **1.** $\frac{1}{10,000,000}$ m **3.** 1 **5.** $\frac{1}{27}$
7. $-\frac{1}{512}$ **9.** 1 **11.** $\frac{1}{16}$ **13.** $\frac{1}{256}$
15. $-\frac{1}{32}$ **17.** $\frac{3}{k^4}$ **19.** $x^{10}d^3$ **21.** $\frac{g^6}{f^4}$
23. $\frac{p^7}{q}$ **25.** 1 **27.** $\frac{1}{81}$ **29.** $-\frac{1}{36}$ **31.** 1
33. $-\frac{1}{3}$ **35.** 4 **37.** $\frac{1}{256}$ **39.** 1 **41.** $\frac{1}{144}$
43. $\frac{1}{k^4}$ **45.** $\frac{b^3}{2}$ **47.** $-\frac{5}{x^3}$ **49.** $\frac{2g^{10}}{7}$
51. $s^5 t^{12}$ **53.** 1 **55.** $\frac{1}{q^2}$ **57.** $\frac{h^3}{6m^2k}$
59. $\frac{1}{16}$ **61.** $-\frac{1}{6}$ **63.** 3 **65.** 3 **67.** $\frac{a^3}{b^2}$
69. $\frac{w^2}{y}$ **71.** $-\frac{5}{y^6}$ **73.** $2a^3b$ **75.** $\frac{1}{3x^8 y^{12}}$
79. never **81.** sometimes
83. sometimes **87.** 81 **89.** 1 **91.** −3
93. −1 **95.** D **97.** A **103.** −2
105. 4 **107.** 28 **111.** $y = \frac{1}{3}x + 5$
113. $y = -4x + 9$

7-2

Check It Out! **1a.** 0.01 **1b.** 100,000
1c. 10,000,000,000 **2a.** 10^8 **2b.** 10^{-4}
2c. 10^{-1} **3a.** 85,340,000 **3b.** 0.00163
4a. 1.43×10^5 km **4b.** 13,000 m/s
5. 2×10^{-12}, 4×10^{-3}, 5.2×10^{-3},
3×10^{14}, 4.5×10^{14}, 4.5×10^{30}

Exercises **3.** 0.00001 **5.** 100,000,000
7. 10^{-6} **9.** 650,300,000 **11.** 0.092
13. 5.85×10^{-3}, 2.5×10^{-1},
8.5×10^{-1}, 3.6×10^8, 8.5×10^8
15. 0.000000001
17. 100,000,000,000,000 **19.** 10^6
21. 92,000 **23.** 0.00042
25. 10,000,000,000,000 **27.** 1.23×10^{-3}, 1.32×10^{-3}, 3.12×10^{-3},
2.13×10^{-1}, 2.13×10^1, 3.12×10^2
29. 2.7×10^7 **31.** 2.35×10^5
33. 6×10^{-7} **35.** 4.12×10^{-2}
37. yes **39.** no; 2.5×10^2 **41.** yes
43. yes **47.** 10^{-3} **51.** F **55.** Let
m = number of minutes; $m \geq 45$
59. $(-2, 1)$ **61.** $\frac{1}{16}$ **63.** $\frac{3}{125}$

7-3

Check It Out! **1a.** 7^{12} **1b.** 3×5^{10}
1c. $\frac{m^5}{n^4}$ **1d.** $\frac{1}{x^7}$ **2.** 6.696×10^8 mi
3a. 3^{20} **3b.** 1 **3c.** a^{18} **4a.** $64p^3$
4b. $25t^4$ **4c.** $\frac{1}{y^4}$

Exercises **1.** 2^5 **3.** n^8 **5.** 7.5×10^8
mi **7.** y^{32} **9.** $\frac{1}{3^4}$, or $\frac{1}{81}$ **11.** $x^7 y^{13}$
13. $36k^2$ **15.** $-8x^{15}$ **17.** b^{10} **19.** 6^8
21. $\frac{x}{y^3}$ **23.** 2^9, or 512 **25.** $\frac{1}{x^2}$ **27.** $\frac{a^{12}}{b^3}$
29. $27x^3$ **31.** $p^{28}q^{14}$ **33.** $-256x^{12}$
35. 6 **37.** 3 **39.** 8 **41.** $2x^3$ **43.** $2m^{10}n^6$
45. $108x^{13}$ **47.** $125x^6$ **49.** $3a^6$
51. 10^3, or 1000 **57.** $\frac{a^7}{b^5}$ **59.** $15m^{12}n^9$
61. $9s^2 t^7$ **63.** t^7 **67.** yes **69.** $17k^2$
71. $6x^4$ **73.** $15a^2 b^3$ **75a.** 6×10^{-7} m
b. 3×10^8 m/s **c.** Associative
and Commutative Properties of
Multiplication **77.** $(6ab)^2$ **79.** $\left(\frac{1}{2kmn}\right)^2$
81. H **83.** F **85.** 3^{2x} **87.** $x + 1$
89. $x^{3y + 3z}$ **91.** x^{x^2} **93.** $x = 4$
95. $x = 4$ **97.** 1.728×10^{-6} **99.** 15
101. no **103.** 7,800,000 **105.** 98.3

7-4

Check It Out! **1a.** $\frac{n^3}{m^5}$ **1b.** $\frac{1}{y^3}$ **1c.** $\frac{n^3}{m^5}$
1d. $\frac{3}{16}$ **2.** 1.1×10^{-2} **3.** $12,800
4a. $\frac{2^6}{3^4}$, or $\frac{64}{81}$ **4b.** $\frac{a^5 b^{20}}{c^{10}d^{15}}$ **4c.** $\frac{a^3}{b^3}$ **5a.** $\frac{9^3}{4^3}$,
or $\frac{729}{64}$ **5b.** $\frac{b^8 c^{12}}{16a^4}$ **5c.** $\frac{t}{s^4}$

Exercises **1.** 25 **3.** 3 **5.** 7×10^2 **7.** 1
9. $\frac{4}{25}$ **11.** $\frac{1}{a^6 b^4}$ **13.** $\frac{16}{9}$ **15.** $\frac{2b^2}{3a^2}$ **17.** 27
19. x^5 **21.** 5×10^{-7} **23.** 7×10^{-3}
25. 2×10^{27} kg **27.** $\frac{a^{12}}{b^6}$ **29.** $\frac{y^3}{x^6}$
31. $\frac{y^{25}}{x^{10}}$ **33.** $\frac{196}{9x^2}$ **35.** $2d^2$ **37.** $\frac{3x^5}{4}$
39. $\frac{c^4}{a^4}$ **41.** $\frac{25}{p^2}$ **43.** $\frac{1}{100}$ **45.** −1

47. 2000: 3 × 10; 1995: 2.84 × 10; 1990: 2.65×10^1 **51.** 3 **53.** 3; 4 **55.** B **57.** A **59.** 3 **61.** m; $(-n)$; m; $-n$; Definition of negative exponent; a^n **63.** 1 **65.** 12 **67** $x = -\frac{1}{2}$ **69.** 1 **71.** $-125x^{12}$

7-5

Check It Out! 1a. 3 **1b.** 15 **2a.** 8 **2b.** 1 **2c.** 81 **3.** 1944 **4a.** xy^3 **4b.** xy

Exercises 1. 5 **3.** 4 **5.** 3 **7.** 6 **9.** 5 **11.** 10 **13.** 4 **15.** 32 **17.** 125 **19.** 256 **21.** 0 **23.** x^2y **25.** x^3y^3 **27.** a^2 **29.** 1 **31.** 10 **33.** 8 **35.** 2 **37.** 2 **39.** 14 **41.** 8 **43.** 8 **45.** 64 **47.** 1000 **49.** 243 **51.** $2g$ **53.** $2m$ **55.** $3x^2$ **57.** ab^4 **59.** a^8b **61.** 1 **63.** 0 **65.** 625 **67.** 3 **69.** $\frac{2}{3}$ **71.** $\frac{1}{4}$ **73.** $\frac{4}{9}$ **75.** $\frac{8}{343}$ **77.** $\frac{1}{27}$ **79.** $\frac{16}{625}$ **81.** 1.86 in. **83.** $n^{\frac{2}{3}}$ will be less than n because $\frac{2}{3} < 1$. $n^{\frac{3}{2}}$ will be greater than n because $\frac{3}{2} > 1$. **85a.** 10 in. **85b.** The distance doubles (20 in.). **87.** B **89.** C **91.** a **93.** x^3 **95.** 3 **97.** 36π cm^2; both volume and surface area are described by 36π (although the units are different). **99.** -1 **101.** $n < 3$ **103.** $y \leq -2$ **105.** D: {−2, −1, −0, 1}; R: {0, 1, 2, 3}; yes; each domain value is paired with exactly one range value. **107.** D: $1 \leq x \leq 4$; R: $2 \leq y \leq 4$; yes; each domain value is paired with exactly one range value.

7-6

Check It Out! 1a. 3 **1b.** 1 **1c.** 3 **2a.** 1 **2b.** 5 **3a.** $x^5 + 9x^3 - 4x^2 + 16$; 1 **3b.** $-3y^8 + 18y^5 + 14y$; -3 **4a.** cubic polynomial **4b.** constant monomial **4c.** 8th degree trinomial **5.** 1606 ft

Exercises 1. d **3.** a **5.** 3 **7.** 0 **9.** 8 **11.** 3 **13.** 4 **15.** $-8a^9 + 9a^8$; -8 **17.** $3x^2 + 2x - 1$; 3 **19.** $5c^4 + 5c^3 + 3c^2 - 4$; 5 **21.** linear binomial **23.** quartic polynomial **25.** quartic trinomial **27.** 4 **29.** 6 **31.** 7 **33.** 1 **35.** 4 **37.** 2 **39.** 3 **41.** $4.9t^3 - 4t^2 + t + 2.5$; 4.9 **43.** $x^{10} + x^7 - x^5 + x^3 - x$; 1 **45.** $5x^3 + 3x^2 + 5x - 4$; 5 **47.** $-d^3 + 3d^2 + 4d + 5$; -1 **49.** $-x^5 - x^3 + 4x^2 + 1$; -1 **51.** linear monomial **53.** quadratic

trinomial **55.** quartic trinomial **57.** quadratic monomial **59.** always **61.** never **63a.** 58.5 in^3 **b.** 66 in^3 **c.** 0 **d.** yes **65.** -48; 0; 3270 **75.** A is incorrect **77.** J **79a.** 58 cm; 65 cm **b.** 50.310 cm **81.** $90 - m$ **83.** inconsistent; no solutions **85.** consistent and independent; one solution **87.** $\frac{x^2}{y^5}$ **89.** $\frac{p^8}{16}$

7-7

Check It Out! 1a. $5s^2 + s$ **1b.** $20z^4 - 6$ **1c.** $x^8 + 6y^8$ **1d.** b^3c^2 **2.** $12a^3 + 15a^2 - 16a$ **3.** $-2x^2 - x$ **4.** $-0.05x^2 + 46x - 3200$

Exercises 1. $-3a^2 + 9a$ **3.** $0.26r^4 + 0.32r^3$ **5.** $3b^3c$ **7.** $23n^3 + 3n + 15$ **9.** $9x^2 - x - 6$ **11.** $4c^4 + 8c + 6$ **13.** $-3r + 11$ **15.** $8a^2 + 5a + 9$ **17.** $12n^2 + 6n - 3m$ **19.** $d^5 + 1$ **21.** $5x$ **23.** $2x^3 - 5$ **25.** $10t^2 + t$ **27.** $x^5 + x^4$ **29.** $-2t^3 + 8t^2$ **31.** $-6m^3 + 2m^2 + 5m + 3$ **33.** $4w^2 + 6w + 4$ **35.** $t - 5$ **37.** $2n - 2$ **39.** $6x^2 - x - 1$ **41.** $-u^3 + 3u^2 + 3u + 6$ **43.** $x = \frac{3}{2}$, or 1.5 **45.** B is incorrect. **47.** $3x + 6$ **49.** $6x + 14$ **51.** $2x^2 + x - 5$ **55.** G **57.** $3x^2 - 2$ **69.** b^{11} **71.** $9z^{12}$

7-8

Check It Out! 1a. $18x^5$ **1b.** $10r^2t^4$ **1c.** $4x^5y^5z^7$ **2a.** $8x^2 + 2x + 6$ **2b.** $15a^3b + 3ab^2$ **2c.** $5r^3s^2 - 15r^2s^3$ **3a.** $a^2 - a - 12$ **3b.** $x^2 - 6x + 9$ **3c.** $2a^2 + 7ab^2 - 4b^4$ **4a.** $x^3 - x^2 - 6x + 18$ **4b.** $3x^3 - 4x^2 + 11x + 10$ **5a.** $x^2 - 4x$ **5b.** 12 m^2

Exercises 1. $14x^6$ **3.** $3r^5s^5t^5$ **5.** $21x^7y^3$ **7.** $4x^2 + 8x + 4$ **9.** $6a^5b^2 + 2a^4b^3$ **11.** $10x^3y^4 - 5x^2y^2$ **13.** $x^2 - x - 2$ **15.** $x^2 - 4x + 4$ **17.** $4a^4 - 2ab - 12a^3b^2 + 6b^3$ **19.** $x^3 + 3x^2 - 7x + 15$ **21.** $-6x^4 + 12x^3 + 4x^2 - 18x + 20$ **23.** $x^3 - 4x^2 - 4x - 5$ **25a.** $2x^2 - 3x$ **b.** 20 in^2 **27.** $-12r^5s^5$ **29.** $10a^4$ **31.** $-6a^5b^6$ **33.** $-12a^7b^7c^8$ **35.** $9s^2 + 54s$ **37.** $27x^3 - 12x^2$ **39.** $10s^3t^3 - 15s^2t^5$ **41.** $-10x^3 + 15x^2 + 5x$ **43.** $-14x^6y^3 + 7x^5y^4$ **45.** $x^2 + 8x + 16$ **47.** $5x^2 + 13x - 6$ **49.** $10x^2 - x - 2$ **51.** $7x^2 - 52x - 32$ **53.** $x^3 - x^2 - x + 10$ **55.** $-10x^4 + 2x^3 + 20x^2 - 19x + 3$

57. $8x^5 - 12x^3 - 2x^4 + 17x^2 - 21$ **59.** $x^3 - 3x - 2$ **61.** $-x^3 + 3x^2 - 3x + 1$ **63.** $16x^2 - 48x + 36$ **65a.** 3; 2; $10x^5 + 5x^3$; 5 **b.** 2; 2; $x^4 - x^3 + 2x^2 - 2x$; 4 **c.** 1; 3; $x^4 - 5x^3 + 6x^2 + x - 3$; 4 **d.** $m + n$ **67.** $12x^2 + 12x + 3$ **69a.** $2x^2$ **b.** 800 m^2 **71.** $2x^2 - 7x - 30$ **73.** $8x^2 - 16xy + 6y^2$ **75.** $6x^2 - 9x - 6$ **77.** $x^3 + 3x^2$ **79.** $2x^3 - 7x^2 - 10x + 24$ **81.** $8p^3 - 36p^2q + 54pq^2 - 27q^3$ **87.** C **89.** D **91.** $-x^2 - 6$ **93. a.** $x^2 - 1$ **b.** $8x + 16$ **95.** $x^3 + 3x^2 + 2x$ **97.** $a = 2$ **99.** 3.61 **101.** 9.49

7-9

Check It Out! 1a. $x^2 + 12x + 36$ **1b.** $25a^2 + 10ab + b^2$ **1c.** $1 + 2c^3 + c^6$ **2a.** $x^2 - 14x + 49$ **2b.** $9b^2 - 12bc + 4c^2$ **2c.** $a^4 - 8a^2 + 16$ **3a.** $x^2 - 64$ **3b.** $9 - 4y^4$ **3c.** $81 - r^2$ **4.** 25

Exercises 3. $4 + 4x + x^2$ **5.** $4x^2 + 24x + 36$ **7.** $4a^2 + 28ab + 49b^2$ **9.** $x^2 - 4x + 4$ **11.** $64 - 16x + x^2$ **13.** $49a^2 - 28ab + 4b^2$ **15.** $x^2 - 36$ **17.** $4x^4 - 9$ **19.** $4x^2 - 25y^2$ **21.** $x^2 + 6x + 9$ **23.** $x^4 + 2x^2y^2 + y^4$ **25.** $4 + 12x + 9x^2$ **27.** $s^4 - 14s^2 + 49$ **29.** $a^2 - 16a + 64$ **31.** $9x^2 - 24x + 16$ **33.** $a^2 - 100$ **35.** $49x^2 - 9$ **37.** $25a^4 - 81$ **39.** $\pi x^2 + 8\pi x + 16\pi$ **41.** $x^2 + 2xy + y^2$ **43.** $x^4 - 16$ **45.** $x^4 - 8x^2 + 16$ **47.** $1 + 2x + x^2$ **49.** $x^6 - 2a^3x^3 + a^6$ **51.** $36a^2 - 25b^2$ **53.** 4; 4 **55.** 25; 25 **57.** 9; 9 **59.** -5; -5 **61.** 840 **65.** 1, 4, 9, 16, 25, 36, 49, 64, 81, 100 **67.** B **69.** D **71.** $x^3 + 4x^2 - 16x - 64$ **73.** $b = \pm 2\sqrt{c}$ **75.** 13 cm

Study Guide: Review

1. cubic **2.** standard form of a polynomial **3.** monomial **4.** trinomial **5.** scientific notation **6.** $\frac{1}{32}$ in. **7.** 1 **8.** 1 **9.** $\frac{1}{125}$ **10.** $\frac{1}{10,000}$, or 0.0001 **11.** $\frac{1}{16}$ **12.** $\frac{1}{256}$ **13.** $\frac{27}{4}$ **14.** $\frac{1}{m^2}$ **15.** b **16.** $-\frac{1}{2x^2y^4}$ **17.** $2b^6c^4$ **18.** $\frac{3a^2}{4c^2}$ **19.** $\frac{s^3}{qr^2}$ **20.** 10,000,000 **21.** 0.00001 **22.** 10^2 **23.** 10^{-11} **24.** 325,000 **25.** 1800 **26.** 0.17 **27.** 0.000299 **28.** 5.8×10^{-7}, 6.3×10^{-3}, 2.2×10^2, 1.2×10^4 **29.** \$38,500,000,000 **30.** 5^9 **31.** $2^3 \cdot 3^4$ **32.** b^{10} **33.** r^5 **34.** x^{12} **35.** 1 **36.** $\frac{1}{2^3}$, or $\frac{1}{8}$ **37.** $\frac{1}{5^4}$, or $\frac{1}{625}$

38. $\frac{1}{16b^6}$ **39.** $g^{12}h^8$ **40.** x^4y^2
41. $-x^4y^2$ **42.** x^6y^{15} **43.** j^6k^9 **44.** $\frac{1}{5}$
45. m^8n^{30} **46.** 8×10^{11} **47.** 9×10^7
48. 1×10^{10} **49.** 2.8×10^{15}
50. 6×10^1 **51.** 1.8×10^{-8}
52. 3.55×10^7 **53.** 64 **54.** m^5 **55.** $\frac{7}{32}$
56. $6b$ **57.** t^3v^4 **58.** 16 **59.** 5×10^1
60. 2.5×10^7 **61.** 9 **62.** 7 **63.** 16
64. 8 **65.** z^2 **66.** $5x^2$ **67.** x^4y^3
68. m^2n^4 **69.** 0 **70.** 3 **71.** 6 **72.** 1
73. $3n^2 + 2n - 4$; 3 **74.** $-a^6 - a^4 + 3a^3 + 2a$; -1 **75.** linear binomial
76. quintic monomial **77.** quartic trinomial **78.** constant monomial
79. $-4t + 3$ **80.** $-6x^6 - x^5$ **81.** $3h^3 - 3h^2 + 5$ **82.** $2m^2 - 5m - 1$ **83.** $p^2 + 5p + 8$ **84.** $-7z^2 - z + 10$ **85.** $3g^2 + 2g + 4$ **86.** $-x^2 + 4x + 8$ **87.** $8r^2$
88. $6a^6b$ **89.** $18x^3y^2$ **90.** $3s^6t^{14}$
91. $2x^2 - 8x + 12$ **92.** $-3a^2b^2 + 6a^3b^2 - 15a^2b$ **93.** $a^2 - 3a - 18$
94. $b^2 - 6b - 27$ **95.** $x^2 - 12x + 20$
96. $t^2 - 1$ **97.** $8q^2 + 34q + 30$
98. $20g^2 - 37g + 8$ **99.** $p^2 - 8p + 16$
100. $x^2 + 24x + 144$ **101.** $m^2 + 12m + 36$ **102.** $9c^2 + 42c + 49$
103. $4r^2 - 4r + 1$ **104.** $9a^2 - 6ab + b^2$ **105.** $4n^2 - 20n + 25$ **106.** $h^2 - 26h + 169$ **107.** $x^2 - 1$ **108.** $z^2 - 225$
109. $c^4 - d^2$ **110.** $9k^4 - 49$

Chapter 8

8-1

Check It Out! **1a.** $2^3 \cdot 5$ **1b.** $3 \cdot 11$
1c. 7^2 **1d.** 19 **2a.** 4 **2b.** 5 **3a.** $9g^2$
3b. 1 **3c.** 1 **4.** 7

Exercises **3.** $3^2 \cdot 2^2$ **5.** $3^3 \cdot 2$ **7.** 7 (prime) **9.** $3 \cdot 5^2$ **11.** 7 **13.** x^2
15. 1 **17.** $2 \cdot 3^2$ **19.** $2^2 \cdot 3$
21. 17 **23.** 7^2 **25.** 9 **27.** 10 **29.** $9s$
31. 5 **33.** $4x^2$ **35.** $2n$ **39.** 15
rows **41.** 8 and 20; 4 **43.** 63 and 105; 21 **45.** 54 and 72; 18 **47.** 36; 2; 9; 3 **49.** 105; 5; 7 **51.** 2; 2; 27; 3
53. 24; 2; 6; 3 **55.** 2; 2; 10, 5 **57.** D
61. $9y$ **63.** $2p^2r$ **65.** $4a^2b^3$ **69.** 3.12 h
71. ≈ 0.10 mi/yr **73.** 40 **75.** $3x^2 + 14x - 3$

8-2

Check It Out! **1a.** $b(5 + 9b^2)$
1b. cannot be factored
1c. $-y^2(18y + 7)$

1d. $2x^2(4x^2 + 2x - 1)$
2. $2x$ cm; $(x + 2)$ cm
3a. $(4s - 5)(s + 6)$ **3b.** $(7x + 1)(2x + 3)$
3c. cannot be factored **3d.** $(5x - 2)^2$
4a. $(2b^2 + 3)(3b + 4)$
4b. $(4r + 1)(r^2 + 6)$
5a. $(5x^2 - 4)(3 - 2x)$
5b. $(8 + x)(y - 1)$

Exercises **1.** $5a(3 - a)$ **3.** $7(-5x + 6)$
5. $2h(6h^3 + 4h - 3)$ **7.** $m(9m + 1)$
9. $3(12f + 6f^2 + 1)$ **11.** $16t(-t + 20)$
13. $(2b + 5)(b + 3)$
15. $(x^2 + 2)(x + 4)$
17. $(2b^2 + 5)(2b - 3)$
19. $(7r^2 + 6)(r - 5)$
21. $2(r - 2)(r - 3)$
23. $(7q - 2)(2q - 3)$
25. $(2m^2 - 3)(m - 3)$ **27.** $9y(y + 5)$
29. $x^2(-14x^2 + 5)$
31. $-d^2(4d^2 - d + 3)$
33. $7c(3c + 2)$ **35.** $-5g^2(g + 3)$
37. cannot be factored
39. $(6y + 1)(y - 7)$
41. $(-3 + 4b)(b + 2)$
43. $(2a^2 + 3)(a - 4)$
45. $(6x^2 + 1)(x + 3)$
47. $(n^2 + 5)(n - 2)$
49. $(2m^2 - 3)(m - 1)$
51. $(2f^2 - 5)(3f - 4)$
53. $(b^2 - 2)(b + 4)$ **55.** $3v$
57. $2k$ **59.** 2; binomial; $x(x + 5)$
61. 3; trinomial; $a^2(a^2 + a + 1)$
63a. $100x^3$; $200x^2$; $400x$
b. $100x^3 + 200x^2 + 400x + 800$
c. $100(x^2 + 4)(x + 2)$; $1603.12
67. The sum of opposite binomials is 0. **69a.** Commutative Property of Addition **b.** Associative Property of Addition **c.** Distributive Property **d.** Distributive Property
71. D **73.** C **75.** $-9ab(8ab + 5)$
77. $(a + c)(b + d)$
79. $(x^2 + 3)(x - 4)$ **81.** 11 **83.** 5

8-3

Check It Out! **1a.** $(x + 4)(x + 6)$
1b. $(x + 4)(x + 3)$ **2a.** $(x + 6)(x + 2)$
2b. $(x - 6)(x + 1)$ **2c.** $(x + 6)(x + 7)$
2d. $(x - 8)(x - 5)$ **3a.** $(x + 5)(x - 3)$
3b. $(x - 4)(x - 2)$ **3c.** $(x - 10)(x + 2)$
4.

n	$n^2 - 7n + 10$
0	$0^2 - 7(0) + 10 = 10$
1	$1^2 - 7(1) + 10 = 4$
2	$2^2 - 7(2) + 10 = 0$
3	$3^2 - 7(3) + 10 = -2$
4	$4^2 - 7(4) + 10 = -2$

n	$(n - 5)(n - 2)$
0	$(0 - 5)(0 - 2) = 10$
1	$(1 - 5)(1 - 2) = 4$
2	$(2 - 5)(2 - 2) = 0$
3	$(3 - 5)(3 - 2) = -2$
4	$(4 - 5)(4 - 2) = -2$

Exercises **1.** $(x + 4)(x + 9)$
3. $(x + 4)(x + 10)$ **5.** $(x + 2)(x + 8)$
7. $(x - 1)(x - 6)$ **9.** $(x - 3)(x - 8)$
11. $(x + 9)(x - 3)$ **13.** $(x - 2)(x + 1)$
15. $(x - 9)(x + 5)$ **17.** $(x + 3)(x + 10)$
19. $(x + 4)(x + 12)$
21. $(x + 2)(x + 14)$ **23.** $(x - 1)(x - 5)$
25. $(x - 4)(x - 8)$ **27.** $(x + 7)(x - 3)$
29. $(x - 13)(x + 1)$ **31.** $(x - 7)(x + 5)$
33. C **35.** D **37.** They are inverse operations. **39.** $(x - 2)(x - 9)$
41. $(x + 1)(x + 9)$ **43.** $(x + 6)(x + 7)$
45. $(x + 2)(x + 9)$ **47.** $(x - 3)(x + 8)$
49. $(x - 5)(x + 9)$ **51.** approximately 1.5 **55.** $x^2 + 6x + 8$; $(x + 4)(x + 2)$
57. Positive; $-$, $-$; Both negative
59. Negative; $+$, $-$; Positive; Negative **61a.** $d = t^2$ **b.** $d = 4t$
c. $t(t - 4)$ **63.** true **65.** false **67.** 4
69. 4 **71a.** $(x + 10)$ ft **b.** $\ell = (x + 14)$ ft; $w = (x + 6)$ ft **c.** $A = (x^2 + 20x + 84)$ ft^2
73. D **75.** C **77.** $(x^2 + 9)(x^2 + 9)$
79. $(d^2 + 21)(d^2 + 1)$
81. $(de - 5)(de + 4)$ **83.** 16; 11; 29
85a. $(x + 7)$ ft **b.** $(4x + 26)$ ft **c.** $92.00
d. $36.96 **e.** $128.96 **87.** x^5 **89.** t^{12}
91. $(x + 2)(x^2 + 5)$
93. $(p - 2)(2p^3 + 7)$

8-4

Check It Out! **1a.** $(3x + 1)(2x + 3)$
1b. $(3x + 4)(x - 2)$
2a. $(2x + 5)(3x + 1)$
2b. $(3x - 4)(3x - 1)$
2c. $(3x + 4)(x + 3)$
3a. $(3x - 1)(2x + 3)$
3b. $(4n + 3)(n - 1)$
4a. $-1(2x + 3)(3x + 4)$
4b. $-1(3x + 2)(x + 5)$

Exercises **1.** $(2x + 5)(x + 2)$
3. $(5x - 3)(x + 2)$ **5.** $(3x + 4)(x - 6)$
7. $(x + 2)(5x + 1)$
9. $(4x - 5)(x - 1)$
11. $(5x + 4)(x + 1)$
13. $(2a - 1)(2a + 5)$
15. $(2x - 3)(x + 2)$
17. $(10x + 1)(x - 1)$
19. $(2x + 3)(4 - x)$

21. $-1(5x + 3)(x - 2)$
23. $-1(2x - 1)(2x + 5)$
25. $(3x + 2)(3x + 1)$
27. $(n + 2)(3n + 2)$
29. $(4c - 5)(c - 3)$
31. $(2x + 5)(4x + 1)$
33. $(5x - 6)(x + 3)$
35. $(10n - 7)(n - 1)$
37. $(7x + 1)(x + 2)$
39. $(3x - 4)(x - 5)$
41. $(x - 7)(4x - 3)$
43. $(4y - 1)(3y + 5)$
45. $(2x - 1)(2x + 3)$
47. $(3x + 5)(x - 3)$
49. $-1(2x - 3)(2x + 5)$
51. $-1(3x - 2)(x + 1)$
53. $2x^2 - 5x + 2;\ (x - 2)(2x - 1)$
55. $(9n + 8)(n + 1)$
57. $(2x - 1)(2x - 5)$
59. $(3x + 8)(x + 2)$
61. $(3x + 4)(2x - 3)$
63. $(2x - 3)(2x - 3)$
65. $(2x + 3)(3x + 2)$
69a. $-16t^2 + 20t + 6$
b. $-2(4t + 1)(2t - 3)$ **c.** 10 ft **71.** D
73. B **77.** B **79.** A
81. $(2x + 1)(2x + 1)$
83. $(9x + 1)(9x + 1)$
85. $(5x + 2)(5x + 2)$ **87.** $-7; -5; 5; 7$
89. $-6; 6$ **95.** $(x + 1)(x - 9)$

8-5

Check It Out! 1a. yes; $(x + 2)^2$
1b. yes; $(x - 7)^2$ **1c.** no; $-6x \neq 2(3x)(2)$ **2.** $4(3x + 1)$ m; 40 m
3a. yes; $(1 - 2x)(1 + 2x)$
3b. yes; $(p^4 + 7q^3)(p^4 - 7q^3)$
3c. No; $4y^5$ is not a perfect square.

Exercises 1. yes; $(x - 2)^2$ **3.** yes; $(3x - 2)^2$ **5.** yes; $(x - 3)^2$
7. $4(x + 12)$; 88 yd **9.** yes; $(s + 4)(s - 4)$ **11.** yes; $(2x^2 + 3y)(2x^2 - 3y)$
13. yes; $x^3 + 3x^3 - 3$ **15.** No; the last term must be positive. **17.** no; $10x \neq 2(5x)(2)$ **19.** yes; $(4x - 5)^2$
21. yes; $(1 + 2x)(1 - 2x)$ **23.** No; $4x$ and $9y$ are not perfect squares.
25. yes; $(9 - 10x^2)(9 + 10x^2)$
27. 49 **29.** $4y^2$
31. $(10x + 9y)(10x - 9y)$; difference of 2 squares
33. $(2r^3 + 5s^3)(2r^3 - 5s^3)$; difference of 2 squares
35. $(x^7 + 12)(x^7 - 12)$; difference of 2 squares **39.** $c = 32$ **41a.** $5z - 4$
b. $20z - 16$ **c.** 11; 44; 121
43a. 0; 0; 100; 100; 0 **b.** 16; 16; 36;

36; −24 **c.** 25; 25; 25; 25; −25
d. 36; 36; 16; 16; −24 **e.** 100; 100; 0; 0; 0 **45.** $a - b; a + b$ **47.** C **49.** 1
51a. $a = 2; b = v + 2$
b. $[2 + (v + 2)][2 - (v + 2)] = (v + 4)(-v) = -v^2 - 4v$ **53.** $a = 3y; b = y;\ (3y - 4)(9y^2 + 12y + 16)$
55. D: {5, 4, 3, 2}; R: {2, 1, 0, −1}; yes **57.** D: {2}; R: {−8, −2, 4, 10}; no
59. $6a^3 + 14a^2 - 10a$ **61.** $t^2 - 8t + 16$
63. 8

8-6

Check It Out! 1a. yes **1b.** no; $4(x + 1)^2$ **2a.** $4x(x + 2)^2$
2b. $2y(x - y)(x + y)$
3a. $(3x + 4)(x + 1)$
3b. $2p^3(p + 6)(p - 1)$
3c. $3q^4(3q + 4)(q + 2)$ **3d.** $2(x^4 + 9)$

Exercises 1. yes **3.** yes **5.** no; $4(2p^2 + 1)(2p^2 - 1)$
7. $3x^3(x + 2)(x - 2)$ **9.** $2p(2q + 1)^2$
11. $mn(n^2 + m)(n^2 - m)$
13. $3x^2(2x - 3)(x + 1)$
15. $(p^3 + 1)(p^2 + 3)$
17. unfactorable **19.** no; $2xy(y^2 - 4y + 5)$
21. no; $3n^2(n + 5)(n - 5)$ **23.** yes
25. $-4x(x - 3)^2$ **27.** $5(d - 3)(d - 9)$
29. $2x(7x + 5y)(7x - 5y)$
31. unfactorable
33. $(p^2 + 4)(p + 2)(p - 2)$
35. $(k^2 + 3)(2k + 3)$ **37.** $x^2 + 12x + 36 = (x + 6)^2$ **39.** $s^2 - 16s + 28 = (s - 2)(s - 14)$ **41.** $b^2 - 49 = (b + 7)(b - 7)$ **45.** $(3x - 1)(x + 7)$
47. $(3x + y - 3)(3x - y - 7)$
53. 8 **55.** C **57.** C **59a.** $V = 8p\left[\pi(3p + 1)^2\right]$ **b.** $r = (3p + 1)$ cm
c. $h = 8$ cm; $V = 128\pi$ cm³
61. $h^2(h^4 + 1)(h^2 + 1)$
63. $x^{n + 3}(x^2 + x + 1)$ **65.** $-2n$
67. $12.3r$ **69.** $\frac{23}{2} = \frac{x}{3}$; 34.5 cm
71. $(2x - 1)(2x + 3)$

Study Guide: Review

1. prime factorization **2.** greatest common factor **3.** $2^2 \cdot 3$ **4.** $2^2 \cdot 5$
5. 2^5 **6.** prime **7.** $2^3 \cdot 5$ **8.** 2^6
9. $2 \cdot 3 \cdot 11$ **10.** $2 \cdot 3 \cdot 19$ **11.** 5
12. 12 **13.** 1 **14.** 27 **15.** 4 **16.** 3
17. $2x$ **18.** $9b^2$ **19.** $25r$ **20.** 6 boxes; 13 rows **21.** $5x(1 - 3x^2)$
22. $16(-b + 2)$ **23.** $-7(2v + 3)$
24. $4(a^2 - 3a - 2)$
25. $5g(g^2 - 3)(g^2 + 1)$

26. $10(4p^2 - p + 3)$
27. $(6x + 5)$ ft by x ft
28. $(2x + 9)(x - 4)$
29. $(t - 6)(3t + 5)$
30. $(5 - 3n)(6 - n)$
31. $(b + 2)(b + 4)$
32. $(x^2 + 7)(x - 3)$
33. $(n^2 + 1)(n - 4)$
34. $(2b + 5)(3b - 4)$
35. $(2h^2 - 7)(h + 7)$
36. $(3t + 1)(t + 6)$
37. $(5m^2 - 1)(2m + 3)$
38. $(4p - 3)(2p^2 + 1)$
39. $-1(r - 5)(r - 2)$
40. $(b^2 - 5)(b - 3)$
41. $(t + 4)(-t^2 + 6)$
42. $-1(3h - 1)(h - 4)$
43. $-1(d - 1)^2$ **44.** $(2 - b)(5b - 6)$
45. $(t + 1)(5 - t)$
46. $(2b^2 + 5)(4 - b)$
47. $-1(3r - 1)(r - 1)$
48. left rectangle: $2x^2 + 3x$; right rectangle: $8x + 12$; combined: $2x^2 + 8x + 3x + 12$; $(2x + 3)(x + 4)$
49. $(x + 1)(x + 5)$ **50.** $(x + 2)(x + 4)$
51. $(x + 3)(x + 5)$ **52.** $(x - 6)(x - 2)$
53. $(x + 5)^2$ **54.** $(x - 2)(x - 11)$
55. $(x + 4)(x + 20)$ **56.** $(x - 6)(x - 20)$
57. $(x + 12)(x - 7)$ **58.** $(x + 3)(x - 8)$
59. $(x + 4)(x - 7)$ **60.** $(x - 1)(x + 5)$
61. $(x + 3)(x - 2)$ **62.** $(x + 5)(x - 4)$
63. $(x - 8)(x + 6)$ **64.** $(x - 9)(x + 4)$
65. $(x - 12)(x + 6)$
66. $(x - 10)(x + 7)$
67. $(x + 20)(x - 6)$
68. $(x + 7)(x - 1)$ **69.** $(y + 3)$ m
70. $(2x + 1)(x + 5)$
71. $(3x + 7)(x + 1)$
72. $(2x - 1)(x - 1)$
73. $(3x + 2)(x + 2)$
74. $(5x + 3)(x + 5)$
75. $(2x - 3)(3x - 5)$
76. $(4x + 5)(x + 2)$
77. $(3x + 4)(x + 2)$
78. $(7x - 2)(x - 5)$
79. $(3x + 2)(3x + 4)$
80. $(2x + 1)(x - 1)$
81. $(3x + 1)(x - 4)$
82. $(2x - 1)(x - 5)$
83. $(7x + 2)(x - 3)$
84. $(5x + 1)(x - 2)$
85. $-1(2x - 1)(3x + 2)$
86. $(6x + 5)(x - 1)$
87. $(3x - 2)(2x + 7)$
88. $-1(2x + 1)(2x - 5)$
89. $-1(2x - 3)(5x + 2)$
90. $12x^2 - 11x - 5;\ (4x - 5)(3x + 1)$

91. yes; $(x+6)^2$ **92.** no; $5x \neq 2(x)(5)$
93. no; $-2x \neq 2(2x)(1)$
94. yes; $(3x+2)^2$ **95.** no; $8x \neq 2(4x)(2)$ **96.** yes; $(x+7)^2$ **97.** yes; $(10x-9)(10x+9)$ **98.** No; 2 is not a perfect square. **99.** No; 5 and 10 are not perfect squares.
100. yes; $(-12+x^3)(-12-x^3)$
101. no; terms must be subtracted
102. yes; $(10p-5q)(10p+5q)$
103. $(x-5)(x+5)$; difference of 2 squares **104.** $(x+10)^2$; perfect-square trinomial **105.** $(j-k^2)(j+k^2)$; difference of 2 squares
106. $(3x-7)^2$; perfect-square trinomial **107.** $(9x+8)^2$; perfect-square trinomial
108. $(4b^2-11c^3)(4b^2+11c^3)$; difference of 2 squares
109. no; $2(2x+3)(x+1)$
110. yes
111. no; $(b^2+9)(b-3)(b+3)$
112. yes **113.** $4(x-4)(x+4)$
114. $3b^3(b-4)(b+2)$
115. $a^2b^3(a-b)(a+b)$
116. $t^4(t^8+1)(t^4+1)(t^2+1)(t+1)(t-1)$ **117.** $5(x+3)(x+1)$
118. $2x^2(x-5)(x+5)$
119. $2(s+4)(t+4)$
120. $5m(5m+2)(m-4)$
121. $4x(4x^2+1)(2x-3)$
122. $6s^2t(s+t^2)$
123. $2(m+3)(m-3)(5m+2)$

Chapter 9

9-1

Check It Out! 1a. Yes; the second differences are constant. **1b.** Yes; the function can be written in the form $y = ax^2 + bx + c$.

2a.

2b.

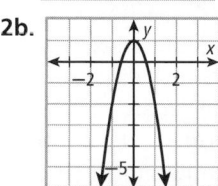

3a. Because $a < 0$, the parabola opens downward. **3b.** Because $a > 0$, the parabola opens upward.

4a. vertex: $(-2, 5)$; maximum: 5
4b. vertex: $(3, -1)$; minimum: -1
5a. D: all real numbers; R: $y \geq 4$
5b. D: all real numbers; R: $y \leq 3$

Exercises 1. minimum **3.** yes
5. no

7.

9.

11. upward; $a > 0$ **13.** upward; $a > 0$ **15.** downward; $a < 0$
17. $(-3, -4)$; minimum: -4 **19.** D: all real numbers; R: $y \leq 4$ **21.** D: all real numbers; R: $y \geq -4$ **23.** yes
25. yes **31.** upward; $a > 0$
33. vertex: $(0, -5)$; minimum: -5
35. D: all real numbers; R: $y \leq 0$
37. D: all real numbers; R: $y \geq -2$
39. never **41.** always
43. sometimes **45.** no **47.** yes
49. yes **53.** quadratic **55.** quadratic
57. neither **59.** linear **61b.** $t \geq 0$
c. 16 ft **d.** 2 s **65.** C **67.** yes
71. $(-2)^4$ **73.** $42\frac{3}{4}$ mi

9-2

Check It Out! 1a. no zeros
1b. 3 **2a.** $x = -3$ **2b.** $x = 1$
3. $x = -\frac{1}{4}$ **4.** $(2, -14)$ **5.** 7 ft

Exercises 3. -1 **5.** no zeros
7. $x = 2$ **9.** $x = -2$ **11.** $x = -\frac{3}{4}$
13. $(1, 8)$ **15.** $(-2, -2)$ **17.** $(-2, -9)$
19. no zeros **21.** $-8, -2$
23. $x = 6$ **25.** $x = -\frac{1}{2}$ **27.** $x = 5$
29. $(-3.5, -12.25)$ **31.** $(-2, 5)$
33. $(1, 4.5)$ **35.** $x = 0$. **37.** 0 **39.** 2
41. B **43.** 2 **45.** 25 ft; 100 ft
47. $y = -2x + 3$ **49.** $y = -4x + 2$
51. yes

9-3

Check It Out!

1a.

1b.

2. maximum height: 16 ft at 0.5 s; time it takes to reach the pool: 1.5 s

Exercises 1.

3.

5.

7. maximum height: 144 ft at 3 s; time in the air: 6 s

9.

11.

13.

15. $x = 4$; $(4, -16)$ **17.** $x = 0$; $(0, 4)$
19. $x = -\frac{1}{2}$; $\left(-\frac{1}{2}, -\frac{15}{4}\right)$ **21.** vertex: $(0, 0)$; axis of symmetry: $x = 0$
23. vertex: $(3, -5)$; axis of symmetry: $x = 3$ **25.** vertex: $(0, -4)$; axis of symmetry: $x = 0$ **27b.** D: $0 \leq x \leq 3.16$; R: $0 \leq y \leq 50$ **c.** about 3.16 s
31. 12 cm/s **35a.** $h(t) = -16t^2 + 45t + 50$ **b.** approximately $(1.4, 81.6)$ **37.** A **39.** D **41.** -1
43. x-intercept: 3; y-intercept: 6

45. no x-intercept; y-intercept: 3
47. $(3, -1)$ **49.** $(-1, -16)$ **51.** $(-1, 4)$

9-4

Check It Out! 1a. $f(x), g(x)$
1b. $g(x), f(x), h(x)$ **2a.** same
width, same axis of symmetry,
opens upward, translated 4 units
down **2b.** narrower, same axis
of symmetry, opens upward,
translated 9 units up **2c.** wider,
same axis of symmetry, opens
upward, translated 2 units up
3a. The graph of the ball that is
dropped from a height of 100 ft is
a vertical translation of the graph
of the ball that is dropped from
a height of 16 ft. The y-intercept
of the graph of the ball that is
dropped from 100 ft is 84 units
higher. **3b.** The ball that is dropped
from 16 ft reaches the ground in
1 s. The ball that is dropped from
100 ft reaches the ground in 2.5 s.

Exercises 1. $f(x), g(x)$ **3.** $h(x)$,
$g(x), f(x)$ **5.** same width, same
axis of symmetry, opens upward,
translated 6 units up **7.** wider,
same axis of symmetry, opens
upward, same vertex
9a. $h_1(t) = -16t^2 + 16, h_2(t) =$
$-16t^2 + 256$; the graph of h_2 is a
vertical translation of the graph
of h_1. The y-intercept of h_2 is 240
units higher. **b.** The baseball that
is dropped from 256 ft reaches the
ground in 4 s. The baseball that
is dropped from 16 ft reaches the
ground in 1 s. **11.** $f(x), g(x)$ **13.** $f(x)$,
$h(x), g(x)$ **19.** always **21.** never
25. $f(x) = 3x^2 - 6$ **29.** B **31.** A
39. D **41.** 0 **43a.** $f(x) = x^2 - 7$
b. $f(x) = -x^2 + 2$ **c.** $f(x) = \frac{1}{2}x^2 + 1$
45. no correlation

9-5

Check It Out! 1a. $x = -4$ **1b.** no
real solutions **1c.** $x = -2$ or
$x = 2$ **2.** 2 s

Exercises 1. zeros, x-intercepts
3. $-4, 4$ **5.** 6 **7.** $-2, 4$ **9.** -1
11. no real solutions **13.** no real
solutions **15.** $x = -4$ or $x = 4$
17. $x = \frac{1}{2}$ or $x = 5$ **19.** $x = -3$
21. no real solutions **23.** no real
solutions **25.** always **27.** always

29. never **31a.** 4 s **b.** 10 ft **33.** 1.4 s
35. $-1, 1$ **41.** C **45.** no real solutions
47. $x \approx -1.6$ or $x \approx 0.86$ **49.** $y - 4 =$
$-3(x + 2)$ **51.** 27 **53.** x^{11} **55.** a^3b^3
57. $\frac{27b^2}{8a^6}$

9-6

Check It Out! 1a. $0, -4$ **1b.** $-4, 3$
2a. 3 **2b.** $1, -5$ **2c.** $-\frac{5}{3}$ **2d.** $\frac{1}{3}, 1$
3. 1.5 s

Exercises 1. $-2, 8$ **3.** $-7, -9$
5. $-11, 0$ **7.** $-6, 2$ **9.** 2, 3
11. $-8, -2$ **13.** 4 **15.** 6 **17.** $-2, -\frac{3}{2}$
19. 1 s **21.** $-4, -7$ **23.** 0, 9
25. $-\frac{1}{2}, \frac{1}{3}$ **27.** $-2, 4$ **29.** $-\frac{1}{3}, 1$
31. -2 **33.** 1 **35.** 1 **37.** 1 **39.** B
41. 6 m **43.** 6 s **45.** no **47a.** 3 s
b. 64 ft **c.** yes **49.** F **51.** $-5, -1$
53. $\frac{1}{2}, -3$ **55.** $-2, 5$ **57.** $-1, 0$
59. $x^2 - x - 12$ **61.** $x^2 - 4x - 12 =$
$48; x = 10$ **63.** -8 **65.** 2 **67.** $(-9,$
$-16)$ **69.** ± 7 **71.** 3, 5

9-7

Check It Out! 1a. ± 11
1b. 0 **1c.** no real solutions
2a. no real solutions **2b.** 9, 1
3a. ± 9.49 **3b.** ± 5.66 **3c.** no real
solutions **4.** 45 ft

Exercises 1. ± 15 **3.** no real
solutions **5.** no real solutions **7.** ± 5
9. no real solutions **11.** 11, -5
13. ± 5.20 **15.** ± 4.47 **17.** ± 13
19. no real solutions **21.** no real
solutions **23.** $\pm \frac{2}{9}$ **25.** $\pm \frac{5}{8}$ **27.** $\pm \frac{13}{7}$
29. ± 4.69 **31.** ± 10.20 **33.** ± 7.07
35. 6.1 s **37.** $t = \sqrt{\frac{2d}{a}}$ **39.** $a = -6$
and $b = -3$ or $a = 6$ and $b = 3$
41. about 4.2 ft by 8.4 ft **43.** A
45. sometimes **47a.** $a > 0$
b. $a = 0$ **c.** $a < 0$ **49.** no; $x =$
$\pm\sqrt{\frac{1}{2}}$, irrational **51.** yes; $x = \pm\frac{1}{2}$,
rational **55.** H **57.** $\pm\frac{1}{4}$ **59.** $\pm\frac{8^2}{11}$
61. 13 **63.** 2, 4 **65.** $-2, 7$

9-8

Check It Out! 1a. 36 **1b.** $\frac{25}{4}$ **1c.** 16
2a. $-9, -1$ **2b.** $4 \pm \sqrt{21}$ **3a.** $-\frac{1}{3}, 2$
3b. no real solutions **4.** 16.4 ft by
24.4 ft

Exercises 3. 4 **5.** $-5, -1$ **7.** $-6, 5$
9. 1, 9 **11.** $\frac{-5 \pm 3\sqrt{5}}{2}$ **13.** no real
solutions **15.** $4 \pm \sqrt{10}$ **17.** 7.2 m;
11.2 m **19.** 1 **21.** $-2, 12$

23. $-13, -2$ **25.** $-6, 8$ **27.** $-2, 3$
29. $\frac{-1 \pm \sqrt{5}}{2}$ **31.** $\frac{-15 \pm \sqrt{105}}{2}$ **33.** 4 in.
35. $1 \pm \sqrt{7}$ **37.** $-3, \frac{1}{2}$ **39.** $-10, 2$
41. 81 **43.** $\frac{49}{4}$ **45.** 9
47a. $(10 + 2x)(24 + 2x) = 640$
b. 3 ft **51.** $-6 \pm \sqrt{26}$ **53.** -6 **55.** no
real solutions **57.** no real solutions
61a. $-16t^2 + 64t + 32 = 0$ **b.** 4
c. 4.4 s **63.** B **65.** B **67.** $-\frac{3}{2}, \frac{2}{3}$
69. $-\frac{2}{3} - \frac{\sqrt{7}}{3}, -\frac{2}{3} + \frac{\sqrt{7}}{3}$ **71.** $0, -\frac{b}{a}$
77. $x^2 - 8x + 16$ **79.** $t^2 - 8t + 16$
81. $64b^4 - 4$ **83.** ± 1 **85.** ± 4 **87.** ± 15
89. ± 1.55 **91.** ± 5.10 **93.** ± 1.48

9-9

Check It Out! 1a. $2, -\frac{1}{3}$ **1b.** $2, -\frac{1}{5}$
2. $\frac{8 - \sqrt{56}}{4} \approx 0.13, \frac{8 + \sqrt{56}}{4} \approx 3.87$
3a. 0 **3b.** 1 **3c.** 2 **4.** No; for the
equation $45 = -16t^2 + 20t + 0$,
the discriminant is negative, so the
weight will not ring the bell.
5a. $-2, -5$ **5b.** $-2, 7$
5c. $\frac{-4 - \sqrt{184}}{4} \approx -4.39, \frac{-4 + \sqrt{184}}{4} \approx$
2.39

Exercises 1. no **3.** $\frac{1}{2}, 3$ **5.** $-4, -10$
7. $-\frac{1}{2}, \frac{3}{2}$ **9.** $\frac{-6 - \sqrt{24}}{2} \approx -5.45$,
$\frac{-6 - \sqrt{24}}{2} \approx -0.55$
11. $\frac{-1 - \sqrt{61}}{6} \approx 1.14, \frac{-1 + \sqrt{61}}{6} \approx$
-1.47 **13.** $\frac{-1 - \sqrt{41}}{4} \approx -1.85$,
$\frac{-1 + \sqrt{41}}{4} \approx 1.35$ **15.** 1 **17.** 0
19. 2 **21.** 0 **23.** yes **25.** -3
27. $-\frac{1}{2}$ **29.** $-3, \frac{3}{2}$ **31.** 1, 9
33. $\frac{4 - \sqrt{12}}{2} \approx 0.27$,
$\frac{4 + \sqrt{12}}{2} \approx 3.73$ **35.** $\frac{-7 - \sqrt{17}}{4} \approx 2.78$,
$\frac{-7 + \sqrt{17}}{4} \approx -0.72$ **37.** 2
39. no **41.** $-5, 3$ **43.** no real
solutions **45.** 2 solutions; $-2, \frac{1}{4}$
47. 1 solution; $\frac{2}{3}$ **49.** 2 x-intercepts;
$\frac{7}{2}, -3$ **51.** 1 x-intercept; 5 **57.** A
59a. 1 **b.** -1 **c.** -1 **d.** -1 **63.** $-10, 4$
65. $(r^3 + t)(s^2 + 5)$
67. $(n^4 - 2)(n - 6)$ **69.** $f(x), g(x)$

Study Guide: Review

1. vertex **2.** minimum; maximum
3. zero of a function **4.** discriminant
5. completing the square **6.** Yes; it
is in standard form. **7.** No; $a = 0$
8. Yes; it is in standard form. **9.** No;
a quadratic function does not have
a power of x greater than 2.

10.

11.

12.

13.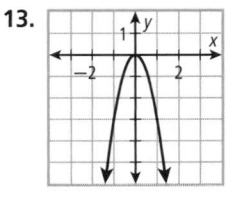

14. upward **15.** downward
16. $(-2, -4)$; minimum: -4
17. -5 and 2 **18.** -1 and 2
19. $x = 6$; $(6, 4)$ **20.** $x = -1$;
$(-1, -18)$

21.

22.

23.

24.

25.

26.

27.

Water Fountain

In 2 seconds, the water reaches its maximum height of 20 meters. It takes a total of 4 seconds for the water to reach the ground. **28.** $g(x)$, $f(x)$ **29.** The graphs have the same width. **30.** $h(x), f(x), g(x)$ **31.** same width, same axis of symmetry, opens upward, vertex translated 5 units up **32.** narrower, same axis of symmetry, opens upward, vertex translated 1 unit down **33.** narrower, same axis of symmetry, opens upward, vertex translated 3 units up **34.** $x = -3$ or $x = -1$ **35.** $x = -3$ **36.** no real solutions **37.** $x = 1$ or $x = 5$ **38.** $x = 4$ **39.** $x = 1$ or $x = -1$ **40.** no real solutions **41.** $x = -5$ or $x = -1$ **42.** $x = -7$ or $x = -2$ **43.** $x = -3$ or $x = 5$ **44.** $x = -1$ or $x = 2$ **45.** $x = -5$ **46.** $x = 4.5$ **47.** $x^2 + 2x = 48$; 6 ft **48.** $x = -8$ or $x = 8$ **49.** $x = -12$ or $x = 12$ **50.** no real solutions **51.** $x = 0$ **52.** $x = -5$ or $x = 5$ **53.** $x = -\frac{5}{2}$ or $x = \frac{5}{2}$ **54.** 4 ft **55.** $x = -8$ or $x = 6$ **56.** $x = -7$ or $x = 3$ **57.** $x = 1$ or $x = 5$ **58.** $x = 5 \pm \sqrt{5}$ **59.** 16 ft by 12 ft **60.** $x = -1$ or $x = 6$ **61.** $x = -\frac{1}{2}$ or $x = 5$ **62.** $x = 1$ **63.** $x = \frac{6 \pm \sqrt{8}}{2}$ **64.** 1 **65.** 0 **66.** 2 **67.** 2

Chapter 10

10-1

Check It Out! **1a.** bread
1b. cheese and mayonnaise
2. 2001, 2002, and 2005; about 13,000 **3.** about 18 °F **4.** Prices increased from January through July or August, and then prices decreased through November.
5. 31.25%
6.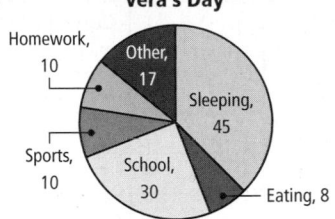

Vera's Day

A circle graph shows parts of a whole.

Exercises **1.** one part of a whole **3.** 82 animals **5.** $15 **7.** Prices at stadium A are greater than prices at stadium B. **9.** between weeks 4 and 5 **11.** 18% **13.** purple **15.** blue and green **17.** 225,000 **19.** Friday **21.** 3.5 times **23.** games 3, 4, and 5 **25.** Stock Y changed the most between April and July of 2004. **27.** $8\frac{1}{3}$% **31.** double line **33.** circle **35a.** Greece; about 40% **b.** United States; about 15% **37.** D **41.** 19 girls **43.** D: $\{-3, -1, 0, 1, 3\}$; R: $\{0, 1, 3\}$; yes **47.** quadratic binomial

10-2

Check It Out!

1.

Temperature (°C)

Stem	Leaves
0	7
1	9
2	2 3 6 7 9
3	0 1 1 2 4 5 6 6

Key: 1|9 means 19

2.

Interval	Frequency
4–6	5
7–9	4
10–12	4
13–15	2

3.

Vacation

4a.

Interval	Frequency	Cumulative Frequency
28–31	2	2
32–35	7	9
36–39	5	14
40–43	3	17

4b. 9

Exercises 1. stem-and-leaf plot

3.

Austin	Stem	New York
9 9 9	1	
4 3 2 1	2	
6 5 3 2 0	3	1 3 3 3 6 6 7 9
	4	1 1 2 2

5.

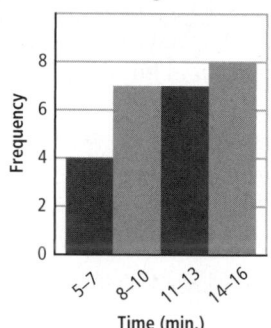

Breathing Intervals

7.

Summer	Stem	Winter
	0	4 9 9
	1	1 2 3 4 9 9
9 7 7 6 5 5 3 3 2 2	2	1 7
	3	0 3 5
	4	
9 7 4 3	5	

Key: |2|1 means 21
7|2| means 27

9.

Interval	Frequency
2.0–2.4	2
2.5–2.9	7
3.0–3.4	5
3.5–3.9	3

11a.

Interval	Frequency	Cumulative Frequency
36–38	4	4
39–41	6	10
42–44	5	15
45–47	1	16

b. 10

15a.

Interval	Frequency
160–169.9	2
170–179.9	4
180–189.9	3
190–199.9	1
200–209.9	2
210–219.9	1

19. G **21.** 8; 8; 41; 66 **23.** −2.3
25. 0.5 in. **27.** books

10-3

Check It Out! 1. mean: 14 lb; median: 14 lb; modes: 12 lb and 16 lb; range: 4 lb **2.** 3; the outlier decreases the mean by 3.7 and increases the range by 18. It has no effect on the median and mode. **3a.** mode: 7 **3b.** Median: 81; the median is greater than either the mean or the mode.

4.

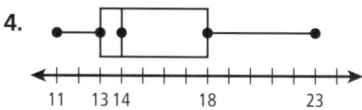

5a. The data set for 2000; the distance between the points for the least and greatest values is less for 2000 than for 2007. **5b.** about $40 million

Exercises 3. mean: 31.5; median: 33.5; mode: 44; range: 32 **5.** mean: 78.25; median: 78; mode: 78; range: 15 **7.** 13; the outlier decreases the mean by 11.15 and the median by 4. It increases the range by 51 and has no effect on the mode. **9.** Median: 83; the median is greater than the mean, and there is no mode. **13.** Simon; about 3000 points **15.** mean: 2.5; median: 2.5; modes: 2 and 3; range: 3 **17.** mean: 60; median: 60; mode: 60; range: 5 **19.** 23; the outlier increases the mean by 3, the median by 2.5, and

the range by 15. It has no effect on the mode. **21.** Mean: 153; the mean is greater than the median, and there is no mode. **25.** Sneaks R Us; the middle half of the data doesn't vary as much at Sneaks R Us as at Jump N Run. **27.** mean: 5.5; median: 5.5; mode: none; range: 9 **29.** mean: 3.5; median: 3.4; mode: none; range: 5.3
31. mean: 24.4; median: 25; modes: 23 and 25; range: 3 **33.** mean: $15\frac{1}{6}$; median: $12\frac{1}{2}$; mode: none; range: 35 **37.** sometimes **39.** always
41. Median; the mean is affected by the outlier of 1218, and there is no mode. **43.** Median or mode; the store wants their prices to seem low, and the median and mode are both $2.80 less than the mean. **49.** Mean: $32,000; median: $25,000; median; the outlier of $78,000 increases the mean significantly. **51.** 96 **53.** increase the mean; decrease the mean **55.** G **57.** The mean decreases by 6.6 lb. **61.** 32; typing speed is 32 words per minute. **63.** 2 **65.** 5 **67.** length: 5 yd; width: 3 yd

10-4

Check It Out! 1. Possible answer: company D; the fertilizer from company D appears to be more effective than the other fertilizers. **2.** Possible answer: taxi drivers; the drivers could justify charging higher rates by using this graph, which seems to show that gas prices have increased dramatically. **3.** Possible answer: Smith; Smith might want to show that he or she got many more votes than Atkins or Napier. **4.** The sample size is much too small.

Exercises 3a. The vertical scale does not start at 0, and the categories on the horizontal scale are not at equal time intervals. **b.** Possible answer: Tourism is decreasing rapidly. **5.** The sample size is too small. **7a.** The vertical scale does not start at 0. **b.** Possible answer: Single men pay significantly more than single women.

9a. The sectors of the graph do not add to 100%.
b. Possible answer: Nearly half of the state's spending was for welfare. **15.** B **19.** $w \le 1500$
21. $b \le 20$ **23.** $t \ge -4$

10-5

Check It Out! 1. sample space: {1, 2, 3, 4, 5, 6}; outcome shown: 3
2. certain **3a.** $\frac{7}{20}$ **3b.** $\frac{13}{20}$ **4a.** 99.8%
4b. 34,930

Exercises 3. sample space: {blue, red, yellow, green}; outcome shown: red **5.** impossible **7.** unlikely
9. $\frac{3}{5}$ **11a.** 30% **b.** 54 **13.** sample space: {blue, red, yellow}; outcome shown: blue **15.** as likely as not
17. likely **19.** $\frac{6}{25}$ **21a.** 5% **b.** 21
27. about 1%; about 57 **29.** B **31.** B
33. as likely as not **35.** unlikely
37a. 7 **b.** 8 **39.** $14 **41.** reflected across the x-axis **43.** mean: 6; median: 5; mode: 5

10-6

Check It Out! 1a. 50% **1b.** $33\frac{1}{3}$%
2. 0.4 **3.** $\frac{1}{25}$

Exercises 1. complement **3.** 25%
5. $\frac{1}{2}$ **7.** $\frac{2}{3}$ **9.** $\frac{9}{10}$ **11.** 1.12 **13.** $\frac{1}{4}$ **15.** 50%
17. $\frac{5}{9}$ **19.** 70% **21.** $\frac{9}{1}$ **23.** $\frac{1}{5}$ **25.** $\frac{4}{5}$
27. 4:1 **31.** $\frac{1}{2}$ **35.** D **37.** B
41. $(4x - 3)(x - 1)$ **43.** $\frac{1}{10}$ **45.** $\frac{13}{20}$

10-7

Check It Out! 1a. Independent; the result of rolling the number cube the first time does not affect the result of the second roll.
1b. Dependent; choosing the first student leaves fewer students to choose from the second time. **2.** $\frac{1}{4}$
3. $\frac{8}{87}$

Exercises 1. dependent
3. independent **5.** independent
7. $\frac{1}{8}$ **9.** $\frac{1}{6}$ **11.** $\frac{1}{16}$ **13.** $\frac{2}{7}$
15. dependent **17.** $\frac{1}{8}$ **19.** $\frac{1}{12}$
21. $\frac{2}{9}$ **23a.** $\frac{27}{64}$ **b.** $\frac{1}{64}$ **25.** dependent
27. independent **29a.** $\frac{3}{20}$ **b.** $\frac{1}{6}$
c. $\frac{9}{100}$ **d.** $\frac{1}{15}$ **31.** $\frac{2}{15}$ **35.** D **37.** A
39. 72.9% **41.** 80% **43.** 48%
45. 24 **47.** wider **49.** $\frac{3}{5}$ **51.** $\frac{5}{26}$

10-8

Check It Out! 1. 15,600
2a. permutation; 6
2b. combination; 6 **3.** 362,880
4. 792

Exercises 1. combination **3.** 8
5. combination; 6 **7.** 20,160 **9.** 35
11. 15,504 **13.** 441,000
15. combination; 10 **17.** 120
19. 133,784,560 **21.** $_nP_r$
25a. $\frac{1}{308,915,776}$ **b.** about 85,810 h
27. J **29.** 260,130 **31.** 168 **33a.** 28
b. 28 **37.** $5x + 5$ **39.** independent: minutes; dependent: volume of water in tub; $f(x) = 15x$
41. independent: hours; dependent: total fee; $f(x) = 300 + 80x$

Study Guide: Review

1. outcome **2.** interquartile range
3. independent events **4.** 2003
5. 14 more boys

6.

Stem	Leaves
0	1 7 9
1	2 4 8 9
2	2 2 4 8

Key: 1|2 means 12

7.

Comedy Camp	Days and Days
2	6
	7
3 1	8 0 2
	9
4 4 2	10 3 5 9
	11
6 2 0	12 8
	13 2 5 9

Key: |12|8 means 128
4|10| means 104

8.

Gas Tank Capacities		
Capacity	Tally	Frequency
10–14	‖‖ I	6
15–19	‖‖ ‖‖	10
20–24	III	3
25–29	III	3

9.

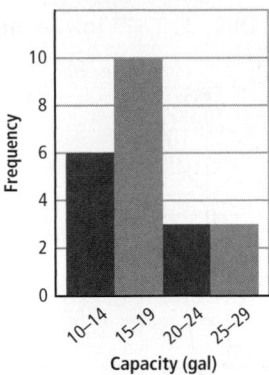

Gas Tank Capacities

10. mean: 14; median: 12; mode: 12; range: 28 **11.** Median; the mean is higher than 4 of the 5 prices; the mode is the lowest price.
12.

13. The scale on the vertical axis is too large. This makes the slopes of the segments less steep.
14. Someone might believe that the price has been relatively stable when in fact it has doubled.
15. 99.5% **16.** 24,875 **17.** 250 **18.** $\frac{1}{2}$
19. $\frac{1}{4}$ **20.** $\frac{5}{8}$ **21.** independent
22. independent **23.** dependent
24. $\frac{2048}{9555}$ **25.** 0 **26.** $\frac{256}{2401}$ **27.** 60
28. permutation; 604,800
29. combination; 220
30. combination; 1365

Chapter 11

11-1

Check It Out! 1a. 80, -160, 320
1b. 216, 162, 121.5 **2.** 7.8125
3. $1342.18

Exercises 3. 25, 12.5, 6.25
5. 1,000,000,000 **7.** 4 **9.** 162, 243, 364.5 **11.** 2058; 14,406; 100,842
13. $\frac{5}{32}, \frac{5}{128}, \frac{5}{512}$ **15.** 0.0000000001, or 1×10^{-10} **17.** 80; 160 **19.** $\frac{1}{3}$ **21.** $\frac{1}{7}; \frac{1}{49}$
23. 6; -48 **25.** 4913 **27.** yes; $\frac{1}{3}$ **29.** no
31. no **33a.** 1.28 cm **b.** 40.96 cm
35. $-2, -8, -32, -128$
37. 2, 4, 8, 16 **39.** 12, 3, $\frac{3}{4}, \frac{3}{16}$
43a. $3993; $4392.30 **b.** 1.1
c. $2727.27 **45.** J **47.** x^4, x^5, x^6
49. 1, y, y^2 **51.** -400 **53.** the 7th term **55.** $b > 10$ **57.** $c < -\frac{1}{3}$
61. $f(x) = x^2 + 4$

11-2

Check It Out! 1. 3.375 in. **2a.** no
2b. yes

3a.

3b.

4a.

4b.

5a.

5b.

6. after about 13 yr

Exercises 1. no **3.** no **17.** about
2023 **19.** 289 ft **21.** yes **23.** no
35. $y = 4.8(2)^x$ **41.** -0.125
43a. $2000 **b.** 8% **c.** $2938.66
45. C **45.** C **47.** D **49.** 3 **51.** The
value of a is the y-intercept.
53. 25 **55.** $9x^2$

11-3

Check It Out! 1. $y = 1200(1.08)^t$;
$1904.25 **2a.** $A = 1200(1.00875)^{4t}$;
$1379.49 **2b.** $A = 4000(1.0025)^{12t}$;
$5083.47 **3.** $y = 48,000(0.97)^t$; 38,783
4a. 1.5625 mg **4b.** 0.78125 g

Exercises 1. exponential growth
3. $y = 300(1.08)^t$; 441 **5.** $A =$
$4200(1.007)^{4t}$; $4965.43 **7.** $y =$
$10(0.84)^t$; 4.98 mg **9.** 5.5 g **11.** $y =$
$1600(1.03)^t$; 2150 **13.** $A = 30(1.078)^t$;
47 members **15.** $A = 7000(1.0075)^{4t}$;
$9438.44 **17.** $A = 12,000(1.026)^t$;
$17,635.66 **19.** $y = 58(0.9)^t$; $24.97
21. growth; 61% **23.** decay; $33\frac{1}{3}$%
25. growth; 10% **27.** growth; 25%
29. $y = 58,000,000(1.001)^t$;
58,174,174 **31.** $y = 8200(0.98)^t$;
$7118.63 **33.** $y = 970(1.012)^t$; 1030
35. B **37.** 18 yr **39.** A; B **45.** D **47.** D
49. about 20 yr **51.** 100 min, or 1 h
40 min **53.** $225,344 **55.** 16 ft

11-4

Check It Out!

1a.

exponential

1b.

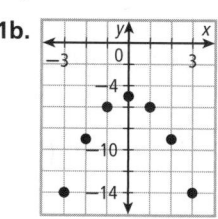

quadratic
2. quadratic **3.** The oven
temperature decreases by 50 °F
every 10 min; $y = -5x + 375$; 75 °F

Exercises 1. exponential
3. linear **5.** exponential **7.** Grapes
cost $1.79/lb; $y = 1.79x$; $10.74
11. linear **13.** exponential
15. $\ell = 6k$; linear **17.** linear
19. $y = 0.2(4)^x$ **21.** linear **27.** C
29. C **33.** $\frac{145}{g}$
35. 5, -5 **37.** $\frac{9}{4}$, $-\frac{9}{4}$

11-5

Check It Out! 1a. 40 ft/s
1b. 30.98 ft/s **2a.** $x \geq \frac{1}{2}$ **2b.** $x \geq \frac{5}{3}$

3a.

3b.

Exercises 1. There is no variable
under the square-root sign.
3. $x \geq -6$ **5.** $x \geq 0$ **7.** $x \geq -3$
15. 49.96 mi/h **17.** $x \geq 0$ **19.** $x \leq \frac{3}{2}$
21. $x \geq -\frac{5}{3}$ **23.** $x \geq 40$ **25.** $x \geq 9$
27. $x \geq -\frac{2}{3}$ **37.** 3.61 units
39. Mercury: 4214 m/s; Venus:
10,361 m/s; Earth: 11,200 m/s;
Mars: 5016 m/s **45.** A **47.** C
49. $x \leq -5$ OR $x \geq 5$
51. $x \leq -4$ OR $x \geq \frac{3}{2}$
53. D: $x \leq 3$; R: $y \leq 4$ **57a.** 2 and 4
b. 3, 1 **59.** $y = -\frac{1}{2}x + 2$
61. $9x^2 - 6x + 1$
63. $a^2 - 2ab^2c + b^4c^2$ **65.** $9r^2 - 4s^2$
67. $A = 42,000(1.0125)^{4t}$; $48,751.69

11-6

Check It Out! 1a. 8 **1b.** 7 **1c.** 13
1d. $|3 - x|$ **2a.** $8\sqrt{2}$ **2b.** $xy\sqrt{x}$
2c. $4a\sqrt{3b}$ **3a.** $\frac{2}{3}$ **3b.** $\frac{6}{x^2}$ **3c.** $\frac{y^3}{2}$
4a. $\frac{2\sqrt{5}}{7}$ **4b.** $\frac{z^2\sqrt{z}}{5y}$ **4c.** $\frac{p^3}{q^5}$ **5.** $60\sqrt{2}$ ft;
84.9 ft

Exercises 1. $3x - 6$ **3.** 7 **5.** $6\sqrt{5}$
7. $18\sqrt{2}$ **9.** $4x^2y\sqrt{2y}$ **11.** $\frac{\sqrt{17}}{5}$ **13.** $\frac{\sqrt{6}}{7}$
15. $\frac{\sqrt{x}}{3}$ **17.** $\frac{6\sqrt{3}}{7}$ **19.** $\frac{16\sqrt{2}}{9}$ **21.** $\frac{5x\sqrt{2}}{13}$
23. $5\sqrt{41}$ mi; 32 mi **25.** 20 **27.** 9
29. $|x + 1|$ **31.** $|x - 3|$ **33.** $20\sqrt{10}$
35. $8rs\sqrt{5}$ **37.** $\frac{3\sqrt{5}}{2}$ **39.** $\frac{\sqrt{14}}{3}$ **41.** $\frac{x\sqrt{x}}{y^3}$
43. $\frac{8s\sqrt{3}}{7}$ **45.** $-20\sqrt{3}$ **47.** $15x\sqrt{7}$
49. x **51.** $\frac{x^3\sqrt{x}}{3}$ **53.** $\sqrt{36}$; 6 **55.** $\sqrt{50}$;
$5\sqrt{2}$ **57.** $\sqrt{3}$ **59.** $\sqrt{20}$; $2\sqrt{5}$ **67.** C
69. C **71.** $x\sqrt{x + 1}$ **73a.** $|x|$ **b.** x^2
c. $|x^3|$ **d.** x^4 **e.** $|x^5|$ **f.** x^n; $|x^n|$
75. no **77.** exponential

11-7

Check It Out! 1a. $-\sqrt{7}$ **1b.** $3\sqrt{3}$
1c. $8\sqrt{n}$ **1d.** $\sqrt{2s} + 8\sqrt{5s}$ **2a.** $5\sqrt{6}$
2b. $12\sqrt{3} - 3\sqrt{2}$ **2c.** $5\sqrt{3y}$
3. $10\sqrt{b}$ in.

Exercises 3. $10\sqrt{5}$ **5.** $3\sqrt{7} + 5\sqrt{2}$
7. $5\sqrt{6a} + 6\sqrt{5a}$ **9.** $13\sqrt{3}$ **11.** $-\sqrt{5x}$
13. $8\sqrt{2t} - 4\sqrt{3t}$ **15.** $6\sqrt{3}$ **17.** $-3\sqrt{11}$
19. $-4\sqrt{n}$ **21.** $7\sqrt{7}$ **23.** $12\sqrt{2}$
25. $3\sqrt{7x} - 12\sqrt{3x}$ **27.** $3\sqrt{5j}$

29. $2\sqrt{3m}$ **31.** $12\sqrt{7}$ **33.** 0 **35.** $7\sqrt{3}$
37. $7\sqrt{2}$ **41.** $2\sqrt{3}+5\sqrt{5}+5$
43. $8\sqrt{7x}-\sqrt{70x}$ **45.** $35\sqrt{5k}$
47. $5\sqrt{3}+5\sqrt{5}$ **51.** 9 **53.** 18
55. $36x^2$ **57.** $16\sqrt{3}$ in.; $8\sqrt{3}$ in.;
$24\sqrt{3}$ in. **59.** B **61.** A **63.** $\sqrt{x}(x+2)$
65. 0 **67.** $(x+2)\sqrt{x-1}$
69. $3\sqrt{x+1}-x\sqrt{x+2}$ **73.** $\frac{1}{12}$
75. $x \geq -3$

11-8

Check It Out! 1a. $5\sqrt{2}$ **1b.** 63
1c. $2m\sqrt{7}$ **2a.** $4\sqrt{3}-3\sqrt{6}$
2b. $5\sqrt{2}+4\sqrt{15}$ **2c.** $7\sqrt{k}-5\sqrt{7k}$
2d. $150-20\sqrt{5}$ **3a.** $21+5\sqrt{3}$
3b. $83+18\sqrt{2}$ **3c.** $11-6\sqrt{2}$
3d. $17-\sqrt{3}$ **4a.** $\frac{\sqrt{65}}{5}$ **4b.** $\frac{\sqrt{21a}}{6}$
4c. $\frac{8\sqrt{35}}{7}$

Exercises 1. $\sqrt{6}$ **3.** 125 **5.** $3\sqrt{30a}$
7. $2\sqrt{6}+\sqrt{42}$ **9.** $\sqrt{35}-\sqrt{21}$
11. $5\sqrt{3y}+4\sqrt{5y}$ **13.** $12+7\sqrt{2}$
15. $-5-2\sqrt{3}$ **17.** $81-30\sqrt{2}$
19. $\frac{\sqrt{26}}{2}$ **21.** $\frac{\sqrt{33}}{18}$ **23.** $\frac{2\sqrt{7}}{7}$
25. $\frac{\sqrt{5x}}{5x}$ **27.** $3\sqrt{10}$ **29.** 8
31. $6d\sqrt{7}$ **33.** $4\sqrt{5}-5\sqrt{2}$
35. $2\sqrt{3}-2\sqrt{5}$ **37.** $3\sqrt{f}+12\sqrt{3f}$
39. $75+19\sqrt{15}$ **41.** $10-\sqrt{2}$
43. $67+16\sqrt{3}$ **45.** $\frac{5\sqrt{6}}{2}$ **47.** $\frac{\sqrt{3x}}{x}$
49. $\frac{7\sqrt{2x}}{2}$ **51.** $2\sqrt{y}$ **53.** 180 in^2
55. $\left(6\sqrt{10}-2\sqrt{5}\right)$ cm^2 **57.** $\sqrt{30}$
59. $-5-2\sqrt{3}$ **61.** $3\sqrt{2}$
63. $134\sqrt{3}+96$ **65.** $x-2\sqrt{xy}+y$
67. $3+2\sqrt{3x}+x$ **69.** $\frac{\pi\sqrt{6}}{4}$ s ≈ 1.9 s
71. 269.5 ft^2 **75.** B **77.** D
79. $-4\sqrt{3}+4\sqrt{5}$ **81.** $-5-2\sqrt{6}$
83. $2-\sqrt{3}$ **85.** $2\sqrt{6}+2\sqrt{5}$
87. translation 4 units down
89. $(x-3)(x+10)$
91. $(x+4)(x-4)$
93. $2(x^2+3)(x^2-3)$
95. $6\sqrt{10}$ **97.** $\frac{7x}{8y^2}$

11-9

Check It Out! 1a. 36 **1b.** 3 **1c.** $\frac{1}{3}$
2a. 9 **2b.** 18 **2c.** 3 **3a.** 121 **3b.** 64
3c. 100 **4a.** 2 **4b.** $\frac{11}{2}$ **5a.** no solution
5b. no solution **5c.** 4 **6.** 8; 3 cm

Exercises 1. No; it does not contain
a variable under the radical sign.
3. -8 **5.** -144 **7.** 27 **9.** 50 **11.** -2
13. 9 **15.** 64 **17.** 16 **19.** 16 **21.** $\frac{4}{9}$
23. 100 **25.** 5 **27.** 13 **29.** 6 **31.** 2

33. no solution **35.** 4 **37.** 2 **39.** no
solution **41.** 48 **43.** -25 **45.** 71
47. -8 **49.** 36 **51.** -16 **53.** 8 **55.** 9
57. 2 **59.** -5 **61.** 5 **63.** 1 **65.** 1
67. $x = 144$; 12 in. **69.** $\sqrt{x}-3 = 4$; 49
71. $x = \sqrt{x+6}$; 3 **73.** 3 in. by 1 in.
75a. 54.88 joules **b.** 0 joules
77. 1690 ft **79.** $x = 25$; $y = 16$
81. sometimes **87.** A **89.** C
91. A **93.** 1, 2 **95.** 2 **97.** 0
101. 51.2 mi **103.** 10,000

Study Guide: Review

1. square-root function
2. exponential decay **3.** common
ratio **4.** exponential function
5. 81, 243, 729 **6.** 48, -96, 192
7. 5, 2.5, 1.25 **8.** -256, -1024, -4096
9. 7,812,500 **10.** 19,131,876 **11.** yes
12. no

13.

14.
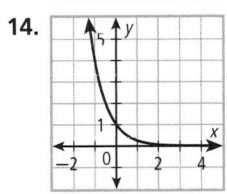

15. $y = 9(1.15)^t$; 24
16. $y = 24{,}500(0.96)^t$; 3182
17. quadratic **18.** linear
19. exponential **20.** exponential
21. quadratic **22.** linear
23. $y = 1.5x$; 15 h **24.** 4.74 cm
25. $x \geq 0$ **26.** $x \geq -4$ **27.** $x \geq 0$
28. $x \geq -2$ **29.** $x \geq \frac{4}{3}$ **30.** $x \geq -3$
31. $x \geq \frac{7}{2}$ **32.** $x \geq -\frac{18}{5}$ **33.** $x \geq \frac{3}{4}$
34. $x \geq 1$

35.

36.

37.

38.

39.

40.

41.

42.

43.

44.

45. 11 **46.** n^2 **47.** $x+3$ **48.** 5
49. $6d$ **50.** $y^3\sqrt{x}$ **51.** $2\sqrt{3}$
52. $4b^2\sqrt{2ab}$ **53.** $\frac{\sqrt{5}}{2}$ **54.** $\frac{t}{10}$ **55.** $\frac{2}{3}$
56. $\frac{4p^2\sqrt{2}}{7}$ **57.** $\frac{t^4\sqrt{t}}{s}$ **58.** $\frac{2b^3\sqrt{2}}{5}$
59. $9\sqrt{7}$ **60.** $3\sqrt{3}$ **61.** $3\sqrt{2}+2\sqrt{3}$
62. $\sqrt{5t}$ **63.** $2\sqrt{2}$ **64.** $2\sqrt{3}+2\sqrt{5}$

65. $-2\sqrt{5x}$ **66.** $10\sqrt{6}$ **67.** $\sqrt{14}$
68. $3\sqrt{2}$ **69.** $6\sqrt{7x}$ **70.** 150
71. $4\sqrt{2}-4$ **72.** $71+16\sqrt{7}$ **73.** $\frac{4\sqrt{5}}{5}$
74. $\frac{3a\sqrt{2}}{2}$ **75.** $\frac{\sqrt{3}}{3}$ **76.** $\frac{\sqrt{10n}}{2n}$ **77.** $\frac{\sqrt{6}}{2}$
78. $-\sqrt{3}$ **79.** 64 **80.** 8 **81.** 3 **82.** 25
83. -81 **84.** 100 **85.** 3 **86.** no
solution **87.** $x=4$ **88.** $x=6$
89. $x=7$ **90.** $x=\frac{19}{2}$ **91.** $x=12$
92. $x=3$ **93.** $x=4$ **94.** $x=5$

Chapter 12

12-1

Check It Out! 1a. No; the product xy is not constant. **1b.** Yes; the product xy is constant. **1c.** No; the equation cannot be written in the form $y=\frac{k}{x}$. **2.** $y=\frac{5}{x}$

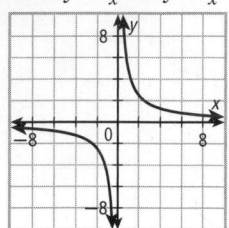

3. D: $x>0$; R: $y>0$; 2.5 mm³

4. 3 **5.** 80.625 lb

Exercises 3. no **5.** yes
7. $y=\frac{-6}{x}$

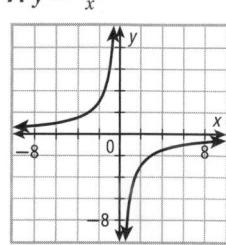

9. 4 **11.** 16 teeth
13. yes **15.** no

17. $y=\frac{2}{x}$

19. 2 **21.** 12 yd **23.** direct; 8
25. neither **27.** inverse; 12
29. inverse; 15 **31.** $d=\frac{10}{n}$; inverse
33. neither **35.** $y=\frac{2000}{x}$; D: natural numbers; R: $y>0$

41. C **43.** C
47. approximately 888.9 watts
49. D: $\{-4, -2, 0, 2, 4\}$; R: $\{1, 3, 5\}$; yes **51.** $-1, 7$ **53.** $2\sqrt{10}$ cm

12-2

Check It Out! 1a. 0 **1b.** 1 **1c.** -4
2a. $x=5$; $y=0$ **2b.** $x=-4$; $y=5$
2c. $x=-77$; $y=-15$

3a.

3b.

4a. D: $x>0$; R: natural numbers > 10
4b.

Exercises 1. excluded value **3.** -3
5. 4 **7.** $x=-5$; $y=0$ **9.** $x=-9$; $y=-10$

11.

13.

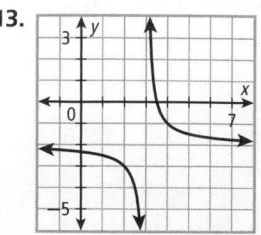

15. 0 **17.** 0 **19.** $x=4$; $y=0$
21. $x=3$; $y=4$
23.

25.

27a. D: $x>0$; R: natural numbers > 5
b.

29. 7 **31.** $-\frac{1}{2}$ **37.** $x=-1$; $y=0$
39. $x=2$; $y=5$ **41.** B **43.** C **51.** D: $x>2$ **53.** D: $x>-\frac{1}{5}$ **55.** I and III; II and IV **59.** J **61a.** yes **b.** D: all real numbers **c.** R: $0<y\le 1$ **d.** no
63. $y=\frac{3}{x+2}+3$ **65.** $-2, 3$
67. 0.46875 cm **69.** no

12-3

Check It Out! 1a. -5 **1b.** 0, -5
1c. $-3, -4$ **2a.** $\frac{m}{3}$; $m\ne 0$ **2b.** $6p$
2c. $\frac{3n}{n-2}$; $n\ne 2$ **3a.** $\frac{1}{r+5}$ **3b.** $\frac{b-5}{b+5}$
4a. $-\frac{3}{4+x}$ **4b.** $-\frac{1}{x+1}$ **4c.** $\frac{3}{x+11}$

5. The barrel cactus with a radius of 3 inches has less of a chance to survive. Its surface-area-to-volume ratio is greater than for a cactus with a radius of 6 inches.

Exercises 3. 0, 8 **5.** $\frac{a}{2}$; $a \neq 0$ **7.** $\frac{2}{y+3}$; $y \neq -3$ **9.** $\frac{h}{h+2}$; $h \neq -2$ **11.** $\frac{1}{b+1}$

13. $\frac{c+2}{c-4}$ **15.** $\frac{j-5}{j-3}$ **17.** $-\frac{2}{8+n}$

21. $-\frac{5}{10+q}$ **23a.** $\frac{b_2}{b_1+b_2}$ **b.** They will be the same: $\frac{b_2}{b_1+b_2}$.

25. 0 **27.** $-\frac{1}{2}$, 4 **29.** already simplified; $m \neq 4$ **31.** $\frac{t}{8}$; $t \neq 0$

33. $\frac{z-1}{z+1}$ **35.** $\frac{p-7}{p-5}$ **37.** $\frac{2}{x-4}$

39. $-\frac{1}{b+7}$ **43.** $\frac{p+6}{12}$ **45.** $\frac{1}{3}$ **47.** $\frac{3w+7}{3}$

49. 1 **51.** $-\frac{5+x}{x+2}$ **53a.** $\frac{6}{s}$

b. 3 **c.** 1 **57.** F **59.** sometimes

61. sometimes **63.** $\frac{a-3}{a+5}$ **65.** ± 14

67. $-2, 0$ **73.** -6

Check It Out! 1a. $-\frac{9}{4}$ **1b.** $\frac{5x^2y^4}{6}$

2. $\frac{3m-15}{m-6}$ **3a.** $\frac{n+4}{n^2+2n}$ **3b.** $\frac{p^2-p-20}{p^3+16p}$

4a. $\frac{3x-15}{x^5}$ **4b.** $\frac{2w^6}{v^2x^3}$ **4c.** $\frac{x}{x^2+5x+6}$

5. approximately 0.23

Exercises 1. $\frac{6h}{5jk^2}$ **3.** $\frac{2r-4}{3}$ **5.** $\frac{a}{6}$

7. $3y-6$ **9.** $\frac{m^2-10m}{2}$ **11.** a^3+10a^2+25a **13.** $\frac{a+6b}{b^2}$ **15.** $\frac{1}{2}$ **17.** $\frac{2r+28}{r-4}$ **19.** b

21. $\frac{1}{3x-15}$ **23.** $-\frac{3p^8q^2}{7r^4}$ **25.** $\frac{10y+20}{3y+15}$

27. $4m^2-4m$ **29.** $\frac{3n^2-3n}{n+8}$ **31.** 1

33. $-\frac{1}{2a^3}$ **35a.** $\frac{x^2}{4(4x^2+8x-1)}$

b. $\frac{9}{236}$ **37.** b **39.** $\frac{1}{2m}$ **41.** $\frac{1}{16x}$

43. 1 **45a.** 64 cm **b.** 80 cm

c. 4 **47.** H **49.** $\frac{1}{3x^2+9x}$ **51.** $\frac{1}{3}$ **53.** $\frac{x}{z^2}$

55. $\frac{1}{2a+2}$ **57.** $m \leq 9$

59. $8\sqrt{3t}$ **61.** $x \neq 3$; $x = 3$ and $y = 0$

63. $x \neq 0$; $x = 0$ and $y = 3$ **65.** $x \neq 0$; $x = 0$ and $y = 0$

Check It Out! 1a. 2 **1b.** $3y$

2a. $\frac{3}{a-2}$ **2b.** $\frac{4b+12}{b^2+3b-4}$ **3a.** $15f^2h^2$

3b. $(x-6)(x+2)(x+5)$ **4a.** $\frac{4d-3}{3d^2}$

4b. $\frac{a+8}{a-2}$ **5.** $\frac{5}{24}$ h or 12.5 min

Exercises 1. $\frac{2}{y}$ **3.** $\frac{1}{x-4}$ **5.** $\frac{2}{a+1}$

7. $6x^3y^2z$ **9.** $(y+4)(y-4)(y+9)$

11. $\frac{x+3}{x+2}$ **13a.** $\frac{260}{r}$ **b.** $6\frac{1}{2}$ h **15.** $a-1$

17. m **19.** $3a+1$ **21.** $36a(3a+1)$

23. $10xy^3z$ **25.** $(y+5)(y+2)(y+4)$ **27.** $\frac{y+2}{3(y-3)}$

29. $\frac{19}{21z}$ **31.** $\frac{-m^2-6m}{4(m-2)^2}$ **33a.** $\frac{700}{r}$

b. 14 h **35.** $\frac{1}{7+c}$ **37.** $\frac{3}{2b^2}$ **39.** $\frac{x-5}{3}$

41. $\frac{8x+20}{(x+4)(x+2)}$ **43.** A

47. $4x^2$; $8x^2$; $8x^3$ **49.** A **51.** D

53. $\frac{x-4y}{(x+y)(x-y)}$; $x \neq y$ and $x \neq -y$

55. $\frac{az+by+cx}{xyz}$; $x \neq 0$, $y \neq 0$, and $z \neq 0$ **61.** $\frac{1}{2}$, 4 **63.** 2; $t \neq \pm 2$

65. $-\frac{1}{x+4}$; $x \neq \pm 4$

Check It Out! 1a. $-2p+1-\frac{3}{p}$

1b. $x^2+\frac{1}{3}-\frac{5}{2x}$ **2a.** $k+5$ **2b.** $b-7$

2c. $s+6$ **3a.** $2y+1$ **3b.** $a-2$

4a. $3m-5+\frac{13}{m+3}$ **4b.** $y+6+\frac{20}{y-3}$

5a. $x^2-2x-4+\frac{-7}{x-2}$

5b. $2p^2-2p+6+\frac{-7}{p+1}$

Exercises 1. $2x-\frac{1}{2}$ **3.** $7b-\frac{14}{3}+\frac{8}{h}$

5. $2x+4+\frac{3}{x}$ **7.** $2x-3$ **9.** $2y+5$

11. $x+1$ **13.** $c+3$ **15.** $x-2$

17. $a+2+\frac{-1}{a+2}$ **19.** $n+4+\frac{-1}{n+4}$

21. $4n-5+\frac{-2}{2n+1}$

23. $-2x^2+6x-15+\frac{35}{x+3}$

25. $m+1+\frac{3}{m-1}$

27. $4k^2-4k+2+\frac{-10}{k+1}$

29. $3t+4-\frac{2}{t}$ **31.** $-4p+1+\frac{2}{p^3}$

33. $4t+3$ **35.** $x-3$ **37.** $3a-1$

39. $3x+4+\frac{14}{x-2}$

41. $3x+1+\frac{-2}{2x-1}$

43. $2t^2-6t+25+\frac{-216}{3t+9}$

45. -20 **47.** $2x-5+\frac{3}{x+1}$

51. $0.5m+1$ **57.** C **59.** B

61. $3x-\frac{1}{2y}+\frac{2y}{x}$ **63.** $x+2$

65. 3 m **67.** $\frac{\sqrt{15}}{15}$

69. $6\sqrt{5}-5\sqrt{2}$ **71.** $4(x+1)$

73. $2k^2+5k+2$

Check It Out! 1a. 2 **1b.** 1 **1c.** $-\frac{7}{6}$

2a. -4 **2b.** -4 **2c.** 1, 3 **3.** $22\frac{2}{9}$ min

4a. 5; 7 is extraneous.

4b. 1 and 5; no extraneous solutions **4c.** 4; 0 is extraneous.

Exercises 1. rational equation

3. -24 **5.** $-\frac{8}{3}$ **7.** $\frac{3}{2}$ **9.** $\frac{3}{5}$ **11.** $-\frac{11}{5}$

13. $\frac{15}{19}$ **15.** $3, -\frac{4}{3}$ **17.** $-2, 3$ **19.** $-1, \frac{3}{2}$

21. $\frac{1}{2}$ h, or 30 min **23.** $-\frac{4}{3}$; 1 is extraneous. **25.** -2 **27.** 0 **29.** $\frac{4}{5}$

31. 5 **33.** $\frac{3}{2}$ **35.** $-4, 3$ **37.** 6 h

39. 2; 3 is extraneous. **41.** No solution; 4 is extraneous.

43. $\frac{240}{t}$; $t-2$; 40 mi/h

45a. $\frac{1}{15}=\frac{1}{24}+\frac{1}{y}$ **b.** 40 cm

c. It will increase to 72 cm. **49.** F

53. Eddie: 6 h; Luke 3 h; Ryan: 4 h

55. $y=-2x$ and $y=\frac{1}{2}x+4$ are perpendicular. **59.** 5

1. rational expression **2.** rational function **3.** rational equation **4.** inverse variation **5.** discontinuous function **6.** Yes; the product xy is constant. **7.** No; the product xy is not constant.

8. $y=-\frac{4}{x}$

9. $y=\frac{1}{x}$

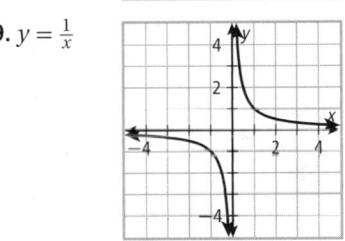

10. -15 **11.** \$13,200 **12.** -4; $x=-4$ and $y=0$ **13.** -1; $x=-1$ and $y=3$ **14.** -3; $x=-3$ and $y=-4$ **15.** $\frac{7}{4}$; $x=\frac{7}{4}$ and $y=5$

16.

17.

18.

19.

20. D: $x > 0$; R: $y > 0$

Length (cm) vs Width (cm) graph

21. 0 **22.** 7 **23.** 0, 1 **24.** $-1, 5$
25. $5, -5$ **26.** 4, 7 **27.** $\frac{1}{3r}$;
$r \neq 0$ **28.** $\frac{1}{2k-3}$; $k \neq 0$ and
$k \neq \frac{3}{2}$ **29.** $\frac{1}{x-2}$; $x \neq -6$ and $x \neq$
2 **30.** $\frac{-2}{x+3}$; $x \neq \pm 3$
31. $\frac{3}{x-1}$; $x \neq -5$ and $x \neq 1$ **32.** $\frac{x+3}{x-5}$;
$x \neq -6$ and $x \neq 5$ **33.** $\frac{4}{\pi}$ **34.** $\frac{2b^2 + 2b}{3}$
35. $\frac{4x^2 - 12x}{3}$ **36.** $\frac{15b^2}{2}$ **37.** $\frac{-3c^3}{4d^2}$
38. $\frac{b+2}{2b^2 + 8b}$ **39.** $\frac{n^2 + 3n + 2}{n^2 - n - 42}$
40. $\frac{1}{b-3}$ **41.** $\frac{y^2}{3}$ **42.** $\frac{12n^3}{m}$ **43.** $\frac{x^2 + 2x - 3}{4x^2 - 16}$
44. $\frac{(b+8)(b+7)}{2(b+4)(2b+7)}$ **45.** $10a^2b^2$
46. $10x(x-3)$ **47.** $\frac{b^2 + 8}{2b}$
48. $\frac{3x^2 + 2x - 4}{x^2 - 2}$ **49.** $\frac{8p - 2}{p^2 - 4p + 2}$
50. $\frac{5b - 1}{7 - b}$ **51.** $\frac{-10}{n^2 - 1}$ **52.** $\frac{7m + 2}{10m^2}$
53. $\frac{h^2 + 5h - 1}{h - 5}$ **54.** $\frac{40}{3r}$ **55.** $2n^2 - 3n - 5$
56. $x - \frac{2}{x} + \frac{5}{x^2}$ **57.** $x + 2$ **58.** $3n + 1$
59. $h + 12$ **60.** $3x + 2$ **61.** $m - 6$
62. $3m + 4$ **63.** $x + 2$ **64.** $x + 6$
65. $p - 2$ **66.** $2x - 1 + \frac{-3}{x+2}$

67. $2n + 7 + \frac{36}{n-5}$ **68.** $3b^2 + 6b +$
$8 + \frac{18}{b-2}$ **69.** $-4x^2 + 10x -$
$17 + \frac{34}{x+2}$ **70.** $-\frac{3}{4}$ **71.** $\frac{12}{7}$ **72.** $-\frac{18}{11}$
73. $-\frac{7}{6}$; 0 is extraneous. **74.** $-\frac{2}{3}$; 1
is extraneous. **75.** $-\frac{1}{3}, 1$
76. -3 **77.** ± 1 **78.** $-\frac{1}{12}$ **79.** -2; 4 is
extraneous. **80.** 4, 5 **81.** $-12, 1$
82. -19 **83.** 0; 2 is extraneous.

Glossary/Glosario

A

ENGLISH	SPANISH	EXAMPLES
absolute value (p. 14) The absolute value of x is the distance from zero to x on a number line, denoted $|x|$. $$|x| = \begin{cases} x & \text{if } x \geq 0 \\ -x & \text{if } x < 0 \end{cases}$$	**valor absoluto** El valor absoluto de x es la distancia de cero a x en una recta numérica, y se expresa $|x|$. $$|x| = \begin{cases} x & \text{si } x \geq 0 \\ -x & \text{si } x < 0 \end{cases}$$	$|3| = 3$ $|-3| = 3$
absolute-value equation (p. 112) An equation that contains absolute-value expressions.	**ecuación de valor absoluto** Ecuación que contiene expresiones de valor absoluto.	$|x + 4| = 7$
absolute-value function (p. 378) A function whose rule contains absolute-value expressions.	**función de valor absoluto** Función cuya regla contiene expresiones de valor absoluto.	$y = |x + 4|$
absolute-value inequality (p. 212) An inequality that contains absolute-value expressions.	**desigualdad de valor absoluto** Desigualdad que contiene expresiones de valor absoluto.	$|x + 4| > 7$
acute angle An angle that measures greater than 0° and less than 90°.	**ángulo agudo** Ángulo que mide más de 0° y menos de 90°.	
acute triangle A triangle with three acute angles.	**triángulo acutángulo** Triángulo con tres ángulos agudos.	
Addition Property of Equality (p. 79) For real numbers a, b, and c, if $a = b$, then $a + c = b + c$.	**Propiedad de igualdad de la suma** Dados los números reales a, b y c, si $a = b$, entonces $a + c = b + c$.	$\begin{array}{r} x - 6 = 8 \\ +6 \quad +6 \\ \hline x \quad\; = 14 \end{array}$
Addition Property of Inequality (p. 176) For real numbers a, b, and c, if $a < b$, then $a + c < b + c$. Also holds true for $>$, $\leq$, $\geq$, and $\neq$.	**Propiedad de desigualdad de la suma** Dados los números reales a, b y c, si $a < b$, entonces $a + c < b + c$. Es válido también para $>$, $\leq$, $\geq$ y $\neq$.	$\begin{array}{r} x - 6 < 8 \\ +6 \quad +6 \\ \hline x \quad\; < 14 \end{array}$
additive inverse (p. 15) The opposite of a number. Two numbers are additive inverses if their sum is zero.	**inverso aditivo** El opuesto de un número. Dos números son inversos aditivos si su suma es cero.	The additive inverse of 5 is −5. The additive inverse of −5 is 5.
algebraic expression (p. 6) An expression that contains at least one variable.	**expresión algebraica** Expresión que contiene por lo menos una variable.	$2x + 3y$ $4x$
algebraic order of operations *See* order of operations.	**orden algebraico de las operaciones** *Ver* orden de las operaciones.	

ENGLISH	SPANISH	EXAMPLES
AND (p. 204) A logical operator representing the intersection of two sets.	**Y** Operador lógico que representa la intersección de dos conjuntos.	$A = \{2, 3, 4, 5\}$ $B = \{1, 3, 5, 7\}$ The set of values that are in A AND B is $A \cap B = \{3, 5\}$.
angle A figure formed by two rays with a common endpoint.	**ángulo** Figura formada por dos rayos con un extremo común.	A
area The number of nonoverlapping unit squares of a given size that will exactly cover the interior of a plane figure.	**área** Cantidad de cuadrados unitarios de un determinado tamaño no superpuestos que cubren exactamente el interior de una figura plana.	The area is 10 square units.
arithmetic sequence (p. 276) A sequence whose successive terms differ by the same nonzero number d, called the *common difference*.	**sucesión aritmética** Sucesión cuyos términos sucesivos difieren en el mismo número distinto de cero d, denominado *diferencia común*.	4, 7, 10, 13, 16, … $+3 +3 +3 +3$ $d = 3$
Associative Property of Addition (p. 46) For all numbers a, b, and c, $(a + b) + c = a + (b + c)$.	**Propiedad asociativa de la suma** Dados tres números cualesquiera a, b y c, $(a + b) + c = a + (b + c)$.	$(5 + 3) + 7 = 5 + (3 + 7)$
Associative Property of Multiplication (p. 46) For all numbers a, b, and c, $(a \cdot b) \cdot c = a \cdot (b \cdot c)$.	**Propiedad asociativa de la multiplicación** Dados tres números cualesquiera a, b y c, $(a \cdot b) \cdot c = a \cdot (b \cdot c)$.	$(5 \cdot 3) \cdot 7 = 5 \cdot (3 \cdot 7)$
asymptote (p. 878) A line that a graph gets closer to as the value of a variable becomes extremely large or small.	**asíntota** Línea recta a la cual se aproxima una gráfica a medida que el valor de una variable se hace sumamente grande o pequeño.	
average *See* mean.	**promedio** *Ver* media.	
axis of a coordinate plane (p. 54) One of two perpendicular number lines, called the x-axis and the y-axis, used to define the location of a point in a coordinate plane.	**eje de un plano cartesiano** Una de las dos rectas numéricas perpendiculares, denominadas eje x y eje y, utilizadas para definir la ubicación de un punto en un plano cartesiano.	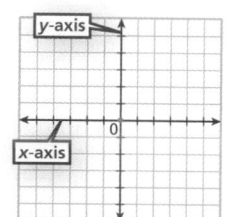
axis of symmetry (p. 378, p. 620) A line that divides a plane figure or a graph into two congruent reflected halves.	**eje de simetría** Línea que divide una figura plana o una gráfica en dos mitades reflejadas congruentes.	

ENGLISH	SPANISH	EXAMPLES

back-to-back stem-and-leaf plot (p. 709) A graph used to organize and compare two sets of data so that the frequencies can be compared. *See also* stem-and-leaf plot.

diagrama doble de tallo y hojas Gráfica utilizada para organizar y comparar dos conjuntos de datos para poder comparar las frecuencias. *Ver también* diagrama de tallo y hojas.

Data set A: 9, 12, 14, 16, 23, 27
Data set B: 6, 8, 10, 13, 15, 16, 21

Set A		Set B
9	0	6 8
6 4 2	1	0 3 5 6
7 3	2	1

Key: $|2|1$ means 21
$7|2|$ means 27

---

bar graph (p. 700) A graph that uses vertical or horizontal bars to display data.

gráfica de barras Gráfica con barras horizontales o verticales para mostrar datos.

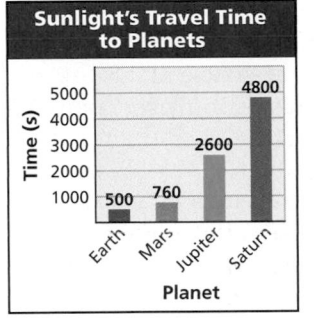

---

base of a power (p. 26) The number in a power that is used as a factor.

base de una potencia Número de una potencia que se utiliza como factor.

$3^4 = 3 \cdot 3 \cdot 3 \cdot 3 - 81$
3 is the base.

---

base of an exponential function (p. 796) The value of b in a function of the form $f(x) = ab^x$, where a and b are real numbers with $a \neq 0$, $b > 0$, and $b \neq 1$.

base de una función exponencial Valor de b en una función del tipo $f(x) = ab^x$, donde a y b son números reales con $a \neq 0$, $b > 0$ y $b \neq 1$.

In the function $f(x) = 5(2)^x$, the base is 2.

---

biased sample (p. 733) A sample that does not fairly represent the population.

muestra no representativa Muestra que no representa adecuadamente una población.

To find out about the exercise habits of average Americans, a fitness magazine surveyed its readers about how often they exercise. The population is all Americans and the sample is readers of the fitness magazine. This sample will likely be biased because readers of fitness magazines may exercise more often than other people do.

---

binomial (p. 497) A polynomial with two terms.

binomio Polinomio con dos términos.

$x + y$
$2a^2 + 3$
$4m^3n^2 + 6mn^4$

---

boundary line (p. 428) A line that divides a coordinate plane into two half-planes.

línea de límite Línea que divide un plano cartesiano en dos semiplanos.

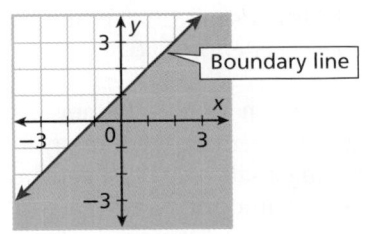

ENGLISH	SPANISH	EXAMPLES

box-and-whisker plot (p. 718) A method of showing how data are distributed by using the median, quartiles, and minimum and maximum values; also called a *box plot*.

gráfica de mediana y rango Método para mostrar la distribución de datos utilizando la mediana, los cuartiles y los valores mínimo y máximo; también llamado *gráfica de caja*.

C

Cartesian coordinate system *See* coordinate plane.

sistema de coordenadas cartesianas *Ver* plano cartesiano.

---

center of a circle The point inside a circle that is the same distance from every point on the circle.

centro de un círculo Punto dentro de un círculo que se encuentra a la misma distancia de todos los puntos del círculo.

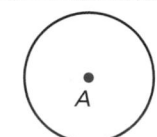

---

central angle of a circle An angle whose vertex is the center of a circle.

ángulo central de un círculo Ángulo cuyo vértice es el centro de un círculo.

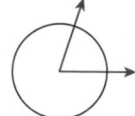

---

circle The set of points in a plane that are a fixed distance from a given point called the center of the circle.

círculo Conjunto de puntos en un plano que se encuentran a una distancia fija de un punto determinado denominado centro del círculo.

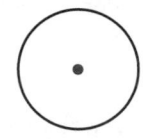

---

circle graph (p. 702) A way to display data by using a circle divided into non-overlapping sectors.

gráfica circular Forma de mostrar datos mediante un círculo dividido en sectores no superpuestos.

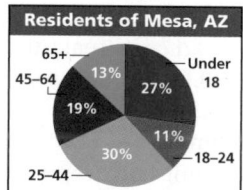

---

circumference The distance around a circle.

circunferencia Distancia alrededor de un círculo.

---

coefficient (p. 48) A number that is multiplied by a variable.

coeficiente Número que se multiplica por una variable.

In the expression $2x + 3y$, 2 is the coefficient of x and 3 is the coefficient of y.

---

combination (p. 761) A selection of a group of objects in which order is *not* important. The number of combinations of r objects chosen from a group of n objects is denoted $_nC_r$.

combinación Selección de un grupo de objetos en la cual el orden *no* es importante. El número de combinaciones de r objetos elegidos de un grupo de n objetos se expresa así: $_nC_r$.

For objects A, B, C, and D, there are 6 different combinations of 2 objects. AB, AC, AD, BC, BD, CD

---

commission (p. 139) Money paid to a person or company for making a sale, usually a percent of the sale amount.

comisión Dinero que se paga a una persona o empresa por realizar una venta; generalmente se trata de un porcentaje del total de la venta.

ENGLISH	SPANISH	EXAMPLES
common difference (p. 276) In an arithmetic sequence, the nonzero constant difference of any term and the previous term.	**diferencia común** En una sucesión aritmética, diferencia constante distinta de cero entre cualquier término y el término anterior.	In the arithmetic sequence 3, 5, 7, 9, 11, ..., the common difference is 2.
common factor (p. 545) A factor that is common to all terms of an expression or to two or more expressions.	**factor común** Factor que es común a todos los términos de una expresión o a dos o más expresiones.	Expression: $4x^2 + 16x^3 - 8x$ Common factor: $4x$ Expressions: 12 and 18 Common factors: 2, 3, and 6
common ratio (p. 790) In a geometric sequence, the constant ratio of any term and the previous term.	**razón común** En una sucesión geométrica, la razón constante entre cualquier término y el término anterior.	In the geometric sequence 32, 16, 8, 4, 2, . . ., the common ratio is $\frac{1}{2}$.
Commutative Property of Addition (p. 46) For any two numbers a and b, $a + b = b + a$.	**Propiedad conmutativa de la suma** Dados dos números cualesquiera a y b, $a + b = b + a$.	$3 + 4 = 4 + 3 = 7$
Commutative Property of Multiplication (p. 46) For any two numbers a and b, $a \cdot b = b \cdot a$.	**Propiedad conmutativa de la multiplicación** Dados dos números cualesquiera a y b, $a \cdot b = b \cdot a$.	$3 \cdot 4 = 4 \cdot 3 = 12$
complement of an event (p. 745) The set of all outcomes that are not the event.	**complemento de un suceso** Todos los resultados que no están en el suceso.	In the experiment of rolling a number cube, the complement of rolling a 3 is rolling a 1, 2, 4, 5, or 6.
complementary angles Two angles whose measures have a sum of 90°.	**ángulos complementarios** Dos ángulos cuyas medidas suman 90°.	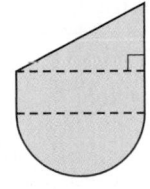
completing the square (p. 663) A process used to form a perfect-square trinomial. To complete the square of $x^2 + bx$, add $\left(\frac{b}{2}\right)^2$.	**completar el cuadrado** Proceso utilizado para formar un trinomio cuadrado perfecto. Para completar el cuadrado de $x^2 + bx$, hay que sumar $\left(\frac{b}{2}\right)^2$.	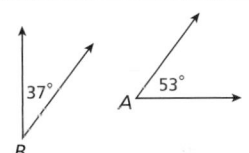 $x^2 + 6x + $ ▓ Add $\left(\frac{6}{2}\right)^2 = 9$. $x^2 + 6x + 9$
complex fraction (p. 904) A fraction that contains one or more fractions in the numerator, the denominator, or both.	**fracción compleja** Fracción que contiene una o más fracciones en el numerador, en el denominador, o en ambos.	$\dfrac{\frac{1}{2}}{1 + \frac{2}{3}}$
composite figure (p. 83) A plane figure made up of triangles, rectangles, trapezoids, circles, and other simple shapes, or a three-dimensional figure made up of prisms, cones, pyramids, cylinders, and other simple three-dimensional figures.	**figura compuesta** Figura plana compuesta por triángulos, rectángulos, trapecios, círculos y otras figuras simples, o figura tridimensional compuesta por prismas, conos, pirámides, cilindros y otras figuras tridimensionales simples.	

ENGLISH	SPANISH	EXAMPLES
compound event (p. 761) An event made up of two or more simple events.	**suceso compuesto** Suceso formado por dos o más sucesos simples.	In the experiment of tossing a coin and rolling a number cube, the event of the coin landing heads and the number cube landing on 3.
compound inequality (p. 204) Two inequalities that are combined into one statement by the word *and* or *or*.	**desigualdad compuesta** Dos desigualdades unidas en un enunciado por la palabra *y* u *o*.	$x \geq 2$ AND $x < 7$ (also written $2 \leq x < 7$) $x < 2$ OR $x > 6$
compound interest (p. 860) Interest earned or paid on both the principal and previously earned interest. The formula for compound interest is $A = P\left(1 + \frac{r}{n}\right)^{nt}$, where A is the final amount, P is the principal, r is the interest rate expressed as a decimal, n is the number of times interest is compounded, and t is the time.	**interés compuesto** Intereses ganados o pagados sobre el capital y los intereses ya devengados. La fórmula de interés compuesto es $A = P\left(1 + \frac{r}{n}\right)^{nt}$, donde A es la cantidad final, P es el capital, r es la tasa de interés expresada como un decimal, n es la cantidad de veces que se capitaliza el interés y t es el tiempo.	If \$100 is put into an account with an interest rate of 5% compounded monthly, then after 2 years, the account will have $100\left(1 + \frac{0.05}{12}\right)^{12 \cdot 2} = \$110.49$.
compound statement (p. 203) Two statements that are connected by the word *and* or *or*.	**enunciado compuesto** Dos enunciados unidos por la palabra *y* u *o*.	The sky is blue and the grass is green. I will drive to school or I will take the bus.
cone (p. 894) A three-dimensional figure with a circular base and a curved surface that connects the base to a point called the vertex.	**cono** Figura tridimensional con una base circular y una superficie lateral curva que conecta la base con un punto denominado vértice.	
congruent Having the same size and shape, denoted by ≅.	**congruente** Que tiene el mismo tamaño y la misma forma, expresado por ≅.	$\overline{PQ} \cong \overline{RS}$
conjugate of an irrational number (p. 845) The conjugate of a number in the form $a + \sqrt{b}$ is $a - \sqrt{b}$.	**conjugado de un número irracional** El conjugado de un número en la forma $a + \sqrt{b}$ es $a - \sqrt{b}$.	The conjugate of $1 + \sqrt{2}$ is $1 - \sqrt{2}$.
consistent system (p. 420) A system of equations or inequalities that has at least one solution.	**sistema consistente** Sistema de ecuaciones o desigualdades que tiene por lo menos una solución.	$\begin{cases} x + y = 6 \\ x - y = 4 \end{cases}$ solution: (5, 1)
constant (p. 6) A value that does not change.	**constante** Valor que no cambia.	$3, 0, \pi$

ENGLISH	SPANISH	EXAMPLES
constant of variation (p. 336) The constant k in direct and inverse variation equations.	**constante de variación** La constante k en ecuaciones de variación directa e inversa.	
continuous graph (p. 235) A graph made up of connected lines or curves.	**gráfica continua** Gráfica compuesta por líneas rectas o curvas conectadas.	Angelique's Heart Rate
convenience sample (p. 733) A sample based on members of the population that are readily available.	**muestra de conveniencia** Una muestra basada en miembros de la población que están fácilmente disponibles.	A reporter surveys people he personally knows.
conversion factor (p. 121) The ratio of two equal quantities, each measured in different units.	**factor de conversión** Razón entre dos cantidades iguales, cada una medida en unidades diferentes.	
coordinate (p. 54) A number used to identify the location of a point. On a number line, one coordinate is used. On a coordinate plane, two coordinates are used, called the x-coordinate and the y-coordinate.	**coordenada** Número utilizado para identificar la ubicación de un punto. En una recta numérica se utiliza una coordenada. En un plano cartesiano se utilizan dos coordenadas, denominadas coordenada x y coordenada y.	The coordinate of A is 2. The coordinates of B are $(-2, 3)$.
coordinate plane (p. 54) A plane that is divided into four regions by a horizontal line called the x-axis and a vertical line called the y-axis.	**plano cartesiano** Plano dividido en cuatro regiones por una línea horizontal denominada eje x y una línea vertical denominada eje y.	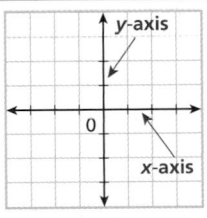
correlation (p. 266) A measure of the strength and direction of the relationship between two variables or data sets.	**correlación** Medida de la fuerza y dirección de la relación entre dos variables o conjuntos de datos.	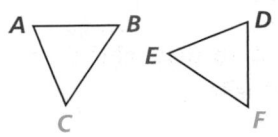
corresponding angles of polygons (p. 127) Angles in the same relative position in polygons with an equal number of angles.	**ángulos correspondientes de los polígonos** Ángulos que se ubican en la misma posición relativa en polígonos que tienen el mismo número de ángulos.	$\angle A$ and $\angle D$ are corresponding angles.

ENGLISH	SPANISH	EXAMPLES
corresponding sides of polygons (p. 127) Sides in the same relative position in polygons with an equal number of sides.	**lados correspondientes de los polígonos** Lados que se ubican en la misma posición relativa en polígonos que tienen el mismo número de lados.	 $\overline{AB}$ and $\overline{DE}$ are corresponding sides.
cosine (p. 928) In a right triangle, the cosine of angle A is the ratio of the length of the leg adjacent to angle A to the length of the hypotenuse.	**coseno** En un triángulo rectángulo, el coseno del ángulo A es la razón entre la longitud del cateto adyacente al ángulo A y la longitud de la hipotenusa.	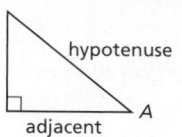 $\cos A = \dfrac{adjacent}{hypotenuse}$
cross products (p. 121) In the statement $\frac{a}{b} = \frac{c}{d}$, bc and ad are the cross products.	**productos cruzados** En el enunciado $\frac{a}{b} = \frac{c}{d}$, bc y ad son productos cruzados.	$\dfrac{1}{2} = \dfrac{3}{6}$ Cross products: $2 \cdot 3 = 6$ and $1 \cdot 6 = 6$
Cross Product Property (p. 121) For any real numbers a, b, c, and d, where $b \neq 0$ and $d \neq 0$, if $\frac{a}{b} = \frac{c}{d}$, then $ad = bc$.	**Propiedad de productos cruzados** Dados los números reales a, b, c y d, donde $b \neq 0$ y $d \neq 0$, si $\frac{a}{b} = \frac{c}{d}$, entonces $ad = bc$.	If $\dfrac{4}{6} = \dfrac{10}{x}$, then $4x = 60$, so $x = 15$.
cube A prism with six square faces.	**cubo** Prisma con seis caras cuadradas.	
cube in numeration (p. 26) The third power of a number.	**cubo en numeración** Tercera potencia de un número.	8 is the cube of 2.
cube root (p. 32) A number, written as $\sqrt[3]{x}$, whose cube is x.	**raíz cúbica** Número, expresado como $\sqrt[3]{x}$, cuyo cubo es x.	$\sqrt[3]{64} = 4$, because $4^3 = 64$; 4 is the cube root of 64.
cubic equation (p. 681) An equation that can be written in the form $ax^3 + bx^2 + cx + d = 0$, where a, b, c, and d are real numbers and $a \neq 0$.	**ecuación cúbica** Ecuación que se puede expresar como $ax^3 + bx^2 + cx + d = 0$, donde a, b, c, y d son números reales y $a \neq 0$.	$4x^3 + x^2 - 3x - 1 = 0$
cubic function (p. 680) A function that can be written in the form $f(x) = ax^3 + bx^2 + cx + d$, where a, b, c, and d are real numbers and $a \neq 0$.	**función cúbica** Función que se puede expresar como $f(x) = ax^3 + bx^2 + cx + d$, donde a, b, c, y d son números reales y $a \neq 0$.	$f(x) = x^3 + 2x^2 - 6x + 8$
cubic polynomial (p. 497) A polynomial of degree 3.	**polinomio cúbico** Polinomio de grado 3.	$x^3 + 4x^2 - 6x + 2$
cumulative frequency (p. 711) The frequency of all data values that are less than or equal to a given value.	**frecuencia acumulativa** Frecuencia de todos los valores de los datos que son menores que o iguales a un valor dado.	For the data set 2, 2, 3, 5, 5, 6, 7, 7, 8, 8, 8, 9, the cumulative frequency table is shown below.

Data	Frequency	Cumulative Frequency
2	2	2
3	1	3
5	2	5
6	1	6
7	2	8
8	3	11
9	1	12

cylinder (p. 894) A three-dimensional figure with two parallel congruent circular bases and a curved surface that connects the bases.

cilindro Figura tridimensional con dos bases circulares congruentes paralelas y una superficie lateral curva que conecta las bases.

data Information gathered from a survey or experiment.

datos Información reunida en una encuesta o experimento.

---

degree measure of an angle A unit of angle measure; one degree is $\frac{1}{360}$ of a circle.

medida en grados de un ángulo Unidad de medida de los ángulos; un grado es $\frac{1}{360}$ de un círculo.

---

degree of a monomial (p. 496) The sum of the exponents of the variables in the monomial.

grado de un monomio Suma de los exponentes de las variables del monomio.

$4x^2y^5z^3$ Degree: $2 + 5 + 3 = 10$
$5 = 5x^0$ Degree: 0

---

degree of a polynomial (p. 496) The degree of the term of the polynomial with the greatest degree.

grado de un polinomio Grado del término del polinomio con el grado máximo.

$3x^2y^2 + 4xy^5 - 12x^3y^2$
Degree 4 Degree 6 Degree 5
Degree 6

---

dependent events (p. 750) Events for which the occurrence or nonoccurrence of one event affects the probability of the other event.

sucesos dependientes Dos sucesos son dependientes si el hecho de que uno de ellos ocurra o no afecta la probabilidad del otro suceso.

From a bag containing 3 red marbles and 2 blue marbles, draw a red marble, and then draw a blue marble without replacing the first marble.

---

dependent system (p. 421) A system of equations that has infinitely many solutions.

sistema dependiente Sistema de ecuaciones que tiene infinitamente muchas soluciones.

$$\begin{cases} x + y = 2 \\ 2x + 2y = 4 \end{cases}$$

---

dependent variable (p. 250) The output of a function; a variable whose value depends on the value of the input, or independent variable.

variable dependiente Salida de una función; variable cuyo valor depende del valor de la entrada, o variable independiente.

For $y = 2x + 1$, y is the dependent variable.
input: x output: y

---

diameter A segment that has endpoints on the circle and that passes through the center of the circle; also the length of that segment.

diámetro Segmento que atraviesa el centro de un círculo y cuyos extremos están sobre la circunferencia; longitud de dicho segmento.

---

difference of two cubes (p. 584) A polynomial of the form $a^3 - b^3$, which may be written as the product $(a - b)(a^2 + ab + b^2)$.

diferencia de dos cubos Polinomio del tipo $a^3 - b^3$, que se puede expresar como el producto $(a - b)(a^2 + ab + b^2)$.

$x^3 - 8 = (x - 2)(x^2 + 2x + 4)$

---

difference of two squares (p. 523) A polynomial of the form $a^2 - b^2$, which may be written as the product $(a + b)(a - b)$.

diferencia de dos cuadrados Polinomio del tipo $a^2 - b^2$, que se puede expresar como el producto $(a + b)(a - b)$.

$x^2 - 4 = (x + 2)(x - 2)$

Glossary/Glosario

ENGLISH	SPANISH	EXAMPLES
dimensional analysis (p. 121) A process that uses rates to convert measurements from one unit to another.	**análisis dimensional** Un proceso que utiliza tasas para convertir medidas de unidad a otra.	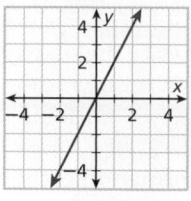 $12 \text{ pt} \cdot \dfrac{1 \text{ qt}}{2 \text{ pt}} = 6 \text{ qt}$
direct variation (p. 336) A linear relationship between two variables, x and y, that can be written in the form $y = kx$, where k is a nonzero constant.	**variación directa** Relación lineal entre dos variables, x e y, que puede expresarse en la forma $y = kx$, donde k es una constante distinta de cero.	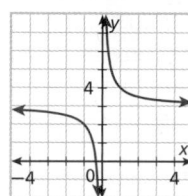 $y = 2x$
discontinuous function (p. 878) A function whose graph has one or more jumps, breaks, or holes.	**función discontinua** Función cuya gráfica tiene uno o más saltos, interrupciones u hoyos.	
discount (p. 145) An amount by which an original price is reduced.	**descuento** Cantidad por la que se reduce un precio original.	
discrete graph (p. 235) A graph made up of unconnected points.	**gráfica discreta** Gráfica compuesta de puntos no conectados.	**Theme Park Attendance**
discriminant (p. 672) The discriminant of the quadratic equation $ax^2 + bx + c = 0$ is $b^2 - 4ac$.	**discriminante** El discriminante de la ecuación cuadrática $ax^2 + bx + c = 0$ es $b^2 - 4ac$.	The discriminant of $2x^2 - 5x - 3 = 0$ is $(-5)^2 - 4(2)(-3)$ or 49.
Distance Formula (p. 331) In a coordinate plane, the distance from (x_1, y_1) to (x_2, y_2) is $$d = \sqrt{(x_2 - x_1)^2 + (y_2 - y_1)^2}.$$	**Fórmula de distancia** En un plano cartesiano, la distancia desde (x_1, y_1) hasta (x_2, y_2) es $$d = \sqrt{(x_2 - x_1)^2 + (y_2 - y_1)^2}.$$	The distance from $(2, 5)$ to $(-1, 1)$ is $$\begin{aligned} d &= \sqrt{(-1 - 2)^2 + (1 - 5)^2} \\ &= \sqrt{(-3)^2 + (-4)^2} \\ &= \sqrt{9 + 16} = \sqrt{25} = 5. \end{aligned}$$
Distributive Property (p. 47) For all real numbers a, b, and c, $a(b + c) = ab + ac$, and $(b + c)a = ba + ca$.	**Propiedad distributiva** Dados los números reales a, b y c, $a(b + c) = ab + ac$, y $(b + c)a = ba + ca$.	$3(4 + 5) = 3 \cdot 4 + 3 \cdot 5$ $(4 + 5)3 = 4 \cdot 3 + 5 \cdot 3$
Division Property of Equality (p. 86) For real numbers a, b, and c, where $c \neq 0$, if $a = b$, then $\frac{a}{c} = \frac{b}{c}$.	**Propiedad de igualdad de la división** Dados los números reales a, b y c, donde $c \neq 0$, si $a = b$, entonces $\frac{a}{c} = \frac{b}{c}$.	$4x = 12$ $\dfrac{4x}{4} = \dfrac{12}{4}$ $x = 3$

ENGLISH	SPANISH	EXAMPLES
Division Property of Inequality (p. 182, p. 183) If both sides of an inequality are divided by the same positive quantity, the new inequality will have the same solution set. If both sides of an inequality are divided by the same negative quantity, the new inequality will have the same solution set if the inequality symbol is reversed.	**Propiedad de desigualdad de la división** Cuando ambos lados de una desigualdad se dividen entre el mismo número positivo, la nueva desigualdad tiene el mismo conjunto solución. Cuando ambos lados de una desigualdad se dividen entra el mismo número negativo, la nueva desigualdad tiene el mismo conjunto solución si se invierte el símbolo de desigualdad.	$4x \geq 12$ $\dfrac{4x}{4} \geq \dfrac{12}{4}$ $x \geq 3$ $-4x \geq 12$ $\dfrac{-4x}{-4} \leq \dfrac{12}{-4}$ $x \leq -3$
domain (p. 240) The set of all first coordinates (or x-values) of a relation or function.	**dominio** Conjunto de todos los valores de la primera coordenada (o valores de x) de una función o relación.	The domain of the function $\{(-5, 3), (-3, -2), (-1, -1), (1, 0)\}$ is $\{-5, -3, -1, 1\}$.

E

ENGLISH	SPANISH	EXAMPLES
element Each member in a set or matrix. *See also* entry.	**elemento** Cada miembro en un conjunto o matriz. *Ver también* entrada.	
elimination method (p. 411) A method used to solve systems of equations in which one variable is eliminated by adding or subtracting two equations of the system.	**eliminación** Método utilizado para resolver sistemas de ecuaciones por el cual se elimina una variable sumando o restando dos ecuaciones del sistema.	
empty set (p. 102) A set with no elements.	**conjunto vacío** Conjunto sin elementos.	The solution set of $|x| < 0$ is the empty set, { }, or $\varnothing$.
entry (p. 770) Each value in a matrix; also called an element.	**entrada** Cada valor de una matriz, también denominado elemento.	3 is the entry in the first row and second column of $A = \begin{bmatrix} 2 & 3 \\ 0 & 1 \end{bmatrix}$, denoted a_{12}.
equally likely outcomes (p. 744) Outcomes are equally likely if they have the same probability of occurring. If an experiment has n equally likely outcomes, then the probability of each outcome is $\frac{1}{n}$.	**resultados igualmente probables** Los resultados son igualmente probables si tienen la misma probabilidad de ocurrir. Si un experimento tiene n resultados igualmente probables, entonces la probabilidad de cada resultado es $\frac{1}{n}$.	If a fair coin is tossed, then $P(\text{heads}) = P(\text{tails}) = \frac{1}{2}$. So the outcome "heads" and the outcome "tails" are equally likely.
equation (p. 77) A mathematical statement that two expressions are equivalent.	**ecuación** Enunciado matemático que indica que dos expresiones son equivalentes.	$x + 4 = 7$ $2 + 3 = 6 - 1$ $(x - 1)^2 + (y + 2)^2 = 4$
equilateral triangle A triangle with three congruent sides.	**triángulo equilátero** Triángulo con tres lados congruentes.	
equivalent ratios (p. 120) Ratios that name the same comparison.	**razones equivalentes** Razones que expresan la misma comparación.	$\frac{1}{2}$ and $\frac{2}{4}$ are equivalent ratios.

Glossary/Glosario

ENGLISH	SPANISH	EXAMPLES
evaluate (p. 7) To find the value of an algebraic expression by substituting a number for each variable and simplifying by using the order of operations.	**evaluar** Calcular el valor de una expresión algebraica sustituyendo cada variable por un número y simplificando mediante el orden de las operaciones.	Evaluate $2x + 7$ for $x = 3$. $2x + 7$ $2(3) + 7$ $6 + 7$ 13
event (p. 737) An outcome or set of outcomes of an experiment.	**suceso** Resultado o conjunto de resultados en un experimento.	In the experiment of rolling a number cube, the event "an odd number" consists of the outcomes 1, 3, and 5.
excluded values (p. 878) Values of x for which a function or expression is not defined.	**valores excluidos** Valores de x para los cuales no está definida una función o expresión.	The excluded values of $$\frac{(x + 2)}{(x - 1)(x + 4)}$$ are $x = 1$ and $x = -4$, which would make the denominator equal to 0.
experiment (p. 737) An operation, process, or activity in which outcomes can be used to estimate probability.	**experimento** Una operación, proceso o actividad en la que se usan los resultados para estimar una probabilidad.	Tossing a coin 10 times and noting the number of heads
experimental probability (p. 738) The ratio of the number of times an event occurs to the number of trials, or times, that an activity is performed.	**probabilidad experimental** Razón entre la cantidad de veces que ocurre un suceso y la cantidad de pruebas, o veces, que se realiza una actividad.	Kendra attempted 27 free throws and made 16 of them. The experimental probability that she will make her next free throw is $P(\text{free throw}) = $ $$\frac{\text{number made}}{\text{number attempted}} = \frac{16}{27} \approx 0.59.$$
exponent (p. 26) The number that indicates how many times the base in a power is used as a factor.	**exponente** Número que indica la cantidad de veces que la base de una potencia se utiliza como factor.	$3^4 = 3 \cdot 3 \cdot 3 \cdot 3 = 81$ 4 is the exponent.
exponential decay (p. 807) An exponential function of the form $f(x) = ab^x$ in which $0 < b < 1$. If r is the rate of decay, then the function can be written $y = a(1 - r)^t$, where a is the initial amount and t is the time.	**decremento exponencial** Función exponencial del tipo $f(x) = ab^x$ en la cual $0 < b < 1$. Si r es la tasa decremental, entonces la función se puede expresar como $y = a(1 - r)^t$, donde a es la cantidad inicial y t es el tiempo.	$f(x) = 3\left(\frac{1}{2}\right)^x$
exponential expression An algebraic expression in which the variable is in an exponent with a fixed number as the base.	**expresión exponencial** Expresión algebraica en la que la variable está en un exponente y que tiene un número fijo como base.	2^{x+1}
exponential function (p. 796) A function of the form $f(x) = ab^x$, where a and b are real numbers with $a \neq 0$, $b > 0$, and $b \neq 1$.	**función exponencial** Función del tipo $f(x) = ab^x$, donde a y b son números reales con $a \neq 0$, $b > 0$ y $b \neq 1$.	$f(x) = 3 \cdot 4^x$

ENGLISH	SPANISH	EXAMPLES
exponential growth (p. 805) An exponential function of the form $f(x) = ab^x$ in which $b > 1$. If r is the rate of growth, then the function can be written $y = a(1 + r)^t$, where a is the initial amount and t is the time.	**crecimiento exponencial** Función exponencial del tipo $f(x) = ab^x$ en la que $b > 1$. Si r es la tasa de crecimiento, entonces la función se puede expresar como $y = a(1 + r)^t$, donde a es la cantidad inicial y t es el tiempo.	$f(x) = 2^x$ 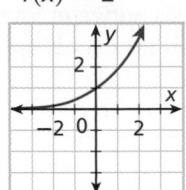
expression (p. 6) A mathematical phrase that contains operations, numbers, and/or variables.	**expresión** Frase matemática que contiene operaciones, números y/o variables.	$6x + 1$
extraneous solution (p. 848) A solution of a derived equation that is not a solution of the original equation.	**solución extraña** Solución de una ecuación derivada que no es una solución de la ecuación original.	To solve $\sqrt{x} = -2$, square both sides; $x = 4$. **Check** $\sqrt{4} = -2$ is false; so 4 is an extraneous solution.

ENGLISH	SPANISH	EXAMPLES
factor (p. 544) A number or expression that is multiplied by another number or expression to get a product. *See also* factoring.	**factor** Número o expresión que se multiplica por otro número o expresión para obtener un producto. *Ver también* factoreo.	$12 = 3 \cdot 4$ 3 and 4 are factors of 12. $x^2 - 1 = (x - 1)(x + 1)$ $(x - 1)$ and $(x + 1)$ are factors of $x^2 - 1$.
factorial (p. 762) If n is a positive integer, then n factorial, written $n!$, is $n \cdot (n - 1) \cdot (n - 2) \cdot \ldots \cdot 2 \cdot 1$. The factorial of 0 is defined to be 1.	**factorial** Si n es un entero positivo, entonces el factorial de n, expresado como $n!$, es $n \cdot (n - 1) \cdot (n - 2) \cdot \ldots \cdot 2 \cdot 1$. Por definición, el factorial de 0 será 1.	$7! = 7 \cdot 6 \cdot 5 \cdot 4 \cdot 3 \cdot 2 \cdot 1$ $= 5040$
factoring (p. 544) The process of writing a number or algebraic expression as a product.	**factorización** Proceso por el que se expresa un número o expresión algebraica como un producto.	$x^2 - 4x - 21 = (x - 7)(x + 3)$
fair (p. 744) When all outcomes of an experiment are equally likely.	**justo** Cuando todos los resultados de un experimento son igualmente probables.	When tossing a fair coin, heads and tails are equally likely. Each has a probability of $\frac{1}{2}$.
family of functions (p. 369) A set of functions whose graphs have basic characteristics in common. Functions in the same family are transformations of their parent function.	**familia de funciones** Conjunto de funciones cuyas gráficas tienen características básicas en común. Las funciones de la misma familia son transformaciones de su función madre.	

ENGLISH	SPANISH	EXAMPLES
first differences (p. 610) The differences between y-values of a function for evenly spaced x-values.	**primeras diferencias** Diferencias entre los valores de y de una función para valores de x espaciados uniformemente.	

first quartile (p. 718) The median of the lower half of a data set, denoted Q_1. Also called *lower quartile*.

primer cuartil Mediana de la mitad inferior de un conjunto de datos, expresada como Q_1. También se llama *cuartil inferior*.

Lower half   Upper half

18, ㉓ 28,   29, 36, 42

First quartile

FOIL (p. 513) A mnemonic (memory) device for a method of multiplying two binomials:

Multiply the **First** terms.

Multiply the **Outer** terms.

Multiply the **Inner** terms.

Multiply the **Last** terms.

FOIL Regla mnemotécnica para recordar el método de multiplicación de dos binomios:

Multiplicar los términos **Primeros** (*First*).

Multiplicar los términos **Externos** (*Outer*).

Multiplicar los términos **Internos** (*Inner*).

Multiplicar los términos **Últimos** (*Last*).

$$(x + 2)(x - 3) = x^2 - 3x + 2x - 6$$
$$= x^2 - x - 6$$

---

formula (p. 107) A literal equation that states a rule for a relationship among quantities.

fórmula Ecuación literal que establece una regla para una relación entre cantidades.

$$A = \pi r^2$$

---

fractional exponent *See* rational exponent.

exponente fraccionario *Ver* exponente racional.

---

frequency (p. 710) The number of times the value appears in the data set.

frecuencia Cantidad de veces que aparece el valor en un conjunto de datos.

In the data set 5, 6, 6, 7, 8, 9, the data value 6 has a frequency of 2.

---

frequency table (p. 710) A table that lists the number of times, or frequency, that each data value occurs.

tabla de frecuencia Tabla que enumera la cantidad de veces que ocurre cada valor de datos, o la frecuencia.

Data set: 1, 1, 2, 2, 3, 4, 5, 5, 5, 6, 6, 6, 6
Frequency table:

Data	Frequency
1	2
2	2
3	1
4	1
5	3
6	4

---

function (p. 241) A relation in which every domain value is paired with exactly one range value.

función Relación en la que a cada valor de dominio corresponde exactamente un valor de rango.

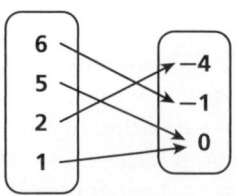

ENGLISH	SPANISH	EXAMPLES
function notation (p. 250) If x is the independent variable and y is the dependent variable, then the function notation for y is $f(x)$, read "f of x," where f names the function.	**notación de función** Si x es la variable independiente e y es la variable dependiente, entonces la notación de función para y es $f(x)$, que se lee "f de x," donde f nombra la función.	equation: $y = 2x$ function notation: $f(x) = 2x$
function rule (p. 250) An algebraic expression that defines a function.	**regla de función** Expresión algebraica que define una función.	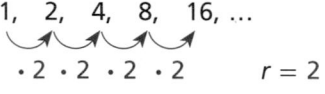
Fundamental Counting Principle (p. 760) If one event has m possible outcomes and a second event has n possible outcomes after the first event has occurred, then there are mn total possible outcomes for the two events.	**Principio fundamental de conteo** Si un suceso tiene m resultados posibles y otro suceso tiene n resultados posibles después de ocurrido el primer suceso, entonces hay mn resultados posibles en total para los dos sucesos.	If there are 4 colors of shirts, 3 colors of pants, and 2 colors of shoes, then there are $4 \cdot 3 \cdot 2 = 24$ possible outfits.

ENGLISH	SPANISH	EXAMPLES
geometric sequence (p. 790) A sequence in which the ratio of successive terms is a constant r, called the common ratio, where $r \neq 0$ and $r \neq 1$.	**sucesión geométrica** Sucesión en la que la razón de los términos sucesivos es una constante r, denominada razón común, donde $r \neq 0$ y $r \neq 1$.	$1, \quad 2, \quad 4, \quad 8, \quad 16, \dots$ $\cdot 2 \cdot 2 \cdot 2 \cdot 2 \qquad r = 2$
graph of a function (p. 256) The set of points in a coordinate plane with coordinates (x, y), where x is in the domain of the function f and $y = f(x)$.	**gráfica de una función** Conjunto de los puntos de un plano cartesiano con coordenadas (x, y), donde x está en el dominio de la función f e $y = f(x)$.	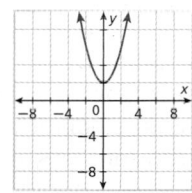
graph of a system of linear inequalities (p. 435) The region in a coordinate plane consisting of points whose coordinates are solutions to all of the inequalities in the system.	**gráfica de un sistema de desigualdades lineales** Región de un plano cartesiano que consta de puntos cuyas coordenadas son soluciones de todas las desigualdades del sistema.	
graph of an inequality in one variable (p. 171) The set of points on a number line that are solutions of the inequality.	**gráfica de una desigualdad en una variable** Conjunto de los puntos de una recta numérica que representan soluciones de la desigualdad.	
graph of an inequality in two variables (p. 428) The set of points in a coordinate plane whose coordinates (x, y) are solutions of the inequality.	**gráfica de una desigualdad en dos variables** Conjunto de los puntos de un plano cartesiano cuyas coordenadas (x, y) son soluciones de la desigualdad.	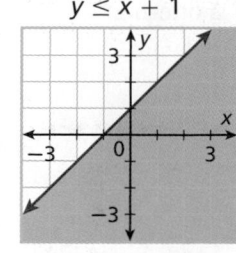

ENGLISH	SPANISH	EXAMPLES
graph of an ordered pair (p. 54) For the ordered pair (x, y), the point in a coordinate plane that is a horizontal distance of x units from the origin and a vertical distance of y units from the origin.	**gráfica de un par ordenado** Dado el par ordenado (x, y), punto en un plano cartesiano que está a una distancia horizontal de x unidades desde el origen y a una distancia vertical de y unidades desde el origen.	$S(2, -4)$
greatest common factor (monomials) (GCF) (p. 575) The product of the greatest integer and the greatest power of each variable that divide evenly into each monomial.	**máximo común divisor (monomios) (MCD)** Producto del entero mayor y la potencia mayor de cada variable que divide exactamente cada monomio.	The GCF of $4x^3y$ and $6x^2y$ is $2x^2y$.
greatest common factor (numbers) (GCF) The largest common factor of two or more given numbers.	**máximo común divisor (números) (MCD)** El mayor de los factores comunes compartidos por dos o más números dados.	The GCF of 27 and 45 is 9.
grouping symbols (p. 40) Symbols such as parentheses ( ), brackets [ ], and braces { } that separate part of an expression. A fraction bar, absolute-value symbols, and radical symbols may also be used as grouping symbols.	**símbolos de agrupación** Símbolos tales como paréntesis ( ), corchetes [ ] y llaves { } que separan parte de una expresión. La barra de fracciones, los símbolos de valor absoluto y los símbolos de radical también se pueden utilizar como símbolos de agrupación.	$6 + \{3 - [(4 - 3) + 2] + 1\} - 5$ $6 + \{3 - [1 + 2] + 1\} - 5$ $6 + \{3 - 3 + 1\} - 5$ $6 + 1 - 5$ 2

H

half-life (p. 807) The half-life of a substance is the time it takes for one-half of the substance to decay into another substance.	**vida media** La vida media de una sustancia es el tiempo que tarda la mitad de la sustancia en desintegrarse y transformarse en otra sustancia.	Carbon-14 has a half-life of 5730 years, so 5 g of an initial amount of 10 g will remain after 5730 years.
half-plane (p. 428) The part of the coordinate plane on one side of a line, which may include the line.	**semiplano** La parte del plano cartesiano de un lado de una línea, que puede incluir la línea.	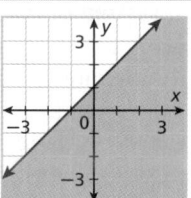
Heron's Formula (p. 834) A triangle with side lengths a, b, and c has area $A = \sqrt{s(s-a)(s-b)(s-c)}$, where s is one-half the perimeter, or $s = \frac{1}{2}(a + b + c)$.	**fórmula de Herón** Un triángulo con longitudes de lado a, b y c tiene un área $A = \sqrt{s(s-a)(s-b)(s-c)}$, donde s es la mitad del perímetro ó $s = \frac{1}{2}(a + b + c)$.	

Glossary/Glosario

ENGLISH	SPANISH	EXAMPLES
histogram (p. 710) A bar graph used to display data grouped in intervals.	**histograma** Gráfica de barras utilizada para mostrar datos agrupados en intervalos de clases.	
horizontal line (p. 316) A line described by the equation $y = b$, where b is the y-intercept.	**línea horizontal** Línea descrita por la ecuación $y = b$, donde b es la intersección con el eje y.	
hypotenuse The side opposite the right angle in a right triangle.	**hipotenusa** Lado opuesto al ángulo recto de un triángulo rectángulo.	

ENGLISH	SPANISH	EXAMPLES
identity (p. 101) An equation that is true for all values of the variables.	**identidad** Ecuación verdadera para todos los valores de las variables.	$3 = 3$ $2(x - 1) = 2x - 2$
inclusive events (p. 758) Events that have one or more outcomes in common.	**sucesos inclusivos** Sucesos que tienen uno o más resultados en común.	In the experiment of rolling a number cube, rolling an even number and rolling a number less than 3 are inclusive events because both contain the outcome 2.
inconsistent system (p. 420) A system of equations or inequalities that has no solution.	**sistema inconsistente** Sistema de ecuaciones o desigualdades que no tiene solución.	$\begin{cases} x + y = 0 \\ x + y = 1 \end{cases}$
independent events (p. 750) Events for which the occurrence or nonoccurrence of one event does not affect the probability of the other event.	**sucesos independientes** Dos sucesos son independientes si el hecho de que se produzca o no uno de ellos no afecta la probabilidad del otro suceso.	From a bag containing 3 red marbles and 2 blue marbles, draw a red marble, replace it, and then draw a blue marble.
independent system (p. 421) A system of equations that has exactly one solution.	**sistema independiente** Sistema de ecuaciones que tiene sólo una solución.	$\begin{cases} x + y = 7 \\ x - y = 1 \end{cases}$ Solution: $(4, 3)$
independent variable (p. 250) The input of a function; a variable whose value determines the value of the output, or dependent variable.	**variable independiente** Entrada de una función; variable cuyo valor determina el valor de la salida, o variable dependiente.	For $y = 2x + 1$, x is the independent variable.

Glossary/Glosario

ENGLISH	SPANISH	EXAMPLES
index (p. 488) In the radical $\sqrt[n]{x}$, which represents the nth root of x, n is the index. In the radical $\sqrt{x}$, the index is understood to be 2.	**índice** En el radical $\sqrt[n]{x}$, que representa la enésima raíz de x, n es el índice. En el radical $\sqrt{x}$, se da por sentado que el índice es 2.	The radical $\sqrt[3]{8}$ has an index of 3.
indirect measurement (p. 128) A method of measurement that uses formulas, similar figures, and/or proportions.	**medición indirecta** Método de medición en el que se usan fórmulas, figuras semejantes y/o proporciones.	
inequality (p. 170) A statement that compares two expressions by using one of the following signs: $<$, $>$, $\leq$, $\geq$, or $\neq$.	**desigualdad** Enunciado que compara dos expresiones utilizando uno de los siguientes signos: $<$, $>$, $\leq$, $\geq$, o $\neq$.	$x \geq 2$ ←++++++●++++→ −4 −3 −2 −1 0 1 2 3 4 5 6
input (p. 55) A value that is substituted for the independent variable in a relation or function.	**entrada** Valor que sustituye a la variable independiente en una relación o función.	For the function $f(x) = x + 5$, the input 3 produces an output of 8.
input-output table A table that displays input values of a function or expression together with the corresponding outputs.	**tabla de entrada y salida** Tabla que muestra los valores de entrada de una función o expresión junto con las correspondientes salidas.	Input x: 1, 2, 3, 4 Output y: 4, 7, 10, 13
integer (p. 34) A member of the set of whole numbers and their opposites.	**entero** Miembro del conjunto de números cabales y sus opuestos.	..., −3, −2, −1, 0, 1, 2, 3, ...
intercept *See* x-intercept and y-intercept.	**intersección** *Ver* intersección con el eje x e intersección con el eje y.	
interest (p. 139) The amount of money charged for borrowing money or the amount of money earned when saving or investing money. *See also* compound interest, simple interest.	**interés** Cantidad de dinero que se cobra por prestar dinero o cantidad de dinero que se gana cuando se ahorra o invierte dinero. *Ver también* interés compuesto, interés simple.	
interquartile range (IQR) (p. 718) The difference of the third (upper) and first (lower) quartiles in a data set, representing the middle half of the data.	**rango entre cuartiles** Diferencia entre el tercer cuartil (superior) y el primer cuartil (inferior) de un conjunto de datos, que representa la mitad central de los datos.	Lower half Upper half 18, ㉓ 28, 29, ㊱ 42 First quartile Third quartile Interquartile range: $36 - 23 = 13$
intersection (p. 205) The intersection of two sets is the set of all elements that are common to both sets, denoted by ∩.	**intersección de conjuntos** La intersección de dos conjuntos es el conjunto de todos los elementos que son comunes a ambos conjuntos, expresado por ∩.	$A = \{1, 2, 3, 4\}$ $B = \{1, 3, 5, 7, 9\}$ $A \cap B = \{1, 3\}$
inverse operations Operations that undo each other.	**operaciones inversas** Operaciones que se anulan entre sí.	Addition and subtraction of the same quantity are inverse operations: $5 + 3 = 8$, $8 - 3 = 5$ Multiplication and division by the same quantity are inverse operations: $2 \cdot 3 = 6$, $6 \div 3 = 2$

ENGLISH	SPANISH	EXAMPLES
inverse variation (p. 871) A relationship between two variables, x and y, that can be written in the form $y = \frac{k}{x}$, where k is a nonzero constant and $x \neq 0$.	**variación inversa** Relación entre dos variables, x e y, que puede expresarse en la forma $y = \frac{k}{x}$, donde k es una constante distinta de cero y $x \neq 0$.	$y = \frac{8}{x}$
irrational number (p. 34) A real number that cannot be expressed as the ratio of two integers.	**número irracional** Número real que no se puede expresar como una razón de enteros.	$\sqrt{2}, \pi, e$
isolate the variable (p. 77) To isolate a variable in an equation, use inverse operations on both sides until the variable appears by itself on one side of the equation and does not appear on the other side.	**despejar la variable** Para despejar la variable de una ecuación, utiliza operaciones inversas en ambos lados hasta que la variable aparezca sola en uno de los lados de la ecuación y no aparezca en el otro lado.	$$10 = 6 - 2x$$ $$\underline{-6} \quad \underline{-6}$$ $$4 = -2x$$ $$\frac{4}{-2} = \frac{-2x}{-2}$$ $$-2 = x$$
isosceles triangle A triangle with at least two congruent sides.	**triángulo isósceles** Triángulo que tiene al menos dos lados congruentes.	

L

leading coefficient (p. 497) The coefficient of the first term of a polynomial in standard form.	**coeficiente principal** Coeficiente del primer término de un polinomio en forma estándar.	$3x^2 + 7x - 2$ Leading coefficient: 3
least common denominator (LCD) (p. 907) The least common multiple of the denominators of two or more given fractions or rational expressions.	**mínimo común denominador (MCD)** Mínimo común múltiplo de los denominadores de dos o más fracciones dadas o expresionnes racionales.	The LCD of $\frac{3}{4}$ and $\frac{5}{6}$ is 12.
least common multiple (monomials) (LCM) (p. 906) The product of the smallest positive number and the lowest power of each variable that divide evenly into each monomial.	**mínimo común múltiplo (monomios) (MCM)** El producto del número positivo más pequeño y la menor potencia de cada variable que divide exactamente cada monomio.	The LCM of $6x^2$ and $4x$ is $12x^2$.
least common multiple (numbers) (LCM) The smallest whole number, other than zero, that is a multiple of two or more given numbers.	**mínimo común múltiplo (números) (MCM)** El menor de los números cabales, distinto de cero, que es múltiplo de dos o más números dados.	The LCM of 10 and 18 is 90.
leg of a right triangle One of the two sides of a right triangle that form the right angle.	**cateto de un triángulo rectángulo** Uno de los dos lados de un triángulo rectángulo que forman el ángulo recto.	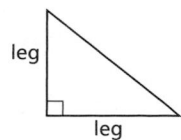

Glossary/Glosario

ENGLISH	SPANISH	EXAMPLES
like radicals (p. 835) Radical terms having the same radicand and index.	**radicales semejantes** Términos radicales que tienen el mismo radicando e índice.	$3\sqrt{2x}$ and $\sqrt{2x}$
like terms (p. 47) Terms with the same variables raised to the same exponents.	**términos semejantes** Términos con las mismas variables elevadas a los mismos exponentes.	$3a^3b^2$ and $7a^3b^2$
line A straight path that has no thickness and extends forever.	**línea** Un trazo recto que no tiene grosor y se extiende infinitamente.	
line graph (p. 701) A graph that uses line segments to show how data changes.	**gráfica lineal** Gráfica que se vale de segmentos de recta para mostrar cambios en los datos.	
linear equation in one variable An equation that can be written in the form $ax = b$ where a and b are constants and $a \neq 0$.	**ecuación lineal en una variable** Ecuación que puede expresarse en la forma $ax = b$ donde a y b son constantes y $a \neq 0$.	$x + 1 = 7$
linear equation in two variables (p. 302) An equation that can be written in the form $Ax + By = C$ where A, B, and C are constants and A and B are not both 0.	**ecuación lineal en dos variables** Ecuación que puede expresarse en la forma $Ax + By = C$ donde A, B y C son constantes y A y B no son ambas 0.	$2x + 3y = 6$
linear function (p. 300) A function that can be written in the form $y = mx + b$, where x is the independent variable and m and b are real numbers. Its graph is a line.	**función lineal** Función que puede expresarse en la forma $y = mx + b$, donde x es la variable independiente y m y b son números reales. Su gráfica es una línea.	$y = x - 1$
linear inequality in one variable An inequality that can be written in one of the following forms: $ax < b$, $ax > b$, $ax \leq b$, $ax \geq b$, or $ax \neq b$, where a and b are constants and $a \neq 0$.	**desigualdad lineal en una variable** Desigualdad que puede expresarse de una de las siguientes formas: $ax < b$, $ax > b$, $ax \leq b$, $ax \geq b$ o $ax \neq b$, donde a y b son constantes y $a \neq 0$.	$3x - 5 \leq 2(x + 4)$
linear inequality in two variables (p. 428) An inequality that can be written in one of the following forms: $Ax + By < C$, $Ax + By > C$, $Ax + By \leq C$, $Ax + By \geq C$, or $Ax + By \neq C$, where A, B, and C are constants and A and B are not both 0.	**desigualdad lineal en dos variables** Desigualdad que puede expresarse de una de las siguientes formas: $Ax + By < C$, $Ax + By > C$, $Ax + By \leq C$, $Ax + By \geq C$ o $Ax + By \neq C$, donde A, B y C son constantes y A y B no son ambas 0.	$2x + 3y > 6$

ENGLISH	SPANISH	EXAMPLES
literal equation (p. 108) An equation that contains two or more variables.	**ecuación literal** Ecuación que contiene dos o más variables.	$d = rt$ $A = \frac{1}{2}h(b_1 + b_2)$
lower quartile *See* first quartile.	**cuartil inferior** *Ver* primer cuartil.	

ENGLISH	SPANISH	EXAMPLES
mapping diagram (p. 240) A diagram that shows the relationship of elements in the domain to elements in the range of a relation or function.	**diagrama de correspondencia** Diagrama que muestra la relación entre los elementos del dominio y los elementos del rango de una función.	**Mapping Diagram** 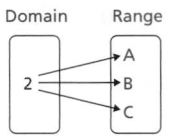
markup (p. 145) The amount by which a wholesale cost is increased.	**margen de ganancia** Cantidad que se agrega a un costo mayorista.	
matrix (p. 770) A rectangular array of numbers.	**matriz** Arreglo rectangular de números.	$\begin{bmatrix} 1 & 0 & 3 \\ -2 & 2 & -5 \\ 7 & -6 & 3 \end{bmatrix}$
maximum of a function (p. 380, p. 612) The *y*-value of the highest point on the graph of the function.	**máximo de una función** Valor de *y* del punto más alto en la gráfica de la función.	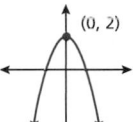 The maximum of the function is 2.
mean (p. 716) The sum of all the values in a data set divided by the number of data values. Also called the *average*.	**media** Suma de todos los valores de un conjunto de datos dividida entre el número de valores de datos. También llamada *promedio*.	Data set: 4, 6, 7, 8, 10 Mean: $\frac{4 + 6 + 7 + 8 + 10}{5}$ $= \frac{35}{5} = 7$
measure of an angle Angles are measured in degrees. A degree is $\frac{1}{360}$ of a complete circle.	**medida de un ángulo** Los ángulos se miden en grados. Un grado es $\frac{1}{360}$ de un círculo completo.	M ∠ 26.8°
measure of central tendency (p. 716) A measure that describes the center of a data set.	**medida de tendencia dominante** Medida que describe el centro de un conjunto de datos.	mean, median, or mode
median (p. 716) For an ordered data set with an odd number of values, the median is the middle value. For an ordered data set with an even number of values, the median is the average of the two middle values.	**mediana** Dado un conjunto de datos ordenado con un número impar de valores, la mediana es el valor medio. Dado un conjunto de datos con un número par de valores, la mediana es el promedio de los dos valores medios.	8, 9, ⑨, 12, 15 Median: 9 4, 6, ⑦, ⑩, 10, 12 Median: $\frac{7 + 10}{2} = 8.5$
midpoint (p. 330) The point that divides a segment into two congruent segments.	**punto medio** Punto que divide un segmento en dos segmentos congruentes.	A ———B——— C Point B is the midpoint of $\overline{AC}$.

ENGLISH	SPANISH	EXAMPLES
minimum of a function (p. 380, p. 612) The *y*-value of the lowest point on the graph of the function.	**mínimo de una función** Valor de *y* del punto más bajo en la gráfica de la función.	$(0, -2)$ The minimum of the function is -2.
mode (p. 716) The value or values that occur most frequently in a data set; if all values occur with the same frequency, the data set is said to have no mode.	**moda** El valor o los valores que se presentan con mayor frecuencia en un conjunto de datos. Si todos los valores se presentan con la misma frecuencia, se dice que el conjunto de datos no tiene moda.	Data set: 3, 6, 8, 8, 10 Mode: 8 Data set: 2, 5, 5, 7, 7 Modes: 5 and 7 Data set: 2, 3, 6, 9, 11 No mode
monomial (p. 496) A number or a product of numbers and variables with whole-number exponents, or a polynomial with one term.	**monomio** Número o producto de números y variables con exponentes de números cabales, o polinomio con un término.	$3x^2y^4$
Multiplication Property of Equality (p. 86) If *a*, *b*, and *c* are real numbers and $a = b$, then $ac = bc$.	**Propiedad de igualdad de la multiplicación** Si *a*, *b* y *c* son números reales y $a = b$, entonces $ac = bc$.	$\frac{1}{3}x = 7$ $(3)\left(\frac{1}{3}x\right) = (3)(7)$ $x = 21$
Multiplication Property of Inequality (p. 182, p. 183) If both sides of an inequality are multiplied by the same positive quantity, the new inequality will have the same solution set. If both sides of an inequality are multiplied by the same negative quantity, the new inequality will have the same solution set if the inequality symbol is reversed.	**Propiedad de desigualdad de la multiplicación** Si ambos lados de una desigualdad se multiplican por el mismo número positivo, la nueva desigualdad tendrá el mismo conjunto solución. Si ambos lados de una desigualdad se multiplican por el mismo número negativo, la nueva desigualdad tendrá el mismo conjunto solución si se invierte el símbolo de desigualdad.	$\frac{1}{3}x > 7$ $(3)\left(\frac{1}{3}x\right) > (3)(7)$ $x > 21$ $-x \leq 2$ $(-1)(-x) \geq (-1)(2)$ $x \geq -2$
multiplicative inverse (p. 21) The reciprocal of the number.	**inverso multiplicativo** Recíproco de un número.	The multiplicative inverse of 5 is $\frac{1}{5}$.
mutually exclusive events (p. 758) Two events are mutually exclusive if they cannot both occur in the same trial of an experiment.	**sucesos mutuamente excluyentes** Dos sucesos son mutuamente excluyentes si ambos no pueden ocurrir en la misma prueba de un experimento.	In the experiment of rolling a number cube, rolling a 3 and rolling an even number are mutually exclusive events.

ENGLISH	SPANISH	EXAMPLES
natural number (p. 34) A counting number.	**número natural** Número que se utiliza para contar.	1, 2, 3, 4, 5, 6, ...
negative correlation (p. 267) Two data sets have a negative correlation if one set of data values increases as the other set decreases.	**correlación negativa** Dos conjuntos de datos tienen una correlación negativa si un conjunto de valores de datos aumenta a medida que el otro conjunto disminuye.	

ENGLISH	SPANISH	EXAMPLES
negative exponent (p. 460) For any nonzero real number x and any integer n, $x^{-n} = \frac{1}{x^n}$.	**exponente negativo** Para cualquier número real distinto de cero x y cualquier entero n, $x^{-n} = \frac{1}{x^n}$.	$x^{-2} = \frac{1}{x^2}$; $3^{-2} = \frac{1}{3^2}$
negative number A number that is less than zero. Negative numbers lie to the left of zero on a number line.	**número negativo** Número menor que cero. Los números negativos se ubican a la izquierda del cero en una recta numérica.	−2 is a negative number. 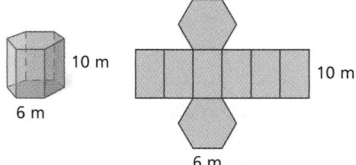
negative square root (p. 32) The opposite of the principal square root of a number a, written as $-\sqrt{a}$.	**raíz cuadrada negativa** Opuesto de la raíz cuadrada principal de un número a, que se expresa como $-\sqrt{a}$.	The negative square root of 9 is $-\sqrt{9} = -3$.
net (p. 894) A diagram of the faces of a three-dimensional figure arranged in such a way that the diagram can be folded to form the three-dimensional figure.	**plantilla** Diagrama de las caras de una figura tridimensional que se puede plegar para formar la figura tridimensional.	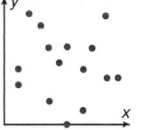
no correlation (p. 267) Two data sets have no correlation if there is no relationship between the sets of values.	**sin correlación** Dos conjuntos de datos no tienen correlación si no existe una relación entre los conjuntos de valores.	
***n*th root** (p. 488) The nth root of a number a, written as $\sqrt[n]{a}$ or $a^{\frac{1}{n}}$, is a number that is equal to a when it is raised to the nth power.	**enésima raíz** La enésima raíz de un número a, que se escribe $\sqrt[n]{a}$ o $a^{\frac{1}{n}}$, es un número igual a a cuando se eleva a la enésima potencia.	$\sqrt[5]{32} = 2$, because $2^5 = 32$.
number line (p. 14) A line used to represent the real numbers.	**recta numérica** Línea utilizada para representar los números reales.	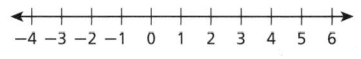
numerical expression (p. 6) An expression that contains only numbers and/or operations.	**expresión numérica** Expresión que contiene únicamente números y operaciones.	$2 \cdot 3 + (4 - 6)$

obtuse angle An angle that measures greater than 90° and less than 180°.	**ángulo obtuso** Ángulo que mide más de 90° y menos de 180°.	
obtuse triangle A triangle with one obtuse angle.	**triángulo obtusángulo** Triángulo con un ángulo obtuso.	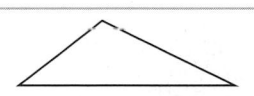
odds (p. 746) A comparison of favorable and unfavorable outcomes. The odds in favor of an event are the ratio of the number of favorable outcomes to the number of unfavorable outcomes. The odds against an event are the ratio of the number of unfavorable outcomes to the number of favorable outcomes.	**probabilidades a favor y en contra** Comparación de los resultados favorables y desfavorables. Las probabilidades a favor de un suceso son la razón entre la cantidad de resultados favorables y la cantidad de resultados desfavorables. Las probabilidades en contra de un suceso son la razón entre la cantidad de resultados desfavorables y la cantidad de resultados favorables.	The odds in favor of rolling a 3 on a number cube are 1:5. The odds against rolling a 3 on a number cube are 5:1.

ENGLISH	SPANISH	EXAMPLES
opposite (p. 15) The opposite of a number a, denoted $-a$, is the number that is the same distance from zero as a, on the opposite side of the number line. The sum of opposites is 0.	**opuesto** El opuesto de un número a, expresado $-a$, es el número que se encuentra a la misma distancia de cero que a, del lado opuesto de la recta numérica. La suma de los opuestos es 0.	←5 units→ ←5 units→ $-6\ -5\ -4\ -3\ -2\ -1\ \ 0\ \ 1\ \ 2\ \ 3\ \ 4\ \ 5\ \ 6$ 5 and -5 are opposites.
opposite reciprocal (p. 364) The opposite of the reciprocal of a number. The opposite reciprocal of any nonzero number a is $-\frac{1}{a}$.	**recíproco opuesto** Opuesto del recíproco de un número. El recíproco opuesto de a es $-\frac{1}{a}$.	The opposite reciprocal of $\frac{2}{3}$ is $-\frac{3}{2}$.
OR (p. 204) A logical operator representing the union of two sets.	**O** Operador lógico que representa la unión de dos conjuntos.	$A = \{2, 3, 4, 5\}$ $B = \{1, 3, 5, 7\}$ The set of values that are in A OR B is $A \cup B = \{1, 2, 3, 4, 5, 7\}$.
order of operations (p. 40) A process for evaluating expressions: First, perform operations in parentheses or other grouping symbols. Second, simplify powers and roots. Third, perform all multiplication and division from left to right. Fourth, perform all addition and subtraction from left to right.	**orden de las operaciones** Regla para evaluar las expresiones: Primero, realizar las operaciones entre paréntesis u otros símbolos de agrupación. Segundo, simplificar las potencias y las raíces. Tercero, realizar todas las multiplicaciones y divisiones de izquierda a derecha. Cuarto, realizar todas las sumas y restas de izquierda a derecha.	$2 + 3^2 - (7 + 5) \div 4 \cdot 3$ $2 + 3^2 - 12 \div 4 \cdot 3$ Add inside parentheses. $2 + 9 - 12 \div 4 \cdot 3$ Simplify the power. $2 + 9 - 3 \cdot 3$ Divide. $2 + 9 - 9$ Multiply. $11 - 9$ Add. 2 Subtract.
ordered pair (p. 54) A pair of numbers (x, y) that can be used to locate a point on a coordinate plane. The first number x indicates the distance to the left or right of the origin, and the second number y indicates the distance above or below the origin.	**par ordenado** Par de números (x, y) que se pueden utilizar para ubicar un punto en un plano cartesiano. El primer número, x, indica la distancia a la izquierda o derecha del origen y el segundo número, y, indica la distancia hacia arriba o hacia abajo del origen.	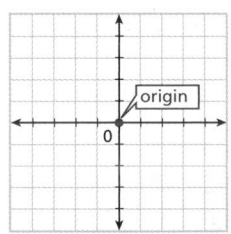 The ordered pair $(-2, 3)$ can be used to locate B.
origin (p. 54) The intersection of the x- and y-axes in a coordinate plane. The coordinates of the origin are $(0, 0)$.	**origen** Intersección de los ejes x e y en un plano cartesiano. Las coordenadas de origen son $(0, 0)$.	origin
outcome (p. 737) A possible result of a probability experiment.	**resultado** Resultado posible de un experimento de probabilidad.	In the experiment of rolling a number cube, the possible outcomes are 1, 2, 3, 4, 5, and 6.
outlier (p. 716) A data value that is far removed from the rest of the data.	**valor extremo** Valor de datos que está muy alejado del resto de los datos.	Most of data Mean Outlier ↓ ↓ ↓
output (p. 55) The result of substituting a value for a variable in a function.	**salida** Resultado de la sustitución de una variable por un valor en una función.	For the function $f(x) = x^2 + 1$, the input 3 produces an output of 10.

ENGLISH	SPANISH	EXAMPLES

P

parabola (p. 611) The shape of the graph of a quadratic function.

parábola Forma de la gráfica de una función cuadrática.

parallel lines (p. 361) Lines in the same plane that do not intersect.

líneas paralelas Líneas en el mismo plano que no se cruzan.

parallelogram A quadrilateral with two pairs of parallel sides.

paralelogramo Cuadrilátero con dos pares de lados paralelos.

parent function (p. 369) The simplest function with the defining characteristics of the family. Functions in the same family are transformations of their parent function.

función madre La función más básica que tiene las características distintivas de una familia. Las funciones de la misma familia son transformaciones de su función madre.

$f(x) = x^2$ is the parent function for $g(x) = x^2 + 4$ and $h(x) = (5x + 2)^2 - 3$.

Pascal's triangle (p. 590) A triangular arrangement of numbers in which every row starts and ends with 1 and each other number is the sum of the two numbers above it.

triángulo de Pascal Arreglo triangular de números en el cual cada fila comienza y termina con 1 y los demás números son la suma de los dos valores que están arriba de cada uno.

```
      1
     1 1
    1 2 1
   1 3 3 1
  1 4 6 4 1
```

percent (p. 133) A ratio that compares a number to 100.

porcentaje Razón que compara un número con 100.

$\frac{17}{100} = 17\%$

percent change (p. 144) An increase or decrease given as a percent of the original amount. *See also* percent decrease, percent increase.

porcentaje de cambio Incremento o disminución dada como un porcentaje de la cantidad original. *Ver también* porcentaje de disminución, porcentaje de incremento.

percent decrease (p. 144) A decrease given as a percent of the original amount.

porcentaje de disminución Disminución dada como un porcentaje de la cantidad original.

If an item that costs $8.00 is marked down to $6.00, the amount of the decrease is $2.00, so the percent decrease is $\frac{2.00}{8.00} = 0.25 = 25\%$.

percent increase (p. 144) An increase given as a percent of the original amount.

porcentaje de incremento Incremento dado como un porcentaje de la cantidad original.

If an item's wholesale cost of $8.00 is marked up to $12.00, the amount of the increase is $4.00, so the percent increase is $\frac{4.00}{8.00} = 0.5 = 50\%$.

perfect square (p. 32) A number whose positive square root is a whole number.

cuadrado perfecto Número cuya raíz cuadrada positiva es un número cabal.

36 is a perfect square because $\sqrt{36} = 6$.

ENGLISH	SPANISH	EXAMPLES
perfect-square trinomial (p. 521) A trinomial whose factored form is the square of a binomial. A perfect-square trinomial has the form $a^2 - 2ab + b^2 = (a - b)^2$ or $a^2 + 2ab + b^2 = (a + b)^2$.	**trinomio cuadrado perfecto** Trinomio cuya forma factorizada es el cuadrado de un binomio. Un trinomio cuadrado perfecto tiene la forma $a^2 - 2ab + b^2 = (a - b)^2$ o $a^2 + 2ab + b^2 = (a + b)^2$.	$x^2 + 6x + 9$ is a perfect-square trinomial, because $x^2 + 6x + 9 = (x + 3)^2$.
perimeter (p. 52) The sum of the side lengths of a closed plane figure.	**perímetro** Suma de las longitudes de los lados de una figura plana cerrada.	Perimeter = 18 + 6 + 18 + 6 = 48 ft
permutation (p. 761) An arrangement of a group of objects in which order is important.	**permutación** Arreglo de un grupo de objetos en el cual el orden es importante.	For objects *A*, *B*, *C*, and *D*, there are 12 different permutations of 2 objects. *AB*, *AC*, *AD*, *BC*, *BD*, *CD* *BA*, *CA*, *DA*, *CB*, *DB*, *DC*
perpendicular Intersecting to form 90° angles.	**perpendicular** Que se cruza para formar ángulos de 90°.	
perpendicular lines (p. 363) Lines that intersect at 90° angles.	**líneas perpendiculares** Líneas que se cruzan en ángulos de 90°.	
plane A flat surface that has no thickness and extends forever.	**plano** Una superficie plana que no tiene grosor y se extiende infinitamente.	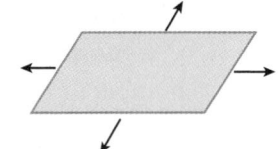
point A location that has no size.	**punto** Ubicación exacta que no tiene ningún tamaño.	*P* • point *P*
point-slope form (p. 351) The point-slope form of a linear equation is $y - y_1 = m(x - x_1)$, where m is the slope and (x_1, y_1) is a point on the line.	**forma de punto y pendiente** La forma de punto y pendiente de una ecuación lineal es $y - y_1 = m(x - x_1)$, donde m es la pendiente y (x_1, y_1) es un punto en la línea.	$y - 3 = 2(x - 3)$
polygon (p. 52) A closed plane figure formed by three or more segments such that each segment intersects exactly two other segments only at their endpoints and no two segments with a common endpoint are collinear.	**polígono** Figura plana cerrada formada por tres o más segmentos tal que cada segmento se cruza únicamente con otros dos segmentos sólo en sus extremos y ningún segmento con un extremo común a otro es colineal con éste.	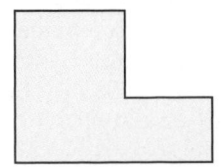
polynomial (p. 496) A monomial or a sum or difference of monomials.	**polinomio** Monomio o suma o diferencia de monomios.	$2x^2 + 3xy - 7y^2$

ENGLISH	SPANISH	EXAMPLES

polynomial long division (p. 914) A method of dividing one polynomial by another.

división larga polinomial Método por el que se divide un polinomio entre otro.

$$x + 2 \overline{)\, x^2 + 3x + 5} \quad \begin{array}{r} x + 1 \end{array}$$
$$\underline{-(x^2 + 2x)}$$
$$x + 5$$
$$\underline{-(x + 2)}$$
$$3$$

$$\frac{x^2 + 3x + 5}{x + 2} = x + 1 + \frac{3}{x + 2}$$

---

population (p. 732) The entire group of objects or individuals considered for a survey.

población Grupo completo de objetos o individuos que se desea estudiar.

In a survey about the study habits of high school students, the population is all high school students.

---

positive correlation (p. 267) Two data sets have a positive correlation if both sets of data values increase.

correlación positiva Dos conjuntos de datos tienen correlación positiva si los valores de ambos conjuntos de datos aumentan.

---

positive number A number greater than zero.

número positivo Número mayor que cero.

2 is a positive number.

---

positive square root (p. 32) The positive square root of a number, indicated by the radical sign.

raíz cuadrada positiva Raíz cuadrada positiva de un número, expresada por el signo de radical.

The positive square root of 36 is $\sqrt{36} = 6$.

---

power (p. 26) An expression written with a base and an exponent or the value of such an expression.

potencia Expresión escrita con una base y un exponente o el valor de dicha expresión.

$2^3 = 8$, so 8 is the third power of 2.

Power of a Power Property (p. 476) If a is any nonzero real number and m and n are integers, then $(a^m)^n = a^{mn}$.

Propiedad de la potencia de una potencia Dado un número real a distinto de cero y los números enteros m y n, entonces $(a^m)^n = a^{mn}$.

$$(6^7)^4 = 6^{7\cdot4}$$
$$= 6^{28}$$

Power of a Product Property (p. 477) If a and b are any nonzero real numbers and n is any integer, then $(ab)^n = a^n b^n$.

Propiedad de la potencia de un producto Dados los números reales a y b distintos de cero y un número entero n, entonces $(ab)^n = a^n b^n$.

$$(2 \cdot 4)^3 = 2^3 \cdot 4^3$$
$$= 8 \cdot 64$$
$$= 512$$

Power of a Quotient Property (p. 483, p. 484) If a and b are any nonzero real numbers and n is an integer, then $\left(\frac{a}{b}\right)^n = \frac{a^n}{b^n}$.

Propiedad de la potencia de un cociente Dados los números reales a y b distintos de cero y un número entero n, entonces $\left(\frac{a}{b}\right)^n = \frac{a^n}{b^n}$.

$$\left(\frac{3}{5}\right)^4 = \frac{3}{5} \cdot \frac{3}{5} \cdot \frac{3}{5} \cdot \frac{3}{5}$$
$$= \frac{3 \cdot 3 \cdot 3 \cdot 3}{5 \cdot 5 \cdot 5 \cdot 5}$$
$$= \frac{3^4}{5^4}$$

---

prediction (p. 739) An estimate or guess about something that has not yet happened.

predicción Estimación o suposición sobre algo que todavía no ha sucedido.

---

prime factorization (p. 544) A representation of a number or a polynomial as a product of primes.

factorización prima Representación de un número o de un polinomio como producto de números primos.

The prime factorization of 60 is $2 \cdot 2 \cdot 3 \cdot 5$.

ENGLISH	SPANISH	EXAMPLES
prime number (p. 544) A whole number greater than 1 that has exactly two positive factors, itself and 1.	**número primo** Número cabal mayor que 1 que es divisible únicamente entre sí mismo y entre 1.	5 is prime because its only positive factors are 5 and 1.
principal (p. 139) An amount of money borrowed or invested.	**capital** Cantidad de dinero que se pide prestado o se invierte.	
prism (p. 894) A polyhedron formed by two parallel congruent polygonal bases connected by faces that are parallelograms.	**prisma** Poliedro formado por dos bases poligonales congruentes y paralelas conectadas por caras laterales que son paralelogramos.	
probability (p. 737) A number from 0 to 1 (or 0% to 100%) that is the measure of how likely an event is to occur.	**probabilidad** Número entre 0 y 1 (o entre 0% y 100%) que describe cuán probable es que ocurra un suceso.	A bag contains 3 red marbles and 4 blue marbles. The probability of randomly choosing a red marble is $\frac{3}{7}$.
Product of Powers Property (p. 474) If a is any nonzero real number and m and n are integers, then $a^m \cdot a^n = a^{m+n}$.	**Propiedad del producto de potencias** Dado un número real a distinto de cero y los números enteros m y n, entonces $a^m \cdot a^n = a^{m+n}$.	$6^7 \cdot 6^4 = 6^{7+4}$ $= 6^{11}$
Product Property of Square Roots (p. 830) For $a \geq 0$ and $b \geq 0$, $\sqrt{ab} = \sqrt{a} \cdot \sqrt{b}$.	**Propiedad del producto de raíces cuadradas** Dados $a \geq 0$ y $b \geq 0$, $\sqrt{ab} = \sqrt{a} \cdot \sqrt{b}$.	$\sqrt{9 \cdot 25} = \sqrt{9} \cdot \sqrt{25}$ $= 3 \cdot 5 = 15$
proportion (p. 120) A statement that two ratios are equal; $\frac{a}{b} = \frac{c}{d}$.	**proporción** Ecuación que establece que dos razones son iguales; $\frac{a}{b} = \frac{c}{d}$.	$\frac{2}{3} = \frac{4}{6}$
pyramid (p. 894) A polyhedron formed by a polygonal base and triangular lateral faces that meet at a common vertex.	**pirámide** Poliedro formado por una base poligonal y caras laterales triangulares que se encuentran en un vértice común.	
Pythagorean Theorem If a right triangle has legs of lengths a and b and a hypotenuse of length c, then $a^2 + b^2 = c^2$.	**Teorema de Pitágoras** Dado un triángulo rectángulo con catetos de longitudes a y b y una hipotenusa de longitud c, entonces $a^2 + b^2 = c^2$.	$5^2 + 12^2 = 13^2$ $25 + 144 = 169$
Pythagorean triple (p. 539) A set of three positive integers a, b, and c such that $a^2 + b^2 = c^2$.	**Tripleta de Pitágoras** Conjunto de tres enteros positivos a, b y c tal que $a^2 + b^2 = c^2$.	The numbers 3, 4, and 5 form a Pythagorean triple because $3^2 + 4^2 = 5^2$.

Q

quadrant (p. 54) One of the four regions into which the x- and y-axes divide the coordinate plane.	**cuadrante** Una de las cuatro regiones en las que los ejes x e y dividen el plano cartesiano.	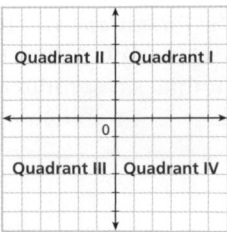

Glossary/Glosario

ENGLISH	SPANISH	EXAMPLES
quadratic equation (p. 642) An equation that can be written in the form $ax^2 + bx + c = 0$, where a, b, and c are real numbers and $a \neq 0$.	**ecuación cuadrática** Ecuación que se puede expresar como $ax^2 + bx + c = 0$, donde a, b y c son números reales y $a \neq 0$.	$x^2 + 3x - 4 = 0$ $x^2 - 9 = 0$
Quadratic Formula (p. 670) The formula $x = \frac{-b \pm \sqrt{b^2 - 4ac}}{2a}$, which gives solutions, or roots, of equations in the form $ax^2 + bx + c = 0$, where $a \neq 0$.	**fórmula cuadrática** La fórmula $x = \frac{-b \pm \sqrt{b^2 - 4ac}}{2a}$, que da soluciones, o raíces, para las ecuaciones del tipo $ax^2 + bx + c = 0$, donde $a \neq 0$.	The solutions of $2x^2 - 5x - 3 = 0$ are given by $x = \dfrac{-(-5) \pm \sqrt{(-5)^2 - 4(2)(-3)}}{2(2)}$ $= \dfrac{5 \pm \sqrt{25 + 24}}{4} = \dfrac{5 \pm 7}{4}$ $x = 3$ or $x = -\dfrac{1}{2}$
quadratic function (p. 610) A function that can be written in the form $f(x) = ax^2 + bx + c$, where a, b, and c are real numbers and $a \neq 0$.	**función cuadrática** Función que se puede expresar como $f(x) = ax^2 + bx + c$, donde a, b y c son números reales y $a \neq 0$.	$f(x) = x^2 - 6x + 8$
quadratic polynomial (p. 497) A polynomial of degree 2.	**polinomio cuadrático** Polinomio de grado 2.	$x^2 - 6x + 8$
quartile The median of the upper or lower half of a data set. *See also* first quartile, third quartile.	**cuartil** La mediana de la mitad superior o inferior de un conjunto de datos. *Ver también* primer cuartil, tercer cuartil.	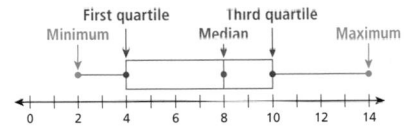
Quotient of Powers Property (p. 481) If a is a nonzero real number and m and n are integers, then $\frac{a^m}{a^n} = a^{m-n}$.	**Propiedad del cociente de potencias** Dado un número real a distinto de cero y los números enteros m y n, entonces $\frac{a^m}{a^n} = a^{m-n}$.	$\dfrac{6^7}{6^4} = 6^{7-4} = 6^3$
Quotient Property of Square Roots (p. 830) For $a \geq 0$ and $b > 0$, $\sqrt{\frac{a}{b}} = \frac{\sqrt{a}}{\sqrt{b}}$.	**Propiedad del cociente de raíces cuadradas** Dados $a \geq 0$ y $b > 0$, $\sqrt{\frac{a}{b}} = \frac{\sqrt{a}}{\sqrt{b}}$.	$\sqrt{\dfrac{9}{25}} = \dfrac{\sqrt{9}}{\sqrt{25}} = \dfrac{3}{5}$

radical equation (p. 846) An equation that contains a variable within a radical.	**ecuación radical** Ecuación que contiene una variable dentro de un radical.	$\sqrt{x + 3} + 4 = 7$
radical expression (p. 829) An expression that contains a radical sign.	**expresión radical** Expresión que contiene un signo de radical.	$\sqrt{x + 3} + 4$
radical symbol (p. 32) The symbol $\sqrt{}$ used to denote a root. The symbol is used alone to indicate a square root or with an index, $\sqrt[n]{}$, to indicate the nth root.	**símbolo de radical** Símbolo $\sqrt{}$ que se utiliza para expresar una raíz. Puede utilizarse solo para indicar una raíz cuadrada, o con un índice, $\sqrt[n]{}$, para indicar la enésima raíz.	$\sqrt{36} = 6$ $\sqrt[3]{27} = 3$

Glossary/Glosario

radicand (p. 829) The expression under a radical sign.

radicando Número o expresión debajo del signo de radical.

Expression: $\sqrt{x+3}$
Radicand: $x+3$

---

radius A segment whose endpoints are the center of a circle and a point on the circle; the distance from the center of a circle to any point on the circle.

radio Segmento cuyos extremos son el centro de un círculo y un punto de la circunferencia; distancia desde el centro de un círculo hasta cualquier punto de la circunferencia.

Radius

---

random sample (p. 727) A sample selected from a population so that each member of the population has an equal chance of being selected.

muestra aleatoria Muestra seleccionada de una población tal que cada miembro de ésta tenga igual probabilidad de ser seleccionada.

Mr. Hansen chose a random sample of the class by writing each student's name on a slip of paper, mixing up the slips, and drawing five slips without looking.

---

range of a data set (p. 716) The difference of the greatest and least values in the data set.

rango de un conjunto de datos La diferencia del mayor y menor valor en un conjunto de datos.

The data set {3, 3, 5, 7, 8, 10, 11, 11, 12} has a range of $12 - 3 = 9$.

---

range of a function or relation (p. 240) The set of all second coordinates (or y-values) of a function or relation.

rango de una función o relación Conjunto de todos los valores de la segunda coordenada (o valores de y) de una función o relación.

The range of the function {(−5, 3), (−3, −2), (−1, −1), (1, 0)} is {−2, −1, 0, 3}.

---

rate (p. 120) A ratio that compares two quantities measured in different units.

tasa Razón que compara dos cantidades medidas en diferentes unidades.

$\dfrac{55 \text{ miles}}{1 \text{ hour}} = 55 \text{ mi/h}$

---

rate of change (p. 314) A ratio that compares the amount of change in a dependent variable to the amount of change in an independent variable.

tasa de cambio Razón que compara la cantidad de cambio de la variable dependiente con la cantidad de cambio de la variable independiente.

The cost of mailing a letter increased from 22 cents in 1985 to 25 cents in 1988. During this period, the rate of change was

$\dfrac{\text{change in cost}}{\text{change in year}} = \dfrac{25 - 22}{1988 - 1985} = \dfrac{3}{3}$

$= 1$ cent per year.

---

ratio (p. 120) A comparison of two quantities by division.

razón Comparación de dos cantidades mediante una división.

$\dfrac{1}{2}$ or $1:2$

---

rational equation (p. 920) An equation that contains one or more rational expressions.

ecuación racional Ecuación que contiene una o más expresiones racionales.

$\dfrac{x + 2}{x^2 + 3x - 1} = 6$

---

rational exponent (p. 489) An exponent that can be expressed as $\frac{m}{n}$ such that if m and n are integers, then $b^{\frac{m}{n}} = \sqrt[n]{b^m} = \left(\sqrt[n]{b}\right)^m$.

exponente racional Exponente que se puede expresar como $\frac{m}{n}$ tal que si m y n son números enteros, entonces $b^{\frac{m}{n}} = \sqrt[n]{b^m} = \left(\sqrt[n]{b}\right)^m$.

$64^{\frac{1}{6}} = \sqrt[6]{64}$

---

rational expression (p. 886) An algebraic expression whose numerator and denominator are polynomials and whose denominator has a degree ≥ 1.

expresión racional Expresión algebraica cuyo numerador y denominador son polinomios y cuyo denominador tiene un grado ≥ 1.

$\dfrac{x + 2}{x^2 + 3x - 1}$

Glossary/Glosario

ENGLISH	SPANISH	EXAMPLES
rational function (p. 878) A function whose rule can be written as a rational expression.	**función racional** Función cuya regla se puede expresar como una expresión racional.	$f(x) = \dfrac{x + 2}{x^2 + 3x - 1}$
rational number (p. 34) A number that can be written in the form $\frac{a}{b}$, where a and b are integers and $b \neq 0$.	**número racional** Número que se puede expresar como $\frac{a}{b}$, donde a y b son números enteros y $b \neq 0$.	$3,\ 1.75,\ 0.\overline{3},\ -\dfrac{2}{3},\ 0$
rationalizing the denominator (p. 842) A method of rewriting a fraction by multiplying by another fraction that is equivalent to 1 in order to remove radical terms from the denominator.	**racionalizar el denominador** Método que consiste en escribir nuevamente una fracción multiplicándola por otra fracción equivalente a 1 a fin de eliminar los términos radicales del denominador.	$\dfrac{1}{\sqrt{2}} \cdot \dfrac{\sqrt{2}}{\sqrt{2}} = \dfrac{\sqrt{2}}{2}$
ray A part of a line that starts at an endpoint and extends forever in one direction.	**rayo** Parte de una recta que comienza en un extremo y se extiende infinitamente en una dirección.	
real number (p. 34) A rational or irrational number. Every point on the number line represents a real number.	**número real** Número racional o irracional. Cada punto de la recta numérica representa un número real.	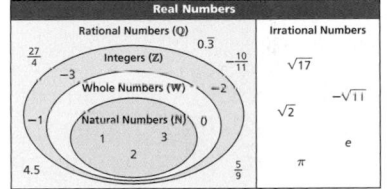
reciprocal (p. 21) For a real number $a \neq 0$, the reciprocal of a is $\frac{1}{a}$. The product of reciprocals is 1.	**recíproco** Dado el número real $a \neq 0$, el recíproco de a es $\frac{1}{a}$. El producto de los recíprocos es 1.	

Number	Reciprocal
2	$\frac{1}{2}$
1	1
-1	-1
0	No reciprocal

ENGLISH	SPANISH	EXAMPLES
rectangle A quadrilateral with four right angles.	**rectángulo** Cuadrilátero con cuatro ángulos rectos.	
rectangular prism (p. 894) A prism whose bases are rectangles.	**prisma rectangular** Prisma cuyas bases son rectángulos.	
rectangular pyramid (p. 894) A pyramid whose base is a rectangle.	**pirámide rectangular** Pirámide cuya base es un rectángulo.	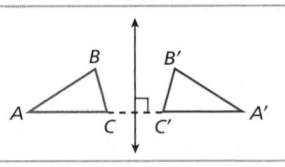
reflection (p. 371) A transformation that reflects, or "flips," a graph or figure across a line, called the line of reflection.	**reflexión** Transformación en la que una gráfica o figura se refleja o se invierte sobre una línea, denominada la línea de reflexión.	
regular polygon A polygon that is both equilateral and equiangular.	**polígono regular** Polígono equilátero de ángulos iguales.	

ENGLISH	SPANISH	EXAMPLES
relation (p. 240) A set of ordered pairs.	**relación** Conjunto de pares ordenados.	$\{(0, 5), (0, 4), (2, 3), (4, 0)\}$
repeating decimal (p. 34) A rational number in decimal form that has a nonzero block of one or more digits that repeat continuously.	**decimal periódico** Número racional en forma decimal que tiene un bloque de uno o más dígitos que se repite continuamente.	$1.\overline{3}, 0.\overline{6}, 2.1\overline{4}, 6.77\overline{3}$
replacement set (p. 8) A set of numbers that can be substituted for a variable.	**conjunto de reemplazo** Conjunto de números que pueden sustituir una variable.	
rhombus A quadrilateral with four congruent sides.	**rombo** Cuadrilátero con cuatro lados congruentes.	
right angle An angle that measures 90°.	**ángulo recto** Ángulo que mide 90°.	
rise (p. 315) The difference in the y-values of two points on a line.	**distancia vertical** Diferencia entre los valores de y de dos puntos de una línea.	For the points $(3, -1)$ and $(6, 5)$, the rise is $5 - (-1) = 6$.
rotation (p. 370) A transformation that rotates or turns a figure about a point called the center of rotation.	**rotación** Transformación que rota o gira una figura sobre un punto llamado centro de rotación.	
run (p. 315) The difference in the x-values of two points on a line.	**distancia horizontal** Diferencia entre los valores de x de dos puntos de una línea.	For the points $(3, -1)$ and $(6, 5)$, the run is $6 - 3 = 3$.

S

ENGLISH	SPANISH	EXAMPLES
sales tax (p. 140) A percent of the cost of an item that is charged by governments to raise money.	**impuesto sobre la venta** Porcentaje del costo de un artículo que cobran los gobiernos para recaudar dinero.	
sample (p. 732) A part of the population.	**muestra** Una parte de la población.	In a survey about the study habits of high school students, a sample is a survey of 100 students.
sample space (p. 737) The set of all possible outcomes of a probability experiment.	**espacio muestral** Conjunto de todos los resultados posibles de un experimento de probabilidad.	In the experiment of rolling a number cube, the sample space is {1, 2, 3, 4, 5, 6}.
scalar (p. 771) A number that is multiplied by a matrix.	**escalar** Número que se multiplica por una matriz.	$3\begin{bmatrix}1 & -2\\2 & 3\end{bmatrix} = \begin{bmatrix}3 & -6\\6 & 9\end{bmatrix}$ scalar
scale (p. 122) The ratio between two corresponding measurements.	**escala** Razón entre dos medidas correspondientes.	1 cm : 5 mi

ENGLISH	SPANISH	EXAMPLES
scale drawing (p. 122) A drawing that uses a scale to represent an object as smaller or larger than the actual object.	**dibujo a escala** Dibujo que utiliza una escala para representar un objeto como más pequeño o más grande que el objeto original.	A blueprint is an example of a scale drawing.
scale factor (p. 129) The multiplier used on each dimension to change one figure into a similar figure.	**factor de escala** El multiplicador utilizado en cada dimensión para transformar una figura en una figura semejante.	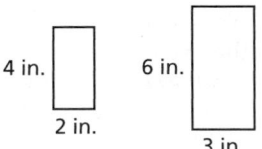 Scale factor: $\frac{3}{2} = 1.5$
scale model (p. 122) A three-dimensional model that uses a scale to represent an object as smaller or larger than the actual object.	**modelo a escala** Modelo tridimensional que utiliza una escala para representar un objeto como más pequeño o más grande que el objeto real.	
scalene triangle A triangle with no congruent sides.	**triángulo escaleno** Triángulo sin lados congruentes.	
scatter plot (p. 266) A graph with points plotted to show a possible relationship between two sets of data.	**diagrama de dispersión** Gráfica con puntos que se usa para demostrar una relación posible entre dos conjuntos de datos.	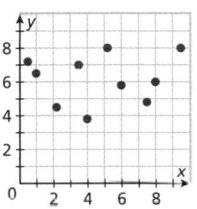
scientific notation (p. 467) A method of writing very large or very small numbers, by using powers of 10, in the form $m \times 10^n$, where $1 \le m < 10$ and n is an integer.	**notación científica** Método que consiste en escribir números muy grandes o muy pequeños utilizando potencias de 10 del tipo $m \times 10^n$, donde $1 \le m < 10$ y n es un número entero.	$12{,}560{,}000{,}000{,}000 = 1.256 \times 10^{13}$ $0.0000075 = 7.5 \times 10^{-6}$
second differences (p. 610) Differences between first differences of a function.	**segundas diferencias** Diferencias entre las primeras diferencias de una función.	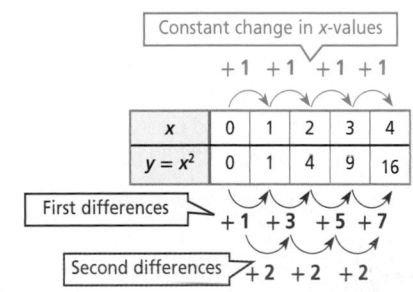
sequence (p. 276) A list of numbers that often form a pattern.	**sucesión** Lista de números que generalmente forman un patrón.	1, 2, 4, 8, 16, …
set-builder notation (p. 170) A notation for a set that uses a rule to describe the properties of the elements of the set.	**notación de conjuntos** Notación para un conjunto que se vale de una regla para describir las propiedades de los elementos del conjunto.	$\{x \mid x > 3\}$ is read "The set of all x such that x is greater than 3."

similar (p. 127) Two figures are similar if they have the same shape but not necessarily the same size.

semejantes Dos figuras con la misma forma pero no necesariamente del mismo tamaño.

---

similarity statement (p. 127) A statement that indicates that two polygons are similar by listing the vertices in the order of correspondence.

enunciado de semejanza Enunciado que indica que dos polígonos son semejantes enumerando los vértices en orden de correspondencia.

quadrilateral $ABCD \sim$ quadrilateral $EFGH$

---

simple event (p. 761) An event consisting of only one outcome.

suceso simple Suceso que tiene sólo un resultado.

In the experiment of rolling a number cube, the event consisting of the outcome 3 is a simple event.

---

simple interest (p. 139) A fixed percent of the principal. For principal P, interest rate r, and time t in years, the simple interest is $I = Prt$.

interés simple Porcentaje fijo del capital. Dado el capital P, la tasa de interés r y el tiempo t expresado en años, el interés simple es $I = Prt$.

If \$100 is put into an account with a simple interest rate of 5%, then after 2 years, the account will have earned $I = 100 \cdot 0.05 \cdot 2 = \$10$ in interest.

---

simplest form of a square root expression (p. 829) A square root expression is in simplest form if it meets the following criteria:
1. No perfect squares are in the radicand.
2. No fractions are in the radicand.
3. No square roots appear in the denominator of a fraction.

See also rationalizing the denominator.

forma simplificada de una expresión de raíz cuadrada Una expresión de raíz cuadrada está en forma simplificada si reúne los siguientes requisitos:
1. No hay cuadrados perfectos en el radicando.
2. No hay fracciones en el radicando.
3. No aparecen raíces cuadradas en el denominador de una fracción.

Ver también racionalizar el denominador.

Not Simplest Form	Simplest Form
$\sqrt{180}$	$6\sqrt{5}$
$\sqrt{216a^2b^2}$	$6ab\sqrt{6}$
$\dfrac{\sqrt{7}}{\sqrt{2}}$	$\dfrac{\sqrt{14}}{2}$

---

simplest form of a rational expression (p. 887) A rational expression is in simplest form if the numerator and denominator have no common factors.

forma simplificada de una expresión racional Una expresión racional está en forma simplificada cuando el numerador y el denominador no tienen factores comunes.

$$\frac{x^2 - 1}{x^2 + x - 2} = \frac{(x - 1)(x + 1)}{(x - 1)(x + 2)}$$
$$= \frac{x + 1}{x + 2}$$

↑ Simplest form

Glossary/Glosario

| | ENGLISH | SPANISH | EXAMPLES |

simplest form of an exponential expression (p. 474) An exponential expression is in simplest form if it meets the following criteria:

1. There are no negative exponents.
2. The same base does not appear more than once in a product or quotient.
3. No powers, products, or quotients are raised to powers.
4. Numerical coefficients in a quotient do not have any common factor other than 1.

forma simplificada de una expresión exponencial Una expresión exponencial está en forma simplificada si reúne los siguientes requisitos:

1. No hay exponentes negativos.
2. La misma base no aparece más de una vez en un producto o cociente.
3. No se elevan a potencias productos, cocientes ni potencias.
4. Los coeficientes numéricos en un cociente no tienen ningún factor común que no sea 1.

Not Simplest Form	Simplest Form
$7^8 \cdot 7^4$	7^{12}
$(x^2)^{-4} \cdot x^5$	$\dfrac{1}{x^3}$
$\dfrac{a^5 b^9}{(ab)^4}$	ab^5

---

simplify (p. 40) To perform all indicated operations.

simplificar Realizar todas las operaciones indicadas.

$$13 - 20 + 8$$
$$-7 + 8$$
$$1$$

---

simulation (p. 736) A model of an experiment, often one that would be too difficult or time-consuming to actually perform.

simulación Modelo de un experimento; generalmente se recurre a la simulación cuando realizar dicho experimento sería demasiado difícil o llevaría mucho tiempo.

---

sine (p. 928) In a right triangle, the ratio of the length of the leg opposite $\angle A$ to the length of the hypotenuse.

seno En un triángulo rectángulo, razón entre la longitud del cateto opuesto a $\angle A$ y la longitud de la hipotenusa.

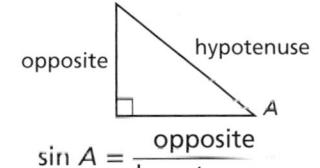

$$\sin A = \frac{\text{opposite}}{\text{hypotenuse}}$$

---

slope (p. 315) A measure of the steepness of a line. If (x_1, y_1) and (x_2, y_2) are any two points on the line, the slope of the line, known as m, is represented by the equation $m = \frac{y_2 - y_1}{x_2 - x_1}$.

pendiente Medida de la inclinación de una línea. Dados dos puntos (x_1, y_1) y (x_2, y_2) en una línea, la pendiente de la línea, denominada m, se representa con la ecuación $m = \frac{y_2 - y_1}{x_2 - x_1}$.

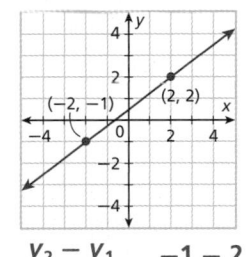

$$m = \frac{y_2 - y_1}{x_2 - x_1} = \frac{-1 - 2}{-2 - 2} = \frac{3}{4}$$

---

slope-intercept form (p. 345) The slope-intercept form of a linear equation is $y = mx + b$, where m is the slope and b is the y-intercept.

forma de pendiente-intersección La forma de pendiente-intersección de una ecuación lineal es $y = mx + b$, donde m es la pendiente y b es la intersección con el eje y.

$$y = -2x + 4$$
The slope is -2.
The y-intercept is 4.

---

solution of a linear equation in two variables An ordered pair or ordered pairs that make the equation true.

solución de una ecuación lineal en dos variables Un par ordenado o pares ordenados que hacen que la ecuación sea verdadera.

$(4, 2)$ is a solution of $x + y = 6$.

ENGLISH	SPANISH	EXAMPLES
solution of a linear inequality in two variables (p. 428) An ordered pair or ordered pairs that make the inequality true.	**solución de una desigualdad lineal en dos variables** Un par ordenado o pares ordenados que hacen que la desigualdad sea verdadera.	$(3, 1)$ is a solution of $x + y < 6$.
solution of a system of linear equations (p. 397) Any ordered pair that satisfies all the equations in a system.	**solución de un sistema de ecuaciones lineales** Cualquier par ordenado que resuelva todas las ecuaciones de un sistema.	$\begin{cases} x + y = -1 \\ -x + y = -3 \end{cases}$ Solution: $(1, -2)$
solution of a system of linear inequalities (p. 435) Any ordered pair that satisfies all the inequalities in a system.	**solución de un sistema de desigualdades lineales** Cualquier par ordenado que resuelva todas las desigualdades de un sistema.	$\begin{cases} y \le x + 1 \\ y < -x + 4 \end{cases}$ (2, 1) is in the overlapping shaded regions, so it is a solution.
solution of an equation in one variable (p. 77) A value or values that make the equation true.	**solución de una ecuación en una variable** Valor o valores que hacen que la ecuación sea verdadera.	Equation: $x + 2 = 6$ Solution: $x = 4$
solution of an inequality in one variable (p. 170) A value or values that make the inequality true.	**solución de una desigualdad en una variable** Valor o valores que hacen que la desigualdad sea verdadera.	Inequality: $x + 2 < 6$ Solution: $x < 4$
solution set (p. 77) The set of values that make a statement true.	**conjunto solución** Conjunto de valores que hacen verdadero un enunciado.	Inequality: $x + 3 \ge 5$ Solution set: $\{x \mid x \ge 2\}$
square A quadrilateral with four congruent sides and four right angles.	**cuadrado** Cuadrilátero con cuatro lados congruentes y cuatro ángulos rectos.	
square in numeration (p. 26) The second power of a number.	**cuadrado en numeración** La segunda potencia de un número.	16 is the square of 4.
square root (p. 32) A number that is multiplied by itself to form a product is called a square root of that product.	**raíz cuadrada** El número que se multiplica por sí mismo para formar un producto se denomina la raíz cuadrada de ese producto.	$\sqrt{16} = 4$, because $4^2 = 4 \cdot 4 = 16$.
square-root function (p. 822) A function whose rule contains a variable under a square-root sign.	**función de raíz cuadrada** Función cuya regla contiene una variable bajo un signo de raíz cuadrada.	$y = \sqrt{3x} - 5$
standard form of a linear equation (p. 302) $Ax + By = C$, where A, B, and C are real numbers and A and B are not both 0.	**forma estándar de una ecuación lineal** $Ax + By = C$, donde A, B y C son números reales y A y B no son ambos cero.	$2x + 3y = 6$

Glossary/Glosario

ENGLISH	SPANISH	EXAMPLES
standard form of a polynomial (p. 497) A polynomial in one variable is written in standard form when the terms are in order from greatest degree to least degree.	**forma estándar de un polinomio** Un polinomio de una variable se expresa en forma estándar cuando los términos se ordenan de mayor a menor grado.	$4x^5 - 2x^4 + x^2 - x + 1$
standard form of a quadratic equation (p. 642) $ax^2 + bx + c = 0$, where a, b, and c are real numbers and $a \neq 0$.	**forma estándar de una ecuación cuadrática** $ax^2 + bx + c = 0$, donde a, b y c son números reales y $a \neq 0$.	$2x^2 + 3x - 1 = 0$
stem-and-leaf plot (p. 709) A graph used to organize and display data by dividing each data value into two parts, a stem and a leaf.	**diagrama de tallo y hojas** Gráfica utilizada para organizar y mostrar datos dividiendo cada valor de datos en dos partes, un tallo y una hoja.	Stem | Leaves 3 | 2 3 4 4 7 9 4 | 0 1 5 7 7 7 8 5 | 1 2 2 3 *Key: 3|2 means 3.2*
stratified random sample (p. 732) A sample in which a population is divided into distinct groups and members are selected at random from each group.	**muestra aleatoria estratificada** Muestra en la que la población está dividida en grupos diferenciados y los miembros de cada grupo se seleccionan al azar.	Ms. Carter chose a stratified random sample of her school's student population by randomly selecting 30 students from each grade level.
substitution method (p. 404) A method used to solve systems of equations by solving an equation for one variable and substituting the resulting expression into the other equation(s).	**sustitución** Método utilizado para resolver sistemas de ecuaciones resolviendo una ecuación para una variable y sustituyendo la expresión resultante en las demás ecuaciones.	
Subtraction Property of Equality (p. 79) If a, b, and c are real numbers and $a = b$, then $a - c = b - c$.	**Propiedad de igualdad de la resta** Si a, b y c son números reales y $a = b$, entonces $a - c = b - c$.	$x + 6 = \ \ 8$ $\underline{\ \ \ -6 \ \ \ -6}$ $x \ \ \ = \ 2$
Subtraction Property of Inequality (p. 176) For real numbers a, b, and c, if $a < b$, then $a - c < b - c$. Also holds true for $>$, $\leq$, $\geq$, and $\neq$.	**Propiedad de desigualdad de la resta** Dados los números reales a, b y c, si $a < b$, entonces $a - c < b - c$. Es válido también para $>$, $\leq$, $\geq$ y $\neq$.	$x + 6 < \ \ 8$ $\underline{\ \ \ -6 \ \ \ -6}$ $x \ \ \ < \ 2$
supplementary angles Two angles whose measures have a sum of 180°.	**ángulos suplementarios** Dos ángulos cuyas medidas suman 180°.	30° ⧹ 150°
surface area (p. 520) The total area of all faces and curved surfaces of a three-dimensional figure.	**área total** Área total de todas las caras y superficies curvas de una figura tridimensional.	 12 cm 6 cm 8 cm Surface area $= 2(8)(12) + 2(8)(6) + 2(12)(6)$ $= 432 \text{ cm}^2$

ENGLISH	SPANISH	EXAMPLES
system of linear equations (p. 397) A system of equations in which all of the equations are linear.	**sistema de ecuaciones lineales** Sistema de ecuaciones en el que todas las ecuaciones son lineales.	$\begin{cases} 2x + 3y = -1 \\ x - 3y = 4 \end{cases}$
system of linear inequalities (p. 435) A system of inequalities in which all of the inequalities are linear.	**sistema de desigualdades lineales** Sistema de desigualdades en el que todas las desigualdades son lineales.	$\begin{cases} 2x + 3y > -1 \\ x - 3y \le 4 \end{cases}$
systematic random sample (p. 732) A sample based on selecting one member of the population at random and then selecting other members by using a pattern.	**muestra sistemática** Muestra en la que se elige a un miembro de la población al azar y luego se elige a otros miembros mediante un patrón.	Mr. Martin chose a systematic random sample of customers visiting a store by selecting one customer at random and then selecting every tenth customer after that.

tangent (p. 928) In a right triangle, the ratio of the length of the leg opposite $\angle A$ to the length of the leg adjacent to $\angle A$.	**tangente** En un triángulo rectángulo, razón entre la longitud del cateto opuesto a $\angle A$ y la longitud del cateto adyacente a $\angle A$.	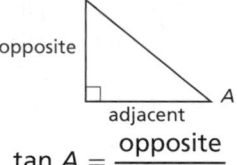 $\tan A = \dfrac{\text{opposite}}{\text{adjacent}}$
term of an expression (p. 47) The parts of the expression that are added or subtracted.	**término de una expresión** Parte de una expresión que debe sumarse o restarse.	$3x^2 + 6x - 8$ Term Term Term
term of a sequence (p. 276) An element or number in the sequence.	**término de una sucesión** Elemento o número de una sucesión.	5 is the third term in the sequence 1, 3, 5, 7, ...
terminating decimal (p. 34) A decimal that ends, or terminates.	**decimal finito** Decimal con un número determinados de posiciones decimales.	1.5, 2.75, 4.0
theoretical probability (p. 744) The ratio of the number of equally likely outcomes in an event to the total number of possible outcomes.	**probabilidad teórica** Razón entre el número de resultados igualmente probables de un suceso y el número total de resultados posibles.	In the experiment of rolling a number cube, the theoretical probability of rolling an odd number is $\frac{3}{6} = \frac{1}{2}$.
third quartile (p. 718) The median of the upper half of a data set. Also called *upper quartile*.	**tercer cuartil** La mediana de la mitad superior de un conjunto de datos. También se llama *cuartil superior*.	Lower half Upper half 18, 23, 28, 29, (36) 42 Third quartile
tip (p. 140) An amount of money added to a bill for service; usually a percent of the bill.	**propina** Cantidad que se agrega a una factura por servicios; generalmente, un porcentaje de la factura.	
transformation (p. 369) A change in the position, size, or shape of a figure or graph.	**transformación** Cambio en la posición, tamaño o forma de una figura o gráfica.	$\triangle ABC \rightarrow \triangle A'B'C'$

ENGLISH	SPANISH	EXAMPLES
translation (p. 369) A transformation that shifts or slides every point of a figure or graph the same distance in the same direction.	**traslación** Transformación en la que todos los puntos de una figura o gráfica se mueven la misma distancia en la misma dirección.	
trapezoid A quadrilateral with exactly one pair of parallel sides.	**trapecio** Cuadrilátero con sólo un par de lados paralelos.	
tree diagram (p. 760) A branching diagram that shows all possible combinations or outcomes of an experiment.	**diagrama de árbol** Diagrama con ramificaciones que muestra todas las combinaciones o resultados posibles de un experimento.	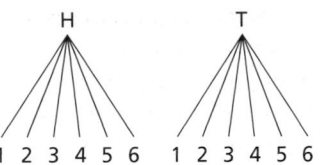 The tree diagram shows the possible outcomes when tossing a coin and rolling a number cube.
trend line (p. 269) A line on a scatter plot that helps show the correlation between data sets more clearly.	**línea de tendencia** Línea en un diagrama de dispersión que sirve para mostrar la correlación entre conjuntos de datos más claramente.	
trial (p. 737) Each repetition or observation of an experiment.	**prueba** Una sola repetición u observación de un experimento.	In the experiment of rolling a number cube, each roll is one trial.
triangle A three-sided polygon.	**triángulo** Polígono de tres lados.	
triangular prism (p. 894) A prism whose bases are triangles.	**prisma triangular** Prisma cuyas bases son triángulos.	
triangular pyramid (p. 894) A pyramid whose base is a triangle.	**pirámide triangular** Pirámide cuya base es un triángulo.	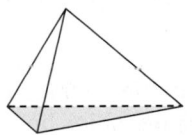
trigonometric ratio (p. 928) Ratio of the lengths of two sides of a right triangle.	**razón trigonométrica** Razón entre dos lados de un triángulo rectángulo.	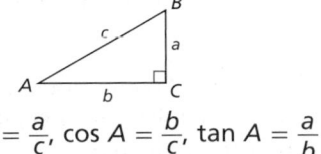 $\sin A = \frac{a}{c}$, $\cos A = \frac{b}{c}$, $\tan A = \frac{a}{b}$
trinomial (p. 497) A polynomial with three terms.	**trinomio** Polinomio con tres términos.	$4x^2 + 3xy - 5y^2$

ENGLISH	SPANISH	EXAMPLES

union (p. 206) The union of two sets is the set of all elements that are in either set, denoted by ∪. | **unión** La unión de dos conjuntos es el conjunto de todos los elementos que se encuentran en ambos conjuntos, expresado por ∪. | $A = \{1, 2, 3, 4\}$
$B = \{1, 3, 5, 7, 9\}$
$A \cup B = \{1, 2, 3, 4, 5, 7, 9\}$

unit rate (p. 120) A rate in which the second quantity in the comparison is one unit. | **tasa unitaria** Tasa en la que la segunda cantidad de la comparación es una unidad. | $\dfrac{30 \text{ mi}}{1 \text{ h}} = 30 \text{ mi/h}$

unlike radicals (p. 835) Radicals with a different quantity under the radical. | **radicales distintos** Radicales con cantidades diferentes debajo del signo de radical. | $2\sqrt{2}$ and $2\sqrt{3}$

unlike terms Terms with different variables or the same variables raised to different powers. | **términos distintos** Términos con variables diferentes o las mismas variables elevadas a potencias diferentes. | $4xy^2$ and $6x^2y$

upper quartile *See* third quartile. | **cuartil superior** *Ver* tercer cuartil. |

value of a function (p. 251) The result of replacing the independent variable with a number and simplifying. | **valor de una función** Resultado de reemplazar la variable independiente por un número y luego simplificar. | The value of the function $f(x) = x + 1$ for $x = 3$ is 4.

value of a variable (p. 7) A number used to replace a variable to make an equation true. | **valor de una variable** Número utilizado para reemplazar una variable y hacer que una ecuación sea verdadera. | In the equation $x + 1 = 4$, the value of x is 3.

value of an expression (p. 7) The result of replacing the variables in an expression with numbers and simplifying. | **valor de una expresión** Resultado de reemplazar las variables de una expresión por un número y luego simplificar. | The value of the expression $x + 1$ for $x = 3$ is 4.

variable (p. 6) A symbol used to represent a quantity that can change. | **variable** Símbolo utilizado para representar una cantidad que puede cambiar. | In the expression $2x + 3$, x is the variable.

Venn diagram A diagram used to show relationships between sets. | **diagrama de Venn** Diagrama utilizado para mostrar la relación entre conjuntos. |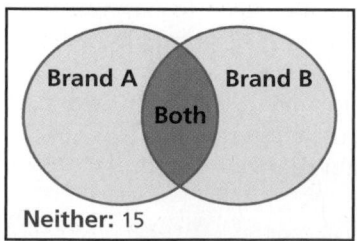

vertex of a parabola (p. 612) The highest or lowest point on the parabola. | **vértice de una parábola** Punto más alto o más bajo de una parábola. |
The vertex is $(0, -2)$.

ENGLISH	SPANISH	EXAMPLES
vertex of an absolute-value graph (p. 378) The point on the axis of symmetry of the graph.	**vértice de una gráfica de valor absoluto** Punto en el eje de simetría de la gráfica.	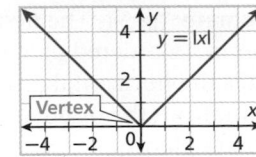
vertical angles The nonadjacent angles formed by two intersecting lines.	**ángulos opuestos por el vértice** Ángulos no adyacentes formados por dos líneas que se cruzan.	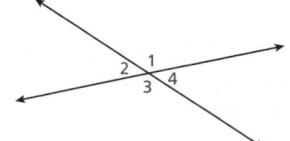 ∠1 and ∠3 are vertical angles. ∠2 and ∠4 are vertical angles.
vertical line (p. 316) A line whose equation is $x = a$, where a is the x-intercept.	**línea vertical** Línea cuya ecuación es $x = a$, donde a es la intersección con el eje x.	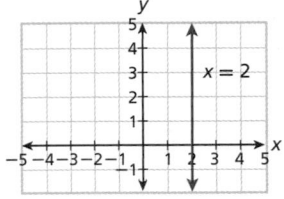
vertical-line test (p. 247) A test used to determine whether a relation is a function. If any vertical line crosses the graph of a relation more than once, the relation is not a function.	**prueba de la línea vertical** Prueba utilizada para determinar si una relación es una función. Si una línea vertical corta la gráfica de una relación más de una vez, la relación no es una función.	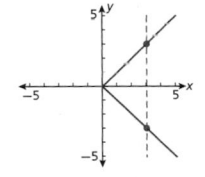 Function Not a function
volume (p. 520) The number of nonoverlapping unit cubes of a given size that will exactly fill the interior of a three-dimensional figure.	**volumen** Cantidad de cubos unitarios no superpuestos de un determinado tamaño que llenan exactamente el interior de una figura tridimensional.	Volume = (3)(4)(12) = 144 ft³
voluntary response sample (p. 733) A sample in which members choose to be in the sample.	**muestra de respuesta voluntaria** Una muestra en la que los miembros eligen participar.	A store provides survey cards for customers who wish to fill them out.

ENGLISH	SPANISH	EXAMPLES
whole number (p. 34) A member of the set of natural numbers and zero.	**número cabal** Miembro del conjunto de los números naturales y cero.	0, 1, 2, 3, 4, 5, …

ENGLISH	SPANISH	EXAMPLES
***x*-axis** (p. 54) The horizontal axis in a coordinate plane.	**eje *x*** Eje horizontal en un plano cartesiano.	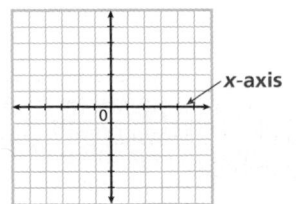

ENGLISH	SPANISH	EXAMPLES

x-coordinate (p. 54) The first number in an ordered pair, which indicates the horizontal distance of a point from the origin on the coordinate plane.

coordenada x Primer número de un par ordenado, que indica la distancia horizontal de un punto desde el origen en un plano cartesiano.

x-intercept (p. 307) The x-coordinate(s) of the point(s) where a graph intersects the x-axis.

intersección con el eje x Coordenada(s) x de uno o más puntos donde una gráfica corta el eje x.

The x-intercept is 2.

y-axis (p. 54) The vertical axis in a coordinate plane.

eje y Eje vertical en un plano cartesiano.

y-coordinate (p. 54) The second number in an ordered pair, which indicates the vertical distance of a point from the origin on the coordinate plane.

coordenada y Segundo número de un par ordenado, que indica la distancia vertical de un punto desde el origen en un plano cartesiano.

y-intercept (p. 307) The y-coordinate(s) of the point(s) where a graph intersects the y-axis.

intersección con el eje y Coordenada(s) y de uno o más puntos donde una gráfica corta el eje y.

The y-intercept is 2.

Z

zero exponent (p. 460) For any nonzero real number x, $x^0 = 1$.

exponente cero Dado un número real distinto de cero x, $x^0 = 1$.

$5^0 = 1$

zero of a function (p. 619) For the function f, any number x such that $f(x) = 0$.

cero de una función Dada la función f, todo número x tal que $f(x) = 0$.

The zeros are −3 and 1.

Zero Product Property (p. 650) For real numbers p and q, if $pq = 0$, then $p = 0$ or $q = 0$.

Propiedad del producto cero Dados los números reales p y q, si $pq = 0$, entonces $p = 0$ o $q = 0$.

If $(x - 1)(x + 2) = 0$, then $x - 1 = 0$ or $x + 2 = 0$, so $x = 1$ or $x = -2$.

Index

Index

Index

Index

Index

Index

Credits

Adams/Getty Images; 558 (tr), © Lee Snider/Photo Images/CORBIS; 559 (cr), © Yann Arthus-Bertrand/CORBIS; 563 (tl), © Stockbyte; 566 (tr), © Robbie Jack/CORBIS; 570 (tl), © Stockbyte; 570 (cl), Sheila Terry/Science Photo Library/Photo Researchers, Inc.; 572 (tl), © Stockbyte; 572 (br), David Young Wolff/Photoedit; 584 (tr), Eric Horan; 584 (br), Eric Horan; 584 (bl), PhotoDisc/Getty Images; 585 (tc), Courtesy Mike Brown/University of South Carolina; 585 (br), Mike Brown/University of South Carolina, University Publications; 585 (cr), John Sanford/Science Photo Library/Photo Researchers, Inc.

Chapter Nine: Page 586–587 (all), © James Randklev/CORBIS; 590 (tr), Aflo Foto Agency; 596 (bl), Sam Dudgeon/HRW; 599 (tr), Gary Crabbe/Alamy; 604 (bl), © Gensaku Izumiya/Sebun Photo/Getty Images; 605 (tl), Sam Dudgeon/HRW; 606 (tr), © Michael S. Yamashita/CORBIS; 610 (tl), AP Photo/Fabio Muzzi; 610 (bl), Sam Dudgeon/HRW; 613 (tr), © Craig Tuttle/CORBIS; 618 (bl), Sam Dudgeon/HRW; 620 (all), Sam Dudgeon/HRW; 622 (tr), © MedioImages/SuperStock; 624 (tr), © Digital Vision; 626 (cl), © Theo Allofs/CORBIS; 626 (bl), PhotoDisc/Getty Images; 626 (bc), © COMSTOCK, Inc.; 630 (tr), Dynamic Graphics Group/IT Stock Free/Alamy; 634 (cr), imagebroker/Alamy; 634 (bl), PhotoDisc/Getty Images; 634 (bc), © COMSTOCK, Inc.; 636 (t), © Gerald French/CORBIS; 640 (cl), Loren Winters/Visuals Unlimited; 640 (bl), PhotoDisc/Getty Images; 640 (bc), © COMSTOCK, Inc.; 645 (tr), The Garden Picture Library/Alamy; 650 (bl), PhotoDisc/Getty Images; 650 (bl), © COMSTOCK, Inc.; 652 (tr), © Powerstock/SuperStock; 656 (bl), Comstock Images/Alamy; 659 (tl), PhotoDisc/Getty Images; 659 (tc), © COMSTOCK, Inc.; 660 (tl), PhotoDisc/Getty Images; 660 (tc), © COMSTOCK, Inc.; 660 (tr), Stuart Franklin/Getty Images; 660 (b), Robert Laberge/Getty Images.

Chapter Ten: Page 672–673 (all), Frans Lanting/Minden Pictures; 678 (tr), Victoria Smith/HRW; 680 (all), Sam Dudgeon/HRW; 687 (tr), © Tom Stewart/CORBIS; 691 (cl), © Reuters/CORBIS; 694 (tr), AP Photo/Dave Martin; 696 (tr), Victoria Smith/HRW; 698 (cr), © Michael Prince/CORBIS; 707 (tl), © Bettmann/CORBIS; 710 (cr), Stuart Franklin/Getty Images; 710 (bl), Stuart Franklin/Getty Images; 712 (tr), Sam Dudgeon/HRW; 713 (tl), Sam Dudgeon/HRW; 713 (tc), United States Mint image; 713 (tc), United States Mint image; 713 (tr), Sam Dudgeon/HRW; 713 (c), United States Mint image; 713 (c), United States Mint image; 713 (bc, br), Sam Dudgeon/HRW; 716 (tl, tc), Sam Dudgeon/HRW; 716 (penny), PhotoDisc/Getty Images; 716 (dime), PhotoDisc/Getty Images; 716 (nickel), PhotoDisc/Getty Images; 716 (bl), PhotoDisc/Getty Images; 716 (bc), Sam Dudgeon/HRW; 716 (br), Victoria Smith/HRW; 717 (bl), Sam Dudgeon/HRW; 718 (cr), © European Communities; 720 (tr), © Warren Faidley/Weatherstock; 721 (bl), Aflo Foto Agency/Alamy; 722 (cr), Victoria Smith/HRW; 724 (bl), Sam Dudgeon/HRW; 727 (tl), David Young-Wolff/Alamy; 728 (tl), Peter Van Steen/HRW; 728 (bl, bc), Victoria Smith/HRW; 729 (tr), Victoria Smith/HRW; 730 (cr), Sam Dudgeon/HRW; 731 (bl), © Jose Luis Pelaez, Inc./CORBIS; 732 (tl), Sam Dudgeon/HRW; 735 (all), Sam Dudgeon/HRW; 736 (all), Sam Dudgeon/HRW; 741 (cr), Sam Dudgeon/HRW; 741 (cl), © Underwood & Underwood/CORBIS; 742 (tl), Sam Dudgeon/HRW; 743 (tr), Foodcollection.com/Alamy; 743 (bl), © Comstock Images; 744 (tl), Sam Dudgeon/HRW; 744 (b), © Handout/Hasbro/Ray Stubblebine/Reuters/CORBIS; 749 (cl), Courtesy of Blue Sky Studios/ZUMA Press; 760 (cr), Blair Seitz; 761 (br), AP Photo/John Heller; 761 (tr, bl), Tom Pawlesh.

Chapter Eleven: Page 762–763 (all), © age fotostock/Superstock; 766 (tr), Randy Lincks/Masterfile; 777 (tl), Lucidio Studio, Inc./Alamy; 781 (tr), © Wendy Stone/CORBIS; 786 (cr), Tom Goskar/Wessex Archaeology Ltd.; 789 (tr), © Stan Liu/Icon SMI/ZUMA Press; 791 (tr), Stephen Dalton/Photo Researchers, Inc.; 792 (cl), age fotostock; 796 (c), Laimute Druskis/Stock Boston/IPN; 796 (bc), © D. Hurst/Alamy; 796 (br), © Brian Hagiwara/Brand X Pictures/Alamy; 798 (tr), NASA; 802 (tl), AP Photo/Andy Eames; 802 (bl), © Brand X Pictures; 805 (tr), Steve Gottlieb/PictureQuest; 809 (bl), © Brand X Pictures; 814 (bl), © Brand X Pictures; 816 (tr), ON-PAGE CREDIT; 820 (tl), © Richard Cummins/SuperStock; 820 (bl), © Brand X Pictures; 827 (bl), AP Photo/Gregory Smith; 828 (bl), © Brand X Pictures; 830 (cr), Walker/PictureQuest; 830 (tl), © Brand X Pictures; 830 (bc), AP Photo/Anna Branthwaite.

Chapter Twelve: Page 846–847 (all), © Robert Daly/Stone/Getty Images; 849 Sam Dudgeon/HRW; 851 (tr), © RubberBall/Alamy; 853 (tl), MedioImages/Alamy; 856 (tl), AP Photo/Robert F. Bukaty; 856 (bl), PhotoDisc/Getty Images; 858 (tr), © Steve Hamblin/Alamy; 864 (bl), PhotoDisc/Getty Images; 866 (tr), Gerald C. Kelley/Photo Researchers, Inc.; 868 (bl), © Paul Barton/CORBIS; 869 (tl), © SuperStock; 871 (cl), AP Photo/Lou Krasky; 871 (bl), PhotoDisc/Getty Images; 876 (tl), PhotoDisc/Getty Images; 876 (br), AP Photo/Tyler Morning Telegraph, Tom Worner; 876 (sky), PhotoDisc/Getty Images; 878 (tr), © Stock Connection Distribution / Alamy; 885 (tr), Philippe Blondel/Photo Researchers, Inc.; 890 (tl), Photo Researchers, Inc.; 893 (tc), AP Photo/Dolores Ochoa; 893 (tr), © Nigel Francis/Robert Harding/Alamy Photos; 898 (cl), AP Photo /NASA, Nick Galante, PMRF; 900 (tr), © Tom Stewart/CORBIS; 904 (br), ON-PAGE CREDIT; 906 (b), © Dynamic Graphics Group/i2i/Alamy; 906 (movie screen), © Ralph Nelson/Imagine Entertainment/ZUMA/CORBIS; 920 (tr), Sam Dudgeon/HRW; 920 (bl), © David Bergman/Corbis; 920 (bc), AP Photo/Al Behrman; 921 (br), Bicycle Museum of America/New Bremen, Ohio/www.bicyclemuseum.com; 921 (tr), Courtesy of the Bicycle Museum of America.

Student Handbook: S2 (tl), PhotoDisc/Getty Images; S3 (hr), Sam Dudgeon/HRW.

Symbols

Relation Symbols

<	is less than
>	is greater than
≤	is less than or equal to
≥	is greater than or equal to
≠	is not equal to
≈	is approximately equal to
≅	is congruent to
~	is similar to

Real Numbers

$\mathbb{R}$	the set of real numbers
$\mathbb{Q}$	the set of rational numbers
$\mathbb{Z}$	the set of integers
$\mathbb{W}$	the set of whole numbers
$\mathbb{N}$	the set of natural numbers

Geometry

$\angle ABC$	angle ABC
$m\angle ABC$	the measure of angle ABC
$\triangle ABC$	triangle ABC
$\overline{AB}$	segment AB

Other

±	plus or minus
$\lvert -4 \rvert$	the absolute value of -4
{	system
π	pi; $\pi \approx 3.14$ or $\pi \approx \frac{22}{7}$
∅	empty set
$f(x)$	function notation; f of x
a_n	the nth term of a sequence
$n!$	n factorial
$P(\text{event})$	the probability of an event

Table of Measures

METRIC

Length

1 kilometer (km) = 1000 meters (m)

1 meter = 100 centimeters (cm)

1 centimeter = 10 millimeters (mm)

Capacity and Volume

1 liter (L) = 1000 milliliters (mL)

Mass

1 kilogram (kg) = 1000 grams (g)

1 gram = 1000 milligrams (mg)

CUSTOMARY

Length

1 mile (mi) = 1760 yards (yd)

1 yard = 3 feet (ft)

1 foot = 12 inches (in.)

Capacity and Volume

1 gallon (gal) = 4 quarts (qt)

1 quart = 2 pints (pt)

1 pint = 2 cups (c)

1 cup = 8 fluid ounces (fl oz)

Weight

1 ton = 2000 pounds (lb)

1 pound = 16 ounces (oz)

TIME

1 year (yr) = 365 days (d)

1 year = 12 months (mo)

1 year = 52 weeks (wk)

1 week = 7 days

1 day = 24 hours (h)

1 hour = 60 minutes (min)

1 minute = 60 seconds (s)